Discovering Psychology Chapter-Program Preview Guide

Textbook Chapter Number	Textbook Chapter Title	Discovering Psychology Video Program	Discovering Psychology Video Program Description
Chapter 1	Psychology and Life	**Program 1:** Past, Present, and Promise	**Program 1** introduces psychology as the scientific study of behavior and mental processes. It looks at how psychologists work from a variety of theoretical models and traditions, record and analyze their observations, and attempt to unravel the mysteries of the mind.
Chapter 2	Research Methods in Psychology	**Program 2:** Understanding Research	**Program 2** demonstrates the hows and whys of psychological research. By showing how psychologists rely on systematic observation, data collection, and analysis to find out the answers to their questions, this program reveals why the scientific method is used in all areas of empirical investigation.
Chapter 3	The Biological and Evolutionary Bases of Behavior	**Program 3:** The Behaving Brain	Psychologists who study the structure and composition of the brain believe that all our thoughts, feelings, and actions have a biological and chemical basis. **Program 3** explains the nervous system and the methods scientists use to explore the link between physiological processes in the brain and psychological experience and behavior.
		Program 4: The Responsive Brain	**Program 4** takes a closer look at the dynamic relationship between the brain and behavior. We'll see how the brain controls behavior and, conversely, how behavior and environment can cause changes in the structure and the functioning of the brain.
		Program 25: Cognitive Neuroscience	**Program 25** introduces cognitive neuroscience and the techniques now available for studying mental processes by studying the brain's activities. Cognitive neuroscience is a highly interdisciplinary field that unites psychologists with brain researchers, biologists, and physicists in what has become the most dramatic advance in the last decade of psychological research.
Chapter 4	Sensation and Perception	**Program 7:** Sensation and Perception	**Program 7** explores how we make contact with the world outside our brain and body. We'll see how biological, cognitive, social, and environmental influences shape our personal sense of reality, and we'll gain an understanding of how psychologists use our perceptual errors to study how the constructive process of perception works.
Chapter 5	Mind, Consciousness, and Alternate States	**Program 13:** The Mind Awake and Asleep	**Program 13** describes how psychologists investigate the nature of sleeping, dreaming, and altered states of conscious awareness. It also explores the ways we use consciousness to interpret, analyze, and even change our behavior.
		Program 14: The Mind Hidden and Divided	**Program 14** considers the evidence that our moods, behavior, and even our health are largely the result of multiple mental processes, many of which are out of conscious awareness. It also looks at some of the most dramatic phenomena in psychology, such as hypnosis and the division of human consciousness into "two minds" when the brain is split in half by surgical intervention.
Chapter 6	Learning and Behavior Analysis	**Program 8:** Learning	Learning is the process that enables humans and other animals to profit from experience, anticipate events, and adapt to changing conditions. **Program 8** explains the basic learning principles and the methods psychologists use to study and modify behavior. It also demonstrates how cognitive processes, such as insight and observation, influence learning.
Chapter 7	Memory	**Program 9:** Remembering and Forgetting	**Program 9** explores memory, the complex mental process that allows us to store and recall our previous experiences. It looks at the ways cognitive psychologists investigate memory as an information-processing task and at the ways neuroscientists study how the structure and functioning of the brain affect how we remember and why we forget.
Chapter 8	Cognitive Processes	**Program 10:** Cognitive Processes	The study of mental processes and structures—perceiving, reasoning, imagining, anticipating, and problem solving—is known as cognition. **Program 10** explores these higher mental processes, offering insight into how the field has evolved and why more psychologists than ever are investigating the way we absorb, transform, and manipulate knowledge.
		Program 11: Judgment and Decision Making	**Program 11** explores the decision-making process and the psychology of risk taking, revealing how people arrive at good and bad decisions. It also looks at the reasons people lapse into irrationality and how personal biases can affect judgment.

Textbook Chapter Number	Textbook Chapter Title	Discovering Psychology Video Program	Discovering Psychology Video Program Description
Chapter 9	Intelligence and Intelligence Assessment	**Program 16:** Testing and Intelligence	Just as no two fingerprints are alike, no two people have the same set of abilities, aptitudes, interests, and talents. **Program 16** explains the tools psychologists use to measure these differences. It also describes the long-standing controversy over how to define intelligence and how IQ tests have been misused and misapplied. Is it wise, accurate, or fair to reduce intelligence to a number? Researchers are currently debating the value of intelligence and personality tests.
Chapter 10	Human Development Across the Life Span	**Program 5:** The Developing Child	**Program 5** looks at how advances in technology and methodology have revealed the abilities of newborn infants, giving researchers a better understanding of the role infants play in shaping their environment. In contrast to the nature-versus-nurture debates of the past, today's researchers concentrate on how heredity and environment interact to contribute to the developmental process.
		Program 6: Language Development	**Program 6** examines how children acquire language and demonstrates the methods psychologists use to study the role of biology and social interaction in language acquisition. It also looks at the contribution of language to children's cognitive and social development.
		Program 18: Maturing and Aging	Thanks to growing scientific interest in the elderly, research on aging has replaced many myths and fears with facts. **Program 18** focuses on what scientists are learning about life cycle development as they look at how aging is affected by biology, environment, and lifestyle.
Chapter 11	Motivation	**Program 12:** Motivation and Emotion	What moves us to act? Why do we feel the way we do? **Program 12** shows how psychologists study the continuous interactions of mind and body in an effort to explain the enormous variety and complexities of human behavior.
		Program 17: Sex and Gender	**Program 17** looks at the similarities and differences between the sexes resulting from the complex interaction of biological and social factors. It contrasts the universal differences in anatomy and physiology with those learned and culturally acquired, and it reveals how roles are changing to reflect new values and psychological knowledge.
Chapter 12	Emotion, Stress, and Health	**Program 23:** Health, Mind, and Behavior	A profound rethinking of the relationship between mind and body has led to an approach to health that assumes that mental and physical processes are constantly interacting. **Program 23** looks at what health psychologists know about the factors that increase our chances of becoming ill and what we can do to improve and maintain our health.
Chapter 13	Understanding Human Personality	**Program 15:** The Self	What makes each of us unique? What traits and experiences make you? **Program 15** describes how psychologists systematically study the origins and development of self-identity, self-esteem, and other aspects of our thoughts, feelings, and behaviors that make up our personalities.
Chapter 14	Psychological Disorders	**Program 21:** Psychopathology	**Program 21** describes the major types of mental illnesses and some of the factors that influence them—both biological and psychological. It also reports on several approaches to classifying and treating mental illness and explains the difficulties of defining abnormal behavior.
Chapter 15	Therapies for Psychological Disorders	**Program 22:** Psychotherapy	**Program 22** looks at psychotherapy and therapists, the professionals trained to help us solve some of our most critical problems. You will learn about different approaches to the treatment of mental, emotional, and behavioral disorders and the kind of helping relationships that therapists provide.
Chapter 16	Social Psychology	**Program 19:** The Power of the Situation	**Program 19** investigates the social and situational forces that influence our individual and group behavior and how our beliefs can be manipulated by other people.
		Program 20: Constructing Social Reality	**Program 20** explores our subjective view of reality and how it influences social behavior. It reveals how our perceptions and reasoning ability can be influenced in positive and negative ways, and it increases our understanding of how psychological processes govern our interpretation of reality.

Why Do You Need this New Edition?

5 Good Reasons Why You Should Buy This New Edition of *Psychology and Life*!

1. This edition of *Psychology and Life* is fresh with the most up-to-date coverage and brimming with over 650 new references. Our goal is to be the most current, most accurate, and most accessible treatment of our discipline today. An in-depth list of updates can be found in the preface.

2. Chapter 16 is a combination of the two Social Psychology chapters from the last edition. We have streamlined content and thoroughly updated this chapter to include new research on a variety of topics.

3. Each chapter of this edition of *Psychology and Life* is tied to one or more programs of the *Discovering Psychology* video series, produced by WGBH Boston with funding by Annenberg Media. Author Phil Zimbardo narrates the video series, as leading researchers, practitioners, and theorists probe the mysteries of the mind and body and bring psychology to life just for you! At the end of each chapter, you'll find a program summary, review questions, and additional questions to answer for each program.

4. In addition to the vast topical updates made to this edition, we have replaced more than 1/3 of the nearly 140 research studies, highlighted with dark red brackets throughout the text. These major studies showcase the *how* and *why* behind key psychological research.

5. Every feature box in each chapter has been taken into consideration during this revision. Many boxes contain updated research, and nearly half of all the *Critical Thinking in Your Life* and *Psychology in Your Life* boxes have been replaced with new topics altogether.

19TH EDITION

PSYCHOLOGY AND LIFE

Global Edition

Richard J. Gerrig
Stony Brook University

WITH

Philip G. Zimbardo
Stanford University

PEARSON

Boston   Columbus   Indianapolis   New York   San Francisco   Upper Saddle River
Amsterdam   Cape Town   Dubai   London   Madrid   Milan   Munich   Paris   Montreal   Toronto
Delhi   Mexico City   Sao Paulo   Sydney   Hong Kong   Seoul   Singapore   Taipei   Tokyo

Editor in Chief: Jessica Mosher
Executive Editor: Stephen Frail
Development Editor: Deb Hanlon
Editorial Assistant: Kerri Hart-Morris
Director of Development: Sharon Geary
Associate Editor: Kara Kikel
Senior Media Editor: Paul DeLuca
Executive Marketing Manager: Jeanette Koskinas
Market Development Manager: Tara Kelly
Director, Market Research and Development: Laura Coaty
Production Supervisor: Roberta Sherman
Cover Designer: Kristina Mose-Libon
Production Service: Nesbitt Graphics, Inc.
Manufacturing Buyer: JoAnne Sweeney
Electronic Composition: Nesbitt Graphics, Inc.
Interior Design: Jerilyn Bockerick, Nesbitt Graphics, Inc.
Photo Research: Katharine S. Cebik

10 9 8 7 6 5 4 3 2 1

ISBN-10: 0-205-71091-3
ISBN-13: 978-0-205-71091-1

We dedicate this book to our daughters
Alex, Zara, and Tanya.

My daughter Alex has become a remarkable young woman. She brings an
articulate passion to a broad range of substantial issues. Alex will soon begin
her college career with an interest in political science.
I have no doubt that she will continue to excel—R. J. G.

My wonderful daughters, Zara Maria and Tanya Lucia, have been a source of
endless delight and personal support over the past three decades. They have
always modeled what is best in students, curiosity in knowing why and how things and
behavior work, while never settling for the obvious simple answers to complex issues.
I look forward to the unfolding of their careers as teachers, social activists,
and Zara as a cultural anthropologist, and Tanya as a museum
curator in media arts—P. G. Z.

Brief Contents

Contents

Meet the Authors

RICHARD J. GERRIG is a professor of psychology at Stony Brook University. Before joining the Stony Brook faculty, Gerrig taught at Yale University, where he was awarded the Lex Hixon Prize for teaching excellence in the social sciences. Gerrig's research on cognitive psychological aspects of language use has been widely published. One line of work examines the mental processes that underlie efficient communication. A second research program considers the cognitive and emotional changes readers experience when they are transported to the worlds of stories. His book *Experiencing Narrative Worlds* was published by Yale University Press. Gerrig is a Fellow of the Society for Text & Discourse, the American Psychological Association, and the Association for Psychological Science. He is also an associate editor of *Psychonomic Bulletin & Review*. Gerrig is the proud father of Alexandra, who at age 18 provides substantial and valuable advice about many aspects of psychology and life. Life on Long Island is greatly enhanced by the guidance and support of Timothy Peterson.

PHILIP G. ZIMBARDO, Stanford University professor emeritus, has taught the introductory psychology course for 50 years and has been writing and coauthoring *Psychology and Life,* as well as the Faculty Guides and Student Workbooks, for the past 38 years. He has been called the "Face and Voice of Psychology" because of his popular PBS-TV series, *Discovering Psychology,* which is used in many high school and university courses both nationally and internationally. Zimbardo also loves to conduct and publish research on a wide variety of subjects, as well as teaching and engaging in public and social service activities. He has published more than 350 professional and popular articles and chapters and 50 books of all kinds. His recent trade book on the psychology of evil, *The Lucifer Effect,* relates his classic Stanford Prison Experiment to the abuses at Iraq's Abu Ghraib Prison. It was a *New York Times* best seller and William James Prize book of the year. Zimbardo has also just published *The Time Paradox,* a summary of research and applications of the psychology of time perspective. He is currently exploring research and developing new educational materials on the topic of the psychology of ordinary heroes. Please see these websites for more information: www.zimbardo.com, www.prisonexp.org, www.lucifereffect.com, and www.everydayheroism.com. Zimbardo now teaches graduate courses at the Pacific Graduate School of Psychology and also at the Naval Postgraduate School in Monterey, CA.

Preface

Teaching introductory psychology is one of the greatest challenges facing any academic psychologist. Indeed, because of the range of our subject matter, it is probably the most difficult course to teach effectively in all of academia. We must cover both the micro-level analyses of nerve cell processes and the macro-level analyses of cultural systems: both the vitality of health psychology and the tragedy of lives blighted by mental illness. Our challenge in writing this text—like your challenge in teaching—is to give form and substance to all this information, to bring it to life for our students.

More often than not, students come into our course filled with misconceptions about psychology that they have picked up from the infusion of "pop psychology" into our society. They also bring with them high expectations about what they want to get out of a course in psychology—they want to learn much that will be personally valuable, that will help them improve their everyday lives. Indeed, that is a tall order for any teacher to fill. But we believe that *Psychology and Life* can help you to fill it.

Our goal has been to design a text that students will enjoy reading as they learn what is so exciting and special about the many fields of psychology. In every chapter, in every sentence, we have tried to make sure that students will want to go on reading. At the same time, we have focused on how our text will work within the syllabi of instructors who value a research-centered, applications-relevant approach to psychology.

This 19th edition of *Psychology and Life* is the fifth collaboration between Richard Gerrig and Philip Zimbardo. Our partnership was forged because we shared a commitment to teaching psychology as a science relevant to human welfare. We both could bring our teaching experience to bear on a text that balances scientific rigor with psychology's relevance to contemporary life concerns. Furthermore, Richard's expertise in cognitive psychology provided an important complement to Phil's expertise in social psychology. With Richard as lead author, *Psychology and Life* has been able to keep pace with rapid changes in psychology, particularly in areas such as cognitive and affective neuroscience. Even so, *Psychology and Life* remains a collaboration of like minds: Together, we celebrate both an ongoing tradition and a continued vision of bringing the most important psychological insights to bear on your students' lives. The 19th edition is a product of this fine collaboration.

Text Theme: The Science of Psychology

The aim of *Psychology and Life* is to use solid scientific research to combat psychological misconceptions. In our experience as teachers, one of the most reliable occurrences on the first day of introductory psychology is the throng of students who push forward at the end of class to ask, in essence, "Will this class teach me what I need to know?":

> My mother is taking Prozac: Will we learn what it does?
> Are you going to teach us how to study better?
> I need to put my son in day care to come back to school.
>   Is that going to be all right for him?
> What should I do if I have a friend talking about suicide?

We take comfort that each of these questions has been addressed by rigorous empirical research. *Psychology and Life* is devoted to providing students with scientific analyses of their foremost concerns. As a result, the features of *Psychology and Life* support a central theme: psychology as a science, with a focus on *applying* that science to your students' lives.

CRITICAL THINKING IN YOUR LIFE

An important goal of *Psychology and Life* is to teach the scientific basis of psychological reasoning. When our students ask us questions—what they need to know—they quite often have acquired partial answers based on the types of information that are available in the popular media. Some of that information is accurate, but often students do not know how to make sense of it. How do they learn to interpret and evaluate what they hear in the media? How can they become wiser consumers of the

overabundance of research studies and surveys cited? How can they judge the credibility of these sources? To counteract this infusion of so-called reliable research, we provide students with the scientific tools to think critically about the information with which they are surrounded and to draw generalizations appropriate to the goals and methods of research.

With a feature we call **Critical Thinking in Your Life,** we seek to confront students directly with the experimental basis of critical conclusions. Our intention is not to maintain that each of these boxes has the definitive answer to a particular research area, but to invite critical thinking and open the door for further questions.

Critical Thinking in Your Life topics, by chapter:

Why Do Friendships End? (Chapter 1)

How Can You Evaluate Psychological Information on the Web? (Chapter 2)

What Does "It's Genetic" Mean? (Chapter 3)

(**NEW!**) Are Drivers Distracted When They Use Their Cell Phones? (Chapter 4)

(**NEW!**) What Can We Learn from "the Munchies"? (Chapter 5)

To Spank or Not to Spank? (Chapter 6)

How Can Memory Research Help You Prepare for Exams? (Chapter 7)

Can Political Experts Predict the Future? (Chapter 8)

Can You Trust Assessment on the Web? (Chapter 9)

How Does Day Care Affect Children's Development? (Chapter 10)

How Does Motivation Affect Academic Achievement? (Chapter 11)

(**NEW!**) Can Health Psychology Help You Get More Exercise? (Chapter 12)

(**NEW!**) How Is Personality Conveyed in Cyberspace? (Chapter 13)

(**NEW!**) How Do Disorders Enter *DSM?* (Chapter 14)

Does Therapy Affect Brain Activity? (Chapter 15)

How Can You Get People to Volunteer? (Chapter 16)

PSYCHOLOGY IN YOUR LIFE

The questions we cited earlier are real questions from real students, and your students will find the answers throughout the book. These questions represent data we collected from students over the years. We told them, "Tell us what you need to know about psychology," and we have placed those questions—your students' own voices—directly into the text in the form of the popular **Psychology in Your Life** sections. Our hope is that your students will see, in each instance, exactly why psychological knowledge is directly relevant to the decisions they make every day of their lives.

Psychology in Your Life topics, by chapter:

(**NEW!**) In What Ways Do Psychologists Participate in the Legal System? (Chapter 1)

Can Survey Research Affect Your Attitudes? (Chapter 2)

(**NEW!**) How Does Your Brain Determine Trust? (Chapter 3)

Why Is Eating "Hot" Food Painful? (Chapter 4)

(**NEW!**) Are You a Morning Type or an Evening Type? (Chapter 5)

How Does Classical Conditioning Affect Cancer Treatment? (Chapter 6)

Why Does Alzheimer's Disease Affect Memory? (Chapter 7)

Why and How Do People Lie? (Chapter 8)

(**NEW!**) How Can You Become More Creative? (Chapter 9)

Will Your Brain Work Differently as You Age? (Chapter 10)

(**NEW!**) How Does the Presence of Others Influence Your Eating? (Chapter 11)

(**NEW!**) Can You Accurately Predict Your Future Emotions? (Chapter 12)

Why Are Some People Shy? (Chapter 13)

How Can We Pinpoint Interactions of Nature and Nurture? (Chapter 14)

Are Lives Haunted by Repressed Memories? (Chapter 15)

(**NEW!**) In What Ways Are You Like a Chameleon? (Chapter 16)

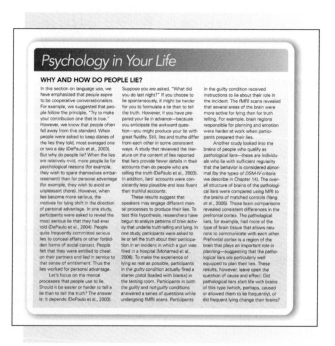

RESEARCH STUDIES

These major studies showcase the *how* and *why* behind key psychological research. These studies have been integrated into the text itself, allowing students to understand their full impact within the context of their reading. Example topics include plasticity in the visual cortex of adult rats, the impact of meditation on brain structure, the impact of culture on judgments of which category members are typical, the impact of mood on people's gullibility, individual differences in intimacy goals, family therapy for children's anxiety disorders, cross-cultural differences in cognitive dissonance, and genetic influences on physical and social aggression. Many of the nearly 140 research studies throughout the text are new or have been revised for this edition.

PEDAGOGICAL FEATURES

Psychology and Life has maintained a reputation for presenting the science of psychology in a way that is challenging, yet accessible, to a broad range of students, and the 19th edition is no exception. To enhance students' experience with the book, we include several pedagogical features:

- *Stop and Review.* This feature appears at the end of every major section and provides students with thought-provoking questions to test their mastery of material before moving on. Answers to these questions can be found in the Answer Appendix at the back of the book. For this edition, we've also included a list of valuable video clips, audio files, and simulations from MyPsychLab at the end of each Stop and Review.
- *Recapping Main Points.* Each chapter concludes with a chapter summary, *Recapping Main Points,* which summarizes the chapter content and is organized according to major section headings.
- *Key Terms.* Key terms are boldfaced in the text as they appear with their definitions at the bottom of each page and are listed, with page references, at the end of each chapter for quick review.
- *Practice Test.* Each chapter concludes with a practice test with 15 multiple choice questions based on the material in both the main text and the boxes. In addition, we've provided sample essay questions that allow students to think more broadly about the content of each chapter. Multiple choice answers can be found in the Answer Appendix, and suggested answers for the essay questions can be found in the Instructor's Manual.

DISCOVERING PSYCHOLOGY VIDEO PROGRAM

We are thrilled to be able to integrate into our textbook the wildly successful video series, *Discovering Psychology: Updated Edition,* produced by WGBH Boston with funding by Annenberg Media. Author Phil Zimbardo narrates the video series, as leading researchers, practitioners, and theorists probe the mysteries of the mind and body and bring psychology to life for introductory students. Each chapter of this textbook ends with a *Discovering Psychology* Viewing Guide that contains program review questions that draw attention to key information presented in the video.

New in the 19th Edition

In addition to the new features mentioned earlier, *Psychology and Life* is fresh with the most up-to-date coverage and brimming with over 650 new references. Our goal is to be the most current, most accurate, and most accessible treatment of our discipline today. The 19th edition of *Psychology and Life* also incorporates new research on the diversity of people's life experiences. We intend our text to have meaning for the whole range of students who enroll in introductory psychology—men and women, members of diverse cultural and racial groups, traditional and nontraditional students. Wherever possible, we have brought new research to bear on cultural issues.

CHAPTER-BY-CHAPTER CHANGES

Chapter 1

- New Psychology in Your Life: In What Ways Do Psychologists Participate in the Legal System?
- Expanded section on women as pioneering researchers
- Updated discussion on psychology's historical foundations—with more information on Plato, Aristotle, John Locke, and Immanuel Kant
- Expanded section on the cognitive perspective—with examples of Noam Chomsky and Jean Piaget

Chapter 2

- New Critical Thinking in Your Life: Why Is Skill with Numbers Important?
- New research studies:
  - "Relational uncertainty and message processing in marriage" (Knobloch et al., 2007)
  - "Memory for 'mean' over 'nice': The influence of threat on children's face memory" (Kinzler & Shutts, 2008)
  - "The face of success: Inferences from chief executive officers' appearance predict company profits" (Rule & Ambady, 2008)
- Discussion on the process of research expanded to include more information on peer review and the need to disseminate research results
- Updated research included on free will versus determinism
- Discussion of third variable added to section on correlational methods
- New discussion of Dorothy Cheney and Robert Seyfarth and their research on the social intelligence of chacma baboons
- Updated information on ethics of animal rights

Chapter 3

- New Psychology in Your Life: How Does Your Brain Determine Trust?
- New research studies:
  - "Heritability of food preferences in young children" (Breen et al., 2006)
  - "Processing nouns and verbs in the left frontal cortex: A transcranial magnetic stimulation study" (Cappelletti, et al., 2008)
- Expanded discussions on human evolution and genetics
- New discussion on glutamate

- Updated information on glial cells
- New research with EEGs explored

Chapter 4

- New Critical Thinking in Your Life: Are Drivers Distracted When They Use Their Cell Phones?
- New research studies:
  - "Domain specificity in the visual cortex" (Downing et al., 2006)
  - "Attention capture by faces" (Langton et al., 2007)
- New discussion on agnosias and simultanagnosia
- New figure on nearsightedness and farsightedness
- Reorganization of some topics for a more coherent flow of information

Chapter 5

- New Psychology in Your Life: Are You a Morning Type or an Evening Type?
- New Critical Thinking in Your Life: What Can We Learn from the "Munchies"?
- New research studies:
  - "Dare to compare: Fact-based versus simulation-based comparison in daily life" (Summerville & Roese, 2007)
  - "Focused analgesia in waking and hypnosis: Effects on pain, memory, and somatosensory event-related potentials" (De Pascalis et al., 2008)
  - "Acute disinhibiting effects of alcohol as a factor in risky driving behavior" (Fillmore et al., 2008)
- New research investigating the cortical thickness in brains as people grow older (2007)
- Expanded section on unattended information and the cocktail party phenomenon
- Updated sections on moral reasoning, nightmares, and night terrors
- Expanded section on the consequences of sleep deprivation
- Updates made to discussions of cannabinoids, OxyContin, depressants, alcohol, methamphetamine, and MDMA

Chapter 6

- Updated research added to Critical Thinking in Your Life: To Spank or Not to Spank?
- New research study: "Flavor preferences produced by backward pairing with wheel running" (Hughes & Boakes, 2008)
- Updated discussion on comparative cognition
- New information on how certain species of birds use cognitive maps

Chapter 7

- Updated research added to Psychology in Your Life: Why Does Alzheimer's Disease Affect Memory?
- New research studies:
  - "For whom the mind wanders, and when: An experience-sampling study of working memory and executive control in daily life" (Kane et al., 2007)
  - "Language contexts guides memory content" (Marian & Kaushanskaya, 2007)
  - "Do you remember proposing to the Pepsi machine? False recollections from a campus walk" (Seamon et al., 2006)
  - "Flashbulb memories are special after all; in phenomenology, not accuracy" (Talarico & Rubin, 2003)

- "'With a little help from my friends . . .': The role of co-witness relationship in susceptibility to misinformation" (Hope et al., 2008)
  - "Implicit memory for novel conceptual associations in amnesia" (Verfaellie et al., 2006)
  - "The spatiotemporal dynamics of autobiographical memory: Neural correlates of recall, emotional intensity, and reliving" (Daselaar et al., 2008)
- New research identifying the specific brain regions that are activated when new memories are formed (Hasson et al., 2008)
- Expanded section on using memory recognitions
- Expanded section on memory disorders

Chapter 8

- New research studies:
  - "Lexical ambiguity in sentence comprehension" (Mason & Just, 2007)
  - "Representational flexibility and specificity following spatial descriptions of real-world environments" (Brunyé et al., 2008)
  - "Framing, intentions, and trust-choice incompatibility" (Keren, 2007)
- New research examining the extent to which members of other species are able to understand the relationship between where people focus their attention and what they can see (Okamoto-Barth et al, 2007)
- New research on linguistic relativity (Kousta et al., 2008)
- Updates made to section on belief-bias effect
- Updated discussion of Heuristics and Judgment

Chapter 9

- New Psychology in Your Life: How Can You Become More Creative?
- New research studies:
  - "Individual differences in attitudes relevant to juror decision making" (Leci & Myers, 2008)
  - "Emotional intelligence and individual performance: Evidence of direct and moderated effects" (Rode et al., 2007)
  - "Longitudinal genetic study of verbal and nonverbal IQ from early childhood to young adulthood" (Hoekstra et al., 2007)
  - "Becoming American: Stereotype threat effects in Afro-Carribbean immigrant groups" (Deaux et al., 2007)
  - "Discernment and creativity: How well can people identify their most creative ideas?" (Silvia, 2008)
- Expanded section on using memory recognitions
- New research cited in section on encoding specifity (Mishra & Backlin, 2007)

Chapter 10

- Updated research in Critical Thinking in Your Life: How Does Day Care Affect Children's Development?
- New research studies:
  - "Age and flexible thinking: An experimental demonstration of the beneficial effects of increased cognitively stimulating activity on fluid intelligence in healthy older adults" (Tranter & Koutstaal, 2008)
  - "A comparison of high- and low-distress marriages that end in divorce" (Amato & Hohmann-Marriott, 2007)

- "Developmental trajectories of sex-typed behavior in boys and girls: A longitudinal general population study of children aged 2.5–8 years" (Golombok et al., 2008)
- "Moral development in a violent society: Colombian children's judgments in the context of survival and revenge" (Posada & Wainryb, 2008)
- Reworked section on physical development in the womb
- Added information on how adolescents tend to engage in risky behavior
- New research on infant cognition (Hamlin et al., 2008)
- New research determining what older adults might do to minimize declines with age ("use it or lose it") (Bielak et al., 2007)
- Updated discussion on how children's early attachment styles predict later behavior and how parenting styles have an impact on children's attachment relationships
- Expanded discussion on "storm and stress" in adolescent development
- Updated discussion on intimacy, including new data on societal support of heterosexual and homosexual couples
- Expanded section on the evolutionary perspective of moral development
- Expanded discussion of gender and cultural perspectives on moral reasoning

Chapter 11

- New Psychology in Your Life: How Does the Presence of Others Influence Your Eating?
- New research studies:
  - "Brains of anorexia nervosa patients process self-images differently from non-self-images: An fMRI study" (Sachdev et al., 2008)
  - "A question of belonging: Race, social fit, and achievement" (Walton & Cohen, 2007)
- Expanded discussion on drives and incentives
- Updated discussion on obesity, including genetic mechanisms that may predispose some individuals to obesity (Farooqi & Rahilly, 2007)
- New discussion on binge eating disorder
- New research on genetic factors causing eating disorders
- Updated discussion on gender and cultural difference in eating disorders
- New research on sexual practices of college students
- Updated research on brain differences between homosexuals and heterosexuals (Savic & Lindström, 2008)

Chapter 12

- New Psychology in Your Life: Can You Accurately Predict Your Future Emotions?
- Updated research in Critical Thinking in Your Life: Can Health Psychology Help You Get More Exercise?
- New research studies:
  - "Do infants show distinct negative facial expressions for fear and anger? Emotional expression in 11-month-old European American, Chinese, and Japanese infants" (Camras et al., 2007)
  - "On being happy and gullible: Mood effects on skepticism and detection of deception" (Forgas & East, 2008)
  - "The role of positive and negative emotions in life satisfaction judgment across nations" (Kuppens et al., 2008)
  - "Lending a hand: Social regulation of the neural response to threat" (Coan et al., 2006)

- "Patient and physician attitudes in the health-care context: Attitudinal symmetry predicts patient satisfaction and adherence" (Cvengros et al., 2007)
- Expanded section on positive psychology
- New research on how life events may affect subjective well-being
- Updates made to Social Readjustment Rating Scale (SRRS)
- New research on how daily hassles may be balanced out by daily positive experiences (Jain et al., 2007)
- New research examining the ways in which women cope with the stress of undergoing surgery for breast cancer (Roussi et al., 2007)
- New research exploring the heritability of why people start smoking (Boardman et al., 2008)
- New research on optimism and immune function (Segerstrom, 2006, 2007)

Chapter 13

- New Critical Thinking in Your Life: How Is Personality Conveyed in Cyberspace?
- New research studies:
  - "Genetic and environmental influences on positive traits of the values in action classification, and biometric covariance with normal personality" (Steger et al., 2007)
  - "Verbal intelligence and self-regulatory competencies: Joint predictors of boys' aggression" (Ayduk et al., 2007)
  - "Using past performance, proxy efficacy, and academic self-efficacy to predict college performance" (Elias & MacDonald, 2007)
  - "She works hard for the money: Valuing effort underlies gender differences in behavioral self-handicapping" (McCrae et al., 2008)
- Extended section on evolutionary perspectives on trait dimensions, with updated research
- New discussion of Rotter's Expectancy Theory
- Updated research on self-esteem
- New information on the MMPI-2-RF

Chapter 14

- New Critical Thinking in Your Life: How Do Disorders Enter the *DSM*?
- New research studies:
  - "Time course of selective attention in clinically depressed young adults: An eye tracking study" (Kellough et al., 2008)
  - "When does the gender difference in rumination begin? Gender and age differences in the use of rumination by adolescents" (Jose & Brown, 2008)
  - "fMRI in patients with motor conversion symptoms and controls with simulated weakness" (Stone, et al., 2007)
  - "Life events and high-trait reactivity together predict psychotic symptom increases in schizophrenia" (Docherty et al., 2008)
- Section on the concept of insanity added
- Updated section on the biological causes of anxiety disorders
- Updated discussion of gender differences in depression
- Updated section on causes of dissociative disorders
- Gender differences in ADHD explored

Chapter 15

- Updated research in Psychology in Your Life: Are Lives Haunted by Repressed Memories?

- Updated research in Critical Thinking in Your Life: Does Therapy Affect Brain Activity?
- New research studies:
  - "Virtual reality exposure therapy and standard (in vivo) exposure therapy in the treatment of fear of flying" (Rothbaum et al., 2006)
  - "A randomized, controlled trial of group cognitive-behavioral therapy for compulsive buying disorder: Posttreatment and 6-month follow-up results" (Mueller et al., 2008)
- New section on diversity issues in psychotherapy
- New research on how exposure therapy has also been used to combat obsessive-compulsive disorder
- Additional updated research on cognitive behavior therapy, including a study on how it was used to treat women with binge eating disorder (Cassin et al., 2008)
- New discussion on the debate on individuals who take antidepressant drugs and a greater risk for suicide
- Mention of a recent study that evaluated the effectiveness of a cingulotomy (Shields et al., 2008)

Chapter 16

- Two social psychology chapters merged into one chapter for the 19th edition
- New Psychology in Your Life: In What Ways Are You Like a Chameleon?
- New research studies:
  - "Going for the gold: Models of agency in Japanese and American contexts" (Markus et al., 2006)
  - "Attributions, deception, and event-related potentials: An investigation of self-serving bias" (Krusemark et al., 2008)
  - "Asking questions changes behavior: Mere measurement effects on frequency of blood donation" (Godin et al., 2008)
  - "Biased assimilation and attitude polarization in response to learning about biological explanations of homosexuality" (Boysen & Vogel, 2007)
  - "Kinship and altruism: A cross-cultural experimental study" (Madsen et al., 2007)
- Expanded discussion on the long-term consequences of the Stanford Prison Experiment
- New research that examined the types of messages that work most effectively to bring about reductions in people's energy consumption (Nolan et al., 2007)
- New section on suicide cults
- New research showing the elaboration likelihood model suggests that you'll often need to expend some effort to avoid being persuaded (Burkley, 2008)

The *Psychology and Life* Teaching and Learning Program

A good textbook is only one part of the package of educational materials that makes an introductory psychology course valuable for students and effective for instructors. To make the difficult task of teaching introductory psychology easier for you and more interesting for your students, we have prepared a number of valuable ancillary materials in both electronic and print form.

The **Instructor's Manual** (**ISBN** 0-205-75720-0), authored by David Ward (Arkansas Tech University), gives you unparalleled access to a huge selection of classroom-proven assets. First-time instructors will appreciate the detailed introduction to teaching the introductory psychology course, with suggestions for preparing for the course, sample syllabi, and current trends and strategies for successful teaching. Each chapter offers integrated teaching outlines to help instructors seamlessly incorporate all the ancillary materials for this book into their lectures. Instructors will also find an extensive bank of lecture launchers, handouts, activities, crossword puzzles, suggestions for integrating third-party videos and web resources, and cross-references to transparencies and the hundreds of multimedia and video assets found in the MyPsychLab course.

The **Test Bank** (**ISBN** 0-205-75721-9), authored by Jacqueline Hess (University of Indianapolis), contains, for each chapter, 100 multiple-choice questions, some of which address myths or factoids from the text, along with 20 true/false questions and 5 to 10 fill-in-the-blank questions. Each multiple choice question has an answer justification, and all questions include a page reference, a difficulty rating (easy/medium/difficult), and skill type (conceptual/factual/analytical). Essay questions and MyPsychLab questions, which deal specifically with critical thinking skills, have also been included, along with sample answers for each. A secondary Test Bank authored by Fred Whitford of Montana State University includes item analysis data based on actual student performance on test items.

The test bank is available in a computerized format called **Pearson MyTest** (**ISBN** 0-205-75015-X). It is a powerful assessment generation program that helps instructors easily create and print quizzes and exams. Questions and tests can be authored online, allowing instructors ultimate flexibility and the ability to efficiently manage assessments anytime, anywhere. Instructors can easily access existing questions, edit, create, and store using simple drag and drop and Word-like controls. Data on each question provide information on difficulty level and page number. For more information, go to www.PearsonMyTest.com

We are pleased to offer a unique and comprehensive collection of PowerPoint presentations for use in your classroom. The PowerPoints are available for download at the Instructor's Resource Center (www.pearsoned.com/IRC) or on the Instructor's

Resource DVD. **A PowerPoint lecture presentation** by Brian Malley (University of Michigan) highlights major topics from the chapter, pairing them with select art images. A **PowerPoint collection of the complete art files** from the text allows customized lectures with any of the figures from the text. Finally, Pearson has developed a set of **interactive PowerPoints** (available only on the Instructor's Resource DVD) with embedded animations, videos and activities, authored by Derek Borman of Mesa Community College in Arizona. Many of the slides include layered art, allowing instructors the ability to highlight specific aspects of a figure, such as identifying each part of the brain.

For instructors using **Clicker student response systems** in their classroom, we offer a collection of text-specific lecture questions for each chapter of the book. These questions can be used to evaluate students' knowledge of material or to enhance classroom discussions. Many of the clicker questions address specific critical thinking skills from the textbook.

Discovering Psychology Telecourse Videos

Written, designed, and hosted by Philip Zimbardo, this set of 26 half-hour videos is available for class use from the Annenberg/CPB collection. The collection includes two completely new programs and more than 15 new sequences that bring students up to date on some of the latest developments in the field. A perfect complement to *Psychology and Life*, this course supplement has won numerous prizes and is widely used in the United States and internationally. Videos are distributed by Annenberg Media at www.learner.org.

Discovering Psychology Telecourse Faculty Guide
(**ISBN** 0205757073)

The Telecourse Faculty Guide provides guidelines for using *Discovering Psychology* as a resource within your course. Keyed directly to *Psychology and Life*, the faculty guide includes the complete Telecourse Study Guide plus suggested activities; suggested essays; cited studies; instructional resources, including books, articles, films, and websites; video program test questions with answer key; textbook test questions with answer key; and a key term glossary.

Discovering Psychology Telecourse Study Guide
(**ISBN** 0205757081)

In this Telecourse Study Guide, each chapter corresponds to one program, expands on the material covered in the program, specifies appropriate reading assignments, and reviews material covered in the text. In addition, the study guide includes learning objectives; reading assignments; key people and terms; video program summaries and test questions with answer key; textbook test questions with answer key; essay questions; student activities; additional book, article, and film resources; and annotated websites. All vocabulary and review questions are keyed to *Psychology and Life*.

SAVE TIME. IMPROVE RESULTS. PUT SCIENTIFIC THINKING TO THE TEST.

Across the country, from small community colleges to large public universities, a trend is emerging. Introductory psychol-ogy enrollments are increasing, and available resources can't keep pace; in some instances, they are even decreasing. The result is instructor time stretched to its limit like never before. At the same time, continual feedback is an important component to successful student progress. The APA strongly recommends student self-assessment tools and the use of embedded questions and assignments (see http://www.apa.org/ed/eval_strategies.html for more information). In response to these demands Pearson's MyPsychLab (MPL) offers students useful and engaging self-assessment tools and instructors flexibility in assessing and tracking student progress.

WHAT IS MYPSYCHLAB?

MyPsychLab is a learning and assessment tool that enables instructors to assess student performance and adapt course content—without investing additional time or resources.

MyPsychLab includes:

- An interactive eBook that allows students to highlight text and instructors to post their own notes for students to read.

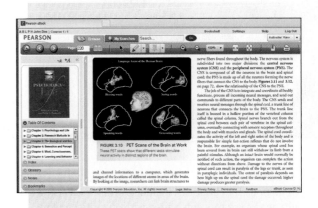

- Customized student Study Plans dynamically generated when students complete the available practice quizzes. Practice quizzes include questions specifically designed to assess students understanding of and ability to use the scientific thinking questions.

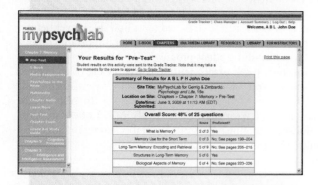

- An interactive time line tool that presents the history of psychology.

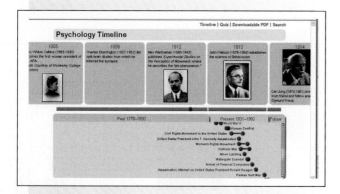

- Interactive mobile-ready flash cards of the key terms from the text—students can build their own stacks, print the cards, or export their flashcards to their cell phone.

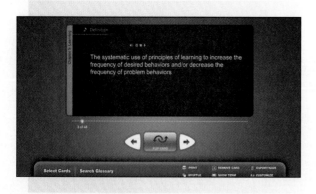

- A Multimedia Library with links to over 200 video clips, animations, and podcasts. Included within each chapter are specific key concepts paired with scientific thinking activities.
- Within each chapter, a **Psychology in the News** activity presents students with a real news story and then asks students to use the six scientific thinking questions to critically about the claims introduced in the story.

- Audio podcasts present a hot topic in the field of psychology and use the scientific thinking framework to critically evaluate the issues.
- A Gradebook for instructors and the availability of full course management capabilities for instructors teaching online or hybrid courses.

Unlimited use of Pearson's MySearchLab™—the easiest way for students to start a research assignment. Complete with extensive help on the research process and four exclusive databases of credible and reliable source material, including the EBSCO Academic Journal and Abstract Database, the New York Times Search by Subject Archive, "Best of the Web" Link Library, and Financial Times Article Archive and Company Financial, MySearchLab helps students quickly and efficiently make the most of their research time.

ASSESSMENT AND ABILITY TO ADAPT

MyPsychLab is designed with instructor flexibility in mind—you decide the extent of integration into your course—from independent self-assessment for students to total course management. By transferring faculty members' most time-consuming tasks—content delivery, student assessment, and grading—to automated tools, MyPsychLab enables faculty to spend more quality time with students. For sample syllabi with ideas on incorporating MPL, see the Instructor's Manual as well as on-line at www.mypsychlab.com.

Instructors are provided with the results of the diagnostic tests—by student as well as an aggregate report of their class.

For more information on MyPsychLab go to www.mypsychlab.com

ADDITIONAL SUPPLEMENTS FOR YOUR INTRODUCTORY PSYCHOLOGY COURSE:

- **Allyn and Bacon Transparencies for Introductory Psychology** (**ISBN:** 0205398626) This set of approximately 200 revised, full-color acetates will enhance classroom lecture and discussion. It includes images from Allyn and Bacon's major introductory psychology texts.
- **Pearson Teaching Films: Introductory Psychology, Instructor's Library** (**ISBN:** 0-13-175432-7) This five-disk DVD series includes 82 segments covering all of the major topics in introductory psychology. All of the segments have been selected from ABC News, Films for Humanities & Sciences, Pearson Education's own assets, and ScienCentral.
- **Pearson Teaching Films: Introductory Psychology, Instructor's Library** ©*2008 UPDATE* (**ISBN:** 0-205-65280-8) This update to the five-disk DVD series offers a fresh new set of video to illustrate key points and enhance your lectures. In particular, this DVD offers some new segments addressing science versus pseudoscience!
- **Insights into Psychology II** (**ISBN II:** 0205402909) **and III** (**ISBN III:** 0205472990) These video programs include two or three short clips per topic, covering such

topics as animal research, parapsychology, health and stress, Alzheimer's disease, bilingual education, genetics and IQ, and much more. A Video Guide containing critical thinking questions accompanies each video and is also available on DVD.

- **STUDY CARD FOR INTRODUCTORY PSYCHOLOGY** (**ISBN:** 0205-43509-2) Colorful, affordable, and packed with useful information, Allyn & Bacon/Longman's Study Cards make studying easier, more efficient, and more enjoyable. Course information is distilled down to the basics, helping students quickly master the fundamentals, review a subject for understanding, or prepare for an exam.
- **THE BLOCKBUSTER APPROACH: A GUIDE TO TEACHING INTRODUCTORY PSYCHOLOGY WITH VIDEO** (**ISBN:** 0-205-47300-8) The Blockbuster Approach is a unique print resource for instructors who enjoy enhancing their classroom presentations with film. With heavy coverage of general, abnormal, social, and developmental psychology, this guide suggests a wide range of films to use in class and provides questions for reflection and other pedagogical tools to make the use of film more effective in the classroom.

ACCESSING ALL RESOURCES:

For a list of all student resources available with *Psychology and Life,* go to www.mypearsonstore.com, enter the text ISBN (0-205-68591-9), and check out the "Everything That Goes with It" section under the book cover.

For access to all instructor supplements for Gerrig/Zimbardo, *Psychology and Life,* **simply go to** http://pearsonhighered.com/irc and follow the directions to register (or log in if you already have a Pearson user name and password).

Once you have registered and your status as an instructor is verified, you will be e-mailed a login name and password. Use your login name and password to gain access to the catalogue. Click on the "online catalogue" link, click on "psychology" followed by "introductory psychology" and then the Gerrig/Zimbardo, *Psychology and Life* text. Under the description of each supplement is a link that allows you to download and save the supplement to your desktop.

For technical support for any of your Pearson products, you and your students can contact http://247.pearsoned.com.

Personal Acknowledgments

Although the Beatles may have gotten by with a little help from their friends, we have survived the revision and production of this edition of *Psychology and Life* only with a great deal of help from many colleagues and friends. We especially thank Brenda Anderson, Stephanie Anderson, Sara Bufferd, Edward Carr, Turhan Canli, Joanne Davila, Anna Floyd, Tony Freitas, Greg Hajcak, Helene Intraub, Paul Kaplan, Sheri Levy, Anne Moyer, Timothy Peterson, Suparna Rajaram, John Robinson, Arthur Samuel, Trish Van Zandt, and Patricia Whitaker.

We would like to thank the following reviewers of both this edition and previous ones, who read drafts of the manuscript and provided valuable feedback:

Debra Ainbinder, Lynn University
Robert M. Arkin, Ohio State University
Trey Asbury, Campbell University
Gordon Atlas, Alfred University
Lori L. Badura, State University of
    New York at Buffalo
David Barkmeier, Northeastern University
Tanner Bateman, Virginia Tech
Darryl K. Beale, Cerritos College
N. Jay Bean, Vassar College
Susan Hart Bell, Georgetown College
Danny Benbassat, George Washington University
Sarah A. Burnett, Rice University
Michael Bloch, University of San Francisco
Richard Bowen, Loyola University
Mike Boyes, University of Calgary
Wayne Briner, University of Nebraska at Kearney
D. Cody Brooks, Denison University
Brad J. Bushman, Iowa State University
Jennifer L. Butler, Case Western Reserve University
James Calhoun, University of Georgia
Timothy Cannon, University of Scranton
John Caruso, University of Massachusetts,
    Dartmouth
Marc Carter, Hofstra University
Dennis Cogan, Texas Tech University
Sheree Dukes Conrad, University of
    Massachusetts, Boston
Randolph R. Cornelius, Vassar College
Leslie D. Cramblet, Northern Arizona University
Catherine E. Creeley, University of Missouri
Lawrence Dachowski, Tulane University
Mark Dombeck, Idaho State University
Dale Doty, Monroe Community College
Victor Duarte, North Idaho College
Tami Egglesten, McKendree College
Kenneth Elliott, University of Maine at Augusta
Matthew Erdelyi, Brooklyn College, CUNY
Michael Faber, University of New Hampshire
Valeri Farmer-Dougan, Illinois State University
Trudi Feinstein, Boston University
Mark B. Fineman, Southern Connecticut
    State University
Diane Finley, Prince George Community College
Kathleen A. Flannery, Saint Anselm College
Lisa Fournier, Washington State University
Traci Fraley, College of Charleston
Rita Frank, Virginia Wesleyan College
Eugene H. Galluscio, Clemson University
Preston E. Garraghty, Indiana University
Adam Goodie, University of Georgia
Peter Gram, Pensacola Junior College
Jeremy Gray, Yale University
W. Lawrence Gulick, University of Delaware
Pryor Hale, Piedmont Virginia Community College
Rebecca Hellams, Southeast Community College
Jacqueline L. Hess, University of Indianapolis
Dong Hodge, Dyersburg State Community College

Mark Hoyert, Indiana University Northwest
Herman Huber, College of St. Elizabeth
Richard A. Hudiburg, University of North Alabama
James D. Jackson, Lehigh University
Stanley J. Jackson, Westfield State College
Matthew Johnson, University of Vermont
Seth Kalichman, Georgia State University
Mark Kline, Indiana University
Stephen La Berge, Stanford University
Andrea L. Lassiter, Minnesota State University
Mark Laumakis, San Diego State University
Charles F. Levinthal, Hofstra University
Suzanne B. Lovett, Bowdoin College
Tracy Luster, Mount San Jacinto College
M. Kimberley Maclin, University of Northern Iowa
Gregory G. Manley, University of Texas
    at San Antonio
Leonard S. Mark, Miami University
Michael R. Markham, Florida International University
Karen Marsh, University of Minnesota, Duluth
Kathleen Martynowicz, Colorado Northwestern
    Community College
Lori Metcalf, Gatson College
Michael McCall, Ithaca College
Mary McCaslin, University of Arizona
David McDonald, University of Missouri
Greg L. Miller, Stanford University
    School of Medicine
Karl Minke, University of Hawaii–Honolulu
Charles D. Miron, Catonsville
    Community College
J. L. Motrin, University of Guelph
Anne Moyer, Stony Brook University
Eric S. Murphy, University of Alaska
William Pavot, Southwest State University
Amy R. Pearce, Arkansas State University
Kelly Elizabeth Pelzel, University of Utah
Linda Perrotti, University of Texas at Arlington
Brady J. Phelps, South Dakota State University
Gregory R. Pierce, Hamilton College
William J. Pizzi, Northeastern Illinois University

Mark Plonsky, University of Wisconsin–Stevens Point
Bret Roark, Oklahoma Baptist University
Cheryl A. Rickabaugh, University of Redlands
Rich Robbins, Washburn University
Daniel N. Robinson, Georgetown University
Michael Root, Ohio University
Nicole Ruffin, Hampton University
Bernadette Sanchez, DePaul University
Patrick Saxe, State University of New York at New Paltz
Mary Schild, Columbus State University
Elizabeth Sherwin, University of Arkansas,
    Little Rock
Norman R. Simonsen, University of
    Massachusetts, Amherst
Peggy Skinner, South Plains College
R. H. Starr, Jr., University of Maryland–Baltimore
Walter Swap, Tufts University
Priscilla Stillwell, Black River Technical College
Charles Strong, Northwest Mississippi
    Community College
Jennifer Trich Kremer, Pennsylvania State University
Jeffrey Wagman, Illinois State University
David Ward, Arkansas Tech University
Douglas Wardell, University of Alberta
Linda Weldon, Essex Community College
Alan J. Whitlock, University of Idaho
Paul Whitney, Washington State University
Allen Wolach, Illinois Institute of Technology
John W. Wright, Washington State University
Jim Zacks, Michigan State University

The enormous task of writing a book of this scope was possible only with the expert assistance of all these friends and colleagues and that of the editorial staff of Allyn & Bacon. We gratefully acknowledge their invaluable contributions at every stage of this project, collectively and, now, individually. We thank the following people at Allyn & Bacon: Stephen Frail, Executive Editor; Deb Hanlon, Development Editor; Kara Kikel, Supplements Editor; Jeanette Koskinas, Senior Marketing Manager, Psychology; Roberta Sherman, Production Editor; Susan McNally, Project Manager; and Kate Cebik, Photo Researcher.

PSYCHOLOGY AND LIFE

Psychology and Life

1

Why should you study psychology? Our answer to that question is quite straightforward: We believe that psychological research has immediate and crucial applications to important issues of everyday experience: your physical and mental health, your ability to form and sustain close relationships, and your capacity for learning and personal growth. One of the foremost goals of *Psychology and Life* is to highlight the personal relevance and social significance of psychological expertise.

Every semester when we begin to teach, we are faced with students who enter an introductory psychology class with some very specific questions in mind. Sometimes those questions emerge from their own experience ("What should I do if I think my mother is mentally ill?" "Will this course teach me how to improve my grades?"); sometimes those questions emerge from the type of psychological information that is communicated through the media ("Do people experience more health problems in tough economic times?" "Is it possible to tell when people are lying?") The challenge for us as we teach the course is to bring the products of scientific research to bear on questions that matter to you.

Research in psychology provides a continuous stream of new information about the basic mechanisms that govern mental and behavioral processes. As new ideas replace or modify old ideas, we are continually intrigued and challenged by the many fascinating pieces of the puzzle of human nature. We hope that, by the end of this journey through psychology, you too will cherish your store of psychological knowledge.

Foremost in the journey will be a scientific quest for understanding. We will inquire about the how, what, when, and why of human behavior and about the causes and consequences of behaviors you observe in yourself, in other people, and in animals. We will explain why you think, feel, and behave as you do. What makes you uniquely different from all other people? Yet why do you often behave so much like others? Are you molded by heredity, or are you shaped more by personal experiences? How can aggression and altruism, love and hate, and mental illness and creativity exist side by side in this complex creature—the human animal? In this opening chapter, we consider how and why all these types of questions have become relevant to psychology's goals as a discipline.

What Makes Psychology Unique?

To appreciate the uniqueness and unity of psychology, you must consider the way psychologists define the field and the goals they bring to their research and applications. By the end of the text, we hope you will think like a psychologist. In this first section, we'll give you a strong idea of what that might mean.

---

psychology The scientific study of the behavior of individuals and their mental processes.

scientific method The set of procedures used for gathering and interpreting objective information in a way that minimizes error and yields dependable generalizations.

behavior The actions by which an organism adjusts to its environment.

DEFINITIONS

Many psychologists seek answers to this fundamental question: What is human nature? Psychology answers this question by looking at processes that occur within individuals as well as forces that arise within the physical and social environment. In this light, we formally define **psychology** as the scientific study of the behavior of individuals and their mental processes. Let's explore the critical parts of this definition: *scientific, behavior, individual,* and *mental.*

The scientific aspect of psychology requires that psychological conclusions be based on evidence collected according to the principles of the scientific method. The **scientific method** consists of a set of orderly steps used to analyze and solve problems. This method uses objectively collected information as the factual basis for drawing conclusions. We will elaborate on the features of the scientific method more fully in Chapter 2, when we consider how psychologists conduct their research.

Behavior is the means by which organisms adjust to their environment. Behavior is action. The subject matter of psychology largely consists of the observable behavior of humans and other species of animals. Smiling, crying, running, hitting, talking, and touching are some obvious examples of behavior you can observe. Psychologists examine what the individual does and how the individual goes about doing it within a given behavioral setting and in the broader social or cultural context.

The subject of psychological analysis is most often an *individual*—a newborn infant, a teenage athlete, a college student adjusting to life in a dormitory, a man facing a midlife career change, or a woman coping with the stress of her husband's deterioration from Alzheimer's disease. However, the subject might also be a chimpanzee learning to use symbols to communicate, a white rat navigating a maze, or a sea slug responding to a danger signal. An individual might be studied in its natural habitat or in the controlled conditions of a research laboratory.

Many researchers in psychology also recognize that they cannot understand human actions without also understanding *mental processes,* the workings of the human mind. Much human activity takes place as private, internal events—thinking, planning, reasoning, creating, and dreaming. Many psychologists believe that mental processes represent the most important aspect of psychological inquiry. As you shall soon see, psychological investigators have devised ingenious techniques to study mental events and processes—to make these private experiences public.

The combination of these concerns defines psychology as a unique field. Within the *social sciences,* psychologists focus largely on the behavior of individuals in various settings, whereas sociologists study social behavior of groups or institutions, and anthropologists focus on the broader context of behavior in different cultures. Even so, psychologists draw broadly from the insights of other scholars. Psychologists share many interests with researchers in *biological sciences,* especially with those who study brain processes and the biochemical bases of behavior. As part of *cognitive science,* psychologists' questions about how the human mind works are related to research and theory in computer science, philosophy, linguistics, and neuroscience. As a *health science*—with links to medicine, education, law, and environmental studies—psychology seeks to improve the quality of each individual's and the collective's well-being.

Most psychological study focuses on individuals—usually human ones, but sometimes those of other species. Is there anything happening in your life that might make you want to conduct a research study?

Although the remarkable breadth and depth of modern psychology are a source of delight to those who become psychologists, these same attributes make the field a challenge to the student exploring it for the first time. There is so much more to the study of psychology than you might expect initially—and, because of that, there will also be much of value that you can take away from this introduction to psychology. The best way to learn about the field is to learn to share psychologists' goals. Let's consider those goals.

THE GOALS OF PSYCHOLOGY

The goals of the psychologist conducting basic research are to describe, explain, predict, and control behavior. These goals form the basis of the psychological enterprise. What is involved in trying to achieve each of them?

Describing What Happens The first task in psychology is to make accurate observations about behavior. Psychologists typically refer to such observations as their *data* (*data* is the plural, *datum* the singular). **Behavioral data** are reports of observations about the behavior of organisms and the conditions under which the behavior occurs. When researchers undertake data collection, they must choose an appropriate *level of analysis* and devise measures of behavior that ensure *objectivity*.

In order to investigate an individual's behavior, researchers may use different *levels of analysis*—from the broadest, most

global level down to the most minute, specific level. Suppose, for example, you were trying to describe a painting you saw at a museum (see **Figure 1.1** on page 4). At a global level, you might describe it by title, *Bathers,* and by artist, Georges Seurat. At a more specific level, you might recount features of the painting: Some people are sunning themselves on a riverbank while others are enjoying the water, and so on. At a very specific level, you might describe the technique Seurat used—tiny points of paint—to create the scene. The description at each level would answer different questions about the painting.

Different levels of psychological description also address different questions. At the broadest level of psychological analysis, researchers investigate the behavior of the whole person within complex social and cultural contexts. At this level, researchers might study cross-cultural differences in violence, the origins of prejudice, and the consequences of mental illness. At the next level, psychologists focus on narrower, finer units of behavior, such as speed of reaction to a stop light, eye movements during reading, and grammatical errors made by children acquiring language. Researchers can study even smaller units of behavior. They might work to discover the biological bases of behavior by identifying the places in the brain where different types of memories are stored, the biochemical changes

---

behavioral data Observational reports about the behavior of organisms and the conditions under which the behavior occurs or changes.

FIGURE 1.1 Levels of Analysis
Suppose you wanted a friend to meet you in front of this painting. How would you describe it? Suppose your friend wanted to make an exact copy of the painting. How would you describe it?

that occur during learning, and the sensory paths responsible for vision or hearing. Each level of analysis yields information essential to the final composite portrait of human nature that psychologists hope ultimately to develop.

However tight or broad the focus of the observation, psychologists strive to describe behavior *objectively*. Collecting the facts as they exist, and not as the researcher expects or hopes them to be, is of utmost importance. Because every observer brings to each observation his or her *subjective* point of view—biases, prejudices, and expectations—it is essential to prevent these personal factors from creeping in and distorting the data. As you will see in the next chapter, psychological researchers have developed a variety of techniques to maintain objectivity.

Explaining What Happens Whereas *descriptions* must stick to perceivable information, *explanations* deliberately go beyond what can be observed. In many areas of psychology, the central goal is to find regular patterns in behavioral and mental processes. Psychologists want to discover *how* behavior works. Why do you laugh at situations that differ from your expectations of what is coming next? What conditions could lead someone to attempt suicide or commit rape?

Explanations in psychology usually recognize that most behavior is influenced by a combination of factors. Some factors operate within the individual, such as genetic makeup, motivation, intelligence level, or self-esteem. These inner determinants tell something special about the organism. Other factors, however, operate externally. Suppose, for example, that a child tries to please a teacher to win a prize or that a motorist trapped in a traffic jam becomes frustrated and hostile. These behaviors are largely influenced by events outside the person. When psychologists seek to explain behavior, they almost always consider both types of explanations. Suppose, for example, psychologists want to explain why some people start smoking. Researchers might examine the possibility that some individuals are particularly prone to risk taking (an internal explanation) or that some individuals experience a lot of peer pressure (an external explanation)—or that both a disposition toward risk taking and situational peer pressure are necessary (a combined explanation).

Often a psychologist's goal is to explain a wide variety of behavior in terms of one underlying cause. Consider a situation in which your professor says that, to earn a good grade, each student must participate regularly in class discussions. Your roommate, who is always well prepared for class, never raises his hand to answer questions or volunteer information. Your professor chides him for being unmotivated and assumes he is not bright. That same roommate also goes to parties but speaks only to people he knows, doesn't openly defend his point of view when it is challenged by someone less informed, and rarely engages in small talk at the dinner table. What is your diagnosis? What underlying cause might account for this range of behavior? How about *shyness?* Like many other people who suffer from intense feelings of shyness, your roommate is unable to behave in desired ways (Zimbardo & Radl, 1999). We can use the concept of shyness to explain the full pattern of your roommate's behavior.

To forge such causal explanations, researchers must often engage in a creative process of examining a diverse collection of data. Master detective Sherlock Holmes drew shrewd conclusions from scraps of evidence. In a similar fashion, every researcher must use an informed imagination, which creatively *synthesizes* what is known and what is not yet known. A well-trained psychologist can explain observations by using her or his insight into the human experience along with the facts previous researchers have uncovered about the phenomenon in question. Much psychological research is an attempt to give accurate explanations for different behavioral patterns.

Predicting What Will Happen Predictions in psychology are statements about the likelihood that a certain behavior will occur or that a given relationship will be found. Often an accurate explanation of the causes underlying some form of behavior will allow a researcher to make accurate predictions about future behavior. Thus, if we believe your roommate to be shy, we could confidently predict that he would be uncomfortable

What causes people to smoke? Can psychologists create conditions under which people will be less likely to engage in this behavior?

A psychological prediction.

broad range of circumstances in which psychologists use their knowledge to control and improve people's lives. In this respect, psychologists are a rather optimistic group; many believe that virtually any undesired behavior pattern can be modified by the proper intervention. *Psychology and Life* shares that optimism.

STOP AND REVIEW

❶ What are the four components of the definition of psychology?
❷ What four goals apply to psychologists who conduct research?
❸ Why is there often a close relationship between the goals of explanation and prediction?

Visit MyPsychLab.com for more review and practice on the following topic:

👁 **Watch:** The Complexity of Humans: Phil Zimbardo

when asked to give a speech in front of a large class. When different explanations are put forward to account for some behavior or relationship, they are usually judged by how well they can make accurate and comprehensive predictions. If your roommate was to speak happily to the class, we would be forced to rethink our diagnosis.

Just as observations must be made objectively, scientific predictions must be worded precisely enough to enable them to be tested and then rejected if the evidence does not support them. Suppose, for example, a researcher predicts that the presence of a stranger will reliably cause human and monkey babies, beyond a certain age, to respond with signs of anxiety. We might want to bring more precision to this prediction by examining the dimension of "stranger." Would fewer signs of anxiety appear in a human or a monkey baby if the stranger were also a baby rather than an adult, or if the stranger were of the same species rather than of a different one? To improve future predictions, a researcher would create systematic variations in environmental conditions and observe their influence on the baby's response.

Controlling What Happens For many psychologists, control is the central, most powerful goal. Control means making behavior happen or not happen—starting it, maintaining it, stopping it, and influencing its form, strength, or rate of occurrence. A causal explanation of behavior is convincing if it can create conditions under which the behavior can be controlled.

The ability to control behavior is important because it gives psychologists ways of helping people improve the quality of their lives. Throughout *Psychology and Life,* you will see examples of the types of *interventions* psychologists have devised to help people gain control over problematic aspects of their lives. Chapter 15, for example, discusses treatments for mental illness. We also describe how people can harness psychological forces to eliminate unhealthy behaviors like smoking and initiate healthy behaviors like regular exercise (see Chapter 12). You will learn what types of parenting practices can help parents maintain solid bonds with their children (Chapter 10); you will learn what forces make strangers reluctant to offer assistance in emergency situations and how those forces can be overcome (Chapter 16). These are just a few examples of the

The Evolution of Modern Psychology

Today, it is relatively easy to define psychology and to state the goals of psychological research. As you begin to study psychology, however, it is important to understand the many forces that led to the emergence of modern psychology. At the core of this historical review is one simple principle: *Ideas matter.* Much of the history of psychology has been characterized by heated debates about what constitutes the appropriate subject matter and methodologies for a science of mind and behavior.

Our historical review will be carried out at two levels of analysis. In the first section, we will consider the period of history in which some of the critical groundwork for modern psychology was laid down. This focus will enable you to witness at close range the battle of ideas. In the second section, we will describe in a broader fashion seven perspectives that have emerged in the modern day. For both levels of focus, you should allow yourself to imagine the intellectual passion with which the theories evolved.

PSYCHOLOGY'S HISTORICAL FOUNDATIONS

In 1908, **Hermann Ebbinghaus** (1858–1909), one of the first experimental psychologists, wrote "Psychology has a long past, but only a short history" (Ebbinghaus, 1908/1973). Scholars had long asked important questions about human nature—about how people perceive reality, the nature of consciousness, and the origins of madness—but they did not possess the means to answer them. Consider the fundamental questions posed in the fourth and fifth centuries B.C. by the classical Greek philosophers, **Plato** (427–347 B.C.) and **Aristotle** (384–322 B.C.): How does the mind work? What is the nature of free will? What is the relationship of individual citizens to their community or state? Although

Critical Thinking in Your Life

WHY DO FRIENDSHIPS END?

An important goal of *Psychology and Life* is to improve your ability to think critically about the world around you: We want to help you "reach intelligent decisions about what [you] should believe and how [you] should act" (Appleby, 2006, p. 61). Let's consider that aim with respect to a question that has often seemed urgent for the students who enroll in our classes: Why do friendships end?

Try to think back to circumstances in which a valued friendship has dissolved. Were you able to understand what had gone wrong? Psychology can provide theoretical analyses to help you understand what goes on in your life. In fact, researchers have studied the types of events that cause friendships to come to an end (Sheets & Lugar, 2005). People report such incidents as romantic competition ("she slept with my boyfriend"), disrespectful behavior ("he let his friends destroy my room"), and betrayals of confidence ("he blabbed all my secrets"). If you understand these different categories, you now have a framework to assess any tensions in your own friendships. The research provides even more specific conclusions: Among about 400 students from the midwestern United States, the most common sources of conflicts—the causes of arguments that ended friendships—were romantic competition and disrespectful behavior. Can you use this information to look more critically at the state of your friendships? This research illustrates how psychology can help you perceive and apply appropriate distinctions for your life experiences.

But there's another aspect of critical thinking you can engage here: You should try to ask yourself how broadly you should apply the information you learn. For example, we asserted that the results about friendship emerged from U.S. students from the Midwest. In this chapter, we've already identified the sociocultural perspective that prompts contemporary researchers always to be mindful of the impact of culture on research results. To assess the cross-cultural generality of their findings, the researchers collected data from a group of students in Russia. Those students collectively reported that the greatest source of conflict with their friends centered on betrayals of confidence. Why might that be the case? The researchers speculated that Russians are more sensitive to these circumstances because of "Russia's totalitarian history, during which a friend's breach of confidence could threaten one's life" (Sheets & Lugar, 2005, p. 391).

There are a couple of noteworthy implications for this cultural difference between U.S. and Russian college students. First, this result reminds you that an important component of critical thinking is to test a conclusion for its soundness and generality. In Chapter 2, we will focus on the scientific method. That discussion will give you an indication of the standards researchers must meet before we report their research in *Psychology and Life*. In addition, throughout the text we will be mindful of how important it is to consider the ways in which culture can affect basic aspects of human existence. The second implication of this difference between U.S. and Russian students refers to how you might behave toward the people around you. Most people now live and work in settings with cultural diversity. Let your education in psychology make you more sensitive to the domains in which culture does and does not matter. Remember, the goal is to have your psychological knowledge help you make more intelligent decisions with respect to your everyday experiences.

- In the study, could it matter that the U.S. sample came from the Midwest?

- What aspects of U.S. history might have an impact on the psychology of U.S. citizens?

---

forms of psychology existed in ancient Indian Yogic traditions, Western psychology traces its origin to the writings of these philosophers. Plato and Aristotle defined opposing views that continue to have an impact on contemporary thinking. Consider how people come to know about the world. On the *empiricist* view, people begin life with their mind as a blank tablet; the mind acquires information through experiences in the world. **John Locke** (1632–1704) articulated this position at length in the 17th century; its roots can be traced to Aristotle. On the *nativist* view, people begin life with mental structures that provide constraints on how they experience the world. **Immanuel Kant** (1724–1804) fully developed this position in the 18th century; its roots can be traced to Plato. (In later chapters, we revisit this theoretical debate in the form of "nature versus nurture.") Toward the end of the 19th century, psychology began to emerge as a discipline when researchers applied the laboratory techniques from other sciences—such as physiology and physics—to the study of such fundamental questions from philosophy.

A critical figure in the evolution of modern psychology was **Wilhelm Wundt,** who, in 1879 in Leipzig, Germany, founded the first formal laboratory devoted to experimental psychology. Although Wundt had been trained as a physiologist, over his research career his interest shifted from questions of body to questions of mind: He wished to understand basic processes of sensation and perception as well as the speed of simple mental processes. By the time he established his psychology laboratory, Wundt had already accomplished a range of research and published the first of several editions of *Principles of Physiological Psychology* (Kendler, 1987). Once Wundt's laboratory was established at Leipzig, he began to train the first graduate students specifically devoted to the emerging field of psychology. Those students often became founders of their own psychology laboratories around the world.

As psychology became established as a separate discipline, psychology laboratories began to appear in universities throughout North America, the first at Johns Hopkins University in 1883. These early laboratories often bore Wundt's impact. For example, after studying with Wundt, **Edward Titchener** became one of the first psychologists in the United States, founding a laboratory at Cornell University in 1892. However, at around the same time, a young Harvard philosophy professor who had studied medicine and had strong interests in literature and religion developed a uniquely American perspective. **William James,** brother of the great novelist Henry James, wrote a two-volume work, *The Principles of Psychology* (1890/1950), which many experts consider to be the most important psychology text ever written. Shortly after, in 1892, G. Stanley Hall founded the American Psychological Association. By 1900 there were more than 40 psychology laboratories in North America (Hilgard, 1986).

Almost as soon as psychology emerged, a debate arose about the proper subject matter and methods for the new discipline. This debate isolated some of the issues that still loom large in psychology. We will describe, specifically, the tension between structuralism and functionalism.

Structuralism: The Contents of the Mind Psychology's potential to make a unique contribution to knowledge became apparent when psychology became a laboratory science organized around experiments. In Wundt's laboratory, experimental participants made simple responses (saying yes or no, pressing a button) to stimuli they perceived under conditions varied by laboratory instruments. Because the data were collected through systematic, objective procedures, independent observers could replicate the results of these experiments. Emphasis on the scientific method (see Chapter 2), concern for precise measurement, and statistical analysis of data characterized Wundt's psychological tradition.

When Titchener brought Wundt's psychology to the United States, he advocated that such scientific methods be used to study consciousness. His method for examining the elements of conscious mental life was **introspection,** the systematic examination by individuals of their own thoughts and feelings about specific sensory experiences. Titchener emphasized the "what" of mental contents rather than the "why" or "how" of thinking. His approach came to be known as **structuralism,** the study of the structure of mind and behavior.

Structuralism was based on the presumption that all human mental experience could be understood as the combination of basic components. The goal of this approach was to reveal the underlying structure of the human mind by analyzing the component elements of sensation and other experiences that form an individual's mental life. Many psychologists attacked structuralism on three fronts: (1) It was *reductionistic* because it reduced all complex human experience to simple sensations; (2) it was *elemental* because it sought to combine parts, or elements, into a whole rather than study complex, or whole, behaviors directly; and (3) it was *mentalistic* because it studied only verbal reports of human conscious awareness, ignoring the study of individuals who could not describe their introspections, including animals, children, and the mentally disturbed.

One important alternative to structuralism, pioneered by the German psychologist **Max Wertheimer,** focused on the way in which the mind understands many experiences as *gestalts*—organized wholes—rather than as the sums of simple parts: Your experience of a painting, for example, is more than the sum of the individual daubs of paint. As we will see in Chapter 4, **Gestalt psychology** continues to have an impact on the study of perception.

A second major opposition to structuralism came under the banner of *functionalism.*

Functionalism: Minds with a Purpose William James agreed with Titchener that consciousness was central to the study of psychology; but, for James, the study of consciousness was not reduced to elements, contents, and structures. Instead, consciousness was an ongoing stream, a property of mind in continual interaction with the environment. Human consciousness facilitated one's adjustment to the environment; thus the acts and functions of mental processes were of significance, not the contents of the mind.

Functionalism gave primary importance to learned habits that enable organisms to adapt to their environment and to

In 1879, Wilhelm Wundt founded the first formal laboratory devoted to experimental psychology. Suppose you decided to found your own psychology laboratory. What one area in your life would you study if you could?

---

introspection Individuals' systematic examination of their own thoughts and feelings.

structuralism The study of the structure of mind and behavior; the view that all human mental experience can be understood as a combination of simple elements or events.

Gestalt psychology A school of psychology that maintains that psychological phenomena can be understood only when viewed as organized, structured wholes, not when broken down into primitive perceptual elements.

functionalism The perspective on mind and behavior that focuses on the examination of their functions in an organism's interactions with the environment.

function effectively. For functionalists, the key question to be answered by research was "What is the function or purpose of any behavioral act?" The founder of the school of functionalism was the American philosopher **John Dewey.** His concern for the practical uses of mental processes led to important advances in education. Dewey's theorizing provided the impetus for *progressive education* in his own laboratory school and more generally in the United States: "Rote learning was abandoned in favor of learning by doing, in expectation that intellectual curiosity would be encouraged and understanding would be enhanced" (Kendler, 1987, p. 124).

Although James believed in careful observation, he put little value on the rigorous laboratory methods of Wundt. In James's psychology, there was a place for emotions, self, will, values, and even religious and mystical experience. His "warm-blooded" psychology recognized a uniqueness in each individual that could not be reduced to formulas or numbers from test results. For James, explanation rather than experimental control was the goal of psychology (Arkin, 1990).

The Legacy of These Approaches Despite their differences, the insights of the practitioners of both structuralism and functionalism created an intellectual context in which contemporary psychology could flourish. Psychologists currently examine *both* the structure and the function of behavior. Consider the process of speech production. Suppose you want to invite a friend over to watch the Superbowl. To do so, the words you speak must serve the right function—*Superbowl, with me, today*—but also have the right structure: It wouldn't do to say, "Would watch Superbowl me the with today you to like?" To understand how speech production works, researchers study the way that speakers fit meanings (functions) to the grammatical structures of their languages (Bock, 1990). (We will describe some of the processes of language production in Chapter 8.) Throughout *Psychology and Life,* we emphasize both structure

Classroom practices in the United States were changed through the efforts of the functionalist John Dewey. As a student, what classroom experiences have you experienced that encouraged your "intellectual curiosity"?

and function as we review both classic and contemporary research. Psychologists continue to employ a great variety of methodologies to study the general forces that apply to all humans as well as unique aspects of each individual.

WOMEN AS PIONEERING RESEARCHERS

It probably won't surprise you to learn that, early in its history, research and practice in psychology were dominated by men. Even when they were still few in numbers, however, women made substantial contributions to the field (Russo & Denmark, 1987; Scarborough & Forumoto, 1987). Let's consider four women who were pioneers in different areas of psychological research.

Mary Whiton Calkins (1863–1930) studied with William James at Harvard University. However, because she was a woman she was allowed to participate only as a "guest" graduate student. Although she completed all the requirements for a PhD with an exceptional record, the Harvard administration refused to grant a PhD to a woman. Despite this insult, Calkins established one of the first psychology laboratories in the United States and invented important techniques for studying memory. In 1905, she became the first woman president of the American Psychological Association.

In 1894, **Margaret Floy Washburn** (1871–1939) graduated from Cornell University to become the first woman to receive a PhD in psychology. She went on to write an influential early textbook, *The Animal Mind,* which was published in 1908. The book provided a review of research on perception, learning, and memory across animal species. In 1921, Washburn became the second woman to lead the American Psychological Association.

Helen Thompson Wooley (1874–1947) accomplished some of the earliest research that examined differences between the sexes (Maracek et al., 2003; Milar, 2000). For her PhD research at the University of Chicago in 1900, Wooley compared the performance of 25 men and 25 women on a battery of tests including tests of intelligence and emotions. The research led her to the conclusion that differences between the sexes arose not from natural ability but rather from differences in men and women's social experiences across their life spans. Wooley also offered a famous critique of "the flagrant personal bias, logic martyred in the cause of supporting a prejudice, unfounded assertions, and even sentimental rot and drivel" (Wooley, 1910, p. 340) that characterized research, largely by men, on differences between the sexes.

Leta Stetter Hollingworth (1886–1939) was inspired by Wooley to bring research data to bear on claims about gender differences (Maracek et al., 2003). In particular, Hollingworth attacked the claim that women were genetically inferior to men with respect to their levels of creativity and intelligence. Hollingworth also conducted some of the earliest research on children who tested at the extremes of intelligence—both those who had mental retardation and those who were gifted. She invented a curriculum to help nurture the talents of gifted children that she was able to implement in school settings in New York City.

Since the days in which these women were pioneers, the field of psychology has changed in the direction of far greater diversity. In fact, in recent years more women than men have earned PhDs in the field (Hoffer et al., 2007). We will highlight the work of diverse researchers throughout *Psychology and Life.*

In 1894, Margaret Washburn became the first woman to receive a PhD in psychology. She went on to write an influential textbook, *The Animal Mind* (1908). What challenges might she have faced as a pioneer woman researcher?

As psychology continues to contribute to the scientific and human enterprise, more people—women and men, and members of all segments of society—are being drawn to its richness.

PERSPECTIVES ON PSYCHOLOGY

Suppose your friend accepts the invitation to join you for the Superbowl. What *perspective* does each of you bring to your viewing of the game? Suppose one of you played football in high school, whereas the other did not. Or suppose one of you has rooted from birth for one of the competing teams, whereas the other has no prior commitments. You can see how these different perspectives would affect the way in which you evaluate the game as it unfolds.

In a similar fashion, psychologists' perspectives determine the way in which they examine behavior and mental processes. The perspectives influence what psychologists look for, where they look, and what research methods they use. In this section, we define seven perspectives—psychodynamic, behaviorist, humanistic, cognitive, biological, evolutionary, and sociocultural. As you read the section, note how each perspective defines the causes and consequences of behavior.

A word of caution: Although each perspective represents a different approach to the central issues of psychology, you should come to appreciate why most psychologists borrow and blend concepts from more than one of these perspectives. Each perspective enhances the understanding of the entirety of human experience.

The Psychodynamic Perspective According to the **psychodynamic perspective,** behavior is driven, or motivated, by powerful inner forces. In this view, human actions stem from inherited instincts, biological drives, and attempts to resolve conflicts between personal needs and society's demands. Deprivation states, physiological arousal, and conflicts provide the power for behavior. According to this model, the organism stops reacting when its needs are satisfied and its drives reduced. The main purpose of action is to reduce tension.

Psychodynamic principles of motivation were most fully developed by the Viennese physician **Sigmund Freud** (1856–1939) in the late 19th and early 20th centuries. Freud's ideas grew out of his work with mentally disturbed patients, but he believed that the principles he observed applied to both normal and abnormal behavior. Freud's psychodynamic theory views a person as pulled and pushed by a complex network of inner and outer forces. Freud's model was the first to recognize that human nature is not always rational and that actions may be driven by motives that are not in conscious awareness.

Many psychologists since Freud have taken the psychodynamic model in new directions. Freud himself emphasized early childhood as the stage in which personality is formed.

Sigmund Freud, photographed with his daughter, Anna, on a trip to the Italian Alps in 1913. Freud suggested that behavior is often driven by motives outside of conscious awareness. What implications does that perspective have for the ways in which you make life choices?

---

psychodynamic perspective A psychological model in which behavior is explained in terms of past experiences and motivational forces; actions are viewed as stemming from inherited instincts, biological drives, and attempts to resolve conflicts between personal needs and social requirements.

Neo-Freudian theorists have broadened psychodynamic theory to include social influences and interactions that occur over the individual's entire lifetime. Psychodynamic ideas have had a great influence on many areas of psychology. You will encounter different aspects of Freud's contributions as you read about child development, dreaming, forgetting, unconscious motivation, personality, and psychoanalytic therapy.

The Behaviorist Perspective Those who take the **behaviorist perspective** seek to understand how particular environmental stimuli control particular kinds of behavior. First, behaviorists analyze the *antecedent* environmental conditions—those that precede the behavior and set the stage for an organism to make a response or withhold a response. Next, they look at the *behavioral response,* which is the main object of study—the action to be understood, predicted, and controlled. Finally, they examine the observable *consequences* that follow from the response. A behaviorist, for example, might be interested in the way in which speeding tickets of varying penalties (the consequences of speeding) change the likelihood that motorists will drive with caution or abandon (behavioral responses).

The behaviorist perspective was pioneered by **John Watson** (1878–1958), who argued that psychological research should seek the laws that govern observable behavior across species. **B. F. Skinner** (1904–1990) extended the influence of behaviorism by expanding its analyses to the consequences of behaviors. Both researchers insisted on precise definitions of the phenomena studied and on rigorous standards of evidence. Both Watson and Skinner believed that the basic processes they investigated with nonhuman animals represented general principles that would hold true for humans as well.

Behaviorism has yielded a critical practical legacy. Its emphasis on the need for rigorous experimentation and carefully defined variables has influenced most areas of psychology. Although behaviorists have conducted much basic research with nonhuman animals, the principles of behaviorism have been widely applied to human problems. Behaviorist principles have yielded a more humane approach to educating children (through the use of positive reinforcement rather than punishment), new therapies for modifying behavior disorders, and guidelines for creating model utopian communities.

The Humanistic Perspective Humanistic psychology emerged in the 1950s as an alternative to the psychodynamic and the behaviorist models. According to the **humanistic perspective,** people are neither driven by the powerful, instinctive forces postulated by the Freudians nor manipulated by their environments, as proposed by the behaviorists. Instead, people are active creatures who are innately good and capable of choice. Humanistic psychologists study behavior, but not by reducing it to components, elements, and variables

John Watson was an important pioneer of the behaviorist perspective. Why did he find it necessary to research behaviors of both humans and nonhuman animals?

in laboratory experiments. Instead, they look for patterns in people's life histories.

According to the humanistic perspective, the main task for humans is to strive for positive development. For example, **Carl Rogers** (1902–1987) emphasized that individuals have a natural tendency toward psychological growth and health—a process that is aided by the positive regard of those who surround them. **Abraham Maslow** (1908–1970) coined the term *self-actualization* to refer to each individual's drive toward the fullest development of his or her potential. In addition, Rogers, Maslow, and their colleagues defined a perspective that strives to deal with the whole person, practicing a *holistic* approach to human psychology. They believed that true understanding requires integrating knowledge of the individual's mind, body, and behavior with an awareness of social and cultural forces.

The humanistic approach expands the realm of psychology to include valuable lessons from the study of literature, history, and the arts. In this manner, psychology becomes a more complete discipline. Humanists suggest that their view is the yeast that helps psychology rise above its focus on negative forces and on the animal-like aspects of humanity. As we shall see in Chapter 15, the humanistic perspective had a major impact on the development of new approaches to psychotherapy.

behaviorist perspective The psychological perspective primarily concerned with observable behavior that can be objectively recorded and with the relationships of observable behavior to environmental stimuli.

behaviorism A scientific approach that limits the study of psychology to measurable or observable behavior.

humanistic perspective A psychological model that emphasizes an individual's phenomenal world and inherent capacity for making rational choices and developing to maximum potential.

Carl Rogers provided foundational ideas for the humanistic perspective. Why did Rogers place an emphasis on positive regard?

The Cognitive Perspective

The cognitive revolution in psychology emerged as another challenge to the limits of behaviorism. The centerpiece of the **cognitive perspective** is human thought and all the processes of knowing—attending, thinking, remembering, and understanding. From the cognitive perspective, people act because they think, and people think because they are human beings, exquisitely equipped to do so.

According to the cognitive model, behavior is only partly determined by preceding environmental events and past behavioral consequences, as behaviorists believe. Some of the most significant behavior emerges from totally novel ways of thinking, not from predictable ways used in the past. Consider how children learn their native language. In his book *Verbal Behavior* (1957), B. F. Skinner suggested that children acquire language through ordinary processes of learning. **Noam Chomsky** (b. 1928) helped originate the cognitive perspective by arguing forcefully against Skinner's claim. Chomsky asserted that even children are able to produce utterances that fall outside the bounds of their previous experience. In his own research with children, the Swiss researcher **Jean Piaget** (1896–1980) used a series of mental tasks to demonstrate qualitative changes over the course of cognitive development. To explain children's growing sophistication, Piaget made reference to children's inner cognitive states.

Cognitive psychologists study higher mental processes such as perception, memory, language use, thinking, problem solving, and decision making at a variety of levels. Cognitive psychologists view thoughts as both results and causes of overt actions. Feeling

regret when you've hurt someone is an example of thought as a result. But apologizing for your actions after feeling regret is an example of thought as a cause of behavior. Within the cognitive perspective, an individual responds to reality not as it is in the objective world of matter but as it is in the *subjective reality* of the individual's inner world of thoughts and imagination. Because of its focus on mental processes, many researchers see the cognitive perspective as the dominant approach in psychology today.

The Biological Perspective

The **biological perspective** guides psychologists who search for the causes of behavior in the functioning of genes, the brain, the nervous system, and the endocrine system. An organism's functioning is explained in terms of underlying physical structures and biochemical processes. Experience and behaviors are largely understood as the result of chemical and electrical activities taking place within and between nerve cells.

Researchers who take the biological perspective generally assume that psychological and social phenomena can be ultimately understood in terms of biochemical processes: Even the most complex phenomena can be understood by analysis, or reduction, into ever smaller, more specific units. They might, for example, try to explain how you are reading the words of this sentence with respect to the exact physical processes in cells in your brain. According to this perspective, behavior is determined by physical structures and hereditary processes. Experience can modify behavior by altering these underlying biological structures and processes. Researchers might ask, "What changes in your brain occurred while you learned to read?" The task of psychobiological researchers is to understand behavior at the most precise level of analysis.

Many researchers who take the biological perspective contribute to the multidisciplinary field of **behavioral neuroscience**. Neuroscience is the study of brain function; behavioral neuroscience attempts to understand the brain processes underlying behaviors such as sensation, learning, and emotion. The advances in the brain imaging techniques that we will describe in Chapter 3 have led to dramatic breakthroughs in the field of **cognitive neuroscience**. Cognitive neuroscience trains a multidisciplinary research focus on the brain bases of higher cognitive functions such as memory and language. As we shall see, brain-imaging techniques allow the biological perspective to be extended into a broad range of human experience.

The Evolutionary Perspective

The **evolutionary perspective** seeks to connect contemporary psychology to a central

---

cognitive perspective The perspective on psychology that stresses human thought and the processes of knowing, such as attending, thinking, remembering, expecting, solving problems, fantasizing, and consciousness.

biological perspective The approach to identifying causes of behavior that focuses on the functioning of the genes, the brain, the nervous system, and the endocrine system.

behavioral neuroscience A multidisciplinary field that attempts to understand the brain processes that underlie behavior.

cognitive neuroscience A multidisciplinary field that attempts to understand the brain processes that underlie higher cognitive functions in humans.

evolutionary perspective The approach to psychology that stresses the importance of behavioral and mental adaptiveness, based on the assumption that mental capabilities evolved over millions of years to serve particular adaptive purposes.

idea of the life sciences, Charles Darwin's theory of evolution by natural selection. The idea of natural selection is quite simple: Those organisms that are better suited to their environments tend to produce offspring (and pass on their genes) more successfully than those organisms with poorer adaptations. Over many generations, the species changes in the direction of the privileged adaptation. The evolutionary perspective in psychology suggests that *mental abilities* evolved over millions of years to serve particular adaptive purposes, just as physical abilities did.

To practice evolutionary psychology, researchers focus on the environmental conditions in which the human brain evolved. Humans spent 99 percent of their evolutionary history as hunter–gatherers living in small groups during the Pleistocene era (the roughly 2-million-year period ending 10,000 years ago). Evolutionary psychology uses the rich theoretical framework of evolutionary biology to identify the central adaptive problems that faced this species: avoiding predators and parasites, gathering and exchanging food, finding and retaining mates, and raising healthy children. After identifying the adaptive problems that these early humans faced, evolutionary psychologists generate inferences about the sorts of mental mechanisms, or psychological adaptations, that might have evolved to solve those problems.

Evolutionary psychology differs from other perspectives most fundamentally in its focus on the extremely long process of evolution as a central explanatory principle. Evolutionary psychologists, for example, attempt to understand the different sex roles assumed by men and women as products of evolution, rather than as products of contemporary societal pressures. Because evolutionary psychologists cannot carry out experiments that vary the course of evolution, they must be particularly inventive to provide evidence in favor of their theories.

The Sociocultural Perspective Psychologists who take a **sociocultural perspective** study *cross-cultural* differences in the causes and consequences of behavior. The sociocultural perspective is an important response to the criticism that psychological research has too often been based on a Western conception of human nature and had as its subject population only white middle-class Americans (Gergen et al., 1996). A proper consideration of cultural forces may involve comparisons of groups within the same national boundaries. For example, researchers may compare the prevalence of eating disorders for white American versus African American teenagers within the United States (see Chapter 11). Cultural forces may also be assessed across nationalities, as in comparisons of media reports in the United States and Japan (see Chapter 16). Cross-cultural psychologists want to determine whether the theories researchers have developed apply to all humans, or only to more narrow, specific populations.

A cross-cultural perspective can be brought to bear on almost every topic of psychological research: Are people's perceptions of the world affected by culture? Do the languages people speak affect the way they experience the world? How does culture affect the way children develop toward adulthood? How do cultural attitudes shape the experience of old age? How does culture affect our sense of self? Does culture influence an individual's likelihood to engage in particular

Bronislaw Malinowski documented the important roles women play in the culture of the Trobriand Islands. Why is cross-cultural research critical to the search for universal psychological principles?

behaviors? Does culture affect the way individuals express emotions? Does culture affect the rates at which people suffer from psychological disorders?

By asking these types of questions, the sociocultural perspective often yields conclusions that directly challenge those generated from the other perspectives. Researchers have claimed, for example, that many aspects of Freud's psychodynamic theories cannot apply to cultures that are very different from Freud's Vienna. This concern was raised as early as 1927 by the anthropologist Bronislaw Malinowski (1927), who soundly critiqued Freud's father-centered theory by describing the family practices of the Trobriand Islanders of New Guinea, for whom family authority resided with mothers rather than with fathers. The sociocultural perspective, therefore, suggests that some universal claims of the psychodynamic perspective are incorrect. The sociocultural perspective poses a continual, important challenge to generalizations about human experience that ignore the diversity and richness of culture.

Comparing Perspectives: Focus on Aggression

Each of the seven perspectives rests on a different set of assumptions and leads to a different way of looking for answers to questions about behavior. **Table 1.1** summarizes the perspectives. As an example, let's briefly compare how psychologists using these models might deal with the question of why people act aggressively. All of the approaches have been used in the effort to understand the nature of aggression and violence. For each perspective, we give examples of the types of claims researchers might make and experiments they might undertake:

- *Psychodynamic.* Analyze aggression as a reaction to frustrations caused by barriers to pleasure, such as unjust authority. View aggression as an adult's displacement of hostility originally felt as a child against his or her parents.
- *Behaviorist.* Identify reinforcements of past aggressive responses, such as extra attention given to a child who hits classmates or siblings. Assert that children learn from physically abusive parents to be abusive with their own children.

---

sociocultural perspective The psychological perspective that focuses on cross-cultural differences in the causes and consequences of behavior.

TABLE 1.1 Comparison of Seven Perspectives on Psychology

Perspective	Focus of Study	Primary Research Topics
Psychodynamic	Unconscious drives Conflicts	Behavior as overt expression of unconscious motives
Behaviorist	Specific overt responses	Behavior and its stimulus causes and consequences
Humanistic	Human experience and potentials	Life patterns Values Goals
Cognitive	Mental processes Language	Inferred mental processes through behavioral indicators
Biological	Brain and nervous system processes	Biochemical basis of behavior and mental processes
Evolutionary	Evolved psychological adaptations	Mental mechanisms in terms of evolved adaptive functions
Sociocultural	Cross-cultural patterns of attitudes and behaviors	Universal and culture-specific aspects of human experience

- *Humanistic.* Look for personal values and social conditions that foster self-limiting, aggressive perspectives instead of growth-enhancing, shared experiences.
- *Cognitive.* Explore the hostile thoughts and fantasies people experience while witnessing violent acts, noting both aggressive imagery and intentions to harm others. Study the impact of violence in films and videos, including pornographic violence, on attitudes toward gun control, rape, and war.
- *Biological.* Study the role of specific brain systems in aggression by stimulating different regions and then recording any destructive actions that are elicited. Also analyze the brains of mass murderers for abnormalities; examine female aggression as related to phases of the menstrual cycle.
- *Evolutionary.* Consider what conditions would have made aggression an adaptive behavior for early humans. Identify psychological mechanisms capable of selectively generating aggressive behavior under those conditions.
- *Sociocultural.* Consider how members of different cultures display and interpret aggression. Identify how cultural forces affect the likelihood of different types of aggressive behavior.

From this example of aggression, you can see how the different perspectives conspire to provide a full understanding of particular domains of psychological research. In contemporary psychology, most research is informed by multiple perspectives. Throughout *Psychology and Life,* you will see how new theories often emerge from combinations of different perspectives. In addition, technological advances have made it easier for researchers to combine perspectives. For example, the innovative brain-imaging techniques you'll learn about in Chapter 3 allow researchers to bring a biological perspective to topics as varied as personality differences (Chapter 13) and therapeutic outcomes (Chapter 15). Moreover, developments such as the Internet have made it easier for researchers to collaborate across the globe. They can bring a sociocultural perspective to topics as diverse as moral reasoning (Chapter 10) and people's body images (Chapter 11). Psychology's diversity of perspectives helps researchers think creatively about core topics of human experience.

STOP AND REVIEW

❶ What are the central concerns of the structuralist and functionalist approaches?

❷ What conclusions did Helen Thompson Wooley draw about differences between the sexes?

❸ How do the psychodynamic and behaviorist perspectives conceptualize the forces that shape people's actions?

❹ What is the purpose of cognitive neuroscience?

❺ How do the evolutionary perspective and sociocultural perspective complement each other?

Visit MyPsychLab.com for more review and practice on the following topics:

Psychology Timeline

👁 **Watch:** Even the Rat Was White: Robert Guthrie

👁 **Explore:** How to Be a Critical Thinker

What Psychologists Do

You now know enough about psychology to formulate questions that span the full range of psychological inquiry. If you prepared such a list of questions, you would be likely to touch on the areas of expertise of the great variety of individuals who call themselves psychologists. In **Table 1.2** on page 14, we provide our own version of such questions and indicate what sort of psychologist might address each one.

As you examine the table, you will note the great many subfields within the profession of psychology. Some of the labels the field uses tell you about the major content of a psychologist's expertise. For example, *cognitive psychologists* focus on basic cognitive processes such as memory and language; *social psychologists* focus on the social forces that shape people's attitudes and behavior. Some of the labels identify the domains in which

TABLE 1.2 The Diversity of Psychological Inquiry

The Question	Who Addresses It?	Focus of Research and Practice
How can people cope better with day-to-day problems?	Clinical psychologists Counseling psychologists Community psychologists Psychiatrists	Study the origins of psychological disorders and day-to-day evaluate treatment options; provide diagnosis and treatment of psychological disorders and other issues of personal adjustment
How can I cope with the aftereffects of a stroke?	Rehabilitation psychologists	Provide assessment and counseling for people with illnesses or disabilities; offer coping strategies and education to affected individuals, caretakers, employers, and community members
How do memories get stored in the brain?	Biological psychologists Psychopharmacologists	Study the biochemical bases of behavior, feelings, and mental processes
How can you teach a dog to follow commands?	Experimental psychologists Behavior analysts	Use laboratory experiments, often with nonhuman participants, to study basic processes of learning, sensation, perception, emotion, and motivation
Why can't I always recall information I'm sure I know?	Cognitive psychologists Cognitive scientists	Study mental processes such as memory, perception, reasoning, problem solving, decision making, and language use
What makes people different from one another?	Personality psychologists Behavioral geneticists	Develop tests and theories to understand differences in personalities and behaviors; study the influence of genetics and environments on those differences
How does peer pressure work?	Social psychologists	Study how people function in social groups as well as the processes by which people select, interpret, and remember social information
What do babies know about the world?	Developmental psychologists	Study the changes that occur in the physical, cognitive, and social functioning of individuals across the life span; study the influence of genetics and environments on those changes
Why does my job make me feel so depressed?	Industrial–organizational psychologists Human factors psychologists	Study the factors that influence performance and morale in the general workplace or on particular tasks; apply those insights in the workplace
How should teachers deal with disruptive students?	Educational psychologists School psychologists	Study how to improve aspects of the learning process; help design school curricular, teaching-training, and child-care programs
Why do I get sick before every exam?	Health psychologists	Study how different lifestyles affect physical health; design and evaluate prevention programs to help people change unhealthy behaviors and cope with stress
Was the defendant insane when she committed the crime?	Forensic psychologists	Apply psychological knowledge to human problems in the field of law enforcement
Why do I always choke during important basketball games?	Sports psychologists	Assess the performance of athletes and use motivational, cognitive, and behavioral principles to help them achieve peak performance levels
How can I make sense of all the numbers people throw at me?	Quantitative psychologists Psychometricians	Develop and evaluate new statistical methods; construct and validate measurement tools
How accurately can psychologists predict how people will behave?	Mathematical psychologists	Develop mathematical expressions that allow for precise predictions about behavior and tests of contrasting psychological theories

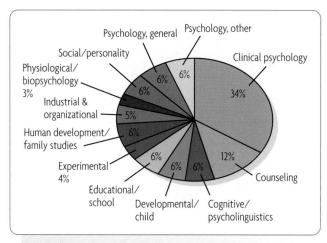

FIGURE 1.2 Distribution of Degrees to Subfields of Psychology

In 2006, roughly 3,300 people received PhDs in the many subfields of psychology (Hoffer et al., 2007). Although the largest percentage of those degrees went to individuals pursuing careers in clinical psychology, students also received advanced training in several other areas of basic and applied research.

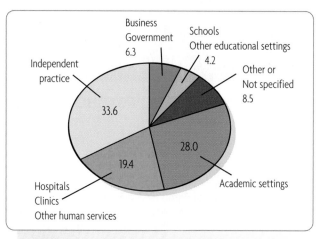

FIGURE 1.3 Work Settings of Psychologists

Shown are percentages of psychologists working in particular settings, according to a survey of American Psychological Association (APA) members holding doctoral degrees in psychology.

psychologists apply their expertise. For example, *industrial–organizational psychologists* focus their efforts on improving people's adjustment in the workplace; *school psychologists* focus on students' adjustment in educational settings.

Each type of psychologist achieves a balance between *research*—seeking new insights—and *application*—putting those insights to use in the world. There's a necessary relationship between those two types of activities. For example, we often think of *clinical psychologists* largely as individuals who apply psychological knowledge to better people's lives. However, as we will see in Chapters 14 and 15, clinical psychologists also have important research functions. Contemporary research continues to improve our understanding of the distinctions among psychological disor-

ders and the treatments that best ease patients' distress. **Figure 1.2** provides information about the numbers of people who pursue PhDs across psychology's many subfields.

Take a look back at Table 1.2. We intended the list of questions to demonstrate why psychology has so many divisions. Did we manage to capture your own concerns? If you have the time, make a list of your own questions. Cross off each question as *Psychology and Life* answers it. If, at the end of the course, you still have unanswered questions, please send them to us! (Our e-mail addresses can be found in the preface.)

Have you begun to wonder exactly how many practicing psychologists there are in the world? Surveys suggest the number is well over 500,000. **Figure 1.3** gives you an idea of the distribution of settings in which psychologists function. Although the percentage of psychologists in the population is greatest in Western industrialized nations, interest in psychology continues to increase in many countries. The International Union of Psychological Science draws together member organizations from 70 countries (Ritchie, 2007). The American Psychological Association (APA), an organization that includes psychologists from all over the world, has 148,000 members. A second international organization, the Association for Psychological Science (APS), with about 20,000 members, focuses more on scientific aspects of psychology and less on the clinical, or treatment, side.

Developmental psychologists may use puppets or other toys in their study of how children behave, think, or feel. Why might it be easier for a child to express his or her thoughts to a puppet than to an adult?

STOP AND REVIEW

❶ What is the relationship between research and application?

❷ In what two settings are most psychologists employed?

Visit MyPsychLab.com for more review and practice on the following topic:

◄● **Explore:** Psychologists at Work

Psychology in Your Life

IN WHAT WAYS DO PSYCHOLOGISTS PARTICIPATE IN THE LEGAL SYSTEM?

An important lesson of *Psychology and Life* is that empirical research provides psychologists with a broad range of expertise. As this text unfolds, we will have a good number of opportunities to demonstrate how research results are applied to important issues in everyday life. In this opening chapter, we'll take an opportunity to provide a concrete example of how psychological expertise functions in the public forum. We focus our attention on some ways in which *forensic psychologists* become involved in important legal decisions.

The legal system relies on forensic psychologists to provide assessments for both civil and criminal proceedings (Packer, 2008). On the civil side, for example, forensic psychologists provide evidence that influences decisions about child custody in divorce hearings. They might also testify about the potential psychological harm workers have sustained in a particular place of employment. On the criminal side, forensic psychologists evaluate people's capacity to understand the acts they have committed and their competence to stand trial. The legal system also asks forensic psychologists to assess whether individuals are a danger to themselves or others. Let's examine that last role more closely.

It's hard to read the news without learning about someone who has committed a violent crime. Suppose that person is sent to prison and, after having served some time, he or she arrives at a parole hearing. An important consideration at that hearing will be what lies in the prisoner's future. What is the likelihood that violent acts will occur again?

In recent years, psychologists have attempted to provide increasingly research-based answers to that question (Fabian, 2006). This type of research often begins with a theoretical analysis of the factors in people's lives that make violence more or less likely. Researchers make an important distinction between *static* and *dynamic* factors (Douglas & Skeem, 2005). Static factors are those that are relatively stable over time (such as gender and age at first conviction); dynamic variables are those that may change over time (such as emotional control and substance abuse). The inclusion of dynamic factors suggests why the risk a particular individual presents changes over time. Past history alone does not provide a valid indication of how a person will behave in the future. It's also important to measure the trajectory of a person's life.

When researchers develop new risk assessment devices, they must provide evidence that those devices are successful at predicting future violence. To do so, researchers often follow groups of individuals over time. For example, Wong and Gordon (2006) evaluated 918 adult male offenders who were incarcerated in the Canadian provinces of Alberta, Saskatchewan, and Manitoba. Each participant was evaluated with the Violence Risk Scale (VRS), a device that measures six static and twenty dynamic variables. To evaluate the validity of the VRS, the researchers followed their participants over several years, to see how often they were convicted of new crimes after they had been released into the community. In both the short term (after one year) and the longer term (after 4.4 years), men who had obtained higher ratings on the VRS were more likely to be convicted of additional violent crimes.

Research results of this sort are quite important because they help forensic psychologists provide more accurate guidance for legal judgments.

How to Use This Text

You are about to embark with us on an intellectual journey through the many areas of modern psychology. Before we start, we want to share with you some important information that will help guide your adventures. "The journey" is a metaphor used throughout *Psychology and Life;* your teacher serves as the tour director, the text as your tour book, and we, your authors, as your personal tour guides. The goal of this journey is for you to discover what is known about the most incredible phenomena in the entire universe: the brain, the human mind, and the behavior of all living creatures. Psychology is about understanding the seemingly mysterious processes that give rise to your thoughts, feelings, and actions.

This guide offers general strategies and specific suggestions about how to use this book to get the quality grade you deserve for your performance and to get the most from your introduction to psychology.

STUDY STRATEGIES

1. *Set aside sufficient time* for your reading assignments and review of class notes. This text contains much new technical information, many principles to learn, and a new glossary of terms to memorize. To master this material, you will need at least three hours of reading time per chapter.
2. *Keep a record of your study time* for this course. Plot the number of hours (in half-hour intervals) you study at

each reading session. Chart your time investment on a cumulative graph. Add each new study time to the previous total on the left-hand axis of the graph and each study session on the baseline axis. The chart will provide visual feedback of your progress and show you when you have not been hitting the books as you should.

3. *Be an active participant.* Optimal learning occurs when you are actively involved with the learning materials. That means reading attentively, listening to lectures mindfully, paraphrasing in your own words what you are reading or hearing, and taking good notes. In the text, underline key sections, write notes to yourself in the margins, and summarize points that you think might be included on class tests.

4. *Space out your studying.* Research in psychology tells us that it is more effective to do your studying regularly rather than cramming just before tests. If you let yourself fall behind, it will be difficult to catch up with all the information included in introductory psychology at last-minute panic time.

5. *Get study-centered.* Find a place with minimal distractions for studying. Reserve that place for studying, reading, and writing course assignments—and do nothing else there. The place will come to be associated with study activities, and you will find it easier to work whenever you are seated at your study center.

Take the teacher's perspective, anticipating the kinds of questions she or he is likely to ask and then making sure you can answer them. Find out what kinds of tests you will be given in this course—essay, fill-in, multiple-choice, or true/false. That form will affect the extent to which you focus on the big ideas and/or on details. Essays and fill-ins ask for recall-type memory; multiple-choice and true/false tests ask for recognition-type memory.

STUDY TECHNIQUES

In this section, we give you specific advice about a technique you can use to learn the material for this course and your other courses. The technique emerged from the principles of human memory we will discuss in Chapter 7. It is called *PQ4R* from the initials of the six phases it suggests for effective study: Preview, Question, Read, Reflect, Recite, and Review (Thomas & Robinson, 1972).

1. *Preview.* Skim through the chapter to get a general sense of the topics the chapter will discuss. Make yourself aware of the organization and major topics. Read the section headings and scan the photos and figures. In fact, your first stop for each chapter should be the section "Recapping Main Points." There you will find the main ideas of the chapter organized under each of the first-level headings, which will give you a clear sense of what the chapter covers.

2. *Question.* For each section, make up questions. You should use the section headings and key terms to help you. For example, you might transform the heading "The Goals of Psychology" into the question "What are the goals of psychology?" You might use the key term *biological perspective* to generate the question, "What is the major focus of the biological perspective?" These questions will help direct your attention as you read.

3. *Read.* Read the material carefully so that you are able to answer the questions you invented.

4. *Reflect.* As you read the text, reflect on it to relate the material to your prior knowledge about the topics. Think of extra examples to enrich the text. Try to link the ideas together across the subsections.

5. *Recite.* After you have read and reflected on a section, try to demonstrate your recall of the material as concretely as possible. For example, answer the questions you invented earlier by producing the material out loud. For later review, write down the ideas you find difficult to remember.

6. *Review.* After you have read the entire chapter, review the key points. If you are unable to recall important points, or you cannot answer the questions you invented, consult the book and repeat the earlier phases (read, reflect, and recite).

Take a moment now to use PQ4R for one of the earlier sections of this chapter to see how each phase works. It will take you some time to master the flow of PQ4R. Make that investment at the beginning of the semester.

You are now prepared to take full advantage of *Psychology and Life.* We hope your journey through this text will be worthwhile, full of memorable moments and unexpected pleasures.

STOP AND REVIEW

❶ What does it mean to be an active participant in a course?

❷ What is the relationship between the *Question* and *Read* phases of PQ4R?

❸ What is the purpose of the *Recite* phase of PQ4R?

Recapping Main Points

What Makes Psychology Unique?

- Psychology is the scientific study of the behavior and the mental processes of individuals.
- The goals of psychology are to describe, explain, predict, and help control behavior.

The Evolution of Modern Psychology

- Structuralism emerged from the work of Wundt and Titchener. It emphasized the structure of the mind and behavior built from elemental sensations.
- Functionalism, developed by James and Dewey, emphasized the purpose behind behavior.
- Taken together, these theories created the agenda for modern psychology.
- Women made substantial research contributions in psychology's early history.
- Each of the seven perspectives on psychology differs in its view of human nature, the determinants of behavior, the focus of study, and the primary research approach.
- The psychodynamic perspective looks at behavior as driven by instinctive forces, inner conflicts, and conscious and unconscious motivations.
- The behaviorist perspective views behavior as determined by external stimulus conditions.

- The humanistic perspective emphasizes an individual's inherent capacity to make rational choices.
- The cognitive perspective stresses mental processes that affect behavioral responses.
- The biological perspective studies relationships between behavior and brain mechanisms.
- The evolutionary perspective looks at behavior as having evolved as an adaptation for survival in the environment.
- The sociocultural perspective examines behavior and its interpretation in cultural context.

What Psychologists Do

- Psychologists work in a variety of settings and draw on expertise from a range of specialty areas.
- Almost any question that can be generated about real-life experiences is addressed by some member of the psychological profession.

How to Use This Text

- Devise concrete strategies for determining how much study time you need and how to distribute the time most efficiently.
- Take an active approach to your lectures and the text. The PQ4R method provides six phases—Preview, Question, Read, Reflect, Recite, and Review—for enhanced learning.

KEY TERMS

behavior (p. 2)
behavioral data (p. 3)
behavioral neuroscience (p. 11)
behaviorism (p. 10)
behaviorist perspective (p. 10)
biological perspective (p. 11)

cognitive neuroscience (p. 11)
cognitive perspective (p. 11)
evolutionary perspective (p. 11)
functionalism (p. 7)
Gestalt psychology (p. 7)
humanistic perspective (p. 10)

introspection (p. 7)
psychodynamic perspective (p. 9)
psychology (p. 2)
scientific method (p. 2)
sociocultural perspective (p. 12)
structuralism (p. 7)

Chapter 1 Practice Test

1. The definition of psychology focuses on both _____ and _____ .
   a. behaviors; structures
   b. behaviors; mental processes
   c. mental processes; functions
   d. mental processes; structures

2. To what goal of psychology is "level of analysis" most relevant?
   a. explaining what happens
   b. describing what happens
   c. predicting what will happen
   d. controlling what happens

3. If you want to _____ what will happen, you first must be able to _____ what will happen.
   a. describe; explain
   b. describe; control
   c. control; predict
   d. explain; predict

4. Experiences with totalitarian regimes may have made Russian students more sensitive to their friends'
   a. betrayals of confidence.
   b. romantic competition.
   c. disrespectful behavior.
   d. jealousy.

5. Who founded the first laboratory that was devoted to experimental psychology?
   a. William James
   b. Wilhelm Wundt
   c. Max Wertheimer
   d. John Dewey

6. A researcher tells you that her main goal is to understand mental experiences as the combination of basic components. It is most likely that she finds the historical roots of her research in
   a. functionalism.
   b. the humanist perspective.
   c. structuralism.
   d. the evolutionary perspective.

7. Who was the first woman to serve as president of the American Psychological Association?
   a. Margaret Washburn
   b. Anna Freud
   c. Jane Goodall
   d. Mary Calkins

8. Two professors at universities in Boston and Mumbai are collaborating on a research project to determine how their students in the United States and India respond to the same reasoning problems. It's likely that they take a _____ perspective in their research.
   a. humanistic
   b. sociocultural
   c. biological
   d. psychodynamic

9. The _____ perspective draws on the ways in which human mental abilities serve adaptive purposes.
   a. cognitive
   b. humanistic
   c. evolutionary
   d. sociocultural

10. When you're home with the flu, you spend a lot of time watching CourtTV. You weren't surprised to see a _____ psychologist testifying during a trial.
    a. health
    b. social
    c. forensic
    d. developmental

11. What type of question would a cognitive psychologist be likely to ask?
    a. Why do children sometimes have imaginary friends?
    b. Why do some students get sick every time they have a major exam?
    c. How can we design a keyboard for a computer that allows people to type more quickly?
    d. How are bilingual individuals able to switch between their two languages?

12. Which type of psychologist is *least* likely to focus on genetic aspects of human psychology?
    a. industrial–organizational psychologists
    b. developmental psychologists
    c. personality psychologists
    d. biological psychologists

13. Individuals with advanced degrees in psychology are most likely to be working in
    a. academic settings.
    b. hospitals and clinics.
    c. business and government.
    d. independent practice.

14. In assessments of violence risk, _____ counts as a dynamic factor.
    a. gender
    b. substance abuse
    c. stability of family upbringing
    d. age at first conviction

15. In what phase of P4QR should you try to relate the textbook material to your prior knowledge about a topic?
    a. Reflect
    b. Recite
    c. Review
    d. Question

Essay Questions

1. With respect to the goals of psychology, why is it appropriate to characterize psychologists as "rather optimistic"?

2. Why is it often good to consider the same research question from several of psychology's seven perspectives?

3. Why does the field of psychology include both research and application?

Discovering Psychology Viewing Guide

Watch the following video by logging on to MyPsychLab (www.mypsychlab.com). After you have watched the video, complete the activities that follow.

Program 1: Past, Present, and Promise

KEY TERMS AND PEOPLE

As you watch the program, pay particular attention to these terms and people in addition to those covered in this textbook.

- *ERP (event-related potentials)*—variations in brain waves as recorded by the electroencephalograph (EEG) that are triggered by specific internal or external events.
- *Heisenberg indeterminacy principle*—principle stating that our impressions of other people are distorted by how we observe and assess them.
- *Mahzarin Banaji*—uses indirect measures of reaction time and brain activity to study prejudice.
- *Emanuel Donchin*—discovered that brains measure surprise before we are aware of it.
- *G. Stanley Hall*—founded the first American psychology lab in 1883.
- *Liz Phelps*—collaborates with M. Banaji in conducting brain-based studies of prejudice.
- *Robert Rosenthal*—showed that body language can reflect what we think and feel.

PROGRAM REVIEW

1. What is the best definition of *psychology?*
   a. the scientific study of how people interact in social groups
   b. the philosophy explaining the relation between brain and mind
   c. the scientific study of the behavior of individuals and of their mental processes
   d. the knowledge used to predict how virtually any organism will behave under specified conditions

2. As scientists, psychologists do which of the following?
   a. develop methods of inquiry that are fundamentally at odds with those of physics and chemistry
   b. test their theories under carefully controlled experimental circumstances
   c. ignore their own observational biases when collecting data
   d. rely completely on introspective techniques

3. What is the main focus of Donchin's research involving the P-300 wave?
   a. the relation between brain and mind
   b. the role of heredity in shaping personality
   c. the development of mental illness
   d. the role of situational factors in perception

4. What is the main goal of psychological research?
   a. to cure mental illness
   b. to find the biological bases of the behavior of organisms
   c. to predict and, in some cases, control behavior
   d. to provide valid legal testimony

5. The reactions of the boys and the girls to the teacher in the *Candid Camera* episode were essentially similar. Professor Zimbardo attributes this reaction to
   a. how easily adolescents become embarrassed.
   b. how an attractive teacher violates expectations.
   c. the way sexual titillation makes people act.
   d. the need people have to hide their real reactions.

6. What do EEGs measure?
   a. heart rate
   b. changes in hormone levels in the body
   c. energy expended in overcoming gravity
   d. brain activity

7. According to Robert Rosenthal's research, you are most likely to detect a liar by
   a. observing eye movements.
   b. listening to tone of voice.
   c. considering sociocultural factors.
   d. looking at body language.

8. Which cluster of topics did William James consider the main concerns of psychology?
   a. reaction times, sensory stimuli, word associations
   b. consciousness, self, emotions
   c. conditioned responses, psychophysics
   d. experimental design, computer models

9. What do we learn from our misreading of the "Paris in the the spring" sign?
   a. We are accustomed to an artist's use of perspective.
   b. Experience disposes us to respond in a particular way.
   c. Unexpected events trigger P-300 waves in the brain.
   d. We laugh at those things that violate our expectations.

10. The amygdala is an area of the brain that processes
    a. sound.
    b. social status.
    c. faces.
    d. emotion.

11. According to Mahzarin Banaji, the IAT could potentially be used for what practical application?
    a. studying latent prejudice in police officers
    b. assessing relationships among family members
    c. evaluating intellectual ability
    d. determining when someone is lying during negotiation

12. Who founded the first psychology laboratory in the United States?
    a. Wilhelm Wundt
    b. William James
    c. G. Stanley Hall
    d. Sigmund Freud

13. How did Wundtian psychologists, such as Hall, react to William James's concept of psychology?
    a. They accepted it with minor reservations.
    b. They expanded it to include consciousness and the self.
    c. They rejected it as unscientific.
    d. They revised it to include the thinking of Sigmund Freud.

14. Which level of analysis concerns a person's behavior within a complex situation?
    a. cosmological level
    b. molar level
    c. molecular level
    d. micro level

15. Which of the following, according to Robert Rosenthal, predicts success in getting alcoholics into treatment?
    a. their income
    b. the number of years they've been drinking
    c. the physical appearance of the doctor recommending treatment
    d. the doctor's tone of voice

16. Which of the following psychologists was the first to study people's sensory processing, judgment, attention, and word associations?
    a. G. Stanley Hall
    b. William James
    c. Wilhelm Wundt
    d. Sigmund Freud

17. Most psychologists study human behavior at which level of analysis?
    a. molecular
    b. macro
    c. micro
    d. molar

18. Who wrote *Principles of Psychology* and thereby became arguably the most influential psychologist of the last century?
    a. G. Stanley Hall
    b. Wilhelm Wundt
    c. William James
    d. Sigmund Freud

19. What assumption underlies the use of reaction times to study prejudice indirectly?
    a. People of certain ethnic backgrounds are quicker intellectually than people of other ethnicities.
    b. Concepts that are associated more strongly in memory are verified more quickly.
    c. Prejudice can't be studied in any other way.
    d. People respond to emotional memories more slowly than emotionless memories.

20. Prejudice can be studied at
    a. the micro level.
    b. the molecular level.
    c. the molar level.
    d. all of the above.

QUESTIONS TO CONSIDER

1. Although psychologists are involved in many different kinds of research and professional activities, there are certain fundamental issues that form the basic foundation of psychology. What are they?

2. Why would the study of normal behavior be more important to the science of psychology than an understanding of abnormal behavior?

3. List as many reasons as you can think of for why people who would benefit from seeing a therapist might not choose to do so.

4. How do your culture, age, gender, education level, and past experience bias your observations about events, your own actions, and the behavior of others?

5. Is thinking a behavior? How can it be studied?

6. Imagine the year 2500. How do you think the boundaries of psychological and biological research might have become redefined by then? Do you think the two fields will have become more integrated or more distinct?

ACTIVITIES

1. Start a personal journal or a log. Make a daily practice of recording events, thoughts, feelings, observations, and questions that catch your attention each day. Include the ordinary and the unusual. Then speculate on the possible forces causing your behavior. As you progress through the course, review your notes and see how your observations and questions reflect what you have learned.

2. Look ahead to one or two psychological principles described in the book. After describing the experimental situation to your friends, ask them to think about what their own data would have shown if they had participated. How closely do their introspections match the actual results of the study? What factors might lead their introspections to be more or less accurate?

3. As you go through your day-to-day life, watching the news, battling traffic, and making decisions about how to spend your time and money, consider all the ways that psychologists might be interested in studying, facilitating, or intervening in human behavior.

2

Research Methods in Psychology

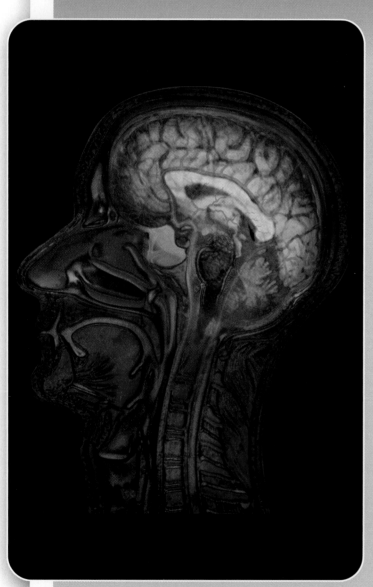

ou may recall that in Chapter 1 we asked you to compose a list of questions that you would like to have answered by the end of *Psychology and Life*. Students who have used the book in the past responded to this request with a range of interesting concerns. Here are some of their questions:

- Why is eating "hot" food painful?
- Is it bad to spank your children?
- Can memory research help me study for exams?
- How can you get people to volunteer?

In this chapter, we describe how psychologists generate answers to questions that matter most to students. We focus on the special way in which psychology applies the scientific method to its domain of inquiry. We want you to understand how psychologists design their research: How can solid conclusions ever be drawn from the complex and often fuzzy phenomena that psychologists study—how people think, feel, and behave? Even if you never do any scientific research in your life, mastering the information in this section will be useful. The underlying purpose here is to help improve your *critical thinking skills* by teaching you how to ask the right questions and evaluate the answers about the causes, consequences, and correlates of psychological phenomena. The mass media constantly release stories that begin with, "Research shows that . . . ." By sharpening your intelligent skepticism, we will help you become a more sophisticated consumer of the research-based conclusions that confront you in everyday life.

The Process of Research

The research process in psychology can be divided into several steps that usually occur in sequence (see **Figure 2.1**). The process typically begins with *Step 1*, in which observations, beliefs, information, and general knowledge lead someone to come up with a new idea or a different way of thinking about a phenomenon. Where do researchers' questions originate? Some come from direct observations of events, humans, and nonhumans in the environment. Other research addresses traditional parts of the field: Some issues are considered to be "great unanswered questions" that have been passed down from earlier scholars. Researchers often combine old ideas in unique ways that offer an original perspective. The hallmark of the truly creative thinker is the discovery of a new truth that moves science and society in a better direction.

As psychologists accumulate information about phenomena, they create theories that become an important context to formulate research questions. A **theory** is an organized set of concepts that *explains* a phenomenon or set of phenomena. At the common core of most psychological theories is the assumption of **determinism,** the idea that all events—physical, mental, and behavioral—are the result of, or determined by, specific causal factors. These causal factors are limited to those in the individual's environment or within the person. Researchers also assume that behavior and mental processes follow *lawful patterns* of relationships, patterns that can be discovered and revealed through research. Psychological theories are typically claims about the causal forces that underlie such lawful patterns.

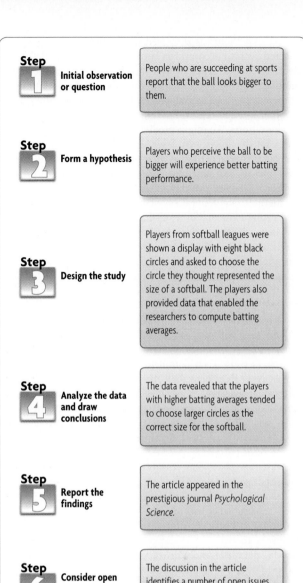

FIGURE 2.1 Steps in the Process of Conducting and Reporting Research

To illustrate the steps in the scientific process, we use a project that sought a relationship between softball players' perceptions of the size of the ball and their actual batting averages (Witt & Proffitt, 2005).

---

theory An organized set of concepts that explains a phenomenon or set of phenomena.

determinism The doctrine that all events—physical, behavioral, and mental—are determined by specific causal factors that are potentially knowable.

When a theory is proposed in psychology, it is generally expected both to account for known facts and, as *Step 2* in the research process, generate new hypotheses. A **hypothesis** is a tentative and testable statement about the relationship between causes and consequences. Hypotheses are often stated as if–then predictions, specifying certain outcomes from specific conditions. We might predict, for example, that *if* children view a lot of violence on television, *then* they will engage in more aggressive acts toward their peers. Research is required to verify the if–then link. For *Step 3*, researchers rely on the *scientific method* to put their hypotheses to the test. The scientific method is a general set of procedures for gathering and interpreting evidence in ways that limit sources of errors and yield dependable conclusions. Psychology is considered a science to the extent that it follows the rules established by the scientific method. Much of this chapter is devoted to describing the scientific method. Once researchers have collected their data, they proceed to *Step 4,* in which they analyze those data and generate conclusions.

If researchers believe that their data will have an impact on the field, they will move on to *Step 5* and submit the paper for publication in a journal. For publication to be possible, researchers must keep complete records of observations and data analyses in a form that other researchers can understand and evaluate. Secrecy is banned from the research procedure because all data and methods must eventually be open for *public verifiability;* that is, other researchers must have the opportunity to inspect, criticize, replicate, or disprove the data and methods.

Much psychological research appears in journals that are published by organizations such as the American Psychological Association or the Association for Psychological Science. When research manuscripts are submitted to most journals, they undergo a process of *peer review.* Each manuscript is typically sent to two to five experts in the field. Those experts provide detailed analyses of the manuscript's rationale, methodology, and results. Only when those experts have been sufficiently satisfied do manuscripts become journal articles. This is a rigorous process. For example, in 2007, journals published by the American Psychological Association (2008) rejected, on average, 76 percent of the manuscripts submitted to them. The process of peer review isn't perfect—no doubt some worthy research projects are overlooked and some uneven ones slip through—but, in general, this process ensures that the research you read in the vast majority of journals has met high standards.

At Step 5, psychologists also often try to disseminate their results to a wider public. In a presidential address to the American Psychological Association, George Miller (1969) reached the celebrated conclusion that the responsibility of professional psychologists "is less to assume the role of experts and try to apply psychology ourselves than to give it away to the people who really need it—and that includes everyone" (p. 1071). Individual psychologists often write books and give lectures that are directed toward broad audiences. Major professional organizations, such as the American Psychological Association and Association for Psychological Science, also issue press releases and create public forums in which researchers can give psychology away.

At *Step 6* of the research process, the scientific community reflects on the research and identifies questions the work leaves unresolved. Most research articles start this process in a *discussion* section in which the researchers lay out the implications and limitations of their work. They might explicitly describe the type of future research they consider desirable. When the data do not fully support a hypothesis, researchers must rethink aspects of their theories. Thus there is continual interaction between theory and research. At *Step 7,* the original researchers or their peers might act on open questions and begin the research cycle again.

This research process is centered around appropriate uses of the scientific method. The goal of the scientific method is to allow researchers to draw conclusions with maximum objectivity. Conclusions are *objective* when they are uninfluenced by researchers' emotions or personal biases. Each of the next two sections begins with a *challenge to objectivity* and then describes the *remedy* prescribed by the scientific method.

OBSERVER BIASES AND OPERATIONAL DEFINITIONS

When different people observe the same events, they don't always "see" the same thing. In this section, we describe the problem of *observer bias* and the steps researchers take as remedies.

The Challenge to Objectivity An **observer bias** is an error due to the personal motives and expectations of the viewer. At times, people see and hear what they expect rather than what is. Consider a rather dramatic example of observer bias. Around the beginning of the 20th century, a leading psychologist, Hugo Munsterberg, gave a speech on peace to a large

Participants, as well as spectators and broadcast viewers, are subject to observer bias. How can you determine what really happened?

---

hypothesis A tentative and testable explanation of the relationship between two (or more) events or variables; often stated as a prediction that a certain outcome will result from specific conditions.

observer bias The distortion of evidence because of the personal motives and expectations of the viewer.

audience that included many reporters. He summarized the news accounts of what they heard and saw in this way:

> The reporters sat immediately in front of the platform. One man wrote that the audience was so surprised by my speech that it received it in complete silence; another wrote that I was constantly interrupted by loud applause and that at the end of my address the applause continued for minutes. The one wrote that during my opponent's speech I was constantly smiling; the other noticed that my face remained grave and without a smile. The one said that I grew purple-red from excitement; and the other found that I grew chalk-white. (1908, pp. 35–36) It would be interesting to go back to the original newspapers, to see how the reporters' accounts were related to their political views—then we might be able to understand why the reporters supposedly saw what they did.

You can look for examples of observer biases in your day-to-day life. Suppose, for example, you are in a close relationship. How might the motives and expectations you bring to that relationship affect the way you view your partner's behavior? Let's consider a study of 125 married couples.

> The couples were videotaped while they had two different 10-minute conversations (Knobloch et al., 2007). For one conversation, the couples discussed a positive aspect of their relationship; for the other, they discussed a recent unexpected event that had changed how sure they were (for better or for worse) about the future of their relationship. After each conversation, the two spouses gave individual ratings about the quality of the interactions along dimensions such as how warm or cold they thought their partner had been and how much their partner attempted to dominate the conversation. The researchers also asked neutral raters—people who had no connections to the couples—to watch and evaluate the conversations. Against the baseline provided by those neutral ratings, the couples' ratings displayed consistent observer bias. The direction of the bias was determined by how certain each member reported him- or herself to be about the future of the relationship. The researchers noted, for example, that "participants who were sure about their marriage had strong positive reactions to conversations that seemed normal to the naked eye" (p. 173).

This study demonstrates how expectations can lead different observers to reach different conclusions. The biases of the observers act as *filters* through which some things are noticed as relevant and significant and others are ignored as irrelevant and not meaningful.

Let's apply this lesson to what happens in psychology experiments. Researchers are often in the business of making observations. Given that every observer brings a different set of prior experiences to making those observations—and often those experiences include a commitment to a particular theory—you can see why observer biases could pose a problem. Researchers must work hard to ensure that they are viewing behavior with a "naked eye," free of biases. What can researchers do to ensure that their observations are minimally affected by prior expectations?

The Remedy To minimize observer biases, researchers rely on standardization and operational definitions. **Standardization** means using uniform, consistent procedures in all phases of data collection. All features of the test or experimental situation should be sufficiently standardized so all research participants experience exactly the same experimental conditions. Standardization means asking questions in the same way and scoring responses according to preestablished rules. Having results printed or recorded helps ensure their comparability across different times and places and with different participants and researchers.

Observations themselves must also be standardized: Scientists must solve the problem of how to translate their theories into concepts with consistent meaning. The strategy for standardizing the meaning of concepts is called *operationalization*. An **operational definition** standardizes meaning within an experiment, by defining a concept in terms of specific operations or procedures used to measure it or to determine its presence. All the variables in an experiment must be given operational definitions. A **variable** is any factor that varies in amount or kind.

In experimental settings, researchers most often wish to demonstrate a cause-and-effect relationship between two types of variables. The **independent variable** is the factor that the researcher manipulates; it functions as the causal part of the relationship. The effect part of the relationship is served by the **dependent variable,** which is what the experimenter measures. If the researcher's claims about cause and effect are correct, the value of the dependent variable will *depend* on the value of the independent variable. Imagine, for example, that you wished to test the hypothesis we mentioned earlier: that children who view a lot of violence on television will engage in more aggressive acts toward their peers. You could devise an experiment in which you manipulated the amount of violence each participant viewed (the independent variable) and then assessed how much aggression he or she displayed (the dependent variable).

Let's take a moment to put these new concepts to use in the context of a real experiment. The research project we will describe begins with a great philosophical question: Do people have free will, or is their behavior determined by forces of genetics and environment outside their control? The study didn't attempt to answer that question. Rather, the researchers argued that the way in which different individuals answer this question—their beliefs in *free will* versus *determinism*—has an impact on how they behave (Vohs & Schooler, 2008). The researchers reasoned that people who are guided by a worldview of determinism would feel less personal responsibility for bad behavior because they'd consider it out of their control. To test this hypothesis, the researchers gave students an opportunity to cheat!

Figure 2.2, on page 26, presents important aspects of the experiment. The researchers recruited roughly 120 college undergraduates to serve as participants. The independent variable for the study was participants' beliefs in free will versus

---

standardization A set of uniform procedures for treating each participant in a test, interview, or experiment, or for recording data.

operational definition A definition of a variable or condition in terms of the specific operation or procedure used to determine its presence.

variable In an experimental setting, a factor that varies in amount and kind.

independent variable In an experimental setting, a variable that the researcher manipulates with the expectation of having an impact on values of the dependent variable.

dependent variable In an experimental setting, a variable that the researcher measures to assess the impact of a variation in an independent variable.

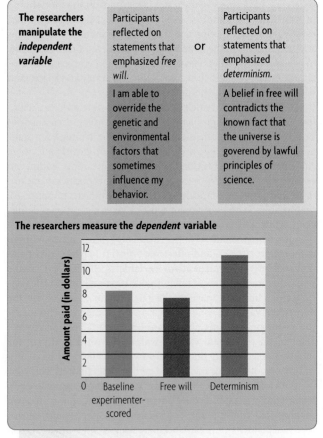

The researchers manipulate the *independent* variable	Participants reflected on statements that emphasized *free will*.	or	Participants reflected on statements that emphasized *determinism*.
	I am able to override the genetic and environmental factors that sometimes influence my behavior.		A belief in free will contradicts the known fact that the universe is goverend by lawful principles of science.

The researchers measure the *dependent* variable

FIGURE 2.2   Elements of an Experiment

To test their hypotheses, researchers create operational definitions for the independent and dependent variables.

From Vohs, K.D. & Schooler, J.W. (2008) The value of believing in free will: Encouraging a belief in determinism increases cheating. *Psychological Science, 19*, pp. 49–54. Reprinted with permission of Wiley-Blackwell.

determinism. To manipulate this variable, the researchers presented students with a series of 15 statements and asked them to think about each statement for one minute. As you might expect, those statements were different for the free will and determinism conditions. We provide examples in Figure 2.2.

To test their hypothesis, the researchers needed to provide the students with an opportunity to cheat. During the experiment, the students attempted to answer 15 problems from Graduate Record Examination practice tests. They could earn $1 for each correct answer. Participants scored their own answers in the absence of the experimenter. That provided the context for cheating: The experimenter would never know if a participant paid him- or herself more money than was due. The dependent variable for the experiment was the amount of money participants paid themselves.

---

experimental method   Research methodology that involves the manipulation of independent variables to determine their effects on the dependent variables.

confounding variable   A stimulus other than the variable an experimenter explicitly introduces into a research setting that affects a participant's behavior.

expectancy effect   Result that occurs when a researcher or observer subtly communicates to participants the kind of behavior he or she expects to find, thereby creating that expected reaction.

Figure 2.2 provides the results of the experiment. To determine how average students would actually score on the 15 GRE questions, the researchers had an extra condition in which they scored participants' performance themselves to see how much money the students would earn. The bar labeled "Baseline Experimenter-Scored" provides that information. As you can see from the other two bars in Figure 2.2, the independent variable had the effect on the dependent variable that the researchers expected. Those students who had been prompted to take the perspective of determinism paid themselves about $4 more than those students who focused on free will. Because of the experimenter-scored baseline—which shows free-will students at the same level as experimenter-scored students—we can infer that the determinism students were cheating. Take a moment to think about other ways in which you might operationalize the experimental variables, to test the same hypothesis by other means. You might, for example, want to measure cheating in some other fashion, to show that the results generalize to other life circumstances. This type of concern provides a transition to our exploration of experimental methods.

EXPERIMENTAL METHODS: ALTERNATIVE EXPLANATIONS AND THE NEED FOR CONTROLS

You know from day-to-day experience that people can suggest many causes for the same outcome. Psychologists face this same problem when they try to make exact claims about causality. To overcome causal ambiguity, researchers use **experimental methods:** They manipulate an independent variable to look for an effect on a dependent variable. The goal of this method is to make strong causal claims about the impact of one variable on the other. In this section, we describe the problem of *alternative explanations* and some steps researchers take to counter the problem.

The Challenge to Objectivity   When psychologists test a hypothesis, they most often have in mind an explanation for why change in the independent variable should affect the dependent variable in a particular way. For example, you might predict, and demonstrate experimentally, that the viewing of television violence leads to high levels of aggression. But how can you know that it was precisely the viewing of *violence* that produced aggression? To make the strongest possible case for their hypotheses, psychologists must be very sensitive to the existence of possible *alternative explanations*. The more alternative explanations there might be for a given result, the less confidence there is that the initial hypothesis is accurate. When something other than what an experimenter purposely introduces into a research setting changes a participant's behavior and adds confusion to the interpretation of the data, it is called a **confounding variable.** When the real cause of some observed behavioral effect is *confounded,* the experimenter's interpretation of the data is put at risk. Suppose, for example, that violent television scenes are louder and involve more movement than do most nonviolent scenes. In that case, the violent and the superficial aspects of the scenes are confounded. The researcher is unable to specify which factor uniquely produces aggressive behavior.

Although each different experimental method potentially gives rise to a unique set of alternative explanations, we can identify two types of confounds that apply to almost all experiments, which we will call *expectancy effects* and *placebo effects*. Unintentional **expectancy effects** occur when a researcher or

Is violent behavior caused by viewing violence on television? How could you find out?

observer subtly communicates to the research participants the behaviors he or she expects to find, thereby producing the desired reaction. Under these circumstances, the experimenter's expectations, rather than the independent variable, actually help trigger the observed reactions.

> In an experiment, 12 students were given groups of rats that were going to be trained to run a maze. Half of the students were told their rats were from a special maze-bright breed. The other students were told their rats were bred to be maze-dull. As you might guess, their rats were actually all the same. Nonetheless, the students' results corresponded with their expectations for their rats. The rats labeled bright were found to be much better learners than those that had been labeled as dull (Rosenthal & Fode, 1963).

How do you suppose the students communicated their expectations to their rats? Do you see why you should worry even more about expectancy effects when an experiment is carried out within species—with a human experimenter and human participants? Expectation effects distort the content of discovery.

A **placebo effect** occurs when experimental participants change their behavior in the *absence* of any kind of experimental manipulation. This concept originated in medicine to account for cases in which a patient's health improved after he or she had received medication that was chemically inert or a treatment that was nonspecific. The placebo effect refers to an improvement in health or well-being related to the individual's *belief* that the treatment will be effective. Some treatments with no genuine medical effects have been shown, even so, to produce good or excellent outcomes for 70 percent of the patients on whom they were used (Roberts et al., 1993).

In a psychological research setting, a placebo effect has occurred whenever a behavioral response is influenced by a person's expectation of what to do or how to feel rather than by the specific intervention or procedures employed to produce that response. Recall the experiment relating television viewing to later aggression. Suppose we discovered that experimental participants who hadn't watched any television at all also showed high levels of aggression. We might conclude that these individuals, by virtue of being put in a situation that allowed them to display aggression, would expect they were *supposed* to behave aggressively and would go on to do so. Experimenters must always be aware that participants change the way they behave simply because they are aware of being observed or tested. For example, participants may feel special about being chosen to take part in a study and thus act differently than they would ordinarily. Such effects can compromise an experiment's results.

The Remedy: Control Procedures Because human and animal behaviors are complex and often have multiple causes, good research design involves anticipating possible confounds and devising strategies for eliminating them. Similar to defensive strategies in sports, good research designs anticipate what the other team might do and make plans to counteract it. Researchers' strategies are called **control procedures**—methods that attempt to hold constant all variables and conditions other than those related to the hypothesis being tested. In an experiment, instructions, room temperature, tasks, the way the researcher is dressed, time allotted, the way the responses are recorded, and many other details of the situation must be similar for all participants, to ensure that their experience is the same. The only differences in participants' experiences should be those introduced by the independent variable. Let's look at remedies for the specific confounding variables, expectancy and placebo effects.

Imagine, for example, that you enriched the aggression experiment to include a treatment group that watched comedy programs. You'd want to be careful not to treat your comedy and violence participants in different ways based on your expectations. Thus, in your experiment, we would want the research assistant who greeted the participants and later assessed their aggression to be unaware of whether they had watched a violent program or a comedy: We would keep the research assistant *blind* to the assignment of participants to conditions. In the best circumstances, bias can be eliminated by keeping *both* experimental assistants and participants blind to which participants get which treatment. This technique is called a **double-blind control.** In our prospective aggression experiment, we couldn't keep participants from knowing whether they had watched comedy or violence. However, we would take great care to ensure that they couldn't guess that our later analyses would focus on their subsequent aggression.

To account for placebo effects, researchers generally include an experimental condition in which the treatment is

---

placebo effect A change in behavior in the absence of an experimental manipulation.

control procedure Consistent procedure for giving instructions, scoring responses, and holding all other variables constant except those being systematically varied.

double-blind control An experimental technique in which biased expectations of experimenters are eliminated by keeping both participants and experimental assistants unaware of which participants have received which treatment.

not administered. We call this a **placebo control.** Placebo controls fall into the general category of controls by which experimenters assure themselves they are making appropriate comparisons. Suppose you see a late-night TV commercial that celebrates the herbal supplement ginkgo biloba as an answer to all your memory problems. What might you expect if you buy a supply of ginkgo and take it weekly? One study demonstrated that university students who took ginkgo every morning for six weeks did, in fact, show improvements in their performance on cognitive tasks (Elsabagh et al., 2005). On one task, people were asked to view a series of 20 pictures on a computer screen, name them, and later recall those names. The participants were 14 percent better at this task after six weeks of ginkgo. However, participants who took a placebo—a pill with no active ingredients—also improved by 14 percent. The placebo control suggests that improvement on the task was the result of practice from the initial session. The data from control conditions provide an important baseline against which the experimental effect is evaluated.

The Remedy: Research Designs To implement control conditions, researchers make decisions about what type of research design best suits their goals. In some research designs, which are referred to as **between-subjects designs,** different groups of participants are *randomly assigned,* by chance procedures, to an experimental condition (exposed to one or more experimental treatments) or to a control condition (not exposed to an experimental treatment). **Random assignment** is one of the major steps researchers take to eliminate confounding variables that relate to individual differences among potential research participants. This is the same procedure we had in mind for the aggression experiment. The random assignment to experimental and control conditions makes it quite likely that the two groups will be similar in important ways at the start of an experiment because each participant has the same probability of being in a treatment condition as in a control condition. We shouldn't have to worry, for example, that everyone in the **experimental group** loves violent television and

everyone in the **control group** hates it. Random assignment should mix both types of people together in each group. If outcome differences are found between conditions, we can be more confident that the differences were caused by a treatment or intervention rather than by preexisting differences.

Researchers also try to approximate randomness in the way they bring participants into the laboratory. Suppose you would like to test the hypothesis that 6-year-old children are more likely to lie than 4-year-old children. At the end of your experiment, you'd like your conclusions to apply to the whole **population** of 4-year-olds and 6-year-olds. However, you can bring only a very small subset—a **sample**—of the world's 4- and 6-year-olds into your laboratory. Typically, psychology experiments use from 20 to 100 participants. How should you choose your group of children? Researchers attempt to construct a **representative sample,** which is a sample that closely matches the overall characteristics of the population with respect, for example, to the distribution of males and females, racial and ethnic groups, and so on. For example, if your study of children's lying only included boys, we wouldn't consider that a representative sample of the full population of 4- and 6-year-olds. To achieve a representative sample, researchers often use the procedure of **random sampling,** which means that every member of a population has an equal likelihood of participating in the experiment.

Another type of experimental design—a **within-subjects design**—uses each participant as his or her own control. For example, the behavior of an experimental participant before getting the treatment might be compared with behavior after. Or, each participant might experience more than one level of the independent variable. Consider an experiment that tested whether children had better memory for "nice" versus "mean" individuals.

As you go through life, you might consider it a good policy to avoid people who are threatening to you. To do so, of course, you need to be able to remember who those people are. Researchers tested the hypothesis that 3- and 4-year-old children already have better memory for the faces of "mean" individuals (Kinzler & Shutts, 2008). In the training phase of the experiment, the children viewed, on a computer screen, a series of faces with slightly positive expressions. For half the faces, the experimenter provided nice facts (for example, "Kevin is always nice. Today he brought in cookies and everyone got some."). For the remaining faces, the experimenter provided mean facts (for example "Kevin is always mean. Today he stole everyone's cookies and no one got any."). In the test phase of the experiment, the children received a memory test. They saw the original faces paired with brand new faces. The children had to indicate which face they had seen before (for example, "Which one is Kevin?"). As shown in **Figure 2.3,** the children showed consistently better memory for the faces with which mean facts had been associated.

Because this study used a within-subjects design, the experiments could draw the strong conclusion that the children's memory was different for faces associated with nice versus mean information. The study indicates that by age 3 you were probably good at remembering which people had been mean to you. We might imagine that the researchers are hard at work to see if the same pattern appears with even younger children.

The research methodologies we have described so far all involve the manipulation of an independent variable to look for an effect on a dependent variable. Although this experimental

---

placebo control An experimental condition in which treatment is not administered; it is used in cases where a placebo effect might occur.

between-subjects design A research design in which different groups of participants are randomly assigned to experimental conditions or to control conditions.

random assignment A procedure by which participants have an equal likelihood of being assigned to any condition within an experiment.

experimental group A group in an experiment that is exposed to a treatment or experiences a manipulation of the independent variable.

control group A group in an experiment that is not exposed to a treatment or does not experience a manipulation of the independent variable.

population The entire set of individuals to which generalizations will be made based on an experimental sample.

sample A subset of a population selected as participants in an experiment.

representative sample A subset of a population that closely matches the overall characteristics of the population with respect to the distribution of males and females, racial and ethnic groups, and so on.

random sampling A procedure that ensures that every member of a population has an equal likelihood of participating in an experiment.

within-subjects design A research design that uses each participant as his or her own control; for example, the behavior of an experimental participant before receiving treatment might be compared to his or her behavior after receiving treatment.

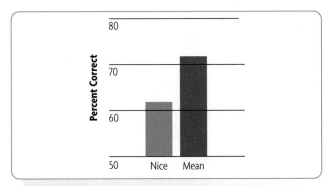

FIGURE 2.3 Children's Memory for Faces of "Mean" and "Nice" Individuals

In the training phase of the experiment, 3- to 4-year-old children acquired "mean" and "nice" information about a series of faces. In the test phase, the children attempted to identify the faces they had seen earlier. Children's memory was better for the faces with which "mean" information had been associated.

From Kinzler, K.D., & Shutts, K., Memory for 'mean' over 'nice': The influence of threat on children's face memory, *Cognition, 107,* pp. 775–783, Copyright (2008), with permission from Elsevier.

method often allows researchers to make the strongest claims about causal relations among variables, several conditions can make this method less desirable. First, during an experiment, behavior is frequently studied in an artificial environment, one in which situational factors are controlled so heavily that the environment may itself distort the behavior from the way it would occur naturally. Critics claim that much of the richness and complexity of natural behavior patterns is lost in controlled experiments, sacrificed to the simplicity of dealing with only one or a few variables and responses. Second, research participants typically know they are in an experiment and are being tested and measured. They may react to this awareness by trying to please the researcher, attempting to "psych out" the research purpose, or changing their behavior from what it would be if they were unaware of being monitored. Third, some important research problems are not amenable to ethical experimental treatment. We could not, for example, try to discover whether the tendency toward child abuse is transmitted from generation to generation by creating an experimental group of children who would be abused and a control group of children who would not be. In the next section, we will turn to a type of research method that often addresses these concerns.

CORRELATIONAL METHODS

Is intelligence associated with creativity? Are optimistic people healthier than pessimists? Is there a relationship between experiencing child abuse and later mental illness? These questions involve variables that a psychologist could not easily or ethically manipulate. To answer these questions, as we do in later chapters, requires research based on **correlational methods.** Psychologists use correlational methods when they want to determine to what extent two variables, traits, or attributes are related.

To determine the precise degree of correlation that exists between two variables, psychologists compute a statistical measure known as the **correlation coefficient (r).** This value can vary between +1.0 and −1.0, where +1.0 indicates a perfect

positive correlation, −1.0 indicates a perfect negative correlation, and 0.0 indicates no correlation at all. A positive correlation coefficient means that as one set of scores increases, a second set also increases. The reverse is true with negative correlations; the second set of scores goes in the opposite direction to the values of the first scores (see **Figure 2.4** on page 30). Correlations that are closer to zero mean that there is a weak relationship or no relationship between scores on two measures. As the correlation coefficient gets stronger, closer to the ±1.0 maximum, predictions about one variable based on information about the other variable become increasingly more accurate.

Suppose, for example, researchers were interested in determining the relationship between students' sleep habits and their success in college. They might operationally define *sleep habits* as the average amount of sleep per night. *Success in college* could be defined as cumulative grade-point average (GPA). The researchers could assess each variable for an appropriate sample of students and compute the correlation coefficient between them. A strongly positive score would mean that the more a student sleeps, the higher his or her GPA is likely to be. Knowing a student's "hours per night" would then allow the researchers to make a reasonable prediction about the student's GPA.

The researchers might want to take the next step and say that the way to improve students' GPAs would be to force them to sleep more. This intervention is misguided. A strong correlation indicates only that two sets of data are related in a systematic way; the correlation does not ensure that one causes the other. *Correlation does not imply causation.* The correlation could reflect any one of several cause-and-effect possibilities. Many of those possibilities involve a *third variable* that works in the background to bring about the correlation. Suppose, for example, that people both sleep better and get higher grades when they take easy courses. Under those circumstances, the difficulty of students' courses would be a third variable that would bring about a positive correlation between amount of sleep and GPA. It could also be that case people who study more efficiently get to bed sooner or that people who experience anxiety about schoolwork cannot fall asleep. You can see from these three possibilities that correlations most often require researchers to probe for deeper explanations.

We don't want to leave you with the impression that correlational methods aren't valuable research tools. Throughout *Psychology and Life,* we will see many correlational studies that have led to important insights. We'll offer just one example here to whet your appetite.

Can you tell whether people will be good leaders just by looking at them? To address this question, a pair of researchers gathered photographs of the CEOs of the companies that were listed as the top 25 and bottom 25 on the Fortune 500 website (Rule & Ambady, 2008). The researchers asked 50 students to view the photographs and answer, on a 7-point scale, "How good would this person be

correlational method Research methodology that determines to what extent two variables, traits, or attributes are related.

correlation coefficient (r) A statistic that indicates the degree of relationship between two variables.

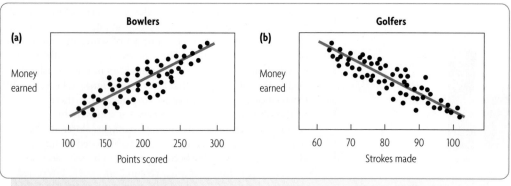

Bowlers (a)

Money earned

100 150 200 250 300
Points scored

Golfers (b)

Money earned

60 70 80 90 100
Strokes made

FIGURE 2.4   Positive and Negative Correlations

These imaginary data display the difference between positive and negative correlations. Each point represents a single bowler or golfer. (a) In general, the more points a professional bowler scores, the more money he or she will earn. Thus, there is a positive correlation between those two variables. (b) The correlation for golf is negative, because golfers earn more money when they make fewer strokes.

at leading a company?" The researchers also collected financial information for each company. The data revealed a positive correlation between participants' judgments and the companies' performance. On the whole, the CEOs who got the highest leadership ratings—again, based only on their photographs—led the most profitable companies. Why might this positive correlation emerge? The researchers were careful to acknowledge that more than one causal pathway is possible: "Of course, we cannot draw any causal inferences as to whether more successful companies choose individuals with a particular appearance to be their CEOs or whether individuals with a particular appearance emerge as more successful in their work as CEOs" (p. 110).

Can you see why a correlational design is appropriate to address this issue? You can't randomly assign people to look like leaders

What procedures might you follow to determine the correlation between students' sleep habits and their success in college? How would you evaluate potential causal relationships underlying any correlation?

or not, nor can you randomly assign companies to be profitable or not. You must wait to see what differences emerge as leadership unfolds in the real world.

SUBLIMINAL INFLUENCE?

To close this section, we offer one concrete example of how psychological research has been used to assess vigorous claims that behavior can be influenced by messages outside conscious awareness—*subliminal* messages. Are there messages hidden on rock albums that encourage teens toward violent acts? The media have reported such claims. Could subliminal advertising affect the outcome of a presidential election? In the 2000 election, the word "RATS" flashed briefly during an ad that criticized the Democratic candidate. Might that have changed votes?

Subliminal influence has a long history. Although it was almost certainly a hoax, a 1957 study made headlines when James Vicary, the "inventor" of subliminal advertising, claimed that the message "Buy Popcorn" flashed on the screen during a movie yielded a 58 percent increase in popcorn sales (Rogers, 1993)! The *Wall Street Journal* once reported that a New Orleans supermarket significantly decreased stealing and cashier shortages after piping the following subliminal message into its music system: "If I steal, I will go to jail." A telephone survey in Toledo, Ohio, showed that nearly 75 percent of the 400 adults surveyed were familiar with subliminal advertising (Rogers & Smith, 1993). Of that group, again, nearly 75 percent believed subliminal advertising was used successfully by marketers. In general, the better educated the respondents were, the more likely they were to believe in the effectiveness of subliminal advertising.

You now have the knowledge to address the critical question: Do subliminal messages really influence mental states and behavior as their advocates claim? Our answer comes from an application of the experimental methods we have described (see **Figure 2.5**).

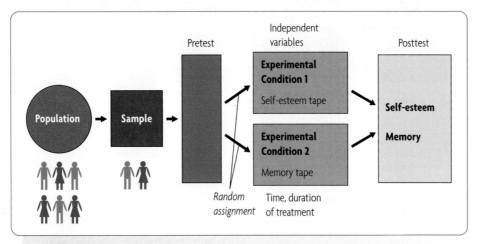

FIGURE 2.5 Experimental Design for Testing Hypotheses about the Effectiveness of Subliminal Messages

In this simplified version of the experiment, a sample of people is drawn from a larger, general population. They are given pretest measures and randomly assigned to receive subliminal tapes. They are then given posttests that objectively assess any changes in the dependent variables, memory, and self-esteem.

A team of experimenters set out to determine the effectiveness of listening to commercially available audiotapes designed to improve self-esteem or memory. The participants were 237 men and women volunteers, ranging from 18 to 60 years of age.

After a pretest session in which their initial self-esteem and memory were measured on standard psychological tests and questionnaires, the participants were randomly assigned to two conditions. Half of them received subliminal memory tapes, and the others received subliminal self-esteem tapes. They listened regularly to the tapes for a five-week period and then returned to the laboratory for a posttest session to evaluate their memories (using four memory tests) and self-esteem (using three self-esteem scales). The researchers were blind to which participants received which treatment (Greenwald et al., 1991).

Did the tapes boost self-esteem and enhance memory? The results from this controlled experiment indicate that no significant improvement was shown on any of the objective measures of either self-esteem or memory. However, one very powerful effect did emerge: the placebo effect of expecting to be helped. Anticipating this placebo effect, the researchers had added another independent variable. Half the participants in each group received memory tapes that were mismarked "self-esteem" and the others received self-esteem tapes in "memory boxes." Participants believed their self-esteem improved if they received tapes with that label or felt their memory improved if their tapes were labeled "memory"—even when they had been listening to the other tape!

This rigorous experiment allows for some very concrete advice: Save your money; subliminal self-help programs offer nothing more than placebo effects. An important goal of *Psychology and Life* is to provide you with such concrete conclusions based on solid experimental methods.

This experiment also gives you a specific example of the types of variables that psychologists measure. In this case, it was partici-

pants' beliefs about improvements in self-esteem and memory as well as objective measures of self-esteem and memory. In the next section, we discuss more generally the way in which psychologists measure important processes and dimensions of experience.

Psychological Measurement

Because psychological processes are so varied and complex, they pose major challenges to researchers who want to measure them. Although some actions and processes are easily seen,

CAN SURVEY RESEARCH AFFECT YOUR ATTITUDES?

Consider this scenario. It's about election time. Just when you've finished eating dinner, the telephone rings. A friendly voice at the other end asks you if you have a few minutes to answer some questions about the candidates. You say, "Why not?" This is an opportunity for you to be a research participant outside the laboratory. But here's an answer to your question, "Why not?" The questions on the survey can have a strong impact on your attitudes.

Let's look at a laboratory study that illustrates this principle. The study took place in England, so it focused on participants' attitudes toward the Prime Minister, Tony Blair (Haddock, 2002). Participants filled out a questionnaire that began with the question, "How interested are you in British politics?" After that, the questionnaire continued in one of four ways. One version asked participants to list two positive characteristics for Blair; a second asked participants for five positive characteristics. The remaining two versions of the questionnaires asked for two or five negative characteristics. The next questions on each questionnaire asked the participants to provide favorability ratings toward Blair on 7-point scales with higher scores reflecting more positive attitudes.

From this description, you can see that one important component of the experiment was the number of characteristics each participant attempted to list. Why might that matter? Suppose you were asked to list negative attributes for a politician such as the president or a senator. You would probably find it easy to generate two negative attributes but relatively hard to generate five. After trying to generate five, you might be thinking, "Hey, if I can't think of five things that are bad about this person, maybe he or she is actually pretty good" (see Schwarz et al., 2003). For that reason, if you try to generate more negative characteristics, you might actually come to like the politician better; if you try to generate more positive characteristics, that effort can have a negative impact on your attitudes.

The results presented in the figure support these predictions for the subset of participants who were relatively uninterested in British politics. For example, those participants' ratings of Blair were relatively more positive when they attempted to recall more negative characteristics. For those students who were already interested in British politics—presumably because they had sufficient knowledge and strong attitudes—the ease with which they could retrieve information about Blair did not have a similar impact on their attitudes.

From this pattern of results, here's what you might anticipate when you get that after-dinner call: The first thing the voice should ask is how interested you are in politics. At that point, the voice will know how easy it might be to alter your attitudes with questions that, on the surface, seem quite reasonable. Would you have anticipated that having people focus at length on Blair's negative characteristics would make them like him more?

So when you answer "research" questions out in the real world, be wary of the true purposes of the enterprise. In the laboratory, researchers must provide you with debriefing information (see p. 37) that helps you understand how research participation might have influenced how you think or feel. Those people who catch you after dinner have no similar responsibilities toward full disclosure. Their major hope is that they can change your attitudes in a way that will affect your behavior when you find yourself in the voting booth.

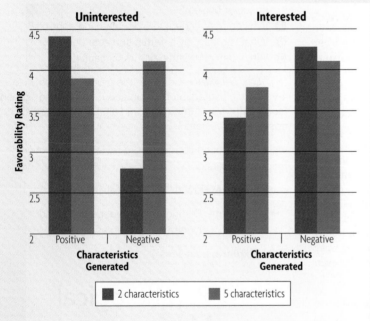

Interest in Politics

many, such as anxiety or dreaming, are not. Thus one task for a psychological researcher is to make the unseen visible, to make internal events and processes external, and to make private experiences public. You have already seen how important it is for researchers to provide operational definitions of the phenomena they wish to study. Those definitions generally provide some procedure for assigning numbers to, or *quantifying,* different levels, sizes, intensities, or amounts of a variable. Many measurement methods are available, each with its particular advantages and disadvantages.

Our review of psychological measurement begins with a discussion of the distinction between two ways of gauging the accuracy of a measure: reliability and validity. We then review different measurement techniques for data collection. By whatever means psychologists collect their data, they must use appropriate statistical methods to verify their hypotheses. A description of how psychologists analyze their data is given in the Statistical Supplement, which follows this chapter. Read it in conjunction with this chapter.

ACHIEVING RELIABILITY AND VALIDITY

The goal of psychological measurement is to generate findings that are both reliable and valid. **Reliability** refers to the consistency or dependability of behavioral data resulting from psychological testing or experimental research. A reliable result is one that will be repeated under similar conditions of testing at different times. A reliable measuring instrument yields comparable scores when employed repeatedly (and when the thing being measured does not change). Consider the experiment we just described, which showed that subliminal audiotapes generate only placebo effects. That experiment used 237 participants. The experimenters' claim that the result was "reliable" means that they should be able to repeat the experiment with any new group of participants of comparable size and generate the same pattern of data.

Validity means that the information produced by research or testing accurately measures the psychological variable or quality it is intended to measure. A valid measure of *happiness,* for example, should allow us to predict how happy you are likely to be in particular situations. A valid experiment means that the researcher can generalize to broader circumstances, often from the laboratory to the real world. When we gave you advice based on the audiotapes experiment, we were accepting the researchers' claim that the results are valid. Tests and experiments can be reliable without being valid. We could, for example, use your shoe size as an index of your happiness. This would be reliable (we'd always get the same answer), but not valid (we'd learn very little about your day-to-day happiness level).

As you now read about different types of measures, try to evaluate them in terms of reliability and validity.

SELF-REPORT MEASURES

Often researchers are interested in obtaining data about experiences they cannot directly observe. Sometimes these experiences are internal psychological states, such as beliefs, attitudes, and feelings. At other times, these experiences are external behaviors but—like sexual activities or criminal acts—not generally appropriate for psychologists to witness. In these cases, investigations rely on self-reports. **Self-report measures** are verbal answers, either written or spoken, to questions the researcher poses. Researchers devise reliable ways to quantify these self-reports so they can make meaningful comparisons between different individuals' responses.

Self-reports include responses made on questionnaires and during interviews. A *questionnaire* or *survey* is a written set of questions, ranging in content from questions of fact ("Are you a registered voter?"), to questions about past or present behavior ("How much do you smoke?"), to questions about attitudes and feelings ("How satisfied are you with your present job?"). *Open-ended* questions allow respondents to answer freely in their own words. Questions may also have a number of *fixed alternatives* such as *yes, no,* and *undecided.*

An *interview* is a dialogue between a researcher and an individual for the purpose of obtaining detailed information. Instead of being completely standardized, like a questionnaire, an interview is *interactive.* An interviewer may vary the questioning to follow up on something the respondent said. Good interviewers are also sensitive to the process of the social interaction as well as to the information revealed. They are trained to establish *rapport,* a positive social relationship with the respondent that encourages trust and the sharing of personal information.

Although researchers rely on a wide variety of self-report measures, there are limits to their usefulness. Obviously, many forms of self-report cannot be used with preverbal children, illiterate adults, speakers of other languages, some mentally disturbed people, and nonhuman animals. Even when self-reports can be used, they may not be reliable or valid. Participants may misunderstand the questions or not remember clearly what they actually experienced. Furthermore, self-reports may be influenced by social desirability. People may give false or misleading answers to create a favorable (or, sometimes, unfavorable) impression of themselves. They may be embarrassed to report their true experiences or feelings. If respondents are aware of a questionnaire's or interview's purpose, they may lie or alter the truth to get a job, to get discharged from a mental hospital, or to accomplish any other goal. An interview situation also allows personal biases and prejudices to affect how the interviewer asks questions and how the respondent answers them.

BEHAVIORAL MEASURES AND OBSERVATIONS

As a group, psychological researchers are interested in a wide range of behaviors. They may study a rat running a maze, a child drawing a picture, a student memorizing a poem, or a worker repeatedly performing a task. **Behavioral measures** are ways to study overt actions and observable and recordable reactions.

---

reliability The degree to which a test produces similar scores each time it is used; stability or consistency of the scores produced by an instrument.

validity The extent to which a test measures what it was intended to measure.

self-report measure A self-behavior that is identified through a participant's own observations and reports.

behavioral measure Overt actions or reaction that is observed and recorded, exclusive of self-reported behavior.

By watching from behind a one-way mirror, a researcher can record observations of a child without influencing or interfering with the child's behavior. Have you ever changed your behavior when you knew you were being watched?

One of the primary ways to study what people do is *observation*. Researchers use observation in a planned, precise, and systematic manner. Observations focus on either the *process* or the *products* of behavior. In an experiment on learning, for instance, a researcher might observe how many times a research participant rehearsed a list of words (process) and then how many words the participant remembered on a final test (product). For *direct observations*, the behavior under investigation must be clearly visible and overt and easily recorded. For example, in a laboratory experiment on emotions, a researcher could observe a participant's facial expressions as the individual looked at emotionally arousing stimuli.

A researcher's direct observations are often augmented by technology. For example, contemporary psychologists often rely on computers to provide very precise measures of the time it takes for research participants to perform various tasks, such as reading a sentence or solving a problem. Although some forms of exact measurement were available before the computer age, computers now provide extraordinary flexibility in collecting and analyzing precise information. In Chapter 3, we will describe the newest types of technologies that allow researchers to produce behavioral measures of a remarkable kind: pictures of the brain at work.

In **naturalistic observation,** some naturally occurring behavior is viewed by a researcher, who makes no attempt to change or interfere with it. For instance, a researcher behind a one-way mirror might observe the play of children who are not aware of being observed. Some kinds of human behavior can be studied only through naturalistic observation because it would be unethical or impractical to do otherwise. For example, it would be unethical to experiment with severe deprivation in early life to see its effects on a child's later development.

When studying behavior in a laboratory setting, researchers are unable to observe the long-term effects of natural habitats in

shaping complex patterns of behavior. To overcome those limitations, researchers may undertake programs of naturalistic observation. Consider the work of biologist **Dorothy Cheney** and psychologist **Robert Seyfarth** who, since 1992, have journeyed repeatedly to Botswana to observe a group of chacma baboons (Cheney & Seyfarth, 2007). Cheney and Seyfarth explain why they chose to study baboons:

> Each animal maintains a complex network of social relationships with relatives and nonrelatives—relationships that are simultaneously cooperative and competitive. Navigating through this network would seem to require sophisticated social knowledge and skills. Moreover, the challenges that baboons confront are not just social but also ecological. Food must be found and defended, predators evaded and sometimes attacked. Studies of baboons in the wild, therefore, allow us to examine how an individual's behavior affects her survival and reproduction. (*Cheney & Seyfarth, 2007, p. 10*)

The data Cheney and Seyfarth have obtained from their ambitious project cast important light on how baboons deploy their social intelligence. Moreover, their analyses allow for a deeper understanding of how evolutionary pressures might have yielded similarities and dissimilarities between human behavior and the behavior of these particular nonhuman primates. For example, Cheney and Seyfarth conclude that, "although their minds have been overwhelmingly shaped by social life, baboons have only a limited ability to recognize the mental states of others": "Unlike humans and even very young children, they feel no urge to gossip or share information" (p. 275).

In the early stages of an investigation, naturalistic observation is especially useful. It helps researchers discover the extent of a phenomenon or to get an idea of what the important variables and relationships might be. The data from naturalistic observation often provide clues for an investigator to use in formulating a specific hypothesis or research plan.

When they wish to test hypotheses with behavioral measures, researchers sometimes turn to *archival data*. Imagine all the types of information you might find in a library or on the Web: birth and death records, weather reports, movie attendance figures, legislators' voting patterns, and so on. Any of those types of information could become valuable to test the right hypothesis. Consider a study that examined whether men and women differ in their level of *heroism* (Becker & Eagly, 2004). To address this question, the researchers couldn't create a laboratory test; they couldn't set a building on fire to see whether more men or women rushed in. Instead, they defined behaviors out in the world that were arguably heroic and then looked to archival records to assess the relative contributions of men and women. For example, the researchers examined participation in "Doctors of the World," an organization that sends medical personnel to all corners of the globe. Personnel in this program assume a "nonnegligible risk [by] delivering health and medical services in environments marked by local violence and unsanitary conditions" (Becker & Eagly, 2004, p. 173). What did the archival data show? More than half of the participants in Doctors of the World (65.8 percent) were women. You can see why archival data are essential to address certain types of questions.

Before we leave the topic of psychological measurement, we must emphasize that many research projects combine both self-report measures and behavioral observations. Researchers

---

naturalistic observation A research technique in which unobtrusive observations are made of behaviors that occur in natural environments.

Robert Seyfarth and Dorothy Cheney have paid repeated visits to Botswana to make naturalistic observations of baboons. What are some advantages of studying animals in their natural habitats?

may, for example, specifically look for a relationship between how people report they will behave and how they actually behave. In addition, rather than involving large numbers of participants, some research projects will focus all their measures on a single individual or small group in a **case study.** Intensive analyses of particular individuals can sometimes yield important insights into general features of human experience. For example, in Chapter 3 you will learn that careful observations of single patients with brain damage provided the basis for important theories of the localization of language functions in the brain.

We have now described several types of procedures and measures that researchers use. Before we move on, we want to give you an opportunity to see how the same issue can be addressed in different research designs. Consider Shakespeare's question, "What's in a name?" In *Romeo and Juliet,* Juliet asserts, "That which we call a rose by any other name would smell as sweet." But is that correct? Do you think your name has an impact on the way other people treat you? Is it better to have a common, familiar name or a rare, distinctive one? Or does your name not matter at all? In **Table 2.1** on page 36 we give examples of combinations of measures and methods that researchers might use to answer those questions. As you read through Table 2.1, ask yourself how willing you would be to participate in each type of study. In the next section, we consider the ethical standards that govern psychological research.

STOP AND REVIEW

❶ Why can some measures be reliable but not valid?

❷ Why is it important for interviewers to establish rapport?

❸ Suppose a researcher spends time observing children's behavior on a playground. What kind of measure would that be?

Visit MyPsychLab.com for more review and practice on the following topics:

❋ **Simulate:** Doing Simple Statistics

❋ **Simulate:** Observational Studies

Ethical Issues in Human and Animal Research

In the study that tested the effectiveness of subliminal messages, the researchers deceived the participants by mislabeling the tapes. They did so to see if the participants' expectations would lead them to believe that the messages were helpful even if objective measures of memory and self-esteem showed no improvement. Deception is always ethically suspect, but in this case, how else could researchers assess the placebo effect of false beliefs held by the participants? How should the *potential gains* of a research project be weighed against the *costs* it incurs to those who are subjected to procedures that are risky, painful, stressful, or deceptive? Psychologists ask themselves these questions all the time (Bersoff, 2008).

Respect for the basic rights of humans and animals is a fundamental obligation of all researchers. Beginning in 1953, the American Psychological Association has published guidelines for ethical standards for researchers. Current research practice is governed by the 2002 revision of those guidelines. Consider the issue of deception in research. The 2002 guidelines assert, "Psychologists do not deceive prospective participants about research that is reasonably expected to cause physical pain or severe emotional distress" (American Psychological Association, 2002, p. 1070). Guidelines of this sort were not always in force. For example, in Chapter 16 we will describe classic experiments on *obedience to authority.* In these experiments, participants were deceived into believing that they were giving dangerous electric shocks to total strangers. Evidence from the experiments suggests that the participants were, in fact, experiencing "severe emotional distress." For that reason—although the research is quite important to an understanding of human nature—no responsible psychologist could advocate replicating the studies today. In fact, researchers no longer make decisions about issues like

---

case study Intensive observation of a particular individual or small group of individuals.

TABLE 2.1 What's in a Name? Methods and Measures

Research Goal	Dependent Measure	
	Self-Report	**Observation**
Correlational Methods To assess the correlation between the frequency of people's names and their experience of happiness.	Each participant's assessment of his or her own happiness.	
To assess the correlation between the frequency of children's names and their acceptance by peers.		Children's amount of social interaction on the playground.
Experimental Methods To determine if people judge identical photos differently when different names are assigned to them.	Participants' ratings of baby pictures to which random names have been assigned.	
To determine if people's actual social interactions change because of name-based expectations.		The number of positive facial expressions people produce in conversation with a stranger who has introduced himself as *Mark* or *Marcus*.

the use of deception in isolation. To guarantee that ethical principles are honored, special committees oversee every research proposal, imposing strict guidelines issued by the U.S. Department of Health and Human Services. Universities and colleges, hospitals, and research institutes each have *review boards* that approve and reject proposals for human and animal research. Let's review some of the factors those review boards consider.

INFORMED CONSENT

At the start of nearly all laboratory research with human subjects, participants undergo a process of **informed consent.** They are *informed* about the procedures they will experience

as well as the potential risks and benefits of participation. Given that information, participants are asked to sign a statement indicating that they *consent* to continue. Participants are also assured that their privacy is protected: All records of their behavior are kept strictly confidential; they must approve any public sharing of them. In addition, participants are told in advance that they may leave an experiment any time they wish, without penalty, and they are given the names and phone numbers of officials to contact if they have any grievances.

RISK/GAIN ASSESSMENT

Most psychology experiments carry little risk to the participants, especially where participants are merely asked to perform routine tasks. However, some experiments that study more personal aspects of human nature—such as emotional reactions, self-images, conformity, stress, or aggression—can be upsetting or psychologically disturbing. Therefore,

---

informed consent The process through which individuals are informed about experimental procedures, risks, and benefits before they provide formal consent to become research participants.

Researchers who use animal subjects are required to provide a humane environment. Do you think scientific gains justify the use of nonhuman animals in research?

whenever a researcher conducts such a study, risks must be minimized, participants must be informed of the risks, and suitable precautions must be taken to deal with strong reactions. Where any risk is involved, it is carefully weighed by each institutional review board in terms of its necessity for achieving the benefits to the participants of the study, to science, and to society.

INTENTIONAL DECEPTION

For some kinds of research, it is not possible to tell the participants the whole story in advance without biasing the results. If you were studying the effects of violence on television on aggression, for example, you would not want your participants to know your purpose in advance. But is your hypothesis enough to justify the deception?

We already noted that the American Psychological Association's (2002) ethical principles give explicit instructions about the use of deception. In addition to the guideline that participants not be misled about the probability of physical or emotional distress, the APA provides other restrictions: (1) The study must have sufficient scientific and educational importance to warrant deception; (2) researchers must demonstrate that no equally effective procedures excluding deception are available; (3) the deception must be explained to the participants by the conclusion of the research; and (4) participants must have the opportunity to withdraw their data once the deception is explained. In experiments involving deception, a review board may impose constraints, insist on monitoring initial demonstrations of the procedure, or deny approval.

DEBRIEFING

Participation in psychological research should always be a mutual exchange of information between researcher and participant. The researcher may learn something new about a behavioral phenomenon from the participant's responses, and

the participant should be informed of the purpose, hypothesis, anticipated results, and expected benefits of the study. At the end of an experiment, each participant must be given a careful **debriefing,** in which the researcher provides as much information about the study as possible and makes sure that no one leaves feeling confused, upset, or embarrassed. If it was necessary to mislead the participants during any stage of the research, the experimenter carefully explains the reasons for the deception. Finally, participants have the right to withdraw their data if they feel they have been misused or their rights abused in any way.

ISSUES IN ANIMAL RESEARCH

Should animals be used in psychological and medical research? This question has often produced very polarized responses. On one side are researchers who point to the very important breakthroughs research with animals has allowed in several areas of behavioral science (Carroll & Overmier, 2001). The benefits of animal research have included discovery and testing of drugs that treat anxiety and mental illnesses as well as important knowledge about drug addiction. Animal research benefits animals as well. For example, psychological researchers have shown how to alleviate the stresses of confinement experienced by zoo animals. Their studies of animal learning and social organization have led to the improved design of enclosures and animal facilities that promote good health (Nicoll et al., 1988).

For defenders of animal rights "ethical concerns about compromised animal welfare cannot be eased by human benefits alone" (Olsson et al., 2007, p. 1680). Ethicists encourage researchers to adhere to the 3 *Rs:* Researchers should devise

---

debriefing A procedure conducted at the end of an experiment in which the researcher provides the participant with as much information about the study as possible and makes sure that no participant leaves feeling confused, upset, or embarrassed.

tests of their hypothesis that enable them to *reduce* the number of animals they require or to *replace* the use of animals altogether; they should *refine* their procedures to minimize pain and distress (Ryder, 2006). Each animal researcher must judge his or her work with heightened scrutiny. The American Psychological Association provides firm ethical guidelines for researchers who use nonhuman animals in their research (American Psychological Association, 2002).

Surveys of 1,188 psychology students and 3,982 American Psychological Association members on their attitudes toward animal research support a criterion of heightened scrutiny (Plous, 1996a, 1996b):

- Roughly 80 percent of the people surveyed believed that observational studies in naturalistic settings were appropriate. Smaller numbers (30 to 70 percent) supported studies involving caging or confinement, depending in part on the type of animal (for example, rats, pigeons, dogs, or primates). Both students and their professors disapproved of studies involving physical pain or death.
- A majority of both groups (roughly 60 percent) supported the use of animals in undergraduate psychology courses, but only about a third of each group felt that laboratory work with animals should be a required part of an undergraduate psychology major.

How do your beliefs compare to those of your peers? How would you make decisions about the costs and benefits of animal research?

A news interview with an expert may include misleading sound bites taken out of context or oversimplified "nutshell" descriptions of research conclusions. How could you become a wiser consumer of media reports?

STOP AND REVIEW

❶ What is the purpose of informed consent?
❷ What is the purpose of debriefing?
❸ What recommendation about research settings do researchers make with respect to the use of nonhuman animals as research participants?

Visit MyPsychLab.com for more review and practice on the following topics:

👁 **Watch:** Drapetomania: Robert Guthrie

✳ **Simulate:** Ethics in Psychological Research

👁 **Watch:** Before Informed Consent: Robert Guthrie

Becoming a Critical Consumer of Research

In the final section of this chapter, we will focus on the kinds of critical thinking skills you need to become a wiser consumer of psychological knowledge. Honing these thinking tools is essential for any responsible person in a dynamic society such as ours—one so filled with claims of truth; with false, supposedly commonsense myths; and with biased conclusions that serve special interests. To be a *critical thinker* is to go beyond the information as given and to delve beneath slick appearances, with the goal of understanding the substance without being seduced by style and image.

Psychological claims are an ever-present aspect of the daily life of any thinking, feeling, and acting person in this psychologically sophisticated society. Unfortunately, much information on psychology does not come from the books, articles, and reports of accredited practitioners. Rather, this information comes from newspaper and magazine articles, TV and radio shows, pop psychology, and self-help books. Return to the idea of subliminal mind control. Although it began as a hoax propagated by profit-minded marketing consultant James M. Vicary (Rogers, 1993)—and, as we have seen, has been rigorously discredited in the laboratory—the idea of subliminal influences on overt behavior continues to exert a pull on people's beliefs—and their wallets!

Studying psychology will help you make wiser decisions based on evidence gathered either by you or by others. Always try to apply the insights you derive from your formal study of psychology to the informal psychology that surrounds you: Ask questions about your own behavior or that of other people, seek answers to these questions with respect to rational psychological theories, and check out the answers against the evidence available to you.

Here are some general rules to keep in mind to be a more sophisticated shopper as you travel through the supermarket of knowledge:

- Avoid the inference that correlation is causation.
- Ask that critical terms and key concepts be defined operationally so that there can be consensus about their meanings.
- Consider first how to disprove a theory, hypothesis, or belief before seeking confirming evidence, which is easy to find when you're looking for a justification.

- Always search for alternative explanations to the obvious ones proposed, especially when the explanations benefit the proposer.
- Recognize how personal biases can distort perceptions of reality.
- Be suspicious of simple answers to complex questions or single causes and cures for complex effects and problems.
- Question any statement about the effectiveness of some treatment, intervention, or product by finding the comparative basis for the effect: compared to what?

- Be open-minded yet skeptical: Recognize that most conclusions are tentative and not certain; seek new evidence that decreases your uncertainty while keeping yourself open to change and revision.
- Challenge authority that uses personal opinion in place of evidence for conclusions and is not open to constructive criticism.

We want you to apply open-minded skepticism while you read *Psychology and Life*. We don't want you to view your study of psychology as the acquisition of a list of facts. Instead, we hope you will participate in the joy of observing and discovering and putting ideas to the test.

Critical Thinking in Your Life

WHY IS SKILL WITH NUMBERS IMPORTANT?

We want you to imagine that you've become a clinical psychologist. You are called upon to make an important judgment (Slovic et al., 2000, p. 287):

A patient—Mr. James Jones—has been evaluated for discharge from an acute civil mental health facility where he has been treated for the past several weeks. A psychologist whose professional opinion you respect has done a state-of-the-art assessment of Mr. Jones. Among the conclusions reached in the psychologist's assessment is the following: Of every 100 patients similar to Mr. Jones, 10% are estimated to commit an act of violence to others during the first several months of discharge.

You must indicate whether Mr. Jones is high risk, medium risk, or low risk for "harming someone other than himself during the first several months following discharge" (p. 286). What judgment would you make? Now consider a slightly different version of the scenario's last sentence:

Of every 100 patients similar to Mr. Jones, 10 are estimated to commit an act of violence to others during the first several months of discharge.

Once again, what judgment would you make with respect to the risk Mr. Jones poses?

If you look closely at the two versions of the scenario, you should see that they describe exactly the same mathematical situation: Ten percent out of 100 equals 10 out of 100. For

that reason, you might expect it to be the case that people's risk assessments would be the same. However, when a sample of professional psychologists responded to the two versions of the scenario, the mathematical format had a major impact (Slovic et al., 2000). Mr. Jones was rated as "low risk" by 30.3% of participants who got the "10% out of 100" version; he was rated as "low risk" by just 19.4% of participants who got the "10 out of 100" version. The researchers suggested that these different responses result from the "frightening images evoked by the frequency format" (p. 290). Specifically, it's relatively hard for you to form a firm mental image of 10%, whereas you can easily imagine looking around a room of 100 people and imagining the 10 who might be dangerous. An important first lesson here is that the format in which a statistic is presented can have a major impact on how people act on the information.

But here's a second important lesson: People who have better numerical skills are less likely to be influenced by a statistic's presentation. In one study, a team of researchers measured students' *numeracy* (a term that parallels *literacy*) by asking them to answer a series of questions that captured knowledge of probability concepts (Peters et al., 2006). The researchers used the students' scores to divide them into groups they called

high numerate and *low numerate*. When students from those groups responded to the scenario with Mr. Jones, the low numerate students gave quite different risk ratings for the two versions of the scenario. However, the high numerate students gave virtually identical ratings. Numeracy also has an impact in real-world settings. For example, people must often evaluate data about factors such as hospital performance and costs as they make critical decisions about medical care. People who are more numerate show better comprehension of such complex data and make higher quality decisions (Hibbard et al., 2007).

The good news is that college provides you with ample opportunities to become more numerate. For example, at most institutions, psychology majors must enroll in a statistics course. In the short term, that course should provide you with a deeper understanding of psychological research. However, as we have just seen, the course should also lay the groundwork for you to make better data-based decisions well beyond your college years.

- In the scenario with Mr. Jones, people perceive more risk when they read "20 out of 100" versus "2 out of 10." Why might that be?

- How might you choose the format in which you present a statistic to influence public opinion?

Recapping Main Points

The Process of Research

- In the initial phase of research, observations, beliefs, information, and general knowledge lead to a new way of thinking about a phenomenon. The researcher formulates a theory and generates hypotheses to be tested.
- To test their ideas, researchers use the scientific method, a set of procedures for gathering and interpreting evidence in ways that limit errors.
- Researchers combat observer biases by standardizing procedures and using operational definitions.
- Experimental research methods determine whether causal relationships exist between variables specified by the hypothesis being tested.
- Researchers rule out alternative explanations by using appropriate control procedures.
- Correlational research methods determine if and how much two variables are related. Correlations do not imply causation.

Psychological Measurement

- Researchers strive to produce measures that are both reliable and valid.
- Psychological measurements include self-reports and behavioral measures.

Ethical Issues in Human and Animal Research

- Respect for the basic rights of human and animal research participants is the obligation of all researchers. A variety of safeguards have been enacted to guarantee ethical and humane treatment.

Becoming a Critical Consumer of Research

- Becoming a wise research consumer involves learning how to think critically and knowing how to evaluate claims about what research shows.

KEY TERMS

behavioral measure (p. 33)

between-subjects design (p. 28)

case study (p. 35)

confounding variable (p. 26)

control group (p. 28)

control procedure (p. 27)

correlation coefficient (r) (p. 29)

correlational method (p. 29)

debriefing (p. 37)

dependent variable (p. 25)

determinism (p. 23)

double-blind control (p. 27)

expectancy effect (p. 26)

experimental group (p. 28)

experimental method (p. 26)

hypothesis (p. 24)

independent variable (p. 25)

informed consent (p. 36)

naturalistic observation (p. 34)

observer bias (p. 24)

operational definition (p. 25)

placebo control (p. 28)

placebo effect (p. 27)

population (p. 28)

random assignment (p. 28)

random sampling (p. 28)

reliability (p. 33)

representative sample (p. 28)

sample (p. 28)

self-report measures (p. 33)

standardization (p. 25)

theory (p. 23)

validity (p. 33)

variable (p. 25)

within-subjects design (p. 28)

Chapter 2 Practice Test

1. A(n) _____ is an organized set of concepts that explains a phenomenon or set of phenomena.
   a. theory
   b. hypothesis
   c. operational definition
   d. correlation

2. When articles are submitted to most journals, they are sent out to experts for detailed analyses. This process is known as
   a. debriefing.
   b. informed consent.
   c. peer review.
   d. control procedures.

3. Professor Peterson is testing the hypothesis that people will cooperate less when a lot of people are in a group. In the experiment he plans, he will vary the number of people in each group. That will be his
   a. placebo control.
   b. independent variable.
   c. double-blind control.
   d. dependent variable.

4. Rahul is serving as a research assistant. In the first phase of the experiment, Rahul gives each participant a can of cola or a can of caffeine-free cola. In the second phase of the experiment, Rahul times the participants with a stopwatch while they play a video game. It sounds like this study is lacking a(n)
   a. placebo control.
   b. correlational design.
   c. operational definition.
   d. double-blind control.

5. Matt is participating in a two-day experiment. On Day 1, he takes a memory test after running on a treadmill for 2 minutes. On Day 2, he takes a similar test after running for 10 minutes. The experimenters plan to compare Matt's performance on the two tests. This sounds like a
   a. within-subjects design.
   b. double-blind control.
   c. between-subjects design.
   d. correlational design.

6. Shirley visits an antique store. The owner explains to her that the smaller an object is, the more he can charge for it. This is an example of a
   a. correlation coefficient.
   b. negative correlation.
   c. positive correlation.
   d. placebo effect.

7. Sally isn't very interested in movies. Her friend Rob wants to get her attitude to be more favorable toward his all-time favorite, *Final Destination*. Rob might be best off asking Sally to generate _____ characteristics for the movie.
   a. two negative
   b. five positive
   c. ten positive
   d. five negative

8. Dr. Paul is developing a new measure of hunger. He says, "I need a measure that will accurately predict how much food people will eat in their next meal." Dr. Paul's statement is about the _____ of the measure.
   a. operational definition
   b. standardization
   c. validity
   d. reliability

9. Giovanna is worried that the results of her experiment may be affected by her participants' desire to provide favorable impressions of themselves. It sounds as if she might be using _____ measures.
   a. valid
   b. self-report
   c. reliable
   d. operational

10. Ben believes that men are more likely to arrive late to classes than are women. To test this hypothesis most effectively, Ben should use
    a. a within-subjects design.
    b. a correlational design.
    c. self-report measures.
    d. naturalistic observation.

11. Andrew wishes to test the hypothesis that people give more freely to charities when the weather is pleasant. To test this hypothesis, Andrew is likely to make use of
    a. double-blind controls.
    b. expectancy effects.
    c. laboratory observation.
    d. archival data.

12. Before you participate in an experiment, the researcher should provide you with information about procedures, potential risks, and expected benefits. This process is called
    a. a risk/gain assessment.
    b. informed debriefing.
    c. informed consent.
    d. operational definitions.

13. When members of the American Psychological Association were surveyed about the uses of nonhuman animals in research, the majority believed that
    a. observational studies in naturalistic settings were appropriate.
    b. nonhuman animals should never be used as replacements for human participants.
    c. intentional deception is unethical for experiments with nonhuman animals.
    d. nonhuman animals should not be used in undergraduate psychology courses.

14. Always search for _____ explanations to the obvious ones proposed.
    a. optimistic
    b. alternative
    c. negative
    d. opposite

15. You ask people to respond to scenarios that describe the risk associated with excess cell phone usage. You expect people to give the highest risk estimates when they read that "_____ people suffer serious vocal chord damage."
    a. 10 of every 100
    b. 10%
    c. 20 of every 100
    d. 20%

Essay Questions

1. Why is it so important that research procedures be open for public verifiability?

2. Suppose you wanted to measure "happiness." What might you do to assess the validity of your measure?

3. With respect to ethical principles, how are risks and gains defined in the context of psychological research?

Discovering Psychology Viewing Guide

Watch the following video by logging on to MyPsychLab (www.mypsychlab.com). After you have watched the video, complete the activities that follow.

Program 2: Understanding Research

KEY TERMS AND PEOPLE

As you watch the program, pay particular attention to these terms and people in addition to those covered in this textbook.

- *burnout*—a work-related condition in which stress, lack of support, and negative self-evaluation disrupt performance and well-being.
- *field study*—research carried on outside the laboratory where naturally occurring, ongoing behavior can be observed.
- *random sample*—an unbiased population selected at random.
- *subjective reality*—the perceptions and beliefs that we accept without question.
- *Daryl Bem*—psychologist who illustrated the importance of critical thinking in scientific experiments.
- *Jerome Frank*—psychiatrist who studies the common features of miracle cures and healings, political and religious conversions, and psychotherapy.
- *Christina Maslach*—uses psychometric research to study job burnout.
- *Leonard Saxe*—studies the use and misuse of polygraphs to detect lying.

PROGRAM REVIEW

1. Which of the following describes a field study?
   a. observing a natural, ongoing situation
   b. randomly assigning participants to treatment groups
   c. randomly assigning participants to a control group
   d. distributing a questionnaire to a large group

2. Which of the following is desirable in research?
   a. having the control and experimental conditions differ on several variables
   b. interpreting correlation as implying causality
   c. systematically manipulate the variable(s) of interest
   d. using samples of participants who are more capable than the population you want to draw conclusions about

3. What is the main reason that the results of research studies are published?
   a. so researchers can prove they earned their money
   b. so other researchers can try to replicate the work
   c. so the general public can understand the importance of spending money on research
   d. so attempts at fraud and trickery are detected

4. Why does the placebo effect work?
   a. because researchers believe it does
   b. because participants believe in the power of the placebo
   c. because human beings prefer feeling they are in control
   d. because it is part of the scientific method

5. What is the purpose of a double-blind procedure?
   a. to test more than one variable at a time
   b. to repeat the results of previously published work
   c. to define a hypothesis clearly before it is tested
   d. to eliminate experimenter bias

6. If you had been one of the participants in the lie detector study, what information would have helped you earn some money?
   a. The results depend on the skill of the person administering the lie detector test.
   b. Lie detectors measure only arousal level, not lying.
   c. The polygraph is used to make millions of decisions each year.
   d. The placebo effect works with lie detectors.

7. According to Jerome Frank, placebos work through
   a. emotional arousal.
   b. brainwashing.
   c. chemical alteration of neural transmission.
   d. cognitive reassessment of the illness.

8. A report on children's television watching found that children who watch more TV have lower grades. What cause–effect conclusion are we justified in making on the basis of this study?
   a. TV watching causes low grades.
   b. Poor school performance causes children to watch more TV.
   c. Cause–effect conclusions can never be based on one study.
   d. None; cause–effect conclusions cannot be based on correlation.

9. What was the major weakness of the Hite Report on women's attitudes toward sex and marriage?
   a. The sample was not representative.
   b. Hypotheses were not clearly stated beforehand.
   c. Experimenter bias arose because the double-blind procedure was not used.
   d. No control group was used.

10. A prediction of how two or more variables are likely to be related is called a
   a. theory.   c. hypothesis.
   b. conclusion.   d. correlation.

11. Imagine a friend tells you that she has been doing better in school since she started taking vitamin pills. When you express disbelief, she urges you to take vitamins too. Why might the pills "work" for her but not necessarily for you?
    a. Healthy people don't need vitamins.
    b. A belief in the power of the vitamins is necessary for any effect to occur.
    c. She is lying.
    d. They would work for her and not for you if she were a poor student and you were a straight-A student.

12. In which experiment would a double-blind test be most appropriate?
    a. a lab experiment by a technician who does not understand the theory under scrutiny
    b. a study designed to test the researcher's own controversial theory
    c. a survey asking subjects how many siblings they have
    d. an experiment on the effect of a drug on maze-running ability in rats

13. What does the "card trick" in the program demonstrate about good science?
    a. Predictions should be made explicitly before data collection.
    b. Chance must be ruled out as an explanation.
    c. The experimenter's effect on the subject must be ruled out as an explanation.
    d. All of the above.

14. When long-term stress and lack of support on the job lead to chronic deficits in a worker's productivity and health, the worker is likely to be suffering from
    a. generalized anxiety disorder.   c. job burnout.
    b. posttraumatic stress.   d. insomnia.

15. Christina Maslach uses all of the following to study job burnout *except*
    a. interviews.   c. surveys.
    b. hospitalization records.   d. psychometric scales.

16. How could you improve on Shere Hite's survey techniques?
    a. Redo her study using her methods, but send the survey to 10 times as many recipients.
    b. Hire one subject, pay her for a full day's work, and spend eight hours interviewing her thoroughly.
    c. Redo her study, using her methods, but send the survey to an equal number of men.
    d. Redo her study, but ensure that the percentage of respondents is much higher and much more representative of the population of interest.

17. Why would other scientists want to replicate an experiment that has already been done?
    a. to have their names associated with a well-known phenomenon
    b. to gain a high-odds, low-risk publication
    c. to ensure that the phenomenon under study is real and reliable
    d. to calibrate their equipment with those of another laboratory

18. Because experiments involve careful manipulation of all factors of interest and careful control of all others, which experiment would not be ethically allowable?
    a. the effect of classical music on the ability to solve crossword puzzles

b. the effect of room lighting on color preference
c. the effect of supplementary vitamins on retirement age
d. the effect of prolonged solitary confinement of toddlers on language development

19. Because of what it actually does measure, under what circumstances would an innocent person likely fail a polygraph test?
    a. if she is extremely worried about the possibility of being found guilty
    b. if she is drunk
    c. if she is acquainted with the actual guilty party
    d. if she is confident in the validity of the polygraph test

QUESTIONS TO CONSIDER

1. If some people really get healed by faith healers, why condemn the practice of faith healing?

2. If there is value in running studies with within-subjects designs, why would an experimenter ever use a between-subjects design?

3. What are some of the practical objections to studying mental processes?

4. What is your reaction to the guidelines prohibiting research if it would require deception and if distress is a likely result? Are there studies you think would be valuable to perform but that could not be? Could the same research questions be answered in some other way?

5. Are animals adequately protected by the APA's guidelines? Why or why not?

6. How could a study be biased simply because it uses volunteer participants?

7. Can the results of experiments conducted mostly on college students, who are among the more highly educated members of our society, really be extended to the rest of society? Which sorts of psychological phenomena would be more likely or less likely to generalize to people of other age groups, socioeconomic status, and education levels?

ACTIVITIES

1. Write operational definitions of the following:

green	thirst	wealth
warm	anger	learning
cleverness	intelligence	jealousy
suffering	comprehension	

2. Design a study that would test whether children come to learn self-control better if they are physically punished vs. receive time-outs for bad behavior. What features of the problem determine whether you can run an experiment to test this? What confounding variables might be present in a study like this? How would you eliminate them as possible alternative explanations?

3. Design an experiment that would allow you to show whether a 2-week-old child knows who her mother is. Be sure that your experimental design can eliminate alternative explanations for your data.

Statistical Supplement
Understanding Statistics: Analyzing Data and Forming Conclusions

A s we noted in Chapter 2, psychologists use statistics to make sense of the data they collect. They also use statistics to provide a quantitative basis for the conclusions they draw. Knowing something about statistics, therefore, can help you appreciate the process by which psychological knowledge is developed. On a more personal level, having a basic understanding of statistics will help you make better decisions when people use data to try to sway your opinions and actions.

Most students perceive statistics as a dry, uninteresting topic. However, statistics have many vital applications in your life. To demonstrate this point, we will follow a single project from its real-world inspiration to the statistical arguments that were used to bolster general conclusions. The project began in response to the types of stories that appear on newspaper front pages, about shy individuals who became *sudden murderers.* Here's an example:

> *Fred Cowan was described by relatives, co-workers, and acquaintances as a "nice, quiet man," a "gentle man who loved children," and a "real pussycat." The principal of the parochial school Cowan had attended as a child reported that his former student had received A grades in courtesy, cooperation, and religion. According to a co-worker, Cowan "never talked to anybody and was someone you could push around." Cowan, however, surprised*

everyone who knew him when, one Valentine's Day, he strolled into work toting a semiautomatic rifle and shot and killed four co-workers, a police officer, and, finally, himself.

This story has a common plot: A shy, quiet person suddenly becomes violent, shocking everyone who knows him. What did Fred Cowan have in common with other people who are suddenly transformed from gentle and caring into violent and ruthless? What personal attributes might distinguish them from us?

A team of researchers had a hunch that there might be a link between shyness and other personal characteristics and violent behavior (Lee et al., 1977). They began to collect some data that might reveal such a connection. The researchers reasoned that seemingly nonviolent people who suddenly commit murders are probably typically shy, nonaggressive individuals who keep their passions in check and their impulses under tight control. For most of their lives, they suffer many silent injuries. Seldom, if ever, do they express anger, regardless of how angry they really feel. On the outside, they appear unbothered, but on the inside they may be fighting to control furious rages. They give the impression that they are quiet, passive, responsible people, both as children and as adults. Because they are shy, they probably do not let others get close to them, so no one knows how they really feel. Then, suddenly, something explodes. At the slightest provocation—one more small insult, one more little rejection, one more bit of social pressure—the fuse is lit, and they release the suppressed violence that has been building up for so long. Because they did not learn to deal with interpersonal conflicts through discussion and verbal negotiation, these sudden murderers act out their anger physically.

The researchers' reasoning led them to the hypothesis that shyness would be more characteristic of *sudden murderers*—people who had engaged in homicide without any prior history of violence or antisocial behavior—than it would of *habitual criminal murderers*—those who had committed homicide but had had a previous record of violent criminal behavior. In addition, sudden murderers should have higher levels of control over their impulses than habitually violent people. Finally, their passivity and dependence would be manifested in more feminine and androgynous (both male and female) characteristics, as measured on a standard sex-role inventory, than those of habitual criminals.

To test their ideas about sudden murderers, the researchers obtained permission to administer psychological questionnaires to a group of inmates serving time for murder in California prisons. Nineteen inmates (all male) agreed to participate in the study. Prior to committing murder, some had committed a series of crimes, whereas the other part of the sample had had no previous criminal record. The researchers collected three kinds of data from these two types of participants: shyness scores, sex-role identification scores, and impulse control scores.

Shyness scores were collected using the Stanford Shyness Survey. The most important item on this questionnaire asked if the individual was shy; the answer could be either yes or no. Other items on the scale tapped degree and kinds of shyness and a variety of dimensions related to origins and triggers of shyness.

The second questionnaire was the Bem Sex-Role Inventory (BSRI), which presented a list of adjectives, such as *aggressive* and *affectionate,* and asked how well each adjective described the individual (Bem, 1974, 1981). Some adjectives were typically associated with being "feminine," and the total score of these adjectives was an individual's femininity score. Other adjectives were considered "masculine," and the total score of those adjectives was an individual's masculinity score. The final sex-role score, which reflected the difference between an individual's femininity and masculinity, was calculated by subtracting the masculinity score from the femininity score. A combination of the masculinity and femininity scores shows up as an individual's androgyny score.

The third questionnaire was the Minnesota Multiphasic Personality Inventory (MMPI), which was designed to measure many different aspects of personality (see Chapter 13). The study used only the "ego-overcontrol" scale, which measures the degree to which a person acts out or controls impulses. The higher the individual's score on this scale, the more ego overcontrol the individual exhibits.

The researchers predicted that, compared with murderers with a prior criminal record, sudden murderers would (1) more often describe themselves as shy on the shyness survey, (2) select more feminine traits than masculine ones on the sex-role scale, and (3) score higher in ego overcontrol. What did they discover?

Before you find out, you need to understand some of the basic procedures that were used to analyze these data. The actual sets of data collected by the researchers are used here as the source material to teach you about some of the different types of statistical analyses and also about the kinds of conclusions they make possible.

Analyzing the Data

For most researchers in psychology, analyzing the data is an exciting step. Statistical analysis allows researchers to discover if their predictions were correct. In this section, we will work step by step through an analysis of some of the data from the Sudden Murderers Study. If you have looked ahead, you will have seen numbers and equations. Keep in mind that mathematics is a tool; mathematical symbols are a shorthand for representing ideas and conceptual operations.

The *raw data*—the actual scores or other measures obtained—from the 19 inmates in the Sudden Murderers Study are listed in **Table S.1** on page 46. As you can see, there were 10 inmates in the sudden murderers group and 9 in the habitual criminal murderers group. When first glancing at these data, any researcher would feel what you probably feel: confusion. What do all these scores mean? Do the two groups of murderers differ from one another on these various personality measures? It is difficult to know just by examining this disorganized array of numbers.

Psychologists rely on two types of statistics to help make sense of and draw meaningful conclusions from the data they collect: descriptive and inferential. **Descriptive statistics** use mathematical procedures in an objective, uniform way to describe different aspects of numerical data. If you have ever computed your GPA, you already have used descriptive statistics. **Inferential statistics** use probability theory to make sound decisions about which results might have occurred simply through chance variation.

DESCRIPTIVE STATISTICS

Descriptive statistics provide a summary picture of patterns in the data. They are used to describe sets of scores collected from one experimental participant or, more often, from different groups of participants. They are also used to describe relationships among variables. Thus, instead of trying to keep in mind all the scores obtained by each of the participants, researchers get indexes of the scores that are most *typical* for each group. They also get measures of how *variable* the scores are with respect to the typical score—whether the scores are spread out or clustered closely together. Let's see how researchers derive these measures.

Frequency Distributions How would you summarize the data in Table S.1? To present a clear picture of how the various scores are distributed, we can draw up a **frequency distribution**— a summary of how frequently each of the various scores occurs. The shyness data are easy to summarize. Of the 19 scores, there are 9 *yes* and 10 *no* responses; almost all the yes responses are in Group 1, and almost all the *no* responses are in Group 2. However, the ego-overcontrol and sex-role scores do not fall into easy *yes* and *no* categories. To see how

---

descriptive statistics Statistical procedures that are used to summarize sets of scores with respect to central tendencies, variability, and correlations.

inferential statistics Statistical procedures that allow researchers to determine whether the results they obtain support their hypotheses or can be attributed just to chance variation.

frequency distribution A summary of how frequently each score appears in a set of observations.

TABLE S.1 Raw Data from the Sudden Murderers Study			
		BSRI	**MMPI**
Inmate	**Shyness**	**Femininity–Masculinity**	**Ego Overcontrol**
		Group 1:	
		Sudden Murderers	
1	Yes	+5	17
2	No	−1	17
3	Yes	+4	13
4	Yes	+61	17
5	Yes	+19	13
6	Yes	+41	19
7	No	−29	14
8	Yes	+23	9
9	Yes	−13	11
10	Yes	+5	14
		Group 2:	
		Habitual Criminal Murderers	
11	No	−12	15
12	No	−14	11
13	Yes	−33	14
14	No	−8	10
15	No	−7	16
16	No	+3	11
17	No	−17	6
18	No	+6	9
19	No	−10	12

TABLE S.2 Rank Ordering of Sex-Role Difference Scores		
Highest	+61	−1
	+41	−7
	+23	−8
	+19	−10
	+6	−12
	+5	−13
	+5	−14
	+4	−17
	+3	−29
		−33 **Lowest**

Note: + scores are more feminine; − scores are more masculine.

TABLE S.3 Frequency Distribution of Sex-Role Difference Scores	
Category	**Frequency**
+60 to +69	1
+50 to +59	0
+40 to +49	1
+30 to +39	0
+20 to +29	1
+10 to +19	1
0 to +9	5
−10 to −1	4
−20 to −11	4
−30 to −21	1
−40 to −31	1

frequency distributions of numerical responses can allow informative comparisons between groups, we will focus on the sex-role scores.

Consider the sex-role data in Table S.1. The highest score is +61 (most feminine) and the lowest is −33 (most masculine). Of the 19 scores, 9 are positive and 10 negative. This means that 9 of the murderers described themselves as relatively feminine and 10 as relatively masculine. But how are these scores distributed between the groups? The first step in preparing a frequency distribution for a set of numerical data is to *rank-order* the scores from highest to lowest. The rank ordering for the sex-role scores is shown in **Table S.2.** The second step is to group these rank-ordered scores into a smaller number of categories called *intervals*. In this study, 10 categories were used, with each category covering 10 possible scores. The third step is to construct a frequency distribution table, listing the intervals from highest to lowest and noting the *frequencies,* the number of scores within each interval. Our frequency distribution shows

us that the sex-role scores are largely between −20 and +9 (see **Table S.3**). The majority of the inmates' scores did not deviate much from zero. That is, they were neither strongly positive nor strongly negative.

The data are now arranged in useful categories. The researchers' next step was to display the distributions in graphic form.

Graphs Distributions are often easier to understand when they are displayed in graphs. The simplest type of graph is a *bar graph.* Bar graphs allow you to see patterns in the data. We can use a bar graph to illustrate how many more sudden murderers than habitual criminal murderers described themselves as shy (see **Figure S.1**).

For more complex data, such as the sex-role scores, we can use a *histogram,* which is similar to a bar graph except that the categories are intervals—number categories instead of the

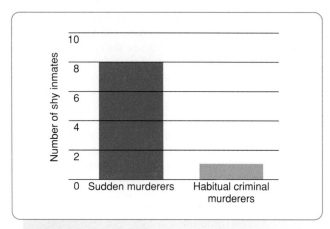

FIGURE S.1   Shyness for Two Groups of Murderers (a Bar Graph)

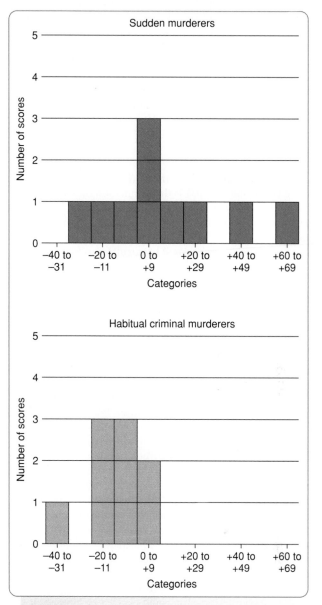

FIGURE S.2   Sex-Role Scores (Histograms)

name categories used in the bar graph. A histogram gives a visual picture of the number of scores in a distribution that are in each interval. It is easy to see from the sex-role scores shown in the histograms (in **Figure S.2**) that the distributions of scores are different for the two groups of murderers.

You can see from Figures S.1 and S.2 that the overall distributions of responses conform to two of the researchers' hypotheses. Sudden murderers were more likely to describe themselves as shy and were more likely to use feminine traits to describe themselves than were habitual criminal murderers.

Measures of Central Tendency So far, we have formed a general picture of how the scores are *distributed*. Tables and graphs increase our general understanding of research results, but we want to know more—for example, the one score that is most typical of the group as a whole. This score becomes particularly useful when we compare two or more groups; it is much easier to compare the typical scores of two groups than their entire distributions. A single *representative* score that can be used as an index of the most typical score obtained by a group of participants is called a **measure of central tendency**. (It is located in the center of the distribution, and other scores tend to cluster around it.) Typically, psychologists use three different measures of central tendency: the *mode,* the *median,* and the *mean.*

The **mode** is the score that occurs more often than any other. For the measure of shyness, the modal response of the sudden murderers was *yes*—8 out of 10 said they were shy. Among habitual criminal murderers, the modal response was *no*. The sex-role scores for the sudden murderers had a mode of +5. Can you figure out what the mode of their ego-overcontrol scores is? The mode is the easiest index of central tendency to determine, but it is often the least useful. You will see one reason for this relative lack of usefulness if you notice that only one overcontrol score lies above the mode of 17, and six lie below it. Although 17 is the score obtained most often, it may not fit your idea of "typical" or "central."

The **median** is more clearly a central score; it separates the upper half of the scores in a distribution from the lower half. The number of scores larger than the median is the same as the number that is smaller. When there are an odd number of scores, the median is the middle score; when there are an even number of scores, researchers most often average the two scores

at the middle. For example, if you rank-order the sex-role scores of only the habitual criminal murderers on a separate piece of paper, you will see that the median score is −10, with four scores higher and four scores lower. For the sudden murderers, the median is +5—the average of the fifth and sixth scores, each of which happens to be +5. The median is not affected by extreme scores. For example, even if the sudden murderers' highest sex-role score had been +129 instead of +61, the median value would still have been +5. That score would still separate the

---

measure of central tendency A statistic, such as a mean, median, or mode, that provides one score as representative of a set of observations.

mode The score appearing most frequently in a set of observations; a measure of central tendency.

median The score in a distribution above and below which lie 50 percent of the other scores; a measure of central tendency.

upper half of the data from the lower half. The median is quite simply the score in the middle of the distribution.

The **mean** is what most people think of when they hear the word *average*. It is also the statistic most often used to describe a set of data. To calculate the mean, you add up all the scores in a distribution and divide by the total number of scores. The operation is summarized by the following formula:

$$M = \frac{(\Sigma X)}{N}$$

In this formula, M is the mean, X is each individual score, Σ (the Greek letter sigma) is the summation of what immediately follows it, and N is the total number of scores. Because the summation of all the sex-role scores (ΣX) is 115, and the total number of scores (N) is 10, the mean (M) of the sex-role scores of the sudden murderers would be calculated as follows:

$$M = \frac{115}{10} = 11.5$$

Try to calculate their mean overcontrol scores yourself. You should come up with a mean of 14.4.

Unlike the median, the mean *is* affected by the specific values of all scores in the distribution. Changing the value of an extreme score does change the value of the mean. For example, if the sex-role score of inmate 4 were +101 instead of +61, the mean for the whole group would increase from 11.5 to 15.5.

Variability In addition to knowing which score is most representative of the distribution as a whole, it is useful to know how representative that measure of central tendency really is. Are most of the other scores fairly close to it or widely spread out? **Measures of variability** are statistics that describe the distribution of scores around some measure of central tendency.

Can you see why measures of variability are important? An example may help. Suppose you are a grade-school teacher. It is the beginning of the school year, and you will be teaching reading to a group of 30 second graders. Knowing that the average child in the class can now read a first-grade-level book will help you to plan your lessons. You could plan better, however, if you knew how *similar* or how *divergent* the reading abilities of the 30 children were. Are they all at about the same level (low variability)? If so, then you can plan a fairly standard second-grade lesson. What if several can read advanced material and others can barely read at all (high variability)? Now the mean level is not so representative of the entire class, and you will have to plan a variety of lessons to meet the children's varied needs.

The simplest measure of variability is the **range,** the difference between the highest and the lowest values in a frequency distribution. For the sudden murderers' sex-role scores, the range is 90: $(+61) - (-29)$. The range of their overcontrol scores is 10: $(+19) - (+9)$. To compute the range, you need to know only two of the scores: the highest and the lowest.

The range is simple to compute, but psychologists often prefer measures of variability that are more sensitive and that take into account *all* the scores in a distribution, not just the extremes. One widely used measure is the **standard deviation (SD),** a measure of variability that indicates the *average* difference between the scores and their mean. To figure out the standard deviation of a distribution, you need to know the mean of the distribution and the individual scores. The general procedure involves subtracting the value of each individual score from the mean and then determining the average of those mean deviations. Here is the formula:

$$SD = \sqrt{\frac{\Sigma (X - M)^2}{N}}$$

You should recognize most of the symbols from the formula for the mean. The expression $(X - M)$ means "individual score minus the mean" and is commonly called the *deviation score*. The mean is subtracted from each score, and each resulting score is squared (to eliminate negative values). Then the mean of these deviations is calculated by summing them up (Σ) and dividing by the number of observations (N). The symbol Σ tells you to take the square root of the enclosed value to offset the previous squaring. The standard deviation of the overcontrol scores for the sudden murderers is calculated in **Table S.4.** Recall that the mean of these scores is 14.4. This, then, is the value that must be subtracted from each score to obtain the corresponding deviation scores.

The standard deviation tells us how variable a set of scores is. The larger the standard deviation, the more spread out the scores are. The standard deviation of the sex-role scores for the sudden murderers is 24.6, but the standard deviation for the habitual criminals is only 10.7. This shows that there was less variability in the habitual criminals group. Their scores clustered more closely about their mean than did those of the sudden murderers. When the standard deviation is small, the mean is a good representative index of the entire distribution. When the standard deviation is large, the mean is less typical of the whole group.

Correlation Another useful tool in interpreting psychological data is the **correlation coefficient,** a measure of the nature and strength of the relationship between two variables (such as height and weight or sex-role score and ego-overcontrol score). It tells us the extent to which scores on one measure are associated with scores on the other. If people with high scores on one variable tend to have *high* scores on the other variable, then the correlation coefficient will be positive (greater than 0). If, however, most people with high scores on one variable tend to have *low* scores on the other variable, then the correlation coefficient will be negative (less than 0). If there is *no* consistent relationship between the scores, the correlation will be close to 0 (see also Chapter 2).

Correlation coefficients range from +1 (perfect positive correlation) through 0 to −1 (perfect negative correlation). The further a coefficient is from 0 in *either* direction, the more closely related the two variables are, positively or negatively. Higher coefficients permit better predictions of one variable, given knowledge of the other.

In the Sudden Murderers Study, the correlation coefficient (symbolized as r) between the sex-role scores and the overcontrol

---

mean The arithmetic average of a group of scores; the most commonly used measure of central tendency.

measure of variability A statistic, such as a range or standard deviation, that indicates how tightly the scores in a set of observations cluster together.

range The difference between the highest and the lowest scores in a set of observations; the simplest measure of variability.

standard deviation (SD) The average difference of a set of scores from their mean; a measure of variability.

correlational coefficient (r) A statistic that indicates the degree of relationship between two variables.

TABLE S.4 Calculating the Standard Deviation of Sudden Murderers' Ego-Overcontrol Scores

Score (X)	Deviation (score minus mean) (X − M)	Deviations Squared (score minus mean)² (X − M)²
17	2.6	6.76
17	2.6	6.76
13	−1.4	1.96
17	2.6	6.76
13	−1.4	1.96
19	4.6	21.16
14	−.4	.16
9	−5.4	29.16
11	−3.4	11.56
14	−.4	.16

$$\text{Standard deviation} = SD = \sqrt{\frac{\Sigma(X-M)^2}{N}}$$

$$\Sigma(X-M)^2 = 86.40$$

$$\sqrt{\frac{86.40}{10}} = \sqrt{8.64} = 2.94$$

$$SD = 2.94$$

scores turns out to be +0.35. Thus the sex-role scores and the overcontrol scores are positively correlated. In general, individuals seeing themselves as more feminine also tend to be higher in overcontrol. However, the correlation is modest, compared with the highest possible value, +1.00, so we know that there are many exceptions to this relationship. If we had also measured the self-esteem of these inmates and found a correlation of −0.68 between overcontrol scores and self-esteem, it would mean that there was a negative correlation. If this were the case, we could say that the individuals who had high overcontrol scores tended to be lower in self-esteem. It would be a stronger relationship than the relationship between the sex-role scores and the overcontrol scores because −0.68 is farther from 0, the point of no relationship, than is +0.35.

INFERENTIAL STATISTICS

We have used a number of descriptive statistics to characterize the data from the Sudden Murderers Study, and now we have an idea of the pattern of results. However, some basic questions remain unanswered. Recall that the research team hypothesized that sudden murderers would be shyer, more overcontrolled, and more feminine than habitual criminal murderers. After we have used descriptive statistics to compare average responses and variability in the two groups, it appears that there are some differences between the groups. But how do we know if the differences are large enough to be meaningful? If we repeated this study, with other sudden murderers and other habitual criminal murderers, would we expect to find the same pattern of results, or could these results have been an outcome of chance?

If we could somehow measure the entire population of sudden murderers and habitual criminal murderers, would the means and standard deviations be the same as those we found for these small samples?

Inferential statistics are used to answer these kinds of questions. They tell us which inferences we *can* make from our samples and which conclusions we can legitimately draw from our data. Inferential statistics use probability theory to determine the likelihood that a set of data occurred simply by chance variation.

The Normal Curve To understand how inferential statistics work, we must look first at the special properties of a distribution called the *normal curve*. When data on a variable (for example, height, IQ, or overcontrol) are collected from a large number of individuals, the numbers obtained often fit a curve roughly similar to that shown in **Figure S.3** on page 50. Notice that the curve is symmetrical (the left half is a mirror image of the right) and bell shaped—high in the middle, where most scores are, and lower the farther you get from the mean. This type of curve is called a **normal curve,** or *normal distribution.* (A *skewed* distribution is one in which scores cluster toward one end instead of around the middle.)

In a normal curve, the median, mode, and mean values are the same. A specific percentage of the scores can be predicted to fall under different sections of the curve. Figure S.3 shows IQ scores on the Stanford-Binet Intelligence Test. These scores have a mean of 100 and a standard deviation of 15. If you indicate standard deviations as distances from the mean along the baseline, you find that a little over 68 percent of all the scores are between the mean of 100 and 1 standard deviation above and below—between IQs of 85 and 115. Roughly another 27 percent of the scores are found between the first and second standard deviations below the mean (IQ scores between 70 and 85) and above the mean (IQ scores between 115 and 130). Less than 5 percent of the scores fall in the third standard deviation above and below the mean, and very few scores fall beyond—only about one quarter of 1 percent.

Inferential statistics indicate the probability that the particular sample of scores obtained is actually related to whatever you are attempting to measure or whether it could have occurred by chance. For example, it is more likely that someone would have an IQ of 105 than an IQ of 140, but an IQ of 140 is more probable than one of 35.

A normal curve is also obtained by collecting a series of measurements whose differences are due only to chance. If you flip a coin 10 times in a row and record the number of heads and tails, you will probably get 5 of each—most of the time. If you keep flipping the coin for 100 sets of 10 tosses, you probably will get a few sets with all heads or no heads, more sets where the number is between these extremes, and, most typically, more sets where the number is about half each way. If you made a graph of your 1,000 tosses, you would get one that closely fits a normal curve, such as the one in the figure.

Statistical Significance A researcher who finds a difference between the mean scores for two samples must ask if it is a *real* difference or if it occurred simply because of chance.

---

normal curve The symmetrical curve that represents the distribution of scores on many psychological attributes; allows researchers to make judgments of how unusual an observation or result is.

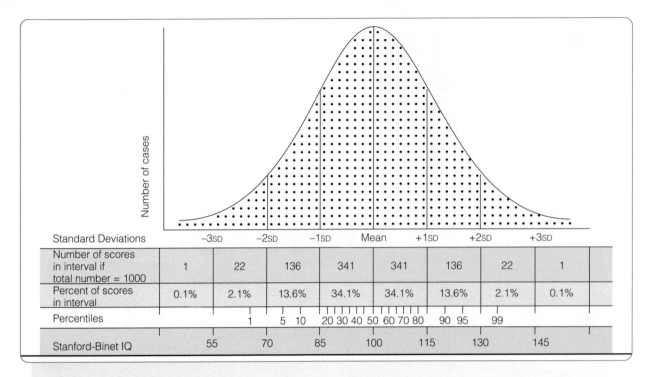

Standard Deviations	−3SD		−2SD		−1SD		Mean		+1SD		+2SD		+3SD	
Number of scores in interval if total number = 1000	1		22		136		341		341		136		22		1
Percent of scores in interval	0.1%		2.1%		13.6%		34.1%		34.1%		13.6%		2.1%		0.1%
Percentiles			1		5 10		20 30 40 50 60 70 80			90 95		99		
Stanford-Binet IQ		55		70		85		100		115		130		145	

FIGURE S.3   A Normal Curve

Because chance differences have a normal distribution, a researcher can use the normal curve to answer this question.

A simple example will help to illustrate the point. Suppose your psychology professor wants to see if the gender of a person overseeing a test makes a difference in the test scores obtained from male and from female students. For this purpose, the professor randomly assigns half of the students to a male teaching assistant and half to a female assistant. The professor then compares the mean score of each group. The two mean scores would probably be fairly similar; any slight difference would most likely be due to chance. Why? Because if only chance is operating and both groups are from the same population (no difference), then the means of male assistant and female assistant samples should be fairly close most of the time. From the percentages of scores found in different parts of the normal distribution, you know that less than a third of the scores in the male assistant condition should be greater than one standard deviation above or below the female assistant mean. The chances of getting a male assistant mean score more than three standard deviations above or below most of your female assistant means would be very small. A professor who *did* get a difference that great would feel fairly confident that the difference is a real one and is somehow related to the gender of the assistant who oversaw the test. The next question would be *how* that variable influences test scores.

If male and female students were randomly assigned to each type of assistant, it would be possible to analyze whether

an overall difference found between the assistant was consistent across both student groups or was limited to only one sex. Imagine that the data show that males grade female students higher than do females, but both grade male students the same. Your professor could use a statistical inference procedure to estimate the probability that an observed difference could have occurred by chance. This computation is based on the size of the difference and the spread of the scores.

By common agreement, psychologists accept a difference as "real" when the probability that it might be due to chance is less than 5 in 100 (indicated by the notation $p < .05$). A **significant difference** is one that meets this criterion. However, in some cases, even stricter probability levels are used, such as $p < .01$ (less than 1 in 100) and $p < .001$ (less than 1 in 1,000).

With a statistically significant difference, a researcher can draw a conclusion about the behavior that was under investigation. There are many different types of tests for estimating the statistical significance of sets of data. The type of test chosen for a particular case depends on the design of the study, the form of the data, and the size of the groups. We will mention only one of the most common tests, the *t-test*, which may be used when an investigator wants to know if the difference between the means of two groups is statistically significant.

We can use a *t*-test to see if the mean sex-role score of the sudden murderers is significantly different from that of the habitual criminal murderers. The *t*-test uses a mathematical procedure to confirm the conclusion you may have drawn from Figure S.2: The distributions of sex-role scores for the two groups is sufficiently different to be "real." If we carry out the appropriate calculations—which evaluate the difference between the two means as a function of the variability around those two means—we find that there is a very slim chance, less than 5 in 100 ($p < .05$), of obtaining such a large *t* value if no true difference exists. The difference is, therefore, statistically significant,

---

significant difference A difference between experimental groups or conditions that would have occurred by chance less than an accepted criterion; in psychology, the criterion most often used is a probability of less than 5 times out of 100, or $p < .05$.

and we can feel more confident that there is a real difference between the two groups. The sudden murderers *did* rate themselves as more feminine than did the habitual criminal murderers. On the other hand, the difference between the two groups of murderers in overcontrol scores turns out not to be statistically significant ($p < .10$), so we must be more cautious in making claims about this difference. There is a trend in the predicted direction—the difference is one that would occur by chance only 10 times in 100. However, the difference is not within the standard 5-in-100 range. (The difference in shyness, analyzed using another statistical test for frequency of scores, is highly significant.)

So, by using inferential statistics, we are able to answer some of the basic questions with which we began, and we are closer to understanding the psychology of people who suddenly change from mild-mannered, shy individuals into murderers. Any conclusion, however, is only a statement of the *probable* relationship between the events that were investigated; it is never one of certainty. Truth in science is provisional, always open to revision by later data from better studies, developed from better hypotheses.

You might take a moment to consider what else you'd like to know, to put these data in a richer context. For example, you might want to know how both types of murderers differ from individuals who have never committed murders on measures such as their sex-role scores. If we collected new data we could use descriptive and inferential statistics to answer such questions as whether all murderers are, on such dimensions, different from those who don't commit murders. What might you expect?

Becoming a Wise Consumer of Statistics

Now that we have considered what statistics are, how they are used, and what they mean, we must talk briefly about how they can be misused. Many people accept unsupported so-called facts that are bolstered by the air of authority of a statistic. Others choose to believe or disbelieve what the statistics say without having any idea of how to question the numbers that are presented in support of a product, politician, or proposal. At the end of Chapter 2, we gave you some suggestions about how you can become a wiser research consumer. Based on this brief survey of statistics, we can extend that advice to situations in which people make specific statistical claims.

There are many ways to give a misleading impression using statistics. The decisions made at all stages of research—from who the participants are to how the study is designed, what statistics are selected, and how they are used—can have a profound effect on the conclusions that can be drawn from the data.

The group of participants can make a large difference that can easily remain undetected when the results are reported. For example, a survey of views on abortion rights will yield very different results if conducted in a small conservative community in the South rather than at a university in New York City. Likewise, a pro-life group surveying the opinions of its membership will very likely arrive at conclusions that differ from those obtained by the same survey conducted by a pro-choice group.

Even if the participants are randomly selected and not biased by the methodology, the statistics can produce misleading results if the assumptions of the statistics are violated. For example, suppose 20 people take an IQ test; 19 of them receive scores between 90 and 110, and 1 receives a score of 220. The mean of the group will be strongly elevated by that one outlying high score. With this sort of a data set, it would be much more accurate to present the median or the mode, which would accurately report the group's generally average intelligence, rather than the mean, which would make it look as if the average member of this group had a high IQ. This sort of bias is especially powerful in a small sample. If, however, the number of people in this group were 2,000 instead of 20, the one extreme outlier would make virtually no difference, and the mean would be a legitimate summary of the group's intelligence.

One good way to avoid falling for this sort of deception is to check on the size of the sample. Large samples are less likely to be misleading than small ones. Another check is to look at the median or the mode as well as the mean. The results can be interpreted with more confidence if they are similar than if they are different. Always closely examine the methodology and results of the research reported. Check to see if the experimenters report their sample size, measures of variability, and significance levels. Try to find out if the methods they used measure accurately and consistently whatever they claim to be investigating.

Statistics are the backbone of psychological research. They are used to understand observations and to determine whether the findings are, in fact, correct. Through the methods we have described, psychologists can prepare a frequency distribution of data and find the central tendencies and variability of the scores. They can use the correlation coefficient to determine the strength and direction of the association between sets of scores. Finally, psychological investigators can then find out how representative the observations are and whether they are significantly different from what would be observed among the general population. Statistics can also be used poorly or deceptively, misleading those who do not understand them. But when statistics are applied correctly and ethically, they allow researchers to expand the body of psychological knowledge.

KEY TERMS

correlation coefficient (*r*) (p. 48)

descriptive statistics (p. 45)

frequency distribution (p. 45)

inferential statistics (p. 45)

mean (p. 48)

measure of central tendency (p. 47)

measure of variability (p. 48)

median (p. 47)

mode (p. 47)

normal curve (p. 49)

range (p. 48)

significant difference (p. 50)

standard deviation (SD) (p. 48)

3

The Biological and Evolutionary Bases of Behavior

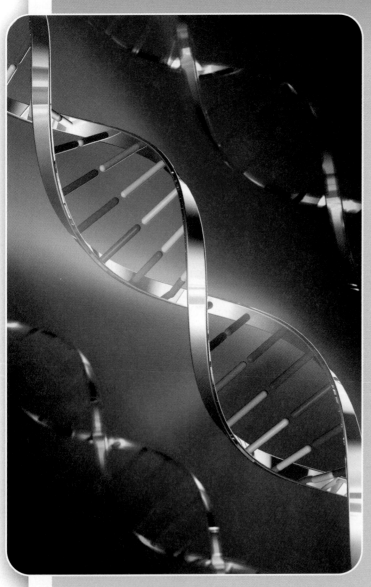

What makes you a unique individual? *Psychology and Life* provides many answers to this question, but in this chapter we will focus on the biological aspects of your individuality. To help you understand what makes you different from the people around you, we will describe the role that heredity plays in shaping your life and in forming the brain that controls your experiences. Of course, you can appreciate these differences only against the background of what you have in common with all other people. You might, therefore, think of this as a chapter about biological potential: What possibilities for behavior define the human species, and how do those possibilities emerge for particular members of that species?

In a way, this chapter stands as proof of one remarkable aspect of your biological potential: Your brain is sufficiently complex to carry out a systematic examination of its own functions. Why is this so remarkable? The human brain is sometimes likened to a spectacular computer: At only 3 pounds, your brain contains more cells than there are stars in our entire galaxy—over 100 billion cells that communicate and store information with astonishing efficiency. But even the world's mightiest computer is incapable of reflecting on the rules that guide its own operation. Thus you are much more than a computer; your consciousness allows you to put your vast computational power to work, trying to determine your species' own rules for operation. The research we describe in this chapter arose from the special human desire for self-understanding.

For many students, this chapter will pose a greater challenge than the rest of *Psychology and Life*. It requires that you learn some anatomy and many new terms that seem far removed from the information you may have expected to get from an introduction to psychology. However, understanding your biological nature will enable you to appreciate more fully the complex interplay among the brain, mind, behavior, and environment that creates the unique experience of being human.

Our goal for this chapter is to help you to understand how biology contributes to the creation of unique individuals against a shared background potential. To approach this goal, we first describe how evolution and heredity determine your biology and behavior. We then see how laboratory and clinical research provide a view into the workings of the brain, the nervous system, and the endocrine system. Finally, we describe the basic mechanisms of communication among cells in your nervous system that produce the full range of complex human behaviors.

Heredity and Behavior

In Chapter 1, we defined one of the major goals of psychology to be the discovery of the causes underlying the variety of human behavior. An important dimension of causal explanation within psychology is defined by the end points of *nature* versus *nurture*, or *heredity* versus *environment*. Consider, as we did in Chapter 1, the question of the roots of aggressive behavior. You might imagine that individuals are aggressive by virtue of some aspect of their biological makeup: They may have inherited a tendency toward violence from one of their parents. Alternatively, you might imagine that all humans are about equally predisposed to aggression and that the degree of aggression individuals display arises in response to features of the environment in which they are raised. The correct answer to

this question has a profound impact on how society treats individuals who are overly aggressive—by focusing resources on changing certain environments or on changing aspects of the people themselves. You need to be able to discriminate the forces of heredity from the forces of environment.

Because the features of environments can be directly observed, it is often easier to understand how they affect people's behavior. You can, for example, actually watch a parent acting aggressively toward a child and wonder what consequences such treatment might have on the child's later tendency toward aggression; you can observe the overcrowded and impoverished settings in which some children grow up and wonder whether these features of the environment lead to aggressive behaviors. The biological forces that shape behavior, by comparison, are never plainly visible to the naked eye. To make the biology of behavior more understandable to you, we will begin by describing some of the basic principles that shape a species potential repertory of behaviors—elements of the theory of evolution—and then describe how behavioral variation is passed from generation to generation.

EVOLUTION AND NATURAL SELECTION

In 1831, **Charles Darwin** (1809–1882), fresh out of college with a degree in theology, set sail from England on HMS *Beagle,* an ocean research vessel, for a five-year cruise to survey the coast of South America. During the trip, Darwin collected everything that crossed his path: marine animals, birds, insects, plants, fossils, seashells, and rocks. His extensive notes became the foundation for his books on topics ranging from geology to emotion to zoology. The book for which he is most remembered is *The Origin of Species,* published in 1859. In this work, Darwin set forth science's grandest theory: the evolution of life on planet Earth.

Natural Selection Darwin developed his theory of evolution by reflecting on the species of animals he had encountered while on his voyage. One of the many places *Beagle* visited was

Psychologists often wish to understand the separate impact of nature and nurture on individuals' courses through life. Why might it be easier to observe the impact of environments versus the impact of heredity?

the Galápagos Islands, a volcanic archipelago off the west coast of South America. These islands are a haven for diverse forms of wildlife, including 13 species of finches, now known as Darwin's finches. Darwin wondered how so many different species of finches could have come to inhabit the islands. He reasoned that they couldn't have migrated from the mainland because those species didn't exist there. He suggested, therefore, that the variety of species reflected the operation of a process he came to call **natural selection.**

Darwin's theory suggests that each species of finch emerged from a common set of ancestors. Originally, a small flock of finches found their way to one of the islands; they mated among themselves and eventually their number multiplied. Over time, some finches migrated to different islands in the archipelago. What happened next was the process of natural selection. Food resources and living conditions—*habitats*—vary considerably from island to island. Some of the islands are lush with berries and seeds, others are covered with cacti, and others have plenty of insects. At first, the populations on different islands were similar—there was *variation* among the groups of finches on each island. However, because food resources on the islands were limited, a bird was more likely to survive and reproduce if the shape of its beak was well suited to the food sources available on the island. For example, birds that migrated to islands rich in berries and seeds were more likely to survive and reproduce if they had thick beaks. On those islands, birds with thinner, more pointed beaks, unsuitable for crushing or breaking open seeds, died. The environment of each island determined which among the original population of finches would live and reproduce and which would more likely perish, leaving no offspring. Over time, this led to very different populations on each island and permitted the different species of Darwin's finches to evolve from the original ancestral group.

In general, the theory of natural selection suggests that organisms well adapted to their environment, whatever it happens to be, will produce more offspring than those less well adapted. Over time, those organisms possessing traits more favorable for survival will become more numerous than those not possessing those traits. In evolutionary terms, an individual's success is measured by the number of offspring he or she produces.

Contemporary research has shown that natural selection can have dramatic effects, even in the short run. In a series of studies by **Peter** and **Rosemary Grant** (Grant & Grant, 2006, 2008), involving several species of Darwin's finches, records were kept of rainfall, food supply, and the population size of these finches on one of the Galápagos Islands. In 1976, the population numbered well over 1,000 birds. The following year brought a murderous drought that wiped out most of the food supply. The smallest seeds were the first to be depleted, leaving only larger and tougher seeds. That year the finch population decreased by more than 80 percent. However, smaller finches with smaller beaks died at a higher frequency than larger finches with thicker beaks. Consequently, as Darwin would have predicted, the larger birds became more numerous in the following years. Why? Because only they, with their larger bodies and thicker beaks, were fit enough to

What observations ultimately led Charles Darwin to propose the theory of evolution?

respond to the environmental change caused by the drought. Interestingly, in 1983, rain was plentiful, and seeds, especially the smaller ones, became abundant. As a result, smaller birds outsurvived larger birds, probably because their beaks were better suited for pecking the smaller seeds. The Grants' study shows that natural selection can have noticeable effects even over short periods. Researchers continue to document the impact of environments on natural selection in diverse species such as fruit flies, mosquitos, flounders, and pygmy possums (Hoffmann & Willi, 2008).

---

natural selection Darwin's theory that favorable adaptations to features of the environment allow some members of a species to reproduce more successfully than others.

Although Darwin provided the foundation for evolutionary theory, researchers continue to study mechanisms of evolutionary change that fell beyond the bounds of Darwin's ideas (Gould, 2002). For example, one important question that Darwin was unable to address fully was how populations with common ancestors evolve so that one species becomes two. As you have already seen in the Grants' research with Darwin's finches, species can change rapidly in response to local environments. One explanation for the appearance of new species is that they emerge when two populations from an original species become geographically separate—and therefore evolve in response to different environmental events. However, contemporary research on evolution has uncovered many examples of new species that have emerged without that type of geographic isolation (Barton, 2000). Researchers are pursuing a variety of explanations for how species arise under those circumstances. These explanations focus, for example, on how subgroups within a species evolve different cues—such as the chemical signals fruit flies use—to recognize appropriate mates (Higgie et al., 2000). If, over time, those cues become distinct, separate species may emerge.

Genotypes and Phenotypes

Let's return our focus to the forces that bring about change within an existing species.

The example of the ebb and flow of finch populations demonstrates why Darwin characterized the course of evolution as *survival of the fittest*. Imagine that each environment poses some range of difficulties for each species of living beings. Those members of the species who possess the range of physical and psychological attributes best adapted to the environment are most likely to survive. To the extent that the attributes that foster survival can be passed from one generation to another—and stresses in the environment endure over time—the species is likely to evolve.

To examine the process of natural selection in more detail, we must introduce some of the vocabulary of evolutionary theory. Let us focus on an individual finch. At conception, that finch inherited a **genotype,** or genetic structure, from its parents. In the context of a particular environment, this genotype determined the finch's development and behavior. The outward appearance and repertory of behaviors of the finch are known as its **phenotype.** For our finch, its genotype may have interacted with the environment to yield the phenotype of *small beak* and *ability to peck smaller seeds.*

If seeds of all types were plentiful, this phenotype would have no particular bearing on the finch's survival. Suppose, however, that the environment provided insufficient seeds to feed the whole population of finches. In that case, the individual finches would be in *competition* for resources. When species function in circumstances of competition, phenotypes help determine which individual members are better adapted to ensure survival. Recall our finch with a small beak. If only small seeds were available, our finch would be at a *selective advantage* with respect to finches with large beaks. If only large seeds were available, our finch would be at a disadvantage.

Only finches that survive can reproduce. Only those animals that reproduce can pass on their genotypes. Therefore, if the environment continued to provide only small seeds, over several generations the finches would probably come to have almost exclusively small beaks—with the consequence that they would be almost exclusively capable of eating only small seeds. In this way, forces in the environment can shape a species

repertory of possible behaviors. **Figure 3.1** on page 56 provides a simplified model of the process of natural selection. Let us now apply these ideas to human evolution.

Human Evolution By looking backward to the circumstances in which the human species evolved, you can begin to understand why certain physical and behavioral features are part of the biological endowment of the entire human species. In the evolution of our species, natural selection favored two major adaptations—bipedalism and encephalization. Together, they made possible the rise of human civilization. *Bipedalism,* which refers to the ability to walk upright, emerged in our evolutionary ancestors 5 to 7 million years ago (Thorpe et al., 2007). As our ancestors evolved the ability to walk upright, they were able to explore new environments and exploit new resources. *Encephalization* refers to increases in brain size. Early human ancestors, who emerged about 4 million years ago (for example, *Australopithecus*), had brains roughly the same size as chimpanzees (see **Figure 3.2** on page 57). In the time from 1.9 million years ago *(Homo erectus)* to 200,000 years ago *(Homo sapiens),* brain size tripled (Gibbons, 2007). As brain size increased, our ancestors became more intelligent and developed capacities for complex thinking, reasoning, remembering, and planning (Sherwood et al., 2008). However, the evolution of a bigger brain did not guarantee that humans would become more intelligent—what was important was the kind of tissue that developed and expanded within the brain (Gibbons, 2002). The genotype coding for mobile and intelligent phenotypes slowly squeezed out other, less well-adapted genotypes from the human gene pool, affording only intelligent bipeds the opportunity to reproduce.

After bipedalism and encephalization, perhaps the most important evolutionary milestone for our species was the advent of *language* (Sherwood et al., 2008). Think of the tremendous adaptive advantages that language conferred on early humans. Simple instructions for making tools, finding a good hunting or fishing spot, and avoiding danger would save time, effort, and lives. Instead of learning every one of life's lessons firsthand, by trial and error, humans could benefit from experiences shared by others. Conversation, even humor, would strengthen the social bonds among members of a naturally gregarious species. Most important, the advent of language would provide for the transmission of accumulated wisdom, from one generation to future generations.

Language is the basis for *cultural evolution,* which is the tendency of cultures to respond adaptively, through learning, to environmental change. Cultural evolution has given rise to major advances in toolmaking, improved agricultural practices, and the development and refinement of industry and technology. Cultural evolution allows our species to make very rapid adjustments to changes in environmental conditions. Adaptations to the use of personal computers, for example, have arisen in only the past few decades. Even so, cultural evolution could not occur without genotype coding for the capacities to learn and to think abstractly.

---

genotype The genetic structure an organism inherits from its parents.

phenotype The observable characteristics of an organism, resulting from the interaction between the organism's genotype and its environment.

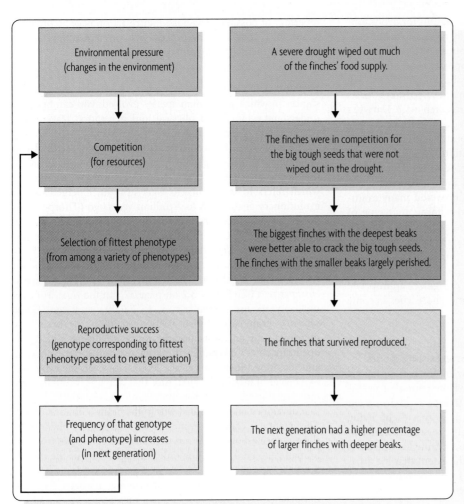

FIGURE 3.1 How Natural Selection Works
Environmental changes create competition for resources among species members. Only those individuals possessing characteristics instrumental in coping with these changes will survive and reproduce. The next generation will have a greater number of individuals possessing these genetically based traits.

Culture—including art, literature, music, scientific knowledge, and philanthropic activities—is possible only because of the potential of the human genotype.

VARIATION IN THE HUMAN GENOTYPE

You have seen that the conditions in which humans evolved favored the evolution of important shared biological potential: for example, bipedalism and the capacity for thought and language. There remains, however, considerable variation within that shared potential. Your mother and father have endowed you with a part of what their parents, grandparents, and all past generations of their family lines have given them, resulting in a unique biological blueprint and timetable for your development. The study of the mechanisms of **heredity**—the inheritance of physical and psychological traits from ancestors—is called **genetics.**

---

heredity The biological transmission of traits from parents to offspring.

genetics The study of the inheritance of physical and psychological traits from ancestors.

DNA (deoxyribonucleic acid) The physical basis for the transmission of genetic information.

gene The biological unit of heredity; discrete section of a chromosome responsible for transmission of traits.

The earliest systematic research exploring the relationship between parents and their offspring was published in 1866 by **Gregor Mendel** (1822–1884). Mendel's studies were carried out on the humble garden pea. He was able to demonstrate that the physical features of peas that emerged from different seeds—for example, whether the peas appeared *round* or *wrinkled*—could be predicted from the physical features of the plants from which the seeds had been obtained. Based on his observations, Mendel suggested that pairs of "factors"—one inherited from each parent—determined the properties of the offspring (Lander & Weinberg, 2000). Although Mendel's work originally received little attention from other scientists, modern techniques have allowed researchers to visualize and study Mendel's "factors," which we now call *genes*.

Basic Genetics In the nucleus of each of your cells is genetic material called **DNA (deoxyribonucleic acid;** see **Figure 3.3** on page 58). DNA is organized into tiny units, called **genes.** Genes contain the instructions for the production of proteins. These proteins regulate the body's physiological processes and the expression of phenotypic traits: body build, physical strength, intelligence, and many behavior patterns.

Genes are found on rodlike structures known as *chromosomes*. At the very instant you were conceived, you inherited from your parents 46 chromosomes—23 from your mother and 23 from your father. Each of these chromosomes

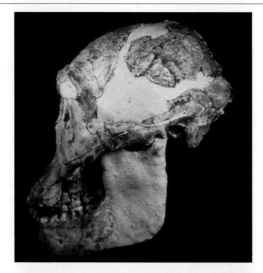

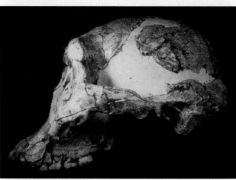

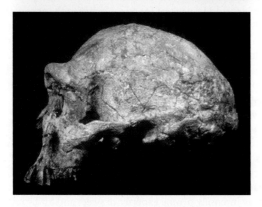

FIGURE 3.2   Increases in Brain Size across Human Evolution

Early in human evolution, brain size doubled from *Australopithecus* (top) to *Homo erectus* (middle). Over the course of evolution, increases continued so that the brains of modern humans, *Homo sapiens* (bottom), are three times larger than those of *Australopithecus*.

codes for development of female characteristics; an XY combination codes for development of male characteristics.

The pairs of genes you inherited—one from your mother and one from your father—provide the genetic starting point for most physical and psychological attributes. In many cases, there are different versions of a particular gene. Your phenotype is determined by the versions you inherited. Consider what happens when people come in contact with poison ivy: One version of a gene makes them immune to its allergic effects; the other version of the same gene will have them breaking out in a rash. However, the gene that makes people immune is the *dominant* version of the gene, whereas the gene that makes people susceptible is the *recessive* version. When people inherit different versions of a gene, the dominant gene wins out. If your skin responds badly to poison ivy, you likely inherited two recessive genes. A range of other physical traits (such as the color of your eyes and hair or the breadth of your lips) is determined by dominant and recessive genes.

As we begin to consider the genetic basis of more complex aspects of human experience, it is important to note that more than one pair of genes contributes to a particular attribute. These characteristics are known as **polygenic traits** because more than one gene influences the phenotype. For example, in Chapter 15 we will discuss the genetic basis of psychological disorders. For each disorder, research suggests that more than one gene influences which individuals will be at risk (Keller & Miller, 2006).

Beginning in 1990, the U.S. government funded an international effort called the *Human Genome Project (HGP)*. The **genome** of an organism is the full sequence of genes found on the chromosomes with the associated DNA. In 2003, the HGP achieved the goal of providing a complete sequencing of the human genome. With that information in hand, researchers have now turned their attention to identifying all 20,500 human genes (Clamp et al., 2007). The ultimate goal is to provide a complete account of the location and functions of that full set of genes.

Genes and Behavior We have seen that evolutionary processes have allowed a considerable amount of variation to remain in human genotypes; the interactions of these genotypes with particular environments produce variation in human phenotypes. Researchers in the field of **human behavior genetics** unite genetics and psychology to explore the causal link between inheritance and behavior (Plomin et al., 2003).

Research in human behavior genetics often focuses on estimating the **heritability** of particular human traits and behaviors. Heritability is measured on a scale of 0 to 1. If an estimate is near 0, it suggests that the attribute is largely a product of environmental influences; if an estimate is near 1, it suggests that the attribute is largely a product of genetic influences.

---

sex chromosome Chromosome that contains the genes that code for the development of male or female characteristics.

polygenic trait Characteristic that is influenced by more than one gene.

genome The genetic information for an organism, stored in the DNA of its chromosomes.

human behavior genetics The area of study that evaluates the genetic component of individual differences in behaviors and traits.

heritability The relative influence of genetics—versus environment—in determining patterns of behavior.

contains thousands of genes—the union of a sperm and an egg results in only one of many billion possible gene combinations. The **sex chromosomes** are those that contain genes coding for development of male or female physical characteristics. You inherited an X chromosome from your mother and either an X or a Y chromosome from your father. An XX combination

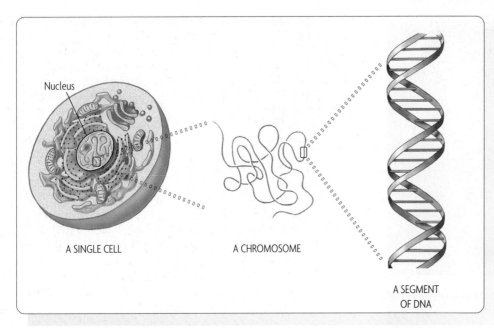

FIGURE 3.3 Genetic Material

The nucleus of each cell in your body contains a copy of the chromosomes that transmit your genetic inheritance. Each chromosome contains a long strand of DNA arranged in a double helix. Genes are segments of the DNA that contain instructions for the production of the proteins that guide your individual development.

From Lefton, *Psychology*, © 2003. Reproduced by permission of Pearson Education, Inc.

To separate environmental influences from genetic influences, researchers often use *adoption studies* or *twin studies*. For adoption studies, researchers obtain as much information as possible about the birth parents of children who are raised in adoptive homes. As the children develop, researchers assess the relative similarity of children to their birth families—representing genetics—and their adoptive families—representing environment.

In twin studies, researchers examine the extent to which *monozygotic (MZ)* twins (also called *identical twins*) and *dizygotic (DZ)* twins (also called *fraternal twins*) show similarity within pairs on particular traits or behaviors. MZ twins share 100 percent of their genetic material, whereas DZ twins share roughly 50 percent. (DZ twins are no more genetically alike than any other pair of brothers and sisters.) Researchers compute heritability estimates by determining how much more alike MZ twins are than DZ twins on a particular attribute. Consider a twin study that assessed genetic impact on people's food preferences:

When you choose a meal at a restaurant, you need to make a series of decisions: Will you order meat or fish? Will you order fruit or vegetables? Will you save room for dessert? If you've eaten meals with friends, you know that people's food preferences vary enormously. To what extent can these preferences be affected by genetic makeup? To address this question, a team of researchers recruited 103 pairs of MZ twins and 111 pairs of DZ twins between the ages of 4 and 5 (Breen et al., 2006). The researchers obtained information about these children's likes and dislikes for 95 foods that clustered into the groups meat and fish, fruit, vegetables, and desserts. **Table 3.1** shows the correlations for each category for the different types of twins as well as heritability estimates. Note that the larger the difference between the two correlations, the larger the heritability estimate. From the table you learn, for example, that there's a larger genetic impact on people's preferences for meat and fish than there is for desserts. The differences in genetic contributions arise, in part, from the particular flavors represented within each category. For example, different genes likely determine how intensely people experience sweet and bitter tastes.

Note that this high heritability estimate does not mean that everyone in a family is going to crave exactly the same foods. Just as the same parents will produce some children with blue eyes and some with brown eyes, the same parents will produce some children who love broccoli and others who avoid it at all costs. Instead, the heritability estimates give a sense of how much room there is for life experiences to affect the food choices you make.

This example of the heritability of food preferences points to some of the ethical issues that have arisen in the wake of the Human Genome Project's successes. Suppose the HGP is able to determine which genes are responsible for the differences in preferences? If you were to become a parent, would you choose only to have children who were likely to eat their vegetables without complaints? Although this question might not seem urgent in the context of food preferences, ethicists have begun to ponder some serious consequences of genetic knowledge (Bostrom, 2005; Liao, 2005). For example, a variety of tech-

Human chromosomes—at the moment of conception, you inherited 23 from your mother and 23 from your father.

TABLE 3.1 The Heritability of Food Preferences

Food Category	Correlations between Twins' Preferences		
	MZ Twins	DZ Twins	Heritability Estimate
Desserts	0.84	0.73	0.22
Vegetables	0.88	0.67	0.42
Fruit	0.82	0.59	0.46
Meat and fish	0.90	0.52	0.76

From Breen, F.M., Plomin, R., & Wardle, J., Heritability of food preferences in young children, *Physiology & Behavior, 88*, pp. 443–447, Copyright (2006), with permission from Elsevier.

niques already allow prospective parents to choose to have a boy or a girl. Should they be willing and able to make that choice? How about choices with respect to a child's intelligence level, sports ability, or criminal inclinations? As the HGP and related efforts continue to yield new insights, such ethical questions will become increasingly prominent in debates over public policy.

Still, it's important to remember that—except in cases such as a child's sex—genes are not destiny. In fact, researchers have begun to document important instances in which both genetics and environments play critical roles to determine organisms' behaviors.

Consider a study that looked at the nature and nurture of aggression among male rhesus macaques (Newman et al., 2005). Let's start with nature. Within the population of 45 monkeys, there was variation with respect to a gene that affected the levels of neurotransmitters (see p. 65) in the brain—some monkeys had the high-activity variation of the gene, whereas other monkeys had the low-activity variation. With respect to nurture, roughly half of the monkeys were raised with their own or a foster mother; the others were raised without early maternal care. The experimenters measured the monkeys' aggression by observing, for example, how effectively they competed for food. These observations suggested that the monkeys' levels of aggression depended on both genetics and environment: The monkeys who had the low-activity variation of the gene and who also had been raised by mothers showed the most aggressive behavior. Monkeys with the same gene variation but who had not experienced maternal contact did not show higher levels of aggression.

From this example you can see why researchers seek to understand how and why certain environments allow genes to be expressed.

The study of human behavior genetics most often focuses on the origins of individual differences: What factors in your individual genetic inheritance help to explain the way you think and behave? To complement human behavior genetics, two other fields have emerged that take a broader focus on how forces of natural selection affected the behavioral repertoire of humans and other species. Researchers in the field of **sociobiology** provide evolutionary explanations for the social behavior and social systems of humans and other animal species. Researchers in **evolutionary psychology** extend those evolutionary explanations to include other aspects of human experience, such as how the mind functions.

Consider the question of happiness: How might an evolutionary perspective explain the human species general ability to experience happiness? Buss (2000) suggested that some limits are

placed on human happiness by the "discrepancies between modern and ancestral environments" (p. 15). For example, although humans evolved in the context of small groups, many people now live in large urban environments in which they are mostly surrounded by large numbers of total strangers. We might no longer have close bonds to the group of individuals that share our space—the types of bonds that could help us weather crises to experience happy lives. What can be done? Although you cannot turn back the tide of cultural evolution that has brought about these changes, you can try to counteract their negative effects by increasing your closeness to your family members and to your friends (Buss, 2000). This example reveals the contrast between the sociobiological emphasis on the human species in a particular environment versus the behavior genetic emphasis on variation within the general pattern for a species. In the remainder of *Psychology and Life,* we will present several more instances in which the evolutionary perspective sheds light on human experience. These examples range from partner choices in relationships (Chapter 11) to emotional expression (Chapter 12).

STOP AND REVIEW

❶ How does the Grants' research on finches illustrate the role of genetic variation in the process of evolution?

❷ What is the difference between a genotype and a phenotype?

❸ What were two evolutionary advances most critical in human evolution?

❹ What is meant by heritability?

CRITICAL THINKING Consider the study on food preferences. Why might preferences for desserts show the smallest impact of genes?

Visit MyPsychLab.com for more review and practice on the following topics:

◄● **Explore:** Building Blocks of Genetics

◉ **Watch:** Junk DNA

◉ **Watch:** Depression among the Amish

---

sociobiology A field of research that focuses on evolutionary explanations for the social behavior and social systems of humans and other animal species.

evolutionary psychology The study of behavior and mind using the principles of evolutionary theory.

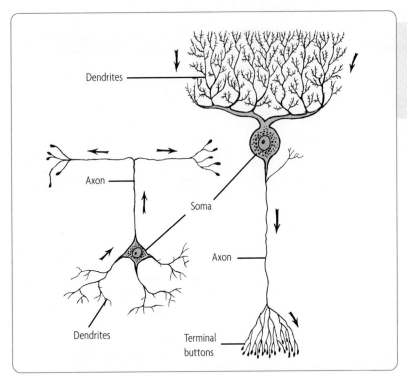

FIGURE 3.4 Two Types of Neurons
Note the differences in shape and dendritic branching. Arrows indicate directions in which information flows. Both cells are types of interneurons.

Dendrites

Axon

Soma

Axon

Dendrites

Terminal buttons

The Nervous System in Action

We turn our attention now to the remarkable products of the human genotype: the biological systems that make possible the full range of thought and performance. Long before Darwin made preparations for his trip aboard *Beagle,* scientists, philosophers, and others debated the role that biological processes play in everyday life. An important figure in the history of brain studies was the French philosopher **René Descartes** (1596–1650). Descartes proposed what at that time was a very new and very radical idea: The human body is an "animal machine" that can be understood scientifically—by discovering natural laws through empirical observation.

Researchers who pursue these natural laws are called *neuroscientists.* Today, **neuroscience** is one of the most rapidly growing areas of research. Important discoveries come with astonishing regularity. Our objective for the remainder of this chapter is to explore how the information available to your senses is ultimately communicated throughout your body and brain by nerve impulses. In this section, we begin that exploration by discussing the properties of the basic unit of the nervous system, the neuron.

---

neuroscience The scientific study of the brain and of the links between brain activity and behavior.

neuron A cell in the nervous system specialized to receive, process, and/or transmit information to other cells.

dendrite One of the branched fibers of neurons that receive incoming signals.

soma The cell body of a neuron, containing the nucleus and cytoplasm.

THE NEURON

A **neuron** is a cell specialized to receive, process, and/or transmit information to other cells within the body. Neurons vary in shape, size, chemical composition, and function, but all neurons have the same basic structure (see **Figure 3.4**). There are between 100 billion and 1 trillion neurons in your brain.

Neurons typically take in information at one end and send out messages from the other. The part of the cell that receives incoming signals is a set of branched fibers called **dendrites,** which extend outward from the cell body. The basic job of the dendrites is to receive stimulation from sense receptors or other neurons. The cell body, or **soma,** contains the nucleus of the cell

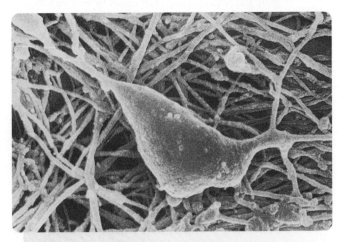

A neuron that affects contractions in the human intestine. What are the roles of the dendrites, soma, and axons in neural transmission?

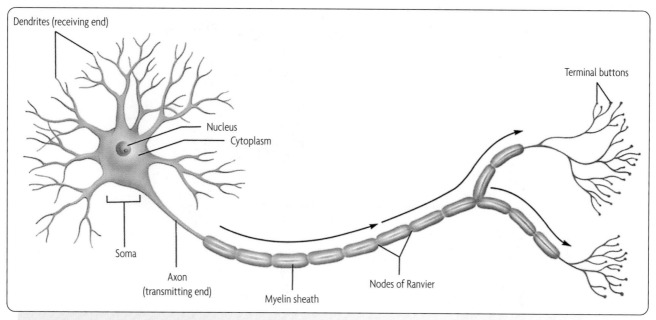

FIGURE 3.5   The Major Structures of the Neuron

The neuron receives nerve impulses through its dendrites. It then sends the nerve impulses through its axon to the terminal buttons, where neurotransmitters are released to stimulate other neurons.

and the cytoplasm that sustains its life. The soma integrates information about the stimulation received from the dendrites (or in some cases received directly from another neuron) and passes it on to a single, extended fiber, the **axon.** In turn, the axon conducts this information along its length—which, in the spinal cord, can be several feet and, in the brain, less than a millimeter. At the other end of axons are swollen, bulblike structures called **terminal buttons,** through which the neuron is able to stimulate nearby glands, muscles, or other neurons. Neurons generally transmit information in only one direction: from the dendrites through the soma to the axon to the terminal buttons (see **Figure 3.5**).

There are three major classes of neurons. **Sensory neurons** carry messages from sense receptor cells *toward* the central nervous system. Receptor cells are highly specialized cells that are sensitive, for example, to light, sound, and body position. **Motor neurons** carry messages *away* from the central nervous system toward the muscles and glands. The bulk of the neurons in the brain are **interneurons,** which relay messages from sensory neurons to other interneurons or to motor neurons. For every motor neuron in the body there are as many as 5,000 interneurons in the great intermediate network that forms the computational system of the brain.

As an example of how these three kinds of neurons work together, consider the pain withdrawal reflex (see **Figure 3.6** on page 62). When pain receptors near the skin's surface are stimulated by a sharp object, they send messages via sensory neurons to an interneuron in the spinal cord. The interneuron responds by stimulating motor neurons, which, in turn, excite muscles in the appropriate area of the body to pull away from the pain-producing object. It is only *after* this sequence of neuronal events has taken place, and the body has been moved away from the stimulating object, that the brain receives information about the situation. In cases such as this, where survival depends on swift action, your perception of pain often occurs

after you have physically responded to the danger. Of course, then the information from the incident is stored in the brain's memory system so that the next time you will avoid the potentially dangerous object altogether, before it can hurt you.

Interspersed among the brain's vast web of neurons are about five to ten times as many glial cells (**glia**). The word *glia* is derived from the Greek word for *glue,* which gives you a hint of one of the major duties performed by these cells: They hold neurons in place. In vertebrates, glial cells have several other important functions. A first function applies during development. Glial cells help guide newborn neurons to appropriate locations in the brain. A second function is housekeeping. When neurons are damaged and die, glial cells in the area multiply and clean up the cellular junk left behind; they can also take up excess neurotransmitters and other substances at the gaps between neurons. A third function is insulation. Glial cells form an insulating cover, called a **myelin sheath,** around some

---

axon The extended fiber of a neuron through which nerve impulses travel from the soma to the terminal buttons.

terminal button A bulblike structure at the branched ending of an axon that contains vesicles filled with neurotransmitters.

sensory neuron Neuron that carries messages from sense receptors toward the central nervous system.

motor neuron Neuron that carries messages away from the central nervous system toward the muscles and glands.

interneuron Brain neuron that relays messages from sensory neurons to other interneurons or to motor neurons.

glia The cells that hold neurons together and facilitate neural transmission, remove damaged and dead neurons, and prevent poisonous substances in the blood from reaching the brain.

myelin sheath Insulating material that surrounds axons and increases the speed of neural transmission.

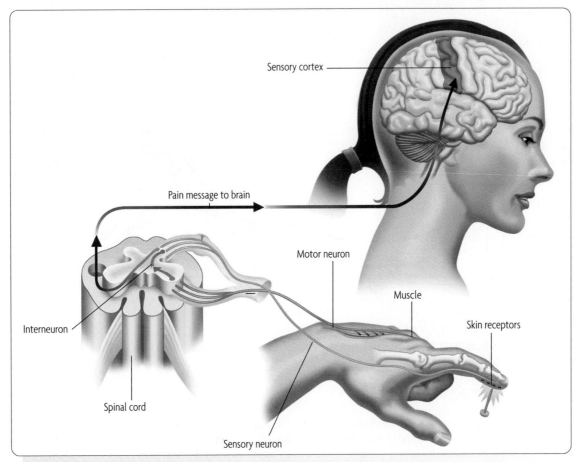

FIGURE 3.6 The Pain Withdrawal Reflex
The pain withdrawal reflex shown here involves only three neurons: a sensory neuron, a motor neuron, and an interneuron.

types of axons. This fatty insulation greatly increases the speed of nerve signal conduction. A fourth function of glial cells is to prevent toxic substances in the blood from reaching the delicate cells of the brain. Specialized glial cells, called astrocytes, make up a *blood–brain barrier,* forming a continuous envelope of fatty material around the blood vessels in the brain. Substances that are not soluble in fat do not dissolve through this barrier, and because many poisons and other harmful substances are not fat soluble, they cannot penetrate the barrier to reach the brain. Finally, neuroscientists have come to believe that glia may play an active role in neural communication. Glia may affect the concentrations of ions that allow for the transmission of nerve impulses (Fields & Stevens-Graham, 2002). In addition, some glia may generate the same types of electrochemical signals that neurons generate (Káradóttir et al., 2008). In the next section, we discuss those signals.

---

excitatory input Information entering a neuron that signals it to fire.

inhibitory input Information entering a neuron that signals it not to fire.

action potential The nerve impulse activated in a neuron that travels down the axon and causes neurotransmitters to be released into a synapse.

ACTION POTENTIALS

So far, we have spoken loosely about neurons "sending messages" or "stimulating" each other. The time has come to describe more formally the kinds of electrochemical signals used by the nervous system to process and transmit information. These signals are the basis of all you know, feel, desire, and create.

This is the basic question asked of each neuron: Should it or should it not *fire*—produce a response—at some given time? In loose terms, neurons make this decision by combining the information arriving at their dendrites and soma (cell body) and determining whether those inputs are predominantly saying "fire" or "don't fire." More formally, each neuron will receive a balance of **excitatory**—fire!—and **inhibitory**—don't fire!—**inputs.** In neurons, the right pattern of excitatory inputs over time or space will lead to the production of an *action potential:* The neuron fires.

The Biochemical Basis of Action Potentials To explain how an **action potential** works, we need to describe the biochemical environment in which neurons draw together incoming information. All neural communication is produced by the flow of electrically charged particles, called *ions,* through the neuron's membrane, a thin "skin" separating the cell's internal

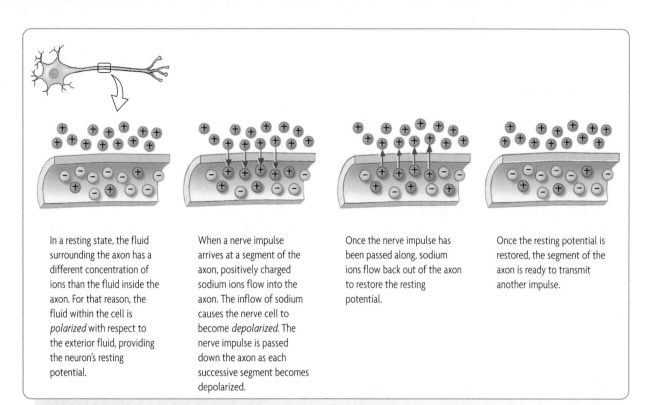

In a resting state, the fluid surrounding the axon has a different concentration of ions than the fluid inside the axon. For that reason, the fluid within the cell is *polarized* with respect to the exterior fluid, providing the neuron's resting potential.

When a nerve impulse arrives at a segment of the axon, positively charged sodium ions flow into the axon. The inflow of sodium causes the nerve cell to become *depolarized*. The nerve impulse is passed down the axon as each successive segment becomes depolarized.

Once the nerve impulse has been passed along, sodium ions flow back out of the axon to restore the resting potential.

Once the resting potential is restored, the segment of the axon is ready to transmit another impulse.

FIGURE 3.7   The Biochemical Basis of Action Potentials

Action potentials rely on an imbalance of the electrical charge of the ions present inside and outside of axons.

From Lefton, *Psychology*, © 2003. Reproduced by permission of Pearson Education, Inc.

and external environments. Think of a nerve fiber as a piece of macaroni, filled with salt water, floating in a salty soup. The soup and the fluid in the macaroni both contain ions—atoms of sodium (Na^+), chloride (Cl^-), and potassium (K^+)—that have either positive (+) or negative (−) charges (see **Figure 3.7**). The membrane, or the surface of the macaroni, plays a critical role in keeping the ingredients of the two fluids in an appropriate balance. When a cell is inactive, or in a resting state, there is a greater concentration of potassium ions inside the axon and a greater concentration of sodium ions outside the axon. The membrane is not a perfect barrier; it "leaks" a little, allowing some sodium ions to slip in while some potassium ions slip out. To correct for this, nature has provided transport mechanisms within the membrane that pump out sodium and pump in potassium. Successful operation of these pumps leaves the fluid inside a neuron with a slightly negative voltage (70/1,000 of a volt) relative to the fluid outside. This means that the fluid inside the cell is *polarized* with respect to the fluid outside the cell. This slight polarization is called the **resting potential.** It provides the electrochemical context in which a nerve cell can produce an action potential.

The nerve cell begins the transition from a resting potential to an action potential in response to the pattern of inhibitory and excitatory inputs. Each kind of input affects the likelihood that the balance of ions from the inside to the outside of the cell will change. They cause changes in the function of **ion channels,** excitable portions of the cell membrane that selectively permit certain ions to flow in and out. Inhibitory inputs cause the ion channels to work harder to keep the inside of the cell negatively charged—this will keep the cell from firing. Excitatory inputs cause the ion channels to begin to allow sodium ions to flow in—this will allow the cell to fire. Because sodium ions have a positive charge, their influx can begin to change the relative balance of positive and negative charges across the cell membrane. An action potential begins when the excitatory inputs are sufficiently strong with respect to inhibitory inputs to *depolarize* the cell from −70 millivolts to −55 millivolts: Sufficient sodium has entered the cell to effect this change.

Once the action potential begins, sodium rushes into the neuron. As a result, the inside of the neuron becomes positive relative to the outside, meaning the neuron has become fully depolarized. A domino effect now propels the action potential down the axon. The leading edge of depolarization causes ion channels in the adjacent region of the axon to open and allow sodium to rush in. In this way—through successive depolarization—the signal passes down the axon (see Figure 3.7).

How does the neuron return to its original resting state of polarization after it fires? When the inside of the neuron becomes positive, the channels that allow sodium to flow in close and the channels that allow potassium to flow out open.

resting potential   The polarization of cellular fluid within a neuron, which provides the capability to produce an action potential.

ion channel   A portion of neurons' cell membranes that selectively permits certain ions to flow in and out.

The outflow of potassium ions restores the negative charge of the neuron. Thus, even while the signal is reaching the far end of the axon, the portions of the cell in which the action potential originated are being returned to their resting balance, so that they can be ready for their next stimulation.

Properties of the Action Potential The biochemical manner in which the action potential is transmitted leads to several important properties. The action potential obeys the **all-or-none law:** The size of the action potential is unaffected by increases in the intensity of stimulation beyond the threshold level. Once excitatory inputs sum to reach the threshold level, a uniform action potential is generated. If the threshold is not reached, no action potential occurs. An added consequence of the all-or-none law is that the size of the action potential does not diminish along the length of the axon. In this sense, the action potential is said to be *self-propagating;* once started, it needs no outside stimulation to keep itself moving. It's similar to a lit fuse on a firecracker.

Different neurons conduct action potentials along their axons at different speeds; the fastest have signals that move at the rate of 200 meters per second, the slowest plod along at 10 centimeters per second. The axons of the faster neurons are covered with a tightly wrapped myelin sheath—consisting, as we explained earlier, of glial cells—making this part of the neuron resemble short tubes on a string. The tiny breaks between the tubes are called *nodes of Ranvier* (see Figure 3.5). In neurons having myelinated axons, the action potential literally skips along from one node to the next—saving the time and energy required to open and close ion channels at every location on the axon. Damage to the myelin sheath throws off the delicate timing of the action potential and causes serious problems. Multiple sclerosis (MS) is a devastating disorder caused by deterioration of the myelin sheath. It is characterized by double vision, tremors, and eventually paralysis. In MS, specialized cells from the body's immune system actually attack myelinated neurons, exposing the axon and disrupting normal synaptic transmission (Joyce, 1990).

After an action potential has passed down a segment of the axon, that region of the neuron enters a **refractory period** (see **Figure 3.8**). During the *absolute refractory period,* further stimulation, no matter how intense, cannot cause another action potential to be generated; during the *relative refractory period,* the neuron will fire only in response to a stimulus stronger than what is ordinarily necessary. Have you ever tried to flush the toilet while it is filling back up with water? There must be a critical level of water for the toilet to flush again. Similarly, for a neuron to be able to generate another action potential, it must "reset" itself and await stimulation beyond its threshold. The refractory period ensures, in part, that the action potential will only travel

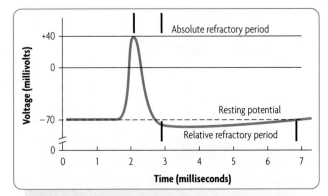

FIGURE 3.8 Timetable for Electrical Changes in the Neuron during an Action Potential
Sodium ions entering the neuron cause its electrical potential to change from slightly negative during its polarized, or resting, state to slightly positive during depolarization. Once the neuron is depolarized, it enters a brief refractory period during which further stimulation will not produce another action potential. Another action potential can occur only after the ionic balance between the inside and the outside of the cell is restored.

in one direction down the axon: It cannot move backward because "earlier" parts of the axon are in a refractory state.

SYNAPTIC TRANSMISSION

When the action potential completes its leapfrog journey down the axon to a terminal button, it must pass its information along to the next neuron. But no two neurons ever touch: They are joined at a **synapse,** with a small gap between the *presynaptic membrane* (the terminal button of the sending neuron) and the *postsynaptic membrane* (the surface of a dendrite or soma of a receiving neuron). When the action potential reaches the terminal button, it sets in motion a series of events called **synaptic transmission,** which is the relaying of information from one neuron to another across the synaptic gap (see **Figure 3.9**). Synaptic transmission begins when the arrival of the action potential at the terminal button causes small round packets, called *synaptic vesicles,* to move toward and affix themselves to the interior membrane of the terminal button. Inside each vesicle are **neurotransmitters,** biochemical substances that stimulate other neurons. The action potential also causes ion channels to open, allowing calcium ions into the terminal button. The influx of calcium ions causes the rupture of the synaptic vesicles and the release of whatever neurotransmitters they contain. Once the synaptic vesicles rupture, the neurotransmitters are dispersed rapidly across the *synaptic cleft,* the gap between the terminal button of one neuron and the cell membrane of the next. To complete synaptic transmission, the neurotransmitters attach to *receptor molecules* embedded in the postsynaptic membrane.

The neurotransmitters will bind to the receptor molecules under two conditions. First, no other neurotransmitters or other chemical substances can be attached to the receptor molecule. Second, the shape of the neurotransmitter must match the shape of the receptor molecule—as precisely as a key fits

---

all-or-none law The rule that the size of the action potential is unaffected by increases in the intensity of stimulation beyond the threshold level.

refractory period The period of rest during which a new nerve impulse cannot be activated in a segment of an axon.

synapse The gap between one neuron and another.

synaptic transmission The relaying information from one neuron to another across the synaptic gap.

neurotransmitter Chemical messenger released from a neuron that crosses the synapse from one neuron to another, stimulating the postsynaptic neuron.

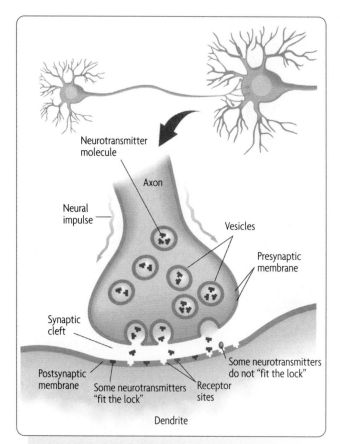

FIGURE 3.9　Synaptic Transmission

The action potential in the presynaptic neuron causes neurotransmitters to be released into the synaptic gap. Once across the gap, they stimulate receptor molecules embedded in the membrane of the postsynaptic neuron. Multiple neurotransmitters can exist within the same cell.

into a keyhole. If either condition is not met, the neurotransmitter will not attach to the receptor molecule. This means that it will not be able to stimulate the postsynaptic membrane. If the neurotransmitter does become attached to the receptor molecule, then it may provide "fire" or "don't fire" information to this next neuron. Once the neurotransmitter has completed its job, it detaches from the receptor molecule and drifts back into the synaptic gap. There it is either decomposed through the action of enzymes or reabsorbed into the presynaptic terminal button for quick reuse.

Depending on the receptor molecule, a neurotransmitter will have either an excitatory or an inhibitory effect. That is, the same neurotransmitter may be excitatory at one synapse but inhibitory at another. Each neuron integrates the information it obtains at synapses with between 1,000 and 10,000 other neurons to decide whether it ought to initiate another action potential. It is the integration of these thousands of inhibitory and excitatory inputs that allows all-or-none action potentials to provide the foundation for all human experience.

You may be wondering why we have taken you so deep into the nervous system. After all, this is a psychology course, and psychology is supposed to be about behavior and thinking and emotion. In fact, synapses are the biological medium in which all of these activities occur. If you change the normal activity of the synapse, you change how people behave, how they think, and how they feel. Understanding the functioning of the synapse has led to tremendous advances in the understanding of learning and memory, emotion, psychological disorders, drug addiction, and, in general, the chemical formula for mental health. You will use the knowledge you have acquired in this chapter throughout *Psychology and Life.*

NEUROTRANSMITTERS AND THEIR FUNCTIONS

Dozens of chemical substances are known or suspected to function as neurotransmitters in the brain. The neurotransmitters that have been studied most intensively meet a set of technical criteria. Each is manufactured in the presynaptic terminal button and is released when an action potential reaches that terminal. The neurotransmitter's presence in the synaptic cleft produces a biological response in the postsynaptic membrane; and, if its release is prevented, no subsequent responses can occur. To give you a sense of the effects different neurotransmitters have on the regulation of behavior, we will discuss a set that has been found to play an important role in the daily functioning of the brain. This brief discussion will also enable you to understand many of the ways in which neural transmission can go awry.

Acetylcholine　*Acetylcholine* is found in both the central and peripheral nervous systems. Memory loss among patients suffering from Alzheimer's disease, a degenerative disease that is increasingly common among older persons, is believed to be caused by the deterioration of neurons that secrete acetylcholine (Herholz et al., 2008). Acetylcholine is also excitatory at junctions between nerves and muscles, where it causes muscles to contract. A number of toxins affect the synaptic actions of acetylcholine. For example, botulinum toxin, often found in food that has been preserved incorrectly, poisons an individual by preventing release of acetylcholine in the respiratory system. This poisoning, known as *botulism,* can cause death by suffocation. Curare, a poison Amazon Indians use on the tips of their blowgun darts, paralyzes lung muscles by occupying critical acetylcholine receptors, preventing the normal activity of the transmitter.

GABA　*GABA* (gamma-aminobutyric acid) is the most common inhibitory neurotransmitter in the brain. GABA may be used as a messenger in as many as a third of all brain synapses. Neurons that are sensitive to GABA are particularly concentrated in brain regions such as the thalamus, hypothalamus, and occipital lobes (see pp. 72–76). GABA appears to play a critical role in some forms of psychopathology by inhibiting neural activity. When levels of this neurotransmitter in the brain become low, people may experience anxiety or depression (Kalueff & Nutt, 2007). Anxiety disorders are often treated with *benzodiazepine* drugs, such as *Valium* or *Xanax,* that increase GABA activity. The *benzodiazepine* drugs do not attach directly to GABA receptors. Instead they allow GABA itself to bind more effectively to postsynaptic receptor molecules.

Glutamate　Glutamate is the brain's most common excitatory neurotransmitter. Because glutamate helps transmit information within the brain, it plays a critical role in processes of emotional response, learning, and memory (Goddyn et al., 2008). Learning proceeds more slowly when glutamate receptors are not functioning properly. In addition, disruptions of brain levels of glutamate have been associated with various psychological disorders, including schizophrenia (Harrison et al., 2008). Glutamate also plays a role in addictions to drugs, alcohol, and nicotine. Researchers are beginning to explore the possibilities of treatments for these addictions that alter the brain's use of glutamate (Markou, 2007).

Dopamine, Norepinephrine, and Serotonin

The *catecholamines* are a class of chemical substances that include two important neurotransmitters, *dopamine* and *norepinephrine*. Both have been shown to play prominent roles in psychological disorders such as mood disturbances and schizophrenia (Sillitoe & Vogel, 2008; Southwick et al., 2005). Norepinephrine appears to be involved in some forms of depression: Drugs that increase brain levels of this neurotransmitter elevate mood and relieve depression. Conversely, higher-than-normal levels of dopamine have been found in persons with schizophrenia. As you might expect, one way to treat people with this disorder is to give them a drug that decreases brain levels of dopamine. In the early days of drug therapy, an interesting but unfortunate problem arose. High doses of the drug used to treat schizophrenia produced symptoms of Parkinson's disease, a progressive disorder involving disruption of motor functioning. (Parkinson's disease is caused by deterioration of neurons that manufacture most of the brain's dopamine.) This finding led to research that improved drug therapy for schizophrenia and to research that focused on drugs that could be used in the treatment of Parkinson's disease.

All the neurons that produce *serotonin* are located in the brain stem (see p. 72), which is involved in arousal and many autonomic processes. The hallucinogenic drug LSD (lysergic acid diethylamide) appears to produce its effects by suppressing the effects of serotonin neurons (Béïque et al., 2007). These serotonin neurons normally inhibit other neurons, but the lack of inhibition produced by LSD creates vivid and bizarre sensory experiences, some of which last for hours. As we'll see in Chapter 14, abnormal levels of serotonin in the brain are associated with mood disorders. For example, reduced levels of serotonin may lead to depression. That's why many antidepressant drugs, such as *Prozac*, enhance the action of serotonin by preventing it from being removed from the synaptic cleft.

Endorphins

The *endorphins* are a group of chemicals that are usually classified as neuromodulators. A **neuromodulator** is any substance that modifies or modulates the activities of the

Roughly 1.5 million people in the United States, including the actor Michael J. Fox, are impaired by Parkinson's disease. Research on the neurotransmitter dopamine has led to advances in understanding this disease. How does basic research in neuroscience allow for improved treatments?

postsynaptic neuron. Endorphins (short for *endogenous morphines*) play an important role in the control of emotional behaviors (anxiety, fear, tension, pleasure) and pain—drugs like opium and morphine bind to the same receptor sites in the brain. Endorphins have been called the "keys to paradise" because of their pleasure–pain controlling properties. Researchers have examined the possibility that endorphins are at least partially responsible for the pain-reducing effects of acupuncture and placebos (Benedetti et al., 2005; Han, 2004). Such tests rely on the drug *naloxone*, whose only known effect is to block morphine and endorphins from binding to receptors. Any procedure that reduces pain by stimulating release of endorphins becomes ineffective when naloxone is administered. With the injection of naloxone, acupuncture and placebos do, in fact, lose their power—suggesting that, ordinarily, endorphins help them do their work.

STOP AND REVIEW

❶ What is the pattern of information flow through the major parts of each neuron?

❷ What is meant by the "all-or-none law"?

❸ How do neurotransmitters pass from one neuron to the next?

❹ What chemical substance is the most common inhibitory neurotransmitter in the brain?

Visit MyPsychLab.com for more review and practice on the following topics:

◀◉ **Explore:** Structure of Neuron

◀◉ **Explore:** The Action Potential

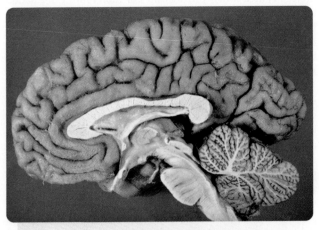

Why might researchers study the brain to understand human psychology?

---

neuromodulator Any substance that modifies or modulates the activities of the postsynaptic neuron.

WHAT DOES "IT'S GENETIC" MEAN?

The Human Genome Project has put the study of genetics very much in the public eye. The media routinely report on the progress researchers have made in understanding genetic contributions to important aspects of human experience such as obesity, sexuality, and mental illness. We want to give you a framework that should help you evaluate those media reports. We are going to focus our discussion on the behavioral trait of *impulsivity*. Researchers have been interested in this dimension because high levels of impulsivity put people at risk for problems such as drug and alcohol addiction (Sher et al., 2000).

Suppose you see a newspaper headline that reads, "Scientists Find Impulsivity Gene." What information should the newspaper article provide? First, it's important to understand exactly what "impulsivity" means in the context of the article. Take a moment to consider how you might define or apply the term: You probably know some people whom you would label as impulsive and others for whom you wouldn't use this label. But what exactly does that mean? Are your acquaintances impulsive because they never plan ahead? Because they can't stop themselves from acting out? Because they take too many risks? If you see the claim "Scientists Find Impulsivity Gene," you need to understand

exactly how the researchers are using the term. This level of specificity is important because it's quite possible that the different behaviors associated with the one concept "impulsivity" could have different genetic bases (Congdon & Canli, 2006). If the newspaper article doesn't offer a careful description of what is meant by "impulsivity," you should be careful about accepting its conclusions.

The next information you need to find is an explanation for why the researchers believe the gene they have identified plays a causal role in producing impulsive behavior. Sometimes, this information will be given as a statement of fact: "People who have variation *A* of this gene are impulsive; those who have variation *B* are not." However, in contemporary research, scientists most often want to provide some sense of the mechanism that allows the gene to influence behavior. What you'll often learn from those accounts is that the gene in question only indirectly has an influence on a trait.

For example, analyses of impulsive behavior have recently focused on the neurotransmitter dopamine. Dopamine functions in regions of the brain that are critical to tasks such as planning—it is the neurotransmitter that helps achieve cognitive stability and flexibility (Bilder et al., 2004). From this characterization, you can see why disruptions in the function of

dopamine could lead people to engage in behaviors that are impulsive or unstable. The implication here is that if you want to find a genetic basis for impulsivity, what you might really seek is a genetic basis for differences in individual brain's uses of dopamine. In fact, researchers have begun to document variations in more than one gene—genes with names such as *DRD4* and *COMT*—that affect the use of dopamine (Congdon & Canli, 2006).

You can start to see how all the pieces fit together. Researchers start with a trait or behavior such as impulsivity that shows variability among individuals. Over time, they begin to have an understanding of what processes in the brain might produce that variability. Then, they can look for genetic variations that might explain why brains perform differently. Thus, although the headline would read "Scientists Find Impulsivity Gene," the real news might be that scientists have discovered how a particular gene—perhaps one of many—has an impact on the brain's use of dopamine. That's a less tidy headline, but it would go closer to the heart of the discovery.

- With respect to genetic research, why is it important to give precise definitions of traits or behaviors?
- Why might the genes that influence impulsivity also have an impact on other behavioral traits?

Biology and Behavior

You now have an understanding of the basic mechanisms that allow nerve cells to communicate. The time has come to assemble those neurons into the larger systems that guide your body and mind. We begin this discussion with an overview of the techniques researchers use to hasten new discoveries. We then offer a general description of the structure of the nervous system, followed by a more detailed look at the brain itself. We discuss the activity of the endocrine system, a second biological control

system that works in cooperation with your nervous system and brain. Finally, we describe ways in which your life experiences continue to modify your brain.

EAVESDROPPING ON THE BRAIN

Neuroscientists seek to understand how the brain works at a number of different levels—from the operation of large structures visible to the naked eye to the properties of individual nerve cells visible only under powerful microscopes.

The techniques researchers use are suited to their level of analysis. Here, we discuss the techniques that have been used most often to attribute functions and behaviors to particular regions of the brain.

Interventions in the Brain Several research methods in neuroscience involve direct intervention with structures in the brain. These methods find their historical roots in circumstances like the story of railroad foreman Phineas Gage, who in September 1848 suffered an accident in which a 3-foot, 7-inch-long pole was blown, as the result of an unexpected explosion, clear through his head. Gage's physical impairment was remarkably slight: He lost vision in his left eye, and the left side of his face was partially paralyzed, but his posture, movement, and speech were all unimpaired. Yet, psychologically, he was a changed man, as his doctor's account made clear:

> The equilibrium or balance, so to speak, between his intellectual faculties and animal propensities seems to have been destroyed. He is fitful, irreverent, indulging at times in the grossest profanity (which was not previously his custom), manifesting but little deference for his fellows, impatient of restraint or advice when it conflicts with his desires. . . . Previous to his injury, though untrained in schools, he possessed a well-balanced mind, and was looked upon by those who knew him as a shrewd, smart businessman, very energetic and persistent in executing all his plans of operation. In this regard his mind was radically changed, so decidedly that his friends and acquaintances said he was "no longer Gage."
> (Harlow, 1868, pp. 339–340)

Gage's injury came at a time when scientists were just beginning to form hypotheses about the links between brain functions and complex behavior. The behavioral changes following the dramatic piercing of his brain prompted his doctor to hypothesize brain bases for aspects of personality and rational behavior.

At about the same time that Gage was convalescing from his injury, **Paul Broca** was studying the brain's role in language. His first research in this area involved an autopsy of a man whose name was derived from the only word he

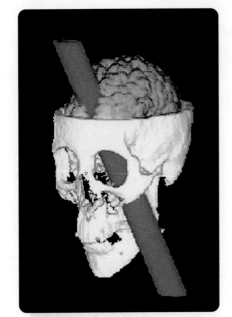

Phineas Gage's skull is preserved in the collections of the Warren Anatomical Museum, Harvard University Medical School. Why were doctors so fascinated by Gage's changes in personality?

had been able to speak, "Tan." Broca found that the left front portion of Tan's brain had been severely damaged. This finding led Broca to study the brains of other persons who suffered from language impairments. In each case, Broca's work revealed similar damage to the same area of the brain, a region now known as **Broca's area.** As you will see as *Psychology and Life* unfolds, contemporary researchers still attempt to correlate patterns of behavior change or impairment with the sites of brain damage.

The problem with studying accidentally damaged brains, of course, is that researchers have no control over the location and extent of the damage. To produce a well-founded understanding of the brain and its relationship to behavioral and cognitive functioning, scientists need methods that allow them to specify precisely the brain tissue that has been incapacitated. Researchers have developed a variety of techniques to produce **lesions,** highly localized brain injuries. They may, for example, surgically remove specific brain areas, cut the neural connections to those areas, or destroy those areas through application of intense heat, cold, or electricity. As you would guess, experimental work with permanent lesions is carried out exclusively with nonhuman animals. (Recall our discussion in Chapter 2 that the ethics of this type of animal research has now come under heightened scrutiny.) Our conception of the brain has been radically changed as researchers have repeatedly compared and coordinated the results of lesioning experiments on animals with the growing body of clinical findings on the effects of brain damage on human behavior. In recent years, scientists have developed a procedure called **repetitive transcranial magnetic stimulation (rTMS),** that uses pulses of magnetic stimulation to create temporary, reversible "lesions" in human participants—without any damage being done to tissue, brain regions can be briefly inactivated. This new technique enables researchers to address a range of questions that would not have been possible with nonhuman experiments. Consider an application of rTMS to study how your brain responds to nouns and verbs.

If you've spent any time studying languages, you're likely aware that nouns and verbs serve very different functions. A team of researchers used rTMS to test the hypothesis that different brain regions are at work when you produce the two parts of speech (Cappelletti et al., 2008). In the experiment, participants completed simple phrases presented by computer. For example, participants would read, "today I walk," and then complete, "yesterday I . . ." Similarly, they would read "one child," and then complete "many. . . ." Under ordinary circumstances, participants should be relatively quick to respond "walked" and "children." Suppose, however, that the researchers are able to

---

Broca's area The region of the brain that translates thoughts into speech or signs.

lesion Injury to or destruction of brain tissue.

repetitive transcranial magnetic stimulation (rTMS) A technique for producing temporary inactivation of brain areas using repeated pulses of magnetic stimulation.

use rTMS to "lesion" brain regions that help make these responses possible. Then, we'd expect participants' responses to be slowed down. In fact, the researchers identified one brain region (in the vicinity of Broca's area) that, when stimulated by rTMS, yielded slower performance for verbs but not for nouns. These data support the hypothesis that your brain processes make distinctions between nouns and verbs.

You can see why this experiment would not be possible with nonhuman participants: Humans are the only species that habitually produces nouns and verbs.

On other occasions, neuroscientists learn about the function of brain regions by directly *stimulating* them. For example, in the mid-1950s, **Walter Hess** (1881–1973) pioneered the use of electrical stimulation to probe structures deep in the brain. For example, Hess put electrodes into the brains of freely moving cats. By pressing a button, he could then send a small electrical current to the point of the electrode. Hess carefully recorded the behavioral consequences of stimulating each of 4,500 brain sites in nearly 500 cats. Hess discovered that, depending on the location of the electrode, sleep, sexual arousal, anxiety, or terror could be provoked by the flick of the switch—and turned off just as abruptly. For example, electrical stimulation of certain regions of the brain led the otherwise gentle cats to bristle with rage and hurl themselves on a nearby object.

Recording and Imaging Brain Activity

Other neuroscientists map brain function by using electrodes to record the electrical activity of the brain in response to environmental stimulation. The brain's electrical output can be monitored at different levels of precision. At the most specific, researchers can insert ultrasensitive microelectrodes into the brain to record the electrical activity of a single brain cell. Such recordings can illuminate changes in the activity of individual cells in response to stimuli in the environment.

For human subjects, researchers often place a number of electrodes on the surface of the scalp to record larger, integrated patterns of electrical activity. These electrodes provide the data for an **electroencephalogram (EEG),** or an amplified tracing of the brain activity. EEGs can be used to study the relationship between psychological activities and brain response. For example, in one experiment, researchers used EEGs to demonstrate that people's brains respond differently when they view emotionally charged images (Hajcak & Olvet, 2008). While their brain activity was being recorded, participants viewed a series of pleasant (e.g., smiling faces), neutral (e.g., household objects), and unpleasant (e.g., violent images) pictures on a computer screen. The EEGs revealed distinct patterns for the neutral versus emotional pictures: Participants appeared to devote more attention to the pleasant and unpleasant pictures, and that greater attention lingered even after the pictures left the computer screen.

Some of the most exciting technological innovations for studying the brain are machines originally developed to help neurosurgeons detect brain abnormalities, such as damage caused by strokes or diseases. These devices produce images of the living brain without invasive procedures that risk damaging brain tissue.

To obtain three-dimensional images of the brain, researchers may use **computerized axial tomography (CT or CAT).** When people undergo a CT scan, their head is placed in

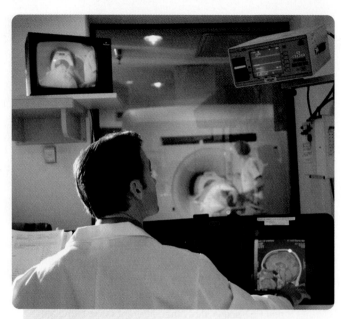

How have new imaging techniques expanded the range of questions researchers can ask?

a doughnut-shaped ring that contains an X-ray source and an X-ray detector. During the scan, focused X-ray beams pass through the individual's head from several different angles. The computer assembles those separate X-ray images into coherent pictures of the brain. Researchers often use CT scans to determine the location and extent of brain damage or brain abnormalities.

In research with **positron emission tomography,** or **PET,** subjects are given different kinds of radioactive (but safe) substances that eventually travel to the brain, where they are taken up by active brain cells. Recording instruments outside the skull can detect the radioactivity emitted by cells that are active during different cognitive or behavioral activities. This information is then fed into a computer that constructs a dynamic portrait of the brain, showing where different types of psychological activities are actually occurring (see **Figure 3.10**).

Magnetic resonance imaging, or **MRI,** uses magnetic fields and radio waves to generate pulses of energy within the brain. As the pulse is tuned to different frequencies, some atoms line up with the magnetic field. When the magnetic pulse is turned off, the atoms vibrate (resonate) as they return to their original positions. Special radio receivers detect this resonance

---

electroencephalogram (EEG) A recording of the electrical activity of the brain.

computerized axial tomography (CT or CAT) A technique that uses narrow beams of X-rays passed through the brain at several angles to assemble complete brain images.

positron emission tomography (PET) scan Brain image produced by a device that obtains detailed pictures of activity in the living brain by recording the radioactivity emitted by cells during different cognitive or behavioral activities.

magnetic resonance imaging (MRI) A technique for brain imaging that scans the brain using magnetic fields and radio waves.

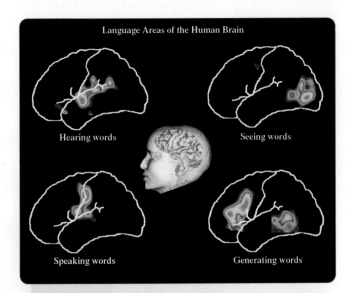

FIGURE 3.10 PET Scans of the Brain at Work
These PET scans show that different tasks stimulate neural activity in distinct regions of the brain.

and channel information to a computer, which generates images of the locations of different atoms in areas of the brain. By looking at the image, researchers can link brain structures to psychological processes.

MRI is most useful for providing clear images of anatomical details; PET scans provide better information about function. A newer technique called **functional MRI,** or **fMRI,** combines some of the benefits of both techniques by detecting magnetic changes in the flow of blood to cells in the brain; fMRI allows more precise claims about both structure and function. Researchers have begun to use fMRI to discover the distributions of brain regions responsible for many of your most important cognitive abilities, such as attention, perception, language processing, and memory (Spiers & Maguire, 2007).

More than 300 years have passed since Descartes sat in his candlelit study and mused about the brain; over 100 years have passed since Broca discovered that brain regions seem to be linked to specific functions. In the time since these developments, cultural evolution has provided neuroscientists with the technology necessary to reveal some of your brain's most important secrets. The remainder of this chapter describes some of those secrets.

THE NERVOUS SYSTEM

The nervous system is composed of billions of highly specialized nerve cells, or *neurons,* that constitute the brain and the

---

functional MRI (fMRI) A brain-imaging technique that combines benefits of both MRI and PET scans by detecting magnetic changes in the flow of blood to cells in the brain.

central nervous system (CNS) The part of the nervous system consisting of the brain and spinal cord.

peripheral nervous system (PNS) The part of the nervous system composed of the spinal and cranial nerves that connect the body's sensory receptors to the CNS and the CNS to the muscles and glands.

nerve fibers found throughout the body. The nervous system is subdivided into two major divisions: the **central nervous system (CNS)** and the **peripheral nervous system (PNS).** The CNS is composed of all the neurons in the brain and spinal cord; the PNS is made up of all the neurons forming the nerve fibers that connect the CNS to the body. **Figures 3.11** and **3.12,** on page 72, show the relationship of the CNS to the PNS.

The job of the CNS is to integrate and coordinate all bodily functions, process all incoming neural messages, and send out commands to different parts of the body. The CNS sends and receives neural messages through the *spinal cord,* a trunk line of neurons that connects the brain to the PNS. The trunk line itself is housed in a hollow portion of the vertebral column called the spinal column. Spinal nerves branch out from the spinal cord between each pair of vertebrae in the spinal column, eventually connecting with sensory receptors throughout the body and with muscles and glands. The spinal cord coordinates the activity of the left and right sides of the body and is responsible for simple fast-action reflexes that do not involve the brain. For example, an organism whose spinal cord has been severed from its brain can still withdraw its limb from a painful stimulus. Although an intact brain would normally be notified of such action, the organism can complete the action without directions from above. Damage to the nerves of the spinal cord can result in paralysis of the legs or trunk, as seen in paraplegic individuals. The extent of paralysis depends on how high up on the spinal cord the damage occurred; higher damage produces greater paralysis.

Despite its commanding position, the CNS is isolated from any direct contact with the outside world. It is the role of the PNS to provide the CNS with information from sensory receptors, such as those found in the eyes and ears, and to relay commands from the brain to the body's organs and muscles. The PNS is actually composed of two sets of nerve fibers (see

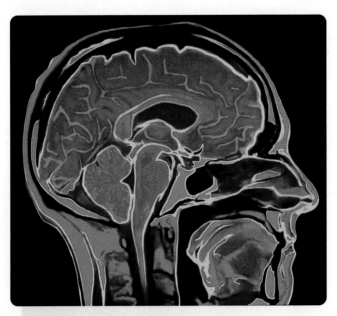

Magnetic resonance imaging (MRI) produces this color-enhanced profile of a normal brain. What is the purpose of trying to identify brain regions that underlie particular functions?

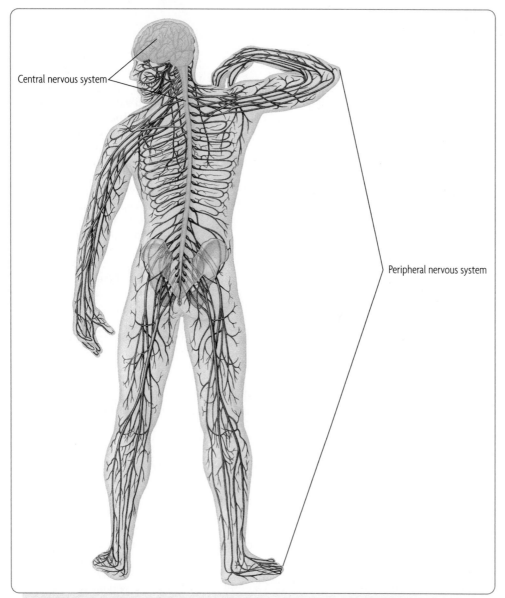

Central nervous system

Peripheral nervous system

FIGURE 3.11 Divisions of the Central and Peripheral Nervous Systems

The sensory and motor nerve fibers that constitute the peripheral nervous system are linked to the brain by the spinal cord.

From Richard D. McAnulty and M. Michele Burnette. *Fundamentals of Human Sexuality*, p. 87. Published by Allyn and Bacon, Boston, MA. Copyright © 2003 by the author. Reproduced by permission of Pearson Education. Inc.

Figure 3.12). The **somatic nervous system** regulates the actions of the body's skeletal muscles. For example, imagine you are typing an e-mail. The movement of your fingers over the keyboard is managed by your somatic nervous system. As you decide what to say, your brain sends commands to your fingers to press certain keys. Simultaneously, the fingers send feedback about their position and movement to the brain. If you strike the wrong key (th**w**), the somatic nervous system informs the brain, which then issues the necessary correction, and, in a fraction of a second, you delete the mistake and hit the right key (th**e**).

The other branch of the PNS is the **autonomic nervous system (ANS),** which sustains basic life processes. This system is on the job 24 hours a day, regulating bodily functions that you usually don't consciously control, such as respiration, digestion, and arousal. The ANS must work even when you are asleep, and it sustains life processes during anesthesia and prolonged coma states.

---

somatic nervous system The subdivision of the peripheral nervous system that connects the central nervous system to the skeletal muscles and skin.

autonomic nervous system (ANS) The subdivision of the peripheral nervous system that controls the body's involuntary motor responses by connecting the sensory receptors to the central nervous system (CNS) and the CNS to the smooth muscle, cardiac muscle, and glands.

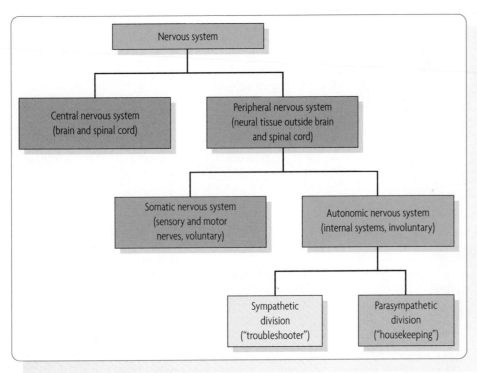

FIGURE 3.12 Hierarchical Organization of the Human Nervous System

The central nervous system is composed of the brain and the spinal cord. The peripheral nervous system is divided according to function: The somatic nervous system controls voluntary actions, and the autonomic nervous system regulates internal processes. The autonomic nervous system is subdivided into two systems: The sympathetic nervous system governs behavior in emergency situations, and the parasympathetic nervous system regulates behavior and internal processes in routine circumstances.

The autonomic nervous system deals with survival matters of two kinds: those involving threats to the organism and those involving bodily maintenance. To carry out these functions, the autonomic nervous system is further subdivided into the sympathetic and parasympathetic nervous systems (see Figure 3.12). These divisions work in opposition to accomplish their tasks. The **sympathetic division** governs responses to emergency situations; the **parasympathetic division** monitors the routine operation of the body's internal functions. The sympathetic division can be regarded as a troubleshooter. In an emergency or stressful situation, it arouses the brain structures that prepare the organism either to fight the threat or flee from it—a pattern of activity called the *fight-or-flight response*. Digestion stops, blood flows away from internal organs to the muscles, oxygen transfer increases, and heart rate increases. After the danger is over, the parasympathetic division takes charge, and the individual begins to calm down. Digestion resumes, heartbeat slows, and breathing is relaxed. The parasympathetic division carries out the body's nonemergency housekeeping chores, such as elimination of bodily wastes, protection of the visual system (through tears and pupil constriction), and long-term conservation of body energy.

The separate duties of the sympathetic and parasympathetic nervous systems are illustrated in **Figure 3.13.**

BRAIN STRUCTURES AND THEIR FUNCTIONS

The brain is the most important component of your central nervous system. The brains of human beings have three interconnected layers. In the deepest recesses of the brain, in a region called the *brain stem,* are structures involved primarily with autonomic processes such as heart rate, breathing, swallowing, and digestion. Enveloping this central core is the *limbic system,* which is involved with motivation, emotion, and memory processes. Wrapped around these two regions is the *cerebrum.* The universe of the human mind exists in this region. The cerebrum, and its surface layer, the *cerebral cortex,* integrates sensory information, coordinates your movements, and facilitates abstract thinking and reasoning (see **Figure 3.14**). Let's look more closely at the functions of the three major brain regions, beginning with the brain stem, thalamus, and cerebellum.

The Brain Stem, Thalamus, and Cerebellum The **brain stem** is found in all vertebrate species. It contains structures that collectively regulate the internal state of the body (see **Figure 3.15** on page 75). The **medulla,** located at the very top of the spinal cord, is the center for breathing, blood pressure, and the beating of the heart. Because these processes are essential for life, damage to the medulla can be fatal. Nerve fibers ascending from the body and descending from the brain cross over at the medulla, which means that the left side of the body is linked to the right side of the brain and the right side of the body is connected to the left side of the brain.

Directly above the medulla is the **pons,** which provides inputs to other structures in the brain stem and to the cerebellum (*pons* is the Latin word for *bridge*). The **reticular formation** is a dense network of nerve cells that serves as the brain's

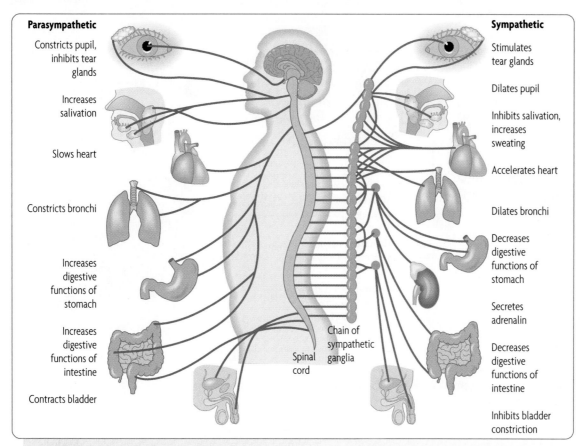

FIGURE 3.13 The Autonomic Nervous System

The parasympathetic nervous system, which regulates day-to-day internal processes and behavior, is shown on the left. The sympathetic nervous system, which regulates internal processes and behavior in stressful situations, is shown on the right. Note that on their way to and from the spinal cord, the nerve fibers of the sympathetic nervous system innervate, or make connections with, ganglia, which are specialized clusters of neuron chains.

sentinel. It arouses the cerebral cortex to attend to new stimulation and keeps the brain alert even during sleep. Massive damage to this area often results in a coma.

The reticular formation has long tracts of fibers that run to the **thalamus,** which channels incoming sensory information to the appropriate area of the cerebral cortex, where that information is processed. For example, the thalamus relays information from the eyes to cortical areas for vision.

Neuroscientists have long known that the **cerebellum,** attached to the brain stem at the base of the skull, coordinates bodily movements, controls posture, and maintains equilibrium. Damage to the cerebellum interrupts the flow of otherwise smooth movement, causing it to appear uncoordinated and jerky. More recent research suggests that the cerebellum also plays an important role in the ability to learn and perform sequences of body movements (Hazeltine & Ivry, 2002; Seidler et al., 2002).

The Limbic System The **limbic system** mediates motivated behaviors, emotional states, and memory processes. It also regulates body temperature, blood pressure, and blood-sugar level and performs other housekeeping activities. The limbic system comprises three structures: the hippocampus, amygdala, and hypothalamus (see **Figure 3.16**).

The **hippocampus,** which is the largest of the limbic system structures, plays an important role in the acquisition of memories. Considerable clinical evidence supports this conclusion, including the notable studies of a patient, H.M., perhaps psychology's most famous subject.

When he was 27, H.M. underwent surgery in an attempt to reduce the frequency and severity of his epileptic seizures. During the operation, parts of his hippocampus were removed. As a result, H.M. could recall only the very distant past; his ability to put new information into long-term memory was gone. Long after his surgery, he

---

thalamus The brain structure that relays sensory impulses to the cerebral cortex.

cerebellum The region of the brain attached to the brain stem that controls motor coordination, posture, and balance as well as the ability to learn control of body movements.

limbic system The region of the brain that regulates emotional behavior, basic motivational urges, and memory, as well as major physiological functions.

hippocampus The part of the limbic system that is involved in the acquisition of explicit memory.

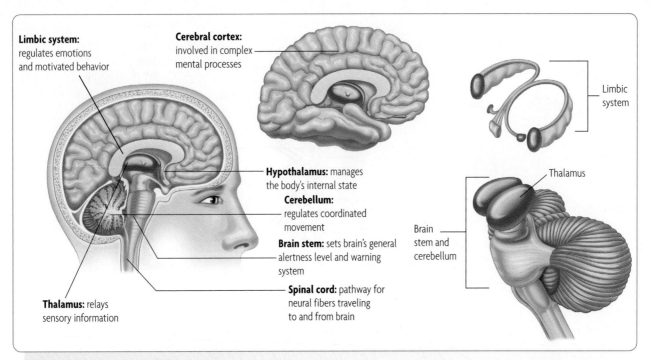

FIGURE 3.14 Brain Structures
The brain contains several major components, including the brain stem, cerebellum, limbic system, and cerebral cortex, all of which fit together in an intricate design.

continued to believe he was living in 1953, which was the year the operation was performed.

H.M. served as a gracious participant for 50 years of research. When he passed away in 2008, he left a remarkable legacy of critical information about brain function. For example, although H.M. always lived in 1953, he was able to form some types of new memories after damage to his hippocampus. For example, he was able to acquire new skills. This pattern suggests that if you were in an accident and sustained damage to your hippocampus, you would still be able to learn some new tasks, but you would not be able to remember having done so! As researchers have continued to focus attention on the hippocampus, they have come to a more detailed understanding of how even different regions of the structure play roles in the acquisition of different types of memories (Zeineh et al., 2003). In Chapter 7, we will return to the functions of the hippocampus for memory acquisition.

The **amygdala** plays a role in emotional control. Because of this control function, damage to areas of the amygdala may have

a calming effect on otherwise mean-spirited individuals. (We discuss *psychosurgery* in Chapter 15.) However, damage to some areas of the amygdala also impairs the ability to recognize when facial expressions communicate negative emotions such as sadness and fear (Adolphs & Tranel, 2004). The amygdala also plays a critical role in the formation and retrieval of memories with emotional content (LaBar, 2007). When people retrieve autobiographical information, activity in the amygdala predicts the emotional intensity of the memories (Daselaar et al., 2008).

The **hypothalamus** is one of the smallest structures in the brain, yet it plays a vital role in many of your most important daily actions. It is actually composed of several nuclei, small bundles of neurons that regulate physiological processes involved in motivated behavior (including eating, drinking, temperature regulation, and sexual arousal). The hypothalamus maintains the body's internal equilibrium, or **homeostasis.** When the body's energy reserves are low, the hypothalamus is involved in stimulating the organism to find food and to eat. When body temperature drops, the hypothalamus causes blood vessel constriction, or minute involuntary movements you commonly refer to as "shivering." The hypothalamus also regulates the activities of the endocrine system.

The Cerebrum In humans, the **cerebrum** dwarfs the rest of the brain, occupying two thirds of its total mass. Its role is to regulate the brain's higher cognitive and emotional functions. The outer surface of the cerebrum, made up of billions of cells in a layer about a tenth of an inch thick, is called the **cerebral cortex.** The cerebrum is also divided into two almost symmetrical halves, the **cerebral hemispheres** (we discuss the two hemispheres at length in a later section of this chapter). The two hemispheres are connected by a thick mass of nerve fibers, collectively referred to as the **corpus callosum.** This pathway sends messages back and forth between the hemispheres.

---

amygdala The part of the limbic system that controls emotion, aggression, and the formation of emotional memory.

hypothalamus The brain structure that regulates motivated behavior (such as eating and drinking) and homeostasis.

homeostasis Constancy or equilibrium of the internal conditions of the body.

cerebrum The region of the brain that regulates higher cognitive and emotional functions.

cerebral cortex The outer surface of the cerebrum.

cerebral hemispheres The two halves of the cerebrum, connected by the corpus callosum.

corpus callosum The mass of nerve fibers connecting the two hemispheres of the cerebrum.

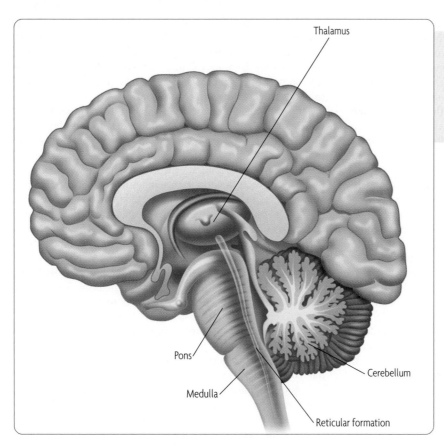

Thalamus

Pons

Medulla

Cerebellum

Reticular formation

FIGURE 3.15 The Brain Stem, Thalamus, and Cerebellum

These structures are primarily involved in basic life processes: breathing, pulse, arousal, movement, balance, and simple processing of sensory information.

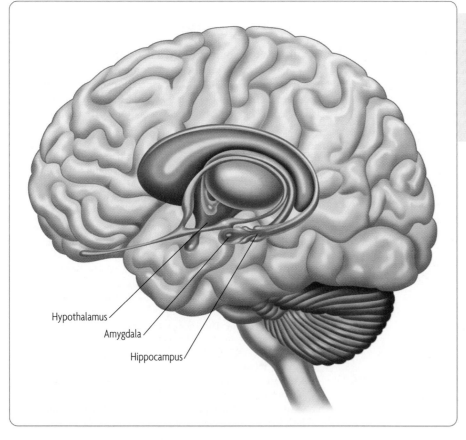

Hypothalamus

Amygdala

Hippocampus

FIGURE 3.16 The Limbic System

The structures of the limbic system, which are present only in mammals, are involved in motivated behavior, emotional states, and memory processes.

Neuroscientists have mapped the brain to define four areas, or lobes, for each hemisphere (see **Figure 3.17**). The **frontal lobe,** involved in motor control and cognitive activities, such as planning, making decisions, and setting goals, is located above the lateral fissure and in front of the central sulcus. Accidents that damage the frontal lobes can have devastating effects on human action and personality. This was the location of the injury that brought about such a dramatic change in Phineas Gage (Damasio et al., 1994). The frontal lobe also includes *Broca's area,* the region of the brain that Paul Broca identified from his research on patients with language disorders.

The **parietal lobe,** responsible for sensations of touch, pain, and temperature, is located directly behind the central sulcus. The **occipital lobe,** the final destination for visual information, is located at the back of the head. The **temporal lobe,** responsible for the processes of hearing, is found below the lateral fissure, on the sides of each cerebral hemisphere. The temporal lobe includes a region called **Wernicke's area.** In 1874, **Carl Wernicke** (1848–1905) discovered that patients who had damage to this region produced speech that was fluent but meaningless and had disrupted language comprehension.

It would be misleading to say that any lobe alone controls any one specific function. The structures of the brain perform their duties in concert, working smoothly as an integrated unit, similar to a symphony orchestra. Whether you are doing the dishes, solving a calculus problem, or carrying on a conversation with a friend, your brain works as a unified whole, each lobe interacting and cooperating with the others. Nevertheless, neuroscientists can identify areas of the four lobes of the cerebrum that are necessary for specific functions, such as vision, hearing, language, and memory. When they are damaged, their functions are disrupted or lost entirely.

The actions of the body's voluntary muscles, of which there are more than 600, are controlled by the **motor cortex,** located just in front of the central sulcus in the frontal lobes. Recall that commands from one side of the brain are directed to muscles on the opposite side of the body. Also, muscles in the lower part of the body—for example, the toes—are controlled by neurons in the top part of the motor cortex. Muscles in the upper part of the body, such as the throat, are controlled by neurons in the lower part of the motor cortex. As you can see in **Figure 3.18,** the upper parts of the body receive far more detailed motor instructions than the lower parts. In fact, the two largest areas of the motor cortex are devoted to the fingers—especially the thumb—and to the muscles involved in speech. Their greater brain area reflects the importance in human activity of manipulating objects, using tools, eating, and talking.

The **somatosensory cortex** is located just behind the central sulcus in the left and right parietal lobes. This part of the cortex processes information about temperature, touch, body position, and pain. Similar to the motor cortex, the upper part of the sensory cortex relates to the lower parts of the body, and the lower part to the upper parts of the body. Most of the area of the sensory cortex is devoted to the lips, tongue, thumb, and index fingers—the parts of the body that provide the most important sensory input (see Figure 3.18). And like the motor cortex, the right half of the somatosensory cortex communicates with the left side of the body, and the left half communicates with the right side of the body.

Auditory information is processed in the **auditory cortex,** which is in the two temporal lobes. The auditory cortex in each hemisphere receives information from *both* ears. One area of the auditory cortex is involved in the production of language, and a different area is involved in language comprehension. Visual input is processed at the back of the brain in the **visual cortex,** located in the occipital lobes. Here the greatest area is devoted to input from the center part of the retina, at the back of the eye, the area that transmits the most detailed visual information.

Not all of the cerebral cortex is devoted to processing sensory information and commanding the muscles to action. In fact, the majority of it is involved in *interpreting* and *integrating* information. Processes such as planning and decision making are believed to occur in the **association cortex.** Association areas are distributed to several areas of the cortex—one region is labeled in Figure 3.18. The association cortex allows you to

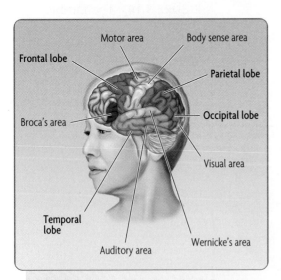

FIGURE 3.17   The Cerebral Cortex

Each of the two hemispheres of the cerebral cortex has four lobes. Different sensory and motor functions are associated with specific parts of each lobe

From Lilienfeld et al, *Psychology: From Inquiry to Understanding,* © 2009. Reproduced by permission of Pearson Education, Inc.

frontal lobe Region of the brain located above the lateral fissure and in front of the central sulcus; involved in motor control and cognitive activities.

parietal lobe Region of the brain behind the frontal lobe and above the lateral fissure; contains somatosensory cortex.

occipital lobe Rearmost region of the brain; contains primary visual cortex.

temporal lobe Region of the brain found below the lateral fissure; contains auditory cortex.

Wernicke's area A region of the brain that allows fluent speech production and comprehension.

motor cortex The region of the cerebral cortex that controls the action of the body's voluntary muscles.

somatosensory cortex The region of the parietal lobes that processes sensory input from various body areas.

auditory cortex The area of the temporal lobes that receives and processes auditory information.

visual cortex The region of the occipital lobes in which visual information is processed.

association cortex The parts of the cerebral cortex in which many high-level brain processes occur.

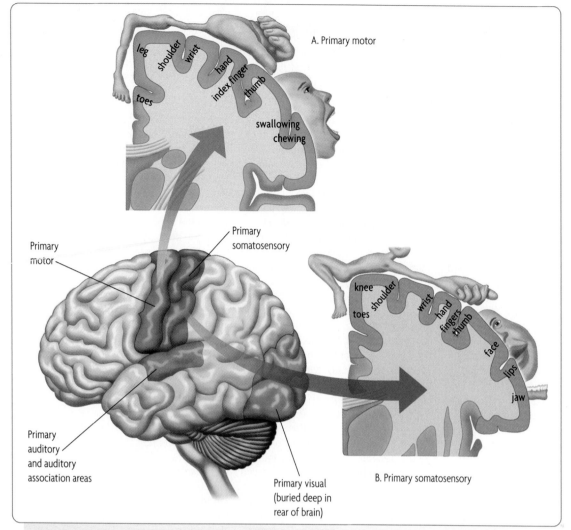

FIGURE 3.18 Motor and Somatosensory Cortex

Different parts of the body are more or less sensitive to environmental stimulation and brain control. Sensitivity in a particular region of the body is related to the amount of space in the cerebral cortex devoted to that region. In this figure, the body is drawn so that the size of body parts is relative to the cortical space devoted to them. The larger the body part in the drawing, the greater its sensitivity to environmental stimulation and the greater the brain's control over its movement.

combine information from various sensory modalities to plan appropriate responses to stimuli in the environment.

We have now reviewed the many important structures in your nervous system. When we began to talk about the cerebrum, we noted that each cerebral structure is represented in both hemispheres of your brain. However, the structures in those two hemispheres play somewhat different functions with respect to many types of behaviors. We turn now to those differences between your brain's two hemispheres.

HEMISPHERIC LATERALIZATION

What types of information originally led researchers to suspect that the functions of the brain's two hemispheres differed? Recall that when Paul Broca carried out his autopsy on Tan, he discovered damage in the left hemisphere. As he followed up this origi-

nal discovery, Broca found that other patients who showed similar disruption of their language abilities—a pattern now known as *Broca's aphasia*—also had damage on the *left* side of their brains. Damage to the same areas on the *right* side of the brain did not have the same effect. What should one conclude?

The chance to investigate hemispheric differences first arose in the context of a treatment for severe epilepsy in which surgeons sever the corpus callosum—the bundle of about 200 million nerve fibers that transfers information back and forth between the two hemispheres (see **Figure 3.19** on page 79). The goal of this surgery is to prevent the violent electrical activity that accompanies epileptic seizures from crossing between the hemispheres. The operation is usually successful, and a patient's subsequent behavior in most circumstances appears normal. Patients who undergo this type of surgery are often referred to as *split-brain* patients.

Psychology in Your Life

HOW DOES YOUR BRAIN DETERMINE TRUST?

Suppose a friend makes you a promise. You worry that the promise is empty, but your friend says, "Trust me!" Should you? In recent years, researchers have begun to understand how your brain responds when you have to make decisions about trust. Much of that research has focused on a hormone called *oxytocin*.

Oxytocin first became the focus of researchers who were interested in the biological mechanisms that prompt nonhuman animals to form social bonds (Bartz & Hollander, 2006; Lim & Young, 2006). Brain levels of oxytocin affect the likelihood that mother rats will bond with their pups and the likelihood that adult rats will engage in social interaction. Research suggests that oxytocin has an impact because it promotes *approach* behavior. Consider again that friend who made you a promise. The decision to trust or not can be boiled down to a choice between approach and avoidance—you decide to continue to interact with this individual or you decide to steer clear. High brain levels of oxytocin tilt the balance toward approach. Oxytocin functions in your brain to make it seem likely that future interactions will continue to be rewarding.

To document the dramatic impact of oxytocin, a team of researchers recruited participants to play a game that focused on trust (Baumgartner et al., 2008). The game required two players to distribute a pool of "money units." In each round, the *investor*

had to decide how many money units, out of 12, to invest. The experimenters provided the *trustee* with returns on those investments. The trustee then had the opportunity to share those returns fairly with the investor or not. In fact, halfway through the game, the investors all got the same feedback: The experimenters told them that they were only getting their fair share about half the time. The trustees could not be trusted!

What happened in the second half of the game depended on the investors' levels of oxytocin. Before the game started, half the investors received a dose of the hormone through a nasal spray. (Once it is absorbed, the hormone is able to cross into the brain.) The other participants received a placebo. For the first half of the game, it made little difference whether investors had inhaled oxytocin or the placebo. The figure plots the average number of money units participants invested in each round. As you can see, before the feedback oxytocin participants invested nearly the same amount as placebo participants. You might expect that the dramatic feedback—Don't trust this person!—would

prompt participants to reduce their investments. That's exactly what the placebo group did. Their investments fell for the second half of the game. However, the oxytocin group didn't reduce their investments. In fact, as you can see in the figure, the trend was in the opposite direction. Apparently, the preexperimental dose of oxytocin prevented participants from acting on the information that the other players had violated their trust.

There's one more element to this project: While the investors were making their decisions they were undergoing fMRI scans. Those brain data enabled the researchers to determine what areas of the brain were affected by the dose of oxytocin. The scans revealed that oxytocin participants showed less brain activity in regions of the brain, such as the amygdala, that are involved in fear responses. The researchers suggested that the oxytocin dampens fear responses and thereby increases participants' ability "to trust in situations characterized by the risk of betrayal" (Baumgartner et al., 2008, p. 645).

After reading about this study, you might wonder about the levels of oxytocin in your own brain: Does your brain chemistry predispose you to trust or distrust your friend? Researchers are starting to consider exactly that question of how individual differences in people's levels of oxytocin may have an important impact on social behavior (Bartz & Hollander, 2006; Lim & Young, 2006).

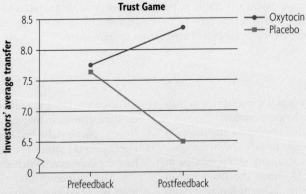

From J.A. Bartz & E. Hollander, The neuroscience of affiliation: Forging links between basic and clinical research on neuropeptides and social behavior, *Hormones and Behavior, 50,* pp. 518–528, Copyright (2006), with permission from Elsevier.

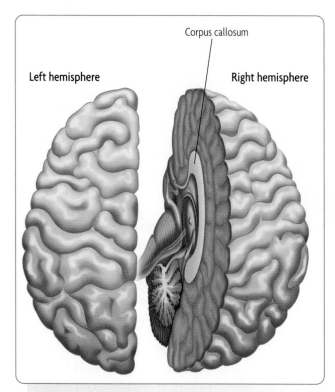

FIGURE 3.19 The Corpus Callosum

The corpus callosum is a massive network of nerve fibers that channels information between the two hemispheres. Severing the corpus callosum impairs this communication process.

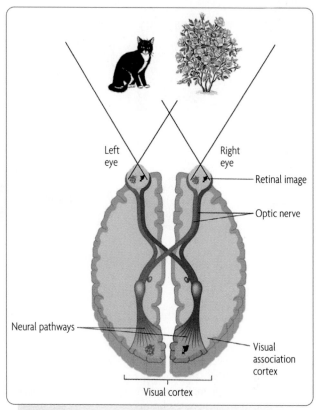

FIGURE 3.20 The Neural Pathways for Visual Information

The neural pathways for visual information coming from the inside portions of each eye cross from one side of the brain to the other at the corpus callosum. The pathways carrying information from the outside portions of each eye do not cross over. Severing the corpus callosum prevents information selectively displayed in the right visual field from entering the right hemisphere, and left visual field information cannot enter the left hemisphere.

To test the capabilities of the separated hemispheres of epileptic patients, **Roger Sperry** (1968) and **Michael Gazzaniga** (1970) devised situations that could allow visual information to be presented separately to each hemisphere. Sperry and Gazzaniga's methodology relies on the anatomy of the visual system (see **Figure 3.20**). For each eye, information from the *right visual field* goes to the left hemisphere, and information from the *left visual field* goes to the right hemisphere. Ordinarily, information arriving from both hemispheres is shared very quickly across the corpus callosum. But because these pathways have been severed in split-brain patients, information presented to the right or left visual field may remain only in the left or right hemisphere (see **Figure 3.21** on page 80).

Because for most people speech is controlled by the left hemisphere, the left hemisphere could "talk back" to the researchers, whereas the right hemisphere could not. Communication with the right hemisphere was achieved by confronting it with manual tasks involving identification, matching, or assembly of objects—tasks that did not require the use of words. Consider the following demonstration of a split-brain subject using his left half brain to account for the activity of his left hand, which was being guided by his right half brain.

> A snow scene was presented to the right hemisphere and a picture of a chicken claw was simultaneously presented to the left hemisphere. The subject selected, from an array of objects, those that "went with" each of the two scenes. With his right hand, the patient pointed to a chicken head; with his left hand, he pointed to a shovel. The patient reported that the shovel was needed to clean out the chicken shed (rather than to shovel snow). Because the left brain was not privy to what the right brain "saw" due to the severed corpus callosum, it needed to explain why the left hand was pointing at a shovel when the only picture the left hemisphere was aware of seeing was a chicken claw. The left brain's cognitive system provided a theory to make sense of the behavior of different parts of its body (Gazzaniga, 1985).

From a variety of research methods in addition to split-brain studies, we now know that, for most people, many language-related functions are *lateralized* to the left hemisphere. A function is considered lateralized when one cerebral hemisphere plays the primary role in accomplishing that function. Speech—the ability to produce coherent spoken language—is perhaps the most highly lateralized of all functions. Neuroscientists have found that only about 5 percent of right-handers and 15 percent of left-handers have speech controlled by the right hemisphere; another 15 percent of left-handers have

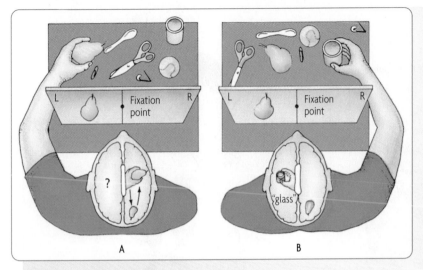

FIGURE 3.21   Testing a Split-Brain Patient

When the split-brain patient uses his left hand to find a match to an object flashed briefly in the left visual field, he is successful because both the visual and tactile (touch) information are registered in the right hemisphere, as shown in A. Nevertheless, the patient cannot name the object, because speech is mainly a left-hemisphere function. Now consider the same patient asked to perform the same task with the right hand, as shown in B. In this case, he is unsuccessful in picking out the object by touch, because the visual information and the tactile information are processed in different hemispheres. In this test, however, the patient is able to name the object in his hand!

From Zimbardo/Johnson/McCann, *Psychology: Core Concepts,* © 2009. Reproduced by permission of Pearson Education, Inc.

speech processes occurring in both sides of the brain (Rasmussen & Milner, 1977). For most people, therefore, speech is a left-hemisphere function. As a consequence, damage to the left side of most people's brains can cause speech disorders. What is interesting is that for users of languages like American Sign Language—which use systems of intricate hand positions and movements to convey meaning—left-brain damage is similarly disruptive (Hickok et al., 2002; Horwitz et al., 2003). What is lateralized, therefore, is not speech as such, but rather, the ability to produce the sequences of gestures—either vocal or manual—that encode communicative meaning.

You should not conclude that the left hemisphere is somehow better than the right hemisphere. Researchers have suggested that each hemisphere has a different style for processing the same information. The left hemisphere tends to be more *analytical:* It processes information bit by bit. The right hemisphere tends to be more *holistic:* It processes information

with respect to global patterns. It is the combined action of the right and left hemispheres—each with its particular processing style—that gives fullness to your experiences. For example, you wouldn't be surprised to learn that the left hemisphere, with its attention to fine detail, plays a key role in most forms of problem solving. However, the function of the right hemisphere becomes more apparent when problems require creative solutions or bursts of insight. Those individuals who show relatively greater activity in their right hemispheres are more likely to have those bursts of insight (Kounios et al., 2008). (If you want to put your right hemisphere to work, you can skip ahead to try some of these types of problems on p. 251 in Chapter 8.)

We have reviewed the many important structures of your nervous system. Now we will consider the endocrine system, a bodily system that functions in close cooperation with the nervous system to regulate bodily functions.

How have studies with individuals who use sign language influenced researchers' beliefs about the lateralization of brain function?

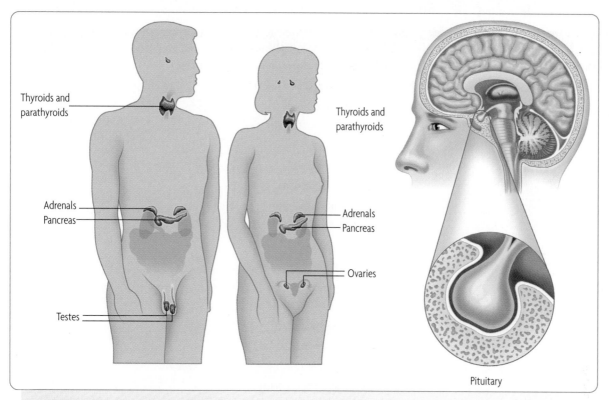

FIGURE 3.22   Endocrine Glands in Males and Females
The pituitary gland is shown at the far right; it is the master gland that regulates the glands shown at the left.
The pituitary gland is under the control of the hypothalamus, an important structure in the limbic system.

THE ENDOCRINE SYSTEM

The human genotype specifies a second highly complex regulatory system, the **endocrine system,** to supplement the work of the nervous system. The endocrine system is a network of glands that manufacture and secrete chemical messengers called **hormones** into the bloodstream (see **Figure 3.22**). Hormones are important in everyday functioning, although they are more vital at some stages of life and in some situations than others. Hormones influence body growth. They initiate, maintain, and stop development of primary and secondary sexual characteristics; influence levels of arousal and awareness; serve as the basis for mood changes; and regulate metabolism, the rate at which the body uses its energy stores. The endocrine system promotes the survival of an *organism* by helping fight infections and disease. It advances the survival of the *species* through regulation of sexual arousal, production of reproductive cells, and production of milk in nursing mothers. Thus you could not survive without an effective endocrine system.

Endocrine glands respond to the levels of chemicals in the bloodstream or are stimulated by other hormones or by nerve impulses from the brain. Hormones are then secreted into the blood and travel to distant target cells that have specific receptors; hormones exert their influence on the body's program of chemical regulation only at the places that are genetically predetermined to respond to them. In influencing diverse, but specific, target organs or tissue, hormones regulate an enormous range of biochemical processes. This multiple-action communication system allows for control of slow continuous processes such as maintenance of blood-sugar levels and calcium levels, metabolism of carbohydrates, and general body growth. But what happens during crises? The endocrine system also releases the hormone adrenaline into the bloodstream; adrenaline energizes your body so that you can respond quickly to challenges.

As we mentioned earlier, the brain structure known as the *hypothalamus* serves as a relay station between the endocrine system and the central nervous system. Specialized cells in the hypothalamus receive messages from other brain cells, commanding it to release a number of different hormones to the pituitary gland, where they either stimulate or inhibit the release of other hormones. Hormones are produced in several different regions of the body. These "factories" make a variety of hormones, each of which regulates different bodily processes, as outlined in **Table 3.2** on page 82. Let's examine the most significant of these processes.

***

endocrine system The network of glands that manufacture and secrete hormones into the bloodstream.

hormone One of the chemical messengers, manufactured and secreted by the endocrine glands, that regulate metabolism and influence body growth, mood, and sexual characteristics.

TABLE 3.2 Major Endocrine Glands and the Functions of the Hormones They Produce

These Glands:	Produce Hormones That Regulate:
Hypothalamus	Release of pituitary hormones
Anterior pituitary	Testes and ovaries
	Breast milk production
	Metabolism
	Reactions to stress
Posterior pituitary	Water conservation
	Breast milk excretion
	Uterus contraction
Thyroid	Metabolism
	Growth and development
Parathyroid	Calcium levels
Gut	Digestion
Pancreas	Glucose metabolism
Adrenals	Fight-or-flight responses
	Metabolism
	Sexual desire in women
Ovaries	Development of female sexual traits
	Ova production
Testes	Development of male sexual traits
	Sperm production
	Sexual desire in men

The **pituitary gland** is often called the master gland, because it produces about ten different kinds of hormones that influence the secretions of all the other endocrine glands, as well as a hormone that influences growth. The absence of this growth hormone results in dwarfism; its excess results in gigantic growth. In males, pituitary secretions activate the testes to secrete **testosterone,** which stimulates production of sperm. The pituitary gland is also involved in the development of male secondary sexual characteristics, such as facial hair, voice change, and physical maturation. Testosterone may even increase aggression and sexual desire. In females, a pituitary hormone stimulates production of **estrogen,** which is essential to the hormonal chain reaction that triggers the release of ova from a woman's ovaries, making her fertile. Certain birth control pills work by blocking the mechanism in the pituitary gland that controls this hormone flow, thus preventing the ova from being released.

PLASTICITY AND NEUROGENESIS: OUR CHANGING BRAINS

You now have a good basic idea of your nervous system at work: At all times, millions of neurons are communicating to do the essential work of your body and mind. What makes the brain even more interesting, however, is one consequence of all that neural communication: The brain itself changes over time. Do you want to take a moment to change your brain? Go back a few pages and memorize the definition of *action potential*. If you are successful at learning that definition—or any other new information—you will have brought about a modification of your brain. Researchers refer to changes in the performance of the brain as **plasticity.** A good deal of research in neuroscience focuses on the physical bases for plasticity. For example, researchers examine how learning arises from the formation of new synapses or from changes in communication across existing synapses (Miyashita et al., 2008).

---

pituitary gland Located in the brain, the gland that secretes growth hormone and influences the secretion of hormones by other endocrine glands.

testosterone The male sex hormone, secreted by the testes, that stimulates production of sperm and is also responsible for the development of male secondary sex characteristics.

estrogen The female sex hormone, produced by the ovaries, that is responsible for the release of eggs from the ovaries as well as for the development and maintenance of female reproductive structures and secondary sex characteristics.

plasticity Changes in the performance of the brain; may involve the creation of new synapses or changes in the function of existing synapses.

Because brain plasticity depends on life experiences, you won't be surprised to learn that brains show the impact of different environments and activities. One line of research, pioneered by **Mark Rosenzweig,** demonstrated the consequences for rats of being raised in impoverished or enriched environments (for reviews, see Rosenzweig, 1996, 1999). Early research demonstrated an advantage for young animals: The average cortex of rats reared in the enriched environments was heavier and thicker—positive attributes—than that of their impoverished littermates. Researchers have now demonstrated that environmental enrichment continues to have an impact on the brains of adult animals.

Twenty-five male rats from the same litter were housed in small groups for their first 120 days—which, for rats, makes them adults. At that point, the rats were moved to one of three environments. In the complex environment condition, the rats were housed together in a cage "filled with a variety of objects such as swings, wooden blocks, plastic cars and trucks, plastic tunnels, and mirrors" (Briones et al., 2004, p. 131). In the inactive condition, the rats were housed individually with no other objects in the cage. In the social condition, the rats were housed in pairs, but otherwise the cages had no other objects. After 30 days, the researchers carried out analyses to determine the environments' impact on neurons in visual cortex. Those analyses demonstrated that the complex environment rats had 21 percent more synapses for each neuron than the social rats; they had 27 percent more synapses for each neuron than the isolated rats. These results confirm that enriched environments continue to bring about changes in the brains of adult rats.

With brain-imaging techniques, it is possible to measure very specific brain differences related to individuals' life experiences. Consider those musicians who play the violin. They are required to control the fingers of their left hands with an extremely delicate touch. If you refer back to Figure 3.18, you'll see that a good deal of sensory cortex is devoted to the fingers. Brain scans reveal that the representation of fingers of the left hand is even more enhanced for violin players, as compared to nonplayers (Elbert et al., 1995). No such increase is found for fingers of the right hand, which do not have as great a sensory role in violin playing. The extra representation of the left fingers was greatest for violinists who took up the instrument before age 12.

One important aspect of research on plasticity concerns circumstances in which humans or animals have sustained injuries to the brain or spinal cord, through strokes, degenerative diseases, or accidents. A good deal of clinical evidence confirms that the brain is sometimes able to heal itself. For example, patients who suffer from strokes that cause disruptions in language often recover over time. In some instances, the damaged brain areas themselves have enough lingering function that recovery is possible; in other cases other brain areas take over the functions of those that were damaged (Kuest & Karbe, 2002). Researchers have also begun to develop techniques to help the brain along in the healing process. In recent years, attention has focused on *stem cells*—unspecialized cells that, under appropriate conditions, can be prompted to function as new neurons (Li et al., 2008). Researchers hope that stem cells may ultimately provide a means to replace damaged tissue in the nervous system with new neural growth. Because the most flexible stem cells come from embryos and aborted fetuses, stem cell research has been subject to political controversy. Still, researchers believe that stem cell research could lead to cures for paralysis and other serious malfunctions in the nervous system. For that reason, the scientific community is highly motivated to discover ways to continue research within accepted societal norms.

Research on brain repair has accelerated in recent years in the face of important new data suggesting that **neurogenesis**—the production of new brain cells from naturally occurring stem cells—occurs in the brains of adult mammals, including humans (Christie & Cameron, 2006; Gould & Gross, 2002). For nearly 100 years, neuroscientists believed that the adult brains of mammals had their full supply of neurons—all that could happen over the adult years was that neurons could die out. However, the new data have challenged that view. Recall, for example, that we identified the hippocampus as an important structure for the formation of certain types of memories. Now that researchers have documented neurogenesis in the adult hippocampus, they are trying to understand how newly born neurons provide a resource for the acquisition of new memories across the life span (Kempermann, 2008).

In this chapter, we have taken a brief peek at the marvelous 3-pound universe that is your brain. It is one thing to recognize that the brain controls behavior and your mental processes but quite another to understand how the brain serves all those functions. Neuroscientists are engaged in the fascinating quest to understand the interplay among brain, behavior, and environment. You now have the type of background that will allow you to appreciate new knowledge as it unfolds.

STOP AND REVIEW

❶ What are the advantages of fMRI over other brain-imaging techniques?

❷ What are the two major divisions of the autonomic nervous system?

❸ What are some of the major functions of the amygdala?

❹ What processing styles are reflected by the two hemispheres of the brain?

❺ Why is the pituitary gland often called the master gland?

❻ What is neurogenesis?

CRITICAL THINKING Consider the study on plasticity in adult rats. Why did the researchers use both the inactive and social controls?

Visit MyPsychLab.com for more review and practice on the following topics:

👁 **Watch:** MKM and Brain Scans

✳ **Simulate:** Hemispheric Experiment

✳ **Simulate:** Split-Brain Experiments

---

neurogenesis The creation of new neurons.

Recapping Main Points

Heredity and Behavior

- Species originate and change over time because of natural selection.
- In the evolution of humans, bipedalism and encephalization were responsible for subsequent advances, including language and culture.
- The basic unit of heredity is the gene. Genes determine the range of effects that environmental factors can have in influencing the expression of phenotypic traits.

The Nervous System in Action

- The neuron, the basic unit of the nervous system, receives, processes, and relays information to other cells, glands, and muscles.
- Neurons relay information from the dendrites through the cell body (soma) to the axon to the terminal buttons.
- Sensory neurons receive messages from specialized receptor cells and send them toward the CNS. Motor neurons direct messages from the CNS to muscles and glands. Interneurons relay information from sensory neurons to other interneurons or to motor neurons.
- Once the summation of inputs to a neuron exceeds a specific threshold, an action potential is sent along the axon to the terminal buttons.
- All-or-none action potentials are created when the opening of ion channels allows an exchange of ions across the cell membrane.
- Neurotransmitters are released into the synaptic gap between neurons. Once they diffuse across the gap, they lodge in the receptor molecules of the postsynaptic membrane.
- Whether these neurotransmitters excite or inhibit the membrane depends on the nature of the receptor molecule.

Biology and Behavior

- Neuroscientists use several methods to research the relation between brain and behavior: studying brain-damaged patients, producing lesions at specific brain sites, electrically stimulating the brain, recording brain activity, and imaging the brain with computerized devices.
- The brain and the spinal cord make up the central nervous system (CNS).
- The peripheral nervous system (PNS) is composed of all neurons connecting the CNS to the body. The PNS consists of the somatic nervous system, which regulates the body's skeletal muscles, and the autonomic nervous system (ANS), which regulates life-support processes.
- The brain consists of three integrated layers: the brain stem, limbic system, and cerebrum.
- The brain stem is responsible for breathing, digestion, and heart rate.
- The limbic system is involved in long-term memory, aggression, eating, drinking, and sexual behavior.
- The cerebrum controls higher mental functions.
- Some functions are lateralized to one hemisphere of the brain. For example, most individuals have speech localized in the left hemisphere.
- Although the two hemispheres of the brain work smoothly in concert, they typically embody different styles of processing: The left hemisphere is more analytic; the right hemisphere is more holistic.
- The endocrine system produces and secretes hormones into the bloodstream.
- Hormones help regulate growth, primary and secondary sexual characteristics, metabolism, digestion, and arousal.
- New cell growth and life experiences reshape the brain after birth.

KEY TERMS

action potential (p. 62)

all-or-none law (p. 64)

amygdala (p. 74)

association cortex (p. 76)

auditory cortex (p. 76)

autonomic nervous system (ANS) (p. 71)

axon (p. 61)

brain stem (p. 72)

Broca's area (p. 68)

central nervous system (CNS) (p. 70)

cerebellum (p. 74)

cerebral cortex (p. 74)

cerebral hemispheres (p. 74)

cerebrum (p. 74)

computerized axial tomography (CT or CAT) (p. 69)

corpus callosum (p. 74)

dendrite (p. 60)

DNA (deoxyribonucleic acid) (p. 56)

electroencephalogram (EEG) (p. 69)

endocrine system (p. 81)

estrogen (p. 82)

evolutionary psychology (p. 59)

excitatory input (p. 62)

frontal lobe (p. 76)

functional MRI (fMRI) (p. 70)

gene (p. 56)

genetics (p. 56)

genome (p. 57)

genotype (p. 55)

glia (p. 61)

heredity (p. 56)

heritability (p. 57)

hippocampus (p. 74)

homeostasis (p. 74)

hormone (p. 81)

human behavior genetics (p. 57)

hypothalamus (p. 74)

inhibitory input (p. 62)

interneuron (p. 61)

ion channel (p. 63)

lesion (p. 68)

limbic system (p. 74)

magnetic resonance imaging (MRI) (p. 69)

medulla (p. 72)

motor cortex (p. 76)

motor neuron (p. 61)

Chapter 3 Practice Test

1. When Peter and Rosemary Grant studied several species of Darwin's finches, they discovered that major climate changes affected which populations of finches survived. This is an example of
   a. heritability.
   b. the all-or-none law.
   c. natural selection.
   d. nature versus nurture.

2. Sharon is involved in a project in which she observes the behaviors of young children. She is most able to directly observe their
   a. genotypes.   c. chromosomes.
   b. phenotypes.   d. DNA.

3. Suppose you carried out a study to assess whether there is a genetic component to "sense of humor." To conclude that genetics plays a role, you would want to find that
   a. DZ twins are more similar in their sense of humor than MZ twins.
   b. DZ twins always have better senses of humor than MZ twins.
   c. MZ twins always have better senses of humor than DZ twins.
   d. MZ twins are more similar in their sense of humor than DZ twins.

4. One of the jobs of _____ is to receive stimulation from other neurons.
   a. axons
   b. terminal buttons
   c. synapses
   d. dendrites

5. After Jonas withdraws money from the bank, he has to wait two minutes before his card will work again. This sounds a lot like the _____ in neural transmission.
   a. all-or-none law
   b. action potential
   c. refractory period
   d. ion channels

6. Wilma is creating an illustration of neural transmission. She leaves a small gap between a terminal button on one neuron and the dendrite of the next. She should label that gap the
   a. ion channel.   c. node of Ranvier.
   b. glia.   d. synapse.

7. Bea has decided to undergo an acupuncture treatment to help her with her back pain. You explain that researchers believe that acupuncture leads to the release of _____ in the brain.
   a. GABA   c. endorphins
   b. acetylcholine   d. dopamine

8. Suppose you want to understand the genetics of impulsivity. You might concentrate your research on variations in genes that affect the brain's use of
   a. glia.   c. GABA.
   b. dopamine.   d. ion channels.

9. Which technique allows researchers to create reversible "lesions"?
   a. fMRI   c. PET scans
   b. rTMS   d. EEG

10. The _____ nervous system processes incoming neural messages and sends commands to different parts of the body.
    a. central   c. somatic
    b. autonomic   d. peripheral

11. After he experienced damage to his _____, H.M. had difficulties acquiring new information.
    a. reticular formation
    b. thalamus
    c. hippocampus
    d. Broca's area

12. After Jeff inhales oxytocin through a nasal spray, you expect him to display _____ trust toward Mona due, in part, to _____ activity in his amygdala.
    a. more; reduced
    b. more; increased
    c. less; reduced
    d. less; increased

13. As you are chatting with Tejus, you noticed that she is right-handed. You think that it's most likely that her ability to produce speech is controlled by
    a. her left hemisphere.
    b. her right hemisphere.
    c. both the left and right hemispheres.
    d. neither the left nor the right hemisphere.

14. Which brain structure serves as a relay station between the brain and the endocrine system?
    a. the hippocampus
    b. the hypothalamus
    c. the pons
    d. the amygdala

15. Brain-imaging techniques reveal that the brain representation of the fingers of the left hand is enhanced for people who play the violin versus nonplayers. This result provides an example of
    a. neurogenesis.
    b. heritability.
    c. lateralization.
    d. brain plasticity.

Essay Questions

1. What important contrasts exist between research in human behavior genetics and research in evolutionary psychology?

2. Why does a neuron's behavior depend on the balance of excitatory and inhibitory inputs it receives?

3. Why are the two hemispheres of the brain often characterized as having distinctive processing styles?

Discovering Psychology Viewing Guide

Watch the following videos by logging on to MyPsychLab (www.mypsychlab.com). After you have watched the videos, complete the activities that follow.

Program 3: The Behaving Brain

Program 4: The Responsive Brain

Program 25: Cognitive Neuroscience

KEY TERMS AND PEOPLE

As you watch the programs, pay particular attention to these terms and people in addition to those covered in this textbook.

- *agonist*—a chemical or drug that mimics the action of a neurotransmitter.
- *antagonist*—a chemical or drug that blocks the action of a neurotransmitter.
- *enzymes*—protein molecules that act as catalysts in body chemistry by facilitating chemical reactions.
- *ERP*—a measure of event-related potentials of single brain cells.
- *IAT (Implicit Attitudes Test)*—uses response time as a means of detecting unconscious prejudice.
- *maternal deprivation*—the lack of adequate affection and stimulation from the mother or mother substitute.
- *phoneme*—the smallest recognizable unit of speech sound.
- *plasticity*—the ability of the brain to restructure itself as a result, for example, of learning.
- *priming*—a speeding up in response time as a function of recent exposure.
- *Mahzarin Banaji*—studies brain processes that appear to underlie prejudice.
- *Russell Fernald*—neuroethologist who studies how the brain, behavior, and the environment interact in animals in their natural habitat.
- *Tiffany Field*—studies the effect of infant massage on the cognitive and motor development of infants.
- *John Gabrieli*—studies amnesic patients to determine how different types of memory are physically stored in and retrieved from the brain.
- *David Heeger*—uses functional MRI to study vision.
- *Nancy Kanwisher*—studies the brain's processing of faces and scenes.
- *Stephen Kosslyn*—studies how mental imagery evokes brain processes similar to those involved in perception.
- *Joseph Martinez*—studies how brain chemicals affect learning and memory.
- *Michael Meaney*—developmental psychologist who studies how early experiences can change the brains and behavior of animals, especially under stress.
- *Robert Sapolsky*—neurobiologist who studies the social structure of baboon communities. Argues that dominance affects physiological functioning, with higher ranks being associated with greater control, predictability, and better physiological functioning.
- *Saul Schanberg*—works with infant rats to demonstrate how touch is a brain-based requirement for normal growth and development. Argues that a mother's touch has real biological value to offspring and is required to maintain normal growth and development.
- *Mieke Verfaellie*—studies the effects of amnesia on memory and cognition.

PROGRAM REVIEW

Programs 3 and 4

1. In general, neuroscientists are interested in the
   a. brain mechanisms underlying normal and abnormal behavior.
   b. biological consequences of stress on the body.
   c. comparison of neurons with other types of cells.
   d. computer simulation of intelligence.

2. Which method of probing the brain produces actual pictures of the brain's inner workings?
   a. autopsies
   b. brain imaging
   c. lesioning
   d. electroencephalograms

3. E. Roy John cites the example of the staff member responding to a personal question to show how imaging can detect
   a. abnormal structure in the brain.
   b. abnormal personality.
   c. abnormal but transient states.
   d. pathological states, such as alcoholism.

4. If a scientist was studying the effects of endorphins on the body, the scientist would be likely to look at a participant's
   a. memory.
   b. ability to learn new material.
   c. mood.
   d. motivation to compete in sports.

5. Joseph Martinez taught rats a maze task and then gave them scopolamine. What effect did the drug have on brain functioning?
   a. It enhanced the rats' memories.
   b. It made the rats forget what they had learned.
   c. It enabled the rats to learn a similar task more quickly.
   d. It had no effect.

6. Research related to acetylcholine may someday help people who
   a. have Alzheimer's disease.
   b. have Parkinson's disease.
   c. suffer spinal cord trauma.
   d. suffer from depression.

7. When we say the relationship between the brain and behavior is reciprocal, we mean that
   a. the brain controls behavior, but behavior can modify the brain.
   b. behavior determines what the brain will think about.
   c. the brain and behavior operate as separate systems with no interconnection.
   d. the brain alters behavior as it learns more about the world.

8. Before an operation, men and women were gently touched by a nurse. What effect did this touch have on the patients' anxiety levels?
   a. It decreased anxiety in both men and women.
   b. It increased anxiety in both men and women.
   c. It decreased anxiety in men, but increased it in women.
   d. It increased anxiety in men, but decreased it in women.

9. A group of people comfortable with touching others is compared with a group uncomfortable with touching others. Those comfortable with touch were generally higher in
   a. self-esteem.   c. social withdrawal.
   b. conformity.   d. suspicion of others.

10. What long-term effect did Tiffany Field find massage had on premature infants?
    a. Massaged infants had better social relationships.
    b. Massaged infants were physically and cognitively more developed.
    c. Massaged infants slept and ate better.
    d. There were no long-term effects noted.

11. What is the relationship between the results of Saul Schanberg's research and that of Tiffany Field?
    a. Their results are contradictory.
    b. The results of Schanberg's research led to Field's research.
    c. Their results show similar phenomena in different species.
    d. Their results are essentially unrelated.

12. What physical change did Mark Rosenzweig's team note when they studied rats raised in an enriched environment?
    a. a thicker cortex   d. no physical changes were
    b. more neurons   noted, only functional
    c. fewer neurotransmitters   changes

13. In Michael Meaney's research on aged rats' performance in a swimming maze, the rats that performed best were those that

    a. had received doses of glucocorticoid.
    b. had been subjected to less stress in their lives.
    c. had been handled early in life.
    d. could use spatial clues for orientation.

14. Repeated exposure to stress hormones
    a. increases the number of glucocorticoid neurons.
    b. has its greatest effect on the brain stem.
    c. affect learning and memory.
    d. makes brain cells live longer.

15. In his study of cichlid fish, Russell Fernald found that there was growth in a specific area of the brain following
    a. improved diet.   c. gentle handling.
    b. social success.   d. loss of territory.

16. In Robert Sapolsky's study of stress physiology among baboons, what is the relationship between high status and "good" physiology?
    a. Animals attain high status because they have good physiology.
    b. Attaining high status leads to good physiology.
    c. Lowering one's status leads to improved physiology.
    d. Animals with high status produce high levels of stress hormone, which break down the immune system.

17. What did Robert Sapolsky discover is the optimal style of behavior for dominant baboons?
    a. unpredictable aggression   c. active curiosity
    b. social style   d. frequent vocalizing

Program 25

18. After a rod was shot through Phineas Gage's skull, what psychological system was most strongly disrupted?
    a. his emotional responses
    b. his ability to sleep and wake
    c. his language comprehension
    d. his ability to count

19. Which of the following does *not* provide information about the structure of the brain?
    a. CAT   c. MRI
    b. EEG   d. fMRI

20. The technique of fMRI measures
    a. distribution of radioactivity throughout the brain.
    b. electrical impulses in neurons.
    c. oxygen in the blood vessels of the brain.
    d. neural cellular growth over time.

21. Which of the following accurately identifies how visual information progresses?
    a. from the retina to the thalamus to the primary visual cortex
    b. from the retina to the primary visual cortex to the thalamus
    c. from the thalamus to the retina to the primary visual cortex
    d. from the primary visual cortex to the retina to the thalamus

22. All of the following areas are specialized for motion, *except*
    a. V1   c. left hemisphere
    b. right hemisphere   d. thalamus

23. The right side of the world is processed by
    a. the left side of the brain.   c. the right side of the brain.
    b. the front of the brain.   d. the brain stem.

24. The brain regions that are involved in identifying human faces will also become active when shown
    a. human hands.
    c. a picture of the moon.
    b. animal faces.
    d. a clock.

25. According to Nancy Kanwisher, why is it important to identify faces?
    a. because it allows us to identify other objects, like alphanumeric characters
    b. because we can then identify people who are familiar and friendly from other people
    c. both of the above
    d. none of the above

26. The way that participants move their eyes in Stephen Kosslyn's studies
    a. is diagnostic of whether they may later develop Alzheimer's disease.
    b. indicates whether they harbor unconscious prejudices.
    c. resembles the patterns of eye movements by participants who are looking at real objects.
    d. reveals which part of the brain they are using to view the stimuli.

27. The formation of mental images _____ the construction of real objects, and the transformation of mental images _____ the transformation of real objects.
    a. follows the same pattern as; does not follow the same pattern as
    b. does not follow the same pattern as; does not follow the same pattern as
    c. does not follow the same pattern as; follows the same pattern as
    d. follows the same pattern as; follows the same pattern as

28. The process of learning how to read shows that the brain is plastic. What does this mean?
    a. The brain is rigid in what it is designed to do.
    b. Learning how to read reorganizes the brain.
    c. The brain cannot be damaged simply by attempting new mental feats.
    d. The brain can be damaged when it attempts new mental feats.

29. For dyslexics who have trouble processing phonemes, which area of the brain is most likely to be damaged?
    a. the thalamus
    c. the parietal lobe
    b. the right hemisphere
    d. the left hemisphere

30. The IAT, administered by Mahzarin Banaji, can detect
    a. flaws in the imaginal system.
    b. unconscious prejudice.
    c. sensorimotor malfunctions.
    d. facial processing deficits.

31. Which area of the brain becomes particularly active when prejudice is aroused?
    a. the hypothalamus
    c. the medulla
    b. the amygdala
    d. the parietal lobe

32. People who show a strong eyeblink response in Banaji's studies also tend to show
    a. a preference for white faces on the IAT.
    b. low activation in the amygdala.
    c. a preference for black faces on the IAT.
    d. no cultural biases.

QUESTIONS TO CONSIDER

1. Considering what is known about the damaging effects of poor nutrition, drugs, cigarettes, and alcohol on the fetus, what can be done to protect a baby from the effects of its mother's activities? Should any legal action be taken?

2. Given the advances being made in the imaging of brain activity, will it ever be possible for scientists to "read someone's mind" or to control someone's thoughts?

3. Speculate on why music, having no survival benefit or pharmacological properties, would have the strong effect on people's emotions and brains that it seems to have.

4. Imagine that you were designing an animal brain. Why would you want to design neurons to have an all-or-none response rather than a graded potential? Why would you want to create a brain that responded to several different neurotransmitters rather than creating one all-purpose neurotransmitter that affected all cells equally?

5. What will our scientific study of the brain, including emotion, social interaction, personality, and moral reason, mean for people's religious beliefs? Will the concept of the soul be seriously challenged?

ACTIVITIES

1. Interview a few parents from different generations and from different cultures about the infancy of their children. Did they read books on child development or follow an expert's advice? Did they sleep with their babies? How did they comfort them? Which early experiences do they believe were most influential in their children's future development?

2. As science enters an era of being able to study the brain's activities, our imaginations about what is possible run much faster than the development of neuroimaging and simulation techniques. Watch films like The Cell, The Matrix, and AI, and identify several ways in which the "science" they portray is impossible given the current state of the field. Think about which aspects will likely remain impossible even hundreds of years from now.

3. Check out a textbook for a neuroscience or medical course that shows brain images of normal people and various clinical populations, such as schizophrenics, Alzheimer's patients, or accident victims. Look to see which areas of loss are associated with the loss of which functions.

4. Go on the Web and look up these terms: *aphasia*, *agnosia*, and *transient ischemic attack*. Compare the types and durations of the deficits, and see if you can come to understand the functions of different parts of the brain by learning what goes wrong with the loss of tissue in different brain areas.

4

Sensation and Perception

Have you ever wondered how your brain—locked in the dark, silent chamber of the skull—experiences the blaze of color in a van Gogh painting, the driving melodies and rhythms of rock 'n' roll, the refreshing taste of watermelon on a hot day, the soft touch of a child's kiss, or the fragrance of wildflowers in the springtime? Our task in this chapter is to explain how your body and brain make sense of the buzz of stimulation—sights, sounds, and so on—constantly around you. You will see how evolution has equipped you with the capability to detect many different dimensions of experience.

In this chapter, we will describe how your experience of the world relies on processes of *perception*. The term **perception,** in its broad usage, refers to the overall process of apprehending objects and events in the environment—to sense them, understand them, recognize and label them, and prepare to react to them. A *percept* is what is perceived—the phenomenological, or experienced, outcome of the process of perception. Your perceptual processes serve the dual functions of *survival* and *sensuality*. These processes help you survive by sounding alarms of danger, priming you to take swift action to ward off hazards, and directing you toward agreeable experiences. These processes also provide you with sensuality. Sensuality is the quality of being devoted to the gratification of the senses; it entails enjoying the experiences that appeal to your various senses of sight, sound, touch, taste, and smell.

The process of perception is best understood when we divide it into three stages: sensation, perceptual organization, and identification (or recognition) of objects. **Sensation** is the process by which stimulation of *sensory receptors*—the structures in your eyes, ears, and so on—produces neural impulses that represent experiences inside or outside the body. For example, sensation provides the basic facts of the visual field. Nerve cells in your eyes pass information along to cells in your brain.

Perceptual organization refers to the stage in which your brain integrates evidence from your senses with prior knowledge of the world to form an internal representation of an external stimulus. With respect to vision, organizational processes provide estimates of an object's likely size, shape, movement, distance, and orientation. These mental activities most often occur swiftly and efficiently, without conscious awareness.

The processes of **identification and recognition** assign meaning to percepts. With respect to vision, earlier stages of perception answer the question "What does the object look like?" At this stage, the questions become those of identification—"What is this object?"—and recognition—"What is the object's function?" You identify circular objects as baseballs, coins, clocks, oranges, and moons; you identify people as male or female, friend or foe, relative or rock star.

We have briefly introduced the stages of processing that enable you to arrive at a meaningful understanding of the world around you. In everyday life, perception seems to be entirely effortless. We will try to convince you that you actually do quite a bit of sophisticated processing, a lot of mental work, to arrive at this "illusion of ease."

What senses are involved in the enjoyment of a slice of watermelon?

Sensory Knowledge of the World

Your experience of external reality must be relatively accurate and error free. If not, you couldn't survive. You need food to sustain you, shelter to protect you, interactions with other people to fulfill social needs, and awareness of danger to keep out of harm's way. To meet these needs, you must get reliable information about the world. In this section, we provide an overview of how your sensory processes address these goals.

THE PROXIMAL AND DISTAL STIMULI

Imagine you are the person in **Figure 4.1A,** surveying a room from an easy chair. Some of the light reflected from the objects

perception The processes that organize information in the sensory image and interpret it as having been produced by properties of objects or events in the external, three-dimensional world.

sensation The process by which stimulation of a sensory receptor gives rise to neutral impulses that result in an experience, or awareness, of conditions inside or outside the body.

perceptual organization The processes that put sensory information together to give the perception of a coherent scene over the whole visual field.

identification and recognition Two ways of attaching meaning to percepts.

in the room enters your eyes and forms images on your retinas. **Figure 4.1B** shows what would appear to your left eye as you sit in the room. (The bump on the right is your nose, and the hand and knee at the bottom are your own.) How does this retinal image compare with the environment that produced it?

One very important difference is that the retinal image is *two dimensional*, whereas the environment is *three dimensional*. This difference has many consequences. For instance, compare the shapes of the physical objects in Figure 4.1A with the shapes of their corresponding retinal images (**Figure 4.1C**). The table, rug, window, and picture in the real-world scene are all rectangular, but only the image of the window actually produces a rectangle in your retinal image. The image of the picture is a trapezoid, the image of the tabletop is an irregular four-sided figure, and the image of the rug is actually three separate regions with more than 20 different sides! Here's our first perceptual puzzle: How do you manage to perceive all of these objects as simple standard rectangles?

The situation, however, is even a bit more complicated. You can also notice that many parts of what you perceive in the room are not actually present in your retinal image. For instance, you perceive the vertical edge between the two walls as going all the way to the floor, but your retinal image of that edge stops at the tabletop. Similarly, in your retinal image parts of the rug are hidden behind the table; yet this does not keep you from correctly perceiving the rug as a single unbroken rectangle. In fact, when you consider all the differences between the environmental objects and the images of them on your retina, you may be surprised that you perceive the scene as well as you do.

The differences between a physical object in the world and its optical image on your retina are so profound and important that psychologists distinguish carefully between them as two different stimuli for perception. The physical object in the world is called the **distal stimulus** (distant from the observer) and the optical image on the retina is called the **proximal stimulus** (proximate, or near, to the observer).

The critical point of our discussion can now be restated more concisely: What you wish to *perceive* is the *distal stimulus*—the "real" object in the environment—whereas the stimulus from which you must derive your information is the *proximal stimulus*—the image on the retina. You can think of the major computational task of perception as the process of determining the distal stimulus from information contained in the proximal stimulus. This is true across perceptual domains. For hearing, touch, taste, and so on, perception involves processes that use information in the proximal stimulus to tell you about properties of the distal stimulus.

To show you how the distal stimulus and proximal stimulus fit with the three stages in perceiving, let's examine one of the objects in the scene from Figure 4.1: the picture hanging on the wall. In the sensory stage, this picture corresponds to a two-dimensional trapezoid in your retinal image; the top and bottom sides converge toward the right, and the left and right sides are different in length. This is the proximal stimulus.

distal stimulus   In the processes of perception, the physical object in the world, as contrasted with the proximal stimulus, the optical image on the retina.

proximal stimulus   The optical image on the retina; contrasted with the distal stimulus, the physical object in the world.

A.

B.

(View from left eye)

(Picture)   (Window)

(Tabletop)

(Rug)

C.

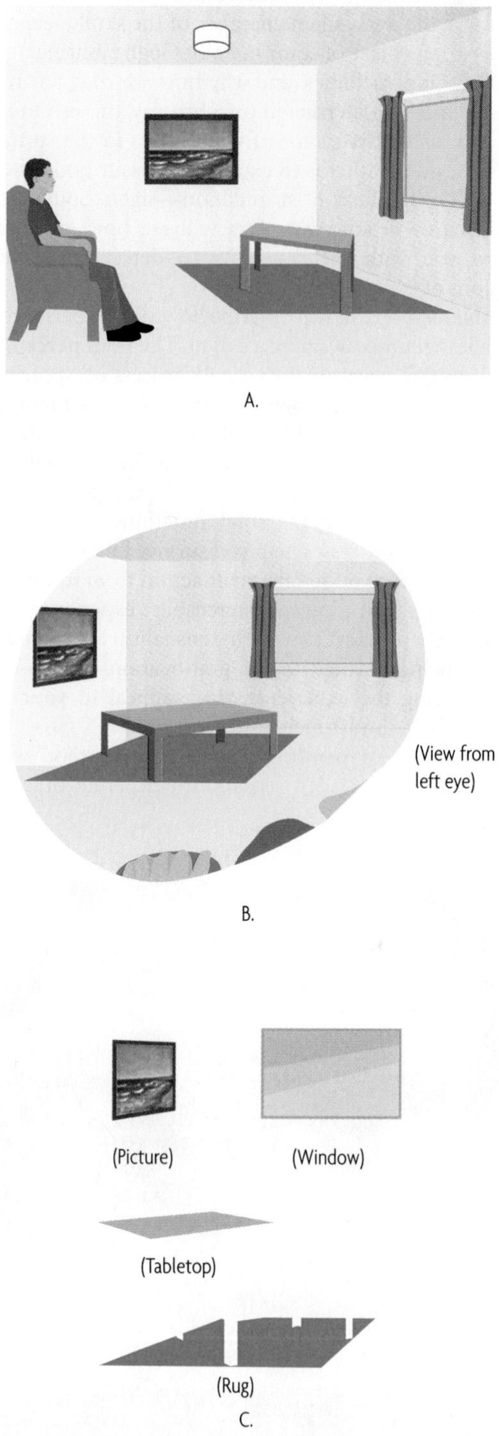

FIGURE 4.1   Interpreting Retinal Images

Suppose you are sitting in an easy chair, looking around a room (A). The light reflected from objects in the room forms images on your retina. Consider the information that arrives at your left eye (B). When you see that information out of context (C), you can appreciate the task that faces your visual system: Your visual perception must interpret or identify distal stimulus, the actual object in the environment, using the information from the proximal stimulus, the retinal image produced by the object.

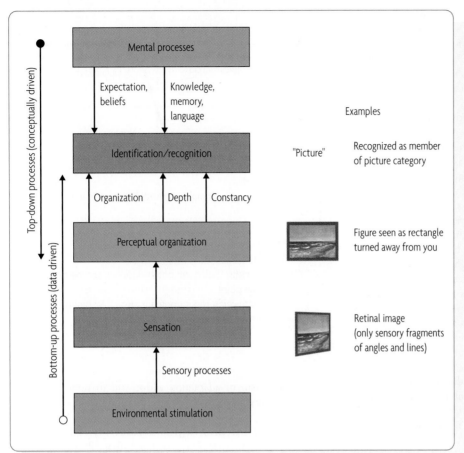

FIGURE 4.2 Sensation, Perceptual Organization, and Identification/Recognition Stages

The diagram outlines the processes that give rise to the transformation of incoming information at the stages of sensation, perceptual organization, and identification/recognition. Bottom-up processing occurs when the perceptual representation is derived from the information available in the sensory input. Top-down processing occurs when the perceptual representation is affected by an individual's prior knowledge, motivations, expectations, and other aspects of higher mental functioning.

In the perceptual organization stage, you see this trapezoid as a rectangle turned away from you in three-dimensional space. You perceive the top and bottom sides as parallel but receding into the distance toward the right; you perceive the left and right sides as equal in length. Your perceptual processes have developed a strong *hypothesis* about the physical properties of the distal stimulus; now it needs an identity. In the recognition stage, you identify this rectangular object as a picture. **Figure 4.2** is a flowchart illustrating this sequence of events. The processes that take information from one stage to the next are shown as arrows between the boxes. By the end of this chapter, we will explain the interactions represented in this figure.

We have defined the task of perception as the identification of the distal stimulus from the proximal stimulus. However, the earliest researchers on sensation recognized that people's experiences of the world have a psychological component. As we'll see next, those researchers examined the relationship between events in the environment and people's experience of those events.

PSYCHOPHYSICS

How loud must a fire alarm at a factory be for workers to hear it over the din of the machinery? How bright does a warning light on a pilot's control panel have to be to appear twice as bright as the other lights? How much sugar do you need to put in a cup of coffee before it begins to taste sweet? To answer these questions, we must be able to measure the intensity of sensory experiences. This is the central task of **psychophysics,** the study of the relationship between physical stimuli and the behavior or mental experiences the stimuli evoke.

The most significant figure in the history of psychophysics was the German physicist **Gustav Fechner** (1801–1887). Fechner coined the term *psychophysics* and provided a set of procedures to relate the intensity of a physical stimulus—measured in physical units—to the magnitude of the sensory experience—measured in psychological units (Fechner, 1860/1966). Fechner's techniques are the same whether the stimuli are for light, sound, taste, odor, or touch: Researchers determine thresholds and construct psychophysical scales relating strength of sensation to strength of stimuli.

Absolute Thresholds and Sensory Adaptation What is the smallest, weakest stimulus energy that an organism can detect? How soft can a tone be, for instance, and still be heard? These questions refer to the **absolute threshold** for stimulation—the minimum amount of physical energy needed to produce a sensory experience. Researchers measure absolute thresholds by

---

psychophysics The study of the correspondence between physical simulation and psychological experience.

absolute threshold The minimum amount of physical energy needed to produce a reliable sensory experience; operationally defined as the stimulus level at which a sensory signal is detected half the time.

asking vigilant observers to perform detection tasks, such as trying to see a dim light in a dark room or trying to hear a soft sound in a quiet room. During a series of many trials, the stimulus is presented at varying intensities, and on each trial the observers indicate whether they were aware of it. (If you've ever had your hearing evaluated, you participated in an absolute threshold test.)

The results of an absolute threshold study can be summarized in a **psychometric function:** a graph that shows the percentage of detections (plotted on the vertical axis) at each stimulus intensity (plotted on the horizontal axis). A typical psychometric function is shown in **Figure 4.3.** For very dim lights, detection is at 0 percent; for bright lights, detection is at 100 percent. If there were a single, true absolute threshold, you would expect the transition from 0 to 100 percent detection to be very sharp, occurring right at the point where the intensity reached the threshold. But this does not happen, for at least two reasons: Viewers themselves change slightly each time they try to detect a stimulus (because of changes in attention, fatigue, and so on), and viewers sometimes respond even in the absence of a stimulus (the type of false alarm we will discuss shortly when we describe signal detection theory). Thus the psychometric curve is usually a smooth *S*-shaped curve, in which there is a region of transition from no detection to occasional detection to detection all the time.

Because a stimulus does not suddenly become clearly detectable at all times at a specific intensity, the operational definition of absolute threshold is *the stimulus level at which a sensory signal is detected half the time.* Thresholds for different senses can be measured using the same procedure, simply by changing the stimulus dimension. **Table 4.1** shows absolute threshold levels for several familiar natural stimuli.

Although it is possible to identify absolute thresholds for detection, it is also important to note that your sensory systems are more sensitive to *changes* in the sensory environment than to steady states. The systems have evolved so that they favor new environmental inputs over old through a process called adaptation. **Sensory adaptation** is the diminishing responsiveness of sensory systems to prolonged stimulus input. You may have noticed, for example, that sunshine seems less blinding after a while outdoors. People often have their most fortunate experiences of adaptation in the domain of smell: You walk into a room, and something really has a foul odor; over time, however, as your smell system adapts, the odor fades out of awareness. Your environment is always full of a great diversity of sensory stimulation.

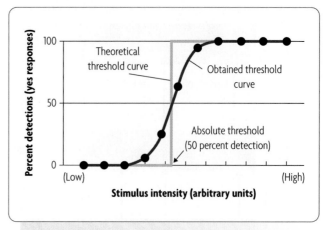

FIGURE 4.3 Calculation of Absolute Thresholds

Because a stimulus does not suddenly become detectable at a certain point, absolute threshold is defined as the intensity at which the stimulus is detected half of the time over many trials.

The mechanism of adaptation allows you to notice and react quickly to the challenges of new sources of information.

Response Bias and Signal Detection Theory In our discussion so far, we have assumed that all observers are created equal. However, threshold measurements can also be affected by **response bias,** the systematic tendency for an observer to favor responding in a particular way because of factors unrelated to the sensory features of the stimulus. Suppose, for example, you are in an experiment in which you

psychometric function A graph that plots the percentage of detections of a stimulus (on the vertical axis) for each stimulus intensity (on the horizon axis).

sensory adaptation A phenomenon in which receptor cells lose their power to respond after a period of unchanged stimulation; allows a more rapid reaction to new sources of information.

response bias The systematic tendency as a result of nonsensory factors for an observer to favor responding in a particular way.

TABLE 4.1 Approximate Thresholds of Familiar Events	
Sense Modality	**Detection Threshold**
Light	A candle flame seen at 30 miles on a dark clear night
Sound	The tick of a watch under quiet conditions at 20 feet
Taste	One teaspoon of sugar in 2 gallons of water
Smell	One drop of perfume diffused into the entire volume of a three-room apartment
Touch	The wing of a bee falling on your cheek from a distance of 1 centimeter

If you decline a dinner invitation, will you be avoiding a dull evening (a correct rejection) or sacrificing the chance for a lifetime of love (a miss)?

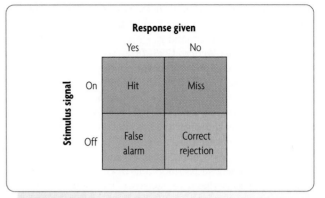

FIGURE 4.4 The Theory of Signal Detection
The matrix shows the possible outcomes when a subject is asked if a target stimulus occurred on a given trial.

must detect a weak light. In the first phase of the experiment, the researcher gives you $5 when you are correct in saying, "Yes, a light was there." In the second phase, the researcher gives you $5 when you are correct in saying, "No, there wasn't any light." In each phase, you are penalized $2 any time you are incorrect. Can you see how this reward structure would create a shift in response bias from phase 1 to phase 2? Wouldn't you say *yes* more often in the first phase—with the same amount of certainty that the stimulus was present?

Signal detection theory (SDT) is a systematic approach to the problem of response bias (Green & Swets, 1966). Instead of focusing strictly on sensory processes, SDT emphasizes the process of making a *judgment* about the presence or absence of stimulus events. Whereas classical psychophysics conceptualized a single absolute threshold, SDT identifies two distinct processes in sensory detection: (1) an initial *sensory process,* which reflects the observer's sensitivity to the strength of the stimulus; and (2) a subsequent separate *decision process,* which reflects the observer's response biases.

SDT offers a procedure for evaluating both the sensory process and the decision processes at once. The basic design is given in **Figure 4.4.** A weak stimulus is presented in half the trials; no stimulus is presented in the other half. In each trial, observers respond by saying *yes* if they think the signal was present and *no* if they think it wasn't. As shown in the figure, each response is scored in one of four ways:

- A response is a *hit* when the signal is present and the observer says "yes."
- A response is a *miss* when the signal is present and the observer says "no."
- A response is a *false alarm* when the signal is absent and the observer says "yes."
- A response is a *correct rejection* when the signal is absent and the observer says "no."

How can we see the impact of the perceivers' decision processes? If Carol is a yea-sayer (she chronically answers *yes*), she will almost inevitably say *yes* when the stimulus was present, so she'll have a large number of hits. However, she'll also

have a high number of false alarms because she'll also say *yes* quite often when the stimulus was absent. If Bob is a naysayer (he chronically answers *no*), he will give a lower number of hits but also a lower number of false alarms.

Working with the percentages of hits and false alarms, researchers use mathematical procedures to calculate separate measures of observers' sensitivity and response biases. This procedure makes it possible to find out whether two observers have the same sensitivity despite large differences in response criterion. By providing a way of separating sensory process from response bias, the theory of signal detection allows an experimenter to identify and separate the roles of the sensory stimulus and the individual's criterion level in producing the final response.

Difference Thresholds Imagine you have been employed by a beverage company that wants to produce a cola product that tastes noticeably sweeter than existing colas, but (to save money) the firm wants to put as little extra sugar in the cola as possible. You are being asked to measure a **difference threshold,** the smallest physical difference between two stimuli that can still be recognized as a difference. To measure a difference threshold, you use pairs of stimuli and ask your observers whether they believe the two stimuli to be the same or different.

For the beverage problem, you would give your observers two colas on each trial, one of some standard recipe and one just a bit sweeter. For each pair, the individual would say *same* or *different*. After many such trials, you would plot a psychometric function by graphing the percent of *different* responses on the vertical axis as a function of the actual differences, plotted on the horizontal axis. The difference threshold is operationally defined as *the point at which the stimuli are recognized as different half of the time.* This difference threshold value is known as a

---

signal detection theory A systematic approach to the problem of response bias that allows an experimenter to identify and separate the roles of sensory stimuli and the individual's criterion level in producing the final response.

difference threshold The smallest physical difference between two stimuli that can still be recognized as a difference; operationally defined as the point at which the stimuli are recognized as different half of the time.

just noticeable difference, or **JND.** The JND is a quantitative unit for measuring the magnitude of the psychological difference between any two sensations.

In 1834, **Ernst Weber** (1795–1878) pioneered the study of JNDs and discovered the important relationship that we illustrate in **Figure 4.5.** This relationship is summarized as **Weber's law:** *The JND between stimuli is a constant fraction of the intensity of the standard stimulus.* Thus, the bigger or more intense the standard stimulus, the larger the increment needed to get a just noticeable difference. The formula for Weber's law is $\Delta I/I = k$, where I is the intensity of the standard and ΔI, or delta I, is the size of the increase that produces a JND. Weber found that each stimulus dimension has a characteristic value for this ratio. In this formula, k is that ratio, or *Weber's constant,* for the particular stimulus dimension. Weber's law provides a good approximation, but not a perfect fit to experimental data, of how the size of JND increases with intensity (most problems with the law arise when stimulus intensities become extremely high).

You see in Table 4.2 that Weber's constant (k) has different values for different sensory dimensions—smaller values mean that people can detect smaller differences. So this table tells you that you can differentiate two sound frequencies more precisely than light intensities, which, in turn, are detectable with a smaller JND than odor or taste differences are. Your beverage company would need a relatively large amount of extra sugar to produce a noticeably sweeter cola!

FROM PHYSICAL EVENTS TO MENTAL EVENTS

Our review of psychophysics has made you aware of the central mystery of sensation: How do physical energies give rise to particular psychological experiences? How, for example, do the various physical wavelengths of light give rise to your experience of viewing a rainbow? Before we consider specific sensory domains, we will give you an overview of the flow of information from physical events—waves of light and sound, complex chemicals, and so on—to mental events—your experiences of sights, sounds, tastes, and smells.

The conversion of one form of physical energy, such as light, to another form, such as neural impulses, is called **transduction.** Because all sensory information is transduced, or converted, into identical types of neural impulses, your brain differentiates sensory experiences by devoting special areas of cortex to each sensory domain. For each domain, researchers try to discover how the transduction of physical energy into the electrochemical activity of the nervous system gives rise to sensations of different quality (red rather than green) and different quantity (loud rather than soft).

Sensory systems share the same basic flow of information. The trigger for any sensing system is the detection of an environmental event, or *stimulus.* Environmental stimuli are detected by specialized **sensory receptors.** Sensory receptors convert the physical form of the sensory signal into cellular

signals that can be processed by the nervous system. These cellular signals contribute information to higher-level neurons that integrate information across different detector units. At this stage, neurons extract information about the basic qualities of the stimulus, such as its size, intensity, shape, and distance. Deeper into the sensory systems, information is combined into even more complex codes that are passed on to specific areas of the sensory and association cortex of the brain.

We move now to specific sensory domains.

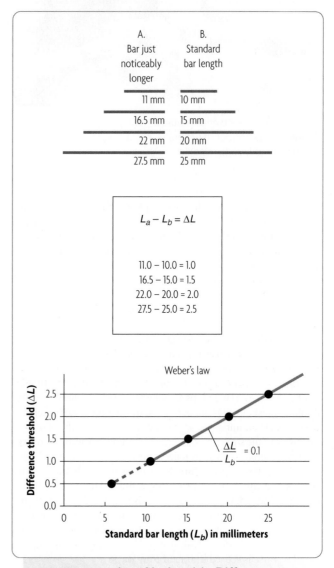

FIGURE 4.5   Just Noticeable Differences and Weber's Law

Suppose you are conducting an experiment in which you challenge participants to detect whether two bars are the same or different in length. The longer the standard bar, the greater the amount you must add (ΔL) to see a just noticeable difference. The difference threshold is the added length detected on half the trials. When these increments are plotted against standard bars of increasing length, the proportions stay the same—the amount added is always one tenth of the standard length. The relationship is linear, producing a straight line on the graph. We can predict that the ΔL for a bar length of 5 will be 0.5.

---

just noticeable difference (JND) The smallest difference between two sensations that allows them to be discriminated.

Weber's law An assertion that the size of a difference threshold is proportional to the intensity of the standard stimulus.

transduction Transformation of one form of energy into another; for example, light is transformed into neutral impulses.

sensory receptor Specialized cell that converts physical signals into cellular signals that are processed by the nervous system.

TABLE 4.2 Weber's Constant Values for Selected Stimulus Dimensions

Stimulus Dimension	Weber's Constant (k)
Sound frequency	0.003
Light intensity	0.01
Odor concentration	0.07
Pressure intensity	0.14
Sound intensity	0.15
Taste concentration	0.20

From Atkinson/Atkinson/Smith/Bern. *Introduction to Psychology*, 10e. © 1989 Wadsworth, a part of Cengage Learning, Inc. Reproduced by permission. www.cengage.com/permissions

STOP AND REVIEW

❶ What is the proximal stimulus?
❷ What is the subject matter of psychophysics?
❸ What is the operational definition of an absolute threshold?
❹ In signal detection theory, what two processes contribute to observers' judgments?
❺ What is a difference threshold?
❻ What is transduction?

Visit MyPsychLab.com for more review and practice on the following topic:

✳ **Simulate:** Weber's Law

The Visual System

Vision is the most complex, highly developed, and important sense for humans and most other mobile creatures. Animals with good vision have an enormous evolutionary advantage. Good vision helps animals detect their prey or predators from a distance. Vision enables humans to be aware of changing features in the physical environment and to adapt their behavior accordingly. Vision is also the most studied of all the senses.

THE HUMAN EYE

The eye is the camera for the brain's motion pictures of the world (see **Figure 4.6**). A camera views the world through a lens that gathers and focuses light. The eye also gathers and focuses light—light enters the *cornea*, a transparent bulge on the front of the eye. Next it passes through the *anterior chamber*, which is filled with a clear liquid called the *aqueous humor*. The light then passes through the *pupil*, an opening in the opaque *iris*. To focus a camera, you move its lens closer to or farther from the object viewed. To focus light in the eye, a bean-shaped crystalline *lens*

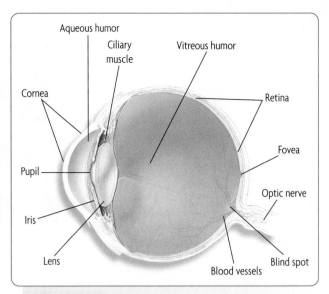

FIGURE 4.6 **Structure of the Human Eye**
The cornea, pupil, and lens focus light onto the retina. Nerve signals from the retina are carried to the brain by the optic nerve.

changes its shape, thinning to focus on distant objects and thickening to focus on near ones. To control the amount of light coming into a camera, you vary the opening of the lens. In the eye, the muscular disk of the iris changes the size of the pupil, the opening through which light passes into the eyeball. At the back of a traditional camera body is the photosensitive film that records the variations in light that have come through the lens. Similarly, in the eye, light travels through the *vitreous humor*, finally striking the *retina*, a thin sheet that lines the rear wall of the eyeball.

As you can see, the features of a camera and the eye are very similar. Now let's examine the components of the vision process in more detail.

THE PUPIL AND THE LENS

The **pupil** is the opening in the iris through which light passes. The iris makes the pupil dilate or constrict to control the amount of light entering the eyeball. Light passing through the pupil is focused by the **lens** on the retina; the lens reverses and inverts the light pattern as it does so. The lens is particularly important because of its variable focusing ability for near and far objects. The ciliary muscles can change the thickness of the lens and hence its optical properties in a process called **accommodation.**

People with normal accommodation have a range of focus from about 3 inches in front of their nose to as far as they can see. However, many people suffer from accommodation problems. For example, people who are nearsighted have their range of accommodation shifted closer to them with the consequence that they cannot focus well on distant objects; those who are farsighted have their range of accommodation shifted farther

---

pupil The opening at the front of the eye through which light passes.

lens The flexible tissue that focuses light on the retina.

accommodation The process by which the ciliary muscles change the thickness of the lens of the eye to permit variable focusing on near and distant objects.

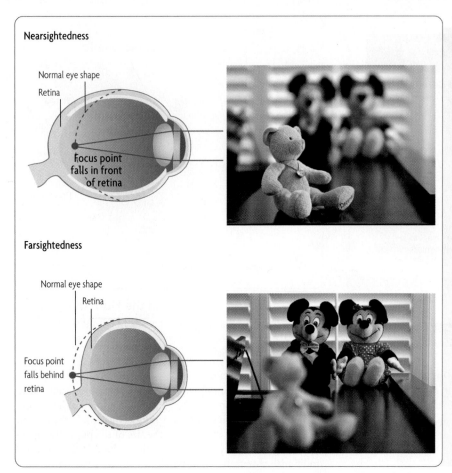

Nearsightedness

Normal eye shape

Retina

Focus point
falls in front
of retina

Farsightedness

Normal eye shape

Retina

Focus point
falls behind
retina

FIGURE 4.7
Nearsightedness and Farsightedness

People experience nearsightedness when light from distant objects focuses in front of the retina. They experience farsightedness when light from near objects focuses behind the retina. The photos suggest how the world might appear to nearsighted and farsighted people if their vision remained uncorrected by glasses or contact lenses.

From Weiten, *Psychology*, 7e. © 2007 Wadsworth, a part of Cengage Learning, Inc. Reproduced by permission. www.cengage.com/permissions

away from them so that they cannot focus normally on nearby objects (see **Figure 4.7**). Aging also leads to problems in accommodation. The lens starts off as clear, transparent, and convex. As people age, however, the lens becomes more amber tinted, opaque, and flattened, and it loses its elasticity. The effect of some of these changes is that the lens cannot become thick enough for close vision. When people age past the 45-year mark, the *near point*—the closest point at which they can focus clearly—gets progressively farther away.

THE RETINA

You look with your eyes but see with your brain. The eye gathers light, focuses it, and starts a neural signal on its way

toward the brain. The eye's critical function, therefore, is to convert information about the world from light waves into neural signals. This happens in the **retina,** at the back of the eye. Under the microscope, you can see that the retina has several highly organized layers of different types of neurons.

The basic conversion from light energy to neural responses is performed in your retina by *rods* and *cones*—receptor cells sensitive to light. These **photoreceptors** are uniquely placed in the visual system between the outer world, ablaze with light, and the inner world of neural processing. Because you sometimes operate in near darkness and sometimes in bright light, nature has provided two ways of processing light, rods and cones (see **Figure 4.8**). The 120 million thin **rods** operate best in near darkness. The 7 million fat **cones** are specialized for the bright, color-filled day.

You experience differences between the functions of your rods and cones each time you turn off the lights to go to sleep at night. You have noticed many times that at first it seems as though you can't see much of anything in the dim light that remains, but over time your visual sensitivity improves again. You are undergoing the process of **dark adaptation**—the gradual improvement of the eyes' sensitivity after a shift in illumination from light to near darkness. Dark adaptation occurs because, as time passes in the dark, your rods become more sensitive than your cones; over time, your rods are able to respond to less light from the environment than your cones are.

retina The layer at the back of the eye that contains photoreceptors and converts light energy to neutral responses.

photoreceptor Receptor cell in the retina that is sensitive to light.

rod One of the photoreceptors concentrated in the periphery of the retina that are most active in dim illumination; rods do not produce sensation of color.

cone One of the photoreceptors concentrated in the center of the retina that are responsible for visual experience under normal viewing conditions for all experiences of color.

dark adaptation The gradual improvement of the eyes' sensitivity after a shift in illumination from light to near darkness.

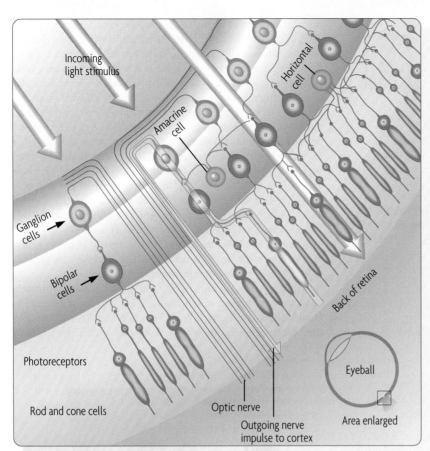

FIGURE 4.8 Retinal Pathways
This is a stylized and greatly simplified diagram showing the pathways that connect three of the layers of nerve cells in the retina. Incoming light passes through all these layers to reach the receptors, at the back of the eyeball, which are pointed away from the source of light. Note that the bipolar cells gather impulses from more than one receptor cell and send the results to ganglion cells. Nerve impulses (blue arrow) from the ganglion cells leave the eye via the optic nerve and travel to the next relay point.

Near the center of the retina is a small region called the **fovea,** which contains nothing but densely packed cones—it is rod free. The fovea is the area of your sharpest vision—both color and spatial detail are most accurately detected there. Other cells in your retina are responsible for integrating information across regions of rods and cones. The **bipolar cells** are nerve cells that combine impulses from many receptors and send the results to ganglion cells. Each **ganglion cell** then integrates the impulses from one or more bipolar cells into a single firing rate. The cones in the central fovea send their impulses to the ganglion cells in that region while, farther out on the periphery of the retina, rods and cones converge on the same bipolar and ganglion cells. The axons of the ganglion cells make up the optic nerve, which carries this visual information out of the eye and back toward the brain.

Your **horizontal cells** and **amacrine cells** integrate information across the retina. Rather than send signals toward the brain, horizontal cells connect receptors to each other, and amacrine cells link bipolar cells to other bipolar cells and ganglion cells to other ganglion cells.

An interesting curiosity in the anatomical design of the retina exists where the optic nerve leaves each eye. This region, called the optic disk, or **blind spot,** contains no receptor cells at all. You do not experience blindness there, except under very special circumstances, for two reasons: First, the blind spots of the two eyes are positioned so that receptors in each eye register what is missed in the other; second, the brain fills in this region with appropriate sensory information from the surrounding area.

To find your blind spot, you will have to look at **Figure 4.9** on page 100 under special viewing conditions. Hold this book at arm's length, close your right eye, and fixate on the bank figure with your left eye as you bring the book slowly closer. When the dollar sign is in your blind spot, it will disappear, but you will experience no gaping hole in your visual field. Instead, your visual system fills in this area with the background whiteness of the surrounding area so you "see" the whiteness, which isn't there, while failing to see your money, which you should have put in the bank before you lost it!

For a second demonstration of your blind spot, use the same procedure to focus on the plus sign in Figure 4.9. As you pull the book closer to you, do you see the gap disappear and the line become whole?

---

fovea Area of the retina that contains densely packed cones and forms the point of sharpest vision.

bipolar cell Nerve cell in the visual system that combines impulses from many receptors and transmits the results to ganglion cells.

ganglion cell Cell in the visual system that integrates impulses from many bipolar cells in a single firing rate.

horizontal cell One of the cells that integrate information across the retina; rather than sending signals toward the brain, horizontal cells connect receptors to each other.

amacrine cell One of the cells that integrate information across the retina; rather than sending signals toward the brain, amacrine cells link bipolar cells to other bipolar cells and ganglion cells to other ganglion cells.

blind spot The region of the retina where the optic nerve leaves the back of the eye; no receptors cells are present in this region.

FIGURE 4.9 Find Your Blind Spot
To find your blind spot, hold this book at arm's length, close your right eye, and fixate on the bank figure with your left eye as you bring the book slowly closer. When the dollar sign is in your blind spot, it will disappear, but you will experience no gaping hole in your visual field. Similarly, if you use the same procedure to focus on the plus sign, the line will appear whole when the gap is in your blind spot. In both cases, your visual system fills in the background whiteness of the surrounding area so you "see" the whiteness, which isn't there.

PROCESSES IN THE BRAIN

The ultimate destination of much visual information is the part of the occipital lobe of the brain known as primary *visual cortex*. However, most information leaving the retinas passes through other brain regions before it arrives at the visual cortex. Let's trace the pathways visual information takes.

The million axons of the ganglion cells that form each **optic nerve** come together in the *optic chiasma*, which resembles the Greek letter χ (*chi*, pronounced *kye*). The axons in each optic nerve are divided into two bundles at the optic chiasma. Half of the fibers from each retina remain on the side of the body from which they originated. The axons from the inner half of each eye cross over the midline as they continue their journey toward the back of the brain (see **Figure 4.10**).

These two bundles of fibers, which now contain axons from both eyes, are renamed *optic tracts*. The optic tracts deliver information to two clusters of cells in the brain. Research supports the theory that visual analysis is largely separated into pathways for *pattern recognition*—how things look—and *place recognition*—where things are (Konen & Kastner, 2008). The division into pattern and place recognition gives you an example of the way in which your visual system consists of several separate subsystems that analyze different aspects of the same retinal image. Although your final perception is of a unified visual scene, your vision of it is accomplished through a host of pathways in your visual system that, under normal conditions, are exquisitely coordinated.

Researchers obtain valuable information about visual processing when this exquisite coordination breaks down. Brain damage can affect either the pattern or place pathways—or communication between the pathways—to yield several different

disorders known as *agnosias*. People who experience an agnosia generally have difficulty recognizing or identifying objects or people. For example, a patient known as K.E. suffered a stroke that produced the specific condition known as *simultanagnosia* (Coslett & Lie, 2008). People with this disorder have difficulty experiencing more than one feature of the visual world simultaneously. For example, K.E. was asked to view color words (e.g., the word *red*) written in different color inks (e.g., *red* would be printed in blue ink). When the researchers asked K.E. to name the color word, he was correct on 47 out of 48 trials. However, when they asked him to name the color of the ink, K.E. was always wrong. In fact, he "explicitly stated that he did not see a color" (p. 41). Note that K.E.'s color vision was perfectly normal. When he was asked to identify the color of color patches, he was 100 percent correct. What K.E., apparently, couldn't do was to experience two attributes of the same perceptual object (e.g., the meaning of a word and the color in which it was written) simultaneously in the same spatial location.

Sensory information from the visual world ultimately arrives at the brain's visual cortex. The sensory physiologists **David Hubel** and **Torsten Wiesel** won a Nobel Prize in 1981 for their pioneering studies of *receptive fields* of cells in the visual

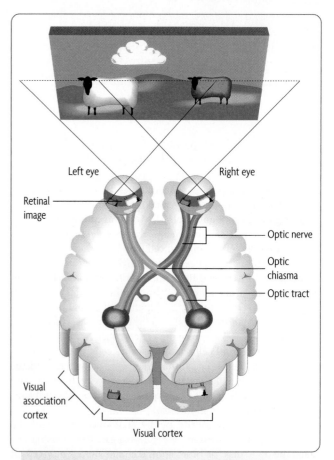

FIGURE 4.10 Pathways in the Human Visual System
The diagram shows the way light from the visual field projects onto the two retinas and the routes by which neural messages from the retina are sent to the two visual centers of each hemisphere.

---

optic nerve The axons of the ganglion cells that carry information from the eye toward the brain.

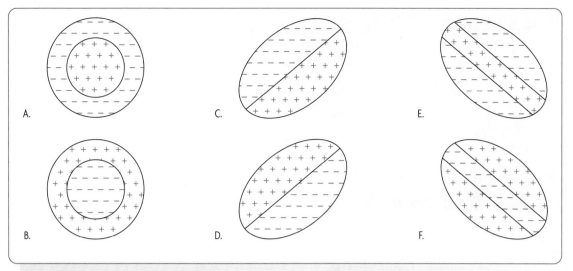

FIGURE 4.11 Receptive Fields of Ganglion and Cortical Cells
The receptive field of a cell in the visual pathway is the area in the visual field from which it receives stimulation. The receptive fields of the ganglion cells in the retina are circular (A, B); those of the simplest cells in the visual cortex are elongated in a particular orientation (C, D, E, F). In both cases, the cell responding to the receptive field is excited by light in the regions marked with plus signs and inhibited by light in the regions marked with minus signs. In addition, the stimulus that most excites the cell is the one in which areas where light is excitatory (marked with plus signs) are illuminated, but areas where light is inhibitory (marked by minus signs) are in darkness.

cortex. The **receptive field** of a cell is the area in the visual field from which it receives stimulation. As shown in **Figure 4.11,** Hubel and Wiesel discovered that cells at different levels of the visual system responded most strongly to different patterns of stimulation. For example, one type of cortical cell, *simple* cells, responded most strongly to bars of light in their "favorite" orientation (see **Figure 4.11**). *Complex* cells also each have a "favorite" orientation, but they require as well that the bar be moving. *Hypercomplex* cells require moving bars of a particular length or moving corners or angles. The cells provide types of information to higher visual centers in the brain that ultimately allow the brain to recognize objects in the visual world.

The advances in imaging techniques we described in Chapter 3 have enabled researchers to discover regions of the cortex that are specially responsive to even more complex environmental images.

Take a moment to look at your hand. Now focus on any other object in the room. If a team of researchers is correct, one particular region of your brain just turned on and off as you shifted your focus from your hand—a body part—to an object from a different category (Downing et al., 2006). To test this hypothesis, the researchers collected fMRI data while participants viewed color pictures of objects from 20 categories, including human faces, human bodies, insects, birds, tools, weapons, clothes, and chairs. The fMRI images demonstrated that specific brain regions were selectively active for different categories. **Figure 4.12,** on page 102, shows, for example, that some brain regions were more active for animate stimuli (such as faces, bodies, insects, and birds) whereas other regions were more active for inanimate stimuli (such as tools, weapons, clothes, and chairs).

Given these brain responses, you might wonder whether these regions have special functions at birth or if those functions are the product of a lifetime of experience. Researchers have begun to undertake projects to sort out the balance of nature and nurture that leads to these brain responses (Baker et al., 2007; McKone et al., 2007).

You have now learned the basics of how visual information is distributed from the eyes to various parts of the brain. Researchers still have more to learn: There are roughly 30 anatomical subdivisions of primate visual cortex, and theories vary about the pattern of communication among those areas (Orban et al., 2004). For now, we turn to particular aspects of the visual world. One of the most remarkable features of the human visual system is that your experiences of form, color, position, and depth are based on processing the same sensory information in different ways. How do the transformations occur that enable you to see these different features of the visual world?

SEEING COLOR

Physical objects seem to have the marvelous property of being painted with color. You most often have the impression of brightly colored objects—red valentines, green fir trees, or blue robins' eggs—but your vivid experience of color relies on the rays of light these objects reflect onto your sensory receptors. Color is created when your brain processes the information coded in the light source.

Wavelengths and Hues The light you see is just a small portion of a physical dimension called the *electromagnetic*

receptive field The area of the visual field to which a neuron in the visual system responds.

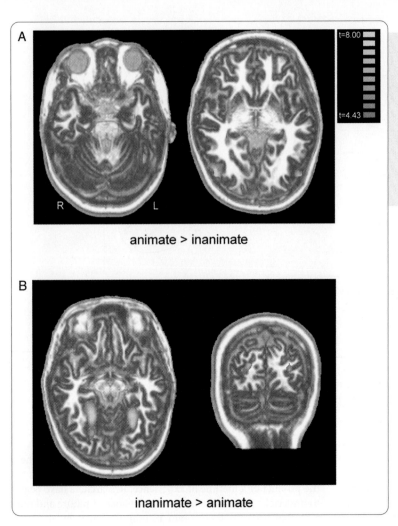

A

t=8.00

t=4.43

R   L

animate > inanimate

B

inanimate > animate

FIGURE 4.12   Brain Regions That Respond to Animate and Inanimate Objects

Researchers used fMRI to assess participants' brain responses to objects from 20 different categories. The fMRI data identified regions in which responses were relatively higher to animate objects (A) and other regions in which responses were relatively higher to inanimate objects (B).

spectrum (see **Figure 4.13**). Your visual system is not equipped to detect other types of waves in this spectrum, such as X-rays, microwaves, and radio waves. The physical property that distinguishes types of electromagnetic energy, including light, is *wavelength,* the distance between the crests of two adjacent waves. Wavelengths of visible light are measured in *nanometers* (billionths of a meter). What you see as light is the range of wavelengths from 400 to about 700 nanometers. Light rays of particular physical wavelengths give rise to experiences of particular colors—for example, violet–blue at the lower end and red–orange at the higher end. Thus light is described physically in terms of wavelengths, not colors; colors exist only in your sensory system's interpretation of the wavelengths.

All experiences of color can be described in terms of three basic dimensions: hue, saturation, and brightness. **Hue** is the dimension that captures the color of a light: red, blue, green, and so on. Hue is largely determined by the wavelength of the light. As shown in **Figure 4.14,** hues can be arranged in a circle. The hues people perceive to be most similar are in adjacent positions. **Saturation** is the dimension that captures the purity of color sensations. Undiluted colors have the most saturation; muted, muddy, and pastel colors have intermediate amounts of saturation; and grays have zero saturation. **Brightness** is the dimension that captures the intensity of a color. White has the most brightness; black has the least. When colors are analyzed along these three dimensions, a remarkable finding emerges: Humans are capable of visually discriminating about 7 million different colors! However, most people can label only a small number of those colors.

Let's explain some facts about your everyday experience of color. At some point in your science education, you may have repeated Sir Isaac Newton's discovery that sunlight combines all wavelengths of light: You repeated Newton's proof by using a prism to separate sunlight into the full rainbow of colors. The prism shows that the right combination of wavelengths yields white light. The combination of wavelengths is called *additive color mixture.* Take another look at Figure 4.14. Wavelengths that appear directly across from each other on the color circle—called **complementary colors**—will create the sensation of

---

hue The dimension of color space that captures the qualitative experience of the color of light.

saturation The dimension of color space that captures the purity and vividness of color sensations.

brightness The dimension of color space that captures the intensity of light.

complementary colors Colors opposite each other on the color circle; when additively mixed, they create the sensation of white light.

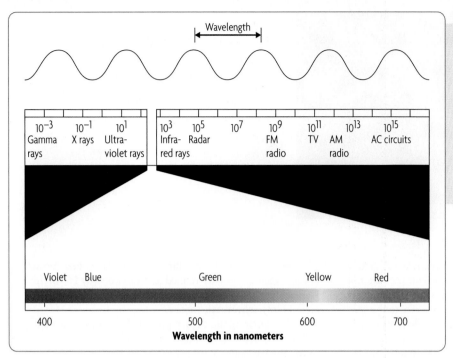

FIGURE 4.13 The Electro-magnetic Spectrum

Your visual system can sense only a small range of wavelengths in the electromagnetic spectrum. You experience that range of wavelengths, which is enlarged in the figure, as the colors violet through red.

Reprinted with permission from R. Sekular & Blake, *Perception*, 3rd ed., pp. 27, 221. Copyright © 1994 by The McGraw-Hill Companies, Inc.

white light when mixed. Do you want to prove to yourself the existence of complementary colors? Consider **Figure 4.15** on page 104. The green–yellow–black flag should give you the experience of a *negative afterimage* (the afterimage is called "negative" because it is the opposite of the original color). For reasons that we will explain when we consider theories of color vision, when you stare at any color long enough to partially fatigue your photoreceptors, looking at a white surface will allow you to experience the complement of the original color.

You have probably noticed afterimages from time to time in your everyday exposure to colors. Most of your experience with colors, however, does not come from complementary lights. Instead, you have probably spent your time at play with colors by combining crayons or paints of different hues.

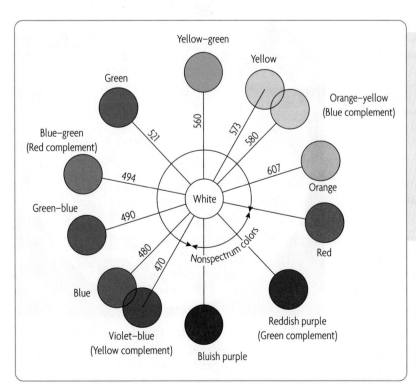

FIGURE 4.14 The Color Circle

Colors are arranged based on similarity. Complementary colors are placed directly opposite each other. Mixing complementary colors yields a neutral gray or white light at the center. The numbers next to each hue are the wavelength values for spectral colors, those colors within the regions of visual sensitivity. Nonspectral hues are obtained by mixing short and long spectral wavelengths.

Reprinted with permission from R. Sekular & Blake, *Perception,* 3rd ed., pp. 27, 221. Copyright 1994 by The McGraw-Hill Companies, Inc.

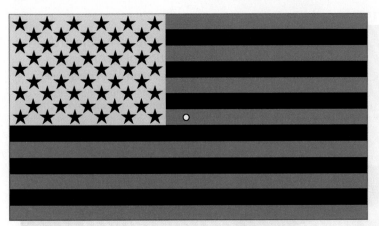

FIGURE 4.15   Color Afterimages
Stare at the dot in the center of the green, black, and yellow flag for at least 30 seconds. Then fixate on the center of a sheet of white paper or a blank wall. Try this aftereffect illusion on your friends.

The colors you see when you look at a crayon mark, or any other colored surface, are the wavelengths of light that are not absorbed by the surface. Although yellow crayon looks mostly yellow, it lets some wavelengths escape that give rise to the sensation of green. Similarly, blue crayon lets wavelengths escape that give rise to the sensations of blue and some green. When yellow and blue crayon are combined, yellow absorbs blue and blue absorbs yellow—the only wavelengths that are not absorbed look green! This phenomenon is called *subtractive color mixture.* The remaining wavelengths that are not absorbed—the wavelengths that are reflected—give the crayon mixture the color you perceive.

Some of these rules about the experience of color do not apply to those people born with a color deficiency. *Color blindness* is the partial or total inability to distinguish colors. The negative afterimage effect of viewing the green, yellow, and black flag will not work if you are color blind. Color blindness is usually a sex-linked hereditary defect associated with a gene on the X chromosome. Because males have a single X chromosome, they are more likely than females to show this recessive trait. Females would need to have a defective gene on both X chromosomes to be color blind. An estimate for color blindness among white males is about 8 percent, but less than .5 percent among females (Coren et al., 1999).

Most color blindness involves difficulty distinguishing red from green, especially at weak saturations. Color blindness of those who confuse yellows and blues is rarer. Rarest of all are those who see no color at all, only variations in brightness. **Figure 4.16** provides an example of the figures researchers use to test for color blindness. Individuals who have appropriate deficiencies in their red–green system will not see the number. Let's see next how scientists have explained facts about color vision such as complementary colors and color blindness.

Theories of Color Vision The first scientific theory of color vision was proposed by **Sir Thomas Young** (1773–1829) around 1800. He suggested that there were three types of color receptors in the normal human eye that produced psychologically primary sensations: red, green, and blue. All other colors, he believed, were additive or subtractive combinations of these three primaries. Young's theory was later refined and extended by **Hermann von Helmholtz** (1821–1894) and came to be known as the Young-Helmholtz **trichromatic theory.**

The trichromatic theory provided a plausible explanation for people's color sensations and for color blindness (according to the theory, color-blind people had only one or two kinds of receptors). However, other facts and observations were not as well explained by the theory. Why did adaptation to one color produce color afterimages that had the complementary hue? Why did color-blind people always fail to distinguish pairs of colors: red and green or blue and yellow?

Answers to these questions became the cornerstones for a second theory of color vision proposed by **Ewald Hering** (1834–1918) in the late 1800s. According to his **opponent-process theory,** all color experiences arise from three

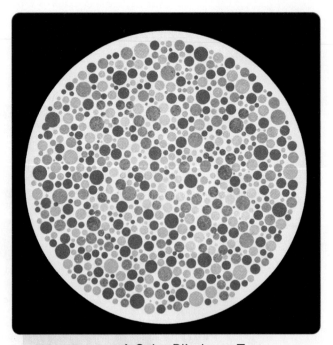

FIGURE 4.16   A Color Blindness Test
Individuals who cannot see a number in this display are unable to discriminate red and green.

---

trichromatic theory The theory that there are three types of color receptors that produce the primary color sensations of red, green, and blue.

opponent-process theory The theory that all color experiences arise from three systems, each of which includes two "opponent" elements (red versus green, blue versus yellow, and black versus white).

underlying systems, each of which includes two opponent elements: red versus green, blue versus yellow, or black (no color) versus white (all colors). Hering theorized that colors produced complementary afterimages because one element of the system became fatigued (from overstimulation) and thus increased the relative contribution of its opponent element. Acccording to Hering's theory, types of color blindness came in pairs because the color system was actually built from pairs of opposites, not from single primary colors.

For many years, scientists debated the merits of the theories. Eventually, scientists recognized that the theories were not really in conflict; they simply described two different stages of processing that corresponded to successive physiological structures in the visual system (Hurvich & Jameson, 1974). We now know, for example, that there are, indeed, three types of cones. Although the three types each respond to a range of wavelengths, they are each *most* sensitive to light at a particular wavelength. The responses of these cone types confirm Young and Helmholtz's prediction that color vision relies on three types of color receptors. People who are color blind lack one or more of these types of receptor cones.

We also now know that the retinal ganglion cells combine the outputs of these three cone types in accordance with Hering's opponent-process theory (De Valois & Jacobs, 1968). According to the contemporary version of opponent-process theory, as supported by **Leo Hurvich** and **Dorothea Jameson** (1974), the two members of each color pair work in opposition (are opponents) by means of neural inhibition. Some ganglion cells receive excitatory input from lights that appear red and inhibitory input from lights that appear green. Other cells in the system have the opposite arrangement of excitation and inhibition. Together, these two types of ganglion cells form the physiological basis of the red/green opponent-process system. Other ganglion cells make up the blue/yellow opponent system. The black/white system contributes to your perception of color saturation and brightness.

We turn now from the world of sight to the world of sound.

STOP AND REVIEW

❶ In the visual system, what is meant by accommodation?

❷ What percentages of rods and cones are found in the fovea?

❸ What patterns of stimulation cause complex cells to respond?

❹ Which theory of color vision explains why you experience a blue afterimage after staring at a patch of yellow?

CRITICAL THINKING Recall the study that contrasted brain responses to objects from animate and inanimate categories. Why was it important to have objects within each category that were not visually similar (such as weapons and chairs)?

Visit MyPsychLab.com for more review and practice on the following topics:

◄●) **Explore:** Light and the Optic Nerve

◄●) **Explore:** Normal Vision, Nearsightedness

◄●) **Explore:** Receptive Fields

Hearing

Hearing and vision play complementary functions in your experience of the world. You often hear stimuli before you see them, particularly if they take place behind you or on the other side of opaque objects such as walls. Although vision is better than hearing for identifying an object once it is in the field of view, you often see the object only because you have used your ears to point your eyes in the right direction. To begin our discussion of hearing, we describe the types of physical energy that arrive at your ears.

THE PHYSICS OF SOUND

Clap your hands. Whistle. Tap your pencil on the table. Why do these actions create sounds? The reason is that they cause objects to vibrate. The vibrational energy is transmitted to the surrounding medium—usually air—as the vibrating objects push molecules of the medium back and forth. The resulting slight changes in pressure spread outward from the vibrating objects in the form of a combination of *sine waves* traveling at a rate of about 1,100 feet per second (see **Figure 4.17**). Sound cannot be created in a true vacuum (such as outer space) because there are no air molecules in a vacuum for vibrating objects to move.

A sine wave has two basic physical properties that determine how it sounds to you: frequency and amplitude. *Frequency* measures the number of cycles the wave completes in a given amount of time. A cycle, as indicated in Figure 4.17, is the left-to-right distance from the peak in one wave to the peak in the next wave. Sound frequency is usually expressed in *hertz* (Hz), which measures cycles per second. *Amplitude* measures the physical property of strength of the sound wave, as shown in its peak-to-valley height. Amplitude is defined in units of sound pressure or energy.

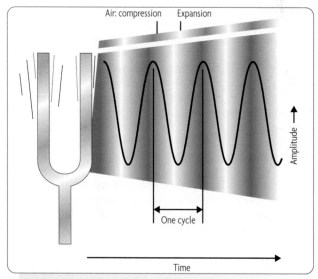

FIGURE 4.17   An Idealized Sine Wave
The two basic properties of sine waves are their *frequency*—the number of cycles in a fixed unit of time—and their *amplitude*—the vertical range of their cycles.

What physical properties of sounds allow you to pick out the timbres of individual instruments from a musical ensemble?

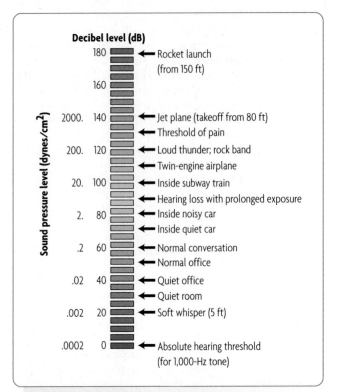

FIGURE 4.18 Decibel Levels of Familiar Sounds

This figure shows the range in decibels of the sounds to which you respond from the absolute threshold for hearing to the noise of a rocket launch. Decibels are calculated from sound pressure, which is a measure of a sound wave's amplitude level and generally corresponds to what you experience as loudness.

PSYCHOLOGICAL DIMENSIONS OF SOUND

The physical properties of frequency and amplitude give rise to the three psychological dimensions of sound: pitch, loudness, and timbre. Let's see how these phenomena work.

Pitch **Pitch** is the highness or lowness of a sound determined by the sound's frequency; high frequencies produce high pitch, and low frequencies produce low pitch. The full range of human sensitivity to pure tones extends from frequencies as low as 20 Hz to frequencies as high as 20,000 Hz. (Frequencies below 20 Hz may be experienced through touch as vibrations rather than as sound.) You can get a sense of how big this range is by noting that the 88 keys on a piano cover only the range from about 30 to 4,000 Hz.

As you might expect from our earlier discussion of psychophysics, the relationship between frequency (the physical reality) and pitch (the psychological effect) is not a linear one. At the low end of the frequency scale, increasing the frequency by just a few hertz raises the pitch quite noticeably. At the high end of frequency, you require a much bigger increase in order to hear the difference in pitch. For example, the two lowest notes on a piano differ by only 1.6 Hz, whereas the two highest ones differ by 235 Hz. This is another example of the psychophysics of just noticeable differences.

Loudness The **loudness,** or physical intensity, of a sound is determined by its amplitude; sound waves with large amplitudes are experienced as loud and those with small amplitudes as soft. The human auditory system is sensitive to an enormous range of physical intensities. At one limit, you can hear the tick of a wristwatch at 20 feet. This is the system's absolute threshold—if it were more sensitive, you would hear the blood flowing in your ears. At the other extreme, a jetliner taking off 100 yards away is so loud that the sound is painful. In terms of physical units of sound pressure, the jet produces a sound wave with more than a billion times the energy of the ticking watch.

Because the range of hearing is so great, physical intensities of sound are usually expressed in ratios rather than absolute amounts; sound pressure—the index of amplitude level that gives rise to the experience of loudness—is measured in units called decibels (dB). **Figure 4.18** shows the decibel measures of some representative natural sounds. It also shows the corresponding sound pressures for comparison. You can see that two sounds differing by 20 dB have sound pressures in a ratio of 10 to 1. Note that sounds louder than about 90 dB can produce hearing loss, depending on how long a person is exposed to them.

Timbre The **timbre** of a sound reflects the components of its complex sound wave. Timbre is what sets apart, for example, the sound of a piano from the sound of a flute. A small number of physical stimuli, such as a tuning fork, produce pure tones consisting of a single sine wave. A *pure tone* has only one

---

pitch Sound quality of highness or lowness; primarily dependent on the frequency of the sound wave.

loudness A perceptual dimension of sound influenced by the amplitude of a sound wave; sound waves in large amplitudes are generally experienced as loud and those with small amplitudes as soft.

timbre The dimension of auditory sensation that reflects the complexity of a sound wave.

frequency and one amplitude. Most sounds in the real world are not pure tones. They are complex waves, containing a combination of frequencies and amplitudes.

The sounds that you call *noise* do not have the clear simple structures of frequencies. Noise contains many frequencies that are not systematically related. For instance, the static noise you hear between radio stations contains energy at all audible frequencies; you perceive it as having no pitch because it has no fundamental frequency.

THE PHYSIOLOGY OF HEARING

Now that you know something about the physical bases of your psychological experiences of sound, let's see how those experiences arise from physiological activity in the auditory system. First, we will look at the way the ear works. Then we will consider some theories about how pitch experiences are coded in the auditory system and how sounds are localized.

The Auditory System You have already learned that sensory processes transform forms of external energy into forms of energy within your brain. For you to hear, as shown in **Figure 4.19**, four basic energy transformations must take place: (1) Airborne sound waves must get translated into *fluid* waves within the *cochlea* of the ear, (2) the fluid waves must then stimulate mechanical vibrations of the *basilar membrane*, (3) these vibrations must be converted into electrical impulses, and (4) the impulses must travel to the *auditory cortex*. Let's examine each of these transformations in detail.

In the first transformation, vibrating air molecules enter the ears (see Figure 4.19). Some sound enters the external

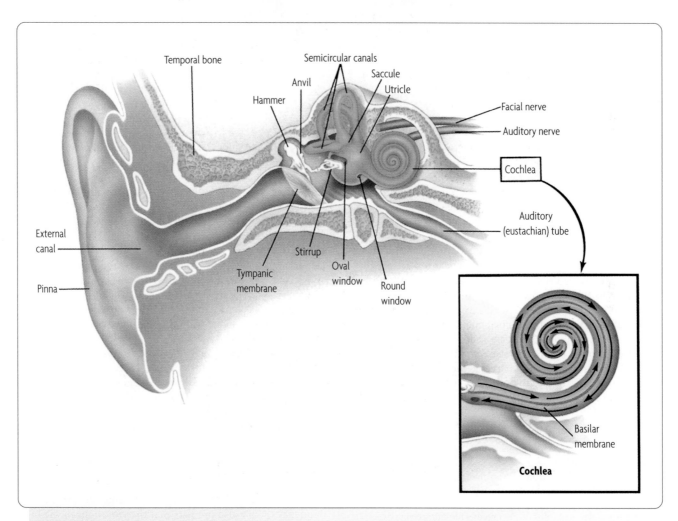

FIGURE 4.19   Structure of the Human Ear

Sound waves are channeled by the external ear, or pinna, through the external canal, causing the tympanic membrane to vibrate. This vibration activates the tiny bones of the inner ear—the hammer, anvil, and stirrup. Their mechanical vibrations are passed along from the oval window to the cochlea, where they set in motion the fluid in its canal. Tiny hair cells lining the coiled basilar membrane within the cochlea bend as the fluid moves, stimulating nerve endings attached to them. The mechanical energy is then transformed into neural energy and sent to the brain via the auditory nerve.

canal of the ear directly, and some enters after having been reflected off the *external ear,* or *pinna.* The sound wave travels along the canal through the outer ear until it reaches the end of the canal. There it encounters a thin membrane called the eardrum, or *tympanic membrane.* The sound wave's pressure variations set the eardrum into motion. The eardrum transmits the vibrations from the outer ear into the middle ear, a chamber that contains the three smallest bones in the human body: the *hammer,* the *anvil,* and the *stirrup.* These bones form a mechanical chain that transmits and concentrates the vibrations from the eardrum to the primary organ of hearing, the *cochlea,* which is located in the *inner ear.*

In the second transformation, which occurs in the cochlea, the airborne sound wave becomes "seaborne." The **cochlea** is a fluid-filled coiled tube that has a membrane, known as the **basilar membrane,** running down its middle along its length. When the stirrup vibrates against the oval window at the base of the cochlea, the fluid in the cochlea causes the basilar membrane to move in a wavelike motion (hence "seaborne"). Researchers speculate that the cochlea's distinctive spiral shape provides greater sensitivity to low-frequency sounds than would be possible without the spiral (Manoussaki et al., 2006).

In the third transformation, the wavelike motion of the basilar membrane bends the tiny hair cells connected to the membrane. The hair cells are the receptor cells for the auditory system. As the hair cells bend, they stimulate nerve endings, transforming the mechanical vibrations of the basilar membrane into neural activity.

Finally, in the fourth transformation, nerve impulses leave the cochlea in a bundle of fibers called the **auditory nerve.** These fibers meet in the *cochlear nucleus* of the brain stem. Similar to the crossing over of nerves in the visual system, stimulation from one ear goes to both sides of the brain. Auditory

Sustained exposure to loud noise can lead to hearing loss. What can people do to avoid such losses?

signals pass through a series of other nuclei on their way to the *auditory cortex,* in the temporal lobes of the cerebral hemispheres. Higher-order processing of these signals begins in the auditory cortex. (As you will learn shortly, other parts of the ear labeled in Figure 4.19 play roles in your other senses.)

The four transformations occur in fully functioning auditory systems. However, millions of people suffer from some form of hearing impairment. The two general types of hearing impairment are each caused by a defect in one or more of the components of the auditory system. The less serious type of impairment is *conduction deafness,* a problem in the conduction of the air vibrations to the cochlea. Often in this type of impairment, the bones in the middle ear are not functioning properly, a problem that may be corrected in microsurgery by insertion of an artificial anvil or stirrup. The more serious type of impairment is *nerve deafness,* a defect in the neural mechanisms that create nerve impulses in the ear or relay them to the auditory cortex. Damage to the auditory cortex can also create nerve deafness.

Theories of Pitch Perception To explain how the auditory system converts sound waves into sensations of pitch, researchers have outlined two distinct theories: place theory and frequency theory.

Place theory was initially proposed by Hermann von Helmholtz in the 1800s and was later modified, elaborated, and tested by **Georg von Békésy** (1899–1972), who won a Nobel Prize for this work in 1961. Place theory is based on the fact that the basilar membrane moves when sound waves are conducted through the inner ear. Different frequencies produce their most movement at particular locations along the basilar membrane. For high-frequency tones, the wave motion is greatest at the base of the cochlea, where the oval and round windows are located. For low-frequency tones, the greatest wave motion of the basilar membrane is at the opposite end. So place theory suggests that perception of pitch depends on the specific location on the basilar membrane at which the greatest stimulation occurs.

The second theory, **frequency theory,** explains pitch by the rate of vibration of the basilar membrane. This theory predicts that a sound wave with a frequency of 100 Hz will set the basilar membrane vibrating 100 times per second. The frequency theory also predicts that the vibrations of the basilar membrane will cause neurons to fire at the same rate, so that rate of firing is the neural code for pitch. One problem with this theory is that individual neurons cannot fire rapidly enough to represent high-pitched sounds because none of them can fire more than 1,000 times per second. This limitation makes it impossible for one neuron to distinguish sounds above 1,000 Hz—which, of course, your auditory system can do quite well. The limitation might be overcome by the

---

cochlea The primary organ of hearing; a fluid-filled coiled tube located in the inner ear.

basilar membrane A membrane in the cochlea that, when set into motion, stimulates hair cells that produce the neural effects of auditory stimulation.

auditory nerve The nerve that carries impulses form the cochlea to the cochlear nucleus of the brain.

place theory The theory that different frequency tones produce maximum activation at different locations along the basilar membrane, with the result that pitch can be coded by the place at which activation occurs.

frequency theory The theory that a tone produces a rate of vibration in the basilar membrane equal to its frequency, with the result that pitch can be coded by the frequency of the neural response.

volley principle, which explains what might happen at such high frequencies. This principle suggests that several neurons in a combined action, or volley, fire at the frequency that matches a stimulus tone of 2,000 Hz, 3,000 Hz, and so on (Wever, 1949).

As with the trichromatic and opponent-process theories of color vision, the place and frequency theories each successfully account for different aspects of your experience of pitch. Frequency theory accounts well for coding frequencies below about 5,000 Hz. At higher frequencies, neurons cannot fire quickly and precisely enough to code a signal adequately, even in volley. Place theory accounts well for perception of pitch at frequencies above 1,000 Hz. Below 1,000 Hz, the entire basilar membrane vibrates so broadly that it cannot provide a signal distinctive enough for the neural receptors to use as a means of distinguishing pitch. Between 1,000 and 5,000 Hz, both mechanisms can operate. Thus a complex sensory task is divided between two systems that, together, offer greater sensory precision than either system alone could provide. We see next that you also possess two converging neural systems to help you localize sounds in the environment.

Sound Localization Suppose you are walking across campus and you hear someone call your name. In most cases, you can readily locate the spatial location of the speaker. This example suggests how efficiently your auditory system carries out the task of **sound localization**—you are able to determine the spatial origins of auditory events. You do so through two mechanisms: assessments of the relative timing and relative intensity of the sounds that arrive at each ear (Recanzone & Sutter, 2008).

The first mechanism involves neurons that compare the relative times at which incoming sound reaches each ear. A sound occurring off to your right side, for example, reaches

Why might bats have evolved the ability to use echolocation to navigate through their environment?

your right ear before your left (see point B in **Figure 4.20**). Neurons in your auditory system are specialized to fire most actively for specific time delays between the two ears. Your brain uses this information about disparities in arrival time to make precise estimates for the likely origins of a sound in space.

The second mechanism relies on the principle that a sound has a slightly greater intensity in the first ear at which it arrives—because your head itself casts a *sound shadow* that weakens the signal. These intensity differences depend on the relative size of the wavelength of a tone with respect to your head. Large-wavelength, low-frequency tones show virtually no intensity differences, whereas small-wavelength, high-frequency tones show measurable intensity differences. Your brain, once again, has specialized cells that detect intensity differences in the signals arriving at your two ears.

But what happens when a sound creates neither a timing nor an intensity difference? In Figure 4.20, a sound originating at point A would have this property. With your eyes closed, you cannot tell its exact location. So you must move your head—to reposition your ears—to break the symmetry and provide the necessary information for sound localization.

It's interesting to note that porpoises and bats use their auditory systems rather than their visual systems to locate objects in dark waters or dark caves. These species use *echolocation*—they emit high-pitched sounds that bounce off objects, giving them feedback about the objects' distances, locations, sizes, textures, and movements. In fact, one species of bat is able to use echolocation to differentiate between objects that are just 0.3 millimeters apart (Simmons et al., 1998).

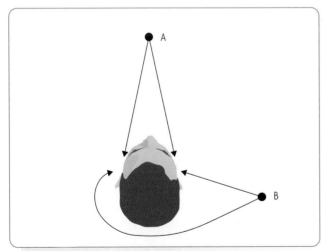

FIGURE 4.20 **Time Disparity and Sound Localization**

The brain uses differences in the time course with which sounds arrive at the two ears to localize the sounds in space.

volley principle An extension of frequency theory, which proposes that when peaks in a sound wave come too frequently for a single neuron to fire at each peak, several neurons fire as a group at the frequency of the stimulus tone.

sound localization The auditory processes that allow the spatial origins of environmental sounds.

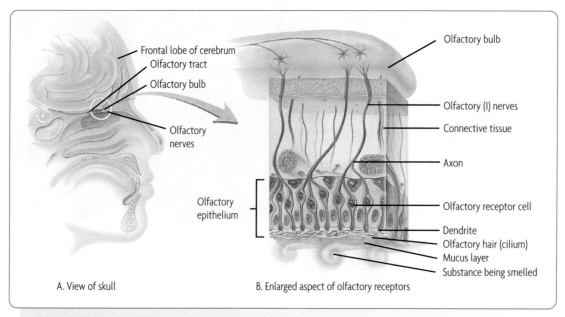

FIGURE 4.21   Receptors for Smell
The olfactory receptor cells in your nasal cavities are stimulated by chemicals in the environment. They send information to the olfactory bulb in your brain.

STOP AND REVIEW

❶ What physical property of a sound produces the perception of pitch?

❷ What role do hair cells play in the auditory system?

❸ Which theory suggests that the perception of pitch depends on the location on the basilar membrane at which the greatest stimulation occurs?

❹ What timing difference would you expect if a sound originated off to your right side?

Visit MyPsychLab.com for more review and practice on the following topic:

◉ **Watch:** Ear Ringing

Your Other Senses

We have devoted the most attention to vision and hearing because scientists have studied them most thoroughly. However, your ability both to survive in and to enjoy the external environment relies on your full repertory of senses. We close our discussion of sensation with brief analyses of several of your other senses.

olfaction The sense of smell.

olfactory bulb The center where odor-sensitive receptors send their signals, located just below the frontal lobes of the cortex.

SMELL

You can probably imagine circumstances in which you'd be just as happy to give up your sense of smell: Did you ever have a family dog that lost a battle with a skunk? But to avoid that skunk experience, you'd also have to give up the smells of fresh roses, hot buttered popcorn, and hot chocolate. Each of these substances releases odors into the air in the form of *odorant molecules*. The process of **olfaction**—the technical term for the sense of smell—begins when those molecules interact with receptor proteins on the membranes of *olfactory cilia* (see **Figure 4.21**). It takes only 8 molecules of a substance to initiate one of these nerve impulses, but at least 40 nerve endings must be stimulated before you can smell the substance. Once initiated, these nerve impulses convey odor information to the **olfactory bulb,** located just above the receptors and just below the frontal lobes of the cerebrum. Odor stimuli start the process of smell by stimulating an influx of chemical substances into ion channels in olfactory neurons, an event that, as you may recall from Chapter 3, triggers an action potential.

The anatomical location of the olfactory nerves and olfactory bulb leaves them vulnerable to damage. For example, when people suffer from blows to the head, the axons of the nerve cells that carry impulses to the olfactory bulb may be damaged. In one sample of 111 patients who had experienced a mild traumatic brain injury, 22 percent experienced *hyposmia* (a diminished sense of smell), and 4 percent experienced *anosmia* (a total loss of smell) two weeks after the traumatic incident (de Kriujk et al., 2003). However, there's some hope for recovery: The olfactory system generates new cells in both olfactory receptors and the olfactory bulb. For that reason, some patients are able to regain some or all of their ability to smell as time passes after brain injury (London et al., 2008).

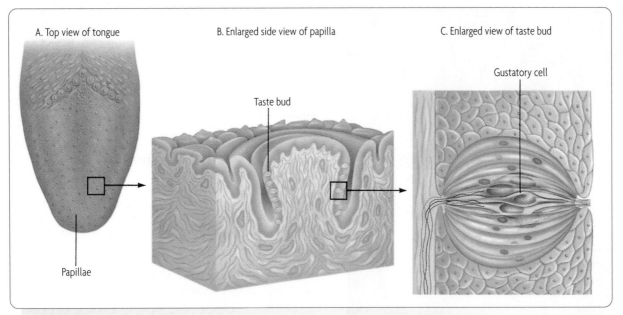

FIGURE 4.22 Receptors for Taste
Part A shows the distribution of the papillae on the upper side of the tongue. Part B shows a single papilla enlarged so that the individual taste buds are visible. Part C shows one of the taste buds enlarged.

The significance of the sense of smell varies greatly across species. Smell presumably evolved as a system for detecting and locating food (Moncrieff, 1951). Humans seem to use the sense of smell primarily in conjunction with taste, to seek and sample food. However, for many species smell is also used to detect potential sources of danger. Dogs, rats, insects, and many other creatures for whom smell is central to survival have a far keener sense of smell than humans do. Relatively more of their brain is devoted to smell. Smell serves these species well because organisms do not have to come into direct contact with other organisms to smell them.

In addition, smell can be a powerful form of active communication. Members of many species communicate by secreting and detecting chemical signals called **pheromones,** chemical substances used within a given species to signal sexual receptivity, danger, territorial boundaries, and food sources (Luo et al., 2003). For example, females of various insect species produce sex pheromones to signal that they are available for mating (Carazo et al., 2004; De Cock & Matthysen, 2005). We revisit the topic of pheromones when we discuss both human and nonhuman sexual behaviors in Chapter 11.

TASTE

Although food and wine gourmets are capable of making remarkably subtle and complex taste distinctions, many of their sensations are really smells, not tastes. **Gustation**—the technical term for the sense of taste—and smell work together closely when you eat. In fact, when you have a cold, food seems tasteless because your nasal passages are blocked and you can't smell

the food. Demonstrate this principle for yourself: Hold your nose and try to tell the difference between foods of similar texture but different tastes, such as pieces of apple and raw potato. Because the sense of smell has such a broad impact on how food tastes, people who suffer from olfactory disorders often experience a loss of appetite.

The surface of your tongue is covered with *papillae,* which give it a bumpy appearance. Many of these papillae contain clusters of taste receptor cells called the *taste buds* (see **Figure 4.22**). Single-cell recordings of taste receptors show that individual receptor cells respond best to one of the four primary taste qualities: sweet, sour, bitter, and saline (salty) (Frank & Nowlis, 1989). In recent years, researchers have found receptors for a fifth basic taste quality, *umami* (McCabe & Rolls, 2007). Umami is the flavor of monosodium glutamate (MSG), the chemical that is often added to Asian foods and occurs naturally in foods rich in protein, such as meat, seafood, and aged cheese. Although receptor cells for the five qualities may produce small responses to other tastes, the "best" response most directly encodes quality. There appear to be separate transduction systems for each of the basic classes of taste (Rolls, 2005).

Taste receptors can be damaged by many things you put in your mouth, such as alcohol, cigarette smoke, and acids. Fortunately, your taste receptors get replaced about every ten

---

pheromone Chemical signal released by an organism to communicate with other members of the species; pheromones often serve as long-distance sexual attractors.

gustation The sense of taste.

Why would a man with a cold be ill-advised to take up wine tasting?

and *Merkel disks* are most active when a small object exerts steady pressure against the skin.

The skin's sensitivity to pressure varies tremendously over the body. For example, you are 10 times more accurate in sensing the position of stimulation on your fingertips than on your back. The variation in sensitivity of different body regions is shown by the greater density of nerve endings in these regions and also by the greater amount of sensory cortex devoted to them. In Chapter 3, you learned that your sensitivity is greatest where you need it most—on your face, tongue, and hands. Precise sensory feedback from these parts of the body permits effective eating, speaking, and grasping.

Suppose someone rubs an ice cube along your arm. You now have some ideas about how you would feel the pressure of the ice cube. But how would you sense that the *temperature* is cold? You may be surprised to learn that you have separate receptors for warmth and coolness. Rather than having one type of receptor that works like a thermometer, your brain integrates separate signals from *cold fibers* and *warm fibers* to monitor changes in environmental temperature.

One aspect of cutaneous sensitivity plays a central role in human relationships: touch. Through touch, you communicate to others your desire to give or receive comfort, support, love, and passion. However, where you get touched or touch someone else makes a difference; those areas of the skin surface that give rise to erotic, or sexual, sensations are called *erogenous zones.* Other touch-sensitive erotic areas vary in their arousal potential for different individuals, depending on learned associations and the concentration of sensory receptors in the areas.

THE VESTIBULAR AND KINESTHETIC SENSES

The next pair of senses we will describe may be entirely new to you because they do not have receptors you can see directly, like eyes, ears, or noses. Your **vestibular sense** tells you how your body—especially your head—is oriented in the world with respect to gravity. The receptors for this information are tiny hairs in fluid-filled sacs and canals in the inner ear. The hairs bend when the fluid moves and presses on them, which is what happens when you turn your head quickly. The *saccule* and *utricle* (shown in Figure 4.19) tell you about acceleration or deceleration in a straight line. The three canals, called the *semicircular canals,* are at right angles to each other and thus can tell you about motion in any direction. They inform you how your head is moving when you turn, nod, or tilt it.

People who lose their vestibular sense because of accidents or disease are initially quite disoriented and prone to falls and dizziness. However, most of these people eventually compensate by relying more heavily on visual information. *Motion sickness* can occur when the signals from the visual system conflict with those from the vestibular system. People feel nauseated when reading in a moving car because the visual signal is of a stationary object while the vestibular signal is of movement. Drivers rarely get motion sickness because they are both seeing and feeling motion.

Whether you are standing erect, drawing pictures, or making love, your brain needs to have accurate information about the current positions and movement of your body parts relative to one another. The **kinesthetic sense** (also called *kinesthesis*)

days—even more frequently than smell receptors (Breslin & Spector, 2008). Indeed, the taste system is the most resistant to damage of all your sensory systems; it is extremely rare for anyone to suffer a total, permanent taste loss.

TOUCH AND SKIN SENSES

The skin is a remarkably versatile organ. In addition to protecting you against surface injury, holding in body fluids, and helping regulate body temperature, it contains nerve endings that produce sensations of pressure, warmth, and cold. These sensations are called the **cutaneous senses** (skin senses).

Consider how you become aware that a stimulus is creating *pressure* on your skin. Because you receive so much sensory information through your skin, different types of receptor cells operate close to the surface of the body. Each type of receptor responds to somewhat different patterns of contact with the skin (Lumpkin & Caterina, 2007). As two examples, *Meissner corpuscles* respond best when something rubs against the skin,

---

cutaneous senses The skin senses that register sensations or pressure, warmth, and cold.

vestibular sense The sense that tells how one's own body is oriented in the world with respect to gravity.

kinesthetic sense The sense concerned with bodily position and movement of the body parts relative to one another.

provides constant sensory feedback about what the body is doing during motor activities. Without it, you would be unable to coordinate most voluntary movements.

You have two sources of kinesthetic information: receptors in the joints and receptors in the muscles and tendons. Receptors that lie in the joints respond to pressures that accompany different positions of the limbs and to pressure changes that accompany movements of the joints. Receptors in the muscles and tendons respond to changes in tension that accompany muscle shortening and lengthening.

The brain often integrates information from your kinesthetic sense with information from touch senses. Your brain, for example, can't grasp the full meaning of the signals coming from each of your fingers if it doesn't know exactly where your fingers are in relation to one another. Imagine that you pick up an object with your eyes closed. Your sense of touch may allow you to guess that the object is a stone, but your kinesthetic sense will enable you to know how large it is.

PAIN

Pain is the body's response to stimulation from harmful stimuli—those that are intense enough to cause tissue damage or threaten to do so. Are you entirely happy that you have such a well-developed pain sense? Your answer probably should be "yes and no." On the "yes" side, your pain sense is critical for survival. People born with congenital insensitivity to pain feel no hurt, but their bodies often become scarred and their limbs deformed from injuries that they could have avoided, had their brains been able to warn them of danger (Cox et al., 2006). Their experience shows that pain serves as an essential defense signal—it warns you of potential harm. On the "no" side, there are certainly times when you would be happy to be able to turn off your pain sense. More than 50 million people in the United States suffer from chronic, persistent pain. Medical treatment for pain and the workdays lost because of pain are esti-

What role does the kinesthetic sense play in the performance of skilled athletes?

mated to cost more than $70 billion annually in the United States (Gatchel, 2004).

Scientists have begun to identify the specific sets of receptors that respond to pain-producing stimuli. They have learned that some receptors respond only to temperature, others to chemicals, others to mechanical stimuli, and still others to combinations of pain-producing stimuli. This network of pain fibers is a fine meshwork that covers your entire body. Peripheral nerve fibers send pain signals to the central nervous system by two pathways: a fast-conducting set of nerve fibers that are covered with myelin and slower, smaller nerve fibers without any myelin coating. Starting at the spinal cord, the impulses are relayed to the thalamus and then to the cerebral cortex, where the location and intensity of the pain are identified, the significance of the injury is evaluated, and action plans are formulated.

Within your brain, *endorphins* have an impact on your experience of pain. Recall from Chapter 3 that pain-killing drugs such as morphine bind to the same receptor sites in the brain—the term *endorphin* comes from *endogenous* (self-produced) *morphines*. The release of endorphins within the brain controls your experience of pain. Researchers believe that endorphins are at least partially responsible for the pain-reducing effects of acupuncture and placebos (Benedetti et al., 2005; Han, 2004).

Your emotional responses, context factors, and your interpretation of the situation can be as important as actual physical stimuli in determining how much pain you experience (Gatchel et al., 2007). How are pain sensations affected by the psychological context? One theory about the way pain may be modulated is known as the **gate-control theory,** developed by **Ronald Melzack** (1973, 1980). This theory

Why would riding in the front seat of a roller coaster be less likely to make you nauseated than riding in the rear?

pain The body's response to noxious stimuli that are intense enough to cause, or threaten to cause, tissue damage.

gate-control theory A theory about pain modulation that proposes that certain cells in the spinal cord act as gates to interrupt and block some pain signals while sending others to the brain.

Individuals taking part in religious rituals, such as walking on a bed of hot coals, are able to block out pain. What does that tell you about the relationship between the physiology and psychology of pain?

suggests that cells in the spinal cord act as neurological gates, interrupting and blocking some pain signals and letting others get through to the brain. Receptors in the skin and the brain send messages to the spinal cord to open or close those gates. Suppose, for example, you bump your shin on a table while running to answer the telephone. As you rub the skin around the bump, you send inhibitory messages to your spinal cord—closing the gates. Messages descending from the brain also can close the gates. If, for example, the phone call includes urgent news, your brain might close the gates to prevent you from experiencing the distraction of pain. Melzack (2005) has proposed an updated *neuromatrix theory* of pain that incorporates the reality that people often experience pain with little or no physical cause: In these cases, the experience of pain originates wholly in the brain.

We've just seen that the way you perceive pain may reveal more about your psychological state than about the intensity of the pain stimulus: What you perceive may be different from, and even independent of, what you sense. This discussion of pain prepares you for the rest of the chapter, in which we discuss the perceptual processes that allow you to organize and label your experiences of the world.

STOP AND REVIEW

❶ What is an important brain structure involved in the sense of smell?

---

attention A state of focused awareness on a subset of the available perceptual information.

goal-directed selection A determinant of why people select some parts of sensory input for further processing; it reflects the choices made as a function of one's own goals.

stimulus-driven capture A determinant of why people select some parts of sensory input for further processing; occurs when features of stimuli—objects in the environment—automatically capture attention, independent of the local goals of a perceiver.

❷ To what basic taste qualities do your taste buds respond?

❸ How does your skin sense temperature?

❹ What is the purpose of the vestibular sense?

❺ What is the goal of gate-control theory?

Visit MyPsychLab.com for more review and practice on the following topic:

⊙ **Watch:** Brain Pain

Organizational Processes in Perception

Imagine how confusing the world would be if you were unable to put together and organize the information available from the output of your millions of retinal receptors. You would experience a kaleidoscope of disconnected bits of color moving and swirling before your eyes. The processes that put sensory information together to give you the perception of coherence are referred to collectively as processes of perceptual organization.

We begin our discussion of perceptual organization with a description of the processes of *attention* that prompt you to focus on a subset of stimuli from your kaleidoscope of experience. We then examine the organizational processes first described by *Gestalt* theorists, who argued that what you perceive depends on laws of organization, or simple rules by which you perceive shapes and forms.

ATTENTIONAL PROCESSES

Take a moment now to find ten things in your environment that had not been, so far, in your immediate awareness. Had you noticed a spot on the wall? Had you noticed the ticking of a clock? If you start to examine your surroundings very carefully, you will discover that there are literally thousands of things on which you could focus. The processes of **attention** enable you to direct your awareness to a subset of all the information available to you. Generally, the more closely you attend to some object or event in the environment, the more you can perceive and learn about it.

What forces determine the objects that become the focus of your attention? The answer to this question has two components, which we will call goal-directed selection and stimulus-driven capture (Yantis, 1993). **Goal-directed selection** reflects the choices that you make about the objects to which you'd like to attend, as a function of your own goals. If, for example, you are contemplating a case full of pastries, you might direct your attention to only those desserts covered in chocolate. You are probably already comfortable with the idea that you can explicitly choose objects for particular scrutiny. **Stimulus-driven capture** occurs when features of the stimuli—objects in the environment—themselves automatically capture your attention, independent of your local goals as a perceiver. You've experienced stimulus-driven

Psychology in Your Life

WHY IS EATING "HOT" FOOD PAINFUL?

Have you ever had this experience? You are eating a very "hot" dish in a Chinese or Mexican restaurant, and you accidentally bite directly into a chili pepper. In just moments you go from enjoyment to intense pain. If this has happened, then you know that, in the realm of taste, there is a fine line between what gives pleasure and what gives pain. Let's explore this relationship.

Physiologically, it's easy to explain why hot pepper can cause you pain. On your tongue, your taste buds have associated with them pain fibers (Bartoshuk, 1993). Thus the very same chemical that can stimulate the receptors in your taste buds can stimulate the closely allied pain fibers (Caterina et al., 2000). In the case of hot pepper, this chemical is *capsaicin*. If you want to enjoy a spicy meal, you have to keep the concentration of capsaicin in your meal sufficiently low so that your taste receptors are more active than your pain receptors.

But why, you might wonder, do different people have such obvious differences in their preferences for hot food? People often find it very difficult to understand how their friends can or cannot eat food that is very spicy. Again, we can look to physiology to explain these differences. The figure shows photographs of tongues from two individuals studied by **Linda Bartoshuk** and her colleagues. You can see that one tongue has considerably more taste buds than the other. If there are more taste buds, there will be more pain receptors. Therefore, people with more taste buds are more likely to get a strong pain response from capsaicin. The group of individuals who have more taste buds have been dubbed *supertasters* (Bartoshuk, 1993). They form a sharp contrast, in the extremes of their sensory experiences, to *nontasters*. For many taste sensations, these two groups are equivalent—you wouldn't know at most times whether you were a supertaster, a nontaster, or somewhere in between. The differences arise only for certain chemicals—capsaicin is an excellent example.

The variations in the density of taste buds on different people's tongues appear to be genetic (Bartoshuk & Beauchamp, 1994). Women are much more likely than men to be supertasters. Supertasters generally have more sensitivity to bitter chemicals—a sensory quality shared by most poisons. You can imagine that if women generally were responsible for nurturing and feeding offspring over the course of evolution, the children of women with greater taste sensitivity would be more likely to survive. Because taster status is genetic, you can find preference differences among children at very young ages (Anliker et al., 1991). Five- to 7-year-old supertasters preferred milk to cheddar cheese. This preference was reversed for nontasters. Why? The supertasters may perceive the milk as sweeter and the cheese as more bitter than do the nontasters. Thus genetic differences may help explain why some young children have such strong (and vocal) taste preferences.

But let's return to the restaurant meal at which you have had your painful accident. What you might have noticed is that the sensation of pain fades over time. In this respect, the pain receptors in your mouth act like other sensory receptors: Over time, you adapt to a constant stimulus. That's good news! You should be glad that your sensory processes offer built-in relief.

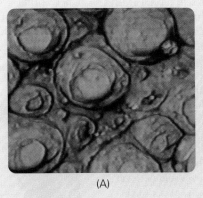 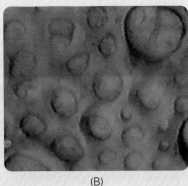

(A)   (B)

(A) The tongue of a supertaster. (B) The tongue of a nontaster.

capture, for example, if you've ever been day-dreaming at a stoplight while out for a drive. The stoplight's abrupt change from red to green will often capture your attention even if you were not particularly focused on it.

You might wonder what the relationship is between these two processes: Research suggests that, at least under some circumstances, stimulus-driven capture wins out over goal-directed selection.

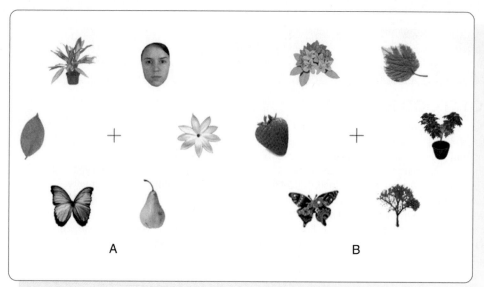

A   B

The researchers began with the hypothesis that "because of their biological and social significance," human faces are likely to capture attention (Langton et al., 2008, p. 331). To test that hypothesis, the researchers asked participants to view the types of displays shown in Parts A and B of **Figure 4.23.** The participants' task, in each case, was to answer as quickly as possible whether a butterfly was present in the display. For both parts of the figure, the answer is "yes." (There were, of course, other displays for which the answer was "no"!) Note that in Part A the the display also includes a human face. The researchers predicted that participants' attention would be captured by such faces. As a consequence, the researchers expected participants to take longer to find the butterflies than when no faces were present (as in Part B of the figure). That prediction was confirmed: The presence of the faces made it more difficult for participants to find the butterflies. To rule out the possibility that the faces were just more visually interesting, the researchers replicated the experiment except that they turned all the stimulus pictures upside down. Under those circumstances, the faces no longer looked facelike. As such, they no longer interfered with the participants' ability to find the butterflies.

You can recognize this phenomenon as stimulus-driven capture because it works in the opposite direction of the perceiver's goals. If participants could ignore the faces, they would perform the task better. Because participants almost always prefer to perform as well as possible on experimental tasks, we can conclude that the faces captured their attention despite their goal-directed desire to attend to the butterflies as efficiently as possible.

Let's suppose that you have focused your attention on some stimulus in the environment. It's time for your processes of perceptual organization to go to work.

Gestalt psychology A school of psychology that maintains that psychological phenomena can be understood only when viewed as organized, structured wholes, not when broken down into primitive perceptual elements.

PRINCIPLES OF PERCEPTUAL GROUPING

Consider the image on the left in **Figure 4.24.** If you're like most people, you'll see a vase as *figure* against a black *ground.* A figure is seen as an objectlike region in the forefront, and ground is seen as the backdrop against which the figures stand out. As you can see on the right of Figure 4.24, it's possible to change the relationship between figure and ground—to see two faces rather than one vase. One of the first tasks your perceptual processes carry out is to decide what in a scene counts as figure and what as ground.

How do your perceptual processes determine what should be gathered together into the figure? The principles of perceptual grouping were studied extensively by proponents of **Gestalt psychology,** such as **Kurt Koffka** (1935), **Wolfgang Köhler** (1947), and **Max Wertheimer** (1923).

FIGURE 4.24 Figure and Ground
An initial step in perceptual grouping is for your perceptual processes to interpret part of a scene as a figure standing out against a ground.

Members of this group maintained that psychological phenomena could be understood only when viewed as organized, structured *wholes* and not when broken down into primitive perceptual elements. The term *gestalt* roughly means "form," "whole," "configuration," or "essence." In their experiments, the Gestalt psychologists studied how perceptual arrays give rise to gestalts: They demonstrated that the whole is often quite different from the sum of its parts. By varying a single factor and observing how it affected the way people perceived the structure of the array, they were able to formulate a set of laws:

1. *The law of proximity.* People group together the nearest (most proximal) elements. That's why you see this display as five columns of objects instead of four rows.

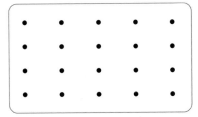

2. *The law of similarity.* People group together the most similar elements. That's why you see a square of *Os* against a field of *Xs* rather than columns of mixed *Xs* and *Os*.

3. *The law of good continuation.* People experience lines as continuous even when they are interrupted. That's why you interpret this display as an arrow piercing the heart rather than as a design with three separate pieces.

4. *The law of closure.* People tend to fill in small gaps to experience objects as wholes. That's why you fill in the missing piece to perceive a whole circle.

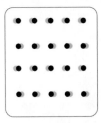

5. *The law of common fate.* People tend to group together objects that appear to be moving in the same direction. That's why you experience this figure as alternating rows moving apart.

SPATIAL AND TEMPORAL INTEGRATION

All the gestalt laws we have presented to you so far should have convinced you that a lot of perception consists of putting the pieces of your world together in the "right way." Often, however, you can't perceive an entire scene in one glance, or *fixation* (recall our discussion of attention). What you perceive at a given time is often a restricted glimpse of a large visual world extending in all directions to unseen areas of the environment. To get a complete idea of what is around you, you must combine information from fixations of different spatial locations—*spatial integration*—at different moments in time—*temporal integration*.

What may surprise you is that your visual system does not work very hard to create a moment-by-moment, integrated picture of the environment. Research suggests that your visual memory for each fixation on the world does not preserve precise details.

Consider the two photos in **Figure 4.25** on page 118: They show the same scene but one in close-up and the other in wide-angle. Suppose we showed you just one of these two photos and, after a brief delay, asked you which one it had been. You might think you'd do quite well at this memory test. However, researchers have demonstrated that participants make systematic errors after a delay of less than 1/20th of a second (Dickinson & Intraub, 2008). In a series of studies, participants viewed three photographs—either close-up or wide-angle—in quick succession. Then, after brief delays, the participants saw either a close-up or wide-angle version of one of the three photos. The participants had to respond whether the view was the one they had seen before on a 5-point scale that ranged from −2 ("much closer up") to 0 ("the same") to +2 ("much farther away"). Participants made a very consistent error in their judgments: They rated identical views as being too close up. The researchers called this error boundary extension because participants regularly believed that the original photos included information beyond the boundaries of the original photo.

Why might boundary extension happen and happen so quickly? Consider what it's like to look out a window. You

| (A)
Wide-Angle View | (B)
Close-Up View |

FIGURE 4.25   Boundary Extension

When people view photographs they are quite likely to use memory processes to extend the boundaries of the scene. For that reason, they often recall seeing a wide-angle view when, in fact, they originally experienced a close-up.

don't believe that the world stops at the window's edges. Instead, you use your world knowledge to extend the view beyond what you can see. In many respects, looking at a photograph is the same as looking out a window. Because you complete the scene around the edges of the photo, you are quite likely to recall that the photo included more than was actually present. This explanation of boundary extension should suggest to you why this "error" makes sense: It's not a bad thing for you to complete the larger scene from the sample of a single glimpse.

Researchers have identified a number of instances in which people have difficulty noticing changes from one view of a scene to the next (Simons & Ambinder, 2005). Some instances of what is often called *change blindness* can be quite dramatic. For example, in one study, participants failed to notice that the person with whom they were having a conversation had changed (Simons & Levin, 1998)! The study unfolded somewhat like a magic trick—the two experimenters changed places as a door passed through the middle of the conversation. In fact, stage magicians have long taken advantage of change blindness to accomplish a variety of their tricks. (For examples of the perceptual basis of several famous illusions, see Macknik et al., 2008.) How is it possible for people to be blind to such large changes in their visual world? Recall our earlier discussion of attention. To notice a change, it is important that you have attended to both the original and changed features of the world. Even then, you often need to expend mental resources to try to detect a change.

MOTION PERCEPTION

One type of perception that does require you to make comparisons across different glimpses of the world is motion perception. Suppose you see a friend across a classroom. If he stands still, the size of his image on your retina will expand as you walk toward him. The rate at which this image has expanded gives you a sense of how quickly you have been approaching (Gibson, 1979).

As we noted, motion perception requires you to combine information from difference glimpses of the world. You can appreciate the consequences of how your perceptual processes combine those glimpses quite strongly when you experience the **phi phenomenon.** This phenomenon occurs when two stationary spots of light in different positions in the visual field are turned on and off alternately at a rate of about four to five times per second. This effect occurs on outdoor advertising signs and in strobe light displays. Even at this relatively slow rate of alternation, it appears that a single light is moving back and forth between the two spots. There are multiple ways to conceive of the path that leads from the location of the first dot to the location of the second dot. Yet human observers normally see only the simplest path, a straight line (Cutting & Proffitt, 1982; Shepard, 1984). This straight-line rule is violated, however, when viewers are shown alternating views of a human body in motion. Then the visual system fills in the paths of normal biological motion (Shiffrar, 1994; Stevens et al., 2000).

DEPTH PERCEPTION

Until now, we have considered only two-dimensional patterns on flat surfaces. Everyday perceiving, however, involves objects in three-dimensional space. Perceiving all three spatial dimensions is absolutely vital for you to approach what you want,

---

phi phenomenon The simplest form of apparent motion, the movement illusion in which one or more stationary lights going on and off in succession are perceived as a single moving light.

What makes you aware that the "protagonist" in this photo is moving—and in what direction is the motion?

with some small object in the distance, holding one finger at arm's length and the other about a foot in front of your face. Now, keeping your fingers stationary, close your right eye and open the left one while continuing to fixate on the distant object. What happened to the position of your two fingers? The second eye does not see them lined up with the distant object because it gets a slightly different view.

This displacement between the horizontal positions of corresponding images in your two eyes is called **retinal disparity.** It provides depth information because the amount of disparity, or difference, depends on the relative distance of objects from you (see **Figure 4.26** on page 120). For instance, when you switched eyes, the closer finger was displaced farther to the side than was the distant finger.

When you look at the world with both eyes open, most objects that you see stimulate different positions on your two retinas. If the disparity between corresponding images in the two retinas is small enough, the visual system is able to fuse them into a perception of a single object in depth. (However, if the images are too far apart, you actually see the double images, as when you cross your eyes.) When you stop to think about it, what your visual system does is pretty amazing: It takes two different retinal images, compares them for horizontal displacement of corresponding parts, and produces a unitary perception of a single object in depth. In effect, the visual system interprets horizontal displacement between the two images as depth in the three-dimensional world.

Other binocular information about depth comes from **convergence.** Your eyes turn inward to some extent whenever they are fixated on an object (see **Figure 4.27** on page 120). When the object is very close—a few inches in front of your face—the eyes must turn toward each other quite a bit for the same image to fall on both foveae. You can actually see the eyes converge if you watch a friend focus first on a distant object and then on one a foot or so away. Your brain uses information from your eye muscles to make judgments about depth. However, convergence information from the eye muscles is useful for depth perception only up to about 10 feet. At greater distances, the angular differences are too small to detect because the eyes are nearly parallel when you fixate on a distant object.

To see how *motion* is another source for depth information, try the following demonstration. As you did before, close one eye and line up your two index fingers with some distant object. Then move your head to the side while fixating on the distant object and keeping your fingers still. As you move your head, you see both your fingers move, but the close finger seems to move farther and faster than the more distant one. The fixated object does not move at all. This source of information about depth is called **motion parallax.** Motion

such as interesting people and good food, and avoid what is dangerous, such as speeding cars and falling pianos. This perception requires accurate information about *depth* (the distance from you to an object) as well as about its *direction* from you. Your ears can help in determining direction, but they are not much help in determining depth. Your interpretation of depth relies on many different information sources about distance (often called *depth cues*)—among them binocular cues, motion cues, and pictorial cues.

Binocular and Motion Cues Have you ever wondered why you have two eyes instead of just one? The second eye is more than just a spare. Your two eyes together provide you with compelling information about depth. Cues to depth that involve comparisons of the visual information that arrives at your two eyes are called **binocular depth cues.** The two sources of binocular depth information are *retinal disparity* and *convergence*.

Because the eyes are about 2 to 3 inches apart horizontally, they receive slightly different views of the world. To convince yourself of this, try the following experiment. First, close your left eye and use the right one to line up your two index fingers

binocular depth cue Depth cue that uses information from both eyes.

retinal disparity The displacement between the horizontal positions of corresponding images in the two eyes.

convergence The degree to which the eyes turn inward to fixate on an object.

motion parallax A source of information about depth in which the relative distances of objects from a viewer determine the amount and direction of their relative motion in the retinal image.

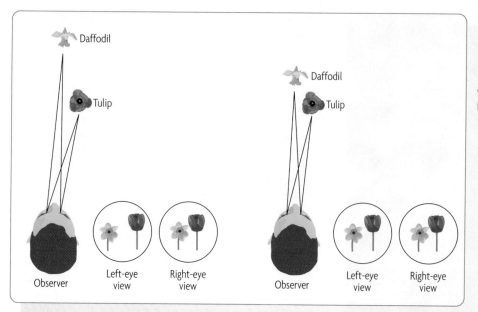

FIGURE 4.26 Retinal Disparity

Retinal disparity increases with the distance in depth between two objects.

parallax provides information about depth because, as you move, the relative distances of objects in the world determine the amount and direction of their relative motion in your retinal image of the scene. Next time you sit in the passenger seat of a car, keep a watch out the window for motion parallax at work. Objects at a distance from the moving car will appear much more stationary than those closer to you.

Monocular Cues But suppose you had vision in only one eye. Would you not be able to perceive depth? In fact, further information about depth is available from just one eye. These sources are called **monocular depth cues** because they require information just from one or the other eye. Artists who create images in what appear to be three dimensions (on the two dimensions of a piece of paper or canvas) make skilled use of monocular depth cues.

Interposition, or *occlusion,* arises when an opaque object blocks out part of a second object (see **Figure 4.28**). Interposition gives you depth information indicating that the occluded object is farther away than the occluding one. Occluding surfaces also block out light, creating shadows that can be used as an additional source of depth information.

Three more sources of pictorial information are all related to the way light projects from a three-dimensional world onto a two-dimensional surface such as the retina: relative size, linear perspective, and texture gradients. *Relative size* involves a basic rule of light projection: Objects of the same size at different distances project images of different sizes on the retina. The closest one projects the largest image and the farthest one the smallest image. This rule is called the *size/distance relation.* As you can see in **Figure 4.29,** if you

look at an array with identical objects, you interpret the smaller ones to be farther away.

Linear perspective is a depth cue that also depends on the size/distance relation. When parallel lines (by definition

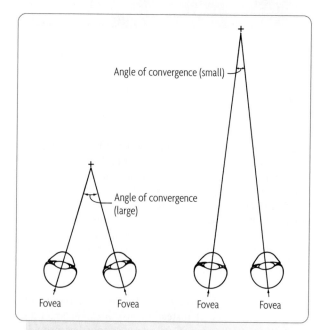

FIGURE 4.27 Convergence Cues to Depth

When an object is close to you, your eyes must converge more than when an object is at a greater distance. Your brain uses information from your eye muscles to use convergence as a cue to depth.

Reprinted with permission from R. Sekular & Blake, *Perception,* 3rd ed., pp. 27, 221. Copyright © 1994 by The McGraw-Hill Companies, Inc.

---

monocular depth cue Depth cue that uses information from only one eye.

FIGURE 4.28 Interposition Cues to Depth
What visual cues tell you whether this woman is behind the bars?

separated along their lengths by the same distance) recede into the distance, they converge toward a point on the horizon in your retinal image (see **Figure 4.30** on page 122). Your visual system's interpretation of converging lines gives rise to the Ponzo illusion. The upper line looks longer because you interpret the converging sides according to linear perspective as parallel lines receding into the distance. In this context, you interpret the upper line as though it were farther away, so you see it as longer—a farther object would have to be longer than a nearer one for both to produce retinal images of the same size.

Texture gradients provide depth cues because the density of a texture becomes greater as a surface recedes in depth. The wheat field in **Figure 4.31** on page 122 is an example of the way texture is used as a depth cue. You can think of this as another consequence of the size/distance relation. In this case, the units that make up the texture become smaller as they recede into the distance, and your visual system interprets this diminishing grain as greater distance in three-dimensional space.

By now, it should be clear that there are many sources of depth information. Under normal viewing conditions, however, information from these sources comes together in a single, coherent three-dimensional interpretation of the environment. You experience depth, not the different cues to depth that existed in the proximal stimulus. In other words, your visual system uses cues such as differential motion, interposition, and

relative size automatically, without your conscious awareness, to make the complex computations that give you a perception of depth in the three-dimensional environment.

PERCEPTUAL CONSTANCIES

To help you discover another important property of visual perception, we are going to ask you to play a bit with your textbook. Put your book down on a table, then move your head closer to it so that it's just a few inches away. Then move your head back to a normal reading distance. Although the book stimulated a much larger part of your retina when it was up close than when it was far away, didn't you perceive the book's size to remain the same? Now set the book upright and try tilting your head clockwise. When you do this, the image of the book rotates counterclockwise on your retina, but didn't you still perceive the book to be upright?

In general, you see the world as *invariant, constant,* and *stable* despite changes in the stimulation of your sensory receptors. Psychologists refer to this phenomenon as **perceptual constancy.** Roughly speaking, it means that you perceive the properties of the distal stimuli, which are usually constant, rather than the properties of proximal stimuli, which change every time you move your eyes or head. For survival, it is critical that you perceive constant and stable properties of objects in the world despite the enormous variations in the properties of the light patterns that stimulate your eyes. The critical task of perception is to discover *invariant* properties of your environment despite the variations in your retinal impressions of them. We see next how this works for size, shape, and orientation.

FIGURE 4.29 Relative Size as a Depth Cue
Objects that are closer project larger images on the retina. As a consequence, when you look at an array with identical objects, you interpret the smaller ones to be at a greater distance.

---

perceptual constancy The ability to retain an unchanging percept of an object despite variations in the retinal image.

FIGURE 4.30   The Ponzo Illusion
The converging lines add a dimension of depth, and therefore the distance cue makes the top line appear larger than the bottom line, even though they are actually the same length.

Size and Shape Constancy What determines your perception of the size of an object? In part, you perceive an object's actual size on the basis of the size of its retinal image. However, the demonstration with your book shows that the size of the retinal image depends on both the actual size of the book and its distance from the eye. As you now know, information about distance is available from a variety of depth cues. Your visual system combines that information with retinal information about image size to yield a perception of an object size that usually corresponds to the actual size of the distal stimulus. **Size constancy** refers to your ability to perceive the true size of an object despite variations in the size of its retinal image.

If the size of an object is perceived by taking distance cues into account, then you should be fooled about size whenever you are fooled about distance. One such illusion occurs in the Ames room shown in **Figure 4.32**. In comparison to the child, the adult looks quite short in the left corner of this room, but he looks enormous in the right corner. The reason for this illusion is that you perceive the room to be rectangular, with the two back corners equally distant from you. Thus you perceive the child's actual size as being consistent with the size of the images on your retina in both cases. In fact, the child is not at the same distance because the Ames room creates a clever illusion. While it appears to be a rectangular room, it is actually made from nonrectangular surfaces at odd angles in depth and height, as you can see in the drawings that accompany the photos. Any person on the right will make a larger retinal image, because he or she is twice as close to the observer. (By the way, to get the illusion you must view the display with a single eye through a peephole—that's the vantage point of the photographs in Figure 4.32. If you could move around while viewing the room, your visual system would acquire information about the unusual structure of the room.)

Another way that the perceptual system can infer objective size is by using prior knowledge about the characteristic size of similarly shaped objects. For instance, once you recognize the shape of a house, a tree, or a dog, you have a good idea of how big each is, even without knowing its distance from you. When past experience does not give you knowledge of what familiar objects look like at extreme distances, size constancy may break down. You have experienced this problem if you have looked down at people from the top of a skyscraper and thought that they resembled ants.

Shape constancy is closely related to size constancy. You perceive an object's actual shape correctly even when the object is slanted away from you, making the shape of the retinal image substantially different from that of the object itself. For instance, a rectangle tipped away projects a trapezoidal image onto your retina; a circle tipped away from you projects an elliptical image (see **Figure 4.33**). Yet you usually perceive the shapes accurately as a circle and a rectangle slanted away in space. When there is good depth information available, your visual system can determine an object's true shape simply by taking into account your distance from its different parts.

FIGURE 4.31   Examples of Texture as a Depth Cue
The wheat field is a natural example of the way texture can be used as a depth cue. Notice the way the wheat slants.

---

size constancy The ability to perceive the true size of an object despite variations in the size of its retinal image.

shape constancy The ability to perceive the true shape of an object despite variations in the size of the retinal image.

lightness constancy The tendency to perceive the whiteness, grayness, or blackness of objects as constant across changing levels of illuminations.

FIGURE 4.32 The Ames Room

The Ames room is designed to be viewed through a peephole with one eye—that is the vantage point from which these photographs were taken. The Ames room is constructed from nonrectangular surfaces at odd angles in depth and height. However, with only the view from the peephole, your visual system interprets it as an ordinary room and makes some unusual guesses about the relative heights of the occupants.

Lightness Constancy Consider the photograph in **Figure 4.34** on page 124. When you look at the brick wall in this picture, you don't perceive some of the bricks to be light red and some of them to be dark red— instead, you perceive this as a wall in which all the bricks are equally light or dark but some of them are in shadow (Goldstein, 1999). This is an example of lightness constancy: **Lightness constancy** is your tendency to perceive the whiteness, grayness, or blackness of objects as constant across changing levels of illumination.

As with the other constancies we have described, you experience lightness constancy quite frequently in everyday life. Suppose, for example, you are wearing a white T-shirt and walk from a dimly lit room outside into a bright sunny day. In bright sun-

shine, the T-shirt reflects far more light into your eyes than it does in the dim room, yet it looks about equally light to you in both contexts. In fact, lightness constancy works because the *percentage* of light an object reflects remains about the same even as the *absolute* amount of light changes. Your bright white T-shirt is going to reflect 80 to 90 percent of whatever light is available; your black jeans are going to reflect only about 5 percent of the available light. That's why—when you see them in the same context—the T-shirt will always look lighter than the jeans.

In this section, we have described a number of organizational processes in perception. In the final section of the chapter, we consider the identification and recognition processes that give meaning to objects and events in the environment.

FIGURE 4.33 Shape Constancy

As a coin is rotated, its image becomes an ellipse that grows narrower and narrower until it becomes a thin rectangle, an ellipse again, and then a circle. At each orientation, however, it is still perceived as a circular coin.

FIGURE 4.34 Lightness Constancy
Lightness constancy helps explain why you perceive all the bricks in the wall to be made of the same material.

ILLUSIONS

We have just reviewed a number of processes that your perceptual system uses to provide you with accurate perception of the world. Even so, occasions remain on which your perceptual systems deceive you: When you experience a stimulus pattern in a manner that is demonstrably incorrect, you are experiencing an **illusion.** The word *illusion* shares the same root as *ludicrous*—both stem from the Latin *illudere,* which means "to mock at." Illusions are shared by most people in the same perceptual situation because of shared physiology in sensory systems and overlapping experiences of the world. (As we will explain in Chapter 5, this sets illusions apart from hallucinations. Hallucinations are nonshared perceptual distortions that individuals experience as a result of unusual physical or mental states.) Examine the classic visual illusions in **Figure 4.35.** Although it is most convenient for us to present you with visual illusions, illusions also exist in other sensory modalities such as hearing (Russo & Thompson, 2005; Sonnadara & Trainor, 2005), taste (Todrank & Bartoshuk, 1991), and touch (Heller et al., 2003).

Researchers often invent new illusions or reconceive old ones to investigate important features of perceptual processes. Consider the first example in Figure 4.35, the Müller-Lyer illusion, which was first given as an illustrating by Franz Müller-Lyer in an 1889 work on optical illusions. Figure 4.35 shows a prominent explanation for this illusion. **Richard Gregory** (1966) suggested that people experience the standard arrow as the exterior corner of a building bulging toward them; people experience the open arrow as an interior corner, farther away. Because of the relationship between size and distance, people experience the arrow that looks like an interior corner as farther away. On this explanation, the Müller-Lyer illusion provides an example of ordinary

processes of depth perception leading to an incorrect percept. However, the matter is far from settled. Contemporary researchers continue to provide evidence that sometimes supports and sometimes contradicts this explanation (Howe & Purves, 2005; Weidner & Fink, 2007)! Fortunately, ongoing investigations of the classic illusions in Figure 4.35 continue to provide researchers with novel insights into perceptual processes.

Illusions are also a basic part of your everyday life. Consider your day-to-day experience of your home planet, Earth. You've seen the sun "rise" and "set" even though you know that the sun is sitting out there in the center of the solar system as decisively as ever. You can appreciate why it was such an extraordinary feat of courage for Christopher Columbus and other voyagers to deny the obvious illusion that Earth was flat and sail off toward one of its apparent edges. Similarly, when a full moon is overhead, it seems to follow you wherever you go even though you know the moon isn't chasing you. What you are experiencing is an illusion created by the great distance of the moon from your eye. When they reach Earth, the moon's light rays are essentially parallel and perpendicular to your direction of travel, no matter where you go.

People can control illusions to achieve desired effects. Architects and interior designers use principles of perception to create objects in space that seem larger or smaller than they really are. A small apartment becomes more spacious when it is painted with light colors and sparsely furnished with low small couches, chairs, and tables in the center of the room instead of against the walls. Psychologists working with NASA in the U.S. space program have researched the effects of environment on perception in order to design space capsules that have pleasant sensory qualities. Set and lighting directors of movies and theatrical productions purposely create illusions on film and on stage.

Despite all of these illusions, you generally do pretty well getting around the environment. That is why researchers typically study illusions to help explain how perception ordinarily works so well. The study of illusions supplements other strands of research on organizational processes in perception.

STOP AND REVIEW

❶ What is meant by stimulus-driven capture?
❷ What is the law of closure?
❸ What visual information allows you to understand that a man is walking toward you?
❹ How does convergence provide cues to depth?
❺ What is shape constancy?

CRITICAL THINKING In the experiment on boundary extension, do you think the results would change if participants were warned about the error?

Visit MyPsychLab.com for more review and practice on the following topics:

✳ **Simulate:** Distinguishing Figure–Ground Relationships

✳ **Simulate:** Gestalt Laws of Perception

◄◉ **Explore:** Five Well-Known Illusions

---

illusion An experience of a stimulus pattern in a manner that is demonstrably incorrect but shared by others in the same perceptual environment.

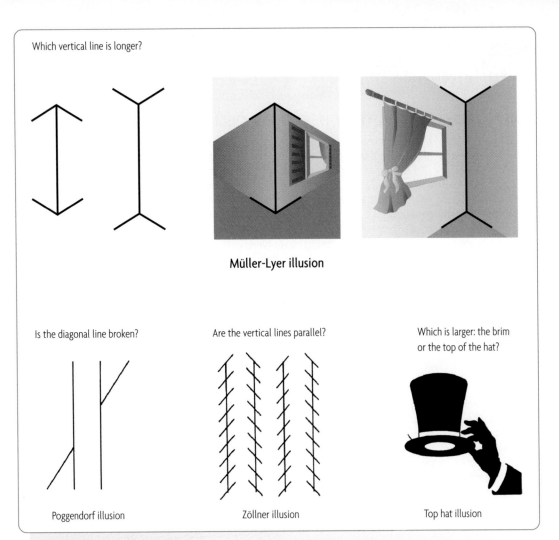

Which vertical line is longer?

Müller-Lyer illusion

Is the diagonal line broken?

Poggendorf illusion

Are the vertical lines parallel?

Zöllner illusion

Which is larger: the brim or the top of the hat?

Top hat illusion

FIGURE 4.35 Four Illusions to Tease Your Brain

Each of these illusions represents circumstances in which perception is demonstrably incorrect. Researchers often use illusions to test their theories. These theories explain why perceptual systems that generally function quite accurately yield illusions in special circumstances.

Identification and Recognition Processes

You can think of all the perceptual processes described so far as providing knowledge about physical properties of the distal stimulus—the position, size, shape, texture, and color of objects in a three-dimensional environment. However, you would not know what the objects were or whether you had seen them before. Your experience would resemble a visit to an alien planet where everything was new to you; you wouldn't know what to eat, what to put on your head, what to run away from, or what to date. Your environment appears nonalien because you are able to recognize and identify most objects as things you have seen before and as members of the meaningful categories that you know about from experience. Identification and recognition attach meaning to what you perceive.

BOTTOM-UP AND TOP-DOWN PROCESSES

When you identify an object, you must match what you see to your stored knowledge. Taking sensory data in from the environment and sending it toward the brain for extraction and analysis of relevant information is called bottom-up processing. **Bottom-up processing** is anchored in empirical reality and deals with bits of information and the transformation of concrete, physical features of stimuli into abstract representations (look back to Figure 4.2 on p. 93). This type of processing is also called *data-driven processing* because your starting point for identification is the sensory evidence you obtain from the environment—the data.

bottom-up processing Perceptual analyses based on the sensory data available in the environment; results of analysis are passed upward toward more abstract representations.

Critical Thinking in Your Life

ARE DRIVERS DISTRACTED WHEN THEY USE THEIR CELL PHONES?

Depending on where you live, it might already be illegal for you to use some types of cell phones while you drive. You probably also have strong opinions about whether such restrictions are necessary. The goal for researchers has been to provide data that can inform what have often been heated public policy debates on this issue. Much of that research has focused on perceptual consequences of cell phone use. In particular, researchers have evaluated drivers' ability to focus their attention both on their phone calls and on the driving environment (Strayer & Drews, 2007).

Consider a study in which participants drove through a suburban environment in a high-fidelity driving simulator (Strayer et al., 2003). The simulation required participants to display the full range of ordinary driving skills (including accelerating, maintaining speed, and braking). Each participant had two different driving experiences. Half the time, participants performed only the single task of navigating the route. At the other times, participants engaged in a second task: As they drove along, they had hands-free cell phone calls about a variety of ordinary topics. At all times, participants drove routes that included several billboards. At the end of the experiment, they were given a surprise memory test on these billboards. Participants recognized 6.9 (out of 15) billboards from times when they were just driving; they recognized just 3.9

billboards from times when they were also having a cell phone conversation.

Let's try to establish the role that attention plays in this result. There are two reasonable explanations for why participants' memory would be less good when they were having their conversations: They might never have looked at the billboards at all or they might have *looked* at the billboards but not have *attended* to them. To understand this latter hypothesis, look up from your textbook at the room around you. As you gaze in a particular direction, there are many objects you can see but to acquire detailed information you must focus your attention directly on an object.

In the driving experiment, the researchers obtained measures of participants' eye movements allowing for precise determination of where they looked. In fact, participants were equally likely to look at each billboard with and without the simultaneous conversation—and they even looked for the same amount of time. What seemed to impair participants' memory was that they looked at the billboards without actually focusing attention on them. Researchers have conducted similar experiments with participants driving real cars out on the road (Harbluk et al., 2007). This work has generated the same strong conclusion that cell phone conversations divert drivers' attention from the environment in which they are driving. In addition, this research documented the behavioral consequences of

diversions of attention: The most distracted drivers also had to engage in the most "hard braking."

Some people are surprised by these results because they reason that engaging in a conversation and attending to the visual environment are two rather different mental activities. Indeed, different areas of your brain are involved in carrying out these two tasks. Consider however an experiment in which participants underwent fMRI scans while they carried out simulated driving (Just et al., 2008). In parallel to the other studies we have described, participants either just drove or they both drove and engaged in language processes. When just driving, participants showed a good deal of activity in regions of their parietal lobes related to spatial processing. However, with the addition of the language task, activity in those parietal regions fell by 37%. The language task apparently put sufficient demands on the brain that the spatial task was left with inadequate resources.

Do these studies convince you that you should discourage people from using even hands-free cell phones while driving? What other data would you want to see?

- Why might the researchers have chosen research designs in which every participant carried out both the single and dual tasks?

- How do ethical considerations constrain the types of studies researchers can carry out on this issue?

In many cases, however, you can use information you already have about the environment to help you make a perceptual identification. If you visit a zoo, for example, you might be better prepared to recognize some types of animals than you otherwise would be. You are more likely to hypothesize that you are seeing a tiger there than you would be in your own backyard. When

your expectations affect perception, the phenomenon is called top-down processing. **Top-down processing** involves your past experiences, knowledge, motivations, and cultural background in perceiving the world. With top-down processing, higher mental functioning influences how you understand objects and events. Top-down processing is also known as conceptually driven (or hypothesis-driven) processing because the concepts you have stored in memory affect interpretation of the sensory data.

For a more detailed example of top-down versus bottom-up processing, we turn to the domain of speech perception. You have undoubtedly had the experience of trying to carry on a conversation at a very loud party. Under those circumstances,

---

top-down processing Perceptual processes in which information from an individual's past experience, knowledge, expectations, motivations, and background influence the way a perceived object is interpreted and classified.

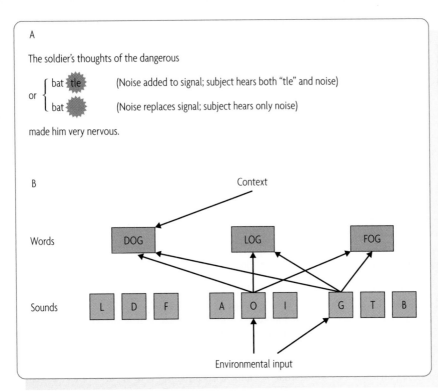

A

The soldier's thoughts of the dangerous

or $\begin{cases} \text{bat} \quad \text{tle} \quad \text{(Noise added to signal; subject hears both "tle" and noise)} \\ \text{bat} \qquad \quad \text{(Noise replaces signal; subject hears only noise)} \end{cases}$

made him very nervous.

B

Context

Words

DOG   LOG   FOG

Sounds

L D F   A O I   G T B

Environmental input

FIGURE 4.36 Phonemic Restoration

(A) Listeners are challenged to say whether noise has been added on top of a syllable or used to replace a syllable. Because of phonemic restoration, they often can't tell. They "hear" the missing information even when the sound is replaced by noise. (B) In this example, noise obscured the /d/ when your friend said "dog." Based only on the environmental input, your perceptual system can come up with several hypotheses: dog, log, fog, and so on. However, top-down information from the context—"I have to go home and walk my . . ."—supports the hypothesis that your friend said "dog."

Reprinted with permission from Irwin Rock, *The Logic of Perception*, Cambridge, MA: The MIT Press. Copyright © 1983.

it's probably true that not all of the physical signal you are producing arrives unambiguously at your acquaintance's ears: Some of what you had to say was almost certainly obscured by coughs, thumping music, or peals of laughter. Even so, people rarely realize that there are gaps in the physical signal they are experiencing. This phenomenon is known as *phonemic restoration* (Warren, 1970). As we explain more fully in Chapter 10, *phonemes* are the minimal, meaningful units of sound in a language; phonemic restoration occurs when people use top-down processes to fill in missing phonemes. Listeners often find it difficult to tell whether they are hearing a word that has a noise replacing part of the original speech signal or whether they are hearing a word with a noise just superimposed on the intact signal (see part A of **Figure 4.36**) (Samuel, 1981, 1991).

Part B of Figure 4.36 shows how bottom-up and top-down processes could interact to produce phonemic restoration (McClelland & Elman, 1986). Suppose part of what your friend says at a noisy party is obscured so the signal that arrives at your ears is "I have to go home to walk my (noise)og." If noise covers the /d/, you are likely to think that you actually heard the full word *dog*. But why? In Figure 4.36, you see two of the types of information relevant to speech perception. We have the individual sounds that make up words and the words themselves. When the sounds /o/ and /g/ arrive in this system, they provide information—in a bottom-up fashion—to the word level (we have given only a subset of the words in English that end with /og/). This provides you with a range of candidates for what your friend might have said. Now top-down processes go to work—the context helps you select *dog* as the most likely word to appear in this utterance. When all of this happens swiftly enough—bottom-up identification of a set of candidate words and top-down selection of the likely correct candidate—you'll never know that the /d/ was missing. Your perceptual processes believe that the word was intact (Samuel, 1997). The next time you're in a noisy environment, you'll be glad your perceptual processes fill sounds in so efficiently!

THE INFLUENCE OF CONTEXTS AND EXPECTATIONS

A primary goal of perception is to get an accurate "fix" on the world. Survival depends on accurate perceptions of objects and events in your environment: Is that motion in the bushes a tiger? However, there are many occasions on which bottom-up perceptual processes leave you with more than one hypothesis about the identity of the stimuli in the world—or in some cases, no particularly good hypotheses at all. In those cases, your top-down processes make use of contexts and expectations to help you get a clear sense of what's out in the world.

Consider **Figure 4.37** on page 128, which provides two examples in which the same sensory information permits two interpretations. The two examples are *ambiguous figures*. **Ambiguity** is an important concept in understanding perception because it shows that a single image can result in *multiple interpretations*. Look at each image until you can see the two alternative interpretations. Notice that once you have seen both of them, your perception flips back and forth between them as you look at the ambiguous figure.

Many prominent artists have used perceptual ambiguity as a central creative device in their works. **Figure 4.38,** on page 128 presents *Slave Market with the Disappearing Bust of Voltaire* by Salvador Dali. This work reveals a complex ambiguity in which a whole section of the picture must be radically reorganized and reinterpreted to allow perception of the "hidden" bust of the French philosopher-writer Voltaire. The white sky under the lower arch is Voltaire's forehead and hair; the white portions of the two ladies' dresses are his cheeks, nose, and chin. (If you have trouble seeing him, try blurring your vision or holding the book at arm's length.) Once you have seen the bust of Voltaire

---

ambiguity Property of perceptual object that may have more than one interpretation.

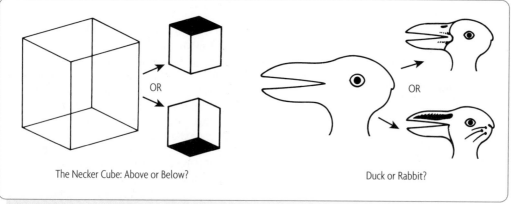

FIGURE 4.37 Perceptual Ambiguities
Each example allows two interpretations, but you cannot experience both at the same time.
Do you notice your perception flipping back and forth between each pair of possibilities?

in this picture, however, you will never be able to look at it without knowing where this Frenchman is hiding.

When the environment provides ambiguous information, you use contextual information as well as prior expectations to help you settle on particular interpretations. Depending on what you already know, where you are, and what else you see around you, your identification may vary. Read the following words:

THE CAT

They say THE CAT, right? Now look again at the middle letter of each word. Physically, these two letters are exactly the same, yet you perceived the first as an *H* and the second as an *A*. Why? Clearly, your perception was affected by what you know about words in English. The context provided by T_E makes an *H* highly likely and an *A* unlikely, whereas the reverse is true of the context of C_T (Selfridge, 1955).

In some cases, you need context to work even a bit harder. Consider **Figure 4.39** on page 129. What do you make of it? Suppose we tell you that it's a view into our neighbor's back-yard, showing a tree around which his Dalmatian routinely sniffs? Now can you see a dog? (The dog's nose is roughly in the middle of the figure.) To perceive the Dalmatian requires the top-down use of information from memory. If you didn't have any prior experiences of sniffing dogs, you'd likely never be able to have an unambiguous percept of this scene.

Contexts and expectations play an important background role throughout your everyday life. Have you ever had the experience of seeing people you knew in places where you didn't expect to see them, such as in a different city or a different social group? It takes much longer to recognize them in such situations, and some-times you aren't even sure that you really know them. The problem is not that they look any different but that the *context* is wrong; you didn't *expect* them to be there. The spatial and temporal context in which objects are recognized provides an important source of information because from the context you generate expectations about what objects you are and are not likely to see nearby.

Researchers have often documented the effects of context and expectation on perception (and response) by studying set. **Set** is a temporary readiness to perceive or react to a stimulus in a particular way. There are three types of set: motor, mental, and perceptual. A *motor set* is a readiness to make a quick, prepared response. A runner trains by perfecting a motor set to come out of the blocks as fast as possible at the sound of the starting gun. A *mental set* is a readiness to deal with a situation, such as a prob-lem-solving task or a game, in a way determined by learned rules, instructions, expectations, or habitual tendencies. A *mental set* can actually prevent you from solving a problem when the old rules don't seem to fit the new situation, as we'll see when we study problem solving in Chapter 9. A *perceptual set* is a readiness to detect a particular stimulus in a given context. A new mother, for example, is perceptually set to hear the cries of her child.

Often a set leads you to change your interpretation of an ambiguous stimulus. Consider these two series of words:

FOX; OWL; SNAKE; TURKEY; SWAN; D?VE
BOB; RAY; TONY; BILL; HENRY; D?VE

FIGURE 4.38 Ambiguity in Art
This painting by Salvador Dali is called *Slave Market with the Disappearing Bust of Voltaire*. Can you find Voltaire? Dali is one of a large number of modern and contemporary artists who have exploited ambiguity in their work.

---

set A temporary readiness to perceive or react to a stimulus in a particular way.

FIGURE 4.39   An Ambiguous Picture

What do you see in this picture?

Reprinted with permission from Irwin Rock, *The Logic of Perception.* Cambridge, MA, The MIT Press. Copyright © 1983.

Did you read through the lists? What word came to mind for D?VE in each case? If you thought DOVE and DAVE, it's because the list of words created a set that directed your search of memory in a particular way.

All the effects of context on perception clearly require that your memory be organized in such a fashion that information relevant to particular situations becomes available at the right times. In other words, to generate appropriate (or inappropriate) expectations, you must be able to make use of prior knowledge stored in memory. Sometimes you "see" with your memory as much as you see with your eyes. In Chapter 7, we discuss the properties of memory that make context effects on perception possible.

FINAL LESSONS

To solidify all that you have learned in this chapter, we suggest that you take a look back at Figure 4.2—you now have the knowledge necessary to understand the whole flowchart. Examination of Figure 4.2 will also confirm that the important lesson to be learned from the study of perception is that a perceptual experience in response to a stimulus event is a response of the whole person. In addition to the information provided when your sensory receptors are stimulated, your final perception depends on who you are, whom you are with, and what you expect, want, and value. A perceiver often plays two different roles that we can compare to gambling and interior design. As a gambler, a perceiver is willing to bet that the present input can be understood in terms of past knowledge and personal theories. As a compulsive interior decorator, a perceiver is constantly rearranging the stimuli so that they fit better and are more coherent. Incongruity and messy perceptions are rejected in favor of those with clear, clean, consistent lines.

If perceiving were completely bottom-up, you would be bound to the same mundane, concrete reality of the here and now. You could register experience but not profit from it on later occasions, nor would you see the world differently under different circumstances. If perceptual processing were completely top-down, however, you could become lost in your own fantasy world of what you expect and hope to perceive. A proper balance between the two extremes achieves the basic goal of perception: to experience what is out there in a way that optimally serves your needs as a biological and social being, moving about and adapting to your physical and social environment.

Recapping Main Points

Perceptual Knowledge of the World

- The task of perception is to determine what the distal (external) stimulus is from the information contained in the proximal (sensory) stimulus.
- Psychophysics investigates psychological responses to physical stimuli. Researchers measure absolute thresholds and just noticeable differences between stimuli.
- Signal detection allows researchers to separate sensory acuity from response biases.
- Researchers in psychophysics have captured the relationship between physical intensity and psychological effect with mathematical functions.
- Sensation translates the physical energy of stimuli into neural codes via transduction.

The Visual System

- Photoreceptors in the retina, called rods and cones, convert light energy into neural impulses.
- Ganglion cells in the retina integrate input from receptors and bipolar cells. Their axons form the optic nerves that meet at the optic chiasma.
- Visual information is distributed to several different areas of the brain that process different aspects of the visual environment such as how things look and where they are.
- The wavelength of light is the stimulus for color.
- Color sensations differ in hue, saturation, and brightness.
- Color vision theory combines the trichromatic theory of three color receptors with the opponent-process theory of color systems composed of opponent elements.

Hearing

- Hearing is produced by sound waves that vary in frequency, amplitude, and complexity.
- In the cochlea, sound waves are transformed into fluid waves that move the basilar membrane. Hairs on the basilar membrane stimulate neural impulses that are sent to the auditory cortex.
- Place theory best explains the coding of high frequencies, and frequency theory best explains the coding of low frequencies.
- To compute the direction from which the sound is arriving, two types of neural mechanisms compute the relative intensity and timing of sounds coming to each ear.

Your Other Senses

- Smell and taste respond to the chemical properties of substances and work together when people are seeking and sampling food.
- Olfaction is accomplished by odor-sensitive cells deep in the nasal passages.
- Taste receptors are taste buds embedded in papillae, mostly in the tongue.
- The cutaneous (skin) senses give sensations of pressure and temperature.
- The vestibular sense gives information about the direction and rate of body motion.
- The kinesthetic sense gives information about the position of body parts and helps coordinate motion.
- Pain is the body's response to potentially harmful stimuli.
- The physiological response to pain involves sensory response at the site of the pain stimulus and nerve impulses moving between the brain and the spinal cord.

Organizational Processes in Perception

- Perceptual processes organize sensations into coherent images and give you perception of objects and patterns.
- Both your personal goals and the properties of the objects in the world determine where you will focus your attention.
- The Gestalt psychologists provided several laws of perceptual grouping, including proximity, similarity, good continuation, closure, and common fate.
- Perceptual processes integrate over both time and space to provide an interpretation of the environment.
- Binocular, motion, and pictorial cues all contribute to the perception of depth.
- You tend to perceive objects as having stable size, shape, and lightness.
- Knowledge about perceptual illusions can provide constraints on ordinary perceptual processes.

Identification and Recognition Processes

- During the final stage of perceptual processing—identification and recognition of objects—percepts are given meaning through processes that combine bottom-up and top-down influences.
- Ambiguity may arise when the same sensory information can be organized into different percepts.
- Context, expectations, and perceptual sets may guide recognition of incomplete or ambiguous data in one direction rather than another equally possible one.

KEY TERMS

absolute threshold (p. 93)

accommodation (p. 97)

amacrine cell (p. 99)

ambiguity (p. 127)

attention (p. 114)

auditory nerve (p. 108)

basilar membrane (p. 108)

binocular depth cue (p. 119)

bipolar cell (p. 99)

blind spot (p. 99)

bottom-up processing (p. 125)

brightness (p. 102)

cochlea (p. 108)

complementary colors (p. 102)

cone (p. 98)

convergence (p. 119)

cutaneous sense (p. 112)

dark adaptation (p. 98)

difference threshold (p. 95)

distal stimulus (p. 92)

fovea (p. 99)

frequency theory (p. 108)

ganglion cell (p. 99)

gate-control theory (p. 113)

Gestalt psychology (p. 116)

goal-directed selection (p. 114)

gustation (p. 111)

horizontal cell (p. 99)

hue (p. 102)

identification and recognition (p. 91)

illusion (p. 124)

just noticeable difference (JND) (p. 96)

kinesthetic sense (p. 112)

lens (p. 97)

lightness constancy (p. 123)

loudness (p. 106)

monocular depth cue (p. 120)

motion parallax (p. 119)

olfaction (p. 110)

olfactory bulb (p. 110)

opponent-process theory (p. 104)

optic nerve (p. 100)

pain (p. 113)

perception (p. 91)

perceptual constancy (p. 121)

perceptual organization (p. 91)

pheromone (p. 111)

phi phenomenon (p. 118)

photoreceptor (p. 98)

pitch (p. 106)

place theory (p. 108)

proximal stimulus (p. 92)

psychometric function (p. 94)

psychophysics (p. 93)

pupil (p. 97)

receptive field (p. 101)

response bias (p. 94)

retina (p. 98)

retinal disparity (p. 119)

rod (p. 98)

saturation (p. 102)

sensation (p. 91)

sensory adaptation (p. 94)

sensory receptor (p. 96)

set (p. 128)

shape constancy (p. 122)

signal detection theory (p. 95)

size constancy (p. 122)

sound localization (p. 109)

stimulus-driven capture (p. 114)

timbre (p. 106)

top-down processing (p. 126)

transduction (p. 96)

trichromatic theory (p. 104)

vestibular sense (p. 112)

volley principle (p. 109)

Weber's law (p. 96)

Chapter 4 Practice Test

1. Suppose you are looking at a globe of the world. Although the _____ is a sphere, you'd expect the _____ to be a circle.
   a. distal; absolute
   b. distal; proximal
   c. threshold; distal
   d. proximal; distal

2. When you first walked into a room, you were overwhelmed by the smell of someone's perfume. Over time, you become less aware of the smell. This is an example of
   a. a psychometric function.
   b. sensory adaptation.
   c. an illusion.
   d. transduction.

3. You are carrying out an experiment in which you want to find a difference threshold for soft drinks that vary in their sugar concentration. You want to find the point at which the stimuli are recognized as different _____ percent of the time.
   a. 50
   b. 25
   c. 100
   d. 75

4. The conversion of one form of physical energy into another is called
   a. sensory adaptation.
   b. transduction.
   c. sensory reception.
   d. photoreception.

5. If you walk into a room that has very low illumination, your _____ are likely to contribute more than your _____ to your visual experience.
   a. rods; amacrine cells
   b. horizontal cells; rods
   c. cones; rods
   d. rods; cones

6. Which of these pairs does not play a role in opponent-process theory?
   a. red versus green
   b. white versus black
   c. yellow versus blue
   d. blue versus green

7. The airborne sound wave becomes "seaborne" when the auditory information reaches the
   a. auditory nerve.
   b. cochlea.
   c. tympanic membrane.
   d. fovea.

8. Which of these is *not* a primary taste quality?
   a. bitter
   b. sweet
   c. tangy
   d. sour

9. The purpose of _____ theory is to explain some aspects of the relationship between physical and psychological experiences of pain.
   a. gate-control
   b. volley
   c. frequency
   d. place

10. In general, you would predict that people with _____ taste buds would experience _____ pain when they eat spicy food.
    a. fewer; more
    b. fewer; no
    c. more; more
    d. more; less

11. When Shirley walks into a party, she looks around the room to find her husband Paul. This is an example of
    a. goal-driven attention.
    b. stimulus-driven capture.
    c. temporal integration.
    d. sensory adaptation.

12. Tomas owns a ring with a very small gap in it. The law of _____ explains why most people perceive his ring to be intact.
    a. similarity
    b. common fate
    c. good continuation
    d. closure

13. While engaging in simulated driving, Michael underwent fMRI scans. On Trial 1 he was just driving; on Trial 2 he was also engaged in a language task.
    a. You expect to see equal amounts of activity in the parietal lobe on both trials.
    b. You expect to see less activity in the parietal lobe on Trial 1.
    c. You expect to see less activity in the parietal lobe on Trial 2.
    d. You cannot make any predictions about activity in the parietal lobe.

14. Just as Chris says, "I love you," a truck sounds its horn. Although the horn covered the *l* sound in *love*, Pat still perceives *love* as intact. This is an example of
    a. bottom-up processing.
    b. perceptual constancy.
    c. top-down processing.
    d. good continuation.

15. For a short while after seeing a horror movie, Calvin perceives every shadow as a monster. It sounds as though he is experiencing
    a. a perceptual set.
    b. shape constancy.
    c. the phi phenomenon.
    d. the law of common fate.

Essay Questions

1. How does signal detection theory explain why people might make different judgments given the same sensory experiences?

2. How do trichromatic theory and opponent-process theory fit together to explain important aspects of color vision?

3. How do ambiguous stimuli demonstrate some of the challenges your sensory and perceptual processes face as they help you interpret the world?

Discovering Psychology Viewing Guide

Watch the following video by logging on to MyPsychLab (www.mypsychlab.com). After you have watched the video, complete the activities that follow.

Program 7: Sensation and Perception

KEY TERMS AND PEOPLE

As you watch the program, pay particular attention to this term and person in addition to those covered in this textbook.

- *receptor*—a specialized nerve cell sensitive to particular kinds of stimulus energy.
- *Misha Pavel*—studies the successive stages of information processing that take place as we continually perceive the world.

PROGRAM REVIEW

1. Imagine that a teaspoon of sugar is dissolved in two gallons of water. Rita can detect this level of sweetness at least half the time. This level is called the
   a. distal stimulus.
   b. perceptual constant.
   c. response bias.
   d. absolute threshold.

2. What is the job of a receptor?
   a. to transmit a neural impulse
   b. to connect new information with old information
   c. to detect a type of physical energy
   d. to receive an impulse from the brain

3. In what area of the brain is the visual cortex located?
   a. in the front   c. in the back
   b. in the middle   d. under the brain stem

4. What is the function of the thalamus in visual processing?
   a. It relays information to the cortex.
   b. It rotates the retinal image.
   c. It converts light energy to a neural impulse.
   d. It makes sense of the proximal stimulus.

5. David Hubel discusses the visual pathway and the response to a line. The program shows an experiment in which the response to a moving line changed dramatically with changes in the line's
   a. thickness.   c. speed.
   b. color.   d. orientation.

6. Misha Pavel used computer graphics to study how
   a. we process visual information.
   b. rods differ from cones in function.
   c. we combine information from different senses.
   d. physical energy is transduced in the visual system.

7. Imagine that a baseball player puts on special glasses that shift his visual field up 10 degrees. When he wears these glasses, the player sees everything higher than it actually is. After some practice, the player can hit with the glasses on. What will happen when the player first tries to hit with the glasses off?
   a. He will think that the ball is lower than it is.
   b. He will think that the ball is higher than it is.
   c. He will accurately perceive the ball's position.
   d. It is impossible to predict an individual's reaction in this situation.

8. Imagine that a dog is walking toward you. As the dog gets closer, the image it casts on your retina
   a. gets larger.   c. gets smaller.
   b. gets darker.   d. stays exactly the same size.

9. You want to paint your room yellow, so you get some samples at the paint store. When you hold the sample against your white wall, it looks different from the way it looks against the green curtain. A psychologist would attribute this to
   a. perceptual constancy.   c. contrast effects.
   b. visual paradoxes.   d. threshold differences.

10. Which of the following phenomena best illustrates that perception is an active process?
    a. bottom-up processing   c. top-down processing
    b. motion parallax   d. parietal senses

11. The program shows a drawing that can be seen as a rat or as a man. People were more likely to identify the drawing as a man if they
    a. were men themselves.
    b. had just seen pictures of people.
    c. were afraid of rats.
    d. looked at the picture holistically rather than analytically.

12. Where is the proximal stimulus to be found?
    a. in the outside world   c. in the occipital lobe
    b. on the retina   d. in the thalamus

13. How is visual information processed by the brain?
    a. It's processed by the parietal lobe, which relays the information to the temporal lobe.
    b. It's processed entirely within the frontal lobe.
    c. It's processed by the occipital lobe, which projects to the thalamus, which projects to a succession of areas in the cortex.
    d. If the information is abstract, it's processed by the cortex; if it's concrete, it's processed by the thalamus.

14. Which of the following is true about the proximal stimulus in visual perception?
    a. It's identical to the distal stimulus because the retina produces a faithful reproduction of the perceptual world.
    b. It's upside-down, flat, distorted, and obscured by blood vessels.
    c. It's black-and-white and consists of very sparse information about horizontal and vertical edges.
    d. It contains information about the degree of convergence of the two eyes.

15. Which of the following is an example of pure top-down processing?
    a. hallucinating
    b. understanding someone else's speech when honking horns are obscuring individual sounds
    c. perceiving a circular color patch that has been painted onto a canvas
    d. enjoying a melody

16. Which sensory information is *not* paired with the cortical lobe that is primarily responsible for processing it?
    a. visual information, occipital lobe
    b. speech, frontal lobe
    c. body senses, parietal lobe
    d. hearing, central sulcus lobe

17. When your eyes are shut, you cannot
    a. hallucinate.
    b. use contextual information from other senses to make inferences about what's there.
    c. transform a distal visual stimulus into a proximal stimulus.
    d. experience perceptual constancy.

18. The researcher David Hubel is best known for
    a. mapping visual receptor cells.
    b. discovering subjective contours.
    c. identifying the neural pathways by which body sensations occur.
    d. realizing that hearing and smell originate from the same brain area.

19. The primary reason why psychologists study illusions is because
    a. they help identify areas of the cortex that have been damaged.
    b. they serve as good "public relations" material for curious novices.
    c. they help us categorize people into good and bad perceivers.
    d. they help us understand how perception normally works.

20. The shrinking-square illusion demonstrated by Misha Pavel relies on the processing of which kinds of feature?
    a. edges and corners
    b. color and texture
    c. torque and angular momentum
    d. density gradients and motion

QUESTIONS TO CONSIDER

1. Why do psychologists identify sensation and perception as two different fields of study? Does this reflect the relative youth of psychology as a science, or does it represent a scientific distinction that will still be favored in 50 years?

2. As the population ages, adapting the environment for people with a range of sensory abilities and deficits will become increasingly important. Architects will need to improve access to and safety of buildings, taking into account that older people need about three times as much light as young people in order to distinguish objects. They also need higher visual contrasts to detect potential hazards, such as curbs or steps. How might you identify some changes you could make in and around your home to create a safer, more comfortable environment for a disabled or visually or hearing-impaired person?

3. Investigations of people who claim to have extrasensory perception reveal that the better controlled the study, the less likely it is to support claims of ESP. Does it do any harm to believe in ESP? Why do most psychologists suggest that we should be skeptical of people who claim to have extrasensory perception?

4. Choose a familiar context, like a grocery store, and describe how the Gestalt principles of perceptual organization are used to help people perceive objects and group them.

5. Describe how film and television directors use sight and sound techniques to create meaning and feeling. As you watch a television commercial, program, or film, notice the way the camera frames the image and how angle and motion create a mood or point of view. Notice the use of sound. Consider how these elements shape viewers' desires, expectations, and feelings.

6. Although the neural pathways serving perception are similar in all of us, our internal perceptual experiences could theoretically differ. What sorts of differences in our experiences can you imagine as being possible? What sorts of differences would you think would be unlikely?

7. Absolute thresholds seem to differ across species. For example, you are much better at detecting degraded visual stimuli than animals of some other species would be, but at the same time you may be much worse than them at smelling faint odors. Why do you think that humans evolved to favor the visual sense?

ACTIVITIES

1. Closure and continuity of line are organizing principles that we use to make sense out of stimuli. Make line drawings of familiar objects by tracing pictures from comics, children's coloring books, or magazines. Leave out sections of the drawing, and ask family members or friends to identify the objects. See how incomplete the line drawing can be and still be identified.

2. Blindfold yourself. (Have someone standing by to prevent injury or damage.) Contrast the experience of moving about in a familiar room, such as your bedroom or kitchen, with the experience of moving about a room in which you spend little time. Note the expectations and significant sensory cues you depend on to avoid tripping and bumping into things. How relaxed or tense were you in each room?

3. Listen to a conversation, trying hard to (a) notice all of the other noise going on around you and (b) notice all the instances of imperfect transmission of speech sounds. For example, the speaker might mispronounce something or say it with his or her mouth full, or an outside noise may obscure the sound coming from the speaker. Is it hard for you to snap out of top-down mode to do this exercise?

4. If you have access to a virtual reality game, try playing it while also monitoring what is going on in the room around you. While interacting with the virtual objects in the game, think about how you must look to passersby, and think about the layout of the objects in the space that physically surrounds you. How good are you at immersing yourself in two worlds at once? Do you find that you have to switch back and forth, or are you able to consider yourself as being in two very different realities simultaneously?

Mind, Consciousness, and Alternate States

As you begin reading this chapter, take a moment to think about a favorite past event. Now think about what you'd like to have happen tomorrow or the next day. Where did these memories of the past and projections into the future *come* from and when did they *arrive*? Although you obviously have a vast body of information stored in your brain, it is very unlikely that the thoughts we asked you to have were "in mind" just as you were sitting down to read your psychology text. Therefore, you might feel comfortable saying that the thoughts arrived in your consciousness—and that they came from some part of your brain that was not then conscious. But how did these particular thoughts come to mind? Did you actually consider several different memories or options for the future? That is, were you consciously aware of making a choice? Or did thoughts somehow just emerge—by virtue of some set of unconscious operations—into your consciousness?

This series of questions provides a preview of the major topics of Chapter 5. We will begin by discussing the contents and functions of your everyday consciousness. We suggest that consciousness both aids survival and provides a sense of who you are and where you fit in the world. We will then move to the changes in consciousness that accompany your daily cycles from waking to sleeping. We will examine the approaches to dreams that have emerged in both Western and non-Western cultures. Finally, we will discuss the many instances in which people intentionally alter their states of consciousness by, for example, engaging in meditation and consuming mind-altering drugs. For all these topics, we will explore the methods researchers use so that aspects of mind can be studied scientifically. We will describe how researchers have learned to externalize the internal, make public the private, and provide precise measures of subjective experiences.

of the conscious mind, and William James observed his own stream of consciousness (see Chapter 1). In fact, on the very first page of his classic 1892 text, *Psychology*, James endorsed as a definition of psychology *"the description and explanation of states of consciousness as such."*

Your ordinary waking consciousness includes your perceptions, thoughts, feelings, images, and desires at a given moment—all the mental activity on which you are focusing your attention. You are conscious of both what you are doing and also of the fact that you are doing it. At times, you are conscious of the realization that others are observing, evaluating, and reacting to what you are doing. A *sense of self* comes out of the experience of watching yourself from this privileged "insider" position. Taken together, these various mental activities form the contents of consciousness—all the experiences you are consciously aware of at a particular time (Legrand, 2007).

We have defined the general types of information that *might* be conscious at a particular place and time, but what determines what is conscious right now? Were you, for example, aware of your breathing just now? Probably not; its control is part of *nonconscious processes*. Were you thinking about your last vacation or about the author of *Hamlet*? Again, probably not; control of such thoughts is part of *preconscious memories*. Were you aware of background noises, such as the ticking of a clock, the hum of traffic, or the buzzing of a fluorescent light? It would be difficult to be aware of all this and still pay full attention to the meaning of the material in this chapter; these stimuli are part of *unattended information*. Finally, there may be types

The Contents of Consciousness

We must start by admitting that the term **consciousness** is ambiguous. We can use the term to refer to a general state of mind *or* to its specific contents: Sometimes you say you were "conscious" in contrast to being "unconscious" (for example, being under anesthesia or asleep); at other times, you say you were conscious—*aware*—of certain information or actions. There is, in fact, a certain consistency here—to be conscious of any particular information, you must be conscious. In this chapter, when we speak of the *contents* of consciousness, we mean the body of information of which you are aware.

AWARENESS AND CONSCIOUSNESS

Some of the earliest research in psychology concerned the contents of consciousness. As psychology gradually diverged from philosophy in the 1800s, it became the science of the mind. Wundt and Titchener used introspection to explore the contents

Why is self-awareness considered such an important aspect of consciousness?

---

consciousness A state of awareness of internal events and the external environment.

At any given time, thoughts about your job, your parents, or your hungry pet may flow below the level of consciousness until something occurs to focus your attention on one of these topics. Why are these memories considered preconscious, not unconscious?

of information that are *unconscious*—not readily accessible to conscious awareness—such as the set of grammatical rules that enable you to understand this sentence. Let's examine each of these types of awareness.

Nonconscious Processes There is a range of **nonconscious** bodily activities that rarely, if ever, impinge on consciousness. An example of nonconscious processes at work is the regulation of blood pressure. Your nervous system monitors physiological information to detect and act on changes continually, without your awareness. At certain times, some ordinarily nonconscious activities can be made conscious: You can, for example, choose to exercise conscious control over your pattern of breathing. Even so, your nervous system takes care of many important functions without requiring conscious resources.

Preconscious Memories Memories accessible to consciousness only after something calls your attention to them are known as **preconscious memories.** The storehouse of memory is filled with an incredible amount of information, such as your general knowledge of language, sports, or geography and recollections of your personally experienced events. Preconscious memories function silently in the background of your mind until a situation arises in which they are consciously necessary (as when we asked you to call to mind a favorite past event). You will learn much more about memory in Chapter 7.

Unattended Information At any given time, you are surrounded by a vast amount of stimulation. As we described in Chapter 4, you can focus your attention only on a small part of it. What you focus on, in combination with the memories it evokes, will determine, to a large extent, what is in consciousness. Still, researchers have long wondered how thoroughly people process perceptual information to which they have not directed conscious attention. A classic hypothesis was formulated

by **Donald Broadbent** (1958), who suggested that the mind has only *limited capacity* to carry out complete processing. On his view, people's processing of unattended stimuli falls short of the point at which they could identify those stimuli. Some researchers have reported phenomena that appeared to contradict this view. Consider what has been called the *cocktail party phenomenon:* People often report that they hear their name being mentioned in a noisy room, even when they are engaged in their own conversation. Laboratory research has confirmed that people are especially likely to notice their own names among unattended information (Wood & Cowan, 1995). However, other researchers have critiqued these experiments by suggesting that participants were actually apportioning some attention to the "unattended" information. On the whole, evidence suggests that Broadbent was correct: People need conscious attention to identify the sights and sounds (and so on) in their environments (Lachter et al., 2004).

The Unconscious You typically recognize the existence of *unconscious* information when you cannot explain some behavior by virtue of forces that were conscious at the time of the behavior. Sigmund Freud developed an initial theory of unconscious forces. As we will describe in Chapter 13, Freud argued that people's psychological well-being is sufficiently threatened by certain life experiences that memories of those experiences are permanently banished from consciousness. Freud believed that when the content of unacceptable ideas or motives is *repressed*—put out of consciousness—the strong feelings associated with the thoughts still remain and influence behavior. Freud's "discovery" of the unconscious contradicted a long tradition of Western thought. From the time the English philosopher

---

nonconscious Not typically available to consciousness or memory.

preconscious memory Memory that is not currently conscious but that can easily be called into consciousness when necessary.

John Locke wrote his classic text on the mind, *An Essay Concerning Human Understanding* (1690/1975), most thinkers firmly believed that rational beings had access to all the activities of their own minds. Freud's initial hypothesis about the existence of unconscious mental processes was considered outrageous by his contemporaries (Dennett, 1987). (We will revisit Freud's ideas when we discuss the origin of your unique personality in Chapter 13.)

Many psychologists now use the term *unconscious* to refer to information and processes that are more benign than the types of thoughts Freud suggested must be repressed (McGovern & Baars, 2007). For example, many types of ordinary language processing rely on unconscious processes. Consider this sentence (Vu et al., 2000):

> *She investigated the bark.*

How did you interpret this sentence? Did you picture some woman looking after a dog or examining a tree? Because the word *bark* is ambiguous—and the sentence context provides little help—you can only guess at what the writer meant. Now consider the same sentence in a slightly larger context:

> *The botanist looked for a fungus. She investigated the bark.*

Did you find the sentence easier to understand in this context? If you did, it's because your unconscious language processes used the extra context to make a very swift choice between the two meanings of *bark*.

With this example, we demonstrate that processes that operate below the level of consciousness often affect your behavior—in this case, the ease with which you came to a clear understanding of the sentence. We have thus shifted subtly from discussing the contents of consciousness to discussing the functions of consciousness. Before we take up that topic in detail, however, we will briefly describe two ways in which the contents of consciousness can be studied.

STUDYING THE CONTENTS OF CONSCIOUSNESS

To study consciousness, researchers have had to devise methodologies to make deeply private experiences overtly measurable. One method is a new variation on Wundt and Titchener's practice of introspection. Experimental participants are asked to speak aloud as they work through a variety of complex tasks. They report, in as much detail as possible, the sequence of thoughts they experience while they complete the tasks. The participants' reports, called *think-aloud protocols,* are used to document the mental strategies and representations of knowledge that the participants employ to do the task. For example, researchers collected think-aloud protocols to understand the different strategies experts and novices bring to their judgments about product designs (Locher et al., 2008).

In the *experience-sampling method,* participants provide information about their thoughts and feelings in the normal course of their daily lives (Hektner et al., 2007). Participants in experience-sampling research often carry devices that signal them when they should provide reports about the contents of their consciousness. For example, in one methodology, participants wear electronic pagers. A radio transmitter activates the pager at various

TABLE 5.1 Types of Comparisons in People's Thoughts

Type	Example
Social	"I'm a better basketball player than Tom."
Counterfactual	"If I'd left earlier, I could have gotten here on time."
Temporal–past	"I got more sleep when I was in high school."
Temporal–future	"My sister is going to start making new friends."

From A. Summerville & N. J. Roese, Dare to compare: Fact-based versus simulation-based comparison in daily life, *Journal of Experimental Social Psychology, 44,* pp. 664–671, Copyright (2008), with permission from Elsevier.

random times each day for a week or more. Whenever the pager signals, participants may be asked to respond to questions such as "How well were you concentrating?" In this way, researchers can keep a running record of participants' thoughts, awareness, and focuses of attention as they go about their everyday lives (Hektner & Csikszentmihalyi, 2002). Consider an experiment that used handheld computers to obtain experience samples.

The researchers wished to determine how often people's thoughts focus on comparisons between their current reality and other possibilities (Summerville & Roese, 2007). At seven random times daily for two weeks, 34 participants were signaled by handheld computers to report what they were thinking in the moment. If the thoughts centered on comparisons, the *participants* placed them in the categories indicated in **Table 5.1**. The researchers found that 12 percent of the participants' thoughts were comparisons, which, as they noted, was "a remarkably large proportion given the sheer variety of mental experience" (p. 668). The comparisons were fairly evenly distributed across the four categories in Table 5.1. In addition, when participants' thoughts turned to changing the past (counterfactual comparisons) or contemplating the future (temporal–future comparisons), they were most often thoughts about how circumstances might have been or still could be better.

Have you ever noticed how often these types of comparisons enter into your consciousness? The experience-sampling method allows researchers to provide a nuanced account of what and how people think about their lives.

If you take a quick look around the room in which you are reading, you can appreciate how many objects in your environment are readily available but are not (until you inspect the room) part of the contents of your consciousness. You can carry out the same quick review of your memory to demonstrate how much you have stored beyond the information that is the particular focus of your conscious attention. Techniques such as think-aloud protocols and experience sampling allow researchers to determine—for particular tasks and for particular times—which subset of all the information that individuals have available is present in consciousness.

STOP AND REVIEW

❶ What is meant by a preconscious memory?

❷ How did Freud believe information became unconscious?

❸ How do researchers obtain think-aloud protocols?

CRITICAL THINKING Recall the experiment on comparisons. Why is it important that the experience samples be taken at random moments?

The Functions of Consciousness

When we address the question of the *functions* of consciousness, we are trying to understand why we *need* consciousness—what does it add to our human experience? In this section, we will describe the importance of consciousness to human survival and social function.

THE USES OF CONSCIOUSNESS

Human consciousness was forged in the crucible of competition with the most hostile force in its evolutionary environment—other humans. The human mind may have evolved as a consequence of the extreme *sociability* of human ancestors, which was perhaps originally a group defense against predators and a means to exploit resources more efficiently. However, close group living then created new demands for cooperative as well as competitive abilities with other humans. Natural selection favored those who could think, plan, and imagine alternative realities that could promote both bonding with kin and victory over adversaries. Those who developed language and tools won the grand prize of survival of the fittest mind—and, fortunately, passed it on to us (Terrace & Metcalfe, 2005).

Because consciousness evolved, you should not be surprised that it provides a range of functions that aid in the survival of the species (Bering & Bjorklund, 2007). Consciousness also plays an important role in allowing for the construction of both personal and culturally shared realities.

Aiding Survival From a biological perspective, consciousness probably evolved because it helped individuals make sense of environmental information and use that information in planning the most appropriate and effective actions. Usually, you are faced with a sensory-information overload. William James described the massive amount of information that strikes the sensory receptors as a "blooming, buzzing confusion" assailing you from all sides. Consciousness helps you adapt to your environment by making sense of this profusion of confusion in three ways.

First, consciousness reduces the flow of stimulus input by restricting what you notice and what you focus on. You might recognize this *restrictive* function of consciousness from the discussion of *attention* in Chapter 4. Consciousness helps you tune out much of the information that is not relevant to your immediate goals and purposes. Suppose you decide to take a walk to enjoy a spring day. You notice trees blooming, birds singing, and children playing. If, all at once, a snarling dog appears on the scene, you use consciousness to restrict your attention to that dog and assess the level of danger. The restrictive function also applies to information you draw from your internal storehouse of information. When, at the outset of this chapter, we asked you to think about a favorite past event, we were asking you to use your consciousness to restrict your mental attention to a single past memory.

A second function of consciousness is *selective storage*. Even within the category of information to which you consciously attend, not all of it has continuing relevance to your ongoing concerns. After your encounter with the snarling dog, you might stop yourself and think, "I want to remember not to walk down this street." Consciousness allows you to selectively store—commit to memory—information that you want to analyze, interpret, and act on in the future; consciousness allows you to classify events and experiences as relevant or irrelevant to personal needs by selecting some and ignoring others. When we consider memory processes in Chapter 7, we will see that not all the information you add to memory requires conscious processing. Still, conscious memories have different properties—and involve different brain regions—than other types of memories.

A third function of consciousness is to make you stop, think, and consider alternatives based on past knowledge and imagine various consequences. This *planning* function enables you to suppress strong desires when they conflict with moral, ethical, or practical concerns. With this kind of consciousness you can plan a route for your next walk that avoids that snarling dog. Because consciousness gives you a broad time perspective in which to frame potential actions, you can call on knowledge of the past and expectations for the future to influence your current decisions. For all these reasons, consciousness gives you great potential for flexible, appropriate responses to the changing demands in your life.

Personal and Cultural Constructions of Reality

No two people interpret a situation in exactly the same way (Higgins & Pittman, 2008). Your *personal construction of reality* is your unique interpretation of a current situation based on your general knowledge, memories of past experiences, current needs, values, beliefs, and future goals. Each person attends more to certain features of the stimulus environment than to others precisely because his or her personal construction of reality has been formed from a selection of unique inputs. When your personal construction of reality remains relatively stable, your *sense of self* has continuity over time.

Individual differences in personal constructions of reality are even greater when people have grown up in different cultures, lived in different environments within a culture, or faced different survival tasks. The opposite is also true—because the people of a given culture share many of the same experiences, they often have similar constructions of reality. *Cultural constructions of reality* are ways of thinking about the world that are shared by most members of a particular group of people. When a member of a society develops a personal construction of reality that fits in with the cultural construction, it is affirmed by the culture and, at the same time, it affirms the cultural construction. In Chapter 13, we will describe more fully the relationship between the personal and the cultural sense of self.

STUDYING THE FUNCTIONS OF CONSCIOUSNESS

People's behavior is most often influenced by both conscious and unconscious processes. Many functions of consciousness include implicit comparisons with what remains unconscious. That is, conscious processes often affect or are affected by unconscious processes. To study the functions of consciousness, researchers often conduct research that demonstrates the different products of conscious and unconscious processes (McGovern & Baars, 2007).

For example, researchers have argued that people may bring either unconscious or conscious processes to bear on the many decisions they face in life (Evans, 2008). Depending on which system of processes they use, people's responses can be quite different. Consider the domain of moral reasoning (to which we will return in Chapter 10). How would you respond to the classic "crying baby" dilemma in which you "must decide whether to smother one's own baby in order to prevent enemy soldiers from finding and killing oneself, one's baby, and several others" (Greene et al., 2008, p. 1147). When people face this dilemma, their gut response—the product of unconscious processes—is that they could never smother their own child. However, when people face this problem with conscious deliberation, they often conclude that they must make the sacrifice to save the larger number of individuals.

To demonstrate that this shift reflects the use of conscious processes, researchers asked participants to consider dilemmas of this sort in two different circumstances (Greene et al., 2008). In one condition, participants read the dilemmas on a computer screen and indicated a "yes" or "no" judgment to a possible response (e.g., "Is it appropriate for you to smother your child in order to save yourself and the other townspeople?") as swiftly as possible. In the second condition, participants also read and responded to the dilemmas. However, they simultaneously had to monitor a stream of numbers scrolling across the computer screen and press a button every time they saw the number 5. The purpose of this second task is to overload participants' conscious processes. This simultaneous task should have made it much more difficult for them to use conscious processes to reason about the moral dilemmas. In fact, when participants had this extra load, it took them much longer to give the "yes" responses to the moral dilemmas that represented the use of conscious reasoning. Thus, one way to study the function of consciousness is to demonstrate how people's responses change when conscious processes are not, in fact, allowed to function normally.

Another way to study the functions of consciousness is to determine which of the many tasks you carry out on a day-to-day basis require conscious intervention. To give you an example, we want you to put your book down for a moment and try to find an object in the room that is *red*. Let's assume that there is, in fact, a red object in your room. Under most circumstances, you should have felt as if your eyes were drawn to that object without any conscious effort. Research confirms that people can carry out a search for certain basic features of objects such as color, shape, and size, with little or no conscious attention (Wolfe, 2003). Suppose, now, that you try to find an object that is both *blue* and *red*. If you take a moment to carry out that task, you should have a very different sense of how much conscious effort is involved. Under most circumstances, you'll have to use conscious attention to find an object that has a combination of two features.

We provide another example of the uses of conscious attention in **Figure 5.1**. In Part A, try to find the yellow and blue item. In Part B, try to find the yellow house with blue windows. Wasn't this second task much easier? Performance is much less affected by all the extra objects in the picture when the two colors are organized into *parts* and *wholes* (Wolfe et al., 1994). Could you feel your conscious attention

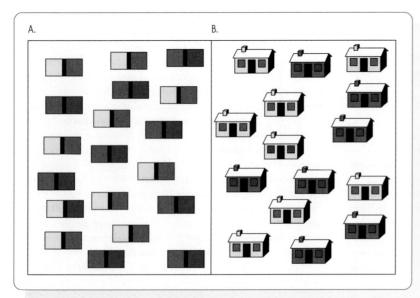

A.   B.

FIGURE 5.1   Search for the Conjunction of Two Colors

(A) Find the yellow and blue item. (B) Find the yellow house with blue windows. (A) Search is very inefficient when the conjunction is between the colors of two parts of a target. (B) However, search is much easier when the conjunction is between the color of the whole item and the color of one of its parts.

Adapted with permission from Jerome Kuhl, from Features and objects in visual processing, by Anne Triesman, *Scientific American*, November 1986, p. 116.

being more engaged when we asked you to find the yellow and blue item? From results of this sort, researchers are assembling a global view of the circumstances in which consciousness functions.

We have seen how the contents and functions of consciousness are defined and studied. We turn now to ordinary and then extraordinary alterations in consciousness.

STOP AND REVIEW

❶ What is the selective storage function of consciousness?

❷ What is a cultural construction of reality?

❸ What role does consciousness play in visual search?

Sleep and Dreams

Almost every day of your life you experience a rather profound change in consciousness: When you decide it's time to end your day, you surrender yourself to sleep—and while you sleep you will undoubtedly dream. A third of your life is spent sleeping, with your muscles in a state of "benign paralysis" and your brain humming with activity. We begin this section by considering the general biological rhythms of wakefulness and sleeping. We then focus more directly on the physiology of sleeping. Finally, we examine the major mental activity that accompanies sleep—dreaming—and explore the role dreams play in human psychology.

CIRCADIAN RHYTHMS

All creatures are influenced by nature's rhythms of day and night. Your body is attuned to a time cycle known as a **circadian rhythm:** Your arousal levels, metabolism, heart rate, body temperature, and hormonal activity ebb and flow according to the ticking of your internal clock. For the most part, these activities reach their peak during the day and hit their low point at night while you sleep. In the *Psychology in Your Life* box on page 142, we discuss individual difference in circadian rhythms.

Research suggests that the clock your body uses is not exactly in synchrony with the clock on the wall: Without the corrective effects of external time cues, the human internal "pacemaker" establishes a 24.18-hour cycle (Czeisler et al., 1999). The exposure to sunlight that you get each day helps you make the small adjustment to a 24-hour cycle. Information about sunlight is gathered through your eyes, but receptors for regulation of circadian rhythms are not the same receptors that allow you to see the world (Vansteensel et al., 2008). For example, animals without rods and cones (see Chapter 4) still sense light in a way that enables them to maintain their circadian rhythms (Van Gelder, 2003).

Life circumstances that bring about a mismatch between your biological clock and your sleep cycle affect how you feel and act (Blatter & Cajochen, 2007). For example, individuals who work night shifts often experience both physical and cognitive difficulties because their circadian rhythms are disrupted (Boivin et al., 2007). Even after long periods on the night shift, most people are unable to adjust their circadian rhythms to overcome these negative effects (Folkard, 2008). People also experience disruptions when they engage in long-distance air travel. When people fly across time zones, they may experience *jet lag,* a condition whose symptoms include fatigue, irresistible sleepiness, and subsequent unusual sleep–wake schedules. Jet lag occurs because the internal circadian rhythm is out of phase with the normal temporal environment (Waterhouse et al., 2007). For example, your body says it's 2 A.M.—and thus is at a low point on many physiological measures—when local time requires you to act as if it is noon.

What variables influence jet lag? The direction of travel and the number of time zones passed through are the most important variables. Traveling eastbound creates greater jet lag than traveling westbound because your biological clock can be more readily extended than shortened, as required on eastbound trips (it is easier to stay awake longer than it is to fall asleep sooner). When healthy volunteers were flown back and forth between Europe and the United States, their peak performance on standard tasks was reached within two to four days after westbound flights but nine days after eastbound travel (Klein & Wegmann, 1974).

If you've ever suffered from jet lag, you might have gotten the advice to take a dose of the hormone *melatonin.* Melatonin acts in the brain to help regulate your cycles of waking and sleep. To determine whether external doses of melatonin might help with jet lag, researchers have studied people who have traveled on flights that crossed several time zones—such as trips from London to San Francisco. On the whole, research suggests that people who take melatonin after these long flights experience fewer sleep disruptions (Arendt & Skene, 2005). The general advice that emerges from various studies is that travelers should take melatonin at bedtime in their new time zone both on the day of the flight and for four or five subsequent days (Pandi-Perumal et al., 2007). Note, however, that there is little evidence to suggest that melatonin helps with jet lag for short stopovers. Researchers have also demonstrated melatonin's potential to help night shift workers adjust their cycles of sleeping and waking (Pandi-Perumal et al., 2007).

Circadian rhythms are also highly affected by exposure to light. For that reason, researchers have explored the possiblities of helping people adjust their circadian rhythms by exposing them to light. These interventions have often proved successful for night shift workers (Fahey & Zee, 2006). For example, night shift workers often suffer from difficulties in paying attention while on the job. In one study, participants experienced several hours of bright light to help them make the transition to a night shift (Santhi et al., 2008). The light treatment helped to reduce the negative impact on the participants' attentional performance.

THE SLEEP CYCLE

About a third of your circadian rhythm is devoted to that period of behavioral quiescence called *sleep*. Most of what is known

---

circadian rhythm A consistent pattern of cyclical body activities, usually lasting 24 to 25 hours and determined by an internal biological clock.

Psychology in Your Life

ARE YOU A MORNING TYPE OR AN EVENING TYPE?

When we introduced the concept of the circadian rhythm, we noted that, as the day unfolds, your body undergoes changes in important biological functions such as arousal levels, metabolism, heart rate, and body temperature. Although those daily rhythms are true across individuals, the exact timing differs greatly from person to person. In fact, researchers have suggested that people can be sorted into *chronotypes*, according to their preferred patterns of sleep and wakefulness.

Consider a study in which a team of researchers asked thousands of European adults to answer a series of questions (such as, When do you go to bed? How long do you need to fall asleep?). On days when participants were not required to get up for work, the most frequent response had people going to sleep just after midnight and rising at about 8:20 A.M. (Roenneberg et al., 2007). How do your own preferences compare to that norm? If you are in and out of bed earlier, you count as a *morning type*. If you habitually choose to go to bed after midnight, you count as an *evening type*. The further from the norm, the more morning or evening type you are. As people move through adulthood, their preferences tend to switch toward morning: Grandparents generally prefer to rise much earlier than their teenage grandchildren. However,

against this overall shift, individual differences seem to remain stable. Those individuals who were relatively more evening type as teenagers are likely to remain later risers relative to their peers as older adults. Now let's see why your chronotype matters.

Researchers have provided abundant demonstrations that circadian rhythms help determine the times of day at which people will experience their peak performance (Blatter & Cajochen, 2007). Given this impact of circadian rhythms, people with different chronotypes will most often peak at different times of day. This rule applies to both physical and cognitive tasks. For example, soccer players demonstrated changes in their sport-related skills—such as their ability to juggle a ball with their feet—depending on the time of day at which they are tested (Reilly et al., 2007). Many of the performance differences were correlated with circadian patterns of temperature changes.

To document the cognitive impact of chronotype, one team of researchers recruited a group of adolescents whose ages ranged from 11 to 14 (Goldstein et al., 2007). The researchers chose 40 participants, each of whom was explicitly morning type or evening type. The adolescents completed a subset of the items from a standard intelligence test (the WISC; see Chapter 9) at either their optimal

or nonoptimal time of day. For example, half of the morning-type students took the test in the morning and half in the afternoon. Those participants who were tested on their preferred time of day scored, on average, 6 points higher on the intelligence measure. (If you turn to Figure 9.2, on p. 277, you'll see how substantial a difference that is.)

The researchers also obtained information from the adolescents' parents and relatives about their day-to-day behavior. On these measures, morning-type students emerged as more socially competent—with fewer reports of attention problems and aggressive behaviors than their evening-type peers. Results of this sort support the idea that evening-type students suffer from a type of "social jet lag" (Wittmann et al., 2006). Because they are roused out of bed by their alarm clocks, they are routinely made to perform at times of day that are out of sync with their personal rhythms. That lack of synchrony has a negative impact on both achievement and behavior.

So, are you definitely a morning type or an evening type? You might consider that question carefully as you plan your days in school and beyond. If you are have a strong chronotype, think how you might arrange work and play to obtain your optimal performance.

---

about sleep concerns the electrical activities of the brain. The methodological breakthrough for the study of sleep came in 1937 with the application of a technology that records brain wave activity of the sleeper in the form of an electroencephalogram (EEG). The EEG provided an objective, ongoing measure of

the way brain activity varies when people are awake or asleep. With the EEG, researchers discovered that brain waves change in form at the onset of sleep and show further systematic, predictable changes during the entire sleep period (Loomis et al., 1937). The next significant discovery in sleep research was that bursts of **rapid eye movements (REM)** occur at periodic intervals during sleep (Aserinsky & Kleitman, 1953). The time when a sleeper is not showing REM is known as **non-REM (NREM) sleep.** We will see in a later section that REM and NREM sleep have significance for one of the night's major activities—dreaming.

Let us track your brain waves through the night. As you prepare to go to bed, an EEG records that your brain waves are

---

rapid eye movements (REM) A behavioral sign of the phase of sleep during which the sleeper is likely to be experiencing dreamlike mental activity.

non-REM (NREM) sleep The period during which a sleeper does not show rapid eye movement; characterized by less dream activity than during REM sleep.

moving along at a rate of about 14 cycles per second (cps). Once you are comfortably in bed, you begin to relax, and your brain waves slow down to a rate of about 8 to 12 cps. When you fall asleep, you enter your *sleep cycle*, each of whose stages shows a distinct EEG pattern. In stage 1 sleep, the EEG shows brain waves of about 3 to 7 cps. During stage 2, the EEG is characterized by *sleep spindles*, minute bursts of electrical activity of 12 to 16 cps. In the next two stages (3 and 4) of sleep, you enter into a very deep state of relaxed sleep. Your brain waves slow to about 1 to 2 cps, and your breathing and heart rate decrease. In a final stage, the electrical activity of your brain increases; your EEG looks very similar to those recorded during stages 1 and 2. It is during this stage that you will experience REM sleep, and you will begin to dream (see **Figure 5.2**). (Because the EEG pattern during REM sleep resembles that of an awake person, REM sleep was originally termed *paradoxical sleep*.)

Cycling through the first four stages of sleep, which are NREM sleep, requires about 90 minutes. REM sleep lasts for about 10 minutes. Over the course of a night's sleep, you pass through this 100-minute cycle four to six times (see **Figure 5.3**). With each cycle, the amount of time you spend in deep sleep (stages 3 and 4) decreases, and the amount of time you spend in REM sleep increases. During the last cycle, you may spend as much time as an hour in REM sleep. NREM sleep accounts for 75 to 80 percent of total sleep time, and REM sleep makes up 20 to 25 percent of sleep time.

Not all individuals sleep for the same amount of time. Although a genetic sleep need is programmed into the human species, the actual amount of sleep each individual obtains is highly affected by conscious actions. People actively control sleep length in a number of ways, such as by staying up late or using alarm clocks. Sleep duration is also controlled by circadian rhythms; that is, the time one goes to sleep influences sleep duration. Getting adequate amounts of NREM and REM sleep is likely only when you standardize your bedtime and rising time across the entire week, including weekends. In that way, the time

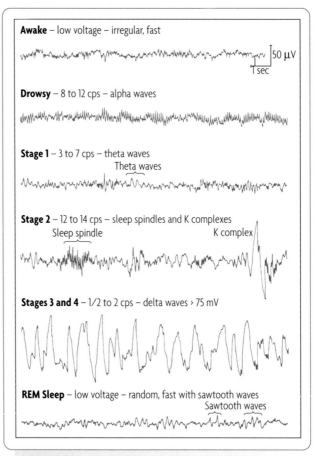

FIGURE 5.2   EEG Patterns Reflecting the Stages of a Regular Night's Sleep

Each sleep stage is defined by characteristic patterns of brain activity.

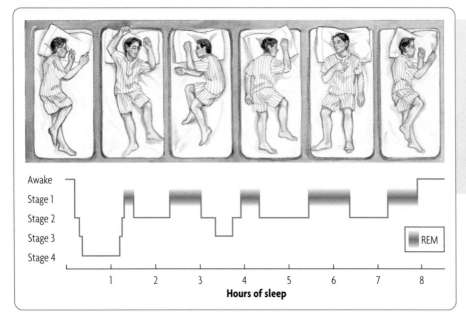

FIGURE 5.3   The Stages of Sleep

A typical pattern of the stages of sleep during a single night includes deeper sleep in the early cycles but more time in REM in the later cycles.

From "The March of Sleep Cycles" from *Sleep* by J. Allan Hobson. Copyright © 1989 by J. Allan Hobson, M.D. Reprinted by permission of Henry Holt and Company, LLC.

you spend in bed is likely to correspond closely to the sleepy phase of your circadian rhythm.

Of further interest is the dramatic change in patterns of sleep that occurs over an individual's lifetime (shown in **Figure 5.4**). You started out in this world sleeping for about 16 hours a day, with nearly half of that time spent in REM sleep. By age 50, you may sleep only 6 hours and spend only about 20 percent of the time in REM sleep. Young adults typically sleep 7 to 8 hours, with about 20 percent REM sleep.

The change in sleep patterns with age doesn't mean that sleep isn't as important as you grow older. One study followed healthy older adults—those in their 60s through 80s—to see if there was a relationship between their sleep behaviors and how long they lived (Dew et al., 2003). The researchers found that people who had higher sleep efficiency—a measure based on the amount of time they were asleep divided by the amount of time they spent in bed—were likely to live longer. This result leads directly to our next question: Why do people need sleep?

WHY SLEEP?

The orderly progression of stages of sleep in humans and other animals suggests that there is an evolutionary basis and a biological need for sleep. People function quite well when they get the time-honored 7 to 8 hours of sleep a night (Foster & Wulff, 2005; Hublin et al., 2007). Why do humans sleep so much, and what functions do types of sleep (NREM and REM) serve?

The two most general functions for NREM sleep may be *conservation* and *restoration* (Siegel, 2005). NREM sleep may have evolved because it enabled animals to conserve energy at times when there was no need to forage for food, search for mates, or work. However, sleep also puts animals at risk for attacks from predators. Researchers speculate that cycles of brain activity across a period of sleep (see Figure 5.2) may have evolved to help animals minimize the risk of predation—some

patterns of brain activity might allow animals to retain relatively greater awareness of activity in the environment even while they were asleep (Lesku et al., 2008). Why would animals put themselves at risk at all? The answer quite likely lies in the restorative properties of NREM sleep. For example, when brains are hard at work during waking states, oxygen metabolism produces by-products that are ultimately damaging to neurons in areas of the brain such as the brain stem, hippocampus, and hypothalamus (see Chapter 3). NREM sleep provides the brain with an opportunity to interrupt that damage and undertake repairs of brain cells (Siegel, 2005).

If you were to be deprived of REM sleep for a night, you would have more REM sleep than usual the next night, suggesting that REM sleep also serves some necessary functions. For example, it appears that, during infancy, the brain activity that defines REM sleep is necessary for the development of normal function in the visual system and perhaps other sensory and motor systems (Siegel, 2005). For adults, research has focused on the role REM sleep plays in learning and memory (Walker & Stickgold, 2006). Consider an experiment that asked participants to learn a new task.

At the beginning of the experiment, 24 participants spent a night in a sleep lab, so that the researchers could obtain a baseline measure for the amount of REM sleep they experienced in a night (Smith et al., 2004). The next evening, 6 participants were assigned to a control group. They spent the evening in the lab, but they carried out no special activities. The other 18 participants were asked to learn a new task—a problem-solving task called the Tower of Hanoi. Participants' REM sleep was then assessed for a second time. On this second night, participants in the task-learning group had more intense REM sleep compared to their baseline—they experienced both more rapid eye movements as a percentage of the number of minutes of REM sleep.

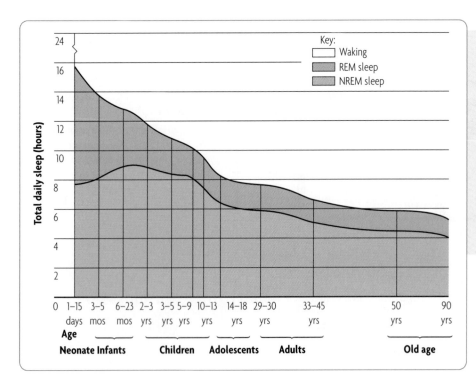

FIGURE 5.4 Patterns of Human Sleep over a Lifetime

The graph shows changes with age in total amounts of daily REM sleep and NREM sleep. Note that the amount of REM sleep decreases considerably over the years, and NREM diminishes less sharply.

From Roffwarg et al., Ontogenetic Development of the human sleep-dream cycle, *Science, 152,* 604-619. Reprinted with permission from AAAS.

What is the relationship between actual sleep patterns and people's perceptions of insomnia?

Members of the control group did not show any comparable changes in their REM sleep. After a week had passed, participants in the training group returned to attempt the Tower of Hanoi once again. The participants generally showed improvement on the task from the initial test to this retest. However, those individuals who showed the greatest intensity of REM sleep after the training session also showed the greatest improvement on the Tower of Hanoi.

This experiment suggests that REM sleep provides a context in which the brain solidifies its attainment of new tasks. It's important to note that NREM sleep also plays a role in the consolidation of learning and memory (Rasch & Born, 2008). Researchers have demonstrated that performance on some tasks is marked by increases in stage 3 and stage 4 sleep early in the night and REM sleep late in the night (Walker & Stickgold, 2006).

After reading about all the important functions that sleep serves, it probably won't surprise you to learn that there are some serious consequences when people get too little sleep. Sleep deprivation has a range of negative effects on cognitive performance including difficulties with attention and working memory (Banks & Dinges, 2007). Sleep deprivation also impairs people's ability to perform motor skills. For example, drivers who have been sleep deprived are more likely to have car accidents than their well-rested peers. This fact has led some commentators to suggest that engineers should invent a measurement device for excess sleepiness that would parallel the breathalyzer for excess alcohol (Yegneswaran & Shapiro, 2007).

SLEEP DISORDERS

It would be great if you could always take a good night's sleep for granted. Unfortunately, many people suffer from sleep disorders that pose a serious burden to their personal lives and careers. Because sleep disorders are important in many students' lives, we review them here. Their origins involve biological, environmental, and psychological forces. As you read, also remember that sleep disorders vary in severity.

Insomnia When people are dissatisfied with their amount or quality of sleep, they are suffering from **insomnia.** This chronic failure to get adequate sleep is characterized by an inability to fall asleep quickly, frequent arousals during sleep, or early-morning awakening. In one sample of 3,643 adults in the United States, 52.5 percent of the participants reported that they had experienced insomnia at least once a month; 7 percent reported that they experienced insomnia almost every night (Hamilton et al., 2007). The study also demonsrated that insomnia had a consistent negative impact on people's sense of well-being.

Insomnia is a complex disorder caused by a variety of psychological, environmental, and biological factors (Drake & Roth, 2006). However, when insomniacs are studied in sleep laboratories, the objective quantity and quality of their actual sleep vary considerably, from disturbed sleep to normal sleep. Research has revealed that many insomniacs who complain of lack of sleep actually show completely normal physiological patterns of sleep—a condition described as *subjective insomnia.* For example, in one study 38 percent of the participants who reported that they suffered from insomnia actually had normal sleep (Edinger et al., 2000). Equally interesting, the same study showed detectable sleep disturbances in 43 percent of the participants who had no complaints of insomnia. The discrepancies may result from differences in the cognitions and emotions

---

insomnia The chronic inability to sleep normally; symptoms include difficulty in falling asleep, frequent waking, inability to return to sleep, and early-morning awakening.

that surround sleep (Espie, 2002). People who experience insomnia—or those who only think they do—may be less able to banish intrusive thoughts and feelings from consciousness even while they are trying to sleep.

Narcolepsy **Narcolepsy** is a sleep disorder characterized by sudden and irresistible instances of sleepiness during the daytime. It is often combined with *cataplexy,* muscle weakness or a loss of muscle control brought on by emotional excitement (such as laughing, anger, fear, surprise, or hunger) that causes the afflicted person to fall down suddenly. When they fall asleep, narcoleptics enter REM sleep almost immediately. This rush to REM causes them to experience—and be consciously aware of—vivid dream images or sometimes terrifying hallucinations. Narcolepsy affects about 1 of every 2,000 individuals. Because narcolepsy runs in families, scientists believe the disease has a genetic basis (Mahowald & Schenck, 2005). Narcolepsy often has a negative social and psychological impact on sufferers because of their desire to avoid the embarrassment caused by sudden bouts of sleep (Ervik et al., 2006).

Sleep Apnea **Sleep apnea** is an upper-respiratory sleep disorder in which the person stops breathing while asleep. When this happens, the blood's oxygen level drops and emergency hormones are secreted, causing the sleeper to awaken and begin breathing again. Although most people have a few such apnea episodes a night, someone with sleep apnea disorder can have hundreds of such cycles every night. Sometimes apnea episodes frighten the sleeper, but often they are so brief that the sleeper fails to attribute accumulating sleepiness to them (Pagel, 2008). Sleep apnea affects roughly 2 percent of adults (Sonnad et al., 2003).

Sleep apnea also occurs frequently among premature infants, who sometimes need physical stimulation to start breathing again. Because of their underdeveloped respiratory system, these infants must remain attached to monitors in intensive care nurseries as long as the problem continues.

Somnambulism Individuals who suffer from **somnambulism,** or *sleepwalking,* leave their beds and wander while still remaining asleep. Sleepwalking is more frequent among children than among adults (Mason & Pack, 2007). For example, studies have found that about 7 percent of children sleepwalk (Nevéus et al., 2001) but only about 2 percent of adults do so (Plazzi et al., 2005). Sleepwalking is associated with NREM sleep. When monitored in a sleep laboratory, adult sleepwalkers demonstrated abrupt arousal—involving movement or speech—during stage 3 and stage 4 sleep (see Figure 5.2) in the first third of their night's sleep (Guilleminault et al., 2001). Contrary to popular conceptions, it is not particularly dangerous to wake

sleepwalkers—they're just likely to be confused by the sudden awakening. Still, sleepwalking in itself can be dangerous because individuals are navigating in their environments without conscious awareness.

Nightmares and Sleep Terrors When a dream frightens you by making you feel helpless or out of control, you are having a **nightmare.** For most people nightmares are relatively infrequent. In one sample of 89 undergraduates who kept dream logs daily for one month, the average number of nightmares reported in the month was 0.48. That monthly average corresponds to a rate of 5.76 nightmares each year (Zadra & Donderi, 2000). However, some people experience nightmares more frequently, sometimes as often as every night. Children, for example, are more likely than adults to experience nightmares. The peak time for nightmares is between ages 3 and 6, when a majority of children have them at least occasionally (Mason & Park, 2007). Also, people who have experienced traumatic events, such as rape or war, may have repetitive nightmares that force them to relive some aspects of their trauma (Davis et al., 2007). College students who experienced a major earthquake in the San Francisco Bay area were about twice as likely to experience nightmares as were a matched group of students who hadn't experienced an earthquake—and, as you might imagine, many of the nightmares were about the devastating effects of earthquakes (Wood et al., 1992).

Sleep terrors (or *night terrors*) are instances in which sleepers wake up suddenly in a state of extreme arousal, often marked by a panicky scream (DSM-IV-TR, 2000). These episodes typically occur during NREM sleep in the first third of a night's sleep. Most people who have sleep terrors have no memory of the episodes. Sleep terrors are most common during childhood, with the greatest number occurring between ages 5 and 7 (Mason & Pack, 2007). Between the ages of 4 and 12, about 3 percent of children experience sleep terrors. They occur in less than 1 percent of adults. Researchers have begun to document distinctive patterns of brain activity that identify children at particular risk for sleep terrors (Bruni et al., 2008).

DREAMS: THEATER OF THE MIND

During every ordinary night of your life, you enter into the complex world of dreams. Once the province only of prophets, psychics, and psychoanalysts, dreams have become a vital area of study for scientific researchers. Much dream research begins in sleep laboratories, where experimenters can monitor sleepers for REM and NREM sleep. Although individuals report more dreams when they are awakened from REM periods—on about 82 percent of their awakenings—dreaming also takes place during NREM periods—on about 54 percent of awakenings (Foulkes, 1962). Dreaming associated with NREM states is less likely to contain story content that is emotionally involving. It is more akin to daytime thought, with less sensory imagery.

Because dreams have such prominence in people's mental lives, virtually every culture has arrived at the same question: Do dreams have significance? The answer that has almost always emerged is *yes.* That is, most cultures encode the belief that, in one way or another, dreams have important personal and cultural meaning. We now review some of the ways in which cultures attach meaning to dreams.

---

narcolepsy A sleep disorder characterized by an irresistible compulsion to sleep during the daytime.

sleep apnea A sleep disorder of the upper respiratory system that causes the person to stop breathing while asleep.

somnambulism A disorder that causes sleepers to leave their beds and wander while still remaining asleep; also known as sleepwalking.

nightmare A frightening dream that usually wakes up the sleeper.

sleep terrors Episodes in which sleepers wake up suddenly in an extreme state of arousal and panic.

Freudian Dream Analysis The most prominent dream theory in modern Western culture was originated by Sigmund Freud. Freud called dreams "transient psychoses" and models of "everynight madness." He also called them "the royal road to the unconscious." He made the analysis of dreams the cornerstone of psychoanalysis with his classic book, *The Interpretation of Dreams* (1900/1965). Freud suggested that all dreams are instances of *wish-fulfillment:* On his view, people's dreams allow them to express powerful unconscious wishes in disguised symbolic form. These wishes appear in disguised form because they harbor forbidden desires, such as sexual yearning for the parent of the opposite sex. The two dynamic forces operating in dreams are thus the *wish* and the *censorship,* a defense against the wish. The censor transforms the hidden meaning, or **latent content,** of the dream into **manifest content,** which appears to the dreamer after a distortion process that Freud referred to as **dream work.** The manifest content is the acceptable version of the story; the latent content represents the socially or personally unacceptable version but also the true, "uncut" one.

According to Freud, the interpretation of dreams requires working backward from the manifest content to the latent content. To the psychoanalyst who uses dream analysis to understand and treat a patient's problems, dreams reveal the patient's unconscious wishes, the fears attached to those wishes, and the characteristic defenses the patient employs to handle the resulting psychic conflict between the wishes and the fears. Freud believed in both idiosyncratic—special to particular individuals—and universal meanings—many of a sexual nature—for the symbols and metaphors in dreams:

> Boxes, cases, chests, cupboards and ovens represent the uterus, and also hollow objects, ships, and vessels of all kinds. Rooms in dreams are usually women; if the various ways in and out of them are represented, this interpretation is scarcely open to doubt. . . . A dream of going through a suite of rooms is a brothel or harem dream. . . . It is highly probable that all complicated machinery and apparatus occurring in dreams stand for the genitals (and as a rule male ones). . . . (Freud, 1900/1965, pp. 389–391)

Freud's theory of dream interpretation related dream symbols to his explicit theory of human psychology. Freud's emphasis on the psychological importance of dreams has pointed the way to contemporary examinations of dream content.

Non-Western Approaches to Dream Interpretation

Many people in Western societies may never think seriously about their dreams until they become students of psychology or enter therapy. By contrast, in many non-Western cultures, dream sharing and interpretation are part of the very fabric of the culture (Wax, 2004). Consider the daily practice of the Archur Indians of Ecuador (Schlitz, 1997, p. 2):

> Like every other morning, the men [of the village] sit together in a small circle. . . . They share their dreams from the night before. This daily ritual of dream-sharing is vital to the life of the Archur. It is their belief that each individual dreams, not for themselves, but for the community as a whole. Individual experience serves collective action.

During these morning gatherings, each dreamer tells his dream story and the others offer their interpretations, hoping to arrive at some consensus understanding of the meaning of the dream.

Contrast the belief that individuals dream "for the community as a whole" with the view articulated by Freud, that dreams are the "royal road" to the individual unconscious.

In many cultures, specific groups of individuals are designated as possessing special powers to assist with dream interpretation. Consider the practices of Mayan Indians who live in various parts of Mexico, Guatemala, Belize, and Honduras. In the Mayan culture, *shamans* function as dream interpreters. In fact, among some subgroups of Mayans, the shamans are selected for these roles when they have dreams in which they are visited by deities who announce the shaman's calling. Formal instruction about religious rituals is also provided to these newly selected shamans by way of dream revelation. Although the shamans, and other religious figures, have special knowledge relevant to dream interpretation, ordinary individuals also recount and discuss dreams. Dreamers commonly wake their bed partners in the middle of the night to narrate dreams; mothers in some communities ask their children each morning to talk about their dreams. In contemporary times, the Mayan people have been the victims of civil war in their homelands; many people have been killed or forced to flee. One important response, according to anthropologist **Barbara Tedlock,** has been "an increased emphasis on dreams and visions that enable them to stay in touch with their ancestors and the sacred earth on which they live" (Tedlock, 1992, p. 471).

The cultural practices of many non-Western groups with respect to dreams also reflect a fundamentally different time perspective. Freud's theory had dream interpretation looking backward in time, toward childhood experiences and repressed wishes. In many other cultures, dreams are believed instead to present a vision of the future (Basso, 1987). For example, among the people of the Ingessana Hills, a region along the border of Ethiopia and the Sudan, the timing of festivals is determined by dream visions (Jedrej, 1995). The keepers of religious shrines are visited in their dreams by their fathers and other ancestors who instruct them to "announce the festival." Other groups have culturally given systems of relationships between dream symbols and meanings. Consider these interpretations from the Kalapalo Indians of central Brazil (Basso, 1987, p. 104):

> When we dream we are burnt by fire, later we will be bitten by a wild thing, by a spider or a stinging ant, for example.
> When [we dream] we are making love to women, we will be very successful when we go fishing.
> When a boy is in seclusion and he dreams of climbing a tall tree, or another one sees a long path, they will live long. This would also be true if we dreamt of crossing a wide stream in a forest.

Note how each interpretation looks to the future. The future orientation of dream interpretation is an important component of a rich cultural tradition.

---

latent content In Freudian dream analysis, the hidden meaning of a dream.

manifest content In Freudian dream analysis, the surface content of a dream, which is assumed to mask the dream's actual meaning.

dream work In Freudian dream analysis, the process by which the internal censor transforms the latent content of a dream into manifest content.

Contemporary Theories of Dream Content The cornerstone of both Western and non-Western approaches to dream interpretation is that dreams provide information that is of genuine value to the person or community. When researchers first began to consider the biological underpinnings of dream they challenged this view. For example, the *activation-synthesis model* suggested that signals emerged from the brain stem that stimulated the forebrain and association areas of the cortex to produce random memories and connections with the dreamer's past experiences (Hobson, 1988; Hobson & McCarley, 1977). According to this view, there are no logical connections, no intrinsic meaning, and no coherent patterns to these random bursts of electrical "signals."

However, contemporary research on dreams contradicts the view that the content emerges from random signals. Brain-imaging studies suggest that the hippocampus—the brain structure critical to the acquisition of certain types of memories (see Chapter 7)—is active during REM sleep (Nielsen & Stenstrom, 2005). Another brain structure that plays an important role for emotional memories—the amygdala—is also quite active during REM sleep. This deeper understanding of the physiological aspects of dreams supports the assertion that one of the functions of sleep is to draw together "an individual's recent experiences of the past few days along with their goals, desires, and problems" (Paller & Voss, 2004, p. 667). According to this view, the story of the dream reflects the brain's attempt to weave a narrative around the recent fragments of a person's life that become most prominent during REM sleep.

Studies of dream content confirm that content of dreams shows a good deal of continuity with dreamers' waking concerns (Domhoff, 2005). For example, research using experience-sampling methods suggested that girls were more likely than boys to be thinking about friends of both sexes, rather than just friends of their own sex (Richards et al., 1998). Dream studies with 9- to 15-year-olds demonstrate similar gender differences in dream content about peers (Strauch, 2005; Strauch & Lederbogen, 1999). Similarly, people who spent more waking time engaged in particular activities (such as sports or reading) reported a higher percentage of dreams that included those activities (Schredl & Erlacher, 2008). In addition, across adulthood, the overall content of each individual's dreams stays very much the same over years or even decades (Domhoff, 1999).

You might consider keeping your own dream log—try to write your dreams as soon as you wake up each morning—to see both how your own dreams relate to daily concerns and how your dream content changes or remains stable over time. Still, we should warn you that some people have more difficulty recalling dreams than other people do (Wolcott & Strapp, 2002). For example, it's easier to recall dreams if you wake up during a REM period or close to one. If you want to recall your dreams, you might consider changing the time you set your alarm. Also, people who have more positive attitudes toward dreaming appear to find it easier to recall their dreams. In that sense, the interest you show in your dreams by undertaking a dream log might help increase your ability to recall them.

We can consider dreams to be at the limit of ordinary consciousness. We turn now to circumstances in which individuals deliberately seek to go beyond those everyday experiences.

---

lucid dreaming The theory that conscious awareness of dreaming is a learnable skill that enables dreamers to control the direction and content of their dreams.

STOP AND REVIEW

❶ Why do you experience jet lag?

❷ How does the balance of NREM and REM sleep change over the course of a night?

❸ What two functions might NREM sleep serve?

❹ What happens to a person who suffers from sleep apnea?

❺ What did Freud mean by the latent content of a dream?

CRITICAL THINKING Consider the study that documented the impact of new task learning on REM sleep. Why was it important to have the control group?

Visit MyPsychLab.com for more review and practice on the following topics:

👁 **Watch:** Insomnia

👁 **Explore:** Theories of Dreaming

Altered States of Consciousness

In every culture, some people have been dissatisfied with ordinary transformations of their waking consciousness. They have developed practices that take them beyond familiar forms of consciousness to experiences of altered states of consciousness. Some of these practices are individual, such as meditation. Others, such as certain religious practices, are shared attempts to transcend the normal boundaries of conscious experience. We survey a variety of such practices in which altered states of consciousness are induced by a range of procedures.

LUCID DREAMING

Is it possible to be aware that you are dreaming while you are dreaming? Proponents of the theory of **lucid dreaming** have demonstrated that being consciously aware that one is dreaming is a learnable skill—perfected with regular practice—that enables dreamers to control the direction of their dreams (LaBerge, 2007).

Stephen LaBerge and his colleagues devised a methodology that enabled them to test the reality of reports of lucid dreaming. The demonstration relied on previous research that had shown that some of the eye movements of REM sleep correspond to the reported direction of the dreamer's gaze. The researchers therefore asked experienced lucid dreamers to execute distinctive patterns of voluntary eye movements when they realized that they were dreaming. The prearranged eye movement signals appeared on the polygraph records during REM, thus demonstrating that the participants had indeed been lucid during REM sleep (LaBerge et al., 1981).

Researchers have documented other physiological markers of lucid dreams: Individuals who performed physical activity during their lucid dreams showed increased heart rates during the dream periods (Erlacher & Schredl, 2008).

A variety of methods have been used to induce lucid dreaming. For example, in some lucid dreaming research, sleepers wear specially designed goggles that flash a red light when they detect REM sleep. The participants have learned previously that the red light is a cue for becoming consciously aware that they are dreaming (LaBerge & Levitan, 1995). Once aware of dreaming, yet still not awake, sleepers move into a state of lucid dreaming in which they can take control of their dreams, directing them according to their personal goals and making the dreams' outcomes fit their current needs. The ability to have lucid dreams reportedly increases when sleepers firmly believe that such dreams are possible and regularly practice the induction techniques (LaBerge & Rheingold, 1990). Researchers such as Stephen LaBerge argue that gaining control over the "uncontrollable" events of dreams is healthy because it enhances self-confidence and generates positive experiences for the individual. However, some therapists who use dream analysis as part of their understanding of a patient's problems oppose such procedures because they feel that they distort the natural process of dreaming.

HYPNOSIS

As portrayed in popular culture, hypnotists wield vast power over their witting or unwitting participants. Is this view of hypnotists accurate? What is hypnosis, what are its important features, and what are some of its valid psychological uses? The term **hypnosis** is derived from Hypnos, the name of the Greek god of sleep. Sleep, however, plays no part in hypnosis, except that people may in some cases give the *appearance* of being in a deeply relaxed, sleeplike state. (If people were really asleep, they could not respond to hypnosis.) A broad definition of hypnosis is that it is an alternative state of awareness characterized by the special ability some people have of responding to suggestion with changes in perception, memory, motivation, and sense of self-control. In the hypnotic state, participants experience heightened responsiveness to the hypnotist's suggestions—they often feel that their behavior is performed without intention or any conscious effort.

Researchers have often disagreed about the psychological mechanisms involved in hypnosis (Lynn & Kirsch, 2006). Some early theorists suggested that hypnotized individuals enter into a *trance* state, far different from waking consciousness. Others argued that hypnosis was nothing more than heightened motivation. Still others believed it to be a type of social role playing, a kind of *placebo* response of trying to please the hypnotist (see Chapter 2). In fact, research has largely ruled out the idea that hypnosis involves a special

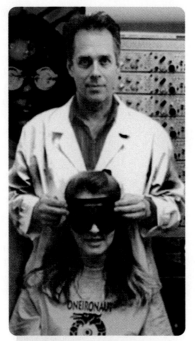

Researcher Stephen LaBerge adjusts the special goggles that will alert the sleeping participant that REM sleep is occurring. The individual is trained to enter into a state of lucid dreaming, being aware of the process and content of dream activity. If you had the ability to experience lucid dreaming, in what ways would you shape your dreams?

trancelike change in consciousness. However, even though nonhypnotized individuals can produce some of the same patterns of behavior that hypnotized individuals can, there appears to be some added effects of hypnosis—beyond motivational or placebo processes. After we discuss hypnotic induction and hypnotizability, we describe some of those effects.

Hypnotic Induction and Hypnotizability Hypnosis begins with a *hypnotic induction,* a preliminary set of activities that minimizes external distractions and encourages participants to concentrate only on suggested stimuli and believe that they are about to enter a special state of consciousness. Induction activities involve suggestions to imagine certain experiences or to visualize events and reactions. When practiced repeatedly, the induction procedure functions as a learned signal so that participants can quickly enter the hypnotic state. The typical induction procedure uses suggestions for deep relaxation, but some people can become hypnotized with an active, alert induction—such as imagining that they are jogging or riding a bicycle (Banyai & Hilgard, 1976).

Hypnotizability represents the degree to which an individual is responsive to standardized suggestions to experience hypnotic reactions. There are wide individual differences in susceptibility, varying from a complete lack of responsiveness to total responsiveness. **Figure 5.5** on page 150 shows the percentage of college-age individuals who presented various levels of hypnotizability the first time they were given a hypnotic induction test. What does it mean to have scored "high" or "very high" on this scale? When the test is administered, the hypnotist makes a series of posthypnotic suggestions, dictating the experiences each individual might have. When the hypnotist suggested that their extended arms had turned into bars of iron, highly hypnotizable individuals were likely to find themselves unable to bend those arms. With the appropriate suggestion, they were likely to brush away a nonexistent fly. As a third example, highly hypnotizable individuals probably couldn't nod their heads "no" when the hypnotist suggested they had lost that ability. Students who scored "low" on the hypnotizability scale experienced few if any of these reactions.

Hypnotizability is a relatively stable attribute. When 50 men and women were retested 25 years after their college

---

hypnosis An altered state of awareness characterized by deep relaxation, susceptibility to suggestions, and changes in perception, memory, motivation, and self-control.

hypnotizability The degree to which an individual is responsive to standardized hypnotic suggestion.

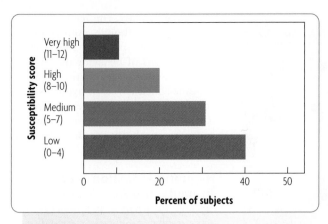

FIGURE 5.5 Level of Hypnosis at First Induction

The graph shows the results for 533 individuals hypnotized for the first time. Hypnotizability was measured on the Stanford Hypnotic Susceptibility Scale, which consists of 12 items.

hypnotizability assessment, the results indicated a remarkably high correlation coefficient of .71 (Piccione et al., 1989). Children tend to be more suggestible than adults; hypnotic responsiveness peaks just before adolescence and declines thereafter. Researchers have identified relatively few personality traits that are correlated with hypnotizability (Kihlstrom, 2007). Highly hypnotizable people are not more likely to be gullible or conformist. In fact, the personality trait that has the highest positive correlation with hypnotizability is *absorption,* which is an individual's "predisposition to become highly involved in imaginative or sensory experiences" (Council & Green, 2004, p. 364). If, for example, you often find yourself losing track of the "real" world while you watch a movie, you might also be highly hypnotizable.

Some evidence indicates genetic determinants of hypnotizability. Early research demonstrated that hypnotizability scores of identical twins are more similar than are those of fraternal twins (Morgan et al., 1970). More recently, studies have begun to focus on the particular genes that underlie individual differences. For example, researchers have identified a gene known as *COMT* that influences the brain's use of the neurotransmitter dopamine. Variations in this gene are related to individual differences in hypnotizability (Raz, 2005).

Effects of Hypnosis In describing the way in which hypnotizability is measured, we already mentioned some of the standard effects of hypnosis: While under hypnosis, individuals respond to suggestions about motor abilities (for example, their arms become unbendable) and perceptual experiences (for example, they hallucinate a fly). How can we be sure, however, that these behaviors arise from special properties of hypnosis and not just a strong willingness on participants' part to please the hypnotist? To address this important question, researchers have often conducted experiments that

contrast the effectiveness of suggestions when participants are in waking or hypnotic states.

Researchers created three groups of participants who tested high, medium, and low on hypnotizability, with 12 individuals in each group (De Pascalis et al., 2008). Before they began the experiment, participants were informed that they were going to receive painful electric stimulation to their fingers. Each participant received the same suggestions about how to lessen the pain both when hypnotized and in a waking state: They were told, for example, to imagine that a glove was covering the finger. In each phase of the experiment, participants provided reports on the amount of pain they were experiencing. For low hypnotizability participants, pain experiences were fairly steady irrespective of their waking or hypnotic state. Medium hypnotizability participants showed some pain relief from hypnosis. High hypnotizability participants provided the clearest evidence that suggestions for pain relief under hypnosis acted more effectively than the exact same suggestion during the waking state.

The researchers also recorded EEG data (see Chapter 3) to determine whether the participants' brain activity would show the impact of the hypnotic suggestions. In fact, when high hypnotizability participants received hypnotic suggestions for pain reduction, they produced more muted brain responses in sensory areas.

This experiment demonstrates the potential for hypnosis to bring about pain relief *(hypnotic analgesia).* Your mind can amplify pain stimuli through anticipation and fear; you can diminish this psychological effect with hypnosis (Chaves, 1999). Pain control is accomplished through a variety of hypnotic suggestions: imagining the part of the body in pain as nonorganic (made of wood or plastic) or as separate from the rest of the body, thus taking one's mind on a vacation from the body and distorting time in various ways. People can control pain through hypnosis even when they banish all thoughts and images from consciousness (Hargadon et al., 1995).

The study also illustrates that people who are high in hypnotizability are able to obtain greater pain relief through hypnosis. Researchers are trying to understand the brain bases for this difference. For example, a brain-imaging study demonstrated that people who were higher in hypnotizability also had larger regions at the front of the corpus callosum (see Chapter 3) (Horton et al., 2004). This area of the corpus callosum plays a role in attention and the inhibition of unwanted stimuli, suggesting that people who are highly hypnotizable may have more brain tissue that allows them to use hypnosis to inhibit pain. Studies with EEG measures also demonstrate—in the context of hypnotic pain reduction—differences in the brain responses of low and high hypnotizable individuals (Ray et al., 2002).

One final note on hypnosis: The power of hypnosis does *not* reside in some special ability or skill of the hypnotist, but rather it resides in the relative hypnotizability of the person or persons being hypnotized. Being hypnotized does not involve giving up one's personal control; instead, the experience of being hypnotized allows an individual to learn new ways to exercise control that the hypnotist—as coach—can train the

How does meditation create an altered state of consciousness?

subject—as performer—to enact. Keep all of this in mind if you watch a stage show in which people perform outlandish acts under hypnosis: Stage hypnotists make a living entertaining audiences by getting highly exhibitionist people to do things in public that most others could never be made to do. As used by researchers and therapists, hypnosis is a technique with the potential to allow you to explore and modify your sense of consciousness.

MEDITATION

Many religions and traditional psychologies of the East work to direct consciousness away from immediate worldly concerns. They seek to achieve an inner focus on the mental and spiritual self.

Meditation is a form of consciousness change designed to enhance self-knowledge and well-being by achieving a deep state of tranquility. During *concentrative* meditation, a person may focus on and regulate breathing, assume certain body positions (yogic positions), minimize external stimulation, generate specific mental images, or free the mind of all thought. By contrast, during *mindfulness* meditation, a person learns to let thoughts and memories pass freely through the mind without reacting to them.

Research has often focused on the ability of meditation to relieve the anxiety of those who must function in stress-filled environments (Oman et al., 2006; Walach et al., 2007). For example, mindfulness meditation has served as the basis for mindfulness-based stress reduction (Kabat-Zinn, 1990). In one study, women suffering from heart disease were given eight weeks of training on mindfulness meditation; at the end of this intervention, the women reported consistently lower feelings of anxiety than they did before the study (Tacon et al., 2003). Women in the control group didn't experience improvement in their anxiety reports. Because feelings of anxiety play a role in the development of heart disease, this result provides evidence that the mind can help to heal the body. (We will return to this theme when we discuss health psychology in Chapter 12.)

Brain-imaging techniques have begun to reveal the ways in which the practice of meditation affects patterns of brain activity (Cahn & Polich, 2006). In fact, recent evidence suggests that, over time, the practice of meditation might have a positive impact on the brain itself.

> The researchers reasoned that the activities associated with meditation—focused attention on internal and external sensations—would bring about positive changes in the brain regions associated with these activities (Lazar et al., 2005). To test this hypothesis, the researchers recruited two groups of participants, 20 individuals with extensive meditation experience and 15 control individuals with no meditation experience. All the participants underwent MRI scans to provide measures of the thickness of relevant areas of the cortex. As the researchers had predicted, these scans revealed that the meditation groups had thicker cortex in areas of auditory and somatosensory cortex (see Chapter 3). The two groups did not differ in areas of the cortex that were not directly relevant to meditation. The researchers carried out further analyses that indicated that those individuals who had the most meditation experience also had the greatest extra thickness in relevant areas of the cortex.

As people grow older, they typically lose cortical thickness. Based on their findings, the researchers speculated that meditation could help slow this natural loss of neurons. Researchers have begun to confirm that speculation. One study compared 13 individuals with three or more years of experience at Zen meditation with 13 control participants who were matched for age, sex, and education level (Pagnoni & Cekic, 2007). Among the control participants, there was a negative correlation such that the older participants had the least brain volume. The participants who meditated regularly showed no such decline with age.

Practicers of meditation have suggested that, when practiced regularly, some forms of meditation can heighten your consciousness and help you achieve enlightenment by enabling you to see familiar things in new ways. This recent research suggests that meditation might also literally be good for your brain.

In this section, we have reviewed several ways in which people achieve altered states of consciousness in their dreaming and waking lives. We conclude this chapter with a discussion of what might be the most common means people use to affect their consciousness: mind-altering drugs.

STOP AND REVIEW

❶ What is the major goal of lucid dreaming?
❷ What does research suggest about the genetics of hypnotizability?
❸ What are two forms of meditation?

---

meditation A form of consciousness alteration designed to enhance self-knowledge and well-being through reduced self-awareness.

CRITICAL THINKING Consider the study that found differences in cortical thickness for meditators versus nonmeditators. Why was it important to demonstrate that the two groups' brains didn't differ in all areas of the cortex?

Visit MyPsychLab.com for more review and practice on the following topics:

- ◉ **Watch:** Lucid Dreaming
- ◉ **Watch:** Hypnosis

Mind-Altering Drugs

Since ancient times, people have taken drugs to alter their perception of reality. Archaeological evidence indicates the uninterrupted use of sophora seed (mescal bean) for over 10,000 years in the southwestern United States and Mexico. The ancient Aztecs fermented mescal beans into a beer. From ancient times, individuals in North and South America also ingested *teonanacatl,* the *Psilocybe* mushroom also known as "the flesh of the gods," as parts of rituals. Small doses of these mushrooms produce vivid hallucinations.

In Western cultures, drugs are associated less with sacred communal rituals than with recreation. Individuals throughout the world take various drugs to relax, cope with stress, avoid facing the unpleasantness of current realities, feel comfortable in social situations, or experience an alternate state of consciousness. Over 100 years ago, William James—whom we have cited several times as a founder of psychology in the United States—reported on his experiments with a mind-altering drug. After inhaling nitrous oxide, James explained that "the keynote of the experience is the tremendously exciting sense of intense metaphysical illumination. Truth lies open to the view in depth beneath depth of almost blinding evidence. The mind sees all the logical relations of being with an apparent subtlety and instantaneity to which its normal consciousness offer no parallel" (James, 1882, p. 186). Thus James's interest in the study of consciousness extended to the study of self-induced alternate states.

As we will see in Chapter 15, drugs that have an impact on an individual's psychological states are often a critical aspect of the treatment of psychological disorders. In fact, as we indicate in **Table 5.2,** many types of drugs have important medical uses. Still, many individuals use drugs that are not prescribed to enhance physical or psychological health. In a 2007 survey of U.S. citizens, with nearly 68,000 respondents age 12 and older, 8.0 percent reported using one or more illicit drugs during the past month (Substance Abuse and Mental Health Services Administration [SAMHSA], 2008). The rate was much higher for people in their late teen years—16.0 percent of 16- to 17-year-olds and 21.6 percent of 18- to 20-year-olds reported some type of illicit drug use. In addition, 51.1 percent of the individuals in the sample consumed alcohol sometime in the month before the survey, and 28.6 percent smoked cigarettes. These figures support the importance of understanding the physiological and psychological consequences of drug use.

DEPENDENCE AND ADDICTION

Psychoactive drugs are chemicals that affect mental processes and behavior by temporarily changing conscious awareness. Once in the brain, they attach themselves to synaptic receptors, blocking or stimulating certain reactions. By doing so, they profoundly alter the brain's communication system, affecting perception, memory, mood, and behavior. However, continued use of a given drug creates **tolerance**—greater dosages are required to achieve the same effect. In Chapter 6, we will discuss learning processes that explain important aspects of the occurrence of drug tolerance (see p. 173). We will describe how repeated episodes of drug use condition the brain to produce responses that push back against the drug's effects. Because the body pushes back, people require increasingly greater doses for the drug to have the same impact.

Hand in hand with tolerance is **physiological dependence,** a process in which the body becomes adjusted to and dependent on the substance, in part because neurotransmitters are depleted by the frequent presence of the drug. The tragic outcome of tolerance and dependence is **addiction.** A person who is addicted requires the drug in his or her body and suffers painful withdrawal symptoms (shaking, sweating, nausea, and, in the case of alcohol withdrawal, even death) if the drug is not present.

When an individual finds the use of a drug so desirable or pleasurable that a *craving* develops, with or without addiction, the condition is known as **psychological dependence,** which can occur with any drug. The result of drug dependence is that a person's lifestyle comes to revolve around drug use so wholly that his or her capacity to function is limited or impaired. In addition, the expense involved in maintaining a drug habit of daily—and increasing—amounts often drives an addict to robbery, assault, prostitution, or drug peddling.

VARIETIES OF PSYCHOACTIVE DRUGS

Table 5.2 lists common psychoactive drugs. (In Chapter 15, we will discuss other types of psychoactive drugs used to relieve mental illness.) Next, we will briefly describe how each class of drugs achieves its physiological and psychological impact. We will also note the personal and societal consequences of drug use.

Hallucinogens The most dramatic changes in consciousness are produced by drugs known as **hallucinogens** or

---

psychoactive drug Chemical that affects mental processes and behavior by temporarily changing conscious awareness of reality.

tolerance A situation that occurs with continued use of a drug in which an individual requires greater dosages to achieve the same effect.

physiological dependence The process by which the body becomes adjusted to or dependent on a drug.

addiction A condition in which the body requires a drug in order to function without physical and psychological reactions to its absence; often the outcome of tolerance and dependence.

psychological dependence The psychological need or craving for a drug.

hallucinogen Drug that alters cognitions and perceptions and causes hallucinations.

TABLE 5.2 Medical Uses of Psychoactive Drugs	
Drug	**Medical Uses**
Hallucinogens	
LSD	None
PCP (Phencyclidine)	Veterinary anesthetic
Cannabis (Marijuana)	Nausea associated with chemotherapy
Opiates (Narcotics)	
Morphine	Painkiller
Heroin	None
Depressants	
Barbiturates (e.g., Seconal)	Sedative, sleeping pill, anesthetic, anticonvulsant
Benzodiazepines (e.g., Valium)	Antianxiety, sedative, sleeping pill, anticonvulsant
Rohypnol	Sleeping pill
GHB	Treatment for narcolepsy
Alcohol	Antiseptic
Stimulants	
Amphetamines	Hyperkinesis, narcolepsy, weight control
Methamphetamines	None
MDMA (Ecstasy)	Potential aid to psychotherapy
Cocaine	Local anesthetic
Nicotine	Nicotine gum for cessation of smoking habit
Caffeine	Weight control, stimulant in acute respiratory failure, analgesic

Cannabis is a plant with psychoactive effects. Its active ingredient is THC, found in both *hashish* (the solidified resin of the plant) and *marijuana* (the dried leaves and flowers of the plant). The experience derived from inhaling THC depends on its dose—small doses create mild, pleasurable highs, and large doses result in long hallucinogenic reactions. Regular users report euphoria, feelings of well-being, distortions of space and time, and, occasionally, out-of-body experiences. However, depending on the context, the effects may be negative—fear, anxiety, and confusion.

Researchers have known for several years that *cannabinoids*, the active chemicals in marijuana, bind to specific receptors in the brain—these cannabinoid receptors are particularly common in the hippocampus, the brain region involved in memory (De Oliveira Alvares et al., 2008). Researchers subsequently discovered substances internal to the brain that bind to the same receptors. The first *endocannabinoid* (from *endogenous cannabinoid*) to be discovered was *anandamide* (named for the Sanskrit word for bliss, *ananda*) (Di Marzo & Cristino, 2008). That discovery led to the insight that cannabinoids achieve their mind-altering effects by binding to brain sites sensitive to naturally occurring substances in the brain. These endocannabinoids function as neuromodulators. For example, they suppress the release of the neurotransmitter GABA (Wilson & Nicoll, 2002). In the *Critical Thinking in Your Life* box on page 154, we discuss the important role these substances play in regulating appetite and feeding behaviors.

Opiates *Opiates*, such as *heroin* and *morphine*, suppress physical sensation and response to stimulation. Pain killers such as *OxyContin* are also opiates and have the same effects. In the last few years, there has been a dramatic increase in the number of people who abuse OxyContin and other prescription opiates (Rawson et al., 2007). In Chapter 3, we noted that the brain contains endorphins (short for *endogenous*

Why does heroin use often lead to addiction?

psychedelics; these drugs alter both perceptions of the external environment and inner awareness. As the name implies, these drugs often create **hallucinations**—vivid perceptions that occur in the absence of objective stimulation. The hallucinations may lead to a loss of boundary between self and nonself. *LSD* and *PCP* are two common hallucinogens that are synthesized in laboratories. Hallucinogenic drugs typically act in the brain by affecting the use of the chemical neurotransmitter serotonin (Béïque et al., 2007). For example, LSD binds very tightly to serotonin receptors so that neurons produce prolonged activation.

hallucination False perception that occurs in the absence of objective stimulation.

WHAT CAN WE LEARN FROM "THE MUNCHIES"?

Even if you've never smoked marijuana you're likely to be familiar with one of the drug's legendary effects: Marijuana gives people intense cravings for food—cravings often called "the munchies." Observations about marijuana's effects on hunger go back at least to 300 A.D. when texts in India recommended that it be used to stimulate the appetite (Cota et al., 2003). Take a moment to consider how you might turn "the munchies" into a research agenda. What questions might you generate? What hypotheses would you like to test?

The first question you might wish to address would perhaps be "Why?": Why does marijuana affect people's appetite? In the text, we've already told you important parts of that story. Researchers determined that the active chemicals—the cannabinoids—in marijuana bind to specific receptors in the brain. As research unfolded, researchers also made the breakthrough discovery of the existence of endocannabinoids (endogenous cannabinoids) in the brain. With that discovery in hand, researchers could test the hypothesis that endocannabinoids play an ongoing role in regulating food consumption. This hypothesis was solidly confirmed (Vemuri et al., 2008). That research even helped to explain observations about the *types* of food people crave when they have the munchies. Besides their role in regulating apetite, endocannabinoids also play a role in

reward systems in the brain (Cota et al., 2006). For that reason, endocannabinoids have the particular effect of making people seek foods that are tasty or sweet. Thus, it's no coincidence that the munchies are best satisfied with junk food. This range of insights has enabled researchers to develop drug therapies to treat people who are reluctant to eat for psychological or medical reasons (Cota et al., 2003).

So, you know that endocannabinoids increase appetite. Here's the next step your thinking might take: Can researchers devise drugs that will use this same system to *suppress* appetite? The goal, in this context, is to find drugs that prevent the endocannabinoids from having their ordinary impact. Over the last several years, researchers have begun to have great successes in this quest (Vemuri et al., 2008). One drug that has demonstrated early promise is called *rimonabant*. Rimonabant blocks the brain's cannabinoid receptors from carrying out their normal functions. In one double-blind study testing the impact of rimonabant treatment, 1,036 overweight and obese individuals were given either a low or high dose of the drug or a placebo (i.e., an inert substance) (Després et al., 2005). Over the course of the year-long study, participants in the placebo group lost about 5 pounds. Participants who got the low dose of rimonabant lost about 9 pounds.

Participants on the high dose lost about 19 pounds! Similarly, high-dose participants took considerably more inches off their waists (3.6 in.) than did low-dose (1.9 in.) or placebo (1.3 in.) participants. With results of this sort in hand, researchers have begun the quest for drugs that achieve the same effects as rimonabant with fewer side effects (such as nausea or insomnia) (Vemuri et al., 2008).

From this example, you can see how research progresses from a real-world observation to a productive research agenda. With the goal of understanding why marijuana has an impact on appetite, researchers have generated insights that have led to successful treatments for both people who eat too little and people who eat too much. In fact, the same course of research points to even greater promise for the future: Because the endocannabinoids have an important impact on the brain's reward circuits, researchers believe that drugs targeting the endocannabinoid system may provide successful treatments for both pain and addiction (Fattore et al., 2007; Hosking & Zajicek, 2008).

- Why was it important for the study testing rimonabant to be double-blind?
- Why might there be a link between the brain systems that regulate appetite and reward?

morphines) that generate powerful effects on mood, pain, and pleasure. These endogenous opiates play a critical role in the brain's response to both physical and psychological stressors (Ribeiro et al., 2005). Drugs like opium and morphine bind to the same receptor sites in the brain as the endorphins (Trescot et al., 2008). Thus both opiates and, as we described in the previous section, marijuana achieve their effects because they have active components that have similar chemical properties to substances that naturally occur in the brain.

The initial effect of an intravenous injection of heroin is a rush of pleasure. Feelings of euphoria supplant all worries and awareness of bodily needs. However, heroin use often leads to addiction. When the neural receptors in the endogenous opiate system are artificially stimulated, the brain loses its subtle balance. People who try to withdraw from opiates often experience harsh physical symptoms (such as vomiting, pain, and insomnia) as well as intense craving for the drug. When people undertake medical assistance to help with withdrawal, they often receive treatments that block the opiates' ability to create pleasure responses in the brain (Grüsser et al., 2006).

Depressants The **depressants** include *barbiturates, benzodiazepines,* and *alcohol.* These substances tend to depress (slow down) the mental and physical activity of the body by inhibiting or decreasing the transmission of nerve impulses in the central nervous system. Depressants achieve this effect, in part, by facilitating neural communication at synapses that use the neurotransmitter GABA (Licata & Rowlett, 2008). GABA often functions to inhibit neural transmission, which explains depressants' inhibiting outcomes. In the past, people were often prescribed barbiturates such as *Nembutol* and *Seconal* to act as sedatives or to treat insomnia. However, because of barbiturates' potential for addiction and overdose, people are now more likely to receive prescriptions for benzodiazepines such as *Valium* or *Xanax.* In Chapter 15, we will see that these drugs are also commonly used to counteract anxiety.

In recent years, two depressants, *Rohypnol* (more commonly known as *roofies*) and *GHB,* have achieved reputations as drugs used to carry out sexual assaults (Maxwell, 2005). These "date rape drugs" can be manufactured as colorless liquids so that they can be added to alcohol or other beverages without detection. In that way, victims can be unknowingly sedated and find themselves vulnerable to rape attacks. In addition, Rohypnol causes amnesia, so that victims may not remember events that occurred while they were under the drug's influence.

Alcohol was apparently one of the first psychoactive substances used extensively by early humans. Under its influence, some people become silly, boisterous, friendly, and talkative; others become abusive and violent; still others become quietly depressed. Alcohol appears to stimulate the release of dopamine, which enhances feelings of pleasure. Also, as with other depressants, it appears to affect GABA activity (Lobo & Harris, 2008). At small dosages, alcohol can induce relaxation and slightly improve an adult's speed of reaction. However, the body can break down alcohol only at a slow rate, and large amounts consumed in a short time period overtax the central nervous system. As the concentration of alcohol increases to 0.05 to 0.10 percent, cognitive, perceptual, and motor processes begin rapidly to deteriorate. When the level of alcohol in the blood reaches 0.15 percent, there are gross negative effects on thinking, memory, and judgment, along with emotional instability and loss of motor coordination.

Excess consumption of alcohol is a major social problem in the United States. When the amount and frequency of drinking interfere with job performance, impair social and family relationships, and create serious health problems, the diagnosis of *alcoholism* is appropriate. Physical dependence, tolerance, and addiction all develop with prolonged heavy drinking. For some individuals, alcoholism is associated with an inability to abstain from drinking. For others, alcoholism manifests itself as an inability to stop drinking once the person takes a few drinks. In a 2007 survey, 14.7 percent of 18- to 25-year-olds reported heavy drinking—defined as drinking five or more drinks on the same occasion on each of five or more days in a 1-month period (SAMHSA, 2008). The peak of heavy drinking was age 21, with 17.9 percent of 21-year-olds reporting heavy alcohol use.

Why does alcohol remain the most popular way in which college students alter their consciousness?

Driving accidents and fatalities occur six times more often to individuals with 0.10 percent alcohol in their bloodstream than to those with half that amount. Alcohol-related automobile accidents are a leading cause of death among people between the ages of 15 and 25. Given these disturbing statistics, researchers have tried to understand the several ways in which alcohol has a negative impact on driving performance. Part of the answer lies in alcohol's effect on drinkers' ability to inhibit bad impulses.

Suppose you are driving to an important appointment for which you can't be late. As you drive, you might have an impulse to indulge in bad driving behaviors such as speeding or reckless lane changes. However, those negative impulses are offset by your knowledge that you might get a ticket, have an accident, and so on. A team of researchers tested the hypothesis that people under the influence of alcohol drive particularly badly when they are driving in those sorts of circumstances—in which there's a conflict between good and bad impulses (Fillmore et al., 2008). The participants in the study engaged in a simulated driving task after consuming either alcohol or a placebo. (You can understand why the researchers couldn't conduct the experiment on real roads.) Participants' driving was considerably worse after alcohol consumption on measures such as failures to stop at red lights and abrupt steering maneuvers. The impact of alcohol was even greater, however, when the researchers increased the participants' sense of response conflict. The researchers offered the participants cash

---

depressant Drug that depresses or slows down the activity of the central nervous system.

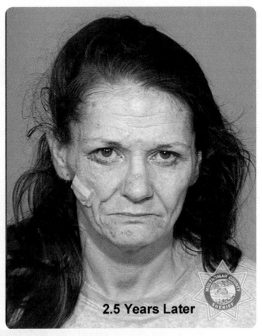

Methamphetamine is so addictive that users will tolerate the physical deterioration that accompanies long-term use. The left photograph shows a 42-year-old woman before she became a methamphetamine addict. The right photo was taken 2 1/2 years later. Why is it so easy for people to become addicted to methamphetamine and other stimulants?

rewards for reaching their destinations quickly, but they lost money if they drove poorly. When they were in this state of conflict, participants' performance was worst of all: Their bad impulses dramatically won out.

You are no doubt familiar with the claim that people will do things while they're drunk that they would never do if they were sober. In the realm of driving, the lack of impulse control can have deadly consequences.

Stimulants Stimulants, such as *amphetamines, methamphetamines,* and *cocaine,* keep the drug user aroused and induce states of euphoria. Stimulants achieve their effects by increasing the brain levels of neurotransmitters such as norepinephrine, serotonin, and dopamine. For example, stimulants act in the brain to prevent the action of molecules that ordinarily remove dopamine from synapses (Martin-Fardon et al., 2005). The serious addition that often accompanies stimulant use may arise because of long-term changes in the neurotransmitter systems (Ahmed & Koob, 2004).

In recent years, research attention has focused on abuse of methamphetamine. Over a period of 10 years, from 1993 to 2003, admissions to facilities for the treatment of methamphetamine addiction increased by 400 percent (Homer et al., 2008). Poll data indicate that the rate of methamphetamine use has held steady, at about 0.2 to 0.3 percent of the U.S. population,

for the period from 2002 to 2007 (SAMHSA, 2008). As with other stimulants, methamphetamine has an impact on the brain's use of dopamine. People who take methamphetamine experience feelings of euphoria, decreased anxiety, and intense sexual craving. However, methamphetamine use very quickly has negative consequences: After only days or weeks of continuous use, people begin to experience frightening hallucinations and develop beliefs that others are out to harm them. These beliefs are known as *paranoid delusions.* Methamphetamine is highly addictive. Chronic use causes several types of damage in the brain, including the loss of nerve terminals in the dopamine system (Rose & Grant, 2008). Damage to brain regions involved in decision making and planning may explain why methamphetamine users become overly aggressive and suffer from social isolation (Homer et al., 2008).

MDMA—more commonly known as *ecstasy*—is a stimulant but also produces hallucinogen-like distortions of time and perception. The stimulant properties of the drug gives users feelings of boundless energy; the hallucinogenic properties make sounds, colors, and emotions more intense. Ecstasy brings about these effects by altering the functioning of neurotransmitters such as dopamine, serotonin, and norepinephrine. Because ecstasy has a broad impact on these neurotransmitter systems considerable research has focused on the drug's long-term impact on the brain (Jager et al., 2008). Researchers have been particularly sensitive to ecstasy's status as a party drug. They have attempted to devise studies that accurately reflect human norms of drug use. Researchers recognize, for example, that ecstasy users often ingest the drug at the same time that they

stimulant Drug that causes arousal, increased activity, and euphoria.

have consumed alcohol. This leads to the question of how alcohol and ecstasy jointly affect the brain. Research suggests that the combination of ecstasy and alcohol produces negative effects in rats' brains that would not have occurred with ecstasy alone (Cassel et al., 2005).

Stimulants have three major effects that users seek: increased self-confidence, greater energy and hyperalertness, and mood alterations approaching euphoria. As we noted for metamphetamine, heavy users often experience hallucinations and paranoid delusions. A special danger with cocaine use is the contrast between euphoric highs and very depressive lows. This leads users to increase uncontrollably the frequency of drug use and the dosage. *Crack,* a crystallized form of cocaine, increases these dangers. Crack produces a swift high that wears off quickly; craving for the drug is intense.

Two stimulants that you may often overlook as psychoactive drugs are *caffeine* and *nicotine.* As you may know from experience, two cups of strong coffee or tea administer enough caffeine to have a profound effect on heart, blood, and circulatory functions and make it difficult for you to sleep. Nicotine, a chemical found in tobacco, is a sufficiently strong stimulant to have been used in high concentrations by Native American shamans to attain mystical states or trances. Unlike some modern users, however, the shamans knew that nicotine is addictive, and they carefully chose when to be under its influence. Like other addictive drugs, nicotine mimics natural chemicals released by the brain. In fact, research has uncovered common regions of brain activation for addiction to nicotine and cocaine (Vezina et al., 2007). Chemicals in nicotine stimulate receptors that make you feel good whenever you have done something right—a phenomenon that aids survival. Unfortunately, nicotine teases those same brain receptors into responding as if it were good for you to be smoking. It's not. As you know, smoking is far from good for your health.

We began this chapter by asking you to remember your past and plan for your future. These ordinary activities allowed us nonetheless to pose some interesting questions about consciousness: Where did your thoughts come from? How did they emerge? When did they arrive? You've now learned some of the theories that apply to these questions and how it has been possible to test those theories. You've seen that consciousness ultimately allows you to have the full range of experiences that define you as human.

We also asked you to consider some increasingly less ordinary uses of consciousness. Why, we asked, do people become dissatisfied with their everyday working minds and seek to alter their consciousness in so many ways? Ordinarily, your primary focus is on meeting the immediate demands of tasks and situations facing you. However, you are aware of these reality-based constraints on your consciousness. You realize they limit the range and depth of your experience and do not allow you to fulfill your potential. Perhaps, at times, you long to reach beyond the confines of ordinary reality. You may seek the uncertainty of freedom instead of settling for the security of the ordinary.

STOP AND REVIEW

❶ What is the definition of drug tolerance?
❷ How do drugs like heroin work in the brain?
❸ To what category of drugs does nicotine belong?

Visit MyPsychLab.com for more review and practice on the following topic:

✳ **Simulate:** General Model of Drug Addiction

Recapping Main Points

The Contents of Consciousness

- Consciousness is an awareness of the mind's contents.
- The contents of waking consciousness contrast with nonconscious processes, preconscious memories, unattended information, the unconscious, and conscious awareness.
- Research techniques such as think-aloud protocols and experience sampling are used to study the contents of consciousness.

The Functions of Consciousness

- Consciousness aids your survival and enables you to construct both personal and culturally shared realities.
- Researchers have studied the relationship between conscious and unconscious processes.

Sleep and Dreams

- Circadian rhythms reflect the operation of a biological clock.
- Patterns of brain activity change over the course of a night's sleep. REM sleep is signaled by rapid eye movements.
- The amount of sleep and relative proportion of REM to NREM sleep change with age.
- REM and NREM sleep serve different functions, including conservation and restoration.
- Sleep disorders such as insomnia, narcolepsy, and sleep apnea have a negative impact on people's ability to function during waking time.
- Freud proposed that the content of dreams is unconscious material slipped by a sleeping censor.
- In other cultures, dreams are interpreted regularly, often by people with special cultural roles.

- Some dream theories have focused on biological explanations for the origins of dreams.

Altered States of Consciousness

- Lucid dreaming is an awareness that one is dreaming, in an attempt to control the dream.
- Hypnosis is an alternate state of consciousness characterized by the ability of hypnotizable people to change perception, motivation, memory, and self-control in response to suggestions.
- Meditation changes conscious functioning by ritual practices that focus attention away from external concerns to inner experience.

Mind-Altering Drugs

- Psychoactive drugs affect mental processes by temporarily changing consciousness as they modify nervous system activity.
- Among psychoactive drugs that alter consciousness are hallucinogens, opiates, depressants, and stimulants.

KEY TERMS

addiction (p. 152)
circadian rhythm (p. 141)
consciousness (p. 136)
depressant (p. 155)
dream work (p. 147)
hallucination (p. 153)
hallucinogen (p. 152)
hypnosis (p. 149)
hypnotizability (p. 149)
insomnia (p. 145)

latent content (p. 147)
lucid dreaming (p. 148)
manifest content (p. 147)
meditation (p. 151)
narcolepsy (p. 146)
nightmare (p. 146)
nonconscious (p. 137)
non-REM (NREM) sleep (p. 142)
physiological dependence (p. 152)
preconscious memory (p. 137)

psychoactive drug (p. 152)
psychological dependence (p. 152)
rapid eye movements (REM) (p. 142)
sleep apnea (p. 146)
sleep terrors (p. 146)
somnambulism (p. 146)
stimulant (p. 156)
tolerance (p. 152)

Chapter 5 Practice Test

1. Freud suggested that some memories are sufficiently threatening that they are forced to reside in
   a. the unconscious.
   b. the preconscious.
   c. consciousness.
   d. manifest content.

2. You have a group of men and women watch the same TV commercial for a new car. If you want to determine what type of information the commercial brings to mind, you could use
   a. meditation.
   b. a visual search experiment.
   c. lucid dreaming.
   d. think-aloud protocols.

3. Which of these is an example of the selective storage function of consciousness?
   a. Rob kept his eye on the hoop while he shot the basketball.
   b. Laura decided to get chocolate ice cream instead of vanilla.
   c. Mel hit the gas pedal as soon as the light turned green.
   d. Salvatore committed to memory the address of his new girlfriend.

4. Because it requires more conscious attention, it is harder to find a _____ object than a _____ object.
   a. red; large and red
   b. green; green and yellow
   c. red and blue; green and yellow
   d. red and blue; red

5. To determine Garrick's chronotype, which question would you be mostly likely to ask him?
   a. How many times a month do you have nightmares?
   b. When do you usually go to bed?
   c. Do you have more NREM sleep or more REM sleep?
   d. Do you smoke marijuana or cigarettes?

6. Both NREM and REM sleep may be important for
   a. conservation.
   b. restoration.
   c. latent and manifest content.
   d. learning and memory.

7. Several times a night, Carolyn stops breathing and then she wakes up. It sounds as if Carolyn suffers from
   a. insomnia.
   b. sleep apnea.
   c. somnambulism.
   d. narcolepsy.

8. The activation-synthesis model claimed that
   a. dreams arise from random brain activity.
   b. manifest content is synthesized from latent content.
   c. dream content reflects people's day-to-day concerns.
   d. girls and boys have different dream content.

9. To demonstrate that _____ is possible, researchers had participants perform distinctive patterns of voluntary eye movements while they were asleep.
   a. lucid dreaming
   b. hypnosis
   c. meditation
   d. activation and synthesis

10. Which of these individuals would you expect to be most responsive to hypnosis?
    a. 19-year-old Paula
    b. 11-year-old Ralph
    c. 24-year-old Jeannine
    d. 46-year-old George

11. Research suggests that people who practice _____ have thicker areas of cortex than individuals who do not.
    a. hypnosis
    b. lucid dreaming
    c. somnambulism
    d. meditation

12. Craving for a drug in the absence of a physical need is the definition of
    a. addiction.
    b. drug tolerance.
    c. psychological dependence.
    d. physiological dependence.

13. Hallucinogens act in the brain by _____ the activation of _____ neurons.
    a. inhibiting; GABA
    b. prolonging; dopamine
    c. prolonging; serotonin
    d. inhibiting; dopamine

14. Heavy use of _____ may lead to paranoid delusions.
    a. stimulants
    b. depressants
    c. opiates
    d. hallucinogens

15. A team of researchers is developing a new drug treatment to help people control their weight. You suspect that the drug might target the brain's _____ system.
    a. barbiturate
    b. opiate
    c. benzodiazepine
    d. cannabinoid

Essay Questions

1. How has the concept of the unconscious been modified in the time since Freud's theory?

2. What practices of dream interpretation are carried out in non-Western cultures?

3. What physiological mechanisms explain why drug use often leads to addiction?

Discovering Psychology Viewing Guide

Watch the following videos by logging on to MyPsychLab (www.mypsychlab.com). After you have watched the videos, complete the activities that follow.

Program 13: The Mind Awake and Asleep

Program 14: The Mind Hidden and Divided

KEY TERMS AND PEOPLE

As you watch the programs, pay particular attention to these terms and people in addition to those covered in this textbook.

- *hypnagogic state*—a period of reverie at the onset of the sleeping state.
- *posthypnotic amnesia*—forgetting selected events by suggestion.
- *Michael Gazzaniga*—conducts research on the psychological study of split-brain phenomena.
- *Ernest Hartmann*—an expert on sleep who believes that it serves a restorative function.
- *Jonathan Schooler*—studies discovered memories in people who previously had no memory of major, traumatic events in their lives.

PROGRAM REVIEW

1. Which of the following is an example of a circadian rhythm?
   a. eating three meals a day at approximately the same time
   b. experiencing alternate periods of REM and non-REM sleep
   c. having systematic changes in hormone levels during 24 hours
   d. having changes in fertility levels during a month

2. How normal is it to experience alternate states of consciousness?
   a. It happens to most people, mainly in times of stress.
   b. It is something we all experience every day.
   c. It is rare and generally indicates a mental disorder.
   d. It is common in childhood and becomes rarer with age.

3. In the program, the part of the brain that is identified as the "interior decorator" imposing order on experience is the
   a. pons.
   b. hippocampus.
   c. limbic system.
   d. cerebral cortex.

4. Which of the following is an example of the lower-level processing of sensory input that is nonconscious?
   a. recognizing a friend's face
   b. detecting edges
   c. working on an assembly line
   d. noticing something tastes good

5. Edward Titchener was the leader of structuralism in the United States. What aspect of the concept of consciousness interested him?
   a. the contents of consciousness
   b. the material repressed from conscious awareness
   c. the uniqueness of consciousness
   d. He viewed consciousness as a scientifically worthless concept.

6. In Donald Broadbent's research, what happened when people heard two stories but were asked to attend to only one?
   a. They comprehended both stories.
   b. They comprehended only the attended story.
   c. They wove bits of the unattended story into the attended story.
   d. They were not able to follow either story.

7. What is a positive function of daydreaming?
   a. It focuses attention on a task.
   b. It reduces demands made on the brain.
   c. It enables us to be mentally active when we are bored.
   d. It provides delta wave activity normally received only in sleep.

8. Ernest Hartmann points out the logic behind Shakespeare's description of sleep. According to Hartmann, a major function of sleep is that it allows the brain to
   a. process material too threatening to be dealt with consciously.
   b. integrate the day's events with previously learned material.
   c. make plans for the day ahead.
   d. discharge a buildup of electrical activity.

9. According to Freud, dreams are significant because they
   a. permit neurotransmitters to be regenerated.
   b. reveal unconscious fears and desires.
   c. forecast the future.
   d. supply a story line to patterns of electrical charges.

10. According to McCarley and Hobson's activation synthesis theory of dreams, what activates dreams?
    a. the needs of the dreamer's unconscious
    b. the sending of electrical charges to the forebrain
    c. the memories contained in the cerebral cortex
    d. the synthesis of chemicals needed for brain function

11. According to McCarley and Hobson, what is true about REM sleep?
    a. Adults spend more time in REM sleep than infants.
    b. REM sleep is an unnecessary physiological function.
    c. The random burst of brain activity occurs first, followed by the dreamer's attempt to make sense of it.
    d. The subconscious expresses its deepest desires during REM sleep.

12. In his work on lucid dreaming, why does LaBerge use a flashing light?
    a. so participants are consciously aware of their dream and can control it
    b. so participants can incorporate the light itself into their dream narrative
    c. so participants get feedback about where they are in the REM sleep cycle
    d. so measurements can be made of physiological response

13. In the experiment described in the program, patients under anesthesia were exposed to a positive or negative message. What effect did getting a positive message have?
    a. It meant less anesthesia was needed.
    b. It shortened patients' hospital stays.
    c. It created more positive attitudes toward surgery.
    d. Positive messages had no effect because patients were unaware of them.

14. Which part of the brain is responsible for conscious awareness?
    a. cerebral cortex   c. limbic system
    b. brain stem   d. hypothalamus

15. When societies around the world were studied, what proportion of them practiced some culturally patterned form of altering consciousness?
    a. practically none   c. about half
    b. about a third   d. the vast majority

16. Edward Titchener is to structuralism as William James is to
    a. introspection.   c. lucid dreaming.
    b. functionalism.   d. discovered memories.

17. According to Freud, how do we feel when painful memories or unacceptable urges threaten to break into consciousness?
    a. relieved   c. sad
    b. guilty   d. anxious

18. What are Freudian slips thought to reveal?
    a. what we have dreamed about
    b. how we really feel
    c. who we would like to be transformed into
    d. why we make certain choices

19. What happens if a hypnotized person who expects to smell cologne actually smells ammonia?
    a. The ammonia smell wakes him from the trance.
    b. He recognizes the ammonia smell, but he remains hypnotized.
    c. He interprets the ammonia smell as a musky cologne.
    d. He overgeneralizes and finds that the cologne smells like ammonia.

20. All of the following appear to fluctuate based on circadian rhythm, *except*
    a. intelligence.   c. blood pressure.
    b. hormone levels.   d. body temperature.

21. Michael Gazzaniga has worked with split-brain, or "broken-brain," patients. What has this led him to believe about our individuality?
    a. It comes from an interpreter in the left hemisphere.
    b. It is an illusion based on our emotional needs.
    c. It derives from our unique set of independent mind-modules.
    d. It is located in the corpus callosum.

22. Consciousness performs all of the following functions, *except*
    a. filtering sensory data.
    b. enabling us to respond flexibly.
    c. allowing us to have a sense of our own mortality.
    d. guiding performance of highly routinized actions.

23. Which of the following people would have the strongest objection to the concept of consciousness?
    a. William James   c. Edward Titchener
    b. John Watson   d. Wilhelm Wundt

24. Instances in which people believe they have remembered long-forgotten traumatic events are known as
    a. repression.   c. recovered memories.
    b. suppression.   d. fugue states.

25. One of the most important techniques that psychologists commonly use to confirm the validity of a recovered memory is to
    a. have the rememberer recount the memory under hypnosis.
    b. subject the rememberer to a lie-detector test.
    c. count the number of details in the rememberer's story.
    d. collect confirming evidence from other people who knew about the event.

26. Sigmund Freud is to the unconscious as _____ is to discovered memories.
    a. B. F. Skinner   c. Michael Gazzaniga
    b. Jonathan Schooler   d. Stephen LaBerge

27. According to Freud, normal people banish undesirable memories from their conscious minds through
    a. repression.   c. anterograde amnesia.
    b. projection.   d. hysteria.

28. According to Freud, the "alarm" that signals that unconscious thoughts or memories are about to break loose to consciousness is
    a. sexual desire.   c. confusion.
    b. lethargy.   d. anxiety.

29. Which topic related to human consciousness is conveyed by the story of Dr. Jekyll and Mr. Hyde?

    a. witchcraft   c. identity transformation

    b. hypnosis   d. sleep disorders

30. Communication between the two hemispheres of the brain is disrupted when

    a. a person is in deep meditation.

    b. a person is in deep Freudian denial.

    c. a person has just recovered an early memory.

    d. the corpus callosum is severed.

31. What occurs about every 90 minutes throughout sleep?

    a. rapid eye movement

    b. rapid irregular changes in brain activity

    c. dreaming

    d. more than one of the above

QUESTIONS TO CONSIDER

1. Donald Broadbent conceived of attention as a selective filter that acts like a tuner on a radio, selecting one message from all the others. According to Broadbent, the unattended sensory information is sent to a buffer, where it either receives attention and gets processed or is ignored and lost. How is this buffer similar to the concept of the sensory memory? What role might it play in subliminal perception?

2. Consider the role of culture and language in structuring consciousness or focused perception. In what ways is awareness culturally determined?

3. How do you experience REM rebound effects when you have been deprived of sleep? Do you begin dreaming soon after falling asleep? Do you experience vivid visual imagery when you are awake?

4. Changes in perceptions, time sense, memory, feelings of self-control, and suggestibility are aspects of an altered state of consciousness. Would you consider illness, love, or grief to be altered states of consciousness?

5. Psychoactive drugs are only partially responsible for the changes in the drug taker's consciousness. Mental sets, expectations, and the context in which the drugs are taken can also have significant influences. What are the implications for alcohol and drug education and treatment?

6. Do you consider television or other electronic media to have mind-altering influence? What do they have in common with other mind-altering substances or experiences? Are children more susceptible to these effects than adults?

7. Do you think you could benefit from hypnosis or meditation? Do you believe you could easily enter these states? If someone finds it difficult to become hypnotized or to meditate, would you advise him or her that it is worth the effort of learning? And how would you suggest the person learn?

ACTIVITIES

1. Keep a pad and pencil by your bed and start a dream journal. Just before you fall asleep, remind yourself to remember your dreams. Immediately upon awakening, record what you remember: images, actions, characters, emotions, events, and settings. Does your ability to recall your dreams improve over time? Does this change if you set your alarm for different times during the sleep cycle? Does your recall become more vivid or more organized? Can you shape your dreams by telling yourself at bedtime what you want to dream about?

2. Make a list of common examples of dissociation and divided consciousness. Do these examples support the concept of mini-minds or different areas of the brain operating independently? What other explanations might account for your ability to divide your consciousness?

3. Try to think of a time when you surprised yourself by having a very strong feeling in response to an incident that didn't seem to warrant such a strong response. Could nonconscious factors have played a role in your response? What did you think about your response at the time? What did you think about it later?

4. Go on the Internet and look up various cultures, religions, and communities that practice altered states of consciousness. See if you can develop any insights into what aspects of their art, social interaction, and values appear to be influenced by such practices.

Learning and Behavior Analysis

Imagine that you are in a movie theater, watching a horror film. As the hero approaches a closed door, the music on the movie's sound track grows dark and menacing. You suddenly feel the urge to yell, "Don't go through that door!" Meanwhile, you find that your heart is racing. But why? If you think about this question formally, you might come to the answer, "I have learned an association between movie music and movie events—and that's what's making me nervous!" But had you ever thought about this relationship before? Probably not. Somehow, by virtue of sitting in enough movie theaters, you have learned the association without any particular thought. The main topic of Chapter 6 is the types of associations that you acquire effortlessly in your day-to-day experience.

Psychologists have long been interested in *learning*, the ways in which organisms learn from experiences in the world. In just a moment, we will offer a more precise definition of learning. We then consider particular types of learning: classical conditioning and operant conditioning. As you will see, each of these types of learning represents a different way in which organisms acquire and use information about the structure of their environments. For each of these types of learning, we will describe both the basic mechanisms that govern its operation in the laboratory and applications to real-life situations.

In this chapter, we also reflect on the way learning is similar and dissimilar across species. You will see that basic processes of conditioning are the same across a wide variety of species. However, we will note that some aspects of learning are constrained by species' particular genetic endowments. In particular, we will see how *cognition*—higher mental processes—affects learning processes in both humans and other species.

in behavior require experience following maturational readiness. For example, consider the timetable that determines when an infant is ready to crawl, stand, walk, run, and be toilet trained. No amount of training or practice will produce those behaviors before the child has matured sufficiently. Psychologists are especially interested in discovering what aspects of behavior can be changed through experience and how such changes come about.

A Change in Behavior or Behavior Potential It is obvious that learning has taken place when you are able to demonstrate the results, such as when you drive a car or use a microwave oven. You can't directly observe learning itself—meaning, you can't ordinarily see the changes in your brain—but learning is apparent from improvements in your *performance*. Often, however, your performance doesn't show everything that you have learned. Sometimes, too, you have acquired general attitudes, such as an *appreciation* of modern art or an *understanding* of Eastern philosophy, that may not be apparent in your measurable actions. In such instances, you have achieved a potential for behavior change because you have learned attitudes and values that can influence the kinds of books you read or the way you spend your leisure time. This is an example of the **learning-performance distinction**—the difference between what has been learned and what is expressed, or performed, in overt behavior.

A Relatively Consistent Change To qualify as learned, a change in behavior or behavior potential must be relatively consistent over different occasions. Thus, once you learn to swim, you will probably always be able to do so. Note that consistent changes are not always permanent changes. You may, for example, have become quite a consistent dart thrower when you practiced every day. If you gave up the sport, however, your skills might have deteriorated toward their original level. But if you have learned once

The Study of Learning

To begin our exploration of learning, we will first define learning itself and then offer a brief sketch of the history of psychological research on the topic.

WHAT IS LEARNING?

Learning is a process based on experience that results in a relatively consistent change in behavior or behavior potential. Let's look more closely at the three critical parts of this definition.

A Process Based on Experience Learning can take place only through experience. Experience includes taking in information (and evaluating and transforming it) and making responses that affect the environment. Learning consists of a response influenced by the lessons of memory. Learned behavior does not include changes that come about because of physical maturation or brain development as the organism ages, nor those caused by illness or brain damage. Some lasting changes

How does consistent form in ballet dancers fit the definition of learning?

---

learning A process based on experience that results in a relatively permanent change in behavior or behavioral potential.

learning-performance distinction The difference between what has been learned and what is expressed in overt behavior.

to be a championship dart thrower, it ought to be easier for you to learn a second time. Something has been "saved" from your prior experience. In that sense, the change may be permanent.

Habituation and Sensitization To help you master the concept of learning, we want to describe two of its most basic forms: *habituation* and *sensitization.* Imagine that you are examining a picture of a pleasant scene—an image, for example, of waterskiing or windsurfing. The first time you see it, you might have a fairly strong emotional response. However, if you view the same image repeatedly in short succession, your emotional response will become weaker over time (Leventhal et al., 2007). This is an example of **habituation:** You show a decrease in behavioral response when a stimulus is presented repeatedly. Habituation helps keep your focus on novel events in the environment—you don't expend behavioral effort to respond repeatedly to old stimuli.

Note how habituation fits the definition of learning. There's a change in behavior (your emotional response is weaker) that is based on experience (you've seen the image repeatedly), and that behavior change is consistent (you do not return to your original level of emotional response). However, the change in emotional response is unlikely to be permanent. If you see the same picture after sufficient time has passed, you might find it emotionally engaging once again.

When **sensitization** occurs, your response to a stimulus becomes stronger, rather than weaker, when it occurs repeatedly. Suppose, for example, you experience the same painful stimulus several times in short succession. Even if the intensity of the stimulus remained constant, you would report greater pain in response to the final stimulus in the series than you would in response to the first stimulus (Farrell & Gibson, 2007). Once again, sensitization fits the definition of learning because experience in the world (repeated experiences of a painful stimulus) leads to a consistent change in behavioral response (reports that the pain is more intense). You might wonder what determines whether people will experience habituation or sensitization in response to different stimuli. In general, sensitization is more likely to occur when stimuli are intense or irritating.

BEHAVIORISM AND BEHAVIOR ANALYSIS

Much of modern psychology's view of learning finds its roots in the work of **John Watson** (1878–1958). Watson founded the school of psychology known as *behaviorism.* For nearly 50 years, American psychology was dominated by the behaviorist tradition expressed in Watson's 1919 book, *Psychology from the Standpoint of a Behaviorist.* Watson argued that introspection—people's verbal reports of sensations, images, and feelings—was *not* an acceptable means of studying behavior because it was too subjective. How could scientists verify the accuracy of such private experiences? But once introspection has been rejected, what should the subject matter of psychology be? Watson's answer was *observable behavior.* In Watson's words, "States of consciousness, like the so-called phenomenon of spiritualism, are not objectively verifiable and for that reason can never become data for science" (Watson, 1919, p. 1). Watson also defined the chief goal of psychology as "the prediction and control of behavior" (Watson, 1913, p. 158).

B. F. Skinner (1904–1990) adopted Watson's cause and expanded his agenda. Skinner began the research that would lead

B. F. Skinner expanded on Watson's ideas and applied them to a wide spectrum of behavior. Why did Skinner's psychology focus on environmental events rather than internal states?

him to formulate this position when, after reading Watson's 1924 book *Behaviorism,* he began his graduate study in psychology at Harvard. Over time, Skinner formulated a position known as *radical behaviorism.* Skinner embraced Watson's complaint against internal states and mental events. However, Skinner focused not so much on their legitimacy as data as on their legitimacy as *causes of behavior* (Skinner, 1990). In Skinner's view, mental events, such as thinking and imagining, do not cause behavior. Rather, they are examples of behavior that are caused by environmental stimuli.

Suppose that we deprive a pigeon of food for 24 hours, place it in an apparatus where it can obtain food by pecking a small disk, and find that it soon does so. Skinner would argue that the animal's behavior can be fully explained by environmental events—deprivation and the use of food as reinforcement. The subjective feeling of hunger, which cannot be directly observed or measured, is not a cause of the behavior but the result of deprivation. It adds nothing to our account to say that the bird pecked the disk because it was hungry or because it wanted to get the food. To explain what the bird does, you need not understand anything about its inner psychological states—you need only understand the principles of learning that allow the bird to acquire the association between behavior and reward. This is the essence of Skinner's brand of behaviorism.

This brand of behaviorism originated by Skinner served as the original philosophical cornerstone of **behavior analysis,** the area of psychology that focuses on discovering environmental determinants of learning and behavior (Cooper et al., 2007). In general, behavior analysts attempt to discover regularities in learning that are universal, occurring in all types of animal

---

habituation A decrease in a behavioral response when a stimulus is presented repeatedly.

sensitization An increase in behavioral response when a stimulus is presented repeatedly.

behavior analysis The area of psychology that focuses on the environmental determinants of learning and behavior.

species, including humans, under comparable situations. That is why studies with nonhuman animals have been so critical to progress in this area. Complex forms of learning represent combinations and elaborations of simpler processes and not qualitatively different phenomena. In the sections that follow, we describe classical conditioning and operant conditioning—two simple forms of learning that give rise to quite complex behaviors.

STOP AND REVIEW

❶ What is meant by the learning-performance distinction?
❷ Why did Watson emphasize the study of observable behavior?
❸ What is a major goal of behavior analysis?
❹ What is the definition of habituation?

Visit MyPsychLab.com for more review and practice on the following topic:

◄•) **Explore:** Three Stages of Classical Conditioning

Classical Conditioning: Learning Predictable Signals

Imagine once more that you are watching that horror movie. Why does your heart race when the sound track signals trouble for the hero? Somehow your body has learned to produce a physiological response (a racing heart) when one environmental event (for example, scary music) is associated with another (scary visual events). This type of learning is known as **classical conditioning,** a basic form of learning in which one stimulus or event predicts the occurrence of another stimulus or event. The organism learns a new *association* between two stimuli—a stimulus that did not previously elicit the response and one that naturally elicited the response. As you shall see, the innate capacity to quickly associate pairs of events in your environment has profound behavioral implications.

PAVLOV'S SURPRISING OBSERVATION

The first rigorous study of classical conditioning was the result of what may well be psychology's most famous accident. The Russian physiologist **Ivan Pavlov** (1849–1936) did not set out to study classical conditioning or any other psychological phenomenon. He happened on classical conditioning while conducting research on digestion, for which he won a Nobel Prize in 1904.

Pavlov had devised a technique to study digestive processes in dogs by implanting tubes in their glands and digestive organs to divert bodily secretions to containers outside their bodies so that

---

classical conditioning A type of learning in which a behavior (conditioned response) comes to be elicited by a stimulus (conditioned stimulus) that has acquired its power through an association with a biologically significant stimulus (unconditioned stimulus).

Physiologist Ivan Pavlov (shown here with his research team) observed classical conditioning while conducting research on digestion. What were some of Pavlov's major contributions to the study of this form of learning?

the secretions could be measured and analyzed. To produce these secretions, Pavlov's assistants put meat powder into the dogs' mouths. After repeating this procedure a number of times, Pavlov observed an unexpected behavior in his dogs—they salivated *before* the powder was put in their mouths! They would start salivating at the mere sight of the food and, later, at the sight of the assistant who brought the food or even at the sound of the assistant's footsteps. Indeed, any stimulus that regularly preceded the presentation of food came to elicit salivation. Quite by accident, Pavlov had observed that learning may result from two stimuli becoming associated with each other.

Fortunately, Pavlov had the scientific skills and curiosity to begin a rigorous attack on this surprising phenomenon. He ignored the advice of the great physiologist of the time, Sir Charles Sherrington, suggesting he give up his foolish investigation of "psychic" secretions. Instead, Pavlov abandoned his work on digestion and, in so doing, changed the course of psychology forever (Pavlov, 1928). For the remainder of Pavlov's life, he continued to search for the variables that influence classically conditioned behavior. Classical conditioning is also called *Pavlovian conditioning* because of Pavlov's discovery of the major phenomena of conditioning and his dedication to tracking down the variables that influence it.

Pavlov's considerable research experience allowed him to follow a simple and elegant strategy to discover the conditions necessary for his dogs to be conditioned to salivate. As shown in **Figure 6.1,** dogs in his experiments were first placed in a restraining harness. At regular intervals, a stimulus such as a tone was presented, and a dog was given a bit of food. Importantly, the tone had no prior meaning for the dog with respect to food or salivation. As you might imagine, the dog's first reaction to the tone was only an *orienting response*—the dog pricked its ears and moved its head to locate the source of the sound. However, with *repeated pairings* of the tone and the food, the orienting response stopped and salivation began. What Pavlov had observed in his earlier research was no accident: The phenomenon could be replicated under controlled conditions. Pavlov demonstrated the generality of this effect by using a variety of other stimuli ordinarily neutral with respect to salivation, such as lights and ticking metronomes.

The main features of Pavlov's classical conditioning procedure are illustrated in **Figure 6.2.** At the core of classical

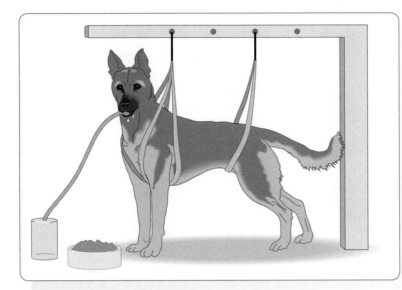

FIGURE 6.1
Pavlov's Original Procedure

In his original experiments, Pavlov used a variety of stimuli such as tones, bells, lights, and metronomes to serve as neutral stimuli. The experimenter presented one of these neutral stimuli and then the food powder. The dog's saliva was collected through a tube.

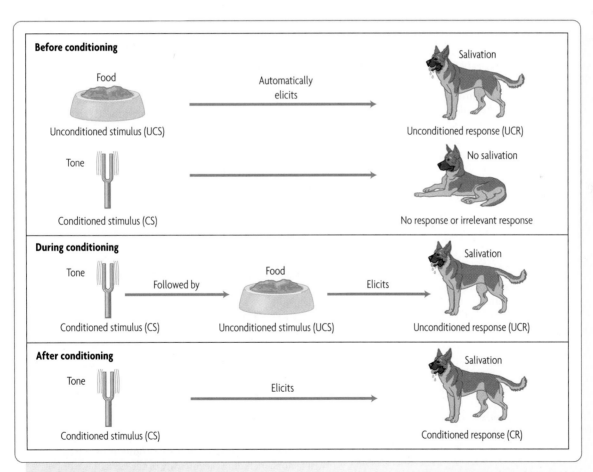

FIGURE 6.2   Basic Features of Classical Conditioning

Before conditioning, the unconditioned stimulus (UCS) naturally elicits the unconditioned response (UCR). A neutral stimulus, such as a tone, has no eliciting effect. During conditioning, the neutral stimulus is paired with the UCS. Through its association with the UCS, the neutral stimulus becomes a conditioned stimulus (CS) and elicits a conditioned response (CR) that is similar to the UCR.

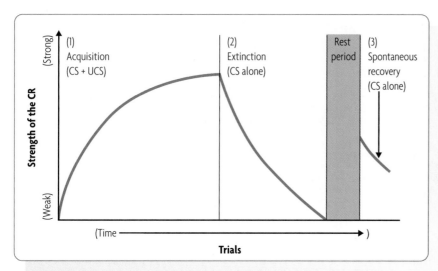

FIGURE 6.3 Acquisition, Extinction, and Spontaneous Recovery in Classical Conditioning

During acquisition (CS + UCS), the strength of the CR increases rapidly. During extinction, when the UCS no longer follows the CS, the strength of the CR drops to zero. The CR may reappear after a brief rest period, even when the UCS is still not presented. The reappearance of the CR is called spontaneous recovery.

conditioning are *reflex* responses such as salivation, pupil contraction, knee jerks, or eye blinking. A **reflex** is a response that is naturally triggered—*elicited*—by specific stimuli that are biologically relevant for the organism. Any stimulus, such as the food powder used in Pavlov's experiments, that naturally elicits a reflexive behavior is called an **unconditioned stimulus (UCS)** because learning is not a necessary condition for the stimulus to control the behavior. The behavior elicited by the unconditioned stimulus is called the **unconditioned response (UCR)**.

In Pavlov's experiments, the stimuli such as lights and tones did not originally trigger the reflex response of salivation. However, over time each neutral stimulus was repeatedly paired with the unconditioned stimulus. This neutral stimulus is called the **conditioned stimulus (CS)**: Its power to elicit behavior is *conditioned* on its association with the UCS. After several trials, the CS will produce a response called the **conditioned response (CR)**. The conditioned response is whatever response the conditioned stimulus elicits as a product of learning—we will provide several examples as this section unfolds. Let's review. Nature provides the UCS–UCR connections, but the learning produced by classical conditioning creates the CS–CR connection. The conditioned stimulus acquires some of the power to influence behavior that was originally limited to the unconditioned stimulus. Let's now look in more detail at the basic processes of classical conditioning.

***

reflex An unlearned response elicited by specific stimuli that have biological relevance for an organism.

unconditioned stimulus (UCS) In classical conditioning, the stimulus that elicits an unconditioned response.

unconditioned response (UCR) In classical conditioning, the response elicited by an unconditioned stimulus without prior training or learning.

conditioned stimulus (CS) In classical conditioning, a previously neutral stimulus that comes to elicit a conditioned response.

conditioned response (CR) In classical conditioning, a response elicited by some previously neutral stimulus that occurs as a result of pairing the neutral stimulus with an unconditioned stimulus.

acquisition The stage in a classical conditioning experiment during which the conditioned response is first elicited by the conditioned stimulus.

PROCESSES OF CONDITIONING

Pavlov's original experiments inspired extensive study of how classically conditioned responses appear and disappear. In this section, we describe several important conclusions researchers have reached about the basic processes of classical conditioning. These conclusions have emerged from hundreds of different studies across a wide range of animal species.

Acquisition and Extinction **Figure 6.3** displays a hypothetical classical conditioning experiment. The first panel displays **acquisition,** the process by which the CR is first elicited and gradually increases in frequency over repeated trials. In general, the CS and UCS must be paired several times before the CS reliably elicits a CR. With systematic CS–UCS pairings, the CR is elicited with increasing frequency, and the organism may be said to have acquired a conditioned response.

In classical conditioning, as in telling a good joke, *timing* is critical. The CS and UCS must be presented closely enough in time to be perceived by the organism as being related. (We will describe an exception to this rule in a later section on *taste-aversion learning*.) Researchers have studied four temporal patterns between the two stimuli, as shown in **Figure 6.4** (Hearst, 1988). The most widely used type of conditioning is called *delay conditioning*, in which the CS comes on prior to and stays on at least until the UCS is presented. In *trace conditioning*, the CS is discontinued or turned off before the UCS is presented. *Trace* refers to the memory that the organism is assumed to have of the CS, which is no longer present when the UCS appears. In *simultaneous conditioning*, both the CS and UCS are presented at the same time. Finally, in the case of *backward conditioning*, the CS is presented after the UCS.

Conditioning is usually most effective in a delayed conditioning paradigm, with a short interval between the onsets of the CS and UCS. However, the exact time interval between the CS and the UCS that will produce optimal conditioning depends on several factors, including the intensity of the CS and the response being conditioned. Let's focus on the response being conditioned. For muscular responses, such as eye blinks, a short interval of a second or less is best. For visceral responses, such as heart rate and salivation, however, longer intervals of 5 to 15 seconds work best.

Conditioning is generally poor with a simultaneous procedure and very poor with a backward procedure. Evidence

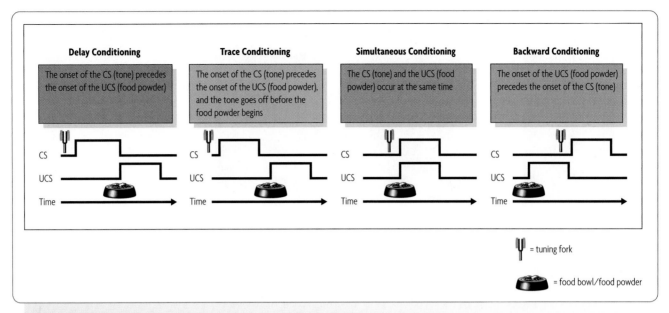

FIGURE 6.4   Four Variations of the CS–UCS Temporal Arrangement in Classical Conditioning

Researchers have explored the four possible timing arrangements between the CS and UCS. Conditioning is generally most effective in a delay conditioning paradigm with a short interval between the onsets of the CS and UCS.

From Baron, *Psychology* 5e, © 2001. Reproduced by permission of Pearson Education, Inc.

of backward conditioning may appear after a few pairings of the UCS and CS but disappear with extended training as the animal learns that the CS is followed by a period free of the UCS. In both cases, conditioning is weak because the CS does not actually predict the onset of the UCS. (We will return to the importance of predictability, or *contingency,* in the next section.)

But what happens when the CS (for example, the tone) no longer predicts the UCS (the food powder)? Under those circumstances, the CR (salivation) becomes weaker over time and eventually stops occurring. When the CR no longer appears in the presence of the CS (and the absence of the UCS), the process of **extinction** is said to have occurred (see Figure 6.3, panel 2). Conditioned responses, then, are not necessarily a permanent aspect of the organism's behavioral repertoire. However, the CR will reappear in a weak form when the CS is presented alone again after extinction (see Figure 6.3, panel 3). Pavlov referred to this sudden reappearance of the CR after a rest period, or time-out, without further exposure to the UCS as **spontaneous recovery** after extinction.

When the original pairing is renewed, postextinction, the CR becomes rapidly stronger. This more rapid relearning is an instance of *savings:* Less time is necessary to reacquire the response than to acquire it originally. Thus some of the original conditioning must be retained by the organism even after experimental extinction appears to have eliminated the CR. In other words, extinction has only weakened performance, not wiped out the original learning. This is why we made a distinction between learning and performance in our original definition of learning.

Stimulus Generalization Suppose we have taught a dog that presentation of a tone of a certain frequency

predicts food powder. Is the dog's response specific to only that stimulus? If you think about this question for a moment, you will probably not be surprised that the answer is no. In general, once a CR has been conditioned to a particular CS, similar stimuli may also elicit the response. For example, if conditioning was to a high-frequency tone, a slightly lower tone could also elicit the response. A child bitten by a big dog is likely to respond with fear even to smaller dogs. This automatic extension of responding to stimuli that have never been paired with the original UCS is called **stimulus generalization.** The more similar the new stimulus is to the original CS, the stronger the response will be. When response strength is measured for each of a series of increasingly dissimilar stimuli along a given dimension, as shown in **Figure 6.5** on page 170, a *generalization gradient* is found.

The existence of generalization gradients should suggest to you the way classical conditioning serves its function in everyday experience. Because important stimuli rarely occur in exactly the same form every time in nature, stimulus generalization builds in a similarity safety factor by extending the range of learning beyond the original specific experience. With this

---

extinction In conditioning, the weakening of a conditioned association in the absence of a reinforcer or unconditioned stimulus.

spontaneous recovery The reappearance of an extinguished conditioned response after a rest period.

stimulus generalization The automatic extension of conditioned responding to similar stimuli that have never been paired with the unconditioned stimulus.

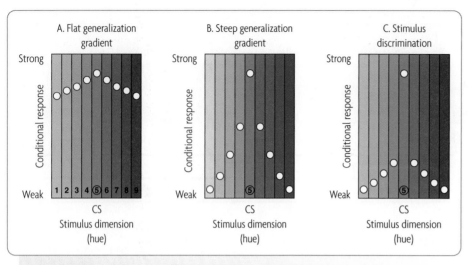

FIGURE 6.5 Stimulus Generalization Gradients

After conditioning to a medium green stimulus, the subject responds almost as strongly to stimuli of similar hues, as shown by the flat generalization gradient in panel A. When the subject is exposed to a broader range of colored stimuli, responses grow weaker as the color becomes increasingly dissimilar to the training stimulus. The generalization gradient becomes very steep, as shown in panel B. The experimenter could change the generalization gradient shown in panel A to resemble the one in panel C by giving the subject discrimination training. In this case, the medium green stimulus would be continually paired with the UCS, but stimuli of all other hues would not.

From *Principles and Methods of Psychology* by Robert B. Lawson, Stephen G. Goldstein, & Richard E. Musty, Copyright © 1975 by Oxford University Press, Inc.

feature, new but comparable events can be recognized as having the same meaning, or behavioral significance, despite apparent differences. For example, even when a predator makes a slightly different sound or is seen from a different angle, its prey can still recognize and respond to it quickly.

Stimulus Discrimination In some circumstances, however, it is important that a response be made to only a very small range of stimuli. An organism should not, for example, exhaust itself by fleeing too often from animals that are only superficially similar to its natural predators. **Stimulus discrimination** is the process by which an organism learns to respond differently to stimuli that are distinct from the CS on some dimension (for example, differences in hue or in pitch). An organism's discrimination among similar stimuli (tones of 1,000, 1,200, and 1,500 Hz, for example) is sharpened with discrimination training in which only one of them (1,200 Hz, for example) predicts the UCS and in which the others are repeatedly presented without it. Early in conditioning, stimuli similar to the CS will elicit a similar response, although not quite as strong. As discrimination training proceeds, the responses to the other, dissimilar stimuli weaken: The organism gradually learns which event-signal predicts the onset of the UCS and which signals do not.

For an organism to perform optimally in an environment, the processes of generalization and discrimination must strike a balance. You don't want to be overselective—it can be quite costly to miss the presence of a predator. You also don't want to be overresponsive—if you are fearful of every shadow, you will waste time and energy to dispel your worry. Classical conditioning provides a mechanism that allows creatures to react efficiently to the structure of their environments (Garcia, 1990).

Why might a child who has been frightened by one dog develop a fear response to all dogs?

---

stimulus discrimination A conditioning process in which an organism learns to respond differently to stimuli that differ from the conditioned stimulus on some dimension.

FOCUS ON ACQUISITION

In this section, we will examine more closely the conditions that are necessary for classical conditioning to take place. So far, we have *described* the acquisition of classically conditioned responses, but we have not yet *explained* it. Pavlov believed that classical conditioning resulted from the mere pairing of the CS and the UCS. In his view, if a response is to be classically conditioned, the CS and the UCS must occur close together in time—that is, be *temporally contiguous*. But as we will see next, contemporary research has modified that view.

Pavlov's theory dominated classical conditioning until the mid-1960s, when **Robert Rescorla** (1966) conducted a very telling experiment using dogs as subjects. Rescorla designed an experiment using a tone (the CS) and a shock (the UCS). For one group of animals the CS and UCS were merely contiguous—which, if Pavlov were correct, would be sufficient to produce classical conditioning. For the other group of animals, the tone reliably predicted the presence of the shock.

FIGURE 6.6   A Shuttlebox
Rescorla used the frequency with which dogs jumped over a barrier as a measure of fear conditioning.

In the first phase of the experiment, Rescorla trained dogs to jump a barrier from one side of a shuttlebox to the other to avoid an electric shock delivered through the grid floor (see **Figure 6.6**). If the dogs did not jump, they received a shock; if they did jump, the shock was postponed. Rescorla used the frequency with which dogs jumped the barrier as a measure of fear conditioning.

When the dogs were jumping across the barrier regularly, Rescorla divided his subjects into two groups and subjected them to another training procedure. To the random group, the UCS (the shock) was delivered randomly and independently of the CS (the tone) (see **Figure 6.7**). Although the CS and the UCS often occurred close together in time—they were, by chance, temporally contiguous—the UCS was as likely to be delivered in the absence of the CS as

it was in its presence. Thus the CS had no predictive value. For the contingency group, however, the UCS always followed the CS. Thus, for this group, the sounding of the tone was a reliable predictor of the delivery of the shock.

Once this training was complete, the dogs were put back into the shuttlebox, but this time with a twist. Now the tone used in the second training procedure occasionally sounded, signaling shock. What happened? **Figure 6.8,** on page 172, indicates that dogs exposed to the *contingent* (predictable) CS–UCS relation jumped more frequently in the presence of the tone than did dogs exposed only to the *contiguous* (associated) CS–UCS relation. Contingency was critical for the signal to serve the dogs as a successful cue for the shock.

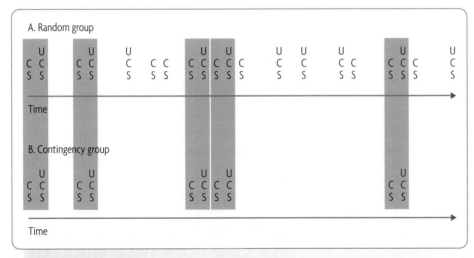

FIGURE 6.7   Rescorla's Procedure for Demonstrating the Importance of Contingency

For the random group, 5-second tones (the CS) and 5-second shocks (the UCS) were distributed randomly through the experimental period. For the contingency group, the dogs experienced only the subset of tones and shocks that occurred in a predictive relationship (the onset of the CS preceded the onset of the UCS by 30 seconds or less). Only the dogs in the contingency group learned to associate the CS with the UCS.

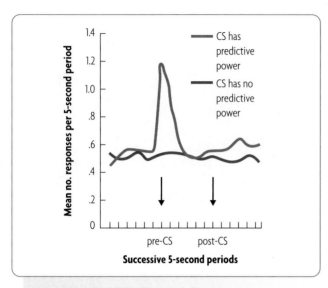

FIGURE 6.8 The Role of Contingency in Classical Conditioning

Rescorla demonstrated that dogs trained under the contingent CS–UCS relation showed more jumping (and thus conditioned fear) than did dogs trained under the contiguous but noncontingent CS–UCS relation. The arrows indicate the onset and offset of the CS tone.

Thus, in addition to the CS being contiguous—occurring close in time—with the UCS, the CS must also *reliably predict* the occurrence of the UCS in order for classical conditioning to occur (Rescorla, 1988). This finding makes considerable sense. After all, in natural situations, where learning enables organisms to adapt to changes in their environment, stimuli come in clusters and not in neat, simple units, as they do in laboratory experiments.

There's one last requirement for a stimulus to serve as a basis for classical conditioning: It must be *informative* in the environment. Consider an experimental situation in which rats have learned that a tone predicts a shock. Now, a light is added into the situation so that both the light and tone precede the shock. However, when the light is subsequently presented alone, the rats do not appear to have learned that the light predicts the shock (Kamin, 1969). For these rats, the previous conditioning to the tone in the first phase of the experiment *blocked* any subsequent conditioning that could occur to the light. From the rat's point of view, the light may as well not have existed; it provided no additional information beyond that already given by the tone. The requirement of informativeness explains why conditioning occurs most rapidly when the CS stands out against the many other stimuli that may also be present in an environment. A stimulus is more readily noticed the more *intense* it is and the more it *contrasts* with other stimuli.

You can see that classical conditioning is more complex than even Pavlov originally realized. A neutral stimulus will become an effective CS only if it is both appropriately contingent and informative. But now let's shift your attention a bit. We want to identify real-life situations in which classical conditioning plays a role.

APPLICATIONS OF CLASSICAL CONDITIONING

Your knowledge of classical conditioning can help you understand significant everyday behavior. In this section, we help you recognize some real-world instances of emotions and preferences as the products of this form of learning. We also explore the role classical conditioning plays in the unfolding of drug addiction.

Emotions and Preferences Earlier we asked you to think about your experience at a horror movie. In that case, you (unconsciously) learned an association between scary music (the CS) and certain likely events (the UCS—the kinds of things that happen in horror movies that cause reflexive revulsion). If you pay careful attention to events in your life, you will discover that there are many circumstances in which you can't quite explain why you are having such a strong emotional reaction or why you have such a strong preference about something. You might take a step back and ask yourself, "Is this the product of classical conditioning?"

Consider these situations (Rozin & Fallon, 1987; Rozin et al., 1986):

- Do you think you'd be willing to eat fudge that had been formed into the shape of dog feces?
- Do you think you'd be willing to drink a sugar-water solution if the sugar was drawn from a container that you knew was incorrectly labeled poison?
- Do you think you would be willing to drink apple juice into which a sterilized cockroach had been dipped?

If each of these situations makes you say "No way!" you are not alone. The classically conditioned response—feelings of disgust or danger—wins out over the knowledge that the stimulus is really OK. Because classically conditioned responses are not built up through conscious thought, they are also hard to eliminate through conscious reasoning!

One of the most extensively studied real-world products of classical conditioning is *fear conditioning* (Delgado et al., 2006; Kim & Jung, 2006). In the earliest days of behaviorism, John Watson and his colleague Rosalie Rayner sought to prove that many fear responses could be understood as the pairing of a neutral stimulus with something naturally fear provoking. To test their idea, they experimented on an infant who came to be called Little Albert.

Watson and Rayner (1920) trained Albert to fear a white rat he had initially liked, by pairing its appearance with an aversive UCS—a loud noise just behind him created by striking a large steel bar with a hammer. The unconditioned startle response and the emotional distress to the noxious noise formed the basis of Albert's learning to react with fear to the appearance of the white rat. His fear was developed in just seven conditioning trials. The emotional conditioning was then extended to behavioral conditioning when Albert learned to escape from the feared stimulus. The infant's learned fear then generalized to other furry objects, such as a rabbit, a dog, and even a Santa Claus mask! (Albert's mother, a wet nurse at the hospital where the study was conducted, took him away before the researchers could try to treat the experimentally conditioned fear. So we don't know whatever happened to Little Albert [Harris, 1979].)

As you'll recall from Chapter 2, researchers in psychology are guided by important ethical principles. Those principles make them look back at Watson and Rayner's experiment with grave discomfort: No ethical researcher would ever replicate an experiment of this type. Concerns about this work are increased by the knowledge that conditioned fear is highly resistant to extinction.

A single traumatic event can condition you to respond with strong physical, emotional, and cognitive reactions—perhaps for a lifetime. For example, one of our friends was in a bad car accident during a rainstorm. Now every time it begins to rain while he is driving, he becomes panic-stricken, sometimes to the extent that he has to pull over and wait out the storm. On one occasion, this rational, sensible man even crawled into the back seat and lay on the floor, face down, until the rain subsided. We will see in Chapter 15 that therapists have designed treatments for these types of fears that are intended to counter the effects of classical conditioning.

We don't want to leave you with the impression that only negative responses are classically conditioned. In fact, we suspect that you will also be able to interpret responses of happiness or excitement as instances of classical conditioning. Certainly toilers in the advertising industry hope that classical conditioning works as a positive force. They strive, for example, to create associations in your mind between their products (for example, jeans, sports cars, and soft drinks) and

How did John Watson and Rosalie Rayner condition Little Albert to fear small, furry objects?

passion. They expect that elements of their advertisements—"sexy" individuals or situations—will serve as the UCS to bring about the UCR—feelings of sexual arousal. The hope then is that the product itself will be the CS, so that the feelings of arousal will become associated with it. To find more examples of the classical conditioning of positive emotions, you should monitor your life for circumstances in which you have a rush of good feelings when you return, for instance, to a familiar location.

Learning to Be a Drug Addict

Consider this scenario. A man's body lies in a Manhattan alley, a half-empty syringe dangling from his arm. Cause of death? The coroner called it an overdose, but the man had ordinarily shot up far greater doses than the one that had supposedly killed him. This sort of incident baffled investigators. How could an addict with high drug tolerance die of an overdose when he didn't even get a full hit?

You now have the concepts to understand a complete version of the explanation we summarized in Chapter 5, on page 152. Some time ago, Pavlov (1927) and later his colleague Bykov (1957) pointed out that tolerance to opiates can develop when an individual anticipates the pharmacological action of a drug. Contemporary researcher **Shepard Siegel** refined these ideas. Siegel suggested that the setting in which drug use occurs acts as a conditioned stimulus for a situation in which the body learns to protect itself by preventing the drug from having its

Tyrese

How do advertisers exploit classical conditioning to make you feel "passion" toward their products?

usual effect. When people take drugs, the drug (UCS) brings about certain physiological responses to which the body responds with countermeasures intended to reestablish homeostasis (see Chapter 3). The body's countermeasures to the drug are the unconditioned response (UCR). Over time, this *compensatory response* also becomes the conditioned response. That is, in settings ordinarily associated with drug use (the CS), the body physiologically prepares itself (the CR) for the drug's expected effects. Tolerance arises because, in that setting, the individual must consume an amount of the drug that overcomes the compensatory response before starting to get any "positive" effect. Increasingly larger doses are needed as the conditioned compensatory response itself grows.

Siegel tested these ideas in his laboratory by creating tolerance to heroin in laboratory rats.

> In one study, Siegel and his colleagues classically conditioned rats to expect heroin injections (UCS) in one setting (CS_1) and dextrose (sweet sugar) solution injections in a different setting (CS_2) (Siegel et al., 1982). In the first phase of training, all rats developed heroin tolerance. On the test day, all animals received a larger-than-usual dose of heroin—nearly twice the previous amount. Half of them received it in the setting where heroin had previously been administered; the other half received it in the setting where dextrose solutions had been given during conditioning. Twice as many rats died in the dextrose-solution setting as in the usual heroin setting: 64 percent versus 32 percent!

Presumably, those receiving heroin in the usual setting were more prepared for this potentially dangerous situation because the context (CS_1) brought about a physiological response (CR) that countered the drug's typical effects.

To find out if a similar process might operate in humans, Siegel and a colleague interviewed heroin addicts who had come close to death from supposed overdoses. In seven out of ten cases, the addicts had been shooting up in a new and unfamiliar setting (Siegel, 1984). Although this natural experiment provides no conclusive data, it suggests that a dose for which an addict has developed tolerance in one setting may become an overdose in an unfamiliar setting. This analysis allows us to suggest that the addict we invoked at the beginning of this section might have died because he was shooting up in an unfamiliar setting.

Although we have mentioned research with heroin, classical conditioning is an important component to tolerance for a variety of drugs, including alcohol (S. Siegel, 2005). Thus the same principles Pavlov observed for dogs, bells, and salivation help explain some of the mechanisms underlying human drug addiction.

STOP AND REVIEW

❶ What is the role of reflexive behaviors in classical conditioning?

❷ What is the difference between the UCS and the CS?

❸ What is meant by stimulus discrimination?

❹ Why is contingency so important in classical conditioning?

❺ What is the conditioned response when classical conditioning plays a role in drug addiction?

CRITICAL THINKING Consider the experiment that demonstrated conditioned heroin tolerance in rats. Why were the rats given twice the normal dose of heroin on the test day?

Visit MyPsychLab.com for more review and practice on the following topic:

◀◉ **Explore:** Classical Conditioning of Little Albert

Operant Conditioning: Learning about Consequences

Let's return to the movie theater. The horror film is now over, and you peel yourself off your seat. Your companion asks you if you're hoping that a sequel will be made. You respond, "I've learned that I shouldn't go to horror films." You're probably right, but what kind of learning is this? Once again our answer begins around the turn of the 20th century.

THE LAW OF EFFECT

At about the same time that Pavlov was using classical conditioning to induce Russian dogs to salivate to the sound of a bell, **Edward L. Thorndike** (1874–1949) was watching American cats trying to escape from puzzle boxes (see **Figure 6.9**). Thorndike (1898) reported his observations and inferences about the kind of learning he believed was taking place in his subjects. The cats at first only struggled against their confinement, but once some "impulsive" action allowed them to open the door "all the other

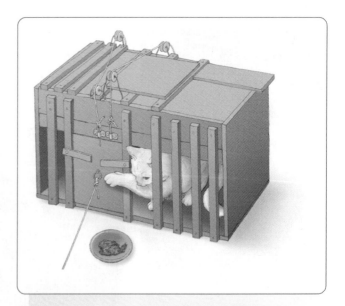

FIGURE 6.9 A Thorndike Puzzle Box

To get out of the puzzle box and obtain food, Thorndike's cat had to manipulate a mechanism to release a weight that would then pull the door open.

From Zimbardo/Johnson/McCann, *Psychology: Core Concepts,* © 2009. Reproduced by permission of Pearson Education, Inc.

Psychology in Your Life

HOW DOES CLASSICAL CONDITIONING AFFECT CANCER TREATMENT?

Medical researchers have made great strides in developing more effective treatments to combat cancers. Many of those treatments involve chemotherapy, drug treatments that kill or greatly weaken cancer cells. People who undergo chemotherapy often experience negative consequences such as fatigue and nausea. You might assume that those side effects would arise from the direct action of the chemotherapy drugs. Although that is partially the case, research suggests that processes of classical conditioning contribute greatly to the persistence of those side effects over time (Bovbjerg, 2006: Stockhorst et al., 2006).

Consider a study that looked at cancer patients' experiences of fatigue. Patients undergoing chemotherapy often report experiencing fatigue and note that the fatigue prevents them from continuing a "normal life" (Curt et al., 2000). To explain the origins of some of those feelings of fatigue, researchers tested a model based on classical conditioning (Bovbjerg et al., 2005). The 82 women in the study repeatedly visited the same outpatient clinic to undergo treatment for breast cancer. In each session, the women received infusions of chemotherapy.

Let's evaluate this situation in terms of classical conditioning. The chemotherapy drugs serve as the unconditioned stimulus (UCS) producing posttreatment fatigue as an unconditioned response (UCR). Then, the researchers suggested that the

clinic environment served as a conditioned stimulus (CS). Over the visits to the clinic—as the CS became paired with the UCS—this model suggests that the women would begin to experience anticipatory fatigue as a conditioned response (CR) as soon as they arrived at the clinic.

To test this idea, the researchers measured how the women's fatigue changed over time. They measured both how the women felt before each session of chemotherapy—their level of preinfusion anticipatory fatigue—and how they felt after each session—their level of postinfusion fatigue. The data showed a clear pattern: Over visits to the clinic, the women experienced increasing levels of anticipatory fatigue. You might think that the fatigue was getting worse just because of the cumulative effect of chemotherapy. However, the women did not report higher levels of postinfusion fatigue. Consistent with the model based on classical conditioning, one important source for the greater levels of anticipatory fatigue seemed to be conditioned associations with the clinic environment. In fact, researchers have produced evidence to support a classical conditioning analysis of other aspects of chemotherapy. Many patients, for example, begin to experience nausea before the chemotherapy sessions—the clinic settings in which they receive treatment begin to function as a conditioned stimulus (Tomoyasu et al., 1996).

This classical conditioning model might help explain why some

of the aftereffects of chemotherapy endure well after the end of treatment. Researchers surveyed a group of 273 Hodgkin's disease survivors who ranged from 1 to 20 years beyond treatment (Cameron et al., 2001). The participants were asked to reflect over the past six months to indicate whether they "had noticed any smell or odor (anything [they had] seen/places [they had] gone to; any foods or drinks)" that had reminded them of treatment and made them "feel good or bad emotionally or physically" (p. 72). More than half of the participants— 55 percent—reported lingering bad responses that were triggered by stimuli associated with their chemotherapy. The researchers suggest that these persistent responses were the result of classically conditioned associations between various aspects of the chemotherapy experience (the CS) and the drug infusions (the UCS).

These studies provide strong evidence for the role of classical conditioning to amplify the negative effects of chemotherapy. The studies also give researchers a context in which they can begin to design treatments. For example, researchers could devise ways to change contextual cues to decrease the likelihood that a clinic environment would become a conditioned stimulus. Interventions of that sort couldn't eliminate negative effects of chemotherapy but they could help stop those negative effects from enduring over time.

---

unsuccessful impulses [were] stamped out and the particular impulse leading to the successful act [was] stamped in by the resulting pleasure" (Thorndike, 1898, p. 13).

What had Thorndike's cats learned? According to Thorndike's analysis, learning was an association between stimuli in the situation and a response that an animal learned to make: a *stimulus–response (S–R) connection*. Thus the cats had learned to produce an appropriate response (for example,

clawing at a button or loop) that in these stimulus circumstances (confinement in the puzzle box) led to a desired outcome (momentary freedom). Note that the learning of these S–R connections occurred gradually and automatically in a mechanistic way as the animal experienced the consequences of its actions through blind *trial and error*. Gradually, the behaviors that had satisfying consequences increased in frequency; they eventually became the dominant response when the animal was placed in the puzzle box. Thorndike referred to this relationship between behavior and its consequences as the **law of effect:** A response that is followed by satisfying consequences becomes more probable and a response that is followed by dissatisfying consequences becomes less probable.

EXPERIMENTAL ANALYSIS OF BEHAVIOR

B. F. Skinner embraced Thorndike's view that environmental consequences exert a powerful effect on behavior. Skinner outlined a program of research whose purpose was to discover, by systematic variation of stimulus conditions, the ways that various environmental conditions affect the likelihood that a given response will occur:

> *A natural datum in a science of behavior is the probability that a given bit of behavior will occur at a given time. An experimental analysis deals with that probability in terms of frequency or rate of responding. . . . The task of an experimental analysis is to discover all the variables of which probability of response is a function. (Skinner, 1966, pp. 213–214)*

Skinner's analysis was experimental rather than theoretical—theorists are guided by derivations and predictions about behavior from their theories, but empiricists, such as Skinner, advocate the bottom-up approach. They start with the collection and evaluation of data within the context of an experiment and are not theory driven.

To analyze behavior experimentally, Skinner developed **operant conditioning** procedures, in which he manipulated the *consequences* of an organism's behavior in order to see what effect they had on subsequent behavior. An **operant** is any behavior that is *emitted* by an organism and can be characterized in terms of the observable effects it has on the environment. Literally, *operant* means *affecting the environment,* or operating on it (Skinner, 1938). Operants are *not elicited* by specific stimuli as classically conditioned behaviors are. Pigeons peck, rats search for food, babies cry and coo, some people gesture while talking, and others stutter. The probability of these behaviors occurring in the future can be increased or decreased by manipulating the effects they have on the environment. If, for example, a baby's coo prompts desirable parental contact, the baby will coo more in the future. Operant conditioning, then, modifies the probability of different types of operant behavior as a function of the environmental consequences they produce.

---

law of effect A basic law of learning that states that the power of a stimulus to evoke a response is strengthened when the response is followed by a reward and weakened when it is not followed by a reward.

operant conditioning Learning in which the probability of a response is changed by a change in its consequences.

operant Behavior emitted by an organism that can be characterized in terms of the observable effects it has on the environment.

reinforcement contingency A consistent relationship between a response and the changes in the environment that it produces.

To carry out his new experimental analysis, Skinner invented an apparatus that allowed him to manipulate the consequences of behavior, the *operant chamber.* **Figure 6.10** shows how the operant chamber works. When, after having produced an appropriate behavior defined by the experimenter, a rat presses a lever, the mechanism delivers a food pellet. This device allows experimenters to study the variables that allow rats to learn—or not to learn—the behaviors they define. For example, if a lever press produces a food pellet only after a rat has turned a circle in the chamber, the rat will swiftly learn (through a process called *shaping* that we will consider shortly) to turn a circle before pressing the lever.

In many operant experiments, the measure of interest is how much of a particular behavior an animal carries out in a period of time. Researchers record the pattern and total amount of behavior emitted in the course of an experiment. This methodology allowed Skinner to study the effect of reinforcement contingencies on animals' behavior.

REINFORCEMENT CONTINGENCIES

A **reinforcement contingency** is a consistent relationship between a response and the changes in the environment that it produces. Imagine, for example, an experiment in which a pigeon's pecking a disk (the response) is generally followed by the presentation of grain (the corresponding change in the environment). This consistent relationship, or reinforcement contingency, will usually be accompanied by an increase in the rate of pecking. For delivery of grain to increase *only* the probability of pecking, it must be contingent *only* on the pecking response—the delivery must occur regularly after that response but not after other responses, such as turning or

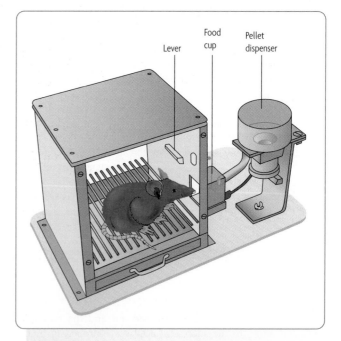

FIGURE 6.10   Operant Chamber
In this specially designed apparatus, typical of those used with rats, a press on the lever may be followed by delivery of a food pellet.

What environmental contingencies might cause babies to smile more often?

bowing. Based on Skinner's work, modern behavior analysts seek to understand behavior in terms of reinforcement contingencies. Let's take a closer look at what has been discovered about these contingencies.

Positive and Negative Reinforcers Suppose you are now captivated by the idea of getting your pet rat to turn a circle in its cage. To increase the probability of circle-turning behavior, you would want to use a **reinforcer,** any stimulus that—when made contingent on a behavior—increases the probability of that behavior over time. *Reinforcement* is the delivery of a reinforcer following a response.

Reinforcers are always defined empirically, in terms of their effects on changing the probability of a response. If you look out at the world, you can probably find three classes of stimuli: those toward which you are neutral, those that you find *appetitive* (you have an "appetite" for them), and those that you find *aversive* (you seek to avoid them). The compositions of these classes of stimuli clearly are not the same for all individuals: What is appetitive or aversive is defined by the behavior of the individual organism. Consider the strawberry. Although many people find strawberries quite delicious, one of your authors finds strawberries virtually inedible. If you intend to use strawberries to change that author's behavior, it's important to know that—for him—they are aversive rather than appetitive.

When a behavior is followed by the delivery of an appetitive stimulus, the event is called **positive reinforcement.** Your

pet rat will turn circles if a consequence of circle turning is the delivery of desirable food. Humans will tell jokes if a consequence of their joke telling is a type of laughter they find pleasurable.

When a behavior is followed by the removal of an aversive stimulus, the event is called **negative reinforcement.** Your author, for example, would be more likely to perform a behavior if it would allow him to cease eating strawberries. There are two general types of learning circumstances in which negative reinforcement applies. In **escape conditioning,** animals learn that a response will allow them to escape from an aversive stimulus. Raising an umbrella during a downpour is a common example of escape conditioning. You learn to use an umbrella to escape the aversive stimulus of getting wet. In **avoidance conditioning,** animals learn responses that allow them to avoid aversive stimuli before they begin. Suppose your car has a buzzer that sounds when you fail to buckle your seat belt. You will learn to buckle up to avoid the aversive noise.

To distinguish clearly between positive and negative reinforcement, remember the following: Both positive reinforcement and negative reinforcement *increase* the probability of the response that precedes them. Positive reinforcement increases response probability by the presentation of an appetitive stimulus following a response; negative reinforcement does the same in reverse, through the removal, reduction, or prevention of an aversive stimulus following a response.

Recall that for classical conditioning, when the unconditioned stimulus is no longer delivered, the conditioned response suffers extinction. The same rule holds for operant conditioning—if reinforcement is withheld, **operant extinction** occurs. Thus, if a behavior no longer produces predictable consequences, it returns to the level it was at before operant conditioning—it is extinguished. You can probably catch your own behaviors being reinforced and then *extinguished.* Have you ever had the experience of dropping a few coins into a soda machine and getting nothing in return? If you kicked the machine one time and your soda came out, the act of kicking would be reinforced. However, if the next few times, your kicking produced no soda, kicking would quickly be extinguished.

As with classical conditioning, *spontaneous recovery* is also a feature of operant conditioning. Suppose you had reinforced a pigeon by providing food pellets when it pecked a key in the presence of a green light. If you discontinued the

---

reinforcer Any stimulus that, when made contingent on a response, increases the probability of that response.

positive reinforcement A behavior is followed by the presentation of an appetitive stimulus, increasing the probability of that behavior.

negative reinforcement A behavior is followed by the removal of an aversive stimulus, increasing the probability of that behavior.

escape conditioning A form of learning in which animals acquire a response that will allow them to escape from an aversive stimulus.

avoidance conditioning A form of learning in which animals acquire responses that allow them to avoid aversive stimuli before they begin.

operant extinction When a behavior no longer produces predictable consequences, its return to the level of occurrence it had before operant conditioning.

reinforcement, the pecking behavior would extinguish. However, the next time you put the pigeon back in the apparatus with the green light on, the pigeon would likely spontaneously peck again. This is called spontaneous recovery. In human terms, you might kick the soda machine again with a time lag after your initial extinction experiences.

Positive and Negative Punishment You are probably familiar with another technique for decreasing the probability of a response—punishment. A **punisher** is any stimulus that—when it is made contingent on a response—decreases the probability of that response over time. *Punishment* is the delivery of a punisher following a response. Just as we could identify positive and negative reinforcement, we can identify positive punishment and negative punishment. When a behavior is followed by the delivery of an aversive stimulus, the event is called **positive punishment** (you can remember *positive* because something is added to the situation). Touching a hot stove, for example, produces pain that punishes the preceding response so that you are less likely next time to touch the stove. When a behavior is followed by the removal of an appetitive stimulus, the event is referred to as **negative punishment** (you can remember *negative* because something is subtracted from the situation). Thus when a parent withdraws a child's allowance after she hits her baby brother, the child learns not to hit her brother in the future. Which kind of punishment explains why you might stay away from horror movies?

Although punishment and reinforcement are closely related operations, they differ in important ways. A good way to differentiate them is to think of each in terms of its effects on behavior. Punishment, by definition, always *reduces* the probability of a response occurring again; reinforcement, by definition, always *increases* the probability of a response recurring. For example, some people get severe headaches after drinking caffeinated beverages. The headache is the stimulus that positively punishes and reduces the behavior of drinking coffee. However, once the headache is present, people often take aspirin or another pain reliever to eliminate the headache. The aspirin's analgesic effect is the stimulus that negatively reinforces the behavior of ingesting aspirin.

Discriminative Stimuli and Generalization You are unlikely to want to change the probability of a certain behavior at all times. Rather, you may want to change the probability of the behavior in a particular context. For example, you often want to increase the probability that a child will sit quietly in

class without changing the probability that he or she will be noisy and active during recess. Through their associations with reinforcement or punishment, certain stimuli that precede a particular response—**discriminative stimuli**—come to set the context for that behavior. Organisms learn that, in the presence of some stimuli but not of others, their behavior is likely to have a particular effect on the environment. For example, in the presence of a green street light, the act of crossing an intersection in a motor vehicle is reinforced. When the light is red, however, such behavior may be punished—it may result in a traffic ticket or an accident. Skinner referred to the sequence of discriminative stimulus–behavior–consequence as the **three-term contingency** and believed that it could explain most human action (Skinner, 1953). **Table 6.1** describes how the three-term contingency might explain several different kinds of human behavior.

Under laboratory conditions, manipulating the consequences of behavior in the presence of discriminative stimuli can exert powerful control over that behavior. For example, a pigeon might be given grain after pecking a disk in the presence of a green light but not a red light. The green light is a discriminative stimulus that sets the occasion for pecking; the red is a discriminative stimulus that sets the occasion for not pecking. Organisms learn quickly to discriminate between these conditions, responding regularly in the presence of one stimulus and not responding in the presence of the other. By manipulating the components of the three-term contingency, you can constrain a behavior to a particular context.

Organisms also generalize responses to other stimuli that resemble the discriminative stimulus. Once a response has been reinforced in the presence of one discriminative stimulus, a similar stimulus can become a discriminative stimulus for that same response. For example, pigeons trained to peck a disk in the presence of a green light will also peck the disk in the presence of lights that are lighter or darker shades of green than the original discriminative stimulus. Similarly, you generalize to different shades of green on stop lights as a discriminative stimulus for your "resume driving" behavior.

Using Reinforcement Contingencies Are you ready to put your new knowledge of reinforcement contingencies to work? Here are some considerations you might have:

- *How can you define the behavior that you would like to reinforce or eliminate?* You must always carefully target the specific behavior whose probability you would like to change. Reinforcement should be contingent on exactly that behavior. When reinforcers are presented so that they are not contingent, their presence has little effect on behavior. For example, if a parent praises poor work as well as good efforts, a child will not learn to work harder in school—but because of the positive reinforcement, other behaviors are likely to increase. (What might those be?)
- *How can you define the contexts in which a behavior is appropriate or inappropriate?* Remember that you rarely want to allow or disallow every instance of a behavior. We suggested earlier, for example, that you might want to increase the probability that a child will sit quietly in class without changing the probability that he or

---

punisher Any stimulus that, when made contingent on a response, decreases the probability of that response.

positive punishment A behavior is followed by the presentation of an aversive stimulus, decreasing the probability of that behavior.

negative punishment A behavior is followed by the removal of an appetitive stimulus, decreasing the probability of that behavior.

discriminative stimulus Stimulus that acts as a predictor of reinforcement, signaling when particular behaviors will result in positive reinforcement.

three-term contingency The means by which organisms learn that, in the presence of some stimuli but not others, their behavior is likely to have a particular effect on the environment.

TABLE 6.1 The Three-Term Contingency: Relationships among Discriminative Stimuli, Behavior, and Consequences

	Discriminative Stimulus	Emitted Response	Stimulus Consequence
1. Positive reinforcement: A response in the presence of an effective signal produces the desired consequence. This response increases.	Soft-drink machine	Put coin in slot	Get drink
2. Negative reinforcement (escape): An aversive situation is escaped from by an operant response. This escape response increases.	Heat	Fan oneself	Escape from heat
3. Positive punishment: A response is followed by an aversive stimulus. The response is eliminated or suppressed.	Attractive matchbox	Play with matches	Get burned or get caught and spanked
4. Negative punishment: A response is followed by the removal of an appetitive stimulus. The response is eliminated or suppressed.	Brussels sprouts	Refusal to eat them	No dessert

she will be noisy and active during recess. You must define the discriminative stimuli and investigate how broadly the desired response will be generalized to similar stimuli. If, for example, the child learned to sit quietly in class, would that behavior generalize to other "serious" settings?

- *Have you unknowingly been reinforcing some behaviors?* Suppose you want to eliminate a behavior. Before you turn to punishment as a way of reducing its probability (more on that in the *Critical Thinking in Your Life* box on page 182), try to determine whether you can identify reinforcers for that behavior. If so, you can try to extinguish the behavior by eliminating those reinforcers. Imagine, for example, that a young boy throws a large number of tantrums. You might ask yourself, "Have I been reinforcing those tantrums by paying the boy extra attention when he screams?" If so, you can try to eliminate the tantrums by eliminating the reinforcement. Even better, you can combine extinction with positive reinforcement of more socially approved behaviors.

It's important to be aware that the reinforcers parents produce can make children's conduct problems, such as tantrums, more likely. In fact, parenting research has identified unknowing reinforcement as one cause of serious behavior problems in children. For example, Gerald Patterson and his colleagues (Granic & Patterson, 2006) have outlined a *coercion model* for antisocial behavior. Family observations suggest that children are put at risk when their parents issue threats in response to small misbehaviors (such as whining,

teasing, or yelling) without following through. At some moments, however, these parents would issue harsh or explosive discipline toward the same behaviors. The children appear to learn the lesson that relatively large acts of aggressive and coercive behavior are appropriate and necessary for achieving goals—leading to a cycle of increase in the severity of the children's antisocial behavior.

Behavior analysts assume that any behavior that persists does so because it results in reinforcement. Any behavior, they argue—even irrational or bizarre behavior—can be understood by discovering what the reinforcement or payoff is. For example, symptoms of mental or physical disorders are sometimes maintained because the person receives attention or sympathy and is excused from normal responsibilities. These *secondary gains* reinforce irrational and sometimes self-destructive behavior. Can you see how shy behaviors can be maintained through reinforcement, even though the shy person would prefer not to be shy? Of course, it is not always possible to know what reinforcers are at work in an environment. However, as a behavior becomes more or less probable, you might try to carry out a bit of behavior analysis.

One final thought. It's often the case that real-life situations will involve intricate combinations of reinforcement and punishment. Suppose, for example, parents use negative punishment by grounding a teenager for two weeks when he stays out past curfew. To soften up his parents, the teen helps more than usual around the house. Assuming his helping behavior appeals to the parents, the teen is trying to reinforce his parents' "reducing the sentence" behavior. If this strategy succeeds in changing the punishment to only one week, the teen's helping behavior will have been negatively reinforced—because helping led to the removal of the aversive stimulus of being grounded. Whenever the teen is grounded again (a discriminative stimulus), his helping behavior should be more likely. Do you see how all the contingencies fit together to change both the teen's and the parents' behaviors?

Let's now take a look at the ways in which various objects and activities may come to function as reinforcers.

PROPERTIES OF REINFORCERS

Reinforcers are the power brokers of operant conditioning: They change or maintain behavior. Reinforcers have a number of interesting and complex properties. They can be learned through experience rather than be biologically determined and can be activities rather than objects. In some situations, even ordinarily powerful reinforcers may not be enough to change a dominant behavior pattern (in this case, we would say that the consequences were not actually reinforcers).

How can parents use reinforcement contingencies to affect their children's behavior?

Conditioned Reinforcers When you came into the world, there were a handful of **primary reinforcers,** such as food and water, whose reinforcing properties were biologically determined. Over time, however, otherwise neutral stimuli have become associated with primary reinforcers and now function as **conditioned reinforcers** for operant responses. Conditioned reinforcers can come to serve as ends in themselves. In fact, a great deal of human behavior is influenced less by biologically significant primary reinforcers than by a wide variety of conditioned reinforcers. Money, grades, smiles of approval, gold stars, and various kinds of status symbols are among the many potent conditioned reinforcers that influence much of your behavior.

Virtually any stimulus can become a conditioned reinforcer by being paired with a primary reinforcer. In one experiment, simple tokens were used with animal learners.

> With raisins as primary reinforcers, chimps were trained to solve problems. Then tokens were delivered along with the raisins. When only the tokens were presented, the chimps continued working for their "money" because they could later deposit the hard-earned tokens in a "chimp-o-mat" designed to exchange tokens for the raisins (Cowles, 1937).

Teachers and experimenters often find conditioned reinforcers more effective and easier to use than primary reinforcers

because (1) few primary reinforcers are available in the classroom, whereas almost any stimulus event that is under control of a teacher can be used as a conditioned reinforcer; (2) they can be dispensed rapidly; (3) they are portable; and (4) their reinforcing effect may be more immediate because it depends only on the perception of receiving them and not on biological processing, as in the case of primary reinforcers.

In some institutions, such as psychiatric hospitals or drug treatment programs, *token economies* are set up based on these principles. Desired behaviors (grooming or taking medication, for example) are explicitly defined, and token payoffs are given by the staff when the behaviors are performed. These tokens can later be exchanged by the patients for a wide array of rewards and privileges (Dickerson et al., 2005; Martin & Pear, 1999). These systems of reinforcement are especially effective in

Inedible tokens can be used as conditioned reinforcers. In one study, chimps deposited tokens in a "chimp-o-mat" in exchange for raisins. What types of conditioned reinforcers function in your life?

---

primary reinforcer Biologically determined reinforcer, such as food and water.

conditioned reinforcer In classical conditioning, a formerly neutral stimulus that has become a reinforcer.

modifying patients' behaviors regarding self-care, upkeep of their environment, and, most important, frequency of their positive social interactions.

Response Deprivation and Positive Reinforcers

Suppose you need to get a child to do something. You don't want to pay her or give her a gold star, so instead you strike this bargain: "When you finish your homework, you can play with your video game." Why might this tactic work? According to *response deprivation theory*, behaviors become preferred and, therefore, reinforcing when an animal is prevented from engaging in them (Timberlake & Allison, 1974). For example, water-deprived rats learned to increase their running in an exercise wheel when their running was followed by an opportunity to drink. Conversely, exercise-deprived rats learned to increase their drinking when that response was followed by a chance to run (Premack, 1965). Can you see how the promise of video games after homework follows this same pattern? For a period of time, the child is video game–deprived—the rate at which the child would ordinarily play the video game is restricted below normal. To overcome that deprivation, she will learn to work on her homework.

This analysis suggests two important lessons. First, these examples remind you why you shouldn't assume that the same activity will function as a reinforcer for an animal at all times. You need to know, for example, whether the animal is food-deprived before you attempt to use food as a reinforcer. Second, these examples suggest why virtually any activity can come to serve as a reinforcer. You can experience deprivation along any number of dimensions. In fact, if you didn't allow a child to do homework for a period of time, she would learn other behaviors to overcome homework-doing deprivation.

SCHEDULES OF REINFORCEMENT

What happens when you cannot, or do not want to, reinforce your pet on every occasion when it performs a special behavior? Consider a story about the young B. F. Skinner. It seems that one weekend he was secluded in his laboratory with not enough of a food-reward supply for his hardworking rats. He economized by giving the rats pellets only after a certain interval of time—no matter how many times they pressed in between, they couldn't get any more pellets. Even so, the rats responded as much with this *partial reinforcement schedule* as they had with continuous reinforcement. And what do you predict happened when these animals underwent extinction training and their responses were followed by no pellets at all? The rats whose lever pressing had been partially reinforced continued to respond longer and more vigorously than did the rats who had gotten payoffs after every response. Skinner was on to something important!

The discovery of the effectiveness of partial reinforcement led to extensive study of the effects of different **schedules of reinforcement** on behavior (see **Figure 6.11**). You have experienced different schedules of reinforcement in your daily life. When you raise your hand in class, the teacher sometimes calls on you and sometimes does not; some slot machine players continue to put coins in the one-armed bandits even though the reinforcers are delivered only rarely. In real life or in the laboratory, reinforcers can be delivered according to either a *ratio schedule,* after a certain number of responses, or an *interval schedule,* after the first response

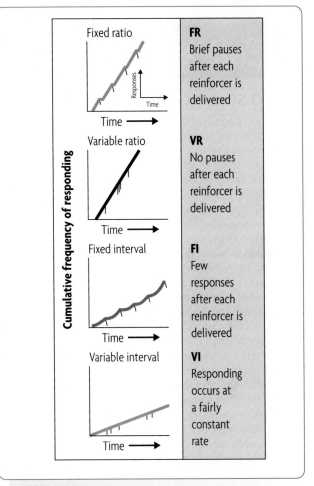

FIGURE 6.11   Reinforcement Schedules
These different patterns of behavior are produced by four simple schedules of reinforcement. The hash marks indicate when reinforcement is delivered.

following a specified interval of time. In each case, there can be either a constant, or *fixed,* pattern of reinforcement or an irregular, or *variable,* pattern of reinforcement, making four major types of schedules in all. So far you've learned about the **partial reinforcement effect:** Responses acquired under schedules of partial reinforcement are more resistant to extinction than those acquired with continuous reinforcement. Let's see what else researchers have discovered about different schedules of reinforcement.

Fixed-Ratio Schedules In **fixed-ratio (FR)** schedules, the reinforcer comes after the organism has emitted a fixed

---

schedule of reinforcement In operant conditioning, a pattern of delivering and withholding reinforcement.

partial reinforcement effect The behavioral principle that states that responses acquired under intermittent reinforcement are more difficult to extinguish than those acquired with continuous reinforcement.

fixed-ratio (FR) schedule A schedule of reinforcement in which a reinforcer is delivered for the first response made after a fixed number of responses.

Critical Thinking in Your Life

TO SPANK OR NOT TO SPANK?

If you plan to become a parent (or if you already are one), you have almost certainly considered the question "To spank or not to spank?" In fact, most parents in the United States make the choice "to spank." In one sample of 962 parents, 64 percent reported that they had spanked their 19- to 35-month old children; 26 percent reported spanking those children frequently (Regalado et al., 2004). Spanking is quite common—but what are the consequences for children who are spanked?

Why is that a difficult question to answer? First, no researchers could ethically conduct an experiment in which they expose children to physical punishment. For that reason, all research on spanking relies on correlational analyses: Researchers try to assess whether a relationship exists between the amount of physical punishment children have experienced and negative aspects of their behavior. This leads to a second problem with research on spanking. Parents may be unwilling or unable to give accurate indications of how often they spanked their children. Researchers can ask the children, but they might also misremember or misrepresent the past. A third problem is getting accurate data on the child behaviors that led parents to spank them: How "bad" were the children before they were spanked? A final problem with research on spanking is understanding its impact as an

element of a larger environment (Kazdin & Benjet, 2003). The households in which parents spank their children the most also tend, for example, to be households with more marital discord. Perhaps it's other factors of that sort that lead children whose parents spanked them to have problems later in life. The spanking itself might have played no causal role.

Despite all these obstacles, researchers have been able to reach important conclusions. An abundance of data confirms that physical punishment leads to negative child outcomes (Gershoff & Bitensky, 2007). For example, one study involving over 1,000 children examined the relationship between the amount of physical punishment the children received as 15-month-olds and the behavior problems they displayed as 36-month-olds and as first graders (Mulvaney & Mebert, 2007). To account for the fact that some children are more difficult than others—and, therefore, might be more likely to elicit punishment—the analyses focused on changes in each child's behavior. The study demonstrated that, for both "easy" and "difficult" children (as reported by their parents), the more the children had been spanked early in life the more likely they were to show increases in, for example, aggressive behaviors as they grew older. Other research has demonstrated a reduction in children's behavior problems after their parents

underwent an intervention program that trained them to forgo spanking and other harsh forms of discipline (Beauchaine et al., 2005).

In light of these findings, people need to give careful consideration to the question of "To spank or not to spank" with respect to their goals as parents (Benjet & Kazdin, 2003). Parents usually turn to physical punishment to stop children from performing unwanted behaviors. However, experts suggest that parents instead use positive reinforcement: "Many undesirable behaviors can be completely suppressed by positive reinforcement of alternative and incompatible behaviors" (Benjet & Kazdin, p. 215). For example, you can praise a child for sitting quietly rather than spanking him for running around. Thus reinforcing children for behaving well is often a better long-term strategy than punishing them for behaving poorly.

As a parent, you presumably want to avoid putting your children at risk. To meet that goal, consider using other strategies besides physical punishment to modify your children's behavior.

- Why would parents be "unwilling or unable" to provide accurate information about their spanking practices?

- Why was it important for the study looking at change over time to consider both "easy" and "difficult" children?

---

number of responses. When reinforcement follows only one response, the schedule is called an FR-1 schedule (this is the original continuous reinforcement schedule). When reinforcement follows only every 25th response, the schedule is an FR-25 schedule. FR schedules generate high rates of responding because there is a direct correlation between responding and reinforcement. A pigeon can get as much food as it wants in a

period of time if it pecks often enough. Figure 6.11 shows that FR schedules produce a pause after each reinforcer. The higher the ratio, the longer the pause after each reinforcement. Stretching the ratio too thin by requiring a great many responses for reinforcement without first training the animal to emit that many responses may lead to extinction. Many salespeople are on FR schedules: They must sell a certain number of units before they can get paid.

variable-ratio (VR) schedule A schedule of reinforcement in which a reinforcer is delivered for the first response made after a variable number of responses whose average is predetermined.

Variable-Ratio Schedules In a **variable-ratio (VR) schedule,** the average number of responses between reinforcers is predetermined. A VR-10 schedule means that, on average, reinforcement follows every 10th response, but it might come after only 1 response or after 20 responses. Variable-ratio schedules generate the highest rate of responding and the greatest resistance to extinction, especially when the VR value is large. Suppose you start a pigeon with a low VR value (for example, VR-5) and then move it toward a higher value. A pigeon on a VR-110 schedule will respond with up to 12,000 pecks per hour and will continue responding for hours even with no reinforcement. Gambling would seem to be under the control of VR schedules. The response of dropping coins in slot machines is maintained at a high, steady level by the payoff, which is delivered only after an unknown, variable number of coins has been deposited. VR schedules leave you guessing when the reward will come—you gamble that it will be after the next response, not many responses later (Rachlin, 1990).

Fixed-Interval Schedules On a **fixed-interval (FI) schedule,** a reinforcer is delivered for the first response made after a fixed period of time. On an FI-10 schedule, the subject, after receiving reinforcement, has to wait 10 seconds before another response can be reinforced irrespective of the number of responses. Response rates under FI schedules show a scalloped pattern. Immediately after each reinforced response, the animal makes few if any responses. As the payoff time approaches, the animal responds more and more. You experience an FI schedule when you reheat a slice of pizza. Suppose you set the oven's timer for 2 minutes. You probably won't check very much for the first 90 seconds, but in the last 30 seconds, you'll peek in more often.

Variable-Interval Schedules For **variable-interval (VI) schedules,** the average interval is predetermined. For example, on a VI-20 schedule, reinforcers are delivered at an average rate of 1 every 20 seconds. This schedule generates a moderate but very stable response rate. Extinction under VI schedules is gradual and much slower than under fixed-interval schedules. In one case, a pigeon pecked 18,000 times during the first 4 hours after reinforcement stopped and required 168 hours before its responding extinguished completely (Ferster & Skinner, 1957). You have experienced a VI schedule if you've taken a course with a professor who gave occasional, irregularly scheduled pop quizzes. Did you study your notes each day before class?

SHAPING

As parts of experiments, we have spoken of rats pressing levers to get food. However, even lever pressing is a learned behavior. When a rat is introduced to an operant chamber, it is quite unlikely it will ever press the lever spontaneously; the rat has learned to use its paws in many ways, but it probably has never pressed a lever before. How should you go about training the rat to perform a behavior that it would rarely, if ever, produce on its own? You've settled on a reinforcer, food, and a schedule of reinforcement, FR-1—now what? To train new or complex behaviors, you will want to use a method called **shaping by successive approximations**—in which you reinforce any responses that successively approximate and ultimately match the desired response.

This woman is assisted by a monkey who has been operantly shaped to perform tasks such as getting food or drink, retrieving dropped or out of reach items, and turning lights on or off. For each of these behaviors, can you think through the successive approximations you would reinforce to arrive at the end point?

Here's how you'd do it. First, you deprive the rat of food for a day. (Without deprivation, food is not likely to serve as a reinforcer.) Then you systematically make food pellets available in the food hopper in an operant chamber so that the rat learns to look there for food. Now you can begin the actual shaping process by making delivery of food contingent on specific aspects of the rat's behavior, such as orienting itself toward the lever. Next, food is delivered only as the rat moves closer and closer to the lever. Soon the requirement for reinforcement is actually to touch the lever. Finally, the rat must depress the lever for food to be delivered. In small increments, the rat has learned that a lever press will produce food. Thus, for *shaping* to work,

fixed-interval (FI) schedule A schedule of reinforcement in which a reinforcer is delivered for the first response made after a fixed period of time.

variable-interval (VI) schedule A schedule of reinforcement in which a reinforcer is delivered for the first response made after a variable period of time whose average is predetermined.

shaping by successive approximations A behavioral method that reinforces responses that successively approximate and ultimately match the desired response.

you must define what constitutes progress toward the target behavior and use *differential reinforcement* to refine each step along the way.

Let's look at another example, in which shaping was used to improve the performance of a Canadian pole vaulter who was an international competitor.

A 21-year-old university pole vaulter sought a research team's assistance to help him correct a technical problem with his vaulting technique (Scott et al., 1997). The vaulter's particular problem was that he didn't sufficiently extend his arms (holding the pole) above his head before he planted the pole to lift himself off. At the beginning of the intervention, the vaulter's average hand-height at takeoff was calculated as 2.25 meters. The goal was set to use a shaping procedure to help him achieve his physical potential of 2.54 meters. A photoelectric beam was set up so that, when the vaulter achieved a desired extension, the beam was broken and equipment produced a beep. The beep served as a conditioned positive reinforcer. At first, the beam was set at 2.30 meters, but once the vaulter was able to reach that height with 90 percent success, the beam was moved to 2.35 meters. Further success brought further increments of 2.40, 2.45, 2.50, and 2.52 meters. In that way, the vaulter's behavior was successfully shaped toward the desired goal.

You can imagine how difficult it would have been for the vaulter to show spontaneous improvement of 0.27 meters. (That's about 10 1/2 inches.) The shaping procedure allowed him to achieve that gain through successive approximations to the desired behavior.

Let's return to your rat. Recall that we suggested you might wish to teach it to turn circles in its cage. Can you devise a plan, using shaping, to bring about this behavior? Think about what each successive approximation would be. At the beginning, for example, you might reinforce the rat if it just turned its head in a particular direction. Next, you would let the rat obtain a food pellet only if it turned its whole body in the right direction. What might you do after that?

The two forms of learning we have examined so far—classical conditioning and operant conditioning—have most often been studied with the assumption that processes of learning are consistent across all animals. In fact, we have cited examples from dogs, cats, rats, mice, pigeons, and humans to show exactly such consistency. However, researchers have come to understand that learning is modified in many situations by the particular biological and cognitive capabilities of individual species. We turn now to the processes that limit the generality of the laws of learning.

STOP AND REVIEW

❶ What is the law of effect?

❷ How do reinforcement and punishment affect the probability of behaviors?

---

biological constraint on learning Any limitation on an organism's capacity to learn that is caused by the inherited sensory, response, or cognitive capabilities of members of a given species.

❸ What is the role of discriminative stimuli in operant conditioning?

❹ What is the difference between fixed-ratio and fixed-interval schedules of reinforcement?

❺ What is meant by shaping?

CRITICAL THINKING In the experiment with chimps, why did the researcher start the training with raisins before moving to tokens?

Visit MyPsychLab.com for more review and practice on the following topic:

✳ **Simulate:** Shaping

Biology and Learning

The contemporary view that a single, general account of the associationist principles of learning is common to humans and all animals was first proposed by English philosopher **David Hume** (1711–1776) in 1748. Hume reasoned that "any theory by which we explain the operations of the understanding, or the origin and connexion of the passions in man, will acquire additional authority, if we find that the same theory is requisite to explain the same phenomena in all other animals" (Hume, 1748/1951, p. 104).

The appealing simplicity of such a view has come under scrutiny since the 1960s as psychologists have discovered certain constraints, or limitations, on the generality of the findings regarding conditioning (Domjan, 2005; Griffin, 2008). In Chapter 3, we suggested that animals have evolved in response to the need for survival: We can explain many of the differences among species as adaptations to the demands of their particular environmental niches. The same evolutionary perspective applies to a species' capacity for learning. **Biological constraints on learning** are any limitations on learning imposed by a species' genetic endowment. These constraints can apply to the animal's sensory, behavioral, and cognitive capacities. We will examine two areas of research that show how behavior–environment relations can be biased by an organism's genotype: instinctual drift and taste-aversion learning.

INSTINCTUAL DRIFT

You have no doubt seen animals performing tricks on television or in the circus. Some animals play baseball or Ping-Pong, and others drive tiny race cars. For years, **Keller Breland** and **Marion Breland** used operant conditioning techniques to train thousands of animals from many different species to perform a remarkable array of behaviors. The Brelands had believed that general principles derived from laboratory research using virtually any type of response or reward could be directly applied to the control of animal behavior outside the laboratory.

At some point after training, though, some of the animals began to "misbehave." For example, a raccoon was trained to pick up a coin, put it into a toy bank, and collect an edible reinforcer. The raccoon, however, would not immediately deposit the coin. Even worse, when there were two coins to be deposited, conditioning broke down completely—the raccoon would not give up the coins at all. Instead, it would rub the coins together, dip them into the bank, and then pull them back out. But is this really so strange? Raccoons often engage in rubbing and washing behaviors as they remove the outer shells of a favorite food, crayfish. Similarly, when pigs were given the task of putting their hard-earned tokens into a large piggy bank, they instead would drop the coins onto the floor, root (poke at) them with their snouts, and toss them into the air. Again, should you consider this strange? Pigs root and shake their food as a natural part of their inherited food-gathering repertory.

These experiences convinced the Brelands that, even when animals have learned to make operant responses perfectly, the "learned behavior drifts toward instinctual behavior" over time. They called this tendency **instinctual drift** (Breland & Breland, 1951, 1961). The behavior of their animals is not explainable by ordinary operant principles, but it is understandable if you consider the species-specific tendencies imposed by an inherited genotype. These tendencies override the changes in behavior brought about by operant conditioning.

The bulk of traditional research on animal learning focused on arbitrarily chosen responses to conveniently available stimuli. The Brelands' theory and demonstration of instinctual drift make it evident that not all aspects of learning are under the control of the experimenters' reinforcers. Behaviors will be more or less easy to change as a function of an animal's normal, genetically programmed responses in its environment. Conditioning will be particularly efficient when you can frame a target response as biologically relevant. For example, what change might you make to get the pigs to place their tokens in a bank? If the token was paired with a water reward for a thirsty pig, it would then not be rooted as food but would be deposited in the bank as a valuable commodity—dare we say a liquid asset?

How does instinctual drift affect the behaviors raccoons can learn to perform?

TASTE-AVERSION LEARNING

Your authors have a pair of confessions to make: One of us still gets a bit queasy at the thought of eating pork and beans; the other has the same response, alas, to popcorn. Why? In each case, we became violently ill after eating one of these foods. Although it's unlikely that it was the food itself that made us sick—and we have tried valiantly, particularly for the popcorn, to convince ourselves of that fact—we nonetheless have this queasy response. We can look to nonhuman animals for a clue to why this is so.

Suppose we asked you to devise a strategy for tasting a variety of unfamiliar substances. If you had the genetic endowment of rats, you would be very cautious in doing so. When presented with a new food or flavor, rats take only a very small sample. Only if it fails to make them sick will they go back for more. To flip that around, suppose we include a substance with the new flavor that does make the rats ill—they'll never consume that flavor again. This phenomenon is known as **taste-aversion learning.** You can see why having this genetic capacity to sample and learn which foods are safe and which are toxic could have great survival value.

Taste-aversion learning is an enormously powerful mechanism. Unlike most other instances of classical conditioning, taste aversion is learned with only one pairing of a CS (the novel flavor) and its consequences (the result of the underlying UCS—the element that actually brings about the illness). This is true even with a long interval, 12 hours or more, between the time the rat consumes the substance and the time it becomes ill. Finally, unlike many classically conditioned associations that are quite fragile, this one is permanent after one experience. Again, to understand these violations of the norms of classical conditioning, consider how dramatically this mechanism aids survival.

John Garcia, the psychologist who first documented taste-aversion learning in the laboratory, and his colleague Robert Koelling used this phenomenon to demonstrate that, in general, animals are biologically prepared to learn certain associations. The researchers discovered that some CS–UCS combinations can be classically conditioned in particular species of animals, but others cannot.

In phase 1 of Garcia and Koelling's experiment, thirsty rats were first familiarized with the experimental situation in which licking a tube produced three CSs: saccharin-flavored water, noise, and bright light. In phase 2, when the rats licked the tube, half of them received only the sweet water and half received only the noise, light, and plain water. Each of these two groups was again divided: Half of each group was given electric shocks that produced pain, and half was given X-ray radiation that produced nausea and illness.

The amount of water drunk by the rats in phase 1 was compared with the amount drunk in phase 2, when pain and illness were involved (see **Figure 6.12**). Big reductions in drinking occurred when flavor was associated with illness (taste aversion) and when noise and light were associated

instinctual drift The tendency for learned behavior to drift toward instinctual behavior over time.

taste-aversion learning A biological constraint on learning in which an organism learns in one trial to avoid a food whose ingestion is followed by illness.

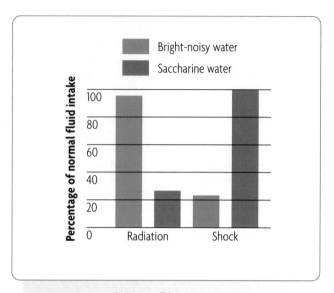

FIGURE 6.12 Inborn Bias

Results from Garcia and Koelling's study (1966) showed that rats possess an inborn bias to associate certain cues with certain outcomes. Rats avoided saccharin-flavored water when it predicted illness but not when it predicted shock. Conversely, rats avoided the "bright-noisy water" when it predicted shock but not when it predicted illness.

with pain. However, there was little change in behavior under the other two conditions—when flavor predicted pain or when the "bright-noisy water" predicted illness.

The pattern of results suggests that rats have an inborn bias to associate particular stimuli with particular consequences (Garcia & Koelling, 1966). Some instances of conditioning, then, depend not only on the relationship between stimuli and behavior but also on the way an organism is genetically predisposed toward stimuli in its environment (Barker et al., 1978). Animals appear to have encoded, within their genetic inheritance, the types of sensory cues—taste, smell, or appearance—that are most likely to signal dimensions of reward or danger. Taste-aversion learning is an example of what researchers call *biological preparedness:* A particular species has evolved so that the members of the species require less learning experience than normal to acquire a conditioned response. Experimenters who try arbitrarily to break these genetic links will look forward to little success. (In Chapter 14, we will see that researchers believe humans are biologically prepared to acquire intense fears—known as *phobias*—to stimuli such as snakes and spiders that provided dangers over the course of human evolution.)

Researchers have put knowledge of the mechanisms of taste-aversion learning to practical use. To stop coyotes from killing sheep (and sheep ranchers from shooting coyotes), John Garcia and colleagues have put toxic lamb burgers wrapped in sheep fur on the outskirts of fenced-in areas of sheep ranches. The coyotes that eat these lamb burgers get sick, vomit, and develop an instant distaste for lamb meat. Their subsequent disgust at the mere sight of sheep makes them back away from the animals instead of attacking.

In the classic research on taste-aversion learning, researchers paired novel flavors with substances that made the rats feel ill. However, there are other circumstances that will lead to taste aversions. Take a moment to consider this scenario: Have you ever undertaken a new exercise program and found yourself feeling ill from the exertion? Suppose you had tried a new sports drink just before you began to exercise. What might the consequences have been? Let's see how researchers have addressed that question in the laboratory.

Before they began running on an exercise wheel, eight rats were allowed to drink a solution that included a novel flavor: Half were introduced to an almond flavor and half to an orange flavor. The rats then had three hours of access to the exercise wheel. At the end of several days of training, the researchers assessed the rats' taste preferences by giving them the opportunity to drink freely from bottles that had the almond and orange flavors. The rats had developed conditioned aversions: They were less likely to drink the solution with the flavor that came before their exercise (Hughes & Boakes, 2008). The researchers also conducted a version of the experiment in which a group of rats were given substantial experience on the wheel before conditioning began. Under those circumstances, the rats didn't develop an aversion to the new flavor. Instead, they actually developed a preference for a new flavor they sampled after they got off the wheel.

If you've gotten to the point where a particular type of exercise feels really good to you, you'll find these results easy to grasp. Once the rats were accustomed to the running wheel, the positive aspects of exercise apparently overcame the original discomfort. Those positive aspects allowed for the conditioning of taste preferences. How might you apply these insights to your own exercise practices?

You have now seen why modern behavior analysts must be attentive to the types of responses each species is best suited to

How have researchers used taste-aversion conditioning to prevent coyotes from killing sheep?

learn. If you want to teach an old dog new tricks, you're best off adapting the tricks to the dog's genetic behavioral repertory! Our survey of learning is not complete, however, because we have not yet dealt with types of learning that might require more complex cognitive processes. We turn now to those types of learning.

STOP AND REVIEW

❶ What is instinctual drift?
❷ What makes taste-aversion learning unusual as a conditioned response?

Visit MyPsychLab.com for more review and practice on the following topic:

◀●▶ **Explore:** Taste Aversion

Cognitive Influences on Learning

Our reviews of classical and operant conditioning have demonstrated that a wide variety of behaviors can be understood as the products of simple learning processes. You might wonder, however, if certain classes of learning require more complex, more cognitive types of processes. *Cognition* is any mental activity involved in the representation and processing of knowledge, such as thinking, remembering, perceiving, and language use. In this section, we look at forms of learning in animals and humans that cannot be explained only by principles of classical or operant conditioning. We suggest, therefore, that the behaviors are partially the product of cognitive processes.

COMPARATIVE COGNITION

In this chapter, we have emphasized that, species-specific constraints aside, rules of learning acquired from research on rats and pigeons apply as well to dogs, monkeys, and humans. Researchers who study **comparative cognition** consider even broader ranges of behavior to trace the development of cognitive abilities across species and the continuity of abilities from nonhuman to human animals (Wasserman & Zentall, 2006). This field is called *comparative cognition* because researchers often compare abilities across different species; because of the focus on nonhuman species, the field is also called *animal cognition*. In his original formulation of the theory of evolution, Charles Darwin suggested that cognitive abilities evolved along with the physical forms of animals. In this section, we will describe two impressive types of animal performance that indicate further continuity in the cognitive capabilities of nonhuman and human animals.

Cognitive Maps Edward C. Tolman (1886–1959) pioneered the study of cognitive processes in learning by inventing experimental circumstances in which mechanical one-to-one associations between specific stimuli and responses could not explain animals' observed behavior. Consider the maze shown in **Figure 6.13.** Tolman and his students demonstrated that, when an original goal path is blocked in a maze, a rat with prior experience in the maze will take the shortest detour around the barrier, even though that particular response was never previously reinforced (Tolman & Honzik, 1930). The rats, therefore, behaved

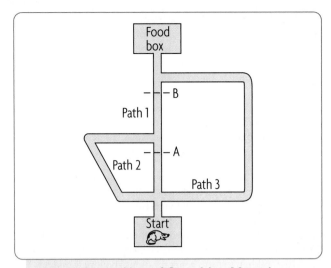

FIGURE 6.13   Use of Cognitive Maps in Maze Learning
Subjects preferred the direct path (Path 1) when it was open. With a block at A, they preferred Path 2. When a block was placed at B, the rats usually chose Path 3. Their behavior seemed to indicate that they had a cognitive map of the best way to get the food.

as if they were responding to an internal **cognitive map**—a representation of the overall layout of the maze—rather than blindly exploring different parts of the maze through trial and error (Tolman, 1948). Tolman's results showed that conditioning involves more than the simple formation of associations between sets of stimuli or between responses and reinforcers. It includes learning and representing other facets of the total behavioral context.

Research in Tolman's tradition has consistently demonstrated an impressive capacity for spatial memory in birds, bees, rats, humans, and other animals (Benhamou & Poucet, 1996; Olton, 1992). To understand the efficiency of spatial cognitive maps, consider the functions they serve (Poucet, 1993):

- Animals use spatial memory to recognize and identify features of their environments.
- Animals use spatial memory to find important goal objects in their environments.
- Animals use spatial memory to plan their route through an environment.

You can see these different functions of cognitive maps at work in the many species of birds that store food over a dispersed area but are able to recover that food with great accuracy when they need it. For example, pinyon jays bury thousands of pine seeds each fall and retrieve them four to seven months later to survive through the winter into the early spring (Stafford et al., 2006). By the time they are 8 months old, these birds appear to have the spatial memory they require to find their way back to their seeds. Other species use their spatial abilities to disperse seeds in ways that protect them against theft by other animals. Coal tits, for example, use their memories for the positions of their old seed caches to make decisions about proper locations for new caches (Male & Smulders, 2007). These

comparative cognition The study of the development of cognitive abilities across species and the continuity of abilities from nonhuman to human animals.

cognitive map A mental representation of physical space.

seed-caching birds do not just roam their environments and come upon the seeds through good fortune. Studies with Clark's nutcrackers demonstrated that they returned, with up to 84 percent accuracy, to the thousands of locations at which they buried their seeds (Kamil & Balda, 1990). They were also able to discriminate sites that still had seeds from those that had been emptied (Kamil et al., 1993). Note that these birds' caching behaviors are not reinforced when they initially bury their seeds. Only if their cognitive maps remained accurate over the winter can they later recover the seeds and survive to reproduce.

Conceptual Behavior We have seen that cognitive maps, in part, help animals preserve details of the spatial locations of objects in their environments. But what other cognitive processes can animals use to find structure, or categories of experiences, in the diverse stimuli they encounter in their environments? In Chapter 10, we will suggest that one of the challenges of language acquisition is for children to form generalizations about new *concepts* and *categories* they are learning, like the words *dog* and *tree*. Human children, however, are not the only animals capable of facing this challenge. Researchers have demonstrated that pigeons also have the cognitive ability to make use of *conceptual* distinctions.

We have seen that cognitive maps, in part, help animals preserve details of the spatial locations of objects in their environments. But what other cognitive processes can animals use to find structure, or categories of experiences, in the diverse stimuli they encounter in their environments? In Chapter 7, we will describe some of the ways in which humans carve up the world. For example, people can think about objects like *chairs* and *cars* both as their own basic categories but also understand that both chairs and cars belong to the higher-order category of artificial, human-made stimuli, whereas *flowers* and *people* belong to the higher-order category of natural stimuli. Humans, however, are not the only animals capable of showing flexibility in the way they carve up the world. Researchers have demonstrated that pigeons as well have the cognitive ability to categorize objects in different ways.

Pigeons viewed color photographs of people, flowers, cars, and chairs (see **Figure 6.14**). For each photograph, the pigeons need to make one of two types of correct responses to obtain food. On half of the trials, the pigeons pecked one of four keys that represented the four basic categories of people, flowers, cars, and chairs. On the other half of the trials, the pigeons pecked one of two keys that represented the higher-order categories of natural stimuli (people and flowers) versus artificial stimuli (cars and chairs). The two types of trials were randomly intermingled: The pigeons could see the same photo and have to categorize it as a "flower" and then as a "natural stimulus" in back-to-back trials. In fact, the pigeons were readily able to learn to respond correctly for both types of category judgments. At the end of the experiment, the researchers tested the pigeons with new photographs—photographs from the same categories that had not been part of the original training set. The pigeons were able to provide correct responses to these new photographs at a level well above chance. The test with novel photographs strongly suggests that the pigeons had learned general categories rather than individual responses to particular stimuli (Lazareva et al., 2004).

observational learning The process of learning new responses by watching the behavior of another.

FIGURE 6.14 Categorization in Pigeons
Pigeons viewed photographs that fit into four basic categories (chairs, cars, flowers, and people) as well as two higher-order categories (artificial stimuli and natural stimuli).

Reprinted with permission from Edward Wasserman, *Categorization in Pigeons*, Department of Psychology, University of Iowa.

We will devote Chapters 7 and 8 to an analysis of cognitive processes in humans. However, this experiment that demonstrates flexible categorization in pigeons should convince you that humans are not the only species with impressive and useful cognitive capabilities. Before we conclude this chapter, let's move to another type of learning that requires cognitive processes.

OBSERVATIONAL LEARNING

To introduce this further type of learning, we'd like you to return for a moment to the comparison of rats' and humans' approaches to sampling new foods. The rats are almost certainly more cautious than you are, but that's largely because they are missing an invaluable source of information—input from other rats. When you try a new food, it's almost always in a context in which you have good reason to believe that other people have eaten and enjoyed the food. The probability of your "food-eating behavior" is thus influenced by your knowledge of patterns of reinforcement for other individuals. This example illustrates your capacity to learn via *vicarious reinforcement* and *vicarious punishment*. You can use your cognitive capacities for memory and reasoning to change your own behaviors in light of the experience of others.

In fact, much *social learning* occurs in situations where learning would not be predicted by traditional conditioning theory because a learner has made no active response and has received no tangible reinforcer. The individual, after simply watching another person exhibiting behavior that was reinforced or punished, later behaves in much the same way, or refrains from doing so. This is known as **observational learning.**

From left to right: Adult models aggression; boy imitates aggression; girl imitates aggression. What does this experiment demonstrate about the role models play in learning?

Cognition often enters into observational learning in the form of expectations. In essence, after observing a model, you may think, "If I do exactly what she does, I will get the same reinforcer or avoid the same punisher." A younger child may be better behaved than his older sister because he has learned from the sister's mistakes.

This capacity to learn from watching as well as from doing is extremely useful. It enables you to acquire large integrated patterns of behavior without going through the tedious trial-and-error process of gradually eliminating wrong responses and acquiring the right ones. You can profit immediately from the mistakes and successes of others. Researchers have demonstrated that observational learning is not special to humans. Among other species, mice (Carlier & Jamon, 2006), ravens (Schwab et al., 2008), and chorus frog tadpoles (Ferrari & Chivers, 2008) are capable of changing their behavior after observing the performance of another member of their species.

A classic demonstration of human observational learning occurred in the laboratory of **Albert Bandura.** After watching adult models punching, hitting, and kicking a large plastic BoBo doll, the children in the experiment later showed a greater frequency of the same behaviors than did children in control conditions who had not observed the aggressive models (Bandura et al., 1963). Subsequent studies showed that children imitated such behaviors just from watching filmed sequences of models, even when the models were cartoon characters.

There is little question now that we learn much—both prosocial (helping) and antisocial (hurting) behaviors—through observation of models, but there are many possible models in the world. What variables are important in determining which models will be most likely to influence you? Research suggests that there are four processes that determine when a model's observed behavior will be most influential (Bandura, 1977):

- *Attention.* The observer must pay attention to the model's behavior and its consequences. This is more likely when there are perceived similarities between features and traits of the model and the observer.
- *Retention.* The observer must store a representation of the model's behavior in memory.
- *Reproduction.* The observer must have the physical or mental ability to reproduce the model's behavior.
- *Motivation.* The observer must have a reason to reproduce the model's behavior. For example, the model's behavior could be seen as having reinforcing consequences.

Imagine yourself in modeling situations and see how each process on the list would apply. Suppose, for example, you were learning to perform surgery by observing an experienced doctor. How would each process affect your ability to learn?

Because people learn so efficiently from models, you can understand why a good deal of psychological research has been directed at the behavioral impact of television: Are viewers affected by what they see being rewarded and punished on TV? Attention has focused on the link between televised acts of violence—murder, rape, assault, robbery, terrorism, and suicide—and children's and adolescents' subsequent behavior. Does exposure to acts of violence foster imitation? The conclusion from psychological research is yes—it does for some people, and particularly in the United States (Comstock & Scharrer, 1999).

The project began in 1977 when a team of researchers measured two years of television viewing for 557 children starting in either first or third grade. In particular, the researchers obtained measures of the extent to which the children watched TV shows with violent content. Fifteen years later, the researchers were able to conduct interviews with 329 of those children, who were now 20 to 22 years old (Huesmann et al., 2003). The researchers sought to determine whether there would be a relationship between the amount of television violence the individuals viewed in childhood and their level of aggression as young adults. Their adult level of aggression was measured both through their own self-reports and through the reports of others, such as spouses. As shown in **Figure 6.15,** on page 190 the men and women who had watched the most violent TV as children also displayed the highest adult levels of aggression. These data suggest that early TV viewing of violence causes later aggression. You might wonder, however, if the causality works in the opposite direction: Could it be that the children destined to be aggressive were already more interested in violent content as children? Fortunately, the researchers collected data that allowed them to argue against this possibility. For example, the data found only a small relationship between childhood aggression and the individuals' viewing of TV violence as adults.

This study argues strongly that children who watch violent TV are at risk to become overly aggressive as adults.

Several decades of research have demonstrated three ways in which television violence has a negative impact on viewers' lives (Smith & Donnerstein, 1998). First, as we have just seen, the viewing of television violence brings about, through the mechanisms of observational learning, increases in aggressive behavior. This causal association has particularly important implications for children: Aggressive habits born of heavy television

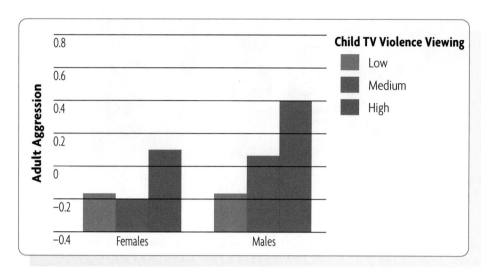

FIGURE 6.15 TV Violence and Aggression

For both men and women, those individuals who had viewed the most violent TV as children also displayed the most aggression as adults. The measure of aggression is a composite score that reflects the individuals' self-ratings and ratings of them by others. Higher scores indicate higher levels of aggression.

viewing early in life may serve as the basis for antisocial behavior later in life. Second, the viewing of television violence leads viewers to overestimate the occurrences of violence in the everyday world. Television viewers may be unduly afraid of becoming victims of real-world violence. Third, the viewing of television violence may bring about *desensitization,* a reduction in both emotional arousal and distress at viewing violent behavior.

Note that research has also shown that children can learn prosocial, helping behaviors when they watch television programs that provide prosocial behavioral models (Mares & Woodard, 2005). You should take seriously the idea that children learn from the television they watch. As a parent or caretaker, you may want to help children select appropriate televised models.

An analysis of observational learning acknowledges both that principles of reinforcement influence behavior and that humans have the capacity to use their cognitive processes to change behaviors with vicarious rewards and punishment. This approach to the understanding of human behavior has proven very powerful. In Chapter 15, we will look at successful programs of therapy that have emerged from the cognitive modification of maladaptive patterns of behavior.

Let's close this chapter by calling back to mind a visit to a horror movie. How can behavior analysis explain your experiences? If you went to the movie because of a friend's recommendation, you have succumbed to vicarious reinforcement. If you made it to the theater, despite having to forgo your normal route, you have shown evidence of a cognitive map. If the sound of scary music made you fear for the hero's well-being, you felt the effects of classical conditioning. If your failure to enjoy the film made you vow never to see a horror movie again, you have discovered the effect a punisher has on your subsequent behavior.

Are you ready to return to the theater?

STOP AND REVIEW

❶ What conclusions did Tolman draw from his pioneering work?

❷ What evidence suggests that pigeons are able to categorize stimuli with some flexibility?

❸ What is meant by vicarious reinforcement?

❹ Why is it important to evaluate children's TV viewing in the context of observational learning?

CRITICAL THINKING Consider the TV viewing study. What steps did the researchers take to assert that they had given the right causal explanation for the correlation revealed in their data?

Visit MyPsychLab.com for more review and practice on the following topics:

👁 **Watch:** Bandura's BoBo Doll Experiment

👁 **Watch:** Television Violence

✳ **Simulate:** Forms of Learning

Recapping Main Points

The Study of Learning

- Learning entails a relatively consistent change in behavior or behavior potential based on experience.
- Behaviorists believe that much behavior can be explained by simple learning processes.
- They also believe that many of the same principles of learning apply to all organisms.

Classical Conditioning: Learning Predictable Signals

- In classical conditioning, first investigated by Pavlov, an unconditioned stimulus (UCS) elicits an unconditioned response (UCR). A neutral stimulus paired with the UCS becomes a conditioned stimulus (CS), which elicits a response, called the conditioned response (CR).
- Extinction occurs when the UCS no longer follows the CS.
- Stimulus generalization is the phenomenon whereby stimuli similar to the CS elicit the CR.
- Discrimination learning narrows the range of CSs to which an organism responds.
- For classical conditioning to occur, a contingent and informative relationship must exist between the CS and UCS.
- Classical conditioning explains many emotional responses and drug tolerance.

Operant Conditioning: Learning about Consequences

- Thorndike demonstrated that behaviors that bring about satisfying outcomes tend to be repeated.
- Skinner's behavior analytic approach centers on manipulating contingencies of reinforcement and observing the effects on behavior.

- Behaviors are made more likely by positive and negative reinforcement. They are made less likely by positive and negative punishment.
- Contextually appropriate behavior is explained by the three-term contingency of discriminative stimulus–behavior–consequence.
- Primary reinforcers are stimuli that function as reinforcers even when an organism has not had previous experience with them. Conditioned reinforcers are acquired by association with primary reinforcers.
- Probable activities function as positive reinforcers.
- Behavior is affected by schedules of reinforcement that may be varied or fixed and delivered in intervals or in ratios.
- Complex responses may be learned through shaping.

Biology and Learning

- Research suggests that learning may be constrained by the species-specific repertoires of different organisms.
- Instinctual drift may overwhelm some response–reinforcement learning.
- Taste-aversion learning suggests that species are genetically prepared for some forms of associations.

Cognitive Influences on Learning

- Some forms of learning reflect more complex processes than those of classical or operant conditioning.
- Animals develop cognitive maps to enable them to function in a complex environment.
- Conceptual behavior allows animals to form generalizations about the structure of the environment.
- Behaviors can be vicariously reinforced or punished. Humans and other animals can learn through observation.

KEY TERMS

acquisition (p. 168)
avoidance conditioning (p. 177)
behavior analysis (p. 165)
biological constraint on learning (p. 184)
classical conditioning (p. 166)
cognitive map (p. 187)
comparative cognition (p. 187)
conditioned reinforcers (p. 180)
conditioned response (CR) (p. 168)
conditioned stimulus (CS) (p. 168)
discriminative stimulus (p. 178)
escape conditioning (p. 177)
extinction (p. 169)
fixed-interval (FI) schedule (p. 183)
fixed-ratio (FR) schedule (p. 181)
habituation (p. 165)

instinctual drift (p. 185)
law of effect (p. 176)
learning (p. 164)
learning-performance distinction (p. 164)
negative punishment (p. 178)
negative reinforcement (p. 177)
observational learning (p. 188)
operant (p. 176)
operant conditioning (p. 176)
operant extinction (p. 177)
partial reinforcement effect (p. 181)
positive punishment (p. 178)
positive reinforcement (p. 177)
primary reinforcer (p. 180)
punisher (p. 178)

reflex (p. 168)
reinforcement contingency (p. 176)
reinforcer (p. 177)
schedule of reinforcement (p. 181)
sensitization (p. 165)
shaping by successive approximations (p. 183)
spontaneous recovery (p. 169)
stimulus discrimination (p. 170)
stimulus generalization (p. 169)
taste-aversion learning (p. 185)
three-term contingency (p. 178)
unconditioned response (UCR) (p. 168)
unconditioned stimulus (UCS) (p. 168)
variable-interval (VI) schedule (p. 183)
variable-ratio (VR) schedule (p. 182)

Chapter 6 Practice Test

1. When Joan first moved to the city, she couldn't sleep because of the traffic noise. Now she hardly hears the traffic at all. This is an example of
   a. sensitization.
   b. habituation.
   c. consistency.
   d. classical conditioning.

2. You would *not* expect a close adherent to Skinner's ideas to focus on
   a. internal states as causes of behavior.
   b. forms of learning conserved across species.
   c. associations between behaviors and rewards.
   d. the environmental stimuli that cause behaviors.

3. In Pavlov's experiments, _____ served as the unconditioned stimulus.
   a. salivation
   b. food powder
   c. the sight of the assistant
   d. tones

4. Six-year-old Pavel has a neighbor with a small dog who barks at him every day. Over time, Pavel has become frightened of all dogs. This is an example of
   a. stimulus discrimination.
   b. backward conditioning.
   c. spontaneous recovery.
   d. stimulus generalization.

5. Peter wishes to use classical conditioning in which a light will be the CS and an electric shock will be the UCS. You tell him that the light must _____ the shock.
   a. be temporally contiguous with
   b. reliably predict
   c. be in a blocking relationship with
   d. occur after

6. When classical conditioning contributes to drug tolerance, the conditioned stimulus is
   a. the setting in which individuals take the drugs.
   b. the body's compensatory reaction to the drug.
   c. the high the drugs give when individuals take them.
   d. the individual's fear of an overdose.

7. For people undergoing chemotherapy, an unconditioned response would be
   a. anticipatory fatigue.
   b. the setting in which the individual receives the treatment.
   c. their body's reaction to the drugs.
   d. the infusion of drugs into their bodies.

8. In an operant conditioning experiment, you offer people expensive chocolate each time they perform a desired behavior. You think it's likely that the chocolate will be a _____ of the people.
   a. reinforcer for all
   b. reinforcer for none
   c. punisher for all
   d. reinforcer for some

9. Carlotta's parents haven't allowed her to watch television for three days. If she eats her brussels sprouts, she'll be allowed to watch TV that night. It sounds as if Carlotta's parents might be familiar with
   a. operant extinction.
   b. conditioned reinforcement.
   c. token economies.
   d. response deprivation theory.

10. In one study, the children who had received the most physical punishment as 15-month-olds showed _____ behavior problems at 36 months and _____ behavior problems in first grade then their less-punished peers.
    a. fewer; fewer
    b. fewer; more
    c. more; more
    d. more; fewer

11. In your new job, you get paid $2 every time you finish polishing 20 apples. This situation puts you on a _____ schedule.
    a. variable-interval
    b. fixed-interval
    c. variable-ratio
    d. fixed-ratio

12. One night after eating a hot dog you get very sick, now you shudder at the idea of eating a hot dog. A friend suggests that extinction trials will allow you to over come this aversion. This means that you should
    a. associate hot dogs with foods you like.
    b. eat some more hot dogs.
    c. make yourself sick eating something else.
    d. use hot dogs as a reward.

13. Birds like Clark's nutcrackers are very successful at finding the seeds they have buried. This provides evidence for species-specific
    a. conditioning processes.
    b. applications of classical conditioning.
    c. spatial memory.
    d. shaping processes.

14. Suppose you showed a pigeon a photograph of a car. Humans can categorize the photograph as both a *car* and an *artificial stimulus*. You believe that you can train a pigeon to categorize the photograph
    a. as both a *car* and an *artificial stimulus*.
    b. only as a *car*.
    c. only as an *artificial stimulus*.
    d. as neither a *car* nor an *artificial stimulus*.

15. Zoe watches her older sister slip on ice and bruise her arm. After that, Zoe is very careful when she walks on ice. This is an example of
    a. observational learning.
    b. classical conditioning.
    c. operant extinction.
    d. sensitization.

Essay Questions

1. What information about classical conditioning might you share with someone who is about to undergo chemotherapy?

2. Why might you choose one schedule of reinforcement (that is, fixed-interval versus variable-interval) over another?

3. What mechanisms explain why viewing of TV violence might cause aggressive behavior?

Discovering Psychology Viewing Guide

Watch the following video by logging on to MyPsychLab (www.mypsychlab.com). After you have watched the video, complete the activities that follow.

Program 8: Learning

KEY TERMS AND PEOPLE

As you watch the program, pay particular attention to this person in addition to those covered in this textbook.

- *Howard Rachlin*—studies how operant principles can be used to train self-control.

PROGRAM REVIEW

1. Which of the following is an example of a fixed-action pattern?
   a. a fish leaping at bait that looks like a fly
   b. a flock of birds migrating in winter
   c. a person blinking when something gets in her eye
   d. a chimpanzee solving a problem using insight

2. What is the basic purpose of learning?
   a. to improve one's genes
   b. to understand the world one lives in
   c. to find food more successfully
   d. to adapt to changing circumstances

3. How have psychologists traditionally studied learning?
   a. in classrooms with children as participants
   b. in classrooms with college students as participants
   c. in laboratories with humans as participants
   d. in laboratories with nonhuman animals as participants

4. In his work, Pavlov found that a metronome could produce salivation in dogs because
   a. it signaled that food would arrive.
   b. it was the dogs' normal reaction to a metronome.
   c. it was on while the dogs ate.
   d. it extinguished the dogs' original response.

5. What is learned in classical conditioning?
   a. a relationship between an action and its consequence
   b. a relationship between two stimulus events
   c. a relationship between two response events
   d. classical conditioning does not involve learning

6. What point is Professor Zimbardo making when he says, "Relax," while firing a pistol?
   a. There are fixed reactions to verbal stimuli.
   b. The acquisition process is reversed during extinction.
   c. Any stimulus can come to elicit any reaction.
   d. Unconditioned stimuli are frequently negative.

7. What point does Ader and Cohen's research on taste aversion in rats make about classical conditioning?
   a. It can be extinguished easily.
   b. It takes many conditioning trials to be effective.
   c. It is powerful enough to suppress the immune system.
   d. It tends to be more effective than instrumental conditioning.

8. What is Thorndike's law of effect?
   a. Learning is controlled by its consequences.
   b. Every action has an equal and opposite reaction.
   c. Effects are more easily changed than causes.
   d. A conditioned stimulus comes to have the same effect as an unconditioned stimulus.

9. According to John B. Watson, any behavior, even strong emotion, could be explained by the power of
   a. instinct.
   b. inherited traits.
   c. innate ideas.
   d. conditioning.

10. In Watson's work with Little Albert, why was Albert afraid of the Santa Claus mask?
    a. He had been classically conditioned with the mask.
    b. The mask was an unconditioned stimulus creating fear.
    c. He generalized his learned fear of the rat.
    d. Instrumental conditioning created a fear of strangers.

11. What was the point of the Skinner box?
    a. It kept animals safe.
    b. It provided a simple, highly controlled environment.
    c. It set up a classical conditioning situation.
    d. It allowed psychologists to use computers for research.

12. Skinner found that the rate at which a pigeon pecked at a target varied directly with
    a. the conditioned stimulus.
    b. the conditioned response.
    c. the operant antecedents.
    d. the reinforcing consequences.

13. Imagine a behavior therapist is treating a person who fears going out into public places. What would the therapist be likely to focus on?
    a. the conditioning experience that created the fear
    b. the deeper problems that the fear is a symptom of
    c. providing positive consequences for going out
    d. reinforcing the patient's desire to overcome the fear

14. When should the conditioned stimulus be presented in order to optimally produce classical conditioning?
    a. just before the unconditioned stimulus
    b. simultaneously with the unconditioned response
    c. just after the unconditioned stimulus
    d. just after the conditioned response

15. Operant conditioning can be used to achieve all of the following, *except*
    a. teaching dogs to assist the handicapped.
    b. teaching infants English grammar.
    c. teaching self-control to someone who is trying to quit smoking.
    d. increasing productivity among factory workers.

16. Which psychologist has argued that in order to understand and control behavior, one has to consider both the reinforcements acting on the selected behavior and the reinforcements acting on the alternatives?
    a. E. Thorndike   c. B. F. Skinner
    b. J. Watson   d. H. Rachlin

17. If given a choice between an immediate small reinforcer and a delayed larger reinforcer, an untrained pigeon will
    a. select the immediate small one.
    b. select the delayed larger one.
    c. experiment and alternate across trials.
    d. not show any signs of perceiving the difference.

18. In order to produce extinction of a classically conditioned behavior, an experimenter would
    a. reward the behavior.
    b. pair the behavior with negative reinforcement.
    c. present the conditioned stimulus in the absence of the unconditioned stimulus.
    d. model the behavior for the organism.

19. In Pavlov's early work, bell is to food as
    a. unconditioned response is to conditioned response.
    b. conditioned stimulus is to unconditioned stimulus.
    c. unconditioned response is to conditioned stimulus.
    d. conditioned stimulus is to conditioned response.

20. Howard Rachlin has discovered that animals can be taught self-control through
    a. reinforcement.
    b. operant conditioning.
    c. instrumental conditioning.
    d. all of the above.

QUESTIONS TO CONSIDER

1. Approximately 2 percent of Americans are hooked on gambling, which experts claim can be just as addictive as drugs. Is compulsive gambling a disease or a learned behavior? Consider the kind of reinforcement gamblers get. Using the terms you learned in this program, how would you characterize the nature of the reinforcement and the reinforcement schedule? What techniques do you predict would work best to help compulsive gamblers change their behavior?

2. You are a school principal, and you are trying to get your students to help clean up the school. Given what you now know about the control of behavior, what sorts of techniques would you use in order to get students to comply?

3. What role does intention to learn play in classical and operant conditioning? Would these techniques work on people who do not know they are being used? Would they work on people who oppose their use?

4. Is it possible that children learn their native language through operant conditioning? When parents and young children interact, do the parents reinforce the use of some grammar and punish others? Are some aspects of language, such as the rules of politeness, more likely to be taught through conditioning than other aspects?

ACTIVITIES

1. Design your own behavior change program based on the learning principles described in Program 8. First, identify a specific behavior. Instead of setting a broad goal, such as becoming more fit, design a strategy to reinforce a desired behavior—going for jogs, cutting out midnight snacks, or taking the stairs rather than the elevator. Analyze the specific behavior you would like to change in terms of antecedents–behavior–consequences. Then get a baseline measurement of the target behavior, try out your plan for a predetermined amount of time, and evaluate the results.

2. Have someone teach you something new, such as how to juggle, play basic guitar chords, or serve a tennis ball. Analyze the teacher's method. How does it apply principles of theories of learning? How would you change the teacher's method to be more effective?

3. Choose a member of your family and some trivial behavioral detail, such as standing still. See if you can train the person to reliably perform the behavior without having him or her catch on to what you're doing.

Memory

How are actors and actresses able to remember all the different aspects—movements, expressions, and words—of their performances?

As you begin this chapter on memory processes, we'd like you to take a moment to recover your own earliest memory. How long ago did the memory originate? How vivid a scene do you recall? Has your memory been influenced by other people's recollections of the same event?

Now, a slightly different exercise. We'd like you to imagine what it would be like if you suddenly had no memory of your past—of the people you have known or of events that have happened to you. You wouldn't remember your mother's face, or your 10th birthday, or your senior prom. Without such time anchors, how would you maintain a sense of who you are—of your self-identity? Or suppose you lost the ability to form any new memories. What would happen to your most recent experiences? Could you follow a conversation or untangle the plot of a TV show? Everything would vanish, as if events had never existed, as if you had never had any thoughts in mind. Is there any activity you can think of that is not influenced by memory?

If you have never given much thought to your memory, it's probably because it tends to do its job reasonably well—you take it for granted, alongside other bodily processes, like digestion or breathing. But as with stomachaches or allergies, the times you notice your memory are likely to be the times when something goes wrong: You forget your car keys, an important date, lines in a play, or the answer to an examination question that you know you "really know." There's no reason you shouldn't find these occasions irritating, but you should also reflect for a moment on the estimate that the average human brain can store 100 trillion bits of information. The task of managing such a vast array of information is a formidable one. Perhaps you shouldn't be too surprised when an answer is sometimes not available when you need it!

Our goal in this chapter is to explain how you usually remember so much and why you forget some of what you have known. We will explore how you get your everyday experiences into and out of memory. You will learn what psychology has discovered about different types of memories and about how those memories work. We hope that in the course of learning the many facts of memory, you will gain an appreciation for how wonderful memory is.

One last thing: Because this is a chapter on memory, we're going to put your memory immediately to work. We'd like you to remember the number 48. Do whatever you need to do to remember 48. And yes, there will be a test!

What Is Memory?

To begin, we will define **memory** as the capacity to encode, store, and retrieve information. In this chapter, we will describe memory as a type of *information processing*. The bulk of our attention, therefore, will be trained on the flow of information in and out of your memory systems. Our examination of the processes that guide the acquisition and retrieval of information will enable you to refine your sense of what *memory* means.

FUNCTIONS OF MEMORY

When you think about memory, what is most likely to come to mind at first are situations in which you use your memory to recall (or try to recall) specific events or information: your favorite movie, the dates of World War II, or your student ID number. In fact, one of the important functions of memory is to allow you to have conscious access to the personal and collective past. But memory does much more for you than that. It also enables you to have effortless continuity of experience from one day to the next. When you drive through your neighborhood, for example, it is this second function of memory that makes the stores along the roadside seem familiar. In defining types of memories, we will make plain to you how hard your memory works to fulfill these functions, often outside of conscious awareness.

Implicit and Explicit Memory Consider **Figure 7.1.** What's wrong with this picture? It probably strikes you as unusual that there's a rabbit in the kitchen. But where does this feeling come from? You probably didn't go through the objects in the picture one by one and ask yourself, "Does the toaster belong?" "Do the cabinets belong?" Rather, the image of the rabbit jumps out at you as being out of place.

This simple example allows you to understand the difference between explicit and implicit uses of memory. For circumstances in which you engage conscious effort to encode or retrieve information, those are **explicit uses of memory.** When

---

memory The mental capacity to encode, store, and retrieve information.

explicit use of memory Conscious effort to encode or recover information through memory processes.

FIGURE 7.1 What's Wrong with This Picture?

Did you think right away, "What's a rabbit doing in the kitchen?" If the image of the rabbit immediately jumped out at you, it is because your memory processes performed an analysis of the scene outside of consciousness and delivered the rabbit as the odd element.

you encode or retrieve information without conscious effort, those are **implicit uses of memory.** Your discovery of the rabbit is implicit because your memory processes brought past knowledge of kitchens to bear on your interpretation of the picture without any particular effort on your part. Suppose now we asked you, "What's missing from the picture?" To answer this second question, you probably have to put explicit memory to work. What appears in the typical kitchen? What's missing? (Did you think of the sink or the stove?) Thus, when it comes to using knowledge stored in memory, sometimes the use will be implicit—the information becomes available without any conscious effort—and sometimes it will be explicit—you make a conscious effort to recover the information.

We can make the same distinction when it comes to the initial acquisition of memories. How do you know what should appear in a kitchen? Did you ever memorize a list of what appears there and what the appropriate configuration should be? Probably not. Rather, it's likely that you acquired most of this knowledge without conscious effort. By contrast, you probably learned the names of many of the objects in the room explicitly. As we shall see in Chapter 10, to learn the association between words and experiences, your younger self needed to engage in explicit memory processes. You learned the word *refrigerator* because someone called your explicit attention to the name of that object.

The distinction between implicit and explicit memory greatly expands the range of questions researchers must address about memory processes (Bowers & Marsolek, 2003). Most early memory research focused on the explicit acquisition of information. Experimenters most frequently provided participants with new information to retain, and theories of memory were directed to explaining what participants could

and could not remember under those circumstances. However, as you will see in this chapter, researchers have now devised methods for studying implicit memory as well. Thus we can give you a more complete account of the variety of uses to which you put your memory. We can acknowledge that most circumstances in which you encode or retrieve information represent a mix of implicit and explicit uses of memory. Let's turn now to a second dimension along which memories are distributed.

Declarative and Procedural Memory Can you whistle? Go ahead and try. Or if you can't whistle, try snapping your fingers. What kind of memory allows you to do these sorts of things? You probably remember having to learn these skills, but now they seem effortless. The examples we gave before of both implicit and explicit memories all involved the recollection of *facts* and *events*, which is called **declarative memory.** Now we see that you also have memories for *how to do things,* which is called **procedural memory.** Because the bulk of this chapter will be focused on how you acquire and use facts, let's take a moment now to consider how you acquire the ability to do things.

Procedural memory refers to the way you remember how things get done. With enough practice, you are able to

---

implicit uses of memory Availability of information through memory processes without conscious effort to encode or recover information.

declarative memory Memory for information such as facts and events.

procedural memory Memory for how things get done; the way perceptual, cognitive, and motor skills are acquired, retained, and used.

acquire, retain, and employ procedural memories for perceptual, cognitive, and motor skills. Theories of procedural memory often concern themselves with how much practice you need and over what period of time: How do you go from a conscious list of declarative facts about some activity to unconscious, automatic performance of that same activity (Anderson et al., 2004)? And why is it that after learning a skill, you often find it difficult to go back and talk about the component declarative facts?

We can see these phenomena at work in even the very simple activity of punching in a phone number that, over time, has become highly familiar. At first, you probably had to think your way through each digit, one at a time. You had to work through a list of declarative facts:

> First, I must punch 2,
> Next, I must punch 0,
> Then I punch 7,
> and so on.

Why does pretending to punch in a number help you to remember it?

However, when you began to punch in the number often enough, you could start to produce it as one unit—a swift sequence of actions on the touch-tone pad. The process at work is called *knowledge compilation* (Anderson, 1987). As a consequence of practice, you are able to carry out longer sequences of the activity without conscious intervention and mental effort. But you also don't have conscious access to the content of these compiled units: Back at the telephone, it's not uncommon to find someone who can't actually remember the phone number without pretending to punch it in. In general, knowledge compilation makes it hard to share your procedural knowledge with others. You may have noticed this if your parents tried to teach you to drive. Although they may be good drivers themselves, they may not have been very good at communicating the content of compiled good-driving procedures.

You may also have noticed that knowledge compilation can lead to errors. If you are a skilled typist, you've probably suffered from the *the* problem: As soon as you hit the *t* and the *h* keys, your finger may fly to the *e*, even if you're really trying to type *throne* or *thistle*. Once you have sufficiently committed the execution of *the* to procedural memory, you can do little else but finish the sequence. Without procedural memory, life would be extremely laborious—you would be doomed to go step by step through every activity. However, each time you mistakenly type *the,* you can reflect on the trade-off between efficiency and potential error. Let's continue now to an overview of the basic processes that apply to all these different types of memory.

---

encoding The process by which a mental representation is formed in memory.

storage The retention of encoded material over time.

retrieval The recovery of stored information from memory.

AN OVERVIEW OF MEMORY PROCESSES

No matter what the category of memory, being able to use knowledge at some later time requires the operation of three mental processes: encoding, storage, and retrieval. **Encoding** is the initial processing of information that leads to a representation in memory. **Storage** is the retention over time of encoded material. **Retrieval** is the recovery at a later time of the stored information. Simply put, encoding gets information in, storage holds it until you need it, and retrieval gets it out. Let's now expand on these ideas.

Encoding requires that you form *mental representations* of information from the external world. You can understand the idea of mental representations if we draw an analogy to representations outside your head. Imagine we wanted to know something about the best gift you got at your last birthday party. (Let's suppose it's not something you have with you.) What could you do to inform us about the gift? You might describe the properties of the object. Or you might draw us a picture. Or you might pretend that you're using the object. In each case, these are representations of the original object. Although none of the representations is likely to be quite as good as having the real thing present, they should allow us to acquire knowledge of the most important aspects of the gift. Mental representations work much the same way. They preserve important features of past experiences in a way that enables you to *re-present* those experiences to yourself.

If information is properly encoded, it will be retained in *storage* over some period of time. Storage requires both short- and long-term changes in the structures of your brain. At the end of the chapter, we will see how researchers are attempting to locate the brain structures that are responsible for storing new and old memories. We will also see what happens in cases of extreme amnesia, where individuals become incapable of storing new memories.

Retrieval is the payoff for all your earlier effort. When it works, it enables you to gain access—often in a split second—to information you stored earlier. Can you remember what comes before storage: decoding or encoding? The answer is simple to retrieve now, but will you still be able to retrieve the concept of encoding as swiftly and with as much confidence when you are tested on this chapter's contents days or weeks from now? Discovering how you are able to retrieve one specific bit of information from the vast quantity of information in your memory storehouse is a challenge facing psychologists who want to know how memory works and how it can be improved.

Although it is easy to define encoding, storage, and retrieval as separate memory processes, the interaction among the three processes is quite complex. For example, to be able to encode the information that you have seen a tiger, you must first retrieve from memory information about the concept

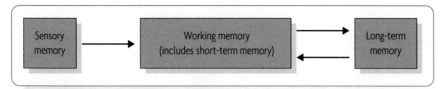

FIGURE 7.2   The Flow of Information In and Out of Long-Term Memory
Memory theories describe the flow of information to and from long-term memory. The theories address initial encodings of information in sensory and working memory, the transfer of information into long-term memory for storage, and the transfer of information from long-term memory to working memory for retrieval.

tiger. Similarly, to commit to memory the meaning of a sentence such as "He's as honest as Benedict Arnold," you must retrieve the meanings of each individual word, retrieve the rules of grammar that specify how word meanings should be combined in English, and retrieve cultural information that specifies exactly how honest Benedict Arnold—a famous Revolutionary War traitor—was.

We are now ready to look in more detail at the encoding, storage, and retrieval of information. Our discussion will start with memory processes that preserve information for the short term such as sensory memory and working memory. We then move to the more permanent forms of long-term memory (see **Figure 7.2**). We will give you an account of how you remember and why you forget. Our plan is to make you forever self-conscious about all the ways in which you use your capacity for memory. We hope this will even allow you to improve some aspects of your memory skills.

STOP AND REVIEW

❶ What is the difference between explicit and implicit uses of memory?

❷ Suppose you are a skilled juggler. Does your skill rely more on declarative or procedural memory?

❸ You suddenly can't remember the password for your e-mail account. Which memory process is most likely to be causing the difficulty?

Visit MyPsychLab.com for more review and practice on the following topic:

◀◉ **Explore:** Key Processes in Stages of Memory

Memory Use for the Short Term

Let's begin with a demonstration of the impermanence of some memories. In **Figure 7.3**, on page 200, we have provided you with a reasonably busy visual scene. We'd like you to take a quick look at it—about 10 seconds—and then cover it up. Suppose we now ask you a series of questions about the scene:

1. What tool is the little boy at the bottom holding?
2. What is the middle man at the top doing?
3. In the lower right-hand corner, does the woman's umbrella handle hook to the left or to the right?

To answer these questions, wouldn't you be more comfortable if you could go back and have an extra peek at the picture?

This quick demonstration reminds you that much of the information you experience never lodges itself securely in your memory. Instead, you possess and use the information only for the short term. In this section, we examine properties of three less permanent uses of memory: *iconic memory, short-term memory,* and *working memory.*

ICONIC MEMORY

When you first covered up Figure 7.3, did you have the impression that you could briefly still "see" the whole picture? This extra peek at the picture is provided by your **iconic memory**—a memory system in the visual domain that allows large amounts of information to be stored for very brief durations (Neisser, 1967). Iconic memory is an example of a *sensory memory:* Researchers have speculated that each sensory system has a memory store that preserves representations of physical features of environmental stimuli for, at most, a few seconds (Radvansky, 2006). For example, people retain brief sensory representations of stimuli that have touched their bodies (Gallace et al., 2008). We focus on iconic memory because it has received the most research attention.

A visual memory, or icon, lasts about half a second. Iconic memory was first revealed in experiments that required participants to retrieve information from visual displays that were exposed for only one twentieth of a second.

---

iconic memory Memory system in the visual domain that allows large amounts of information to be stored for very brief durations.

FIGURE 7.3 How Much Can You Remember from This Scene?

After viewing this scene for about 10 seconds, cover it up and try to answer the questions in the text. Under ordinary circumstances, iconic memory preserves a glimpse of the visual world for a brief time after the scene has been removed.

George Sperling (1960, 1963) presented participants with arrays of three rows of letters and numbers.

7	1	V	F
X	L	5	3
B	4	W	7

Participants were asked to perform two different tasks. In a *whole-report procedure,* they tried to recall as many of the items in the display as possible. Typically, they could report only about four items. Other participants underwent a *partial-report procedure,* which required them to report only one row rather than the whole pattern. A signal of a high, medium, or low tone was sounded immediately after the presentation to indicate which row the participants were to report. Sperling found that regardless of which row he asked for, the participants' recall was quite high.

Because participants could accurately report any of the three rows in response to a tone, Sperling concluded that all of the information in the display must have gotten into iconic memory. That is evidence for its large capacity. At the same time, the difference between the whole- and partial-report procedures suggests that the information fades rapidly: The participants in

the whole-report procedure were unable to recall all the information present in the icon. This second point was reinforced by experiments in which the identification signal was slightly delayed. **Figure 7.4** shows that as the delay interval increases from 0 seconds to 1 second, the number of items accurately reported declines steadily. Researchers have measured quite accurately the time course with which information must be transferred from the fading icon (Becker et al., 2000; Tijus & Reeves, 2004). To take advantage of the "extra peek" at the visual world, your memory processes must very quickly transfer information to more durable stores.

Note that iconic memory is not the same as the "photographic memory" that some people claim to have. The technical term for "photographic memory" is *eidetic imagery:* People who experience eidetic imagery are able to recall the details of a picture, for periods of time considerably longer than iconic memory, as if they were still looking at a photograph. "People" in this case really means children: Researchers have estimated that roughly 8 percent of preadolescent children are eidetickers, but virtually no adults (Neath & Surprenant, 2003). No satisfactory theory has been proposed for why eidetic imagery fades over time. However, if you are reading this book as a high school or college student, you almost certainly have iconic memory but not eidetic images.

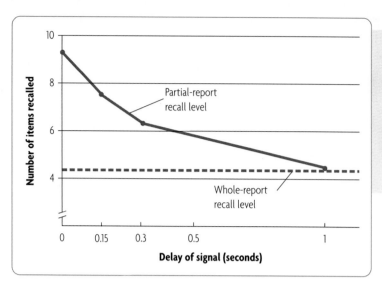

FIGURE 7.4 Recall by the Partial-Report Method

The solid line shows the average number of items recalled using the partial-report method, both immediately after presentation and at four later times. For comparison, the dotted line shows the number of items recalled by the whole-report method.

Adapted from Sperling, 1960.

SHORT-TERM MEMORY

Before you began to read this chapter, you may not have been aware that you had iconic memory. It is very likely, however, that you were aware that there are some memories that you possess only for the short term. Consider the common occurrence of consulting a telephone book to find a friend's number and then remembering the number just long enough to punch it in. If the number turns up busy, you often have to go right back to the phone book. When you consider this experience, it's easy to understand why researchers have hypothesized a special type of memory called **short-term memory (STM).**

You shouldn't think of short-term memory as a particular place that memories go to, but rather as a built-in mechanism for focusing cognitive resources on some small set of mental representations (Shiffrin, 2003). But the resources of STM are fickle. As even your experience with phone numbers shows, you have to take some special care to ensure that memories become encoded into more permanent forms.

The Capacity Limitations of STM In Chapter 4, we described how your attentional resources are devoted to selecting the objects and events in the external world on which you will expend your mental resources. Just as there are limits on your capacity to attend to more than a small sample of the available information, there are limits on your ability to keep more than a small sample of information active in STM. The limited capacity of STM enforces a sharp focus of mental attention.

To estimate the capacity of STM, researchers at first turned to tests of *memory span*. At some point in your life, you have probably been asked to carry out a task like this one:

Read the following list of random numbers once, cover them, and write down as many as you can in the order they appear:

8 1 7 3 4 9 4 2 8 5

How many did you get correct?

Now read the next list of random letters and perform the same memory test:

J M R S O F L P T Z B

How many did you get correct?

If you are like most individuals, you probably could recall somewhere in the range of five to nine items. **George Miller** (1956) suggested that seven (plus or minus two) was the "magic number" that characterized people's memory performance on random lists of letters, words, numbers, or almost any kind of meaningful, familiar item.

Tests of memory span, however, overestimate the true capacity of STM because participants are able to use other sources of information to carry out the task. When other sources of memory are factored out, researchers have estimated the pure contribution of STM to your seven (or so) item memory span to be only between three and five items (Cowan, 2001). But if that's all the capacity you have to commence the acquisition of new memories, why don't you notice your limitations more often? Despite the capacity limitations of STM, you function efficiently for at least two reasons. As we will see in the next two sections, the encoding of information in STM can be enhanced through rehearsal and chunking.

Rehearsal You probably know that a good way to keep your friend's telephone number in mind is to keep repeating the digits in a cycle in your head. This memorization technique is called *maintenance rehearsal*. The fate of unrehearsed information was demonstrated in an ingenious experiment.

Participants heard three consonants, such as *F*, *C*, and *V*. After a delay of 3 to 18 seconds, the participants heard a signal that instructed them to recall the consonants. To prevent rehearsal, a *distractor task* was put between the stimulus input and the recall signal—the participants were given a three-digit number and told to count backward from it by 3s until the recall signal was presented. Many different consonant

---

short-term memory (STM) Memory processes associated with preservation of recent experiences and with retrieval of information from long-term memory; short-term memory is of limited capacity and stores information for only a short length of time without rehearsal.

What role does short-term memory play when you punch in your ATM password?

you wish to acquire is, at least at first, too cumbersome to be rehearsed? You might turn to the strategy of chunking.

Chunking A *chunk* is a meaningful unit of information (Anderson, 1996). A chunk can be a single letter or number, a group of letters or other items, or even a group of words or an entire sentence. For example, the sequence 1–9–8–4 consists of four digits that could exhaust your STM capacity. However, if you see the digits as a year or the title of George Orwell's book *1984,* they constitute only one chunk, leaving you much more capacity for other chunks of information. **Chunking** is the process of reconfiguring items by grouping them on the basis of similarity or some other organizing principle, or by combining them into larger patterns based on information stored in long-term memory (Chen & Cowan, 2005).

See how many chunks you find in this sequence of 20 numbers: 19411917186118121776. You can answer "20" if you see the sequence as a list of unrelated digits, or "5" if you break down the sequence into the dates of major wars in U.S. history. If you do the latter, it's easy for you to recall all the digits in proper sequence after one quick glance. It would be impossible for you to remember them all from a short exposure if you saw them as 20 unrelated items.

Your memory span can always be greatly increased if you can discover ways to organize an available body of information into smaller chunks. A famous subject, S.F., was able to memorize 84 digits by grouping them as racing times (S.F. was an avid runner):

S.F.'s memory protocols provided the key to his mental wizardry. Because he was a long-distance runner, S.F.

sets were given, and several short delays were used over a series of trials with a number of participants.

As shown in **Figure 7.5,** recall became increasingly poorer as the time required to retain the information became longer. After even 3 seconds, there was considerable memory loss, and by 18 seconds, loss was nearly total. In the absence of an opportunity to rehearse the information, short-term recall was impaired with the passage of time (Peterson & Peterson, 1959).

Performance suffered because information could not be rehearsed. It also suffered because of interference from the competing information of the distractor task. (We will discuss interference as a cause of forgetting later in this chapter.) You may have noticed how often a new acquaintance says his or her name—and then you immediately forget it. One of the most common reasons for this is that you are distracted from performing the type of rehearsal you need to carry out to acquire a new memory. As a remedy, try to encode and rehearse a new name carefully before you continue with a conversation.

Our conclusion so far is that rehearsal will help you to keep information from fading out of STM. But suppose the information

chunking The process of taking single items of information and recoding them on the basis of similarity or some other organizing principle.

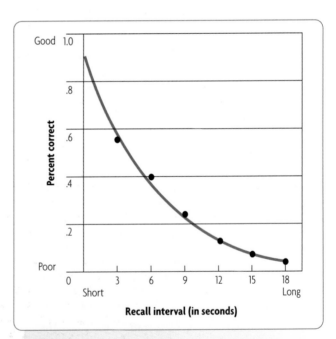

FIGURE 7.5 Short-Term Memory Recall without Rehearsal

When the interval between stimulus presentation and recall was filled with a distracting task, recall became poorer as the interval grew longer.

How can you put chunking to good use while listening to a lecture?

noticed that many of the random numbers could be grouped into running times for different distances. For instance, he would recode the sequence 3, 4, 9, 2, 5, 6, 1, 4, 9, 3, 5 as 3:49.2, near record mile; 56:14, 10-mile time; 9:35, slow 2 miles. Later, S.F. also used ages, years of memorable events, and special numerical patterns to chunk the random digits. In this way, he was able to use his long-term memory to convert long strings of random input into manageable and meaningful chunks. S.F.'s memory for letters was still about average, however, because he had not developed any chunking strategies to recall alphabet strings (Chase & Ericsson, 1981; Ericsson & Chase, 1982).

Like S.F., you can structure incoming information according to its personal meaning to you (linking it to the ages of friends and relatives, for example); or you can match new stimuli with various codes that have been stored in your long-term memory. Even if you can't link new stimuli to rules, meanings, or codes in your long-term memory, you can still use chunking. You can simply group the items in a rhythmical pattern or temporal group (181379256460 could become 181, pause, 379, pause, 256,

In what ways is retrieval from STM analogous to retrieval from a vast research library?

pause, 460). You know from everyday experience that this grouping principle works well for remembering telephone numbers.

WORKING MEMORY

Our focus so far has been on short-term memory, and specifically the role that STM plays in the explicit acquisition of new memories. However, you need more memory resources on a moment-by-moment basis than those that allow you to acquire facts. For example, you also need to be able to retrieve preexisting memories. At the start of this chapter, we asked you to commit a number to memory. Can you remember now what it was? If you can remember (if not, peek), you have made your mental representation of that memory active once more—that's another memory function. If we ask you to do something more complicated—suppose we ask you to toss a ball from hand to hand while you count backward by 3s from 132—you'll put even more demands on your memory resources.

Based on an analysis of the memory functions you require to navigate through life, researchers have articulated theories of **working memory**—the memory resource that you use to accomplish tasks such as reasoning and language comprehension. Suppose you are trying to remember a phone number while you search for a pencil and pad to write it down. Whereas your short-term memory processes allow you to keep the number in mind, your more general working memory resource allows you to execute the mental operations to accomplish an efficient search. Working memory provides a foundation for the moment-by-moment fluidity of thought and action.

Alan Baddeley (2002, 2003) has provided evidence for four components of working memory:

- A *phonological loop*. This resource holds and manipulates speech-based information. The phonological loop overlaps most with short-term memory, as we have described it in the earlier sections. When you rehearse a telephone number by "listening" to it as you run it through your head, you are making use of the phonological loop.
- A *visuospatial sketchpad*. This resource performs the same types of functions as the phonological loop for visual and spatial information. If, for example, someone asked you how many desks there are in your psychology classroom, you might use the resources of the visuospatial sketchpad to form a mental picture of the classroom and then estimate the number of desks from that picture.
- The *central executive*. This resource is responsible for controlling attention and coordinating information from the phonological loop and the visuospatial sketchpad. Any time you carry out a task that requires a combination of mental processes—imagine, for example, you are asked to describe a picture from memory—you rely on the central executive function to apportion your mental resources to different aspects of the task (we return to this idea in Chapter 8).

---

working memory A memory resource that is used to accomplish tasks such as reasoning and language comprehension; consists of the phonological loop, visuospatial sketchpad, and central executive.

- The *episodic buffer* is a storage system with limited capacity that is controlled by the central executive. The episodic buffer allows you to retrieve information from long-term memory and combine it with information from the current situation. Most life events include a complex array of sights, sounds, and so on. The episodic buffer provides a resource to integrate those different types of perceptual stimulation with past experiences to provide a unified interpretation of each situation.

The incorporation of short-term memory into the broader context of working memory should help reinforce the idea that STM is not a place but a process. To do the work of cognition—to carry out cognitive activities like language processing or problem solving—you must bring a lot of different elements together in quick succession. You can think of working memory as short-term special focus on the necessary elements. If you wish to get a better look at a physical object, you can shine a brighter light on it; working memory shines a brighter mental light on your mental objects—your memory representations. Working memory also coordinates the activities required to take action with respect to those objects.

Researchers have demonstrated that working memory capacity differs among individuals. They have devised several procedures to measure those differences (Conway et al., 2005). We will give you an example of one of those measures, which is called *operation span* (Turner & Engle, 1989). Take a look at **Table 7.1.** To determine operation span, researchers ask participants to read each math problem aloud and then answer "yes" or "no" to indicate whether the equation was correct. After solving each problem, participants try to memorize the word that comes after it. (In the real version of the test, participants get the words only after they've solved the problems, and they get the problems one at a time.) After completing a whole group of problems, participants try to recall all the words in the correct order. Try to get a feel for the task by working through Table 7.1. Operation span requires people to carry out one task (such as solving math problems) while maintaining a second task (such as remembering words). For that reason, it provides an index of individual differences in the efficiency of the central executive to apportion mental resources to different tasks.

Because working memory span is a measure of the resources individuals have available to carry out short-term

cognitive processes, researchers can use it to predict performance on a variety of tasks. For example, working memory allows individuals to keep their attention focused on the tasks they need to accomplish. In general, the greater the working memory capacity, the more information individuals should be able to keep their minds from wandering.

To demonstrate the relationship between working memory capacity and mind wandering, a team of researchers recruited 124 college undergraduates for a study using experience sampling (Kane et al., 2007). At the start of the experiment, participants all completed measures of working memory capacity similar to the operations span task. In the experiment's next phase, participants carried handheld computers for a week. The computers signaled them eight times each day, between noon and midnight, to fill out a questionnaire. The questionnaires gathered information about the tasks on which the participants had been engaged when the beeps sounded. Participants indicated, for example, how challenging they had found the task at hand. The questionnaires also asked participants to report the extent to which their minds had wandered from each task. For nonchallenging tasks, participants' working memory capacity had no impact on the amount of mind wandering. However, when participants were engaged with challenging tasks, people with higher working memory capacity reported much less mind wandering than people with lower working memory capacity.

Recall that one component of working memory is the central executive. This experiment suggests that people with higher working memory capacity are better able to use that central executive resource: They can keep their attention tightly focused on the challenging tasks for which they need it most.

A final note on working memory: Working memory helps maintain your psychological present. It is what sets a context for new events and links separate episodes together into a continuing story. It enables you to maintain and continually update your representation of a changing situation and to keep track of topics during a conversation. All of this is true because working memory serves as a conduit for information coming and going to long-term memory. Let's turn our attention now to the types of memories that can last a lifetime.

STOP AND REVIEW

❶ Why do researchers believe that the capacity of iconic memory is large?

❷ What is the contemporary estimate of the capacity of short-term memory?

❸ What does it mean to *chunk* some group of items?

❹ What are the components of working memory?

CRITICAL THINKING Recall the study that demonstrated the importance of rehearsal to maintain information in short-term memory. In that study, why were participants asked to count backward by 3s (for example, 167, 164, 161 . . .) rather than by 1s (167, 166, 165 . . .)?

Visit MyPsychLab.com for more review and practice on the following topic:

✴ **Simulate:** Delay and Interference in Short-Term Memory

TABLE 7.1   Sample Items for a Test of Operation Span

Try to answer "yes" or "no" to each math problem and then memorize the words at the end of each problem. Once you're done with all four problems, cover them up and try to recall the four words.

IS $(6 \div 2) - 2 = 2$? SNOW
IS $(8 \times 1) - 5 = 3$? TASTE
IS $(9 \times 2) - 6 = 12$? KNIFE
IS $(8 \div 4) + 3 = 6$? CLOWN

Long-Term Memory: Encoding and Retrieval

How long can memories last? At the chapter's outset, we asked you to recall your own earliest memory. How old is that memory? Fifteen years? Twenty years? Longer? When psychologists speak of *long-term memory,* it is with the knowledge that memories often last a lifetime. Therefore, whatever theory explains how memories are acquired for the long term must also explain how they can remain accessible over the life course. **Long-term memory (LTM)** is the storehouse of all the experiences, events, information, emotions, skills, words, categories, rules, and judgments that have been acquired from sensory and short-term memories. LTM constitutes each person's total knowledge of the world and of the self.

Psychologists know that it is often easier to acquire new long-term information when an important conclusion is stated in advance. With that conclusion in place, you have a framework for understanding the incoming information. For memory, the conclusion we will reach is this: Your ability to remember will be greatest when there is a good match between the circumstances in which you encoded information and the circumstances in which you attempt to retrieve it. We will see over the next several sections what it means to have a "good match."

RETRIEVAL CUES

To begin our exploration between encoding and retrieval, let's consider this general question: How do you "find" a memory? The basic answer is that you use retrieval cues. **Retrieval cues** are the stimuli available as you search for a particular memory. These cues may be provided externally, such as questions on a quiz ("What memory concepts do you associate with the research of Baddeley and Sperling?"), or generated internally ("Where have I met her before?"). Each time you attempt to retrieve an explicit memory, you do so for some purpose, and that purpose often supplies the retrieval cue. It won't surprise you that memories can be easier or harder to retrieve depending on the quality of the retrieval cue. If a friend asks you, "Who's the one Roman emperor I can't remember?" you're likely to be involved in a guessing game. If she asks instead, "Who was the emperor after Claudius?" you can immediately respond "Nero."

To give you a full sense of the importance of retrieval cues, we will attempt to replicate classic memory experiments by asking you to learn some word pairs. Keep working at it until you can go through the six pairs three times in a row without an error.

Apple–Boat
Hat–Bone
Bicycle–Clock
Mouse–Tree
Ball–House
Ear–Blanket

Now that you've committed the pairs to memory, we want to make the test more interesting. We need to do something to give you a *retention interval*—a period of time over which you must keep the information in memory. Let's spend a moment, therefore, discussing some of the procedures we might use to test your memory. You might assume that you either know something or you don't and that any method of testing what you know will give the same results. Not so. Let's consider two tests for explicit memory, recall and recognition.

Recall and Recognition When you **recall,** you reproduce the information to which you were previously exposed. "What are the components of working memory?" is a recall question. **Recognition** refers to the realization that a certain stimulus event is one you have seen or heard before. "Which is the term for a visual sensory memory: (1) echo; (2) chunk; (3) icon; or (4) abstract code?" is a recognition question. You can relate recall and recognition to your day-to-day experiences of explicit memory. When trying to identify a criminal, the police would be using a recall method if they asked the victim to describe, from memory, some of the perpetrator's distinguishing features: "Did you notice anything unusual about the attacker?" They would be using the recognition method if they showed the victim photos, one at a time, from a file of criminal suspects or if they asked the victim to identify the perpetrator in a police lineup.

Let's now use these two procedures to test you on the word pairs you learned a few moments ago. What words finished the pairs?

Hat–?   Bicycle–?   Ear–?

Can you select the correct pair from these possibilities?

Apple–Baby	Mouse–Tree	Ball–House
Apple–Boat	Mouse–Tongue	Ball–Hill
Apple–Bottle	Mouse–Tent	Ball–Horn

Was the recognition test easier than the recall test? It should be. Let's try to explain this result with respect to retrieval cues.

Both recall and recognition require a search using cues. The cues for recognition, however, are much more useful. For recall, you have to hope that the cue alone will help you locate the information. For recognition, part of the work has been done for you. When you look at the pair *Mouse–Tree,* you only have to answer *yes* or *no* to "Did I have this experience?" rather than, in response to *Mouse–?* "What was the experience I had?" In this light, you can see that we made the recognition test reasonably easy for you. Suppose we had given you, instead, recombinations of the original pairs. Which of these are correct?

Hat–Clock   Ear–Boat
Hat–Bone   Ear–Blanket

Now you must recognize not just that you saw the word before, but that you saw it in a particular context. (We will return to the idea of context shortly.) If you are a veteran of difficult multiple-choice exams, you have come to learn how tough even recognition situations can be. However, in most cases, your recognition performance will be better than your recall because retrieval cues are more straightforward for recognition. Let's look at some other aspects of retrieval cues.

---

long-term memory (LTM) Memory processes associated with the preservation of information for retrieval at any later time.

retrieval cue Internally or externally generated stimulus available to help with the retrieval of a memory.

recall A method of retrieval in which an individual is required to reproduce the information previously presented.

recognition A method of retrieval in which an individual is required to identify stimuli as having been experienced before.

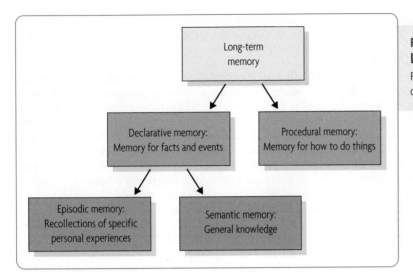

FIGURE 7.6 Dimensions of Long-Term Memory
Researchers have suggested that people store different types of memories.

Episodic and Semantic Memories When we discussed the functions of memories earlier in the chapter, we made a distinction between declarative and procedural memories. We can define another dimension along which declarative memories differ with respect to the cues that are necessary to retrieve them from memory. Canadian psychologist **Endel Tulving** (1972) first proposed the distinction between *episodic* and *semantic* types of declarative memories (see **Figure 7.6**).

Episodic memories preserve, individually, the specific events that you have personally experienced. For example, memories of your happiest birthday or of your first kiss are stored in episodic memory. To recover such memories, you need retrieval cues that specify something about the time at which the event occurred and something about the content of the events. Depending on how the information has been encoded, you may or may not be able to produce a specific memory representation for an event. For example, do you have any specific memories to differentiate the tenth time ago you brushed your teeth from the eleventh time ago?

Everything you know, you began to acquire in some particular context. However, there are large classes of information that, over time, you encounter in many different contexts. These classes of information come to be available for retrieval without reference to their multiple times and places of experience. These **semantic memories** are generic, categorical memories, such as the meanings of words and concepts. For most people, facts like the formula $E = MC^2$ and the capital of France don't require retrieval cues that make reference to the episodes, the original learning contexts, in which the memory was acquired.

Of course, this doesn't mean that your recall of semantic memories is foolproof. You know perfectly well that you can forget many facts that have become dissociated from the contexts in which you learned them. A good strategy when you can't recover a semantic memory is to treat it like an episodic memory again. By thinking to yourself, "I know I learned the names of the Roman emperors in my Western civilization course," you may be able to provide the extra retrieval cues that will shake loose a memory.

CONTEXT AND ENCODING

To continue our exploration of encoding and retrieval, we want you to consider a phenomenon that you might call "context shock." You see someone across a crowded room, and you know that you know the person but you just can't place her. Finally, after staring for longer than is absolutely polite, you remember who it is—and you realize you were having difficulty identifying her because you have never seen her in this particular context. What is the woman who delivers your mail doing at your best friend's party? Whenever you have this type of experience, you have rediscovered the

Events of personal importance, like seeing a good friend for the first time after a year's separation, are retained in *episodic* memory. What types of information from *semantic* memory might contribute to a reunion?

---

episodic memory Long-term memory for an autobiographical event and the context in which it occurred.

semantic memory Generic, categorical memory, such as the meaning of words and concepts.

After receiving a traffic warning from this man, why might you not recognize him if you ran into him at a party?

Why was recall better than recognition? Tulving and Thomson suggested that what mattered was the change in context. After the participants had studied the word *black* in the context of *train*, it was hard to recover the memory representation when the context was changed to *white*. Given the significant effect of even these minimal contexts, you can anticipate that richly organized real-life contexts would have an even greater effect on your memory.

Researchers have provided several remarkable demonstrations of *context-dependent* memory. In one experiment, scuba divers learned lists of words either on a beach or under water. They were then tested for retention of those words, again in one of those two contexts. Performance was nearly 50 percent better when the context at encoding and recall matched—even though the material had nothing at all to do with water or diving (Godden & Baddeley, 1975). Similarly, piano students performed a brief composition more accurately when they played it on the same piano on which they had first learned it (Mishra & Backlin, 2007). In another study, memory performance was improved over the span of four weeks when the same odor—either lemon or lavender—was present at both encoding and recall (Parker et al., 2001).

In each of the examples we have provided so far, memories are encoded with respect to a context in the external environment—for example, the type of piano or an odor in the air. However, encoding specificity also occurs based on people's internal states. For example, in one study participants drank either alcohol or a placebo before the study and test sessions for a free recall task (Weissenborn & Duka, 2000). In general, alcohol impaired memory performance. However, participants who drank alcohol at both study and test were able to retrieve information that eluded participants who drank alcohol at only study or test alone. When internal states provide the basis for encoding specificity, those effects are called *state-dependent memory*. Researchers have demonstrated that state-dependent memory occurs for other drugs such as marijuana and amphetamine. Also, if you take antihistamines for allergies, you might be interested to learn that they lead to state-dependent memory (Carter & Cassaday, 1998). How might you use that information when allergy season roles around?

As a final example of encoding specificity, we want you to consider the experience of individuals who are bilingual and, thus, acquire information in more than one language. Research suggests that memory performance can be strongly *language-dependent:* People find it easier to recall information when the language at encoding matches the language at retrieval.

principle of **encoding specificity:** Memories emerge most efficiently when the context of retrieval matches the context of encoding. Let's see how researchers have demonstrated that principle.

Encoding Specificity What are the consequences of learning information in a particular context? Endel Tulving and Donald Thomson (1973) first demonstrated the power of encoding specificity by reversing the usual performance relationship between recall and recognition.

Participants were asked to learn pairs of words like *train–black,* but they were told that they would be responsible for remembering only the second word of the pair. In a subsequent phase of the experiment, participants were asked to generate four free associates to words like *white.* Those words were chosen so that it was likely that the original to-be-remembered words (like *black*) would be among the associates. The participants were then asked to check off any words on their associates lists that they recognized as to-be-remembered words from the first phase of the experiment. They were able to do so 54 percent of the time. However, when the participants were later given the first words of the pair, like *train,* and asked to recall the associate, they were 61 percent accurate.

Twenty Mandarin–English bilinguals agreed to participate in a study that tested their general world knowledge (Marian & Kaushanskaya, 2007). For one task, the experimenter asked each participant to name four examples from categories such as "tourist attractions" and "famous actors." The questions were posed in either Mandarin or English. Participants' responses demonstrated language dependence: Although they could name, for example, tourist

encoding specificity The principle that subsequent retrieval of information is enhanced if cues received at the time of recall are consistent with those present at the time of encoding.

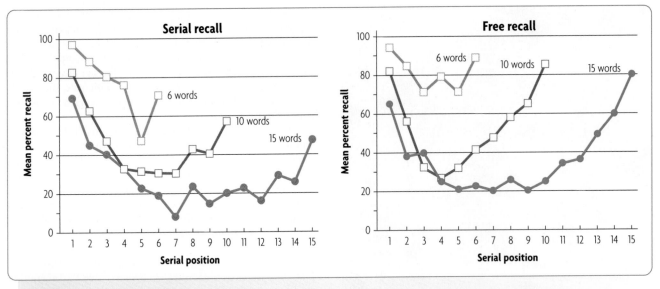

FIGURE 7.7 The Serial Position Effect

This figure shows the generality of the serial position effect. Students were asked to try to remember word lists of varying lengths (6, 10, and 15 words) using either *serial recall* ("Recite the words in the order you heard them") or *free recall* ("Recite as many words as you can"). Each curve shows better memory for both the beginning (the *primacy* effect) and end (the *recency* effect) of the list.

attractions in both China and the United States, they were more likely to provide answers that matched the language in which the experimenter had posed the question. In a second task, participants received questions that each had two possible answers. Consider the question, "In a famous love story, what were the names of two lovers who died because of family disapproval?" The answer can be either *Romeo and Juliet* or *Liang Shanbo and Zhu Yingtai*. Again, the participants' responses showed the impact of the language in which the question was posed: They provided more answers that matched the language of the question.

As you consider these results, recall that all the information is stored in the same brain! What makes the information more or less accessible is the entry point provided by each language. That same conclusion holds true for all these varieties of encoding specificity. It's easiest to find your way back to information when you can reinstate the original context in which you encoded it.

The Serial Position Effect We can also use changes in context to explain one of the classic effects in memory research: the **serial position effect.** Suppose we required you to learn a

list of unrelated words. If we asked you to recall those words in order, your data would almost certainly conform to the pattern shown in **Figure 7.7:** You would do very well on the first few words (the **primacy effect**) and very well on the last few words (the **recency effect**) but rather poorly on the middle part of the list. Figure 7.7 shows the generality of this pattern when students are asked to try to remember word lists of varying lengths (6, 10, and 15 words) using either *serial recall* ("Recite the words in the order you heard them") or *free recall* ("Recite as many words as you can") (Jahnke, 1965). Researchers have found primacy and recency in a wide variety of test situations (Neath & Surprenant, 2003). What day is it today? Do you believe that you would be almost a second faster to answer this question at the beginning or end of the week than in the middle (Koriat & Fischoff, 1974)?

The role context plays in producing the shape of the serial position curve has to do with the **contextual distinctiveness** of different items on a list, different experiences in your life, and so on (Neath et al., 2006). To understand contextual distinctiveness, you can ask the question, "How different were the contexts in which I learned this information from the context in which I will try to recall it?" Let's focus on recency. **Figure 7.8** is a visual representation of distinctiveness. Imagine, in Part A, that you are looking at train tracks. What you can see is that they look as if they clump together at the horizon—even though they are equally spaced apart. We could say that the nearest tracks stand out most—are most distinctive—from your context. Imagine now that you are trying to remember the last 10 movies you've seen. The movies are like the train tracks. Under most circumstances, you should remember the last movie best because you share the most overlapping context with the experience—it is "closest" to the context of your current experiences. This logic

serial position effect A characteristic of memory retrieval in which the recall of beginning and end items on a list is often better than recall of items appearing in the middle.

primacy effect Improved memory for items at the start of a list.

recency effect Improved memory for items at the end of a list.

contextual distinctiveness The assumption that the serial position effect can be altered by the context and the distinctiveness of the experience being recalled.

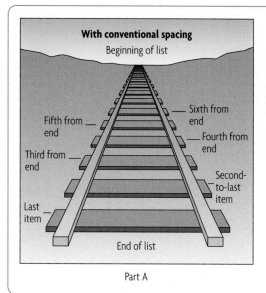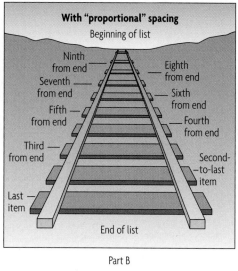

FIGURE 7.8 Contextual Distinctiveness

You can think of items you put into memory as train tracks. In Part A, you can imagine that memories farther back in time become blurred together, just like train tracks in the distance. In Part B, you see that one way to combat this effect is to make the earlier tracks physically farther apart, so the distances look proportional. Similarly, you can make early memories more distinctive by moving them apart psychologically.

suggests that "middle" information will become more memorable if it is made more distinctive. The idea with respect to our analogy, as shown in Part B of Figure 7.8, is to make the train tracks seem equally far apart.

> To make the train tracks seem evenly spaced, engineers would have to make the more distant ones actually be farther apart. Researchers have used the same logic for a memory test, by exploiting the analogy between space and time. They had participants try to learn lists of letters, but they manipulated how far apart in time the letters were made to seem. This manipulation was accomplished by asking participants to read out some number of random digits that appeared on a computer screen between the letters. In the *conventional* condition (like Part A of Figure 7.8), each pair of letters was separated by two digits. In the *proportional* condition (like Part B), the first pair had four digits and the last pair had zero digits; this should have the effect of making the early digits more distinctive, just like moving distant train tracks farther apart. Participants, in fact, showed better memory for early items on the list when those items had been made more separate (Neath & Crowder, 1990).

This experiment suggests that the standard recency effect arises because the last few items are almost automatically distinctive. The same principle may explain primacy—each time you begin something new, your activity establishes a new context. In that new context, the first few experiences are particularly distinctive. Thus you can think of primacy and recency as two views of the same set of train tracks—one from each end!

THE PROCESSES OF ENCODING AND RETRIEVAL

We have seen so far that a match between the context of encoding and of retrieval is beneficial to good memory performance. We will now refine this conclusion somewhat by considering the actual processes that are used to get information to and from long-term memory. We will see that memory functions best when encoding and retrieval processes make a good match as well.

Levels of Processing Let's begin with the idea that the type of processing you perform on information—the type of attention you pay to information at time of encoding—will have an influence on your memory for the information. **Levels-of-processing theory** suggests that the deeper the level at which information was processed, the more likely it is to be committed to memory (Craik & Lockhart, 1972; Lockhart & Craik, 1990). If processing involves more analysis, interpretation, comparison, and elaboration, it should result in better memory.

The depth of processing is often defined by the types of judgments participants are required to make with respect to experimental materials. Consider the word *GRAPE*. We could ask you to make a physical judgment—is the word in capital letters? Or a rhyme judgment—does the word rhyme with *tape*? Or a meaning judgment—does the word represent a type of

---

levels-of-processing theory A theory that suggests that the deeper the level at which information was processed, the more likely it is to be retained in memory.

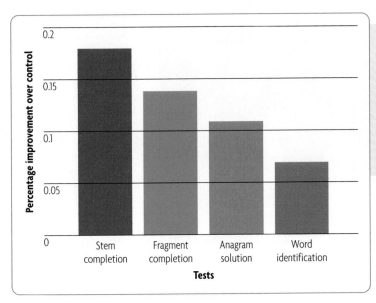

FIGURE 7.9 Priming on Implicit Memory Tests

Priming indicates improvement on the various tasks over performance on control words. Some implicit memory tests demonstrate that priming can last a week or more.

Adapted with permission from Table 1 in "Direct Comparison of Four Implicit Memory Tests" by Suparna Rajaram & H. L. Roediger III.

fruit? Do you see how each of these questions requires you to think a little bit more deeply about *GRAPE?* In fact, the deeper the original processing participants carry out, the more words they remember (Lockhart & Craik, 1990).

A difficulty of the levels-of-processing theory, however, is that researchers have not always been able to specify exactly what makes certain processes "shallow" or "deep." Even so, results of this sort confirm that the way in which information is committed to memory—the mental processes that you use to encode information—has an effect on whether you can retrieve that information later. However, so far we have discussed only explicit memory. We will now see that the match between processes at encoding and retrieval is particularly critical for implicit memory.

Processes and Implicit Memory Earlier, we defined the explicit versus implicit dimension for memories as a distinction that applies both at encoding and at retrieval (Bowers & Marsolek, 2003). Under many circumstances, for example, you will retrieve implicitly memories that you originally encoded explicitly. This is true when you greet your best friend by name without having to expend any particular mental effort. Even so, implicit memories are often most robust when there is a strong match between the processes at implicit encoding and the processes at implicit retrieval. This perspective is called **transfer-appropriate processing:** Memory is best when the type of processing carried out at encoding *transfers* to the processes required at retrieval (Roediger et al., 2002). To support this perspective, we will first describe some of the methodologies that are used to demonstrate implicit memories. Then we will show how the match between encoding and retrieval processes matters.

Let's consider a typical experiment in which implicit memory is assessed. The researchers presented students with

lists of concrete nouns and asked them to judge the pleasantness of each word on a 1 (least pleasant) to 5 (most pleasant) scale (Rajaram & Roediger, 1993). The pleasantness ratings required participants to think about the meaning of a word without explicitly committing it to memory. After this study phase, participants' memory was assessed using one of four implicit memory tasks (suppose that a word on one list was *unicorn*):

- *Word fragment completion.* The participant is given fragments of a word, like ____ *ni____or____*, and asked to complete the fragments with the first word that comes to mind.
- *Word stem completion.* The participant is asked to complete a stem, like *uni____*, with the first word that comes to mind.
- *Word identification.* Words are flashed on a computer screen in such a fashion that participants cannot see them clearly. They must try to guess each word that is flashed. In this case, one of the words would be *unicorn.*
- *Anagrams.* Participants are given a scrambled word, like *corunni,* and asked to give the first unscrambled word that comes to mind.

Just like our example with *unicorn,* correct responses to each of the tasks can be provided by words from the earlier lists. What is critical, however, is that the experimenters have not called attention to the relationship between the words on the earlier list and appropriate responses on these new tasks—that's why the use of memory is implicit.

To assess the degree of implicit memory, the researchers compared the performance of participants who had seen a particular word, like *unicorn,* on the pleasantness lists with those who had not. **Figure 7.9** plots the improvement brought about by implicit memory for a word—percentage correct when the word had appeared on the participant's list minus percentage correct when it had not. (Different participants experienced different word lists.) You can see that for each task there was an advantage to having seen a word before, even though participants had been asked only to say whether the word had a pleasant meaning. This advantage is known as **priming** because the first experience of the word *primes* memory for later experiences. For some memory tasks, like word fragment completion,

---

transfer-appropriate processing The perspective that suggests that memory is best when the type of processing carried out at encoding matches the processes carried out at retrieval.

priming In the assessment of implicit memory, the advantage conferred by prior exposure to a word or situation.

researchers have found priming effects lasting a week and beyond (Sloman et al., 1988).

Let's turn now to the nature of the match between encoding and retrieval. The four implicit memory tests we've mentioned so far all rely on a *physical* match between the original stimulus and the information given at test. In a sense, whatever processes allow you to encode *unicorn* also make that word available when you are asked to complete the stem *uni_____*, and so on. We can, however, introduce another test, *general knowledge,* that relies on *meaning* or *concepts* instead of on a physical match. Imagine we gave you the question, "What mythological creature had a single horn?" You might very well say "unicorn." However, if you became more likely to say unicorn because you had seen the word on an earlier list, in a different context, that would be evidence of implicit memory.

Using two different types of implicit memory tests based on priming—by physical features or by meaning—we can look for a relationship between encoding and retrieval.

> Memory researchers designed a levels-of-processing experiment to demonstrate that different implicit memories rely on different types of processes. Participants were asked to respond to each word on a list. For *deep* judgments, they responded to the words' meanings—for example, "Can you buy this?" For *shallow* judgments, they responded to the words' physical features—for example, "Does this word contain a *c*?" The researchers assessed implicit memory by using general knowledge questions and word fragment completion. Let's examine the tasks with an eye to transfer-appropriate processing. The deep judgments engage conceptual processes at encoding, but the shallow judgments do not. The general knowledge questions engage conceptual processes at retrieval, but word fragment completion does not. Accordingly, the researchers predicted that they should find a priming advantage for deep judgments when processes at encoding and retrieval matched (deep judgments with general knowledge questions) versus when they mismatched (deep judgments with fragment completion). The results confirmed the prediction (Hamilton & Rajaram, 2001).

This type of research supports the idea of transfer-appropriate processing: If you use a certain type of processing—for example, physical or meaning analysis—to encode information, you will retrieve that information most efficiently when the processing uses the same type of analysis.

Earlier we made this assertion: Your ability to remember will be greatest when there is a good match between the circumstances in which you encode information and the circumstances in which you attempt to retrieve it. This section provided the research evidence for this assertion. Note that this analysis defines both when your memory processes will function relatively well (when circumstances of encoding and retrieval match) and when those processes will function relatively less well (when there is a mismatch). In that sense, we've already provided you with some initial ideas about why you might not be capable of retrieving memories when you need them. Let's now look more generally at circumstances in which your memory processes fall short.

WHY WE FORGET

Much of the time, your memory works just fine. You see a new acquaintance walking toward you, and you retrieve his name from memory without hesitation. Unfortunately, every once in a while, you end up greeting him in awkward silence—with that awful realization that you can't remember his name. How does that happen? Sometimes the answer will reside with the forces we've already discussed. It could be the case, for example, that you're trying to recall the name in a context that's very different from the one in which you learned it. However, researchers have studied other explanations for forgetting. In fact, the earliest formal body of research on memory, published in 1885, focused directly on that topic. Let's begin with that work.

Ebbinghaus Quantifies Forgetting See if this statement rings true: "Facts crammed at examination time soon vanish, if they were not sufficiently grounded by other study and later subjected to a sufficient review." In other words, if you cram for a test, you're not likely to remember very much a few days later. This astute observation was made in 1885 by the German psychologist **Hermann Ebbinghaus** (1850–1909), who outlined a series of such phenomena to motivate his new science of memory. Ebbinghaus's observations added up to a convincing argument in favor of an empirical investigation of memory. What was needed was a methodology, and Ebbinghaus invented a brilliant one. Ebbinghaus used nonsense syllables—meaningless three-letter units consisting of a vowel between two consonants, such as *CEG* or *DAX*. He used nonsense syllables, rather than meaningful words, like *DOG*, because he hoped to obtain a "pure" measure of memory—one uncontaminated by previous learning or associations that a person might bring to the experimental memory task. Not only was Ebbinghaus the researcher, he was also his own subject. He performed the research tasks himself and measured his own performance. The task he assigned himself was memorization of lists of varying length. Ebbinghaus chose to use *rote learning,* memorization by mechanical repetition, to perform the task.

Ebbinghaus started his studies by reading through the items one at a time until he finished the list. Then he read through the list again in the same order, and again, until he could recite all the items in the correct order—the *criterion performance.* Then he distracted himself from rehearsing the original list by forcing himself to learn many other lists. After this interval, Ebbinghaus measured his memory by seeing how many trials it took him to *relearn* the original list. If he needed fewer trials to relearn it than he had needed to learn it initially, information had been *saved* from his original study. (This concept should be familiar from Chapter 6. Recall that there is often a savings when animals relearn a conditioned response.)

> For example, if Ebbinghaus took 12 trials to learn a list and 9 trials to relearn it several days later, his savings score for that elapsed time would be 25 percent (12 trials − 9 trials = 3 trials; 3 trials ÷ 12 trials = 0.25, or 25 percent). Using savings as his measure, Ebbinghaus recorded the degree of memory retained after different time intervals. The curve he obtained is shown in **Figure 7.10** on page 212. As you can see, he found a rapid initial loss of memory. In fact, after one hour Ebbinghaus already had to spend half the original time to relearn the list. This initial period of rapid loss was followed by a gradually declining rate of loss.

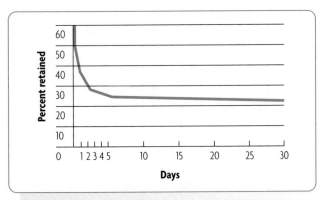

FIGURE 7.10 Ebbinghaus's Forgetting Curve
Ebbinghaus calculated his retention of nonsense syllables over a 30-day period using the savings method. The curve shows rapid forgetting and then reaches a plateau of little change.

You have experienced the pattern revealed in Ebbinghaus's forgetting curve countless times in your life. Consider, for example, how reluctant you'd be to take an exam a week after you studied for it. You know from experience that much of what you learned will no longer be accessible. Similarly, you might find it easy to recall a name right after you've learned it, but if a week goes by when you don't use it, you might find yourself thinking, "I know I knew his name!"

Interference Why else might you forget a name that you knew a week ago? One important answer is that you didn't learn that name in isolation. Before you learned it, you had lots of other names in your head; after you learned it, you probably acquired a few more new ones. All those other names can have a negative impact on your ability to retrieve the one name you need in the moment. To make this point more formally, we want you to try to learn some new word pairs. Once again, keep working on these word pairs until you can repeat them three times in a row without an error.

> Apple–Robe
> Hat–Circle
> Bicycle–Roof
> Mouse–Magazine
> Ball–Baby
> Ear–Penny

How did it go? Examine the list. You can see what we've done—each old prompt is paired with a new response. Was it harder for you to learn these new pairs? Do you think it would now be harder for you to recall the old ones? (Go ahead and try.) The answer in both cases is typically "yes." This brief exercise should give you a sense of how memories can compete—or provide *interference*—with each other.

We have already given you a real-life example of the problem of interference when we asked you to try to differen-

tiate your recollections of your episodes of toothbrushing. All of the specific memories interfere with each other. **Proactive interference** (*proactive* means "forward acting") refers to circumstances in which information you have acquired in the past makes it more difficult to acquire new information (see **Figure 7.11**). **Retroactive interference** (*retroactive* means "backward acting") occurs when the acquisition of new information makes it harder for you to remember older information. The word lists we've provided demonstrate both of these types of interference. You've also experienced both proactive and retroactive interference if you've ever moved and had to change your phone number. At first, you probably found it hard to remember the new number—the old one kept popping out (proactive interference). However, after finally being able to reliably reproduce the new one, you may have found yourself unable to remember the old number—even if you had used it for years (retroactive interference).

As with many other memory phenomena, Hermann Ebbinghaus was the first researcher to document interference rigorously through experiments. Ebbinghaus, after learning dozens of lists of nonsense syllables, found himself forgetting about 65 percent of the new ones he was learning. Fifty years later, students at Northwestern University who studied Ebbinghaus's lists had the same experience—after many trials with many lists, what the students had learned earlier interfered proactively with their recall of current lists (Underwood, 1948, 1949).

In this section, we've suggested some reasons why you might forget information. It seems fitting that we move now to research that gives advice on how to make memory function better.

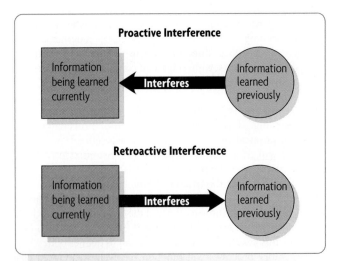

FIGURE 7.11 Proactive and Retroactive Interference
Proactive and retroactive interference help explain why it can be difficult to encode and retrieve memories. What you have learned in the past can make it more difficult for you to encode new information (proactive interference). What you are learning now can make it more difficult for you to retrieve old information (retroactive interference).
From Baron, *Psychology* 5e, © 2001. Reproduced by permission of Pearson Education, Inc.

---

proactive interference Circumstances in which past memories make it more difficult to encode and retrieve new information.

retroactive interference Circumstances in which the formation of new memories makes it more difficult to recover older memories.

IMPROVING MEMORY FOR UNSTRUCTURED INFORMATION

After reading this whole section, you should have some concrete ideas about how you could improve your everyday memory performance—how you can remember more and forget less. (*The Critical Thinking in Your Life* box, later in the chapter, will help you solidify those ideas with respect to school work.) You know, especially, that you're best off trying to recover a piece of information in the same context, or by performing the same types of mental tasks, as when you first acquired it. But there's a slightly different problem with which we still must give you some help. It has to do with encoding unstructured or arbitrary collections of information.

For example, imagine that you are working as a clerk in a store. You must try to commit to memory the several items that each customer wants: "The woman in the green blouse wants hedge clippers and a garden hose. The man in the blue shirt wants a pair of pliers, six quarter-inch screws, and a paint scraper." This scenario, in fact, comes very close to the types of experiments in which researchers ask you to memorize paired associates. How did you go about learning the word pairs we presented earlier? The task probably was somewhat of a chore because the pairs were not particularly meaningful for you—and information that isn't meaningful is hard to remember. To find a way to get the right items to the right customer, you need to make associations seem less arbitrary. Let's explore *elaborative rehearsal* and *mnemonics*.

Elaborative Rehearsal A general strategy for improving encoding is called **elaborative rehearsal.** The basic idea of this technique is that while you are rehearsing information—while you are first committing it to memory—you elaborate on the material to enrich the encoding. One way to do this is to invent a relationship that makes an association seem less arbitrary. For example, if you wanted to remember the pair *Mouse–Tree,* you might conjure up an image of a mouse scurrying up a tree to look for cheese. Recall is enhanced when you encode separate bits of information into this type of miniature story line. Can you imagine, in the clerk situation, swiftly making up a story to link each customer with the appropriate items? (It will work with practice.) You may have already guessed that it is also often helpful to supplement your story line with a mental picture—a visual image—of the scene you are trying to remember. Visual imagery can enhance your recall because it gives you codes for both verbal and visual memories simultaneously (Paivio, 2006).

Elaborative rehearsal can also help save you from what has been called the *next-in-line effect:* When, for example, people are next in line to speak, they often can't remember what the person directly before them said. If you've ever had a circle of people each give his or her name, you're probably well acquainted with this effect. What was the name of the person directly in front of you? The origin of this effect appears to be a shift in attention toward preparing to make your own remarks or to say your own name (Bond et al., 1991). To counter this shift, you should use elaborative rehearsal. Keep your attention focused on the person in front of you and enrich your encoding of his or her name: *Deb—I'm caught in her web!*

Mnemonics Another memory-enhancing option is to draw on special mental strategies called *mnemonics* (from the Greek word meaning "to remember"). **Mnemonics** are devices that

How might a server use elaborative rehearsal or mnemonics to get the right meals to the right customers?

encode a long series of facts by associating them with familiar and previously encoded information. Many mnemonics work by giving you ready-made retrieval cues that help organize otherwise arbitrary information. These mnemonics also encourage you to use visual imagery which, as we noted earlier, provides effective elaboration as you rehearse new information.

Consider the *method of loci*, first practiced by ancient Greek orators. The singular of *loci* is *locus*, and it means "place." The method of loci is a means of remembering the order of a list of names or objects—or, for the orators, the individual sections of a long speech—by associating them with some sequence of places with which you are familiar. To remember a grocery list, you might mentally put each item sequentially along the route you take to get from home to school. To remember the list later, you mentally go through your route and find the item associated with each spot (see **Figure 7.12** on page 214).

The *peg-word method* is similar to the method of loci, except that you associate the items on a list with a series of cues rather than with familiar locations. Typically, the cues for the peg-word method are a series of rhymes that associate numbers with words. For example, you might memorize "one is a *bun,*" "two is a *shoe,*" "three is a *tree,*" and so on. Then you would associate each item on your list interacting with the appropriate cue. Suppose a history professor asked you to memorize, in order, the rulers of the Roman empire. You might have Augustus eating a platter of buns, Tiberius wearing oversized shoes, Caligula sitting in a tree, and so on. You can see that the key to learning arbitrary information is to encode the information in such a fashion that you provide yourself with efficient retrieval cues.

METAMEMORY

Suppose you're in a situation in which you'd really like to remember something. You're doing your best to use retrieval cues that reflect the circumstances of encoding, but you just

---

elaborative rehearsal A technique for improving memory by enriching the encoding of information.

mnemonic Strategy or device that uses familiar information during the encoding of new information to enhance subsequent access to the information in memory.

Bread

Orange juice

Ice cream

Bananas

FIGURE 7.12   The Method of Loci

In the method of loci, you associate the items you wish to remember (such as the items on a grocery list) with locations along a familiar path (such as your route to and from school).

can't get the bit of information to emerge. Part of the reason you're expending so much effort is that you're sure that you are in possession of the information. But are you correct to be so confident about the contents of your memory? Questions like this one—about how your memory works or how you know what information you possess—are questions of **metamemory.** One major question on metamemory has been when and why *feelings-of-knowing*—the subjective sensations that you do have information stored in memory—are accurate.

Research on feelings-of-knowing was pioneered by **J. T. Hart** (1965), who began his studies by asking students a series of general knowledge questions. Suppose, for example, we asked you, "What planet is the largest in our solar system?" Do you know the answer? If you don't, how would you respond to this question: "Even though I don't remember the answer now, do I know the answer to the extent that I could pick the correct answer from among several wrong answers?" This was the question Hart put to his participants. He allowed them to give ratings from 1, to say they were quite sure they wouldn't

choose correctly on the multiple choice, to 6, to say they were quite sure they would choose correctly. What would your rating be? Now here are your alternatives:

a.   Mars
b.   Venus
c.   Earth
d.   Jupiter

If you made an accurate feeling-of-knowing judgment, you should have been less likely to get the correct answer, d, if you gave a 1 rating than if you gave a 6. (Of course, to have a fair test, we'd want to give you a long series of questions.) Hart found that when participants gave 1 ratings, they answered the questions correctly only 30 percent of the time, whereas 6 ratings predicted 75 percent success. That's pretty impressive evidence that feelings-of-knowing can be accurate.

Research on metamemory focuses on both the processes that give rise to feelings-of-knowing and on how their accuracy is ensured (Benjamin, 2005; Koriat & Levy-Sadot, 2001; Metcalfe, 2000):

• The *cue familiarity hypothesis* suggests that people base their feelings-of-knowing on their familiarity with the

---

metamemory Implicit or explicit knowledge about memory abilities and effective memory strategies; cognition about memory.

Critical Thinking in Your Life

HOW CAN MEMORY RESEARCH HELP YOU PREPARE FOR EXAMS?

One important use of critical thinking is to apply new knowledge to your life's important tasks. As you read about memory, you should ask yourself questions of this sort: "How can I put the information to immediate use? How will this research help me prepare for my next exam?" Let's see what advice can be generated from this type of critical thinking:

- *Encoding specificity.* As you'll recall, the principle of encoding specificity suggests that the context of retrieval should match the context of encoding. In school settings, "context" often will mean "the context of other information." If you always study material in the same context, you may find it difficult to retrieve it in a different context—so, if a professor's questions approach a topic in a slightly unusual way, you might be entirely at a loss. As a remedy, you should change contexts even while you study. Rearrange the order of your notes. Ask yourself questions that mix different topics together. Try to make your own novel combinations. But if you get stuck while you're taking an exam, try to generate as many retrieval cues as you can that reinstate the original context: "Let's see. We heard about this in the same lecture we learned about short-term memory. . . ."

- *Serial position.* You know from the serial position curve that, under very broad circumstances, information presented in the "middle" is least well remembered. In fact, college students fail more exam items on material from the middle of a lecture than on material from the start or end of the lecture (Holen & Oaster, 1976; Jensen, 1962). When you're listening to a lecture, you should remind yourself to pay special attention in the middle of the session. When it comes time to study, you should devote some extra time and effort to that material—and make sure not to study the material in the same order each time. You might also note that the chapter you're reading now is about at the middle of *Psychology and Life*. If you have a final examination that covers all the course material, you're going to want to make an especially careful review of this chapter.

- *Elaborative rehearsal and mnemonics.* Sometimes when you study for exams, you will feel as if you are trying to acquire "unstructured information." You might, for example, be asked to memorize the functions of different parts of the brain. Under these circumstances, you need to find ways to provide the structure yourself. Try to form visual images or make up sentences or stories that use the concepts in creative ways. One of your authors still remembers his mnemonic from introductory psychology to remember the function of the *ventromedial hypothalamus*, which is often abbreviated VMH: Very Much Hungry (however, as you will learn in Chapter 11, research in the 30 intervening years has made that mnemonic less accurate). Elaborative rehearsal allows you to use what you know already to make new material more memorable.

- *Metamemory.* Research on metamemory suggests that people generally have good intuitions about what they know and what they don't know. If you are in an exam situation in which there is time pressure, you should allow those intuitions to guide how you allocate your time. You might, for example, read the whole test over quickly and see which questions give you the strongest feelings-of-knowing. If you are taking an exam on which you lose points for giving wrong answers (which happens, for example, on SAT and some GRE exams), you should be particularly attentive to your metamemory intuitions, so you can avoid answering those questions on which you "sense" you are most likely to be incorrect.

As you read the basic facts from memory research, you might not have immediately seen how to put the information to use. We've given you these concrete ideas so you can see how critical thinking will allow you to apply psychological knowledge directly to your life.

- Why might it be a good idea to shuffle your notes before you study for an exam?

- What could a professor do to help students overcome the impact of serial position on lecture material?

---

retrieval cue. Suppose you were asked, "Who played Han Solo in the first *Star Wars* movie?" If you have prior familiarity with *Star Wars* you might think that you probably would be able to recognize the correct alternative when given the multiple choice.
- The *accessibility hypothesis* suggests that people base their judgments on the accessibility, or availability, of partial information from memory. Thus, if the question "Who

played Han Solo in the first *Star Wars* movie?" calls quite easily to mind information you believe to be related to the correct answer, you are likely to think that you will be able to recognize the correct answer as well.

Both of these theories have obtained empirical support—and both suggest that you can generally trust your instincts when you believe that you know something. (Later in the chapter, we will describe research on eyewitness testimony, which provides some exceptions to this general rule.)

You have now learned quite a bit about how you get information in and out of memory. You know what we mean by a "good match" between the circumstances of encoding and of retrieval. In the next section, we will shift our focus from your memory processes to the content of your memories.

STOP AND REVIEW

❶ Do circumstances of recall or recognition generally provide more retrieval cues?

❷ At a party, why might you have the best recall of the first person to whom you spoke?

❸ What does the perspective known as transfer-appropriate processing suggest?

❹ For your English class, you memorize "The Raven." When you're done, you can no longer recite last week's assignment. Is this an example of proactive or retroactive interference?

❺ How could you use the method of loci to remember the order of elements in the periodic table?

❻ What two types of information contribute to feelings of knowing?

CRITICAL THINKING Recall the experiment that tested Mandarin–English bilinguals. What would you expect to find if you tested the participants' episodic memories?

Visit MyPsychLab.com for more review and practice on the following topic:

✳ **Simulate:** Serial Position Effect

Structures in Long-Term Memory

We have focused so far on how you encode and later retrieve information from memory. In this section we focus on an important aspect of memory storage: the way in which the information you acquire over time becomes represented in large bodies of *organized knowledge*. Recall, for example, that we asked you to consider whether *grape* is a fruit. You could say *yes* very quickly. How about *porcupine*? Is it a fruit? How about *tomato*? In this section, we will examine how the difficulty of these types of judgments relates to the way information is structured in memory. We will also discuss how memory organization allows you to make a best guess at the content of experiences you can't remember exactly.

MEMORY STRUCTURES

An essential function of memory is to draw together similar experiences, to enable you to discover patterns in your interactions with the environment. You live in a world filled with countless individual events, from which you must continually extract information to combine them into a smaller, simpler set

that you can manage mentally. But apparently you don't need to expend any particular conscious effort to find structure in the world. Just as we suggested when we defined the implicit acquisition of memories, it's unlikely that you ever formally thought to yourself something like, "Here's what belongs in a kitchen." It is through ordinary experience in the world that you have acquired mental structures to mirror environmental structures. Let's look at the types of memory structures you have formed in your moment-by-moment experience of the world.

Categories and Concepts We will begin by previewing one of the topics we will discuss in Chapter 10—the mental effort a child must go through to acquire the meaning of a word, such as *doggie*. For this word to have meaning, the child must be able to store each instance in which the word *doggie* is used, as well as information about the context. In this way, the child finds out what common core experience—a furry creature with four legs—is meant by *doggie*. The child must acquire the knowledge that *doggie* applies not just to one particular animal, but to a *whole category* of creatures. This ability to categorize individual experiences—to take the same action toward them or give them the same label—is one of the most basic abilities of thinking organisms (Murphy, 2002).

The mental representations of the categories you form are called **concepts.** The concept *doggie*, for example, names the set of mental representations of experiences of dogs that a young child has gathered together in memory. (As we will see in Chapter 10, if the child hasn't yet refined his or her meaning for *doggie*, the concept might also include features that adults wouldn't consider to be appropriate.) You have acquired a vast array of concepts. You have categories for *objects* and *activities*, such as *barns* and *baseball*. Concepts may also represent *properties*, such as *red* or *large; abstract ideas*, such as *truth* or *love*; and *relations*, such as *smarter than* or *sister of*. Each concept represents a summary unit for your experience of the world.

As you consider the many categories you experience in the world, you will recognize that some category members are more or less typical. You can develop this intuition if you think about a category like *bird*. You would probably agree that a robin is a typical bird, whereas an ostrich or a penguin is atypical. The degree of typicality of a category member has real-life

How does the formation of categories—such as what constitutes a healthy head of lettuce, a sweet melon, or a flavorful tomato—help you make daily decisions like what to buy for dinner?

---

concept Mental representation of a kind or category of items and ideas.

consequences. Classic research has shown, for example, that people respond more quickly to typical members of a category than to its more unusual ones. Your reaction time to determine that a robin is a bird would be quicker than your reaction time to determine that an ostrich is a bird (Rosch et al., 1976). But what makes people consider a robin to be a typical bird, rather than an ostrich? Answers to this question have often focused on *family resemblance*—typical category members have attributes that overlap with many other members of the category (Rosch & Mervis, 1975). Robins have most of the attributes you associate with birds—they are about the right size, they fly, and so on. Ostriches, by contrast, are unusually large, and they do not fly. These examples suggest that family resemblance plays a role in judgments of typicality. However, recent research suggests that the most typical category members are also the *ideal* category members.

A team of researchers recruited individuals from two communities who had several decades of fishing experience: One group was Native American Menominee Indians from northern central Wisconsin; the second group was European Americans from roughly the same geographical location (Burnett et al., 2005). The experiment used these two groups because they differ with respect to the species of fish they consider to be most desirable or ideal. For example, the Menominee people consider sturgeon to be sacred. The researchers presented the participants with a group of 44 cards printed with the names of local fish. Participants sorted these cards into groups—the researchers used the participants' verbal justifications (for example, "good eating") for which fish they grouped together as an index of desirability. Also, the participants rated the extent to which each species was a good example of the "fish" category. The researchers found a 0.80 correlation between desirability and typicality. (Recall from Chapter 2 that correlations range from −1.0 to +1.0.) That's impressive evidence that the participants' notions of the "ideal" fish played a role in their judgments of typicality. In addition, the ratings were influenced by cultural differences in desirability. For example, the Menominee group rated sturgeon as even more typical than did the European American group.

If you don't have a lot of fishing experience, you might have less of a sense than these participants did about which fish are desirable. However, you can think about categories with which you have a lot of experience to see how your notions of what is ideal inform your judgments about what is typical.

Hierarchies and Basic Levels Concepts do not exist in isolation. As shown in **Figure 7.13**, concepts can often be arranged into meaningful organizations. A broad category like *animal* has several subcategories, such as *bird* and *fish*, which in turn contain exemplars such as *canary, ostrich, shark,* and *salmon.* The animal category is itself a subcategory of the still larger category of *living beings.* Concepts are also linked to other types of information: You store the knowledge that some birds are *edible*, some are *endangered*, some are *national symbols.*

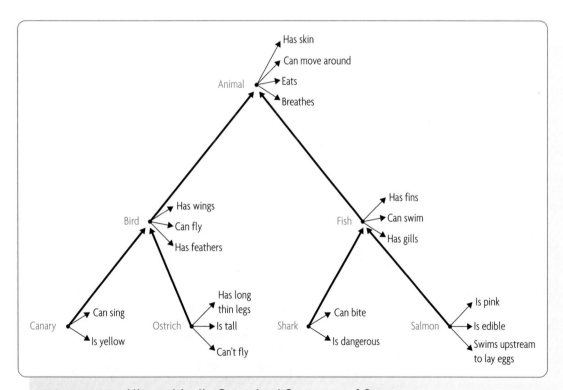

FIGURE 7.13 Hierarchically Organized Structure of Concepts
The category *animal* can be divided into subcategories such as *bird* and *fish;* similarly, each subcategory can be further divided. Some information (such as *"has skin"*) applies to all concepts in the hierarchy; other information (such as *"can sing"*) applies only to concepts at lower levels (for example, a *canary*).

There seems to be a level in such hierarchies at which people best categorize and think about objects. This has been called the **basic level** (Rosch, 1973, 1978). For example, when you buy an apple at the grocery store, you could think of it as a *piece of fruit*—but that seems imprecise—or a *Golden Delicious*—but that seems too specific or narrow. The basic level is just *apple*. If you were shown a picture of such an object, that's what you'd be likely to call it. You would also be faster to say that it was an apple than that it was a piece of fruit (Rosch, 1978). The basic level emerges through your experience of the world. You are more likely to encounter the term *apple* than its more or less specific alternatives. If you became an apple grower, however, you might find yourself having daily conversations about *Cortlands* or *Granny Smiths*. With those experiences, your basic level would probably shift lower in the hierarchy.

Schemas We have seen that concepts are the building blocks of memory hierarchies. They also serve as building blocks for more complex mental structures. Recall Figure 7.1 on page 197. Why did you instantly know that the rabbit didn't belong in the kitchen? We suggested earlier that this judgment relied on implicit memory—but we didn't say what type of memory structure you were using. Clearly, what you need is some representation in memory that combines the individual concepts of a kitchen—your knowledge about ovens, sinks, and refrigerators—into a larger unit. We call that larger unit a schema. **Schemas** are conceptual frameworks, or clusters of knowledge, regarding objects, people, and situations. Schemas are "knowledge packages" that encode complex generalizations about your experience of the structure of the environment. You have schemas for kitchens and bedrooms, race car drivers and professors, surprise parties and graduations. In later chapters, we'll provide more illustrations of the types of schemas that shape your day-to-day experiences. For example, in Chapter 10, we'll see that the attachment relationships children form with their parents provide schemas for later social interactions. In Chapter 13, we'll see that you possess a *self-schema*—a memory structure that allows you to organize information about yourself.

One thing you may have guessed is that your schemas do not include all the individual details of all your varied experiences. A schema represents your average experience of situations in the environment. Thus your schemas are not permanent but shift with your changing life events. Your schemas also include only those details in the world to which you have devoted sufficient attention. For example, when asked to draw the information on the head sides of U.S. coins, college students virtually never filled in the word *Liberty*, although it appears on every coin (Rubin & Kontis, 1983). Check a coin! Thus your schemas provide an accurate reflection of what you've *noticed* about the world. Let's now look at all the ways in which you use your concepts and schemas.

Using Memory Representations Let's consider some instances of memory structures in action. To begin, consider

the picture in Part A of **Figure 7.14.** What is it? Although we purposefully chose an unusual member of the category, you probably reached the conclusion "It's a chair" with reasonable ease. However, to do so, you needed to draw on your memory representations of members of that category. You can say "It's a chair" because the object in the figure calls to mind your past experiences of chairs.

Researchers have provided two theories of how people use concepts in memory to categorize the objects they encounter in the world. One theory suggests that, for each concept in memory, you encode a **prototype**—a representation of the most central or average member of a category (Rosch, 1978). On this view, you recognize objects by comparing them to prototypes in memory. Because the picture in Part A of Figure 7.14 matches many of the important attributes of the prototype in Part B, you can recognize the picture as a chair.

An alternative theory suggests that people retain memories of the many different **exemplars** they experience for each category. In Part C of Figure 7.14, we give you a subset of the exemplars of chairs you might have seen. On the exemplar view, you recognize an object by comparing it to the exemplars you have stored in memory. You recognize the picture as a chair because it is similar to several of those exemplars. Researchers have conducted a large number of studies to contrast prototype and exemplar accounts of categorization. The data largely support the exemplar view: People appear to categorize the objects they encounter by comparing them to multiple representations in memory (Nosofsky & Stanton, 2005; Voorspoels et al., 2008).

We intended the picture in Figure 7.14 to be an unusual chair but clearly a chair nonetheless. However, as we saw in Chapter 4, sometimes the world provides ambiguous stimuli—and you use prior knowledge to help interpret those stimuli. Do you remember **Figure 7.15?** Do you see a duck or a rabbit? Let's suppose we give you the expectation that you're going to see a duck. If you match the features of the picture against the features of a duck present in exemplars in memory, you're likely to be reasonably content. The same thing would happen if we told you to expect a rabbit. You use information from memory to generate—and confirm—expectations.

As we've previously noted, memory representations also allow you to understand when something is unusual in the world. That's why you could quickly notice the anomalous rabbit in the center of Figure 7.1. Because the rabbit is inconsistent with your kitchen schema, you'd also be particularly likely to remember seeing it in the picture. That claim is supported by a study in which researchers filled a graduate student office with both typical objects (such as notebook, pencil) and atypical objects (such as harmonica, toothbrush) (Lampinen et al., 2001). Participants spent 1 minute in the room. Later in the experiment, the participants indicated which items on a list had been present in the room. Their memory was consistently more accurate for the atypical items than for the typical items. This study illustrates how memory structures direct your attention to unusual aspects of a scene.

Taken together, these examples demonstrate that the availability of memory representations influences the way you think about the world. Your past experiences color your present experiences and provide expectations for the future. You will see shortly that, for much the same reasons, concepts and schemas can sometimes work against accurate memory.

---

basic level The level of categorization that can be retrieved from memory most quickly and used most efficiently.

schema General conceptual framework, or cluster of knowledge, regarding objects, people, and situations; knowledge package that encodes generalizations about the structure of the environment.

prototype The most representative example of a category.

exemplar Member of a category that people have encountered.

FIGURE 7.14   Theories of Categorization
A. What is this unusual object? B. One theory suggests that you categorize this object as
a chair by comparing it to a single prototype stored in memory. C. An alternative theory suggests
that you categorize this object by comparing it to the many exemplars you have in memory.

REMEMBERING AS A RECONSTRUCTIVE PROCESS

Let's turn now to another important way in which you use memory structures. In many cases, when you are asked to remember a piece of information, you can't remember the information directly. Instead, you *reconstruct* the information based on more general types of stored knowledge. To experience **reconstructive memory,** consider this trio of questions:

- Did Chapter 3 have the word *the* in it?
- Did 1991 contain the day July 7?
- Did you breathe yesterday between 2:05 and 2:10 P.M.?

You probably were willing to answer "Yes!" to each of these questions without much hesitation, but you almost certainly don't have specific, episodic memories to help you (unless, of course, something happened to fix these events in memory—perhaps July 7 is your birthday or you crossed out all the *the*'s in Chapter 3 to curb your boredom). To answer these questions, you must use more general memories to reconstruct what is likely to have happened. Let's examine this process of reconstruction in a bit more detail.

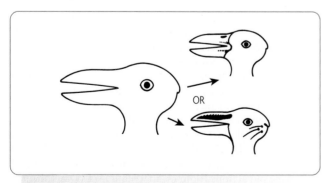

FIGURE 7.15   Recognition Illusion
Duck or rabbit?

---

reconstructive memory The process of putting information together
based on general types of stored knowledge in the absence of a specific
memory representation.

The Accuracy of Reconstructive Memory If people reconstruct some memories, rather than recovering a specific memory representation for what happened, then you might expect that you could find occasions on which the reconstructed memory differed from the real occurrence—distortions. One of the most impressive demonstrations of memory distortions is also the oldest. In his classic book *Remembering: A Study in Experimental and Social Psychology* (1932), **Sir Frederic Bartlett** (1886–1969) undertook a program of research to demonstrate how individuals' prior knowledge influenced the way they remembered new information. Bartlett studied the way British undergraduates remembered stories whose themes and wording were taken from another culture. His most famous story was "The War of the Ghosts," an American Indian tale.

Bartlett found that his readers' reproductions of the story were often greatly altered from the original. The distortions Bartlett found involved three kinds of reconstructive processes:

- *Leveling*—simplifying the story.
- *Sharpening*—highlighting and overemphasizing certain details.
- *Assimilating*—changing the details to better fit the participant's own background or knowledge.

Thus readers reproduced the story with words familiar in their culture taking the place of those unfamiliar: *Boat* might replace *canoe* and *go fishing* might replace *hunt seals*. Bartlett's participants also often changed the story's plot to eliminate references to supernatural forces that were unfamiliar in their culture.

Following Bartlett's lead, contemporary researchers have demonstrated a variety of memory distortions that occur when people use constructive processes to reproduce memories (Bergman & Roediger, 1999). How, for example, do you remember what you did as a child? Participants in one experiment were asked to indicate whether, before the age of 10, they had "Met and shook hands with a favorite TV character at a theme resort" (Braun et al., 2002, p. 7). After answering that question—as part of a larger life-experiences inventory—some of the participants read an advertisement for Disneyland that evoked the idea of a family visit: "Go back to your childhood . . . and remember the characters of your youth, Mickey, Goofy, and Daffy Duck." Later the ad described circumstances in which the visitor was able to shake hands with a childhood hero: "Bugs Bunny, the character you've idolized on TV, is only several feet away. . . . You [reach up] to grab his hand" (p. 6). After reading this type of ad, participants were now more likely to indicate—though they hadn't before—that they shook a character's hand. Moreover, they were more likely to report a specific memory that they had shaken Bugs Bunny's hand at Disneyland: Sixteen percent of the participants in this advertisement group remembered having done so versus 7 percent of the participants in a group that hadn't read the autobiographical ad. Of course, none of these memories can be accurate: Bugs Bunny isn't a Disney character!

This study suggests how even memories for your own life events are reconstructed from various sources. The study also illustrates the fact that people are not always accurate at recalling the original sources for various components of their memories (Mitchell & Johnson, 2000). In fact, researchers have demonstrated that individuals will sometimes come to believe that they actually carried out actions that they, in fact, only accomplished in their imaginations.

Suppose, while you were at this party, someone told you the man on your left was a millionaire. How would this affect your memories for his actions at the party? What if you had been told he only had delusions of being a millionaire?

A group of 40 college students participated in an experiment that had three sessions. In session 1, the students joined an experimenter for a one-hour walk around campus. The pair stopped 48 times during the walk. At each stop, the experimenter read an action statement such as "Check the Pepsi machine for change." After hearing each statement, the students did one of four things: They performed the actions themselves, they watched the experimenter perform the actions, they imagined that they were performing the actions, or they imagined that the experimenter was performing them. In addition, half the actions were bizarre. For example, rather than "Check the Pepsi machine for change," half the students got "Get down on one knee and propose marriage to the machine." The experimenter and the participants took a second walk during session 2, which took place 24 hours later. On the second walk, the students imagined themselves or the experimenter performing some new and some old actions (both ordinary and bizarre) at locations that were also divided between new and old. In session 3, which took place two weeks after session 2, the students were asked to think back to the first session. They tried to recall whether each action had been performed or imagined. For both ordinary and bizarre actions, the same finding held true: Students often recalled that the actions they had only been asked to imagine had actually been performed by them or the experimenter. Thus, some participants agreed that they had actually proposed marriage to a Pepsi machine or patted a dictionary to ask how it was doing when they had only imagined doing so (Seamon et al., 2006).

Can you find applications of this result in your own life? Suppose you keep reminding yourself to set your alarm clock before you go to bed. Each time you remind yourself, you form a picture in your head of the steps you must go through. If you imagine setting the clock often enough, you might mistakenly come to believe that you actually did so!

It is important to keep in mind, however, that just as in Chapter 4, when we discussed perceptual illusions, psychologists often infer the normal operation of processes by demonstrating circumstances in which the processes lead to errors. You can think of these memory distortions as the consequences of processes that usually work pretty well. In fact, a lot of the time, you don't need to remember the exact details of a particular episode. Reconstructing the gist of events will serve just fine.

Flashbulb Memories For most of your past life experiences, you would probably agree that you need to reconstruct the memories. For example, if we asked you to tell us how you celebrated your birthday three years ago, you'd likely count backwards and try to reconstruct the context. However, there are some circumstances in which people believe that their memories remain completely faithful to the original events. These types of memories—which are called **flashbulb memories**—arise when people experience emotionally charged events: People's memories are so vivid that they seem almost to be photographs of the original incident. The first research on flashbulb memories focused on people's recollections of public events (Brown & Kulik, 1977). For example, the researchers asked participants if they had specific memories of how they first learned about the assassination of President John F. Kennedy. All but one of the 80 participants reported vivid recollections.

The concept of flashbulb memory applies to both private and public events. People might have vivid memories, for example, of an accident they experienced or how they learned about the September 11 attacks. However, research on flashbulb memories has largely focused on public events. To conduct these studies, researchers recruit participants and ask them to share their memories of emotionally resonant events. For different age groups, such events might be the *Challenger* explosion, the death of Princess Diana, or the attack on Pearl Harbor. The content of flashbulb memories reflects how people learned about the events. For example, people who acquired their information from the media tend to include more event facts in their memory reports than do people who acquired information from another individual (Bohannon et al., 2007). U.S. citizens had more specific recollections of the September 11 attacks than did citizens of other countries such as Italy, the Netherlands, and Japan (Curci & Luminet, 2006).

Research on these public events confirms that people acquire flashbulb memories. The question remains, however, whether these memories are as accurate as people believe them to be. To address the question of accuracy, researchers recruit participants directly after the events and then assess their mem-

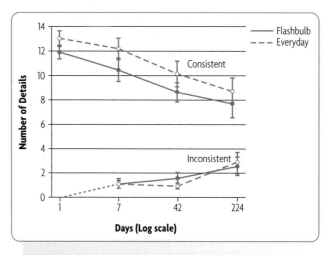

FIGURE 7.16 Students' Recall of Flashbulb and Everyday Memories

On September 12, 2001, students reported details of their memories of the September 11 attack as well as an everyday memory that occurred in the few days preceding that event. When they were tested for the memories 1, 6, or 32 weeks later, the students' performance was highly similar for both types of memories. Over time, they reported fewer details consistent with their first reports and more details that were inconsistent.

From J.M. Talarico & D.C. Rubin (2003). Confidence, not consistency, characterizes flashbulb memories. *Psychological Science, 14,* pp. 445–461. Reprinted with permission of Wiley-Blackwell.

ories at one or more points later in time. One such study began on September 12, 2001.

The day after the September 11 attacks, students provided answers to a series of questions, including "Where were you when you first heard the news?" and "Were there others with you and, if so, who?" (Talarico & Rubin, 2003). For purposes of comparison, the students also reported memories for an everyday event (such as a party or sporting event) that occurred in the few days before the attack. The students answered the same types of questions for those everyday memories (for example, "Where were you physically?" and "Were there others present and, if so, who?"). The researchers called the students back to the laboratory 1, 6, or 32 weeks after the initial memory test. At each delay, the students answered the same series of memory questions they had answered on September 12. The researchers determined which details were consistent with the original reports and which were inconsistent. As you can see in **Figure 7.16,** there were no differences between September 11 memories and everyday memories. The students recalled consistent details and introduced inconsistent details at nearly the same rate for both types of memories.

The researchers extended their project by inviting the original participants for another memory test after a full year had passed (Talarico & Rubin, 2007). The conclusions remained the

---

flashbulb memory People's vivid and richly detailed memory in response to personal or public events that have great emotional significance.

same: In a pattern that was quite similar for both types of memories, the participants' ability to provide correct details decreased, whereas their tendency to introduce incorrect details increased. There was, however, one feature that set flashbulb memories apart from everyday memories: For their flashbulb memories, participants were considerably more confident that they were providing accurate memories.

That final result indicates why it is often difficult for people to accept the results of research on flashbulb memories. How could memories that feel so vivid and true actually be inaccurate (or, at least, be no more accurate than other less vivid memories)? The same processes of reconstruction we discussed earlier apply to flashbulb memories. However, people's desire to hold tight to their memories for particularly emotional events makes it quite difficult for them to consider the possibility that those memories might not be accurate.

We turn now to a domain in which people's overconfidence in their memories can have negative real-world consequences. In the domain of eyewitness testimony, people are always held responsible for reporting *exactly* what happened.

Eyewitness Memory A witness in a courtroom swears "to tell the truth and nothing but the truth." Throughout this chapter, however, we have seen that whether a memory is accurate or inaccurate depends on the care with which it was encoded and the match of the circumstances of encoding and retrieval. Consider the cartoon of a crowd scene we asked you to examine earlier in the chapter. Without looking back, try to write down or think through as much as you can about the scene. Now turn back to p. 200. How did you do? Was everything you recalled accurate? Because researchers understand that people may not be able to report "the truth," even when they genuinely wish to do so, they have focused a good deal of attention on the topic of *eyewitness memory*. The goal is to help the legal system discover the best methods for ensuring the accuracy of witnesses' memories.

Influential studies on eyewitness memory were carried out by **Elizabeth Loftus** (1979; Wells & Loftus, 2003) and her colleagues. The general conclusion from their research was that eyewitnesses' memories for what they had seen were quite vulnerable to distortion from *postevent information*. For example, participants in one study were shown a film of an automobile accident and were asked to estimate the speeds of the cars involved (Loftus & Palmer, 1974). However, some participants were asked, "How fast were the cars going when they smashed into each other?" while others were asked, "How fast were the cars going when they contacted each other?" *Smash* participants estimated the cars' speed to have been over 40 miles per hour; *contact* participants estimated the speed at 30 miles per hour. About a week later, all the eyewitnesses were asked, "Did you see any broken glass?" In fact, no broken glass had appeared in the film. However, about a third of the *smash* participants reported that there had been glass, whereas only 14 percent of the *contact* eyewitnesses did so. Thus postevent information had a substantial effect on what eyewitnesses reported they had experienced.

This experiment represents what is probably the real-life experience of most eyewitnesses: After the events, they have a lot of opportunities to acquire new information that can interact with their original memories. In fact, Loftus and her colleagues demonstrated that participants often succumb to a *misinformation effect* (Loftus, 2005). For example, in one study participants watched a slide show of a traffic accident. They were then asked a series of questions. For half of the participants, one question was, "Did

another car pass the red Datsun while it was stopped at the stop sign?" For the other half, the question read, "Did another car pass the red Datsun while it was stopped at the yield sign?" The original slide show displayed a stop sign. Still, when participants were asked to recognize the original slide between options with a stop sign or a yield sign, those who had been asked about the stop sign were 75 percent correct, whereas those who had been asked about a yield sign were only 41 percent correct (Loftus et al., 1978). That's a large impact of misinformation.

Research on eyewitness memory has evolved to capture a broader range of the experiences of real eyewitnesses. For example, researchers have turned their attention to circumstances in which witnesses discuss events with other people who saw the same events, co-witnesses, before they provide testimony. Survey data confirm the importance of this question: In one sample, 86 percent of the individuals who had witnessed serious events such as physical assault and property vandalism had discussed the events with a co-witness (Paterson & Kemp, 2006). When people spoke to the police about the events, they were discouraged only 14 percent of the time from having such conversations. This is problematic because co-witnesses may serve as a source of information that taints the witnesses' own memories.

A team of researchers sought to demonstrate that people's memory performance can be harmed if they discuss events with co-witnesses (Hope et al., 2008). The researchers also wished to assess the impact of the relationship between the co-witnesses by using pairs that were strangers, friends, or romantic partners. The participants watched a video of a girl entering an office at a university. The events were filmed from two different angles so that some actions (such as the girl's theft of money) were visible from one angle but not the other. The members of each pair watched one or the other versions of the events. They then worked their way through a questionnaire that asked them to recall the events as if "they were real witnesses waiting for the police to arrive" (p. 478). Finally, the participants completed separate memory questionnaires that instructed them to report only information that they themselves had witnessed. Even so, when participants interacted with strangers, 29 percent reported information they had obtained from their co-witness. When participants interacted with friends or romantic partners, 58 percent reported such information.

Why might the different words eyewitnesses use to describe an accident affect their later recall?

This experiment suggests that, after discussing events with co-witnesses, people may find it difficult to isolate their own eyewitness memories from what they have learned from others. This may be particularly if they have a prior relationship with the co-witnesses. Such results are important because, when people testify in court, they swear to report just information they obtained from their own experience of the events.

We have now considered several important features of the encoding, storage, and retrieval of information. In the final section of the chapter, we discuss the brain bases of these memory functions.

STOP AND REVIEW

❶ What is the relationship between categories and concepts?

❷ What claim is made by the exemplar theory of categorization?

❸ On Frederic Bartlett's account, what three processes create distortions in reconstructive memory?

❹ How did Elizabeth Loftus and her colleagues demonstrate misinformation effects?

CRITICAL THINKING Recall the study that investigated the typicality of fish. Why might the researchers have used two groups from the same geographical region?

Visit MyPsychLab.com for more review and practice on the following topic:

◉ **Watch:** Memory: Elizabeth Loftus

Biological Aspects of Memory

The time has come, once again, for us to ask you to recall the number you committed to memory at the beginning of the chapter. Can you still remember it? What was the point of this exercise? Think for a minute about biological aspects of your ability to look at an arbitrary piece of information and commit it instantly to memory. How can you do that? To encode a memory requires that you instantly change something inside your brain. If you wish to retain that memory for at least the length of a chapter, the change must have the potential to become permanent. Have you ever wondered how memory storage is possible? Our excuse for having you recall an arbitrary number was so that we could ask you to reflect on how remarkable the biology of memory really is. Let's take a closer look inside the brain.

SEARCHING FOR THE ENGRAM

Let's consider your memory for the number 48 or, more specifically, your memory that the number 48 was the number we asked you to remember. How could we determine where in your brain that memory resides? **Karl Lashley** (1929, 1950), who performed pioneering work on the anatomy of memory, referred to this question as the search for the **engram,** the physical memory representation. Lashley trained rats to learn mazes, removed varying-size portions of their cortexes, and then retested their

memories for the mazes. Lashley found that memory impairment from brain lesioning was proportional to the amount of tissue removed. The impairment grew worse as more of the cortex was damaged. However, memory was not affected by *where* in the cortex the tissue was removed. Lashley concluded that the elusive engram did not exist in any localized regions but was widely distributed throughout the entire cortex.

Perhaps Lashley could not localize the engram partly because of the variety of types of memories that are called into play even in an apparently simple situation. Maze learning, in fact, involves complex interactions of spatial, visual, and olfactory signals. Neuroscientists now believe that memory for complex sets of information is distributed across many neural systems, even though discrete types of knowledge are separately processed and localized in limited regions of the brain (Markowitsch, 2000; Rolls, 2000).

Five major brain structures are involved in memory:

- The *cerebellum,* essential for procedural memory, memories acquired by repetition, and classically conditioned responses
- The *striatum,* a complex of structures in the forebrain; the likely basis for habit formation and for stimulus response connections
- The *cerebral cortex,* responsible for sensory memories and associations between sensations
- The *hippocampus,* largely responsible for declarative memory of facts, dates, and names, and the consolidation of spatial memories
- The *amygdala,* which plays a critical role in the formation and retrieval of memories with emotional significance

Other parts of the brain, such as the thalamus, the basal forebrain, and the prefrontal cortex, are involved also as way stations for the formation of particular types of memories (see **Figure 7.17** on page 224).

In Chapter 3, we focused directly on brain anatomy. Here, let's take a look at the methods that neuroscientists use to draw conclusions about the role of specific brain structures for memory. We will examine two types of research. First, we consider the insights generated by "experiments of nature"—circumstances in which individuals who have suffered brain damage volunteer to further memory research. Second, we describe the ways in which researchers are applying new brain-imaging techniques to improve their understanding of memory processes in the brain.

MEMORY DISORDERS

In 1960, Nick A., a young Air Force radar technician, experienced a freak injury that permanently changed his life. Nick had been sitting at his desk while his roommate played with a miniature fencing foil. Then, suddenly, Nick stood up and turned around—just as his buddy happened to lunge with the sword. The foil pierced Nick's right nostril and continued to cut into the left side of his brain. The accident left Nick seriously disoriented. His worst problem was **amnesia,** the failure of memory over a prolonged period. Because of Nick's amnesia, he forgets many events immediately after they happen. After he reads a few paragraphs of writing, the first sentences slip from his memory. He cannot remember the plot of a television show unless, during commercials, he actively thinks about and rehearses what he was just watching.

---

engram The physical memory trace for information in the brain.

amnesia A failure of memory caused by physical injury, disease, drug use, or psychological trauma.

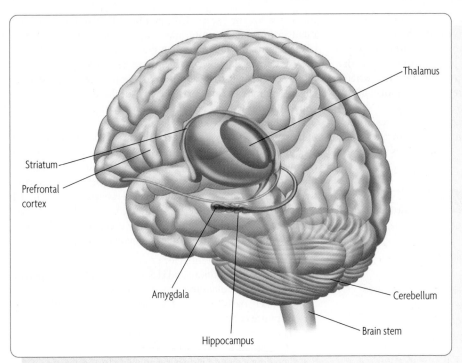

FIGURE 7.17 Brain Structures Involved in Memory
This simplified diagram shows some of the main structures of the brain that are involved in the formation, storage, and retrieval of memories.

The particular type of amnesia from which Nick suffers is called **anterograde amnesia.** This means that Nick can no longer form explicit memories for events that occur after the time at which he suffered physical damage. One consequence of chronic alcoholism is *Korsakoff's syndrome,* for which anterograde amnesia is a prominent symptom. Other patients suffer from **retrograde amnesia.** In those cases, brain damage prevents access to memories that preceded the moment of injury. If you've ever had the misfortune of receiving a sharp blow to the head (during, for example, a car crash), you're likely to have experienced retrograde amnesia for the events leading up to the accident.

Researchers are grateful to patients like Nick for allowing themselves to be studied as "experiments of nature." By relating the locus of brain injuries like Nick's to patterns of performance deficit, researchers have begun to understand the mapping between the types of memories we have introduced you to in this chapter and regions of the brain (O'Connor & Lafleche, 2005). Nick still remembers how to do things—his procedural knowledge appears to be intact even in the absence of declarative knowledge. So, for example, he remembers how to mix, stir, and bake the ingredients in a recipe, but he forgets what the ingredients are.

The selective impairment of explicit memory of the sort demonstrated by Nick is one of the major facts of the biology of memory: There is abundant evidence to support the conclusion that different brain regions underlie explicit and implicit uses of memory (Voss & Paller, 2008). However, researchers continue to explore exactly what types of implicit memory processes are left intact when people acquire anterograde amnesia. Is it possible, for example, for people with amnesia to learn new associations between words?

Twenty people with amnesia and 21 control individuals participated in a study that assessed their explicit and implicit memory ability (Verfaellie et al., 2006). In the experiment, participants read aloud word pairs such as *moss–newspaper* and also read statements that provided a relation between the words, such as "Adding moss to compost helps decompose newspaper." Later, the participants performed explicit and implicit memory tasks. For the explicit task, participants were presented with the first word in each pair and asked to recall the second. By comparison to the control individuals, the people with amnesia performed quite poorly on this explicit task. For the implicit memory task, participants were given the first word from a pair (for example, *moss* or *banana*) and then asked to generate four words from a category (such as "reading material"). Both the control individuals and the people with amnesia were more likely to generate words as examples of categories if they had seen the word earlier in the experiment. This result illustrates that the people with amnesia were able to acquire new information. However, the responses of the people with amnesia didn't show evidence that they learned any new associations. For example, if participants had encoded a new association between *moss* and *newspaper,* we would expect that they would be even more likely to generate *newspaper* among their four examples of "reading material" than they would have been without that association. In fact, the control individuals generated *newspaper* more often in the context of *moss*—but the people with amnesia did not.

This experiment demonstrates some of the subtle differences between the implicit memory processes that are spared and disrupted when people experience anterograde amnesia. People with amnesia are able to learn information about single items (so that, for example, *newspaper* is more accessible when they

anterograde amnesia An inability to form explicit memories for events that occur after the time of physical damage to the brain.

retrograde amnesia An inability to retrieve memories from the time before physical damage to the brain.

Psychology in Your Life

WHY DOES ALZHEIMER'S DISEASE AFFECT MEMORY?

In recent years, researchers have acquired a deeper understanding of how memories are formed in the brain. This knowledge has allowed for focused attention on *Alzheimer's disease*—a biological condition in which memory function gradually breaks down. This disease afflicts about 5 percent of Americans ages 65 to 74. Beyond age 65, the risk of the disease doubles every five years—it affects nearly 50 percent of individuals over 85 (National Institute on Aging, 2006). Alzheimer's disease onset is deceptively mild—in early stages the only observable symptom may be memory impairment. However, its course is one of steady deterioration. Individuals with Alzheimer's disease may show gradual personality changes, such as apathy, lack of spontaneity, and withdrawal from social interactions. In advanced stages, people with Alzheimer's disease may become completely mute and inattentive, even forgetting the names of their spouse and children.

The symptoms of Alzheimer's disease were first described in 1906 by the German psychiatrist Alois Alzheimer. In those earliest investigations, Alzheimer noted that the brains of individuals who had died from the disease contained unusual tangles of neural tissue and sticky deposits called plaques. Still, Alzheimer could not determine whether those brain changes were the cause of the disease or its products. (As you might recall from Chapter 2, correlation does not necessarily imply causation.) Only in the past 15 to 20 years have researchers been able to assemble the evidence that the plaques themselves cause the brain to deteriorate (Hardy & Selkoe, 2002). The plaques are formed from a substance called *amyloid β-peptide (Aβ)*. Ordinary processes in the human brain that aid in the growth and maintenance of neurons create Aβ as a by-product. Normally, Aβ dissolves in the fluid surrounding neurons, without any consequences. However, in Alzheimer's disease, Aβ becomes deadly to neurons: Aβ forms plaques and causes brain cells to self-destruct (Li et al., 2007).

This understanding of the role of Aβ in the progress of Alzheimer's disease has led to important recent breakthroughs. For example, researchers are beginning to improve their ability to diagnose the disease. As we will see in Chapter 10, human aging is accompanied by some ordinary changes in memory function. To make a timely diagnosis of Alzheimer's disease, doctors need a way to determine whether older adults' memory impairments are something more than ordinary change. For most of the past 100 years that was a difficult task. Alzheimer's disease could be definitively diagnosed only when doctors could see the patients' brains—something that was not possible while the patients were living. However, researchers have begun to develop applications of PET scans (see Chapter 3) that enable them to detect the presence of Aβ in the living brain (Nordberg, 2008). The key advance was the manufacture of a radioactive marker that attaches itself to the Aβ plaques. This radioactive marker becomes visible through PET scans—providing a mechanism for early diagnosis of ominous patterns of Aβ in the brain.

Early diagnosis would allow early treatment, with the goal of minimizing the negative impact of the disease. Although scientists are pursuing a number of preventive measures and treatments, several lines of research once again focus on Aβ (Salloway et al., 2008). For example, researchers are seeking methods to interrupt the biochemical processes that produce Aβ in the first place. They are also exploring techniques to destroy the Aβ plaques once they have begun to form. Taken together, these approaches hold out great hope that Alzheimer's disease will be less devastating for future generations.

---

provide examples of "reading material"). However, implicit memory processes do not generally allow people with amnesia to learn new associations.

The cases in which people lose the ability to recall past information or acquire new information are the most dramatic forms of memory disorders. However, people experience less extensive memory disruptions as a result of injury or disease. For example, the *Psychology in Your Life* box describes the progressive course of Alzheimer's disease. Researchers study individuals who are at high risk for Alzheimer's disease to understand the biological basis for successive changes in memory function (Murphy et al., 2008). Researchers often seek out people who have damage in particular brain regions to test specific theories about the biology of memory processes. Recall, for example, our discussion of metamemory which revealed that people's feeling-of-knowing judgments are often reasonably accurate. Researchers suggested that regions of the prefrontal cortex (PFC) (see Figure 7.17) provide the brain basis for those judgments (Modirrousta & Fellows, 2008). To test that claim, the researchers identified five individuals who had damage in those PFC regions. These individuals with PFC damage and matched controls all tried to learn new associations between faces and names. Even when the two participant groups performed equally well on a recognition test, the individuals with PFC damage were consistently less accurate on their feeling-of-knowing judgments. This experiment supports the claim that the prefrontal cortex plays a role in metamemory. It also provides an example of the value of research that examines more subtle forms of memory disorder.

BRAIN IMAGING

Psychologists have gained a great deal of knowledge about the relationship between anatomy and memory from the amnesic patients who generously serve as participants in these experiments. However, the advent of brain-imaging techniques has enabled researchers to study memory processes in individuals without brain damage (Nyberg & Cabeza, 2000). (You may want to review the section on imaging techniques in Chapter 3.) For example, using positron emission tomography (PET), Endel Tulving and his colleagues (Habib et al., 2003) have identified a difference in activation between the two brain hemispheres in the encoding and retrieval of episodic information. Their studies parallel standard memory studies, except that the participants' cerebral blood flow is monitored through PET scans during encoding or retrieval. As you can see in **Figure 7.18,** these researchers discovered disproportionately high brain activity in the left prefrontal cortex for encoding of episodic information and in the right prefrontal cortex for retrieval of episodic information. Thus the processes show some anatomical distinctions in addition to the conceptual distinctions made by cognitive psychologists.

Research with functional magnetic resonance imaging (fMRI) has also provided remarkable detail about the way that memory operations are distributed in the brain. For example, studies with fMRI have begun to identify the specific brain regions that are activated when new memories are formed. Consider a study in which participants underwent fMRI scans while watching an episode of the sitcom "Curb Your Enthusiasm" that was new to them (Hasson et al., 2008). Over the course of 27 minutes, the main character engaged in a series of events such as attending a dinner party and arguing with friends. Three weeks later, the participants returned to the laboratory to take a 77-question memory test on the episode. Each participant remembered some details but not others. The researchers analyzed the fMRI data to identify those brain regions that were particularly active when information was successfully encoded. As shown in **Figure 7.19,** several brain regions emerged from that analysis. Unless you pursue studies in cognitive neuroscience, you needn't worry why it is activity in exactly this set of structures that predicts later recall. Figure 7.19 should suggest to you that researchers are making progress toward the goal of witnessing the birth and consolidation of new memories.

Brain scans also provide information about how memory processes unfold in time. If you try to recall the capital of France, the answer might present itself to you (or not) rather quickly. However, if you try to recall what happened the first time you met someone from France, you'll likely need more time to retrieve and elaborate that memory. For those sorts of rich autobiographical memories, the role of different regions of the brain changes over time.

A team of researchers asked participants to retrieve autobiographical memories while undergoing fMRI scans (Daselaar et al., 2008). Participants heard a cue word, such as *tree,* and

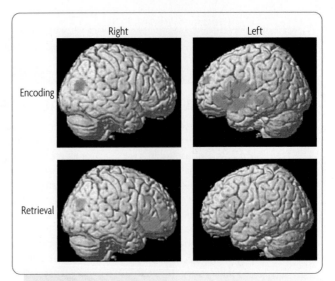

FIGURE 7.18 **Brain Activity for Encoding and Retrieval**

The figure displays the regions of the brain that were most highly activated for encoding versus retrieval. The PET scans display disproportionately high brain activity in the left prefrontal cortex for the encoding of episodic information and in the right prefrontal cortex for the retrieval of episodic information.

Reprinted from *Trends in Cognitive Sciences,* 7(6), Reza Habib, Lars Nyberg, and Endel Tulving, "Brain activity for encoding versus retrieval," p. 241, copyright © 2003, with permission from Elsevier.

attempted to bring a specific event to mind that was associated with the word. Participants pushed a button on a response box to indicate when they had retrieved a memory. Because this process unfolded over several seconds, the researchers were able to determine how different brain areas became involved in different aspects of autobiographical memory. For example, early on, structures like the hippocampus were active as participants searched their episodic memories. As participants elaborated their memories, activity in other areas became more prominent. For example, participants' visual cortex became more active as they enriched their memories with visual images. When the visual cortex was particularly active, participants reported the strongest sense that they were actually reliving the memory.

Take a moment to retrieve your own memory in response to *tree.* Do you feel your recollection of the event become more elaborate over time? The fMRI scans provide a moment-by-moment account of where and how that elaboration occurs in your brain.

The results from imaging studies illustrate why researchers from different disciplines must work closely together in the quest for a full understanding of memory processes. Psychologists provide the data on human performance that become fuel for neurophysiologists' detection of specialized brain structures. At the same time, the realities of physiology con-

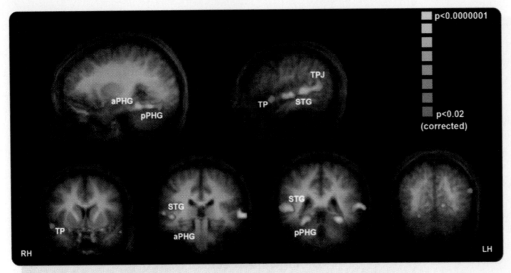

FIGURE 7.19 Brain Regions That Predict Successful Memory
When this set of brain regions was particularly active at time of encoding, people were more likely to remember details from their viewing of a sitcom. The areas are the right temporal pole (TP), superior temporal gyrus (STG), anterior parahippocampal cortex (aPHG), posterior parahippocampal gyrus (pPHG), and temporal parietal junction (TPJ). RH and LH refer to the right and left hemispheres.

strain psychologists' theories of the mechanisms of encoding, storage, and retrieval. Through shared effort, scientists in these fields of research provide great insight into the operation of memory processes.

STOP AND REVIEW

1 What did Karl Lashley conclude about the location of the engram?

2 What has been learned about the impairment of implicit memory for individuals with amnesia?

3 What have PET studies indicated about the brain bases of encoding and retrieval of episodic information?

CRITICAL THINKING Recall the study that looked at memory for sitcom details. Why was it important that participants hadn't seen the episode before?

Recapping Main Points

What Is Memory?

- Cognitive psychologists study memory as a type of information processing.
- Memories involving conscious effort are explicit. Unconscious memories are implicit.
- Declarative memory is memory for facts; procedural memory is memory for how to perform skills.
- Memory is often viewed as a three-stage process of encoding, storage, and retrieval.

Memory Use for the Short Term

- Iconic memory has large capacity but very short duration.

- Short-term memory (STM) has a limited capacity and lasts only briefly without rehearsal.
- Maintenance rehearsal can extend the presence of material in STM indefinitely.
- STM capacity can be increased by chunking unrelated items into meaningful groups.
- The broader concept of working memory includes STM.
- The four components of working memory provide the resources for moment-by-moment experiences of the world.

Long-Term Memory: Encoding and Retrieval

- Long-term memory (LTM) constitutes your total knowledge of the world and of yourself. It is nearly unlimited in capacity.

- Your ability to remember information relies on the match between circumstances of encoding and retrieval.
- Retrieval cues allow you to access information in LTM.
- Episodic memory is concerned with memory for events that have been personally experienced. Semantic memory is memory for the basic meaning of words and concepts.
- Similarity in context between learning and retrieval aids retrieval.
- The serial position curve is explained by distinctiveness in context.
- Information processed more deeply is typically remembered better.
- For implicit memories, it is important that the processes of encoding and retrieval be similar.
- Ebbinghaus studied the time course of forgetting.
- Interference occurs when retrieval cues do not lead uniquely to specific memories.
- Memory performance can be improved through elaborative rehearsal and mnemonics.
- In general, feelings-of-knowing accurately predict the availability of information in memory.

Structures in Long-Term Memory
- Concepts are the memory building blocks of thinking. They are formed when memory processes gather together classes of objects or ideas with common properties.

- Concepts are often organized in hierarchies, ranging from general, to basic level, to specific.
- Schemas are more complex cognitive clusters.
- All these memory structures are used to provide expectations and a context for interpreting new information.
- Remembering is not simply recording but is a constructive process.
- People encode flashbulb memories in response to events with great emotional significance, but those memories may not be more accurate than everyday memories.
- New information can bias recall, making eyewitness memory unreliable when contaminated by postevent input.

Biological Aspects of Memory
- Different brain structures (including the hippocampus, the amygdala, the cerebellum, the striatum, and the cerebral cortex) have been shown to be involved in different types of memories.
- Experiments with individuals with memory disorders have helped investigators understand how different types of memories are acquired and represented in the brain.
- Brain-imaging techniques have extended knowledge about the brain bases of memory encoding and retrieval.

KEY TERMS

amnesia (p. 223)
anterograde amnesia (p. 224)
basic level (p. 218)
chunking (p. 202)
concept (p. 216)
contextual distinctiveness (p. 208)
declarative memory (p. 197)
elaborative rehearsal (p. 213)
encoding (p. 198)
encoding specificity (p. 207)
engram (p. 223)
episodic memory (p. 206)
exemplar (p. 218)
explicit use of memory (p. 196)

flashbulb memory (p. 221)
iconic memory (p. 199)
implicit use of memory (p. 197)
levels-of-processing theory (p. 209)
long-term memory (LTM) (p. 205)
memory (p. 196)
metamemory (p. 214)
mnemonic (p. 213)
primacy effect (p. 208)
priming (p. 210)
proactive interference (p. 212)
procedural memory (p. 197)
prototype (p. 218)
recall (p. 205)

recency effect (p. 208)
recognition (p. 205)
reconstructive memory (p. 219)
retrieval (p. 198)
retrieval cue (p. 205)
retroactive interference (p. 212)
retrograde amnesia (p. 224)
schema (p. 218)
semantic memory (p. 206)
serial position effect (p. 208)
short-term memory (STM) (p. 201)
storage (p. 198)
transfer-appropriate processing (p. 210)
working memory (p. 203)

Chapter 7 Practice Test

1. At her school's talent show, Noa answers questions about politics while spinning basketballs on her fingers. The question and answering mostly require _____ memory, whereas the ball spinning mostly requires _____ memory.
   a. implicit; procedural
   b. declarative; procedural
   c. procedural; declarative
   d. implicit; declarative

2. To demonstrate the capacity of iconic memory, George Sperling showed that participants performed better with the _____ procedure.
   a. whole-report
   b. procedural memory
   c. partial-report
   d. implicit memory

3. Mark looks a number up in a phone book, but he forgets it before he has a chance to make the call. It sounds like Mark should have spent more effort on
   a. rehearsal.
   b. chunking.
   c. memory span.
   d. iconic memory.

4. Which of these is not a component of working memory?
   a. the iconic memory buffer
   b. the phonological loop
   c. the central executive
   d. the visuospatial sketchpad

5. Because of the usefulness of the retrieval cues, _____ is usually easier than _____.
   a. recall; episodic memory
   b. recognition; recall
   c. semantic memory; recognition
   d. recall; recognition

6. After Meghan meets a group of people, she can only remember the name of the last person she met. This is an example of a(n) _____ effect.
   a. primacy
   b. contextual distinctiveness
   c. encoding specificity
   d. recency

7. Consider the word *Mississippi*. Which of these questions asks you to process that word at the deepest level of processing?
   a. How many times does the letter *s* appear in the word?
   b. Is this word the name of a river?
   c. How many syllables does the word have?
   d. What is the word's first letter?

8. You've just memorized a list of nonsense words. You are going to try to recall the words every day for the next 30 days (without looking back at the list). You would expect to show the most forgetting between
   a. day 1 and day 2.
   b. day 3 and day 5.
   c. day 5 and day 10.
   d. day 10 and day 30.

9. Pavel needs to learn the order of the planets with respect to their distance from the sun. To begin, he imagines Mercury as a giant bun and Venus shaped like a shoe. It sounds like Pavel is using
   a. the method of loci.
   b. the peg-word method.
   c. metamemory.
   d. iconic memory.

10. At the start of each exam, Sarah reads over the full set of questions to determine which ones she feels pretty sure she'll get right. To make these judgments, Sarah is using
    a. encoding specificity.
    b. mnemonics.
    c. elaborative rehearsal.
    d. metamemory.

11. At the petting zoo, Tabitha sees a lamb and a bear cub. When she gets home, Tabitha will probably find it easier to remember the _____ because it was schema _____.
    a. bear cub; inconsistent
    b. lamb; inconsistent
    c. bear cub; consistent
    d. lamb; inconsistent

12. Karl Lashley carried out his search for the engram by training rats on mazes and then removing different amounts of the
    a. cortex.
    b. cerebellum.
    c. striatum.
    d. amygdala.

13. Constantine suffers from amnesia. You would expect to find that his ability to acquire _____ memories is more impaired than his ability to acquire _____ memories.
    a. declarative; explicit
    b. explicit; implicit
    c. implicit; procedural
    d. implicit; declarative

14. If you were asked to identify the brain bases of the encoding and retrieval of episodic memories, you should point to
    a. the striatum.
    b. the cerebellum.
    c. prefrontal cortex.
    d. the amygdala.

15. Alois Alzheimer was able to demonstrate that
    a. plaques in the brain caused Alzheimer's disease.
    b. amyloid β-peptide caused Alzheimer's disease.
    c. plaques in the brain could be used to prevent Alzheimer's disease.
    d. people who died of Alzheimer's disease had plaques in their brains.

Essay Questions

1. What are the relationships among encoding, storage, and retrieval?

2. What are the primary functions of working memory?

3. In what ways have brain-imaging techniques helped confirm some of the theoretical distinctions made by memory researchers?

Discovering Psychology Viewing Guide

Watch the following video by logging on to MyPsychLab (www.mypsychlab.com). After you have watched the video, complete the activities that follow.

Program 9: Remembering and Forgetting

KEY TERMS AND PEOPLE

As you watch the program, pay particular attention to these people in addition to those covered in this textbook.

- *Gordon Bower*—studies how mnemonic techniques can enhance learning and retrieval.
- *Richard Thompson*—studies the brain mechanisms underlying classical conditioning.
- *Diana Woodruff-Pak*—uses eyeblink classical conditioning to detect early-onset dementia.

PROGRAM REVIEW

1. What pattern of remembering emerged in Hermann Ebbinghaus's research?
   a. Loss occurred at a steady rate.
   b. A small initial loss was followed by no further loss.
   c. There was no initial loss, but then there was a gradual decline.
   d. A sharp initial loss was followed by a gradual decline.

2. The way psychologists thought about and studied memory was changed by the invention of
   a. television.
   b. electroconvulsive shock therapy.
   c. the computer.
   d. the electron microscope.

3. What do we mean when we say that memories must be encoded?
   a. They must be taken from storage to be used.
   b. They must be put in a form the brain can register.
   c. They must be transferred from one network to another.
   d. They must be put in a passive storehouse.

4. About how many items can be held in short-term memory?
   a. three
   b. seven
   c. eleven
   d. an unlimited number

5. Imagine you had a string of 20 one-digit numbers to remember. The best way to accomplish the task, which requires increasing the capacity of short-term memory, is through the technique of
   a. selective attention.
   b. peg words.
   c. rehearsing.
   d. chunking.

6. According to Gordon Bower, what is an important feature of good mnemonic systems?
   a. There is a dovetailing between storage and retrieval.
   b. The acoustic element is more important than the visual.
   c. The learner is strongly motivated to remember.
   d. Short-term memory is bypassed in favor of long-term memory.

7. According to Freud, what is the purpose of repression?
   a. to protect the memory from encoding too much material
   b. to preserve the individual's self-esteem
   c. to activate networks of associations
   d. to fit new information into existing schemas

8. In an experiment, people spent a few minutes in an office. They were then asked to recall what they had seen. They were most likely to recall objects that
   a. fit into their existing schema of an office.
   b. carried little emotional content.
   c. were unusual within that particular context.
   d. related to objects they owned themselves.

9. The paintings Franco Magnani made of an Italian town were distorted mainly by
   a. repression, causing some features to be left out.
   b. a child's perspective.
   c. sensory gating, changing colors.
   d. false memories of items that were not really there.

10. What was Karl Lashley's goal in teaching rats mazes and then removing part of their cortexes?
    a. finding out how much tissue was necessary for learning to occur
    b. determining whether memory was localized in one area of the brain
    c. discovering how much tissue loss led to memory loss
    d. finding out whether conditioned responses could be eradicated

11. What has Richard Thompson found in his work with rabbits conditioned to a tone before an air puff?
    a. Rabbits learn the response more slowly after lesioning.
    b. Eyelid conditioning involves several brain areas.
    c. The memory of the response can be removed by lesioning.
    d. Once the response is learned, the memory is permanent, despite lesioning.

12. What is the chief cause of functional amnesia?
   a. Alzheimer's disease
   b. substance abuse
   c. traumatic injury to the brain
   d. severe anxiety

13. The best way to keep items in short-term memory for an indefinite length of time is to
   a. chunk.
   b. create context dependence.
   c. use the peg-word system.
   d. rehearse.

14. Long-term memory is organized as
   a. a complex network of associations.
   b. a serial list.
   c. a set of visual images.
   d. a jumble of individual memories with no clear organizational scheme.

15. You remember a list of unrelated words by associating them, one at a time, with images of a bun, a shoe, a tree, a door, a hive, sticks, Heaven, a gate, a line, and a hen. What mnemonic technique are you using?
   a. method of loci
   b. peg-word
   c. link
   d. digit conversion

16. What did Karl Lashley conclude about the engram?
   a. It is localized in the brain stem.
   b. It is localized in the right hemisphere only.
   c. It is localized in the left hemisphere only.
   d. Complex memories cannot be pinpointed within the brain.

17. Long-term memories appear to be stored in the
   a. cortex.
   b. occipital lobe.
   c. hippocampus.
   d. parietal lobe.

18. How has Diana Woodruff-Pak utilized Richard Thompson's work on eyeblink conditioning?
   a. as a precursor to early-onset dementia
   b. as a predictor of musical genius
   c. as a mechanism for growing brain cells in intact animals
   d. as a tool for training long-term visual memories

19. Which neurotransmitter(s) is/are disrupted in Alzheimer's patients?
   a. scopolamine
   b. acetylcholine
   c. both of the above
   d. none of the above

20. Alzheimer's disease is associated with the loss of
   a. memory.
   b. personality.
   c. life itself.
   d. all of the above.

QUESTIONS TO CONSIDER

1. What memory strategies can you apply to help you better retain the information in this course? Why is rote rehearsal not the optimal strategy?

2. What is your earliest memory? How accurate do you think it is? Can you recall an experience that happened before you could talk? If not, why not? How does language influence what we remember? How do photographs and other mementos aid memory?

3. Most American kids learn their ABCs by singing them. Why does singing the ABCs make it easier to remember them?

4. Many quiz shows and board games, like Trivial Pursuit, are based on recalling items of general knowledge that we do not use every day. Why is it so much fun to recall such trivia?

5. As a member of a jury, you are aware of the tendency to reconstruct memories. How much weight do you give to eyewitness testimony? Is it possible ever to get "the whole truth and nothing but the truth" from an eyewitness? Do you think memory distortions (for details of what was said during a trial) occur in jurors as well?

6. Why might metamemory, one's knowledge of the capabilities of and principles governing one's memory, be an important skill when one is studying for a test?

ACTIVITIES

1. Do you have an official family historian? In individual interviews, ask family members to recall and describe their memories of a shared past event, such as a wedding or holiday celebration. Perhaps a photograph or memento will trigger a story. Compare how different people construct the event and what kind of details are recalled. What are different people revealing about their personal interests, needs, and values when they describe the experience?

2. Try to recall an experience from your childhood that at least one friend or family member would also have a memory of. Have each person write down details of their memories, and then compare notes. Are there any details you hadn't remembered that you now do, based on other people's mention of them? Are there any details that you have contradictory memories for? How do you resolve the disagreement?

3. Make up a list of 10 unrelated words. Have 5 friends study the list for one minute with only the instruction to "remember as many of them as you can." After one minute, have them write down as many as they can remember. Have another 5 friends learn the list for one minute after you teach them the peg-word mnemonic. Do they outperform the control group? What sort of strategies, if any, did the control group tend to use?

8

Cognitive Processes

It is midnight. There's a knock on your door. When you answer, no one is there, but you see an envelope on the floor. Inside the envelope is a single sheet of paper with a handwritten message: "The cat is on the mat." What do you make of this?

You must now begin to engage a variety of cognitive processes. You will need language processes to put together some basic meanings for the words, but what then? Can you find any episode in memory to which these words are relevant? (Recall that in Chapter 7 we discussed memory as a type of cognitive processing.) If you can't, you'll have to give other types of thought to the matter. Is the message a code? What kind of code? Whom do you know who might encode a message? Does the fate of civilization rest in your hands?

Perhaps we're getting a bit carried away, but we want to make plain to you what kinds of activities count as **cognitive processes** and why they might interest you. The capacity to use language and to think in abstract ways has often been cited as the essence of the human experience. You tend to take cognition for granted because it's an activity you do continually during your waking hours. Even so, when a carefully crafted speech wins your vote or when you read a detective story in which the sleuth combines a few scraps of apparently trivial clues into a brilliant solution to a crime, you are forced to acknowledge the intellectual triumph of cognitive processes.

Cognition is a general term for all forms of knowing: As shown in **Figure 8.1,** the study of cognition is the study of your mental life. (Note that Chapters 4 and 7 already discussed some of the topics shown in Figure 8.1.) Cognition includes both contents and processes. The *contents* of cognition are *what* you know—concepts, facts, propositions, rules, and memories: "A dog is a mammal." "A red light means stop." "I first left home at

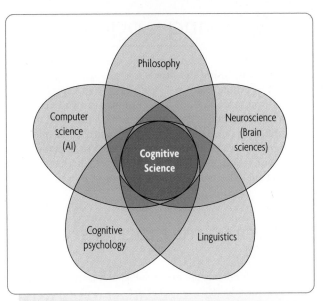

FIGURE 8.2   The Domain of Cognitive Science

The domain of cognitive science occupies the intersection of philosophy, neuroscience, linguistics, cognitive psychology, and computer science (artificial intelligence).

age 18." Cognitive *processes* are *how* you manipulate these mental contents—in ways that enable you to interpret the world around you and to find creative solutions to your life's dilemmas.

Within psychology, the study of cognition is carried out by researchers in the field of **cognitive psychology.** Over the past three decades, the field of cognitive psychology has been supplemented by the interdisciplinary field of **cognitive science** (see **Figure 8.2**). Cognitive science focuses the collected knowledge of several academic specialties on the same theoretical issues. It benefits the practitioners of each of these fields to share their data and insights. You saw this cognitive science philosophy at work in Chapter 7, when we described how studies of the biology of memory can be used to constrain—limit and refine—theories of memory processes. Many of the theories we will describe in this chapter have similarly been shaped through the interactions of researchers from a number of disciplinary perspectives.

We will begin our study of cognition with a brief description of the ways in which researchers try to measure the inner, private processes involved in cognitive functioning. Then we will examine, at some length, topics in cognitive psychology that generate much basic research and practical application: language use, visual cognition, problem solving, reasoning, judging, and decision making.

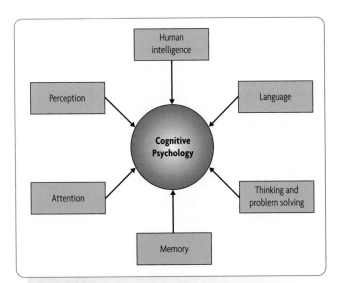

FIGURE 8.1   The Domain of Cognitive Psychology

Cognitive psychologists study higher mental functions with particular emphasis on the ways in which people acquire knowledge and use it to shape and understand their experiences in the world.

From Solso, Robert L., *Cognitive Psychology*, 3e, & Copyright © 1991. Reprinted by permission Pearson Education, Inc.

cognitive process One of the higher mental processes, such as perception, memory, language, problem solving, and abstract thinking.

cognition Processes of knowing, including attending, remembering, and reasoning; also the content of the processes, such as concepts and memories.

cognitive psychology The study of higher mental processes such as attention, language use, memory, perception, problem solving, and thinking.

cognitive science The interdisciplinary field of study of the approach systems and processes that manipulate information.

Studying Cognition

How can you study cognition? The challenge, of course, is that it goes on inside the head. You can see the input—for example, in a note that says, "Call me"—and experience the output—you make a phone call—but how can you determine the series of mental steps that connected the note to your response? How can you reveal what happened in the middle—the cognitive processes and the mental representations on which your action relies? In this section, we describe the types of logical analyses that have made possible the scientific study of cognitive psychology.

DISCOVERING THE PROCESSES OF MIND

One of the fundamental methodologies for studying mental processes was devised, in 1868, by the Dutch physiologist **F. C. Donders** (1818–1889). To study the "speed of mental processes," Donders invented a series of experimental tasks that he believed were differentiated by the mental steps involved for successful performance (Lachman et al., 1979). **Table 8.1** provides a paper-and-pencil experiment that follows Donders's logic. Before reading on, please take a moment to complete each task.

How long did you take to do task 1? Suppose you wanted to give a list of the steps you carried out to perform the task. It might look something like this:

a. Determine whether a character is a capital letter or a lowercase letter.
b. If it is a capital letter, draw a *C* on top.

How long did you take for task 2? When we have used this exercise, students have often taken an additional half minute or more. You can understand why, once we spell out the necessary steps:

a. Determine whether a character is a capital letter or a lowercase letter.
b. Determine whether each capital letter is a vowel or a consonant.
c. If it is a consonant, draw a *C* on top. If it is a vowel, draw a *V*.

Thus, going from task 1 to task 2, we add two mental steps, which we can call *stimulus categorization* (vowel or consonant?) and *response selection* (draw a *C* or draw a *V*). Task 1 requires one stimulus categorization step. Task 2 requires two such categorizations. Task 2 also requires selecting between two responses. Because task 2 requires you to do everything you did for task 1 and more, it takes you more time. That was Donders's fundamental insight: Extra mental steps will often result in more time to perform a task.

You may be wondering why we included task 3. This is a necessary procedural control for the experiment. We have to ensure that the time difference between tasks 1 and 2 does not

---

serial processes Two or more mental processes that are carried out in order, one after the other.

parallel processes Two or more mental processes that are carried out simultaneously.

TABLE 8.1 Donders's Analysis of Mental Processes

Note how long (in seconds) it takes you to complete each of these three tasks. Try to complete each task accurately, but as quickly as possible.

Task 1: Draw a *C* on top of all the capitalized letters:
TO Be, oR noT To BE: tHAT Is thE qUestioN:
WhETher 'Tis noBlEr In tHE MINd tO SuFfER
tHe SLings AnD ARroWS Of OUtrAgeOUs forTUNe,
or To TAke ARmS agaINST a sEa Of tROUBleS,
AnD by oPPOsinG END theM. TIME: _____

Task 2: Draw a *V* on top of the capitalized vowels and a *C* on top of the capitalized consonants:
TO Be, oR noT To BE: tHAT Is thE qUestioN:
WhETher 'Tis noBlEr In tHE MINd tO SuFfER
tHe SLings AnD ARroWS Of OUtrAgeOUs forTUNe,
or To TAke ARmS agaINST a sEa Of tROUBleS,
AnD by oPPOsinG END theM. TIME: _____

Task 3: Draw a *V* on top of all the capitalized letters:
TO Be, oR noT To BE: tHAT Is thE qUestioN:
WhETher 'Tis noBlEr In tHE MINd tO SuFfER
tHe SLings AnD ARroWS Of OUtrAgeOUs forTUNe,
or To TAke ARmS agaINST a sEa Of tROUBleS,
AnD by oPPOsinG END theM. TIME: _____

---

stem from the fact that it takes much longer to draw *V*s than to draw *C*s. Task 3 should still be much swifter than task 2. Was it?

Researchers still follow Donders's basic logic. They frequently use *reaction time*—the amount of time it takes experimental participants to perform particular tasks—as a way of testing specific accounts of how some cognitive process is carried out. Donders's basic premise that extra mental steps will result in extra time is still fundamental to a great deal of cognitive psychological research. Let's see how this successful idea has been developed over the past 135 years.

MENTAL PROCESSES AND MENTAL RESOURCES

When cognitive psychologists break down high-level activities, like language use or problem solving, into their component processes, they often act as if they are playing a game with blocks. Each block represents a different component that must be carried out. The goal is to determine the shape and size of each block and to see how the blocks fit together to form the whole activity. For the Donders tasks, you saw that the blocks can be laid out in a row (see **Figure 8.3,** part A). Each step comes directly after another. The block metaphor allows you to see that we could also stack the blocks so more than one process occurs simultaneously (part B). These two pictures illustrate the distinction between **serial** and **parallel processes.** Processes are *serial* when they take place one after the other. Suppose you're in a restaurant and you need to decide what to order. You

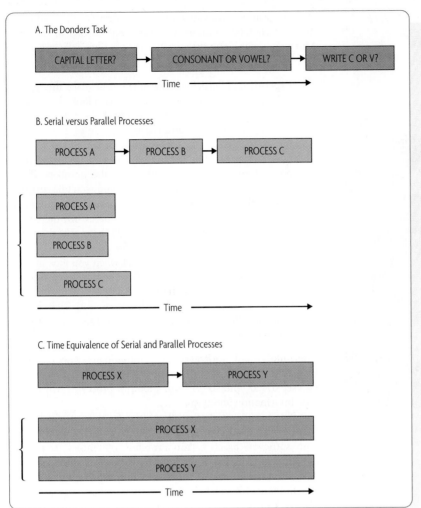

A. The Donders Task

CAPITAL LETTER? → CONSONANT OR VOWEL? → WRITE C OR V?

Time

B. Serial versus Parallel Processes

PROCESS A → PROCESS B → PROCESS C

PROCESS A

PROCESS B

PROCESS C

Time

C. Time Equivalence of Serial and Parallel Processes

PROCESS X → PROCESS Y

PROCESS X

PROCESS Y

Time

FIGURE 8.3 Breaking Down High-Level Cognitive Activities

Cognitive psychologists attempt to determine the identity and organization of the mental processes that are the building blocks of high-level cognitive activities.

(A) Our version of the Donders task requires that at least three processes be carried out one after the other.

(B) Some processes are carried out serially, in sequence; others are carried out in parallel, all at the same time.

(C) The time taken to perform a task does not always allow researchers to conclude whether serial or parallel processes were used.

focus on entries one at a time and then judge whether they qualify as "yes," "no," or "maybe." For each entry, your judgment processes follow your reading processes. Processes are *parallel* when they overlap in time. When it comes time to place your order, the language processes that enable you to understand the waiter's question ("What can I get for you?") are likely to operate at the same time as the processes that allow you to formulate your reply ("I'd like the osso buco"). That's why you're ready to respond as soon as the waiter finishes his question.

Cognitive psychologists often use reaction times to determine whether processes are carried out in parallel or serially. However, the examples in part C of Figure 8.3 should convince you that this is a tricky business. Imagine that we have a task that we believe can be broken down into two processes, *X* and *Y*. If the only information we have is the total time needed to complete the process, we can never be sure if processes *X* and *Y* happen side by side or one after the other. Much of the challenge of research in cognitive psychology is to invent task circumstances that allow the experimenter to determine which of many possible configurations of blocks is correct. In task 2 of the exercise you just did, we could be reasonably certain that the processes were serial because some activities logically required others. For example, you couldn't execute your response

(prepare to draw a *C* or a *V*) until you had determined what the response might be.

In many cases, theorists try to determine if processes are serial or parallel by assessing the extent to which the processes place demands on *mental resources.* Suppose, for example, you are walking to class with a friend. Ordinarily, it should be easy for you to walk a straight path at the same time you carry on a conversation—your navigation processes and your language processes can go on in parallel. But what would happen if you suddenly get to a patch of sidewalk that's dotted with puddles? As you pick your way among the puddles, you may have to stop talking. Now your navigation processes require extra resources for planning, and your language processes are momentarily squeezed out.

A key assumption in this example is that you have *limited* processing resources that must be spread over different mental tasks (Logan, 2002). Your *attentional processes* are responsible for distributing these resources. In Chapter 4, we discussed attention as the set of processes that allow you to select, for particular scrutiny, some small subset of available perceptual information. Our use of *attention* here preserves the idea of selectivity. The decision now, however, concerns which mental processes will be selected as the recipients of processing resources.

Why is it difficult to carry on a conversation while you are trying to avoid puddles?

We have one more complication to add: Not all processes put the same demands on resources. We can, in fact, define a dimension that goes from processes that are *controlled* to those that are *automatic* (Shiffrin & Schneider, 1977). **Controlled processes** require attention; **automatic processes** generally do not. It is often difficult to carry out more than one controlled process at a time because they require more resources; automatic processes can often be performed alongside other tasks without interference.

TABLE 8.2 Size Judgments

Your task is to circle the number that is *physically* larger in each pair. Try to judge which list is harder.

List A

61 —67	22 —28	25 —29	47 —41
68 —64	27 —23	43 —49	44 —48

List B

47 —41	61 —67	27 —23	25 —29
22 —28	68 —64	43 —49	44 —48

We want to give you an example of an automatic process. To get started, take a moment to carry out the task in **Table 8.2.** Make sure you circle the number that is *physically* larger. Did you find one list to be somewhat harder?

Experimental participants were asked to make the types of judgments illustrated in Table 8.2. If you look closely at the table, you'll see that the items on List A present a mismatch between physical size and the magnitude of each number (i.e., 61 is physically larger but it's a number of smaller magnitude than 67). On List B, there is a match between the physical size and the magnitude of the numbers. If you worked your way through Table 8.2, you won't be surprised to learn that participants took longer to make size judgments when there was a mismatch (List A) than when there was a match (List B) (Ganor-Stern et al., 2007). But why should the magnitude of the numbers matter for a judgment of *physical* size? The researchers suggested that when you look at 61 or 67 you can't help but think of the quantity it represents—even when the quantity, in this case, impairs performance on the task you've been asked to carry out. That is, you *automatically* access the meaning of a number, even when you don't need (or want) to do so.

This number task illustrates that automatic processes rely heavily on the efficient use of memory (Barrett et al., 2004). When you see 61, 67, and so on, your memory processes swiftly provide information about quantity.

The number task also illustrates the way in which tasks that first involved controlled processes can become automatic with sufficient practice. You probably remember, as a small child, having to learn how numbers work. Now, the association between numbers and the quantities they represent has become so automatic, you can't shut off the association. You can probably think of other instances in which you've practiced enough to make tasks automatic. Did you learn to play an instrument? Can you type without looking at the keyboard?

Let's apply this knowledge of controlled and automatic processes back to the situation of walking and talking. When you are walking a straight route, you feel little interference between the two activities, suggesting that maintaining your path and planning your utterances are each relatively automatic activities. The situation changes, however, when the puddles force you to choose between a greater number of options for your path. Now you must select where to go and what to say. Because you can't make both choices simultaneously, you have come up against the limits of your processing resources (Tombu & Jolicoeur, 2005). This example shows why controlled and automatic processes are defined along a dimension, rather than constituting strict categories. When circumstances become challenging, what before seemed automatic now requires controlled attention. Thus processes may require more or less attention, depending on the context.

You now know a lot about the logic of mental processes. To explain how complex mental tasks are carried out, theorists propose models that combine serial and parallel and controlled and automatic processes. The goal of much cognitive psychological research is to invent experiments that confirm each of the

---

controlled process Process that requires attention; it is often difficult to carry out more than one controlled process at a time.

automatic process Process that does not require attention; it can often be performed along with other tasks without interference.

components of such models. Now that you understand some of the logic behind cognitive psychological research into mental processes, it is time to move to more specific domains in which you put cognitive processes to work. We begin with language use.

STOP AND REVIEW

❶ What was Donders's goal when he had participants carry out different experimental tasks?

❷ What is the distinction between serial and parallel processes?

❸ What types of processes do not generally require attentional resources?

Language Use

Let's return to the message you received at midnight, "The cat is on the mat." What could we do to change the situation so that this message immediately made sense to you? The easiest step we could take would be to introduce appropriate background knowledge. Suppose you are a secret agent who always gets instructions in this curious fashion. You might know that "the cat" is your contact and that "on the mat" means in the wrestling arena. Off you go.

But you don't have to be a spy for "The cat is on the mat" to take on a variety of meanings:

- Suppose your cat waits on a mat by the door when she wants to be let out. When you say to your roommate, "The cat is on the mat," you use those words to communicate, "Could you get up and let the cat out?"
- Suppose your friend is worried about pulling the car out of the driveway because she's uncertain where the cat is. When you say, "The cat is on the mat," you use those words to communicate, "It's safe to pull out of the driveway."
- Suppose you are trying to have a race between your cat and your friend's dog. When you say, "The cat is on the mat," you use those words to communicate, "My cat won't race!"

These examples illustrate the difference between *sentence meaning*—the generally simple meaning of the combined words of a sentence—and *speaker's meaning*—the unlimited number of meanings a speaker can communicate by putting a sentence to good use (Grice, 1968). When psychologists study language use, they want to comprehend both the *production* and the *understanding* of speakers' meaning:

- How do speakers produce the right words to communicate the meaning they intend?
- How do listeners recover the messages the speakers wished to communicate?

We will examine each of these questions in turn. We also consider the evolutionary and cultural context of language use.

LANGUAGE PRODUCTION

Look at **Figure 8.4.** Try to formulate a few sentences about this picture. What did you think to say? Suppose now we asked you

FIGURE 8.4 Language Production
How would you describe this person to a friend? How might your description change if your friend were blind?

to describe the person for someone who was blind. How would your description change? Does this second description seem to require more mental effort? The study of **language production** concerns both what people say—what they choose to say at a given time—and the processes they go through to produce the message. Note that language users need not produce language out loud. Language production also includes both signing and writing. For convenience, however, we will call language producers *speakers* and language understanders *listeners*.

Audience Design We asked you to imagine the different descriptions you'd give of Figure 8.4 to a sighted and a blind person as a way of getting you to think about **audience design** in language production. Each time you produce an utterance, you must have in mind the audience to whom the utterance will be directed, and what knowledge you share with members of that audience (Clark, 1996; Clark & Van Der Wege, 2002). For example, it won't do you the least bit of good to say, "The cat is on the mat" if your listener does not know that the cat sits on the mat only when she wishes to be let out. An overarching rule of audience design, the *cooperative principle*, was first proposed by the philosopher **H. Paul Grice** (1975). Grice phrased the cooperative principle as an instruction to speakers

---

language production What people say, sign, and write, as well as the processes they go through to produce these messages.

audience design The process of shaping a message depending on the audience for which it is intended.

TABLE 8.3 Grice's Maxims in Language Production

1. *Quantity:* Make your contribution as informative as is required (for the current purposes of the exchange). Do not make your contribution more informative than is required.
   The consequence for the speaker: You must try to judge how much information your audience really needs. Often this judgment will require you to assess what your listener is likely to know already.

2. *Quality:* Try to make your contribution one that is true. Do not say what you believe to be false. Do not say that for which you lack adequate evidence.
   The consequence for the speaker: When you speak, listeners will assume that you can back up your assertions with appropriate evidence. As you plan each utterance, you must have in mind the evidence on which it is based.

3. *Relation:* Be relevant.
   The consequence for the speaker: You must make sure that your listeners will see how what you are saying is relevant to what has come before. If you wish to shift the topic of conversation—so that your utterance is not directly relevant—you must make that clear.

4. *Manner:* Be perspicacious. Avoid obscurity of expression. Avoid ambiguity. Be brief. Be orderly.
   The consequence for the speaker: It is your responsibility to speak in as clear a manner as possible. Although you will inevitably make errors, as a cooperative speaker you must ensure that your listeners can understand your message.
   In this conversation, can you see how Chris follows (or violates) Grice's maxims?

What Is Said	What Chris Might Be Thinking
Pat: *Have you ever been to New York City?* Chris: *I was there once in 2002.*	I don't know why Pat is asking me this question, so I probably should say a little more than just "yes."
Pat: *I'm supposed to visit, but I'm worried about being mugged.* Chris: *I think a lot of areas are safe.*	I can't say that he shouldn't worry because he won't believe me. What can I say that will sound true but make him feel OK?
Pat: *How was your hotel?* Chris: *We didn't stay overnight.*	If I say, "We didn't stay in a hotel," that might suggest we stayed somewhere else. I need to say something relevant that will make clear why I can't answer the question.
Pat: *Would you like to go to New York with me?* Chris: *I'd have to find a way to see if it would be possible for me to leave without it being too impossible.*	I don't want to go, but I don't want to seem rude. Will Pat notice that I'm being evasive in my response?
Pat: *Huh?* Chris: *Well. . . .*	Trapped.

that they should produce utterances appropriate to the setting and meaning of the ongoing conversation. To expand on this instruction, Grice defined four maxims that cooperative speakers live by. In **Table 8.3** we present each of those maxims, as well as an invented conversation that illustrates the effect the maxims have on moment-by-moment choices in language production.

As you can see from Table 8.3, being a cooperative speaker depends, in large part, on having accurate expectations about what your listener is likely to know and understand. Thus you certainly wouldn't tell a friend "I'm having lunch with Alex" if you didn't have good reason to believe that your friend knew who Alex was. You also must assure yourself that, of all the Alexes your friend might know and that she knows that you know, only one would come to mind as the specific Alex you would mention in these circumstances. More formally, we can say that there must be some Alex who is prominent in the *common ground*—common knowledge—you share with your friend.

Herbert Clark (1996) suggested that language users have different bases for their judgments of common ground:

- *Community membership.* Language producers often make strong assumptions about what is likely to be mutually known based on shared membership in communities of various sizes.
- *Copresence for actions.* Language producers often assume that the actions and events they have shared with other conversationalists become part of common ground. This includes information discussed in earlier parts of a conversation (or in past conversations).
- *Perceptual copresence.* Perceptual copresence exists when a speaker and a listener share the same perceptual events (sights, sounds, and so on).

Thus your use of Alex in "I'm having lunch with Alex" might succeed because your friend and you are part of a small community (for example, roommates) that includes only one Alex (community membership). Or it might succeed because you've introduced the existence of Alex earlier in the conversation (copresence for actions). Or Alex might be standing right there in the room (perceptual copresence). You can see from this example why judgments of common ground often rely on the ability of your memory processes to provide information about individuals and communities (Horton, 2007; Horton & Gerrig, 2005b).

Let's focus a bit more on community membership. Take a moment to think about this question: What information would you expect the community members of your college or university to know? What information would you expect students to know—but not the professors? Researchers have examined the extent to which people's estimates of community knowledge are accurate and useful.

In a first experiment, undergraduates in Hong Kong viewed a series of slides of 30 landmarks from Hong Kong, Macau, and New York City (Lau et al., 2001). The participants were asked whether they recognized each landmark and whether they could name it. In addition, the participants tried to estimate what percentage of their classmates would recognize each landmark. The results from this experiment indicated that the students were pretty accurate at guessing what members of their own communities were likely to know: Their estimates were reasonably close to the actual percentages of students who got the landmarks correct. However, the students also tended to err in the direction of believing other people knew the same things they did: They gave higher estimates for those landmarks they themselves knew. In a second experiment, a new group of participants were asked to provide descriptions of each of the 30 landmarks. Their goal was to provide a description that would allow one of their classmates to choose correctly each landmark from among the 30 pictures. The researchers demonstrated that the length of the descriptions was related to community knowledge: Participants generally used more words to describe the landmarks that the first experiment showed to be the least recognizable.

You can think about these results with respect to your own day-to-day experiences. If you are talking to a classmate, you can probably say something like "Meet me at the Union for lunch." If you're expecting a visit from a friend for whom the campus is new, you would probably say something more, like, "It's the red building on the left, about 100 yards beyond the fountain." The comparative lengths of your descriptions suggest that you're using community membership to plan your utterances.

Our discussion so far has focused on language production at the level of the message: How you shape what you wish to say will depend on the audience to whom you are speaking. Let's turn now to a discussion of the mental processes that allow you to produce these messages.

Speech Execution and Speech Errors Would you like to be famous for tripping over your tongue? Consider the Reverend W. A. Spooner of Oxford University, who lent his name to the term *spoonerism:* an exchange of the initial sounds of two or more words in a phrase or sentence. Reverend Spooner came by this honor honestly. When, for example, he was tongue-lashing a lazy student for wasting the term, Reverend Spooner said, "You have tasted the whole worm!" A spoonerism is one of the limited types of speech errors that language producers make. These errors give researchers insight

---

TABLE 8.4 Errors in Planning Speech Production

Types of Planning:

- Speakers must choose the content words that best fit their ideas.

  If the speaker has two words in mind, such as *grizzly* and *ghastly,* a blend like *grastly* might result.

- Speakers must put the chosen words in the right places in the utterance.

  Because speakers plan whole units of their utterances while they produce them, content words will sometimes become misplaced.

  a tank of gas → a gas of tank

  wine is being served at dinner → dinner is being served at wine

- Speakers must fill in the sounds that make up the words they wish to utter.

  Once again, because speakers plan ahead, sounds will sometimes get misplaced.

  left hemisphere → heft lemisphere

  pass out → pat ous

---

into the planning that goes on as speakers produce utterances. As you can see in **Table 8.4,** you need to engage in several types of planning, and speech errors give evidence for each type (Dell, 2004). What should impress you about all these examples of errors is that they are not just random—they make sense given the structure of spoken English. Thus a speaker might exchange initial consonants—"tips of the slung" for "slips of the tongue"—but would never say, "tlips of the sung," which would violate the rule of English that "tl" does not occur as an initial sound (Fromkin, 1980).

Given the importance of speech errors to developing theoretical models of speech production, researchers have not always been content just to wait around for errors to happen naturally. Instead, researchers have explored a number of ways to produce artificial errors in controlled experimental settings (e.g., Hartsuiker et al., 2003; Warker & Dell, 2006). One classic technique is called SLIP (for "spoonerisms of laboratory-induced predisposition"; Baars, 1992). In this procedure, participants are asked to read silently lists of word pairs that provide models for the sound structure of a target spoonerism: *ball doze, bash door, bean deck, bell dark.* They then are required to pronounce out loud a word pair like *darn bore,* but under the influence of the earlier pairs it will sometimes come out *barn door.*

With this technique, researchers can study the factors that affect the likelihood that speakers will produce errors. For example, a spoonerism is more likely when the error will still result in real words (Baars et al., 1975). Thus an error on *darn bore* (to produce *barn door*) is more likely than an error on *dart board* (to produce *bart doard*). Findings like this one suggest that while you are producing utterances, some of your cognitive processes are devoted to detecting and editing potential errors (Nooteboom & Quené, 2008). Those processes are reluctant to let you pronounce sounds like *doard,* which are not real English words.

Contemporary theories of speech production attempt to predict how people's utterances unfold in time for sounds, words, and structures. For example, researchers might study why speakers find it easier to produce some sounds than others in ongoing speech (Goldrick & Larson, 2008). The analyses focus on such factors as the relative frequency of certain sounds in particular positions (for example, an *s* sound is more likely than a *z* sound to occur at the beginning of an English word). Other projects examine the time course with which people produce the particular words of an utterance. Researchers have demonstrated, for example, that people find it harder to produce a word (such as *cow*) when they have recently spoken another word with which it is associated (such as *milk*). Such results are explained as a consequence of different memory representations competing to be included in an utterance (Rahman & Melinger, 2007).

For structures, researchers often examine the factors that lead speakers to choose one or another way of expressing the same idea. Consider **Figure 8.5.** If you described this scene, you might either say "The girl was frightened by the jack-in-the-box" or "The jack-in-the-box frightened the girl." To understand why speakers choose a particular structure, researchers point to such factors as the recent language that the speaker has heard and understood (Bock et al., 2007). If, for example, you have recently heard a sentence such as "The embassy staff isn't being evacuated by the government," you would be more likely to produce an utterance that has the same global structure (such as "The girl was frightened by the jack-in-the-box").

We have now looked at some of the forces that lead speakers to produce particular utterances and at some of the processes that allow them to do so. We turn next to the listeners, who are responsible for understanding what speakers intend to communicate.

LANGUAGE UNDERSTANDING

Suppose a speaker has produced the utterance "The cat is on the mat." You already know that, depending on the context, this utterance can be used to communicate any number of different meanings. How, as a listener, do you settle on just one meaning? We will begin this discussion of language understanding by considering more fully the problem of the ambiguity of meaning.

Resolving Ambiguity What does the word *bank* mean? You can probably think of at least two meanings, one having to do with rivers and the other having to do with money. Suppose you hear the utterance "He came from the bank." How do you know which meaning is intended? You need to be able to resolve the *lexical ambiguity* between the two meanings. (*Lexical* is related to *lexicon,* a synonym for *dictionary.*) If you think about this problem, you'll realize that you have some cognitive processes that allow you to use surrounding context to eliminate the ambiguity—to *disambiguate*—the word. Have you been talking about rivers or about money? That broader context should enable you to choose between the two meanings. But how?

Before we answer that question, we'd like to introduce another type of ambiguity. What does this sentence mean: "The mother of the boy and the girl will arrive soon?" You may detect only one meaning right off, but there is a *structural ambiguity* here (Akmajian et al., 1990). Take a look at **Figure 8.6.** Linguists often represent the structure of sentences with tree diagrams to show how the various words are gathered together into grammatical units. In part A, *we've shown you an analysis of "The cat is on the mat." The structure is pretty simple: a noun phrase made up of an article and a noun, plus a verb phrase made up of a verb and a prepositional phrase. In the other two parts, you see the more complex structures for the two different meanings of "The mother . . . ." In part B, the analysis shows that the whole phrase "of the boy and the girl" applies to the mother. One person—the mother of two children—will arrive soon. In part C, the analysis shows that there are two noun phrases, "the mother of the boy" and "the girl." There are two people, both of whom will arrive soon. Which understanding of the sentence did you come to when you first read it? Now that you can see that two meanings are possible, we arrive at the same question we did for lexical ambiguity: How does prior context enable you to settle on one meaning when more than one is possible?

Let's return to lexical ambiguity (an ambiguity of word meaning). Consider this sentence (from Mason & Just, 2007):

To their surprise, the bark was unusual because it sounded high-pitched and hoarse.

When you read this sentence, how do you interpret the word *bark?* If you imagine that you have a dictionary in your head, your entry for bark might look something like this:

Definition 1. The exterior covering of a tree.
Definition 2. The sound a dog makes.

Research suggests that both definitions become accessible in memory when you first encounter such an ambiguous word, but

FIGURE 8.5 Selecting a Sentence Structure

How would you describe this scene?

Reprinted from *Cognition, 104,* Bock, K., Dell, G.S., Chang, F., & Onishi, K. H., Persistent Structural Priming From Language Comprehension to Language Production, 437-458, Copyright (2007), with permission from Elsevier.

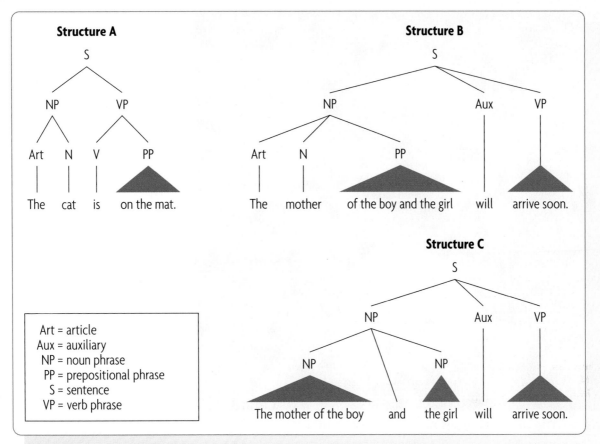

FIGURE 8.6 Sentence Structures

Linguists use tree diagrams to display the grammatical structure of sentences. Part A shows the structure of "The cat is on the mat." Parts B and C show that the sentence "The mother of the boy and the girl will arrive soon" can be represented by two different structural analyses. Who will arrive soon, one person (structure B) or two (structure C)?

you swiftly use contextual information to determine which definition is appropriate. The word *bark* is called a *balanced ambiguity* because people use its two meanings with roughly equal frequency. Now consider this sentence:

Last year the pen was abandoned because it was too dirty for the animals to live in.

Did that sentence give you any trouble? *Pen* also has two definitions:

Definition 1. An implement for writing with ink.
Definition 2. An enclosure for animals.

Pen is called a *biased ambiguity* because people use one meaning (that is, Definition 1) much more often than the other. You may have experienced some momentary trouble understanding this sentence because your initial bias toward understanding *pen* to mean "an implement for writing with ink" was proved wrong by the context that followed its use. Research suggests that your brain responds differently to these two types of ambiguity.

Twelve participants read sentences while undergoing fMRI scans. The sentences included balanced or biased ambiguities or were matched control sentences (Mason & Just, 2007). For example, in the sentence "To their surprise, the bark was

Now that you are looking at a picture of an animal pen, what comes to mind when you think of the word *pen?*

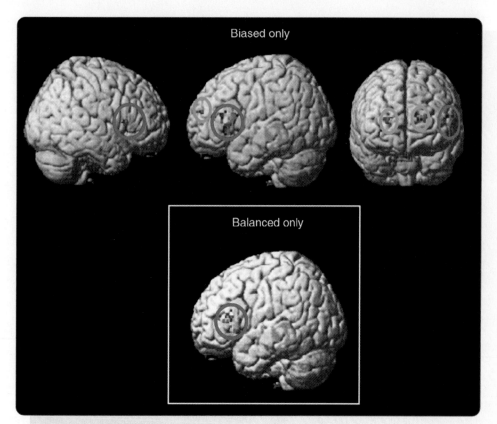

FIGURE 8.7 The Brain Bases of Ambiguity Resolution

Participants underwent fMRI scans while reading sentences with balanced or biased ambiguities or matched control sentences. The brain region circled in red showed greater activity for both types of ambiguity (with respect to the control sentences). The brain region circled in green only showed more activity for the sentences with biased ambiguities.

unusual because it sounded high-pitched and hoarse," *howl* replaced *bark* (that is, "the howl was unusual . . .) to provide an unambiguous sentence. The researchers predicted that, because participants need to select between meanings, ambiguous sentences would produce different patterns of brain activity than control sentences. As seen in **Figure 8.7**, that prediction was confirmed. The reseachers also predicted that, because participants need to recover from their biased interpretations, the biased ambiguities would produce different brain activity than balanced ambiguities. Again, the brain scans shown in Figure 8.7 confirm that prediction.

This experiment identifies brain regions that help you understand an ambiguous word: You put contextual information to swift and efficient use to arrive at a single meaning. Context wields a similar influence on structural ambiguities (Farmer et al., 2007; Grodner et al., 2005). Contextual information speeds decisions when you must choose among different possible grammatical structures.

The overall conclusion you can draw is that your language processes use context powerfully and efficiently to resolve ambiguities. In a way, this shows that there is a good match between production and understanding. When we discussed language production, we emphasized audience design—the processes by which speakers try to make their utterances appropriate in the current context. Our analysis of understanding suggests that listeners expect speakers to have done their jobs well. Under those

circumstances, it makes sense for listeners to let context guide their expectations about what speakers will have meant.

The Products of Understanding Our discussion of ambiguity resolution focused on the *processes* of understanding. In this section, we shift our attention to the *products* of understanding. The question now is: What *representations* result in memory when listeners understand utterances or texts? What, for example, would be stored in memory when you hear our old standby "The cat is on the mat"? Research has suggested that meaning representation begins with basic units called *propositions* (Clark & Clark, 1977; Kintsch, 1974). Propositions are the main ideas of utterances. For "The cat is on the mat," the main idea is that something is on something else. When you read the utterance, you will extract the proposition *on* and understand the relationship that it expresses between *the cat* and *the mat*. Often propositions are written like this: *ON (cat, mat)*. Many utterances contain more than one proposition. Consider "The cat watched the mouse run under the sofa." We have as the first component proposition *UNDER (mouse, sofa)*. From that, we build up *RUN (mouse, UNDER [mouse, sofa])*. Finally, we get to *WATCH (cat, RUN [mouse, UNDER (mouse, sofa)])*.

How can we test whether your mental representations of meaning really work this way? Some of the earliest experiments in the psychology of language were devoted to showing the importance of propositional representations in understanding (Kintsch, 1974). Research has shown that if two words in an utterance belong to the same proposition, they will be represented together in memory even if they are not close together in the actual sentence.

Consider the sentence "The mausoleum that enshrined the tzar overlooked the square." Although *mausoleum* and *square* are far apart in the sentence, a propositional analysis suggests that they should be gathered together in memory in the proposition *OVERLOOKED (mausoleum, square)*. To test this analysis, researchers asked participants to read lists of words and say whether each had appeared in the sentence. Some participants saw *mausoleum* directly after *square* on the list. Other participants saw *mausoleum* after a word from another proposition. The response "Yes, I saw *mausoleum*" was swifter when *mausoleum* came directly after *square* than when its predecessor came from another proposition. This finding suggests that the concepts *mausoleum* and *square* had been represented together in memory (Ratcliff & McKoon, 1978).

Have you ever noticed how hard it is to remember *exactly* what someone said? You might, for example, have tried to remember a line from a movie word-for-word—but you realized when you got home that you could only remember the general sense of what was said. This experiment indicates why word-for-word memory isn't so good: Because one of the main operations your language processes carry out is the extraction of propositions, the exact form with which those propositions were rendered gets lost pretty quickly (for example, "The cat chased the mouse" versus "The mouse was chased by the cat").

Not all the propositions listeners store in memory are made up of information directly stated by the speaker. Often listeners fill gaps with **inferences**—logical assumptions made possible by information in memory. Consider this pair of utterances:

I'm heading to the deli to meet Donna.
She promised to buy me a sandwich for lunch.

To understand how these sentences go together, you must draw at least two important inferences. You must figure out both who *she* is in the second sentence and how going to a deli is related to a promise to buy a sandwich. Note that a friend who actually uttered this pair of sentences would be confident you could figure these things out. You'd never expect to hear this:

I'm heading to the deli to meet Donna. She—and by *she* I mean Donna—promised to buy me a sandwich—and a *deli* is a place where you can buy a sandwich—for lunch.

Speakers count on listeners to draw inferences of this sort.

A great deal of research has been directed toward determining what types of inferences listeners draw on a regular basis (Gerrig & O'Brien, 2005). The number of potential inferences after any utterance is unlimited. For example, because you know that Donna is likely to be a human, you could infer that she has a heart, a liver, a pair of lungs, and so on (and on), but it's unlikely that you would feel compelled to call any of those (perfectly valid) inferences to mind when you heard "I'm heading to the deli to meet Donna."

Research suggests, in fact, that the models readers develop for the whole situation of a text affects which inferences they encode. For example, read the text numbered 1 in **Table 8.5**. At the end of this text, did you encode the inference that Carol is

---

TABLE 8.5 Text Situations and Inferences

1. Carol was a single mother with two young children. She had to work two jobs to make ends meet. She worked full-time as a teacher and part-time as a waitress. She hated not having much free time. Carol was known for her short temper and her tendency to act without thinking. She never thought about the consequences of her actions, so she often suffered negative repercussions. She refused to let people walk all over her. In fact, she had just gotten a ticket for road rage. She decided she would never put up with anyone that was not nice to her. One particular night, Carol had an extremely rude customer. He complained about the spaghetti, and he yelled at Carol as if it were her fault. Carol lifted the spaghetti above his head.

2. Carol was a single mother with two young children. She had to work two jobs to make ends meet. She worked full-time as a teacher and part-time as a waitress. She hated not having much free time. Carol had just come back to work after having had shoulder surgery. She needed to be careful whenever raising anything from a customer's table. Every time she did, it would hurt so much that she thought she might faint. If she raised something too high, she was extremely uncomfortable all night. But, usually, she asked for help when she needed to clear a table. One particular night, Carol had an extremely rude customer. He complained about the spaghetti, and he yelled at Carol as if it were her fault. Carol lifted the spaghetti above his head.

---

likely to dump the spaghetti on the customer? Research suggests that readers consistently draw that inference (Guéraud et al., 2008). Now read the text numbered 2. In this latter case, readers now infer that Carol will experience pain.

Our discussion of language use has demonstrated how much work a speaker does to produce the right sentence at the right time and how much work a listener does to figure out exactly what the speaker meant. You usually aren't aware of all this work! Does this give you a greater appreciation for the elegant efficiency of your cognitive processes?

LANGUAGE AND EVOLUTION

We just concluded you have a range of processes that are working diligently in the background to help you produce and understand language. A question that has long fascinated researchers is whether any other species possesses the same range of processes. We know of no other species that uses a language as complex as any human language. That observation raises an interesting question: What processes did humans evolve that make human language possible? To answer that question, researchers have

---

inference Missing information filled in on the basis of a sample of evidence or on the basis of prior beliefs and theories.

largely turned to research with other species: They attempt to define what makes humans and human languages special. We will focus on *language structure* and *audience design*.

One property that makes human language special is that people can produce an unlimited number of messages with a limited number of words: You follow the grammatical rules of your language—of the types represented by the structures in Figure 8.6—to produce as many sentences as you'll ever need from the set of words you know. Researchers have suggested that humans are the only species that can apply rules of the complexity found in human languages (Fitch & Hauser, 2004; Saffran et al., 2008). This conclusion has been reached after several decades of research in which people have tried to teach nonhuman species languages with humanlike structure.

Beginning as early as the 1920s, psychologists tried to address this question by attempting to teach language to chimpanzees. Chimps don't have the appropriate vocal apparatus to produce spoken language, so researchers had to devise other methods of communication. For example, a chimp named Washoe was taught a highly simplified version of American Sign Language (Gardner & Gardner, 1969); a chimp named Sarah was taught to manipulate plastic symbols (which stood for concepts like *apple* and *give*) on a magnetic board (Premack, 1971). The results of these experiments inspired great controversy (Seidenberg & Petitto, 1979). Skeptics asked whether the chimps' occasional combinations of gestures or symbols (for example, *Washoe sorry. You more drink*) constituted any meaningful kind of language use. They also wondered whether most of the meaning attributed to the chimps' utterances wasn't arising in the heads of the humans rather than in the heads of the chimps.

Sue Savage-Rumbaugh and her colleagues (Savage-Rumbaugh et al., 1998) have conducted research that has provided more solid insights into the language capabilities of chimps. Savage-Rumbaugh works primarily with *bonobos,* a species of great ape that is evolutionarily more similar to humans even than common chimpanzees. Rather remarkably, two of the bonobos in her studies, Kanzi and Mulika, acquired the meanings of plastic symbols (similar to the ones the chimp Sarah had used) with no explicit training: They acquired the symbols *spontaneously* by observing others (humans and bonobos) using them to communicate. Moreover, Kanzi and Mulika were able to understand some *spoken* English. For example, when Kanzi heard a spoken word, he was able to locate either the symbol for the word or a photograph of the object. Kanzi was also able to follow simple commands such as "Take off Sue's shoe." Kanzi's performance strongly suggests that some aspects of human language performance can be found in other species. However, Kanzi still falls short of human abilities: He wasn't able to acquire the type of rule system that would allow him to produce an unlimited number of utterances. Other cross-species research reinforces the conclusion that humans alone evolved the processes to produce and understand appropriately complex grammatical structures (Fitch & Hauser, 2004).

Another focus of cross-species comparison has been on what we earlier called *audience design*. When you are successful at audience design, you take into account what your listener does and doesn't know. Are nonhuman animals able to modify their messages based on what members of their audience know? Researchers have set out to answer this question. For example, **Dorothy Cheney** and **Robert Seyfarth** (1990) have done extensive research on the communicative capabilities of

Some bonobos have learned the meanings of words without explicit training. What other abilities must these animals demonstrate before it can be said that they have genuinely acquired a human language?

vervet monkeys. Vervet monkeys make distinct *calls* to signal the presence of different dangers, such as leopards, eagles, and snakes. These monkeys are able to modify their calls depending on their audience: Female monkeys gave alarms at much higher rates when they were with their own offspring than when they were with monkeys unrelated to them. However, the vervets do not modify their calls based on what their audience knows: In an experimental setting, mother vervets produced the same calls irrespective of whether their offspring had also witnessed the events that evoked the calls.

Researchers continue to try to understand exactly what sets humans apart from other species with respect to their ability to engage in audience design (Hare, 2007). For example, one study examined the extent to which members of other species are able to understand the relationship between where people focus their attention and what they can see (Okamoto-Barth et al., 2007). In the study, experimenters directed their gaze toward a barrier that was either solid or had a window. Imagine yourself in that situation. You would quickly infer that the experimenter's gaze could only indicate the presence of an object on the *far side* of the barrier when the barrier had a window. Bonobos, chimpanzees, and gorillas constructed the same inference, but orangutans did not. When confronted with the solid barrier, bonobos and chimpanzees were more sophisticated in their visual search than were gorillas. These data illustrate some steps in the evolution of humans' ability to take the perspective of others.

An evolutionary perspective on language examines the critical processes humans evolved to make language possible. However, that general set of processes allows a wide variety of languages to emerge. In the next section, we will discuss some potential consequences of the differences among languages.

LANGUAGE, THOUGHT, AND CULTURE

Have you had the opportunity to learn more than one language? If so, do you believe that you *think* differently in the two languages? Does language affect thought? This question is one that researchers have addressed in a variety of ways. Let us give you a cross-linguistic example to make this question more concrete. Consider the words *dog, skunk,* and *monkey.* Which two seem most similar to you? When you approach this question as an English speaker, you might not have a very clear-cut answer to this question. But suppose you speak Italian, a language that assigns nouns *grammatical gender: Cane* (dog) is marked as masculine; *puzzola* (skunk) and *scimmia* (monkey) are marked as feminine. Many languages of the world, such as French and Spanish, mark nouns as masculine or feminine in a similar fashion. Could it be the case that, because of grammatical gender, Italian speakers would experience a puzzola and a scimmia as more similar than English speakers would experience a skunk and a monkey? This question provides a good example of why people have so often been intrigued by the potential of language to influence thought.

Scholarly work on this question was originated by **Edward Sapir** and his student **Benjamin Lee Whorf,** whose cross-linguistic explorations led them to the somewhat radical conclusion that differences in language would create differences in thought. Here's how Sapir put it:

> We see and hear and otherwise experience very largely as we do because the language habits of our community predispose certain choices of interpretation. (Sapir, 1941/1964, p. 69)

For Sapir and Whorf, this conclusion emerged directly from relationships they believed to exist in their own data. From the hypotheses that Sapir and Whorf proposed, the one that has received the most attention is called **linguistic relativity** (Brown, 1976). According to this hypothesis, the structure of the language an individual speaks has an impact on the way in which that individual thinks about the world. Contemporary researchers in psychology, linguistics, and anthropology have attempted to create rigorous tests of these ideas (Gentner & Goldin-Meadow, 2003). Let's look at a particular domain in which researchers have demonstrated an impact of language on thought.

You may be surprised to learn that languages of the world differ with respect to the number of basic color terms they use. As determined by linguistic analysis, English has 11 (*black, white, red, yellow, green, blue, brown, purple, pink, orange,* and *gray*); some languages of the world, such as the language spoken by the Dani people of Papua New Guinea, have only two, a simple distinction between *black* and *white* (or *light* and *dark*) (Berlin & Kay, 1969). Whorf had suggested that language users "dissect nature along the lines laid down by [their] native languages" (1956, p. 213). Researchers speculated that the category structure implied by color terms might influence the ways in which speakers of different languages were able to think about colors:

Researchers asked 12 speakers of Himba from northern Namibia to examine triads of color chips all taken from the blue–green continuum. The participants' task was to indicate "which of these three colors look most like each other, in the way that brothers look like each other?" (Roberson et al., 2005, p. 395). Unlike English, the Himba language doesn't make a lexical distinction between *blue* and *green.* Instead, Himba speakers use the term *borou* that covers most green and blue hues. The researchers looked for evidence of *categorical perception:* They assessed the extent to which Himba speakers perceived hues to be more similar within the categories marked by the language than

The Dani people of Papua New Guinea speak a language with only two basic color terms—they make a distinction between black and white (or light and dark). English, by comparison, has 11 basic color terms. Could this language difference affect the way people experience the world?

between categories. Indeed, the Himba participants' similarity judgments showed a clear impact of the categorical structure of their language.

The results provide support for the claim of linguistic relativity—that language may, in some circumstances, have an impact on thought.

As a second example of research on linguistic relativity, let's return to the contrast between English and Italian with which we opened this section. To assess the impact of grammatical gender, researchers asked English monolinguals, Italian monolinguals, and English–Italian bilinguals to perform a task in which they tried to name the animals in pictures flashed for, on average, less than a second (Kousta et al., 2008). Because the task was difficult, participants sometimes made errors by giving the wrong animal name. However English and Italian monolinguals produced different patterns of errors: Italian speakers were more likely to produce incorrect names that had the same grammatical gender as the correct name. The bilinguals made English-type errors when they performed the task in English and Italian-type errors when they performed the task in Italian!

There are thousands of languages in the world, which provide many interesting distinctions. As researchers have examined a broader range of those distinctions, they find the hypothesis of linguistic relativity is better supported in some domains than in others (see January & Kako, 2007; Papafragou et al., 2007). Still, interesting hypotheses about the link between language and thought have yet to be tested. As we describe cultural differences throughout *Psychology and Life,* it is worth keeping an open mind about linguistic relativity. Given the many situations in which members of different cultures speak very different languages, we can wonder to what extent language plays a causal role in bringing about cultural differences.

---

linguistic relativity The hypothesis that the structure of the language an individual speaks has an impact on the way in which that individual thinks about the world.

Psychology in Your Life

WHY AND HOW DO PEOPLE LIE?

In this section on language use, we have emphasized that people aspire to be cooperative conversationalists. For example, we suggested that people follow the principle, "Try to make your contribution one that is true." However, we know that people often fall away from this standard. When people were asked to keep diaries of the lies they told, most averaged one or two a day (DePaulo et al., 2003). But why do people lie? When the lies are relatively mild, more people lie for psychological reasons (for example, they wish to spare themselves embarrassment) than for personal advantage (for example, they wish to avoid an unpleasant chore). However, when lies become more serious, the motives for lying shift in the direction of personal advantage. In one study, participants were asked to reveal the most serious lie that they had ever told (DePaulo et al., 2004). People quite frequently committed serious lies to conceal affairs or other forbidden forms of social contact. People felt that they were entitled to cheat on their partners and lied in service to that sense of entitlement. Thus the lies worked for personal advantage.

Let's focus on the mental processes that people use to lie. Should it be easier or harder to tell a lie than to tell the truth? The answer is: It depends (DePaulo et al., 2003).

Suppose you are asked, "What did you do last night?" If you choose to lie spontaneously, it might be harder for you to formulate a lie than to tell the truth. However, if you have prepared your lie in advance—because you anticipate the awkward question—you might produce your lie with great fluidity. Still, lies and truths differ from each other in some consistent ways. A study that reviewed the literature on the content of lies reported that liars provide fewer details in their accounts than do people who are telling the truth (DePaulo et al., 2003). In addition, liars' accounts were consistently less plausible and less fluent than truthful accounts.

These results suggest that speakers may engage different mental processes to produce their lies. To test this hypothesis, researchers have begun to analyze patterns of brain activity that underlie truth-telling and lying. In one study, participants were asked to lie or tell the truth about their participation in an incident in which a gun was fired in a hospital (Mohamed et al., 2006). To make the experience of lying as real as possible, participants in the *guilty* condition actually fired a starter pistol (loaded with blanks) in the testing room. Participants in both the *guilty* and *not-guilty* conditions answered a series of questions while undergoing fMRI scans. Participants in the guilty condition received instructions to lie about their role in the incident. The fMRI scans revealed that several areas of the brain were more active for lying than for truth telling. For example, brain regions responsible for planning and emotion were harder at work when participants prepared their lies.

Another study looked into the brains of people who qualify as *pathological liars*—these are individuals who lie with sufficient regularity that the behavior is considered abnormal (by the types of *DSM-IV* criteria we describe in Chapter 14). The overall structure of brains of the pathological liars were compared using MRI to the brains of matched controls (Yang et al., 2005). Those brain comparisons revealed consistent differences in the prefrontal cortex. The pathological liars, for example, had more of the type of brain tissue that allows neurons to communicate with each other. Prefrontal cortex is a region of the brain that plays an important role in planning—suggesting that the pathological liars are particularly well equipped to plan their lies. These results, however, leave open the question of cause and effect: Did pathological liars start life with brains of this type (which, perhaps, caused or allowed them to lie frequently), or did frequent lying change their brains?

Let's turn now from circumstances in which meaning is communicated through words to those in which meaning relies also on pictures.

STOP AND REVIEW

❶ What is the relationship between the cooperative principle and audience design?

❷ Suppose you are trying to pronounce "big pet" and "bird pen." Why would you be more likely to commit the speech error "pig bet" than "pird ben"?

❸ How would you detect inferences in people's representations?

❹ What are two language abilities that researchers suggest might set humans apart from other species?

❺ What does the linguistic relativity hypothesis suggest?

CRITICAL THINKING Recall the study on community membership. Why might the researchers have used landmarks from three different cities?

Visit MyPsychLab.com for more review and practice on the following topic:

◉ **Watch:** Birds and Language

Visual Cognition

In **Figure 8.8,** we give you two choices for visual representations of the sentence "The cat is on the mat." Which one seems right? If you think in terms of language-based propositions, each alternative captures the right meaning—the cat *is* on the mat. Even so, you're probably happy only with option A because it matches the scene you likely called to mind when you first read the sentence (Searle, 1979). How about option B? It probably makes you somewhat nervous because it seems as if the cat is going to tip right over. This anxious feeling must arise because you can think with pictures. In a sense, you can *see* exactly what's going to happen. In this section, we will explore some of the ways in which visual images and visual processes contribute to the way you think.

USING VISUAL REPRESENTATIONS

History is full of examples of famous discoveries apparently made on the basis of mental imagery (Shepard, 1978). Frederich Kekulé, the discoverer of the chemical structure of benzene, often conjured up mental images of dancing atoms that fastened themselves into chains of molecules. His discovery of the benzene ring occurred in a dream in which a snakelike molecule chain suddenly grabbed its own tail, thus forming a ring. Michael Faraday, who discovered many properties of magnetism, knew little about mathematics, but he had vivid mental images of the properties of magnetic fields. Albert Einstein claimed to have thought entirely in terms of visual images, translating his findings into mathematical symbols and words only after the work of visually based discovery was finished.

We have given you these examples to encourage you to try to indulge in visual thinking. But even without trying, you regularly use your capabilities for manipulating visual images. Consider a classic experiment in which participants were asked to transform images in their heads.

> Researchers presented students with examples of the letter *R* and its mirror image that had been rotated various amounts, from 0 to 180 degrees (see **Figure 8.9** on page 248). As the letter appeared, the student had to identify it as either the normal *R* or its mirror image. The reaction time taken to make that decision was longer in direct proportion to the amount the figure had been rotated. This finding indicated that a subject was imagining the figure in his or her "mind's eye" and rotating the image into an upright position at some fixed rate before deciding whether the figure was an *R* or a mirror image. The consistency of the rate of rotation suggested that the process of mental rotation was very similar to the process of physical rotation (Shepard & Cooper, 1982).

You put this ability for mental rotation to very good use. You often see objects in the environment from unfamiliar points of view. Mental rotation allows you to transform the image to one that matches representations stored in memory (Lloyd-Jones & Luckhurst, 2002).

You can also use visual images to answer certain types of questions about the world. Suppose, for example, we asked you whether a golf ball is bigger than a Ping-Pong ball. If you can't retrieve that fact directly from memory, you might find it convenient to form a visual image of them side by side. Your mental images also allow you to recover visual properties of objects

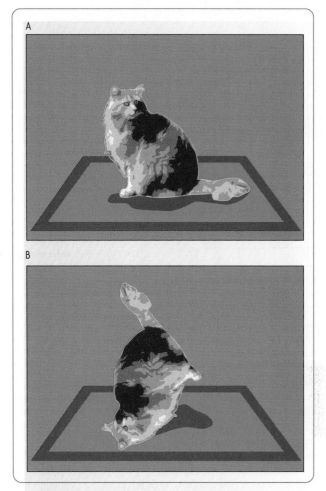

FIGURE 8.8 Visual Representations
Are both of these cats on the mat?

that might have escaped your attention when you first saw them (Thompson et al., 2008). For example, try to create a mental image of the first letter of the English alphabet as a capital letter. Does your image include a diagonal line? Does your image have an enclosed space? Did you get the sense of zooming in on the image to answer these different questions? Once again, this use of an image has much in common with the properties of real visual perception. When an object is physically present, you can refocus your attention to acquire more information. The same is true for visual images.

There are, of course, limits to the use of your visual imagination. Consider this problem:

Imagine that you have a large piece of blank paper. In your mind, fold it in half (making two layers), fold it in half again (four layers), and continue folding it over 50 times. About how thick is the paper when you are done? (Adams, 1986)

The actual answer is about 50 million miles ($2^{50} \times 0.028$ inches, the thickness of a piece of paper), approximately half the distance between Earth and the sun. Your estimate was probably considerably lower. Your mind's eye was overwhelmed by the information you asked it to represent.

We want you to try one last exercise using visual imagery. Find any object in your environment and examine it for a few

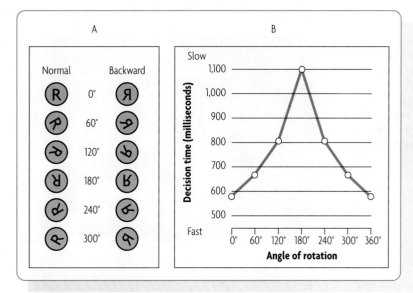

FIGURE 8.9 Rotated *R* Used to Assess Mental Imagery

Participants presented with these figures in random order were asked to say, as quickly as possible, whether each figure was a normal *R* or a mirror image. The more the figure was rotated from upright, the longer the reaction time was.

seconds. Now, close your eyes and try to create a visual image of the same object. Consider this question: How much overlap was there in the brain regions that were active when you engaged in visual perception versus visual imagery? To answer this question, researchers had participants learn a series of line drawings of common objects such as a tree (Ganis et al., 2004). In the next phase of the experiment, participants underwent fMRI scans while they either inspected the same drawings on a computer screen or generated visual images of the drawings. For each drawing, they answered a simple question such as whether the object contained circular parts. **Figure 8.10** presents the results of the fMRI scans from different regions of the brain. The left and middle columns show the regions of the brain that differed for each task from the baseline condition (that is, when participants were not engaged in a task). The right column shows the brain regions that were particular to the perception task. These data support two important conclusions. First, there was substantial overlap between brain processes for perception and imagery. Second, brain regions for imagery were a subset of those for perception—participants didn't use any special regions to create a visual image. With respect to brain activity, you use much the same resources to encode the visual world as to re-create a visual representation.

COMBINING VERBAL AND VISUAL REPRESENTATIONS

Our discussion so far has largely focused on the types of visual representations that you form by committing to memory—or in the case of imagery, retrieving from memory—visual stimuli from the environment. However, you often form visual images based on verbal descriptions. You can, for example, create a mental picture of a cat with three tails, although you've almost certainly never seen one. The verbal description enables you to form a visual representation. Your ability to produce a mental image of a verbal scene is particularly useful when you read works of fiction that involve spatial details. Consider this passage from the James Bond short story "From a View to a Kill":

> *The clearing was about as big as two tennis courts and floored in thick grass and moss. There was one large patch of lilies of the valley and, under the bordering trees, a*

> *scattering of bluebells. To one side there was a low mound . . . completely surrounded and covered with brambles and briar roses now thickly in bloom. Bond walked round this and gazed in among the roots, but there was nothing to see except the earthy shape of the mound. (Fleming, 1959, pp. 19–20)*

Did you try to imagine the scene—and help Bond search for danger? (He will find it.) When you read, you can form a *spatial mental model* to keep track of the whereabouts of characters (Rinck, 2008). Researchers have often focused on the ways in which spatial mental models capture properties of real spatial experiences.

Suppose, for example, you read a passage of a text that places you in the middle of an interesting environment.

> *You are hob-nobbing at the opera. You came tonight to meet and chat with interesting members of the upper class. At the moment, you are standing next to the railing of a wide, elegant balcony overlooking the first floor. Directly behind you, at your eye level, is an ornate lamp attached to the balcony wall. The base of the lamp, which is attached to the wall, is gilded in gold. (Franklin & Tversky, 1990, p. 65)*

In a series of experiments, readers studied descriptions of this sort that vividly described the layout of objects around the viewer (Franklin & Tversky, 1990). The researchers wished to show that readers were faster or slower to access information about the scene, depending on where the objects were in the mental space around them. Readers, for example, were quicker to say what object was in front of them in the scene than what object was behind them, even though all objects were introduced equally carefully in the stories (see **Figure 8.11**). It's easiest to understand this result if you believe that the representation you form while reading actually places you, in some sense, in the scene. You are able to transform a verbal experience into a visual, spatial experience.

You also regularly combine verbal and visual representations when you attempt to find your way to a new destination. Suppose you want to drive from your hometown to Darwin, Minnesota, site of the world's largest ball of twine. Nowadays, you'd probably go to a website like MapQuest or GoogleMaps to get your directions. However, research suggests that some types of directions immediately yield more flexible spatial mental models than do others.

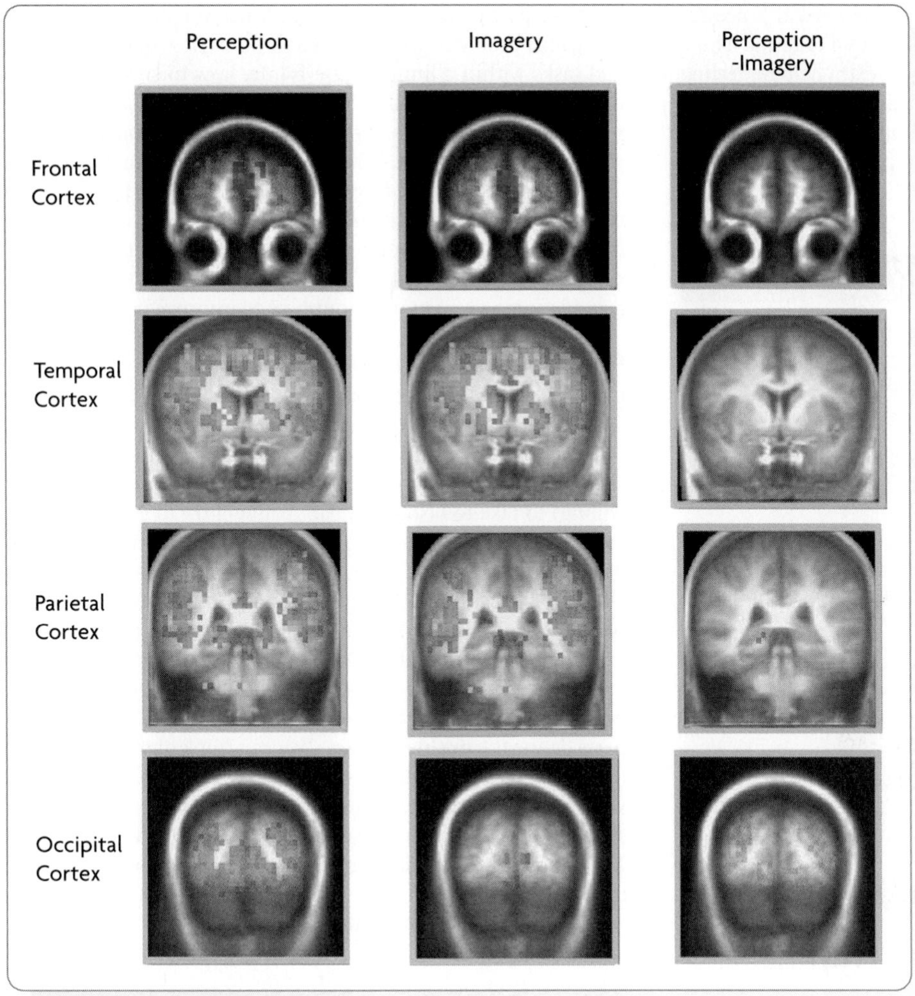

Perception   Imagery   Perception-Imagery

Frontal Cortex

Temporal Cortex

Parietal Cortex

Occipital Cortex

FIGURE 8.10 The Brain Bases of Visual Imagery
The figure shows the results of fMRI scans when participants were engaged in either a perception task or an imagery task. The left and middle columns show brain activity for each task: Regions marked with red, orange, and yellow were more active with respect to a no-task baseline; regions marked in blues were less active. The right column shows the brain regions that were affected by the perception task but not the imagery task. These fMRI scans demonstrate that much the same brain regions are used for perception and imagery.

Reprinted from *Cognitive Brain Research, 20,* G. Ganis et al., "Brain areas underlying visual mental imagery and visual perception: An fMRI study," pp. 226–241, copyright © 2004, with permission from Elsevier.

Participants learned descriptions for a pair of neighborhoods (adapted from areas of Pittsburgh, PA, and Detroit, MI) (Brunyé et al., 2008). The descriptions had two different formats. The *survey descriptions* provided a "bird's-eye view," as if the person providing the information were hovering above the neighborhood: "From Moore Field Playground, Pioneer Avenue runs south. Portions of Pioneer Avenue have been blocked off due to repair. Capital Avenue heads east from Pioneer Avenue." The *route descriptions* moved readers through the neighborhoods on mental tours: "Turn left from Moore Field Playground to Pioneer Avenue heading south. Portions of Pioneer Avenue have been blocked off due to repair. Head left on Capital Avenue driving from Pioneer Avenue." After learning the descriptions, participants responded to a series of questions that tested their knowledge of the neighborhoods. Participants' performance was affected by the type of description they had learned: They were more flexible in their ability to answer questions when they had formed spatial mental models based on survey information.

The researchers suggested that survey descriptions allow readers to get a better sense of how the various parts of a neighborhood fit together. By contrast, route descriptions focus attention on a single path through the neighborhood. If you've ever downloaded directions that mistakenly led you to a dead end, you'll know how inflexible your mental models based on route descriptions can be: It's hard to find your own path around the obstacle!

FIGURE 8.11 Spatial Mental Models
You can use imagination to project yourself into the middle of a scene. Just as if you were really standing in the room, you would take less time to say what is in front of you (the lamp) than what is behind you (the bust).

In this section, we have seen that you have visual processes and representations to complement your verbal abilities. These two types of access to information give you extra help in dealing with the demands and tasks of your life. We turn now to domains in which you put both visual and verbal representations to use in coping with your life's complexities: *problem solving* and *reasoning*.

STOP AND REVIEW

❶ How similar are the processes of physical rotation and mental rotation?

❷ What has research shown about the brain bases of visual images?

❸ If you're imagining yourself in a scene, does it matter how you place yourself in the room?

CRITICAL THINKING Consider the experiment that contrasted types of descriptions. If you receive directions as a route description, how could you transform them into a survey description?

Visit MyPsychLab.com for more review and practice on the following topic:

✴ **Simulate:** Mental Rotation

Problem Solving and Reasoning

Let's return for a minute to your mysterious message, "The cat is on the mat." If you've come to understand the message, what do you do next? For those of you whose lives are less filled with mystery, consider a more common situation: You've accidentally locked yourself out of your home, room, or car. Again, what do you do next? For both situations, reflect on the types of mental steps you might take to overcome your difficulty. Those mental steps will almost certainly include the cognitive processes that make up **problem solving** and **reasoning.** Both of these activities require you to combine current information with information stored in memory to work toward some particular goal: a conclusion or a solution. We will look at aspects of problem solving and at two types of reasoning, deductive and inductive.

PROBLEM SOLVING

What goes on four legs in the morning, on two legs at noon, and on three legs in the twilight? According to Greek mythology, this was the riddle posed by the Sphinx, an evil creature who threatened to hold the people of Thebes in tyranny until someone could solve the riddle. To break the code, Oedipus had to recognize elements of the riddle as metaphors. Morning, noon, and twilight represented different periods in a human life. A baby crawls and so (effectively) has four legs, an adult walks on two legs, and an older person walks on two legs but uses a cane, making a total of three legs. Oedipus's solution to the riddle was *humans.*

Although your daily problems may not seem as monumental as the one faced by young Oedipus, problem-solving activity

is a basic part of your everyday existence. You continually come up against problems that require solutions: how to manage work and tasks within a limited time frame, how to succeed at a job interview, how to break off a relationship, and so on. Many problems involve discrepancies between what you know and what you need to know. When you solve a problem, you reduce that discrepancy by finding a way to get the missing information. To get into the spirit of problem solving, try the problems in **Figure 8.12.** After you're done, we'll see how psychological research can shed light on your performance—and, perhaps, provide some suggestions about how to improve it.

Problem Spaces and Processes How do you define a problem in real-life circumstances? You usually perceive the difference between your current state and a desired goal: For example, you are broke, and you'd like to have some money. You are also usually aware of some of the steps you would be able (or willing) to take to bridge the gap: You will try to get a part-time job, but you won't become a pickpocket. The formal definition of a *problem* captures these three elements (Newell & Simon, 1972). A problem is defined by (1) an *initial state*—the incomplete information or unsatisfactory conditions you start with; (2) a *goal state*—the information or state of the world you hope to obtain; and (3) a *set of operations*—the steps you may take to move from an initial state to a goal state. Together, these three parts define the **problem space.** You can think of solving a problem as walking through a maze (the problem space) from where you are (the initial state) to where you want to be (the goal state), making a series of turns (the allowable operations).

Much of the initial difficulty in solving a problem will arise if any of these elements are not well defined (Simon, 1973). A *well-defined problem* is similar to a textbook problem in which the initial state, the goal state, and the operations are all clearly specified. Your task is to discover how to use allowable, known operations to get the answer. By contrast, an *ill-defined problem* is similar to designing a home, writing a novel, or finding a cure for AIDS. The initial state, the goal state, and/or the operations may be unclear and vaguely specified. In such cases, the problem solver's first task is to work out, as much as possible, exactly what the problem is—to make explicit a beginning, an ideal solution, and the possible means to achieve it.

As you know from your own experience, even when the initial and goal states are well defined, it can still be difficult to find the right set of operations to get from the beginning to the end. If you think back to your experience in math classes, you know that this is true. Your teacher gave you a formula like $x^2 + x - 12 = 0$ and asked you to solve for possible values of *x.* What do you do next? To solve this algebra problem, you can use an **algorithm:** a step-by-step procedure that always provides the right answer for

---

problem solving Thinking that is directed toward solving specific problems and that moves from an initial state to a goal state by means of a set of mental operations.

reasoning The process of thinking in which conclusions are drawn from a set of facts; thinking directed toward a given goal or objective.

problem space The elements that make up a problem: the initial state, the incomplete information or unsatisfactory conditions the person starts with; the goal state, the set of information or state the person wishes to achieve; and the set of operations, the steps the person takes to move from the initial state to the goal state.

algorithm A step-by-step procedure that always provides the right answer for a particular type of problem.

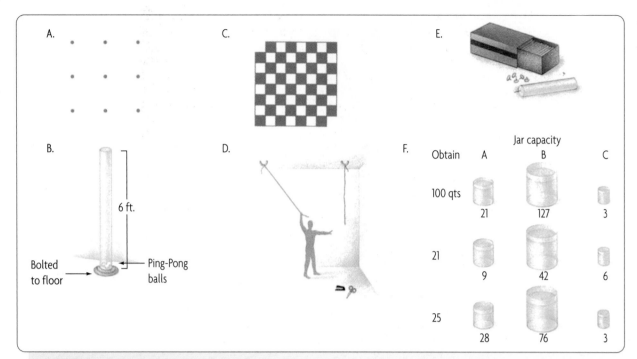

FIGURE 8.12 Can You Solve It? (Part I)

Try to solve each of these problems (the answers are given in Figure 8.13 on page 252, but don't look until you try to solve them all).

(A) Can you connect all the dots in the pattern by drawing four straight, connected lines without lifting your pen from the paper?

(B) A prankster has put three Ping-Pong balls into a 6-foot-long pipe that is standing vertically in the corner of the physics lab, fastened to the floor. How would you get the Ping-Pong balls out?

(C) The checkerboard shown has had two corner pieces cut out, leaving 62 squares. You have 31 dominoes, each of which covers exactly two checkerboard squares. Can you use them to cover the whole checkerboard?

(D) You are in a room with two strings hanging from the ceiling and scissors and a stapler at your feet. Your task is to tie the 2 strings together. If you hold one string, the other is out of reach. Can you do it?

(E) You are given the objects shown (a candle, tacks, matches in a matchbox). The task is to mount a lighted candle on a door. Can you do it?

(F) You are given three "water-jar" problems. Using only the three containers (water supply is unlimited), can you obtain the exact amount specified in each case?

a particular type of problem. If you apply the rules of algebra correctly, you are guaranteed to obtain the correct values of x (3 and −4). If you've ever forgotten the combination to a lock, you may also have engaged in behavior guided by an algorithm. If you try solutions systematically (for example, 1, 2, 3; 1, 2, 4) you will definitely arrive at the right combination—though you may be at it for a good long while! Because well-defined problems have clear initial states and goal states, algorithms are more likely to be available for them than for ill-defined problems. When algorithms are unavailable, problem solvers often rely on **heuristics,** which are strategies or "rules of thumb." Suppose, for example, you are reading a mystery and you'd like to solve the problem of who murdered an e-commerce tycoon. You might rule out the possibility that "the butler did it" because you use the heuristic that authors wouldn't use such a trite plot line. As we shall see shortly, heuristics are also a critical aspect of *judgment* and *decision making.*

Researchers have been interested in understanding the way people apply both algorithms and heuristics as they make their way through a problem space. To study the steps problem solvers take, researchers have often turned to **think-aloud protocols.** In this procedure, participants are asked to verbalize their ongoing thoughts (Ericsson & Simon, 1993). For example, a pair of researchers were interested in capturing the mental processes that enable participants to solve the mutilated checkerboard problem that is part C of Figure 8.12 (Kaplan & Simon, 1990). Here is one of their participants having the crucial breakthrough that the

---

heuristic Cognitive strategies, or "rules of thumb," often used as shortcuts in solving a complex inferential task.

think-aloud protocol Report made by an experimental participant of the mental processes and strategies he or she uses while working on a task.

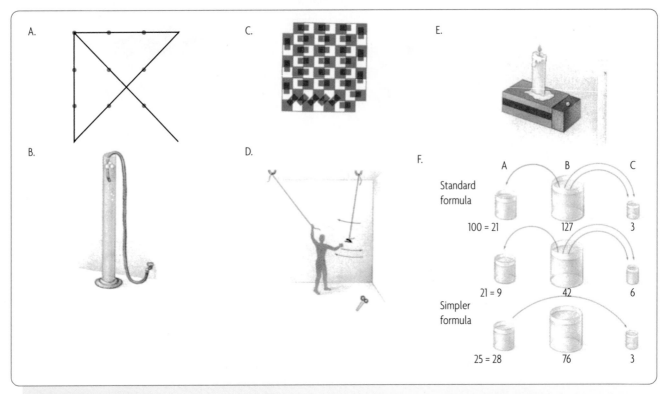

FIGURE 8.13 Can You Solve It? (Part II)

Here are the solutions to the problems. How did you do? As the section on problem solving and reasoning unfolds, we will talk about what makes these problems hard.

From *How to Solve Problems* by Wickelgren, Wayne. Copyright 1974 by Wayne Wickelgren, Rightsholder. Reproduced with permission of Wayne Wickelgren, Rightsholder in the format Textbook via Copyright Clearance Center.

problem cannot be solved with only horizontal and vertical placement of pieces (the checkerboard was pink and black):

> *So you're leaving . . . it's short—how many, you're leaving uhhhh . . . there's more pinks than black, and in order to complete it you'd have to connect two pinks but you can't because they are diagonally . . . is that getting close?*
> (Kaplan & Simon, 1990, p. 388)

The solver has just realized that the goal cannot be accomplished if the dominoes can just be placed horizontally or vertically. Researchers have often used participants' own accounts of their thinking as the starting point for more formal models of problem solving (Simon, 1979, 1989).

Improving Your Problem Solving What makes problem solving hard? If you reflect on your day-to-day experience, you might come up with the answer, "There are too many things to consider all at once." Research on problem solving has led to much the same conclusion. What often makes a problem difficult to solve is that the mental requirements for solving a particular problem overwhelm processing resources (Cho et al., 2007; Kershaw & Ohlsson, 2004). To solve a problem, you need to plan the series of operations you will take. If that series becomes too complex, or if each operation itself is too complex, you may be unable to see your way through from the initial state to the goal state. How might you overcome this potential limitation?

An important step in improving problem solving is to find a way to represent a problem so that each operation is possible, given your processing resources. If you must habitually solve similar

problems, a useful procedure is to practice each of the components of the solution so that, over time, those components require fewer resources (Kotovsky et al., 1985). Suppose, for example, you were a cab driver in New York City and were faced with daily traffic jams. You might mentally practice your responses to jams at various points in the city, so that you'd have ready solutions to components of the overall problem of getting your fare from a pickup spot to a destination. By practicing these component solutions, you could keep more of your attention on the road!

Sometimes, finding a useful representation means finding a whole new way to think about the problem (Novick & Bassok, 2005). Read the puzzle given in **Table 8.6.** How would you go about offering this proof? Think about it for a few minutes before you read on. How well did you do? If the word *proof* suggested to you something mathematical, you probably didn't make much progress. A better way to think about the problem is to imagine two monks, one starting at the top and another starting at the bottom (Adams, 1986). As one climbs and one descends, it's clear that they will pass at some point along the mountain, right (see **Figure 8.14** on page 254)? Now replace the pair of monks with just the one—conceptually it's the same—and there's your proof. What makes this problem suddenly very easy is using the right sort of representation: visual rather than verbal or mathematical.

If you go back to the problems in Figure 8.12 you have other good examples of the importance of an appropriate representation of the problem space. To get the Ping-Pong balls out of the pipe, you had to realize that the solution did not involve reaching into the pipe. To connect the two strings, you had to see one of the tools on the floor as a weight. To mount the

How do scientists approach the ill-defined problem of curing AIDS?

candle on the door, you had to alter your usual perspective and perceive the matchbox as a platform instead of as a container, and you had to perceive the candle as a tool as well as the object to be mounted on the door. The last two problems show a phenomenon called functional fixedness (Duncker, 1945; Maier, 1931). **Functional fixedness** is a mental block that adversely affects problem solving by inhibiting the perception of a new function for an object that was previously associated with some other purpose. Whenever you are stuck on a problem, you should ask yourself, "How am I representing the problem? Are there different or better ways that I can think about the problem or components of its solution?" If words don't work, try drawing a picture. Or try examining your assumptions and see what "rules" you can break by making novel combinations.

Often, when you try to solve problems, you engage in special forms of thinking that are called reasoning. Let's turn now to a first type of reasoning you use to solve problems, deductive reasoning.

DEDUCTIVE REASONING

Suppose you are on your way to a restaurant and you want to pay for your meal with your only credit card, American Express. You call the restaurant and ask, "Do you accept American Express?" The restaurant's hostess replies, "We accept all major credit cards." You can now safely conclude that they accept American Express. To see why, we can reformulate your interchange to fit the structure of the *syllogism*, introduced by the Greek philosopher Aristotle over 2,000 years ago:

Premise 1. The restaurant accepts all major credit cards.
Premise 2. American Express is a major credit card.
Conclusion. The restaurant accepts American Express.

Aristotle was concerned with defining the logical relationships between statements that would lead to *valid* conclusions. **Deductive reasoning** involves the correct application of such logical rules. We gave the credit-card example to show that you are quite capable of drawing conclusions that have the form of logical, deductive proofs. Even so, psychological research has focused on the question of whether you actually have the formal rules of deductive reasoning represented in your mind (Evans, 2008; Goel, 2007). This body of research suggests that you may have some general, abstract sense of formal logic, but your real-world deductive reasoning is affected both by the specific knowledge you possess about the world and the representational resources you can bring to bear on a particular reasoning problem. Let's expand on these conclusions.

How does knowledge influence deductive reasoning? Consider this syllogism:

Premise 1. All things that have a motor need oil.
Premise 2. Automobiles need oil.
Conclusion. Automobiles have motors.

Is this a valid conclusion? According to the rules of logic, it is *not* because Premise 1 leaves open the possibility that some things that don't have motors will also need oil. The difficulty is that what is invalid in a logic problem is not necessarily untrue in real life. That is, if you take Premises 1 and 2 to be all the information in your possession—as you should if you accept this simply as an exercise in formal logic—the conclusion is not valid.

---

functional fixedness An inability to perceive a new use for an object previously associated with some other purpose; adversely affects problem solving and creativity.

deductive reasoning A form of thinking in which one draws a conclusion that is intended to follow logically from two or more statements or premises.

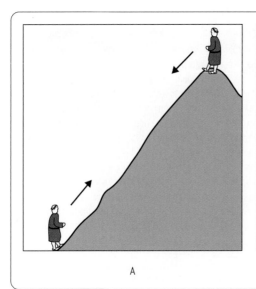

FIGURE 8.14 A "Proof" for the Monk Puzzle

Panel A shows two monks, one who starts at the bottom of the mountain and one who starts at the top. Panel B shows that they must meet at some time during the day. Replace the two monks with a single monk, and you have your proof!

From *How to Solve Problems* by Wickelgren, Wayne. Copyright 1974 by Wayne Wickelgren, Rightsholder. Reproduced with permission of Wayne Wickelgren, Rightsholder in the format Textbook via Copyright Clearance Center.

This example illustrates the **belief-bias effect:** People tend to judge as valid those conclusions that they find believable and judge as invalid those conclusions they find unbelievable (Janis & Frick, 1943). Research suggests that belief bias represents a conflict between two types of mental processes you apply when you engage in deductive reasoning (Evans, 2008). One set of processes uses past experiences to provide rapid, automatic responses to the problems. (These are the heuristic processes we'll explore at greater length when we discuss judgment and decision making.) The other set of processes allows for slower, conscious applications of formal logic. Suppose you judge "Automobiles have motors" to be a valid conclusion. That suggests that the processes that bring past experience to bear on the judgment are winning the conflict with the processes responsible for logical analysis. Researchers have confirmed this account of belief bias by, for example, forcing experimental participants to respond to syllogisms within 10 seconds (Evans & Curtis-Holmes, 2005). Under time pressure, people showed more belief bias. That result supports the idea that people require conscious effort to apply the rules of formal logic.

In some cases, your ability to apply past experience helps you to perform better on reasoning tasks. Imagine that you are given the array of four cards pictured in **Figure 8.15,** which have printed on them *A, D, 4,* and *7.* Your task is to determine which cards you must turn over to test the rule "If a card has a vowel on one side, then it has an even number on the other side" (Johnson-Laird & Wason, 1977). What would you do? Most people say that they would turn over the *A,* which is correct, and the *4*—which is incorrect. No matter what character appears on the flip side of the *4,* the rule will not be invalidated. (Can you see why that is true?) Instead, you must flip the *7.* If you were to find a vowel there, you would have invalidated the rule.

The original research on this task, which is often called the *Wason selection task,* prompted doubts about people's ability to reason effectively. However, deductive reasoning is improved when participants are able to apply their real-world knowledge to the Wason task. Suppose you were asked to perform what is a logically comparable task, on the lower set of cards in Figure 8.15. In this case, however, you are asked to evaluate the rule "If a customer is to drink an alcoholic beverage, then she *must* be at least 18" (Cheng & Holyoak, 1985). Now you can probably see immediately which are the correct cards to turn over: *17* and *drinking beer.* If you look at Figure 8.15, you'll see that 7 and 17 have the same

---

belief-bias effect A situation that occurs when a person's prior knowledge, attitudes, or values distort the reasoning process by influencing the person to accept invalid arguments.

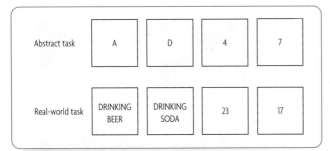

FIGURE 8.15 Abstract versus Real-World Reasoning

In the top row, you are required to say which cards you must turn over to test the rule "If a card has a vowel on one side, then it has an even number on the other side." In the bottom row, you must say which cards you need to turn over to test the rule "If a customer is to drink an alcoholic beverage, then she *must* be at least 18." People typically do better on the second task, which allows them to use real-world strategies.

logical function. You need to turn 17 over for the same reasons of logic you need to turn 7 over. However, your real-world experience helps you appreciate why turning 17 over is logically necessary.

This example of age and alcohol comes from the more general category of permission situations. You probably have a good deal of experience with these sorts of situations—recall all the times you were given conditions like, "You can't watch television unless you do your homework." You most likely never recognized that deductive inference was involved in such circumstances! However, the experience you've accumulated with these situations now allows you to make correct judgments without much difficulty.

To begin this section on deductive reasoning, we described a situation in which you drew a valid deductive inference about your ability to use your American Express card to buy a meal. Unfortunately, life provides many occasions on which you cannot be so certain that you have drawn valid inferences from valid premises. We turn now to a version of the restaurant scenario that requires you to use a different form of reasoning.

INDUCTIVE REASONING

Let's suppose that you have arrived outside the restaurant and only then think to check to see if you have enough cash. Once again you find that you'll want to use your American Express card, but there's no helpful sign on the outside. You peek through the restaurant's windows and see well-dressed clientele. You look at the expensive prices on the menu. You consider the upscale quality of the neighborhood. All these observations lead you to believe that the restaurant is likely to take your credit card. This is not deductive reasoning because your conclusion is based on probabilities rather than logical certainties. Instead, this is **inductive reasoning**—a form of reasoning that uses available evidence to generate likely, but not certain, conclusions.

Although the name might be new, we have already described to you several examples of inductive reasoning. We saw repeatedly, in Chapters 4 and 7, that people use past information stored as schemas to generate expectations about the present and future. You are using inductive reasoning, for example, if you decide that

a certain odor in the air indicates that someone is making popcorn; you are using inductive reasoning if you agree that the words on this page are unlikely to suddenly become invisible (and that, if you study, your knowledge of this material won't become invisible on test day). Finally, earlier in this chapter, we discussed the types of inferences people draw when they use language. Your belief that *she* must be *Donna* in the sequence of utterances we gave you relies on inductive inference.

In real-life circumstances, much of your problem-solving ability relies on inductive reasoning. Return to our opening example: You have accidentally locked yourself out of your home, room, or car. What should you do? A good first step is to call up from memory solutions that worked in the past. This process is called *analogical problem solving:* You establish an analogy between the features of the current situation and the features of previous situations (Christensen & Schunn, 2007; Lee & Holyoak, 2008). In this case, your past experiences of "being locked out" may have allowed you to form the *generalization* "find other people with keys." With that generalization in hand, you can start to figure out who those individuals might be and how to find them. This task might require you to retrieve the method you developed for tracking down your roommates at their afternoon classes. If this problem seems easy to you, it's because you have grown accustomed to letting your past inform your present: Inductive reasoning allows you to access tried-and-true methods that speed current problem solving.

We have one caution to add about inductive reasoning. Often a solution that has worked in the past can be reused for a successful solution. But sometimes you must recognize that reliance on the past can hamper your problem-solving ability when there is a critical difference between the old and current situations. The water-jar problem given in Figure 8.12 is a classic example of circumstances in which reliance on the past may cause you to miss a solution to a problem (Luchins, 1942). If you had discovered, in the first two problems in part F, the conceptual rule that $B - A - 2(C) = answer,$ you probably tried the same formula for the third problem and found it didn't work. Actually, simply filling jar A and pouring off enough to fill jar C would have left you with the right amount. If you were using your initial formula, you probably did not notice this simpler possibility—your previous success with the other rule would have given you a mental set. A **mental set** is a preexisting state of mind, habit, or attitude that can enhance the quality and speed of perceiving and problem solving under some conditions. However, the same set may inhibit or distort the quality of your mental activities at times when old ways of thinking and acting are nonproductive in new situations. When you find yourself frustrated in a problem-solving situation, you might take a step back and ask yourself, "Am I allowing past successes to narrow my focus too much?" Try to make your problem solving more creative by considering a broader spectrum of past situations and past solutions.

Before we leave this discussion of reasoning, we're going to turn once more to your brain. In this section, we've made a rather strong distinction between deductive and inductive reasoning. Research suggests that separation also exists in the way your brain accomplishes the two types of reasoning.

---

inductive reasoning A form of reasoning in which a conclusion is made about the probability of some state of affairs, based on the available evidence and past experience.

mental set The tendency to respond to a new problem in the manner used to respond to a previous problem.

Deductive reasoning:	Inductive reasoning:
Either he likes country music or he listens to opera.	If he is either an accountant or a librarian he listens to opera.
He does not like country music.	He listens to opera.
He listens to opera.	He is an accountant.
Is the conclusion valid?	**Is the conclusion more likely to be true than false?**

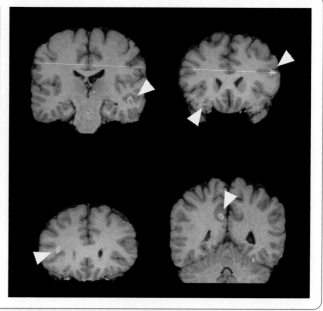

FIGURE 8.16 Reasoning in the Brain

When students were asked to carry out deductive reasoning, brain structures on the right sides of their brain were relatively more active. (Those areas are shown in green.) When students were asked to carry out inductive reasoning, brain structures on the left sides of their brain were relatively more active. (Those areas are shown in yellow.)

Participants carried out two types of reasoning tasks while their brains were undergoing PET scans. As shown in the top portion of **Figure 8.16,** one type of problem required deduction. Participants viewed classic syllogisms and assessed whether the conclusions were valid or not. A second type of problem provided premises that left conclusions uncertain. For that reason, the problems required participants to engage in inductive reasoning. Participants indicated whether the arguments were more likely to be true than false. As shown in the bottom portion of Figure 8.16, the two types of reasoning brought about different patterns of activation. The data are easy to summarize: Deductive reasoning produced greater activation in the right hemisphere; inductive reasoning produced greater activation in the left hemisphere (Parsons & Osherson, 2001).

To make sense of this result, think back to Chapter 3. Recall that your left hemisphere plays a large role in language processing whereas your right hemisphere does not. The results of this study on reasoning suggest that deductive reasoning involves a type of logical analysis that is relatively independent of language. Inductive reasoning calls upon the language-based comprehension and inferencing processes we described earlier in the chapter.

In this section, we have examined a range of types of problem solving and reasoning—and have suggested, in each case, concrete steps you can take to improve your performance in real-world circumstances. We follow the same strategy in the final section of the chapter. We describe some major research findings on the processes of *judgment* and *decision making* and then suggest how you can apply those findings to important situations in your life.

STOP AND REVIEW

❶ With respect to problem solving, what is an algorithm?
❷ What does it mean to overcome functional fixedness?
❸ What happens when people succumb to the belief-bias effect?
❹ What role does memory play in inductive reasoning?

CRITICAL THINKING Consider the experiment on the brain bases of reasoning processes. For the inductive reasoning problems, why did participants judge likely rather than absolute truth or falsehood?

Visit MyPsychLab.com for more review and practice on the following topics:

◀◉ **Explore:** The Two-String Problem
✳ **Simulate:** Anchoring and Adjustment

Judgment and Decision Making

For a final time, we're back to "The cat is on the mat." Let's engage the processes of *judgment* and *decision making.* How likely is it that the message was just a prank? How likely is it that the message has some real importance that has eluded you? Should you just give up and go to sleep?

This series of questions illustrates one of the great truths of your day-to-day experience: You live in a world filled with *uncertainty*. Here are some more questions, of a sort that will be entirely familiar. Should you spend $10 on a movie you may or may not enjoy? Before an exam, would you be better off studying your notes or rereading the chapter? Are you ready to commit yourself to a long-term relationship? Because you can only guess at the future, and because you almost never have full knowledge of the past, very rarely can you be completely certain that you have made a correct judgment or decision. Thus the processes of judgment and decision making must operate in a way that allows you to deal efficiently with uncertainty. As **Herbert Simon,** one of the founding figures of cognitive psychology, put it: Because "human thinking powers are very modest when compared with the complexities of the environments in which human beings live," they must be content "to find 'good enough' solutions to their problems and 'good enough' courses of action" (1979, p. 3). In this light, Simon suggested that thought processes are guided by *bounded rationality*. Your judgments or decisions might not be as good—as "rational"—as they always could be, but you should be able to see how they result from your applying limited resources to situations that require swift action.

Before we move to a closer analysis of the products of bounded rationality, let's quickly distinguish between the two processes of judgment and decision making. **Judgment** is the process by which you form opinions, reach conclusions, and make critical evaluations of events and people. You often make judgments spontaneously, without prompting. **Decision making** is the process of choosing between alternatives, selecting and rejecting available options. Judgment and decision making are interrelated processes. For example, you might meet someone at a party and, after a brief discussion and a dance together, *judge* the person to be intelligent, interesting, honest, and sincere. You might then *decide* to spend most of your party time with that person and to arrange a date for the next weekend; decision making is more closely linked to behavioral actions. Let's turn now to research on these two types of thinking.

HEURISTICS AND JUDGMENT

What's the best way to make a judgment? Suppose, for example, you are asked whether you enjoyed a movie. To answer this question, you could fill out a chart with two columns, "What I liked about the movie" and "What I didn't like about the movie," and see which column came out longer. To be a bit more accurate, perhaps you'd weight the entries in each list according to their importance (thus you might weight "the actors' performances" as more important on the plus side than "the blaring sound track" on the minus side). If you went through this whole procedure, you'd probably be pretty confident of your judgment—but you know already that this is an exercise you rarely undertake. In real-life circumstances, you have to make judgments frequently and rapidly. You don't have the time—and often you don't have sufficient information—to use such a formal procedure.

What do you do instead? An answer to this question was pioneered by **Amos Tversky** and **Daniel Kahneman,** who argued that people's judgments often rely on heuristics rather than on formal methods of analysis. As we noted in our discussion of problem solving, heuristics are informal rules of thumb

What processes influence your decision that you are ready to commit to a long-term relationship?

that provide shortcuts, reducing the complexity of making judgments. Following the lead of Tversky and Kahneman, researchers have suggested that humans evolved an *adaptive toolbox*: a repertory of "fast and frugal" heuristics that yield judgments that are most often likely to be correct (Gigerenzer, 2008; Todd & Gigerenzer, 2007). The important claim is that the ability to make correct judgments quickly (fast) and with limited resources (frugal) is adaptive—the ability has survival value. Researchers have defined a number of fast and frugal heuristics and demonstrated that they often lead to correct judgments (Hertwig et al., 2008).

Even so, research on heuristics has typically focused on circumstances in which they lead to *incorrect* judgments. There are two explanations for this focus. To begin, the research follows a logic that might sound familiar from earlier chapters: Just as you can understand perception by studying perceptual illusion and memory by studying memory failures, you can understand judgment processes by studying judgment errors. In addition, there's value in being able to recognize circumstances in which heuristics might lead to errors. That gives people the opportunity to engage other mental properties to make better judgments.

---

judgment The process by which people form opinions, reach conclusions, and make critical evaluations of events and people based on available material; also, the product of the mental activity.

decision making The process of choosing between alternatives; selecting or rejecting available options.

We already provided you with one such example, when we described the belief-bias effect. In general, it's a good thing to bring past experience to bear on current judgments. However, in the context of deductive logic, that practice can lead to incorrect responses. To make correct deductive judgments, you sometimes need to slow yourself down and effortfully apply your knowledge of logical rules. This example of deductive logic illustrates why many researchers embrace *dual-process models* of judgment and decision making (Evans, 2008). Those models suggest that people have two sets of mental processes: Fast, automatic, and unconscious processes (embodied in heuristics) versus slower, effortful, and conscious processes. As we've noted, your heuristic processes often provide correct judgments. Much of the time you should let those processes operate without conscious intervention. However, as you read about three heuristics—availability, representativeness, and anchoring—try to get some concrete ideas about circumstances in which conscious intervention may be necessary.

Availability Heuristic We'll begin by asking you to make a rather trivial judgment. Suppose we were to give you a few pages from a novel. Do you believe more words in the excerpt would begin with the letter *k* (for example, *kangaroo*) or have *k* in third position (for example, *duke*)? If you are like the participants in a study by Tversky and Kahneman (1973), then you probably judged that *k* is found more often at the beginning of words. In fact, *k* appears about twice as often in the third position.

Why do most people believe that *k* is more likely to appear in first position? The answer has to do with the *availability* of information from memory. It's much easier to think of words that begin with *k* than to think of those in which *k* comes third. Your judgment, thus, arises from use of the **availability heuristic:** You base your judgment on information that is readily available in memory. This heuristic has two components. The first component is the relative ease or *fluency* with which you can retrieve information. Suppose, for example, we asked you to judge which sport is more dangerous, bowling or hang gliding? If you're like us, you'll probably find it easier to retrieve memories of hang gliding accidents than memories of bowling accidents. If you based your judgment on the ease of retrieval, you'd be likely to conclude that hang gliding is more dangerous. The second component of availability is the content of the memories you find it easy to retrieve. Suppose we asked you to share the first five memories that come to mind about bowling. If all those memories were unhappy memories, you'd likely conclude that bowling might not be your best choice for a leisure time activity. Let's see how each of these components of availability can lead to potential problems.

Recall from Chapter 7 the discussion of how retrieval cues function to give you access to memories. We concluded that the same retrieval cues will be more or less effective, depending on the context in which you put them to use. Suppose, before we asked you the *k* question, we started you out with some examples of *k* in the third position (such as *bike, cake, poke,* and *take*). By changing the context of retrieval, we could possibly change your judgment. In that way, the fluency of information—the ease with which you can retrieve information from memory—will vary from context to context. Consider a study in which

participants provided typicality ratings for exemplars from categories (Oppenheimer & Frank, 2008). In some cases, the exemplars appeared in easy-to-read fonts:

hummingbird

In other cases, the exemplars were hard to read:

hummingbird

Participants gave higher typicality ratings to the same exemplars when they appeared in the easy-to-read fonts! An explanation for this result is that participants' assessments of fluency—the difficulty they experienced making their way from the printed word to their representations in memory—contributed to their judgments of typicality. This study illustrates how judgments you make based on fluency may depend on context. Different contexts may yield different judgments (as with the change in font). When you are making important judgments, ask yourself, "How might this context affect the ease with which I can retrieve particular information?"

You may also experience difficulties with availability when the information you have stored in memory has a bias to it. Consider people's judgments of the populations of various countries (Brown & Siegler, 1992). See if you can order these four countries from smallest to largest population:

a. Sweden
b. Indonesia
c. Israel
d. Nigeria

Researchers demonstrated that, in general, the more participants knew about a country, the higher their population estimates. Furthermore, there was a sizable correlation between participants' rated knowledge about a country and the number of times it had been mentioned in *New York Times* articles in a given year. (The right answer, by the way, is Israel, Sweden, Nigeria, Indonesia. Did availability lead you astray?)

You might not be terribly concerned that your estimates of population size are affected by a flawed database. We'll offer a second example that should strike you as more urgent: Many students show a bias in the way they commit information to memory that has a negative impact on test performance. Suppose you are taking a multiple-choice exam. You answer a question, but then, after giving it some additional thought, you decide to change your answer. Are you more likely to change from wrong to right or right to wrong? If you are like most students, you probably believe that you should stick with your first answer—it probably makes you nervous to change your answer. But should it?

Researchers inspected the multiple-choice exams of a group of 1,561 students to determine the consequences of answer changes (Kruger et al., 2005). Of the 3,291 answers those students changed, 23 percent were from one wrong answer to another wrong answer. Of the remaining changes, 51 percent made a wrong answer right; 25 percent made a right answer wrong. This pattern suggests that you shouldn't be reluctant to consider changing an answer. However, when a subset of this group were asked about the wisdom of changing answers, 75 percent indicated that it's a better idea to stick with one's original answer. The researchers argued that students' prejudice against changing answers comes from a memory bias: They suggested

---

availability heuristic A judgment based on the information readily available in memory.

that students find more memorable instances in which changed answers led to negative outcomes than when they led to positive outcomes. How many times have you complained to yourself, "I had that one right!" Now, how many times have you complained, "I had that one wrong!" To test the hypothesis that students are more likely to commit negative outcomes to memory, the researchers carried out a second experiment. In this case, the researchers gave students feedback on correct and incorrect answers shortly after they completed a multiple-choice exam. Four to six weeks later, the researchers asked the participants to try to recall the instances in which they had considered changing their answers, what they had decided, and the consequences of those decisions. A student might, for example, have reported that she had deliberated on three problems and always stuck with her original answer. The memory data showed a consistent bias: Participants *overestimated* how often they switched an answer and then got the question wrong; they *underestimated* how often they switched an answer and then got the question right.

Put yourself in a classroom while you are taking a test. You get to a moment at which you're trying to decide whether to change an answer. These data suggest that you make this judgment with respect to a biased database: You have committed more negative outcomes to memory than positive outcomes—those are the outcomes that are available. This analysis certainly doesn't mean that you should *always* change your answers. However, you should be aware now of why your feelings of distress arise when you contemplate a change.

Representativeness Heuristic When you make judgments based on the **representativeness heuristic,** you assume that if something has the characteristics considered typical of members of a category, it is, in fact, a member of that category. This heuristic will seem familiar to you because it captures the idea that people use past information to make judgments about similar circumstances in the present. That is the essence of inductive reasoning. Under most circumstances—as long as you have unbiased ideas about the features and categories that go together—making judgments along the lines of similarity will be quite reasonable. Thus, if you are deciding whether to begin a new activity like hang gliding, it makes sense to determine how representative that sport is of the category of activities you have previously enjoyed.

Representativeness will lead you astray, however, when it causes you to ignore other types of relevant information, as you will now see (Kahneman & Frederick, 2002; Kahneman & Tversky, 1973). Consider, for example, the description of a successful attorney, given in **Figure 8.17.**

In one experiment, researchers provided their participants with a list of options, including those in Figure 8.17, and gave them the chance to win $45—real money—by ranking the correct option as number 1. Which option seems correct to you? If you're like a majority of the original participants, you'll lose the $45 because you'll say *tennis* rather than *a ball game.* The lower part of Figure 8.17 shows why *tennis* could never be as good a bet: It is included within the category *a ball game.* Participants judge *tennis* to be a better answer because it seems to have all the features of the sport the attorney is likely to play. However, this judgment by

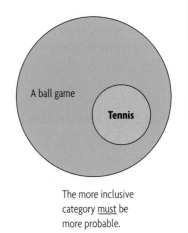

A successful Jerusalem attorney. Colleagues say his whims prevent him from being a team worker, attributing his success to competitiveness and drive. Slim and not tall, he watches his body and is vain. Spends several hours a week on his favorite sport. What sport is that?

a. Fast walking
b. A ball game
c. Tennis
d. A track and field sport

The more inclusive category <u>must</u> be more probable.

FIGURE 8.17 Using the Representativeness Heuristic

When asked to choose the attorney's favorite sport, the representativeness heuristic leads most people to choose "tennis." However, as shown in the bottom part of the figure, the more probable answer is "a ball game," because that includes within it "tennis."

representativeness causes participants to neglect another sort of information—category structure. In this case, the measurable cost is $45 (Bar-Hillel & Neter, 1993).

The implication for your day-to-day life is that you should not be fooled into grabbing at a representative alternative before you consider the structure of all the alternatives.

Let's look at another use of representativeness. Consider the last time you went to hear live music. Suppose we ask you, "How much did you enjoy the concert?" How do you answer such a question? Most live performances unfold over a period of time; they have some good moments and some not-so-good moments. To answer the global question (that is, "How much . . . ?"), you need to provide a value that is representative of all those various moments. Research suggests that representative values often reflect an average of an event's moment of peak intensity and the intensity at the event's end (Kahneman & Frederick, 2002). For example, in one study participants experienced two trials in which they immersed their hands in painfully cold water (Kahneman et al., 1993). In the *short* trial, they kept their hand in 14°C water for 60 seconds. In the *long* trial, after that first 60 seconds, they kept their hand immersed for 30 seconds more as the water gradually warmed to 15 °C. (Participants were able to notice the 1° change.) When asked whether they would

---

representativeness heuristic A cognitive strategy that assigns an object to a category on the basis of a few characteristics regarded as representative of that category.

prefer to repeat the short or the long trial, a majority of participants chose the longer trial! Are you surprised that participants preferred 90 seconds of pain to 60 seconds of pain? The researchers explained that the peak-end average is lower for the short trial (for which the peak equals the end so that 14° and 14° are averaged) than for the long trial (for which 15° and 14° are averaged). The higher value that represents the long trial makes that trial seem less painful in retrospect. The same pattern applies to positive experiences (Do et al., 2008). In one study, people were happier when they received *less* candy if the single piece of "peak" candy was better than the average of the "peak" candy and the "end" candy. Can you see how you might apply this peak-end rule to your own life? To influence people's evaluation of an event, you should think about how to arrange the components of the event so that people encode the desired representative value.

Anchors Aweigh! To introduce you to a third heuristic, we need you to try a thought experiment. First take 5 seconds to estimate the following mathematical product and write down your answer:

$$1 \times 2 \times 3 \times 4 \times 5 \times 6 \times 7 \times 8 = \underline{\qquad}$$

In 5 seconds, you can probably make only a couple of calculations. You get a partial answer, perhaps 24, and then adjust up from there. Now try this series of numbers:

$$8 \times 7 \times 6 \times 5 \times 4 \times 3 \times 2 \times 1 = \underline{\qquad}$$

Even if you notice that this is the same list in reverse, you can see how the experience of carrying out the multiplication would feel quite different. You'd start with 8 × 7, which is 56, and then attempt 56 × 6, which already feels quite large. Once again, you can only make a partial guess and then adjust upward. When Tversky and Kahneman (1974) gave these two arrangements of the identical problem to experimental participants, the 1 to 8 order produced median estimates of 512, and the 8 to 1 group produced estimates of 2,250 *(the real answer is 40,320)*. Apparently, when participants adjusted up from their 5-second estimates, the higher partial solutions led to higher estimates.

Performance on this simple multiplication task provides evidence for the **anchoring heuristic:** People's judgments of the probable value of some event or outcome represent insufficient adjustments—either up or down—from an original starting value. In other words, your judgment is "anchored" too firmly to an original guess. People show a strong tendency to be influenced by an anchor, even when the information is clearly of little or no use. For example, in one study students were given an arbitrary identification number (in the range 1,928 to 1,935) that they were instructed to copy onto their questionnaires. Subsequently, the students estimated the number of physicians listed in the local Yellow Pages. Students in the control group—who hadn't received an ID anchor—produced an average estimate of 219 physicians. Students with the ID anchors produced an estimate of 539—even though they had been specifically warned that the ID number might

affect their judgments (Wilson et al., 1996). You can see how hard it is not to let an anchor have an impact.

Why do people make insufficient adjustments from anchors? Researchers have begun to address this question in real-life circumstances—in which people produce their own anchors before beginning the adjustment process. Consider this question: What is the duration of Mars's orbit around the sun? How might you answer that question? Research suggests that you start with the duration of Earth's orbit of 365 days as an anchor. What next? You might use the knowledge that Mars is farther from the sun than Earth is to adjust away from the 365-day anchor toward a larger value. In fact, participants in an experiment estimated Mars's orbit to be about 492 days (Epley & Gilovich, 2006). This estimate is still short of the actual value, which is 869 days. What people appeared to do in the experiment was to start with a reasonable anchor (365 days) and keep adjusting until they reached a value that seemed *plausible*. When you find yourself in situations of anchoring and adjustment, put this result to use: You should expend some extra effort to confirm that a plausible value is, in fact, the right answer.

You employ judgmental heuristics like availability, representativeness, and anchoring because, in most situations, they allow you to make efficient, acceptable judgments. In a sense, you are doing the best you can, given the uncertainties of situations and constraints on your processing resources. We have shown you, however, that heuristics can lead to errors. Try to use this knowledge to examine your own thought processes when the time comes to make important judgments. Be especially critical when you feel others might be trying to bias your judgments. Let's move now to the decisions you make, often on the basis of those judgments.

THE PSYCHOLOGY OF DECISION MAKING

Let us begin with a powerful example of the way that psychological factors affect the decisions people make. Consider the problem given in part 1 of **Table 8.7.** Read the instructions and then make your choice between Spot A and Spot B. Now read the version of the problem given in part 2. Would you like to change your choice?

In an experiment, students read one version of this problem (Shafir, 1993). When they were asked in part 1 which option they preferred, 67 percent of the students opted for Spot B. However, when students were asked in part 2 to cancel an option, this figure fell to 52 percent (that is, 48 percent said they would cancel Spot B). Why is this change odd? If you take a close look at the "prefer" and "cancel" versions of the problem, you will see that there is no difference in the information available in the two cases. On first pass, you might expect that the same information would lead to the same decision. But that's not what people do. It seems that the "prefer" question focuses people's attention on positive features of options—you're gathering evidence in favor of something—whereas the "cancel" question focuses attention on negative features of options—you're gathering evidence against something. Your decision may shift.

This straightforward example demonstrates that the way in which a question is phrased can have great consequences for the decision you will make. This is why you need to understand the

---

anchoring heuristic An insufficient adjustment up or down from an original starting value when judging the probable value of some event or outcome.

TABLE 8.7 The Effect of Psychological Factors on Decision Making

Part 1: Prefer Version		Part 2: Cancel Version	
1. Imagine that you are planning a week-long vacation in a warm spot over spring break. You currently have two options that are reasonably priced, but the travel brochure gives only a limited amount of information about the two options. Given the information available, which vacation spot would you prefer?		**2.** Imagine that you are planning a week-long vacation in a warm spot over spring break. You currently have two options that are reasonably priced, but you can no longer retain your reservation for both. The travel brochure gives only a limited amount of information about the two options. Given the information available, which reservation do you decide to cancel?	
Spot A	average weather average beaches medium-quality hotel medium-temperature water average nightlife	Spot A	average weather average beaches medium-quality hotel medium-temperature water average nightlife
Spot B	lots of sunshine gorgeous beaches and coral reefs ultramodern hotel very cold water very strong winds no nightlife	Spot B	lots of sunshine gorgeous beaches and coral reefs ultramodern hotel very cold water very strong winds no nightlife

psychological aspects of decision making: You need to be able to test your own decisions to see whether they hold up under careful analysis. In this case, you might ask yourself, "How would my choice change if I were asked to reject an option rather than to choose one?" If you find that your top preference is also your top candidate for rejection, you will have learned that the option has both many positive and many negative features. Now ask, "Is that acceptable?" This is a key step in developing your critical thinking skills.

The Framing of Decisions One of the most natural ways to make a decision is to judge which option will bring about the biggest gain or which option will bring about the smallest loss. Thus, if we offer you $5 or $10, you will feel very little uncertainty that the better option is $10. What makes the situation a bit more complicated, however, is that the perception of a gain or a loss often depends on the way in which a decision is *framed*. A **frame** is a particular description of a choice. Suppose, for example, you were asked how happy you would be to get a $1,000 raise in your job. If you were expecting no raise at all, this would seem like a great gain, and you'd probably be quite happy. But suppose you'd been told several times to expect a raise of $10,000. Now how do you feel? Suddenly, you may feel as if you've lost money because the $1,000 is less than what you had expected. You're not happy at all! In either case, you'd be getting $1,000 more a year—objectively, you'd be in exactly the same position—but the psychological effect is very different. That's why *reference points* are important in decision making (Kahneman, 1992). What seems like a gain or a loss will be determined in part by the expectations—a $0 raise or a $10,000 raise—to which a decision maker refers. (The decision, in this case, might be whether to stay in the job.)

Let's now take a look at a slightly more complex example in which framing has a sizable impact on the decisions people make. In **Table 8.8** on page 262, you are asked to imagine making a choice between surgery and radiation for treatment of lung cancer. First, read the *survival* frame for the problem and choose your preferred treatment; then read the *mortality* frame and see if you feel like changing your preference. Note that the data are objectively the same in the two frames. The only difference is whether statistical information about the consequences of each treatment is presented in terms of survival rates or of mortality rates. When this decision was presented to participants, the focus on relative gains and losses had a marked effect on choice of treatment. Radiation therapy was chosen by only 18 percent of the participants who were given the survival frame but by 44 percent of those given the mortality frame. This framing effect held equally for a group of clinic patients, statistically sophisticated business students, and experienced physicians (McNeil et al., 1982).

Now that you know about frames, you should start to look for them in your everyday life. You're especially likely to find them when people are trying to get you to buy their products. Consider a study that looked at people's judgments about the choices they would make between two butchers.

> The participants in an experiment read a brief scenario that described two neighborhood butchers (Keren, 2007). Butcher A advertised his meat as 25 percent fat; Butcher B

---

frame A particular description of a choice; the perspective from which a choice is described or framed affects how a decision is made and which option is ultimately exercised.

TABLE 8.8	The Effect of Framing

Survival Frame

Surgery. Of 100 people having surgery, 90 live through the postoperative period, 68 are alive at the end of the first year, and 34 are alive at the end of five years.

Radiation therapy. Of 100 people having radiation therapy, all live through the treatment, 77 are alive at the end of one year, and 22 are alive at the end of five years.

What do you choose: surgery or radiation?

Mortality Frame

Surgery. Of 100 people having surgery, 10 die during surgery or the postoperative period, 32 die by the end of one year, and 66 die by the end of five years.

Radiation therapy. Of 100 people having radiation therapy, none dies during treatment, 23 die by the end of one year, and 78 die by the end of five years.

What do you choose: surgery or radiation?

approaches, the opposing candidates compete to have their framings of themselves and of the issues prevail among the voters. One candidate might say, "I believe in sticking with policies that have been successful." His opponent might counter, "He is afraid of new ideas." One candidate might say, "That policy will bring about economic growth." Her opponent might counter, "That policy will bring about environmental destruction." Often both claims are true—the same policy often will bring about both economic good and environmental harm. In this light, whichever frame seems more compelling may be largely a matter of personal history. Thus your knowledge of framing effects can help you understand how people can come to such radically different decisions when they are faced with exactly the same evidence. If you want to understand other people's actions, try to think about how those individuals have framed a decision.

Consequences of Decision Making What happens when you make a decision? In the best of all possible worlds, everything goes well—and you never look back. However, as you likely know, not all decisions yield the best of all possible worlds. When decisions turn out badly, you will likely experience *regret*. Studies suggest that the categories in which people express the greatest regret is their decisions with respect to their education and careers (Roese & Summerville, 2005). To explain this finding, researchers point to the fact that these two domains provide a particularly wide range of opportunities: There are many ways to pursue an education and many careers to which someone might aspire. That range of opportunities makes it quite easy for people to wonder, "Did I make the right decision?"

People also experience more regret when they are clear on the costs associated with particular decisions (van Dijk & Zeelenberg, 2005). Consider a moment on a game show when a contestant must choose between *Box A* and *Box B*. If the contestant chooses the box with $10 instead of $10,000, it's easy to understand why he would experience regret. Some decisions in life are like the game show. You have the apple pie. Your friend has the pecan pie. After you each take one bite, you know that you made the wrong decision. You experience regret because

advertised his meat as 75 percent lean. Participants imagined that they were preparing for a large dinner party and had to buy their meat from one of the two butchers. Which would they choose? The majority of the participants (82 percent) went with Butcher B. You can probably see why: The meat that's 75 percent lean *sounds* much healthier. Of course, the two butchers are actually offering the same product (because meat that is 75 percent lean would have 25 percent fat). Despite that math, the frame has a large impact. Now consider a judgment made by a second group of participants: They indicated which of the two butchers they would trust more. For trust judgments, participants' preferences were reversed: A majority (73 percent) said they trusted more the butcher who told them how much fat the meat had!

This experiment illustrates that the same frame can have an opposite impact on different judgments. Do you suppose the butchers would be happier to be trusted by their customers or to sell their products? As you think about frames in the real world, you should consider what judgments people are trying to affect.

These results we've shared with you should encourage you to think about important decisions from the perspective of different frames. Suppose, for example, you are going to buy a new car. The salesperson will be inclined to frame everything as a gain: "Seventy-eight percent of the Xenons require no repairs in the first year!" You can reframe that to "Twenty-two percent require some repairs in the first year!" Would the new frame change how you feel about the situation? It's an exercise worth trying in real life.

The car salesperson is a good example of a situation in which someone is trying to frame information in a fashion that will have a desired effect on your decision. This, of course, is a regular part of your life. For example, as each election

In what ways can salespeople frame their products to get prospective customers to consider them in a positive light?

you have a clear grasp on what you gave up. In other cases, you have a much vaguer grasp on the consequences of your decision. If you choose a poodle as a pet, you'll never know exactly how different your life would have been had you gone for a bulldog. In that type of situation, it's less likely that you will experience regret.

When people anticipate regret, they are likely to be more deliberate in the way they face decisions—they will take more time and gather more information (Reb, 2008). In fact, under some circumstances, people will try hard to avoid making any decision at all. In **Table 8.9**, we provide an example of circumstances that can bring about an increasing unwillingness to make a decision. Consider the scenario in part A. Which would you choose? Researchers found that only 34 percent of their participants said they would wait for more information (Tversky & Shafir, 1992). Now consider the slightly altered scenario given in part B. Do you want to change your choice? In fact, 46 percent of the participants who read this version said they would wait for new information. How could this be? Ordinarily, you would expect that adding an option would decrease the share of the other options. If, for example, a third candidate enters a political race, you would expect that candidate to pull votes away from the original pair. Here, however, the addition of a third possibility increases the share of one of the original choices by 12 percent. What's going on?

The key to obtaining this effect is to make the decision hard. When the researchers tested participants on a version of the problem that provided a low-quality CD player as an extra option, only 24 percent said they would wait for more information—a decrease rather than an increase—which reflects the ease of choosing the Sony. The decision between the less expensive Sony model and the top-quality Aiwa, however, is hard. It's convenient to put the hard decision off, to wait for more information.

One final observation: Not all decision makers are created equal. Suppose you go to a video store to choose a DVD for a Saturday night rental. If you are a *satisficer*, you would likely browse the DVDs until you got to one that struck you as interesting enough. If you are a *maximizer*, you would likely browse all the DVDs until you had convinced yourself that you'd found exactly the best one. Researchers have demonstrated that there are both satisficers and maximizers in the world—and that the style of decision making has important consequences (Parker et al., 2007; Schwartz et al., 2002).

One study followed a group of 548 students from 11 colleges and universities as they went onto the job market (Iyengar et al., 2006). The students completed a questionnaire that revealed the extent to which they were satisficers or maximizers: They indicated their agreement with statements such as "When shopping, I have a hard time finding clothes that I really love." The researchers contacted the students three months and six months after they completed the initial questionnaire—at those points in time, the students were interviewing and then accepting jobs. The researchers collected a variety of data to determine how the students experienced the process. Those data showed a clear pattern: The maximizers had accepted jobs that, on average, provided 20 percent higher salaries—yet they were miserable. As the researchers put it, "Despite their relative success, maximizers [were] less satisfied with the outcomes of the job search, and more pessimistic, stressed, tired, anxious, worried, overwhelmed, and depressed throughout the process" (Iyengar et al., 2006, p. 147). Apparently, the quest for an elusive "best" outcome provided the maximizers with a substantial psychological burden.

We imagine that most people would like to have a good job without making themselves miserable. As you undertake your own job searches, you might think back to this distinction between maximizers and satisficers—to consider how you might achieve a decision that affords your life a sense of balance.

Throughout this chapter, we've asked you to imagine the mysterious midnight message, "The cat is on the mat." Our goal has been to get you to consider your many types of cognitive processing—language use, visual cognition, problem solving, reasoning, judging, and deciding. Now that this chapter has come to an end, we hope that the example will stick with you—so that you'll never take your cognitive processes for granted. Every chance you get, give some thought to your thought, reason about your reasoning, and so on. You will be reflecting on the essence of the human experience.

STOP AND REVIEW

❶ Why do people rely on heuristics when they are making judgments?

❷ What heuristic might you use to answer the question, "What is the age of the oldest living human being?"

❸ Why do frames play such a large role in the psychology of decision making?

❹ What is the distinction between satisficers and maximizers?

CRITICAL THINKING Recall the study on representativeness. Why did the researchers offer participants $45 if they got the right answer?

CAN POLITICAL EXPERTS PREDICT THE FUTURE?

Here's an exercise you might try: Spend about 15 minutes on the Web gathering experts' predictions about what lies in the political future: Will one party gain a new majority in the next election? Will the Middle East become more democratic? You are likely to find a diversity of opinions on every issue. So, who should you believe? According to a long-term study conducted by psychologist **Philip Tetlock** (2005), the safest answer is that you shouldn't believe anyone—or, more exactly, you can't know whom to believe. Let's see why.

To study the collective wisdom of experts, Tetlock recruited a sample of 284 individuals who had strong credentials for making political predictions with respect to certain countries or regions of the world. (Tetlock assured his participants anonymity, so he was unable to reveal exactly who any of his experts were.) He asked individuals to make predictions of this sort: "How likely is it that after the next election, the party that currently has the most representatives in the legislative branch of government will *retain this status . . .* , *will lose this status*, or *will strengthen this position*?" (p. 46). The questions were made concrete for different countries and regions. The participants were officially experts for some of the questions, whereas for other questions they had to rely on more general knowledge. For example, one participant might be an expert on questions about Russia but not for

questions about Italy. The participants were asked to rate each of the three options (retain this status, lose this status, strengthen this position) on a scale from a likelihood of 0 percent ("impossible") to a likelihood of 100 percent ("certainty"). Tetlock examined the accuracy of 27,451 political forecasts by waiting long enough to see, in each case, what actually happened.

Because there were three options for each question, participants should have been right one third of the time just by chance. If they had true expertise, they should have been right much more often than that. But they weren't. In fact, in some comparisons experts did worse than chance. Moreover, the participants overall did no better in their official areas of expertise than when they just used their general knowledge to answer questions. That is, in general, experts on Russia and experts on Italy did just about as well answering questions on Russia (and Italy). You might wonder if fame played a role. Did better-known experts outperform their lesser-known peers? The answer is decidedly no. As Tetlock put it, "experts in demand were more overconfident than their colleagues who eked out existences far from the limelight" (p. 63).

If experts fare so poorly in their predictions, why does anyone still listen to them? An important reason is that experts aren't generally held accountable for their predictions: The media rarely tracks down the expert

who made the confident prediction that Smith would win, to ask her why Jones is now president. But Tetlock *did* ask his experts to explain why they had been wrong. The experts provided explanations in categories that will likely be familiar to you from your own life. They explained, for example, why they were "almost right" or why they were "wrong for the right reasons." They identified "out of the blue" forces that no one could have foreseen in advance of the outcome they had predicted.

Here's a safe conclusion from Tetlock's research: With respect to politics, no one can routinely predict the future. Some people do a bit better than others, but you can't use their confidence or fame to know who those people are. Still, it's important to note that this research is about a particular type of expert and a particular type of prediction. You shouldn't discount all experts. For example, when you consult medical doctors, they should be able to make their predictions—"Here's the likely impact of treatment"—based on years of education and prior experience. Also, they are regularly held accountable for the accuracy of those predictions!

- Why might Tetlock have given the participants three explicit options for each prediction?

- Why might overconfidence help people become or stay famous, even if their predictions are incorrect?

Recapping Main Points

Studying Cognition

- Cognitive psychologists study the mental processes and structures that enable you to perceive, use language, reason, solve problems, and make judgments and decisions.
- Researchers use reaction time measures to break up complex tasks into underlying mental processes.

Language Use

- Language users both produce and understand language.
- Speakers design their utterances to suit particular audiences.
- Speech errors reveal many of the processes that go into speech planning.
- Much of language understanding consists of using context to resolve ambiguities.
- Memory representations of meaning begin with propositions supplemented with inferences.
- Studies of language evolution have focused on grammatical structure and audience design.
- The language individuals speak may play a role in determining how they think.

Visual Cognition

- Visual representations can be used to supplement propositional representations.

- Visual representations allow you to think about visual aspects of your environment.
- People form visual representations that combine verbal and visual information.

Problem Solving and Reasoning

- Problem solvers must define initial state, goal state, and the operations that get them from the initial to the goal state.
- Deductive reasoning involves drawing conclusions from premises based on rules of logic.
- Inductive reasoning involves inferring a conclusion from evidence based on its likelihood or probability.

Judgment and Decision Making

- Much of judgment and decision making is guided by heuristics—mental shortcuts that can help individuals reach solutions quickly.
- Availability, representativeness, and anchoring can all lead to errors when they are misapplied.
- Decision making is affected by the way in which different options are framed.
- The possibility of regret makes some decisions hard, particularly for individuals who are maximizers rather than satisficers.

KEY TERMS

algorithm (p. 250)

anchoring heuristic (p. 260)

audience design (p. 237)

automatic process (p. 236)

availability heuristic (p. 258)

belief-bias effect (p. 254)

cognition (p. 233)

cognitive process (p. 233)

cognitive psychology (p. 233)

cognitive science (p. 233)

controlled process (p. 236)

decision making (p. 257)

deductive reasoning (p. 253)

frame (p. 261)

functional fixedness (p. 253)

heuristic (p. 251)

inductive reasoning (p. 255)

inference (p. 243)

judgment (p. 257)

language production (p. 237)

linguistic relativity (p. 245)

mental set (p. 255)

parallel processes (p. 234)

problem solving (p. 250)

problem space (p. 250)

reasoning (p. 250)

representativeness heuristic (p. 259)

serial processes (p. 234)

think-aloud protocol (p. 251)

Chapter 8 Practice Test

1. According to the logic of Donders's analysis,
   a. categorization is among the hardest mental processes.
   b. it should always take longer to draw a capital *C* than a capital *V*.
   c. extra mental steps often result in more time to complete a task.
   d. reaction time is useful for understanding the order of mental processes.

2. When Jerry goes with friends to a fast-food restaurant, they each wait in a different line to see who gets to the counter first. That's a good example of _____ processing.
   a. serial
   b. automatic
   c. parallel
   d. ambiguity

3. Lauren can juggle and talk at the same time. Warren cannot. It sounds as if juggling is more of a(n) _____ process for Lauren than for Warren.
   a. controlled
   b. automatic
   c. parallel
   d. serial

4. A friend walks up to you and says, "Remember what I said yesterday? Well, forget about it." If you understand all of this, it's because your friend has made an appropriate assessment of common ground based on
   a. copresence for actions.
   b. perceptual copresence.
   c. community membership.
   d. linguistic membership.

5. Research has demonstrated that _____ can learn the meanings of plastic symbols without any explicit training.
   a. vervet monkeys
   b. orangutans
   c. chimpanzees
   d. bonobos

6. The hypothesis of linguistic relativity suggests that
   a. languages can carve up the color spectrum in any way they choose.
   b. the languages individuals speak affect the way they think about the world.
   c. people have evolved to use languages with greater complexity than other species.
   d. some languages do not allow people to engage in audience design.

7. People's motive for mild lies is more likely to be _____, whereas for serious lies the motive is more likely to be _____.
   a. selfishness; psychological reasons
   b. personal advantage; vanity
   c. psychological reasons; personal advantage
   d. personal advantage; selfishness

8. You are lying on your side when a friend walks up to say hello. To recognize your friend, you might have to use
   a. mental rotation.
   b. mental scanning.
   c. a spatial mental model.
   d. a problem space.

9. Suppose you study a text that inserts you into the middle of a room with objects around you. It should take you the least time to verify that object that is
   a. in front of you.
   b. behind you.
   c. on your left side.
   d. on your right side.

10. A(n) _____ is *not* one component of the definition of a problem space.
    a. algorithm
    b. set of operations
    c. goal state
    d. initial state

11. You are asked to enforce the rule, "If a card has a vowel on one side, it has an even number on the other side." Which of these cards should you turn over to see if the rule has been violated?
    a. F
    b. H
    c. 9
    d. 16

12. When you are engaging in _____ reasoning, you should be wary of a (n) _____.
    a. inductive reasoning; algorithm
    b. inductive reasoning; mental set
    c. deductive reasoning; premise
    d. deductive reasoning; think-aloud protocol

13. Suppose you are asked to estimate whether Hollywood releases more comedies or horror flicks each year. To answer this question, you are most likely to use the _____ heuristic.
    a. anchoring
    b. adjustment
    c. representativeness
    d. availability

14. Because Paul is a satisficer, you would expect him to
    a. watch the first TV channel that catches his interest.
    b. be unhappy even though he recently obtained a high-paying job.
    c. test drive dozens of new cars before making a purchase.
    d. try every flavor of coffee at the new corner market.

15. Suppose you asked an expert on the United States and an expert on Mexico to make predictions about an upcoming election in Mexico. According to Philip Tetlock's research, you would expect that
    a. their predictions would be about equally accurate.
    b. the predictions of the U.S. expert would be better.
    c. the predictions of the Mexico expert would be better.
    d. only one of them would be correct.

Essay Questions

1. Why is ambiguity an important problem for language comprehension?

2. What factors affect your ability to engage in accurate deductive reasoning?

3. Under what circumstances are decisions most likely to cause people regret?

Discovering Psychology Viewing Guide

Watch the following videos by logging on to MyPsychLab (www.mypsychlab.com). After you have watched the videos, complete the activities that follow.

Program 10: Cognitive Processes

Program 11: Judgment and Decision Making

KEY TERMS AND PEOPLE

As you watch the programs, pay particular attention to these terms and people in addition to those covered in this textbook.

- *dread factor*—the fear of unfamiliar or potentially catastrophic events that make us judge these to be riskier than familiar events.
- *framing*—the way information is presented, which tends to bias how it is interpreted.
- *invariance*—the principle stating that preferences between options should be independent of different representations.
- *similarity heuristic*—an error based on the tendency to see a connection between belonging to a certain category and having the characteristics considered typical of members of that category.
- *Max Bazerman*—discusses the five most common cognitive mistakes that negotiators make.
- *Leon Festinger*—developed cognitive dissonance theory.
- *Robert Glaser*—studies learning.
- *Irving Janis*—studied the Cuban Missile Crisis and looked at distorted "groupthink" reasoning.
- *Michael Posner*—uses brain imaging techniques to explore what parts of the brain are used in accomplishing specific cognitive tasks.

PROGRAM REVIEW

Program 10

1. Michael Posner's work on brain imaging showed
   a. major differences between the brains of young and old adults, with cognitive processes more localized in brains of the elderly.
   b. that blood flow decreases in the brain as thinking becomes more efficient.
   c. that electrical stimulation of the brain can enhance performance on logic puzzles reliably.
   d. that patterns of brain activity differ in predictable ways when people see words, versus read them aloud, versus name the function of the objects to which they refer.

2. The movement in psychology known as cognitive psychology developed primarily
   a. at the turn of the century.
   b. in the 1920s.
   c. after World War II.
   d. during the last five years.

3. What analytic tool did Donald Broadbent use to model the process by which information is perceived and stored in memory?
   a. statistical analysis on a computer
   b. a flowchart
   c. a set of categories
   d. an analogy to a steam engine

4. A cognitive psychologist would be most interested in which one of the following issues?
   a. how you decide which answer is correct for this question
   b. how pain stimuli are processed
   c. maturation of the efferent system
   d. how to distinguish mania from schizophrenia

5. When we distinguish between groups of letters on the basis of the kinds of lines that form them, we are performing the mental process of
   a. relating.
   b. categorizing.
   c. creating prototypes.
   d. activating schema.

6. Concepts are mental representations. Which is a concept of an attribute?
   a. bed
   b. jumping
   c. slow
   d. courage

7. What is our prototype of a tree most likely to be similar to?
   a. a maple tree
   b. a palm tree
   c. a Christmas tree
   d. a dead tree

8. According to the program, why do we assume that Montreal is farther north than Seattle?
   a. because we have learned it
   b. because we are less familiar with Montreal than with Seattle
   c. because Canada is north of the United States in our mental maps
   d. because we are not good at making such judgments

9. When Steve Kosslyn asked people about the picture of a motorboat, he was primarily interested in
   a. how they scanned a mental image.
   b. how much detail they noted.
   c. how they compared a new picture with a prototype.
   d. how sure they felt about what they had seen.

10. What is one way in which human problem solving appears to be quite different from the way computers solve problems?
    a. Humans can solve problems that don't involve numbers.
    b. Humans are more logical in their approach to problems.
    c. Humans have trouble when content is unfamiliar.
    d. Humans are less likely to be misled by bias.

11. What did Michael Posner find when he conducted PET scans of people reading a word and associating it with a function?
    a. Localized activity occurred, but the location varied widely.
    b. Similar localized activity was seen in all the participants.
    c. Brain activity was general, rather than localized.
    d. No general pattern of activity was observed.

12. According to Robert Glaser, what is the general purpose of the research at the University of Pittsburgh's Learning and Research Development Center?
    a. to create new types of computers
    b. to model the organic functions of the brain
    c. to classify errors and mistakes
    d. to improve the way people use their intelligence

13. What is a cognitive illusion?
    a. a mental map that we can scan for information
    b. a biased mental strategy
    c. a concept formed on the basis of a perceptual illusion
    d. a decision motivated by emotion

14. How did Freud explain the fact that human beings sometimes make irrational decisions?
    a. They are driven by primitive needs.
    b. They are influenced by the emotions of the crowd.
    c. They are basing their decisions on availability.
    d. They are using standard human mental processes.

15. Why did the people questioned assume that there were more words beginning with k than with k as the third letter?
    a. There is a general tendency to favor the initial position.
    b. The anchoring effect biased their answers.
    c. It's easier to find examples of words beginning with k.
    d. It seems less risky as an answer.

16. A heuristic is a kind of
    a. mistake.
    b. meaning.
    c. mathematical model.
    d. shortcut.

17. When people were confronted with a choice of a sure loss of $85 or an 85 percent chance of losing $100, how did most people react?
    a. They chose the loss.
    b. They chose the chance.
    c. They pointed out the statistical equivalence of the alternatives.
    d. They revised to make the choice.

18. Why would smokers be likely to underestimate the chance of developing lung cancer?
    a. They do not dread the disease.
    b. It is an unfamiliar risk.
    c. It is not representative.
    d. It represents a delayed consequence.

19. Irving Janis studied how the decision to invade Cuba was made during the Kennedy administration. What advice does Janis offer to promote better decision making?
    a. Encourage groupthink by team-building exercises.
    b. Appoint one group member to play devil's advocate.
    c. Restrict the size of the group.
    d. Assume that silence means consent on the part of all group members.

20. Imagine that you are a business leader who has been to a negotiating workshop led by Max Bazerman and Lawrence Susskind. Which statement shows something you should have learned from the experience?
    a. "I will escalate conflict."
    b. "I know this is a zero-sum game."
    c. "I will enlarge my frame of reference."
    d. "I am confident that I am right and will prevail."

21. How does cognitive dissonance make us feel?
    a. We are so uncomfortable that we try to reduce the dissonance.
    b. We enjoy it so much that we actively seek dissonance.
    c. Our reaction to dissonance depends largely on personality.
    d. It creates boredom, which we try to overcome.

22. In Festinger's experiment, which students felt dissonance?
    a. both the students who got $20 and those who got $1
    b. the students who got $20 but not those who got $1
    c. the students who got $1 but not those who got $20
    d. neither the students who got $1 nor those who got $20

23. Read the following sentences: "Mary heard the ice cream truck. She remembered her birthday money and ran into the house." What allowed you to understand how these sentences are related?
    a. a cognitive illusion
    b. reasoning by analogy
    c. a schema
    d. the anchoring heuristic

24. Which of the following is true of groupthink?
    a. Groupthink is characterized by people's strong motivation to provide their colleagues with information that will change their minds.
    b. To avoid groupthink, a company should hire people who were all trained in the same business philosophy.
    c. Groupthink occurs only in the political world, and not in other domains.
    d. Groupthink is characterized by a self-censorship of one's doubts.

25. According to Howard Gardner, which popular approach to psychology did the field of cognitive science overthrow?
    a. functionalism
    b. structuralism
    c. behaviorism
    d. evolutionism

26. All of the following are true about our representation of schema, except that
    a. memory errors can stem from activating inappropriate schema.
    b. schema are complex concepts.
    c. they can be used to understand language.
    d. their use is limited to decision making.

27. According to Robert Glaser, intelligence
    a. is a skill and can be developed.
    b. is genetically determined.
    c. is a myth.
    d. is no higher in humans than it is in chimpanzees and bonobos.

28. Jim has greater dread of the possible consequences for him of a small meteorite impact on Earth than of the consequences of jaywalking across a busy street. According to the program, this difference is likely because
    a. the consequences of the meteorite impact are less familiar.
    b. the consequences of the meteorite impact are less immediate.
    c. the consequences of jaywalking are smaller for him than of a meteorite impact somewhere on Earth.
    d. the anchoring heuristic leads to greater attention for perceptual events.

29. According to Max Bazerman, all of the following are mistakes commonly made during negotiation, *except*
    a. being willing to compromise on points of lesser importance.
    b. failure to consider the judgments made by one's counterpart.
    c. limiting one's thinking to the specific points of conflict.
    d. assuming that whenever one side wins, the other must lose.

30. Which of these is a likely consequence of cognitive dissonance?
    a. becoming more entrenched in one's beliefs
    b. increasing the behavior that is causing dissonance
    c. becoming more sociable
    d. changing an attitude

31. Al's parents are paying for his college tuition. Joe is working two jobs to put himself through college. Both are taking a fairly dry chemistry course together. Who is more likely to say he likes the course, and why?
    a. Al, because of cognitive dissonance
    b. Joe, because of cognitive dissonance
    c. Al, because of the availability heuristic
    d. Joe, because of the availability heuristic

32. Why is the normative approach to decision making different from the descriptive approach?
    a. because people are not rational
    b. because the normative approach is interested in cross-cultural effects, while the descriptive approach is not
    c. because the normative approach studies framing effects, while the descriptive approach does not
    d. because the descriptive approach is a less scientifically rigorous study of human cognition than the normative approach

QUESTIONS TO CONSIDER

1. Where does the poem "Jabberwocky," by Lewis Carroll, get its meaning? Read the excerpt below and consider the concepts and rules of language and underlying structure that help you make sense of it. Can you paraphrase it?

'Twas brillig, and the slithy toves
Did gyre and gimble in the wabe;
All mimsy were the borogoves,
And the mome raths outgrabe.

Beware the Jabberwock, my son!
The jaws that bite, the claws that catch!
Beware the Jubjub bird, and shun
The frumious Bandersnatch!

2. Think of all the ways you can categorize people (for example, by their gender, their age, their ethnicity, their intelligence, their taste in music). Do you have different schemas for people who belong to these various groups? How does your schema influence your behavior toward people?

3. Knowing about problem-solving strategies and using them are two different things. Based on the information in the program and in your text, what are some of the pitfalls you need to avoid in both day-to-day problem solving and decision making about major life changes? How optimistic are you that you can really learn to consistently avoid these pitfalls?

4. How does the framing effect, which shows how the description of a situation can heavily influence decision making, jibe with the evidence encountered in the previous chapter that the limitations inherent in one's native language only weakly limits one's thinking?

5. How might cognitive heuristics, like representativeness and availability, perpetuate ethnic stereotypes?

ACTIVITIES

1. All of us tend to categorize the world into convenient units and to use common labels for our categories. Often those labels become permanent, and we tend to view our world in a rigid or stereotypical way. When this stops us from producing new ideas, it is called functional fixedness. Can you overcome it?

   Try this: How many uses can you think of for an empty milk carton, a brick, a sock with a hole in it, a paper clip, a bandanna, or another ordinary household object? After you feel you've exhausted all possibilities, list as many attributes of the object as possible. Draw a picture of the object from various points of view. Then see if you can generate any new uses.

2. Draw a map of the United States from memory, in as much detail as possible. Then compare it to a real map of the United States. Where is your map systematically distorted or simplified?

3. Go to a busy intersection and observe pedestrian street-crossing behavior. Observe the kinds of risks people take crossing the street. What do you consider risky behavior? Who is most likely to engage in it? Why do you suppose certain people take more risks than others?

9

Intelligence and Intelligence Assessment

Suppose you were asked to define the word *intelligence*. What types of behaviors would you include in your definition? Think back on your own experiences. What was it like when you first started school? What was it like when you labored at your first job? It's very likely that you heard your behaviors labeled as intelligent or unintelligent— smart or not so smart—in those and other situations. When those labels are applied in casual conversation, they have relatively few consequences. However, there are many settings in which it matters whether your behaviors are considered intelligent or not. For example, if you grew up in the United States, it is likely that your "potential" was measured at an early age. In most school districts, teachers and administrators attempt, very early in your life, to measure your *intelligence*. The goal, most often, is to match students with classroom work that makes appropriate demands. However, as you've almost certainly observed, people's lives often seem to be affected by intelligence testing in areas well outside the classroom.

In this chapter, we will examine the foundations and uses of intelligence assessment. We will review the contributions psychologists have made to the understanding of individual differences in the areas of intelligence. We will also discuss the types of controversies that almost inevitably arise when people begin to interpret these differences. Our focus will be on how intelligence tests work, what makes any test useful, and why they do not always do the job they were intended to do. Finally, we will conclude on a personal note, by considering the role of psychological assessment in society.

We begin now with a brief overview of the general practice of psychological assessment.

What Is Assessment?

Psychological assessment is the use of specified testing procedures to evaluate the abilities, behaviors, and personal qualities of people. Psychological assessment is often referred to as the measurement of *individual differences* because the majority of assessments specifies how an individual is different from or similar to other people on a given dimension. Before we examine in detail the basic features of psychological testing, let's outline the history of assessment. This historical overview will help you to understand both the uses and limitations of assessment, as well as prepare you to appreciate some current controversies.

HISTORY OF ASSESSMENT

The development of formal tests and procedures for assessment is a relatively new enterprise in Western psychology, coming into wide use only in the early 1900s. However, long before Western psychology began to devise tests to evaluate people, assessment techniques were commonplace in ancient China. In fact, China employed a sophisticated program of civil service testing over 4,000 years ago—officials were required to demonstrate their competence every third year at an oral examination. Two thousand years later, during the Han Dynasty, written civil service tests were used to measure competence in the areas of law, the military, agriculture, and geography. During the Ming Dynasty

(A.D. 1368–1644), public officials were chosen on the basis of their performance at three stages of an objective selection procedure. During the first stage, examinations were given at the local level. The 4 percent who passed these tests had to endure the second stage: 9 days and nights of essay examinations on the classics. The 5 percent who passed the essay exams were allowed to complete a final stage of tests conducted at the nation's capital.

China's selection procedures were observed and described by British diplomats and missionaries in the early 1800s. Modified versions of China's system were soon adopted by the British and later by the Americans for the selection of civil service personnel (Wiggins, 1973).

The key figure in the development of Western intelligence testing was an upper-class Englishman, **Sir Francis Galton** (1822–1911). His book *Hereditary Genius*, published in 1869, greatly influenced subsequent thinking on the methods, theories, and practices of testing. Galton, a half cousin to Charles Darwin, attempted to apply Darwinian evolutionary theory to the study of human abilities. He was interested in how and why people differ in their abilities. He wondered why some people were gifted and successful—like him—while many others were not.

Galton was the first to postulate four important ideas about the assessment of intelligence. First, differences in intelligence were *quantifiable* in terms of degrees of intelligence. In other words, numerical values could be assigned to distinguish among different people's levels of intelligence. Second, differences among people formed a *bell-shaped curve*, or *normal distribution*. On a bell-shaped curve, most people's scores cluster in the middle, and fewer are found toward the two extremes of genius and mental deficiency (we will return to the bell-shaped curve later in the chapter). Third, intelligence, or mental ability, could be measured by objective tests, tests on which each question had only one "right" answer. And fourth, the precise extent to which two sets of test scores were related could be determined by a statistical procedure he called *co-relations*, now known as *correlations*. These ideas proved to be of lasting value.

Unfortunately, Galton postulated a number of ideas that proved considerably more controversial. He believed, for example, that genius was inherited. In his view, talent, or eminence, ran in families; nurture had only a minimal effect on intelligence. In his view, intelligence was related to Darwinian species' fitness and, somehow, ultimately to one's moral worth. Galton attempted to base public policy on the concept of genetically superior and inferior people. He started the *eugenics* movement, which advocated improving the human species by applying evolutionary theory to encouraging biologically superior people to interbreed while discouraging biologically inferior people from having offspring. Galton wrote, "There exists a sentiment, for the most part quite unreasonable, against the gradual extinction of an inferior race" (Galton, 1883/1907, p. 200).

These controversial ideas were endorsed and extended later by many who argued forcefully that the intellectually superior race should propagate at the expense of those with inferior minds. Among the proponents of these ideas were American psychologists Goddard and Terman, whose theories we review later, and, of course, Nazi dictator Adolf Hitler. We will also see later in the chapter that remnants of these elitist ideas are still being proposed today.

---

psychological assessment The use of specified procedures to evaluate the abilities, behaviors, and personal qualities of people.

What important ideas about the assessment of intelligence are credited to Sir Francis Galton (1822–1911)?

Sir Francis Galton's work created a context for contemporary intelligence assessment. Let's now see what features define circumstances of formal assessment.

BASIC FEATURES OF FORMAL ASSESSMENT

To be useful for classifying individuals or for selecting those with particular qualities, a **formal assessment** procedure should meet three requirements. The assessment instrument should be (1) reliable, (2) valid, and (3) standardized. If it fails to meet these requirements, we cannot be sure whether the conclusions of the assessment can be trusted. Although this chapter focuses on intelligence assessment, formal assessment procedures apply to all types of psychological testing. To ensure that you'll understand the broad application of these principles, we will draw on examples both from intelligence testing and other domains of psychological assessment.

---

formal assessment The systematic procedures and measurement instruments used by trained professionals to assess an individual's functioning, aptitudes, abilities, or mental states.

test–retest reliability A measure of the correlation between the scores of the same people on the same test given on two different occasions.

parallel forms Different versions of a test used to assess test reliability; the change of forms reduces effects of direct practice, memory, or the desire of an individual to appear consistent on the same items.

internal consistency A measure of reliability; the degree to which a test yields similar scores across its different parts, such as odd versus even items.

split-half reliability A measure of the correlation between test takers' performance on different halves (such as odd- and even-numbered items) of a test.

Reliability As you'll recall from Chapter 2, *reliability* is the extent to which an assessment instrument can be trusted to give consistent scores. If you stepped on your bathroom scale three times in the same morning and it gave you a different reading each time, the scale would not be doing its job. You would call it *unreliable* because you could not count on it to give consistent results. Of course, if you ate a big meal in between two weighings, you wouldn't expect the scale to produce the same result. That is, a measurement device can be considered reliable or unreliable only to the extent that the underlying concept it is measuring should remain unchanged.

One straightforward way to find out if a test is reliable is to calculate its **test–retest reliability**—a measure of the correlation between the scores of the same people, on the same test, given on two different occasions. A perfectly reliable test will yield a correlation coefficient of +1.00. This means that the identical pattern of scores emerges both times. The same people who got the highest and lowest scores the first time do so again. A totally unreliable test results in a 0.00 correlation coefficient. That means there is no relationship between the first set of scores and the second set. Someone who initially got the top score gets a completely different score the second time. As the correlation coefficient moves higher (toward the ideal of +1.00), the test is increasingly reliable.

There are two other ways to assess reliability. One is to administer alternate, **parallel forms** of a test instead of giving the same test twice. Using parallel forms reduces the effects of direct practice of the test questions, memory of the test questions, and the desire of an individual to appear consistent from one test to the next. Reliable tests yield comparable scores on parallel forms of the test. The other measure of reliability is the **internal consistency** of responses on a single test. For example, we can compare a person's score on the odd-numbered items of a test with the score on the even-numbered items. A reliable test yields the same score for each of its halves. It is then said to have high internal consistency on this measure of **split-half reliability.** In most circumstances, not only should the measurement device itself be reliable, but so should the method for using the device. Suppose researchers wished to observe children in a classroom in order to assess different levels of aggressive play. The researchers might develop a *coding scheme* that would allow them to make appropriate distinctions. The scheme would be reliable to the extent that all the people who viewed the same behavior would give highly similar ratings to the same children. This is one of the reasons that quite a bit of training is required before individuals can carry out accurate psychological assessment. They must learn to apply systems of distinctions in a reliable fashion.

The researchers who develop and administer assessment devices work hard to ensure reliability. Did you take the SAT I exam for college admissions? You may not know this, but one section of the exam you took did not have an impact on your score. The questions on this unscored section were most likely being considered for future exams. The researchers who develop the exam can compare performance on the scored questions to performance on the unscored questions to ensure that people's scores on future exams are comparable to the scores on the exam that you took. For that reason, if you took the SAT I, you provided some of the information that helps to make the test reliable.

Validity Recall from Chapter 2 that the *validity* of a test is the degree to which it measures what an assessor intends it to measure. A valid test of intelligence measures that trait and predicts performance in situations where intelligence is important.

Scores on a valid measure of creativity reflect actual creativity, not drawing ability or moods. In general, then, validity reflects a test's ability to make accurate predictions about behaviors or outcomes related to the purpose or design of the test. Three important types of validity are *content validity, criterion validity,* and *construct validity.*

A test has **content validity** if it measures the full range of the domain of interest. Suppose you wanted to assess people's satisfaction with their lives. It wouldn't be enough to focus, for example, on success in school. To develop a measure that had content validity, you'd want to sample broadly from the different domains of people's lives. You would ask people if they were satisfied with their jobs, their relationships, and so on.

To assess the **criterion validity** (also known as **predictive validity**) of a test, psychologists compare a person's score on the test with his or her score on some other standard, or *criterion,* associated with what the test measures. For example, if a test is designed to predict success in college, then college grades would be an appropriate criterion. If the test scores correlate highly with college grades, then the test has criterion validity. A major task of test developers is to find appropriate, measurable criteria. Let's see how researchers demonstrated the criterion validity of a measure of juror bias.

The wrong way to measure split-half reliability.

When people become members of juries they are supposed to consider the evidence without any biases. A pair of researchers sought to demonstrate the validity of a measurement device—the *Pretrial Juror Attitude Questionnaire (PJAQ)*—that would enable them to identify potential jurors who could not meet that unbiased standard (Lecci & Myers, 2008). The PJAQ consists of a series of 29 statements (for example, "If a suspect runs from police, then he probably committed the crime," "Many accident claims filed against insurance companies are phony"). People who take the PJAQ indicate their agreement to each statement on a 5-point scale ranging from *strongly disagree* to *strongly agree.* To assess the predictive validity of the PJAQ, the researchers asked 617 participants to complete the measure. Next, they had the same group of participants read summaries of trials for murder, rape, and armed robbery cases. The participants indicated what verdict they thought was appropriate for each case. When participants arrive at more *guilty* verdicts than the majority of their peers, that pattern suggests that some prior bias may be at work. The PJAQ successfully predicted which participants were likely to provide a high number of *guilty* verdicts.

Once criterion validity has been demonstrated for an assessment device, researchers feel confident using the device to make future predictions.

For many personal qualities of interest to psychologists, no ideal criterion exists. No single behavior or objective measure of performance can indicate, for example, how anxious, depressed, or aggressive a person is overall. Psychologists have theories, or *constructs,* about these abstract qualities—what

causes them, how they affect behavior, and how they relate to other variables. The **construct validity** of a test is the degree to which it adequately measures the underlying construct. For example, a new measure of depression has construct validity if the scores it produces correlate highly with valid measures of the features that define the construct of depression. In addition, the new measure should not show relationships with features that fall outside the construct of depression.

The conditions under which a test is valid may be very specific, so it is always important to ask about a test, "For what purpose is it valid?" Knowing which other measures a test does and does not correlate with may reveal something new about the measures, the construct, or the complexity of human behavior. For example, suppose you design a test to measure the ability of medical students to cope with stress. You then find that scores on that test correlate well with students' ability to cope with classroom stress. You presume your test will also correlate with students' ability to deal with stressful hospital emergencies, but you discover it does not. Because you have demonstrated some validity, you have learned something both about your test—the circumstances in which it is valid—and about your construct—different categories of stressors have different consequences. You would then modify your test to take account of the kinds of special stressors found in hospital emergencies.

Consider for a moment the relationship between validity and reliability. Whereas reliability is measured by the degree to which a test correlates with itself (administered at different times or using different items), validity is measured by the degree to which the test correlates with something external to it (another test, a behavioral criterion, or judges' ratings). Usually, a test that is not reliable is also not valid because a test that cannot predict itself will be unable to predict anything else. For example, if your class took a test of aggressiveness today and scores were uncorrelated with scores from a parallel form of the test tomorrow (demonstrating unreliability), it is unlikely that the scores from either day would predict which students had fought or argued most frequently over a week's time: After all, the two sets of test scores would not even make the same prediction! Conversely, it is quite possible for a test to be highly reliable without being valid. Suppose, for example, we decided to use your current height as a measure of intelligence. Do you see why that would be reliable but not valid?

---

content validity The extent to which a test adequately measures the full range of the domain of interest.

criterion validity The degree to which test scores indicate a result on a specific measure that is consistent with some other criterion of the characteristic being assessed; also known as predictive validity.

predictive validity The degree to which test scores indicate a result on a specific measure that is consistent with some other criterion of the characteristic being assessed; also known as criterion validity.

construct validity The degree to which a test adequately measures an underlying construct.

How would you feel if someone used your adult height to assess intelligence? The measure would be reliable, but would it be valid?

Norms and Standardization So we have a reliable and valid test, but we still need *norms* to provide a context for interpreting different test scores. Suppose, for example, you get a score of 18 on a test designed to reveal how depressed you are. What does that mean? Are you a little depressed, not at all depressed, or about averagely depressed? To find out what your score means, you would want to compare your individual score with typical scores, or statistical **norms,** of other students. You would check the test norms to see what the usual range of scores is and what the average is for students of your age and sex. That would provide you with a context for interpreting your depression score.

You probably encountered test norms when you received your scores on aptitude tests, such as the SAT I. The norms told you how your scores compared with those of other students and helped you interpret how well you had done relative to that *normative population.* Group norms are most useful for interpreting individual scores when the comparison group shares important qualities with the individuals tested, such as age, social class, culture, and experience.

For norms to be meaningful, everyone must take the same test under standardized circumstances. **Standardization** is the administration of a testing device to all persons, in the same way, under the same conditions. The need for standardization sounds obvious, but it does not always occur in practice. Some people may be allowed more time than others, be given clearer or more detailed instructions, be permitted to ask questions, or be motivated by a tester to perform better. When procedures do not include explicit instructions about the way to administer a test or the way to score the results, it is difficult to interpret what a given test score means or how it relates to any comparison group.

We have now reviewed some of the concerns researchers have when they construct a test and find out whether it is indeed testing what they wish to test. They must assure themselves

that the test is reliable and valid. They must also specify the standard conditions under which it should be administered, so that resulting norms have meaning. Therefore, you should evaluate any test score you get in terms of the test's reliability and validity, the norms of performance, and the degree of standardization of the circumstances in which you took the test.

We are now ready to turn to the measurement of intelligence.

STOP AND REVIEW

❶ What overarching ideas did Sir Francis Galton contribute to the study of intelligence?
❷ What is meant by split-half reliability?
❸ How would a researcher determine whether a measure has predictive validity?
❹ Why is it important to have norms for measures?

CRITICAL THINKING Recall the study that assessed the criterion validity of the Pretrial Juror Attitude Questionnaire. How might you assess the PJAQ's validity in the context of real-world trials?

Intelligence Assessment

How intelligent are you or your friends? To answer this question, you must begin by defining **intelligence.** Doing so is not an easy task, but a group of 52 intelligence researchers concurred on this general definition: "Intelligence is a very general mental capability that, among other things, involves the ability to reason, plan, solve problems, think abstractly, comprehend complex ideas, learn quickly and learn from experience" (Gottfredson, 1997, p. 13). Given this range of capabilities, it should be clear immediately why controversy has almost always surrounded how intelligence is measured. The way in which theorists conceptualize intelligence and higher mental functioning greatly influences the way they try to assess it (Sternberg, 1994). Some psychologists believe that human intelligence can be quantified and reduced to a single score. Others argue that intelligence has many components that should be separately assessed. Still others say that there are actually several distinct kinds of intelligence, across different domains of experience.

In this section, we will describe how tests of intelligence mesh with these different conceptions of intelligence. Let's begin by considering the historical context in which interest in intelligence and intelligence testing first arose.

THE ORIGINS OF INTELLIGENCE TESTING

The year 1905 marked the first published account of a workable intelligence test. **Alfred Binet** (1857–1911) had responded to the call of the French minister of public instruction for the creation of more effective teaching methods for developmentally disabled children. Binet and his colleague **Theodore Simon** (1873–1961) believed that measuring a child's intellectual ability was necessary for planning an instructional program. Binet attempted to devise an objective test of intellectual performance that could be used to classify and separate developmentally

---

norm Standard based on measurement of a large group of people; used for comparing the scores of an individual with those of others within a well-defined group.

standardization A set of uniform procedures for treating each participant in a test, interview, or experiment, or for recording data.

intelligence The global capacity to profit from experience and to go beyond given information about the environment.

disabled from normal schoolchildren. He hoped that such a test would reduce the school's reliance on the more subjective, and perhaps biased, evaluations of teachers.

To *quantify*—measure—intellectual performance, Binet designed age-appropriate problems or test items on which many children's responses could be compared. The problems on the test were chosen so that they could be scored objectively as correct or incorrect, could vary in content, were not heavily influenced by differences in children's environments, and assessed judgment and reasoning rather than rote memory (Binet, 1911).

Children of various ages were tested, and the average score for normal children at each age was computed. Each individual child's performance was then compared with the average for other children of his or her age. Test results were expressed in terms of the average age at which normal children achieved a particular score. This measure was called the **mental age.** For instance, when a child's score equaled the average score of a group of 5-year-olds, the child was said to have a *mental age* of 5, regardless of his or her actual **chronological age,** the number of years since birth.

Binet's successful development of an intelligence test had great impact in the United States. A unique combination of historical events and social-political forces had prepared the United States for an explosion of interest in assessing mental ability. At the beginning of the 20th century, the United States was a nation in turmoil. As a result of global economic, social, and political conditions, millions of immigrants entered the country. New universal education laws flooded schools with students. Some form of assessment was needed to identify, document, and classify immigrant adults and schoolchildren (Chapman, 1988). When World War I began, millions of volunteers marched into recruiting stations. Recruiters needed to determine who of these many people had the ability to learn quickly and benefit from special leadership training. New nonverbal, group-administered tests of mental ability were used to evaluate over 1.7 million recruits. A group of prominent psychologists, including Lewis Terman, Edward Thorndike, and Robert Yerkes, responded to the wartime emergency and designed these tests in only one month's time (Lennon, 1985).

One consequence of this large-scale testing program was that the American public came to accept the idea that intelligence tests could differentiate people in terms of leadership ability and other socially important characteristics. This acceptance led to the widespread use of tests in schools and industry. Assessment was seen as a way to inject order into a chaotic society and as an inexpensive, democratic way to separate those who could benefit from education or military leadership training from those who could not. To facilitate the wide-scale use of intelligence testing, researchers strove for more broadly applicable testing procedures.

IQ TESTS

Although Binet began the standardized assessment of intellectual ability in France, U.S. psychologists soon took the lead. They also developed the IQ, or intelligence quotient. The IQ was a numerical, standardized measure of intelligence. Two families of individually administered IQ tests are used widely today: the Stanford–Binet scales and the Wechsler scales.

The Stanford–Binet Intelligence Scale Stanford University's **Lewis Terman,** a former public school administrator,

appreciated the importance of Binet's method for assessing intelligence. He adapted Binet's test questions for U.S. schoolchildren, he standardized the administration of the test, and he developed age-level norms by giving the test to thousands of children. In 1916, he published the Stanford Revision of the Binet Tests, commonly referred to as the *Stanford–Binet Intelligence Scale* (Terman, 1916).

With his new test, Terman provided a base for the concept of the **intelligence quotient,** or **IQ** (a term coined by William Stern, 1914). The IQ was the ratio of mental age to chronological age multiplied by 100 to eliminate decimals:

$$\text{IQ} = \text{mental age} \div \text{chronological age} \times 100$$

A child with a chronological age of 8 whose test scores revealed a mental age of 10 had an IQ of 125 ($10 \div 8 \times 100 = 125$), whereas a child of that same chronological age who performed at the level of a 6-year-old had an IQ of 75 ($6 \div 8 \times 100 = 75$). Individuals who performed at the mental age equivalent to their chronological age had IQs of 100. Thus the score of 100 was considered to be the average IQ.

The new Stanford–Binet test soon became a standard instrument in clinical psychology, psychiatry, and educational counseling. The Stanford–Binet contains a series of subtests, each tailored for a particular mental age. Since it was first introduced, the Stanford–Binet has undergone a series of revisions (Terman & Merrill, 1937, 1960, 1972; Thorndike et al., 1986). Through those revisions, the range of the test has been extended to measure the IQ of very young children and very intelligent adults. In addition, the revisions have provided updated norms for age-appropriate average scores. The most recent, fifth edition of the Stanford–Binet test provides IQ estimates for individuals in the normal range of performance as well as for those individuals who are either mentally impaired or mentally gifted (Roid, 2003).

The Wechsler Intelligence Scales David Wechsler of Bellevue Hospital in New York set out to correct the dependence on verbal items in the assessment of adult intelligence. In 1939, he published the Wechsler–Bellevue Intelligence Scale, which combined verbal subtests with nonverbal, or performance, subtests. Thus, in addition to an overall IQ score, people were given separate estimates of verbal IQ and nonverbal IQ. After a few changes, the test was retitled the *Wechsler Adult Intelligence Scale*—the WAIS—in 1955. Today, you would take the WAIS-IV (Wechsler, 1997).

The WAIS-IV has ten core subtests and five supplemental subtests that span several aspects of IQ. **Table 9.1**, on page 276, provides examples of the types of questions you would find on the test. As you can see in the table, the WAIS-IV organizes the subtests into four scales that measure verbal comprehension, perceptual reasoning, working memory, and processing speed.

---

mental age In Binet's measure of intelligence, the age at which a child is performing intellectually, expressed in terms of the average age at which normal children achieve a particular score.

chronological age The number of months or years since an individual's birth.

intelligence quotient (IQ) An index derived from standardized tests of intelligence; originally obtained by dividing an individual's mental age by chronological age and then multiplying by 100; now directly computed as an IQ test score.

TABLE 9.1	Questions and Problems Similar to Those on the WAIS-IV
Verbal Comprehension Scale	
Similarities	In what ways are airplanes and submarines alike?
Vocabulary	What does *emulate* mean?
Perceptual Reasoning Scale	
Block Design	The test taker uses patterned blocks to reproduce designs provided by the examiner.
Picture Completion	The test taker examines a picture and says what is missing (for example, a horse without a mane).
Working Memory Scale	
Digit Span	Repeat the following numbers: 3 2 7 5 9.
Arithmetic	If you paid $8.50 for a movie ticket and $2.75 for popcorn, how much change would you have left from a $20 bill?
Processing Speed Scale	
Symbol Search	The test taker tries to determine whether one of two abstract symbols (such as Θ, ∀) appears on a longer list of symbols.
Cancellation	The test taker looks at visual displays and carries out the examiner's instructions (for example, "Draw a line through each blue square and green triangle").

If you were to take the WAIS-IV, you could receive an overall, or Full Scale, IQ as well as separate measures for each of the four scales.

The WAIS-IV is designed for people age 16 years and older, but similar tests have been developed for children (see **Figure 9.1**). *The Wechsler Intelligence Scale for Children—Fourth Edition* (WISC-IV; Wechsler, 2003) is suited for children ages 6 to 16, and the *Wechsler Preschool and Primary Scale of Intelligence—Third Edition* (WPPSI-III; Wechsler, 2002) for children ages 2½ to 7¼ years. The recent revisions of both of these tests have made the materials more colorful, more contemporary, and more enjoyable for children.

The WAIS-IV, the WISC-IV, and the WPPSI-III form a family of intelligence tests that yield Full Scale IQ scores at all age levels. In addition, they provide comparable subtest scores that allow researchers to track the development over time of more specific intellectual abilities. For this reason, the Wechsler scales are particularly valuable when the same individual is to be tested at different ages—for example, when a child's progress in response to different educational programs is monitored.

EXTREMES OF INTELLIGENCE

IQ scores are no longer derived by dividing mental age by chronological age. If you took the test today, your score would be added up and directly compared with the scores of other people your age. An IQ of 100 is "average" and would indicate that 50 percent of those your age had earned lower scores. As you can see in **Figure 9.2,** scores between 90 and 110 are labeled "normal." In this section, we consider the individuals whose IQ scores fall on either side of this range.

Intellectual Disability and Learning Disorders When individuals below the age of 18 obtain valid IQ scores that are approximately two standard deviations below the mean on an intelligence test, they meet one criterion for a classification of **intellectual disability.** For the WAIS, that criterion would

FIGURE 9.1 Intelligence Testing

A psychologist administers an intelligence test to a 4-year-old child. The performance part of the test includes sorting an array of colored candy. Why is performance an important component of an IQ assessment?

---

intellectual disability Condition in which individuals have IQ scores of 70 to 75 or below and also demonstrate limitations in the ability to bring adaptive skills to bear on life tasks.

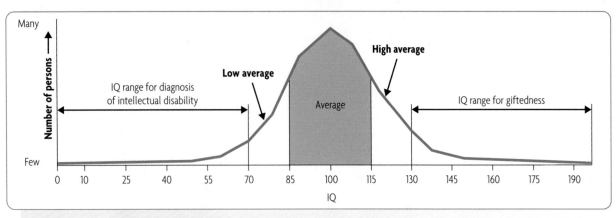

FIGURE 9.2 Distribution of IQ Scores among a Large Sample

IQ scores are normed so that a score of 100 is the population average (as many people score below 100 as score above 100). Scores between 85 and 115 are labeled average. Scores above 130 may indicate that an individual is gifted; scores below 70 contribute to a diagnosis of intellectual disability.

represent an IQ score of 70. However, as shown in **Table 9.2,** to be considered intellectually disabled, individuals must also demonstrate limitations "in adaptive behavior as expressed in

conceptual, social, and adaptive skills" (American Association on Mental Retardation, 2002, p. 73). In earlier times, the term *mental retardation* was used to refer to people with IQs 70 to 75 and below. However, because of the expanded definition that includes consideration of adaptive behavior, intellectual disability has become the more appropriate term (Schalock et al., 2007). When clinicians diagnose individuals with intellectual disability, they attempt to understand as much as possible what limitations each individual has with adaptive skills. Rather than categorizing people just on IQ, the contemporary goal is to provide environmental and social supports that are closely matched to each individual's needs.

Intellectual disability can be brought about by a number of genetic and environmental factors. For example, individuals with *Down syndrome*—a disorder caused by extra genetic material on the 21st chromosome—often have low IQs. Another genetic disorder, known as *phenylketonuria* (PKU), also has a potential negative impact on IQ (Gassió et al., 2005). However, through strict adherence to a special diet, people can control the negative effects of PKU if it is diagnosed in infancy. Family studies suggest that genetic inheritance likely plays a role only in the range of what historically would have been called mild retardation (see Figure 9.2) (Plomin & Spinath, 2004). The more severe forms of retardation appear to be caused by the occurrence of spontaneous genetic abnormalities in an individual's development that are not heritable. The environment that is most often critical for intellectual disability is the prenatal environment. Pregnant women who suffer diseases such as rubella and syphilis are at risk for having children with intellectual disabilities. In addition, pregnant women who consume alcohol or other drugs, particularly during the early weeks of pregnancy, also increase the likelihood of having children with cognitive deficits (Bennett et al., 2008; Huizink & Mulder, 2006).

Historically, individuals with intellectual disabilities were educated—to the extent that they were educated—almost entirely in separate facilities. However, because evidence accumulated that these separate programs were not effective, the U.S. government passed legislation requiring that students

TABLE 9.2 Diagnosis of Intellectual Disability

Intellectual disability is diagnosed if:

- The individual's IQ is approximately two standard deviations below the mean on an intelligence test.
- The individual demonstrates limitations in adaptive behavior, such as

Conceptual

Language use

Reading and writing

Money concepts

Social

Responsibility for actions

Gullibility

Avoid victimization

Practical

Meal preparation and eating

Dressing

Occupational skills

- The age of onset is below 18.

Source: Excerpted from American Association on Mental Retardation, 2002, p. 42.

with disabilities be educated to the greatest extent possible in general classrooms (Williamson et al., 2006). The law recognizes that some levels of impairment skill require students to receive separate instruction. However, about 45 percent of students diagnosed with an intellectual disability spend some or much of each school day in classrooms with their peers.

IQ scores give general information about how well people are able to perform—with respect to age-appropriate norms—on a variety of verbal and nonverbal tasks. In some instances, there is cause for concern when IQ scores and performance fail to match up. People who present a sufficiently large discrepancy between their achievement and their measured IQ might be diagnosed with a learning disorder. Before clinicians diagnose a **learning disorder,** they need to rule out other factors that can lead to poor performance such as low motivation, mediocre teaching, or physical problems (such as visual deficits). Many schools provide special assistance to students who have been diagnosed with learning disorders.

Giftedness Individuals are most likely to be labeled as *gifted* if they have an IQ score above 130. However, as with the definition of intellectual disability, researchers have suggested that the conception of giftedness is not adequately captured just by IQ. For example, **Joseph Renzulli** (2005) has argued in favor of a "three-ring" conception of giftedness that characterizes giftedness along the dimensions of ability, creativity, and task commitment (see **Figure 9.3**). On this view, individuals can be considered gifted with IQs that are above average but not necessarily superior. In addition, they need to show high levels of creativity and exert high levels of commitment to particular problems or domains of performance. This expanded definition of giftedness explains why people often are not gifted across the academic spectrum (Winner, 2000). Abilities, creativity, and task commitment may all differ, for example, between verbal and mathematical domains.

What qualities do gifted children generally possess? The formal study of gifted children began in 1921 when Lewis Terman (1925) began a long-term study of a group of over 1,500 boys and girls who tested in the top 1 percent of their school populations. This group of individuals was followed all the way into their 80s (Holahan & Sears, 1995). Terman and his successors wanted to see how these children fared as they made their way through life. The questions Terman asked continue to shape the research agenda. For example, Terman explored the myth that gifted children have problems with social and emotional adjustment. Terman concluded just the opposite: He found his sample to be better adjusted than their less gifted peers. However, more contemporary studies support the conclusion that gifted children are more introverted—more internally oriented (see p. 410)—than their peers (Sak, 2004). That orientation toward their own inner lives supports, in part, the task commitment that helps define

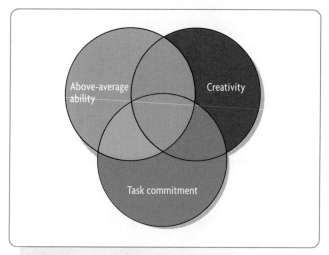

FIGURE 9.3 The Three-Ring Conception of Giftedness

According to the three-ring conception, gifted individuals are found at the intersection of above-average ability, high levels of creativity, and high levels of task commitment.

From Renzulli, J.S. (1978). What makes giftedness? Re-examining a definition. *Phi Delta Kappan, 60,* 180–184. Reprinted with permission.

giftedness. Still, gifted students report a reasonable level of participation in school activities. For example, 230 students attending a summer gifted program reported sports as their most frequent extracurricular or out-of-school activity (Olszewski-Kubilius & Lee, 2004). They were also involved in many academic clubs and competitions, with particular emphasis on mathematics.

Terman also documented that the gifted children were largely successful in life. This is not surprising because, as we'll note again later in the chapter, IQ is a good predictor of occupational status and income. Thus the concern about gifted individuals is not that they aren't doing well. The concern, instead, is that they don't receive sufficient educational support to allow them to develop their gifts fully (Briggs et al., 2008; Sternberg & Grigorenko, 2003). When giftedness is recognized as a multidimensional construct, gifted education must also have the flexibility to address individual students' particular talents.

STOP AND REVIEW

❶ What measures were originally used to compute the intelligence quotient?

❷ What type of subtests did David Wechsler introduce to the measurement of IQ?

❸ How has the diagnosis of intellectual disability changed over the last 20 years?

❹ What dimensions define giftedness in the "three-ring" conception?

---

learning disorder A disorder defined by a large discrepancy between individuals' measured IQ and their actual performance.

Theories of Intelligence

So far, we have seen some of the ways in which intelligence has been measured. You are now in a position to ask yourself: Do these tests capture everything that is meant by the word *intelligence*? Do these tests capture all abilities you believe constitute your own intelligence? To help you to think about those questions, we now review theories of intelligence. As you read about each theory, ask yourself whether its proponents would be comfortable using IQ as a measure of intelligence.

PSYCHOMETRIC THEORIES OF INTELLIGENCE

Psychometric theories of intelligence originated in much the same philosophical atmosphere that gave rise to IQ tests. **Psychometrics** is the field of psychology that specializes in mental testing in any of its facets, including personality assessment, intelligence evaluation, and aptitude measurement. Thus psychometric approaches are intimately related to methods of testing. These theories examine the *statistical relationships* between different measures of ability, such as the 14 subtests of the WAIS-III, and then make inferences about the nature of human intelligence on the basis of those relationships. The technique used most frequently is called *factor analysis,* a statistical procedure that detects a smaller number of dimensions, clusters, or factors within a larger set of independent variables. The goal of factor analysis is to identify the basic psychological dimensions of the concept being investigated. Of course, a statistical procedure only identifies statistical regularities; it is up to psychologists to suggest and defend interpretations of those regularities.

Charles Spearman carried out an early and influential application of factor analysis in the domain of intelligence. Spearman discovered that the performance of individuals on each of a variety of intelligence tests was highly correlated. From this pattern he concluded that there is a factor of *general intelligence,* or *g,* underlying all intelligent performance (Spearman, 1927). Each individual domain also has associated with it specific skills that Spearman called *s.* For example, a person's performance on tests of vocabulary or arithmetic depends both on his or her general intelligence and on domain-specific abilities. Researchers have used MRI scans to identify the basis for *g* in the brain. **Figure 9.4** displays some of the regions of the brain in which people who were relatively high on general intelligence had more brain tissue than people who were lower on general intelligence (Haier et al., 2004).

Raymond Cattell (1963), using more advanced factor analytic techniques, determined that general intelligence can be broken down into two relatively independent components, which he called crystallized and fluid intelligence. **Crystallized intelligence** involves the knowledge a person has already acquired and the ability to access that knowledge; it is measured by tests of vocabulary, arithmetic, and general information. **Fluid intelligence** is the ability to see complex relationships and solve problems; it is measured by tests of block designs and spatial visualization in which the background information needed to solve a problem is included or readily apparent. Crystallized intelligence allows you to cope well with your life's recurring, concrete challenges; fluid intelligence helps you attack novel, abstract problems.

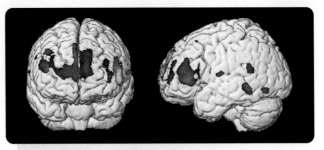

FIGURE 9.4   The Brain Bases of General Intelligence

After completing the WAIS to measure general intelligence, individuals underwent MRI scans to reveal the structure of their brains. The colored regions are areas in which individuals with relatively higher general intelligence had more brain tissue.

Reprinted from *NeuroImage, 23,* R. J. Haier et al., "Structural brain variation and general intelligence," pp. 425–433, copyright © 2004, with permission of Elsevier.

Since Cattell, many psychologists have broadened their conceptions of intelligence to include much more than performance on traditional IQ tests. We now examine two types of theories that go beyond IQ.

STERNBERG'S TRIARCHIC THEORY OF INTELLIGENCE

Robert Sternberg (1999) also stresses the importance of cognitive processes in problem solving as part of his more general theory of intelligence. Sternberg outlines a triarchic—three-part—theory. His three types of intelligence, analytical, creative, and practical, all represent different ways of characterizing effective performance.

Analytical intelligence provides the basic information-processing skills that people apply to life's many familiar tasks. This type of intelligence is defined by the components, or mental processes, that underlie thinking and problem solving. Sternberg identifies three types of components that are central to information processing: (1) knowledge acquisition components, for learning new facts; (2) performance components, for problem-solving strategies and techniques; and (3) metacognitive components, for selecting strategies and monitoring progress toward success. To put some of your analytical intelligence to work, we'd like you now to try the exercise in **Table 9.3** on page 280.

---

psychometrics The field of psychology that specializes in mental testing.

g According to Spearman, the factor of general intelligence underlying all intelligent performance.

crystallized intelligence The facet of intelligence involving the knowledge a person has already acquired and the ability to access that knowledge; measures by vocabulary, arithmetic, and general information tests.

fluid intelligence The aspect of intelligence that involves the ability to see complex relationships and solve problems.

Critical Thinking in Your Life

CAN YOU TRUST ASSESSMENT ON THE WEB?

After reading a chapter on intelligence, students often wonder how they would do if they took an IQ test. Nowadays, it's pretty easy for you to visit one of several websites to click through a test and get some IQ score. Do the numbers you get mean much of anything? We'll answer that question by reviewing some of the concepts we've introduced in this chapter.

To give our analysis, we needed some data—so we asked a friend, whom we'll call Poindexter, to take some online IQ tests for us. The first site he visited had four different tests, which gave us the opportunity to assess reliability. Recall that reliability is about consistency: Does each test, which claims to be measuring the same thing, yield very nearly the same score? In fact, Poindexter's four scores were 116, 117, 129, and 130. If you refer back to Figure 9.2, you'll see that all these scores indicate that Poindexter is above average (how nice for Poindexter), but two place him in "bright normal" and two place him right at the border of "superior"

and "very superior." These supposed IQ tests are not particularly reliable.

If the tests aren't reliable, they can't be valid. But let's suppose they were reliable. Let's consider why, in any case, we'd be concerned about their validity: To what extent do the tests measure what they're supposed to measure? The IQ scores at the site Poindexter visited were calculated by comparing his performance (the number he got right out of 20 questions) to the performance of those individuals who had preceded him to the site. By assuming a bell-shaped distribution like the one shown in Figure 9.2, the site estimates IQ. Can you see the problems here? First, we have no reason to believe that, for the people who visit this site, the average IQ (measured by a traditional, reliable offline test) would be, as it should be, 100. Doesn't it seem likely that there would be self-selection among the people who would take IQ tests on the Web? Second, we have no reason to believe that everyone took the tests under the same standard

circumstances. For example, the tests rely somewhat on vocabulary questions. How can we be sure that people didn't pull out a handy dictionary (or access one online) to enhance their scores? ("Look, Ma, I always told you I was a genius!")

The World Wide Web provides a vast number of opportunities for you to assess IQ as well as other performance and personality constructs. Use the knowledge you've gained in this chapter to do your own careful assessment of the reliability and validity of any scores you obtain on the Web.

Meanwhile, Poindexter has become something of an online IQ addict. His best score so far is a 159 on a "European IQ test." Poindexter is convinced that 159 is a valid measure of his IQ. Are you convinced too?

- Besides comparing overall scores, how might you assess the reliability of different IQ tests on the Web?

- What could you do to standardize conditions for test taking on the Web?

TABLE 9.3 Using Analytical Intelligence

The following is a list of *anagrams*—scrambled words. As quickly as possible, try to find a solution for each anagram

1. H-U-L-A-G _____
2. P-T-T-M-E _____
3. T-R-H-O-S _____
4. T-N-K-H-G-I _____
5. T-E-W-I-R _____
6. L-L-A-O-W _____
7. R-I-D-E-V _____
8. O-C-C-H-U _____
9. T-E-N-R-E _____
10. C-I-B-A-S _____

Turn to page 293 for the solutions.

From Sternberg, 1986

How did you do on the anagrams? To solve these anagrams, you mostly needed to use performance components and metacognitive components. The performance components are what allowed you to manipulate the letters in your head; the metacognitive components are what allowed you to have strategies for finding solutions. Consider T-R-H-O-S. How did you mentally transform that into SHORT? A good strategy to get started is to try consonant clusters that are probable in English—such as S-H and T-H. Selecting strategies requires metacognitive components; carrying them out requires performance components. Note that a good strategy will sometimes fail. Consider T-N-K-H-G-I. What makes this anagram hard for many people is that K-N is not a very likely combination to start a word, whereas T-H is. Did you stare at this anagram for a while, trying to turn it into a word beginning with T-H?

By breaking down various tasks into their components, researchers can pinpoint the processes that differentiate the performance outcomes of individuals with different IQs. For example, researchers might discover that the metacognitive components of high-IQ students prompt them to select different strategies to solve a particular type of problem than do their lower-IQ peers. The difference in strategy selection accounts for the high-IQ students' greater problem-solving success.

Creative intelligence captures people's ability to deal with novel problems. Sternberg (2006) suggests that "creative intelligence involves skills used to create, invent, discover, imagine, suppose, or hypothesize" (p. 325). Suppose, for example, a group of individuals found themselves stranded after an accident. You would credit with intelligence the person in the group who could most quickly help the group find its way home.

Practical intelligence is reflected in the management of day-to-day affairs. It involves your ability to *adapt* to new and different contexts, *select* appropriate contexts, and effectively *shape* your environment to suit your needs. Practical intelligence is bound to particular contexts. To measure practical intelligence, researchers must immerse themselves in those contexts.

A team of researchers set the goal of measuring practical intelligence among adolescents from the Yup'ik Eskimo group in Alaska (Grigorenko et al., 2004). Although the Yup'ik people live in modern houses with electricity, oil, and telephones, many communities can only be reached by airplane during the long harsh winters. For that reason, the measure of practical intelligence focused on the types of knowledge that remain relevant to survival in Yup'ik communities. Consider this question:

Uncle Markus knows a lot about hunting wolverines. He is most likely to catch a wolverine when he sets his trap:

    a. on a slanted tree.
    b. in the hollow of a dead tree.
    c. far from any water.
    d. near a frozen river.

Did you choose (a) as the correct answer? The practical intelligence test consisted of 36 items of this sort. The adolescent students in the sample completed this test. In addition, the researchers gathered evaluations from other members of the group, including adults and elders, about which adolescents they thought could be best described as, for example, *umyuartuli*—"a good thinker, one who comes up with novel solutions to problems and uses the mind to survive" (p. 191). The Yup'ik adolescents produced a range of scores on the measure of practical intelligence. In general, those who lived in urban environments had less practical intelligence than those who lived in rural environments. In addition, the adolescents who had the highest levels of practical intelligence also earned the most positive evaluation for traits such as umyuartuli.

You can see from this example why the concept of practical intelligence has different meanings in different contexts. However, the general idea remains the same: People can bring more or less practical intelligence to bear on their day-to-day tasks.

GARDNER'S MULTIPLE INTELLIGENCES AND EMOTIONAL INTELLIGENCE

Howard Gardner (1999, 2006) has also proposed a theory that expands the definition of intelligence beyond those skills covered on an IQ test. Gardner identifies numerous intelligences that cover a range of human experience. The value of any of the abilities differs across human societies, according to what is needed by, useful to, and prized by a given society. As shown in **Table 9.4** on page 282, Gardner identified eight intelligences.

Gardner argues that Western society values logical–mathematical and linguistic intelligence, whereas non-Western societies often value other types of intelligence. For example, in the Caroline Island of Micronesia, sailors must be able to navigate long distances without maps, using only their spatial intelligence and bodily kinesthetic intelligence. Such abilities count more in that society than the ability to write a term paper. In Bali, where artistic performance is part of everyday life, musical intelligence and talents involved in coordinating intricate dance steps are highly valued. Interpersonal intelligence is more central to collectivist societies such as Japan, where cooperative action and communal life are emphasized, than it is in individualistic societies such as the United States (Triandis, 1990).

Assessing these kinds of intelligence demands more than paper-and-pencil tests and simple quantified measures. Gardner's theory of intelligence requires that the individual be observed and assessed in a variety of life situations as well as in the small slices of life depicted in traditional intelligence tests. If people underwent completed valid tests on all eight intelligences, we'd expect to see great variation in patterns of strengths and weaknesses. However, Gardner suggests that people often differ with respect to the number of intelligences that dominate their life experiences. He draws attention to a major contrast between *searchlight* and *laser* profiles (Gardner, 2006). People with searchlight profiles show balanced strength across several intelligences. Gardner suggests that this profile is common among politicians and businesspeople. People with laser profiles show particular strength in one or two intelligences. Gardner suggests that this profile is common among artists and scientists.

In recent years, researchers have begun to explore a type of intelligence—*emotional intelligence*—that is related to Gardner's concepts of *interpersonal* and *intrapersonal* intelligence (see Table 9.4). On one prominent view, **emotional intelligence** has four major components (Mayer et al., 2008a, 2008b):

- The ability to perceive, appraise, and express emotions accurately and appropriately
- The ability to use emotions to facilitate thinking
- The ability to understand and analyze emotions and to use emotional knowledge effectively
- The ability to regulate one's emotions to promote both emotional and intellectual growth

This definition reflects a view of the positive role of emotion as it relates to intellectual functioning—emotions can make thinking more intelligent, and people can think intelligently about their emotions and those of others.

Researchers have begun to demonstrate that emotional intelligence has important consequences for everyday life. Consider the emotional experiences students have in school settings. Suppose Poindexter does poorly on an exam. If he can prevent himself from being overwhelmed by negative emotions, he's likely to fare better in the future. In general, higher emotional intelligence should allow students to deal more successfully with emotional aspects of academic performance. Let's see how researchers have tested that hypothesis.

TABLE 9.4 Gardner's Eight Intelligences

Intelligence	End States	Core Components
Logical–mathematical	Scientist Mathematician	Sensitivity to, and capacity to discern, logical or numerical patterns; ability to handle long chains of reasoning.
Linguistic	Poet Journalist	Sensitivity to the sounds, rhythms, and meanings of words; sensitivity to the different functions of language.
Naturalist	Biologist Environmentalist	Sensitivity to the differences among diverse species; abilities to interact subtly with living creatures.
Musical	Composer Violinist	Abilities to produce and appreciate rhythm, pitch, and timbre; appreciation of the forms of musical expressiveness.
Spatial	Navigator Sculptor	Capacities to perceive the visual–spatial world accurately and to perform transformations on one's initial perceptions.
Bodily kinesthetic	Dancer Athlete	Abilities to control one's body movements and to handle objects skillfully.
Interpersonal	Therapist Salesperson	Capacities to discern and respond appropriately to the moods, temperaments, motivations, and desires of other people.
Intrapersonal	Person with detailed, accurate self-knowledge	Access to one's own feelings and the ability to discriminate among them and draw upon them to guide behavior; knowledge of one's own strengths, weaknesses, desires, and intelligences.

From *Frames of Mind* by Howard Gardner. Copyright © 1983 by Basic Books. Reprinted by permission of Basic Books, a member of Perseus Books Group.

A team of researchers had a group of 378 students complete a measure of emotional intelligence (EI) (Rode et al., 2007). The measure required the students, for example, to view color photographs of faces and indicate which emotions the faces portrayed. As a measure of academic performance, the researchers obtained the cumulative GPA of each student. In addition, the researchers videotaped the students giving three-minute speeches during group discussions. Judges viewed the videotapes to determine features such as the quality of each student's arguments. When the researchers assessed the relationship between EI and performance, they discovered that high-EI students were more effective public speakers. For other academic measures, the students' relative motivation affected the importance of EI. For example, only those high-EI students who reported themselves to be thorough and careful had higher GPAs than their peers.

These results confirm the importance of emotional intelligence. They also illustrate a conclusion to which we'll return in Chapter 11: Both knowledge and motivation underlie students' success.

Our review of intelligence testing and theories of intelligence sets the stage for a discussion of the societal circumstances that make the topic of intelligence so controversial.

STOP AND REVIEW

❶ Why did Spearman come to believe in *g*, general intelligence?

❷ What are the three types of intelligence in Sternberg's triarchic theory?

❸ In Gardner's theory, what kind of intelligence might determine whether someone could be a successful sculptor?

CRITICAL THINKING Consider the study relating emotional intelligence to everyday well-being. Why is it important to obtain measures of the participants' success from their bosses?

Visit MyPsychLab.com for more review and practice on the following topics:

⊙ **Watch:** Practical Intelligence

✷ **Simulate:** Gardner's Theory of Intelligence

✷ **Simulate:** Explore Your Mental Space

---

emotional intelligence Type of intelligence defined as the abilities to perceive, appraise, and express emotions accurately and appropriately, to use emotions to facilitate thinking, to understand and analyze emotions, to use emotional knowledge effectively, and to regulate one's emotions to promote both emotional and intellectual growth.

The Politics
of Intelligence

We have seen that contemporary conceptions of intelligence reject the narrow linking of a score on an IQ test with a person's intelligence. Even so, IQ tests remain the most frequent measure of "intelligence" in Western society. Because of the prevalence of IQ testing and the availability of IQ scores, it becomes easy to compare different groups according to their "average" IQ. In the United States, such ethnic and racial group comparisons have often been used as evidence for the innate genetic inferiority of members of minority groups. We will briefly examine the history of this practice of using IQ test scores to index the alleged mental inferiority of certain groups. Then we will look at current evidence on the nature and nurture of intelligence and IQ test performance. You will see that this is one of the most politically volatile issues in psychology because public policies about immigration quotas, educational resources, and more may be based on how group IQ data are interpreted.

Why were IQ tests given to immigrants as they arrived at Ellis Island? How were these tests used to draw conclusions about genetic inferiority?

THE HISTORY OF GROUP COMPARISONS

In the early 1900s, psychologist **Henry Goddard** (1866–1957) advocated mental testing of all immigrants and the *selective exclusion* of those who were found to be "mentally defective." Such views may have contributed to a hostile national climate against admission of certain immigrant groups (Zenderland, 1998). Indeed, Congress passed the 1924 Immigration Restriction Act, which made it national policy to administer intelligence tests to immigrants as they arrived at Ellis Island in New York Harbor. Vast numbers of Jewish, Italian, Russian, and immigrants of other nationalities were classified as "morons" on the basis of IQ tests. Some psychologists interpreted these statistical findings as evidence that immigrants from Southern and Eastern Europe were genetically inferior to those from the hardy Northern and Western European stock (see Ruch, 1937). However, these "inferior" groups were also least familiar with the dominant language and culture, embedded in the IQ tests, because they had immigrated most recently. (Within a few decades, these group differences completely disappeared from IQ tests, but the theory of racially inherited differences in intelligence persisted.)

The argument for genetic inferiority advanced by Goddard (1917) and others was reinforced by World War I Army Intelligence tests on which African Americans and other racial minorities scored lower than the White majority. Louis Terman, whom as we saw promoted IQ testing in the United States, commented in this unscientific manner on the data he had helped collect on U.S. racial minorities:

> *Their dullness seems to be racial. . . . There seems no possibility at present of convincing society that they should not be allowed to reproduce, although from a eugenics point of view, they constitute a grave problem because of their unusually prolific breeding. (Terman, 1916, pp. 91–92)*

The names have changed, but the problem remains the same. In the United States today, African Americans and Latinos score, on average, lower than Asian Americans and Whites on standardized intelligence tests. Of course, there are individuals in all groups who score at the highest (and the lowest) extremes of the IQ scale. How should these group differences in IQ scores be interpreted? One tradition has been to attribute these differences to genetic inferiority (nature). After we discuss the evidence for genetic differences in IQ, we will consider a second possibility, that differences in environments (nurture) exert a significant impact on IQ. The validity of either explanation, or some combination of them, has important social, economic, and political consequences.

HEREDITY AND IQ

How can researchers assess the extent to which intelligence is genetically determined? Any answer to this question requires that the researcher choose some measure as an index of intelligence. Thus the question becomes not whether "intelligence," in the abstract, is influenced by heredity but, in most cases, whether IQs are similar within family trees. To answer this more limited question, researchers need to tease apart the effects of shared genes and shared environment. One method is to compare functioning in identical twins (monozygotic), fraternal twins (dizygotic), and relatives with other degrees of genetic overlap. **Figure 9.5,** on page 284, presents correlations between IQ scores of individuals on the basis of their degree of genetic relationship (Plomin & Petrill, 1997). As you can see, the greater the genetic similarity, the greater the IQ similarity. (Note in these data that the impact of environment is also revealed in the greater IQ similarities among those who have been reared together.)

Researchers use results of this sort to try to estimate the *heritability* of IQ. A **heritability estimate** of a particular trait,

---

heritability estimate A statistical estimate of the degree of inheritance of a given trait or behavior, assessed by the degree of similarity between individuals who vary in their extent of genetic similarity.

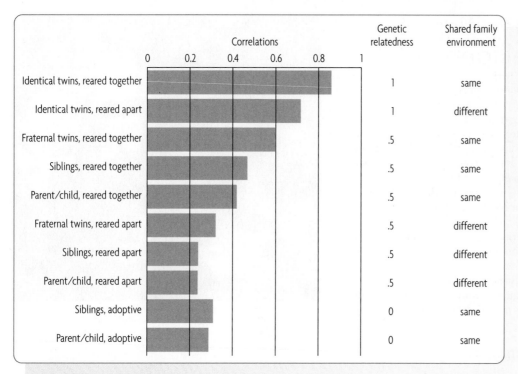

FIGURE 9.5 IQ and Genetic Relationship

This figure presents the correlations between the IQ scores of identical (monozygotic) and fraternal (dizygotic) twins reared together (in the same home environments) or reared apart (in different home environments). For comparison, it also includes data for siblings (brothers and sisters) and parents and children, both biological and adoptive. The data demonstrate the importance of both genetic factors (the numbers under "genetic relatedness" specify the overlap of genetic material) and environmental factors. For example, identical twins show higher correlations between their IQs than do fraternal twins—a genetic influence. However, both types of twins show higher correlations when raised together—an environmental influence.

Reprinted from *Intelligence, 24,* R. Plomin & S. A. Petrill, "Genetics and Intelligence: What's New?" pp. 53–77, copyright © 1997, with permission from Elsevier.

such as intelligence, is based on the proportion of the variability in test scores on that trait that can be traced to genetic factors. The estimate is found by computing the variation in all the test scores for a given population (college students or psychiatric patients, for example) and then identifying what portion of the total variance is due to genetic or inherited factors. This is done by comparing individuals who have different degrees of genetic overlap. Researchers who have reviewed the variety of studies on heritability of IQ conclude that about 50 percent of the variance in IQ scores is due to genetic makeup (Grigorenko, 2000).

What is perhaps even more interesting, however, is that heritability *increases* across the life span: To document this increase, researchers have often assessed twins' IQ repeatedly over several years. Let's consider a study that took 13 years to complete.

A team of researchers began their study by recruiting 209 pairs of 5-year-old twins (Hoekstra et al., 2007). At age 5, the children completed an IQ test that provided estimates for both verbal and nonverbal IQ. The researchers measured the twins' IQs again at ages 7, 10, 12, and 18 years. Given the duration of the study, you won't be surprised that some twins dropped out over time. However, the researchers were able to obtain IQs for 115 pairs at all five ages. The data

analyses showed that the twins' IQs were reasonably stable over time. Across all the twin pairs, the correlations between scores at age 5 and scores at age 18 were 0.51 for verbal IQ and 0.47 for nonverbal IQ. To estimate heritability, the researchers compared the correlations between MZ and DZ twins at each age. For verbal IQ, the heritability estimate was 46 percent at age 5 and increased to 84 percent at age 18. For nonverbal IQ, the heritability estimate was 64 percent at age 5 and increased to 74 percent at age 18.

Many people are surprised by a result of this sort, because it seems that environments should have more, not less, of an effect as people get older. Here's how researchers explain such counterintuitive findings: "It is possible that genetic dispositions nudge us toward environments that accentuate our genetic propensities, thus leading to increased heritability throughout the life span" (Plomin & Petrill, 1997, p. 61).

Let's return now to the point at which genetic analysis becomes controversial: test score differences between African Americans and White Americans. Several decades ago, the gap between the scores of Whites and Blacks was roughly 15 IQ points. However, researchers estimated that the gap closed by 4 to 7 points in the 30 years from 1972 to 2002 (Dickens

This photo shows Nobel Prize–winning chemist Marie Curie with her daughters Irene (on the left) and Eve (on the right). Irene also won a Nobel Prize in chemistry, and Eve became a famous author. Why do families like this one encourage researchers to attempt to understand the impact of heredity and environment on IQ?

& Flynn, 2006). Although the close in the gap suggests environmental influences, the lingering difference has prompted many people to suggest that there are unbridgeable genetic differences between the races (Hernnstein & Murray, 1994). However, even if IQ is highly heritable, does this difference reflect genetic inferiority of individuals in the lower-scoring group? The answer is no. Heritability is based on an estimate *within* one given group. It cannot be used to interpret differences *between* groups, no matter how large those differences are on an objective test.

Heritability estimates pertain only to the average in a given population of individuals. We know, for instance, that the heritability estimate for height is quite high—in the range of 0.93 to 0.96 (Silventoinen et al., 2006). Still, you cannot determine how much of your height is due to genetic influences. The same argument is true for IQ; despite high heritability estimates, we cannot determine the specific genetic contribution to any individual's IQ or to mean IQ scores among groups. The fact that on an IQ test one racial or ethnic group scores lower than another group does not mean that the difference between these groups is genetic in origin, even if the heritability estimate for IQ scores is high as assessed within a group (Hunt & Carlson, 2007).

Another point of controversy is the concept of race itself. When people assert that an IQ gap is caused by genetics, they make the strong assumption that genetic analysis permits clear distinctions among races. Researchers on IQ generally acknowledge that race is both a *biological* and a *social* construct. For example, the social convention in the United States is typically to call people who have any African ancestry Black. Consider the remarkable golfer Tiger Woods, who has often been labeled—and discriminated against—as African American even though his

actual heritage is much more complex (his ancestors were White, Black, Thai, Chinese, and Native American). Woods provides an excellent example of circumstances in which social judgments do not follow biological reality. Even so, some intelligence researchers argue that the races are sufficient genetic differences among races that meaningful comparisons can be made (Hunt & Carlson, 2007). Other researchers argue just as strenuously that the concept of race is so driven by social circumstances that group comparisons are useless (Sternberg & Grigorenko, 2007; Sternberg et al., 2005).

Surely genetics plays a sizable role in influencing individuals' scores on IQ tests, as it does on many other traits and abilities. We have argued, however, that heredity does not constitute an adequate explanation for IQ differences between racial and ethnic groups. It has a necessary, but not sufficient, role in our understanding of such performance effects. Let's turn now to the role the environment may play in creating the IQ gap.

ENVIRONMENTS AND IQ

Because heritability estimates are less than 1.0, we know that genetic inheritance is not solely responsible for anyone's IQ. Environments must also affect IQ. But how can we assess what aspects of the environment are important influences on IQ? What features of your environment affect your potential to score well on an IQ test (Kristensen & Bjerkedal, 2007; van der Sluis et al., 2008)? Environments are complex stimulus packages that vary on many dimensions, both physical and social, and may be experienced in different ways by those within them. Even children in the same family setting do not necessarily share the same critical, psychological environment. Think back to growing up in your family. If you had siblings, did they all get the same attention from your parents? Did conditions of stress change over the course of time? Did your family's financial resources change? Did your parents' marital status change? It is obvious that environments are made up of many components that are in a dynamic relationship and that change over time. So it becomes difficult for psychologists to say what kinds of environmental conditions— attention, stress, poverty, health, war, and so on—actually have an impact on IQ.

Tiger Woods has ancestors who were White, African American, Thai, Chinese, and Native American. What does that suggest about the construct of race in the United States?

The personal attention children receive can affect their intelligence. In the "separate but equal" schoolroom of 1940s Tennessee shown at left, African American children received little attention. In contrast, the parent shown at right is deeply involved in her child's education. How do these types of environmental differences affect IQ?

Researchers have most often focused on more global measures of environment, like the socioeconomic status of the family. For example, in a large-scale longitudinal study of more than 26,000 children, the best predictors of a child's IQ at age 4 were the family's socioeconomic status and the level of the mother's education. This was equally true for African American and White children (Broman et al., 1975). Similarly, **Figure 9.6** shows an overall impact of social class on IQ.

Why does social class affect IQ? Wealth versus poverty can affect intellectual functioning in many ways, health and educational resources being two of the most obvious. Poor health during pregnancy and low birth weight are solid predictors of a child's lowered mental ability. Children born into impoverished families often suffer from poor nutrition; many go to school hungry and thus less able to concentrate on learning tasks. Furthermore, impoverished homes may suffer from a lack of books, written media, computers, and other materials that add to one's mental stimulation. The "survival orientation" of poor parents, especially in single-parent families, that leaves parents little time or energy to play with and intellectually stimulate their children is detrimental to performance on tasks such as those on standard IQ tests.

Researchers have spent the past 40 years developing programs intended to counteract the effects of impoverished environments. The Head Start program was first funded by the federal government in 1965 to address the "physical health, developmental, social, educational, and emotional needs of low-income children and to increase the capacity of the families to care for their children, through empowerment and supportive services" (Kassebaum, 1994, p. 123). The idea of Head Start and similar programs was not to move children to privileged environments but to improve the environments into which they were born. Children are exposed to special preschool education, they receive decent daily meals, and their parents are given advice on health and other aspects of child rearing.

Consider a program started in 1962 at the High/Scope Perry preschool in Ypsilanti, Michigan (Schweinhart, 2004). The program focused on a group of 3- and 4-year-old low-income African American children who had been evaluated as being at risk for school failure. The High/Scope Perry program provided

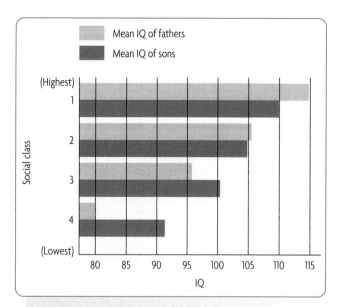

FIGURE 9.6 The Relationship among Heredity, Environment, and IQ

This chart shows evidence for the contribution of heredity and environment to IQ scores. There are similar IQs for fathers and sons (influence of heredity), but the IQs of both fathers and sons are related to social class (influence of environment).

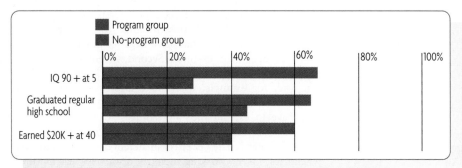

FIGURE 9.7 The Impact of a Preschool Intervention

Students who participated in the High/Scope Perry preschool program had better outcomes than students who were not participants.

From Lawrence J. Schweinhart, "The High/Scope Perry Preschool Study through Age 40."

the children with a classroom environment that focused on *participatory education*—children were encouraged to initiate and plan their own activities and activities for the classroom group. In addition, the program involved parents in the children's educations through home visits and parent group meetings. The researchers followed the students who participated in the program for the next 40 years. **Figure 9.7** compares the outcomes of participants to a group of students from the same population who did not. As you can see, High/Scope Perry students had higher IQs at age 5 than their peers outside the program. They were also considerably more likely to graduate from a regular high school and have higher paying jobs at age 40.

Similar data have emerged from an early intervention program in Chicago: Fifteen years after participating in a preschool program, students saw many of the same advantages as the High/Scope Perry group including much higher rates of high school graduation (Ou & Reynolds, 2006). These studies provide strong evidence for the importance of the environment for intellectual development. They also provide concrete models for programs that can change the lives of children who are at risk.

CULTURE AND THE VALIDITY OF IQ TESTS

People would probably care much less about IQ scores if they didn't allow for such useful predictions: Extensive research shows that IQ scores are valid predictors of school grades from elementary school through college, of occupational status, and of performance in many jobs (Gottfredson, 2002; Nettelbeck & Wilson, 2005). These patterns of results suggest that IQ tests validly measure intellectual abilities that are very basic and important toward the types of success that are valued in Western cultures—intelligence, as measured by IQ, directly affects success. IQ distinctions can also affect academic and job performance indirectly by changing one's motives and beliefs. Those with higher IQ scores are likely to have had more success experiences in school, become more motivated to study, develop an achievement orientation, and become optimistic about their chances of doing well. Also, children scoring low on IQ tests may get "tracked" into schools, classes, or programs that are inferior and may even be stigmatizing to the students' sense of self-competence. In this way, IQ can be affected by environment and, in turn, can create new environments for the child—some better, some worse. IQ assessment may thus become destiny—whatever the child's underlying genetic endowment for intelligence.

Even though IQ tests have proven to be valid for mainstream uses, many observers still question their validity for comparisons among different cultural and racial groups (Greenfield, 1997; Serpell, 2000). To make meaningful comparisons, researchers must use tests that have been validated for each separate group (Hunt & Carlson, 2007). However, critics have often argued that there are systematic biases in IQ tests that make them invalid across cultures. For example, questions on IQ tests that assess verbal comprehension presuppose that certain types of knowledge will have been accessible to all test takers (see Table 9.2). In reality, people from different cultures often have quite different background knowledge that affects the difficulty of those questions (Fagan & Holland, 2007). In addition, forms of tests and testing may not match cultural notions of intelligence or appropriate behavior (Sternberg, 2007). Consider one case of negative evaluations in the classroom:

> *When children of Latino immigrant parents go to school, the emphasis on understanding rather than speaking, on respecting the teacher's authority rather than expressing one's own opinions leads to negative academic assessment. . . . Hence, a valued mode of communication in one culture—respectful listening—becomes the basis for a rather sweeping negative evaluation in the school setting where self-assertive speaking is the valued mode of communication. (Greenfield, 1997, p. 1120)*

These immigrant children must learn how they must behave in U.S. classrooms to make their teachers understand the extent of their intelligence.

Although concerns about cross-cultural comparisons often focus on the *content* of tests, major problems also lie in the *context* of intelligence testing. **Claude Steele** (1997; Steele & Aronson, 1995, 1998) has argued that people's performance on ability tests is influenced by **stereotype threat**—the threat of being at risk for confirming a negative stereotype of one's group. Research suggests that a person's belief that a negative stereotype is relevant in a situation can function to bring about the poor performance encoded in the stereotype. Let's consider an example of stereotype threat at work.

The study focused on first- and second-generation immigrants from the West Indies (Deaux et al., 2007). The researchers hypothesized that first-generation immigrants, who were born in the West Indies, would not generally have had enough U.S. cultural experience to acquire the negative stereotypes about their intellectual abilities. By contrast, the researchers expected that second-generation immigrants, who had been born in the United States, would possess

stereotype threat The threat associated with being at risk for confirming a negative stereotype of one's group.

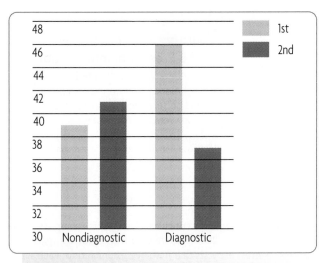

FIGURE 9.8 Stereotype Threat
The study contrasted second-generation immigrants—who possessed a negative stereotype about their group's intellectual ability—with first-generation immigrants—who did not posses that stereotype. Because the second-generation immigrants possessed the stereotype, their performance was impaired when they believed a test was diagnostic of their intellectual ability.

From Deaux, L., Bikmen, N., Gilkes, A., Venuneac, A., Joseph, Y., Payne, Y.A., & Steele, C.A. (2007) Becoming American: Stereotype threat effects in Afro-Carribean immigrant groups. *Social Psychological Quarterly*, 70, 384–404. Copyright © 2007 by the American Sociological Association. Reprinted with permission.

these stereotypes. That prediction was upheld when groups of students who were first- and second-generation immigrants completed scales that assessed their knowledge of the stereotypes. To demonstrate the consequences of this distribution of knowledge, the researchers had both types of immigrants complete a series of questions from the verbal portion of a GRE practice test. The researchers led half the students to believe that their performance was *diagnostic* of their verbal abilities. The researchers told the other half that they were only answering the questions to assist with test development. As you can see in **Figure 9.8,** for the second-generation immigrants who possessed the negative stereotype, performance was impaired in the diagnostic condition: When the situation made the stereotype relevant, stereotype threat had a negative impact. However, because the first-generation immigrants didn't possess the stereotype, they didn't suffer the effects of stereotype threat.

We want to emphasize again that what affected the performance to the second-generation immigrants was how they defined the situation. Only when people believe the situation is relevant to the stereotype—because, for example, they believe that the test measures their intelligence—does knowledge of the stereotype impair performance. Given results of this type, do you think it would be possible to measure IQ without invoking stereotype threat?

Why does stereotype threat have a negative impact? Researchers have identified three mechanisms that disrupt

performance (Schmader et al., 2008). First, stereotype threat produces a physiological stress response (of the type we will describe in Chapter 12) that has a negative impact on people's ability to focus their attention. Second, stereotype threat leads people to monitor their performance more closely in ways that can lead, for example, to more cautious and less creative responses. Third, when people experience stereotype threat they have to expend mental resources to suppress negative thoughts and feelings. Recall our discussion of working memory in Chapter 7. The net effect of stereotype threat is to overwhelm test takers' working memory resources—leaving them less able to succeed on the problems at hand.

One final thought on intelligence and culture. Taken as a whole, the United States demonstrates a cultural bias toward genetic explanations of individual differences. **Harold Stevenson** and his colleagues (1993) spent several years tracking the mathematics achievement of Chinese, Japanese, and U.S. children. In 1980, Asian children on the average vastly outperformed their U.S. peers. In 1990, the gap remained: "Only 4.1% of the Chinese children and 10.3% of the Japanese children . . . had scores as low as those of the average American child" (p. 54). Are Asian children genetically superior in their mathematical abilities? People in the United States are more likely to answer *yes* to this question. When Stevenson and his colleagues asked Asian and U.S. students, teachers, and parents to contrast the importance of "studying hard" versus "innate intelligence," Asian respondents emphasized hard work. U.S. respondents emphasized innate ability. Do you see how this perspective could lead to the conclusion by Americans that Asians must be genetically superior in mathematics? Because such beliefs have public policy implications—how much money should be expended on teaching mathematics if Americans cannot learn math anyway?—it is important to examine rigorous research to sort out what can and cannot be changed with respect to intellectual performance.

Creativity

Before we leave the area of intelligence and its assessment, we turn to the topic of creativity. **Creativity** is an individual's

---

creativity The ability to generate ideas or products that are both novel and appropriate to the circumstances.

(A)   (B)

FIGURE 9.9 **Making Judgments about Creativity**
Hypothetical photography class assignment: Take the best picture you can of a tree.
(A) A noncreative response; (B) a creative response.

ability to generate ideas or products that are both *novel* and *appropriate* to the circumstances in which they were generated (Sternberg & Lubart, 1999). Consider the invention of the wheel. The device was novel because no one before its unknown inventor had seen the application of rolling objects. It was appropriate because the use to which the novel object could be put was very clear. Without appropriateness, new ideas or objects are often considered strange or irrelevant.

Our discussion of creativity falls within a chapter on intelligence because many people believe that there is a strong relationship between intelligence and creativity. To determine if this is the case, we need to be able first to test creativity and then to determine the relationship between creativity and intelligence. Thus we will first discuss methods for judging ideas or products to be creative and then look at the link to intelligence. Next, we will look at situations of exceptional creativity and evaluate the relationship between creativity and madness. We will see what lessons you can learn from people who are possessed of exceptional creative abilities.

ASSESSING CREATIVITY AND THE LINK TO INTELLIGENCE

How might you go about rating individuals as (relatively) creative or uncreative? Researchers have used tasks that measure both *divergent* and *convergent thinking* (Nielsen et al., 2008; Runco, 2007). Many approaches focus on **divergent thinking,** which is defined as the ability to generate a variety of unusual solutions to a problem. Questions that test divergent thinking give the test taker the opportunity to demonstrate *fluid* (swift) and *flexible* thinking (Torrance, 1974; Wallach & Kogan, 1965):

- Name all the things you can think of that are square.
- List as many white edible things as you can in 3 minutes.
- List all the uses that you can think of for a *brick*.

Responses are scored along such dimensions as *fluency,* the overall number of distinct ideas; *uniqueness,* the number of ideas that were given by no other person in an appropriate sample; and *unusualness,* the number of ideas that were given by, for example, less than 5 percent of a sample (Runco, 1991).

Convergent thinking is defined as the ability to gather together different sources of information to solve a problem. We would credit people as being creative if they can put information together in a way that produces novel solutions. One test researchers use to study convergent thinking is called the *remote associates test*. Test takers are challenged to find the term that provides a link for other words (Bowden & Beeman, 2003):

- What word are all three of these words related to? *Cottage, Swiss, cake*
- What word are all three of these words related to? *Fish, mine, rush*
- What word are all three of these words related to? *Flower, friend, scout*

(We'll give you the answers at the end of this section.) Other measures of convergent thinking focus on **insight,** which is defined as circumstances in which solutions suddenly come to mind. Do you recall the problem in Chapter 8 in which you were asked how you would get a Ping-Pong ball out of a 6-foot-tall pipe? That problem required insight. We would credit people whose bursts of insight give rise to novel solutions as being creative.

A different approach to judging some individuals as creative or uncreative is to ask them specifically to generate a creative product—a drawing, a poem, or a short story. Judges then rate the creativity of each of the products. Consider the two photographs shown in **Figure 9.9.** Which do you think is more creative? Could you explain why you think so? Do you think your friends would agree? Research has shown that agreement is quite high when judges rank products for creativity (Amabile, 1983). People can be reliably identified across judges as being high or low in creativity. In fact, people are also pretty accurate at judging whether their own efforts are creative.

---

divergent thinking An aspect of creativity characterized by an ability to produce unusual but appropriate responses to problems.

convergent thinking An aspect of creativity characterized by the ability to gather together different sources of information to solve a problem.

insight Circumstances of problem solving in which solutions suddenly come to mind.

In one study, 226 students completed a test of divergent thinking (Slivia, 2008a). For example, the students tried to generate unusual uses for a knife. After completing each task, the participants read their responses and chose the two they thought showed the most creativity. The participants' responses were also evaluated by a group of three judges. On the whole, the participants and the judges showed good agreement about which responses counted as the most creative. Still, some students were better than others at judging their own products. In particular, those students who judged themselves as being particularly creative and open to new experiences were also best at identifying their most creative responses. The researcher concluded that "creative people are doubly skilled: they are better at generating creative ideas and at discerning which ones are the best" (p. 145).

You might be happy to know that others are likely to agree with your judgments when you believe you have been creative.

Researchers have often tried to assess the relationship between creativity and intelligence. For example, one study obtained measures of IQ and divergent thinking for German school children who ranged in age from 12 to 16 (Preckel et al., 2006). In that sample, the correlation between IQ and divergent thinking was 0.54, suggesting that students with higher IQs also generally showed greater divergent thinking. Similar results have been found with U.S. college students (Slivia, 2008b). These studies measure creativity with divergent thinking tasks which, as we have noted, only represent one way of assessing creativity (Runco, 2008). We know less about the relationship of IQ to other measures of creativity. On balance, as one researcher suggested, "intelligence appears to enable creativity to some extent but not to promote it" (Perkins, 1988, p. 319). In other words, a certain level of intelligence gives a person the opportunity to be creative, but the person may not avail himself or herself of that opportunity. In the *Psychology in Your Life* box on page 292, we review research on how you might increase your creativity.

How did you do on the convergent thinking problems? The answers were *cheese, gold,* and *girl.*

EXTREMES OF CREATIVITY

There are some exceptional individuals who would emerge from assessments of creativity as almost off the scale. Whom do you think of when you are asked to name someone who is exceptionally creative? Your answer is likely to depend partly on your own areas of expertise and your own preferences. Psychologists might nominate Sigmund Freud. Those people interested in fine art, music, or dance might mention Pablo Picasso, Igor Stravinsky, or Martha Graham. Is it possible to detect the commonalities in the personalities or backgrounds of such individuals that could be predictive of exceptional creativity? Howard Gardner (1993) chose a selection of individuals whose extraordinary abilities were relevant to the eight types of intelligence we described earlier, including Freud, Picasso, Stravinsky, and Graham. Gardner's analysis allows him to yield a portrait of the life experiences of the *exemplary creator,* whom he dubs E.C.:

> *E.C. discovers a problem area or realm of special interest, one that promises to [lead] into uncharted waters. This is a highly charged moment. At this point E.C. becomes isolated from her peers and must work mostly on her own. She senses that she is on the verge of a breakthrough that is as yet little understood, even by her. Surprisingly, at this crucial moment,*

> *E.C. craves both cognitive and affective support, so that she can retain her bearings. Without such support, she might well experience some kind of breakdown. (Gardner, 1993, p. 361)*

What lessons are there for you in tales of exceptional creativity that would allow you to be more creative? You can emulate a pattern of *risk taking.* Highly creative individuals are willing to go into "uncharted waters" (Gardner, 1993; Sternberg & Lubart, 1996). There is a pattern of *preparation.* Highly creative individuals typically have spent years acquiring expertise in the domains in which they will excel (Weisberg, 1986). There is a pattern of *intrinsic motivation.* Highly creative individuals pursue their tasks because of the enjoyment and satisfaction they take in the products they generate (Collins & Amabile, 1999). If you can bring all these factors together in your own life, you should be able to increase your personal level of creative performance.

Before we leave the topic of creativity, we want to consider one of the most common stereotypes of exemplary creators: Their life experiences border on—or include the experience of—madness. The idea that great creativity is intimately related to madness has a history that has been traced as far back as Plato (Kessel, 1989). In more modern times, Kraepelin (1921) argued that the manic phases of individuals who suffer from "manic-depressive insanity," or bipolar disorder, provide a context of free-flowing thought processes that facilitate great creativity. Mania, as we will see in Chapter 15, is characterized by periods of enduring excitedness; the person generally acts and feels elated and expansive. There is little doubt that many great figures in the

Art historians have often speculated that Vincent van Gogh's creativity as an artist was influenced by mental illness. What, in general, have researchers discovered about the link between creativity and madness?

arts and humanities have suffered from such mood disorders (Keiger, 1993). However, to establish a link between creativity and mental illness, researchers have attempted to go beyond those anecdotal reports. More controlled studies support at least a weak association between some forms of mental illness—such as bipolar disorder—and creativity (Lauronen et al., 2004; Santosa et al., 2007). However, as always, a correlation doesn't indicate whether there is a causal relationship. It could be the case that some forms of mental illness allow people to be more creative (Akiskal & Akiskal, 2007). It could also be the case that the effort to be highly creative increases the likelihood that people will experience mental illness (Ramey & Weisberg, 2004). There could also be some features of people's brains that make them highly creative and also more prone to mental illness—with no causal link between the two phenomena (Dietrich, 2004).

You have now learned some of the ways in which psychologists assess and interpret individual differences in intelligence and creativity. You have a good understanding of how researchers have tried to measure and understand these difficult concepts. In this chapter's final section, we will consider why psychological assessment can sometimes generate controversy.

STOP AND REVIEW

❶ What are two important criteria for judging ideas or products as creative?

❷ What is divergent thinking?

❸ What three factors appear to play a role in exceptional creativity?

Visit MyPsychLab.com for more review and practice on the following topic:

✳ **Simulate:** Creativity

Assessment and Society

The primary goal of psychological assessment is to make accurate assessments of people that are as free as possible of errors of assessors' judgments. This goal is achieved by replacing subjective judgments of teachers, employers, and other evaluators with more objective measures that have been carefully constructed and are open to critical evaluation. This is the goal that motivated Alfred Binet in his pioneering work. Binet and others hoped that testing would help democratize society and minimize decisions based on arbitrary criteria of sex, race, nationality, privilege, or physical appearance. However, despite these lofty goals, there is no area of psychology more controversial than assessment. Three ethical concerns that are central to the controversy are the fairness of test-based decisions, the utility of tests for evaluating education, and the implications of using test scores as labels to categorize individuals.

Critics concerned with the fairness of testing practices argue that the costs or negative consequences may be higher for some test takers than for others (Helms, 2006). The costs are quite high, for example, when tests on which minority groups receive low scores are used to keep them out of certain jobs. Sometimes, minority group members test poorly because their scores are evaluated relative to inappropriate norms. To address these issues, researchers have studied methods of personnel selection that combine assessments of an array of cognitive and noncognitive skills (De Corte et al., 2007). The goal is to predict job success with composite measures that recognize group differences in test scores.

A second ethical concern is that testing not only helps evaluate students; it may also play a role in the shaping of education. The quality of school systems and the effectiveness of teachers are frequently judged on the basis of how well their students score on standardized achievement tests (Crocco & Costigan, 2007). Local support of the schools through tax levies, and even individual teacher salaries, may ride on test scores. The high stakes associated with test scores may lead to cheating. For example, one study analyzed standardized test scores for public elementary schools in Chicago. The researchers estimated that serious cases of administrator or teacher cheating occur in at least 4 to 5 percent of the classrooms (Jacob & Levitt, 2003). In Potomac, Maryland, an elementary school principal resigned when strong evidence suggested that fifth-graders at her school had been given several types of assistance, including extra time and second chances, to improve their test scores (Thomas & Wingert, 2000). The evidence against the school had come from the students themselves. The 10-year-olds reported to their parents that they had been asked or allowed to cheat: They wondered why the adults at the school had insisted that they do so. These circumstances illustrate how damaging it can be when test scores are taken to matter more than education.

A third ethical concern is that test outcomes can take on the status of unchangeable labels. People too often think of themselves as being an IQ of 110 or a B student, as if the scores were labels stamped on their foreheads. Such labels may become barriers to advancement as people come to believe that their mental and personal qualities are fixed and unchangeable—that they cannot improve their lot in life. For those who are negatively assessed, the scores can become self-imposed motivational limits that lower their sense of self-efficacy and restrict the challenges they are willing to tackle. That is another insidious consequence of pronouncements about group deficiencies in IQ. Those stigmatized publicly in this way come to believe what the "experts" are saying about them, and so disidentify with schools and education as means to improve their lives.

When schools are rewarded for high scores on standardized tests, are teachers likely to place more emphasis on test-taking skills than on broader learning goals?

HOW CAN YOU BECOME MORE CREATIVE?

When researchers measure creativity, some people always display more creativity than others (Runco, 2007). That doesn't mean, however, that any individual can't become more creative. In fact, researchers have begun to demonstrate how contexts greatly influence the quality of people's creative products. We're going to describe three manipulations that researchers have invented that make people more creative. As you read about each project, think how you might apply the insights in your own everyday life.

In the first study, researchers demonstrated the positive impact of multicultural experience on students' creativity (Leung et al., 2008). The researchers reasoned that exposure to another culture gives people experience, for example, in recruiting "ideas from unfamiliar sources and places" and synthesizing "seemingly incompatible ideas from diverse cultures" (p. 173). However, to demonstrate the impact of culture, the researchers didn't send their experimental participants overseas. Instead, they had participants watch different versions of a 45-minute slide show. One version focused only on Chinese culture (which was unfamiliar to the participants). The other version juxtaposed Chinese and American cultures. After each slideshow, the participants attempted to write a creative version of the Cinderella story. Those participants who watched the slideshow

juxtaposing the two cultures were consistently more creative in their stories. The key to increased creativity was that the students experienced the two cultures side-by-side.

A second method to increase creativity comes from a study that contrasted people's thoughts about the near and distant future (Förster et al., 2004). Suppose we asked you how you might plan a party either for tomorrow or for a year from now. When you consider the near future, you're likely to focus on concrete details; when you consider the far future, your thoughts are likely to be more abstract. When you thought about planning a party, did you experience that shift from concrete to abstract? The researchers predicted that they could get participants to be more creative if they could get them thinking in that more abstract fashion. To test that prediction, the researchers began by prompting participants to adopt a near or distant future time perspective. They asked participants to spend two minutes imagining their lives either "tomorrow" or "one year from now." After a brief interval, participants responded to this scenario: "Ms. Miller likes her plants. Please help her to find as many creative ways as you can regarding how she can further improve her room" (p. 184). Participants who had imagined what their lives would be like in a year consistently provided more creative responses to the scenario.

A third method to increase creativity focuses on how people ponder what might have been (Markman et al., 2007). When people think back on their lives, they often contemplate counterfactual thoughts (for example, "If I had left a few minutes earlier, I wouldn't have gotten in that traffic jam"). Some of those counterfactuals are *additive* because they encode a broader range of possible actions with respect to a negative outcome (such as, "If I had done. . . , the outcome would have been better"). Some of the counterfactuals are *subtractive* because they encode a narrower range of actions (such as, "If I had *not* done. . . , the outcome would have been better"). The researchers asked some participants to construct additive counterfactuals and some to construct subtractive counterfactuals with respect to a negative outcome in their lives. The researchers reasoned that "additive counterfactuals—those that add new . . . elements to reconstruct reality—evoke an expansive processing style that facilitates creative generation" (p. 322). In fact, participants who constructed additive counterfactuals produced more short-term creative behavior (for example, they were able to generate more creative novel uses for a brick) than participants who generated subtractive counterfactuals.

Can you see how you might apply each of these projects to improve your everyday creativity?

In this chapter, we've reviewed important aspects of intelligence and creativity. You've learned how researchers have defined and redefined these concepts to recognize important aspects of human performance. You've also seen why the measure of IQ remains controversial. People must give careful consideration of the broader context in which people take tests before they make claims about the abilities of particular individuals and groups.

STOP AND REVIEW

❶ Why might assessment have negative consequences for particular groups of individuals?

❷ Why might assessment play a role in shaping education?

❸ Why might test scores become labels that have broad consequences?

Recapping Main Points

What Is Assessment?

- Psychological assessment has a long history, beginning in ancient China. Many important contributions were made by Sir Francis Galton.
- A useful assessment tool must be reliable, valid, and standardized. A reliable measure gives consistent results. A valid measure assesses the attributes for which the test was designed.
- A standardized test is always administered and scored in the same way; norms allow a person's score to be compared with the averages of others of the same age, sex, and culture.

Intelligence Assessment

- Binet began the tradition of objective intelligence testing in France in the early 1900s. Scores were given in terms of mental ages and were meant to represent children's current level of functioning.
- In the United States, Terman created the Stanford–Binet Intelligence Scale and popularized the concept of IQ.
- Wechsler designed intelligence tests for adults, children, and preschoolers.
- The definitions of both intellectual disability and giftedness focus both on IQ scores and day-to-day performance.

Theories of Intelligence

- Psychometric analyses of IQ suggest that several basic abilities, such as fluid and crystallized aspects of intelligence, contribute to IQ scores.
- Contemporary theories conceive of and measure intelligence very broadly by considering the skills and insights people use to solve the types of problems they encounter.
- Sternberg differentiates analytical, creative, and practical aspects of intelligence.
- Gardner identifies eight types of intelligence that both include and go beyond the types of intelligence assessed by standard IQ measures. Recent research has focused on emotional intelligence.

The Politics of Intelligence

- Almost from the outset, intelligence tests have been used to make negative claims about ethnic and racial groups.
- Because of the reasonably high heritability of IQ, some researchers have attributed the lower scores of some racial and cultural groups to innate inferiority.
- Environmental disadvantages and stereotype threat appear to explain the lower scores of certain groups. Research shows that group differences can be affected through environmental interventions.

Creativity

- Creativity is often assessed using tests of divergent and convergent thinking.
- Exceptionally creative people take risks, prepare, and are highly motivated.
- Although there is an association between creativity and some forms of mental illness, a causal link has not been established.

Assessment and Society

- Though often useful for prediction and as an indication of current performance, test results should not be used to limit an individual's opportunities for development and change.
- When the results of an assessment will affect an individual's life, the techniques used must be reliable and valid for that individual and for the purpose in question.

Solutions to the anagrams in Table 9.3:

1. laugh
2. tempt
3. short
4. knight
5. write
6. allow
7. drive
8. couch
9. enter
10. basic

KEY TERMS

chronological age (p. 275)
construct validity (p. 273)
content validity (p. 273)
convergent thinking (p. 289)
creativity (p. 288)
criterion validity (p. 273)
crystallized intelligence (p. 279)
divergent thinking (p. 289)
emotional intelligence (p. 282)
fluid intelligence (p. 279)

formal assessment (p. 272)
g (p. 279)
heritability estimate (p. 283)
insight (p. 289)
intellectual disability (p. 276)
intelligence (p. 274)
intelligence quotient (IQ) (p. 275)
internal consistency (p. 272)
learning disorder (p. 278)
mental age (p. 275)

norm (p. 274)
parallel forms (p. 272)
predictive validity (p. 273)
psychological assessment (p. 271)
psychometrics (p. 279)
split-half reliability (p. 272)
standardization (p. 274)
stereotype threat (p. 287)
test–retest reliability (p. 272)

Chapter 9 Practice Test

1. Which of these was *not* one of the ideas Sir Francis Galton formulated about intelligence assessment?
   a. Differences in intelligence are quantifiable.
   b. Intelligence could be measured by objective tests.
   c. Intelligence scores followed a bell-shaped curve.
   d. Intelligence scores change over the life span.

2. Martin filled out a test to measure his happiness. He got a score of 72. To interpret that score, Martin needs to consult the _____ the test.
   a. norms for
   b. split-half reliability for
   c. standardization of
   d. predictive validity of

3. Deborah is 10 years old, but she has a mental age of 12. Using the original method for calculating IQ, you conclude that Deborah has an IQ of
   a. 90.
   b. 120.
   c. 150.
   d. 100.

4. Which cause of intellectual disability is easiest to treat?
   a. Down syndrome
   b. The mother's prenatal consumption of alcohol.
   c. The mother's prenatal consumption of cocaine.
   d. PKU

5. Which of these qualities is *not* part of the "three-ring" conception of giftedness?
   a. creativity
   b. mathematical genius
   c. task commitment
   d. high ability

6. When Poindexter took IQ tests on the Web, he took four tests at the same site and obtained scores of 116, 117, 129, and 130. Given these scores, you conclude that the IQ tests are
   a. both reliable and valid.
   b. neither reliable nor valid.
   c. reliable but not valid.
   d. valid but not reliable.

7. _____ intelligence is defined as the knowledge a person has already acquired.
   a. Fluid
   b. Analytical
   c. Crystallized
   d. Creative

8. Felix is applying for chef school. He takes an entrance exam that poses a series of questions on food preparation. This sounds most like a test of _____ intelligence.
   a. practical
   b. analytic
   c. fluid
   d. creative

9. Julian is rarely aware when the people around him are upset. You suspect that Julian is not very high on _____ intelligence.
   a. naturalist
   b. spatial
   c. emotional
   d. bodily kinesthetic

10. Goneril and Regan are sisters. You would expect them to have the most similar IQs if they
    a. are fraternal twins.
    b. are identical twins.
    c. grew up in the same home.
    d. were adopted before age 2.

11. Stereotype threat has an impact on people's test performance when they believe that
    a. the testing situation is relevant to the stereotype.
    b. the stereotype is widespread in a culture.
    c. the testing situation is unfair to certain ethnic groups.
    d. stereotypes change over time.

12. A test of _____ might include a question like, "Name all the things you can think of that are round."
    a. analytic intelligence
    b. crystallized intelligence
    c. convergent thinking
    d. divergent thinking

13. If you want to understand the origins of "Exceptional Creators," you *don't* need to focus on
    a. preparation.
    b. intrinsic motivation.
    c. IQ.
    d. risk taking.

14. Suppose you wanted to provide a short-term boost to the creativity of your friend Constance. You ask her to think about a negative event in her life and construct _____ counterfactuals about it.
    a. additive
    b. near
    c. distant
    d. subtractive

15. When Cyrus was 12, he was told he was a genius. As an adult, he never feels as if he is living up to his potential. This is a good example of circumstances in which assessment has
    a. generated an incorrect outcome.
    b. yielded a label that has personal implications.
    c. shaped the educational experiences of an individual.
    d. had negative consequences for Cyrus's group.

Essay Questions

1. What is the goal of Howard Gardner's theory of multiple intelligences?

2. How have Head Start and other early intervention programs demonstrated the impact of environments on IQ?

3. Why is it difficult to establish a causal link between mental illness and creativity?

Discovering Psychology Viewing Guide

Watch the following video by logging on to MyPsychLab (www.mypsychlab.com). After you have watched the video, complete the activities that follow.

Program 16: Testing and Intelligence

KEY TERMS AND PEOPLE

As you watch the program, pay particular attention to this person in addition to those covered in this textbook.

• *W. Curtis Banks*—an expert on psychological testing.

PROGRAM REVIEW

1. What is the goal of psychological assessment?
   a. to derive a theory of human cognition
   b. to see how people vary in ability, behavior, and personality
   c. to measure the stages of growth in intellectual abilities
   d. to diagnose psychological problems

2. You are taking a test in which you are asked to agree or disagree with statements, such as "I give up too easily when discussing things with others." Which test would this be?
   a. the Scholastic Aptitude Test
   b. the Rorschach test
   c. the Strong Interest Inventory
   d. the Minnesota Multiphasic Personality Inventory

3. What was Binet's aim in developing a measure of intelligence?
   a. to identify children in need of special help
   b. to show that intelligence is innate
   c. to weed out inferior children
   d. to provide an empirical basis for a theory of intelligence

4. How were the results of Binet's test expressed?
   a. in terms of general and specific factors
   b. as an intelligence quotient
   c. as a mental age related to a norm
   d. as a percentile score

5. What formula did Terman create to express intelligence?
   a. $MA/CA = IQ$
   b. $MA \times CA = IQ$
   c. $CA/MA \times 100 = IQ$
   d. $MA/CA \times 100 = IQ$

6. In 1939, David Wechsler designed a new intelligence test. What problem of its predecessors was the test designed to overcome?
   a. bias in favor of minority groups
   b. unreliable scores
   c. dependence on language
   d. norms based on a restricted population

7. A test for prospective firefighters has been shown to predict success on the job. Which statement about the test is true?
   a. The test is reliable.
   b. The test is valid.
   c. The test is standardized.
   d. The test is unbiased.

8. Cultural biases in tests can lead to the overvaluing of some attributes and the undervaluing of others. Which of the following is likely to be overvalued in the United States?
   a. common sense
   b. motivation
   c. creativity
   d. verbal ability

9. Imagine that anyone who wants a job as a hospital orderly has to take a test. The test is valid for its norm group, White men. Imagine a Black woman is taking the test. Which statement about the woman's score is most likely to be accurate?
   a. It will accurately predict her job performance.
   b. It will be lower than that of White men.
   c. It may indicate she is not capable when she in fact is capable.
   d. It cannot indicate anything about her because there were no Blacks or women in the norm group.

10. What new perspective did Howard Gardner introduce to the study of intelligence?
   a. He redefined intelligence as "practical intelligence."
   b. He expanded intelligence to include other types.
   c. He argued for a biological basis for describing intelligence in terms of brain waves.
   d. He argued that the term *intelligence* should be abolished.

11. Robert Sternberg has devised a test for managers. How does its prediction of success compare with predictions from a standard IQ test?
   a. They predict equally well and are not correlated.
   b. They predict equally well, probably because they are measuring the same thing.
   c. Sternberg's test predicts twice as well as IQ and is not correlated with IQ.
   d. Sternberg's test predicts twice as well as IQ and is moderately correlated with IQ.

12. The attempt by neuroscientists to find biologically based measures of intelligence rests on the assumption that intelligence involves
   a. multiple factors.
   b. cultural learning.
   c. speed of adaptation.
   d. high excitability.

13. Standardized intelligence tests typically
    a. overvalue verbal ability.
    b. give too much value to creative problem solving.
    c. are biased to give exceptionally high scores to people from other cultures.
    d. are the best available predictors of life success.

14. Which of these is a self-fulfilling prophesy that can be based on age, race, or gender?
    a. test–retest reliability
    b. stereotype threat
    c. crystallized intelligence
    d. criterion validity

15. The growing practice of "teaching for tests" creates the possibility of
    a. lessened ecological validity.
    b. eliminating stereotype threat.
    c. lowered reliability.
    d. eliminating genetic influences on intelligence.

16. Which of the following is an innovation in intelligence assessment that David Wechsler introduced?
    a. displaying physical coordination
    b. demonstrating social sensitivity
    c. producing appropriate verbal metaphors
    d. putting pictures in a logical sequence

17. William Curtis Banks argued for the importance of all of the following, *except*
    a. correlating intelligence measures with vocational success.
    b. ensuring validity of intelligence tests.
    c. being confident that our assessment measures are reliable.
    d. standardizing assessment measures with respect to the larger population.

18. Which is the most effective way to break the influence of stereotype threat?
    a. Assure the test taker that the test cannot discriminate between members of his or her own group and members of other groups.
    b. Provide the test taker with a visualization exercise ahead of time to enhance his or her self-esteem.
    c. Provide the test taker with a very simple task beforehand in order to boost confidence.
    d. Suggest that the test taker should try to make his or her minority group proud.

19. Stereotype threat requires that the test taker
    a. believes in the stereotype.
    b. is of relatively high intelligence.
    c. knows that others believe in the stereotype.
    d. is of relatively low intelligence.

20. What we have learned about intelligence over the years is that it is *not*
    a. complex.
    b. influenced by environment.
    c. a singular process.
    d. culturally defined.

QUESTIONS TO CONSIDER

1. Does evidence of a genetic basis for intelligence mean that intelligence is unchangeable?

2. What would happen if everyone knew everyone else's IQ scores? How might it affect decisions about whom to marry or hire?

3. Would you rather score high on a standardized test of intelligence or a test of creativity?

4. What are some of the ethical questions related to intelligence testing and psychological assessment?

5. Does it seem reasonable that you can score very high on one type of intelligence and very low on others? Does that change your view of what it means to be "intelligent"?

ACTIVITIES

1. Pick a special interest of yours, such as cooking, baseball, woodworking, dancing, or traveling. Design a test that includes both questions and tasks that would measure knowledge and ability in that area. How would you ensure the test's validity?

2. Consider the possibility that intelligence could be improved. Design a one-year plan to improve your intelligence. What would be the most important components of your plan? Would the plan you devised work equally well for someone else?

3. Talk to an elementary school teacher about his or her experience with children's intellectual development under different kinds of teaching conditions. In his or her view, is it a good idea to "teach to the test" when the teacher knows his or her students will be given standardized tests later on that will determine whether they are "advanced," "average," or "below average"? In his or her experience, what happens to students with respect to educational opportunities and attention after they are categorized in these different ways?

Human Development across the Life Span

Imagine you are holding a newborn baby. How might you predict what this child will be like as a 1-year-old? At 5 years? At 15? At 50? At 70? At 90? Your predictions would almost certainly consist of a mixture of the general and the specific—the child is extremely likely to learn a language but might or might not be a gifted author. Your predictions would also rely on considerations of heredity and of environment—if both of the child's parents were gifted authors, you might be willing to guess that the child would also show literary talent; if the child was to be educated in an enriched environment, you might predict that the child's accomplishments would exceed those of the parents. In this chapter, we describe the theories of developmental psychology that enable us to think systematically about the types of predictions we can make for the life course of a newborn child.

Developmental psychology is the area of psychology that is concerned with changes in physical and psychological functioning that occur from conception across the entire life span. The task of developmental psychologists is to find out how and why organisms change over time—to document and explain development. Investigators study the time periods in which different abilities and functions first appear and observe how those abilities are modified. The basic premise is that mental functioning, social relationships, and other vital aspects of human nature develop and change throughout the entire life cycle. **Table 10.1** presents a rough guide to the major periods of the life span.

In this chapter we will provide a general account of how researchers document development and the theories they use to explain patterns of change over time. We will then divide your life experiences into different domains and trace development in each domain. Early in the chapter, we focus on physical, cognitive, and language development. We then shift our attention to the changing nature of social relationships over the life span as well as the specific tasks individuals face at different moments in their lives. Let's begin now with the question of what it means to study development.

Studying Development

Suppose we ask you to make a list of all the ways in which you believe you have changed in the last year. What sorts of things would you put on the list? Have you undertaken a new physical fitness program? Or have you let an injury heal? Have you developed a range of new hobbies? Or have you decided to focus on just one interest? Have you developed a new circle of friends? Or have you become particularly close to one individual? When we describe development, we will conceptualize it in terms of *change.* We have asked you to perform this exercise of

TABLE 10.1 Stages in Life Span Development

Stage	Age Period
Prenatal	Conception to birth
Infancy	Birth at full term to about 18 months
Early childhood	About 18 months to about 6 years
Middle childhood	About 6 years to about 11 years
Adolescence	About 11 years to about 20 years
Early adulthood	About 20 years to about 40 years
Middle adulthood	About 40 years to about 65 years
Late adulthood	About 65 years and older

thinking about your own changes to make the point that change almost always involves trade-offs.

Often people conceptualize the life span as mostly *gains*—changes for the better—in childhood and mostly *losses*—changes for the worse—over the course of adulthood. However, the perspective on development we will take here emphasizes that *options,* and therefore gains and losses, are features of all development (Dixon, 2003; Lachman, 2004). When, for example, people choose a lifetime companion, they give up variety but gain security. When people retire, they give up status but gain leisure time. It is also important that you not think of development as a *passive* process. You will see that many developmental changes require an individual's *active* engagement with his or her environment (Bronfenbrenner, 2004).

To document change, a good first step is to determine what an average person is like—in physical appearance, cognitive abilities, and so on—at a particular age. **Normative investigations** seek to describe a characteristic of a specific age or developmental stage. By systematically testing individuals of different ages, researchers can determine developmental landmarks. These data provide *norms,* standard patterns of development or achievement, based on observation of many people.

Normative standards allow psychologists to make a distinction between chronological age—the number of months or years since a person's birth—and **developmental age**—the chronological age at which most people show the particular level of physical or mental development demonstrated by that child. A 3-year-old child who has verbal skills typical of most 5-year-olds is said to have a developmental age of 5 for verbal skills. Norms provide a standard basis for comparison both between individuals and between groups.

Developmental psychologists use several types of research designs to understand possible mechanisms of change. In a **longitudinal design,** the same individuals are repeatedly observed and tested over time, often for many years (see **Figure 10.1**). Recall the study on the effectiveness of the Hope/Perry preschool program described in Chapter 9. The researchers first collected data on a group of children when they were 3 and 4 years old (Schweinhart, 2004). To assess the long-term impact of the preschool program, the researchers studied the children every year until age 11, and then again at ages 14, 15, 19, 27, and 40. This longitudinal data

---

developmental psychology The branch of psychology concerned with interaction between physical and psychological processes and with stages of growth from conception throughout the entire life span.

normative investigation Research effort designed to describe what is characteristic of a specific age or developmental stage.

developmental age The chronological age at which most children show a particular level of physical or mental development.

longitudinal design A research design in which the same participants are observed repeatedly, sometimes over many years.

In a longitudinal design, observations are made of the same individual at different ages, often for many years. This well-known woman might be part of a longitudinal study of British children born in 1926. How might she be similar to and different from other children in that cohort?

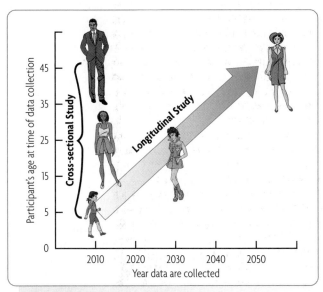

FIGURE 10.1 Longitudinal and Cross-Sectional Research

In longitudinal studies, researchers follow the same group of individuals over days, months, or years. In cross-sectional studies, researchers test individuals of different ages at the same moment in time.

collection allowed the researchers to draw strong conclusions about the program's lifelong benefits. Researchers also often use longitudinal designs to study *individual differences*. To understand the life outcomes of different people, researchers may assess a range of potential causal factors early in life and see how those factors influence each individual's life course.

A general advantage of longitudinal research is that because the participants have lived through the same socioeconomic period, age-related changes cannot be confused with variations in differing societal circumstances. A disadvantage, however, is that some types of generalizations can be made only to the same *cohort*, the group of individuals born in the same time period as the research participants. Suppose, for example, we discovered that current 50-year-olds showed a gain in happiness in the years after their children left home. That result might not apply to a future cohort of 50-year-olds who grew up with different expectations about how long children would remain in their parents' homes. Also, longitudinal studies are costly because it is difficult to keep track of the participants over extended time, and data are easily lost because participants quit or disappear.

Much research on development uses a **cross-sectional design,** in which groups of participants, of different chronological ages, are observed and compared at one and the same time. A researcher can then draw conclusions about behavioral differences that may be related to age changes. For example, researchers who wanted to determine how children learn to walk without falling down tested children of ages 15, 21, 27, 33, and 39 months on the same laboratory task (Joh & Adolph, 2006). A disadvantage of cross-sectional designs comes from comparing individuals who differ by year of birth as well as by chronological age. Age-related changes are confounded by differences in the social or political conditions experienced by different birth cohorts. Thus a study comparing samples of 10- and 18-year-olds now might find that the participants differ from 10- and 18-year-olds who grew up in the 1970s, in ways related to their different eras as well as to their developmental stages.

Each methodology gives researchers the opportunity to document change from one age to another. Researchers use these methodologies to study development in each of several domains. As we now consider some of those domains—physical, cognitive, and social development—you'll come to appreciate and understand some of the vast changes you've already experienced.

---

cross-sectional design A research method in which groups of participants of different chronological ages are observed and compared at a given time.

A drawback of cross-sectional research is the cohort effect. What differences might exist between these two groups of women as a result of the eras in which they lived?

STOP AND REVIEW

❶ What is developmental age?
❷ Why are longitudinal designs often used to study individual differences?
❸ What is the relevance of birth cohorts to cross-sectional designs?

Visit MyPsychLab.com for more review and practice on the following topic:

◀◉ **Explore:** Cross-Sectional and Longitudinal Research Designs

Physical Development across the Life Span

Many of the types of development we describe in this chapter require some special knowledge to detect. For example, you might not notice landmarks in social development until you read about them here. We will begin, however, with a realm of

development in which changes are often plainly visible to the untrained eye: **physical development.** There is no doubt that you have undergone enormous physical change since you were born. Such changes will continue until the end of your life. Because physical changes are so numerous, we will focus on the types that have an impact on psychological development.

PRENATAL AND CHILDHOOD DEVELOPMENT

You began life with unique genetic potential: At the moment of conception a male's sperm cell fertilized a female's egg cell to form the single-cell **zygote;** you received half of the 46 chromosomes found in all normal human body cells from your mother and half from your father. In this section, we outline physical development in the *prenatal period,* from the moment of conception until the moment of birth. We also describe some of the sensory abilities children have obtained even before birth. Finally, we describe the important physical changes that you experienced during childhood.

Physical Development in the Womb The first two weeks after formation of the zygote are known as the **germinal stage** of prenatal development. During this stage, cells begin to divide rapidly; after about one week a mass of microscopic cells attaches itself to the mother's uterine wall. The third through eighth week of prenatal development is called the **embryonic stage.** During this stage, rapid cell division continues, but the cells begin to become specialized to form different organs. As these organs develop, the first heartbeat occurs. Responses to stimulation have been observed as early as the sixth week, when the *embryo* is not yet an inch long. Spontaneous movements are observed by the eighth week (Kisilevsky & Low, 1998).

The **fetal stage** lasts from the end of the eighth week through the birth of the child. The mother will feel the *fetus*

---

physical development The bodily changes, maturation, and growth that occur in an organism starting with conception and continuing across the life span.

zygote The single cell that results when a sperm fertilizes an egg.

germinal stage The first two weeks of prenatal development following conception.

embryonic stage The second stage of prenatal development, lasting from the third through eight weeks after conception.

fetal stage The third stage of prenatal development, lasting from the ninth week through birth of the child.

move in about the sixteenth week after conception. At this point, the fetus is about 7 inches long (the average length at birth is 20 inches). As the brain grows in utero, it generates new neurons at the rate of 250,000 per minute, reaching a full complement of over 100 billion neurons by birth (Cowan, 1979). In humans and many other mammals, most of this cell proliferation and migration of neurons to their correct locations take place before birth; the development of the branching processes of axons and dendrites largely occurs after birth (Kolb, 1989). The sequence of brain development, from 30 days to 9 months, is shown in **Figure 10.2.**

Over the course of pregnancy, environmental factors such as infection, radiation, or drugs can prevent the normal formation of organs and body structures. Any environmental factor that causes structural abnormalities in the fetus is called a **teratogen.** For example, when mothers are infected with rubella (German measles), their children often suffer negative consequences such as mental retardation, eye damage, deafness, or heart defects. When the infection occurs in the first six weeks after conception, the probability of birth defects may be 100 percent (De Santis et al., 2006). If exposure occurs later in the pregnancy, the probability of adverse effects becomes lower (for example, 50 percent in the fourth month; 6 percent in the fifth month). Mothers who consume alcohol during sensitive periods put their unborn children at risk for brain damage and other impairments (Bailey & Sokol, 2008). *Fetal alcohol syndrome* is the most serious consequence of a mother's alcohol consumption during pregnancy. Children with fetal alcohol syndrome often have small heads and bodies and facial abnormalities. Disruptions of the central nervous system cause cognitive and behavioral problems (Niccols, 2007).

Pregnant women who smoke also put their children at risk. Smoking during pregnancy increases the risk of miscarriage, premature births, and low-birth-weight babies (Salihu & Wilson, 2007). In fact, women who are exposed to secondhand smoke during pregnancy are also more likely to have babies with low birth weights (Dejin-Karlsson et al., 1998). Finally, almost all illicit drugs cause damage to the fetus. Cocaine, for example, travels through the placenta and can affect fetal development directly. In adults, cocaine causes blood vessels to constrict; in pregnant

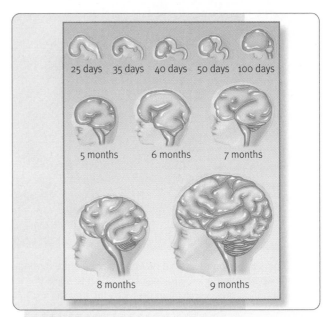

FIGURE 10.2 The Development of the Human Brain

During the nine months before birth, the brain reaches its complement of over 100 billion neurons.

Adapted from *The Brain* by R. Restak. Copyright © 1984. Bantam Books.

women, cocaine restricts placental blood flow and oxygen supply to the fetus. If severe oxygen deprivation results, blood vessels in the fetus's brain may burst. Such prenatal strokes can lead to lifelong mental handicaps (Bennett et al., 2008; Singer et al., 2002). Research suggests that the brain systems most damaged by cocaine are those responsible for controlling attention: Children exposed to cocaine in the womb may spend their lives overcome by the distractions of irrelevant sights and sounds.

Babies Prewired for Survival What capabilities were programmed into your body and brain at birth? We are accustomed to thinking about newborns as entirely helpless. John Watson, the founder of behaviorism, described the human infant as "a lively, squirming bit of flesh, capable of making a few simple responses." If that sounds right, you might be surprised to learn that, moments out of the womb, infants reveal remarkable abilities. They might be thought of as *prewired for survival,* well suited to respond to adult caregivers and to influence their social environments.

To begin, infants are born with a repertoire of reflexes that provide many of their earliest behavioral responses to the environment. Recall from Chapter 6 that a *reflex* is a response that is naturally triggered by specific stimuli that are biologically relevant for the organism. Consider two reflexes that quite literally prewire infants for survival. When something brushes against infants' cheeks, they turn their head in that direction. This *rooting reflex* allows newborns to find their mothers' nipples. When an object is placed in their mouths, infants begin to

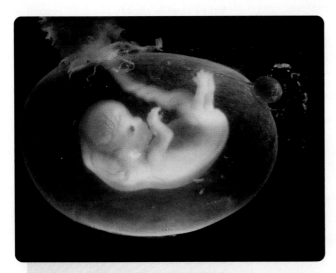

As the brain grows in the developing fetus, it generates 250,000 new neurons per minute. What must the brain be prepared to do, as soon as the child enters the world?

teratogen Environmental factors such as diseases and drugs that cause structural abnormalities in a developing fetus.

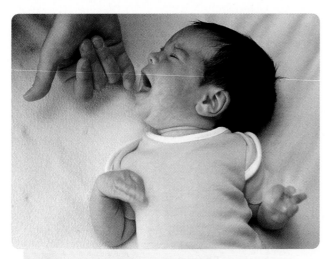

When something touches a newborn's cheek, the rooting reflex prompts the baby to seek something to suck. In what other ways are children prewired for survival?

suck. This *sucking reflex* allows infants to begin feeding. Reflexes of this sort keep infants alive in the early months of their lives.

For example, infants can hear even before birth. Researchers have demonstrated that what infants hear while in the womb has consequences. Newborns prefer to listen to their mothers' voices rather than the voices of other women (Spence & DeCasper, 1987; Spence & Freeman, 1996). In fact, research suggests that children recognize their mothers' voices even before they are born: In one study, the heart rate of fetuses increased in response to recordings of their mothers' voices and decreased in response to strangers' voices (Kisilevsky et al., 2003). Given these strong results favoring mothers, you might wonder whether children also respond more to their fathers' voices. Unfortunately, research so far indicates that children don't seem to have enough auditory experience with their dads. Newborns show no preference for their fathers' voices (DeCasper & Prescott, 1984). Even at age 4 months, infants still do not prefer their fathers' voices to strangers' voices (Ward & Cooper, 1999).

Infants also put their visual systems to work almost immediately: A few minutes after birth, a newborn's eyes are alert, turning in the direction of a voice and searching inquisitively for the source of certain sounds. Even so, vision is less well developed than the other senses at birth. The visual acuity of adults is roughly 40 times better than the visual acuity of newborns (Sireteanu, 1999). However, visual acuity improves rapidly over the first six months of a baby's life. Newborns also are ill equipped to experience the world in three dimensions. Recall from Chapter 4 that you use a great variety of cues to experience depth. Researchers have begun to document the time course with which infants are able to interpret each type of cue. For

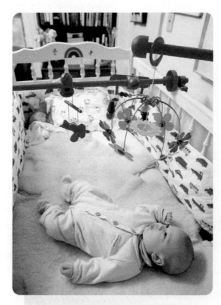

Early on, infants can perceive large objects that display a great deal of contrast. What visual experiences do newborns find particularly appealing?

example, at 4 months, infants start being able to use cues such as relative motion and interposition to infer three-dimensional structures from two-dimensional images of objects (Shuwairi et al., 2007; Soska & Johnson, 2008).

Even without perfect vision, however, children have visual preferences. Pioneering researcher **Robert Fantz** (1963) observed that babies as young as 4 months old preferred looking at objects with contours rather than those that were plain, complex ones rather than simple ones, and whole faces rather than faces with features in disarray. More recent research suggests that—by the age of 3 days—infants have a preference for *top-heavy patterns* (Macchi Cassia et al., 2004). To experience a top-heavy pattern, take a look at your face in a mirror—notice that your eyes, eyebrows, and so on, take up much more space than your lips. The fact that faces are top-heavy might explain why infants prefer to look at human faces versus other types of visual displays.

Once children start to move around in their environment, they quickly acquire other perceptual capabilities. For example, classic research by **Eleanor Gibson** and **Richard Walk** (1960) examined how children respond to depth information. This research used an apparatus called a *visual cliff*. The visual cliff had a board running across the middle of a solid glass surface. As shown in **Figure 10.3,** checkerboard cloth was used to create a deep end and a shallow end. In their original research, Gibson and Walk demonstrated that children would readily leave the center board to crawl across the shallow end, but they were reluctant to crawl across the deep end. Subsequent research has demonstrated that fear of the deep end depends on crawling experience: Children who have begun to crawl experience fear of the deep end, whereas their noncrawling same-age peers do not (Campos et al., 1992; Witherington et al., 2005). Thus wariness of heights is not quite "prewired," but it develops quickly as children begin to explore the world under their own power.

Growth and Maturation in Childhood Newborn infants change at an astonishing rate but, as shown in **Figure 10.4,** physical growth is not equal across all physical structures. You've probably noticed that babies seem to be all head. At birth, a baby's head is already about 60 percent of its adult size and measures a quarter of the whole body length (Bayley, 1956). An infant's body weight doubles in the first six months and triples by the first birthday; by the age of 2, a child's trunk is about half of its adult length. Genital tissue shows little change until the teenage years and then develops rapidly to adult proportions.

For most children, physical growth is accompanied by the maturation of motor ability. **Maturation** refers to the process of growth typical of all members of a species who are reared in the species's usual habitat. The characteristic maturational sequences newborns experience are determined by the interaction of inherited biological boundaries and environmental inputs. For example, in the sequence for locomotion, as shown in **Figure 10.5** on page 304, a child learns to walk without special training. This sequence applies to the great majority of babies; a minority of children skip a step or develop their

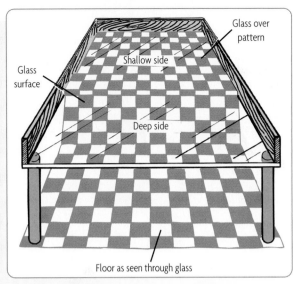

FIGURE 10.3 The Visual Cliff
Once children have gained experience crawling around their environment, they show fear of the deep side of the visual cliff.

own original sequences. Even so, in cultures in which there is less physical stimulation, children begin to walk later. The Native American practice of carrying babies in tightly bound back cradles retards walking, but, once released, the child goes through the same sequence. Therefore, you can think of all unimpaired newborn children as possessing the same potential for physical maturation.

PHYSICAL DEVELOPMENT IN ADOLESCENCE

The first concrete indicator of the end of childhood is the *pubescent growth spurt*. At around age 10 for girls and age 12 for

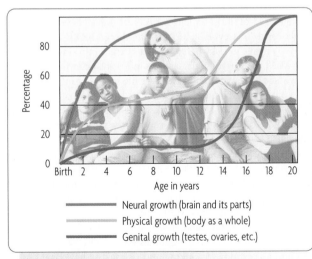

FIGURE 10.4 Growth Patterns across the First Two Decades of Life
Neural growth occurs very rapidly in the first year of life. It is much faster than overall physical growth. By contrast, genital maturation does not occur until adolescence.

boys, growth hormones flow into the bloodstream. For several years, the adolescent may grow 3 to 6 inches a year and gain weight rapidly as well. The adolescent's body does not reach adult proportions all at once. Hands and feet grow to full adult size first. The arms and legs come next, with the torso developing most slowly. Thus an individual's overall shape changes several times over the teenage years.

Another important process that occurs during adolescence is **puberty,** which brings about sexual maturity. (The Latin word *pubertas* means "covered with hair" and signifies the growth of hair on the arms and legs, under the arms, and in the genital area.) Puberty for males brings about the production of live sperm; for girls it leads to **menarche,** the onset of menstruation. In the United States, the average time for menarche is between the ages of 12 and 13, although the normal range extends from 11 to 15. For boys, the production of live sperm first occurs, on average, between the ages of 12 and 14, but again there is considerable variation in this timing. These physical changes often bring about an awareness of sexual feelings. In Chapter 11, we will discuss the onset of sexual motivation.

Some other important physical changes happen inside adolescents' brains. Researchers once thought that most brain growth was over within the first few years of life. However, recent studies using brain imaging techniques have demonstrated continuing development within the adolescent brain (Paus, 2005). Researchers have documented particularly important changes in the *limbic system*—which regulates emotional processes—and the *frontal lobes*—the areas responsible for planning and control of emotions (see Chapter 3). However, maturation of the limbic system precedes maturation of the frontal lobes. The relative timing of changes within those regions may

---

maturation The continuing influence of heredity throughout development, the age-related physical and behavioral changes characteristic of a species.

puberty The process through which sexual maturity is attained.

menarche The onset of menstruation.

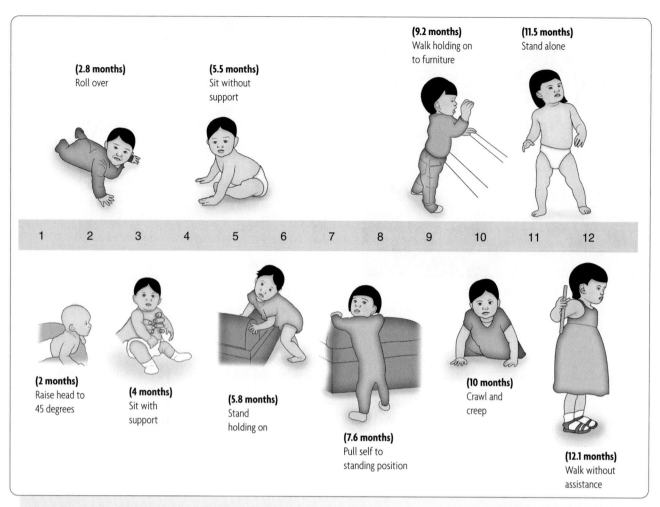

FIGURE 10.5 Maturational Timetable for Locomotion
The development of walking requires no special teaching. It follows a fixed, time-ordered sequence that is typical of all physically capable members of our species.

What effect does a cradleboard have on the infant's ability to learn to walk?

explain one of most salient aspects of social development in adolescence (Casey et al., 2008; Steinberg, 2008): Adolescents tend to engage in risky behavior. Let's explore this insight.

We'll return to social aspects of risky behavior when we review social development across the life span. For now, our focus is on physical development. Researchers speculate that maturation of the limbic system readies adolescents to go out into the world: "Evolutionarily speaking, adolescence is the period in which independence skills are acquired to increase success upon separation from the protection of the family" (Casey et al., 2008, p. 70). In that evolutionary context, it makes sense that regions of the frontal cortex that inhibit and control the emotional drive toward independence would mature somewhat later in life. To survive apart from their families, adolescents would have to take some initial risks. The difficulty is that in contemporary times people no longer typically leave their families during adolescence. Thus, the evolutionary impulse toward novelty seeking and risk taking no longer has an adaptive function. Fortunately, as people develop from adolescence into adulthood, the frontal lobes achieve maturity (Steinberg, 2008). New connections form between the frontal lobes and limbic system. Those new connections enable individuals to exercise more cognitive control over their emotional impulses.

Why do researchers give the advice "Use it or lose it"?

at some changes that are largely unavoidable and frequently have an impact on the way adults think about their lives.

Vision   Beginning at ages 40 to 50, most people begin experiencing changes in the function of their visual system: The lenses of their eyes become less flexible and the muscles that change the thickness of the lens become less effective. These changes can make seeing objects at close range difficult. Lens rigidity also affects dark adaptation, making night vision a problem for older people. Many of these normal visual changes can be aided with corrective lenses. With age, the lenses of people's eyes also become yellowed. The yellowing of the lens is thought to be responsible for diminished color vision experienced by some older people. Colors of lower wavelengths—violets, blues, and greens—are particularly hard for some older adults to discriminate. By age 65, the vast majority of people experience some loss of visual function (Carter, 1982; Pitts, 1982).

Hearing   Hearing loss is common among those 60 and older. The average older adult has difficulty hearing high-frequency sounds (Corso, 1977). This impairment is usually greater for men than for women. Older adults can have a hard time understanding speech—particularly that spoken by high-pitched voices. (Oddly enough, with age, people's speaking voices increase in pitch due to stiffening of the vocal cords.) Deficits in hearing can be gradual and hard for an individual to notice until they are extreme. In addition, even when individuals become aware of hearing loss, they may deny it because it is perceived as an undesirable sign of aging. Some of the physiological aspects of hearing loss can be overcome with the help of hearing aids. You should also be aware, as you grow older or interact with older adults, that it helps to speak in low tones, enunciate clearly, and reduce background noise.

Reproductive and Sexual Functioning   We saw that puberty marks the onset of reproductive functioning. In middle and late adulthood, reproductive capacity diminishes. Around age

With the passing of adolescence, your body once again reaches a period of the life span in which biological change is comparatively minimal. You may affect your body in a variety of ways—by diet and exercise, for example—but the next striking set of changes that are consistent consequences of aging occurs in middle and late adulthood.

PHYSICAL CHANGES IN ADULTHOOD

Some of the most obvious changes that occur with age concern your physical appearance and abilities. As you grow older, you can expect your skin to wrinkle, your hair to thin and gray, and your height to decrease an inch or two. You can also expect some of your senses to become less acute. These changes do not appear suddenly at age 65. They occur gradually, beginning as soon as early adulthood. However, before we describe some common age-related changes, we want to make a more general point: Many physical changes arise not from aging but from *disuse;* research supports a general belief in the maxim "Use it or lose it." Older adults who maintain (or renew) a program of physical fitness may experience fewer of the difficulties that are often thought to be inevitable consequences of aging. (Note that we will explore the same claim when we discuss cognitive and social aspects of middle and late adulthood.) Let's now look, however,

Older adults can and do enjoy the many benefits of intimacy and sexual relationships. Why does this image clash with stereotypes of late adulthood?

50, most women experience *menopause,* the cessation of menstruation and ovulation. For men, changes are less abrupt, but the quantity of viable sperm falls off after age 40, and the volume of seminal fluid declines after age 60. Of course, these changes are relevant primarily to reproduction. Increasing age and physical change do not necessarily impair other aspects of sexual experience (DeLamater & Sill, 2005; Lindau et al., 2007). Indeed, sex is one of life's healthy pleasures that can enhance successful aging because it is arousing, provides aerobic exercise, stimulates fantasy, and is a vital form of social interaction.

You have had a brief review of the landmarks of physical development. Against that background, let's turn now to the ways in which you developed an understanding of the world around you.

STOP AND REVIEW

❶ How does experience with crawling influence children's performance on the visual cliff?

❷ What have recent studies demonstrated with respect to brain development in adolescence?

❸ Why does increasing age often have an effect on color vision?

CRITICAL THINKING Consider the study on prenatal voice recognition. Why did the researchers have mothers tape-record the poems rather than having them read them "live"?

Visit MyPsychLab.com for more review and practice on the following topics:

👁 **Watch:** Prenatal Programming: Christopher Coe

👁 **Watch:** The Newborn's Reflexes

✳ **Simulate:** The Visual Cliff

Cognitive Development across the Life Span

How does an individual's understanding of physical and social reality change across the life span? **Cognitive development** is the study of the processes and products of the mind as they emerge and change over time. Because researchers have been particularly fascinated by the earliest emergence of cognitive capabilities, we will focus much of our attention on the earliest stages of cognitive development. However, we will also describe some of the discoveries researchers have made about cognitive development across the adult years.

---

cognitive development The development of processes of knowing, including imagining, perceiving, reasoning, and problem solving.

scheme Piaget's term for a cognitive structure that develops as infants and young children learn to interpret the world and adapt to their environment.

assimilation According to Piaget, the process whereby new cognitive elements are fitted in with old elements or modified to fit more easily; this process works in tandem with accommodation.

accommodation According to Piaget, the process of restructuring or modifying cognitive structures so that new information can fit into them more easily; this process works in tandem with assimilation.

As we begin this discussion of cognitive development, we want to remind you of a distinction we introduced in Chapter 3—*nature versus nurture.* The question is how best to account for the profound differences between a newborn and, for example, a 10-year-old: To what extent is such development determined by heredity (nature), and to what extent is it a product of learned experiences (nurture)? The debate concerning nature and nurture has a long history among philosophers, psychologists, and educators. On one side of this debate are those who believe that the human infant is born without knowledge or skills and that experience, in the form of human learning, etches messages on the blank tablet (in Latin, the *tabula rasa*) of the infant's unformed mind. This view, originally proposed by British philosopher **John Locke,** is known as *empiricism.* It credits human development to experience. Empiricists believe that what directs human development is the stimulation people receive as they are *nurtured.* Among the scholars opposing empiricism was French philosopher **Jean-Jacques Rousseau.** He argued the *nativist* view that *nature,* or the evolutionary legacy that each child brings into the world, is the mold that shapes development. Our discussion of cognitive development should lead you to see that there is truth to both sides of the debate. Children have innate preparation to learn from their experiences in the world.

We begin our discussion of cognitive development with the pioneering work of the late Swiss psychologist Jean Piaget.

PIAGET'S INSIGHTS INTO MENTAL DEVELOPMENT

For nearly 50 years, **Jean Piaget** (1929, 1954, 1977) developed theories about the ways that children think, reason, and solve problems. Perhaps Piaget's interest in cognitive development grew out of his own intellectually active youth: Piaget published his first article at age 10 and was offered a post as a museum curator at age 14 (Brainerd, 1996). Piaget used simple demonstrations and sensitive interviews with his own children and with other children to generate complex theories about early mental development. His interest was not in the amount of information children possessed but in the ways their thinking and inner representations of physical reality changed at different stages in their development.

Building Blocks of Developmental Change Piaget gave the name **schemes** to the mental structures that enable individuals to interpret the world. Schemes are the building blocks of developmental change. Piaget characterized the infant's initial schemes as *sensorimotor intelligence*—mental structures or programs that guide sensorimotor sequences, such as sucking, looking, grasping, and pushing. With practice, elementary schemes are combined, integrated, and differentiated into ever-more-complex, diverse action patterns, as when a child pushes away undesired objects to seize a desired one behind him or her. According to Piaget, two basic processes work in tandem to achieve cognitive growth—assimilation and accommodation. **Assimilation** modifies new environmental information to fit into what is already known; the child accesses existing schemes to structure incoming sensory data. **Accommodation** restructures or modifies the child's existing schemes so that new information is accounted for more completely.

Consider the transitions a baby must make from sucking at a mother's breast, to sucking the nipple of a bottle, to sipping through a straw, and then to drinking from a cup. The initial sucking response is a reflex action present at birth, but it must be modified somewhat so that the child's mouth fits the shape and size of the mother's nipple. In adapting to a bottle, an infant still uses many parts of the sequence unchanged (assimilation) but must grasp and draw on the rubber nipple somewhat differently from before and learn to hold the bottle at an appropriate angle (accommodation). The steps from bottle to straw to cup require more accommodation but continue to rely on earlier skills. Piaget saw cognitive development as the result of exactly this sort of interweaving of assimilation and accommodation. The balanced application of assimilation and accommodation permits children's behavior and knowledge to become less dependent on concrete external reality, relying more on abstract thought.

Stages in Cognitive Development Piaget believed that children's cognitive development could be divided into a series of four ordered, discontinuous stages (see **Table 10.2**). All children are assumed to progress through these stages in the same sequence, although one child may take longer to pass through a given stage than does another.

Sensorimotor Stage The sensorimotor stage extends roughly from birth to age 2. In the early months, much of an infant's behavior is based on a limited array of inborn schemes, like sucking, looking, grasping, and pushing. During the first year, sensorimotor sequences are improved, combined, coordinated, and integrated (sucking and grasping, looking and manipulating, for example). They become more varied as infants discover that their actions have an effect on external events.

The most important cognitive acquisition of the infancy period is the ability to form mental representations of absent objects—those with which the child is not in direct sensorimotor contact. **Object permanence** refers to children's understanding that objects exist and behave independently of their actions or awareness. In the first months of life, children follow objects with their eyes, but, when the objects disappear from view, they turn away as if the objects had also disappeared from their minds. At around 3 months of age, however, they keep looking at the place where the objects had disappeared. Between 8 and 12 months, children begin to search for those disappearing objects. By age 2 years, children have no remaining uncertainty that "out of sight" objects continue to exist (Flavell, 1985).

Preoperational Stage The preoperational stage extends roughly from 2 to 7 years of age. The big cognitive advance in this developmental stage is an improved ability to represent mentally objects that are not physically present. Except for this development, Piaget characterizes the preoperational stage according to what the child *cannot* do. For example, Piaget believed that young children's preoperational thought is marked by **egocentrism,** the child's inability to take the perspective of another person. You have probably noticed egocentrism if you've heard a 2-year-old's conversations with other children. Children at this age often seem to be talking to themselves rather than interacting.

Preoperational children also experience **centration**—they tend to focus (center) their attention on only one aspect of a situation and disregard other relevant aspects. Centration is illustrated by Piaget's classic demonstration of a child's inability to understand that the amount of a liquid does not change as a function of the size or shape of its container.

When an equal amount of lemonade is poured into two identical glasses, children of ages 5 and 7 report that the glasses contain the same amount. When, however, the lemonade from one glass is poured into a tall, thin glass, their opinions diverge. The 5-year-olds know that the

TABLE 10.2	Piaget's Stages of Cognitive Development
Stage/Ages	**Characteristics and Major Accomplishments**
Sensorimotor (0–2)	Child begins life with small number of sensorimotor sequences. Child develops object permanence and the beginnings of symbolic thought.
Preoperational (2–7)	Child's thought is marked by egocentrism and centration. Child has improved ability to use symbolic thought.
Concrete operations (7–11)	Child achieves understanding of conservation. Child can reason with respect to concrete, physical objects.
Formal operations (11→)	Child develops capacity for abstract reasoning and hypothetical thinking.

lemonade in the tall glass is the same lemonade, but they report that it now is *more*. The 7-year-olds correctly assert that there is no difference between the amounts.

In Piaget's demonstration, the younger children center on a single, perceptually noticeable dimension—the height of the lemonade in the glass. The older children take into account both height and width and correctly infer that appearance is not reality.

Concrete Operations Stage The concrete operations stage goes roughly from 7 to 11 years of age. At this stage, the child has become capable of mental operations, actions performed in the mind that give rise to logical thinking. The preoperational and concrete operations stages are often put in contrast because children in the concrete operation stage are now capable of what they failed earlier on. Concrete operations allow children to replace physical action with mental action. For example, if a child sees that Adam is taller than Zara and, later, that Zara is taller than Tanya, the child can reason that Adam is the tallest of the three—without physically manipulating the three individuals. However, the child still cannot draw the appropriate inference ("Adam is tallest") if the problem is just stated with a verbal description. Children only become able to solve problems of this sort with abstract thought when they arrive at the stage of concrete operations.

---

object permanence The recognition that objects exist independently of an individual's action or awareness; an important cognitive acquisition of infancy.

egocentrism In cognitive development, the inability of a young child at the preoperational stage to take the perspective of another person.

centration Preoperational children's tendency to focus their attention on only one aspect of a situation and disregard other relevant aspects.

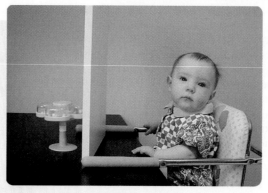

Piaget observed that the typical 6-month-old will attend to an attractive toy (left) but will quickly lose interest if a screen blocks the toy from view (right). What understanding about objects will the child achieve by age 2?

The lemonade study illustrates another hallmark of the concrete operations period. The 7-year-olds have mastered what Piaget called **conservation:** They know that the physical properties of objects do not change when nothing is added or taken away, even though the objects' appearances change. **Figure 10.6** presents examples of Piaget's tests of conservation for different dimensions. One of the newly acquired operations children can bring to bear on conservation tasks is reversibility. *Reversibility* is the child's understanding that both physical actions and mental operations can be reversed: The child can reason that the amount of lemonade *couldn't* have changed because when the physical action is reversed—when the lemonade is poured back into the original glass—the two volumes will once again look identical.

Formal Operations Stage The formal operations stage covers a span roughly from age 11 on. In this final stage of cognitive growth, thinking becomes abstract. Adolescents can see how their particular reality is only one of several imaginable realities, and they begin to ponder deep questions of truth, justice, and existence. They seek answers to problems in a systematic fashion: Once they achieve formal operations, children can start to play the role of scientist, trying each of a series of possibilities in careful order. Adolescents also begin to be able to use the types of advanced deductive logic we described in Chapter 8. Unlike their younger siblings, adolescents have the ability to reason from abstract premises ("If *A,* then *B*" and "not *B*") to their logical conclusions ("not *A*").

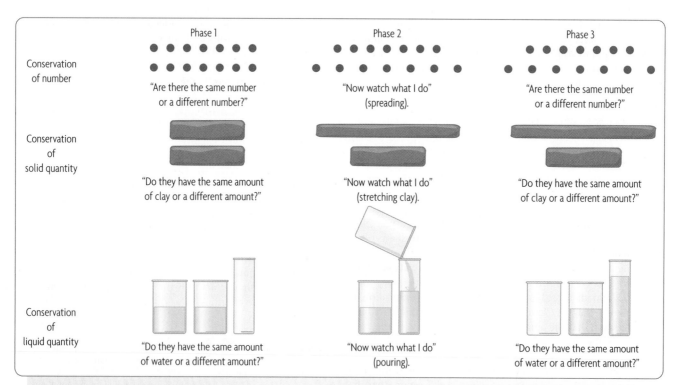

FIGURE 10.6 Tests of Conservation

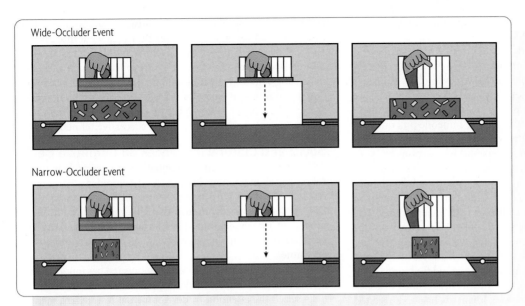

FIGURE 10.7 Four-Month-Olds and Object Permanence

Four-month-olds watched an experimenter lower a rectangular object (shown in brown) behind a wide occluder or a narrow occluder (each shown in patterned green). As the event unfolded, a screen appeared to mask the moment at which the object passed behind the occluder. When the screen disappeared, the experimenter's hand was empty. The infants who saw the narrow-occluder event spent more time looking at the display, suggesting they were surprised that a wide object could be hidden behind a narrow occluder. The infants' surprise suggests they have attained some aspects of object permanence: The rectangular object was out of sight but not out of mind.

From *Cognition, 93,* Su-hua Wang et al., "Young infants' reasoning about hidden objects: Evidence from violation-of-expectation tasks with test trials only," pp. 167–198, Copyright © 2004, with permission from Elsevier.

CONTEMPORARY PERSPECTIVES ON EARLY COGNITIVE DEVELOPMENT

Piaget's theory remains the classic reference point for the understanding of cognitive development (Feldman, 2004; Flavell, 1996). However, contemporary researchers have come up with more flexible ways of studying the development of the child's cognitive abilities.

Infant Cognition We've already detailed some of the tasks Piaget used to draw conclusions about cognitive development. However, contemporary researchers have developed innovative techniques that have allowed them to reevaluate some of Piaget's conclusions. Consider object permanence, which Piaget suggested was the major accomplishment of the 2-year-old child. Contemporary research techniques suggest that infants as young as 3 months old have already developed aspects of this concept. This important finding has been shown with different tasks devised by researcher **Renée Baillargeon** and her colleagues.

> In one study, 4-month-old infants watched while an experimenter lowered a wide rectangular object (see **Figure 10.7**) (Wang et al., 2004). In one condition, the path of the object would put it behind a *wide occluder*—a barrier wide enough to hide the rectangular object completely. In the other condition, the object was destined to pass behind a *narrow occluder*—a barrier too narrow to occlude the object fully. As this event unfolded, a screen appeared that hid the final moment in which the object was lowered. When the screen disappeared, the object was fully hidden. How did the infants respond in the two conditions? If they didn't have object permanence, we would expect them to be equally unbothered in both cases—once the rectangular object was gone, we would expect them to have no recollection that it had ever existed. Suppose they did have some recollection of the object. In that case, we would expect that they—like adults who watched the events—would be rather surprised that a wide object could be hidden by a narrow occluder. To assess the infants' degree of surprise, the researchers recorded how long infants looked at the displays after the screen disappeared. The infants who saw the narrow occluder event looked at the display for about 16 seconds longer than their peers who saw the wide occluder event.

We can't take the infants' surprise as evidence that they have acquired the full concept of object permanence—they may only know that something is wrong without knowing exactly what that something is (Lourenço & Machado, 1996). Even so, the research by Baillargeon and her colleagues suggests that event

---

conservation According to Piaget, the understanding that physical properties do not change when nothing is added or taken away, even though appearances may change.

very young children have acquired important knowledge of the physical world.

The innovative methods researchers have developed to penetrate infants' minds continue to transform our understanding of what infants know and how they know it. Consider the relationship between actions and goals. As an adult, you are accustomed to inferring people's goals when you watch them perform actions. For example, if you see someone pull out a set of keys, you easily infer that he or she needs to unlock something. When did you start to understand how actions relate to goals? Research suggests that 7-month-olds have begun to divide the world up into actions that are goal-directed and those that are not (Hamlin et al., 2008). Consider an experiment in which infants sat in front of a display with a pair of toys. The infants watched an experimenter perform one of two actions with respect to the toys: Some infants watched the researcher grasp a toy; other infants watched her touch a toy with the back of her hand. An adult watching the scene would find it relatively easy to interpret the grasp, but not the touch, as related to a specific goal (that is, to acquire the toy). Infants' behaviors suggested that they also interpreted the actions differently. After the infants viewed the experimenter's actions, she told them "Now it's your turn!" and put the toys within their reach. Infants who had viewed the grasping action were likely to touch the same toy the experimenter had grasped; infants who had viewed the back-of-the-hand contact didn't show a preference for touching one toy over the other. This pattern suggests that the infants interpreted only the grasping action as having goal-directed significance for just one of the two toys. This study illustrates how carefully infants attend to the world around them to understand the origins of other people's behaviors.

Children's Foundational Theories

Piaget's theory is built around stages in which landmark changes take place in children's ways of thinking. More recently, researchers have explored the idea that changes occur separately, in each of several major domains, as children develop **foundational theories**— frameworks for initial understanding—to explain their experiences of the world (Gelman & Raman, 2002; Wellman & Inagaki, 1997). For example, children accumulate their experiences of the properties of mental states into a *theory of mind,* or naive psychology. By doing so, they are better able to understand the thought processes of themselves and others.

Researchers have formally studied the development of scientific concepts, such as the way in which children project biological properties from one species to another. When asked which of a series of animals sleep or have bones, 4-year-old children were inclined to make their judgments based on their perceptions of the similarity of the animal to humans (Carey, 1985). For example, more 4-year-olds attributed these properties (that is, "sleep" and "have bones") to dogs than they did to fish, and attributions to fish were, in turn, greater than those to flies. Over time, children must replace a theory based on similarity to humans with one that acknowledges more structure in the animal kingdom—for example, they must acquire the formal distinction between *vertebrates* and *invertebrates* that defines which types of animals have bones. Similarly, 3- and 4-year-old

children understand that what is inside objects affects their functions—although they have no clear idea what those insides are (Gelman, 2003; Gelman & Wellman, 1991). Thus although 3- and 4-year-olds aren't entirely sure what kinds of things are inside dogs, they are quite certain that a dog would cease to be a dog if you removed whatever is inside. In each domain, you see that children begin to develop a general theory and then use a range of new experiences to provide successive refinements.

Social and Cultural Influences on Cognitive Development Another focus of contemporary research is on the role of social interactions in cognitive development. Much of this research has its origins in the theories of Russian psychologist **Lev Vygotsky.** Vygotsky argued that children develop through a process of **internalization:** They absorb knowledge from their social context that has a major impact on how cognition unfolds over time.

The social theory that Vygotsky pioneered has found support in cross-cultural studies of development. As Piaget's theory initially seized the attention of developmental researchers, many of them sought to use his tasks to study the cognitive achievements of children in diverse cultures (Rogoff, 2003; Rogoff & Chavajay, 1995). These studies began to call into question the universality of Piaget's claims because, for example, people in many cultures failed to show evidence that they had acquired formal operations. Late in his life, Piaget himself began to speculate that the specific achievements he characterized as formal operations may rely

How do children begin to form generalizations about the world based on what they have experienced and observed?

---

foundational theory Framework for initial understanding formulated by children to explain their experiences of the world.

internalization According to Vygotsky, the process through which children absorb knowledge from the social context.

more on the particular type of science education children obtain rather than on an unfolding of biologically predetermined stages of cognitive development (Lourenço & Machado, 1996).

Vygotsky's concept of internalization helps explain the effect culture has on cognitive development. Children's cognition develops to perform culturally valued functions (Serpell, 2000; Serpell & Boykin, 1994). Piaget, for example, invented tasks that reflected his own preconceptions about appropriate and valuable cognitive activities. Other cultures prefer their children to excel in other ways. If Piaget's children had been evaluated with respect to their understanding of the cognitive complexities of weaving, they probably would have appeared to be retarded in their development relative to Mayan children in Guatemala (Rogoff, 1990). Cross-cultural studies of cognitive development have quite often demonstrated that type of schooling plays a large role in determining children's achievement on Piagetian tasks (Rogoff & Chavajay, 1995). Psychologists must use these types of findings to sort out the nature and nurture of cognitive development.

The developmental changes we have documented so far are very dramatic. It's easy to tell that a 12-year-old has all sorts of cognitive capabilities unknown to a 1-year-old. We now shift to the more subtle changes that take place throughout adulthood.

COGNITIVE DEVELOPMENT IN ADULTHOOD

As we have traced cognitive development across childhood into adolescence, "change" has usually meant "change for the better." When we arrive at the period of late adulthood, though, cultural stereotypes suggest that "change" means "change for the worse" (Parr & Siegert, 1993). However, even when people believe that the course of adulthood brings with it general decline, they still anticipate certain types of gains very late into life (Dixon & de Frias, 2004). We will look at intelligence and memory to see the interplay of losses and gains.

Intelligence There is little evidence to support the notion that general cognitive abilities decline among the healthy elderly. Only about 5 percent of the population experiences major losses in cognitive functioning. When age-related decline in cognitive functioning occurs, it is usually limited to only some abilities. When intelligence is separated into the components that make up your verbal abilities (*crystallized intelligence*) and those that are part of your ability to learn quickly and thoroughly (*fluid intelligence*), fluid intelligence shows the greater decline with age (Baltes & Staudinger, 1993; Singer et al., 2003). Much of the decrease in fluidity has been attributed to a general slowing down of processing speed: Older adults' performance on intellectual tasks that require many mental processes to occur in small amounts of time is greatly impaired (Sheppard & Vernon, 2008).

Researchers who study cognitive performance have been quite interested in determining what older adults might do to minimize declines with age. Much research attention has considered the maxim "use it or lose it." One study, for example, focused on a group of older adults whose average age was 69 (Bielak et al., 2007). The adults whose everyday lives had the highest levels of social, physical, and intellectual activities also showed the fastest processing speed on cognitive tasks. These results appear to support "use it or lose it." However interpretation of results of this sort is muddied by a concern we introduced in Chapter 2: Correlation is not causation (Salthouse, 2006). The result *could* indicate that a high level of activity causes processing speed to remain relatively high. However, we must also consider the possibility that a smaller decline in processing speed allows some older adults to remain more active.

Even if it proves difficult to demonstrate that "using it" prevents "losing it," researchers have provided evidence that "using it more" can bring about better intellectual functioning. They have devised training programs that are able to reverse older adults' decline in some cognitive abilities (Schaie, 2005). Let's consider an intervention that had a positive impact on measures of fluid intelligence.

> Participants whose ages ranged from 60 to 75 were assigned either to an experimental or control group (Tranter & Koutstaal, 2008). Participants in the experimental group spent 10 to 12 weeks engaging in mentally stimulating tasks such as creative drawing activities and identification of mystery photographs; participants in the control group did not engage in special tasks. The researchers measured fluid intelligence both at the beginning of the experiment and again after the 10 to 12 week intervention. As the researchers predicted, participants in the experimental group showed greater gains in fluid intelligence compared to the control participants.

These results might encourage you to remain cognitively active across your life span. Meanwhile, if you're obtaining a college education you might already be giving yourself a long-term advantage. Research using fMRI scans has suggested that older adults with more education are better able to compensate for natural decline in their aging brains than are their less educated peers (Springer et al., 2005). There's another good reason to continue your education.

Many prominent figures, such as Nelson Mandela, continue to make important professional contributions through their 70s and beyond. How can some aspects of intellectual performance be kept from decline through late adulthood?

TABLE 10.3 Features of Wisdom

- *Rich factual knowledge.* General and specific knowledge about the conditions of life and its variations

- *Rich procedural knowledge.* General and specific knowledge about strategies of judgment and advice concerning life matters

- *Life span contextualism.* Knowledge about the contexts of life and their temporal (developmental) relationships

- *Uncertainty.* Knowledge about the relative indeterminacy and unpredictability of life and ways to manage it

We close this section by noting that there's one intelligence measure on which people show improvement over the life span. Psychologists have demonstrated age-related gains in **wisdom**— expertise in the fundamental practices of life (Baltes & Kunzmann, 2003; Baltes & Staudinger, 2000). **Table 10.3** presents some of the types of knowledge that define wisdom (Smith & Baltes, 1990). You can see that each type of knowledge is best acquired over a long and thoughtful life.

Memory A common complaint among the elderly is the feeling that their ability to remember things is not as good as it used to be. On a number of tests of memory, adults over 60 *do* perform worse than young adults in their 20s (Hess, 2005). People experience memory deficits with advancing age, even when they have been highly educated and otherwise have good intellectual skills (Zelinski et al., 1993). Aging does *not* seem to diminish elderly individuals' ability to access their general knowledge store and personal information about events that occurred long ago. In a study of name and face recognition, middle-aged adults could identify 90 percent of their high school classmates in yearbooks 35 years after graduation; older adults were still able to recognize 70 to 80 percent of their classmates some 50 years later (Bahrick et al., 1975). However, aging affects the processes that allow new information to be effectively organized, stored, and retrieved (Buchler & Reder, 2007).

As yet, researchers have been unable to develop a wholly adequate description of the mechanisms that underlie memory impairment in older adults—perhaps because the impairment has multiple sources (Hess, 2005). Some theories focus on differences between older and younger people in their efforts to organize and process information. Other theories point to elderly people's reduced ability to pay attention to information. Another type of theory looks to neurobiological changes in the brain systems that produce the physical memory traces. We explore those ideas in the *Psychology in Your Life* box. Note that these brain changes are not the same as the abnormal tangles of neural tissue and plaques that cause the memory loss of Alzheimer's disease (see Chapter 7). Researchers also believe that older adults' performance may be impaired by their very belief that their memory will be poor (Hess & Hinson, 2006).

---

wisdom Expertise in the fundamental pragmatics of life.

Researchers continue to evaluate the relative contributions of each of these factors.

Let's now narrow our focus from general cognitive development to the more specific topic of the acquisition of language.

STOP AND REVIEW

❶ In Piaget's theory, what is the relationship between assimilation and accommodation?

❷ What does it mean when a child is able to overcome centration?

❸ How has contemporary research modified conclusions about object permanence?

❹ What was the major emphasis of Lev Vygotsky's theory?

❺ What happens to processing speed across the life span?

CRITICAL THINKING Recall the experiment that looked at object permanence in 4-month-olds. Why was looking time an appropriate measure to test the researchers' hypothesis?

Visit MyPsychLab.com for more review and practice on the following topics:

- **Explore:** Piaget's Stages of Cognitive Development

- **Explore:** Learning, Categorizing, and Remembering in Infancy

Acquiring Language

Here's a remarkable fact: By the time they are 6 years old, children can analyze language into its units of sound and meaning, use the rules they have discovered to combine sounds into words and words into meaningful sentences, and take an active part in coherent conversations. Children's remarkable language accomplishments have prompted most researchers to agree that the ability to learn language is biologically based—that you are born with an innate language capacity (Tomasello, 2008). Even so, depending on where a child happens to be born, he or she may end up as a native speaker of any one of the world's 4,000 different languages. In addition, children are prepared to learn both spoken languages and gestural languages, like American Sign Language. This means that the innate predisposition to learn language must be both quite strong and quite flexible (Schick et al., 2006).

To explain how it is that infants are such expert language learners, we will describe the evidence that supports the claim of an innate language capacity. But we will also discuss the role that the environment plays—after all, children learn the particular languages that are being used in the world around them. **Table 10.4**, on page 314, outlines the various types of knowledge children must acquire for their particular signed or spoken language. You might review the language use section of Chapter 8 (pages 237–246) to remind yourself how adults put all these types of knowledge to use in fluent conversation.

PERCEIVING SPEECH AND PERCEIVING WORDS

Imagine you are a newborn child, hearing a buzz of noise all around you. How do you start to understand that some of those

Psychology in Your Life

WILL YOUR BRAIN WORK DIFFERENTLY AS YOU AGE?

If you've spent time with older adults, you've probably heard them make casual claims like, "My brain just doesn't work as well as it used to work." Researchers have believed for a long time that older brains function differently from younger brains. However, as brain-imaging techniques have become more available as research tools, an understanding of those changes has grown. Images of the brain at work reveal consistent differences in patterns of brain activity over the adult years.

Let's consider brain activity related to two tasks that should be roughly familiar from earlier chapters. One task assessed participants' ability to use working memory: They attempted to commit four words to working memory and then indicated whether a subsequent probe word had been among that original group. A second task assessed participants' ability to engage visual attention: They monitored a video display of the letter *B* to determine whether it had briefly disappeared zero, once, or two times over the course of a trial. The participants for the two tasks were younger adults (with an average age of 22.6 years) and older adults (with an average age of 70.3 years). The two groups were equally accurate on the two tasks, although the younger adults were faster.

The figure reveals the results of fMRI scans participants underwent as they performed each task (Cabeza et al., 2004). The colored areas are the regions that were most active for each task. What you can see, as indicated by the arrows, is that the older adults showed a pattern of brain activity in which both hemispheres of the brain were more active.

To understand these results, recall from Chapter 3 the finding that the brain's two hemispheres typically carry out different types of processes. The fMRI scans in the figure indicate that the brains of older adults become more symmetrical with respect to the functions in which they play a role (Cabeza, 2002). Researchers have offered two general explanations for this developmental change in the way that processes are distributed to the brain's two hemispheres. Some researchers have argued that when older brains recruit different areas from those used by younger brains, that activity represents *compensations* for other aging-related changes in the brain. Other researchers have argued that brain activation unique to older adults reflects *distraction*—an inability to inhibit unnecessary brain activity.

In fact, researchers have found evidence suggesting that both

compensation and distraction are at work in the aging brain. To provide evidence for compensation, a study using PET scans examined the relationship between individual differences in brain activity and recognition memory performance (Grady et al., 2005). As in earlier studies, older adults were likely to show activity in brain areas that were mostly not active for younger adults. Moreover, there was a positive correlation such that the *more* active those areas were, the *better* the older adults performed on recognition memory. That result supports the idea that the use of these brain areas yields an advantage for older adults. However, researchers have also carried out fMRI studies spanning several memory tasks to demonstrate that there are certain areas that older brains appear unable to turn off (Grady et al., 2006). The consistent appearance of brain activity that is not task relevant provides evidence that some age-related differences in brain function result in distraction from the task at hand.

This body of research supports the conclusion that your brain will, in fact, work differently as you age. The changes in function reflect compensation and distraction with respect to day-to-day cognitive tasks.

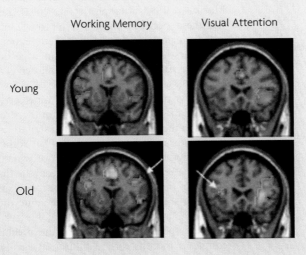

Working Memory   Visual Attention

Young

Old

From R. Cabeza et al., "Task-independent and task-specific age effects in brain activity during working memory, visual attention, and episodic retrieval," *Cerebral Cortex* (2004) *14*, 372. By permission of Oxford University Press, Inc.

TABLE 10.4 The Structure of Language

Grammar is the field of study that seeks to describe the way language is structured and used. It includes several domains:

Phonology—the study of the sounds that are put together to form words.

A **phoneme** is the smallest unit of speech that distinguishes between any two utterances. For example, *b* and *p* distinguish *bin* from *pin*.

Phonetics is the study and classification of speech sounds.

Syntax—the way in which words are strung together to form sentences. For example, subject *(I)* + verb *(like)* + object *(you)* is standard English word order.

A **morpheme** is the minimum distinctive unit of grammar that cannot be divided without losing its meaning. The word *bins* has two morphemes, *bin* and *s*, indicating the plural.

Semantics—the study of the meanings of words and their changes over time.

Lexical meaning is the dictionary meaning of a word. Meaning is sometimes conveyed by the *context* of a word in a sentence ("Run *fast*" versus "Make the knot *fast*") or the *inflection* with which it is spoken (try emphasizing different words in *white house cat*).

Pragmatics—rules for participation in conversations; social conventions for communicating, sequencing sentences, and responding appropriately to others.

Using principles of operant conditioning we described in Chapter 5, researchers condition infants to turn their head toward a sound source when they detect a change from one speech sound to another. The reward that reinforces this behavior is an illuminated box that contains a clapping and drumming toy animal. The procedure ensures that, if the children detect changes, they are very likely to turn toward the sound source. To measure the children's ability to perceive a distinction, researchers monitor how frequently the children turn their heads when a change is present.

Janet Werker and her colleagues (Werker, 1991; Werker & Lalond, 1988) have used this technique to examine the innate basis of speech perception abilities, a version of the /r/–/l/ question we posed earlier. Werker studied sound distinctions that are used in Hindi, but not in English—distinctions that make it difficult for adult English speakers to learn Hindi. Werker and her colleagues measured the ability of infants learning English or Hindi, as well as adults who spoke English or Hindi, to hear the differences between the Hindi phonemes. She found that all the infants, regardless of which language they were learning, could hear the differences until the age of 8 months. However, of the infants older than 8 months and of the adults, only the Hindi speakers or speakers-to-be could hear the Hindi contrasts.

Research of this type strongly suggests that you started out with an innate ability to perceive sound contrasts that are important for spoken languages. However, you swiftly lose the ability to perceive some of the contrasts that are not present in the language you begin to acquire (Werker & Tees, 1999).

Along with this biological head start for speech perception, many children also get an environmental head start. When adults in many cultures speak to infants and young children, they use a special form of language that differs from language addressed to adults. For example, when talking to infants and children, adults tend to slow down their rate of speech and use an exaggerated, high-pitched intonation; they tend to produce utterances that are shorter and have simpler structures (Soderstrom, 2007). Depending on the age of the child, researchers call the forms of speech either **infant-directed speech** or **child-directed speech.** The features that define infant- and child-directed speech appear in many but not all cultures (Fernald & Morikawa, 1993; Kitamura et al., 2002). Researchers suggest that these special forms of speech provide infants and children with information that makes them better able to acquire phonemes and words from the language being used around them (Fernald & Hurtado, 2006; Thiessen et al., 2005; Vallabha et al., 2007).

At what age are children able to perceive the repetition of patterns of sounds—words—within the stream of speech directed to them? This is the first big step toward acquiring language: You can't learn that *doggie* has something to do with the shaggy thing in the corner until you recognize that the sound pattern *doggie* seems to recur in that shaggy thing's presence. Infants, on average, appear to gain the insight that repeated sounds have significance somewhere between ages 6 and $7\frac{1}{2}$ months (Jusczyk, 2003; Jusczyk & Aslin, 1995). For one special word, however, the breakthrough comes a couple of months early: Children at age $4\frac{1}{2}$ months already show a recognition preference for their own names (Mandel et al., 1995)!

---

sounds are relevant to communicating with other people? A child's first step in acquiring a particular language is to take note of the sound contrasts that are used meaningfully in that language. (For signed languages, the child must attend to contrasts in hand positions, for example.) Each spoken language samples from the set of possible distinctions that can be produced by the human vocal tract; no language uses all of the speech–sound contrasts that can be made. The minimal meaningful units of speech that allow people to distinguish one word from another are called **phonemes.** There are about 45 distinct phonemes in English. Imagine you heard someone speak the words *right* and *light*. If you are a native speaker of English, you would have no trouble hearing the difference—/r/ and /l/ are different phonemes in English. If your only language experience was with Japanese, however, you would not be able to hear the difference between these two words because /r/ and /l/ are not distinct phonemes in Japanese. Do English speakers acquire the ability to make this distinction, or do Japanese speakers lose it?

To answer this type of question, researchers needed to develop methods to obtain linguistic information from prelinguistic children.

---

phoneme Minimal unit of speech in any given language that makes a meaningful difference in speech and production and reception; *r* and *l* are two distinct phonemes in English but variations of one in Japanese.

infant-directed speech A form of speech addressed to infants that includes slower speed, distinctive intonation, and structural simplifications.

child-directed speech A form of speech addressed to children that includes slower speed, distinctive intonation, and structural simplifications.

LEARNING WORD MEANINGS

Once you could detect the co-occurrence of sounds and experiences, you were prepared to start learning word meanings. There's no denying that children are excellent word learners. At around 18 months, children's word learning often takes off at an amazing rate. Researchers have called this phase the *naming explosion* because children begin to acquire new words, especially names for objects, at a rapidly increasing rate (see **Figure 10.8**). By the age of 6, the average child is estimated to understand 14,000 words (Templin, 1957). Assuming that most of these words are learned between the ages of 18 months and 6 years, this works out to about nine new words a day or almost one word per waking hour (Carey, 1978). Children have an ability that researchers call *fast mapping*: They are able to learn the meanings of new words with minimal experience—sometimes with only a single exposure to a word and its referent (Gershkoff-Stowe & Hahn, 2007). How is this possible?

Imagine a straightforward situation in which a child and her father are walking through a park and the father points and says, "That's a doggie." The child must decide to which piece of the world *doggie* applies. This is no easy feat (Quine, 1960). Perhaps *doggie* means "any creature with four legs" or "the animal's fur" or "the animal's bark" or any of the other large set of meanings that will be true each time someone points toward a dog. Given all the possibilities, how are children able to fix the meanings of individual words?

Researchers suggest that children act like scientists—developing *hypotheses* about what each new word might mean. You can, for example, see children's scientific minds actively at work when they *overextend* words, using them incorrectly to cover a wide range of objects. They may use the word *doggie* to refer to all animals or the word *moon* to refer to all round objects, including clocks and coins. Other times, children might *underextend* a word—believing, for example, that *doggie* refers only to their own family dog.

The view that children form hypotheses, however, does not explain how children acquire particular meanings in particular contexts. Researchers have suggested that children's hypotheses are guided by expectations such as the *principle of contrast*. This principle suggests that differences in *forms* signal differences in *meaning*: When children hear new words, they should look for meanings that contrast with those for the words they already know (Clark, 2003). Suppose, for example, a father and daughter are watching a TV scene in which a kangaroo is jumping. The child knows the word *jump* but not the word *kangaroo*. Suppose the parent says, "Kangaroo!" What might happen next? Because the child knows *jump*, she supposes that her parent would just say *jump* if *kangaroo* just meant "jump"—different forms should signal contrasts in meaning. The child can now hypothesize that *kangaroo* must label the object rather than the action. She is on her way to acquiring a meaning for *kangaroo*. If you've spent time around small children, you've probably noticed the principle of contrast at work. For example, a child will often become upset if his mother calls his fire *engine* a fire *truck!*

ACQUIRING GRAMMAR

To explain how children acquire meanings, we characterized children as scientists whose hypotheses are constrained by innate principles. We can use the same analogy to describe how children acquire the rules by which units of meaning are combined into larger units—in other words, grammar. The challenge for the child is that different languages follow different rules. For example, in English the typical ordering of units in a sentence is subject-verb-object, but in Japanese the ordering is subject-object-verb. Children must discover what order is present in the language being used around them. How do they do that?

Most researchers now believe that a large part of the answer resides in the human genome. Linguist **Noam Chomsky** (1965, 1975), for example, argued that children are born with mental structures that facilitate the comprehension and production of language. Some of the best evidence for such a biological basis for grammar comes from children who acquire complete grammatical structure in the absence of well-formed input. For example, researchers have studied deaf children whose hearing loss was sufficiently severe that they could not acquire spoken language but whose parents did not expose them to full-fledged signed languages such as American Sign Language (Goldin-Meadow, 2003). These children began to invent signing systems of their own and—despite the lack of environmental support for these invented languages—the gestural systems came to have regular, grammatical structure: "With or without an established language as a guide, children appear to be 'ready' to seek structure at least at word and sentence levels when developing systems for communication" (Goldin-Meadow & Mylander, 1990, p. 351).

But how can researchers go about specifying exactly what knowledge is innately given? The most productive approach to this question is to study language acquisition across many languages—*cross-linguistically*. By examining what is hard and what is easy for children to acquire across the world's many languages, researchers can determine what aspects of grammar are most likely to be supported by innate predispositions.

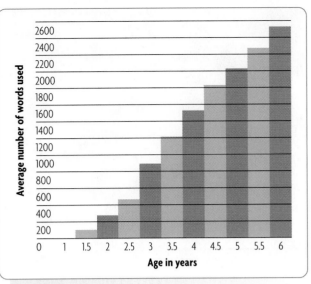

FIGURE 10.8 Children's Growth in Vocabulary
The number of words a child can use increases rapidly between the ages of 18 months and 6 years. This study shows children's average vocabularies at intervals of 6 months.

Children develop linguistic fluency by listening to the speech patterns of those around them. What are the roles of nature and nurture in the acquisition of grammar?

Here we arrive back at the child as scientist. Children bring innate constraints to the task of learning a particular language. **Dan Slobin** has defined these guidelines as a set of *operating principles* that together constitute the child's **language-making capacity.** According to Slobin's (1985) theory, the operating principles take the form of directives to the child. Here, for example, is an operating principle that helps children discover the words that go together to form a grammatical unit: "store together ordered sequences of word classes and functor classes that co-occur in the expression of a particular proposition type, along with a designation of the proposition type" (p. 1252). In simpler language, this operating principle suggests that children must keep track of the relationship between the order in which words appear and the meanings they express. Slobin derived the operating principles by summarizing across the data provided by a large number of other researchers, who examined a variety of different languages. We will use English examples to demonstrate the principles at work.

Consider what English-speaking children can do when they begin, at about age 2, to use combinations of words—the *two-word stage.* Children's speech at this point has been characterized as *telegraphic* because it is filled with short, simple sequences using mostly nouns and verbs. Telegraphic speech lacks function words, such as *the, and,* and *of,* which help express the relationships between words and ideas. For example, "Allgone milk" is a telegraphic message.

For adults to understand two-word utterances, they must know the context in which the words are spoken. "Tanya ball," for example, could mean, among other things, "Tanya wants the ball" or "Tanya throws the ball." Even so, children at the two-word stage show evidence that they have already acquired some knowledge of the grammar of English. Operating principles allow them to discover that word order is important in English and that the three critical elements are actor-action-object (subject-verb-object), arranged in that order. Evidence for this "discovery" comes when children misinterpret a sentence such as "Mary was followed by her little lamb to school" as *Mary* (actor) *followed* (action) *her lamb* (object) (see **Figure 10.9**). Over time, children must apply other operating principles to discover that there are exceptions to the actor-action-object rule.

Consider now an operating principle, which Slobin calls *extension,* that requires children to try to use the same unit of meaning, or *morpheme,* to mark the same concept. Examples of such concepts are possession, past tense, and continuing action. In English, each of these concepts is expressed by adding a grammatical morpheme to a content word, such as *-'s* (as in *Maria's*), *-ed* (as in *called*), and *-ing* (as in *laughing*). Note how the addition of each of these sounds to a noun or verb changes its meaning.

Children use operating principles like extension to form hypotheses about how these morphemes work. Because this principle requires that the child try to mark all cases in the same way, however, the error of **overregularization** often results. For example, once children learn the past-tense rule (adding *-ed* to the verb), they add *-ed* to all verbs, forming words such as *doed* and *breaked.* As children learn the rule for plurals (adding the sound *-s* or *-z* to the end of a word), they again overextend the rule, creating words such as *foots* and *mouses.* Overregularization is an especially interesting error because it usually appears *after* children have learned and used the correct forms of verbs and nouns. The children first use the correct verb forms (for example, *came* and *went*), apparently because they learned them as separate vocabulary items; but

---

language-making capacity The innate guidelines or operating principles that children bring to the task of learning a language.

overregularization A grammatical error, usually appearing during early language development, in which rules of the language are applied too widely, resulting in incorrect linguistic forms.

FIGURE 10.9 Acquiring Grammar
Many toddlers would interpret "Mary was followed by the lamb" and "Mary followed the lamb" to have identical meanings.

when they learn the general rule for the past tense, they extend it even to verbs that are exceptions to the rule—words that they previously used correctly. Over time, children use other operating principles to overcome this temporary overapplication.

Children's acquisition of language has a major impact on their ability to participate in social interactions. Keep them in mind as we shift our focus now to social development across the life span.

STOP AND REVIEW

❶ What are some ways in which infant- and child-directed speech differ from adult-directed speech?

❷ Why do children overextend word meanings?

❸ How does research with deaf children support the idea that aspects of grammar are innate?

❹ How would you notice when a child is overregularizing English past tense constructions?

CRITICAL THINKING Consider the study on children's ability to perceive sound distinctions. Why was it important to compare English-speaking adults with infants who are English speakers-to-be?

Visit MyPsychLab.com for more review and practice on the following topics:

👁 **Watch:** Stimulating Language Development

👁 **Watch:** Child-Directed Language

Social Development across the Life Span

We have seen so far how radically you change as a physical and cognitive being from birth to older adulthood. In this section of the chapter we explore **social development:** how individuals' social interactions and expectations change across the life span. We will see that social and cultural environment interacts with biological aging to provide each period of the life span with its own special challenges and rewards.

As we discuss social development, it is particularly important for you to consider the way in which culture and environment affect certain aspects of our lives. For example, people who live in circumstances of economic hardship undergo types of stresses that are absent from the "normal" course of development (Kohen et al., 2008; Scaramella et al., 2008). Current trends in the United States and in other countries throughout the world make it imperative for developmental psychologists to consider the difficult circumstances in which many children, adolescents, and adults are forced to live—circumstances that continually put their sanity, safety, and survival at risk (Huston, 2005). U.S. culture also enforces different outcomes for men and for women and for individuals who belong to minority groups. For example, in 2006 12 percent of women over 65 were living in poverty compared to 7 percent of men in this age range; 27 percent of African American women over 65 were living in poverty compared to 9 percent of White women over 65 (Federal Interagency Forum on Aging-Related Statistics, 2008).

These differences are direct products of structural inequities in contemporary U.S. society.

When we draw conclusions about the "average" life course, keep in mind that culture dictates that some individuals will depart from this average; as we describe the psychological challenges facing the "ordinary" individual, bear in mind that many individuals face extraordinary challenges. It is the role of researchers to document the impact of contemporary problems—and to design interventions to alleviate their harshest consequences.

As you read the remainder of this chapter, keep in mind how the tasks of life are jointly determined by a biological accumulation of years and a social accumulation of cultural experiences. To begin our discussion of social development, we will describe Erik Erikson's life span theory, which makes explicit the challenges and rewards in each of life's major periods.

ERIKSON'S PSYCHOSOCIAL STAGES

Erik Erikson (1902–1994), who was trained by Sigmund Freud's daughter, Anna Freud, proposed that every individual must successfully navigate a series of **psychosocial stages,** each of which presented a particular conflict or crisis. Erikson (1963) identified eight stages in the life cycle. At each stage, a particular crisis comes into focus, as shown in **Table 10.5** on page 318. Although each conflict never completely disappears, it needs to be sufficiently resolved at a given stage if an individual is to cope successfully with the conflicts of later stages.

Trust vs. Mistrust In Erikson's first stage, an infant needs to develop a basic sense of *trust* in the environment through interaction with caregivers. Trust is a natural accompaniment to a strong attachment relationship with a parent who provides food, warmth, and the comfort of physical closeness. But a child whose basic needs are not met, who experiences inconsistent handling, lack of physical closeness and warmth, and the frequent absence of a caring adult, may develop a pervasive sense of mistrust, insecurity, and anxiety.

Autonomy vs. Self-doubt With the development of walking and the beginnings of language, there is an expansion of a child's exploration and manipulation of objects (and sometimes people). With these activities should come a comfortable sense of *autonomy,* or independence, and of being a capable and worthy person. Excessive restriction or criticism at this second stage may lead instead to self-doubts, whereas demands beyond the child's ability, as in too-early or too-severe toilet training, can discourage the child's efforts to persevere in mastering new tasks.

Initiative vs. Guilt Toward the end of the preschool period, a child who has developed a basic sense of trust, first in the immediate environment and then in himself or herself, can now *initiate* both intellectual and motor activities. The ways that

---

social development The ways in which individuals' social interactions and expectations change across the life span.

psychosocial stage Proposed by Erik Erikson, one of the successive developmental stages that focus on an individual's orientation toward the self and others; these stages incorporate both the sexual and social aspects of a person's developmental and the social conflicts that arise from the interaction between the individual and the social environment.

parents respond to the child's self-initiated activities either encourage the sense of freedom and self-confidence needed for the next stage or produce guilt and feelings of being an inept intruder in an adult world.

Competence vs. Inferiority

During the elementary school years, the child who has successfully resolved the crises of the earlier stages is ready to go beyond random exploring and testing to the systematic development of *competencies*. School and sports offer arenas for learning intellectual and motor skills, and interaction with peers offers an arena for developing social skills. Successful efforts in these pursuits lead to feelings of competence. Some youngsters, however, become spectators rather than performers or experience enough failure to give them a sense of inferiority, leaving them unable to meet the demands of the next life stages.

Identity vs. Role Confusion

Erikson believed that the essential crisis of adolescence is discovering one's true *identity* amid the confusion created by playing many different roles for the different audiences in an

Erik Erikson's psychosocial stage model is a widely used tool for understanding human development over the life span. What crisis did Erikson suggest dominates individuals of your age?

expanding social world. Resolving this crisis helps the individual develop a sense of a coherent self; failing to do so adequately may result in a self-image that lacks a central, stable core.

Intimacy vs. Isolation The essential crisis for the young adult is to resolve the conflict between *intimacy* and *isolation*—to develop the capacity to make full emotional, moral, and sexual commitments to other people. Making that kind of commitment requires that the individual compromise some personal preferences, accept some responsibilities, and yield some degree of privacy and independence. Failure to resolve this crisis adequately leads to isolation and the inability to connect to others in psychologically meaningful ways.

Generativity vs. Stagnation The next major opportunity for growth, which occurs during adult midlife, is known as *generativity*. People in their 30s and 40s move beyond a focus on self and partner to broaden their commitments to family, work, society, and future generations. Those people who haven't resolved earlier developmental tasks are still self-indulgent, question past decisions and goals, and pursue freedom at the expense of security.

TABLE 10.5	Erikson's Psychosocial Stages		
Approximate Age	**Crisis**	**Adequate Resolution**	**Inadequate Resolution**
0–1½	Trust vs. mistrust	Basic sense of safety	Insecurity, anxiety
1½–3	Autonomy vs. self-doubt	Perception of self as agent capable of controlling own body and making things happen	Feelings of inadequacy to control events
3–6	Initiative vs. guilt	Confidence in oneself as initiator, creator	Feelings of lack of self-worth
6–puberty	Competence vs. inferiority	Adequacy in basic social and intellectual skills	Lack of self-confidence, feelings of failure
Adolescent	Identity vs. role confusion	Comfortable sense of self as a person	Sense of self as fragmented; shifting, unclear sense of self
Early adult	Intimacy vs. isolation	Capacity for closeness and commitment to another	Feeling of aloneness, separation; denial of need for closeness
Middle adult	Generativity vs. stagnation	Focus of concern beyond oneself to family, society, future generations	Self-indulgent concerns; lack of future orientation
Later adult	Ego integrity vs. despair	Sense of wholeness, basic satisfaction with life	Feelings of futility, disappointment

From *Childhood and Society* by Erik H. Erikson. Copyright © 1950, 1963 by W.W. Norton & Company, Inc., renewed © 1978, 1991 by Erik H. Erikson. Used with permission of W.W. Norton & Company, Inc.

Ego Integrity vs. Despair The crisis in later adulthood is the conflict between *ego integrity* and *despair*. Resolving the crises at each of the earlier stages prepares the older adult to look back without regrets and to enjoy a sense of wholeness. When previous crises are left unresolved, aspirations remain unfulfilled, and the individual experiences futility, despair, and self-depreciation.

You will see that Erikson's framework is very useful for tracking individuals' progress across the life span. We will begin with childhood.

SOCIAL DEVELOPMENT IN CHILDHOOD

Children's basic survival depends on forming meaningful, effective relationships with other people. **Socialization** is the lifelong process through which an individual's behavior patterns, values, standards, skills, attitudes, and motives are shaped to conform to those regarded as desirable in a particular society. This process involves many people—relatives, friends, teachers—and institutions—schools, houses of worship—that exert pressure on the individual to adopt socially approved values and standards of conduct. The family, however, is the most influential shaper and regulator of socialization. The concept of family itself is being transformed to recognize that many children grow up in circumstances that include either less (a single parent) or more (an extended household) than a mother, father, and siblings. Whatever the configuration, though, the family helps the individual form basic patterns of responsiveness to others—and these patterns, in turn, become the basis of the individual's lifelong style of relating to other people.

Temperament Even as infants begin the process of socialization, they do not all start at the same place. Children begin life with differences in **temperament**—biologically based levels of emotional and behavioral response to the environment (Thomas & Chess, 1977). Researcher **Jerome Kagan** and his colleagues have demonstrated that some infants are "born shy" and others are "born bold" (Kagan & Snidman, 2004). These groups of children differ in sensitivity to physical and social stimulation: The shy or *inhibited* babies are consistently "cautious and emotionally reserved when they confront unfamiliar persons or contexts"; the bold or *uninhibited* babies are consistently "sociable, affectively spontaneous, and minimally fearful in the same unfamiliar situations" (Kagan & Snidman, 1991, p. 40). In one sample, about 10 percent of the infants were inhibited and about 25 percent were uninhibited; the rest of the infants fell in between those end points (Kagan & Snidman, 1991). Researchers have begun to explore the genetic variations that bring about these temperamental differences (Rothbart, 2007).

Longitudinal studies have demonstrated the long-term impact of early temperament. Children who, at age 4 months, displayed inhibited and uninhibited temperaments continue to behave differently as they get older (Kagan & Snidman, 2004). At age 2, the inhibited children generally showed the most fear—and the uninhibited children the least fear—when they were faced with unfamiliar events. At age 4, the uninhibited children were considerably more likely to be sociable when interacting with unfamiliar children. However, not all children who start out at the extreme ends of the dimension of inhibited versus uninhibited remain at those extremes—some children become less shy or more bold as they age (Pfeifer et al., 2002). However, even when children's responses become less extreme, they very rarely shift from one category to the other. For example, a child who started out life as inhibited might become less shy over time, but he or she would rarely switch over to being a bold child.

Infant temperament sets the stage for later aspects of social development. Next, we consider the *attachment* bonds children form as their first social relationships.

Attachment Social development begins with the establishment of a close emotional relationship between a child and a mother, father, or other regular caregiver. This intense, enduring, social–emotional relationship is called **attachment.** Because children are incapable of feeding or protecting themselves, the earliest function of attachment is to ensure survival. In some species, the infant automatically becomes *imprinted* on the first moving object it sees or hears (Bolhuis & Honey, 1998). **Imprinting** occurs rapidly during a critical period of development and cannot easily be modified. The automaticity of imprinting can sometimes be problematic. Ethologist **Konrad Lorenz** demonstrated that young geese raised by a human imprint on the human instead of on one of their own kind. In nature, fortunately, young geese mostly see other geese first.

Konrad Lorenz, the researcher who pioneered the study of imprinting, graphically demonstrates what can happen when young animals become imprinted on someone other than their mother. Why is imprinting important for many animal species?

---

socialization The lifelong process whereby an individual's behavioral patterns, values, standards, skills, attitudes, and motives are shaped to conform to those regarded as desirable in a particular society.

temperament A child's biologically based level of emotional and behavioral response to environmental events.

attachment Emotional relationship between a child and the regular caregiver.

imprinting A primitive form of learning in which some infant animals physically follow and form an attachment to the first moving object they see and/or hear.

Why is it important for a child to develop a secure attachment to a parent or other caregiver?

You won't find human infants imprinting on their parents. Even so, **John Bowlby** (1973), an influential theorist on human attachment, suggested that infants and adults are biologically predisposed to form attachments. That attachment relationship has broad consequences. Beginning with Bowlby (1973), theorists have suggested that the experiences that give rise to an attachment relationship provide individuals with a lifelong schema for social relationships called an *internal working model* (Bretherton, 1996). An internal working model is a memory structure that gathers together a child's history of interactions with his or her caretakers, the interactions that yielded a particular pattern of attachment. The internal working model provides a template that an individual uses to generate expectations about future social interactions.

One of the most widely used research procedures for assessing attachment is the *Strange Situation Test,* developed by **Mary Ainsworth** and her colleagues (Ainsworth et al., 1978). In the first of several standard episodes, the child is brought into an unfamiliar room filled with toys. With the mother present, the child is encouraged to explore the room and to play. After several minutes, a stranger comes in, talks to the mother, and approaches the child. Next, the mother exits the room. After this brief separation, the mother returns, there is a reunion with her child, and the stranger leaves. The researchers record the child's behaviors at separation and reunion. Researchers have found that children's responses on this test fall into three general categories (Ainsworth et al., 1978):

- *Securely attached* children show some distress when the parent leaves the room; seek proximity, comfort, and contact upon reunion; and then gradually return to play.

---

parenting style The manner in which parents rear their children; an authoritative parenting style, which balances demandingness and responsiveness, is seen as the most effective.

- *Insecurely attached–avoidant* children seem aloof and may actively avoid and ignore the parent upon her return.
- *Insecurely attached–ambivalent/resistant* children become quite upset and anxious when the parent leaves; at reunion, they cannot be comforted, and they show anger and resistance to the parent but, at the same time, express a desire for contact.

In middle-class U.S. samples, about 70 percent of babies are classified as securely attached; among the insecurely attached children, about 20 percent are classified as avoidant and 10 percent as resistant. Cross-cultural research on attachment relationships—in countries as diverse as Sweden, Israel, Japan, and China—reveals reasonable consistency in the prevalence of types of attachments (van IJzendoorn & Kroonenberg, 1988). In every country, the majority of children are securely attached; most of the cultural differences occur with respect to the prevalence of different types of insecure attachments.

Categorizations based on the Strange Situation Test have proven to be highly predictive of a child's later behavior in a wider variety of settings, particularly the overall division between children who are securely and insecurely attached. For example, children who were securely attached at 12 months played more comfortably with their mothers at 24 months than did their insecurely attached peers (Donovan et al., 2007). Similarly, research has revealed that children who showed secure or insecure behavior in the Strange Situation at 15 months differed widely in their school behavior at age 8 to 9 years (Bohlin et al., 2000). Those children who had been securely attached at 15 months were more popular and less socially anxious than their peers who had been insecurely attached. Similar continuity from the quality of attachment to later years has been demonstrated in 10-year-olds (Urban et al., 1991) and adolescents (Weinfield et al., 1997). Researchers have also developed measures that assess attachment beyond infancy. Those measures also predict individual's social functioning (Shmueli-Goetz et al., 2008). In Chapter 16, we will see that researchers also use attachment measures to predict the quality of adults' loving relationships.

Attachment relationships are quite important in young lives. Secure attachment to adults who offer dependable social support enables the child to learn a variety of prosocial behaviors, to take risks, to venture into novel situations, and to seek and accept intimacy in personal relationships.

Parenting Styles As we noted earlier, children bring individual temperaments to their interactions with their parents. Children's temperaments may make parents' best (or worst) efforts at parenting have unexpected consequences. Researchers recognize that children's temperaments and parents' behaviors each influence the other to yield developmental outcomes such as the quality of attachment relationships: As much as parents change their children, children change their parents (Collins et al., 2000).

Even so, researchers have located a **parenting style** that is generally most beneficial. This style resides at the intersection of the two dimensions of *demandingness* and *responsiveness* (Maccoby & Martin, 1983): "Demandingness refers to the parent's willingness to act as a socializing agent, whereas responsiveness refers to the parent's recognition of the child's individuality" (Darling & Steinberg, 1993, p. 492). As shown in **Figure 10.10,** *authoritative* parents make appropriate demands on their children—they demand that their children conform to appropriate rules of behavior—but are also responsive to their

Critical Thinking in Your Life

HOW DOES DAY CARE AFFECT CHILDREN'S DEVELOPMENT?

If you plan to have both children and a career, you're likely to face a difficult question: Is it wise to put your children in day care? This is an issue that receives a lot of attention—with highly polarized views—in the popular press. To make this important judgment, you need to get beyond the false dichotomy of "day care is good" versus "day care is bad." Rather, you should formulate the more specific questions that allow you to put the decision in perspective. Let us suggest two of those questions: In what ways is day care better or worse for the developing child? What is the optimal form of day care?

To provide rigorous answers to questions of "better or worse," a team of researchers has been studying a group of 1,364 children since they were 1 month old; the children have now completed sixth grade (Belsky et al., 2007). Some children in the sample were tended by their mothers for the whole period before they started school; many others experienced various types of day care for small or large parts of each day. The research team's earliest publications focused on day care's impact on children's attachment security. The data indicated that children who attended day care were at risk for insecure attachments but only if it was also true that their mothers were insensitive to their needs (NICHD Early Child Care Research Network, 1997). Otherwise, children who attended day care had equally secure attachments as their peers who remained at home.

As the children have gotten older, the research team has measured both their intellectual and social development. Those studies have confirmed both positive and negative consequences of time spent in day care. On the positive side, the children who experienced day care have often performed better on standardized tests of, for example, memory and vocabulary (Belsky et al., 2007). On the negative side, the children who experienced day care have often had more social and behavior problems in their classrooms. However, the likelihood of social problems depends on the exact type of day care the child experienced. That's why data from this "better or worse" project informs the issue of what constitutes quality care for particular children.

Alison Clarke-Stewart (1993; Clarke-Stewart & Alhusen, 2005), an expert on day care, has summarized the research literature to provide a series of guidelines for quality day care. Some of her recommendations relate to the physical comfort of the children:

- The day care center should be physically comfortable and safe.

- There should be at least one caretaker for every six or seven children (more for children under age 3).

Other recommendations cover educational and psychological aspects of the day care curriculum:

- Children should have a free choice of activities intermixed with explicit lessons.

- Children should be taught social problem-solving skills.

Clarke-Stewart has also suggested that day care providers should share the qualities of good parents:

- Caregivers should be responsive to the children's needs and actively involved in their activities.

- Caregivers should not put undue restrictions on the children.

- Caregivers should have sufficient flexibility to recognize differences among the needs of individual children.

If these guidelines are followed, quality day care can be provided to all children whose parents work outside the home. As psychologists spread the message that day care does not harm, and may even enhance, children's development, parents should feel less distress about the necessity of a dual-career family. Such a reduction in stress could only improve the child's overall psychological environment.

- If you are trying to compare outcomes for children who do and do not participate in day care, on what dimensions should you try to match the children?

- How might you assess whether day care providers interact with children in appropriate ways?

---

children. They keep channels of communication open to foster their children's ability to regulate themselves (Gray & Steinberg, 1999). This authoritative style is most likely to produce an effective parent–child bond. The contrast, as seen in Figure 10.10, is to parenting styles that are *authoritarian*—parents apply discipline with little attention to the child's autonomy—or *indulgent*—parents are responsive, but they fail to help children learn about the structure of social rules in which they must live—or *neglecting*—parents neither apply discipline nor are they responsive to their children's individuality.

As you might expect, parenting styles have an impact on children's attachment relationships. Children whose parents use an authoritative style are more likely to be securely attached through childhood into adolescence (Karavasilis et al., 2003). In addition, research suggests that children's outcomes can improve when parenting improves. For example, one study followed over 1,000 children and their mothers from when the children were 15 months old until they began first grade (NICHD Early Child Care Research Network, 2006). The researchers assessed the children's attachment relationships

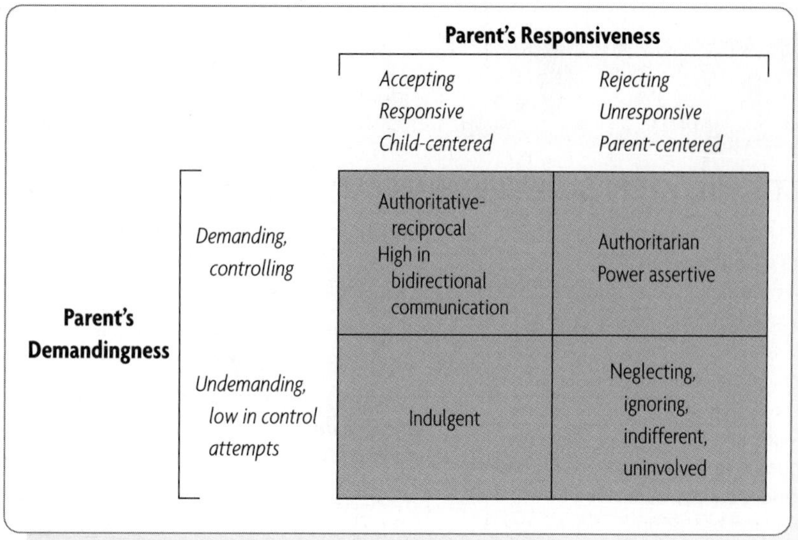

FIGURE 10.10 A Classification of Parenting Styles

Parenting styles can be classified with respect to the two dimensions of demandingness—the parent's willingness to act as a socializing agent—and responsiveness—the parent's recognition of the child's individuality. The authoritative style is most likely to produce an effective parent–child bond.

		Parent's Responsiveness	
		Accepting Responsive Child-centered	Rejecting Unresponsive Parent-centered
Parent's Demandingness	Demanding, controlling	Authoritative-reciprocal High in bidirectional communication	Authoritarian Power assertive
	Undemanding, low in control attempts	Indulgent	Neglecting, ignoring, indifferent, uninvolved

at 15 months in the Strange Situation. Evaluations of the mothers' parenting styles were based on videotapes of their interactions with their children. The researchers analyzed the videotapes to see whether the mothers' parenting styles changed over the course of the three-year project. In parallel to the studies we cited earlier, children who were identified as insecurely attached at 15 months had lower social competence and showed more behavior problems in first grade. However, changes in mothers' parenting style also had an impact on the fates of the insecurely attached children: When parenting quality improved, children's outcomes were consistently better than when parenting quality decreased. Results of this sort encourage researchers to design interventions to improve parenting practices (Van Zeijl et al., 2006).

A close interactive relationship with loving adults is a child's first step toward healthy physical growth and normal socialization. As the original attachment to the primary caregiver extends to other family members, they too become models for new ways of thinking and behaving. From these early attachments, children develop the ability to respond to their own needs and to the needs of others.

Contact Comfort and Social Experience What do children obtain from the attachment bond? Sigmund Freud and other psychologists argued that babies become attached to their parents because the parents provide them with food—their most basic physical need. This view is called the *cupboard theory* of attachment. If the cupboard theory were correct, children should thrive as long as they are adequately fed. Does this seem right?

Harry Harlow (1958) did not believe that the cupboard theory explained the importance of attachment. He set out to test the cupboard theory against his own hypothesis that infants might also attach to those who provide **contact comfort** (Harlow & Zimmerman, 1959). Harlow separated macaque monkeys from their mothers at birth and placed them in cages, where they had access to two artificial "mothers": a wire one and a terry cloth one. Harlow found that the baby monkeys nestled close to the terry cloth mother and spent little time on the wire one. They did this even when only the wire mother

gave milk! The baby monkeys also used the cloth mother as a source of comfort when frightened and as a base of operations when exploring new stimuli. When a fear stimulus (for example, a toy bear beating a drum) was introduced, the baby monkeys would run to the cloth mother. When novel and intriguing stimuli were introduced, the baby monkeys would gradually venture out to explore and then return to the terry cloth mother before exploring further.

Further studies by Harlow and his colleagues found that the monkeys' formation of a strong attachment to the mother substitute was not sufficient for healthy social development. At first, the experimenters thought the young monkeys with terry cloth mothers were developing normally, but a very different picture emerged when it was time for the female monkeys who had been raised in this way to become mothers. Monkeys who had been deprived of chances to interact with other responsive monkeys in their early lives had trouble forming normal social and sexual relationships in adulthood.

Let's see now what lessons research with monkeys holds for human deprivation.

Human Deprivation Tragically, human societies have sometimes created circumstances in which children are deprived of contact comfort. Many studies have shown that a lack of close, loving relationships in infancy affects physical growth and even survival. In 1915, a doctor at Johns Hopkins Hospital reported that, despite adequate physical care, 90 percent of the infants admitted to orphanages in Baltimore died within the first year. Studies of hospitalized infants over the next 30 years found that, despite adequate nutrition, the children often developed respiratory infections and fevers of unknown origin, failed to gain weight, and showed general signs of physiological deterioration (Bowlby, 1969; Spitz & Wolf, 1946).

Contemporary studies continue to demonstrate patterns of disruption. For example, one study compared attachment

---

contact comfort Comfort derived from an infant's physical contact with the mother or caregiver.

How did Harlow demonstrate the importance of contact comfort for normal social development?

outcomes for children raised at home to those for children largely (90 percent of their lives) raised in institutions (Zeanah et al., 2005). The researchers found that 74 percent of the home-reared children had secure attachments; for institution-reared children, only 20 percent had secure attachments. Moreover, a lack of normal social contact may have a long-lasting effect on children's brain development. One study compared a group of children who had spent about their first $1\frac{1}{2}$ years in orphanages to those who had been raised by their biological parents (Wismer Fries et al., 2005). At age $4\frac{1}{2}$, the two groups of children interacted with a stranger. The children who spent their earliest days in orphanages failed to show a normal pattern of brain response—as indicated by brain hormone levels— to the interaction with the stranger.

Unfortunately, no matter what the setting in which children live, there is a potential for abuse. In a recent analysis, the U.S. government found that 144,800 children experienced physical abuse in a single year, and roughly 80,000 experienced sexual abuse (U.S. Department of Health and Human Services, 2008). In one sample of 375 young adults, nearly 11 percent reported having endured some type of physical or sexual abuse. Of that group, about 80 percent presented symptoms of one or more psychiatric disorders (Silverman et al., 1996). Instances of child abuse provide psychologists with a very important agenda: to determine what types of interventions are in the best interest of the child. In the United States, roughly 513,000 children and youths have been removed from their homes and

placed in some type of foster care (such as a foster home or group residence) (Child Welfare Information Gateway, 2007). Are these children always happy to be removed from their abusive homes? The answer is complex because even abused children have often formed an attachment to their caretakers: The children may remain loyal to their natural family and hope that everything could be put right if they were allowed to return. This is one reason that much research attention is focused on designing intervention programs to reunite families (Miller et al., 2006).

In this section, you have seen how experiences during childhood have an impact on later social development. We will now shift our focus to later periods of life, beginning with adolescence.

SOCIAL DEVELOPMENT IN ADOLESCENCE

Earlier in the chapter, we defined adolescence by physical changes. In this section, those changes will serve as background to social experiences. Because the individual has reached a certain level of physical and mental maturity, new social and personal challenges present themselves. We will first consider the general experience of adolescence and then turn to the individual's changing social world.

The Experience of Adolescence The traditional view of adolescence predicts a uniquely tumultuous period of life, characterized by extreme mood swings and unpredictable, difficult behavior: "storm and stress." This view can be traced back to romantic writers of the late 18th and early 19th centuries, such as Goethe. The storm-and-stress conception of adolescence was strongly propounded by **G. Stanley Hall,** the first psychologist of the modern era to write at length about adolescent development (1904). Following Hall, the major proponents of this view have been psychoanalytic theorists working within the Freudian tradition (for example, Blos, 1965; Freud, 1946, 1958). Some of them have argued that not only is extreme turmoil a normal part of adolescence but that failure to exhibit such turmoil is a sign of arrested development. **Anna Freud** wrote that "to be normal during the adolescent period is by itself abnormal" (1958, p. 275).

Two early pioneers in cultural anthropology, **Margaret Mead** (1928) and **Ruth Benedict** (1938), argued that the storm-and-stress theory is not applicable to many non-Western cultures. They described cultures in which children gradually take on more and more adult responsibilities without any sudden stressful transition or period of indecision and turmoil. Contemporary research has confirmed that the experience of adolescence differs across cultures (Arnett, 1999). Those cross-cultural differences argue against strictly biological theories of adolescent experience. Instead, researchers focus on the transitions children are expected to make in different cultures.

Most researchers reject "storm and stress" as a biologically programmed aspect of development. Nonetheless, people typically do experience more extreme emotions and more conflict as they pass from childhood into adolescence. When we discussed physical development we noted that brain areas that control emotional responses show growth during adolescence. That brain maturation may explain why adolescents experience both extreme positive and extreme negative emotions (Casey et al., 2008; Steinberg, 2008). You can understand the conflicts adolescents have with their parents if you recall Erikson's claim that the essential task of adolescence is to discover one's true identity. For cultures like the majority culture in the United States, one consequence is that children attempt to achieve *independence* from their parents. Parents and their adolescent children must weather a transition in their relationship from one in which a parent has unquestioned authority to one in which the adolescent is granted reasonable independence to make important decisions (Allen & Land, 1999; Holmbeck & O'Donnell, 1991). Consider the results of a study that followed 1,330 adolescents from age 11 to age 14 (McGue et al., 2005). As 14-year-olds, these adolescents reported greater conflict with their parents than they had at age 11. At age 14, the adolescents' parents were less involved in their lives; the adolescents had less positive regard for their parents and they believed that their parents had less positive regard for them. These data illustrate some of the relationship costs that arise when children strive for independence.

Still, adolescents' conflicts with their parents often do not lead to harmful outcomes. Most adolescents at most times are able to use their parents as ready sources of practical and emotional support (Smetana et al., 2006). For that reason, many adolescents have conflicts with their parents that leave their basic relationship unharmed. When conflict occurs in the context of otherwise positive relationships, there may be few negative consequences. However, in the context of negative relationships, adolescent conflict can lead to other problems such as social withdrawal and delinquency (Adams & Laursen, 2007). Thus, family contexts may explain why some adolescents experience unusual levels of "storm and stress."

Now that we've considered the general adolescent experience, let's turn to the increasing importance of peers in adolescents' social experience.

Peer Relationships Much of the study of social development in adolescence focuses on the changing roles of family (or adult caretakers) and friends (Smetana et al., 2006). We have already seen that attachments to adults form soon after birth. Children also begin to have friends at very young ages. Adolescence, however, marks the first period in which peers appear to compete with parents to shape a person's attitudes and behaviors. Adolescents participate in peer relations at the three levels of friendships, cliques, and crowds (Brown & Klute, 2003). Over the course of these years, adolescents come to count increasingly on their one-on-one *friendships* to provide them with help and support (Bauminger et al., 2008; Branje et al., 2007). *Cliques* are groups that most often consist of 6 to 12 individuals. Membership in these groups may change over time, but they tend to be drawn along lines of, for example, age and race (Smetana et al., 2006). Finally, *crowds* are the larger groups such as "jocks" or "nerds" that exist more loosely among individuals of this age. Through interaction with peers at these three levels, adolescents gradually define the social component of their developing identities, determining the kinds of people they chose to be and the kinds of relationships they choose to pursue.

The peer relationships that adolescents form are quite important to social development. They give individuals opportunities to learn how to function in what can often be

demanding social circumstances. In that sense, peer relationships play a positive role in preparing adolescents for their futures. At the same time, parents often worry—with reasonable cause—about negative aspects of peer influence. We noted earlier that adolescents are likely to engage in risky behavior. That tendency increases when adolescents are under the influence of their peers.

> To study developmental changes in peer influence, researchers recruited three groups of participants: Adolescents (age 13 to 16), young adults (ages 18 to 22), and adults (ages 24 and older) (Gardner & Steinberg, 2005). Participants in each age range played a video game called "Chicken." In this game, players act as drivers. They must decide how soon to stop their car when a light changes from green to yellow. Their goal is to achieve as much distance as they can before the light turns red and a wall pops up. If they don't stop in time, they'll crash into the wall. About half of the participants played the game alone. The other half played in groups of three—each participant played in turn while the other two watched. **Figure 10.11** presents the results of the experiment. As you can see, adolescents were far more likely to engage in risky driving (within the context of the video game) when in the presence of their peers.

This study confirms a general tendency for adolescents to demonstrate peer influence as a shift toward riskier behaviors. However, some adolescents are more susceptible to peer influence than others—and that susceptibility has consequences. In a longitudinal study, students who were more susceptible to their close friends' influence at the study's outset were more likely to have problems with drugs and alcohol 1 year later (Allen et al., 2006). We note, once again, that adolescence need not be a time of storm and stress. However, research of this type indicates the patterns of behavior that indicate some adolescents are at risk.

SOCIAL DEVELOPMENT IN ADULTHOOD

Erikson defined two tasks of adulthood as intimacy and generativity. Freud identified the needs of adulthood as *Lieben und Arbeiten,* or love and work. Abraham Maslow (1968, 1970) described the needs of this period of life as love and belonging, which, when satisfied, develop into the needs for success and esteem. Other theorists label these needs as affiliation or social acceptance and achievement or competence needs. The shared core of these theories is that adulthood is a time in which both social relationships and personal accomplishments take on special priority. In this section, we will track these themes across the breadth of adulthood.

Intimacy Erikson described **intimacy** as the capacity to make a full commitment to another person. Intimacy, which can occur in both friendships and romantic relationships, requires openness, courage, ethical strength, and usually some compromise of one's personal preferences. Research has consistently confirmed Erikson's supposition that social intimacy is a prerequisite for a sense of psychological well-being across the adult life stages (Kesebir & Diener, 2008). In Chapters 11 and 16, we

---

intimacy The capacity to make a full commitment—sexual, emotional, and moral—to another person.

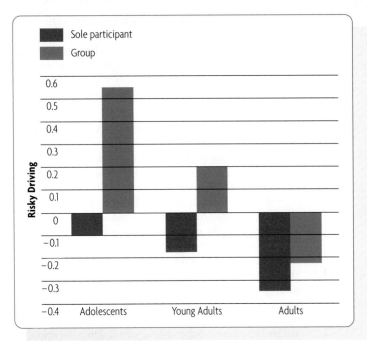

Sole participant
Group

Risky Driving (y-axis: 0.6, 0.5, 0.4, 0.3, 0.2, 0.1, 0, −0.1, −0.2, −0.3, −0.4)

Adolescents   Young Adults   Adults

FIGURE 10.11   Peer Influence on Risky Behavior

Adolescents, young adults, and adults played a video game called "Chicken" by themselves or in a group setting. The video game allowed participants to take risks while driving. The *y*-axis plots a measure of risky driving: Larger positive scores indicate higher risk. Adolescents showed the largest impact of the presence of peers.

From Margo Gardner and Laurence Steinberg, "Peer Influence on Risk Taking, Risk Preference, and Risky Decision Making in Adolescence and Adulthood: An Experimental Study," *Developmental Psychology, 41*(4), 625–635. Copyright © 1997 by the American Psychological Association. Reprinted with permission.

discuss the forces that affect people's particular choices for friends, romantic partners, and sexual partners. Here, we focus on the role intimate relationships play in social development.

Young adulthood is the period in which many people enter into marriages or other stable relationships. In 2007, 14.7 percent of 20- to 24-year-olds were married; among 25- to 29-year-olds that figure increased to 41.2 percent (U.S. Census Bureau, 2008b). In addition, many other individuals live with partners to whom they are not married. In 2007, 4.9 percent of U.S. households had opposite-sex partners, and 0.7 percent of households had same-sex partners (U.S. Census Bureau, 2008a). In recent years, some states have allowed same-sex couples to enter into civil commitments or legal marriages. Researchers try to understand the consequences of all these types of relationships for social development in adulthood. For example, research attention has focused on differences and similarities between heterosexual and homosexual couples (Balsam et al., 2008; Roisman et al., 2008). Studies suggest that the strategies heterosexuals and homosexuals use to maintain relationships over time have much in common: Both types of couples try to remain close by, for example, sharing tasks and activities together (Haas & Stafford, 2005). However, heterosexual couples obtain more societal support for their relationships (Herek, 2006). To combat a lack of social acceptance, homosexual couples often take special measures to maintain relationships, such as being publicly "out" as a couple.

Each of these types of relationships increases the role of family in adults' social lives. Families also grow when individuals decide to include children in their lives. What may surprise you, however, is that the birth of children can often pose a threat to the overall happiness of a couple (Lawrence et al., 2007; Twenge et al., 2003). Why might that be? Researchers have focused on differences in the way that men and women make the transition to parenthood in heterosexual relationships (Cowan & Cowan, 2000). In contemporary Western society,

marriages are more often founded on notions of equality between men and women than was true in the past. However, children's births can have the effect of pushing husbands and wives in the direction of more traditional gender roles. The wife may feel too much of the burden of child care; the husband may feel too much pressure to support a family. The net effect may be that, following the birth of a child, the marriage changes in ways that both spouses find to be negative. In recent years, researchers have begun to study gay male and lesbian couples raising children. As you might expect, homosexual relationships are less troubled by concerns about gender roles in the context of parenting (Goldberg & Perry-Jenkins, 2007; Patterson, 2002). Even so, in parallel to results for heterosexual couples, a study of lesbian couples found decreasing love and increasing conflict across the transition to parenthood (Goldberg & Sayer, 2006).

For many couples, satisfaction with the marriage continues to decline because of conflicts as the child or children pass through their adolescent years. Contrary to the cultural stereotype, many parents look forward to the time when their youngest child leaves home and leaves them with an "empty nest" (Dennerstein et al., 2002; White & Edwards, 1990). Parents may enjoy their children most when they are no longer under the same roof (Levenson et al., 1993). Have we discouraged you from having children? We certainly hope not! Our goal, as always, is to make you aware of research that can help you anticipate and interpret the patterns in your own life.

You've now learned that marriages are happier, on the whole, when the spouses reach late adulthood. However, you're certainly aware that many marriages end in divorce long before late adulthood arrives. Researchers would like to be able to determine which couples are fundamentally mismatched and which couple could avoid divorce (Orbuch et al., 2002; Story & Bradbury, 2004). Let's consider a longitudinal study that examined factors that preceded the divorces of several hundred couples.

Statistically speaking, which spouse is likely to outlive the other? What effect might the quality of the marriage have on this outcome?

The researchers obtained information from 4,460 couples in 1987–1988 and then again in 1992–1994 (Amato & Hohmann-Marriott, 2007). In that period of time, 509 of the couples had divorced or separated. To understand why relationships had ended, the researchers examined data from the study's outset. Participants had reported on their marital quality (such as their happiness with the relationship and the amount of conflict in the relationship). They also reported on their commitment to the marriage (for example, their barriers to leaving the marriage or their alternatives to the marriage). The researchers' analyses revealed two clusters of people who ended relationships. One cluster had been in *high-distress* relationships in 1987–1988. They had reported low-quality relationships, which they brought to an end. Couples in the other cluster had been *low-distress* relationships. Their marriage quality was about average. So why did they divorce? These couples had low barriers to ending the marriage and attractive alternatives beyond it.

These results suggest why you cannot always predict which couples are headed for divorce based on surface aspects of the relationships such as open conflict. When people have other alternatives, they may end relationships in which they are at least moderately happy.

Let's conclude this section where we began, with the idea that social intimacy is a prerequisite for psychological well-being. What matters most is not the quantity of social interaction but the quality (particularly, in U.S. culture, for women). As you grow into older adulthood, you will begin to protect your need for intimacy by selecting those individuals who provide the most direct emotional support.

Let's turn now to a second aspect of adult development, generativity.

Generativity Those people who have established an appropriate foundation of intimate relationships are most often able to turn their focus to issues of **generativity.** This is a commitment beyond oneself to family, work, society, or future generations—typically a crucial step in development in one's 30s and 40s (McAdams & de St. Aubin, 1998). An orientation toward the greater good allows adults to establish a sense of psychological well-being that offsets any longing for youth.

George Vaillant studied the personality development of 95 highly intelligent men through interviews and observations over a 30-year period following their graduation from college in the mid-1930s. Many of the men showed great changes over time, and their later behavior was often quite different from their behavior in college. The interviews covered the topics of physical health, social relationships, and career achievement. At the end of the 30-year period, the 30 men with the best outcomes and the 30 with the worst outcomes were identified and compared (see **Table 10.6**). By middle life, the best-outcome men were carrying out generativity tasks, assuming responsibility for others, and contributing in some way to the world. Their maturity even seemed to be associated with the adjustment of their children—the more mature fathers were better able to give children the help they needed in adjusting to the world (Vaillant, 1977).

This study illustrates the prerequisites for generativity: For the best-outcome men, other aspects of their lives were sufficiently stable to allow them to direct their resources outwards, toward generations to come. When asked what it means to be well

TABLE 10.6 Differences between Best- and Worst-Outcome Subjects on Factors Related to Psychosocial Maturity		
	Best Outcomes (30 Men)	**Worst Outcomes (30 Men)**
Personality integration rated in bottom fifth percentile during college	0%	33%
Dominated by mother in adult life	0	40
Bleak friendship patterns at 50	0	57
Failure to marry by 30	3	37
Pessimism, self-doubt, passivity, and fear of sex at 50	3	50
Childhood environment poor	17	47
Current job has little supervisory responsibility	20	93
Subjects whose career choice reflected identification with father	60	27
Children's outcome described as good or excellent	66	23

generativity A commitment beyond one's self and one's partner to family, work, society, and future generations; typically, a crucial state in development in one's 30s and 40s.

adjusted, middle-aged adults (average age 52) and older adults (average age 74) gave the same response as their most frequent answer. Both groups suggested that adjustment relies on being "others oriented"—on being a caring, compassionate person and having good relationships (Ryff, 1989). This is the essence of generativity.

Let us also note that most older adults looking back on their lives do so with a degree of well-being that is unchanged from earlier years of adulthood (Carstensen & Freund, 1994). As we have seen with respect to social relationships, late adulthood is a time when goals are shifted; priorities change when the future does not apparently flow as freely. Across that change in priorities, however, older adults preserve their sense of the value of their lives. Erikson defined the last crisis of adulthood to be the conflict between ego integrity and despair. The data suggest that few adults look back over their lives with despair. Most older adults review their lives—and look to the future—with a sense of wholeness and satisfaction.

We have worked our way through the life span by considering social and personal aspects of childhood, adolescence, and adulthood. To close out the chapter, we will trace two particular domains in which experience changes over time, the domains of sex and gender differences and moral development.

STOP AND REVIEW

❶ At what life stage did Erik Erikson suggest people navigate the crisis of intimacy versus isolation?

❷ What long-term consequences have been demonstrated for children's early attachment quality?

❸ What dimensions define parenting styles?

❹ In what levels of peer relationships do adolescents engage?

❺ What impact does the birth of a child often have on marital satisfaction?

CRITICAL THINKING Recall the study that examined risk-taking in a video game. Why was it important that all three group members had a turn at the game?

Visit MyPsychLab.com for more review and practice on the following topic:

✳ **Simulate:** Baumrind's Parenting Styles

Sex and Gender Differences

One type of information most children begin to acquire in the first few months in life is that there are two categories of people in their social world: males and females. Over time, children learn that there are many respects in which the psychological experiences of males and females are quite similar. However, when differences do occur, children acquire an understanding that some of those differences arise from biology and others arise from cultural expectations. Biologically based characteristics that distinguish males and females are referred to as **sex**

differences. These characteristics include different reproductive functions and differences in hormones and anatomy. However, the first differences children perceive are entirely social: They begin to sense differences between males and females well before they understand anything about anatomy. In contrast to biological sex, **gender** is a psychological phenomenon referring to learned sex-related behaviors and attitudes. Cultures vary in how strongly gender is linked to daily activities and in the amount of tolerance for what is perceived as cross-gender behavior. In this section, we consider both sex differences and gender development: the nature and nurture of children's sense of maleness or femaleness.

SEX DIFFERENCES

Starting at about six weeks after conception, male fetuses begin to diverge from female fetuses when the male testes develop and begin to produce the hormone *testosterone*. The presence or absence of testosterone plays a critical role in determining whether a child will be born with male or female anatomy. Testosterone also has an impact on brain development: Experiments with nonhuman animals have demonstrated that sex differences in neural structure are largely brought about by this hormone (Morris et al., 2004).

The exact role of testosterone is less clear for the development of the human brain. However, brain scans have revealed consistent structural differences between men's and women's brains (Goldstein et al., 2001). Men typically have bigger brains than women—appropriate comparisons across the sexes adjust for that overall variation. The differences that remain after those adjustments are intriguing with respect to behavioral dissimilarities between men and women. For example, MRI scans reveal that the regions of the frontal lobe that play an important role in regulating social behavior and emotional functioning are relatively bigger in women than in men (Gur et al., 2002). To confirm that sex differences of this type are biological—rather than the product of a lifetime of experience as men or women in particular cultural roles—researchers have undertaken similar studies with children and adolescents (Lenrout et al., 2007). Those studies confirm that sex differences emerge in the brain as a part of ordinary biological development.

Other analyses of sex differences focus on the distinct ways in which men's and women's brains accomplish cognitive and emotional tasks (Kimura, 1999). Consider the brain processes engaged when the two sexes view emotionally charged pictures.

Twelve men and twelve women underwent fMRI scans while viewing 96 pictures that ranged from neutral (for example, a book or a fork) to negative (for example, an autopsy or a gravestone) (Canli et al., 2002a). As the participants viewed the pictures, they provided ratings of the intensity of their emotional experience on a scale ranging from 0 ("not emotionally intense at all") to 3 ("extremely emotionally intense"). Three weeks after this initial experience, the participants completed a test of recognition

---

sex difference One of the biologically based characteristics that distinguish males from females.

gender A psychological phenomenon that refers to learned sex-related behaviors and attitudes of males and females.

How do parents and peers influence children's acquisition of gender roles?

memory for the pictures—they had not been warned when they first viewed the pictures that this test was forthcoming. The researchers assessed the relationship between brain activity at the time of encoding and subsequent memory performance. They found distinct patterns of activity for men and for women. For example, greater activity in the left amygdala (see Chapter 3) preceded recognition success for women; greater activity in the right amygdala preceded success for men.

Further studies of the brain at work confirm sex differences in the encoding and recognition of emotionally arousing stimuli (Cahill et al., 2004). These studies suggest that some of the behavioral differences that set men and women apart can be traced to biological differences rather than to cultural roles.

Most research on the biology of sex differences with human subjects focuses on global differences between men and women. However, researchers have recently begun to look at the biological origins of more fine-grained differences among individuals. These studies turn once again to the impact of the hormone testosterone on later development. In this case, the researchers determined the level of testosterone in the amniotic fluid of each individual participant. The researchers correlated those fetal testosterone levels with, for example, the quality of each boy's or girl's social relationships when they were 4 years old (Knickmeyer et al., 2005). In general, boys had higher levels of fetal testosterone than girls. Against that background, individuals' higher levels of fetal testosterone were associated with poorer social relationships for both boys and girls. These results suggest that the extent to which individuals conform to expectations for male and female behavior may depend, in part, on their prenatal hormonal environment (Morris et al., 2004).

gender identity One's sense of maleness or femaleness; usually includes awareness and acceptance of one's biological sex.

gender stereotype Belief about attributes and behaviors regarded as appropriate for males and females in a particular culture.

GENDER IDENTITY AND GENDER STEREOTYPES

You have just seen that important aspects of men's and women's behavior are shaped by biological differences. However, cultural expectations also have an important impact on **gender identity**—an individual's sense of maleness or femaleness. Very early in life, children start to understand that the world is divided into two genders (Martin & Ruble, 2004; Martin et al., 2002). For example, 10- to 14-month-old children already demonstrate a preference for a video showing the abstract movements of a child of the same sex (Kujawski & Bower, 1993). In their earliest years, children begin to understand that they are either boys or girls—they settle into their gender identity. At the same time, they acquire knowledge of **gender stereotypes,** which are beliefs about attributes behaviors regarded as appropriate for males and females in a particular culture.

Researchers have documented the time course with which most children acquire those gender stereotypes (Martin & Ruble, 2004). Through the preschool years, children's experience in the world provides them with knowledge about cultural expectations for men and women. Between ages 5 and 7, children consolidate that knowledge into gender stereotypes. In fact, those are the years of the children's greatest rigidity with respect to those stereotypes. For example, one study assessed children's gender stereotypes by asking them to indicate which children "like to play toy shop" or "are cruel and hurt others on purpose" (Trautner et al., 2005). For each statement, children dropped cards into different boxes that represented *only males, more males than females, equal numbers of males and females, more females than males,* or *only females.* Children of ages 5 to 7 gave the most "only" responses, indicating the strongest gender stereotypes. Older children showed more flexibility in their thinking about gender and behavior. That is, they were more likely to indicate that both males and females engage in a variety of behaviors. Thus, by around age 8, children have begun to understand that there are also similarities between boys and girls.

How do children acquire the information that leads to gender identity and gender stereotypes? Parents provide one ready source. Parents dress their sons and daughters differently, give them different kinds of toys to play with, and communicate with them differently. When parents play with their children, they consider some toys to be "masculine" and some to be "feminine." When they play with their children, they are more likely to choose gender-appropriate toys—though that preference may be stronger for play with boys than for play with girls (Wood et al., 2002). In general, children receive encouragement from their parents to engage in sex-typed activities (McHale et al., 2003).

Peers provide another important sources of gender socialization. **Eleanor Maccoby** (2002) argues, for example, that young children are segregationists—they seek out peers of the same sex even when adults are not supervising them or in spite of adult encouragement for mixed-group play. Maccoby believes that many of the differences in gender behavior among children are the results of peer relationships. In fact, boys and girls show consistent differences in their patterns of social interaction. Some differences relate to the structure of those interactions. For example, at least by the age of 6, boys prefer to interact in groups, whereas girls prefer one-on-one interactions (Benenson et al., 1997; Benenson & Heath, 2006). Other differences between boys and girls relate to the content of their play (Rose & Rudolph, 2006). Girls are more likely than boys to engage in social conversations and disclose information about themselves. Boys are more likely than girls to engage in rough-and-tumble play. These differences become more prominent as children grow older.

We have been describing factors that affect gender development across all children. However, as with other domains of development, it's important to acknowledge individual differences among children. Consider a study that examined children's gender-typed behaviors over a six-year period.

The mothers of 5,501 children provided information about their gender-typed behaviors when the children were aged $2\frac{1}{2}$ (Golombok et al., 2008). The mothers completed the *Preschool Activities Inventory* (PSAI), which asked them to indicate, for example, how often their children had played with jewelry or engaged in fighting in the last month. The mothers provided PSAI ratings again when their children were $3\frac{1}{2}$ and 5 years old. When the children were 8, they reported their own behavior by completing the *Children's Activities Inventory* (CAI). For this inventory, children listened to pairs of statements that described different types of children: "Some children play with jewelry . . . . but other children don't play with jewelry" (p. 1586). The children indicated how similar they felt to the two types of children. Based on these longitudinal assessments, the researchers concluded that the likelihood that individual children will engage in gender-typed behavior remains very stable over time. For example, **Figure 10.12** plots children's PSAI scores at age $3\frac{1}{2}$ against their CAI scores at age 8. You can see a strong match between children's scores at the two ages.

Why is the children's behavior so stable? The researchers pointed to both nature and nurture. With respect to nature, the researchers suggested that children may experience prenatal environments that cause their brains to be relatively more masculine or feminine. With respect to nurture, the researchers considered differences among the behaviors of both parents and peers. Parents who have less flexible gender

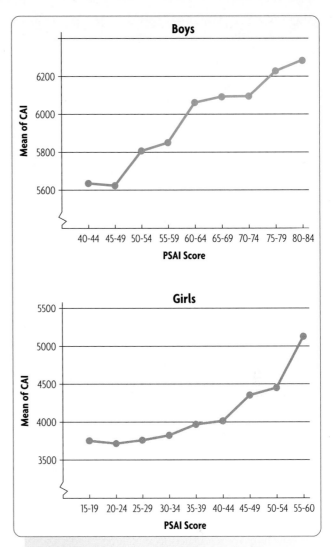

FIGURE 10.12 The Stability of Gender-Typed Behavior over Time

Mothers indicated children's gender-typed behavior on the PSAI at age $3\frac{1}{2}$, and children indicated their own behaviors at age 8. For each group of children who scored in a particular PSAI range at age $3\frac{1}{2}$; (with lower scores indicated more stereotypically feminine behavior), the researchers calculated their mean CAI value at age 8. The plot shows that children's levels of gender-typed behavior were quite similar at the two points in time.

From Golombok, S., Rust, J., Zervoulis, K., Croudace, T., Golding J., & Hines, M. Developmental trajectories of sex-typed behavior in boys and girls: A longitudinal general population study of children aged 2.5–8 yrs. *Child Development*. Copyright © 2008 by Blackwell Publishing, Ltd. Reprinted with permission.

stereotypes may also have children who produce more gender-typed behavior. In addition, children may seek friends who are similar to them with respect to their levels of gender-typed behavior—creating a context for those behaviors to be stable over time.

We have briefly considered how and why it is that boys and girls experience social development in different fashions. Let's now consider moral development.

❶ What is the distinction between sex differences and gender differences?

❷ What does research suggest about differences between men and women for the processing of emotional stimuli?

❸ In what ways are young children "segregationists"?

CRITICAL THINKING Recall the experiment that examined children's understanding of sex differences. Why might the researchers have identified Chris or Pat specifically as a 10-year-old?

Visit MyPsychLab.com for more review and practice on the following topic:

👁 **Watch:** Early Gender Typing

Moral Development

So far we have seen, across the life span, how important it is to develop close social relationships. Let's now consider another aspect of what it means to live as part of a social group: On many occasions you must judge your behavior according to the needs of society, rather than just according to your own needs. This is the basis of *moral behavior*. **Morality** is a system of beliefs, values, and underlying judgments about the rightness or wrongness of human acts.

Before we consider how moral development unfolds for each individual, we want to consider the question for the whole human species: How did morality evolve? To answer that question, contemporary researchers have built on Charles Darwin's foundational observations about how humans function as a social species (Krebs, 2008). From an evolutionary perspective, moral behaviors are consequences of adaptive solutions to situations that have recurred across human history. For example, many early human endeavors (such as killing large game or defending territory) required cooperation among large groups of people. Thus, it was adaptive for humans to evolve a disposition "to resolve fundamental social dilemmas in cooperative ways" (Krebs, p. 154). In contemporary times, moral questions often have a dimension of self-interested versus cooperative behavior: Should a person drive his or her car less so that everyone can breathe cleaner air? The evolutionary perspective suggests that our reflexive responses to such questions is part of our genetic inheritance (Haidt, 2007).

However, even if people share some evolved moral responses, what constitutes moral and immoral behavior in particular situations can become a matter of heated public debate. Perhaps it is no coincidence, therefore, that the study of moral development has also proved to be controversial. The controversy begins with the foundational research of Lawrence Kohlberg.

---

morality A system of beliefs and values that ensures that individuals will keep their obligations to others in society and will behave in ways that do not interfere with the rights and interests of others.

KOHLBERG'S STAGES OF MORAL REASONING

Lawrence Kohlberg (1964, 1981) founded his theory of moral development by studying *moral reasoning*—the judgments people make about what courses of action are correct or incorrect in particular situations. Kohlberg's theory was shaped by the earlier insights of Jean Piaget (1965), who sought to tie the development of moral judgment to a child's general cognitive development. In Piaget's view, as the child progresses through the stages of cognitive growth, he or she assigns differing relative weights to the *consequences* of an act and to the actor's *intentions*. For example, to the preoperational child, someone who breaks ten cups accidentally is "naughtier" than someone who breaks one cup intentionally. As the child gets older, the actor's intentions weigh more heavily in the judgment of morality.

Children ages 3, 4, and 5 years old were asked to make moral judgments about people's behavior that varied along three dimensions: actions, outcomes, and intentions. The *actions* were defined as either positive or negative within a particular scenario (such as petting versus hitting an animal) as were the *outcomes* (such as the animal either cried or smiled). To vary *intentions*, the experimenters described some behaviors as intentional and others as accidental (such as the actor hit the pet either on purpose or by mistake). The children were asked to rate the *acceptability* of the behavior by choosing one of a series of five faces that represented values from "really, really bad" to "really, really good." The younger children based their acceptability ratings almost entirely on the outcome; only the 5-year-olds took intention into account. However, when children were asked whether the actor should be *punished,* more of the younger children took the actor's intention into account (Zelazo et al., 1996).

These results suggest that as children become more sophisticated cognitively, they are able to shift their focus from just outcomes to consideration of both outcomes and intentions together. However, the difference between acceptability judgments and punishment judgments suggests that some types of moral judgments allow children to consider more factors at an earlier age. As we saw earlier in the chapter, what children are specifically asked to do determines, in part, how "mature" they seem.

Kohlberg expanded Piaget's view to define stages of moral development. Each stage is characterized by a different basis for making moral judgments (see **Table 10.7**). The lowest level of moral reasoning is based on self-interest; higher levels center on social good, regardless of personal gain. To document these stages, Kohlberg used a series of dilemmas that pit different moral principles against one another:

In one dilemma, a man named Heinz is trying to help his wife obtain a certain drug needed to treat her cancer. An unscrupulous druggist will only sell it to Heinz for ten times more than what the druggist paid. This is much more money than Heinz has and more than he can raise. Heinz becomes desperate, breaks into the druggist's store, and steals the drug for his wife.

TABLE 10.7 Kohlberg's Stages of Moral Reasoning

Levels and Stages	Reasons for Moral Behavior
I Preconventional morality	
Stage 1 Pleasure/pain orientation	To avoid pain or not to get caught
Stage 2 Cost–benefit orientation; reciprocity—an eye for an eye	To get rewards
II Conventional morality	
Stage 3 Good-child orientation	To gain acceptance and avoid disapproval
Stage 4 Law and order orientation	To follow rules, avoid censure by authorities
III Principled morality	
Stage 5 Social contract orientation	To promote the society's welfare
Stage 6 Ethical principle orientation	To achieve justice and avoid self-condemnation
Stage 7 Cosmic orientation	To be true to universal principles and feel oneself part of a cosmic direction that transcends social norms

Should Heinz have done that? Why? An interviewer probes the participant for the reasons for the decision and then scores the answers.

The scoring is based on the *reasons* the person gives for the decision, not on the decision itself. For example, someone who says that the man should steal the drug because of his obligation to his dying wife or that he should not steal the drug because of his obligation to uphold the law (despite his personal feelings) is expressing concern about meeting established obligations and is scored at Stage 4.

Four principles govern Kohlberg's stage model: (1) An individual can be at only one stage at a given time; (2) everyone goes through the stages in a fixed order; (3) each stage is more comprehensive and complex than the preceding; and (4) the same stages occur in every culture. Kohlberg inherited much of this stage philosophy from Piaget, and, in fact, the progression from Stages 1 to 3 appears to match the course of normal cognitive development. The stages proceed in order, and each can be seen to be more cognitively sophisticated than the preceding. Almost all children reach Stage 3 by the age of 13.

Much of the controversy with Kohlberg's theory occurs beyond Stage 3. In Kohlberg's original view, people would continue their moral development in a steady progression beyond level 3. However, not all people attain Stages 4 to 7. In fact, many adults never reach Stage 5, and only a few go beyond it. The content of Kohlberg's later stages appears to be subjective, and it is hard to understand each successive stage as more comprehensive and sophisticated than the preceding. For example, "avoiding self-condemnation," the basis for moral judgments at Stage 6, does not seem obviously more sophisticated than "promoting society's welfare," the basis for Stage 5. Furthermore, Kohlberg's own research ultimately demonstrated that the higher stages are not found in all cultures (Gibbs et al., 2007). We turn now to contemporary research that enlarges Kohlberg's theory to include considerations of gender and culture.

GENDER AND CULTURAL PERSPECTIVES ON MORAL REASONING

Most critiques of Kohlberg's theory take issue with his claims of universality: Kohlberg's later stages have been criticized because they fail to recognize that adult moral judgments may reflect different, but equally moral, principles. In a well-known critique, **Carol Gilligan** (1982) argued that Kohlberg overlooked potential differences between the habitual moral judgments of men and women. Gilligan proposed that women's moral development is based on a standard of *caring for others* and progresses to a stage of self-realization, whereas men base their reasoning on a standard of *justice*. Research has confirmed that concerns about caring and justice are relevant to moral reasoning—but not that these concerns are found especially in women or in men (Jaffee & Hyde, 2000). When asked to reason about the same moral dilemmas, men and women gave highly similar patterns of care and justice responses (Clopton & Sorell, 1993).

Cross-cultural research has also expanded researchers' understanding about the range of concerns that contribute to moral reasoning (Gibbs et al., 2007). One analysis has identified three types of concern (Jensen, 2008). The first set of concerns relates to *autonomy:* "A focus on people who have needs, desires, and preferences"; "the moral goal is to recognize" people's right "to the fulfillment of these needs and desires" (Jensen, 2008, p. 296). The second set of concerns relates to *community:* A focus on people "as members of social groups such as family, school, and nation"; the moral goal is "the fulfillment of role-based duties to others, and the protections and positive functioning of social groups." The third set of concerns relates to *divinity:* A focus "on people as spiritual or religious entities"; "the moral goal is for the self to become increasingly connected to . . . . [the] pure or divine."

If you think through these three types of concerns you can see how their importance might vary cross-culturally. Consider this situation: You see a stranger at the side of the road with a flat tire. Should you stop to help? Suppose you say no. Is that immoral? If you have grown up in the United States, you probably think helping, under these circumstances, is a matter of personal choice, so it isn't immoral. But if you had grown up in India, in a culture that puts considerably more emphasis on interdependence and mutual assistance, you probably *would* view a failure to help as immoral (Miller et al., 1990).

It's also important to recognize that people's life experiences will have an impact on their judgments. Consider individuals who have grown up in circumstances of great violence.

> The researchers recruited a group of children and adolescents from a highly impoverished area in Bogotá, Columbia (Posada & Wainryb, 2008). A large majority of the participants (88 percent) had witnessed or experienced some severe type of violence: They had, for example, seen people shot at, shot, or killed. The researchers first asked the participants to share their moral judgments in the abstract. The participants answered questions like, "Is it okay or not okay to take other people's things?" On such abstract questions, all the participants presented responses based on norms of justice. They indicated, for example, that it would not be okay to steal. However, the pattern changed when the participants made similar judgments in concrete contexts. For example, the participants read a scenario in which 15-year-old Julio had the opportunity to steal a bicycle from one of "the people who hurt his father and his brother and forced his family to move" (p. 886). After hearing that scenario, participants often indicated their belief that Julio would steal the bicycle. In addition, despite their general aversion to stealing, many participants approved of that behavior in this concrete instance.

The researchers note that the participants' violent life experiences have not completely overwhelmed ordinary moral development: "Even the impoverished environments of war and displacement present youths with opportunities for reflecting on the intrinsic features of actions that harm others" (p. 896). Still, the researchers speculate that, because of their impact on moral judgments, "contexts underscoring revenge might give rise to cycles of violence" (p. 896). The same behavior that seems very wrong framed against one set of moral concerns may look very right framed against another.

We have now described several domains in which people undergo developmental change. In the final section of the chapter, we offer some thoughts for your future.

STOP AND REVIEW

❶ What are the three major levels of moral reasoning in Kohlberg's theory?

❷ What distinction did Carol Gilligan believe separates the moral reasoning of men and women?

❸ What are three types of concerns people may bring to circumstances of moral reasoning?

CRITICAL THINKING Consider the study that looked at moral judgments by children and adolescents in Columbia. Why might the researchers have chosen scenarios that involved revenge?

Learning to Age Successfully

Let us now review some of the themes of this chapter, to form a prescription for successful aging. Early in the chapter, we encouraged you to think of development as a type of change that always brings with it gains and losses. In this light, the trick to prospering across the life span is to solidify one's gains and minimize one's losses. Many of the changes that are stereotypically associated with aging are functions of disuse rather than decay. Our first line of advice is straightforward: Keep at it!

How can older adults cope successfully with whatever changes inevitably accompany increasing age? Successful aging might consist of making the most of gains while minimizing the impact of the normal losses that accompany aging. This strategy for successful aging, proposed by psychologists **Paul Baltes** and **Margaret Baltes,** is called **selective optimization with compensation** (Baltes et al., 1992; Freund & Baltes, 1998). *Selective* means that people scale down the number and extent of their goals for themselves. *Optimization* refers to people exercising or training themselves in areas that are of highest priority to them. *Compensation* means that people use alternative ways to deal with losses—for example, choosing age-friendly environments. Let's consider an example:

> *When the concert pianist [Arthur] Rubinstein was asked, in a television interview, how he managed to remain such a successful pianist in his old age, he mentioned three strategies: (1) In old age he performed fewer pieces, (2) he now practiced each piece more frequently, and (3) he produced more ritardandos [slowings of the tempo] in his playing before fast segments, so that the playing speed sounded faster than it was in reality. These are examples of selection (fewer pieces), optimization (more practice), and compensation (increased use of contrast in speed). (Baltes, 1993, p. 590)*

This example provides a template for how you might think about your own life. Although the selective optimization perspective originated in research on the aging process, it is a good way to characterize the choices you must make throughout your life span. You should always try to select the goals most important to you, optimize your performance with respect to those goals, and compensate when progress toward those goals is blocked. That's our final bit of advice about life span development. We hope you will age wisely and well.

---

selective optimization with compensation A strategy for successful aging in which one makes the most gains while minimizing the impact of losses that accompany normal aging.

Recapping Main Points

Studying Development

- Researchers collect normative, longitudinal, and cross-sectional data to document change.

Physical Development across the Life Span

- Environmental factors can affect physical development while a child is still in the womb.
- Newborns and infants possess a remarkable range of capabilities: They are prewired for survival.
- Through puberty, adolescents achieve sexual maturity.
- Some physical changes in late adulthood are consequences of disuse, not inevitable deterioration.

Cognitive Development across the Life Span

- Piaget's key ideas about cognitive development include development of schemes, assimilation, accommodation, and the four-stage theory of discontinuous development. The four stages are sensorimotor, preoperational, concrete operational, and formal operational.
- Many of Piaget's theories are now being altered by ingenious research paradigms that reveal infants and young children to be more competent than Piaget had thought.
- Researchers suggest that children develop foundational theories that change over time.
- Cross-cultural research has questioned the universality of cognitive developmental theories.
- Age-related declines in cognitive functioning are typically evident in only some abilities.

Acquiring Language

- Many researchers believe that humans have an inborn language-making capacity. Even so, interactions with adult speakers is an essential part of the language acquisition process.
- Like scientists, children develop hypotheses about the meanings and grammar of their language. These hypotheses are often constrained by innate principles.

Social Development across the Life Span

- Social development takes place in a particular cultural context.
- Erik Erikson conceptualized the life span as a series of crises with which individuals must cope.
- Children begin the process of social development with different temperaments.
- Socialization begins with an infant's attachment to a caregiver.
- Failure to make this attachment leads to numerous physical and psychological problems.
- Adolescents must develop a personal identity by forming comfortable social relationships with parents and peers.
- The central concerns of adulthood are organized around the needs of intimacy and generativity.
- People become less socially active as they grow older because they selectively maintain only those relationships that matter most to them emotionally.
- People assess their lives, in part, by their ability to contribute positively to the lives of others.

Sex and Gender Differences

- Research has revealed biologically based sex differences between the brains of men and women.
- Children's gender stereotypes are most rigid between ages 5 and 7.
- Beginning at birth, parents and peers help bring about the socialization of gender roles.

Moral Development

- Kohlberg defined stages of moral development.
- Subsequent research has evaluated gender and cultural differences in moral reasoning.

Learning to Age Successfully

- Successful cognitive aging can be defined as people optimizing their functioning in select domains that are of highest priority to them and compensating for losses by using substitute behaviors.

KEY TERMS

accommodation (p. 306)

assimilation (p. 306)

attachment (p. 319)

centration (p. 307)

child-directed speech (p. 314)

cognitive development (p. 306)

conservation (p. 308)

contact comfort (p. 322)

cross-sectional design (p. 299)

developmental age (p. 298)

developmental psychology (p. 298)

egocentrism (p. 307)

embryonic stage (p. 300)

fetal stage (p. 300)

foundational theory (p. 310)

gender (p. 327)

gender identity (p. 328)

gender stereotype (p. 328)

generativity (p. 326)

germinal stage (p. 300)

imprinting (p. 319)

infant-directed speech (p. 314)

internalization (p. 310)

intimacy (p. 324)

language-making
    capacity (p. 316)

longitudinal design (p. 298)

maturation (p. 302)

menarche (p. 303)

morality (p. 330)

normative investigation (p. 298)

object permanence (p. 307)

overregularization (p. 316)

parenting style (p. 320)

physical development (p. 300)

phoneme (p. 314)

psychosocial stage (p. 317)

puberty (p. 303)

scheme (p. 306)

selective optimization with
    compensation (p. 332)

sex difference (p. 327)

social development (p. 317)

socialization (p. 319)

temperament (p. 319)

teratogen (p. 301)

wisdom (p. 312)

zygote (p. 300)

Chapter 10 Practice Test

1. Rachel just turned 4, but she has the language ability of a 6-year-old. For language ability, Rachel's _____ age is greater than her _____ age.
   a. chronological; normative
   b. developmental; cross-sectional
   c. developmental; chronological
   d. chronological; developmental

2. Your friend Pat says, "I'm sure Caroline recognized my voice as soon as she was born." If Pat is Caroline's _____, Pat's claim is probably correct.
   a. mother
   b. father
   c. mother or father
   d. sister

3. Jack and Jill are twins. Under most circumstances, you would expect that Jack would begin his pubescent growth spurt _____ Jill.
   a. at the same time as
   b. earlier than
   c. a year before
   d. later than

4. Tamara is a child whose thought is marked by egocentrism and centration. With respect to Piaget's theory, you infer that Tamara is in the _____ stage.
   a. sensorimotor
   b. preoperational
   c. concrete operations
   d. formal operations

5. You are testing 20-year-old Keith and his 45-year-old father, Matthew. If they are both average members of their age groups, you'd expect Keith to show more _____ and Matthew to show more _____.
   a. crystallized intelligence; fluid intelligence
   b. wisdom; crystallized intelligence
   c. wisdom; fluid intelligence
   d. fluid intelligence; wisdom

6. You are looking at fMRI scans from an experiment on working memory. Compared to his 38-year-old son Max, you would expect to see _____ for 68-year-old Tony.
   a. more symmetry in activations across brain hemispheres
   b. less activation of brain areas irrelevant to the task
   c. more activation in the left hemisphere
   d. less symmetry in activations across hemispheres

7. You are examining data from an experiment on speech perception. Participant 27 was able to hear a sound distinction that is used in Hindi but not in English. You conclude the Participant 27 is *least* likely to be an
   a. infant in a Hindi language environment.
   b. adult who is a Hindi speaker.
   c. infant in an English language environment.
   d. adult who is an English speaker.

8. If Siyun believes that "mommy" applies to all women, that is an _____. If she believes that "mommy" applies only to her own mother, that is an _____.
   a. contrast; overextension
   b. underextension; hypothesis
   c. overextension; underextension
   d. hypothesis; contrast

9. According to Erik Erikson, the major crisis of age 6 to puberty is
   a. autonomy versus self-doubt.
   b. identity versus role confusion
   c. generativity versus stagnation.
   d. initiative versus guilt.

10. As a mother, Lisbeth is high on the dimension of demandingness and low on the dimension of responsiveness. This combination would be described as a(n) _____ style of parenting.
   a. indulgent
   b. authoritative
   c. neglecting
   d. authoritarian

11. Which of these statements was *not* mentioned as a recommendation for quality day care?
   a. Children should be taught social problem-solving skills.
   b. Children should have similar levels of intellectual development.
   c. Caregivers should not put undue restrictions on the children.
   d. Children should have a free choice of activities intermixed with explicit lessons.

12. Whereas _____ differences are affected by culture, _____ differences are affected by biology.
   a. gender; sex
   b. generativity; gender
   c. sex; identity
   d. sex; gender

13. You are asked to guess whether 6-year-old Chris is a girl or boy. Which observation would most lead you to believe that Chris is a girl?
   a. Chris enjoys rough-and-tumble play.
   b. Chris doesn't like to engage in social conversations.
   c. Chris most enjoys one-on-one relationships.
   d. Chris prefers to have social interactions in groups.

14. For moral behavior, Gracie is most concerned about following rules and avoiding the censure of authorities. She is at the stage of _____ morality.
   a. principled
   b. cultural
   c. preconventional
   d. conventional

15. Carol Gilligan criticized Kohlberg's theory by arguing that women are more focused on the standard of _____, whereas men are more focused on the standard of _____.
   a. caring for others; avoiding pain
   b. caring for others; justice
   c. justice; caring for others
   d. avoiding self-condemnation; justice

Essay Questions

1. Why do researchers believe that some aspects of cognitive development occur within specific domains of knowledge?

2. Why does deprivation and abuse have consequences for social development?

3. Why is it sometimes difficult to discriminate between sex differences and gender differences?

Discovering Psychology Viewing Guide

Watch the following videos by logging on to MyPsychLab (www.mypsychlab.com). After you have watched the videos, complete the activities that follow.

Program 5: The Developing Child

Program 18: Maturing and Aging

Program 6: Language Development

KEY TERMS AND PEOPLE

As you watch the programs, pay particular attention to these terms and people in addition to those covered in this textbook.

- *psycholinguists*—researchers who study the structure of language and communication.
- *senile dementia*—biochemical and neuronal changes in the brain that lead to a gradual reduction in mental efficiency.
- *stage theory*—a theory that describes development as a fixed sequence of distinct periods of life.
- *Judy DeLoache*—studies cognitive development in older children and how they come to understand symbols.
- *Jean Berko Gleason*—developmental psychologist who studies the central impact of social interaction on language acquisition.
- *Jerome Kagan*—studies the inherited behavioral differences between bold and timid children.
- *Daniel Levinson*—studies the life course as a sequence of developmental experiences.
- *Pat Moore*—reporter who disguised herself as an 85-year-old woman to find out more about the experience of being old in America.
- *Werner Schaie*—studies the long-term effects of aging.
- *Steven Suomi*—studies the behavior of genetically shy monkeys. Argues that at least some shyness is an inherited tendency.
- *Sherry Willis*—uses new educational training methods to help the elderly function more effectively.

PROGRAM REVIEW

Program 5

1. What task of infancy is aided by a baby's ability to recognize his or her mother's voice?
   a. avoiding danger
   b. seeking sustenance
   c. forming social relationships
   d. learning to speak

2. A toy company wants to use Robert Fantz's research to design a new mobile for babies to look at in their cribs. The research suggests that the mobile should
   a. be as simple as possible.
   b. use soft colors such as pink.
   c. be made of a shiny material.
   d. have a complex design.

3. Which of a baby's senses is least developed at birth?
   a. hearing   c. sight
   b. taste   d. touch

4. A baby is shown an orange ball a dozen times in a row. How would you predict the baby would respond?
   a. The baby will make the same interested response each time.
   b. The baby will respond with less and less interest each time.
   c. The baby will respond with more and more interest each time.
   d. The baby will not be interested at any time.

5. Renée Baillargeon and other researchers have investigated object permanence in babies. How do their results compare with Piaget's views?
   a. They show Piaget's age estimates for achieving object permanence were too high.
   b. They contradict Piaget's concept of what object permanence consists of.
   c. They support Piaget's timetable.
   d. They indicate that babies show more variation than Piaget found.

6. When Judy DeLoache hid the small and large toy dogs, what was she investigating?
   a. stranger anxiety
   b. activity level
   c. conservation of volume
   d. symbolic representation

7. At what stage in their development do babies refuse to cross the visual cliff?
   a. as soon as their eyes can focus on it
   b. when they develop conditioned fears
   c. just before they are ready to walk
   d. about a month after they learn to crawl

8. What conclusion has Jerome Kagan come to about shyness in young children?
   a. It is inherent but can be modified by experience.
   b. It is created by parents who misunderstand their child's temperament.
   c. It is an inherited trait that cannot be changed.
   d. It is normal for all children to be shy at certain stages.

9. How does Steven Suomi modify shyness reactions in young monkeys?
   a. by putting them in an enriched environment
   b. by providing highly supportive foster mothers
   c. by placing a shy monkey with other shy monkeys
   d. by administering drugs that reduce the level of social anxiety

10. Which of the following is *not* a method that measures what a 2-month-old is interested in?
    a. asking questions in very short, simple sentences
    b. measuring looking time
    c. examining dishabituation
    d. recording heart rate

11. Which of the following developmental psychologists made the mistake of confusing children's physical ability with their cognitive ability and thus believed children were cognitively less capable than they actually are?
    a. Robert Fantz   c. Renée Baillargeon
    b. Jean Piaget   d. Eleanor Gibson

12. Which of the following is last to emerge in children?
    a. fear of heights
    b. preference for mother's voice over other people's voices
    c. temperament
    d. ability to see analogies between a real situation and a scale model of it

Program 6

13. Before Chomsky's work, what assumption was generally made about language acquisition?
    a. Babies have an innate capacity for extracting meaning.
    b. There is a built-in language acquisition device.
    c. Language development varies widely, depending on culture.
    d. Language is a skill learned by imitating parents.

14. How does an infant react when his or her mother's voice is paired with the face of a stranger?
    a. The infant becomes upset.
    b. The infant laughs.
    c. The infant pays closer attention.
    d. An infant is not capable of noting any discrepancy.

15. How does the development of language competence compare from culture to culture?
    a. It varies greatly.
    b. It is remarkably similar.
    c. Western cultures are similar to each other, whereas Eastern cultures are very different.
    d. This topic is just beginning to be explored by researchers.

16. Jean Berko Gleason has studied mothers and their babies. Her major focus is on the role of
    a. neurological maturation in language development.
    b. melodic patterns used by mothers in different cultures.
    c. social interaction in language development.
    d. parental patterning of conversational conventions.

17. A 7-month-old American child with American parents is babbling. The sounds that the child produces include
    a. sounds from many different languages.
    b. only sounds used in English.
    c. only sounds found in Western languages.
    d. sounds unlike those of any language.

18. When Anne Fernald says "the melody is the message," she means that
    a. babies take meaning from pitch contours.
    b. mothers need to sing to their babies.
    c. babies need to learn the intonation patterns of their native language.
    d. mothers speak slowly and clearly to their babies.

19. What mental ability must a child have developed in order to use words as symbols?
    a. storing and retrieving memory codes
    b. recognizing the letters of the alphabet
    c. composing questions
    d. recognizing the spatial relationships between objects

20. The earliest form of communication that children engage in is
    a. telegraphic speech.   c. babbling.
    b. cooing.   d. crying.

21. Which of the following stages of communication consists of simple sentences that lack plurals, articles, and tenses, but tend to have the constituent words in the order appropriate to the child's native language?
    a. telegraphic speech   c. question asking
    b. babbling   d. ritualistic speech

22. According to Chomsky, what might be necessary to activate the innate language acquisition device in the brain?
    a. sex hormones
    b. social interaction
    c. exposure to multiple languages
    d. the child's own vocalizations

23. According to Dan Slobin, a 2-year-old who is not speaking in full sentences yet
    a. cannot know the complex social rules of conversation, like turn taking.
    b. is more able than 10-month-olds to pronounce speech sounds that aren't native to her language.
    c. is considered to be speech delayed.
    d. will nonetheless still use the correct word order when speaking telegraphic sentences.

Program 18

24. What personal experience does Erik Erikson cite as leading to his redefinition of himself?
    a. having a religious conversion
    b. being an immigrant
    c. surviving a major illness
    d. getting married

25. According to Erikson, the young adult faces a conflict between
    a. isolation and intimacy.
    b. heterosexuality and homosexuality.

c. autonomy and shame.

d. wholeness and futility.

26. Daniel Levinson divides the life cycle into a series of eras. For which era is a major problem the hazard of being irrelevant?

a. childhood   c. middle adulthood

b. early adulthood   d. late adulthood

27. When Pat Moore transformed herself into an 85-year-old woman, she was surprised by the

a. compassion with which others treated her.

b. lack of facilities designed to accommodate the aged.

c. extent of ageism in our society.

d. poverty faced by many older people.

28. What has Sherry Willis found about the abilities of older people with regard to spatial orientation tasks?

a. Irreversible decline is inevitable.

b. Training programs yield improved skills.

c. Skills can be maintained but not improved.

d. If memory loss occurs, other skills deteriorate.

29. There is a(n) _____ in paranoid disorders with age largely because _____.

a. decrease; people have become more at peace with their lives.

b. decrease; life becomes more sheltered and more predictable during retirement.

c. increase; life becomes more chaotic during retirement.

d. increase; hearing and vision losses make the world harder to process.

30. Assuming that a person remains healthy, what happens to the ability to derive sexual pleasure as one ages?

a. It does not change.

b. It gradually diminishes.

c. It abruptly ceases.

d. It depends on the availability of a suitable partner.

31. In general, how does the view of the elderly among the population at large compare with the actuality?

a. It is more negative.

b. It is more positive.

c. It is generally accurate.

d. It is more accurate for men than for women.

32. The results of the long-term study by Werner Schaie suggest that the people who do best in the later stages of life are people with

a. high incomes.   c. flexible attitudes.

b. advanced degrees.   d. large, close-knit families.

33. In nursing homes, the staff often behave in ways that treat the elderly like children. What is the effect of this treatment on most older people?

a. It makes them feel more secure.

b. It makes them behave in dependent, childlike ways.

c. It increases their sense of autonomy and control.

d. It improves their health by reducing their stress levels.

34. Cognitive agility in the elderly

a. is considered to have completely disappeared in the average 85-year-old person.

b. tends to improve radically in the years just before death.

c. is one of the most predictable outcomes of the aging process.

d. does not necessarily decline.

35. The elderly are particularly adept at processing information with

a. emotional content.   c. mathematical content.

b. spatial content.   d. folkloric content.

QUESTIONS TO CONSIDER

1. Can some of the measures used to determine the cognitive capabilities of preverbal infants be applied to nonhuman animals? What would we be able to conclude from patterns of results that are similar to or different from those found in human infants?

2. As people age and restructure their lives based on gains and losses in what they are capable of doing, do you think their values change to fit their capabilities? For example, do you think they come to value physical activity less as they become physically more restricted?

3. Is language unique to humans? Although chimps and gorillas lack the vocal apparatus for spoken language, they can use symbols and signs for communication. Consider your textbook's definition of language. Why is there so much resistance to the idea that animals use language?

ACTIVITIES

1. Recall your earliest memory. Speculate as to why you recall it, what you might have distorted in your memory, and what effects the event has had on your development.

2. Interview an elderly person to find out what his or her experiences have been of the costs and benefits, both cognitively and socially, of aging in this country. Does the elder ever find that he or she is discriminated against? Does the elder find that people are more generous with him or her than with other people?

3. In what ways do television programs designed for adults vs. children differ? Is children's programming superior in any way for helping viewers learn new words or learn other aspects of grammar? Watch a children's program such as *Sesame Street* and identify features that may be designed to help specifically with language development.

4. Keep track of the images of people over 60, over 70, and over 80 that you encounter during an average day. Notice how older adults are depicted in television programs and advertisements. What stereotypes persist? Is there evidence that images are changing?

Motivation

Your alarm clock went off this morning. You would have loved to hit the snooze button to get a few extra minutes of sleep, but you dragged yourself right out of bed. Why? Were you desperately hungry? Did you have to complete some important assignment? Had you made a date with someone who has captured your heart? When you consider the question "Why did I get out of bed this morning?" you have arrived directly at the core question of *motivation:* What makes you act as you do? What makes you persistently try to attain some goals despite the high effort, pain, and financial costs involved? Why, conversely, do you sometimes procrastinate too long before attempting to achieve other goals or give in and quit too soon?

It is the task of psychological researchers to bring theoretical rigor to such questions of motivation. How might motivational states affect the outcome of a sports competition or an exam? Why do some people become overweight and others starve themselves to death? Are our sexual behaviors determined by our genetic heritage? In this chapter, you will learn that human actions are motivated by a variety of needs—from fundamental physiological needs like hunger and thirst to psychological needs like personal achievement. But you will see that physiology and psychology are often not easy to separate. Even a seemingly biological drive such as hunger competes with an individual's need for personal control and social acceptance to determine patterns of eating.

We begin the chapter by providing you with a framework to understand general issues about the nature and study of motivation. In the second part of the chapter, we will look in depth at three types of motivation, each important in a different way and each varying in the extent to which biological and psychological factors operate. These three are hunger, sex, and personal achievement.

What different motivational questions might be asked of this individual's behavior?

Understanding Motivation

Motivation is the general term for all the processes involved in starting, directing, and maintaining physical and psychological activities. The word *motivation* comes from the Latin *movere,* which means "to move." All organisms move toward some stimuli and activities and away from others, as dictated by their appetites and aversions. Theories of motivation explain both the general patterns of "movement" of each animal species, including humans, and the personal preferences and performances of the individual members of each species. Let's begin our analysis of motivation by considering the different ways in which motivation has been used to explain and predict species and individual behavior.

FUNCTIONS OF MOTIVATIONAL CONCEPTS

Psychologists have used the concept of motivation for five basic purposes:

- *To relate biology to behavior.* As a biological organism, you have complex internal mechanisms that regulate

your bodily functioning and help you survive. Why did you get out of bed this morning? You may have been hungry, thirsty, or cold. In each case, internal states of deprivation trigger bodily responses that motivate you to take action to restore your body's balance.

- *To account for behavioral variability.* Why might you do well on a task one day and poorly on the same task another day? Why does one child do much better at a competitive task than another child with roughly the same ability and knowledge? Psychologists use motivational explanations when the variations in people's performance in a constant situation cannot be traced to differences in ability, skill, practice, or chance. If you were willing to get up early this morning to get in some extra studying but your friend was not, we would be comfortable describing you as being in a different motivational state than your friend.

- *To infer private states from public acts.* You see someone sitting on a park bench, chuckling. How can you explain this behavior? Psychologists and laypersons are alike in typically moving from observing some behavior to inferring some internal cause for it. People are continually interpreting behavior in terms of likely reasons for why it occurred as it did. The same rule applies to your own behaviors. You often seek to discover whether your own actions are best understood as internally or externally motivated.

- *To assign responsibility for actions.* The concept of personal responsibility is basic in law, religion, and ethics. Personal responsibility presupposes inner motivation and the ability to control your actions. People are judged less responsible for their actions when (1) they did not intend negative consequences to occur, (2) external forces were powerful enough to provoke the behaviors, or (3) the actions were influenced by drugs, alcohol, or intense emotion. Thus a theory of motivation must be able to discriminate among the different potential causes of behavior.

motivation The process of starting, directing, and maintaining physical and psychological activities; includes mechanisms involved in preferences for one activity over another and the vigor and persistence of responses.

- *To explain perseverance despite adversity.* A final reason psychologists study motivation is to explain why organisms perform behaviors when it might be easier not to perform them. Motivation gets you to work or class on time even when you're exhausted. Motivation helps you persist in playing the game to the best of your ability even when you are losing and realize that you can't possibly win.

You now have a general sense of the circumstances in which psychologists might invoke the concept of motivation to explain and predict behavior. Before we turn to specific domains of experience, let's consider general sources of motivation.

SOURCES OF MOTIVATION

In 1999, cyclist Lance Armstrong won the Tour de France—completing one of the most remarkable comebacks in sports history. In 1996, Armstrong had been diagnosed with testicular cancer that had spread to his lungs and brain. After enduring aggressive chemotherapy, Armstrong chose to go back into training. Within three years, he was victorious in his sport's most prestigious event. In 2005, Armstrong won the Tour de France for the seventh time in a row. Detractors had claimed that the field he beat in 1999 was weak; his six additional victories proved that he could repeatedly beat the world's best cyclists.

Could you do what Lance Armstrong did? Could you come back from a serious illness to challenge your body again? Do you think that whatever motivated his behavior was something *internal* to him? Would it take a special set of life experiences for someone to persevere in this manner? Or was it something *external,* something about the situation? Would many or most people behave in this way if they were put in the same situation? Or does his behavior represent an *interaction* of aspects of the person and features of the situation? To help you think about the sources of motivation, we will explore this distinction between internal and external forces. Let's begin with theories that explain certain types of behavior as arising from internal biological drives.

Drives and Incentives Some forms of motivation seem very basic: If you feel hungry, you eat; if you feel thirsty, you drink. The theory that much important behavior was motivated by internal drives was most fully developed by theorist **Clark Hull** (1884–1952). In Hull's (1943, 1952) view, **drives** are internal states that arise in response to an animal's physiological needs. Organisms seek to maintain a state of equilibrium, or **homeostasis,** with respect to biological conditions (see Chapter 3, p. 74). Consider how your body responds to keep your temperature close to 98.6 °F: If you get too hot, you begin to sweat; if you get too cold, you start to shiver. These mechanisms serve to restore equilibrium. Now consider what happens when an animal has been deprived of food for several hours. On Hull's view, such deprivation creates disequilibrium or *tension* which arouses a drive. This drive activates the organism toward *tension reduction;* when the drive is satisfied or reduced—when homeostasis is restored—the organism ceases to act. Thus, according to Hull, the food-deprived animal experiences a drive that motivates food-seeking and eating behaviors. The animal's responses that have led to the food goal will be reinforced because they are associated with the tension reduction that eating produces.

Can tension reduction explain all motivated behavior? Apparently not. Let's consider an experiment that demon-

What combination of internal and external motivational forces may have helped cyclist Lance Armstrong to overcome cancer and win the Tour de France?

strated that hunger and thirst are not always rats' most important motivation.

> Groups of either food- or water-deprived rats were placed in a square maze that consisted of nine equally sized units with doorways that allowed passage between the units (Zimbardo & Montgomery, 1957). Each unit of the maze had a sunken bowl that could contain either water or food. Drive theory would predict that the rats experiencing deprivation would eat or drink at their first opportunity. However, rather than immediately reducing that tension, the rats often chose to explore the maze instead. For example, rats that had been deprived of food for 48 or 72 hours spent 80 percent of their first two minutes in the maze exploring the maze; they spent only 20 percent of their time eating.

In this experiment, it appeared that the rats began to satisfy their hunger or thirst only once they had first satisfied their curiosity. Researchers have provided several similar examples of instances in which other motivational forces prevail over drive reduction (Berlyne, 1960; Fowler, 1965).

These results demonstrate that behavior is not only motivated by internal drives: Behavior is also motivated by

---

drive Internal state that arises in response to a disequilibrium in an animal's physiological needs.

homeostasis Constancy or equilibrium of the internal conditions of the body.

incentives—external stimuli or rewards that do not relate directly to biological needs. When the rats were attuned to objects in the environment rather than to their own internal states, they demonstrated that their behavior was controlled by incentives. Human behavior is also controlled by a variety of incentives. Why do you stay up late watching YouTube videos instead of getting a good night's sleep? Why do you watch a movie that you know will make you feel anxious or frightened? Why do you eat junk food at a party even when you're already feeling full? In each case, elements of the environment serve as incentives to motivate your behavior.

You can see already that behaviors find their origins in a mixture of internal and external sources of motivation. Even though rats might feel biological pressure to eat or drink, they also indulge an impulse to explore a new environment. We turn now to a different tradition of research on motivation, one that focuses on species-specific *instinctual* behaviors.

Instinctual Behaviors and Learning Why do organisms behave the way they do? Part of the answer is that some aspects of a species's behavior are governed by **instincts,** preprogrammed tendencies that are essential for the survival of their species. Instincts provide repertoires of behavior that are part of each animal's genetic inheritance. Salmon swim thousands of miles back to the exact stream where they were spawned, leaping up waterfalls until they come to the right spot, where the surviving males and females engage in ritualized courtship and mating. Fertilized eggs are deposited, the parents die, and, in time, their young swim downstream to live in the ocean until, a few years later, it is time for them to return to complete their part in this continuing drama. Similarly remarkable activities can be reported for most species of animals. Bees communicate the location of food to other bees, army ants go on highly synchronized hunting expeditions, birds build nests, and spiders spin complex webs—exactly as their parents and ancestors did.

Early theories of human function tended to overestimate the importance of instincts for humans. William James, writing in 1890, stated his belief that humans rely even more on instinctual behaviors than other animals (although human instincts were generally not carried out with fixed-action patterns). He argued, for example, that humans have a host of social instincts for sympathy, modesty, sociability, and love. By the 1920s, psychologists had compiled lists of over 10,000 human instincts (Bernard, 1924). At this same time, however, the notion of instincts as universal explanations for human behavior was beginning to stagger under the weight of critical attacks. Cross-cultural anthropologists, such as Ruth Benedict (1959) and Margaret Mead (1939), found enormous behavioral variation between cultures. Their observations contradicted theories that considered only the universals of inborn instincts.

Within psychology, behaviorists objected to the circular reasoning that often gave rise to claims about human instincts: People are sympathetic because they have an instinct to be sympathetic; sympathetic behavior confirms the existence of the instinct. In addition, as we saw in Chapter 6, the behaviorists provided empirical demonstrations that important behaviors and emotions were learned rather than inborn. These types of

Instinctive behaviors, like the nest-building practices of the African masked weaver, are motivated by genetic inheritance. What instincts have theorists attributed to human practice?

demonstrations should be familiar to you from Chapter 6. We saw there that human and nonhuman animals alike are highly sensitive to the ways in which stimuli and responses are associated in the environment. If you want to explain why one animal performs a behavior and another does not, you may need to know nothing more than that one animal's behavior was reinforced and the other's was not. Under those circumstances, you don't need a separate account of motivation at all (that is, it would be a mistake to say that one animal is "motivated" and the other is not). Recall, however, that in Chapter 6 we also saw that the types of behaviors animals will most readily learn are determined, in part, by species-specific instincts. That is, each animal displays a combination of learned and instinctive behaviors.

One final look back to Chapter 6: We saw there that cognitively oriented researchers have challenged the belief that instincts and reinforcement history are sufficient to explain all the details of an animal's behavior. Let's turn now to the role of expectations and cognition in motivation.

Expectations and Cognitive Approaches to Motivation Consider *The Wizard of Oz* as a psychological study of motivation. Dorothy and her three friends work hard to get to the Emerald City, overcoming barriers, persisting against

---

incentive External stimulus or reward that motivates behavior although it does not relate directly to biological needs.

instinct Preprogrammed tendency that is essential to a species's survival.

all adversaries. They do so because they expect the Wizard to give them what they are missing. Instead, the wonderful (and wise) Wizard makes them aware that they, not he, always had the power to fulfill their wishes. For Dorothy, *home* is not a place but a feeling of security, of comfort with people she loves; it is wherever her heart is. The courage the Lion wants, the intelligence the Scarecrow longs for, and the emotions the Tin Man dreams of are attributes they already possess. They need to think about these attributes not as internal conditions but as positive ways in which they are already relating to others. After all, didn't they demonstrate those qualities on the journey to Oz, a journey motivated by little more than an *expectation*, an idea about the future likelihood of getting something they wanted? The Wizard of Oz was clearly among the first cognitive psychologists because he recognized the importance of people's thought processes in determining their goals and behaviors to reach them.

Contemporary psychologists use cognitive analyses to explore the forces that motivate a variety of personal and social behaviors. These psychologists share the Wizard's point of view that significant human motivation comes not from objective realities in the external world but from subjective interpretations of reality. The reinforcing effect of a reward is lost if you don't perceive that your actions obtained it. What you do now is often controlled by what you think was responsible for your past successes and failures, by what you believe is possible for you to do, and by what you anticipate the outcome of an action will be. Cognitive approaches explain why human beings are often motivated by expectations of future events.

The importance of *expectations* in motivating behavior was developed by **Julian Rotter** (1954) in his **social-learning theory** (we touched on social learning in our discussion of observational learning in Chapter 6). For Rotter, the probability that you will engage in a given behavior (studying for an exam instead of partying) is determined by your *expectation* of attaining a goal (getting a good grade) that follows the activity and by the *personal value* of that goal. A *discrepancy* between expectations and reality can motivate an individual to perform corrective behaviors (Festinger, 1957; Lewin, 1936). Suppose you find that your own behaviors do not match the standards or values of a group to which you belong—you might be motivated to change your behaviors to achieve a better fit with the group. You might, for example, be motivated to change your style of dress or the music to which you listen to reduce the discrepancy between expectations and reality.

Fritz Heider (1896–1988) outlined how expectations relate to internal and external forces of motivation. Heider (1958) postulated that the outcome of your behavior (a poor grade, for example) can be attributed to *dispositional forces,* such as lack of effort or insufficient intelligence, or to *situational forces,* such as an unfair test or a biased teacher. These attributions influence the way you will behave. You are likely to try harder next time if you see your poor grade as a result of your lack of effort, but you may give up if you see it as resulting from injustice or lack of ability (Dweck, 1975). Thus the identification of a source of motivation as internal or external may depend, in part, on your own subjective interpretation of reality.

Let's review the various sources of motivation. We began with the observation that researchers can differentiate internal and external factors that bring about behaviors. Drives, instincts, and histories of learning are all internal sources of motivation that affect behaviors in the presence of appropriate external stimuli. Once organisms begin to think about their behaviors—something humans are particularly prone to do—expectations

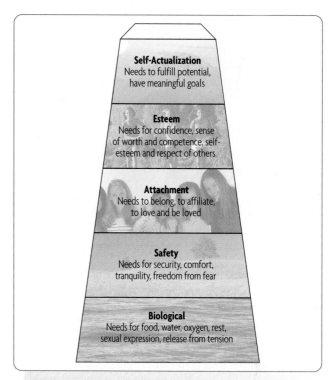

FIGURE 11.1   Maslow's Hierarchy of Needs
According to Maslow, needs at the lower level of the hierarchy dominate an individual's motivation as long as they are unsatisfied. Once these needs are adequately met, the higher needs occupy the individual's attention.

about what should or should not happen also begin to provide motivation. Thinking animals can choose to attribute some motivations to themselves and others to the outside world.

A HIERARCHY OF NEEDS

We have now reviewed several sources of motivation. As a preview for the rest of the chapter, we want to return to a more global account of the domains in which motivational concepts apply. Our intent is to give you a general sense of the forces that could guide your life.

Humanist psychologist **Abraham Maslow** (1908–1970) formulated the theory that basic motives form a **hierarchy of needs,** as illustrated in **Figure 11.1.** In Maslow's (1970) view, the needs at each level of the hierarchy must be satisfied—the needs are arranged in a sequence from primitive to advanced—before the next level can be achieved. At the bottom of this hierarchy are the basic *biological needs,* such as hunger and thirst. They must be met before any other needs can begin to operate. When biological needs are pressing, other needs are put on hold and

---

social-learning theory The learning theory that stresses the role of observation and the imitation of behaviors observed in others.

hierarchy of needs Maslow's view that basic human motives form a hierarchy and that the needs at each level of the hierarchy must be satisfied before the next level can be achieved; these needs progress from basic biological needs to the need for self-actualization.

Where does the need to belong, to form attachments and experience love, fit in Maslow's hierarchy?

are unlikely to influence your actions. When they are reasonably well satisfied, the needs at the next level—*safety needs*—motivate you. When you are no longer concerned about danger, you become motivated by *attachment needs*—needs to belong, to affiliate with others, to love, and to be loved. If you are well fed and safe and if you feel a sense of social belonging, you move up to *esteem needs*—to like oneself, to see oneself as competent and effective, and to do what is necessary to earn the esteem of others.

At the top of the hierarchy are people who are nourished, safe, loved and loving, secure, thinking, and creating. These people have moved beyond basic human needs in the quest for the fullest development of their potentials, or *self-actualization*. A self-actualizing person is self-aware, self-accepting, socially responsive, creative, spontaneous, and open to novelty and challenge, among other positive attributes.

Maslow's theory is a particularly upbeat view of human motivation. At the core of the theory is the need for each individual to grow and actualize his or her highest potential. However, you know from your own experience that Maslow's strict hierarchy breaks down. You may, for example, have skipped a meal so that you could help out a friend. You may have endured the danger of a wilderness trek to boost your self-esteem. Even so, we hope Maslow's scheme will enable you to bring some order to different aspects of your motivational experiences.

We have now given you a general framework for understanding motivation. In the remainder of the chapter, we will take a closer look at three different types of behaviors that are influenced by interactions of motives: eating, sexual performance, and personal achievement.

STOP AND REVIEW

❶ As you're sitting on a bench, you see another student go running by. Which function of motivational concepts applies to how you interpret the situation?

❷ What does it mean for an organism to achieve homeostasis?

❸ Why did cross-cultural research cast doubt on claims about human instincts?

❹ What distinction did Fritz Heider make with respect to explanations for outcomes?

❺ What did Abraham Maslow mean by attachment needs?

CRITICAL THINKING Recall the experiment on food- or water-deprived rats. Why was it important that each unit of the maze could contain food or water?

Visit MyPsychLab.com for more review and practice on the following topics:

◀⦿ **Explore:** Maslow's Hierarchy of Needs

◀⦿ **Explore:** Evolutionary Drive, Arousal, Cognitive, and Humanistic Theories of Motivation

Eating

We'd like to ask you to make a prediction. We are about to offer a slice of pizza to a student enrolled in an introductory psychology course. How likely do you think it is that the student will eat the slice of pizza? Are you willing to make a guess? Your response should probably be, "I need more information." In the last section, we gave you a way of organizing the extra information you need to acquire before making such a prediction. You would want to know about *internal* information. How much has the student eaten already? Is the student trying to diet? You would also want to know about *external* information. Is the pizza tasty? Are friends there to share the pizza and conversation? You can see already that we have some work to do to explain the types of forces that might influence even a simple outcome, such as whether someone is going to eat a slice of pizza. Let's begin with some of the physiological processes that evolution has provided to regulate eating.

THE PHYSIOLOGY OF EATING

When does your body tell you it's time to eat? You have been provided with a variety of mechanisms that contribute to your physical sense of hunger or satiety (Logue, 1991). To regulate food intake effectively, organisms must be equipped with mechanisms that accomplish four tasks: (1) detect internal food need, (2) initiate and organize eating behavior, (3) monitor the quantity and quality of the food eaten, and (4) detect when enough food has been consumed and stop eating. Researchers have tried to understand these processes by relating them either to *peripheral* mechanisms in different parts of the body, such as stomach contractions, or to *central* brain mechanisms, such as the functioning of the hypothalamus. Let's look at these processes in more detail.

Peripheral Responses Where do sensations of hunger come from? Does your stomach send out distress signals to indicate that it is empty? A pioneering physiologist, **Walter Cannon** (1871–1945), believed that gastric activity in an empty stomach was the sole basis for hunger. To test this hypothesis, Cannon's intrepid student A. L. Washburn trained himself to swallow an uninflated balloon attached to a rubber tube. The other end of the tube was attached to a device that recorded changes in air pressure. Cannon then inflated the balloon in Washburn's stomach. As the student's stomach contracted, air was expelled from the balloon and activated the recording device. Reports of Washburn's hunger pangs were correlated with periods when the record showed his stomach was severely contracted. Cannon thought he had proved that stomach cramps were responsible for hunger (Cannon, 1934; Cannon & Washburn, 1912).

Although Cannon and Washburn's procedure was ingenious, later research showed that stomach contractions are not even a necessary condition for hunger. Injections of sugar into the bloodstream will stop the stomach contractions but not the hunger of an animal with an empty stomach. Human patients who have had their stomachs entirely removed still experience hunger pangs (Janowitz & Grossman, 1950), and rats without stomachs still learn mazes when rewarded with food (Penick et al., 1963). So, although sensations originating in the stomach may play a role in the way people usually experience hunger, they do not fully explain how the body detects its need for food and is motivated to eat.

Your empty stomach may not be necessary to feel hungry, but does a "full" stomach terminate eating? Research has shown that gastric pressure caused by food—but not by an inflated balloon—will cause an individual to end a meal (Logue, 1991). Thus the body is sensitive to the source of pressure in the stomach. The oral experience of food also provides a peripheral source of *satiety* cues—cues relevant to feelings of satiation or fullness. You may have noticed that you become less enthusiastic about the tastes of even your favorite foods over the course of a meal, a phenomenon called *sensory-specific satiety* (Raynor & Epstein, 2001). This reduction in interest for foods as you eat them may be one way in which your body regulates intake. However, the "specific" in sensory-specific satiety means that the satiety applies to specific flavors and not to the food itself. In one experiment, participants had reached satiety for particular foods, such as pineapple or cucumber. However, when the flavors of the food were slightly altered—by the addition of vanilla-flavored whipped cream or salt and pepper—people showed renewed interest in the foods (Romer et al., 2006). This body of research suggests that variety in food tastes—as is common in many multicourse meals—might counteract other bodily indications that you've already had enough to eat.

Let's turn now to the brain mechanisms involved in eating behaviors, where information from peripheral sources is gathered together.

Central Responses As is often the case, simple theories about the brain centers for the initiation and cessation of eating have given way to more complex theories. The earliest theories of the brain control of eating were built around observations of the *lateral hypothalamus (LH)* and the *ventromedial hypothalamus (VMH).* (The location of the hypothalamus is shown in Figure 3.16 on page 75.) Research showed that if the VMH was lesioned (or the LH stimulated), the animal consumed more food. If the procedure was reversed, so that the LH was lesioned (or the VMH stimulated), the animal consumed less food. These observations gave rise to the *dual-center model,* in which the LH was thought to be the "hunger center" and the VMH the "satiety center."

Over time, however, researchers provided additional data to suggest that this simple theory was incomplete (Gao & Horvath, 2007). For example, rats with VMH lesions only overate foods they find palatable; they strongly avoid foods that don't taste good. Thus the VMH could not just be a simple center for signaling "eat more" or "don't eat more"—the signal depends on the type of food. In fact, destruction of the VMH may, in part, have the effect of exaggerating ordinary reflex responses to food

Why do people tend to eat more food when a variety of tastes are available?

(Powley, 1977). If the rat's reflex response to good-tasting food is to eat it, its exaggerated response will be to overeat. If the rat reflexively avoids bad-tasting food by gagging or vomiting, its exaggerated response could keep the rat from eating altogether. Researchers have also discovered that two other regions of the hypothalamus, known as the *arcuate nucleus* (ARC) and the *paraventricular nucleus* (PVN), supplement the roles of the VMH and LH to regulate eating.

Some of the most important information these hypothalamic regions use to regulate eating comes from your bloodstream (Gao & Horvath, 2007). Sugar (in the form of glucose in the blood) and fat are the energy sources for metabolism. The two basic signals that initiate eating come from receptors that monitor the levels of sugar and fat in the blood. When stored glucose is low or unavailable for metabolism, signals from liver cell receptors are sent to the LH, where neurons acting as glucose detectors change their activity to initiate eating behavior. Other hypothalamic neurons gather information that indicates high blood levels of glucose or fatty acids and use that information to terminate eating behavior. The hypothalamic circuits also monitor more long-term aspects of the body's state of satiety. For example, fat cells release substances that provide signals to the ARC to decrease eating.

We have seen so far that you have body systems that are dedicated to getting you to start and to stop eating. You almost certainly know, however, from an enormous amount of personal experience, that your need for food depends on more than just the cues generated by your body. Let's look now at psychological factors that motivate you to eat more food or less food.

THE PSYCHOLOGY OF EATING

You know now that your body is equipped with a variety of mechanisms that regulate the amount of food you eat. But do you eat only in response to hunger? You are likely to respond, "Of course not!" If you think back over the last couple of days, you can probably recall several occasions on which when and what you ate had little to do with hunger. In this section on the psychology of eating, we will begin by reviewing the impact of culture on what and how much you eat. Next we will focus on ways in which people attempt to control their eating to have an impact on body shape and size—we explore some of the roots and consequences of obesity and dieting. We will then describe how eating disorders may arise as an extreme response to concerns about body image and weight.

Cultural Impact on Eating How do you decide when and what you should eat? To answer this question, first think about the impact of culture. For example, people in the United States typically eat three daily meals at set times; the timing of those meals relies more on social norms than on body cues. Moreover, people often choose what to eat based on social or cultural norms. Would you say yes if you were offered a free lobster dinner? Your answer might depend on whether, for example, you are an observant Jew (in which case you would say no) or a vegetarian (in which case your answer would still depend on whether you are the type of vegetarian who eats seafood). These examples suggest immediately why culture can trump your body's cues.

Let's look more closely at the culture of eating in the United States. One important source of information is the U.S. government, which serves a number of functions. First, the government regulates what counts as a "serving size" and what types of nutritional information food manufacturers must provide to their customers. Second, the government provides periodic advice on the components of a healthy diet. For example, the U.S. Department of Agriculture (2005) issues publications such as *Dietary Guidelines for Americans*. This publication provides general advice about weight management and physical exercise as well as specific recommendations about how individuals can maintain a healthy diet. The government's publications reflect the current state of scientific knowledge: Recommendations change over time as research advances. You can be quite certain that the dietary guidelines will change again in your lifetime. As with any other type of research-based advice, it's important for you to understand how data support the recommendations as they evolve.

Unfortunately, other aspects of U.S. culture work against recommendations for healthy eating. For example, unhealthy food is relatively inexpensive compared to healthy food. People with limited amounts of money might find a healthy diet relatively unaffordable. This observation has led to the suggestion that people's nutrition would improve if the price differential between healthy and unhealthy food changed (Epstein et al., 2006). Consider a study in which researchers worked with an Alabama deli to decrease prices on healthy foods (Horgen & Brownell, 2002). When the healthy food cost less, people ate more of it. This type of research supports the conclusion that some barriers to healthy eating are the product of economic constraints.

Obesity and Dieting Psychologists have spent a good deal of time considering circumstances that have given rise to what has often been labeled an "epidemic" of obesity. To determine who is overweight and who is obese, researchers often turn to a measure called *body mass index (BMI)*. To calculate BMI, one divides an individual's weight in kilograms by the square of height in meters. For example, someone who weighed 154 lb and was 5′7″ would have a BMI of 24.2. (154 lb = 69.8 kilograms. 5′7″ = 1.70 meters. $69.8/(1.70)^2 = 24.2$.) (You can also use Google to find a BMI calculator on the Web.) In most instances, individuals who have BMIs between 25 to 29.9 are considered overweight. Those individuals with BMIs 30 and above are considered obese. By those standards, roughly 71 percent of adult men and 62 percent of the adult women in the United States are overweight or obese (Ogden et al., 2006). Among children and adolescents, 18.2 percent of boys and 16.0 percent of girls are overweight or obese.

These figures suggest why there's a certain urgency to answer the question, Why do people become overweight? It probably will not surprise you that, as you have seen throughout *Psychology and Life,* the answer lies partly in nature: Some people have a genetic predisposition toward obesity. Researchers have provided ample evidence that people are born with innate tendencies to be lighter or heavier. For example, studies of monozygotic (identical) twins reveal higher correlations for BMI and other measures of body size than those for dizygotic (fraternal) twins (Schousboe et al., 2004; Silventoinen et al., 2007). That consistent pattern provides strong evidence for a genetic influence on people's weight.

Researchers have begun to discover some of the genetic mechanisms that may predispose some individuals to obesity (Farooqi & O'Rahilly, 2007). For example, a gene has been isolated that appears to control signals to the brain that enough fat has been stored in the body in the course of a meal—so the individual should stop eating (Dahlman & Arner, 2007). The gene influences the production of a hormone called *leptin*. Recall from Chapter 5 that cannabinoids in your brain play a role in stimulating appetite (Kirkham, 2005). Leptin works in opposition to those cannabinoids to keep appetite under control (Jo et al., 2005). If leptin is not available to balance these cannabinoids, it is likely that individuals will continue to eat. Thus the gene that controls leptin appears to have a critical influence on weight regulation and the potential for obesity. Research continues to reveal additional genes that influence the likelihood of obesity (Boutin & Frougel, 2005).

However, even a biological predisposition may not be enough to "cause" a particular person to become overweight. What matters, in addition, is the way in which an individual *thinks* about food and eating behaviors. Early research on psychological aspects of eating focused on the extent to which overweight individuals are attentive to their bodies' internal hunger cues versus food in the external environment (Schachter, 1971b). The suggestion was that, when food is available and prominent, overweight individuals ignore the cues their bodies give them. This theory proved to be insufficient, however, because weight itself does not always predict eating patterns. That is, not all people who are overweight have the same psychological makeup with respect to eating behaviors. Let's see why.

Janet Polivy and **Peter Herman** have proposed that the critical dimension that underlies the psychology of eating behaviors is *restrained* versus *unrestrained* eating (Polivy & Herman, 1999). *Restrained* eaters put constant limits on the amount of food they will let themselves eat: They are chronically on diets; they constantly worry about food. Although obese people may be more likely to report these kinds of thoughts and behaviors, individuals can be restrained eaters whatever their

Psychology in Your Life

HOW DOES THE PRESENCE OF OTHERS INFLUENCE YOUR EATING?

We'd like you to think back to the last meal you shared with other people. Do you think you ate more, less, or about the same amount you would have eaten if you'd been eating alone? In the chapter so far, we hope we've convinced you that the amount people eat is only partially determined by internal hunger cues. Research suggests that the social context—the presence of others—is an important external cue that affects people's eating. In fact, when you eat with others your most important motive may be to produce a positive impression (Herman et al., 2003). Let's see what impact that motive has.

Consider a study in which college students had ten-minute conversations with their romantic partners, friends, or strangers (Salvy et al., 2007). To make the conversations more "convivial," the researchers provided bowls of cookies and crackers. At the end of each conversation, the researchers determined how much food each participant had consumed. The amounts differed substantially across the different pairings: Males chatting with male friends ate the most; females chatting with male strangers ate the least. Can you see how those results might emerge if the participants were motivated to make a positive impression? The women, for example, might not have wanted to cast themselves in a negative light by appearing gluttonous in front of male strangers.

A similar study examined the impact of social context on food consumption for overweight and normal-weight children (Salvy et al., 2008). The 10- to 12-year-old participants visited the laboratory for two sessions. In one session, the children played and ate snacks on their own. In the other session, the children played and ate snacks in a peer's company. The normal-weight children ate about the same amount of food in both sessions. However, the overweight children consistently ate *less* while they were with a peer. The researchers provided two explanations for this pattern. First, they suggested that the overweight children might have eaten less "to avoid incurring the stigmas attributed to overweight individuals" (p. 195). Second, they suggested that the children might have eaten less to match the consumption of the normal-weight children. Both these explanations support the general conclusion that the overweight children controlled their eating to make a positive impression.

The researchers also discussed their results in the context of changes that have taken place in family's eating patterns over the last decades—the "trend away from family meals towards grazing and eating alone" (p. 195). They suggested that, historically, children may have learned to limit food consumption in the context of meals with parents and siblings. The absence of

that social context could explain some aspects of the increase in childhood obesity. The researchers suggest that social interventions—returning to circumstances in which children eat in the presence of others—could help overweight children eat less.

A final thought on the social context of eating: People tend to underestimate greatly its influence. In one study, pairs of students were able to eat pizza while watching a video together. Within the pairs, the correlation for pizza consumption was 0.64. Even so, when asked why they had eaten the amount they had, only 3 out of 122 participants mentioned being influenced by their companion's consumption (Vartanian et al., 2008). The participants were much more likely to mention other factors such as how hungry they felt, the time since the last meal, or how good the food tasted. However, a second study found that those factors were not actually correlated with the amount that students ate in social circumstances!

Let's return to the question with which we began: The last time you ate with other people, do you think you ate more, less, or about the same amount you would have eaten if you'd been eating alone? To provide the right answer, you must really address a different question: How might you have adjusted your eating to provide a particular impression?

---

body size. How do people gain weight if they are constantly on a diet? Research suggests that when restrained eaters become *disinhibited* —when life circumstances cause them to let down their restraints—they tend to indulge in high-calorie binges. Unfortunately, many types of life circumstances appear to lead restrained eaters to become disinhibited. Disinhibition will occur, for example, when restrained eaters are made to feel stress about their capabilities and self-esteem (Tanofsky-Kraff et al., 2000; Wallis & Hetherington, 2004). In fact, one type of stress is the *anticipation* of being on a strict diet.

Based on self-evaluations of their behaviors and thoughts with respect to food and dieting, female college students were classified as either restrained (17 women) or unrestrained (24 women) eaters. The students were told they were taking part in a study "investigating the effects of food deprivation on taste perception" (Urbszat et al., 2002, p. 398). When they arrived for the experiment, half of the students were asked to undertake a low-calorie diet—approved by "the Canadian Government and the University of Toronto"—for one week. Before they left the laboratory, participants in both the *diet* and *no-diet* conditions were then asked to perform taste tests on three plates of cookies. The participants believed that these taste tests were the baseline data for the study of taste perception. In fact, the researchers were measuring the total grams of cookies each participant consumed. The results of the study are shown in **Figure 11.2**. For unrestrained eaters, it made no difference whether they were anticipating a strict diet. However, for the restrained eaters, anticipation of the diet led them to eat more than twice as much of the cookies.

This result suggests why diets are often unsuccessful for restrained eaters. As the researchers note, their diets can be broken even "by the prospect of not being able to eat forbidden food" (Urbszat et al., 2002, p. 399).

You see now why it might be difficult for people to lose weight once they have become overweight. Many overweight people report themselves as constantly on diets—they are often restrained eaters. If stressful life events occur that cause these eaters to become disinhibited, binge eating can easily lead to weight gain. Thus the psychological consequences of being constantly on a diet can, paradoxically, create circumstances that are more likely to lead to weight gain than to weight loss. In the next section, we will see how these same psychological forces can lead to health- and life-threatening eating disorders.

Eating Disorders We have already seen that people's internal cues—the hunger they experience—only partially determines how much they eat. For people with *eating disorders*, the mismatch between their body's internal signals and their eating behavior becomes particularly dramatic. **Anorexia nervosa** is diagnosed when an individual weighs less than 85 percent of her or his expected weight but still expresses an intense fear of becoming fat (*DSM-IV-TR*, 2000). The behavior of people diagnosed with **bulimia nervosa** is characterized by binges—periods of intense, out-of-control eating—followed by measures to purge the body of the excess calories—self-induced vomiting, misuse of laxatives, fasting, and so on (*DSM-IV-TR*, 2000). Sufferers from anorexia nervosa may also binge and then purge as a way of minimizing calories absorbed. Both of these syndromes can have serious medical consequences. In the worst cases, sufferers may starve to death.

Binge eating disorder is diagnosed when people engage in regular episodes of binge eating without the purges that accompany bulimia nervosa. People who suffer from this disorder feel, during their binges, that they have lost control; the binges cause them great distress. Compared to anorexia and bulimia, binge eating disorder is a relatively new diagnostic category. In Chapter 14, we will present a *Critical Thinking in Your Life* box that discusses its emergence. For now, we focus on anorexia and bulimia because larger bodies of research have examined their causes.

In **Table 11.1,** we present the prevalence for each eating disorder. These data are drawn from face-to-face interviews

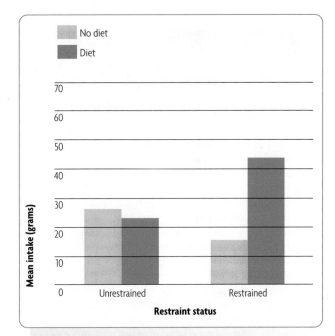

FIGURE 11.2 The Effects of Anticipated Diets
Restrained and unrestrained eaters sampled cookies to rate their taste. Half of the women in each group had agreed to undertake a reduced-calorie diet for one week. For unrestrained eaters, the amount of cookies (in grams) they ate while making the taste ratings was unaffected by the anticipation of a diet. However, those restrained eaters who anticipated dieting ate more than twice as much as their no-diet peers.

of 9,282 men and women in the United States, ages 18 and over (Hudson et al., 2007). Table 11.1 shows that women suffer from these disorders more then men. However, the difference in prevalence has become smaller in the last few years. Earlier estimates suggested that women suffered from anorexia and bulimia at approximately 10 times the rate of men (*DSM-IV-TR*, 2000). However, the data in Table 11.1 show only a three-to-one ratio between women and men. As we describe the causes of eating disorders, we will consider why the gap might be closing.

Research on the causes of eating disorders has confirmed the importance of genetic factors. There is evidence that a predilection toward eating disorders may be genetically transmitted (Kortegaard et al., 2001). One study followed pairs of female twins longitudinally from ages 11 to 18 (Klump et al., 2007). The researchers made comparisons between monozygotic (MZ) and dizygotic (DZ) twins of the sort you have encountered several times before. The data revealed that genetics played a larger role as the twins got older: Over the seven-year period, MZ twins tended to remain similar whereas, by mid- to late adolescence, greater differences emerged within the pairs of the DZ twins. This pattern suggests that genetic risk mattered more as the young girls passed through puberty. Researchers have also conducted twin studies to explore personality variables that may put people at risk for eating disorders. For example, female twins who had high levels of perfectionism (such as concerns over mistakes or doubts about actions) were also more likely to be diagnosed with anorexia (Wade et al., 2008).

anorexia nervosa An eating disorder in which an individual weighs less than 85 percent of her or his expected weight but still expresses intense fear of becoming fat.

bulimia nervosa An eating disorder characterized by binge eating followed by measures to purge the body of excess calories.

binge eating disorder An eating disorder characterized by out of control binge eating without subsequent purges.

What do these photographs of Keira Knightley and Marilyn Monroe suggest about changes over time in how thin women must be for the media to promote them as sexy?

If this general drive for perfection leads people to seek a "perfect" body, eating disorders may be a consequence.

In fact, high levels of *body dissatisfaction*—discomfort with weight, body shape, and appearance—put people at risk for eating disorders (Lynch et al., 2008). For many people with eating disorders, body dissatisfaction is not related to their actual bodies but to their own inaccurate perceptions of their bodies. People with anorexia who are perceived by others as dangerously thin often look in the mirror and still perceive themselves as overweight. Consider a study that looks at the brain bases of these misperceptions.

Ten women with anorexia and ten control women (without the disorder) underwent fMRI scans while they viewed a series of digital images (Sachdev et al., 2008). Each participant had a personalized set of images: Half of the images showed each woman herself; the other half were images of another woman matched for age and body mass index. The women were all photographed wearing the same outfit that made the body's contour easy to detect.

Finally, so that participants would pay most attention to the bodies, the faces in the images were obscured. As they viewed each image, participants were told whether it was a self-image or an other-image. For women in the control group, the fMRI scans revealed the same patterns of brain activity when they studied both types of images. However, for the women with anorexia the patterns for self-images and other-images were quite distinct. For example, when viewing self-images, women with anorexia showed less activity in brain regions that allow people to obtain accurate information from the external world.

An important aspect of this result is that the women with anorexia showed entirely normal patterns of brain activity when looking at the bodies of other women. Only the self-images yielded unusual patterns of brain activity.

Research on body dissatisfaction has yielded consistent group differences in judgments about body size (Roberts et al., 2006). For example, in one study, White college students revealed themselves to be less satisfied with their bodies than did their Black peers. In addition, when asked to choose a drawing to represent their preferred size, White students chose smaller figures than Black students (Aruguete et al., 2005). Similarly, when Black and White college women rated photographs of thin, average, and large models, only the White women rated the large models lower (compared to the thin and average models) on dimensions such as attractiveness, intelligence, and popularity (Hebl & Heatherton, 1998). To explain these differences between Black and White women, researchers often call attention to the role cultural norms and media plays in shaping White women's expectations for their ideal weight and ideal bodies (Durkin & Paxton, 2002; Striegel-Moore & Bulik, 2007). For example, women who make negative comparisons between their own bodies and those of their favorite celebrities are at risk for eating disorders

TABLE 11.1	Prevalence of Eating Disorders	
	Women	**Men**
Anorexia nervosa	0.9%	0.3%
Bulimia nervosa	1.5	0.5
Binge eating disorder	3.5	2.0

Note: Each figure is the percent of the sample of 9,282 U.S. adults who had experienced the disorder in his or her lifetime.

(Shorter et al., 2008). Perhaps because the media provides relatively more images of thin White women, those media images have a greater impact on body dissatisfaction for White women than for their Black peers.

Against this background, you will probably not be surprised to learn that White females are also more likely to suffer from eating disorders than are Black females. One study involved 985 White women and 1,061 Black women who were all about 21 years of age (Striegel-Moore et al., 2003). In those groups, 1.5 percent of the White women had suffered from anorexia nervosa at some point in their lives; no Black women had experienced that disorder. Bulimia nervosa had affected 2.3 percent of the White women but only 0.4 percent of the Black women. Fewer studies have examined other racial and ethnic groups, but evidence to date suggests that eating disturbances are also less frequent in Asian Americans than Whites but equally as common among Hispanic females as among whites. For each of these findings, researchers try to draw a link between cultural values about body size and dieting behaviors.

To close out this section, let's return to the decreasing gap in the prevalence of eating disorders for women and for men. Researchers have begun to study the impact of media images on men's body dissatisfaction. That research interest has emerged because, in the last decade, the number of media images of thin, muscular men has grown considerably. In general, men who view images of ideal male bodies experience increases in body dissatisfaction (Blond, 2008). One study, for example, measured the extent to which Euro-American and Hispanic men in the United States agreed with statements such as "I believe that clothes look better on men that are in good physical shape" and "I wish I looked like men pictured in magazines who model underwear" (Warren, 2008, p. 260). The men from both groups who most agreed with media norms for male appearance, also reported the most body dissatisfaction. Although a causal link must still be demonstrated, these studies support the speculation that changes in media representations of men's bodies have led to the increasing prevalence of male eating disorders.

STOP AND REVIEW

❶ What is sense-specific satiety?

❷ What evidence suggests that the VMH plays a different role in eating from that suggested by the dual-center model?

❸ What pattern of eating do restrained eaters generally follow?

❹ What are the symptoms of bulimia nervosa?

CRITICAL THINKING Recall the study that demonstrated the impact of anticipated diets on food consumption. Why did the researchers lead the students to believe that the study was focused on taste perception?

Visit MyPsychLab.com for more review and practice on the following topics:

◉ **Watch:** Eating Disorders: Nutritionist Alise Thresh

◉ **Watch:** Eating Disorders

Sexual Behaviors

Your body physiology makes it essential that you think about food every day. But what about sex? It's easy to define the biological function of sex—reproduction—but does that explain the frequency with which you think about sexual behaviors? When asked how often they think about sex, 54 percent of adult men and 19 percent of adult women report they think about sex at least once every day (Michael et al., 1994). How can we explain the frequency with which people think about sex? How do thoughts about sex relate to sexual behaviors?

The question of motivation, once again, is the question of why people carry out certain ranges of behavior. As we already acknowledged, sexual behaviors are biologically necessary only for reproduction. Thus, although eating is essential to individual survival, sex is not. Some animals and humans remain celibate for a lifetime without apparent detriment to their daily functioning. But reproduction is crucial to the survival of the species as a whole. To ensure that effort will be expended toward reproduction, nature has made sexual stimulation intensely pleasurable. An orgasm serves as the ultimate reinforcer for the energy expended in mating.

This potential for pleasure gives to sexual behaviors motivating power well beyond the need for reproduction. Individuals will perform a great variety of behaviors to achieve sexual gratification. But some sources of sexual motivation are external. Cultures establish norms or standards for what is acceptable or expected sexual behavior. Whereas most people may be motivated to perform behaviors that accord with those norms, some people achieve their sexual satisfaction primarily by violating them.

In this section, we will first consider some of what is known about the sex drive and mating behavior in nonhuman animals. Then we shift our attention to selected issues in human sexuality.

NONHUMAN SEXUAL BEHAVIORS

The primary motivation for sexual behaviors in nonhuman animals is reproduction. For species that use sex as a means of reproduction, evolution has generally provided two sexual types, males and females. The female produces relatively large eggs (which contain the energy store for the embryo to begin its growth), and the male produces sperm that are specialized for motility (to move into the eggs). The two sexes must synchronize their activity so that sperm and egg meet under the appropriate conditions, resulting in conception.

Sexual arousal is determined primarily by physiological processes. Animals become receptive to mating largely in response to the flow of hormones controlled by the pituitary gland and secreted from the *gonads,* the sex organs. In males, these hormones are known as *androgens,* and they are continuously present in sufficient supply so that males are hormonally ready for mating at almost any time. In the females of many species, however, the sex hormone *estrogen* is released according to regular time cycles of days or months, or according to seasonal changes. Therefore, the female is not always hormonally receptive to mating.

These hormones act on both the brain and genital tissue and often lead to a pattern of predictable *stereotyped sexual behavior* for all members of a species. If, for example, you've seen one pair of rats in their mating sequence, you've seen them all. Much of the sequence is taken up by the male chasing the female. Every so often the female makes herself available, and the pair

What factors determine the sexual behaviors of most species?

copulates briefly. Apes also copulate only briefly (for about 15 seconds). For sables, copulation is slow and long, lasting for as long as 8 hours. Predators, such as lions, can afford to indulge in long, slow copulatory rituals—as much as every 30 minutes over 4 consecutive days. Their prey, however, such as antelope, copulate for only a few seconds, often on the run (Ford & Beach, 1951).

Sexual arousal is often initiated by stimuli in the external environment. In many species, the sight and sound of ritualized display patterns by potential partners is a necessary condition for sexual response. Furthermore, in species as diverse as sheep, bulls, and rats, the novelty of the female partner affects a male animal's behavior. A male that has reached sexual satiation with one female partner may renew sexual activity when a new female is introduced (Dewsbury, 1981). Touch, taste, and smell can also serve as external stimulants for sexual arousal. As we described in Chapter 4, some species secrete chemical signals, called *pheromones,* that attract suitors, sometimes from great distances (Carazo et al., 2004; De Cock & Matthysen, 2005). In many species, the female emits pheromones when her fertility is optimal (and hormone level and sexual interest are peaking). These secretions are unconditioned stimuli for arousal and attraction in the males of the species, who have inherited the tendency to be aroused by the stimuli. When captive male rhesus monkeys smell the odor of a sexually receptive female in an adjacent cage, they respond with a variety of sex-related physiological changes, including an increase in the size of their testes (Hopson, 1979).

Although sexual response in nonhuman animals is largely determined by innate biological forces, this still leaves room for "cultural" aspects to affect choices of mate. Consider the sailfin molly, a particular species of fish.

Under most circumstances, the female sailfin mollies from the Comal River in Texas show a mating preference for larger males. However, what happens when a female sailfin molly observes another female showing a preference for a smaller male? To answer this question, researchers arranged a set of tanks so that female sailfin mollies swam in a large tank that had two smaller tanks at each end (Witte & Noltemeier, 2002). In the initial phase of the experiment, a large and a small male fish were put into small tanks at either end. As seen in **Figure 11.3,** the females spent considerably more time swimming in proximity to the larger male. In the second phase of the experiment, a second female was placed in another small tank so that she appeared to be swimming near the smaller of the two males. The original females had 20 minutes to observe the second female fraternizing with the smaller male. In the final phase of the experiment, the researchers removed the second female and again observed the original females' preferences. As seen in Figure 11.3, in the second preference test the pattern had largely reversed. The female sailfin mollies were now spending most of their time swimming near the smaller males.

Are you surprised to learn that innocent fish swimming in aquariums are paying attention to which fish have been judged desirable and undesirable? This experiment sets the stage for our discussion of human sexuality. We will soon see that researchers believe that human sexual response is also shaped both by our evolutionary history and the preferences of those around us.

HUMAN SEXUAL AROUSAL AND RESPONSE

Hormonal activity, so important in regulating sexual behavior among other animal species, has relatively little effect on sexual receptiveness or gratification in the majority of men and women. Individual differences in hormone levels, within normal limits,

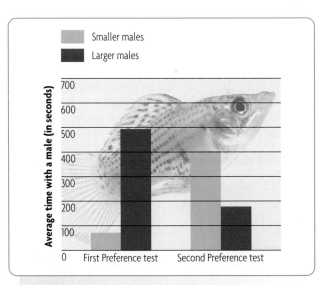

FIGURE 11.3 Female Sailfin Mollies' Mate Selection
Researchers calculated how long female sailfin mollies swam in proximity to larger versus smaller male fish. In the first preference test, the females spent much more time swimming near the larger fish. Next, the original females observed a second female swim close to the smaller male for 20 minutes. In the second preference test, which took place after those 20 minutes, the original females reversed their original pattern to spend more time close to the smaller males.

How did William Masters and Virginia Johnson legitimize the study of human sexuality?

are not predictive of the frequency or quality of sexual activity. However, when hormone levels fall below normal levels because of illness or aging, there is often a negative impact on sexual desire. This is particularly true for the hormone *testosterone*. Both men and women experience restored sexual desire when they undergo treatments that supplement low testosterone levels (Abdallah & Simon, 2007; Allan et al., 2008). Still, men who have undergone surgical castration (and, therefore, no longer produce testosterone) often continue to experience some level of sexual desire, illustrating that human sexuality is motivated by more than hormones (Weinberger et al., 2005).

Sexual arousal in humans is the motivational state of excitement and tension brought about by physiological and cognitive reactions to erotic stimuli. *Erotic stimuli*, which may be physical or psychological, give rise to sexual excitement or feelings of passion. Sexual arousal induced by erotic stimuli is reduced by sexual activities that are perceived by the individual as satisfying, especially by achieving orgasm.

Researchers have studied sexual practices and sexual responses in nonhuman animals for several decades, but for many years studies of similar behaviors in humans were off limits. **William Masters** and **Virginia Johnson** (1966, 1970, 1979) broke down this traditional taboo. They legitimized the study of human sexuality by directly observing and recording, under laboratory conditions, the physiological patterns involved in ongoing human sexual performance. By doing so, they explored not what people said about sex but how individuals actually reacted or performed sexually.

For their direct investigation of the human response to sexual stimulation, Masters and Johnson conducted controlled laboratory observations of thousands of volunteer males and females during tens of thousands of sexual response cycles of intercourse and masturbation. Four of the most significant conclusions drawn from this research are that (1) men and women have similar patterns of sexual response; (2) although the sequence of phases of the sexual response cycle is similar in the two sexes, women are more variable, tending to respond more slowly but often remaining aroused longer; (3) many

women can have multiple orgasms, whereas men rarely do in a comparable time period; and (4) penis size is generally unrelated to any aspect of sexual performance (except in the male's attitude toward having a large penis).

Four phases were found in the human sexual response cycle: excitement, plateau, orgasm, and resolution (see **Figure 11.4**).

- In the excitement phase (lasting from a few minutes to more than an hour), there are vascular (blood vessel) changes in the pelvic region. The penis becomes erect and the clitoris swells; blood and other fluids become congested in the testicles and vagina; a reddening of the body, or sex flush, occurs.
- During the plateau phase, a maximum (though varying) level of arousal is reached. There are rapidly increased heartbeat, respiration, and blood pressure, increased glandular secretions, and both voluntary and involuntary muscle tension throughout the body. Vaginal lubrication increases, and the breasts swell.
- During the orgasm phase, males and females experience a very intense, pleasurable sense of release from the sexual tension that has been building. Orgasm is characterized by rhythmic contractions that occur approximately every eight-tenths of a second in the genital areas. Respiration and blood pressure reach very high levels in both men and women, and heart rate may double. In men, throbbing contractions lead to ejaculation.
- During the resolution phase, the body gradually returns to its normal preexcitement state, with both blood pressure and heartbeat slowing down. After one orgasm, most men enter a refractory period, lasting anywhere from a few minutes to several hours, during which no further orgasm is possible. With sustained arousal, some women are capable of multiple orgasms in fairly rapid succession.

Although Masters and Johnson's research focused on the physiology of sexual response, perhaps their most important discovery was the central significance of *psychological* processes in both arousal and satisfaction. They demonstrated that problems in sexual response often have psychological, rather than physiological, origins and can be modified or overcome

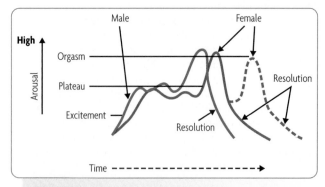

FIGURE 11.4 Phases of Human Sexual Response

The phases of human sexual response in males and females have similar patterns. The primary differences are in the time it takes for males and females to reach each phase and in the greater likelihood that females will achieve multiple orgasms.

---

sexual arousal The motivational state of excitement and tension brought about by physiological and cognitive reactions to erotic stimuli.

through therapy. Of particular concern is the inability to complete the response cycle and achieve gratification. Often the source of the inability is a preoccupation with personal problems, fear of the consequences of sexual activity, anxiety about a partner's evaluation of one's sexual performance, or unconscious guilt or negative thoughts. However, poor nutrition, fatigue, stress, and excessive use of alcohol or drugs can also diminish sexual drive and performance.

We have now reviewed some physiological aspects of human sexuality and sexual arousal. But we have not yet considered the forces that give rise to *differences* in sexual expression. We begin with the idea that the goal of reproduction ensures different patterns of sexual behavior for men and for women.

THE EVOLUTION OF SEXUAL BEHAVIORS

For nonhuman animals, we have already seen that the pattern of sexual behaviors was largely fixed by evolution. The main goal is reproduction—preservation of the species—and sexual behaviors are highly ritualized and stereotyped. Can the same claim be made for general patterns of human sexual behaviors?

Evolutionary psychologists have explored the idea that men and women have evolved to have different *strategies* that underlie sexual behavior (Buss, 2008). To describe these strategies, we have to remind you of some of the realities of human reproduction. Human males could reproduce hundreds of times a year if they could find enough willing mates. To produce a child, all they need to invest is a few minutes of intercourse. Women can reproduce at most about once a year, and each child then requires a huge investment of time and energy. (Incidentally, the world record for the number of times a woman has given birth falls short of 50, but men have fathered many more children. A Moroccan despot, King Ismail the Blood-Thirsty, fathered over 700 children, and the first emperor of China is said to have fathered over 3,000; both had large harems.)

Thus, when reproduction is a objective, eggs are the limited resource and males compete for opportunities to fertilize them. The basic goal for a male animal is to maximize the number of offspring he produces, by mating with the largest number of females possible. But the basic goal for a female animal is to find a high-quality male to ensure the best, healthiest offspring from her limited store of eggs. Furthermore, human offspring take so long to mature and are so helpless while growing that substantial **parental investment** is required (Bell, 2001; Sear & Mace, 2008). Mothers and fathers must spend time and energy raising the children—unlike fish or spiders, which simply lay eggs and depart. Females thus have the problem of selecting not just the biggest, strongest, smartest, highest-status, most thrilling mate but also the most loyal, committed partner to help raise their children.

One evolutionary psychologist, **David Buss** (2008), has suggested that men and women evolved different strategies, emotions, and motivations for short-term mating versus long-term mating. The male strategy of seducing and abandoning as many women as possible—showing signs of loyalty and commitment and then leaving—is a short-term strategy. The male strategy of staying committed to the female and investing in the offspring is a long-term strategy. The female strategy of attracting a loyal male who will stay to help raise her children is a long-term strategy. The female strategy of acquiring resources or obtaining men of high status is a short-term strategy. Because these claims about

TABLE 11.2 Questions for an Unfaithful Partner		
Emotional involvement questions		
Other referent	Do you love him?	
	Have you fallen in love with her?	
Self-referent	Do you still love me?	
	Don't you love me anymore?	
Sexual infidelity questions	Did you have sex?	
	Have you slept with him?	

Adapted from a study by Achim Schützwohl, "Sex differences in jealousy: Information search and cognitive preoccupation," *Personality and Individual Differences*, Science Direct online.

men's and women's differing strategies are based on evolutionary analyses, researchers have sought cross-cultural data to support them. For example, one study involved over 16,000 participants from 52 nations (Schmitt, 2003). The men and women in the study provided information about their interest in short-term sexual relationships. Across the whole sample, men consistently reported greater desire for sexual variety than did women. This result supports the evolutionary claim that men's and women's different reproductive roles has an impact on sexual behavior.

Researchers have provided a variety of types of evidence to support predictions of evolutionary theory. Consider how men's and women's mating strategies could give rise to different experiences of jealousy. According to evolutionary theory, a woman should experience jealousy when she suspects that her partner might no longer feel committed to providing resources to raise her children—these concerns focus on *emotional involvement*. By contrast, a man should experience jealousy when he suspects that he is being burdened by children with whom he has no genetic relationship—these concerns focus on *sexual infidelity*.

To test evolutionary theory's predictions about men's and women's experiences of jealousy, a researcher asked male and female participants to recall or imagine a committed heterosexual relationship (Schützwohl, 2006). The participants were then asked to consider this scenario, with sex-appropriate terms: "Imagine that of late your partner is frequently tardy in coming home. At your insistence, s/he admits meeting another man/woman." Participants then generated a list of questions—under these circumstances, what would they ask their partners? The participants' questions fell into several categories. **Table 11.2** presents the categories relevant to evolutionary theory: Emotional involvement questions and sexual infidelity questions. **Figure 11.5** on page 354 shows the percentage of men and women who wished to ask each type of question. As you can see, women were much more likely to devise questions based on emotional involvement; men were much more likely to devise questions based on sexual infidelity.

---

parental investment The time and energy parents must spend raising their offspring.

Although sex fulfills the biological function of reproduction, most humans engage in sex many more times than they reproduce. Even so, how does the evolutionary perspective explain contemporary sexual strategies?

Does this pattern seem familiar from your own experiences of jealousy? This research illustrates how important aspects of human lives may be guided by our evolutionary history.

Although research supports many of the predictions of the evolutionary account of human sexual behaviors, other theorists believe that the account greatly underestimates the role of culture (Eastwick et al., 2006; Baumeister & Twenge, 2002). For example, women demonstrate greater *erotic plasticity* than men: Women show greater variation in sexual responses and sexual behaviors than men do (Baumeister, 2000). These variations appear, in large part, to be a consequence of cultural constraints (Hyde & Durik, 2000). Consider the "sexual revolution" of the 1960s: Changes in sexual behavior were brought about by women's increased willingness to engage in casual sexual relations. What had changed was not, of course, women's evolutionary history but, rather, cultural attitudes toward the expression of sexuality.

Although the evolutionary approach explains some aspects of human sexual behavior, the critique calls attention to variability imposed by culture. Norms of sexual behavior are highly sensitive to time and place. We turn now to sexual norms.

SEXUAL NORMS

What is an average sex life like? Scientific investigation of human sexual behavior was given the first important impetus by the work of **Alfred Kinsey** and his colleagues beginning in the 1940s (1948, 1953). They interviewed some 17,000 Americans about their sexual behavior and revealed—to a generally shocked public—that certain behaviors, previously considered rare and even abnormal, were actually quite widespread—or at least were reported to be. The norms for sexual behavior have changed over the years, in part because of scientific advances. For example, the availability of birth control pills in the early 1960s allowed women more sexual freedom because it reduced the likelihood of pregnancy. The arrival of Viagra in 1998 allowed men to prolong their years of sexual activity. Alongside the impact of science, there has been a general trend in many cultures toward more open discourse about

sexual issues. **Table 11.3** provides data from a study that surveyed members of the classes of 1950, 1975, and 2000 from the same high school in the northeastern United States with respect to their sexual experiences in high school (Caron & Moskey, 2002). You can see that there have been general trends for people to talk more openly with their families about sexual issues at the same time that actual sexual experiences have increased.

These sexual norms are part of what you acquire as a member of a culture. We already suggested that some general "male" and "female" aspects of sexual behavior may be products of the evolution of the human species. Even so, different cultures define ranges of behavior that are considered to be appropriate for expressing sexual impulses. **Sexual scripts** are socially learned programs of sexual responsiveness that include prescriptions, usually unspoken, of what to do; when, where, and how to do it; with whom, or with what, to do it; and why it should be done (Krahé et al., 2007; Seal et al., 2008). Different aspects of these scripts are assembled through social interaction over your lifetime. The attitudes and values embodied in your sexual script are an external source of sexual motivation: The script suggests the types of behaviors you might or should undertake.

Let's focus more specifically on the sexual practices of college students. Researchers have often been interested in understanding the decisions students make about their sexual activities—and how students feel about those decisions. For example, in one sample of 152 sexually active college women, 77 percent expressed at least "a few" regrets about their sexual decisions (Eshbaugh & Gute, 2008). Two particular behaviors prompted the most intense regret. First, "engaging in intercourse with someone once and only once" (p. 83), something 36 percent of the women reported having done. Second, "engaging in intercourse with someone known for less than 24 [hours]" (p. 83), something 29 percent of the women

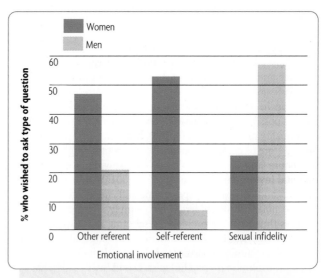

FIGURE 11.5 Sex Differences in Jealousy

Heterosexual men and women wrote questions they imagined asking if they learned their partners had been unfaithful. Women devised more questions that focused on emotional involvement. Men devised more questions focused on sexual infidelity.

Adapted from a study by Achim Schützwohl, "Sex differences in jealousy: Information search and cognitive preoccupation," *Personality and Individual Differences,* Science Direct online.

---

sexual script Socially learned program of sexual responsiveness.

TABLE 11.3 Sexual Experiences of the Classes of 1950, 1975, and 2000			
	1950	**1975**	**2000**
In high school, how much did you discuss sexual intercourse, birth control, sexually transmitted diseases, or pregnancy with your parents/family?			
We never talked about sex issues.	65%	50%	15%
We talked about sex occasionally/a few times.	25%	41%	45%
We talked about sex many times/regularly.	10%	9%	40%
Which statement *best* describes your sexual experience while in high school?			
I did not think about sex.	25%	2%	6%
I had never kissed someone.	41%	9%	3%
I had "made out" with someone.	10%	24%	22%
I had sex 1–3 times.	8%	13%	11%
I had sex more than 3 times.	16%	52%	58%

Adapted from Sandra L. Caron and Eilean G. Moskey, "Changes over time in teenage sexual relationships: Comparing the high school class of 1950, 1975, and 2000." University of Maine.

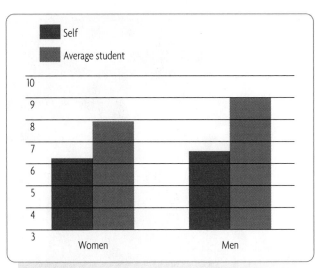

FIGURE 11.6 Judgments about Hooking Up

College students provided ratings on a scale of 1 (not at all comfortable) to 11 (very comfortable) to two questions about "hooking up." For the self ratings, they indicated how comfortable they personally were with the amount of hooking up that went on at their school. For the average student ratings, they indicated how comfortable they believed the average student was with the amount of hooking up.

From *Journal of Sex Research* by Lambert, T.A., Kahn A.S., & Apple, K.J. Copyright 2003 by Taylor & Francis Informa UK Ltd–Journals. Reproduced with permission of Taylor & Francis Informa UK Ltd–Journals in the format Textbook via Copyright Clearance Center.

said they had done. You may recognize those behaviors as part of the definition of "hooking up" (Bogle, 2008). Another study of 327 college undergraduates defined "hooking up" as "a sexual encounter between two people who may or may not know each other well, but who usually are *not* seriously dating" (Lambert et al., 2003, p. 131). Given that definition, 78 percent of the women and 84 percent of the men reported that they had hooked up. The researchers also asked the students who had hooked up to make two judgments: The students rated how comfortable they personally were with the amount of hooking up that went on at their school; they also rated how comfortable the *average* student was with the amount of hooking up. As you can see in **Figure 11.6,** men reported themselves more comfortable with hooking up than did women. However, what you also see is that people's self-ratings were consistently lower than their guesses about others' comfort levels. Thus, the true norm for comfort level (which is the average of people's self-reports) was lower than what the students perceived the norm to be! How might this perception affect people's behaviors?

Research into the sexual experience of college students has revealed an area in which male and female sexual scripts come into devastating conflict: *rape*. In one study, researchers asked 4,446 women at two- or four-year colleges and universities to provide information about their experiences of sexual aggression in seven months of a school year (Fisher et al., 2000). In that reference period, 1.7 percent had experienced rape and 1.1 percent of the women had experienced attempted rape. The

researchers extended those numbers to estimate the likelihood that a woman would experience rape or attempted rape during her college career: They concluded that the number of victimized women might climb to 20 to 25 percent. The researchers also examined a particular type of rape: **date rape.** Date rape applies to circumstances in which someone is coerced into sexual activity by a social acquaintance. For this sample of women, 12.8 percent of rapes and 35.0 percent of attempted rapes occurred on dates. Researchers have documented that men and women have different *date rate scripts*. In one study, college men and women read the same account of a scenario in which a woman had resisted having sex (Clark & Carroll, 2008). Male participants were less likely than female participants to label the incident as a rape. Male participants were also more likely to place responsibility on the victim.

Throughout most of our discussion of sexual motivation, we have been ignoring a major category of sexual experience: homosexuality. We conclude this section on sexual motivation with a discussion of lesbians and gay men. This discussion will give us another opportunity to see how sexual behavior is controlled by the interplay of internal and external motivational forces.

HOMOSEXUALITY

Our discussion so far has focused on the motivations that cause people to perform a certain range of sexual behaviors. In this

---

date rape Unwanted sexual violation by social acquaintance in the context of a consensual dating situation.

How might instances of sexual harassment arise from conflicting sexual scripts?

same context we can discuss the existence of homosexuality. That is, rather than presenting homosexuality as a set of behaviors that is "caused" by a deviation from heterosexuality, our discussion of sexual motivation should allow you to see that all sexual behavior is "caused." In this view, homosexuality and heterosexuality result from similar motivational forces. Neither of them represents a motivated departure from the other.

Most surveys of sexual behavior have tried to obtain an accurate estimate of the incidence of homosexuality. In his early research, Alfred Kinsey found that 37 percent of men in his sample had had at least some homosexual experience and that about 4 percent were exclusively homosexual (percentages for women were somewhat smaller). One major project found that that about 4 percent of women in their sample were sexually attracted to individuals of the same gender, but only 2 percent of the sample had actually had sex with another woman in the past year. Similarly, 6 percent of the men in their survey were sexually attracted to other men, but again only 2 percent of the sample had actually had sex with another man in the past year (Michael et al., 1994). In a recent survey of over 2,000 adults in the United States, 3.2 percent of the men and 2.5 percent of the women reported same-sex activity in the previous year (Turner et al., 2005). Are these figures correct? As long as there is societal hostility directed toward acting on homosexual desires, it may be impossible to get entirely accurate estimates of the incidence of homosexuality because of people's reluctance to confide in researchers.

In this section we consider the origins of homosexuality and heterosexuality. We also review research on societal and personal attitudes toward homosexual behavior.

The Nature and Nurture of Homosexuality After our discussion of evolution and sexual behaviors, it should not surprise you to learn that research evidence suggests that sexual preference has a genetic component. As is often the case, researchers have made this assertion based on studies that compare concordance rates of *monozygotic* (MZ) twins (those who are genetically identical) and *dizygotic* (DZ) twins (those who, like siblings, share only half their genes). When both members of a pair of twins have the same orientation—homosexual or heterosexual—they are concordant. If one twin is homosexual and the other is heterosexual, they are discordant. Studies of both gay men and lesbians have demonstrated considerably higher concordance rates for MZ than for DZ twins (Rahman & Wilson, 2003). For example, in one sample of roughly 750 pairs of twins, 32 percent of the MZ twins were concordant for non-heterosexual orientations versus 8 percent of DZ twins (Kendler et al., 2000a). Although MZ twins may also be reared in more similar environments than DZ twins—they may be treated more similarly by their parents—this pattern strongly suggests that sexuality may, in part, be genetically determined.

Researchers have also begun to document brain differences between homosexuals and heterosexuals. For example, one study used MRI and PET scans to compare brain shape and volumes (Savic & Lindström, 2008). The brain images revealed that heterosexual men had asymmetric brains, with slightly larger right cerebral hemispheres—as did homosexual women. Both the heterosexual women and the homosexual men had symmetrical cerebral hemispheres. The study also identified patterns of connections between the amygdala (which, as you might recall, plays an important role in emotional control and memories) and other brain regions. Once again, the patterns of connections in the homosexual participants' brains were more similar to those in the opposite-sex heterosexual participants. Further research may strengthen or weaken the case for such broad brain differences. Still, it seems clear that some aspects of homosexuality and heterosexuality emerge in response to purely biological forces. Further research may strengthen or weaken the case, but it seems clear that some aspects of homosexuality and heterosexuality emerge in response to purely biological forces.

Social psychologist **Daryl Bem** (1996, 2000) has suggested that biology does not affect sexual preference directly but rather

What evidence suggests that sexual orientation has a genetic component?

has an indirect impact by influencing the temperaments and activities of young children. Recall from Chapter 10 that researchers have suggested that boys and girls engage in different activities—boys' play, for example, tends to be more rough-and-tumble. According to Bem's theory, depending on whether they engage in sex-typical or sex-atypical play, children come to feel dissimilar to either their same-sex or opposite-sex peers. In Bem's theory, "exotic becomes erotic": Feelings of dissimilarity lead to emotional arousal; over time this arousal is transformed into erotic attraction. For example, if a young girl feels dissimilar from other girls because she does not wish to engage in girl-typical activities, over time her emotional arousal will be transformed into homosexual feelings. Note that Bem's theory supports the assertion that homosexuality and heterosexuality arise from the same causal forces: In both cases, the gender the child perceives as dissimilar becomes, over time, eroticized.

Society and Homosexuality Suppose Bem is correct to argue that childhood experiences matter enormously. Does everyone act on the urgings set down in childhood? What, perhaps, most sets homosexuality apart from heterosexuality is the continuing hostility toward homosexual behaviors in many corners of society. In one survey, a sample of 1,335 heterosexual men and women were asked how uncomfortable they would feel being around "a man who is homosexual" or "a woman who is a lesbian" (Herek, 2002). **Figure 11.7** presents the percentage who responded that they would be "somewhat" or "very" uncomfortable. You can see that both men and women anticipate more discomfort being around homosexuals who match their own sex. Researchers have labeled highly negative attitudes toward gay people *homophobia*.

Most homosexuals come to the realization that they are motivated toward same-sex relationships in the hostile context of societal homophobia. Even so, research suggests that many individuals begin to recognize those feelings at quite young ages. For example, researchers asked students from the southeastern United States attending a conference for gay, lesbian, bisexual, and transgendered youth to indicate the age at which they became aware of their sexual orientation (Maguen et al., 2002). Among the gay men, the mean age was 9.6 years; among the lesbians the mean age was 10.9 years. The men reported having same-sex sexual contact at 14.9 years, and the women reported same-sex contact at 16.7 years. These data suggest that many people become aware of their homosexual orientation at a time when they must still function in school environments that are often quite hostile to homosexuality (Espelage et al., 2008). In addition, homosexual youths must often make the difficult decision of whether to disclose their sexual orientation to their parents (Heatherington & Lavner, 2008). Most adolescents rely on their parents for both emotional and financial support; to disclose their homosexuality puts them at risk to lose both types of sustenance. In fact, parental rejection is related to increases in suicide attempts (D'Augelli et al., 2001).

These findings for adolescents reinforce the point that most gay and lesbian individuals find homophobia more psychologically burdensome than homosexuality itself. In 1973, the American Psychiatric Association voted to remove homosexuality from the list of psychological disorders; the American Psychological Association followed in 1975 (Morin & Rothblum, 1991). Spurring this action were research reports suggesting that, in fact, most gay men and lesbians are happy and productive. Contemporary research suggests that much of the stress associated

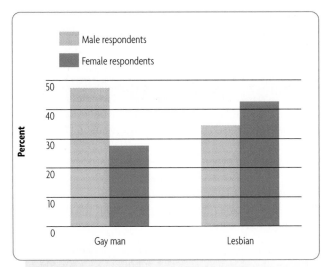

FIGURE 11.7 Attitudes toward Homosexuality

Participants were asked how uncomfortable they would feel being around "a man who is homosexual" or "a woman who is a lesbian." The figure indicates the percentage of men and women who responded that they would be "somewhat" or "very" uncomfortable.

From Gregory M. Herek, "Gender Gaps in Public Opinion about Lesbians and Gay Men," *Public Opinion Quarterly, 66,* 40–66, by permission of Oxford University Press and the American Association for Public Opinion Research.

with homosexuality arises not from the sexual motivation itself—gay people are happy with their orientations—but from the way in which people respond to the revelation of that sexual motivation. Much of lesbians' and gay men's anxiety about homosexuality arises not from being homosexual, but from an ongoing need either to reveal ("come out") to or conceal ("stay in the closet") their sexual identity from family, friends, and coworkers (D'Augelli et al., 2005b). More generally, homosexuals experience distress because they can't speak openly about their lives (Lewis et al., 2006). As you might expect, gay men and lesbians also spend time worrying about establishing and maintaining loving relationships, just as heterosexuals do.

The willingness of lesbians and gay men to "come out" may serve as a first step toward decreasing societal hostility. Research has shown that people's attitudes toward gay men and lesbians are much less negative when they actually *know* individuals in these groups; in fact, on average the more gay men and lesbians a person knows, the more favorable is his or her attitude (Liang & Alimo, 2005; Vonofakou et al., 2007). (When we turn to the topic of prejudice in Chapter 16, we will see there again how experiences with members of minority groups can lead to more positive attitudes.)

This brief review of homosexuality allows us to reinforce our main conclusions about human sexual motivation. Some of the impetus for sexual behaviors is internal—genetic endowment and species evolution provide internal models for both heterosexual and homosexual behaviors. But the external environment also gives rise to sexual motivation. You learn to find some stimuli particularly alluring and some behaviors culturally acceptable. In the case of homosexuality, external societal norms may work against the internal dictates of nature.

Let's move now to our third example of important motivation: the forces that set an individual's course for relative success or failure.

STOP AND REVIEW

❶ What is meant by stereotyped sexual behavior?

❷ What four phases did Masters and Johnson identify for human sexual response?

❸ According to evolutionary theories, why do men desire more sexual variety than do women?

❹ What are sexual scripts?

❺ What does twin research suggest about the genetics of homosexuality?

CRITICAL THINKING Recall the study that looked at jealousy in men and women. Why was it important to break the emotional involvement category of questions into smaller categories that referred to the self and to the other?

Visit MyPsychLab.com for more review and practice on the following topic:

👁 **Watch:** Evolution and Sex: Michael Bailey

These men are participating in the International Games for the Disabled. How can motivation explain variability among individuals—the fact, for example, that some people do better in competition than others?

Motivation for Personal Achievement

Why do some people succeed, whereas other people, relatively speaking, fail? Why, for example, are some people able to swim the English Channel, whereas other people just wave woefully from the shore? You are likely to attribute some of the difference to genetic factors like body type, and you're correct to do so. But you also know that some people are simply much more interested in swimming the English Channel than are others. So we are back at one of our core reasons for studying motivation. We want, in this case, to understand the motivational forces that lead different people to seek different levels of personal achievement. Let's begin with a construct that's actually called the *need for achievement*.

NEED FOR ACHIEVEMENT

As early as 1938, **Henry Murray** had postulated a need to achieve that varied in strength in different people and influenced their tendency to approach success and evaluate their own performances. **David McClelland** and his colleagues (1953) devised a way to measure the strength of this need and then looked for relationships between strength of achievement

motivation in different societies, conditions that had fostered the motivation, and its results in the work world. To gauge the strength of the need for achievement, McClelland used his participants' fantasies. On what is called the **Thematic Apperception Test (TAT),** participants were asked to generate stories in response to a series of ambiguous drawings. Participants shown TAT pictures were asked to make up stories about them—to say what was happening in the picture and describe probable outcomes. Presumably, they projected into the scene reflections of their own values, interests, and motives. According to McClelland, "If you want to find out what's on a person's mind, don't ask him, because he can't always tell you accurately. Study his fantasies and dreams. If you do this over a period of time, you will discover the themes to which his mind returns again and again. And these themes can be used to explain his actions" (McClelland, 1971, p. 5).

From participant responses to a series of TAT pictures, McClelland worked out measures of several human needs, including needs for power, affiliation, and achievement. The **need for achievement** was designated as *n Ach.* It reflected individual differences in the importance of planning and working toward attaining one's goals. The caption for **Figure 11.8** shows an example of how a high *n Ach* individual and a low *n Ach* individual might interpret a TAT picture. Studies in both laboratory and real-life settings have validated the usefulness of this measure.

For example, high-scoring *n Ach* people were found to be more upwardly mobile than those with low scores; sons who had high *n Ach* scores were more likely than sons with low *n Ach* measures to advance above their fathers' occupational status (McClelland et al., 1976). Men and women who measured high on *n Ach* at age 31 tended to have higher salaries than their low *n Ach* peers by age 41 (McClelland & Franz, 1992). Do these findings indicate that high *n Ach* individuals are always willing to work harder? Not really. In the face of a task that they are led to believe will be difficult, high *n Ach* individuals quit early on (Feather, 1961). What, in fact, seems to typify high *n Ach* individuals is a need for *efficiency*—a need to get the same result for less effort. If they outearn their peers, it might be because they also value concrete feedback on how well they

---

Thematic Apperception Test (TAT) A projective test in which pictures of ambiguous scenes are presented to an individual, who is encouraged to generate stories about them.

need for achievement (n Ach) An assumed basic human need to strive for achievement of goals that motivates a wide range of behavior and thinking.

FIGURE 11.8   Alternative Interpretations of a TAT Picture

***Story Showing High* n Ach**

This boy has just finished his violin lesson. He's happy at the progress he is making and is beginning to believe that all his progress is making the sacrifices worthwhile. To become a concert violinist, he will have to give up much of his social life to practice for many hours each day. Although he knows he could make more money by going into his father's business, he is more interested in being a great violinist and giving people joy with his music. He renews his personal commitment to whatever it takes to make it.

***Story Showing Low* n Ach**

This boy is holding his brother's violin and wishes he could play it. But he knows it is not worth the time, energy, and money for lessons. He feels sorry for his brother; he has given up all the enjoyable things in life to practice, practice, practice. It would be great to wake up one day and be a top-notch musician, but it doesn't work that way. The reality is boring practice, no fun, and the strong possibility of becoming just another guy playing a musical instrument in a small-town band.

are doing. As a measure of progress, salary is very concrete (McClelland, 1961; McClelland & Franz, 1992).

How does a high need for achievement arise? Researchers have considered whether parenting practices can bring about a high or low need for achievement. Data come from a longitudinal analysis of a group of Boston-area children.

David McClelland and Carol Franz (1992) compared measures of parenting practice, collected in 1951 when the children were about 5 years old, with measures of *n Ach* and earnings, collected in 1987–1988, when the children were 41. In 1951, the parents were asked to indicate their practices with respect to feeding and toilet training the child. McClelland and Franz considered children to have experienced a high degree of *achievement pressure* when their parents had fed and toilet trained them by strict rules. Overall, there was a positive correlation between early parental achievement pressure and subsequent adult *n Ach*. Furthermore, children who had experienced a high degree of achievement pressure were earning about $10,000 more annually than their peers who had experienced little such pressure.

These data suggest that the degree to which you experience a need to achieve may have been established in the first few years of your life.

ATTRIBUTIONS FOR SUCCESS AND FAILURE

Need for achievement is not the only variable that affects motivation toward personal success. To see why, let's begin with a hypothetical example. Suppose you have two friends who are taking the same class. On the first midterm, each gets a *C.* Do you think they would be equally motivated to study hard for the second midterm? Part of the answer will depend on the *attributions* they each made to explain the C to themselves. **Attributions** are judgments about the causes of outcomes. (We will develop attribution theory at length in Chapter 16.) Attributions can have an important impact on motivation. Let's see why.

Suppose that one friend attributed her performance to construction noise during the exam, whereas the other attributed his performance to poor memory. These attributions provide an answer to the question, "To what extent does a causal factor reside within an individual, or is it a general factor in the environment?" In this example, one friend made an external attribution (construction noise) whereas the other made an internal attribution (poor memory). These attributions would often have an effect on motivation. If your friend attributes her performance to construction noise, she is likely to study hard for the next midterm. If your other friend thinks the fault lies in his poor memory, he's more likely to give up.

The internal-external dimension is one of three dimensions along which attributions can vary. We can also ask: "To what extent is a causal factor likely to be stable and consistent over time, or unstable and varying?" The answer gives us the dimension of *stability* versus *instability.* Or we can ask: "To what extent is a causal factor highly specific, limited to a particular task or situation, or global, applying widely across a variety of settings?" This gives us the dimension of *global* versus *specific.*

An example of how two of these dimension can interact is given in **Figure 11.9** on page 360. Let's stay with the example of attributions about exam grades. Students can interpret their grades as the result of internal factors, such as ability (a stable personality characteristic) or effort (a varying personal quality). Or they may view the grades as caused primarily by external factors such as the difficulty of the task, the actions of others (a stable situational problem), or luck (an unstable external feature). Depending on the nature of the attribution students make for this success or failure, they are likely to experience one of the emotional responses depicted in **Table 11.4** on page 360. What is important here is that the type of interpretation will influence both their emotions and subsequent motivation—to study harder or blow off work—regardless of the true reason for the success or failure.

Let's return to your two friends. We suggested that one friend made an external attribution (construction noise) whereas the other made an internal attribution (poor memory). Researchers have shown that the way people explain events in their lives—from winning at cards to being turned down for a date—can become lifelong, habitual *attributional styles* (Cole et al., 2008). The way people account for their successes and

---

attribution Judgment about the causes of outcomes.

FIGURE 11.9 Attributions Regarding Causes for Behavioral Outcomes

Four possible outcomes are generated with just two sources of attributions about behavior. Ability attributions are made for the internal–stable combination, effort for the internal but unstable combination, a difficult task (test) when external–stable forces are assumed to be operating, and luck for the unstable–external combination.

failures along the three dimensions we've identified can influence motivation, mood, and even ability to perform appropriately. Attributional style affects people's activity and passivity, whether they persist or give up easily, take risks, or play it safe (Seligman, 1991).

In Chapter 14, we will see that an internal–global–stable attributional style ("I never do anything right") puts individuals at risk for depression (and one of the symptoms of depression is impaired motivation). For now, however, let's focus on the way in which attributional style might lead one of your friends to have an *A* and the other an *F* by the end of the semester. The key ingredient to their success and failure might turn out to be familiar and seemingly simple: *optimism* versus *pessimism* (Seligman, 1991). These two divergent ways of looking at the world influence motivation, mood, and behavior.

The *pessimistic attributional style* focuses on the causes of failure as internally generated. Furthermore, the bad situation and the individual's role in causing it are seen as stable and global—"It won't ever change, and it will affect everything." The *optimistic attributional style* sees failure as the result of external causes—"The test was unfair"—and of events that are unstable or modifiable and specific—"If I put in more effort next time, I'll do better, and this one setback won't affect how I perform any other task that is important to me."

These causal explanations are reversed when it comes to the question of success. Optimists take full, personal internal–stable–global credit for success. However, pessimists attribute their success to external–unstable–global or specific factors. Because they believe themselves to be doomed to fail, pessimists perform worse than others would expect, given objective measures of their talent. A body of research supports these generalizations about optimists and pessimists. For example, one study measured the explanatory styles of 130 male salespeople in a leading United Kingdom insurance company (Corr & Gray, 1996). In the study, salespeople with more positive attributional styles were also likely to have higher sales. In everyday life, interpretations of events affect both optimists' and pessimists' levels of motivation for future performance.

To close this section, let's look at a research example of the powerful impact of causal attributions in an academic setting.

> When minority group students attend college, they often report that they do not feel socially comfortable in their new environment. Those feelings of social displacement can undermine students' achievement motivation. A pair of researchers predicted that they could improve Black students' academic performance if they changed the students' attributions about their lack of social belonging (Walton & Cohen, 2007). Participants in the study read survey material about college experiences. For the experimental group, some of that material provided a new way to make attributions about difficulties with social belonging: The survey asserted, for example, that "quantitative statistics indicated that most upperclassmen had 'worried [as 1st-year students] whether other students would accept them,' but that now most are sure 'that other students accept them' " (p. 88). The control group did not read this type of information. To test the impact of this brief intervention, the researchers obtained participants' grades for the following semester. They calculated whether each student's grades were higher or lower than would be expected based on earlier semesters. Participants in the experimental group obtained grades that were better than expected; participants in the control group did worse than expected.

Because of the way in which attributions affect motivation, a small amount of information about feelings of social belonging had a lasting effect on students' performance.

TABLE 11.4 Attribution-Dependent Emotional Responses

Your feelings in response to success and failure depend on the kinds of attributions you make regarding the cause of those outcomes. For example, you take pride in success when you attribute it to your ability but are depressed when you perceive lack of ability to cause failure. Or you feel gratitude when you attribute your success to the actions of others but anger when they are seen as contributing to your failure.

	Emotional Responses	
Attribution	**Success**	**Failure**
Ability	Competence	Incompetence
	Confidence	Resignation
	Pride	Depression
Effort	Relief	Guilt
	Contentment	Shame
	Relaxation	Fear
Action of others	Gratitude	Anger
	Thankfulness	Fury
Luck	Surprise	Surprise
	Guilt	Astonishment

We believe that there is much value to you in this line of psychological research. You can work at developing an optimistic explanatory style for your successes and failures. You can avoid making negative, stable, dispositional attributions for your failures by examining possible causal forces in the situation. Finally, don't let your motivation be undermined by momentary setbacks. You can apply this research-based advice to better your life—a recurring theme of *Psychology and Life.*

WORK AND ORGANIZATIONAL PSYCHOLOGY

Now suppose your positive philosophy has helped you to get a job in a big corporation. Can we predict exactly how motivated you'll be just by knowing about you, as an individual—your *n Ach* score or your explanatory style? Your individual level of motivation will depend, in part, on the overall context of people and rules in which you work. Recognizing that work settings are complex social systems, **organizational psychologists** study various aspects of human relations, such as communication among employees, socialization or enculturation of workers, leadership, attitudes and commitment toward a job and/or an organization, job satisfaction, stress and burnout, and overall quality of life at work (Blustein, 2008; Hodgkinson & Healey, 2008). As consultants to businesses, organizational psychologists may assist in recruitment, selection, and training of employees. They also make recommendations about job redesign—tailoring a job to fit the person. Organizational psychologists apply theories of management, decision making, and development to improve work settings.

Let's look at a pair of theories organizational psychologists have developed to understand motivation in the workplace. *Equity theory* and *expectancy theory* attempt to explain and predict how people will respond under different working conditions. These theories assume that workers engage in certain cognitive activities, such as assessing fairness through processes of social comparison with other workers or estimating expected rewards associated with their performance. Although both equity theory and expectancy theory originated over 40 years ago, researchers continue to use these perspectives to understand workplace motivation (for example, Bolino & Turnley, 2008; Grant, 2008; Siegel et al., 2008).

Equity theory proposes that workers are motivated to maintain fair or equitable relationships with other relevant persons (Adams, 1965). Workers take note of their inputs (investments or contributions they make to their jobs) and their outcomes (what they receive from their jobs), and then they compare these with the inputs and outcomes of other workers. When the ratio of outcomes to inputs for Worker *A* is equal to the ratio for Worker *B* (outcome *A* ÷ input *A* = outcome *B* ÷ input *B*), then Worker *A* will feel satisfied. Dissatisfaction will result when these ratios are not equal. Because feeling this inequity is aversive, workers will be motivated to restore equity by changing the relevant inputs and outcomes. These changes could be behavioral (for example, reducing input by working less, increasing outcome by asking for a raise). Or they could be psychological (for example, reinterpreting the value of the inputs—"My work isn't really that good"—or the value of the outcome—"I'm lucky to have a weekly paycheck I can count on").

Have you noticed the consequences of equity or inequity in your own work situations? Consider a situation in which a coworker leaves for a better job. How does that make you feel?

How does expectancy theory explain some players' choice to favor hitting home runs over achieving a higher batting average?

Equity theory suggests that you may feel like you have been unfairly left behind in an undesirable job. In fact, when coworkers leave in circumstances in which they have expressed dissatisfaction, the people remaining tend to become less productive in their jobs—they decrease productivity to restore their sense of equity (Sheehan, 1993). If you end up in a management position, you should try to prevent this pattern by addressing the psychological needs of your employees with respect to equity. For example, keep in mind the benefit of adequate explanations for changes in the relationship of inputs to outcomes.

Expectancy theory proposes that workers are motivated when they expect that their effort and performance on the job will result in desired outcomes (Harder, 1991; Porter & Lawler, 1968; Vroom, 1964). In other words, people will engage in work they find attractive (leading to favorable consequences) and achievable. Expectancy theory emphasizes

organizational psychologist Psychologist who studies various aspects of the human work environment, such as communication among employees, socialization or enculturation of workers, leadership, job satisfaction, stress and burnout, and overall quality of life.

equity theory A cognitive theory of work motivation that proposes that workers are motivated to maintain fair and equitable relationships with other relevant persons; also, a model that postulates that equitable relationships are those in which the participants' outcomes are proportional to their inputs.

expectancy theory A cognitive theory of work motivation that proposes that workers are motivated when they expect their efforts and job performance to result in desired outcomes.

Critical Thinking in Your Life

HOW DOES MOTIVATION AFFECT ACADEMIC ACHIEVEMENT?

Suppose you've signed up for your introductory psychology course with two friends, Angela and Blake. On the first day of class, Angela says, "I want to get the top grade in the class." Blake replies, "I'll be happy if I just don't get an *F*." Can you see how Angela's and Blake's goals would motivate them to engage in very different behaviors? One of them is likely to spend much more time reading this text! We can develop the contrast between Angela and Blake to examine, more generally, what researchers have learned about how students' goals affect their motivation and classroom performance. The purpose of this review is to allow you to think critically about your own goals and motivation.

Analyses of students' performance have identified three general types of achievement goals (Meece et al., 2006). Angela is representative of a student who has *performance-approach goals.* She focuses on appearing more competent than others. Blake is representative of a student who has *performance-avoidance goals.* He focuses on avoiding being judged as less competent than others. The third type of goals is *mastery goals.* Students who are motivated by mastery goals focus on mastering new skills: "Success is evaluated in terms of self-improvement, and students derive satisfaction from the inherent qualities of the task, such as its interest and challenge" (Meece et al., p. 490). Researchers measure

students' goal orientation by asking them to agree with statements such as "I desire to completely master the material presented in this class" and "I just want to avoid doing poorly in this class" (McGregor & Elliott, 2002, p. 381).

In general, students with mastery goals are most highly motivated to engage in the behaviors that help ensure academic achievement. One study assessed students' behaviors two weeks before an introductory psychology exam and then immediately before the exam (McGregor & Elliott, 2002). Those students with performance-avoidance goals also avoided studying: Two weeks before the exam, they admitted that they hadn't yet done much to prepare; immediately before the exam they admitted that they didn't feel ready. Students with mastery goals and performance-approach goals all started preparing for the exam well in advance. However, students with mastery goals were distinguished by the calm with which they anticipated the exam: From two weeks before the exam to immediately before the exam, they became less concerned about avoiding it.

As you examine the goals that underlie your own academic achievement, also think back to your classroom experiences: Teachers differ with respect to the goals they instill (Meece et al., 2006). Teachers can emphasize mastery goals by acknowledging students' effort and enjoyment when acquiring new abilities; teachers

can emphasize performance goals by identifying students whose test scores are highest or ignoring poor students. In general, students' goals tend to mirror their teachers' goals. Students may not always have had opportunities to develop mastery goals.

In addition, teachers observe students' behavior to make attributions about their motivation. Suppose you do poorly on an exam. As we noted in the text, you can explain your performance with respect to dimensions such as stability and controllability. Teachers use the same dimensions to respond to their students (Reyna & Weiner, 2001; Weiner, 2006). Consider controllability. Suppose a professor believes that Blake failed an exam because he never works, whereas Angela failed an exam because she transferred late into the class. The professor is likely to be considerably more sympathetic toward Angela than toward Blake. It will be to Blake's advantage to change his professor's attributions!

When students do poorly in our classes, we encourage them to examine the goals they bring to the course and how those goals motivate their behavior. We hope you can see the importance of undertaking this exercise.

- Why might students with mastery goals grow increasingly calm as an exam approaches?
- What could students do to change a professor's attributions about their performance?

three components: expectancy, instrumentality, and valence. *Expectancy* refers to the perceived likelihood that a worker's efforts will result in a certain level of performance. *Instrumentality* refers to the perception that performance will lead to certain outcomes, such as rewards. *Valence* refers to the perceived attractiveness of particular outcomes. With respect to a particular work situation, you can imagine different probabilities for these three components. You might, for example, have a job in which there is a high likelihood of reward

if performance is successful (high instrumentality) but a low likelihood that performance will be successful (low expectancy) or a low likelihood that the reward will be worthwhile (low valence). According to expectancy theory, workers assess the probabilities of these three components and combine them by multiplying their individual values. Highest levels of motivation, therefore, result when all three components have high probabilities, whereas lowest levels result when any single component is zero.

Can you see how an expectancy theory analysis might help you if you were in a management position? You should be able to think more clearly about expectancy, instrumentality, and valence. You should be able to determine if one piece of the picture is out of kilter. Suppose, for example, your employees came to believe that there wasn't enough of a relationship between their efforts and how much they are rewarded. What could you do to change the workplace to restore high values for instrumentality?

As a conclusion to this section, we offer a cautionary note on achievement and motivation in work settings. When you make a personal choice about how hard you can work at a career, keep a careful watch on other aspects of your life. As we will see in the next chapter, aggressive striving for success may, in some respects, work counter to the goal of having a long and healthy life.

We have come a long way since we asked you to consider why you got out of bed this morning. We have described the biology and psychology of hunger and eating, and the evolutionary and social dimensions of human sexuality. We have explored individual differences in people's need to achieve and explain personal success. Throughout this discussion, you have seen the intricate interplay of nature and nurture, at the level of both the species and the individual. So, with all this information in hand, why *did* you get out of bed this morning?

STOP AND REVIEW

❶ What is need for achievement?
❷ Along what dimensions do people make attributions?
❸ How does expectancy theory explain motivation in the workplace?

CRITICAL THINKING Consider the study that demonstrated the impact of attributions on academic performance. How might your own college or university apply the study's findings?

Recapping Main Points

Understanding Motivation

- Motivation is a dynamic concept used to describe the processes directing behavior.
- Motivational analysis helps explain how biological and behavioral processes are related and why people pursue goals despite obstacles and adversity.
- Drive theory conceptualizes motivation as tension reduction.
- People are also motivated by incentives, external stimuli that are not related to physiological needs.
- Instinct theory suggests that motivation often relies on innate stereotypical responses.
- Social and cognitive psychologists emphasize the individual's perception of, interpretation of, and reaction to a situation.
- Abraham Maslow suggested that human needs can be organized hierarchically.
- Although real human motivation is more complex, Maslow's theory provides a useful framework for summarizing motivational forces.

Eating

- The body has a number of mechanisms to regulate the initiation and cessation of eating.
- Cultural norms have an impact on what and how much people eat.
- If individuals become restrained eaters, their diets may result in weight gain rather than weight loss.

- Eating disorders are life-threatening illnesses that may arise from genetic factors, misperceptions of body image and cultural pressures.

Sexual Behaviors

- From an evolutionary perspective, sex is the mechanism for producing offspring.
- In animals, the sex drive is largely controlled by hormones.
- The work of Masters and Johnson provided the first hard data on the sexual response cycles of men and women.
- Evolutionary psychologists suggest that much of human sexual behavior reflects different mating strategies for men and women.
- Sexual scripts define culturally appropriate forms of sexual behavior.
- Homosexuality and heterosexuality are determined both by genetics and personal and social environments.

Motivation for Personal Achievement

- People have varying needs for achievement. Motivation for achievement is influenced by how people interpret success and failure.
- Two attributional styles, optimism and pessimism, lead to different attitudes toward achievement and influence motivation.
- Organizational psychologists study human motivation in work settings.

KEY TERMS

anorexia nervosa (p. 348)

attribution (p. 359)

binge eating disorder (p. 348)

bulimia nervosa (p. 348)

date rape (p. 355)

drive (p. 341)

equity theory (p. 361)

expectancy theory (p. 361)

hierarchy of needs (p. 343)

homeostasis (p. 341)

incentive (p. 342)

instinct (p. 342)

motivation (p. 340)

need for achievement *(n Ach)* (p. 358)

organizational psychologist (p. 361)

parental investment (p. 353)

sexual arousal (p. 352)

sexual script (p. 354)

social-learning theory (p. 343)

Thematic Apperception Test (TAT)
    (p. 358)

Chapter 11 Practice Test

1. You are watching your friend Carlos play tennis with little success. At the end of the match, he comes over and says, "I just couldn't get motivated today." How is Carlos using the concept of motivation?
   a. to infer private states from public acts
   b. to relate biology to behavior
   c. to account for behavioral variability
   d. to explain perseverance despite adversity

2. A(n) _____ is a preprogrammed tendency that is essential for the survival of a species.
   a. incentive   c. metamotivational state
   b. drive   d. instinct

3. According to Maslow, you should always try to satisfy your _____ needs before you satisfy your _____ needs.
   a. attachment; biological
   b. esteem; attachment
   c. safety; esteem
   d. self-actualization; esteem

4. At every meal, Jonah eats food with only one flavor. Because of _____, this should generally _____ the amount of food Jonah eats.
   a. stomach contractions; increase
   b. lateral hypothalamus stimulation; decrease
   c. sensory-specific satiety; increase
   d. sensory-specific satiety; decrease

5. When restrained eaters become disinhibited, they tend to
   a. engage in high-calorie binges.
   b. reduce their food consumption further.
   c. go off their diets permanently.
   d. behave more like unrestrained eaters.

6. Which of these statements is *not* true?
   a. Anorexia is diagnosed when people weigh less than 85 percent of their expected body weight.
   b. Men and women suffer from anorexia at the same rate.
   c. Bulimia is characterized by binging and purging.
   d. Bulimia occurs more often than anorexia.

7. Barney and Wilma have just watched a movie together while eating popcorn. Suppose you asked Barney why he ate the amount of popcorn he ate. It's least likely that he would mention
   a. how hungry he had been.
   b. being influenced by the amount that Wilma ate.
   c. how long it had been since he had eaten a meal.
   d. the taste of the popcorn.

8. Because of the action of _____, you would expect _____ of many species not always to be receptive to mating.
   a. androgens; females   c. androgens; males
   b. estrogen; males   d. estrogen; females

9. According to Masters and Johnson's research on human sexual arousal, the _____ phase precedes the _____ phase.
   a. resolution; plateau   c. plateau; orgasm
   b. plateau; excitement   d. resolution; orgasm

10. You have a friend who focuses a lot of energy on having brief sexual relationships. This sounds like a _____ mating strategy for a _____.
    a. long-term; female   c. long-term; male
    b. short-term; male   d. short-term; female

11. According to research, which pair of siblings should be most likely to share the same sexual orientation?
    a. Larry and John, DZ twins
    b. Deborah and Patty, MZ twins
    c. Rose and Leo, DZ twins
    d. Anne and Charlotte, DZ twins

12. Which of these statements is *not* true for individuals high in need for achievement?
    a. They always complete their tasks.
    b. They like work to go efficiently.
    c. They like to attain their goals.
    d. They spend time on planning.

13. Every day, Victor gets a perfect score on his local newspaper's trivia quiz. Victor thinks this is possible because the trivia questions are really easy. This is an _____ for his performance.
    a. internal-stable   c. external-stable
    b. external-unstable   d. external-unstable

14. During a lecture, your professor talks a lot about "valence" and "instrumentality." The lecture most likely concerns
    a. attributions.
    b. equity theory.
    c. need for achievement.
    d. expectancy theory.

15. On the way into an exam, you overhear Trudy say, "I'm going to get a perfect score on this exam." You suspect that Trudy is motivated by _____ goals.
    a. performance-approach
    b. mastery
    c. performance-avoidance
    d. equity

Essay Questions

1. How does culture affect the development of eating disorders?

2. What is the origin of sexual scripts?

3. What impact do optimistic versus pessimistic attributional styles have on people's lives?

Discovering Psychology Viewing Guide

Watch the following videos by logging on to MyPsychLab (www. mypsychlab. com). After you have watched the videos, complete the activities that follow.

Program 12: Motivation and Emotion

Program 17: Sex and Gender

KEY TERMS AND PEOPLE

As you watch the programs, pay particular attention to these terms and people in addition to those covered in this textbook.

- *androgynous*—having both masculine and feminine traits.
- *arousal*—a heightened level of excitation or activation.
- *cognitive developmental theory*—the theory stating that children use "male" and "female" as fundamental categories and actively sex-type themselves to achieve cognitive consistency.
- *developmental strategies*—behaviors that have evolved to conform to the sex roles typical of the adult members of a species.
- *optimism*—the tendency to attribute failure to external, unstable, or changeable factors and to attribute success to stable factors.
- *pessimism*—the tendency to attribute failure to stable or internal factors and to attribute success to global variables.
- *sex typing*—the psychological process by which boys and girls become masculine or feminine.
- *social learning theory*—the theory stating that children are socialized by observing role models and are rewarded or punished for behaving appropriately.
- *stereotype*—the belief that all members of a group share common traits.
- *Norman Adler*—studies the physiological and behavioral mechanisms of sexual behavior.
- *Michael Meaney*—developmental neuroscientist who studies the interaction of biology and psychology in the development of sex differences.

PROGRAM REVIEW

Program 12

1. What is the general term for all the physical and psychological processes that start behavior, maintain it, and stop it?
   a. explanatory style
   b. repression
   c. addiction
   d. motivation

2. Phoebe has a phobia regarding cats. What is her motivation?
   a. environmental arousal
   b. overwhelming fear

   c. repressed sexual satisfaction
   d. a need for attachment to others

3. What is the role of the pleasure-pain principle in motivation?
   a. We repress our pleasure in others' pain.
   b. We seek pleasure and avoid pain.
   c. We persist in doing things, even when they are painful.
   d. We are more intensely motivated by pain than by pleasure.

4. Which activity most clearly involves a "reframing" of the tension between desire and restraint?
   a. eating before you feel hungry
   b. seeking pleasurable physical contact with others
   c. working long hours for an eventual goal
   d. getting angry at someone who interferes with your plans

5. Freud thought there were two primary motivations. One of these is
   a. expressing aggression.
   b. seeking transcendence.
   c. fulfilling creativity.
   d. feeling secure.

6. Compared with Freud's view of human motivation, that of Abraham Maslow could be characterized as being more
   a. negative.
   b. hormonally based.
   c. optimistic.
   d. pathologically based.

7. Behaviors, such as male peacocks displaying their feathers or male rams fighting, are related to which part of sexual reproduction?
   a. providing a safe place for mating
   b. focusing the male's attention on mating
   c. selecting a partner with good genes
   d. mating at the correct time of year

8. In Norman Adler's research on mating behavior in rats, what is the function of the 10 or so mountings?
   a. to trigger hormone production
   b. to prepare the male for ejaculation
   c. to cause fertilization
   d. to impress the female

9. Darwin cited the similarity of certain expressions of emotions as evidence that
   a. all species learn emotions.
   b. emotions are innate.

c. emotions promote survival of the fittest.

d. genetic variability is advantageous.

10. Pictures of happy and sad U.S. workers are shown to American college students and to Italian workers. Based on your knowledge of Paul Ekman's research, what would you predict about how well the groups would identify the emotions?
    a. Both groups will identify the emotions correctly.
    b. Only the Americans will identify the emotions correctly.
    c. Only the Italians will identify the emotions correctly.
    d. Neither group will identify the emotions correctly.

11. Why does Martin Seligman believe that it might be appropriate to help children who develop a pessimistic explanatory style?
    a. These children are unpleasant to be around.
    b. These children lack contact with reality.
    c. These children are at risk for depression.
    d. Other children who live with these children are likely to develop the same style.

12. All of the following are possible origins of a pessimistic explanatory style, *except*
    a. assessments by important adults in our lives.
    b. the reality of our first major negative life event.
    c. our mother's pessimism level.
    d. our level of introversion/extraversion.

13. Which theorist is best known for positing a hierarchy of needs that humans strive to meet?
    a. Freud
    b. Rogers
    c. Maslow
    d. Seligman

14. Although motivation can lead to unpleasant states (such as hunger or frustration), it seems to have evolved because of its benefits to
    a. survival.
    b. propagation of the species.
    c. health.
    d. all of the above

15. What has Robert Plutchik argued about emotions?
    a. There are three basic types of emotions: happiness, sadness, and anger.
    b. There are eight basic emotions, consisting of four pairs of opposites.
    c. Love is not a universal emotion; some cultures do not show signs of having it.
    d. Emotional experience is determined by physiology alone.

16. Wolves and squirrels are most likely to show which of the following in their mating patterns?
    a. romantic love
    b. competition by females for males
    c. competition by males for females
    d. a preference for mating in the autumn so that the offspring will be born during the winter

Program 17

17. According to research by Zella Lurin and Jeffrey Rubin, the difference in the language parents use to describe their newborn sons or daughters is primarily a reflection of
    a. actual physical differences in the newborns.
    b. differences in the way the newborns behave.
    c. the way the hospital staff responds to the babies.
    d. the parents' expectations coloring their perceptions.

18. Michael Meaney attributes the differences in the behavior of male and female rats to the fact that these behaviors "feel good" to the animals. The reason for this is that the behaviors
    a. increase hormone production.
    b. prepare the organism for its life tasks.
    c. stimulate certain brain regions.
    d. fit the preferred pattern of motor activity.

19. How does the health of men compare with the health of women throughout the life cycle?
    a. Men are more vulnerable throughout the life cycle.
    b. Women are more vulnerable throughout the life cycle.
    c. Women are more vulnerable only during their childbearing years.
    d. There is no consistent sex difference in health.

20. What is the likeliest source of the behavioral difference between the sexes regarding crying?
    a. It is an innate difference.
    b. Initial innate differences are reinforced by parents.
    c. It is learned during the socialization process.
    d. We do not know the source.

21. According to Jeanne Block, the sociopsychological contexts for boys and girls tend to be different. One such difference is that the context for girls tends to be more
    a. home centered.
    b. achievement oriented.
    c. filled with risk.
    d. involved with same-sex peers.

22. According to Jeanne Block, the sociopsychological context typically provided to boys is
    a. less protective than for girls.
    b. more supervised than for girls.
    c. less likely to provide opportunities for inventing and discovering than for girls.
    d. more restricted in the network of friends they come into contact with.

23. What is one of the negative consequences of the masculine gender role?
    a. It makes men more vulnerable to depression.
    b. It imposes limits on intellectual development.
    c. It provides little sense of belonging.
    d. It encourages risk-taking behaviors.

24. According to Eleanor Maccoby, at about what age do children begin to prefer same-sex playmates?
    a. 2 years old
    b. 3 years old
    c. 4 years old
    d. 5 years old

25. Which is true about gender roles in children?
    a. Girls tend to be the first to segregate themselves and play among members of their own gender.
    b. Girls are more aggressive in their physical behavior.
    c. Boys and girls will develop strong gender role stereotypes and will segregate themselves based on gender only if adults strongly encourage that.
    d. none of the above

26. According to the film, boys' greater propensity for rough-and-tumble play is likely the result of
    a. biological differences between boys and girls.
    b. different cultural treatment of boys and girls.

c. both of the above
d. neither of the above

27. Boys tend to have _____ friends than girls and tend to be _____ intimate with their friends than girls are.
   a. more; more
   b. more; less
   c. less; more
   d. less; less

28. Because of the way we socialize our children, men tend to experience more freedom to _____, while women tend to experience more freedom to _____.
   a. explore; criticize
   b. withdraw; invent
   c. discover; express themselves
   d. express themselves; explore

29. Which of the following appears in children by 6 years of age?
   a. gender role–related depression
   b. sexual desire
   c. secondary sexual characteristics
   d. extreme gender–based segregation

30. Imagine that a set of parents avoids using gender role stereotypes in the house and that they encourage their son to play with other neighborhood children of both genders. What can we expect will happen?
   a. The boy will show no signs of gender role stereotypes and will be happy playing with both trucks and dolls.
   b. The boy will develop cooperative play patterns that are typical of little girls.
   c. Through social pressure, the boy will develop male gender role–stereotypic behavior.
   d. The boy will be about 10 percent less competent in physical tasks than his male peers.

QUESTIONS TO CONSIDER

1. Human sexual motivation expresses itself in sexual scripts that include attitudes, values, social norms, and expectations about patterns of behavior. Consider how males and females might develop different sexual scripts. How might lack of synchronization affect a couple? How might sexual scripts change as the bad news about sexually transmitted diseases and AIDS increases?

2. If degree of self-restraint and stress determine how likely it is that people will "cheat" on their diets, what sorts of psychological supports would you build into a diet plan?

3. Consider how eating disorders, such as anorexia and bulimia, contradict the pain–pleasure principle.

4. Research suggests that androgynous people are better adjusted than those who are traditionally sex-role stereotyped. But critics contend that the masculine traits lead to higher self-esteem and better adjustment than a combination of masculine and feminine traits. How can having masculine traits enhance a woman's self-esteem?

ACTIVITIES

1. Are we sad because we cry, or do we cry because we are sad? Can making a sad face make us feel sad? Does going through the motions trigger the emotion?

   Try this: Set aside from 10 to 15 minutes for this experiment. Write down the words, *happy, sad, angry,* and *fearful* on slips of paper. In front of a mirror, select one of the slips, and watch yourself as you create the facial expression for it. Hold the expression for at least a minute. Note the thoughts and physical reactions that seem to accompany your facial expression. Then relax your face and repeat the exercise with another slip of paper. Which theories does your experience support or challenge?

2. Observe the activities on which you need to concentrate when your hunger has been satisfied, compared with when you are very hungry. How well can you focus on more abstract motivations when your biological motivations have been left unmet?

3. Pick three close relatives or friends. How would your relationship with them be different if you were of the opposite sex? Which aspects of your personal identity and behavior would change? Which would stay the same?

Emotion, Stress, and Health

S uppose we asked you right now, "How are you feeling?" How would you answer that question? There are at least three different types of information you might provide. First, you might reveal to us the mood you are in—the *emotions* you are feeling. Are you happy because you know you can finish reading this chapter in time to go to a party? Are you angry because your boss just yelled at you over the telephone? Second, you might tell us something more general about the amount of *stress* you are experiencing. Do you feel as if you can cope with all the tasks you have to get done? Or are you feeling a bit overwhelmed? Third, you might report on your psychological or physical *health*. Do you feel some illness coming on? Or do you feel an overall sense of wellness?

This chapter will explore interactions among these three ways in which you might answer the question "How are you feeling?"—in relation to your emotions, stress, and health. *Emotions* are the touchstones of human experience. They give richness to your interactions with people and nature and significance to your memories. In this chapter, we will discuss the experience and functions of emotions. But what happens if the emotional demands on your biological and psychological functioning are too great? You may become overwhelmed and unable to deal with the stressors of your life. This chapter will also examine how *stress* affects you and how you can combat it. Finally, we will broaden our focus to consider psychology's contributions to the study of health and illness. *Health psychologists* investigate the ways in which environmental, social, and psychological processes contribute to the development of disease. Health psychologists also use psychological processes and principles to help treat and prevent illness while also developing strategies to enhance personal wellness.

We begin now by looking at the content and meaning of emotions.

Emotions

Just imagine what your life would be like if you could think and act but not feel. Would you be willing to give up the capacity to experience fear if you would also lose the passion of a lover's kiss? Would you give up sadness at the expense of joy? Surely these would be bad bargains, promptly regretted. We will soon see that emotions serve a number of important functions. Let us begin, however, by offering a definition of emotion and by describing the roots of your emotional experiences.

Although you might be tempted to think of emotion as only a feeling— "I feel happy" or "I feel angry"—we need a more inclusive definition of this important concept that involves both the body and the mind. Contemporary psychologists define **emotion** as a complex pattern of bodily and mental changes that includes physiological arousal, feelings, cognitive processes, visible expressions (including face and posture), and specific behavioral reactions made in response to a situation perceived as personally significant. To see why all of these components are

emotion A complex pattern of changes, including physiological arousal, feelings, cognitive processes, and behavioral reactions, made in response to a situation perceived to be personally significant.

necessary, imagine a situation in which you would feel a surge of happiness. Your physiological arousal might include a gently beating heart. Your feeling would be positive. The associated cognitive processes include interpretations, memories, and expectations that allow you to label the situation as happy. Your overt behavioral reactions might be expressive (smiling) and/or action-oriented (embracing a loved one).

Before we provide an account that unites arousal, feelings, thoughts, and actions, we need to make a distinction between emotions and moods. We have defined emotions as specific responses to specific events—in that sense, emotions are typically relatively short lived and relatively intense. By contrast, *moods* are often less intense and may last several days. There's often a weaker connection between moods and triggering events. You might be in a good or bad mood without knowing exactly why. Keep this distinction between emotions and moods in mind as we describe the theories that explain them.

BASIC EMOTIONS AND CULTURE

Suppose you could gather together in one room representatives from a great diversity of human cultures. What would be common in their experiences of emotion? For an initial answer, you might look to Charles Darwin's book *The Expression of Emotions in Man and Animals* (1872/1965). Darwin believed that emotions evolve alongside other important aspects of human and nonhuman structures and functions. He was interested in the *adaptive* functions of emotions, which he thought of not as vague, unpredictable, personal states but as highly specific, coordinated modes of operation of the human brain. Darwin viewed emotions as inherited, specialized mental states designed to deal with a certain class of *recurring situations* in the world. Over the history of our species, humans have been attacked by predators, fallen in love, given birth to children, fought each other, confronted their mates' sexual infidelity, and witnessed the death of loved ones—innumerable times. We might expect, therefore, that certain types of emotional responses would emerge in all members of the human species. Researchers have tested this claim of the *universality of emotions* by looking at the emotional responses of newborn children as well as the consistency of facial expressions across cultures.

Are Some Emotional Responses Innate? If the evolutionary perspective is correct, we would expect to find much the same patterns of emotional responses in children all over the world (Izard, 1994). **Silvan Tomkins** (1911–1991) was one of the first psychologists to emphasize the pervasive role of immediate, unlearned affective (emotional) reactions. Tomkins (1962, 1981) pointed out that, without prior learning, infants respond to loud sounds with fear or with difficulties in breathing. They seem "prewired" to respond to certain stimuli with an emotional response general enough to fit a wide range of circumstances.

Cross-cultural research has confirmed the expectation that some emotional responses are quite similar in children from very different cultures.

A team of researchers wished to determine how 11-month-old infants from the United States, Japan, and China display anger and fear (Camras et al., 2007). To elicit anger responses, the researchers grasped each infant's wrists and held them against a tray table so that the infants could not

Charles Darwin was one of the first to use photographs in the study of emotion. These plates are from *The Expression of Emotions in Man and Animals* (1872/1965). Why did Darwin believe that emotions were the product of evolution?

move their arms. To elicit fear responses, the researchers presented each infant with "a disembodied toy gorilla head that could be remotely activated to emit loud unpleasant growling noises while its eyes lit up and its lips moved" (p. 136). The infants produced different behavioral responses to the two procedures. For example, they were more likely to increase their breathing rate as an indication of fear versus anger. Those behavioral responses were similar across cultures. In addition, the infants' facial expressions were similar across the cultures. However, those facial expressions were not consistently different for fear and anger. Apparently, children's ability to display distinct facial expressions for negative emotions emerges after the first year of life.

Although this study demonstrated important cross-cultural consistency, there were also subtle differences among the facial expressions for the infants from the three countries. For example, U.S. children were more likely to produce facial expressions that combined *lowered eyebrows* and a *cry mouth* than were their Chinese peers. Such results suggest that culture acts very early in life to have an impact on emotional responses (Camras et al., 1998).

Note that infants also seem to have an innate ability to interpret the facial expressions of others. In one experiment, 5-month-old infants habituated—they showed decreasing interest —to repeated presentations of an adult face showing smiles of different intensities (Bornstein & Arterberry, 2003). The infants were subsequently shown two new photographs: One photograph showed the same adult with a novel smile (that is, a smile with a different intensity); the second photograph showed the same adult with a fearful expression. The infants consistently spent more time looking at the fearful expression—suggesting both that they experienced the fearful expression as something new and also that they sorted the different smiles into the same category. Other research has demonstrated that patterns of brain activity for 7-month-old infants are different in response to angry and fearful expressions (Kobiella et al., 2008). Thus, infants have distinctive responses to facial expressions that, as we just saw for 11-month-olds, they are not yet able to produce.

Are Emotional Expressions Universal?

We have seen that infants produce and perceive standard emotional expressions. If that is so, we might also expect to find adult members of even vastly different cultures showing reasonable agreement in the way they believe emotion is communicated by facial expressions.

According to **Paul Ekman,** the leading researcher on the nature of facial expressions, all people share an overlap in "facial language" (Ekman, 1984, 1994). Ekman and his associates have demonstrated what Darwin first proposed—that a set of emotional expressions is universal to the human species, presumably because they are innate components of our evolutionary heritage. Before you read on, take a look at **Figure 12.1** on page 372 to see how well you can identify these seven universally recognized expressions of emotion (Ekman & Friesen, 1986).

There is considerable evidence that these seven expressions are recognized and produced worldwide in response to the emotions of happiness, surprise, anger, disgust, fear, sadness, and contempt. Cross-cultural researchers have asked people from a variety of cultures to identify the emotions associated with expressions in standardized photographs. Individuals are generally able to identify the expressions associated with the seven emotions.

In one study, members of a preliterate culture in New Guinea (the Fore culture), who had had almost no exposure to Westerners or to Western culture prior to this experiment, accurately identified the emotions expressed in the White faces shown in Figure 12.1. They did so by referring to situations in which they had experienced the same emotion. For example, photo 5 (fear) suggested being chased by a wild boar when you didn't have your

Why do researchers believe that some emotional responses are innate?

  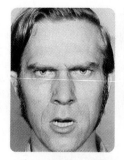 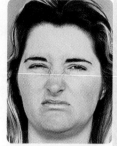

 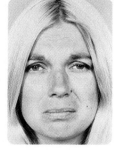 

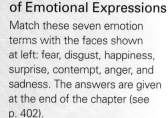

FIGURE 12.1 Judgments of Emotional Expressions

Match these seven emotion terms with the faces shown at left: fear, disgust, happiness, surprise, contempt, anger, and sadness. The answers are given at the end of the chapter (see p. 402).

spear, and photo 6 (sadness) suggested your child had died. Their only confusion came in distinguishing surprise, photo 2, from fear, perhaps because these people are most fearful when taken by surprise.

Next, researchers asked other members of the culture (who had not participated in the first study) to model the expressions that they used to communicate six of the emotions (excluding contempt). When U.S. college students viewed videotapes of the facial expressions of the Fore people, they were able to identify their emotions accurately—with one exception. Not surprisingly, the Americans had difficulty distinguishing between the Fore poses of fear and surprise, the same emotions that the Fore had confused in the Western poses (Ekman & Friesen, 1971).

More recent research has compared judgments of facial expressions across individuals in Hungary, Japan, Poland, Sumatra, the United States, and Vietnam—high agreement was found across these diverse populations (Biehl et al., 1997). The general conclusion is that people all over the world, regardless of cultural differences, race, sex, or education, express basic emotions in much the same way and are able to identify the emotions others are experiencing by reading their facial expressions.

Note that the claim of universality is focused on the basic set of seven emotions. Ekman and his colleagues make no claim that all facial expressions are universal or that cultures express all emotions in the same way (Ekman, 1994). In fact, Ekman (1972) called his position on universality the *neuro-cultural* theory, to reflect the joint contributions of the brain (the product of evolution) and culture in emotional expression. The brain specifies which facial muscles move to produce a particular expression when a particular emotion is aroused. Different cultures, however, impose their own constraints beyond universal biology. We reported some cultural effects in the description of the research comparing responses of members of the Fore culture and U.S. college students. The six-country comparison we cited earlier also produced some differences among the

countries, against the general background of agreement (Biehl et al., 1997). For example, Japanese adults were worse at identifying anger than were U.S., Hungarian, Polish, and Vietnamese adults. Vietnamese adults were worse at identifying disgust than the participants from all the other countries.

Why might these differences arise? Let's now look directly at cultural influences on emotionality.

How Does Culture Constrain Emotional Expression? We've just seen that some aspects of emotional expression are universal. Even so, different cultures have different standards for how emotion should be managed. Some forms of emotional response, even facial expressions, are unique to each culture. Cultures establish social rules for when people may show certain emotions and for the social appropriateness of certain types of emotional displays by given types of people in particular settings (Mesquita & Leu, 2007). Let's look at three examples of cultures that express emotions in manners different from the Western norm.

The Wolof people of Senegal live in a society where status and power differences among people are rigidly defined. High-caste members of this culture are expected to show great restraint in their expressions of emotionality; low-caste individuals are expected to be more volatile, particularly a caste called the *griots*. The griots, in fact, are often called upon to express the "undignified" emotions of the nobility:

One afternoon, a group of women (some five nobles and two griots) were gathered near a well on the edge of town when another woman strode over to the well and threw herself down it. All the women were shocked at the apparent suicide attempt, but the noblewomen were shocked in silence. Only the griot women screamed, on behalf of all. (Irvine, 1990, p. 146)

Can you imagine how you would respond in this situation? It might be easier to put yourself in the place of the griots rather than in the place of the noblewomen: How could you help but

In what ways do cultures constrain emotional expressions in situations like funerals?

scream? The answer, of course, is that the noblewomen have acquired cultural norms for emotional expression that require them not to show any overt response.

A second example of cultural variation in emotional expression arose in the life of one of your authors. At the funeral of an American friend of Syrian descent, he was surprised to see and hear a group of women shrieking and wailing when a visitor entered the funeral parlor. They then stopped just as suddenly until the next visitor arrived, when once again they started their group wailing. What is the explanation for this behavior? Because it is difficult for the family members of the deceased to sustain a high emotional pitch over the three days and nights of such wakes, they hire these professional criers to display, on their behalf, appropriately strong emotions to each newcomer. This is an expected practice among a number of Mediterranean and Near Eastern cultures.

For our third example, we turn to a cross-cultural difference in norms for emotional displays related to pain. Recall from Chapter 4 that psychological context has a major impact on the extent to which people experience pain. Similarly, the cultural context has an impact on the extent to which it is considered appropriate for people to perform behaviors that reveal they are experiencing pain. For example, one study demonstrated a contrast between what people in the United States and Japan consider proper behavioral displays for pain (Hobara, 2005). Participants in both cultures completed the Appropriate Pain Behavior Questionnaire (APBQ) that includes such items as "Women should be able to tolerate pain in most circumstances" and "It is acceptable for men to cry when in pain." In general, Japanese participants provided lower scores on the APBQ: They indicated less approval for open emotional expressions of pain. In addition, both cultural groups suggested more approval for women's emotional displays than men's displays. The researcher attributed the cultural difference to the "traditional stocisim . . . of many Asian cultures" (Hobara, 2005, p. 392).

When you think about the types of emotional patterns that may have evolved over the course of human experience, always bear in mind that culture may have the last word. Western notions of what is necessary or inevitable in emotional expression are as bound to U.S. culture as those of any other societies. Can you see how different standards for emotional expression could cause misunderstandings between people of different cultural origins?

We have seen so far that some physiological responses to emotional situations—such as smiles and grimaces—may be innate. Let's turn now to theories that consider the link between other physiological responses and their psychological interpretations.

THEORIES OF EMOTION

Theories of emotion generally attempt to explain the relationship between physiological and psychological aspects of the experience of emotion. We will begin this section by discussing the responses your body gives in emotionally relevant situations. We will then review theories that explore the way these physiological responses contribute to your psychological experience of emotion.

Physiology of Emotion What happens when you experience a strong emotion? Your heart races, your respiration goes up, your mouth dries, your muscles tense, and maybe you even shake. In addition to these noticeable changes, many others occur beneath the surface. All these responses are designed to mobilize your body for action to deal with the source of the emotion. Let's look at their origins.

The *autonomic nervous system* (ANS) prepares the body for emotional responses through the action of both its sympathetic and parasympathetic divisions (see Chapter 3). The balance between the divisions depends on the quality and intensity of the arousing stimulation. With mild, *unpleasant* stimulation, the *sympathetic* division is more active; with mild, *pleasant* stimulation, the *parasympathetic* division is more active. With more intense stimulation of either kind, both divisions are increasingly involved. Physiologically, strong emotions such as fear or anger activate the body's *emergency reaction system*, which swiftly and silently prepares the body for potential danger. The sympathetic nervous system takes charge by directing the release of hormones (epinephrine and norepinephrine) from the adrenal glands, which in turn leads the internal organs to release blood sugar, raise blood pressure, and increase sweating and salivation. To calm you after the emergency has passed, the parasympathetic nervous system inhibits the release of the activating hormones. You may remain aroused for a while after an experience of strong emotional activation because some of the hormones continue to circulate in your bloodstream.

As we will see when we describe specific theories of emotion, researchers have debated the question, "Do particular emotional experiences give rise to distinct patterns of activity in the autonomic nervous system?" Cross-cultural research suggests that the answer to the question is *yes*. A team of researchers measured autonomic responses such as heart rate and skin temperature while men and women from the United States and Minangkabau men from West Sumatra generated emotions and emotional expressions. Members of the Minangkabau culture are socialized not to display negative emotions. Would they, even so, show the same underlying autonomic patterns for negative emotions as did the U.S. participants? The data revealed a high level of similarity across the two cultures, leading the researchers to suggest that patterns of autonomic activity are "an important part of our common evolved biological heritage" (Levenson et al., 1992, p. 986).

Let's move now from the autonomic nervous system to the central nervous system. Integration of both the hormonal and the neural aspects of arousal is controlled by the *hypothalamus* and the *limbic system*, control systems for emotions and for patterns of attack, defense, and flight. Neuroanatomy research has particularly focused on the *amygdala* as a part of the limbic system that acts as a gateway for emotion and as a filter for memory. The amygdala does this by attaching significance to the information it receives from the senses. It plays an especially strong role in attaching meaning to negative experiences. For example, when people view pictures of fearful facial expressions, the left amygdala (each side of your brain has a separate amygdala) shows increasing activity as the intensity of the expression increases; by contrast, happy facial expressions produce less activity in the same structure the more intensely happy the face becomes (Morris et al., 1996).

In Chapter 10, we described research demonstrating that the left and right amygdala take on different processing roles when men and women encounter and remember emotionally charged pictures (Cahill et al., 2004; Canli et al., 2002a). Recent evidence from PET scans suggests that men's and women's brains are organized differently for emotions even when they are not actively engaged with a task (Kilpatrick et al., 2006). Paralleling the results for emotional memories, men show greater resting activity in the right amygdala, whereas women show more activity in the left amygdala. However, men and women also differ with respect to patterns of connections to other brain regions. For men, the right amygdala communicates extensively with brain regions such as areas of the motor and visual cortex that are oriented toward the external environment. For women, the left amygdala communicates extensively with regions such as the hypothalamus that are oriented toward the body's inner environment. These data suggest that men and women may be biologically predisposed to respond differently to emotional events.

The *cortex* is involved in emotional experiences through its internal neural networks and its connections with other parts of the body. The cortex provides the associations, memories, and meanings that integrate psychological experience and biological responses. Research using brain-scanning techniques has begun to map particular responses for different emotions. For example, positive and negative emotions are not just opposite responses in the same portions of the cortex. Rather, opposite emotions lead to greatest activity in quite different parts of the brain. Consider a study in which participants underwent fMRI scans while viewing positive pictures (such as puppies, brownies, and sunsets) and negative pictures (angry people, spiders, and guns). The scans showed greater activity in the brain's left hemisphere for positive pictures and in the right hemisphere for negative pictures (Canli et al., 1998). In fact, researchers have suggested that there are two distinct systems in the brain that handle *approach-related* and *withdrawal-related* emotional responses (Davidson et al., 2000; Maxwell & Davidson, 2007). Consider puppies and spiders. It is likely that most people would want to approach the puppies but withdraw from the spiders. Research suggests that different brain circuits—apportioned to the different hemispheres of the brain—underlie those responses.

We have seen so far that your body provides many responses to situations in which emotions are relevant. But how do you know which feeling goes with which physiological response? We now review three theories that attempt an answer to this question.

James–Lange Theory of Body Reaction

You might think, at first, that everyone would agree that emotions precede responses: For example, you yell at someone (response) because you feel angry (emotion). However, over 100 years ago, William James argued, as Aristotle had much earlier, that the sequence was reversed—you feel *after* your body reacts. As James put it, "We feel sorry because we cry, angry because we strike, afraid because we tremble" (James, 1890/1950, p. 450). This view that emotion stems from *bodily feedback* became known as the **James–Lange theory of emotion** (Carl Lange was a Danish scientist who presented similar ideas the same year as James). According to this theory, perceiving a stimulus causes autonomic arousal and other bodily actions that lead to the experience of a specific emotion (see **Figure 12.2**). The James–Lange theory is considered a *peripheralist* theory because it assigns the most prominent role in the emotion chain to visceral reactions, the

---

James–Lange theory of emotion A peripheral-feedback theory of emotion stating that an eliciting stimulus triggers a behavioral response that sends different sensory and motor feedback to the brain and creates the feeling of a specific emotion.

How does the brain respond differently to experiences of puppies and spiders?

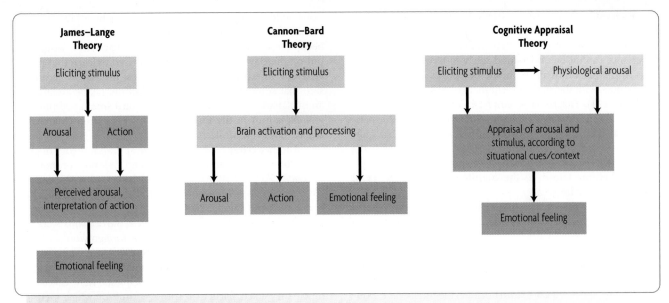

FIGURE 12.2 Comparing Three Theories of Emotion

These classic theories of emotion propose different components of emotion. They also propose different process sequences by which a stimulus event results in the experience of emotion. In the James–Lange theory, events trigger both autonomic arousal and behavioral action, which are perceived and then result in a specific emotional experience. In the Cannon–Bard theory, events are first processed at various centers in the brain, which then direct the simultaneous reactions of arousal, behavioral action, and emotional experience. In the cognitive appraisal theory, both stimulus events and physiological arousal are cognitively appraised at the same time according to situational cues and context factors, with the emotional experience resulting from the interaction of the level of arousal and the nature of appraisal.

From Rathus, *Psychology*, 3E. © 1987 Wadsworth, a part of Cengage Learning, Inc. Reproduced by permission. www.cengage.com/permissions

actions of the autonomic nervous system that are peripheral to the central nervous system.

Cannon–Bard Theory of Central Neural Processes

Physiologist Walter Cannon (1927, 1929) rejected the peripheralist theory in favor of a *centralist* focus on the action of the central nervous system. Cannon (and other critics) raised a number of objections to the James–Lange theory (Leventhal, 1980). They noted, for example, that visceral activity is irrelevant for emotional experience—experimental animals continue to respond emotionally even after their viscera are separated surgically from the CNS. They also argued that ANS responses are typically too slow to be the source of split-second elicited emotions. According to Cannon, emotion requires that the brain intercede between the input stimulation and the output response. Signals from the thalamus get routed to one area of the cortex to produce emotional feeling and to another for emotional expressiveness.

Another physiologist, Philip Bard, also concluded that visceral reactions were not primary in the emotion sequence. Instead, an emotion-arousing stimulus has two simultaneous effects, causing both bodily arousal via the sympathetic nervous system and the subjective experience of emotion via the cortex. The views of these physiologists were combined in the **Cannon–Bard theory of emotion.** This theory states that an emotion stimulus produces two concurrent reactions, arousal and experience of emotion, that do not cause each other (see Figure 12.2). If something makes you angry, your heartbeat increases at

the same time as you think "I'm ticked off!"—but neither your body nor your mind dictates the way the other responds.

The Cannon–Bard theory predicts independence between bodily and psychological responses. We will see next that contemporary theories of emotion reject the claim that these responses are necessarily independent.

Cognitive Appraisal Theories of Emotion Because arousal symptoms and internal states are similar for many different emotions, it is possible to confuse them at times when they are experienced in ambiguous or novel situations. **Stanley Schachter** (1922–1997) originated the **two-factor theory of emotion** to explain how people deal with such uncertainty. According to Schachter (1971a), the experience of emotion is the joint effect of the two factors of physiological arousal and cognitive appraisal. Both parts are necessary for an emotion to occur. On this view, all arousal is assumed to be general and undifferentiated, and arousal is the first step in the emotion sequence. You appraise your physiological arousal in an effort to discover what you are feeling, what emotional label best fits, and what your reaction means in the particular setting in which it is being experienced.

Cannon–Bard theory of emotion A theory stating that an emotional stimulus produces two co-occurring reactions—arousal and experience of emotion—that do not cause each other.

two-factor theory of emotion The theory that emotional experiences arise from autonomic arousal and cognitive appraisal.

Richard Lazarus (1922–2002) was another leading proponent of the importance of cognitive appraisal. Lazarus (1991, 1995; Lazarus & Lazarus, 1994) maintained that "emotional experience cannot be understood solely in terms of what happens in the person or in the brain, but grows out of ongoing transactions with the environment that are evaluated" (Lazarus, 1984a, p. 124). Lazarus also emphasized that appraisal often occurs without conscious thought. When you have past experiences that link emotions to situations—here comes that bully I've clashed with before!—you need not explicitly search the environment for an interpretation of your arousal. This position has become known as the **cognitive appraisal theory of emotion** (see Figure 12.2).

To test this theory, experimenters have sometimes created situations in which environmental cues were available to provide a label for an individual's arousal.

A female researcher interviewed male participants who had just crossed one of two bridges in Vancouver, Canada. One bridge was a safe, sturdy bridge; the other was a wobbly, precarious bridge. The researcher pretended to be interested in the effects of scenery on creativity and asked the men to write brief stories about an ambiguous picture that included a woman. She also invited them to call her if they wanted more information about the research. Those men who had just crossed the dangerous bridge wrote stories with more sexual imagery, and four times as many of those men called the female researcher than did those who had crossed the safe bridge. To show that arousal was the independent variable influencing the emotional misinterpretation, the research team also arranged for another group of men to be interviewed 10 minutes or more after crossing the dangerous bridge, enough time for their physical arousal symptoms to be reduced. These nonaroused men did not show the signs of sexual response that the aroused men did (Dutton & Aron, 1974).

In this situation, the male participants came to an emotional judgment ("I am interested in this woman") based on a *misattribution* of the source of arousal (the woman rather than the danger of the bridge). In a similar experiment, students who performed two minutes of aerobic exercise reported less extreme emotions just after the exercise—when they could easily attribute their arousal to the exercise rather than to an emotional state—by comparison to the emotions they reported after a brief delay that made the exercise seem less relevant to continuing arousal (Sinclair et al., 1994).

Some of the specific aspects of the cognitive appraisal theory have been challenged. For example, you learned earlier that arousal states—the activity of the autonomic nervous system—accompanying different emotions are not identical (Levenson et al., 1992). Therefore, interpretations of at least some emotional experiences may not require appraisal. Furthermore, experiencing strong arousal without any obvious cause does not lead to a neutral, undifferentiated state, as the theory assumes. Stop for a moment and imagine that, right now, your heart suddenly starts beating quickly, your breathing becomes fast and shallow, your chest muscles tighten, and your palms become drenched with sweat. What interpretation would you put on these symptoms? Are you surprised to learn that people generally interpret *unexplained* physical arousal as *negative*, a sign that something is wrong? In addition, people's search for an explanation tends to be biased toward finding stimuli that will explain or justify this negative interpretation (Marshall & Zimbardo, 1979; Maslach, 1979).

Another critique of the cognitive appraisal theory of emotion comes from researcher **Robert Zajonc** (pronounced *Zy-Onts*). Zajonc demonstrated conditions under which people have preferences—emotional responses to stimuli—without knowing why (Zajonc, 2000, 2001). In an extensive series of experiments on the *mere exposure effect*, participants were presented with a variety of stimuli, such as foreign words, Chinese characters, sets of numbers, and strange faces. These stimuli were flashed so briefly that participants could not consciously recognize the items. Later on, participants were asked how much they liked particular stimuli, some of which were old (that is, those stimuli had been flashed below the threshold of consciousness) whereas some were new. The participants tended to give higher ratings to the old items. Because participants experienced these positive emotions without conscious awareness of their origins, the emotional response could not emerge from an appraisal process.

It is probably safest to conclude that cognitive appraisal is an important process of emotional experience but not the only one (Izard, 1993). Under some circumstances, you will, in fact, look to the environment (at least unconsciously) to try to interpret why you feel the way you do. Under other circumstances, however, your emotional experiences may be under the control of the innate links provided by evolution. The physiological response will not require any interpretation. These different routes to emotional experiences suggest that emotions may have a variety of impacts on your day-to-day experiences. We will now consider some of those consequences of moods and emotions.

THE IMPACT OF MOOD AND EMOTIONS

Let's begin by considering the impact of mood and emotion on social interactions. As a positive social glue, they bind you to some people; as a negative social repellent, they distance you from others. You back off when someone is bristling with anger, and you approach when another person signals receptivity with a smile, dilated pupils, and a "come hither" glance. You might suppress strong negative emotions out of respect for another person's status or power. Consider D.R., a woman who lost the function of her amygdala—and with it the ability to perceive anger and fear (Scott et al., 1997). Imagine what life would be like if you couldn't understand when people were trying to communicate negative emotions. For example, what would it be like not to be able to learn from others that a situation was dangerous? Or that your actions had given rise to an angry response? When D.R. lost function in her amygdala, she also lost her ability to function fully in her social world.

The moods you experience have a strong impact on how you function in social settings. Researchers have demonstrated that positive and negative moods affect the way in which people

---

cognitive appraisal theory of emotion A theory stating that the experience of emotion is the joint effect of physiological arousal and cognitive appraisal, which serves to determine how an ambiguous inner state of arousal will be labeled.

What emotions would you be likely to feel if people all around you were wildly cheering your favorite team?

process information (Clore & Huntsinger, 2007; Forgas, 2008). In particular, people in negative moods tend to process information in a more detailed and effortful fashion than their peers in positive moods. Consider the consequences of people's positive or negative moods on the ways they made judgments of guilt or innocence.

Participants in an experiment watched short films that put them in happy, neutral, or sad moods (Forgas & East, 2008). Once the mood was established, participants watched four videotapes of people denying that they had stolen a movie ticket. In fact, two people were being truthful (that is, they hadn't stolen the ticket) and two were not (that is, they had stolen the ticket)—but participants did not have that information. After watching each videotape, the participants judged each person's guilt or innocence. In general, participants in sad moods were more likely to believe that people were being dishonest. In addition, mood had a major impact on participants' ability to make correct judgments of guilt: Participants in sad moods performed better than chance whereas participants in neutral and happy moods did not.

In discussing their results, the researchers suggest that negative moods may make people less gullible. Think about your own life: Are you more skeptical when you are in a sad mood?

We've just illustrated how the global mood you are in may have an impact on the judgments you make. In addition, researchers have explored ways in which thoughts and feelings interact to yield behavioral responses (Storbeck & Clore, 2007). Consider the two reasoning problems given in **Table 12.1.** How would you answer the question at the end of each problem? If you analyze the situations carefully—trying to stick only to the outcomes—you'll see that in each case one person dies so that five others might live. However, most people respond differently to the scenarios: They believe it is appropriate to flip the switch, but they find it difficult to agree that they would actually push a stranger onto trolley tracks. One hypothesis for this difference is that the first type of problem engages emotional

processing. It's hard to be unemotional about the idea of actually *pushing* someone onto the tracks. Evidence in favor of this hypothesis comes directly from the brain. In one study, researchers asked participants to consider moral reasoning problems while undergoing fMRI scans (Greene et al., 2001). As in example 1, some of the problems were *personal*—they asked participants to consider actions that required direct personal involvement. The contrasting problems, as in example 2, were relatively *impersonal.* The two types of problems led to quite different responses in the brain. In particular, for the personal problems the fMRI scans showed considerably more activity in those brain regions that had been associated, in prior research, with emotional processing. This study provides strong evidence that the content of the problems you face in life determines the way in which cognition and emotion interact to yield solutions.

One final note about the relationship between mood and cognition: Researchers have consistently demonstrated that people in positive moods produce more efficient and more creative thinking and problem solving than people in more neutral moods (Baas et al., 2008). Consider a study in which physicians were asked to solve problems that required a certain level of creativity. Those who had been placed in a mildly pleasant mood (the experimenters gave the doctors a small gift of candy) performed reliably better on the creativity test than did those doctors in the control group (who got no prior gift) (Estrada et al., 1994). You can see an immediate application of these types of findings: You are likely to carry out your schoolwork more efficiently and creatively if you can maintain a happy mood. You might be thinking, "How am I supposed to stay happy with all the work I have to do?" We will now consider research that addresses individual differences in people's long-term feelings of happiness.

TABLE 12.1 Moral Reasoning Problems

1. A runaway trolley is heading down the tracks toward five workmen who will be killed if the trolley proceeds on its present course. You are on a footbridge over the tracks, in between the approaching trolley and the five workmen. Next to you on this footbridge is a stranger who happens to be very large.

The only way to save the lives of the five workmen is to push this stranger off the bridge and onto the tracks below where his large body will stop the trolley. The stranger will die if you do this, but the five workmen will be saved.

Is it appropriate for you to push the stranger onto the tracks in order to save the five workmen?

2. You are at the wheel of a runaway trolley quickly approaching a fork in the tracks. On the tracks extending to the left is a group of five railway workmen. On the tracks extending to the right is a single railway workman.

If you do nothing the trolley will proceed to the left, causing the deaths of the five workmen. The only way to avoid the deaths of these workmen is to hit a switch on your dashboard that will cause the trolley to proceed to the right, causing the death of the single workman.

Is it appropriate for you to hit the switch in order to avoid the deaths of the five workmen?

Why might you worry that a positive mood could make you more gullible?

SUBJECTIVE WELL-BEING

At the outset of the chapter, we asked you to consider the question, "How are you feeling?" So far, our focus has been on the present moment: What mood or emotion are you experiencing *now*? However, we can also extend the question over time, to ask "How are you feeling about your life in general?" This question addresses **subjective well-being**—individuals' overall evaluation of life satisfaction and happiness. In recent years, psychologists have paid considerable research attention to the factors that contribute to people's judgments about their own subjective well-being (Kesebir & Diener, 2008). This research focus reflects, in part, the emergence of **positive psychology** as an important movement within the profession of psychology. The goal of positive psychology is to provide people with the knowledge and skills that allow them to experience fulfilling lives. Positive psychology asks this question: "Can psychologists take what they have learned about the science and practice of treating mental illness and use it to create a practice of making people lastingly happier?" (Seligman et al., 2005, p. 410). Much of the research on subjective well-being focuses on trying to determine why some people are happier than others. As is true in most psychological domains, researchers have tried to assess the impact of genetics and environment.

To understand the impact of genetics, researchers have conducted studies using the classic methodology of behavior genetics: They have examined the extent to which monozygotic (MZ) twins and dizygotic (DZ) twins show similar reports of subjective well-being. For example, in one study, researchers obtained measures of subjective well-being from 4,322 Norwegian twins (Nes et al., 2006). Comparisons

subjective well-being Individuals' overall evaluation of life satisfaction and happiness.

positive psychology A movement within psychology that applies research to provide people with the knowledge and skills that allow them to experience fulfilling lives.

between MZ and DZ twins revealed that genetic factors accounted for 51 percent of the variance in subjective well-being for men and 49 percent of the variance for women. The researchers also gathered subjective well-being judgments at two points in time, six years apart. Genetic factors accounted for 85 percent of the correlation across time for men and 78 percent of that correlation for women. Research with a sample of 973 U.S. twin pairs also indicated a large impact of genetics on subjective well-being (Weiss et al., 2008). However, those data also suggested that personality plays an important role in these genetic effects. In Chapter 13, we will discuss the evidence that personality traits are highly heritable. Results from the U.S. twin sample suggest that differences in subjective well-being are consequences of the personality traits people inherit at birth. For example, people who are high in emotional stability and social engagement are also more likely to report high subjective-well being.

We have just seen that genetics has an important impact on individual differences in subjective well-being. Still, life experiences also matter. An important component of people's judgments of subjective well-being is the balance of positive and negative emotions in their lives.

A team of researchers obtained data from 8,557 participants across 46 countries (Kuppens et al., 2008). Participants provided ratings of their life satisfaction by responding to statements such as "In most ways, my life is close to my ideal" (p. 71) on a 7-point scale that ranged from "strongly disagree" to "strongly agree." They used a 9-point scale—ranging from "not at all" to "all the time"—to indicate how often they had felt positive emotions (such as pride, gratitude, and love) and negative emotions (such as guilt, shame, and jealousy) in the last week. The researchers' analyses disclosed consistent relationships among these measures. In general, participants reported higher levels of life satisfaction when they had more positive emotional experiences and fewer negative emotional experiences. However, positive emotions had about twice as much impact on life satisfaction judgments as did negative emotions. The analyses also revealed somewhat different patterns across cultures. For example, cultures differ with respect to the amount of effort people need to expend to ensure their day-to-day survival. For cultures in which survival is an issue, judgments of life satisfaction depended less on positive emotional experiences.

You can probably relate these results to your own feelings of subjective well-being: As you cast your thoughts over the last week, what types of emotional experiences come readily to mind?

You might also think about the features of your life that gave rise to that particular assortment of emotional experiences. Researchers have tested a variety of hypotheses about life events that may affect subjective well-being. For example, major negative life events, such as the loss of a job or the death of a spouse often have a damaging impact on subjective well-being (Lucas, 2007). Researchers have also looked at ongoing differences in the circumstances of people's lives. For example, researchers have suggested that "the single most important source of happiness" is good social relationships (Kesebir & Diener, 2008, p. 122). That conclusion should be familiar from earlier sections of *Psychology and Life;* later in this chapter, we'll emphasize social support as an important resource for coping with stress.

Researchers have also tried to understand the relationship between wealth and subjective well-being. When people struggle to meet their basic needs, they often report low levels of life satisfaction and happiness (Howell & Howell, 2008). However, once people pass the threshold at which those basic needs are secure, the correlation between wealth and subjective well-being is quite modest. If you must make a choice between more money and more friends, the results of positive psychology suggest that you should most often opt for more friends.

We have now explored important short- and long-term consequences of moods and emotions. In the next section, we turn to the topic of stress and how to cope with it. You will learn how to take cognitive control over how you are "feeling."

STOP AND REVIEW

❶ What has cross-cultural research revealed about the recognition of facial expressions?

❷ What role does the autonomous nervous system play in experiences of emotion?

❸ What is the main claim of the Cannon–Bard theory of emotion?

❹ What is the general impact of mood on information processing?

❺ What might be the single most important source of happiness?

CRITICAL THINKING Recall the study that examined mood effects on judgments of guilt. Why was it important that the videotapes showed people that were genuinely innocent and guilty?

Visit MyPsychLab.com for more review and practice on the following topics:

❋ **Simulate:** Transfer of Emotions

◉ **Watch:** Interaction of Cognition and Emotion: Jutta Joormann

◉ **Watch:** Emotion Regulation: James Coan

Stress of Living

Suppose we asked you to keep track of how you are "feeling" over the course of a day. You might report that for brief periods, you felt happiness, sadness, anger, astonishment, and so on. There is one feeling, however, that people often report as a kind of background noise for much of their day-to-day experience, and that is stress (Sapolsky, 1994). Modern industrialized society sets a rapid, hectic pace for living. People often have too many demands placed on their time, are worried about uncertain futures, and have little time for family and fun. But would you be better off without stress? A stress-free life would offer no challenge—no difficulties to surmount, no new fields to conquer, and no reasons to sharpen your wits or improve your abilities. Every organism faces challenges from its external environment and from its personal needs. The organism must solve these problems to survive and thrive.

Stress is the pattern of responses an organism makes to stimulus events that disturb its equilibrium and tax or exceed its ability to cope. The stimulus events include a large variety of external and internal conditions that collectively are called stressors. A **stressor** is a stimulus event that places a demand on an organism for some kind of adaptive response: a bicyclist swerves in front of your car, your professor moves up the due date of your term paper, you're asked to run for class president. An individual's response to the need for change is made up of a diverse combination of reactions taking place on several levels, including physiological, behavioral, emotional, and cognitive. People typically associate stress with *distress*—and assume that all stress is bad. However, you also experience *eustress*. (*Eu* is an ancient Greek suffix meaning "good.") As you'll see by the end of this section, in many circumstances stress can bring about positive changes in your life.

Figure 12.3 on page 381 diagrams the elements of the stress process. Our goal for this section is to give you a clear understanding of all the features represented in this figure. We will begin by considering general physiological responses to stressors. We then describe the particular effects of different categories of stressors. Finally, we explore different methods you can use to cope with the stress in your life.

PHYSIOLOGICAL STRESS REACTIONS

How would you respond if you arrived at a class and discovered that you were about to have a pop quiz? You would probably agree that this would cause you some stress, but what does that mean for your body's reactions? Many of the physiological responses we described for emotional situations are also relevant to day-to-day instances of stress. Such transient states of arousal, with typically clear onset and offset patterns, are examples of **acute stress** Chronic stress**, in contrast, is a state of enduring arousal, continuing over time, in which demands are perceived as greater than the inner and outer resources available for dealing with them. An example of chronic stress might be a continuous frustration with your inability to find time to do all the things you want to do. Let's see how your body responds to these different types of stresses.

Emergency Reactions to Acute Threats In the 1920s, Walter Cannon outlined the first scientific description of the way animals and humans respond to danger. He found that a sequence of activity is triggered in the nerves and glands to prepare the body either to defend itself and struggle or to run away to safety. Cannon called this dual stress response the **fight-or-flight response.** At the center of this stress response is the *hypothalamus,* which is involved in a variety of emotional

---

stress The pattern of specific and nonspecific responses an organism makes to stimulus events that disturb its equilibrium and tax or exceed its ability to cope.

stressor An internal or external event or stimulus that induces stress.

acute stress A transient state of arousal with typically clear onset and offset patterns.

chronic stress A continuous state of arousal in which an individual perceives demands as greater than the inner and outer resources available for dealing with them.

fight-or-flight response A sequence of internal activities triggered when an organism is faced with a threat; prepares the body for combat and struggle or for running away to safety; recent evidence suggests that the response is characteristic only of males.

Psychology in Your Life

CAN YOU ACCURATELY PREDICT YOUR FUTURE EMOTIONS?

Suppose you're about to submit an assignment. A researcher stops you and asks you to look into the future. First, he asks you to predict what grade you think you'll get. Next, he asks you to predict how you imagine you will feel—on the dimensions of rejoicing and regret—if your actual grade were higher or lower than that prediction or pretty much accurate. Take a minute to consider how you might respond.

When researchers conducted this experiment, their goal was to compare students' predictions about their emotional responses to their actual responses (Sevdalis & Harvey, 2007). After the students' received their grades, the researchers found them again to ask them how the outcomes made them feel. On average, the students did somewhat better on their assignments than they had predicted. However, those better-than-expected outcomes didn't make them nearly as happy as they thought they would: The students experienced much less rejoicing than they predicted they would.

Before we consider why people's predictions about their future emotions might be inaccurate, let's consider a second example. Here's a situation that will be familiar to many city dwellers: You dash down a stairway just in time to watch the doors close on your subway car. How would you feel? Suppose you missed the train by a wider margin of time. Now how would you feel? A team of researchers conducted exactly that study (Gilbert et al., 2004). They approached people on a subway platform in Cambridge, Massachusetts, and offered them $1 to fill out a brief questionnaire. One group of participants were *Experiencers*. The researchers provided them with accurate information that they had missed a train by either a narrow margin (one minute) or a wide margin (five minutes). The participants indicated how regretful they felt about missing the train by providing a rating on a scale ranging from "not at all" to "extremely." Participants cast in the role of *Forecasters* used the same scale to predict how regretful they imagined they would feel had they missed the train by a narrow or wide margin (that is, each forecaster answered the question for just one margin).

Earlier, we cast you in the role of forecasters by asking you "How would you feel?" If your responses were similar to those of the experimental participants, you likely had the same expectations as the Forecasters: They predicted that people would experience more regret for the narrow margin than for the wide margin. However, the Experiencers actually reported nearly the same regret for the narrow margin and the wide margin. Once again, we see that people's predictions about their future feelings aren't very accurate.

Why do people have difficulty predicting how they might respond to particular outcomes? In large part, it seems that people are better than they anticipate at putting outcomes into a broader perspective (Kermer et al., 2006). When people actually miss a subway train, they are able to take that outcome in stride by putting it in the larger context of their unfolding day. They don't dwell on the isolated event in a way that makes them continue to feel negative emotions. By contrast, when people predict how they're going to feel they aren't able to interpret the outcome in the fuller context. The same is true for positive emotions. You might not rejoice as much as you predict to a better-than-expected grade because that outcome occurs as part of your whole on-going life.

You often make important decisions based on how you anticipate particular outcomes will make you feel. As you make your decisions, try to be aware why your predictions of future feelings may not be accurate.

---

responses. The hypothalamus has sometimes been referred to as the stress center because of its twin functions in emergencies: (1) It controls the autonomic nervous system (ANS) and (2) it activates the pituitary gland.

The ANS regulates the activities of the body's organs. In stressful conditions, breathing becomes faster and deeper, heart rate increases, blood vessels constrict, and blood pressure rises. In addition to these internal changes, muscles open the passages of the throat and nose to allow more air into the lungs while also producing facial expressions of strong emotion. Messages go to smooth muscles to stop certain bodily functions, such as digestion, that are irrelevant to preparing for the emergency at hand.

Another function of the ANS during stress is to get adrenaline flowing. It signals the inner part of the adrenal glands, the *adrenal medulla,* to release two hormones, *epinephrine* and *norepinephrine,* which, in turn, signal a number of other organs to perform their specialized functions. The spleen releases more red blood corpuscles (to aid in clotting if there is an injury), and the bone marrow is stimulated to make more white corpuscles (to combat possible infection). The liver is stimulated to produce more sugar, building up body energy.

---

tend-and-befriend response A response to stressors that is hypothesized to be typical for females; stressors prompt females to protect their offspring and join social groups to reduce vulnerability.

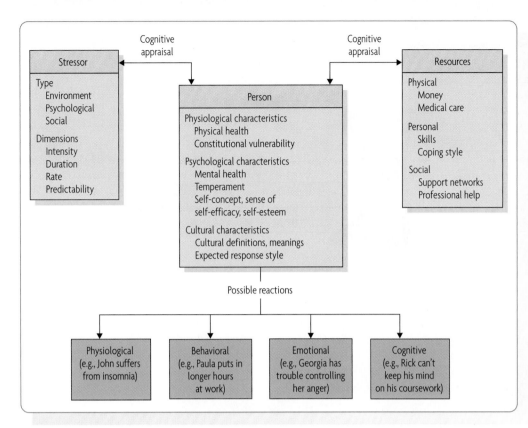

FIGURE 12.3 A Model of Stress
Cognitive appraisal of the stress situation interacts with the stressor and the physical, social, and personal resources available for dealing with the stressor. Individuals respond to threats on various levels: physiological, behavioral, emotional, and cognitive. Some responses are adaptive, and others are maladaptive or even lethal.

The *pituitary gland* responds to signals from the hypothalamus by secreting two hormones vital to the stress reaction. The *thyrotropic hormone* (TTH) stimulates the *thyroid gland,* which makes more energy available to the body. The *adrenocorticotropic hormone* (ACTH), known as the "stress hormone," stimulates the outer part of the adrenal glands, the *adrenal cortex,* resulting in the release of hormones that control metabolic processes and the release of sugar from the liver into the blood. ACTH also signals various organs to release about 30 other hormones, each of which plays a role in the body's adjustment to this call to arms. A summary of this physiological stress response is shown in **Figure 12.4** on page 382.

An analysis by health psychologist **Shelley Taylor** and her colleagues (2000; Taylor, 2006) suggests that these physiological responses to stress may have different consequences for females than for males. Taylor and her colleagues suggest that females do not experience *fight-or-flight.* Rather, these researchers argue that stressors lead females to experience a **tend-and-befriend response:** In times of stress, females ensure the safety of their offspring by tending to their needs;

Whether at work or play, individuals in contemporary society are likely to encounter a stressful environment. What situations in your life do you find most stressful?

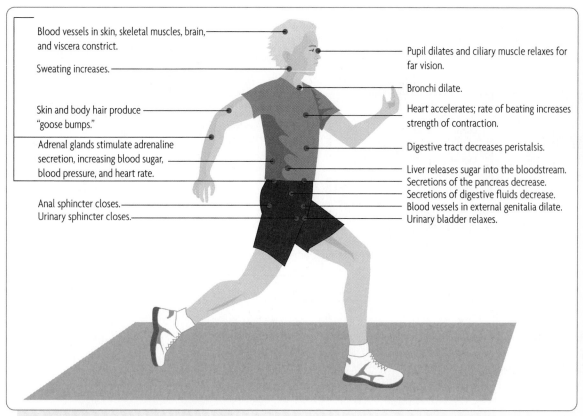

FIGURE 12.4 The Body's Reaction to Stress
Stress produces a wide range of physiological changes in your body.

Blood vessels in skin, skeletal muscles, brain, and viscera constrict.

Sweating increases.

Skin and body hair produce "goose bumps."

Adrenal glands stimulate adrenaline secretion, increasing blood sugar, blood pressure, and heart rate.

Anal sphincter closes.
Urinary sphincter closes.

Pupil dilates and ciliary muscle relaxes for far vision.

Bronchi dilate.

Heart accelerates; rate of beating increases strength of contraction.

Digestive tract decreases peristalsis.

Liver releases sugar into the bloodstream.
Secretions of the pancreas decrease.
Secretions of digestive fluids decrease.
Blood vessels in external genitalia dilate.
Urinary bladder relaxes.

females befriend other members of their social group with the same goal of reducing the vulnerability of their offspring. You can see how this analysis of sex differences in stress responses fits with our earlier discussions of evolutionary perspectives on human behavior. For example, when we discussed human sexual behaviors in Chapter 11, we noted that men and women's *mating strategies* differ, in part, because of the relative roles men and women have played—over the course of evolution—in child rearing. The idea here is very much the same: Because of men and women's different evolutionary niches with respect to nurturing offspring, the same initial physiological responses to stress ultimately produce quite different behaviors.

Unfortunately, neither the fight-or-flight nor the tend-and-befriend response is entirely useful for contemporary lives. Many of the stressors both men and women experience on a day-to-day basis make the physiological stress responses fairly maladaptive. Suppose, for example, you are taking a difficult exam and the clock is swiftly ticking away. Although you might value the heightened attentiveness brought about by your stress response, the rest of the physiological changes do you no good: There's no one to fight or to tend, and so on. The responses that developed in the species as adaptive preparations for dealing with external dangers are counterproductive for dealing with many contemporary types of psychological stressors. This is

particularly true because, as we will see next, many people live their lives under circumstances of chronic stress.

The General Adaptation Syndrome (GAS) and Chronic Stress The first modern researcher to investigate the effects of continued severe stress on the body was **Hans Selye** (1907–1982), a Canadian endocrinologist. Beginning in the late 1930s, Selye reported on the complex response of laboratory animals to damaging agents such as bacterial infections, toxins, trauma, forced restraint, heat, cold, and so on. According to Selye's theory of stress, many kinds of stressors can trigger the same reaction or general bodily response. All stressors call for *adaptation:* An organism must maintain or regain its integrity and well-being by restoring equilibrium, or homeostasis. The response to stressors was described by Selye as the **general adaptation syndrome (GAS).** It includes three stages: an alarm reaction, a stage of resistance, and a stage of exhaustion (Selye, 1976a, 1976b). *Alarm reactions* are brief periods of bodily arousal that prepare the body for vigorous activity. If a stressor is prolonged, the body enters a stage of *resistance*—a state of moderate arousal. During the stage of resistance, the organism can endure and *resist* further debilitating effects of prolonged stressors. However, if the stressor is sufficiently long lasting or intense, the body's resources become depleted and the organism enters the stage of *exhaustion*. The three stages are diagrammed and explained in **Figure 12.5.**

Selye identified some of the dangers associated with the stage of exhaustion. Recall, for example, that ACTH plays a role in the short-term response to stress. In the long term, however, its action reduces the ability of natural killer cells to destroy

general adaptation syndrome (GAS) The pattern of nonspecific adaptational physiological mechanisms that occurs in response to continuing threat by almost any serious stressor.

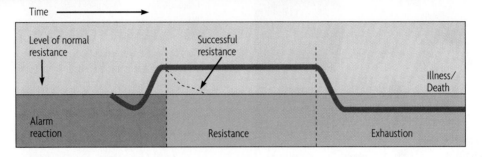

Stage I: Alarm reaction (continuously repeated throughout life)	Stage II: Resistance (continuously repeated throughout life)	Stage III: Exhaustion
• Enlargement of adrenal cortex • Enlargement of lymphatic system • Increase in hormone levels • Response to specific stressor • Epinephrine release associated with high levels of physiological arousal and negative affect • Greater susceptibility to increased intensity of stressor • Heightened susceptibility to illness (If prolonged, the slower components of the GAS are set into motion, beginning with Stage II.)	• Shrinkage of adrenal cortex • Return of lymph nodes to normal size • Sustaining of hormone levels • High physiological arousal • Counteraction of parasympathetic branch of ANS • Enduring of stressor; resistance to further debilitating effects • Heightened sensitivity to stress (If stress continues at intense levels, hormonal reserves are depleted, fatigue sets in, and individual enters Stage III.)	• Enlargement/dysfunction of lymphatic structures • Increase in hormone levels • Depletion of adaptive hormones • Decreased ability to resist either original or extraneous stressors • Affective experience—often depression • Illness • Death

Time →

Level of normal resistance → Successful resistance / Illness/Death

Alarm reaction | Resistance | Exhaustion

FIGURE 12.5   The General Adaptation Syndrome (GAS)
Following exposure to a stressor, the body's resistance is diminished until the physiological changes of the corresponding alarm reaction bring it back up to the normal level. If the stressor continues, the bodily signs characteristic of the alarm reaction virtually disappear; resistance to the particular stressor rises above normal but drops for other stressors. This adaptive resistance returns the body to its normal level of functioning. Following prolonged exposure to the stressor, adaptation breaks down; signs of alarm reaction reappear, the stressor effects are irreversible, and the individual becomes ill and may die.

cancer cells and other life-threatening infections. When the body is stressed chronically, the increased production of "stress hormones" compromises the integrity of the immune system. This application of the general adaptation syndrome has proven valuable to explain **psychosomatic disorders**—illnesses that could not be wholly explained by physical causes—that had baffled physicians who had never considered stress as a cause for illness and disease. What serves the body well in adapting to acute stress impairs the body's response to chronic stress.

Selye's research makes disease seem an inevitable response to stress. We will see, however, that your psychological interpretation of what is stressful and what is not stressful—the way in which you appraise potentially stressful events—has an impact on your body's physiological response. To give a full account of the effect of stress on your body, we will have to combine Selye's foundational physiological theory with later research on psychological factors.

PSYCHOLOGICAL STRESS REACTIONS

Your physiological stress reactions are automatic, predictable, built-in responses over which you normally have no conscious control. However, many psychological reactions are learned. They depend on perceptions and interpretations of the world. In this section, we discuss psychological responses to different categories of stressors, such as major life events and traumatic experiences.

Major Life Events The influence of life events on subsequent mental and physical health has been a target of considerable research. It started in the 1960s with the development of the Social Readjustment Rating Scale (SRRS), a simple measure for rating the degree of adjustment required by the various life changes, both pleasant and unpleasant, that many people experience. The scale was developed from the responses of adults, from all walks of life, who were asked to identify from a list those life events that applied to them. These adults rated the amount of readjustment required for each change by comparing each to marriage, which was arbitrarily assigned a value of 50 life-change units. Researchers then calculated the total number of **life-change units (LCUs)** an individual had undergone, using

---

psychosomatic disorder Physical disorder aggravated by or primarily attributable to prolonged emotional stress or other psychological causes.

life-change unit (LCU) In stress research, the measure of the stress levels of different types of change experienced during a given period.

What are the physiological consequences of chronic stress?

TABLE 12.2 Life-Change Units for Major Life Events	
Event	**Life-Change Units**
Death of spouse	119
Divorce	98
Death of a close family member	92
Marital separation	79
Fired from work	79
Major personal injury or illness	77
Jail term	75
Death of a close friend	70
Pregnancy	66
Major business readjustment	62
Foreclosure on mortgage or loan	61
Marital reconciliation	57
Gain of new family member	57
Change in health or behavior of family member	56
Change in financial state	56
Retirement	54
Change to different line of work	51
Change in number of arguments with spouse	51
Marriage	50
Spouse begins or ends work	46
Sexual difficulties	45
Mortgage or loan greater than $10,000	44
Child leaving home	44
Change in responsibilities at work	43
Change in living conditions	42
Change in residence	41
Trouble with in-laws	38
Begin or end school	38
Outstanding personal achievement	37
Change in work hours or conditions	36
Change in schools	35
Christmas	30
Change in recreation	29
Trouble with boss	29
Mortgage or loan less than $10,000	28
Change in social activities	27
Change in personal habits	27
Change in eating habits	27
Change in sleeping habits	26
Change in number of family get-togethers	26
Vacation	25
Change in church activities	22
Minor violations of the law	22

Adapted from M.A. Miller and R.H. Rahe. Life changes scaling for the 1990s. *Journal of Psychosomatic Research, 43* (3): 279–292, Copyright (1997), with permission from Elsevier.

the units as a measure of the amount of stress the individual had experienced (Holmes & Rahe, 1967).

The SRRS was updated in the 1990s (see **Table 12.2**). The researchers used the same procedure of asking participants to rate the stress of life events as compared to marriage (Miller & Rahe, 1997). In this update, the LCU estimates went up 45 percent over the original values—that is, participants in the 1990s reported that they were experiencing overall much higher levels of stress than their peers had in the 1960s. Women in the 1990s also reported experiencing more stress in their lives than did men. Researchers continue to relate reports on the SRRS to mental and physical health outcome. Consider a study in which 268 people completed the scale (Lynch et al., 2005). There was a positive correlation between SRRS scores and participants' total number of medical visits in the following six months: In general, the participants who had the highest SRRS scores also visited their doctors most often.

Researchers have found a variety of ways to examine the relationship between life events and health outcomes. In one study, participants volunteered to be exposed to viruses that cause the common cold. Those participants who reported a rate of negative life events above the group's average were about 10 percent more likely to actually come down with a cold (Cohen et al., 1993). Consider another study that should have immediate relevance to the choices you make about how to organize your schoolwork.

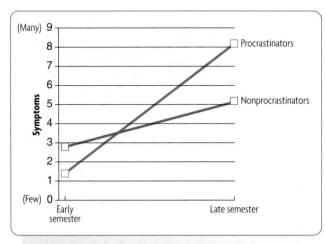

FIGURE 12.6 The Health Costs of Procrastination

Researchers identified students who were, generally, procrastinators and nonprocrastinators. The students were asked to report, early and late in the semester, how many symptoms of physical illness they had experienced. By late in the semester all students showed increases in symptoms. However—as all their work came due—procrastinators were reporting even more symptoms than their nonprocrastinating peers.

When a professor gives you an assignment—a stressful life event in every student's life—do you try to take care of it as soon as possible, or do you put it off to the very last minute? Psychologists have developed a measurement device called the General Procrastination Scale (Lay, 1986) to differentiate those individuals who habitually put things off—*procrastinators*—from those who don't—*nonprocrastinators*. A pair of researchers administered this scale to students in a health psychology course who had a paper due late in the semester. The students were also asked to report, early and late in the semester, how many symptoms of physical illness they had experienced. Not surprisingly, procrastinators, on average, turned their papers in later than did nonprocrastinators; procrastinators also, on average, obtained lower grades on those papers. **Figure 12.6** displays the effect of procrastination on physical health. As you can see, early in the semester, procrastinators reported fewer symptoms, but by late in the semester, they were reporting more symptoms than their nonprocrastinating peers (Tice & Baumeister, 1997).

You see in this study why not all life events have the same impact on all people. The nonprocrastinators got to work right away and so experienced stress and symptoms early in the semester. However, the consequence for the procrastinators of avoiding the early semester stress was a great increase in physical illness toward the end of the semester. Therefore, they were likely to be feeling ill just at the point in the semester when they needed to be in good health to complete all the work they had put off! Think about these results as you develop your own plan for navigating each semester. If you believe that you habitually procrastinate, consider consulting with a psychologist or school counselor to modify your behavior. Your grades and health are at stake!

Traumatic Events An event that is negative but also uncontrollable, unpredictable, or ambiguous is particularly stressful. These conditions hold especially true in the case of *traumatic events*. Some traumatic events, such as rape and automobile crashes, affect individuals. Others, such as earthquakes and tornadoes, have a broader impact. In recent years, no traumatic event has had as widespread consequences as the events of September 11, 2001. On that day, attacks on the World Trade Center and the Pentagon with commercial aircraft led to the deaths of almost 3,000 people. With the goal of providing appropriate mental health care, researchers moved swiftly to assess the psychological aftermath of the attacks.

One particular focus was on the prevalence of **posttraumatic stress disorder (PTSD).** PTSD is a stress reaction in which individuals suffer from persistent reexperiences of the traumatic event in the form, for example, of flashbacks or nightmares (*DSM-IV*, 1994). Sufferers experience an emotional numbing in relation to everyday events and feelings of alienation from other people. Finally, the emotional pain of this reaction can result in an increase in various symptoms, such as sleep problems, guilt about surviving, difficulty in concentrating, and an exaggerated startle response.

Why might TV viewing have an impact on people's experiences of PTSD?

posttraumatic stress disorder (PTSD) An anxiety disorder characterized by the persistent reexperience of traumatic events through distressing recollections, dreams, hallucinations, or dissociative flashbacks; develops in response to rapes, life-threatening events, severe injury, and natural disasters.

In October and November 2001, a team of researchers conducted a Web-based survey of 2,273 adults across the United States (Schlenger et al., 2002). The survey assessed both the participants' exposure to the incidents and their mental health symptoms. As seen in **Table 12.3,** greater exposure made it more likely that people would experience PTSD. The group most affected were those who lived in the New York City metropolitan area. Those individuals were most likely to have been personally involved in the tragedy. As seen in Table 12.3, the events didn't have extra impact on people in the Washington, D.C. area. The researchers suggested that the difference between New York and D.C. might reflect the difference between attacks on a civilian target (the World Trade Center) and a military target (the Pentagon). Table 12.3 also shows that individuals who watched the most television coverage of the events also reported higher levels of symptoms of PTSD. Researchers will continue to assess the mental health consequences of September 11: They attempt to form generalizations from people's responses to catastrophes so that they can alleviate the worst consequences when new circumstances present themselves.

As we noted earlier, people also suffer from individual traumatic events with a negative impact on their psychological health. For example, rape victims often show many of the signs of posttraumatic stress (Ullman et al., 2007). In assessments two weeks

TABLE 12.3 The Psychological Impact of Exposure to the Events of September 11, 2001	Probable PTSD
PROXIMITY TO CRASH SITES	
New York City metropolitan area	11.2
District of Columbia metropolitan area	2.7
Other major metropolitan area	3.6
Remainder of the United States	4.0
TELEVISION VIEWING PER DAY (in hours)	
Less than 4	0.8
4–7	3.9
8–11	4.2
12 or more	10.1

after being assaulted, 94 percent of rape victims were diagnosed with PTSD; 12 weeks after the assault, 51 percent of the victims still met diagnostic criteria (Foa & Riggs, 1995). These data illustrate that the emotional responses of posttraumatic stress can occur in an acute form immediately following a trauma and can subside over a period of several months. We will return to the topic of PTSD when we discuss anxiety disorders in Chapter 14.

Chronic Stressors In our discussion of physiological responses to stress, we made a distinction between stressors that are acute, with clear onsets and offsets, versus those that are chronic—that is, endure over time. With psychological stressors, it's not always easy to draw a sharp distinction. Suppose, for example, your bicycle is stolen. Originally, this is an acute source of stress. However, if you begin to worry constantly that your new bike will also be stolen, the stress associated with this event can become chronic. Researchers have found this pattern in people who suffer from serious illnesses like cancer (Kangas et al., 2005; Stanton et al., 2007). The chronic stress of coping with the anxiety of a cancer diagnosis and treatment may impair health more rapidly than the disease alone would.

For many people, chronic stress arises from conditions in society and the environment. What cumulative effects do overpopulation, crime, economic conditions, pollution, AIDS, and the threat of terrorism have on you? How do these and other environmental stressors affect your mental well-being? Some groups of people suffer chronic stress by virtue of their socioeconomic status or racial identity, with stark consequences for overall well-being (Gallo & Matthews, 2003; Mays et al., 2007). Consider a study that measured economic hardships for more than a thousand participants over three decades (Lynch et al., 1997). Economic hardship was defined as household income of less than 200 percent of the federal poverty level. As assessed in 1994, the more periods of economic hardship adults experienced between 1965 and 1983, the more difficulties they had with physical functioning related to basic activities of daily living, such as cooking, shopping, and bathing. Similar effects were found for psychological and cognitive

This trader on the floor of the New York Stock Exchange has likely experienced chronic stress as a result of the uncertain economy. What are some possible consequences for his physical and mental health?

functioning. Compared to those with no period of economic hardship, people with three episodes of poverty were three times more likely to have experienced symptoms of clinical depression, they were more than five times more likely to be assessed as cynically hostile and lacking optimism, and they were more than four times more likely to report difficulties with cognitive functioning. To confirm that these results were caused by economic hardship and not by initial poor health, the researchers demonstrated comparable patterns of disability among those participants whose health at the initial measurement in 1965 had been good or excellent.

Daily Hassles You may agree that the end of a relationship, an earthquake, or prejudice might cause stress, but what about the smaller stressors you experience on a day-to-day basis? What happened to you yesterday? You probably didn't get a divorce or survive a plane crash. You're more likely to have lost your notes or textbook. Perhaps you were late for an important appointment, or you got a parking ticket, or a noisy neighbor ruined your sleep. These are the types of recurring day-to-day stressors that confront most people, most of the time.

In a diary study, a group of White middle-class middle-aged men and women kept track of their daily hassles over a one-year period (along with a record of major life changes and physical symptoms). A clear relationship emerged between hassles and health problems: The more frequent and intense the hassles people reported, the poorer was their health, both physical and mental (Lazarus, 1981, 1984b). Consider a study that demonstrated the impact of daily hassles in the workplace.

Participants in the study worked full time in university administration, with their effort largely focused on the quality of student life (Luong & Rogelberg, 2005). For a period of five days, participants kept records of their number of meetings. An interaction counted as a meeting if it involved two or more people and was more than a brief chat or five-minute phone call. Participants also provided daily accounts of well-being: They recorded their levels of *fatigue* (such as the extent to which they were worn out at the present moment) and their levels of *subjective workload* (such as the extent to which they felt busy or rushed). The results demonstrated positive correlations between the number of meetings and both of these measures: More meetings were associated with greater fatigue and higher subjective workload.

If you've ever worked in an office, these results probably have a familiar ring: The more often you are interrupted for meetings, the less you feel as though you're making progress on your work.

We have been focusing largely on day-to-day hassles. It is worth noting, however, that for many people daily hassles may be balanced out by daily positive experiences (Lazarus & Lazarus, 1994). For example, one study asked 132 men and women to report the frequency and intensity of the hassles (that is, irritating events) and uplifts (that is, happy events) in their lives (Jain et al., 2007). The researchers also measured the participants' blood levels of substances (such as inflammatory factors) that are indicators of risk for cardiovascular disease. Higher levels of reported hassles were associated with higher levels of these risk indicators; higher levels of reported uplifts were associated with lower levels. Therefore, if we want to predict your life course based on daily hassles, we also need to know something about the daily uplifts your life provides (Lyubomirsky et al., 2005).

We have just reviewed many sources of stress in people's lives. Psychologists have recognized for quite a long time that the impact of these different types of stressors depends in large part on how effectively people can cope with them. Let's now consider how people cope successfully and unsuccessfully with stress.

COPING WITH STRESS

If living is inevitably stressful, and if chronic stress can disrupt your life and even kill you, you need to learn how to manage stress. **Coping** refers to the process of dealing with internal or external demands that are perceived as straining or exceeding an individual's resources (Lazarus & Folkman, 1984). Coping may consist of behavioral, emotional, or motivational responses and thoughts. We begin this section by describing how cognitive appraisal affects what you experience as stressful. We then consider types of coping responses; we describe both general principles of coping and specific interventions. Finally, we onsider some individual differences in individuals' ability to cope with stress.

Appraisal of Stress When you cope with stressful situations, your first step is to define in what ways they are, in fact, stressful. Cognitive appraisal is the cognitive interpretation and evaluation of a stressor. Cognitive appraisal plays a central role in defining the situation—what the demand is, how big a threat it is, and what resources you have for meeting it (Lazarus, 1993; Lazarus & Lazarus, 1994). Some stressors, such as undergoing bodily injury or finding one's house on fire, are experienced as threats by almost everyone. However, many other stressors can be defined in various ways, depending on your personal life situation, the relation of a particular demand to your central goals, your competence in dealing with the demand, and your self-assessment of that competence. The situation that causes acute distress for another person may be all in a day's work for you. Try to notice, and understand, the life events that are different for you and your friends and family: Some situations cause you stress but not your friends and family; other events cause them stress but not you. Why?

Richard Lazarus, whose general theory of appraisal we addressed in our discussion of emotions, distinguished two stages in the cognitive appraisal of demands. *Primary appraisal* describes the initial evaluation of the seriousness of a demand. This evaluation starts with the questions "What's happening?" and "Is this thing good for me, stressful, or irrelevant?" If the answer to the second question is "stressful," you appraise the potential impact of the stressor by determining whether harm has occurred or is likely to and whether action is required (see **Table 12.4** on page 388). Once you decide something must be done, *secondary appraisal* begins. You evaluate the personal and social resources that are available to deal with the stressful circumstance and consider the action options that are needed. Appraisal continues as coping responses are tried; if the first ones don't work and the stress persists, new responses are initiated, and their effectiveness is evaluated.

Cognitive appraisal is an example of a stress moderator variable. **Stress moderator variables** are those variables that change the impact of a stressor on a given type of stress reaction. Moderator variables filter or modify the usual effects of stressors on the

---

coping The process of dealing with internal or external demands that are perceived to be threatening or overwhelming.

stress moderator variable Variable that changes the impact of a stressor on a given type of stress reaction.

TABLE 12.4 Stages in Stable Decision Making/Cognitive Appraisal

Stage	Key Questions
1. Appraising the challenge	Are the risks serious if I don't change?
2. Surveying alternatives	Is this alternative an acceptable means for dealing with the challenge? Have I sufficiently surveyed the available alternatives?
3. Weighing alternatives	Which alternative is best? Could the best alternative meet the essential requirements?
4. Deliberating about commitment	Will I implement the best alternative and allow others to know?
5. Adhering despite negative feedback	Are the risks serious if I *don't* change? Are the risks serious if I *do* change?

individual's reactions. For example, your level of fatigue and general health status are moderator variables influencing your reaction to a given psychological or physical stressor. When you are in good shape, you can deal with a stressor better than when you aren't. You can see how cognitive appraisal also fits the definition of a moderator variable. The way in which you appraise a stressor will determine the types of coping responses you need to bring to it. Let's now consider general types of coping responses.

Types of Coping Responses Suppose you have a big exam coming up. You've thought about it—you've appraised the situation—and you're quite sure that this is a stressful situation. What can you do? It's important to note that coping can precede a potentially stressful event in the form of **anticipatory coping** (Folkman, 1984). How do you deal with the stress of the upcoming exam? How do you tell your parents that you are dropping out of school or your lover that you are no longer in love? Anticipating a stressful situation leads to many thoughts and feelings that themselves may be stress inducing, as in the cases of interviews, speeches, or blind dates. You need to know how to cope.

The two main ways of coping are defined by whether the goal is to confront the problem directly—*problem-directed coping*—or to lessen the discomfort associated with the stress—*emotion-focused coping* (Billings & Moos, 1982; Lazarus & Folkman, 1984). Several subcategories of these two basic approaches are shown in **Table 12.5.**

Let's begin with problem-directed coping. "Taking the bull by the horns" is how we usually characterize the strategy of facing up to a problem situation. This approach includes all strategies

---

anticipatory coping Efforts made in advance of a potentially stressful event to overcome, reduce, or tolerate the imbalance between perceived demands and available resources.

---

designed to deal *directly* with the stressor, whether through overt action or through realistic problem-solving activities. You face up to a bully or run away; you try to win him or her over with bribes or other incentives. Your focus is on the problem to be dealt with and on the agent that has induced the stress. You acknowledge the call to action, you appraise the situation and your resources for dealing with it, and you undertake a response that is appropriate for removing or lessening the threat. Such problem-solving efforts are useful for managing *controllable stressors*—those stressors that you can change or eliminate through your actions, such as overbearing bosses or underwhelming grades.

The emotion-focused approach is useful for managing the impact of more *uncontrollable stressors*. Suppose you are responsible for the care of a parent with Alzheimer's. In that situation, there is no "bully" you can eliminate from the environment; you cannot make the disease go away. Even in this situation, some forms of problem-directed coping would be useful. For example, you could modify your work schedule to make it easier to provide care. However, because you cannot eliminate the source of stress, you also can try to change your feelings and thoughts about the disease. For example, you might take part in a support group for Alzheimer's caregivers or learn relaxation techniques. These approaches still constitute a coping strategy because you are acknowledging that there is a threat to your well-being and you are taking steps to modify that threat.

You will be better off if you have multiple strategies to help you cope in stressful situations (Fresco et al., 2006; Tennen et al., 2000). For coping to be successful, your resources need to match the perceived demand. Thus the availability of multiple coping strategies is adaptive because you are more likely to achieve a match and manage the stressful event. Consider a study that examined the ways in which women cope with the stress of undergoing surgery for breast cancer (Roussi et al., 2007). The women reported their distress levels and coping strategies (such as problem-directed and/or emotion-focused strategies) a day before the surgeries, three days after the procedure, and again three month later. The women who reported that they were using multiple coping strategies in the days after their surgeries reported less distress three months later.

Researchers who study coping have discovered that some individuals meet stressors with a particular degree of resilience—they are able to achieve positive outcomes despite serious threats to their well-being (Bonanno & Mancini, 2008). Research has focused on the types of coping skills that resilient individuals have acquired and how they have acquired them. An important part of the answer is that children who become resilient have been raised by supportive parents with good parenting skills (see Chapter 10). In addition, resilient children appear to have developed coping skills that relate to their ability to regulate their own behavior (Buckner et al., 2003). They can stay focused on tasks (which allows for problem-directed coping) and control their emotional responses (which allows for emotion-focused coping) in ways that better their life outcomes.

Up to now, we have been discussing general approaches to coping with stressors. Now we review specific cognitive and social approaches to successful coping.

Modifying Cognitive Strategies A powerful way to adapt to stress is to change your evaluations of stressors and your self-defeating cognitions about the way you are dealing with them. You need to find a different way to think about a given situation, your role in it, and the causal attributions you make to

TABLE 12.5 Taxonomy of Coping Strategies

Type of Coping Strategy	Example
PROBLEM-DIRECTED COPING	
Change stressor or one's relationship to it through	Fight (destroy, remove, or weaken the threat) direct actions and/or problem-solving activities
	Flight (distance oneself from the threat)
	Seek options to fight or flight (negotiating, bargaining, compromising)
	Prevent future stress (act to increase one's resistance or decrease strength of anticipated stress)
EMOTION-FOCUSED COPING	
Change self through activities that make one feel	Somatically focused activities (use of antianxiety medication, relaxation, biofeedback) better but do not change the stressor
	Cognitively focused activities (planned distractions, fantasies, thoughts about oneself)
	Therapy to adjust conscious or unconscious processes that lead to additional anxiety

explain the undesirable outcome. Two ways of mentally coping with stress are *reappraising* the nature of the stressors themselves and *restructuring* your cognitions about your stress reactions.

We have already described the idea that people control the experience of stress in their lives in part by the way they appraise life events (Lazarus & Lazarus, 1994). Learning to think

Why are multiple coping strategies beneficial for individuals such as Alzheimer's caregivers?

differently about certain stressors, to relabel them, or to imagine them in a less-threatening (perhaps even funny) context is a form of cognitive reappraisal that can reduce stress. Worried about giving a speech to a large, forbidding audience? One stressor reappraisal technique is to imagine your potential critics sitting there in the nude—this surely takes away a great deal of their fearsome power. Anxious about being shy at a party you must attend? Think about finding someone who is shier than you and reducing his or her social anxiety by initiating a conversation.

You can also manage stress by changing what you tell yourself about it and by changing your handling of it. Cognitive-behavior therapist **Donald Meichenbaum** (1977, 1985, 1993) has proposed a three-phase process that allows for such *stress inoculation*. In Phase 1, people work to develop a greater awareness of their actual behavior, what instigates it, and what its results are. One of the best ways of doing this is to keep daily logs. By helping people redefine their problems in terms of their causes and results, these records can increase their feelings of control. You may discover, for example, that your grades are low (a stressor) because you always leave too little time to do a good job on your class assignments. In Phase 2, people begin to identify new behaviors that negate the maladaptive, self-defeating behaviors. Perhaps you might create a fixed "study time" or limit your phone calls to 10 minutes each night. In Phase 3, after adaptive behaviors are being emitted, individuals appraise the consequences of their new behaviors, avoiding the former internal dialogue of put-downs. Instead of telling themselves, "I was lucky the professor called on me when I happened to have read the text," they say, "I'm glad I was prepared for the professor's question. It feels great to be able to respond intelligently in that class."

This three-phase approach means initiating responses and self-statements that are incompatible with previous defeatist cognitions. Once started on this path, people realize that they are changing—and can take full credit for the change, which promotes further successes. **Table 12.6**, on page 390, gives examples of the new kinds of self-statements that help in dealing with stressful situations. *Stress inoculation training* has been used successfully in a wide variety of domains.

TABLE 12.6 Examples of Coping Self-Statements

Preparation

I can develop a plan to deal with it.

Just think about what I can do about it. That's better than getting anxious.

No negative self-statements, just think rationally.

Confrontation

One step at a time; I can handle this situation.

This anxiety is what the doctor said I would feel; it's a reminder to use my coping exercises.

Relax; I'm in control. Take a slow, deep breath.

Coping

When fear comes, just pause.

Keep focused on the present; what is it I have to do?

Don't try to eliminate fear totally; just keep it manageable.

It's not the worst thing that can happen.

Just think about something else.

Self-Reinforcement

It worked; I was able to do it.

It wasn't as bad as I expected.

I'm really pleased with the progress I'm making.

This study involved 22 students who were beginning their first year of law school (Sheehy & Horan, 2004). The students received stress inoculation training that was specifically geared to the types of stressors that arise in law school. For example, the training focused on the anxiety students experience when they interact with professors and compete with peers. In addition, the students learned cognitive restructuring techniques to combat negative self-statements and irrational beliefs. Although all of the students ultimately received the training, roughly half began training immediately at the start of the study, whereas the other half waited several weeks to begin. That research design gave the researchers the opportunity to demonstrate the benefits of the stress inoculation training (by comparing the immediate group to the delayed group) without denying some students those benefits. In fact, participants who completed immediate training reported lower levels of stress at the end of the delay period than their classmates whose training was delayed. In addition, several of the students who completed

---

perceived control The belief that one has the ability to make a difference in the course of the consequences of some event or experience; often helpful in dealing with stressors.

social support Resources, including material aid, socioemotional support, and informational aid, provided by others to help a person cope with stress.

---

the training outperformed expectations (based on their LSAT scores) when the semester's grades were posted.

The whole law school class of 158 students had the opportunity to participate in the stress inoculation training. Only this small subset was wise enough to reap the benefits.

Another main component of successful coping is for you to establish **perceived control** over the stressor, a belief that you can make a difference in the course or the consequences of some event or experience (Endler et al., 2000; Roussi, 2002). If you believe that you can affect the course of an illness or the daily symptoms of a disease, you are probably adjusting well to the disorder. However, if you believe that the source of the stress is another person whose behavior you cannot influence or a situation that you cannot change, chances increase for a poor psychological adjustment to your chronic condition. Consider a study of women who had undergone surgery for breast cancer (Bárez et al., 2007). The women who reported higher levels of perceived control experienced the least physical and psychological distress over the whole year following surgery.

While you file away these control strategies for future use, we will turn to a final aspect of coping with stress—the social dimension.

Social Support as a Coping Resource Social support refers to the resources others provide, giving the message that one is loved, cared for, esteemed, and connected to other people in a network of communication and mutual obligation. In addition to these forms of *emotional support,* other people may provide *tangible support* (money, transportation, housing) and *informational support* (advice, personal feedback, information). Anyone with whom you have a significant social relationship—such as family members, friends, coworkers, and neighbors—can be part of your social support network in time of need.

Much research points to the power of social support in moderating the vulnerability to stress (Kim et al., 2008). When people have other people to whom they can turn, they are better able to handle job stressors, unemployment, marital disruption, and serious illness, as well as their everyday problems of living. Consider individuals who serve as peacekeepers in the world's many troubled regions. The traumas associated with life in battle zones often leads to posttraumatic stress disorder. However, a study of Dutch peacekeepers who served in Lebanon demonstrated that those individuals who experienced higher levels of positive social interactions had fewer symptoms of PTSD (Dirkzwager et al., 2003).

Researchers are trying to identify which types of social supports provide the most benefit for specific life events. One study examined the impact of informational support and emotional support for men and women who were undergoing facial surgery (Krohne & Slangen, 2005). Overall, people who had more social support anticipated their surgery with less anxiety, required less anesthesia during surgery, and had briefer hospital stays. However, the more specific results differed for men and women. Although patients of both sexes obtained an advantage from greater informational support, only women were much affected by the level of emotional support. More generally, what appears to matter is the match between the type of support an individual needs and what that individual gets. As shown in **Figure 12.7,** there are four different possibilities for how desires and reality can be related (Reynolds & Perrin, 2004). People are best off when there's a match between what they want and what they get. For a sample of women with breast cancer, they had

Support is	wanted	not wanted
received	positive congruent support	support commission
not received	support omission	null support

FIGURE 12.7 Matches and Mismatches for Social Support

When people need to cope with difficult situations, there can be matches or mismatches between the social support they want and the social support they need.

From Julie S. Reynolds and Nancy Perrin, "Matches and Mismatches for Social Support and Psychosocial Adjustment to Breast Cancer," *Health Psychology, 23*(4), 425–430. Copyright © 2004 by the American Psychological Association. Reprinted with permission.

the worst psychological outcomes when they received support they did not want ("support commission") (Reynolds & Perrin, 2004). This pattern might have emerged because the unwanted assistance made it difficult for women to obtain the emotional support they really needed.

Researchers are also trying to determine how social support changes the way people's bodies and brains respond to stressors. Let's consider a study that demonstrated consistent changes in brain response that resulted from simple acts of hand holding.

> Sixteen married women underwent fMRI scans while under threat to receive electric shocks: Whenever a red *X* appeared on a screen in front of them, there was a 20 percent chance of a shock to their ankle; all the women received some shocks as the study unfolded (Coan et al., 2006). Each woman completed three blocks of trials. For one block, she held her husband's hand. For a second block, she held a male stranger's hand. The third control block did not have any hand holding. When the women were holding their husbands' hands, their brains showed greatly reduced activity in brain regions that typically register and respond to threat (as compared to brain activity in the control block). This reduction in threat response was greater for women who reported themselves as being in better relationships. Holding a stranger's hand also reduced the women's brain responses to threat, but not as much as holding their husband's hand.

In this study, the very literal social support of holding their spouse's hand (or even a stranger's hand) had the impact of making the women's brains respond as if a threat were less threatening. In this case, social support directly influenced how the women's brains perceived a stressor.

Being part of an effective social support network means that you believe others will be there for you if you need them—even if you don't actually ask for their help when you experience stress. One of the most important take-home messages from *Psychology and Life* is that you should always work at being part of a social support network and never let yourself become socially isolated.

POSITIVE EFFECTS OF STRESS

In this section, we have focused largely on the potential for stress to bring about negative life outcomes. This focus reflects the great effort researchers have expended to help people prevent and overcome those negative outcomes. However, in recent years, psychologists have turned more attention to the potential for stress to have positive effects in people's lives. This new focus is another outcome of the positive psychology movement that we introduced when we discussed subjective well-being. Let's consider stress and coping from a positive psychology perspective.

When we first defined stress, we made a distinction between distress and eustress. It's probably easy for you to generate circumstances in which you experienced distress—but what about eustress? Consider the last time you watched any kind of running race. Did you enjoy the experience of seeing who would win? Did you feel your heart race as the runners approached the finish line? Researchers have demonstrated that eustress—the experience of excitement and anxiety—is often an important motivation for people to watch, for example, sporting events (Cohen & Avrahami, 2005; Wann et al., 2002). If a team or competitor you favor ultimately loses, you may experience some distress. However, along the way, you probably have a more positive emotional experience when competitions stimulate eustress. Search your life for other circumstances in which the experience of stressful events gives you pleasure. We'll offer one more example: Why do you feel happy while you're riding a roller coaster?

For some types of stressful events, it might be hard to anticipate how any positive effects could emerge. However,

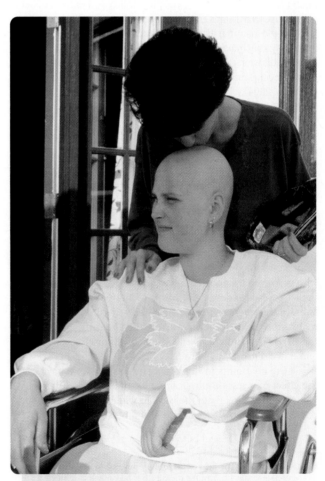

Why are some forms of social support more welcome than others?

research has demonstrated that people can experience positive outcomes and personal growth from deeply negative events. One type of research focuses on *benefit finding*—people's ability to identify positive aspects of negative life events (Helgeson et al., 2006; Littlewood et al., 2008). Consider a study of women with early-stage breast cancer.

> Researchers recruited a group of women who had been diagnosed with breast cancer, on average, about a half year earlier. The women were asked, "Have there been any benefits that have resulted from your experience with breast cancer?" (Sears et al., 2003, p. 491). Of the 92 women in the study, 83 percent were able to report benefits. The women provided responses such as "My husband and I have gotten a lot closer since this happened" and "When you come close to death, life becomes more real to you." The researchers followed the women over the course of a year to determine how their mental and physical health evolved. In general, the women who were doing the best were the ones who were able to use perceived benefits to engage in *positive reappraisal coping*. That is, some women were able to cope with the consequences of their illness by attempting to reappraise the situation in terms of its positive impact.

We noted earlier that reappraisal is an important tool for coping with stress. In this case, people's ability to perceive benefits of negative events aids in that process of reappraisal.

People also may experience *posttraumatic growth*—positive psychological change—in response to serious illnesses, accidents, natural disasters, and other traumatic events. Posttraumatic growth occurs in five domains (Cryder et al., 2006; Tedeschi & Calhoun, 2004):

- New possibilities: "I have new things that I like to do."
- Relating to others: "I feel closer to other people than I did before."
- Personal strength: "I learned I can count on myself."
- Appreciation of life: "I learned that life is important."
- Spiritual change: "I understand religious ideas more."

Not everyone who experiences trauma will experience posttraumatic growth. For example, one study focused on a group of 6- to 15-year-old children who had survived Hurricane Floyd in North Carolina (Cryder et al., 2006). The children who experienced the most posttraumatic growth were the ones who perceived themselves to have the best array of strategies (of the sort we have described in this section) to cope with problems. More generally, people seem likely to experience posttraumatic growth when they frequently turn their thoughts back to the original traumatic events, to help themselves understand and make sense of those events.

At many points in this discussion of stress, we have noted the effect of stress on physical or psychological well-being. We will now turn directly to the ways in which psychologists apply their research knowledge to issues of illness and health.

---

health psychology The field of psychology devoted to understanding the ways people stay healthy, the reasons they become ill, and the ways they respond when they become ill.

health A general condition of soundness and vigor of body and mind; not simply the absence of illness or injury.

Health Psychology

How much do your psychological processes contribute to your experiences of illness and wellness? We have already given you reason to believe that the right answer may be "quite a bit." This acknowledgment of the importance of psychological and social factors in health has spurred the growth of a new field, health psychology. **Health psychology** is the branch of psychology devoted to understanding the way people stay healthy, the reasons they become ill, and the way they respond when they do get ill. **Health** refers to the general condition of the body and mind in terms of soundness and vigor. It is not simply the absence of illness or injury, but is more a matter of how well all the body's component parts are working together. We will begin our discussion of health psychology by describing how the field's underlying philosophy departs from a traditional Western medical model of illness. We then consider the contributions of health psychology to the prevention and treatment of illness and dysfunction.

THE BIOPSYCHOSOCIAL MODEL OF HEALTH

Health psychology is guided by a *biopsychosocial model* of health. We can find the roots of this perspective in many non-Western cultures. To arrive at a definition of the biopsychosocial model, we will start with a description of some of these non-Western traditions.

Traditional Health Practices Psychological principles have been applied in the treatment of illness and the pursuit of health for all of recorded time. Many cultures understand the importance of communal health and relaxation rituals in the enhancement of the quality of life. Among the Navajo, for example, disease, illness, and well-being have been attributed to social

The Navajo, like people in many other cultures around the world, place a high value on aesthetics, family harmony, and physical health. What do the Navajo people consider to be the origins of illness?

harmony and mind–body interactions. The Navajo concept of **hozho** (pronounced *whoa-zo*) means harmony, peace of mind, goodness, ideal family relationships, beauty in arts and crafts, and health of body and spirit. Illness is seen as the outcome of any *disharmony,* caused by evil introduced through violation of taboos, witchcraft, overindulgence, or bad dreams. Traditional healing ceremonies seek to banish illness and restore health, not only through the medicine of the shaman but also through the combined efforts of all family members, who work together with the ill person to reachieve a state of hozho. The illness of any member of a tribe is seen not as his or her individual responsibility (and fault) but rather as a sign of broader disharmony that must be repaired by communal healing ceremonies. This cultural orientation guarantees that a powerful social support network will automatically come to the aid of the sufferer.

Toward a Biopsychosocial Model We have just seen that healing practices in non-Western cultures often assumed a link between the body and the mind. By contrast, modern Western scientific thinking has relied almost exclusively on a *biomedical model* that has a dualistic conception of body and mind. According to this model, medicine treats the physical body as separate from the psyche; the mind is important only for emotions and beliefs and has little to do with the reality of the body. Over time, however, researchers have begun to document types of interactions that make the strict biomedical model unworkable. You have already seen some of the evidence: Good and bad life events can affect immune function; people are more or less resilient with respect to the negative consequences of stress; adequate social support can decrease the probability of death. These realizations yield the three components of the **biopsychosocial model.** The *bio* acknowledges the reality of biological illness. The *psycho* and the *social* acknowledge the psychological and social components of health.

The biopsychosocial model links your physical health to your state of mind and the world around you. Health psychologists view health as a dynamic, multidimensional experience. Optimal health, or **wellness,** incorporates physical, intellectual, emotional, spiritual, social, and environmental aspects of your

life. When you undertake an activity for the purpose of preventing disease or detecting it in the asymptomatic stage, you are exhibiting health behavior. The general goal of health psychology is to use psychological knowledge to promote wellness and positive health behaviors. Let's now consider theory and research relevant to this goal.

HEALTH PROMOTION

Health promotion means developing general strategies and specific tactics to eliminate or reduce the risk that people will get sick. The prevention of illness in the 21st century poses a much different challenge than it did at the beginning of the 20th century. In 1900, the primary cause of death was infectious disease. Health practitioners at that time launched the first revolution in American public health. Over time, through the use of research, public education, the development of vaccines, and changes in public health standards (such as waste control and sewage), they were able to reduce substantially the deaths associated with such diseases as influenza, tuberculosis, polio, measles, and smallpox.

If researchers wish to contribute to the trend toward improved quality of life, they must attempt to decrease those deaths associated with lifestyle factors (see **Table 12.7** on page 394). Smoking, being overweight, eating foods high in fat and cholesterol, drinking too much alcohol, driving without seat belts, and leading stressful lives all play a role in heart disease, cancer, strokes, accidents, and suicide. Changing the behaviors associated with these diseases of civilization will prevent much illness and premature death.

Based on this knowledge, it's easy to make some recommendations. You are more likely to stay well if you practice good health habits, such as those listed in **Table 12.8** on page 394. Many of these suggestions probably are familiar to you already. However, health psychologists would like to use psychological principles to increase the probability that you will actually do the things you know are good for you. To show you how that works, we now consider a pair of concrete domains: smoking and AIDS.

Smoking It would be impossible to imagine that anyone reading this book wouldn't know that smoking is extremely dangerous. Roughly 438,000 people die each year from smoking-related illnesses (Armour et al., 2005). Even so, 60.1 million people in the United States still smoke cigarettes (Substance Abuse and Mental Health Services Administration, 2008). Health psychologists would like to understand both why people begin to smoke—so that the psychologists can help prevent it—and how to assist people in quitting—so they can reap the substantial benefits of becoming ex-smokers.

---

hozho A Navajo concept referring to harmony, peace of mind, goodness, ideal family relationships, beauty in arts and crafts, and health of body and spirit.

biopsychosocial model A model of health and illness that suggests links among the nervous system, the immune system, behavioral styles, cognitive processing, and environmental domains of health.

wellness Optimal health, incorporating the ability to function fully and actively over the physical, intellectual, emotional, spiritual, social, and environmental domains of health.

health promotion The development and implementation of general strategies and specific tactics to eliminate or reduce the risk that people will become ill.

TABLE 12.7　Leading Causes of Death, United States

Rank	Percentage of Deaths	Cause of Death	Contributors to Cause of Death*
1	25.9	Heart disease	D, S
2	23.1	Cancer	D, S
3	5.6	Stroke	D, S
4	5.1	Respiratory diseases	S
5	4.8	All accidents	A/DA
6	3.0	Alzheimer's disease	
7	3.0	Diabetes	D
8	2.3	Influenza and pneumonia	S
9	1.8	Kidney diseases	D
10	1.4	Septicemia (bacteria in the blood)	A/DA

* D = diet; S = smoking; A/DA = alcohol/drug abuse.

Source: Heron et al., 2008.

Analyses of why some people start smoking have focused on interactions of nature and nurture. Studies comparing monozygotic and dizygotic twins for the similarity of their tobacco use consistently find heritability estimates of 0.50 or higher (Munafò & Johnstone, 2008). Consider one study that examined the smoking behavior of 1,198 pairs of adolescent siblings (that is, identical twins, fraternal twins, and nontwin pairs) (Boardman et al., 2008). The researchers reported heritability estimates of 0.51 for whether individuals began to smoke and 0.58 for how much they smoked each day. The study also documented an impact of the environment. For example, when the adolescents attended schools in which the popular students were also smokers, genes mattered more: Apparently, in that social context, students could realize their "genetic potential."

To understand the link between genes and smoking, researchers have often focused on personality differences that predict which people will start smoking. One personality type that has been associated with the initiation of smoking is called *sensation seeking* (Zuckerman, 2007). Individuals characterized as sensation seeking are more likely to engage in risky activities. One study compared personality assessments of men and women in the mid-1960s (1964–1967) with their smoking or nonsmoking behavior in the late 1980s (1987–1991). Both men and women who had revealed themselves to be sensation seeking in the 1960s were more likely to be smoking 20 to 25 years later (Lipkus et al., 1994). Health psychologists understand that successful interventions to prevent the initiation of smoking must address the aspects of individuals' personalities that make smoking attractive to them.

The best approach to smoking is never to start at all. But for those of you who have begun to smoke, what has research revealed about quitting? Although many people who try to quit have relapses, an estimated 35 million Americans have quit. Ninety percent have done so on their own, without professional treatment programs. Researchers have identified stages people pass through that represent increasing readiness to quit (Norman et al., 1998, 2000):

- *Precontemplation.* The smoker is not yet thinking about quitting.
- *Contemplation.* The smoker is thinking about quitting but has not yet undertaken any behavioral changes.
- *Preparation.* The smoker is getting ready to quit.
- *Action.* The smoker takes action toward quitting by setting behavioral goals.
- *Maintenance.* The smoker is now a nonsmoker and is trying to stay that way.

TABLE 12.8　Ten Steps to Personal Wellness

1. Exercise regularly.
2. Eat nutritious, balanced meals (high in vegetables, fruits, and grains; low in fat and cholesterol).
3. Maintain proper weight.
4. Sleep 7 to 8 hours nightly; rest/relax daily.
5. Wear seat belts and bike helmets.
6. Do not smoke or use drugs.
7. Use alcohol in moderation, if at all.
8. Engage only in protected, safe sex.
9. Get regular medical/dental checkups; adhere to medical regimens.
10. Develop an optimistic perspective and friendships.

This analysis suggests that not all smokers are psychologically equivalent in terms of readiness to quit. Interventions can be designed that nudge smokers up the scale of readiness, until, finally, they are psychologically prepared to take healthy action (Velicer et al., 2007).

Successful smoking-cessation treatment requires that both smokers' physiological and psychological needs be met (Fiore et al., 2008). On the physiological side, smokers are best off learning an effective form of *nicotine replacement therapy,* such as nicotine patches or nicotine gum. On the psychological side, smokers must understand that there are huge numbers of ex-smokers and realize that it is possible to quit. Furthermore, smokers must learn strategies to cope with the strong temptations that accompany efforts to quit. Treatments often incorporate the types of cognitive coping techniques we described earlier, which allow people to alleviate the effects of a wide range of stressors. For smoking, people are encouraged to find ways to avoid or escape from situations that may bring on a renewed urge to smoke.

AIDS AIDS is an acronym for *acquired immune deficiency syndrome.* Although hundreds of thousands are dying from this virulent disease, many more are now living with HIV infection. **HIV** *(human immunodeficiency virus)* is a virus that attacks the white blood cells (T lymphocytes) in human blood, thus damaging the immune system and weakening the body's ability to fight other diseases. The individual then becomes vulnerable to infection by a host of other viruses and bacteria that can cause such life-threatening illnesses as cancer, meningitis, and pneumonia. The period of time from initial infection with the virus until symptoms occur (incubation period) can be five years or longer. Although most of the estimated millions of those infected with the HIV virus do not have AIDS (a medical diagnosis), they must live with the continual stress that this life-threatening disease might suddenly emerge. At the present time, there are treatments that delay the onset of full-blown AIDS, but there is neither a cure for AIDS nor a vaccine to prevent its spread.

The HIV virus is not airborne; it requires direct access to the bloodstream to produce an infection. The HIV virus is generally passed from one person to another in one of two ways: (1) the exchange of semen or blood during sexual contact and (2) the sharing of intravenous needles and syringes used for injecting drugs. The virus has also been passed through blood transfusions and medical procedures in which infected blood or organs are unwittingly given to healthy people. Many people suffering from hemophilia have gotten AIDS in this way. However, everyone is at risk for AIDS.

The only way to protect oneself from being infected with the AIDS virus is to change those lifestyle habits that put one at risk. This means making permanent changes in patterns of sexual behavior and use of drug paraphernalia. Health psychologist **Thomas Coates** is part of a multidisciplinary research team that is using an array of psychological principles in a concerted effort to prevent the further spread of AIDS (Coates & Szekeres, 2004). The team is involved in many aspects of applied psychology, such as assessing psychosocial risk factors, developing behavioral interventions, training community leaders to be effective in educating people toward healthier patterns of sexual and drug behavior, assisting with the design of media advertisements and community information campaigns, and systematically evaluating changes in relevant attitudes, values, and behaviors (Fernández-Dávila et al., 2008; Hendriksen et al., 2007). Successful AIDS interventions require three components (Starace et al., 2006):

- *Information.* People must be provided with knowledge about how AIDS is transmitted and how its transmission may be prevented; they should be counseled to practice safer sex (for example, use condoms during sexual contact) and use sterile needles.
- *Motivation.* People must be motivated to practice AIDS prevention.
- *Behavioral skills.* People must be taught how to put the knowledge to use.

Why are all three of these components necessary? People might be highly motivated but uninformed, or vice versa. They may have both sufficient knowledge and sufficient motivation but lack requisite skills. In addition, information must be delivered in a fashion that does not undermine people's motivation. For example, people were more likely to participate in HIV-prevention counseling when information was framed so that the participants felt in control of their own behavior (Albarracín et al., 2008).

TREATMENT

Treatment focuses on helping people adjust to their illnesses and recover from them. We will look at three aspects of treatment.

Why should interventions recognize that not all smokers are the same with respect to their readiness to quit?

AIDS Acronym for acquired immune deficiency syndrome, a syndrome caused by a virus that damages the immune system and weakens the body's ability to fight infection.

HIV Human immunodeficiency virus, a virus that attacks white blood cells (T lymphocytes) in human blood, thereby weakening the functioning of the immune system; HIV causes AIDS.

First, we consider the role of psychologists in encouraging patients to adhere to the regimens prescribed by health-care practitioners. Next, we look at techniques that allow people to explicitly use psychological techniques to take control over the body's responses. Finally, we examine instances in which the mind can contribute to the body's cure.

Patient Adherence Patients are often given a *treatment regimen*. This might include medications, dietary changes, prescribed periods of bed rest and exercise, and follow-up procedures such as return checkups, rehabilitation training, and chemotherapy. Failing to adhere to treatment regimens is one of the most serious problems in health care (Christensen & Johnson, 2002; Quittner et al., 2008). The rate of patient nonadherence is estimated to be as high as 50 percent for some treatment regimens.

What factors affect the likelihood that patients will adhere to prescribed treatments? One type of research has focused on the relationship between patients' perceptions of the severity of their disease. As you might expect, people who perceive greater threat from a disease also show greater likelihood to adhere to treatments (DiMatteo et al., 2007). However, the relationship becomes more complicated when researchers consider patients' objective health (rather, that is, than patients' subjective perceptions). Patients who face serious diseases that leave them in poor physical health show lower levels of adherence than patients who are less debilitated by the same diseases. This lack of adherence may reflect growing pessimism about the likelihood that the treatment will succeed. A second type of research has demonstrated the importance of social support for patient adherence (DiMatteo, 2004). Patients obtain the greatest benefits when they receive practical support that allows them to accomplish their regimens correctly.

Research has shown that health-care professionals can take steps to improve patient adherence. Consider a study that demonstrated the importance of a match between patients' and physicians' attitudes.

A team of researchers recruited 146 patients and the 16 physicians who had most recently provided them with medical care (Cvengros et al., 2007). Both the patients and the physicians completed a questionnaire that assessed their attitudes about the role patients play in their own health outcomes. Patients responded to statements such as "I am in control of my own health" and "When I get sick it is my own behavior which determines how soon I get well." The physicians responded to a version of the questionnaire that focused on the patients (for example, "Patients are in control of their own health."). The patients also reported their satisfaction with their physician and the extent to which they had adhered to the regimen the physician had provided. The results indicated that patients were both more satisfied and more likely to adhere when their attitudes matched their physicians' attitudes.

Why does relaxation through meditation have health benefits?

To understand this result, imagine what might happen when, for example, a patient who believes she is in control of her own health faces a physician who believes otherwise. That mismatch is likely to undermine the patient's trust in her physician. The researchers suggest that physicians should try to understand their patients' attitudes—and modify their behaviors to match those attitudes.

Harnessing the Mind to Heal the Body More and more often, the treatments to which patients must adhere involve a psychological component. Many investigators now believe that psychological strategies can improve well-being. For example, many people react to stress with tension, resulting in tight muscles and high blood pressure. Fortunately, many tension responses can be controlled by psychological techniques, such as *relaxation* and *biofeedback*.

Relaxation through meditation has ancient roots in many parts of the world. In Eastern cultures, ways to calm the mind and still the body's tensions have been practiced for centuries. Today, Zen discipline and yoga exercises from Japan and India are part of daily life for many people both there and, increasingly, in the West. Growing evidence suggests that complete relaxation is a potent antistress response (Dusek et al., 2002). The **relaxation response** is a condition in which muscle tension, cortical activity, heart rate, and blood pressure all decrease and breathing slows (Benson, 2000). There is reduced electrical activity in the brain, and input to the central nervous system from the outside environment is lowered. In this low level of arousal, recuperation from stress can take place. Four conditions are regarded as necessary to produce the relaxation response: (1) a quiet environment, (2) closed eyes, (3) a comfortable position, and (4) a repetitive mental device such as the chanting of a brief phrase over and over again. The first three conditions lower input to the nervous system, and the fourth lowers its internal stimulation.

relaxation response A condition in which muscle tension, cortical activity, heart rate, and blood pressure decrease and breathing slows.

Critical Thinking in Your Life

CAN HEALTH PSYCHOLOGY HELP YOU GET MORE EXERCISE?

An important goal of health psychology is to increase the likelihood that people will engage in behaviors that are good for their health. High on that list is exercise: There is abundant evidence that people who get enough exercise experience better health. How much is "enough"? The U.S. government makes these recommendations (U.S. Department of Health and Human Services, 2008, p. vii):

- "For substantial health benefits, adults should do at least 150 minutes (2 hours and 30 minutes) a week of moderate-intensity, or 75 minutes (1 hour and 15 minutes) a week of vigorous-intensity aerobic physical activity, or an equivalent combination of moderate- and vigorous-intensity aerobic activity. Aerobic activity should be performed in episodes of at least 10 minutes, and preferably, it should be spread throughout the week."

- "Adults should also do muscle-strengthening activities that are moderate or high intensity and involve all major muscle groups on 2 or more days a week, as these activities provide additional health benefits."

The activities in these recommendations lead to increased fitness of the heart and respiratory systems, improvement of muscle tone and strength, and many other health benefits. So, how can your knowledge of health psychology help people reap these benefits?

Researchers have explored the questions of who exercises regularly and why. They are trying to determine what programs or strategies are most effective in getting people to start and continue exercising (Nigg et al., 2008). In fact, much the same model that we outlined for people's readiness to *quit* smoking applies to people's readiness to *begin* exercising (Buckworth et al., 2007). In the *precontemplation* stage, an individual is still more focused on the barriers to exercise (for example, too little time, no exercise partners) rather than the benefits (for example, helps relaxation, improves appearance). As the individual moves through the *contemplation* and *preparation* stages, the emphasis shifts from barriers to benefits. People who have been exercising for less than six months are in the *action* stage; those who have exercised regularly for over six months are in the *maintenance* stage.

If you do not exercise regularly now, how can you get beyond precontemplation? Research suggests that individuals can learn strategies that allow them to overcome obstacles to exercise (Scholz et al., 2008). One strategy is to formulate *action plans:* You should create specific plans about when, where, and how you foresee becoming physically active. Another strategy is to formulate *coping plans:* You should anticipate what obstacles might arise to interfere with your action plans and determine how best to cope with those obstacles. In one study, researchers taught patients with coronary heart disease how to formulate these types of plans (Sniehotta et al., 2006). Two months later, patients who combined both types of planning had engaged in considerably more physical activity than patients in the control group (who did not receive the training).

Studies of this sort indicate why you can treat exercise like any other situation in which you use cognitive appraisal to cope with stress. When you read that the U.S. government suggests 150 minutes of moderate-intensity aerobic exercise a week, you might want to cope with recommendation by avoiding the topic altogether. Don't let yourself be overwhelmed! Instead, use action plans and coping plans to work your way toward your goals for healthy living.

- Why might the same stages apply to undertaking healthy behaviors and overcoming unhealthy behaviors?

- Why is it stressful to contemplate healthy behaviors such as regular exercise?

Biofeedback is a self-regulatory technique used for a variety of special applications, such as control of blood pressure, relaxation of forehead muscles (involved in tension headaches), and even diminishment of extreme blushing. As pioneered by psychologist **Neal Miller** (1978), biofeedback is a procedure that makes an individual aware of ordinarily weak or internal responses by providing clear external signals. The patient is allowed to "see" his or her own bodily reactions, which are monitored and amplified by equipment that transforms them into lights and sound cues of varying intensity. The patient's task is then to control the level of these external cues.

Let's consider one application of biofeedback. Participants who suffered from either high or low blood pressure were brought into a laboratory (Rau et al., 2003). Feedback from equipment measuring an index of the participants' blood pressure on each heart cycle was delivered to a computer screen so that growing green bars indicated changes in the right direction and growing red bars indicated changes in the wrong direction.

---

biofeedback A self-regulatory technique by which an individual acquires voluntary control over nonconscious biological processes.

In addition, the researchers provided verbal reinforcement: "You did it the right way!" After three training sessions, the participants were able to raise or lower their blood pressure, as desired. If you ever become concerned about your blood pressure or other physical disorders, results of this sort might encourage you to seek a course of biofeedback to complement a drug regimen.

Psychoneuroimmunology In the early 1980s, researchers made a series of discoveries that confirmed another way in which the mind affects the body: Psychological states can have an impact on immune function. Historically, scientists had assumed that immunological reactions—rapid production of antibodies to counterattack substances that invade and damage the organism—were automatic biological processes that occurred without any involvement of the central nervous system. However, conditioning experiments of the type we described in Chapter 6 proved that assumption to be incorrect.

> Groundbreaking researchers **Robert Ader** and **Nicholas Cohen** (1981) taught one group of rats to associate sweet-tasting saccharin with cyclophosphamide (CY), a drug that weakens immune response. A control group received only the saccharin. Later, when both groups of rats were given only saccharin, the animals that had been conditioned to associate saccharin with CY produced significantly fewer antibodies to foreign cells than those rats in the control group. Thus the learned association alone was sufficient to elicit suppression of the immune system, making the experimental rats vulnerable to a range of diseases. The learning effect was so powerful that, later in the study, some of the rats died after drinking only the saccharin solution.

Results like this strongly suggested that immune function can be modified by psychological states. A new field of study, **psychoneuroimmunology,** has emerged to explore these types of results that involve psychology, the nervous system, and the immune system (Ader & Cohen, 1993; Coe, 1999).

Research over the past 25 years has confirmed that stressors—and how people cope with them—have a consistent impact on the ability of the immune system to function effectively (Kiecolt-Glaser et al., 2002). Consider one of the immune system's basic functions, to heal small wounds in your skin. In one study, a research team led by **Janet Kiecolt-Glaser** gave 13 caretakers for relatives with Alzheimer's disease (see Chapter 7) and 13 control participants standardized small wounds to their skin. On average, the Alzheimer's caretakers, who experience chronic stress, took nine days longer for their wounds to heal (Kiecolt-Glaser et al., 1995)! People can also experience chronic stress as a consequence of their own personalities—with similar implications for immune function. For example, individuals who reported having difficulty controlling their anger generally took more days to heal the same type of standardized wounds than individuals with better anger control (Gouin et al., 2008).

psychoneuroimmunology The research area that investigates interactions between psychological processes, such as responses to stress, and the functions of the immune system.

You can see from these data how small differences in stress level may affect the speed with which a person's body can heal even the smallest scratch or scrape. From that basic insight, you can understand why research suggests that stress responses play an even more profound role with respect to the progression of serious medical conditions such as infectious diseases and cancer. Researchers wish to understand how the mind affects immune function so they can harness that power to slow these serious illnesses.

Psychological Impact on Health Outcomes One last note on treatment. Have you ever had a secret too shameful to tell anyone? If so, talking about the secret could very well improve your health. That is the conclusion from a large body of research by health psychologist **James Pennebaker** (1990, 1997; Petrie et al., 1998), who has shown that suppressing thoughts and feelings associated with personal traumas, failures, and guilty or shameful experiences takes a devastating toll on mental and physical health. Such inhibition is psychologically hard work and, over time, it undermines the body's defenses against illness. The experience of letting go often is followed by improved physical and psychological health weeks and months later. Consider the effects of emotional disclosure on health outcomes for people with HIV infection.

> Thirty-seven adults with HIV infection participated in this study. Roughly half of the patients were assigned to an emotional writing group. In four 30-minute sessions on consecutive days, participants wrote about "the most traumatic and emotional experiences of their lives" (Petrie et al., 2004, p. 273). The control group spent the same amount of time on a neutral task, writing accounts, for example, about what they had done in the previous day. To assess the impact of emotional writing, the researchers measured *HIV viral load*—the number of HIV copies in a milliliter of blood. **Figure 12.8** displays the dramatic impact of emotional writing. Those participants who had engaged in emotional writing had consistently lower viral loads two weeks, three months, and six months after the writing sessions.

This result is consistent with other data indicating that individuals' stress level has an impact on the course of HIV infection. Emotional writing helped participants cope with some negative psychological consequences of the infection.

PERSONALITY AND HEALTH

Do you know a person like this: someone who is driven to succeed, no matter what obstacles; someone whose high school class voted him or her "most likely to have a heart attack before age 20"? Are you that person? As you've observed the way in which some people charge through life while others take a more relaxed pace, you may have wondered whether these different personalities affect health. Research in health psychology strongly suggests that the answer is yes.

In the 1950s, Meyer Friedman and Ray Rosenman reported what had been suspected since ancient times: There was a relationship between a constellation of personality traits and the probability of illness, specifically coronary heart disease

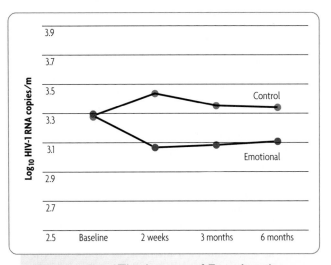

FIGURE 12.8 The Impact of Emotional Writing on HIV Infection

Participants engaged in four sessions of either emotional or neutral writing. Their HIV viral load was assessed two weeks, three months, and six months after the writing sessions. Participants who had engaged in emotional writing had consistently lower viral loads.

From Figure "Viral Load" in "Effect of Written Emotional Expression on Immune Function in Patients with Human Immunodeficiency Virus Infection: A Randomized Trial" by Keith J. Petrie et al., *Psychosomatic Medicine, (66)*: pp. 272–275, © 2004 by the American Psychosomatic Society. Reprinted with permission of the author.

(Friedman & Rosenman, 1974). These researchers identified two behavior patterns that they labeled Type A and Type B. The **Type A behavior pattern** is a complex pattern of behavior and emotions that includes being excessively competitive, aggressive, impatient, time urgent, and hostile. Type A people are often dissatisfied with some central aspect of their lives, are highly competitive and ambitious, and often are loners. The **Type B behavior pattern** is everything Type A is not—individuals are less competitive, less hostile, and so on. Importantly, these behavior patterns have an impact on health. In their original discussion, Friedman and Rosenman reported that people who showed Type A behavior patterns were stricken with coronary heart disease considerably more often than individuals in the general population.

Because the Type A behavior pattern has many components, researchers have focused their attention on identifying the specific Type A elements that most often put people at risk. The personality trait that has emerged most forcefully as "toxic" is hostility.

A longitudinal study began in 1986, with 774 men in the sample who were free of any evidence of cardiovascular disease (Niaura et al., 2002). In 1986, each participant's

level of hostility was measured (using a set of questions from the Minnesota Multiphasic Personality Inventory, a device we will describe in Chapter 13). Hostility is defined as the consistency with which individuals look at the world and other people in a cynical and negative manner. To display the relationship between hostility and coronary heart disease, the researchers divided the hostility scores into percentile groups. As shown in **Figure 12.9**, those individuals whose hostility scores were in the upper 20 percent had a dramatically larger number of episodes of incident coronary heart disease in the subsequent years. In this sample of men, hostility was a better predictor of future illness than several behavioral risk factors such as smoking and drinking.

Hostility may affect health for both physiological reasons—by leading to chronic overarousal of the body's stress responses—and psychological reasons—by leading hostile people to practice poor health habits and avoid social support (Smith & Ruiz, 2002).

The good news is that researchers have begun to implement behavioral treatments to reduce hostility and other aspects of the Type A behavior pattern (Pischke et al., 2008). For example, one intervention was directed toward high-hostile men who had been diagnosed with coronary heart disease (Gidron et al., 1999). As part of the intervention, the men were taught how to use problem-focused coping to reduce anger; they were taught how to use cognitive restructuring to reduce cynicism. After eight weeks, men in the intervention group reported consistently lower levels of hostility than their peers in the control (nonintervention) group. In addition, the men in the intervention group had lower average blood pressure than their control peers. Do you recognize yourself in the definition of hostility? If you do, protect your health by seeking out this type of intervention.

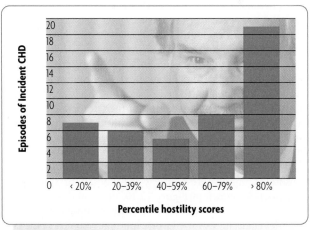

FIGURE 12.9 Hostility Predicts Coronary Heart Disease

Study participants were divided into percentile groups based on their self-reports of hostility. Men whose scores placed them in the top 20 percent on the measure (that is, the group greater than 80 percent) had the highest levels of coronary heart disease.

Type A behavior pattern A complex pattern of behaviors and emotions that includes excessive emphasis on competition, aggression, impatience, and hostility; hostility increases the risk of coronary heart disease.

Type B behavior pattern As compared to Type A behavior pattern, a less competitive, less aggressive, less hostile pattern of behavior and emotion.

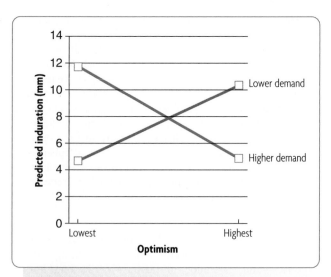

FIGURE 12.10 Optimism and Immune Function

Students with the highest levels of optimism showed better immune response in the face of lower demands. However, they showed worse immune response in the face of higher demands.

From S.C. Segerstrom, "Stress, energy and immunity." *Current Directions in Psychological Science.* Copyright © 2007 by Blackwell Publishers Ltd. Reprinted with permission.

To round out this section on personality and health we want to remind you of the concept of *optimism* we introduced in Chapter 11. We saw there that optimistic individuals attribute failures to external causes and to events that were unstable or modifiable (Seligman, 1991). This style of coping has a strong impact on the optimist's well-being. The particular impact depends on the difficulty of the stressor (Segerstrom, 2005). Because optimists believe they can prevail over stressors, they tend to engage them head on. When the stressor is difficult, this strategy of continued engagement may have negative physiological consequences. Consider a study that assessed the health impact of optimism for students making the transition to law school (Segerstrom, 2006, 2007). For some students this transition was relatively more stressful—because they had social and family demands on top of their academic demands. Each student completed a test that measured optimism. Each student also underwent a procedure to assess immune response. They received an injection of a preparation that tests susceptibility to mumps. In response to the injection, the skin swells. The measure of immune response is the amount of swelling or *induration*. As shown in **Figure 12.10,** those students with the highest optimism showed better immune response in the face of lower demands; they showed worse immune response in the face of higher demands. These data suggest that optimists must recognize that there are some stressors for which the best style of coping is not to engage them directly.

job burnout The syndrome of emotional exhaustion, depersonalization, and reduced personal accomplishment, often experienced by workers in high-stress jobs.

JOB BURNOUT AND THE HEALTH-CARE SYSTEM

One final focus of health psychology is to make recommendations about the design of the health-care system. Researchers, for example, have examined the stress associated with being a health-care provider. Even the most enthusiastic health-care providers run up against the emotional stresses of working intensely with large numbers of people suffering from a variety of personal, physical, and social problems.

The special type of emotional stress experienced by these professional health and welfare practitioners has been termed *burnout* by **Christina Maslach,** a leading researcher on this widespread problem. **Job burnout** is a syndrome of emotional exhaustion, depersonalization, and reduced personal accomplishment that is often experienced by workers in professions that demand high-intensity interpersonal contact with patients, clients, or the public. Health practitioners begin to lose their caring and concern for patients and may come to treat them in detached and even dehumanized ways. They feel bad about themselves and worry that they are failures. Burnout is correlated with greater absenteeism and turnover, impaired job performance, poor relations with coworkers, family problems, and poor personal health (Maslach & Leiter, 2008).

Job burnout in today's workforce is reaching ever higher levels because of the effects of organizational downsizing, job restructuring, and greater concerns for profits than for employee morale and loyalty. Burnout then is not merely a concern of workers and health caregivers, but it also reveals organizational dysfunction that needs to be corrected by reexamining

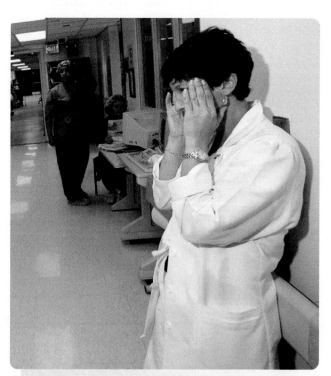

Why are health-care providers particularly prone to job burnout?

goals, values, workloads, and reward structures (Leiter & Maslach, 2005).

What recommendations can be made? Several social and situational factors affect the occurrence and level of burnout and, by implication, suggest ways of preventing or minimizing it (Leiter & Maslach, 2005; Prosser et al., 1997). For example, the quality of the patient–practitioner interaction is greatly influenced by the number of patients for whom a practitioner is providing care—the greater the number, the greater the cognitive, sensory, and emotional overload. Another factor in the quality of that interaction is the amount of direct contact with patients. Longer work hours in continuous direct contact with patients are correlated with greater burnout. This is especially true when the nature of the contact is difficult and upsetting, such as contact with patients who are dying (Jackson et al., 2008). The emotional strain of such prolonged contact can be eased by a number of means. For example, practitioners can modify their work schedules to withdraw temporarily from such high-stress situations. They can use teams rather than only individual contact. They can arrange opportunities to get positive feedback for their efforts.

A TOAST TO YOUR HEALTH

It's time for some final advice. Instead of waiting for stress or illness to come and then reacting to it, set goals and structure your life in ways that are most likely to forge a healthy foundation. The following nine steps to greater happiness and better mental health are presented as guidelines to encourage you to take a more active role in your own life and to create a more positive psychological environment for yourself and others. Think of the steps as *year-round resolutions.*

1. Never say bad things about yourself. Look for sources of your unhappiness in elements that can be modified by future actions. Give yourself and others only *constructive criticism*—what can be done differently next time to get what you want?
2. Compare your reactions, thoughts, and feelings with those of friends, coworkers, family members, and others so that you can gauge the appropriateness and relevance of your responses against a suitable social norm.
3. Have several close friends with whom you can share feelings, joys, and worries. Work at developing, maintaining, and expanding your social support networks.
4. Develop a sense of *balanced time perspective* in which you can flexibly focus on the demands of the task, the situation, and your needs; be future oriented when there is work to be done, present oriented when the goal is achieved and pleasure is at hand, and past oriented to keep you in touch with your roots.
5. Always take full credit for your successes and happiness (and share your positive feelings with other people). Keep an inventory of all the qualities that make you special and unique—those qualities you can offer others. For example, a shy person can provide a talkative person with the gift of attentive listening. Know your sources of personal strength and available coping resources.
6. When you feel you are losing control over your emotions, distance yourself from the situation by physically leaving it, role-playing the position of another person in the situation or conflict, projecting your imagination into the future to gain perspective on what seems an overwhelming problem now, or talking to a sympathetic listener. Allow yourself to feel and express your emotions.
7. Remember that failure and disappointment are sometimes blessings in disguise. They may tell you that your goals are not right for you or may save you from bigger letdowns later on. Learn from every failure. Acknowledge setbacks by saying, "I made a mistake," and move on. Every accident, misfortune, or violation of your expectations is potentially a wonderful opportunity in disguise.
8. If you discover you cannot help yourself or another person in distress, seek the counsel of a trained specialist in your student health department or community. In some cases, a problem that appears to be psychological may really be physical, and vice versa. Check out your student mental health services before you need them and use them without concern about being stigmatized.
9. Cultivate healthy pleasures. Take time out to relax, to meditate, to get a massage, to fly a kite, and to enjoy hobbies and activities you can do alone and that help you get in touch with and better appreciate yourself.

So how are you feeling? If the stressors in your life have the potential to put you in a bad mood, we hope you'll be able to use cognitive reappraisal to minimize their impact. If you are feeling ill, we hope you'll be able to use your mind's healing capacity to speed your way back toward health. Never underestimate the power of these different types of "feelings" to exercise control over your life. Harness that power!

STOP AND REVIEW

❶ What has research revealed about the genetics of smoking?
❷ What are the three components of successful AIDS interventions?
❸ What conditions are necessary to produce the relaxation response?
❹ What is the central goal for researchers who study psychoneuroimmunology?
❺ What is the "toxic" aspect of Type A personalities?
❻ How is job burnout defined?

CRITICAL THINKING   Consider the study that examined the health impact of emotional disclosure. Why did the researchers ask participants in the control group to write texts?

Visit MyPsychLab.com for more review and practice on the following topic:

◉ **Watch:** Adjustment to Physical Illness/HIV Positive: Julia

Recapping Main Points

Emotions

- Emotions are complex patterns of changes made up of physiological arousal, cognitive appraisal, and behavioral and expressive reactions.
- As a product of evolution, all humans may share a basic set of emotional responses.
- Cultures, however, vary in their rules of appropriateness for displaying emotions.
- Classic theories emphasize different parts of emotional response, such as peripheral bodily reactions or central neural processes.
- More contemporary theories emphasize the appraisal of arousal.
- Moods and emotions effect information processing and decision making.
- Subjective well-being is influenced by both genetics and life experiences.

Stress of Living

- Stress can arise from negative or positive events. At the root of most stress are change and the need to adapt to environmental, biological, physical, and social demands.
- Physiological stress reactions are regulated by the hypothalamus and a complex interaction of the hormonal and nervous systems.
- Depending on the type of stressor and its effect over time, stress can be a mild disruption or lead to health-threatening reactions.
- Cognitive appraisal is a primary moderator variable of stress.
- Coping strategies either focus on problems (taking direct actions) or attempt to regulate emotions (indirect or avoidant).

- Cognitive reappraisal and restructuring can be used to cope with stress.
- Social support is also a significant stress moderator, as long as it is appropriate to the circumstances.
- Stress can lead to positive changes such as posttraumatic growth.

Health Psychology

- Health psychology is devoted to treatment and prevention of illness.
- The biopsychosocial model of health and illness looks at the connections among physical, emotional, and environmental factors in illness.
- Illness prevention focuses on lifestyle factors such as smoking and AIDS-risk behaviors.
- Psychological factors influence immune function.
- Psychosocial treatment of illness adds another dimension to patient treatment.
- Individuals who are characterized by Type A (especially hostile), Type B, and optimistic behavior patterns will experience different likelihoods of illness.
- Health-care providers are at risk for burnout, which can be minimized by appropriate situational changes in their helping environment.

Answers for Figure 12.1 (p. 372)

1. happiness
2. surprise
3. anger
4. disgust
5. fear
6. sadness
7. contempt

KEY TERMS

acute stress (p. 379)
AIDS (p. 395)
anticipatory coping (p. 388)
biofeedback (p. 397)
biopsychosocial model (p. 393)
Cannon–Bard theory of emotion (p. 375)
chronic stress (p. 379)
cognitive appraisal theory of emotion (p. 376)
coping (p. 387)
emotion (p. 370)
fight-or-flight response (p. 379)
general adaptation syndrome (GAS) (p. 382)

health (p. 392)
health promotion (p. 393)
health psychology (p. 392)
HIV (p. 395)
hozho (p. 393)
James–Lange theory of emotion (p. 374)
job burnout (p. 400)
life-change unit (LCU) (p. 383)
perceived control (p. 390)
positive psychology (p. 378)
posttraumatic stress disorder (PTSD) (p. 385)
psychoneuroimmunology (p. 398)

psychosomatic disorder (p. 383)
relaxation response (p. 396)
social support (p. 390)
stress (p. 379)
stress moderator variable (p. 387)
stressor (p. 379)
subjective well-being (p. 378)
tend-and-befriend response (p. 381)
two-factor theory of emotion (p. 375)
Type A behavior pattern (p. 399)
Type B behavior pattern (p. 399)
wellness (p. 393)

Chapter 12 Practice Test

1. Which statement is true of moods, but not emotions?
   a. They may last several days.
   b. They can be either positive or negative.
   c. They may arise from specific events.
   d. They are relatively intense.

2. Which of these facial expressions is *not* among the seven universally recognized expressions of emotion?
   a. concern   c. disgust
   b. contempt   d. happiness

3. The _____ prepares the body for physiological aspects of emotional responses.
   a. hypothalamus
   b. amygdala
   c. autonomous nervous system
   d. hippocampus

4. According to the _____ theory of emotion, you feel after your body reacts.
   a. Cannon–Bard   c. James–Lange
   b. cognitive appraisal d. approach-related

5. If Your friend Yasumasa just found out he did better than expected on a calculus exam. An experimenter asks you to predict how happy Yasumasa is feeling. The experimenter also asks Yasumasa the same question. It would probably be the case that your rating would be _____ Yasumas's rating.
   a. equal to   c. higher than
   b. lower than   d. much lower than

6. The brain structure that plays an important role in the fight-or-flight response is the
   a. pituitary gland.   c. hypothalamus.
   b. amygdala.   d. thyroid gland.

7. If you are faced by _____ stressors, the type of coping that is likely to be most useful is _____ coping.
   a. uncontrollable; problem-directed
   b. controllable; emotion-focused
   c. controllable; delay-based
   d. uncontrollable; emotion-focused

8. When May was diagnosed with skin cancer, Al searched the Web to help her learn more about treatment options. This type of social support is _____ support.
   a. tangible   c. emotional
   b. informational   d. inoculation

9. A few months after surviving a tornado, Judy says, "I am grateful for every new day." It sounds like Judy experienced posttraumatic growth in which domain?
   a. spiritual change   c. appreciation of life
   b. relating to others   d. personal strength

10. Consider the stages people pass through as they attempt to quit smoking. Which of these pairs is in the wrong order?
    a. preparation; contemplation
    b. contemplation; action

    c. action; maintenance
    d. preparation; maintenance

11. Marsea is participating in a laboratory study. Every time her blood pressure goes up, she sees a "sad face" on a computer display. It seems that Marsea is learning how to use
    a. the relaxation response.
    b. biofeedback.
    c. anticipatory coping.
    d. stress inoculation.

12. Researchers gave caretakers of Alzheimer's patients and control individuals standardized wounds. What was the result of the study?
    a. The wounds of the Alzheimer's caretakers took longer to heal.
    b. The wounds of the control individuals took longer to heal.
    c. There was no difference in the time it took the wounds to heal.
    d. The wounds of the control individuals were larger.

13. The aspect of the _____ behavior pattern that has the greatest impact on health is _____.
    a. Type B; hostility   c. Type B; pessimism
    b. Type A; optimism   d. Type A; hostility

14. Which of these features is *not* part of the definition of job burnout?
    a. depersonalization
    b. disharmony
    c. emotional exhaustion
    d. reduced personal accomplishment

15. Evanthia is using coping strategies to increase her level of physical activities. Which of these sounds most like a coping plan?
    a. "I will do sit-ups every day before I eat breakfast."
    b. "I will learn how to use an elliptical trainer."
    c. "I will join a gym."
    d. "I will read my textbook while I'm on the treadmill."

Essay Questions

1. What evidence suggests that some emotional responses are innate while others are not?

2. Why does perceived control have an impact on people's ability to cope with stress?

3. What factors affect the likelihood that patients will adhere to treatment regimens?

Discovering Psychology Viewing Guide

Watch the following video by logging on to MyPsychLab (www.mypsychlab.com). After you have watched the video, complete the activities that follow.

Program 23: Health, Mind, and Behavior

KEY TERMS AND PEOPLE

As you watch the program, pay particular attention to these terms and people in addition to those covered in this textbook.

- *psychic numbing*—being emotionally unaffected by an upsetting or alarming event.
- *psychogenic*—organic malfunction or tissue damage caused by anxiety, tension, or depression.
- *Richard Lazarus*—studies cognitive appraisal and the effects of stress.
- *Judith Rodin*—through her study of aging and mind-body relationships, Rodin investigates how subtle psychological factors bring about significant physiological change.

PROGRAM REVIEW

1. How are the biopsychosocial model and the Navaho concept of *hozho* alike?
   a. Both are dualistic.
   b. Both assume individual responsibility for illness.
   c. Both represent holistic approaches to health.
   d. Both are several centuries old.

2. Dr. Wizanski told Thad that his illness was psychogenic. This means that
   a. Thad is not really sick.
   b. Thad's illness was caused by his psychological state.
   c. Thad has a psychological disorder, not a physical one.
   d. Thad's lifestyle puts him at risk.

3. Headaches, exhaustion, and weakness
   a. are not considered to be in the realm of health psychology.
   b. are considered to be psychological factors that lead to unhealthful behaviors.
   c. are usually unrelated to psychological factors.
   d. are considered to be symptoms of underlying tension and personal problems.

4. When Judith Rodin talks about "wet" connections to the immune system, she is referring to connections with the
   a. individual nerve cells.   c. sensory receptors.
   b. endocrine system.   d. skin.

5. What mind–body question is Judith Rodin investigating in her work with infertile couples?
   a. How do psychological factors affect fertility?
   b. Can infertility be cured by psychological counseling?
   c. What effect does infertility have on marital relationships?
   d. Can stress cause rejection of in vitro fertilization?

6. When Professor Zimbardo lowers his heart rate, he is demonstrating the process of
   a. mental relaxation.
   b. stress reduction.
   c. biofeedback.
   d. the general adaptation syndrome.

7. Psychologist Neal Miller uses the example of the blindfolded basketball player to explain
   a. the need for information to improve performance.
   b. how chance variations lead to evolutionary advantage.
   c. the correlation between life-changing events and illness.
   d. how successive approximations can shape behavior.

8. In which area of health psychology has the most research been done?
   a. the definition of health
   b. stress
   c. biofeedback
   d. changes in lifestyle

9. Imagine a family is moving to a new and larger home in a safer neighborhood with better schools. Will this situation be a source of stress for the family?
   a. No, because the change is a positive one.
   b. No, because moving is not really stressful.
   c. Yes, because any change requires adjustment.
   d. Yes, because it provokes guilt that the family does not really deserve this good fortune.

10. Which response shows the stages of the general adaptation syndrome in the correct order?
    a. alarm reaction, exhaustion, resistance
    b. resistance, alarm reaction, exhaustion
    c. exhaustion, resistance, alarm reaction
    d. alarm reaction, resistance, exhaustion

11. What important factor in stress did Hans Selye *not* consider?
    a. the role of hormones in mobilizing the body's defenses
    b. the subjective interpretation of a stressor
    c. the length of exposure to a stressor
    d. the body's vulnerability to new stressors during the resistance stage

12. Today, the major causes of death in the United States are
    a. accidents.
    b. infectious diseases.
    c. sexually transmitted diseases.
    d. diseases related to lifestyle.

13. When Thomas Coates and his colleagues studying AIDS carry out interview studies, they want to gain information that will help them
    a. design interventions at a variety of levels.
    b. determine how effective mass media advertisements are.
    c. motivate AIDS victims to take good care of themselves.
    d. stop people from using intravenous drugs.

14. The body's best external defense against illness is the skin, whereas its best internal defense is
    a. the stomach.
    b. the heart.
    c. T-cells.
    d. the spinal cord.

15. In which stage of the general adaptation syndrome are the pituitary and adrenals stimulated?
    a. exhaustion
    b. alarm
    c. reaction
    d. resistance

16. Which stage of the general adaptation syndrome is associated with the outcome of disease?
    a. alarm
    b. reaction
    c. exhaustion
    d. resistance

17. What claim is Richard Lazarus most closely associated with?
    a. The individual's cognitive appraisal of a stressor is critical.
    b. The biopsychosocial model is an oversimplified view.
    c. Peptic ulcers can be healed through biofeedback.
    d. The general adaptation syndrome can account for 80 percent of heart attacks in middle-aged men.

18. Thomas Coates and Neal Miller are similar in their desire to
    a. eradicate AIDS.
    b. outlaw intravenous drug use.
    c. institute stress management courses as part of standard insurance coverage.
    d. teach basic skills for protecting one's health.

19. How should an advertising campaign ideally be designed in order to get people to use condoms and avoid high-risk sexual activities?
    a. It should be friendly, optimistic, and completely nonthreatening.
    b. It should have enough threat to arouse emotion but not so much that viewers will go into denial.
    c. It should contain a lot of humor.
    d. It should feature an older, white, male doctor and a lot of scientific terminology.

20. Neal Miller is to biofeedback as Judith Rodin is to
    a. analgesics.
    b. meditation.
    c. a sense of control.
    d. social support.

QUESTIONS TO CONSIDER

1. How can you help another person cope with stress?

2. How can a voodoo curse lead to death?

3. How do defense mechanisms help you deal with stress?

4. How can self-deprecating thoughts and behavior increase stress?

5. How might perfectionism lead to stress?

6. What common lifestyle differences might make men or women more susceptible to different kinds of health problems?

7. Is there a likely health benefit to practicing meditation or yoga?

ACTIVITIES

1. Sort the following behaviors into two categories: Category A, stress warning signals; and Category B, signs of successful coping. (You may add others from your own experience.)

Indigestion	Ability to sleep
Fatigue	Tolerance for frustration
Loss of appetite	Constipation
Indecision	Overeating
Sense of belonging	Overuse of drugs or alcohol
Sense of humor	Adaptability to change
Irritability	Optimism
Reliability	Cold hands
Sexual problems	Ulcers
Frequent urination	Sleep problems
Migraine headaches	Difficulty concentrating
Boredom	Free-floating anxiety
Temper tantrums	Frequent colds

2. Use the Student Stress Scale on page 384 in this book to rate the stress in your life. Are you at risk for stress-related problems? Do you need to make your life less stressful? What can you do to reduce the amount of stress in your life?

3. Consider three periods in history: Prehistoric cultures, 0 B.C., and 21st century America. Compare these three moments in history for the impact on health of (a) the reigning understanding of Illness and health and (b) the demands of everyday living. What trade-offs do you see?

13

Understanding Human Personality

Suppose we asked you to compare and contrast your two closest friends. In what ways are they similar? In what ways are they different? It seems likely that your analysis would very quickly come to focus on your friends' *personalities*. You might, for example, assert that one is friendlier than the other or one has more self-confidence than the other. Assertions of this sort would suggest that you've brought your own personality theory to bear on your relationships—you have your own system for appraising personality. You use your beliefs to determine who in a new class would be friend or foe; you worked out techniques for dealing with your parents or teachers based on the way you read their personalities.

Psychologists define personality in many different ways, but common to all of the ways are two basic concepts: *uniqueness* and *characteristic patterns of behavior*. We define **personality** as the complex set of psychological qualities that influence an individual's characteristic patterns of behavior across different situations and over time.

Theories of personality are hypothetical statements about the structure and functioning of individual personalities. They help to achieve two major goals: (1) understanding the structure, origins, and correlates of personality; and (2) predicting behavior and life events based on personality assessments. Different theories make different predictions about the way people will respond and adapt to certain conditions.

Before we examine some of the major theoretical approaches, we should ask why there are so many different (often competing) theories. Theorists differ in their approaches to personality by varying their starting points and sources of data and by trying to explain different types of phenomena. Some are interested in the structure of individual personality and others in how that personality developed and will continue to grow. Some are interested in what people do, either in terms of specific behaviors or important life events; others study how people feel about their lives. Finally, some theories try to explain the personalities of people with psychological problems, whereas others focus on healthy individuals. Thus each theory can teach something about personality, and together they can teach much about human nature.

Our goal for this chapter is to provide you with a framework for understanding your everyday experience of personality. However, before we begin, consider this series of questions: If psychologists studied *you*, what portrait of your personality would they draw? What early experiences might they identify as contributing to the way you now act and think? What conditions in your current life exert strong influences on your thoughts and behaviors? What makes you different from other individuals who are functioning in many of the same situations as you? This chapter should help you formulate specific answers to these questions.

Type and Trait Personality Theories

Two of the oldest approaches to describing personality involve classifying people into a limited number of *distinct types* and scaling the degree to which they can be described by *different*

traits. There seems to be a natural tendency for people to place their own and others' behavior into different categories. Let's examine the formal theories psychologists have developed to capture these differences in types and traits.

CATEGORIZING BY TYPES

We are always categorizing people according to distinguishing features. These include college class, academic major, sex, and race. Some personality theorists also group people into distinct, nonoverlapping categories that are called **personality types.** Personality types are all-or-none phenomena, not matters of degree: If a person is assigned to one type, he or she could not belong to any other type within that system. Many people like to use personality types in everyday life because they help simplify the complex process of understanding other people.

One of the earliest type theories was originated in the 5th century B.C. by **Hippocrates,** the Greek physician who gave medicine the Hippocratic oath. He theorized that the body contained four basic fluids, or *humors*, each associated with a particular *temperament*, a pattern of emotions and behaviors. In the 2nd century A.D., a later Greek physician, **Galen,** suggested that an individual's personality depended on which humor was predominant in his or her body. Galen paired Hippocrates's body humors with personality temperaments according to the following scheme:

- *Blood.* Sanguine temperament: cheerful and active
- *Phlegm.* Phlegmatic temperament: apathetic and sluggish
- *Black bile.* Melancholy temperament: sad and brooding
- *Yellow bile.* Choleric temperament: irritable and excitable

The theory proposed by Galen was believed for centuries, up through the Middle Ages, although it has not held up to modern scrutiny. (We will, however, see a modern echo of these temperaments in Hans Eysenck's trait theory, which we present on p. 410.)

In modern times, **William Sheldon** (1898–1977) originated a type theory that related physique to temperament. Sheldon (1942) assigned people to three categories based on their body builds: *endomorphic* (fat, soft, round), *mesomorphic* (muscular, rectangular, strong), or *ectomorphic* (thin, long, fragile). Sheldon believed that endomorphs are relaxed, fond of eating, and sociable. Mesomorphs are physical people, filled with energy, courage, and assertive tendencies. Ectomorphs are brainy, artistic, and introverted; they would think about life, rather than consuming it or acting on it. For a period of time, Sheldon's theory was sufficiently influential that nude "posture" photographs were taken of thousands of students at U.S. colleges like Yale and Wellesley to allow researchers to study the relationships between body type and life factors. However, like Hippocrates's much earlier theory, Sheldon's notion of body types has proven to be of very little value in predicting an individual's behavior (Tyler, 1965).

---

personality The psychological qualities of an individual that influence a variety of characteristic behavior patterns across difference situations and over time.

personality type Distinct pattern of personality characteristics used to assign people to categories; qualitative differences, rather than differences in degree, used to discriminate among people.

Hippocrates theorized that the body contained four essential fluids, or humors, each associated with a particular temperament. Clockwise: a melancholy patient suffers from an excess of black bile; blood impassions a sanguine lutenist to play; a maiden, dominated by phlegm, is slow to respond to her lover; choler, too much yellow bile, makes an angry master. Do you believe Hippocrates's personality types apply to the people you know?

More recently, **Frank Sulloway** (1996) has proposed a contemporary type theory based on *birth order*. Are you the *firstborn* child (or *only* child) in your family, or are you a *laterborn* child? Because you can take on only one of these birth positions, Sulloway's theory fits the criteria for being a type theory. (For people with unusual family constellations—for example, a very large age gap between two children—Sulloway still provides ways of categorizing individuals.) Sulloway makes birth-order predictions based on Darwin's idea that organisms diversify to find niches in which they will survive. According to Sulloway, firstborns have a ready-made niche: They immediately command their parents' love and attention; they seek to maintain that initial attachment by identifying and complying with their parents. By contrast, laterborn children need to find a different niche—one in which they don't so clearly follow their parents' example. As a consequence, Sulloway characterizes laterborns as "born to rebel": "they seek to excel in those domains where older siblings have not already established superiority. Laterborns typically cultivate openness to experience—a useful strategy for anyone who wishes to find a novel and successful niche in life" (Sulloway, 1996, p. 353). To test the prediction that laterborns embrace innovation, whereas firstborns prefer the status quo, Sulloway examined scientific, historical, and cultural revolutions and determined the birth position of large numbers of historical and contemporary figures who had supported or opposed those revolutions. **Figure 13.1** presents data on the extent to which firstborn and laterborn scientists supported 23 innovative theories in science. As you can see, for all of the family sizes, laterborns were more likely to support the innovative theory than were firstborns. Do you have brothers or sisters? Can you find this pattern in your own family?

Do you know people whom you would label as particular "types"? Does the "type" include all there is to know about the person? Type theories often don't seem to capture more subtle aspects of people's personalities. Let's turn now to theories that allow more flexibility by differentiating individuals according to traits rather than types.

DESCRIBING WITH TRAITS

Type theories presume that there are separate, discontinuous categories into which people fit, such as firstborn or laterborn. By contrast, trait theories propose *continuous dimensions*, such as intelligence or friendliness. **Traits** are enduring qualities or attributes that predispose individuals to behave consistently across situations. For example, you may demonstrate honesty on one day by returning a lost wallet and on another day by not

---

trait Enduring personal quality or attribute that influences behavior across situations.

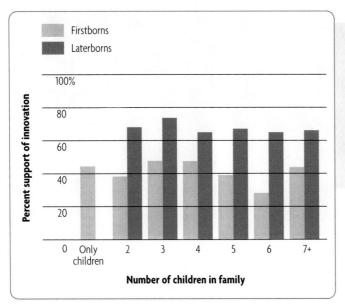

FIGURE 13.1 Birth Position and Support for Scientific Innovation

Frank Sulloway examined 23 innovative scientific theories and determined the birth positions of 1,218 scientists who had adopted or rejected those theories. For every family size, laterborns were more likely to adopt the innovative theory than were firstborns.

From *Born to Rebel* by Frank J. Sulloway, Copyright © 1966 by Frank J. Sulloway. Used by permission of Pantheon Books, a division of Random House, Inc.

cheating on a test. Some trait theorists think of traits as *predispositions* that cause behavior, but more conservative theorists use traits only as *descriptive dimensions* that simply summarize patterns of observed behavior. Let's examine prominent trait theories.

Allport's Trait Approach Gordon Allport (1897–1967) viewed traits as the building blocks of personality and the source of individuality. According to Allport (1937, 1961, 1966), traits produce coherence in behavior because they connect and unify a person's reactions to a variety of stimuli. Traits may act as *intervening variables*, relating sets of stimuli and responses that might seem, at first glance, to have little to do with each other (see **Figure 13.2**).

Allport identified three kinds of traits: cardinal traits, central traits, and secondary traits. *Cardinal traits* are traits around which a person organizes his or her life. For Mother Teresa, a cardinal trait might have been self-sacrifice for the good of others. However, not all people develop such overarching cardinal traits. Instead, *central traits* are traits that represent major characteristics of a person, such as honesty or optimism. *Secondary traits* are specific personal features that help predict an individual's behavior but are less useful for understanding an individual's personality. Food or dress preferences are examples of secondary traits. Allport was interested in discovering the unique combination of these three types of traits that make each person a singular entity and championed the use of case studies to examine these unique traits.

Allport saw *personality structures*, rather than *environmental conditions*, as the critical determiners of individual behavior. "The same fire that melts the butter hardens the egg" was a phrase he used to show that the same stimuli can have different effects on different individuals. Many contemporary trait theories have followed in Allport's tradition.

Identifying Universal Trait Dimensions In 1936, a dictionary search by Gordon Allport and his colleague H. S. Odbert found 17,953 adjectives in the English language to describe individual differences. Researchers since that time have attempted to identify the fundamental dimensions that underlie that enormous trait vocabulary. They have tried to determine how many dimensions exist and which ones will allow psychologists to give a useful, universal characterization of all individuals.

Raymond Cattell (1979) used Allport and Odbert's list of adjectives as a starting point in his quest to uncover the appropriate small set of basic trait dimensions. His research led him to propose that 16 factors underlie human personality. Cattell called these 16 factors *source traits* because he believed they provide the underlying source for the surface behaviors we think of as personality. Cattell's 16 factors included important behavioral oppositions such as *reserved* versus *outgoing*, *trusting* versus *suspicious*, and *relaxed* versus *tense*. Even so, contemporary trait theorists argue that even fewer dimensions than 16 capture the most important distinctions among people's personalities.

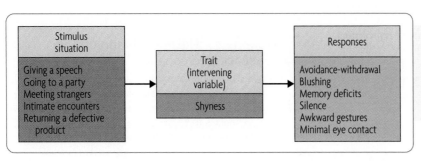

FIGURE 13.2 Shyness as a Trait

Traits may act as intervening variables, relating sets of stimuli and responses that might seem, at first glance, to have little to do with each other.

In the absence of personality test results, traits can be inferred from observed behavior. For example, Martin Luther King Jr. (left) would be thought to have the cardinal trait of peacefully resisting injustice; honesty would be one of Abraham Lincoln's (center) central traits; and Madonna's (right) predilection for changeable styles would be a secondary trait. What do you think may be your cardinal, central, and secondary traits?

Hans Eysenck (1973, 1990) derived just three broad dimensions from personality test data: *extraversion* (internally versus externally oriented), *neuroticism* (emotionally stable versus emotionally unstable), and *psychoticism* (kind and considerate versus aggressive and antisocial). As shown in **Figure 13.3,** Eysenck plotted the two dimensions of extraversion and neuroticism to form a circular display. He suggested that each quadrant of the display represents one of the four personality types associated by Galen with Hippocrates's humors. Eysenck's trait theory, however, allows for individual variation within these categories. Individuals can fall anywhere around the circle, ranging from very introverted to very extraverted and from very unstable (neurotic) to very stable. The traits listed around the circle describe people with combinations of these two dimensions. For example, a person who is very extraverted and somewhat unstable is likely to be impulsive.

Five-Factor Model Research evidence supports many aspects of Eysenck's theory. However, in recent years, a consensus has emerged that five factors, which overlap imperfectly with Eysenck's three dimensions, best characterize personality structure. The five dimensions are very broad because each brings into one large category many traits that have unique connotations but a common theme. These five dimensions of personality are now called the **five-factor model,** or, more informally, the *Big Five* (McCrae & Costa, 1999). The five factors are summarized in **Table 13.1.** You'll notice again that each dimension has two poles—terms that are similar in meaning to the name of the dimension describe the high pole, and terms that are opposite in meaning describe the low pole.

The movement toward the five-factor model represented attempts to find structure among the large list of traits that Allport and Odbert (1936) had extracted from the dictionary. The traits were boiled down into about 200 synonym clusters

that were used to form trait dimensions that have a high pole and a low pole, such as *responsible* versus *irresponsible*. Next, people were asked to rate themselves and others on the bipolar dimensions, and the ratings were subjected to statistical procedures to determine how the synonym clusters were interrelated.

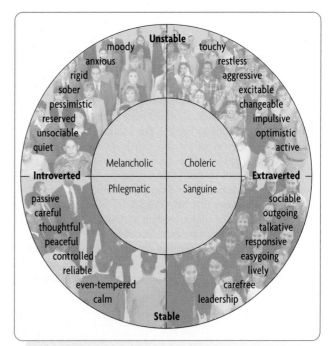

FIGURE 13.3 The Four Quadrants of Eysenck's Personality Circle

The two dimensions of extraversion and neuroticism yield a circular display. Eysenck related each quadrant of the display to one of the four personality types defined by Galen. Eysenck's trait theory, however, allows for individual variation within these categories.

---

five-factor model A comprehensive descriptive personality system that maps out the relationships among common traits, theoretical concepts, and personality scales; informally called the Big Five.

TABLE 13.1	The Five-Factor Model
Factor	**End Points of the Dimension**
Extraversion	Talkative, energetic, and assertive versus quiet, reserved, and shy
Agreeableness	Sympathetic, kind, and affectionate versus cold, quarrelsome, and cruel
Conscientiousness	Organized, responsible, and cautious versus careless, frivolous, and irresponsible
Neuroticism	Stable, calm, and contented versus anxious, unstable, and temperamental
Openness to experience	Creative, intellectual, and open-minded versus simple, shallow, and unintelligent

Using this method, several independent research teams came to the same conclusion: that there are only *five basic dimensions* underlying the traits people use to describe themselves and others (Norman, 1963, 1967; Tupes & Christal, 1961).

Since the 1960s, very similar dimensions have also been found in personality questionnaires, interviewer checklists, and other data (Costa & McCrae, 1992; Digman, 1990; Wiggins & Pincus, 1992). To demonstrate the universality of the five-factor model, researchers have broadened their studies beyond the English language: The five-factor structure has been replicated in a number of languages, including German, Portuguese, Hebrew, Chinese, Korean, and Japanese (McCrae & Costa, 1997). The five factors are not meant to replace the many specific trait terms that carry their own nuances and shades of meaning. Rather, they outline a taxonomy—a classification system—that allows you to give a description of all the people you know in ways that capture the important dimensions on which they differ.

We have emphasized that the five-factor model originally emerged from statistical analyses of clusters of trait terms, rather than from a theory that said, "These are the factors that must exist" (Ozer & Reise, 1994). However, researchers have started to demonstrate that there are differences in the ways that individuals' brains function that correspond to trait differences in the five-factor model.

Recall from Chapter 12 that a brain structure called the amygdala plays an important role in the processing of emotional stimuli. However, researchers had begun to suspect that not all amygdalas—and, therefore, not all people—responded to stimuli in the same way. To test this idea, a team of researchers recruited 15 participants who differed in their level of extraversion (Canli et al., 2002b). The researchers predicted that extraversion would have an impact on emotional processing because that trait captures important aspects of people's emotional lives. To look for individual differences, the researchers had the participants view fearful, happy, and neutral faces while they underwent fMRI scans. **Figure 13.4** displays the correlation between participants' self-reports of extraversion and activity in the left and right amygdalas: The areas in red are those areas

for which high levels of extraversion were associated with high levels of brain activity. As you can see, extraversion was not correlated with the brains' responses to fearful faces (that is, there are no areas in red). In fact, fearful faces activated both the left and right amygdalas, but more or less equally across all levels of extraversion. By contrast, for happy faces the highly extraverted individuals showed abundant activity in their left amygdala.

You might recall from Chapter 12 that researchers have characterized emotions as either *approach-related* or *withdrawal-related*. This study suggests that people who are most content to approach other people—that's what makes them extraverted—have more activation in brain regions that support approach-related emotions.

Evolutionary Perspectives on Trait Dimensions

Supporters of the five-factor model have tried to explain why exactly these five dimensions emerge by looking to evolution: They try to relate the five dimensions to consistent types of interactions that people had with each other and with the external world over the course of human evolution (Buss, 1995; Costa & McCrae, 1992; McCrae et al., 2000). Because, for example, humans are essentially a social species, we can view variation on the five dimensions as answers to fundamental social questions: "who is good company (Extraversion), who is kind and supportive (Agreeableness), who puts in sustained effort (Conscientiousness), who is emotionally undependable (Neuroticism), and who has ideas that pan out (Openness [to experience])" (Bouchard & Loehlin, 2001, p. 250). This evolutionary analysis

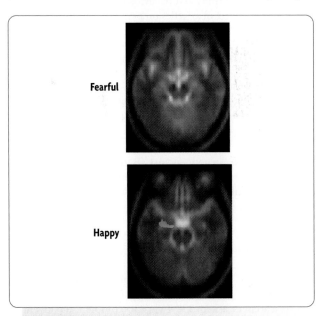

FIGURE 13.4 Extraversion Affects the Function of the Left Amygdala

Participants viewed fearful and happy faces. The figure displays in red those areas of the brain for which there was a positive correlation between extraversion and amygdala activity. For the fearful faces, there was no correlation. However, for happy faces, the most extraverted participants also showed the highest levels of activity in their left amygdalas.

would help explain the universality of the five factors across diverse cultures (Yamagata et al., 2006).

Researchers who take this evolutionary approach have also considered why there is such great variation along these dimensions (Penke et al., 2007). Consider extraversion. As we just noted, humans are a highly social species. For that reason, it might seem maladaptive for an individual to be unsociable and reserved rather than sociable and active. However, we need to factor in differences among environments. People who are highly extraverted are more likely to engage risky behaviors than those who are not (Nettle, 2006). In particularly dangerous environments, people who were relatively more cautious about social interactions would be more likely to survive. The diversity of environments over human evolution explains why people embody both low and high values on each of the five dimensions. If this explanation is correct, we might also expect that, like other aspects of human experience that have been shaped by evolution, traits can be passed from one generation to the next. We turn now to that claim.

TRAITS AND HERITABILITY

You've probably heard people say things such as "Jim's artistic, like his mother" or "Mary's as stubborn as her grandfather." Or maybe you've felt frustrated because the characteristics that you find irritating in your siblings are those you would like to change in yourself. Let's look at the evidence that supports the heritability of personality traits.

Recall that *behavioral genetics* is the study of the degree to which personality traits and behavior patterns are inherited. To determine the effect of genetics on personality, researchers study the personality traits of family members who share different proportions of genes and who have grown up in the same or different households. For example, if a personality characteristic such as *sociability* is passed on genetically, then sociability should correlate more highly between identical, *monozygotic* (MZ) twins (who share 100 percent of their genes) than between fraternal, *dizygotic* (DZ) twins or other siblings (who share, on average, 50 percent of their genes).

Heritability studies show that almost all personality traits are influenced by genetic factors (Bouchard, 2004). The findings are the same with many different measurement techniques, whether they measure broad traits, such as extraversion and neuroticism, or specific traits, such as self-control or sociability. Let's consider one sample study.

Recall from Chapter 12 that researchers in the field of positive psychology wish to identify factors that determine positive features of people's lives. To understand the genetic basis of positive personality traits, researchers asked 336 twins to complete an inventory that listed statements related to 24 traits such as *bravery*, *kindness*, and *fairness* (Steger et al., 2007). For each statement (for example, "I am never too busy to help a friend"), the participants responded on a scale ranging from "very much like me" to "very much unlike me." The researchers' analyses showed a strong genetic impact for 21 out of the positive 24 traits. For example, for the trait of bravery, MZ twins yielded a 0.50 correlation between their responses whereas DZ twins yielded a 0.19 correlation.

These data illustrate the general conclusion that genetics have a strong impact on personality. Look back to Table 13.1. Which poles of the five factors seem to apply best to you? Can you find similarities between you and your parents?

DO TRAITS PREDICT BEHAVIORS?

Suppose we ask you to choose some trait terms that you believe apply particularly well to yourself. You might tell us, for example, that you are *very friendly*. What do we now know? If personality theories allow us to make predictions about behaviors, what can we predict from knowing that you rate yourself as being very friendly? How can we determine the validity of your belief? Let's explore this question.

One idea you might have is that knowing that a person can be characterized by a particular trait would enable you to predict his or her behavior across different *situations*. Thus, we would expect you to produce friendly behaviors in all situations. However, in the 1920s, several researchers who set out to observe trait-related behaviors in different situations were surprised to find little evidence that behavior was consistent across situations. For example, two behaviors presumably related to the trait of honesty—lying and cheating on a test—were only weakly correlated among schoolchildren (Hartshorne & May, 1928). Similar results were found by other researchers who examined the *cross-situational consistency* for other traits such as introversion or punctuality (Dudycha, 1936; Newcomb, 1929).

If trait-related behaviors are not cross-situationally consistent—that is, if people's behavior changes in different situations—why do you perceive your own and others' personalities to be relatively stable? Even more puzzling, the personality ratings of observers who know an individual from one situation correlate with the ratings of observers who know the individual from another situation. The observation that personality ratings across time and among different observers *are consistent*, whereas behavior ratings of a person across situations *are*

Research with identical twins demonstrates the heritability of personality traits. Are there personality traits you believe run in your family?

Assuming you could afford either one, which of these vacations would you prefer? What might that tell us about the ways in which personality traits interact with features of situations?

not consistent, came to be called the **consistency paradox** (Mischel, 1968).

The identification of the consistency paradox led to a great deal of research (Mischel, 2004). Over time, the consensus emerged that the appearance of behavioral inconsistency arose, in large part, because situations had been categorized in the wrong way: The paradox fades away once theorists can provide an appropriate account of the *psychological features* of situations (Mischel & Shoda, 1995, 1999). Suppose, for example, you want to try to assess behavioral consistency by determining if a friend acts in much the same way at every party she attends. You're likely to discover that her behavior varies widely if your level of analysis is just "parties." What you need to determine is what psychologically relevant features separate parties into different categories. Perhaps your friend feels uncomfortable in situations in which she is expected to disclose personal information to strangers. As a consequence, she might seem very unfriendly at some parties (where she is expected to disclose personal information) but quite friendly at others (where she is not). Meanwhile, other situations that require her to be disclosing—such as job interviews—might also bring out negative behaviors. Thus we find consistency in the way that features of situations elicit people's distinctive responses.

Researchers have described the knowledge people have of the relationships between dispositions and situations as *if . . . then . . . personality signatures: If* an individual brings a particular disposition to a specific situation *then* he or she will behave in a particular way (Mischel, 2004). Consider a study that demonstrated the richness of participants' *if . . . then . . .* knowledge.

The researchers asked participants to imagine a college student named Jane (Kammrath et al., 2005). However, different subsets of the participants imagined that Jane was a friendly person, a kiss-up, a flirtatious person, a shy person, or an unfriendly person. After spending a few moments contemplating Jane with that disposition, participants provided judgments of how much warmth they believed Jane would display in six situations: interacting with peers or with professors, with women or with men, with people she was meeting for the first time or with people she has known for a long time. **Figure 13.5** shows participants' warmth predictions for the contrast between new acquaintances (*unfamiliar*) and old acquaintances (*familiar*). You can see that people made very different predictions for different situations. For example, they expected *if* Jane were shy *then* she would be far less warm with unfamiliar than with familiar individuals.

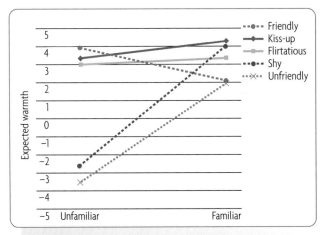

FIGURE 13.5 Students' Knowledge of *If . . . Then . . .* Personality Signatures

Participants imagined a student named Jane as a friendly person, a kiss-up, a flirtatious person, a shy person, or an unfriendly person. They were asked to imagine how warmly Jane would behave on a scale from −5 (Jane feels basically cold and indifferent) to +5 (Jane feels genuine warmth and caring). The participants' predictions for how warmly each version of Jane would behave differed greatly when they imagined her interacting with unfamiliar versus familiar individuals.

From L. K. Kammrath, R. Mendoza-Denton, and W. Mischel, *Journal of Personality and Social Psychology, 88*(4), Copyright © 2005 by the American Psychological Association. Adapted with permission.

consistency paradox The observation that personality ratings across time and among different observers are consistent while behavior ratings across situations are not consistent.

Take a moment to trace through the rest of the data in Figure 13.5. You should be able to convince yourself that you also possess a good deal of knowledge of the *if . . . then . . .* relationships that explain the interactions of dispositions and situations.

EVALUATION OF TYPE AND TRAIT THEORIES

We have seen that type and trait theories allow researchers to give concise descriptions of different people's personalities. These theories have been criticized, however, because they do not generally explain how behavior is generated or how personality develops; they identify and describe only characteristics that are correlated with behavior. Although contemporary trait theorists have begun to address these concerns, trait theories typically portray a *static*, or at least stabilized, view of *personality structure* as it currently exists. By contrast, psychodynamic theories of personality, to which we next turn, emphasize conflicting forces within the individual that lead to change and development.

STOP AND REVIEW

❶ How are personality types defined?

❷ What are the end points of the trait dimension of neuroticism?

❸ How have researchers assessed the heritability of traits?

❹ What is the consistency paradox?

CRITICAL THINKING Recall the study that looked at *if . . . then . . .* knowledge. Why was it important for each participant to make predictions for a range of situations?

Visit MyPsychLab.com for more review and practice on the following topic:

◄●● **Explore:** The Five-Factor Model

Psychodynamic Theories

Common to all **psychodynamic personality theories** is the assumption that powerful inner forces shape personality and motivate behavior. Sigmund Freud, the originator of psychodynamic theories, was characterized by his biographer Ernest Jones as "the Darwin of the mind" (1953). Freud's theory of personality boldly attempts to explain the origins and course of personality development, the nature of mind, aspects of abnormal personality, and the way personality can be changed by therapy. Here we will focus only on normal personality; Freud's

---

psychodynamic personality theory Theory of personality that shares the assumption that personality is shaped by and behavior is motivated by inner forces.

libido The psychic energy that drives individuals toward sensual pleasures of all types, especially sexual ones.

views on psychopathology and treatment will be treated in Chapters 14 and 15. After we explore Freud, we will describe some criticisms and reworkings of his theories.

FREUDIAN PSYCHOANALYSIS

According to psychoanalytic theory, at the core of personality are events within a person's mind *(intrapsychic events)* that motivate behavior. Often, people are aware of these motivations; however, some motivation also operates at an unconscious level. The *psychodynamic* nature of this approach comes from its emphasis on these inner wellsprings of behavior, as well as the clashes among these internal forces. For Freud, *all behavior was motivated.* No chance or accidental happenings cause behavior; all acts are determined by motives. Every human action has a cause and a purpose that can be discovered through analysis of thought associations, dreams, errors, and other behavioral clues to inner passions. The primary data for Freud's hypotheses about personality came from clinical observations and in-depth case studies of individual patients in therapy. He developed a theory of normal personality from his intense study of those with mental disorders. Let's look at some of the most important aspects of Freud's theory.

Drives and Psychosexual Development Freud's medical training as a neurologist led him to postulate a common biological basis for the behavioral patterns he observed in his patients. He ascribed the source of motivation for human actions to *psychic energy* found within each individual. Each person was assumed to have inborn instincts or drives that were *tension systems* created by the organs of the body. These energy sources, when activated, could be expressed in many different ways.

Freud postulated two basic drives. One he saw as involved with *self-preservation* (meeting such needs as hunger and thirst). The other he called *Eros*, the driving force related to sexual urges and preservation of the species. Freud greatly expanded the notion of human sexual desires to include not only the urge for sexual union but all other attempts to seek pleasure or to make physical contact with others. He used the term **libido** to identify the source of energy for sexual urges—a psychic energy that drives us toward sensual pleasures of all types. Sexual urges demand immediate satisfaction, whether through direct actions or through indirect means such as fantasies and dreams.

According to Freud, Eros, as a broadly defined sexual drive, does not suddenly appear at puberty but operates from birth. Eros is evident, he argued, in the pleasure infants derive from physical stimulation of the genitals and other sensitive areas, or *erogenous zones.* Freud's five stages of *psychosexual development* are shown in **Table 13.2**. Freud believed that the physical source of sexual pleasure changed in this orderly progression. One of the major obstacles of psychosexual development, at least for boys, occurs in the phallic stage. Here, the 4- or 5-year-old child must overcome the *Oedipus complex.* Freud named this complex after the mythical figure Oedipus, who unwittingly killed his father and married his mother. Freud believed that every young boy has an innate impulse to view his father as a sexual rival for his mother's attentions. Because the young boy cannot displace his father, the Oedipus complex is generally resolved when the boy comes to *identify* with his father's power. (Freud was inconsistent with respect to his theoretical account of the experiences of young girls.)

According to Freud, either too much gratification or too much frustration at one of the early stages of psychosexual

Psychology in Your Life

WHY ARE SOME PEOPLE SHY?

Surveys reveal that more than 50 percent of college students consider themselves to be "currently shy" (Carducci & Zimbardo, 1995). Most of them say that shyness is an undesirable condition that has negative personal and social consequences. Another group of students say that they are "situationally shy." They feel "shy" in certain situations that are novel, awkward, or socially pressured, such as blind dates, singles bars, or being put on the spot to perform in public without preparation. Researchers investigating shyness in adults were surprised to discover that it is the "not shy" person who is the rare, unusual breed in the United States and in every other country surveyed (Zimbardo, 1991).

Shyness may be defined as an individual's discomfort and/or inhibition in interpersonal situations that interferes with pursuing one's interpersonal or professional goals. Shyness can be the mild reticence and social awkwardness many people feel in new situations, but it can escalate into the extreme of a totally inhibiting fear of people (we will discuss this social phobia in Chapter 14). Many shy people are also introverted; they prefer solitary, nonsocial activities. Others are "shy extraverts," publicly outgoing yet privately shy, preferring to engage in social activities, having the social skills to do so effectively, yet doubting that others will really like or respect them (Pilkonis & Zimbardo, 1979).

So why are some people shy and others are not? One explanation may be nature. Research evidence

suggests that about 10 percent of infants are "born shy" (Kagan, 1994). From birth, these children are unusually cautious and reserved when they interact with unfamiliar people or situations. A complementary explanation focuses on nurture. As children, some individuals are ridiculed, laughed at, or singled out for public shame; others grow up in families that make "being loved" contingent on competitive success in appearance and performance.

A third explanation focuses on culture. Shyness is highest in some Asian countries, notably Japan and Taiwan, and lowest in Israel, among nine countries studied (Zimbardo, 1991). This difference is attributed in part to cultural emphases on shame for social failure and obedience to authority in these Asian countries versus encouragement for taking risks and externalizing blame in Israel (Pines & Zimbardo, 1978). A fourth explanation accounts, in part, for a recent rise in reported prevalence of shyness in the United States: Young people are intensively involved with electronic technology. Spending long hours, typically alone, watching TV, playing video games, surfing the Web, and doing e-mail is socially isolating and reduces daily face-to-face contact. Heavy use of the Internet has the potential to make people feel lonely, isolated, and shyer (Shaw & Black, 2008).

As shyness gets more extreme, it intrudes on ever more aspects of one's life to minimize social pleasures and maximize social discomfort and isolation. There are some simple

concepts and tactics we suggest for shy students to think about and try out (Zimbardo, 1991):

- Realize that you are not alone in your shyness; every person you see is more like you than different from you in his or her shyness.

- Shyness can be modified, even when there is a genetic component, but it takes dedication and a resolve to change, as with any long-standing habit you want to break.

- Practice smiling and making eye contact with most people you meet.

- Talk up; speak in a loud, clear voice, especially when giving your name or asking for information.

- Be the first to ask a question or make a comment in a new social situation. Be prepared with something interesting to say and say it first; everyone appreciates an "ice breaker."

- Never put yourself down. Instead, think about what you can do next time to gain the outcome you want.

- Focus on making others feel comfortable, especially searching out those other shy people. Doing so lowers your self-consciousness.

If you are shy, we hope you will adopt these suggestions. Other students who have followed them have been released from the prison of shyness into a life filled with new-found liberties.

---

development leads to **fixation,** an inability to progress normally to the next stage of development. As shown in Table 13.2, fixation at different stages can produce a variety of adult characteristics. The concept of fixation explains why Freud put such emphasis on early experiences in the continuity of personality. He believed that experiences in the early stages of psychosexual

shyness An individual's discomfort and/or inhibition in interpersonal situations that interferes with pursuing an interpersonal professional goal.

fixation A state in which a person remains attached to objects or activities more appropriate for an earlier stage of psychosexual development.

TABLE 13.2 Freud's Stages of Psychosexual Development

Stage	Age	Erogenous Zones	Major Developmental Task (Potential Source of Conflict)	Some Adult Characteristics of Children Who Have Been Fixated at This Stage
Oral	0–1	Mouth, lips, tongue	Weaning	Oral behavior, such as smoking, overeating; passivity and gullibility
Anal	2–3	Anus	Toilet training	Orderliness, parsimoniousness, obstinacy, or the opposite
Phallic	4–5	Genitals	Oedipus complex	Vanity, recklessness, or the opposite
Latency	6–12	No specific area	Development of defense mechanisms	None: Fixation does not normally occur at this stage
Genital	13–18	Genitals	Mature sexual intimacy	Adults who have successfully integrated earlier stages should emerge with a sincere interest in others and a mature sexuality

development had a profound impact on personality formation and adult behavior patterns.

Psychic Determinism The concept of fixation gives us a first look at Freud's belief that early conflicts help *determine* later behaviors. **Psychic determinism** is the assumption that all mental and behavioral reactions (symptoms) are determined by earlier experiences. Freud believed that symptoms were not arbitrary. Rather, symptoms were related in a meaningful way to significant life events.

Freud's belief in psychic determinism led him to emphasize the **unconscious**—the repository of information that is unavailable to conscious awareness (see **Figure 13.6**). Other writers had discussed this construct, but Freud put the concept of the unconscious determinants of human thought, feeling, and action at center stage in the human drama. According to Freud, behavior can be motivated by drives of which a person is not aware. You may act without knowing why or without direct access to the true cause of your actions. There is a *manifest* content to your behavior—what you say, do, and perceive—of which you are fully aware, but there is also a concealed, *latent* content. The meaning of neurotic (anxiety-based) symptoms, dreams, and slips of the pen and tongue is found at the unconscious level of thinking and information processing. Many psychologists today consider this concept of the unconscious to be Freud's most important contribution to the science of psychology. Much modern literature and drama, as well, explores the implications of unconscious processes for human behavior.

According to Freud, impulses within you that you find unacceptable still strive for expression. A *Freudian slip* occurs when an unconscious desire is betrayed by your speech or behavior. For example, one of your authors felt obligated to write a thank-you note although he hadn't much enjoyed the weekend he'd spent at a friend's home. He intended to write, "I'm glad we got to spend a chunk of time together." However, in a somewhat testy phone call, the friend informed him that he'd actually written "I'm glad we got to spend a *junk* of time together." Do you see how the substitution of *junk* for *chunk*

could be the expression of an unconscious desire? The concept of unconscious motivation adds a new dimension to personality by allowing for greater complexity of mental functioning.

We've now reviewed some basic aspects of Freud's theory. Let's see how they contribute to the structure of personality.

The Structure of Personality In Freud's theory, personality differences arise from the different ways in which people deal with their fundamental drives. To explain these differences, Freud pictured a continuing battle between two antagonistic parts of the personality—the *id* and the *superego*—moderated by a third aspect of the self, the *ego*. Although we will refer to these three

Why did Freud believe that eating is motivated not only by the self-preservation drive to satisfy hunger but also by the "erotic" drive to seek oral gratification?

psychic determinism The assumption that mental and behavioral reactions are determined by previous experiences.

unconscious The domain of the psyche that stores repressed urges and primitive impulses.

FIGURE 13.6 Freud's Conception of the Human Mind

Freudian theory likens the human mind to an iceberg. The tip of the iceberg, which you can see, represents consciousness. The unconscious is the vast bulk of the iceberg, which remains hidden beneath the water.

aspects almost as if they are separate creatures, keep in mind that Freud believed them all to be just different mental *processes.* He did not, for example, identify specific brain locations for the id, ego, and superego.

The **id** is the storehouse of the fundamental drives. It operates irrationally, acting on impulse and pushing for expression and immediate gratification without considering whether what is desired is realistically possible, socially desirable, or morally acceptable. The id is governed by the *pleasure principle,* the unregulated search for gratification—especially sexual, physical, and emotional pleasures—to be experienced here and now without concern for consequences.

The **superego** is the storehouse of an individual's values, including moral attitudes learned from society. The superego corresponds roughly to the common notion of *conscience.* It develops as a child comes to accept as his or her own values the prohibitions of parents and other adults against socially undesirable actions. It is the inner voice of *oughts* and *should nots.* The superego also includes the *ego ideal,* an individual's view of the kind of person he or she should strive to become. Thus the superego is often in conflict with the id. The id wants to do what feels good, whereas the superego insists on doing what is right.

The **ego** is the reality-based aspect of the self that arbitrates the conflict between id impulses and superego demands. The ego represents an individual's personal view of physical and social reality—his or her conscious beliefs about the causes and consequences of behavior. Part of the ego's job is to choose actions that will gratify id impulses without undesirable consequences. The ego is governed by the *reality principle,* which puts reasonable choices before pleasurable demands. Thus the ego would block an impulse to cheat on an exam because of concerns about the consequences of getting caught, and it would substitute the resolution to study harder the next time or solicit the teacher's sympathy. When the id and the superego are in conflict, the ego arranges a compromise that at least partially satisfies both. However, as id and superego pressures intensify, it becomes more difficult for the ego to work out optimal compromises.

Repression and Ego Defense Sometimes this compromise between id and superego involves "putting a lid on the id." Extreme desires are pushed out of conscious awareness into the privacy of the unconscious. **Repression** is the psychological process that protects an individual from experiencing extreme anxiety or guilt about impulses, ideas, or memories that are unacceptable and/or dangerous to express. The ego remains unaware of both the mental content that is censored and the process by which repression keeps information out of consciousness. Repression is considered to be the most basic of the various ways in which the ego defends against being overwhelmed by threatening impulses and ideas.

Ego defense mechanisms are mental strategies the ego uses to defend itself in the daily conflict between id impulses that seek expression and the superego's demand to deny them (see **Table 13.3** on page 418). In psychoanalytic theory, these mechanisms are considered vital to an individual's psychological coping with powerful inner conflicts. By using them, a person is able to maintain a favorable self-image and to sustain an acceptable social image. For example, if a child has strong feelings of hatred toward his father—which, if acted out, would be dangerous—repression may take over. The hostile impulse is then no longer consciously pressing for satisfaction or even recognized as existing. However, although the impulse is not seen or heard, it is not gone; these feelings continue to play a role in personality functioning. For example, by developing a strong *identification* with his father, the child may increase his sense of self-worth and reduce his unconscious fear of being discovered as a hostile agent.

In Freudian theory, **anxiety** is an intense emotional response triggered when a repressed conflict is about to emerge into consciousness. Anxiety is a danger signal: Repression is not working! Red alert! More defenses needed! This is the time for a second line of defense, one or more additional ego defense mechanisms that will relieve the anxiety and send the distressing impulses back

---

id The primitive, unconscious part of the personality that represents the internalization of society's values, standards, and morals.

superego The aspect of personality that represents the internalization of society's values, standards, and morals.

ego The aspect of personality involved in self-preservation activities and in directing instinctual drives and urges into appropriate channels.

repression The basic defense mechanism by which painful or guilt-producing thoughts, feelings, or memories are excluded from conscious awareness.

ego defense mechanism Mental strategy (conscious or unconscious) used by the ego to defend itself against conflicts experienced in the normal course of life.

anxiety An intense emotional response caused by the preconscious recognition that a repressed conflict is about to emerge into consciousness.

Why might a person's enthusiasm for boxing suggest the use of displacement as an ego defense mechanism?

down into the unconscious. For example, a mother who does not like her son and does not want to care for him might use *reaction formation*, which transforms her unacceptable impulse into its opposite: "I don't hate my child" becomes "I love my child. See how I smother the dear little thing with love?" Such defenses serve the critical coping function of alleviating anxiety.

If defense mechanisms defend you against anxiety, why might they still have negative consequences for you? Useful as they are, ego mechanisms of defense are ultimately self-deceptive. When overused, they create more problems than they solve. It is psychologically unhealthy to spend a great deal of time and psychic energy deflecting, disguising, and rechanneling unacceptable urges in order to reduce anxiety. Doing so leaves little energy for productive living or satisfying human relationships. Some forms of mental illness result from excessive reliance on

defense mechanisms to cope with anxiety, as we will see in a later chapter on mental disorders.

EVALUATION OF FREUDIAN THEORY

We have devoted a great deal of space to outlining the essentials of psychoanalytic theory because Freud's ideas have had an enormous impact on the way many psychologists think about normal and abnormal aspects of personality. However, there probably are more psychologists who criticize Freudian concepts than who support them. What is the basis of some of their criticisms?

First, psychoanalytic concepts are vague and not operationally defined; thus much of the theory is difficult to evaluate scientifically. Because some of its central hypotheses cannot be disproved, even in principle, Freud's theory remains questionable. How can the concepts of libido, the structure of personality, and repression of infantile sexual impulses be studied in any direct fashion?

A second, related criticism is that Freudian theory is good history but bad science. It does not reliably *predict* what will occur; it is applied *retrospectively*—after events have occurred. Using psychoanalytic theory to understand personality typically involves historical reconstruction, not scientific construction of probable actions and predictable outcomes. In addition, by overemphasizing historical origins of current behavior, the theory directs attention away from the current stimuli that may be inducing and maintaining the behavior.

There are three other major criticisms of Freudian theory. First, it is a developmental theory, but it never included observations or studies of children. Second, it minimizes traumatic experiences (such as child abuse) by reinterpreting memories of them as fantasies (based on a child's desire for sexual contact with a parent). Third, it has an *androcentric* (male-centered) bias because it uses a male model as the norm without trying to determine how females might be different.

TABLE 13.3	Major Ego Defense Mechanisms
Denial of reality	Protecting self from unpleasant reality by refusing to perceive it
Displacement	Discharging pent-up feelings, usually of hostility, on objects less dangerous than those that initially aroused the emotion
Fantasy	Gratifying frustrated desires in imaginary achievements ("daydreaming" is a common form)
Identification	Increasing feelings of worth by identifying self with another person or institution, often of illustrious standing
Isolation	Cutting off emotional charge from hurtful situations or separating incompatible attitudes into logic-tight compartments (holding conflicting attitudes that are never thought of simultaneously or in relation to each other); also called compartmentalization
Projection	Placing blame for one's difficulties on others or attributing one's own "forbidden" desires to others
Rationalization	Attempting to prove that one's behavior is "rational" and justifiable and thus worthy of the approval of self and others
Reaction formation	Preventing dangerous desires from being expressed by endorsing opposing attitudes and types of behavior and using them as "barriers"
Regression	Retreating to earlier developmental levels involving more childish responses and usually a lower level of aspiration
Repression	Pushing painful or dangerous thoughts out of consciousness, keeping them unconscious; this is considered to be the most basic of the defense mechanisms
Sublimation	Gratifying or working off frustrated sexual desires in substitutive nonsexual activities socially accepted by one's culture.

Some aspects of Freud's theory, however, continue to gain acceptance as they are modified and improved through empirical scrutiny. For example, in Chapter 5, we saw that the concept of the unconscious is being systematically explored by contemporary researchers (McGovern & Baars, 2007). This research reveals that much of your day-to-day experience is shaped by processes outside of your awareness. These results support Freud's general concept but weaken the link between unconscious processes and psychopathology: Little of your unconscious knowledge will cause you anxiety or distress. Similarly, researchers have found evidence for some of the habits of mind Freud characterized as defense mechanisms. We suggested earlier that individuals are most likely to use defense mechanisms when they are experiencing anxiety. Researchers have tested this hypothesis in a variety of ways.

> One study focused on a group of 9- to 11-year-old girls (Sandstrom & Cramer, 2003). The researchers carried out interviews with their peers to determine who among the group of 50 girls was relatively popular and who was relatively unpopular. Each of the 50 girls underwent a laboratory experience in which they were rejected by another young girl. The researchers reasoned that—because of their history of negative social interactions—the unpopular girls would experience more anxiety than the popular girls in the face of this rejection. The researchers suggested that, to cope with that anxiety, the unpopular girls would show evidence for more frequent use of defense mechanisms. To test this hypothesis, the researcher asked the girls to tell stories based on cards from the *Thematic Apperception Test* (see p. 435). The stories were analyzed for evidence of the defense mechanisms *denial* and *projection* (see Table 13.3). These analyses supported the hypothesis: The unpopular girls used more defense mechanisms than the popular girls after the episode of peer rejection.

Some of the styles for coping with stress we described in Chapter 12 fall within the general category of defense mechanisms. You might recall, for example, that inhibiting the thoughts and feelings associated with personal traumas or guilty or shameful experiences can take a devastating toll on mental and physical health (Pennebaker, 1997; Petrie et al., 2004). These findings echo Freud's beliefs that repressed psychic material can lead to psychological distress.

Freud's theory is the most complex, comprehensive, and compelling view of normal and abnormal personality functioning—even when its predictions prove wrong. However, like any other theory, Freud's is best treated as one that must be confirmed or disconfirmed element by element. Freud retains his influence on contemporary psychology because some of his ideas have been widely accepted. Others have been abandoned. Some of the earliest revisions of Freud's theory arose from within his own original circle of students. Let's see how they sought to amend Freud's views.

EXTENDING PSYCHODYNAMIC THEORIES

Some of those who came after Freud retained his basic representation of personality as a battleground on which unconscious primal urges conflict with social values. However, many of Freud's intellectual descendants made major adjustments in the psychoanalytic view of personality. In general, these post-Freudians have made the following changes:

- They put greater emphasis on ego functions, including ego defenses, development of the self, conscious thought processes, and personal mastery.
- They view social variables (culture, family, and peers) as playing a greater role in shaping personality.
- They put less emphasis on the importance of general sexual urges, or libidinal energy.
- They have extended personality development beyond childhood to include the entire life span.

We will now see how these themes emerged in the theories of Alfred Adler, Karen Horney, and Carl Jung.

Alfred Adler (1870–1937) rejected the significance of Eros and the pleasure principle. Adler (1929) believed that as helpless, dependent, small children, people all experience feelings of *inferiority*. He argued that all lives are dominated by the search for ways to overcome those feelings. People compensate to achieve feelings of adequacy or, more often, overcompensate in an attempt to become *superior*. Personality is structured around this underlying striving; people develop lifestyles based on particular ways of overcoming their basic, pervasive feelings of inferiority. Personality conflict arises from incompatibility between external environmental pressures and internal strivings for adequacy, rather than from competing urges within the person.

Karen Horney (1885–1952) was trained in the psychoanalytic school but broke from orthodox Freudian theory in several ways. She challenged Freud's phallocentric emphasis on the importance of the penis, hypothesizing that male envy of pregnancy, motherhood, breasts, and suckling is a dynamic force in the unconscious of boys and men. This "womb envy" leads men to devalue women and to overcompensate by unconscious impulses toward creative work. Horney also placed greater emphasis than did Freud on cultural factors and focused on present character structure rather than on infantile sexuality (Horney, 1937, 1939). Because Horney also had influence on the development of humanistic theories, we will return to her ideas in the next section.

Carl Jung (1875–1961) greatly expanded the conception of the unconscious. For Jung (1959), the unconscious was not limited to an individual's unique life experiences but was filled with fundamental psychological truths shared by the whole human race, a **collective unconscious.** The collective unconscious explains your intuitive understanding of primitive myths, art forms, and symbols, which are the universal archetypes of existence. An **archetype** is a primitive symbolic representation of a particular experience or object. Each archetype is associated with an instinctive tendency to feel and think about it or experience it in a special way. Jung postulated many archetypes that give rise to myths and symbols: the sun god, the hero, the earth mother. *Animus* was the male archetype, *anima* was the female archetype, and all men and women experienced both archetypes in varying degrees. The archetype of the self is

---

collective unconscious The part of an individual's unconscious that is inherited, evolutionarily developed, and common to all members of the species.

archetype A universal, inherited, primitive, and symbolic representation of a particular experience or object.

Jung recognized creativity as a means to release images from both the personal and collective unconscious. Why did Jung believe in the two types of unconscious?

CRITICAL THINKING   Recall the study on the use of defense mechanisms. Why might the researchers have specifically used a rejection episode to produce anxiety?

Visit MyPsychLab.com for more review and practice on the following topics:

◄⦿ **Explore:** The Id, Ego, and Superego

◄⦿ **Explore:** Defense Mechanisms

⦿ **Watch:** Shyness: Phil Zimbardo

the *mandala,* or magic circle; it symbolizes striving for unity and wholeness (Jung, 1973).

Jung saw the healthy, integrated personality as balancing opposing forces, such as masculine aggressiveness and feminine sensitivity. This view of personality as a constellation of compensating internal forces in dynamic balance was called **analytic psychology.** In addition, Jung rejected the primary importance of libido, so central to Freud's own theory. Jung added two equally powerful unconscious instincts: the need to create and the need to become a coherent, whole individual. In the next section on humanist theories, we will see this second need paralleled in the concept of *self-actualization.*

STOP AND REVIEW

❶ According to Freud's theory, what behaviors might arise if an individual became fixated at the oral stage of development?

❷ How is the ego guided by the reality principle?

❸ Although Leon is highly aggressive, he always blames others for starting fights. What defensive mechanism might be at work here?

❹ According to Alfred Adler's view, what drive motivates much of people's behavior?

---

analytic psychology A branch of psychology that views the person as a constellation of compensatory internal forces in a dynamic balance.

self-actualization A concept in personality psychology referring to a person's constant striving to realize his or her potential and to develop inherent talents and capabilities.

unconditional positive regard Complete love and acceptance of an individual by another person, such as a parent for a child, with no conditions attached.

Humanistic Theories

Humanistic approaches to understanding personality are characterized by a concern for the integrity of an individual's personal and conscious experience and growth potential. The key feature of all humanistic theories is an emphasis on the drive toward self-actualization. **Self-actualization** is a constant striving to realize one's inherent potential—to fully develop one's capacities and talents. In this section, you will see how humanistic theorists have developed this concept of self-actualization. You will learn, in addition, what additional features set humanistic theories apart from other types of personality theories.

FEATURES OF HUMANISTIC THEORIES

Humanistic personality theorists, such as Carl Rogers, Abraham Maslow, and Karen Horney, believed that the motivation for behavior comes from a person's unique tendencies, both innate and learned, to develop and change in positive directions toward the goal of self-actualization. Recall from Chapter 11 that Maslow placed self-actualization at the pinnacle of his hierarchy of needs. The striving toward self-fulfillment is a constructive, guiding force that moves each person toward generally positive behaviors and enhancement of the self.

The drive for self-actualization at times comes into conflict with the need for approval from the self and others, especially when the person feels that certain obligations or conditions must be met in order to gain approval. For example, Carl Rogers (1947, 1951, 1977) stressed the importance of **unconditional positive regard** in raising children. By this, he meant that children should feel they will always be loved and approved of, in spite of their mistakes and misbehavior—that they do not have to earn their parents' love. He recommended that, when a child misbehaves, parents should emphasize that it is the behavior they disapprove of, not the child. Unconditional positive regard is important in adulthood, too, because worrying about seeking approval interferes with self-actualization. As an adult, you need to give and receive unconditional positive regard from those to whom you are close. Most important, you need to feel unconditional positive *self-regard,* or acceptance of yourself, in spite of the weaknesses you might be trying to change.

Although not often given due credit, Karen Horney was another major theorist whose ideas created the foundation of humanistic psychology (Frager & Fadiman, 1998). Horney came to believe that people have a "real self" that requires favorable environmental circumstances to be actualized, such as an

Why did Carl Rogers emphasize parents' unconditional positive regard for their children?

atmosphere of warmth, the goodwill of others, and parental love of the child as a "particular individual" (Horney, 1945, 1950). In the absence of those favorable nurturing conditions, the child develops a basic anxiety that stifles spontaneity of expression of real feelings and prevents effective relations with others. To cope with their basic anxiety, individuals resort to interpersonal or intrapsychic defenses. Interpersonal defenses produce movement toward others (through excessive compliance and self-effacing actions), against others (by aggressive, arrogant, or narcissistic solutions), and away from others (through detachment). Intrapsychic defenses operate to develop for some people an unrealistic idealized self-image that generates a "search for glory" to justify it and a pride system that operates on rigid rules of conduct to live up to a grandiose self-concept. Such people often live by the "tyranny of shoulds," self-imposed obligations, such as "I should be perfect, generous, attractive, brave," and so forth. Horney believed that the goal of a humanistic therapy was to help the individual achieve the joy of self-realization and promote the inherent constructive forces in human nature that support a striving for self-fulfillment.

An important aspect of each of the theories of Maslow, Rogers, and Horney is the emphasis on self-actualization or progress toward the real self. In addition, humanistic theories have been described as being holistic, dispositional, and phenomenological. Let's see why.

Humanistic theories are *holistic* because they explain people's separate acts in terms of their entire personalities; people are not seen as the sum of discrete traits that each influence behavior in different ways. Maslow believed that people are intrinsically motivated toward the upper levels of the hierarchy of needs

(discussed in Chapter 11), unless deficiencies at the lower levels weigh them down.

Humanistic theories are *dispositional* because they focus on the innate qualities within a person that exert a major influence over the direction behavior will take. Situational factors are seen as constraints and barriers (like the strings that tie down balloons). Once freed from negative situational conditions, the actualizing tendency should actively guide people to choose life-enhancing situations. However, humanistic theories are not dispositional in the same sense as trait theories or psychodynamic theories. In those views, personal dispositions are recurrent themes played out in behavior again and again. Humanistic dispositions are oriented specifically toward creativity and growth. Each time a humanistic disposition is exercised, the person changes a little, so that the disposition is never expressed in the same way twice. Over time, humanistic dispositions guide the individual toward self-actualization, the purest expression of these motives.

Humanistic theories are *phenomenological* because they emphasize an individual's frame of reference and subjective view of reality—not the objective perspective of an observer or of a therapist. Thus a humanistic psychologist always strives to see each person's unique point of view. This view is also a present-oriented view; past influences are important only to the extent that they have brought the person to the present situation, and the future represents goals to achieve. Thus, unlike psychodynamic theories, humanistic theories do not see people's present behaviors as unconsciously guided by past experiences.

The upbeat humanist view of personality was a welcome treat for many psychologists who had been brought up on a diet of bitter-tasting Freudian medicine. Humanistic approaches focus directly on improvement—on making life more palatable—rather than dredging up painful memories that are sometimes better left repressed. The humanist perspective emphasizes each person's ability to realize his or her fullest potential.

EVALUATION OF HUMANISTIC THEORIES

Freud's theory was often criticized for providing the too-pessimistic view that human nature develops out of conflicts, traumas, and anxieties. Humanistic theories arose to celebrate the healthy personality that strives for happiness and self-actualization. It is difficult to criticize theories that encourage and appreciate people, even for their faults. Even so, critics have complained that humanistic concepts are fuzzy and difficult to explore in research. They ask, "What exactly is self-actualization? Is it an inborn tendency, or is it created by the cultural context?" Humanistic theories also do not traditionally focus on the particular characteristics of individuals. They are more theories about human nature and about qualities all people share than about the individual personality or the basis of differences among people. Other psychologists note that, by emphasizing the role of the self as a source of experience and action, humanistic psychologists neglect the important environmental variables that also influence behavior.

Despite these limitations, a type of contemporary research can be traced in part to the humanist tradition that focuses directly on individual *narratives* or *life stories* (McAdams, 2001). The tradition of using psychological theory to understand the details of an individual's life—to produce a *psychobiography*—can be traced back to Freud's analysis of Leonardo da Vinci (Freud,

1910/1957; see Elms, 1988, for a critique of Freud's work). **Psychobiography** is defined as "the systematic use of psychological (especially personality) theory to transform a life into a coherent and illuminating story" (McAdams, 1988, p. 2). Consider the great artist Pablo Picasso. Picasso suffered a series of traumas as a young child, including a serious earthquake and the death of a young sister. A psychobiography might attempt to explain some of Picasso's vast artistic creativity as the lifelong residue of his responses to these early traumas (Gardner, 1993). When a well-known or historical figure is the subject of a psychobiography, a researcher may turn to published work, diaries, and letters as sources of relevant data. For more ordinary individuals, researchers may directly elicit narratives of life experiences. The request might be, for example, for participants to reflect on key events in their lives: "Why do you think this [was] an important event in your life story? What does this event say about who you are, who you were, who you might be, or how you have developed over time?" (McAdams et al., 2006, p. 1379). The characteristic themes that emerge over series of narrative accounts support the holistic and phenomenological version of personality that was put forth by the early humanists: People construct their identities by weaving life stories out of the strands of narrative. Personal accounts provide a window on people's views of themselves and interpersonal relationships.

Humanistic theorists emphasized each individual's drive toward self-actualization. This group recognized, however, that people's progress toward this goal is determined, in part, by realities of their environments. We turn now to theories that directly examine how individuals' behaviors are shaped by their environments.

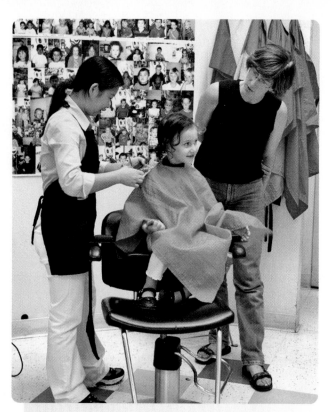

If your parents complimented you every time you got a new haircut, how might that affect your confidence about your appearance and grooming as an adult? Suppose they were regularly critical. What effect could that have?

STOP AND REVIEW

❶ What is self-actualization?
❷ In what ways are humanistic theories dispositional?
❸ What is a psychobiography?

Social-Learning and Cognitive Theories

Common to all the theories we have reviewed so far is an emphasis on hypothesized inner mechanisms—traits, instincts, impulses, tendencies toward self-actualization—that propel behavior and form the basis of a functioning personality. What most of these theories lacked, however, was a solid link between personality and particular behaviors. Psychodynamic and humanistic theories, for example, provide accounts of the total personality but do not predict specific actions. Another tradition of personality theory emerged from a more direct focus on individual differences in behavior. Recall from Chapter 6 that much of a person's behavior can be predicted from contingencies in the environment. Psychologists with a *learning theory* orientation look to the environmental circumstances that control behavior. Personality is seen as the sum of the overt and covert responses that are reliably elicited by an

individual's *reinforcement history*. Learning theory approaches suggest that people are different because they have had different histories of reinforcement.

The theories we will review have as a shared starting point that behavior is influenced by environmental contingencies. However, these contemporary social-learning and cognitive theories go one step further to emphasize the importance of cognitive processes as well as behavioral ones. Those who have proposed cognitive theories of personality point out that there are important individual differences in the way people think about and define any external situation. Like humanistic theories, cognitive theories emphasize that you participate in creating your own personality. For example, you actively *choose* your own environments to a great extent; you do not just react passively. You weigh alternatives and select the settings in which you act and are acted upon—you choose to enter situations that you expect to be reinforcing and to avoid those that are unsatisfying and uncertain.

Let's look now at more concrete embodiments of these ideas. We examine the theories of Julian Rotter, Walter Mischel, Albert Bandura, and Nancy Cantor.

ROTTER'S EXPECTANCY THEORY

Julian Rotter (1954) focused his theory on **expectancy,** which is the extent to which people believe that their behaviors in particular situations will bring about rewards. Suppose, for example, that you need to decide how much to practice before a presentation in class. You'd like to get at least a *B*. Having a high

psychobiography The use of psychological (especially personality) theory to describe and explain an individual's course through life.

expectancy The extent to which people believe that their behaviors in particular situations will bring about rewards.

expectancy means that you think it's very likely that extra practice will lead to a *B* or better; having a low expectancy means that you're not at all confident that extra practice will help with your grade. Your expectancies arise, in part, because of your own history of reinforcement: If practice has led to rewards in the past, you'll have a stronger expectancy that it will lead to a reward again. Rotter also emphasized *reward value*—the value that an individual assigns to a particular reward. If you've had a tough semester, a *B* might have more value to you than it would in a different context. On Rotter's view, you can only begin to predict people's behavior if you can assess both their expectancy with respect to a reward and the extent to which they value a reward.

Rotter emphasized that people bring specific expectancies to the many situations they face in life. However, Rotter also believed that people develop a more general expectancy about the extent to which they can control the rewards they obtain. Rotter (1966) defined a dimemsion of **locus of control:** Some people—known as *internals*—believe more strongly that the outcomes of their actions are contingent on what they do; other people—known as *externals*—believe that the outcomes of their actions are contingent on environmental factors. In **Table 13.4,** we've given you sample items from Rotter's *Internal-External Scale*. To complete the scale, you choose (a) or (b) from each item as the statement you believe to be more accurate. These examples should give you a sense of some differences in the ways that internals and externals generate expectancies about life outcomes. Researchers have consistently demonstrated the importance of people's locus of control orientations. For example, one study examined the relationship between people's locus of control orientation at age 10 and their mental and physical health at age 30 (Gale et al., 2008). The 30-year-olds who had been more internally oriented as children were, on the whole, in better health. They were, for example, at lower risk for obesity, high blood pressure, and psychological distress. The researchers suggested that people with external orientations might be in poorer shape because they believe that their health is outside their control—and therefore they take few actions to better their health.

MISCHEL'S COGNITIVE–AFFECTIVE PERSONALITY THEORY

Walter Mischel developed an influential theory of the cognitive basis of personality. Mischel emphasizes that people actively participate in the cognitive organization of their interactions with the environment. His approach emphasizes the importance of understanding how behavior arises as a function of interactions between persons and situations (Mischel, 2004). Consider this example:

> *John's unique personality may be seen most clearly in that he is always very friendly when meeting someone for the first time, but that he also predictably becomes rather abrupt and unfriendly as he begins to spend more time with that person. Jim, on the other hand, is unique in that he is typically shy and quiet with people who he does not know well but becomes very gregarious once he begins to know someone well. (Shoda et al., 1993a, p. 1023)*

If we were to average John's and Jim's overall friendliness, we would probably get about the same value on this trait—but that would fail to capture important differences in their behavior.

TABLE 13.4 Sample Items from the Internal-External Scale

1. a. In the long run people get the respect they deserve in the world.
   b. Unfortunately, an individual's worth often passes unrecognized no matter how hard he tries.

2. a. Without the right breaks, one cannot be an effective leader.
   b. Capable people who fail to become leaders have not taken advantage of their opportunities.

3. a. Most people don't realize the extent to which their lives are controlled by accidental happenings.
   b. There really is no such thing as "luck."

4. a. What happens to me is my own doing.
   b. Sometimes I feel that I don't have enough control over the direction my life is taking.

Note: 1a, 2b, 3b, and 4a indicate a more internal locus of control orientation.

From J. B. Rotter, Generalized expectancies for internal versus external locus of control of reinforcement, Table 1. *Psychological Monographs, 80* (1):11-12. Copyright © 1966 by the American Psychological Association. Adapted with permission.

According to Mischel (1973, 2004), how you respond to a specific environmental input depends on the variables defined in **Table 13.5** on page 424. Do you see how each variable listed would affect the way in which a person would behave in particular situations? We have given you examples for each variable. Try to invent a situation in which you would produce behavior different from the characters listed in the table because you contrast on the particular variable. You may wonder what determines the nature of these variables for a specific individual. Mischel believes that they result from his or her history of observations and interactions with other people and with inanimate aspects of the physical environment (Mischel, 1973).

We want to provide you with a concrete example of how the variables in Mischel's theory explain differences with respect to the particular behaviors people produce in the same situations. Let's consider a study that documented how interactions of competencies and self-regulatory plans (see Table 13.4) interact to predict aggressive behavior among 10-year-old boys.

The study focused on 59 boys who were attending a summer camp (Ayduk et al., 2007). To measure their competencies, the researchers gave each boy a test of verbal intelligence. To measure their self-regulatory abilities, the researchers had each boy engage in a task that measured his capacity to delay his gratification. The boys were brought into a room with a small and large pile of food of a type they particularly enjoyed (for example, M&M candies). To obtain the

---

locus of control People's general expectancy about the extent to which the rewards they obtain are contingent on their own actions or on environmental factors.

TABLE 13.5 Person Variables in Mischel's Cognitive-Affective Personality Theory

Variable	Definition	Example
Encodings	The way you categorize information about yourself, other people, events, and situations	As soon as Bob meets someone, he tries to figure out how wealthy he or she is.
Expectancies and beliefs	Your beliefs about the social world and likely outcomes for given actions in particular situations; your beliefs about your ability to bring outcomes about	Greg invites friends to the movies, but he never expects them to say "yes."
Affects	Your feelings and emotions, including physiological responses	Cindy blushes very easily.
Goals and values	The outcomes and affective states you do and do not value; your goals and life projects	Peter wants to be president of his college class.
Competencies and self-regulatory plans	The behaviors you can accomplish and plans for generating cognitive and behavioral outcomes	Jan can speak English, French, Russian, and Japanese and expects to work for the United Nations.

larger pile, the boys had to wait 25 minutes without ringing a bell to call a researcher back—if they used the bell, they got only the small pile. To endure the 25-minute wait, the boys needed to be able to regulate their own behavior. In particular, to make the time pass more easily, they needed to be able to divert their attention from the candy and the bell. For that reason, the researchers used the boys' ability to control their attention as a measure of self-regulatory ability. Finally, to measure aggression, the researchers obtained multiple assessments from the camp counselors about the boys' verbal and physical aggression during group activities. As you can see in **Figure 13.7,** to predict the boys' levels of aggression it's important to know both about competencies and self-regulatory abilities. In particular, boys with high verbal intelligence but low ability to control their attention were substantially more aggressive than their peers who had both high intelligence and high ability to control their attention.

You might expect that more intelligent boys would have knowledge that would allow them to function in social environments without resorting to aggression. This study demonstrates that knowledge alone is not sufficient—the boys also need to have the ability and motivation to perform alternative behaviors. The results allow you to understand why Mischel's personality theory focuses on the interactions among several different types of variables.

BANDURA'S COGNITIVE SOCIAL-LEARNING THEORY

Through his theoretical writing and extensive research with children and adults, Albert Bandura (1986, 1999) has been an eloquent champion of a social-learning approach to understanding personality (recall from Chapter 6 his studies of aggressive behavior in children). This approach combines principles of learning with an emphasis on human interactions in social settings. From a social-learning perspective, human beings are not driven by inner forces, nor are they helpless pawns of environmental influence.

The social-learning approach stresses the cognitive processes that are involved in acquiring and maintaining patterns of behavior and, thus, personality.

Bandura's theory points to a complex interaction of individual factors, behavior, and environmental stimuli. Each can influence or change the others, and the direction of change is rarely one way—it is *reciprocal.* Your behavior can be influenced by your attitudes, beliefs, or prior history of reinforcement as well as by stimuli available in the environment. What you do can have an effect on the environment, and important aspects of your personality can be affected by the environment or by

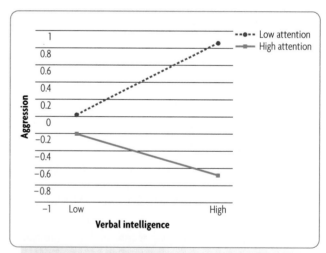

FIGURE 13.7 Boys' Levels of Aggressive Behavior

Boys' levels of aggressive behavior at a summer camp reflected an interaction between their verbal intelligence and their ability to control their attention to delay gratification.

Reprinted from O. Ayduk, M. L. Rodriguez, W. Mischel, Y. Shoda, & J. Wright. Verbal intelligence and self-regulatory competencies: Joint predictors of boys' aggression, *Journal of Research in Personality (41):* 374-388, Copyright © 2007, with permission from Elsevier.

Would you feel comfortable making personality judgments about these boys from this one snapshot? Why might you want to know their patterns of behavior across different types of situations?

events, you can foresee the possible consequences of your actions without having to actually experience them. You may acquire skills, attitudes, and beliefs simply by watching what others do and the consequences that follow.

As his theory developed, Bandura (1997) elaborated self-efficacy as a central construct. **Self-efficacy** is the belief that one can perform adequately in a particular situation. Your sense of self-efficacy influences your perceptions, motivation, and performance in many ways. You don't even try to do things or take chances when you expect to be ineffectual. You avoid situations when you don't feel adequate. Even when you do, in fact, have the ability—and the desire—you may not take the required action or persist to complete the task successfully, if you think you lack what it takes.

Beyond actual accomplishments, there are three other sources of information for *self-efficacy judgments:*

- vicarious experience—your observations of the performance of others
- persuasion—others may convince you that you can do something, or you may convince yourself
- monitoring of your emotional arousal as you think about or approach a task—for example, anxiety suggests low expectations of efficacy; excitement suggests expectations of success

Self-efficacy judgments influence how much effort you expend and how long you persist when faced with difficulty in a wide range of life situations (Bandura, 1997; 2006). For example, how vigorously and persistently you study this chapter may depend more on your sense of self-efficacy than on actual ability (Zimmerman et al., 1992).

Let's consider the impact of self-efficacy in academic settings. Research suggests, for example, that how vigorously

feedback from your behavior. This important concept, **reciprocal determinism,** implies that you must examine all components if you want to completely understand human behavior, personality, and social ecology (Bandura, 1999; see **Figure 13.8).** So, for example, if you don't generally think of yourself as an athlete, you may not choose to be active in track-and-field events, but if you live near a pool, you may nonetheless spend time swimming. If you are outgoing, you'll talk to others sitting around the pool and thereby create a more sociable atmosphere, which, in turn, makes it a more enjoyable environment. This is one instance of reciprocal determinism among person, place, and behavior.

You may recall from Chapter 6 that Bandura's social-learning theory emphasizes observational learning as the process by which a person changes his or her behavior based on observations of another person's behavior. Through observational learning, children and adults acquire an enormous range of information about their social environment. Through observation, you learn what is appropriate and gets rewarded and what gets punished or ignored. Because you can use memory and think about external

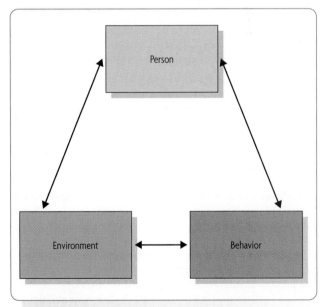

FIGURE 13.8 Reciprocal Determinism

In reciprocal determinism, the individual, the individual's behavior, and the environment all interact to influence and modify the other components.

reciprocal determinism A concept of Albert Bandura's social-learning theory that refers to the notion that a complex reciprocal interaction exists among the individual, his or her behavior, and environmental stimuli and that each of these components affects the others.

self-efficacy The set of beliefs that one can perform adequately in a particular situation.

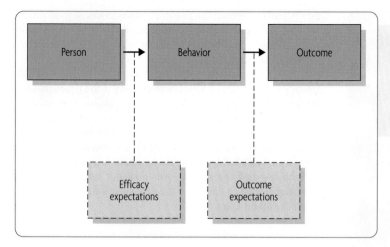

FIGURE 13.9 Bandura's Self-Efficacy Model

This model positions efficacy expectations between the person and his or her behavior; outcome expectations are positioned between behavior and its anticipated outcomes.

and persistently you study this chapter may depend more on your sense of self-efficacy than on actual ability.

> A group of 202 students participated in a study that examined the impact of self-efficacy beliefs on college performance (Elias & MacDonald, 2007). Each student completed a measure of academic self-efficacy: They used a 10-point scale ranging from "no confidence at all" to "complete confidence" to indicate their sense of the likelihood they would, for example, "Successfully pass all classes enrolled in over the next three semesters" and "Complete a course in biology with a grade of *B*" (p. 2531). The students also reported their high school and college GPAs. As you might guess, students' high school GPAs were good predictors of their college GPAs. High school GPAs were also good predictors of students' reports of self-efficacy: Students who had been more successful in the past expected to be more successful in the future. However, self-efficacy still mattered over and above past performance. Students who had higher self-efficacy did better than their peers with equal past performance but lower self-efficacy.

Based on this study, you might wonder if it's possible for students to increase their beliefs of self-efficacy—with the potential to improve their grades. As we'll see in Chapter 15 (page 492), the answer is "yes, it is possible." Researchers have designed interventions that successfully increase self-efficacy.

Bandura's theory of self-efficacy also acknowledges the importance of the environment. Expectations of failure or success—and corresponding decisions to stop trying or to persevere—may be based on perceptions of the supportiveness or unsupportiveness of the environment, in addition to perceptions of one's own adequacy or inadequacy. Such expectations are called *outcome-based expectancies*. **Figure 13.9** displays how the parts of Bandura's theory fit together. Behavioral outcomes depend both on people's perceptions of their own abilities and their perceptions of the environment.

CANTOR'S SOCIAL INTELLIGENCE THEORY

Building on these earlier cognitive and social theories, **Nancy Cantor** and her colleagues have outlined a *social intelligence* theory of personality (Cantor & Kihlstrom, 1987; Kihlstrom & Cantor, 2000). **Social intelligence** refers to the expertise people bring to their experience of life tasks. The theory defines three types of individual differences:

- *Choice of life goals.* People differ as to which life goals or life tasks are most important to them. People's goals may also change over time.
- *Knowledge relevant to social interactions.* People differ with respect to the expertise they bring to tasks of social and personal problem solving.
- *Strategies for implementing goals.* People have different characteristic problem-solving strategies.

Can you see how these three dimensions interact to give rise to the different patterns of behavior you would recognize as personality? You might, for example, have two friends—one of whom is more concerned about "getting and keeping friends," whereas the other one gives more weight to "getting good grades." Or suppose two other friends both value getting good grades. Depending on what they know and how they are able to put that knowledge to use, the moment-by-moment decisions they make about how to behave could be very different. One may have been taught explicit strategies for studying, and the other muddles through without special help. The theory of social intelligence gives a new perspective on how personality predicts consistency: For a given period of time, consistency is found in people's goals, knowledge, and strategies.

Let's examine concrete circumstances in which people's disparate goals yield different outcomes: Researchers have demonstrated that *intimacy goals* have an impact on relationship satisfaction.

> When people enter into friendships, they differ in the extent to which they have *intimacy* as a goal—some people strongly seek to foster interdependence and engage in self-disclosure, whereas other people don't bring those needs to friendships. One study with 80 participants (40 men and 40 women)

---

social intelligence A theory of personality that refers to the expertise people bring to their experience of life tasks.

examined how the strength of intimacy goals affects the way in which people deal with conflict in their close same-sex friendships (Sanderson et al., 2005). The researchers hypothesized that those individuals with strong intimacy goals would have more constructive responses to conflict and, therefore, be more likely to have their friendships endure. To measure the importance of intimacy as a goal, the researchers asked the participants to respond to statements such as "In my close friendship, I want to share my thoughts and feelings." Participants indicated the ways in which they cope with conflict by responding to statements such as "My friend and I always express our feelings in an open and honest manner that prevents little problems from becoming big ones." In keeping with the researchers' hypothesis, students with strong intimacy goals were most likely to endorse responses to conflicts that helped minimize those conflicts. Because of those constructive responses, students with strong intimacy goals also reported greater satisfaction with their friendships.

Do you see how this pattern could follow from the individuals' goals? People with stronger intimacy goals are highly motivated to behave in ways that will help preserve the friendships. In this case, you recognize personality in the consistent way in which people's goals lead them to behave.

EVALUATION OF SOCIAL-LEARNING AND COGNITIVE THEORIES

One set of criticisms leveled against social-learning and cognitive theories is that they often overlook emotion as an important component of personality. In psychodynamic theories, emotions like anxiety play a central role. In social-learning and cognitive theories, emotions are perceived merely as by-products of thoughts and behavior or are just included with other types of thoughts rather than being assigned independent importance. For those who feel that emotions are central to the functioning of human personality, this is a serious flaw. Cognitive theories are also attacked for not fully recognizing the impact of unconscious motivation on behavior and affect.

A second set of criticisms focuses on the vagueness of explanations about the way personal constructs and competencies are created. Cognitive theorists have often had little to say about the developmental origins of adult personality; their focus on the individual's perception of the current behavior setting obscures the individual's history.

Despite these criticisms, cognitive personality theories have made major contributions to current thinking. Mischel's awareness of situation has brought about a better understanding of the interaction between what a person brings to a behavior setting and what that setting brings out of the person. Bandura's ideas have led to improvements in the way teachers educate children and help them achieve as well as new treatments in the areas of health, business, and sports performance. Finally, Cantor's theory shifts the search for personality consistency to the level of life goals and social strategies.

Do these cognitive personality theories provide you with insights about your own personality and behaviors? You can start to see how you define yourself in part through interactions with the environment. We turn now to theories that can add even further to your definition of self.

STOP AND REVIEW

❶ In Julian Rotter's theory, what does it mean to have an external locus of control orientation?
❷ In Walter Mischel's theory, what five types of variables explain individual differences?
❸ What three components are involved in Albert Bandura's theory of reciprocal determinism?
❹ How is social intelligence defined?

CRITICAL THINKING Recall the study that examined boys' aggression in summer camp. Why was it important that the researchers obtained multiple assessments of the boys' levels of aggression?

Visit MyPsychLab.com for more review and practice on the following topic:

Explore: Mischel's Theory of Personality

Self Theories

We have arrived now at theories of personality that are most immediately personal: They deal directly with how each individual manages his or her sense of *self*. What is your conception of your *self*? Do you think of your *self* reacting consistently to the world? Do you try to present a consistent *self* to your friends and family? What impact do positive and negative experiences have on the way you think about your *self*? We will begin our consideration of these questions with a brief historical review.

The concern for analysis of the self found its strongest early advocate in William James (1892). James identified three components of self-experience: the *material me* (the bodily self, along with surrounding physical objects), the *social me* (your awareness of how others view you), and the *spiritual me* (the self that monitors private thoughts and feelings). James believed that everything that you associate with your identity becomes, in some sense, a part of the self. This explains why people may react defensively when their friends or family members—a part of the self—have been attacked. The concept of self was also central to psychodynamic theories. Self-insight was an important part of the psychoanalytic cure in Freud's theory, and Jung stressed that to fully develop the self, one must integrate and accept all aspects of one's conscious and unconscious life.

How has the self been treated in contemporary theory? We will first describe cognitive aspects of the self: self-concepts and possible selves. We then examine the way people present their selves to the world. Finally, we look at the important topic of how views of the self differ across cultures.

DYNAMIC ASPECTS OF SELF-CONCEPTS

The **self-concept** is a dynamic mental structure that motivates, interprets, organizes, mediates, and regulates intrapersonal and

---

self-concept A person's mental model of his or her abilities and attributes.

Imagine for a moment your different "possible selves." What effect might consideration of possible selves have on your behavior?

interpersonal behaviors and processes. The self-concept includes many components. Among them are your memories about yourself; beliefs about your traits, motives, values, and abilities; the ideal self that you would most like to become; the possible selves that you contemplate enacting; positive or negative evaluations of yourself (self-esteem); and beliefs about what others think of you (Chen et al., 2006). In Chapter 7, we discussed *schemas* as "knowledge packages" that embody complex generalizations about the structure of the environment. Your self-concept contains schemas about the self—*self-schemas*—that allow you to organize information about yourself, just as other schemas allow you to manage other aspects of your experience. However, self-schemas influence more than just the way you process information about yourself. Research indicates that these schemas, which you frequently use to interpret your own behavior, influence the way you process information about other people as well (Krueger & Stanke, 2001; Mussweiler & Bodenhausen, 2002). Thus you interpret other people's actions in terms of what you know and believe about yourself.

Another important component of your cognitive sense of self may be the other *possible selves* to which you compare your current self-concept. **Hazel Markus** and her colleagues have defined **possible selves** as "the ideal selves that we would very much like to become. They are also the selves we could become, and the selves we are afraid of becoming" (Markus & Nurius, 1986, p. 954). Possible selves play a role in motivating behavior—they spur action by allowing you to consider what directions your "self" could take, for better or for worse.

Consider a study that explored individuals' ideas about whether they are prepared to become parents.

> A team of researchers developed an assessment device intended to measure the extent to which young adults could imagine themselves becoming parents (Bloom et al., 1999). The 683 college students who participated in the study responded on a scale of *not at all like me* to *very much like me* for statements such as "In the future I see myself as the kind of person who would get married but choose not to have children." To discourage students from guessing the study's purpose, the items relevant to parenting were dispersed into a longer questionnaire. After completing the

questionnaire, each student was assigned a *parent possible-self score* (PPS). On average, men and women did not differ on these scores. However, the researchers defined subsets of both men and women who were particularly high and low on the scale. The individuals in those subsets rated their perceptions of videotaped infants whose behavior ranged from happy to fussy. The high-PPS students gave consistently more favorable ratings to the infants than the low-PPS students did.

Can you think of reasons why a person's ability to envision him- or herself as a parent might have an impact on that person's interpretations of an infant's behavior?

SELF-ESTEEM

A person's **self-esteem** is a *generalized* evaluation of the self. People differ in their levels of self-esteem. Because we have described the importance of genetics for other aspects of personality, you may not be surprised to learn that individual differences in self-esteem have a genetic component: People inherit a tendency toward high or low self-esteem (Neiss et al., 2006). However, environmental factors also have important effects. For example, people's satisfaction or dissatisfaction with their physical appearance has a major impact on their reports of self-esteem (Donnellan et al., 2007). Self-esteem also varies with respect to people's perceptions of their ability to navigate in the social world. People who are high in self-esteem typically feel that they will function well in social relationships; people with low self-esteem have doubts about their social value (Anthony et al., 2007).

Self-esteem can strongly influence people's thoughts, moods, and behavior (Swann et al., 2007). In fact, researchers have linked a number of negative outcomes to low levels of self-esteem. For example, among adolescents and college students, low self-esteem was related to aggression and antisocial behavior (Donnellan et al., 2005). Similarly, people who reported low self-esteem as adolescents had poorer mental and physical health as well as more financial problems as adults (Orth et al., 2008; Trzeniewski et al., 2006). These results suggest that having low self-esteem can undermine people's ability to set goals for positive outcomes and cope with negative life events.

Some people clearly experience low self-esteem. However, evidence suggests that most people go out of their way to maintain self-esteem and to sustain the integrity of their self-concept (Vignoles et al., 2006). To preserve their self-image, people engage in a variety of forms of *self-enhancement*: People take steps to view their own actions and behaviors as consistently positive (Sedikides

---

possible self One of the ideal selves that a person would like to become, the selves a person could become, and the selves a person is afraid of becoming; components of the cognitive sense of self.

self-esteem A generalized evaluative attitude toward the self that influences both moods and behavior and that exerts a powerful effect on a range of personal and social behaviors.

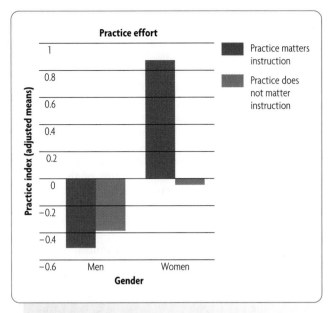

Practice effort

Practice index (adjusted means)

Legend:
- Practice matters instruction
- Practice does not matter instruction

Gender (Men, Women)

FIGURE 13.10 Men's and Women's Self-Handicapping

The *practice index* combined the number of practice items a student completed and the amount of time he or she spent practicing into a single measure. Positive scores indicate more than average practice; negative scores indicate less than average practice. When instructions suggested that practice didn't matter, the difference between men's and women's practice was small. However, when students believed their practice did matter, women practiced considerably more than the men.

Reprinted from S. M. McCrae, E. R. Hirt, & B. J. Milner, She works hard for the money: Valuing effort underlies gender differences in behavioral self-handicapping, *Journal of Experimental Social Psychology (44)*: 292-311, Copyright © 2008, with permission from Elsevier.

& Gregg, 2008). For example, when people doubt their ability to perform a task, they may engage in **self-handicapping** behavior. They deliberately sabotage their performance! The purpose of this strategy is to have a ready-made excuse for failure that does not imply *lack of ability* (McCrae & Hirt, 2001). Thus, a student might party with friends instead of studying for an important exam. That way, if he doesn't succeed, he can blame his failure on low effort rather than low aptitude. Note that our use of "he" in this example is deliberate. Research suggests that men consistently engage in more self-handicapping than do women.

Before taking an intelligence test, male and female psychology students were given the opportunity to work through 18 practice items (McCrae et al., 2008). The researchers gave half the students *practice matters* instructions: Those students were told that without appropriate practice their intelligence tests scores would not be valid. The other students received *practice does not matter* instructions: Those students were told that practice would likely have no effect on

self-handicapping The process of developing, in anticipation of failure, behavioral reactions and explanations that minimize ability deficits as possible attributions for the failure.

their test scores. Suppose you were in the *practice matters* condition. If you wanted to have a ready excuse for your (potentially) low intelligence score, you might choose not to practice very much. As you can see in **Figure 13.10,** that's, on average, what the men chose to do. Women who were told that practiced mattered, practiced quite a bit. Men who had the same instructions practiced least of all. To understand this difference, the researchers asked the participants to complete a scale that had items such as "I try to devote my full effort to every class I take" and "I pride myself in being a hard worker" (p. 309). The women consistently agreed more with such statements than did their male peers.

These results support the researchers' claim that women put too much value on effort to engage in self-handicapping. The effort women expend is an important contributor to their self-esteem.

In this section, we've emphasized that people engage in behaviors such as self-handicapping to maintain a high sense of self-esteem. For that reason, you might not be surprised to learn that people's global ratings of self-esteem are often not a good predictor of their performance across domains (Baumeister et al., 2003). Instead, people's self-views with respect to more specific domains of performance (such as particular academic subjects) provide better predictive information about their likely performance (Swann et al., 2007). Similarly, programs to boost self-esteem are best targeted toward particular domains in which people can learn strategies that actually change performance.

THE CULTURAL CONSTRUCTION OF SELF

Our discussion so far has focused on constructs relevant to the self, such as self-esteem and possible selves, that apply quite widely across individuals. However, researchers on the self have also begun to study the way in which self-concepts and self-development are affected by differing cultural constraints. If you have grown up in a Western culture, you are likely to be

Self-handicapping behavior in action: Instead of studying for tomorrow's exam, you fall asleep in the library, thereby enabling yourself to say, "Well, I didn't really study" if you don't ace the test. Are there situations in which you resort to self-handicapping?

In what ways is an individual's sense of self different when he or she is a member of a culture with an interdependent construal of self rather than an independent construal of self?

pretty comfortable with the research we have reviewed so far: The theories and constructs match the ways that Western cultures conceptualize the *self*. However, the type of culture from which the Western self emerges—an *individualistic* culture—is in the minority with respect to the world's population, which includes about 70 percent *collectivist* cultures. Individualistic cultures emphasize individuals' needs, whereas collectivist cultures emphasize the needs of the group (Triandis, 1994, 1995). This overarching emphasis has important implications for how each member of these cultures conceptualizes his or her *self*: Hazel Markus and Shinobu Kitayama (1991; Kitayama et al., 1995; Markus et al., 1997) have argued that each culture gives rise to different interpretations of the meaning of self—or different *construals* of self:

- Individualistic cultures encourage **independent construals of self**—"Achieving the cultural goal of independence requires construing oneself as an individual whose behavior is organized and made meaningful primarily by reference to one's own internal repertoire of thoughts, feelings, and action, rather than by reference to the thoughts, feelings, and actions of others" (Markus & Kitayama, 1991, p. 226).
- Collectivist cultures encourage **interdependent construals of self**—"Experiencing interdependence entails seeing oneself as part of an encompassing social relationship and recognizing that one's behavior is determined, contingent on, and, to a large extent organized by what the actor perceives to be the thoughts, feelings, and actions of *others* in the relationship" (Markus & Kitayama, 1991, p. 227).

Researchers have documented the reality and implications of these distinctions in a number of ways.

---

independent construal of self Conceptualization of the self as an individual whose behavior is organized primarily by reference to one's own thoughts, feelings, and actions, rather than by reference to the thoughts, feelings, and actions of others.

interdependent construal of self Conceptualization of the self as part of an encompassing social relationship; recognizing that one's behavior is determined, contingent on, and, to a large extent organized by what the actor perceived to be the thoughts, feelings, and actions of others.

One type of cross-cultural research on the self has used a measurement device called the *Twenty Statements Test* (TST) (Kuhn & McPartland, 1954). When they take this test, participants are asked to give 20 different answers to the question "Who am I?" Take a moment to reflect on that question. As shown in **Table 13.6,** responses typically fall into six different categories. Culture has an impact on the categories that are most likely for people's responses. For example, one study had roughly 300 students from the United States and India perform the TST procedure (Dhawan et al., 1995). In keeping with their independent sense of self, about 65 percent of the responses of U.S. women and 64 percent of the responses of U.S. men fell into the category of *self-evaluations*. For the Indian students, 33 percent of women's responses and 35 percent of men's responses fell into this category. Thus the Indian students were about half as likely to produce self-evaluations. Note that differences between men and women overall were rather small—culture mattered more.

You might wonder how the export of Western culture affects the self-concepts of members of collectivist cultures. One study compared the TST responses of Kenyans who had virtually no exposure to Western culture—members of pastoral Samburu and Maasai tribes—to those who had moved to the Westernized capital city of Nairobi. Roughly 82 percent of the tribe members' responses on the TST were social responses; workers in Nairobi gave only 58 percent social responses, and students at the University of Nairobi gave only 17 percent social responses (Ma & Schoeneman, 1997). This pattern suggests that when a nation imports Western products, they may also import a Western sense of self.

These studies illustrate that the cultures to which people belong have a strong impact on the way they construe their selves. You have already read about some consequences of these construals. These studies illustrate that the cultures to which people belong have a strong impact on the way they construe their selves. You will encounter this distinction again in Chapter 16 when we consider, for example, how ideas about *love* are

TABLE 13.6	Categories of Twenty Statements Test Responses
Category	**Examples**
Social identity	I'm a student. I am a daughter.
Ideological beliefs	I believe that all human beings are good. I believe in God.
Interests	I like playing the piano. I enjoy visiting new places.
Ambitions	I want to become a doctor. I want to learn more psychology.
Self-evaluations	I am honest and hardworking. I am a tall person. I worry about the future.
Other	I have noisy friends. I own a dog.

TABLE 13.7 Self-Enhancement across Cultures

	BEHAVIORS	
Culture	**Individualist**	**Collectivist**
American	1.28	−0.45
Japanese	0.06	0.63

Adapted from C. Sedikides & A. P. Gregg (2008). Self-enhancement: Food for thought. *Perpsectives on Psychological Science, 3*, 102-116, table 3.

influenced by construals of the self. For now, consider a study that has particular relevance to theories about the self.

Earlier we reviewed evidence that people are concerned with *self-enhancement*—bringing about positive changes in self-esteem. However, people in different cultures have different interpretations of the *self* in self-enhancement. For that reason, a team of researchers predicted that students from the United States would be more likely to choose individualistic behaviors for self-enhancement, whereas students from Japan would choose collectivist behaviors (Sedikides et al., 2003). To test that idea, the researchers asked each student from the United States and Japan to spend 10 minutes imagining that he or she was part of a task force responsible for solving business problems. The students were asked to consider a range of issues and write down their ideas on those issues. After performing this exercise, the students made predictions about how likely it was that they would outperform the other (imaginary) task force members on a range of behaviors. Some of those behaviors were individualistic: Would they "disagree with [their] group when [they] believe the group is wrong?" Some of those behaviors were collectivist: Would they "avoid open confrontation with [their] group?" For each behavior, the students gave responses ranging from −5 ("much less likely than the typical group member") to +5 ("much more likely than the typical group member"). As shown in **Table 13.7**, the students predicted that they would outperform their peers—the more positive numbers indicate more self-enhancement—with respect to those behaviors that were matched with their construals of self.

Over the next few days, you might try to experience both construals of self by trying to attend to how the events that happen around you have an impact both on your self as an individual and your self as a member of a larger social structure.

EVALUATION OF SELF THEORIES

Self theories succeed at capturing people's own concepts of their personalities and the way they wish to be perceived by others. Furthermore, examinations of cross-cultural construals of the self have had great influence on the way psychologists assess the universality of their theories. However, critics

of self theory approaches to personality argue against its limitless boundaries. Because so many things are relevant to the self and to the self-concept, it is not always clear which factors are most important for predicting behavior. In addition, the emphasis on the self as a social construct is not entirely consistent with evidence that some facets of personality may be inherited. As with the other theories we have described, self theories capture some but not all of what you think of as personality.

STOP AND REVIEW

❶ What role do possible selves play for motivation?
❷ What is self-handicapping?
❸ What does it mean to have an interdependent construal of self?

CRITICAL THINKING Recall the study that demonstrated gender differences in self-handicapping. Why was it important that participants completed the worker scale before they had the opportunity to practice?

Comparing Personality Theories

There is no unified theory of personality that a majority of psychologists can endorse. Several differences in basic assumptions have come up repeatedly in our survey of the various theories. It may be helpful to recap five of the most important differences in assumptions about personality and the approaches that advance each assumption:

1. *Heredity versus environment.* As you have learned throughout *Psychology and Life*, this difference is also referred to as *nature versus nurture*. What is more important to personality development: genetic and biological factors or environmental influences? Trait theories have been split on this issue; Freudian theory depends heavily on heredity; humanistic, social-learning, cognitive, and self theories all emphasize either environment as a determinant of behavior or interaction with the environment as a source of personality development and differences.

2. *Learning processes versus innate laws of behavior.* Should emphasis be placed on the view that personalities are modified through learning or on the view that personality development follows an internal timetable? Again, trait theories have been divided. Freudian theory has favored the inner determinant view, whereas humanists postulate an optimistic view that experience changes people. Social-learning, cognitive, and self theories clearly support the idea that behavior and personality change as a result of learned experiences.

3. *Emphasis on past, present, or future.* Trait theories emphasize past causes, whether innate or learned; Freudian theory stresses past events in early childhood; social-learning theories focus on past reinforcements and present contingencies; humanistic theories emphasize present reality or

HOW IS PERSONALITY CONVEYED IN CYBERSPACE?

Let's start with a straightforward question: Does your e-mail address allow people to make accurate guesses about your personality? To address that question, a team of researchers used a web-based survey to obtain e-mail addresses and self-reports of personality from 599 individuals (Back et al., 2008). Next, the researchers asked a different group of 100 students to make personality judgments on the same personality dimensions—based only on the e-mail addresses. Consider the researchers' example, honey.bunny77@hotmail.de. How aggreeable and conscientious would you imagine the person with that e-mail address to be?

The researchers found that personality ratings based on just the e-mail addresses were quite consistent among the group of 100 raters. The researchers also found positive correlations between the raters' assessments and the e-mail users' self-reports on most of the personality dimensions. That is, the raters were able to make reasonably valid personality judgments based on just the e-mail addresses! The raters appeared to be using a number of features of the addresses to make their judgments. For example, the raters gave higher conscientiousness ratings to addresses with a larger number of

characters; they gave lower conscientiousness ratings to addresses with a larger number of digits.

Of course, if you are like many students, your e-mail address is only one of a very large number of decisions you need to make to determine your exact presence in cyberspace. Suppose, for example, you have a page on a social networking site such as MySpace or Facebook. To manage the impression you make on people who visit your page, you need to make decisions about any number of variables including how many friends you have, how much personal detail you provide, and what types of photos you download (Krämer & Winter, 2008). These variables contribute to how the people who visit your page perceive you. For example, one study varied the number of friends (102, 302, 502, 702, or 902) on a mock Facebook page (Tong et al., 2008). Participants rated the *social attractiveness* of the page's owner. Those ratings were highest for 302 friends: Both too few and too many friends counted against the owner. Why 302? The median number of friends reported by the participants themselves was 300. Perhaps participants gave the highest ratings when they thought the page owner was similar to them.

Another study examined the way in which the photographs on Facebook

pages contributed to judgments on the particular personality trait of *narcissism* (Buffardi & Campbell, 2008). People who are narcissistic have an overly positive self-image. Take a moment to consider how that trait might be expressed through Facebook photos. The researchers found that participants rated page owners as being particularly narcissistic when the main photo on their Facebook pages was attractive and self-promoting (that is, the photo seemed dedicated to "persuading others about [the page owner's] own positive qualities," p. 1307). Raters also gave higher judgments of narcissism to owners whose pages indicated a large amount of social interaction. Finally, there was a positive correlation between raters' judgments and the page owner's self-reports of narcissism: The Facebook pages communicated valid information on this trait!

Do these results make you want to rethink how you present yourself in cyberspace?

- Why might people be comfortable making personality judgments based on Facebook content?

- How might you determine other circumstances in which similarity has an impact on people's judgments of Facebook pages?

future goals; and cognitive and self theories emphasize past and present (and the future if goal setting is involved).

4. *Consciousness versus unconsciousness.* Freudian theory emphasizes unconscious processes; humanistic, social-learning, and cognitive theories emphasize conscious processes. Trait theories pay little attention to this distinction; self theories are unclear on this score.

5. *Inner disposition versus outer situation.* Social-learning theories emphasize situational factors; traits play up dispositional factors; and the others allow for an interaction between person-based and situation-based variables.

Each type of theory makes different contributions to the understanding of human personality. Trait theories provide a catalog that describes parts and structures. Psychodynamic theories add a powerful engine and the fuel to get the vehicle moving. Humanistic theories put a person in the driver's seat. Social-learning theories supply the steering wheel, directional signals, and other regulation equipment. Cognitive theories add reminders that the way the trip is planned, organized, and remembered will be affected by the mental map the driver chooses for the journey. Finally, self theories remind the driver to consider the image his or her driving ability is projecting to backseat drivers and pedestrians.

To complete our discussion of personality, we will now consider personality assessment. We will describe some of the ways in which psychologists obtain information about the range of personality attributes that make each individual unique.

STOP AND REVIEW

❶ In what ways do personality theories differ on the dimension of heredity versus environment?

❷ Does Freud's theory of personality focus most directly on the past, present, or future?

❸ Which dimension of personality theories refers to people's awareness of the forces that shape their behaviors?

Visit MyPsychLab.com for more review and practice on the following topic:

◄● **Explore:** Psychodynamic, Behavioral, Trait and Type, Humanistic, and Cognitive Approaches to Personality

Assessing Personality

Think of all the ways in which you differ from your best friend. Psychologists wonder about the diverse attributes that characterize an individual, set one person apart from others, or distinguish people in one group from those in another (for example, shy people from outgoing or depressed individuals from happy). Two assumptions are basic to these attempts to understand and describe human personality: first, that there are personal characteristics of individuals that give coherence to their behavior and, second, that those characteristics can be assessed or measured. Personality tests must meet the standards of reliability and validity (see Chapter 9). In addition, clinicians and researchers receive thorough training to administer and interpret the tests. We will describe *objective* and *projective* personality tests. Psychologists often combine different measures to obtain a full understanding of an individual's personality.

OBJECTIVE TESTS

Objective tests of personality are those in which scoring and administration are relatively simple and follow well-defined rules. Some objective tests are scored by computer programs. The final score is usually a single number, scaled along a single dimension (such as *adjustment* versus *maladjustment*), or a set of scores on different traits (such as impulsiveness, dependency, or extraversion) reported in comparison with the scores of a normative sample.

A *self-report inventory* is an objective test in which individuals answer a series of questions about their thoughts, feelings, and actions. One of the first self-report inventories, the *Woodworth Personal Data Sheet* (written in 1917) asked questions such as "Are you often frightened in the middle of the night?" (see DuBois, 1970). Today, a person taking a **personality inventory** reads a series of statements and indicates whether each one is true or typical for him- or herself.

The most frequently used personality inventory is the *Minnesota Multiphasic Personality Inventory,* or MMPI (Dahlstrom et al., 1975). It is used in many clinical settings to aid in the diagnosis of patients and to guide their treatment. After reviewing its features and applications, we will briefly discuss the *NEO Personality Inventory* (NEO-PI), which is used widely with nonpatient populations.

The MMPI The MMPI was developed at the University of Minnesota during the 1930s by psychologist Starke Hathaway and psychiatrist J. R. McKinley (Hathaway & McKinley, 1940, 1943). Its basic purpose is to diagnose individuals according to a set of psychiatric labels. The first test consisted of 550 items, which individuals determined to be either true or false for themselves or to which they responded, "Cannot say." From that item pool, scales were developed that were relevant to the kinds of problems patients showed in psychiatric settings.

The MMPI scales were unlike other existing personality tests because they were developed using an *empirical* strategy rather than the intuitive, theoretical approach that dominated at the time. Items were included on a scale only if they clearly distinguished between two groups—for example, schizophrenic patients and a normal comparison group. Each item had to demonstrate its validity by being answered similarly by members within each group but differently between the two groups. Thus the items were not selected on a theoretical basis (what the content seemed to mean to experts) but on an empirical basis (did they distinguish between the two groups?).

The MMPI has 10 *clinical scales,* each constructed to differentiate a special clinical group (such as individuals with schizophrenia) from a normal comparison group. The test also includes *validity scales* that detect suspicious response patterns, such as blatant dishonesty, carelessness, defensiveness, or evasiveness. When an MMPI is interpreted, the tester first checks the validity scales to be sure the test is valid and then looks at the rest of the scores. The pattern of the scores—which are highest, how they differ—forms the "MMPI profile." Individual profiles are compared with those common for particular groups, such as felons and gamblers.

In the mid-1980s, the MMPI underwent a major revision, and it is now called the *MMPI-2* (Butcher et al., 2001). The MMPI-2 has updated language and content to better reflect contemporary concerns, and new populations provided data for norms. The MMPI-2 also adds 15 new *content scales* that were derived using, in part, a theoretical method. For each of 15 clinically relevant topics (such as anxiety or family problems), items were selected on two bases: if they seemed theoretically related to the topic area and if they statistically formed a *homogeneous scale,* meaning that each scale measures a single, unified concept. The clinical and content scales of the MMPI-2 are given in **Table 13.8** and **Table 13.9** on page 434. You'll notice that most of the clinical scales measure several related concepts and that the names of the content scales are simple and self-explanatory.

Because the MMPI-2 plays such a critical role in clinical research and practice, researchers continue to assess the test's reliability and validity to make appropriate clinical judgments. Important aspects of that research were incorporated into the

---

personality inventory A self-report questionnaire used for personality assessment that includes a series of items about personal thoughts, feelings, and behaviors.

TABLE 13.8	MMPI-2 Clinical Scales

Hypochondriasis (Hs): Abnormal concern with bodily functions

Depression (D): Pessimism; hopelessness; slowing of action and thought

Conversion hysteria (Hy): Unconscious use of mental problems to avoid conflicts or responsibility

Psychopathic deviate (Pd): Disregard for social custom; shallow emotions; inability to profit from experience

Masculinity–femininity (Mf): Differences between men and women

Paranoia (Pa): Suspiciousness; delusions of grandeur or persecution

Psychasthenia (Pt): Obsessions; compulsions; fears; guilt; indecisiveness

Schizophrenia (Sc): Bizarre, unusual thoughts or behavior; withdrawal; hallucinations; delusions

Hypomania (Ma): Emotional excitement; flight of ideas; overactivity

Social introversion (Si): Shyness; disinterest in others; insecurity

MMPI-2-RF (for "revised form") which appeared in 2008 (Tellegen & Ben-Porath, 2008). The MMPI-2-RF features revised clinical scales that supplement the MMPI-2 clinical scales. The goal of these revised scales is to allow better discrimination among people with different types of psychological disorders. The revised clinical scales have begun to undergo tests of reliability and validity that will allow psychologists to put the MMPI-2-RF to appropriate uses (Hoelzle & Meyer, 2008; Rouse et al., 2008).

The MMPI was designed to assess individuals with clinical problems. In the next section, we'll describe devices more suited to assess personality in the general, nonpatient population.

The NEO-PI The NEO Personality Inventory (NEO-PI) was designed to assess personality characteristics in nonclinical adult populations. It measures the five-factor model of personality we discussed earlier. If you took the NEO-PI, you would receive a profile sheet that showed your standardized scores relative to a large normative sample on each of the five major dimensions: Neuroticism, Extraversion, Openness, Agreeableness, and Conscientiousness (Costa & McCrae, 1985). The recent NEO-PI-3 assesses 30 separate traits organized within the five major factors (McCrae et al., 2005). For example, the Neuroticism dimension is broken down into six facet scales: Anxiety, Angry hostility, Depression, Self-consciousness, Impulsiveness, and Vulnerability. Much research has demonstrated that the NEO-PI dimensions

are homogeneous, highly reliable, and show good criterion and construct validity (Furnham et al., 1997; McCrae et al., 2004). The NEO-PI is being used to study personality stability and change across the life span as well as the relationship of personality characteristics to physical health and various life events, such as career success or early retirement.

PROJECTIVE TESTS

Have you ever looked at a cloud and seen a face or the shape of an animal? If you asked your friends to look, too, they may have seen a reclining nude or a dragon. Psychologists rely on a similar phenomenon in their use of projective tests for personality assessment.

As we just saw, objective tests take one of two forms: Either they provide test takers with a series of statements and ask them to give a simple response (such as "true," "false," or "cannot say") or they ask test takers to rate themselves with respect to some dimension (such as "anxious" versus "nonanxious"). Thus the respondent is constrained to choose one of the predetermined responses. *Projective tests*, by contrast, have no predetermined range of responses. In a **projective test,** a person is given a series of stimuli that are purposely ambiguous, such as abstract patterns, incomplete pictures, or drawings that can be interpreted in many ways. The person may be asked to describe the patterns, finish the pictures, or tell stories about the drawings. Projective tests were first used by psychoanalysts, who hoped that such tests would reveal their patients' unconscious personality dynamics. Because the stimuli are ambiguous, responses to them are determined partly by what the person brings to the situation—namely, inner feelings, personal motives, and conflicts from prior life experiences. These personal, idiosyncratic aspects, which are *projected* onto the stimuli, permit the personality assessor to make various interpretations.

Projective tests are among the assessment devices most commonly used by psychological practitioners (Butcher & Rouse, 1996). They have also been used more often outside the United

TABLE 13.9	MMPI-2 Content Scales	
Anxiety	Antisocial practices
Fears	Type A (workaholic)
Obsessiveness	Low self-esteem
Depression	Social discomfort
Health concerns	Family problems
Bizarre mentation (thoughts)	Work interference
Anger and cynicism	Negative treatment indicators (negative attitudes about doctors and treatment)

Excerpted from the MMPI-2™ (Minnesota Multiphasic Personality Inventory-2)™ Manual for Administration, Scoring, and Interpretation, Revised Edition. Copyright © 2001 by the Regents of the University of Minnesota. All rights reserved. Used by permission of the University of Minnesota Press. "MMPI-2" and "Minnesota Multiphasic Personality-2" are trademarks owned by the Regents of the University of Minnesota.

projective test A method of personality assessment in which an individual is presented with a standardized set of ambiguous, abstract stimuli and asked to interpret their meanings; the individual's responses are assumed to reveal inner feelings, motives, and conflicts.

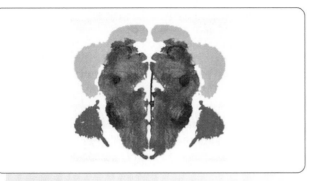

FIGURE 13.11   An Inkblot Similar to Those Used in the Rorschach Test
What do you see? Does your interpretation of this inkblot reveal anything about your personality?

States, such as in the Netherlands, Hong Kong, and Japan, than objective tests like the MMPI (Piotrowski et al., 1993). Objective tests often fail to be adequately translated or standardized for non–U.S. populations. Projective tests are less sensitive to language variation. However, because projective tests are so widespread, critics have often worried that they are used in ways that are not valid. As we examine two of the most common projective tests, the Rorschach test and the Thematic Apperception Test, we will discuss those issues of validity.

The Rorschach In the Rorschach test, developed by Swiss psychiatrist **Hermann Rorschach** in 1921, the ambiguous stimuli are symmetrical inkblots (Rorschach, 1942). Some are black and white, and some are colored (see **Figure 13.11**). During the test, a respondent is shown an inkblot and asked, "What might this be?" Respondents are assured that there are no right or wrong answers (Exner, 1974). Testers record verbatim what people say, how much time they take to respond, the total time they take per inkblot, and the way they handle the inkblot card. Then, in a second phase called an *inquiry,* the respondent is reminded of the previous responses and asked to elaborate on them.

The responses are scored on three major features: (1) the *location,* or part of the card mentioned in the response—whether the respondent refers to the whole stimulus or to part of it and the size of the details mentioned; (2) the *content* of the response—the nature of the object and activities seen; and (3) the *determinants*—which aspects of the card (such as its color or shading) prompted the response. Scorers may also note whether responses are original and unique or popular and conforming.

You might think that ambiguous inkblots would give rise to an uninterpretable diversity of responses. In fact, researchers have devised a comprehensive scoring system for Rorschach responses that allows for meaningful comparisons among different test takers (Exner, 2003; Exner & Weiner, 1994). For example, the scoring system specifies content categories that frequently appear in people's responses. Those categories include *whole human* (the response mentions or implies a whole human form) and *blood* (the response mentions blood, either human or animal). Researchers have developed training procedures to ensure that clinicians can learn to use the comprehensive scoring system reliably (Hilsenroth et al., 2007). In addition, the Rorschach has proven to be valid for diagnosing specific psychological disorders such as abnormal patterns of thought (Dean et al., 2007). However, practitioners also make diagnoses based on people's Rorschach

responses without any formal evidence that supports the validity of the practitioners' inferences. For that reason, the Rorschach test remains controversial (Garb et al., 2005).

The TAT In the Thematic Apperception Test (TAT), developed by **Henry Murray** in 1938, respondents are shown pictures of ambiguous scenes and asked to generate stories about them, describing what the people in the scenes are doing and thinking, what led up to each event, and how each situation will end (see **Figure 13.12**). The person administering the TAT evaluates the structure and content of the stories as well as the behavior of the individual telling them, in an attempt to discover some of the respondent's major concerns, motivations, and personality characteristics. For example, an examiner might evaluate a person as conscientious if his or her stories concerned people who lived up to their obligations and if the stories were told in a serious, orderly way. As with the Rorschach test, critics have suggested that the TAT is often used for purposes for which its validity remains uncertain (Lilienfeld et al., 2001). In Chapter 11, we noted one use of the TAT that has received research support: The TAT has often been used to reveal individual differences in dominant needs, such as needs for power, affiliation, and achievement (McClelland, 1961). Over several decades of research, the TAT has proven to be a valid measure of the need for achievement (Spangler, 1992).

Let us offer some concluding remarks on the subject of personality assessment. Did you see the relationship between

FIGURE 13.12   A Sample Card from the TAT Test
What story do you want to tell? What does your story reveal about your personality?

Reprinted by permission of the publishers from Henry A. Murray, *Thematic Apperception Test,* Plate 12 F, Cambridge, Mass.: Harvard University Press, Copyright © 1943 by the President and Fellows of Harvard College, © by Henry A. Murray.

these personality assessment devices and the theories of personality we reviewed earlier? The conclusion we reached was that each of the types of theories illuminated test different aspects of human experience. We can reach much the same conclusions for personality tests: Each has the potential to provide unique insights into an individual's personality. Clinicians most often use a combination of tests when they carry out a personality assessment. Under many circumstances, the profiles that arise from objective, even computer-based analyses may allow accurate predictions to be made for specific outcomes. Under other circumstances, clinical expertise and skilled intuition must supplement objective norms. In practice, the best predictions are made when the strengths of each approach are combined.

To close the chapter, we would like you to consider a series of questions in light of what you have just learned: If psychologists studied you, what portrait of your personality would they draw? Which early experiences might they identify as contributing to how you now act and think? What conditions in your current life exert strong influences on your thoughts and behaviors? What makes you different from other individuals who are functioning in many of the same situations as you? You now can see that each type of personality theory provides a framework against which you can begin to form your answers to these questions. Suppose the time has really come to paint your psychological portrait. Where would you begin?

STOP AND REVIEW

❶ What is the purpose of the MMPI's 10 clinical scales?
❷ What is the purpose of the NEO Personality Inventory (NEO-PI)?
❸ What three major features do clinicians use to interpret Rorschach responses?

Visit MyPsychLab.com for more review and practice on the following topics:

✴ **Simulate:** Overview of Clinical Assessment Tools

◀◉ **Explore:** Personality Assessment

Recapping Main Points

Type and Trait Personality Theories

- Some theorists categorize people by all-or-none types, assumed to be related to particular characteristic behaviors.
- Other theorists view traits—attributes along continuous dimensions—as the building blocks of personality.
- The five-factor model is a personality system that maps out the relationships among common trait words, theoretical concepts, and personality scales.
- Twin and adoption studies reveal that personality traits are partially inherited.
- People display behavioral consistency when situations are defined with respect to relevant psychological features.

Psychodynamic Theories

- Freud's psychodynamic theory emphasizes instinctive biological energies as sources of human motivation.
- Basic concepts of Freudian theory include psychic energy as powering and directing behavior, early experiences as key determinants of lifelong personality, psychic determinism, and powerful unconscious processes.
- Personality structure consists of the id, the superego, and the reconciling ego.
- Unacceptable impulses are repressed and ego defense mechanisms are developed to lessen anxiety and bolster self-esteem.
- Post-Freudians like Adler, Horney, and Jung put greater emphasis on ego functioning and social variables and less on sexual urges. They saw personality development as a lifelong process.

Humanistic Theories

- Humanistic theories focus on self-actualization—the growth potential of the individual.
- These theories are holistic, dispositional, and phenomenological.
- Contemporary theories in the humanist tradition focus on individuals' life stories.

Social-Learning and Cognitive Theories

- Social-learning theorists focus on understanding individual differences in behavior and personality as a consequence of different histories of reinforcement.
- Cognitive theorists emphasize individual differences in perception and subjective interpretation of the environment.
- Julian Rotter emphasized people's expectancies about rewards including general internal or external locus of control orientations.
- Walter Mischel explored the origins of behaviors as interactions of persons and situations.
- Albert Bandura described the reciprocal determinism among people, environments, and behaviors.
- Nancy Cantor's theory emphasized the impact of goals, knowledge, and strategies on people's behavior.

Self Theories

- Self theories focus on the importance of the self-concept for a full understanding of human personality.
- People engage in behaviors such as self-handicapping to maintain self-esteem.

- Cross-cultural research suggests that individualistic cultures give rise to independent construals of self, whereas collectivist cultures give rise to interdependent construals of self.

Comparing Personality Theories

- Personality theories can be contrasted with respect to the emphasis they put on heredity versus environment; learning processes versus innate laws of behavior; the past, present, or future; consciousness versus unconsciousness; and inner dispositions versus outer situations.
- Each theory makes different contributions to the understanding of human personality.

Assessing Personality

- Personality characteristics are assessed by both objective and projective tests.
- The most common objective test, the MMPI-2, is used to diagnose clinical problems.
- The NEO-PI is an objective test that measures five major dimensions of personality.
- Projective tests of personality ask people to respond to ambiguous stimuli.
- Two important projective tests are the Rorschach test and the TAT.

KEY TERMS

analytic psychology (p. 420)

anxiety (p. 417)

archetype (p. 419)

collective unconscious (p. 419)

consistency paradox (p. 413)

ego (p. 417)

ego defense mechanism (p. 417)

expectancy (p. 422)

five-factor model (p. 410)

fixation (p. 415)

id (p. 417)

independent construal of self (p. 430)

interdependent construal of self (p. 430)

libido (p. 414)

locus of control (p. 423)

personality (p. 407)

personality inventory (p. 433)

personality type (p. 407)

possible self (p. 428)

projective test (p. 434)

psychic determinism (p. 416)

psychobiography (p. 422)

psychodynamic personality theory (p. 414)

reciprocal determinism (p. 425)

repression (p. 417)

self-actualization (p. 420)

self-concept (p. 427)

self-efficacy (p. 425)

self-esteem (p. 428)

self-handicapping (p. 429)

shyness (p. 415)

social intelligence (p. 426)

superego (p. 417)

trait (p. 408)

unconditional positive regard (p. 420)

unconscious (p. 416)

Chapter 13 Practice Test

1. William Sheldon predicted that _____ would be brainy, artistic, and introverted.
   a. endomorphs
   b. ectomorphs
   c. mesomorphs
   d. polymorphs

2. Which of these factors is *not* a trait dimension in the five-factor model?
   a. creativeness
   b. neuroticism
   c. agreeableness
   d. extraversion

3. Which of these is a *nature* explanation for why people are shy?
   a. Many of the activities people carry out on the Internet are socially isolating.
   b. Some cultures put a greater emphasis on obedience to authority.
   c. Some children are more reserved with unfamiliar people from birth.
   d. Parents may withhold love if children are not successful.

4. According to Freud, at ages 4 to 5 children are in the _____ stage of development.
   a. genital
   b. oral
   c. phallic
   d. anal

5. You attend a lecture that is focusing on archetypes in the collective unconscious. The lecture seems to be about the ideas of
   a. Carl Jung.
   b. Sigmund Freud.
   c. Karen Horney.
   d. Alfred Adler.

6. One of the most important claims of humanistic theories of personality is that people strive for
   a. superiority.
   b. erogenous zones.
   c. self-preservation.
   d. self-actualization.

7. Humanistic theories are _____ because they emphasize an individual's subjective view of reality.
   a. holistic
   b. deterministic
   c. phenomenological
   d. dispositional

8. With respect to Walter Mischel's personality theory, which of these statements relates to the variable of goals and values?
   a. Bart wants to graduate from college before he turns 30.
   b. Reese thinks she can persuade her brother to lend her his car.
   c. Piper sweats a lot before she takes an exam.
   d. Vito can do multiplication without a calculator.

9. Jason's best friend Buffy is trying to convince him that he can get a new job. If Buffy is successful, that could have an impact on Jason's sense of
   a. self-efficacy.
   b. self-regulation.
   c. reciprocal determinism.
   d. libido.

10. Brian spends the whole night before he is going to compete in a triathalon reviewing the notes for his philosophy class. This might be an example of
    a. self-efficacy.
    b. psychic determinism.
    c. self-handicapping.
    d. neuroticism.

11. Because Miriam lives in a _____ culture she is likely to have an _____ construal of self.
    a. collectivist; dependent
    b. collectivist; interdependent
    c. individualistic; interdependent
    d. collectivist; independent

12. Which features of Facebook pages were *not* related to judgments of narcissism?
    a. The number of funny quotations.
    b. The attractiveness of the main photograph.
    c. The self-promotion of the main photograph.
    d. The owner's amount of social interaction.

13. Chad and Jeremy are both personality theorists. Chad believes that personalities are largely determined before birth. Jeremy believes that personalities arise from life experiences. The dimension on which they disagree is
    a. learning processes versus innate laws of behavior.
    b. consciousness versus unconsciousness.
    c. inner disposition versus outer situation.
    d. heredity versus environment.

14. The personality test that most directly assesses the dimensions of the five-factor model is the
    a. Rorschach.
    b. NEO-PI.
    c. TAT.
    d. MMPI-2.

15. If you wanted to measure need for achievement, your first choice might be the
    a. Rorschach.
    b. TAT.
    c. MMPI-2.
    d. NEO-PI.

Essay Questions

1. How do traits and situations interact to affect predictions of behaviors?

2. How do humanistic theories give rise to a focus on life stories and psychobiography?

3. What theoretical ideas led to the development of projective personality tests?

Discovering Psychology Viewing Guide

Watch the following video by logging on to MyPsychLab (www.mypsychlab.com). After you have watched the video, complete the activities that follow.

Program 15: The Self

KEY TERMS AND PEOPLE

As you watch the programs, pay particular attention to these terms and people in addition to those covered in this textbook.

- *reference standard*—a norm or model of behavior that we use to decide how to behave in a situation.
- *status transaction*—a form of interpersonal communication in which we establish relative degrees of social status and power.
- *Teresa Amabile*—studies the psychology of creativity.
- *Mark Snyder*—studies strategic self-presentation and behavioral confirmation.

PROGRAM REVIEW

1. What name did William James give to the part of the self that focuses on the images we create in the mind of others?
   a. the material self
   b. the spiritual self
   c. the social self
   d. the outer self

2. Gail is a toddler who is gradually separating from her mother. This process is called
   a. identification.
   b. individuation.
   c. self-presentation.
   d. self-consciousness.

3. In Freudian theory, the part of the person that acts as a police officer restraining drives and passions is called the
   a. superego.
   b. ego.
   c. id.
   d. libido.

4. Which statement reflects the humanistic view of the self, according to Carl Rogers?
   a. Our impulses are in constant conflict with society's demands.
   b. We have a capacity for self-direction and self-understanding.
   c. We form an image of ourselves that determines what we can do.
   d. Our views of ourselves are created by how people react to us.

5. When we characterize self-image as a schema, we mean that
   a. we use it to organize information about ourselves.
   b. other people see us in terms of the image we project.
   c. it is a good predictor of performance in specific situations.
   d. we rationalize our behavior to fit into an image.

6. In Albert Bandura's research, people were given the task of improving production at a model furniture factory. They performed best when they believed that performance
   a. depended on their intelligence.
   b. related mainly to how confident they felt.
   c. would be given a material reward.
   d. was based on learning an acquirable skill.

7. Which of the following behaviors signals low status in a status transaction?
   a. maintaining eye contact
   b. using complete sentences
   c. moving in slow, smooth way
   d. touching one's face or hair

8. According to the principles of behavioral confirmation, what reaction do people generally have to a person who is depressed?
   a. People sympathetically offer help to the person.
   b. People regard the person as inadequate.
   c. People act falsely cheerful to make the person happy.
   d. People treat a depressed person the same as anybody else.

9. What was referred to in the film as a type of psychological genocide?
   a. drugs   c. prejudice
   b. falling emphasis on education   d. immigration

10. What is the relevance of schemas to the self?
    a. We try to avoid schemas in constructing our sense of self.
    b. We organize our beliefs about ourselves in terms of schemas.
    c. Schemas are what makes us individuals.
    d. Schemas are always negative because they underlie prejudice.

11. In Teresa Amabile's work on creativity, how did being in a competitive situation affect creativity?
    a. It reduced creativity.
    b. It increased creativity.
    c. Its effects varied depending on the person's innate creativity.
    d. There was no effect.

12. According to Hazel Markus, culture is what you
  a. think.   c. do.
  b. see.   d. hate.

13. The phrase *mutual constitution* refers to which two components, according to Hazel Markus?
  a. parent and child
  b. art and scholarship
  c. religion and society
  d. self and culture

14. In which culture are you most likely to find a definition of the person as a part of the group?
  a. Japanese
  b. American
  c. Portugese
  d. Russian

15. The high rate of alcoholism among Native Americans was cited as an example of
  a. individualism.
  b. social handicapping.
  c. mutual constitution.
  d. striving for superiority.

16. According to William James, which part of the self serves as our inner witness to outside events?
  a. the material self
  b. the spiritual self
  c. the social self
  d. the outer self

17. Of the following psychologists, who is considered to be the least optimistic about the human condition?
  a. Freud
  b. Adler
  c. Rogers
  d. Maslow

18. Which of the following refers to how capable we believe we are of mastering challenges?
  a. self-efficacy
  b. self-handicapping
  c. confirmatory behavior
  d. status transaction

19. Amabile is to creativity as _____ is to behavioral confirmation.
  a. Alfred Adler
  b. Patricia Ryan
  c. Mark Snyder
  d. Albert Bandura

20. Who is credited as being responsible for psychology's return to the self?
  a. William James
  b. B.F. Skinner
  c. Patricia Ryan
  d. Carl Rogers

QUESTIONS TO CONSIDER

1. Different kinds of standardized tests have been criticized over the years because they may not apply equally well to people of different genders, socioeconomic status, or cultural backgrounds. Speculate on what sorts of problems might arise when standardized personality tests (such as the MMPI-2) are used. Think about what sorts of items might lead to problems, and think about what sorts of consequences might arise from the use of a biased instrument.

2. How is Seligman's concept of pessimism related to shyness?

3. What are some of the positive and negative aspects of the id, according to Freud?

4. Do you have higher self-esteem in some situations than in others? How do different environments and conditions affect you? Do you think that self-esteem is constant or variable?

5. Compare the social skills of your friends and yourself to people who did not grow up with computers and the Internet playing a central role in their lives. Do you see systematic differences in sociability, shyness, and apparent self-concept?

ACTIVITIES

1. How do you recognize extroverts and introverts? Observe people on television, in a public place, or at home. Rate their behavior on a continuum between the opposites of extrovert and introvert. How helpful is the distinction? Do these qualities seem to be a primary dimension of personality?

2. Describe yourself by highlighting your special abilities, admirable qualities, and accomplishments. Write a brief description of your parents, spouse, children, or a close friend. Consider how often you appreciate the positive aspects of your own or another's personality and how often you focus on the negatives. How does your focus affect your own self-esteem and your relationships?

3. Take some characteristic about yourself that you have never liked (such as the tendency to interrupt or to become tongue-tied around people of higher status than you). Spend the next month seeing if you can completely rid yourself of that characteristic. If you are successful, how would you describe the shift? Was it a change in your personality, or was it a change in behavior despite the underlying traits that used to produce it?

4. Interview a new parent and find out how his or her attitudes and behavior toward small children have changed.

Psychological Disorders

onsider these words, written by a 30-year-old woman who was receiving treatment for schizophrenia:

I want to let you know what it is like to be a functional person with schizophrenia in these days and times and what someone with my mental illness faces. . . . I live pretty normal and no one can tell [I'm] mentally ill unless I tell them. . . . The delusions before I got my medicine picked any story line it chose, and changed it at will. As time went by before help, I felt it was taking over my whole brain, and I'd cry wanting my mind and life back.

What are your reactions as you read this young woman's words, an excerpt from a letter to your authors?

If your reactions are similar to ours, you feel a mixture of sadness at her plight, of delight in her willingness to do all she can to cope with the many problems her mental illness creates, of anger toward those who stigmatize her because she may act differently at times, and of hope that, with medication and therapy, her condition may improve. These are but a few of the emotions that clinical and research psychologists and psychiatrists feel as they try to understand and treat mental disorders.

This chapter focuses on the nature and causes of psychological disorders: what they are, why they develop, and how we can explain their causes. The next chapter builds on this knowledge to describe the strategies used to treat, and to prevent, mental illness. Research indicates that 46.4 percent of individuals over age 18 in the United States have suffered from a psychological disorder at some point in their lives (Kessler et al., 2005a). Thus many of you who read this text are likely to benefit directly from knowledge about psychopathology. Facts alone, however, will not convey the serious impact psychological disorders have on the everyday lives of individuals and families. Throughout this chapter, as we discuss categories of psychological disorders, try to envision the real people who live with such a disorder every day. We will share with you their words and lives, as we did at the start of the chapter. Let's begin now with a discussion of the concept of abnormality.

The Nature of Psychological Disorders

Have you ever worried excessively? Felt depressed or anxious without really knowing why? Been fearful of something you rationally knew could not harm you? Had thoughts about suicide? Used alcohol or drugs to escape a problem? Almost everyone will answer yes to at least one of these questions, which means that almost everyone has experienced the symptoms of a psychological disorder. This chapter looks at the range of psychological functioning that is considered unhealthy or abnormal,

often referred to as *psychopathology* or *psychological disorder*. **Psychopathological functioning** involves disruptions in emotional, behavioral, or thought processes that lead to personal distress or that block one's ability to achieve important goals. The field of **abnormal psychology** is the area of psychological investigation most directly concerned with understanding the nature of individual pathologies of mind, mood, and behavior.

We begin this section by exploring a more precise definition of abnormality and then look at problems of objectivity. We then examine how this definition evolved over hundreds of years of human history.

DECIDING WHAT IS ABNORMAL

What does it mean to say someone is *abnormal* or *suffering from a psychological disorder?* How do psychologists and other clinical practitioners decide what is abnormal? Is it always clear when behavior moves from the normal to the abnormal category? The judgment that someone has a mental disorder is typically based on the evaluation of the individual's *behavioral* functioning by people with some special authority or power. The terms used to describe these phenomena—*mental disorder, mental illness,* or *abnormality*—depend on the particular perspective, training, and cultural background of the evaluator, the situation, and the status of the person being judged.

Let's consider seven criteria you might use to label behavior as "abnormal" (Butcher et al., 2008):

1. *Distress or disability.* An individual experiences personal distress or disabled functioning, which produces a risk of

What do you imagine the lives of people with mental illnesses are like?

---

psychopathological functioning Disruptions in emotional, behavioral, or thought processes that lead to personal distress or block one's ability to achieve important goals.

abnormal psychology The area of psychological investigation concerned with understanding the nature of individual pathologies of mind, mood, and behavior.

physical or psychological deterioration or loss of freedom of action. For example, a man who cannot leave his home without weeping would be unable to pursue ordinary life goals.

2. *Maladaptiveness.* An individual acts in ways that hinder goals, do not contribute to personal well-being, or interfere strongly with the goals of others and the needs of society. Someone who is drinking so heavily that she cannot hold down a job or who is endangering others through her intoxication is displaying maladaptive behavior.

3. *Irrationality.* An individual acts or talks in ways that are irrational or incomprehensible to others. A man who responds to voices that do not exist in objective reality is behaving irrationally.

4. *Unpredictability.* An individual behaves unpredictably or erratically from situation to situation, as if experiencing a loss of control. A child who smashes his fist through a window for no apparent reason displays unpredictability.

5. *Unconventionality and statistical rarity.* An individual behaves in ways that are statistically rare and that violate social standards of what is acceptable or desirable. Just being statistically unusual, however, does not lead to a psychological judgment of abnormality. For example, possessing genius-level intelligence is extremely rare, but it is also considered desirable. Conversely, having extremely low intelligence is also rare but is considered undesirable; thus it has often been labeled abnormal.

6. *Observer discomfort.* An individual creates discomfort in others by making them feel threatened or distressed in some way. A woman walking down the middle of the sidewalk, having a loud conversation with herself, creates observer discomfort in other pedestrians trying to avoid her.

7. *Violation of moral and ideal standards.* An individual violates expectations for how one ought to behave with respect to societal norms. Thus, if people generally think it is important to provide care to one's offspring, parents who abandoned their children might be considered abnormal.

Can you see why most of these indicators of abnormality may not be immediately apparent to all observers? Consider just the last criterion. Are you mentally ill if you don't wish to work, even if that is abnormal with respect to the norms of society? Or consider a more serious symptom. It is "bad" to have hallucinations in our culture because they are taken as signs of mental disturbance, but it is "good" in cultures in which hallucinations are interpreted as mystical visions from spirit forces. Whose judgment is correct? At the end of this chapter, we will consider some negative consequences and dangers associated with such socially regulated judgments and the decisions based on them.

We are more confident in labeling behavior as "abnormal" when more than just one of the indicators is present and valid. The more extreme and prevalent the indicators are, the more confident we can be that they point to an abnormal condition. None of these criteria is a *necessary* condition shared by all cases of abnormality. For example, during his murder trial, a Stanford University graduate student who had killed his math professor with a hammer, and then taped to his office door a note that read "No office hours today," reported feeling neither guilt nor remorse. Despite the absence of personal suffering, we would not hesitate to label his overall behavior as abnormal. It is also true that no single criterion, by itself, is a *sufficient* condition that distinguishes all cases of abnormal behavior from normal variations in behavior. The distinction between normal and abnormal is not so much a difference between two independent types of behaviors as it is a matter of the degree to which a person's actions resemble a set of agreed-upon criteria of abnormality. Mental disorder is best thought of as a *continuum* that varies between *mental health* and *mental illness.*

How comfortable do you feel with these ideas about abnormality? Although the criteria seem fairly clear-cut, psychologists still worry about the problem of objectivity.

THE PROBLEM OF OBJECTIVITY

The decision to declare someone psychologically disordered or abnormal is always a *judgment* about behavior: The goal for many researchers is to make these judgments *objectively,* without any type of bias. For some psychological disorders, like depression or schizophrenia, diagnosis often easily meets the standards of objectivity. Other cases are more problematic. As we have seen throughout our study of psychology, the meaning of behavior is jointly determined by its *content* and by its *context.* The same act in different settings conveys very different meanings. A man kisses another man; it may signify a gay relationship in the United States, a ritual greeting in France, or a Mafia "kiss of death" in Sicily. The meaning of a behavior always depends on context.

Let's see why objectivity is such an important issue. History is full of examples of situations in which judgments of abnormality were made by individuals to preserve their moral or political power. Consider an 1851 report, entitled "The Diseases and Physical Peculiarities of the Negro Race," published in a medical journal. Its author, Dr. Samuel Cartwright, had been appointed by the Louisiana Medical Association to chair a committee to investigate the "strange" practices of African American slaves. "Incontrovertible scientific evidence" was amassed to justify the practice of slavery. Several "diseases" previously unknown to the White race were discovered. One finding was that Blacks allegedly suffered from a sensory disease that made them insensitive "to pain when being punished" (thus no need to spare the whip). The committee also invented the disease *drapetomania,* a mania to seek freedom—a mental disorder that caused certain slaves to run away from their masters. Runaway slaves needed to be caught so that their illness could be properly treated (Chorover, 1981)!

Once an individual has obtained an "abnormal" label, people are inclined to interpret later behavior to confirm that judgment. **David Rosenhan** (1973, 1975) and his colleagues demonstrated that it may be impossible to be judged "sane" in an "insane place."

Rosenhan and seven other sane people gained admission to different psychiatric hospitals by pretending to have a single symptom: hallucinations. All eight of these *pseudopatients* were diagnosed on admission as having either paranoid schizophrenia or bipolar disorder. Once admitted, they behaved normally in every way. Rosenhan observed, however, that when a sane person is in an insane place, he or she is likely to be judged insane, and any behavior is likely to be reinterpreted to fit the context. If the pseudopatients discussed their situation in a rational way with the staff, they were reported to be using "intellectualization" defenses, while their taking notes of their observations were evidence of "writing behavior." The pseudopatients remained on the wards for almost three weeks, on average, and not one was identified by the staff as sane. When they were finally released—only with the help of spouses or colleagues—their discharge diagnosis was still "schizophrenia" but "in remission." That is, their symptoms were no longer active.

Rosenhan's research demonstrates how judgments of abnormality rely on factors beyond behavior itself.

In the view of psychiatrist **Thomas Szasz,** mental illness does not even exist—it is a "myth" (1974, 2004). Szasz argues that the symptoms used as evidence of mental illness are merely medical labels that sanction professional intervention into what are social problems—deviant people violating social norms. Once labeled, these people can be treated either benignly or harshly for their problem "of being different," with no threat of disturbing the existing status quo.

Few clinicians would go this far, in large part because the focus of much research and treatment is on understanding and alleviating personal distress. For most of the disorders we will describe in this chapter, individuals experience their own behavior as abnormal, or poorly adapted to the environment. Even so, this discussion suggests that there can be no altogether objective assessments of abnormality. As we describe each type of psychological disorder, try to understand why clinicians believe the cluster of symptoms represents behavior patterns that are more serious for the individual than mere violations of social norms.

CLASSIFYING PSYCHOLOGICAL DISORDERS

Why is it helpful to have a classification system for psychological disorders? What advantages are gained by moving beyond a global assessment that abnormality exists to distinguish among different types of abnormalities? A **psychological diagnosis** is the label given to an abnormality by classifying and categorizing the observed behavior pattern into an approved diagnostic system. Such a diagnosis is in many ways more difficult to make than a medical diagnosis. In the medical context, a doctor can rely on physical evidence, such as X-rays, blood tests, and biopsies, to inform a diagnostic decision. In the case of psychological disorders, the evidence for diagnosis comes from interpretations of a person's actions. To create greater consistency among clinicians and coherence in their diagnostic evaluations, psychologists have helped to develop a system of diagnosis and classification that provides precise descriptions of symptoms, as well as other criteria to help practitioners decide whether a person's behavior is evidence of a particular disorder.

To be most useful, a diagnostic system should provide the following three benefits:

- *Common shorthand language.* To facilitate a quick and clear understanding among clinicians or researchers working in the field of psychopathology, practitioners seek a common set of terms with agreed-upon meanings. A diagnostic category, such as *depression,* summarizes a large and complex collection of information, including characteristic symptoms and the typical course of the disorder. In clinical settings, such as clinics and hospitals, a diagnostic system allows mental health professionals to communicate more effectively about the people they are helping. Researchers studying different aspects of psychopathology or evaluating treatment programs must agree on the disorder they are observing.

- *Understanding of causality.* Ideally, a diagnosis of a specific disorder should make clear the causes of the symptoms. As is the case for physical illness, the same symptoms may arise for more than one disorder. A goal of a classification system is to indicate why practitioners should interpret particular patterns of symptoms as evidence for specific underlying disorders.

- *Treatment plan.* A diagnosis should also suggest what types of treatments to consider for particular disorders. Researchers and clinicians have found that certain treatments or therapies work most effectively for specific kinds of psychological disorders. For example, drugs that are quite effective in treating schizophrenia do not help and may even hurt people with depression. Further advances in knowledge about the effectiveness and specificity of treatments will make fast and reliable diagnosis even more important.

Historical Perspectives on Classification Throughout history, humans have feared psychological disorders, often associating them with evil. Because of this fear, people have reacted aggressively and decisively to any behaviors they perceived as bizarre or abnormal. People who have exhibited such behaviors have been imprisoned and made subject to radical medical treatments. Until the end of the 18th century, the mentally ill in Western societies were perceived as mindless beasts who could be controlled only with chains and physical discipline.

In the latter part of the 18th century, a new perspective about the origins of abnormal behavior emerged—people began to perceive those with psychological problems as *sick,* suffering from illness, rather than as *possessed* or *immoral.* As a result, a number of reforms were gradually implemented in the facilities for the insane. **Philippe Pinel** (1745–1826) was one of the first clinicians to use these ideas to attempt to develop a classification system for psychological difficulties based on the idea that disorders of thought, mood, and behavior are similar in many ways to the physical, organic illnesses. According to such a system, each disorder has a group of characteristic symptoms that distinguishes it from other disorders and from healthy functioning. Disorders are classified according to the patterns of observed symptoms, the circumstances surrounding the onset of the disturbance, the natural course of the disorder, and its response to treatment. Such classification systems are modeled after the biological classification systems naturalists use and are intended to help clinicians identify common disorders more easily.

In 1896, **Emil Kraepelin** (1855–1926), a German psychiatrist, was responsible for creating the first truly comprehensive *classification system* of psychological disorders. Strongly motivated by a belief that there was a physical basis to psychological problems, he gave the process of psychological diagnosis and

---

psychological diagnosis The label given to psychological abnormality by classifying and categorizing the observed behavior pattern into an approved diagnostic system.

TABLE 14.1 The Five Axes of *DSM-IV-TR*

Axis	Classes of Information	Description
Axis I	Clinical disorders	These mental disorders present symptoms or patterns of behavioral or psychological problems that typically are painful or impair an area of functioning. Included are disorders that emerge in infancy, childhood, or adolescence.
Axis II	(a) Personality disorders (b) Mental retardation	These are dysfunctional patterns of perceiving and responding to the world.
Axis III	General medical conditions	This axis codes physical problems relevant to understanding or treating an individual's psychological disorders on Axes I and II.
Axis IV	Psychosocial and environmental problems	This axis codes psychosocial and environmental stressors that may affect the diagnosis and treatment of an individual's disorder and the likelihood of recovery.
Axis V	Global assessment of functioning	This axis codes the individual's overall level of current functioning in the psychological, social, and occupational domains.

classification the flavor of medical diagnosis. That flavor remains today in the diagnostic system we now review.

DSM-IV-TR In the United States, the most widely accepted classification scheme is one developed by the American Psychiatric Association. It is called the *Diagnostic and Statistical Manual of Mental Disorders*. The most recent version, published in 2000 as a revision of the fourth edition, is known by clinicians and researchers as **DSM-IV-TR.** It classifies, defines, and describes over 200 mental disorders.

To reduce the diagnostic difficulties caused by variability in approaches to psychological disorders, *DSM-IV-TR* emphasizes the *description* of patterns of symptoms and courses of disorders rather than etiological theories or treatment strategies. The purely descriptive terms allow clinicians and researchers to use a common language to describe problems while leaving room for disagreement and continued research about which theoretical models best *explain* the problems.

The first version of *DSM*, which appeared in 1952 *(DSM-I)*, listed several dozen mental illnesses. *DSM-II*, introduced in 1968, revised the diagnostic system to make it more compatible with another popular system, the World Health Organization's *International Classification of Diseases (ICD)*. The fourth edition of the *DSM* (*DSM-IV*, 1994) emerged after several years of intense work by committees of scholars. To make their changes (from the *DSM-III-Revised*, which appeared in 1987), these committees carefully scrutinized large bodies of research on psychopathology and also tested proposed changes for workability in actual clinical settings. *DSM-IV* is also fully compatible with the 10th edition of the *ICD. DSM-IV-TR* (2000) incorporated a review of the research literature that had accumulated since *DSM-IV*. Because the changes largely affected the supporting text, rather than the system of classification, the revision was termed a "text revision," which yielded the name *DSM-IV-TR*. After this brief history of the *DSM*, you probably won't be surprised to learn that committees are meeting to bring the newest research to bear on *DSM-V*, which is scheduled to appear in 2012. In the *Critical Thinking in Your Life* box, we give you a sense of the process that could lead to the inclusion of new disorders in *DSM-V*.

To encourage clinicians to consider the psychological, social, and physical factors that may be associated with a psychological disorder, *DSM-IV-TR* uses dimensions, or *axes,* that portray information about all these factors (see **Table 14.1**). Most of the principal clinical disorders are contained on Axis I. Included here are all disorders that emerge in childhood, except for mental retardation. Axis II lists mental retardation as well as personality disorders. These problems may accompany Axis I disorders. Axis III incorporates information about general medical conditions, such as diabetes, that may be relevant to understanding or treating an Axis I or II disorder. Axes IV and V provide supplemental information that can be useful when planning an individual's treatment or assessing the *prognosis* (predictions of future change). Axis IV assesses psychosocial and environmental problems that may explain patients' stress responses or their resources for coping with stress. On Axis V, a clinician evaluates the global level of an individual's functioning. A full diagnosis in the *DSM-IV-TR* system would involve consideration of each of the axes.

Throughout this chapter, we will provide estimates of the frequency with which individuals experience particular psychological disorders. These estimates arise from research projects in which mental health histories are obtained from large samples of the population. Figures are available for the prevalence of different disorders over one-year and lifetime periods (Kessler et al., 2005a, 2005b). The figures we will generally cite come from the *National Comorbidity Study (NCS),* which sampled 9,282 U.S. adults ages 18 and older (Kessler et al., 2005a). It is important to emphasize that often the same individuals have experienced more than one disorder simultaneously at some point in their life span, a phenomenon known as **comorbidity.** (*Morbidity* refers to the occurrence of disease. *Comorbidity* refers to the co-occurrence of diseases.) The NCS found that 45 percent of the people who had experienced one disorder in a 12-month period had actually experienced two or more. Researchers have begun to study

---

DSM-IV-TR The current diagnostic and statistical manual of the American Psychological Association that classifies, defines, and describes mental disorders.

comorbidity The experience of more than one disorder at the same time.

The Salem witchcraft trials were an outgrowth of a desperate attempt to affix blame for frighteningly bizarre behavior among the Puritan colonists. The colonists theorized that the symptoms were the work of the devil, who, through the efforts of earthbound witches, had taken over the minds and bodies of young women.

intensively the patterns of comorbidity of different psychological disorders (Kessler et al., 2005b).

Evolution of Diagnostic Categories The diagnostic categories and the methods used to organize and present them have shifted with each revision of the *DSM*. These shifts reflect changes in the opinions of a majority of mental health experts about exactly what constitutes a psychological disorder and where the lines between different types of disorders should be drawn. They also reflect changing perspectives among the public about what constitutes *abnormality*.

In the revision process of each *DSM*, some diagnostic categories were dropped, and others were added. For example, with the introduction of *DSM-III*, in 1980, the traditional distinction between *neurotic* and *psychotic* disorders was eliminated. **Neurotic disorders,** or *neuroses*, were originally conceived of as relatively common psychological problems in which a person did not have signs of brain abnormalities, did not display grossly irrational thinking, and did not violate basic norms; but he or she did experience subjective distress or a pattern of self-defeating or inadequate coping strategies. **Psychotic disorders,** or *psychoses*, were thought to differ in both quality and severity from neurotic problems. It was

believed that psychotic behavior deviated significantly from social norms and was accompanied by a profound disturbance in rational thinking and general emotional and thought processes. The *DSM-III* advisory committees felt that the terms *neurotic disorders* and *psychotic disorders* had become too general in their meaning to have much usefulness as diagnostic categories (however, they continue to be used by many psychiatrists and psychologists to characterize the general level of disturbance in a person).

We want to note a final aspect of classification that has evolved over time. Historically, people with mental illnesses were often labeled with the name of their disorder. For example, clinicians referred to people as "schizophrenics" or "phobics." That didn't happen for physical illnesses—people with cancer were never known as "cancerics." Clinicians and researchers now take care to separate the person from the diagnosis. People have schizophrenic disorders or phobias, just as they have cancer or the flu. The hope is that appropriate treatments can alleviate each condition so they no longer apply to the person.

The Concept of Insanity Before we turn to the causes of mental illness, we want to turn our attention briefly to the concept of insanity. **Insanity** is not defined in *DSM-IV-TR*; there is no accepted clinical definition of insanity. Rather, insanity is a concept that belongs to popular culture and to the legal system. The treatment of insanity in the law dates back to England in 1843, when Daniel M'Naghten was found not guilty of murder by reason of insanity. M'Naghten's intended victim was the British prime minister—M'Naghten believed that God had instructed him to commit the murder. (He accidentally killed the prime minister's secretary instead.) Because of M'Naghten's delusions, he was sent to a mental hospital rather than to prison.

The anger surrounding this verdict—even Queen Victoria was infuriated—prompted the House of Lords to articulate a guideline, known as the *M'Naghten rule,* to limit claims of insanity. This rule specifies that a criminal must not "know the nature and quality of the act he was doing; or, if he did know it, that he did not know he was doing what was wrong." Does the M'Naghten rule seem like a fair test of guilt or innocence? With advances in the understanding of mental illness, researchers became more aware of circumstances in which a criminal might know right from wrong—a criminal might understand that what he or she was doing was illegal or immoral—but still might not be able to suppress the actions.

Despite the great attention that insanity pleas receive in the media—and, thus, the public's great awareness of them—such pleas are quite rare (Kirschner & Galperin, 2001). For example, one study found that in 60,432 indictments in Baltimore, Maryland, only 190 defendants (0.31 percent) entered insanity pleas; of the 190 pleas, only 8 (4.2 percent) were successful (Janofsky et al., 1996). Thus the likelihood that you will ever be asked to sit on a jury and judge another person as sane or insane is quite low.

THE ETIOLOGY OF PSYCHOPATHOLOGY

Etiology refers to the factors that cause or contribute to the development of psychological and medical problems. Knowing why the disorder occurs, what its origins are, and how it affects

---

neurotic disorder Mental disorder in which a person does not have signs of brain abnormalities and does not display grossly irrational thinking or violate basic norms but does experience subjective distress; a category dropped from *DSM-III*.

psychotic disorder Severe mental disorder in which a person experiences impairments in reality testing manifested through thought, emotional, or perceptual difficulties; no longer used as diagnostic category after *DSM-III*.

insanity The legal (not clinical) designation for the state of an individual judged to be legally irresponsible or incompetent.

etiology The causes of, or factor related to, the development of a disorder.

thought and emotional and behavioral processes may lead to new ways of treating and, ideally, preventing it. An analysis of causality will be an important part of our discussion of each individual disorder. Here we introduce two general categories of causal factors: biological and psychological.

Biological Approaches Building on the heritage of the medical model, modern biological approaches assume that psychological disturbances are directly attributable to underlying biological factors. Biological researchers and clinicians most often investigate structural abnormalities in the brain, biochemical processes, and genetic influences.

The brain is a complex organ whose interrelated elements are held in delicate balance. Subtle alterations in its chemical messengers—the neurotransmitters—or in its tissue can have significant effects. Genetic factors, brain injury, and infection are a few of the causes of these alterations. We have seen in earlier chapters that technological advances in brain-imaging techniques allow mental health professionals to view the structure of the brain and specific biochemical processes in living individuals without surgery. Using these techniques, biologically oriented researchers are discovering new links between psychological disorders and specific abnormalities in the brain. In addition, continuing advances in the field of behavioral genetics have improved researchers' abilities to identify the links between specific genes and the presence of psychological disorders. We will look to these different types of biological explanations throughout the chapter as we try to understand the nature of various forms of abnormality.

Psychological Approaches Psychological approaches focus on the causal role of psychological or social factors in the development of psychopathology. These approaches perceive personal experiences, traumas, conflicts, and environmental factors as the roots of psychological disorders. We will outline four dominant psychological models of abnormality: the psychodynamic, the behavioral, the cognitive, and the sociocultural.

Psychodynamic Like the biological approach, the psychodynamic model holds that the causes of psychopathology are located inside the person. However, according to Sigmund Freud, who developed this model, the internal causal factors are psychological rather than biological. As we noted in earlier chapters, Freud believed that many psychological disorders were simply an extension of "normal" processes of psychic conflict and ego defense that all people experience. In the psychodynamic model, early childhood experiences shape both normal and abnormal behavior.

In psychodynamic theory, behavior is motivated by drives and wishes of which people are often unaware. Symptoms of psychopathology have their roots in *unconscious conflict* and thoughts. If the unconscious is conflicted and tension filled, a

In 2001, Andrea Yates drowned her five children in a bathtub. Five years later, a jury found her not guilty by reason of insanity. Why has the legal definition of "insanity" changed over time?

person will be plagued by anxiety and other disorders. Much of this psychic conflict arises from struggles between the irrational, pleasure-seeking impulses of the *id* and the internalized social constraints imposed by the *superego*. The *ego* is normally the arbiter of this struggle; however, its ability to perform its function can be weakened by abnormal development in childhood. Individuals attempt to avoid the pain caused by conflicting motives and anxiety with *defense mechanisms,* such as repression or denial. Defenses can become overused, distorting reality or leading to self-defeating behaviors. The individual may then expend so much psychic energy in defenses against anxiety and conflict that there is little energy left to provide a productive and satisfying life.

Behavioral Because of their emphasis on observable responses, behavioral theorists have little use for hypothetical psychodynamic processes. These theorists argue that abnormal behaviors are acquired in the same fashion as healthy behaviors—through learning and reinforcement. They do not focus on internal psychological phenomena or early childhood experiences. Instead, they focus on the *current* behavior and the *current* conditions or reinforcements that sustain the behavior. The symptoms of psychological disorders arise because an individual has learned self-defeating or ineffective ways of behaving. By discovering the environmental contingencies that maintain any undesirable, abnormal behavior, an investigator or clinician can then recommend treatment to change those contingencies and extinguish the unwanted behavior. Behaviorists rely on both classical and operant conditioning models (recall Chapter 6) to understand the processes that can result in maladaptive behavior.

Cognitive Cognitive perspectives on psychopathology are often used to supplement behavioral views. The cognitive perspective suggests that the origins of psychological disorders cannot always be found in the objective reality of stimulus environments, reinforcers, and overt responses. What matters as well is the way people perceive or think about themselves and about their relations with other people and the environment. Among the cognitive variables that can guide—or misguide—adaptive responses are a person's perceived degree of control over important reinforcers, a person's beliefs in his or her ability to cope with threatening events, and interpretations of events in terms of situational or personal factors. The cognitive approach suggests that psychological problems are the result of distortions in perceptions of the reality of a situation, faulty reasoning, or poor problem solving.

Sociocultural The sociocultural perspective on psychopathology emphasizes the role culture plays in both the diagnosis and etiology of abnormal behavior. We already gave you a taste of the impact of culture on diagnosis when we described the problem of objectivity. We suggested that behaviors are interpreted in different ways in different cultures: the threshold at which a certain type of behavior will cause an individual problems in adjustment will depend, in part, on how that behavior is viewed in its cultural context. With respect to etiology, the particular cultural circumstances in which people live may define an environment that helps bring about distinctive types or subtypes of psychopathology.

We have now given you a general sense of the types of explanations researchers give for the emergence of mental illness. It is worth noting that contemporary researchers increasingly take an *interactionist* perspective on psychopathology, seeing it as the product of a complex interaction between a number of biological and psychological factors. For example, genetic predispositions may make a person vulnerable to a psychological disorder by affecting neurotransmitter levels or hormone levels, but psychological or social stresses or certain learned behaviors may be required for the disorder to develop fully.

Now that we have given you a basic framework for thinking about abnormality, we get to the core information that you will want to know—the causes and consequences of major psychological disorders, such as anxiety, depression, and schizophrenia. For each category, we will begin by describing what sufferers experience and how they appear to observers. Then we will consider how each of the major biological and psychological approaches to etiology explains the development of these disorders.

There are many other categories of psychopathology that we will not have time to examine. However, what follows is a capsule summary of some of the most important we must omit:

- *Substance-use disorders* include both dependence on and abuse of alcohol and drugs. We discussed issues of substance abuse in the broader context of states of consciousness (see Chapter 5, pages 152 to 157).
- *Sexual disorders* involve problems with sexual inhibition or dysfunction and deviant sexual practices.
- *Eating disorders,* such as anorexia and bulimia, were discussed in Chapter 11 (see pages 348 to 350).

As you read about the symptoms and experiences that are typical of the various psychological disturbances, you may begin to feel that some of the characteristics seem to apply to you—at least part of the time—or to someone you know. Some of the disorders that we will consider are not uncommon, so it would be surprising if they sounded completely alien. Many people have human frailties that appear on the list of criteria for a particular psychological disorder. Recognition of this familiarity can further your understanding of abnormal psychology, but remember that a diagnosis for any disorder depends on a number of criteria and requires the judgment of a trained mental health professional. Please resist the temptation to use this new knowledge to diagnose friends and family members as pathological. However, if the chapter leaves you uneasy about mental health issues, please note that most colleges and universities have counseling centers for students with such concerns.

---

anxiety disorder Mental disorder marked by psychological arousal, feeling of tension, and intense apprehension without apparent reason.

generalized anxiety disorder An anxiety disorder in which an individual feels anxious and worried most of the time for at least six months when not threatened by any specific danger or object.

STOP AND REVIEW

❶ Jerry has such an overwhelming fear of spiders that he will not enter a room until someone he trusts assures him the room has no spiders in it. By what criteria might we decide that Jerry's behavior is abnormal?

❷ What are three important benefits provided by the classification of mental disorders?

❸ Why does culture play a role in the diagnosis of psychopathology?

CRITICAL THINKING Consider the study in which David Rosenhan and seven other people were admitted to psychiatric hospitals. Why might they have chosen "hallucinations" as their pretend symptom?

Visit MyPsychLab.com for more review and practice on the following topic:

◀◉ **Explore:** The Axes of the *DSM*

Anxiety Disorders

Everyone experiences anxiety or fear in certain life situations. For some people, however, anxiety becomes problematic enough to interfere with their ability to function effectively or enjoy everyday life. It has been estimated that 28.8 percent of the adult population has, at some time, experienced symptoms characteristic of the various **anxiety disorders** (Kessler et al., 2005a). Although anxiety plays a key role in each of these disorders, they differ in the extent to which anxiety is experienced, the severity of the anxiety, and the situations that trigger the anxiety. In this section, we will review five major categories: generalized anxiety disorder, panic disorder, phobic disorder, obsessive-compulsive disorder, and posttraumatic stress disorder. We will then consider the causes of these disorders.

GENERALIZED ANXIETY DISORDER

When a person feels anxious or worried most of the time for at least six months, when not threatened by any specific danger, clinicians diagnose **generalized anxiety disorder.** The anxiety is often focused on specific life circumstances, such as unrealistic concerns about finances or the well-being of a loved one. The way the anxiety is expressed—the specific symptoms—varies from person to person, but for a diagnosis of generalized anxiety disorder to be made, the patient must also suffer from at least three other symptoms, such as muscle tension, fatigue, restlessness, poor concentration, irritability, or sleep difficulties. Among U.S. adults, 5.7 percent have experienced generalized anxiety disorder (Kessler et al., 2005a).

Generalized anxiety disorder leads to impaired functioning because the person's worries cannot be controlled or put aside. With the focus of attention on the sources of anxiety, the individual cannot attend sufficiently to social or job obligations. These difficulties are compounded by the physical symptoms associated with the disorder.

Critical Thinking in Your Life

HOW DO DISORDERS ENTER THE *DSM?*

As this chapter unfolds, you will read several descriptions of psychological disorders that are outlined in *DSM-IV-TR* (2000). Before you consider these disorders, we'd like you to reflect on the process through which clinicians achieve consensus that a particular disorder belongs in the *DSM.* For each disorder, this process begins with close observation: Therapists and researchers pay careful attention to people's symptoms and how those symptoms cluster together. Even for diagnostic categories that are well established—such as the mood disorders that we discuss later in the chapter—researchers continue to collect new data with the goal of improving the reliability and validity of the system of classification (Klein, 2008).

Although *DSM-IV-TR* is a formidable volume, clinical observations continue to lead to proposals for new disorders. An appendix in *DSM-IVs* (1994) briefly described about 20 disorders that had been proposed but required "further study": *DSM-IV's* authors asserted that, given the state of research knowledge, insufficient evidence supported the disorders' inclusion at that moment in time. To provide you with a concrete example of how researchers build the case for a new disorder, we will explore one disorder from that list: *binge eating disorder.*

You already had a brief encounter with binge eating disorder (BED) in Chapter 11. There, we defined BED partially in contrast to another eating disorder: We suggested that BED is diagnosed when people engage in regular episodes of binge eating without the purges that accompany bulimia nervosa. In addition, we suggested that people who suffer from BED experience a loss of control during these binges and that the binges cause them great distress.

Note two important features of this definition (Striegel-Moore & Franko, 2008). First, the definition suggests how BED is different from other eating disorders, despite the overlap in some symptoms (that is, binging). When clinicians propose a new diagnostic category, they must firmly establish that the new disorder is distinct from well-established disorders. Second, the definition of BED mentions a cluster of symptoms. When clinicians propose a new diagnostic category, they are making a strong assertion that a particular set of experiences regularly co-occur.

The definition of a disorder serves, in a sense, as a hypothesis: The clinicians who propose the disorder are predicting that data will confirm that people experience this distinctive constellation of symptoms. For BED, this has proven to be the case. In one study, researchers engaged in face-to-face interviews with 9,282 adults in the United States (Hudson et al., 2007). To determine whether people suffered from BED, they used the major criteria from *DSM-IV.* In their sample, 3.5 percent of the women and 2.0 percent of the men met those criteria. Data of this type support the hypothesis that BED exists as a disorder with a unique set of symptoms and consequences.

Still, some data on BED has encouraged researchers to reexamine features of the diagnosis (Striegel-Moore & Franko, 2008). For example, the definitions of other eating disorders include the diagnostic feature "undue influence of body weight or shape on self-evaluation" (*DSM-IV*, 1994, p. 545). Researchers have begun to consider whether this feature should also be included for BED (Grilo et al., 2008). Studies suggest that people who meet the criteria for BED and who also show "undue influence," experience greater distress than people who do not show this influence. However, researchers have yet to reach consensus on how the inclusion of this feature would affect diagnoses of BED.

The goal of research on BED—as well as on other disorders, old and new—is to provide the most valid possible diagnoses. Researchers labor so that the *DSM* will provide valid diagnoses that allow for the provision of appropriate treatments—and, ultimately, for a minimization of people's distress.

- Why do the defintions of disorders include clusters of symptoms?

- Why does improved diagnosis often allow improved treatment?

PANIC DISORDER

In contrast to the chronic presence of anxiety in generalized anxiety disorder, sufferers of **panic disorder** experience unexpected, severe *panic attacks* that may last only minutes. These attacks begin with a feeling of intense apprehension, fear, or terror. Accompanying these feelings are physical symptoms of anxiety, including autonomic hyperactivity (such as rapid heart rate), dizziness, faintness, or sensations of choking or smothering. The attacks are unexpected in the sense that they are not brought about by something concrete in the situation. A panic disorder is diagnosed when an individual has recurrent unexpected panic attacks and also begins to have persistent concerns about the possibility of having more attacks. Research suggests that 4.7 percent of U.S. adults have experienced panic disorder (Kessler et al., 2006b).

---

panic disorder An anxiety disorder in which sufferers experience unexpected, severe panic attacks that begin with a feeling of intense apprehension, fear, or terror.

Why might agoraphobia cause people to become "prisoners" in their own homes?

In *DSM-IV-TR*, panic disorder must be diagnosed as occurring with or without the simultaneous presence of agoraphobia. **Agoraphobia** is an extreme fear of being in public places or open spaces from which escape may be difficult or embarrassing. Individuals with agoraphobia usually fear such places as crowded rooms, malls, and buses. They are often afraid that, if they experience some kind of difficulty outside the home, such as a loss of bladder control or panic attack symptoms, help might not be available or the situation will be embarrassing to them. These fears deprive individuals of their freedom, and, in extreme cases, they become prisoners in their own homes.

Can you see why agoraphobia is related to panic disorder? For some (but not all) people who suffer from panic attacks, the dread of the next attack—the helpless feelings it engenders—can be enough to imprison them. The person suffering from agoraphobia may leave the safety of home but almost always with extreme anxiety.

PHOBIAS

Fear is a rational reaction to an objectively identified external danger (such as a fire in one's home or a mugging attack) that may induce a person to flee or to attack in self-defense. In contrast, a person with a **phobia** suffers from a persistent and irrational fear of a specific object, activity, or situation that is excessive and unreasonable given the reality of the threat.

Many people feel uneasy about spiders or snakes (or even multiple-choice tests). These mild fears do not prevent people from carrying out their everyday activities. Phobias, however,

---

agoraphobia An extreme fear of being in public places or open spaces from which escape may be difficult or embarrassing.

fear A rational reaction to an objectively identified external danger that may induce a person to flee or attack in self-defense.

phobia A persistent and irrational fear of a specific object, activity, or situation that is excessive and unreasonable, given the reality of the threat.

social phobia A persistent, irrational fear that arises in anticipation of a public situation in which an individual can be observed by others.

specific phobia Phobia that occurs in response to a specific type of object or situation.

interfere with adjustment, cause significant distress, and inhibit necessary action toward goals. Even a very specific, apparently limited phobia can have a great impact on one's whole life. *DSM-IV-TR* defines two categories of phobias: *social phobias* and *specific phobias* (see **Table 14.2**).

Social phobia is a persistent, irrational fear that arises in anticipation of a public situation in which an individual can be observed by others. A person with a social phobia fears that he or she will act in ways that could be embarrassing. The person recognizes that the fear is excessive and unreasonable yet feels compelled by the fear to avoid situations in which public scrutiny is possible. Social phobia often involves a self-fulfilling prophecy. A person may be so fearful of the scrutiny and rejection of others that enough anxiety is created to actually impair performance. Even positive social exchanges cause anxiety for people with social phobia: They worry that they have set standards that they will not be able to meet in the future (Weeks et al., 2008).

Among U.S. adults, 12.1 percent have experienced a social phobia (Ruscio et al., 2008).

Specific phobias occur in response to several different types of objects or situations. As shown in Table 14.2, specific phobias are further categorized into several subtypes. For example, an individual suffering from an *animal-type specific phobia* might have a phobic response to spiders. In each case, the phobic response is produced either in the presence of or in anticipation of the feared specific object or situation. Research suggests that 12.5 percent of adults in the United States have experienced a specific phobia (Kessler et al., 2005a).

OBSESSIVE-COMPULSIVE DISORDER

Some people with anxiety disorders get locked into specific patterns of thought and behavior. Consider the following case:

TABLE 14.2   Common Phobias

Social phobias (fear of being observed doing something humiliating)
Specific phobias
Animal type
Cats (ailurophobia)
Dogs (cynophobia)
Insects (insectophobia)
Spiders (arachnophobia)
Snakes (ophidiophobia)
Rodents (rodentophobia)
Natural environment type
Storms (brontophobia)
Heights (acrophobia)
Blood–injection–injury type
Blood (hemophobia)
Needles (belonephobia)
Situational type
Closed spaces (claustrophobia)
Railways (siderodromophobia)

Only a year or so ago, 17-year-old Jim seemed to be a normal adolescent with many talents and interests. Then, almost overnight, he was transformed into a lonely outsider, excluded from social life by his psychological disabilities. Specifically, he developed an obsession with washing. Haunted by the notion that he was dirty—in spite of what his senses told him—he began to spend more of his time cleansing himself of imaginary dirt. At first, his ritual washings were confined to weekends and evenings, but soon they began to consume all his time, forcing him to drop out of school. (Rapoport, 1989)

Jim is suffering from a condition known as **obsessive-compulsive disorder (OCD),** which has been estimated to affect 1.6 percent of U.S. adults at some point during their lives (Kessler et al., 2005a). *Obsessions* are thoughts, images, or impulses (such as Jim's belief that he is unclean) that recur or persist despite a person's efforts to suppress them. Obsessions are experienced as an unwanted invasion of consciousness, they seem to be senseless or repugnant, and they are unacceptable to the person experiencing them. You probably have had some sort of mild obsessional experience, such as the intrusion of petty worries—"Did I really lock the door?" or "Did I turn off the oven?" The obsessive thoughts of people with obsessive-compulsive disorder are much more compelling, cause much more distress, and may interfere with their social or occupational functioning.

Compulsions are repetitive, purposeful *acts* (such as Jim's washing) performed according to certain rules or in a ritualized manner in response to an obsession. Compulsive behavior is performed to reduce or prevent the discomfort associated with some dreaded situation, but it is either unreasonable or clearly excessive. Typical compulsions include irresistible urges to clean, to check that lights or appliances have been turned off, and to count objects or possessions.

At least initially, people with obsessive-compulsive disorder resist carrying out their compulsions. When they are calm, they view their compulsion as senseless. When anxiety rises, however, the power of the ritual compulsive behavior to relieve tension seems irresistible. Part of the pain experienced by people with this mental problem is created by their frustration at

recognizing the irrationality or excessive nature of their obsessions without being able to eliminate them.

POSTTRAUMATIC STRESS DISORDER

In Chapter 12, we described one psychological consequence of traumatic events: People experience posttraumatic stress disorder (PTSD), an anxiety disorder that is characterized by the persistent reexperience of those traumatic events through distressing recollections, dreams, hallucinations, or flashbacks. Individuals may develop PTSD in response to rape, life-threatening events or severe injury, and natural disasters. People develop PTSD both when they themselves have been the victim of the trauma and when they have witnessed others being victimized. People who suffer from PTSD are also likely to suffer simultaneously from other psychopathologies, such as major depression, substance-abuse problems, and sexual dysfunction (Kilpatrick et al., 2003).

Research suggests that about 6.8 percent of adults in the United States will experience PTSD at some point during their lifetime (Kessler et al., 2005a). Studies consistently reveal that most adults have experienced an event that could be defined as traumatic, such as a serious accident, a tragic death, or physical or sexual abuse (Widom et al., 2005). One study with 1,824 Swedish adults found that 80.8 percent had experienced at least one traumatic event (Frans et al., 2005). In this sample, men had experienced more traumatic events than women, but women were twice as likely to develop PTSD. The researchers suggested that women's greater distress in response to traumatic events helped explain this difference.

Much attention has focused on the prevalence of PTSD in the wake of traumas with widespread impact. For example, one study evaluated Pentagon employees for symptoms of PTSD two years after the terrorist attack on September 11, 2001 (Grieger et al., 2005). Among the employees in the sample, 14 percent reported symptoms of PTSD. Individuals who had actually been injured or who had witnessed dead bodies were the most affected. Another study focused on the soldiers who served in the subsequent war in Iraq (Hoge et al., 2004). Before they were deployed for combat, 5.0 percent of the soldiers met the diagnostic criteria for PTSD. Three to 4 months after returning from Iraq, 12.9 percent of army soldiers and 12.2 percent of Marines were experiencing PTSD.

Posttraumatic stress disorder severely disrupts sufferers' lives. How do researchers go about the complex task of exploring the origins of PTSD and other anxiety disorders? Understanding the origins gives hope to eliminating the psychological distress.

CAUSES OF ANXIETY DISORDERS

How do psychologists explain the development of anxiety disorders? Each of the four etiological approaches we have outlined (biological, psychodynamic, behavioral, and cogni-

Why do people with obsessive-compulsive disorder engage in behaviors such as repetitive hand-washing?

---

obsessive-compulsive disorder (OCD) A mental disorder characterized by obsessions—recurrent thoughts, images, or impulses that recur or persist despite efforts to suppress them—and compulsions—repetitive, purposeful acts performed according to certain rules or in a ritualized manner.

tive) emphasizes different factors. Let's analyze how each adds something unique to the understanding of anxiety disorders.

Biological Various investigators have suggested that anxiety disorders have biological origins. One theory attempts to explain why certain phobias, such as those for spiders or heights, are more common than fears of other dangers, such as electricity. Because many fears are shared across cultures, it has been proposed that, at one time in the evolutionary past, certain fears enhanced our ancestors' chances of survival. Perhaps humans are born with a predisposition to fear whatever is related to sources of serious danger in the evolutionary past. This *preparedness hypothesis* suggests that we carry around an evolutionary tendency to respond quickly and "thoughtlessly" to once-feared stimuli (LoBue & DeLoache, 2008; Öhman & Mineka, 2001). However, this hypothesis does not explain types of phobias that develop in response to objects or situations that would not have had survival meaning over evolutionary history, like fear of needles or driving or elevators.

The ability of certain drugs to relieve and of others to produce symptoms of anxiety offers evidence of a biological role in anxiety disorders (Hoffman & Mathew, 2008; Kalueff & Nutt, 2007). For example, recall from Chapter 3 that when the level of the neurotransmitter GABA in the brain becomes low, people often experience feelings of anxiety. Disorders in the brain's use of the neurotransmitter serotonin are also associated with some anxiety disorders. As we'll see in Chapter 15, drugs that affect GABA or serotonin levels are used as successful treatments for some types of anxiety disorders.

Researchers are also using imaging techniques to examine the brain bases of these disorders. Consider a study of posttraumatic stress disorder.

> Some people who suffer traumatic events develop PTSD, whereas others do not. A team of researchers used fMRI scans to explore differences in patterns of brain activity for individuals in those two categories (Lanius et al., 2003). The study focused on the brain activity that arose when the individuals recalled memories of sad, anxious, and traumatic events. As shown in **Figure 14.1,** those individuals who had experienced a trauma but not developed PTSD showed more activity in areas of the brain that play a role in emotional processing compared to individuals whose traumatic experiences led to PTSD. These differences in brain activity applied for all three types of memories (that is, sad, anxious, and traumatic). The generality of the finding suggests that the traumatic experiences for the individuals who developed PTSD led to a broad disruption of the way in which their brains respond to emotional events.

This study illustrates why brain-imaging techniques can help deepen the understanding of the biological bases of anxiety disorders. Similar results have emerged for other disorders. For example, PET scans have revealed a difference in the function of serotonin receptors between the brains of individuals who suffer from panic disorder and those of control individuals (Nash et al., 2008). These differences may help explain the onset of panic disorder. MRI techniques have revealed very widespread abnormalities in OCD patients' brains. For example, patients with OCD have greater cortical thickness in areas of

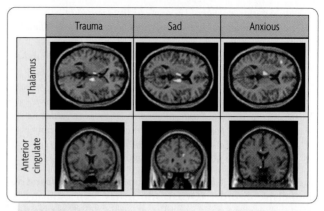

FIGURE 14.1 Brain Activity and Emotional Memories

The study compared individuals who developed PTSD in response to traumatic experiences with those who did not. Members from each group recalled emotional memories while undergoing fMRI scans. The figure shows more brain activity for the group of individuals without PTSD across memories of traumatic, sad, and angry events.

the brain that normally allow people to inhibit behaviors (Narayan et al., 2008). This brain abnormality which potentially hinders communication among neurons may partially explain why people with OCD have difficulty controlling their behavioral compulsions.

Finally, family and twin studies suggest that there is a genetic basis for the predisposition to experience anxiety disorders (Hettema et al., 2005). For example, the probability that a pair of male identical twins both suffered from a social or specific phobia was consistently greater than the probability that both male fraternal twins were sufferers (Kendler et al., 2001). Still, it's important to remember that nature and nurture always interact. For example, recall from Chapter 13 that many aspects of personality are heritable. Research suggests that part of the influence of genes on PTSD arises because people with different personality traits make life choices that decrease or increase the probability that they will experience traumas (Stein et al., 2002).

Psychodynamic The psychodynamic model begins with the assumption that the symptoms of anxiety disorders come from underlying psychic conflicts or fears. The symptoms are attempts to protect the individual from psychological pain. Thus panic attacks are the result of unconscious conflicts bursting into consciousness. Suppose, for example, a child represses conflicting thoughts about his or her wish to escape a difficult home environment. In later life, a phobia may be activated by an object or situation that symbolizes the conflict. A bridge, for example, might come to symbolize the path that the person must traverse from the world of home and family to the outside world. The sight of a bridge would then force the unconscious conflict into awareness, bringing with it the fear and anxiety common to phobias. Avoiding bridges would be a symbolic attempt to stay clear of anxiety about the childhood experiences at home.

In obsessive-compulsive disorders, the obsessive behavior is seen as an attempt to displace anxiety created by a related but far more feared desire or conflict. By substituting an obsession that symbolically captures the forbidden impulse, a person gains some relief. For example, the obsessive fears of dirt experienced by Jim, the adolescent we described earlier, may have their roots in the conflict between his desire to become sexually active and his fear of "dirtying" his reputation. Compulsive preoccupation with carrying out a minor ritualistic task also allows the individual to avoid the original issue that is creating unconscious conflict.

Behavioral Behavioral explanations of anxiety focus on the way symptoms of anxiety disorders are reinforced or conditioned. Investigators do not search for underlying unconscious conflicts or early childhood experiences because these phenomena can't be observed directly. As we saw in Chapter 6, behavioral theories are often used to explain the development of phobias, which are seen as classically conditioned fears: Recall Little Albert, in whom John Watson and Rosalie Rayner instilled a fear of a white rat (see page 172). The behavioral account suggests that a previously neutral object or situation becomes a stimulus for a phobia by being paired with a frightening experience. For example, a child whose mother yells a warning when he or she approaches a snake may develop a phobia about snakes. After this experience, even thinking about snakes may produce a wave of fear. Phobias continue to be maintained by the reduction in anxiety that occurs when a person withdraws from the feared situation.

A behavioral analysis of obsessive-compulsive disorders suggests that compulsive behaviors tend to reduce the anxiety associated with obsessive thoughts—thus reinforcing the compulsive behavior. For example, if a woman fears contamination by touching garbage, then washing her hands reduces the anxiety and is therefore reinforcing. In parallel to phobias, obsessive-compulsive disorders continue to be maintained by the reduction in anxiety that follows from the compulsive behaviors.

Cognitive Cognitive perspectives on anxiety concentrate on the perceptual processes or attitudes that may distort a person's estimate of the danger that he or she is facing. A person may either overestimate the nature or reality of a threat or underestimate his or her ability to cope with the threat effectively. For example, before delivering a speech to a large group, a person with a social phobia may feed his or her anxiety:

> What if I forget what I was going to say? I'll look foolish in front of all these people. Then I'll get even more nervous and start to perspire, and my voice will shake, and I'll look even sillier. Whenever people see me from now on, they'll remember me as the foolish person who tried to give a speech.

People who suffer from anxiety disorders may often interpret their own distress as a sign of impending disaster. Their reaction may set off a vicious cycle in which the person fears disaster, which leads to an increase in anxiety, which in turn worsens the anxiety sensations and confirms the person's fears (Beck & Emery, 1985).

Psychologists have tested this cognitive account by measuring *anxiety sensitivity*: individuals' beliefs that bodily symptoms—such as shortness of breath or heart palpitations—may

have harmful consequences. People high in anxiety sensitivity are likely to agree with statements such as "When I notice that my heart is beating rapidly, I worry that I might have a heart attack." In one study, researchers assessed the anxiety sensitivity of a group of 68 children, ages 10 to 17, all of whom had been exposed to traumatic events (for example, they had witnessed people being killed) (Leen-Feldner et al., 2008). The researchers found a positive correlation between anxiety sensitivity and the children's symptoms of posttraumatic stress disorder: The children who reported the highest levels of anxiety sensitivity were also most likely to report PTSD symptoms. The researchers suggested that high levels of anxiety sensitivity would make reexperience of traumatic events (such as flashbacks) even more frightening.

Research has also found that anxious patients contribute to the *maintenance* of their anxiety by employing cognitive biases that highlight the threatening stimuli. For example, one study examined people's ability to name either body-related words (such as *dizzy, fainting,* and *breathless*) versus control words (such as *delicate, slow,* and *friendly*) when they were presented on a computer screen for only 1/100th of a second. Individuals who suffered from panic disorder showed much greater ability to recognize the body-related words than did the healthy controls (Pauli et al., 1997). Similarly, patients whose symptoms of obsessive-compulsive disorder focused on issues of cleanliness watched a researcher touch a series of objects with a "clean and unused" tissue or a "dirty and already used" tissue. In a later memory test, these OCD patients showed greater ability to recall which objects were "dirty" than which were "clean" (Ceschi et al., 2003). Studies of this type confirm that people suffering from anxiety disorders focus their attention on aspects of the world that may help to sustain their anxiety.

Each of the major approaches to anxiety disorders may explain part of the etiological puzzle. Continued research of each approach will clarify causes and, therefore, potential avenues for treatment. Now that you have this basic knowledge about anxiety disorders, we'd like you to consider the next of the three major categories of abnormality we are covering in some detail—*mood disorders*.

STOP AND REVIEW

❶ What is the relationship between fear and phobias?

❷ What is the difference between an obsession and a compulsion?

❸ With respect to phobias, what is the preparedness hypothesis?

❹ What is the impact of anxiety sensitivity?

CRITICAL THINKING Recall the study in which participants were asked to retrieve memories while undergoing fMRI. Why might the researchers have chosen the three categories of sad, anxious, and traumatic memories?

Visit MyPsychLab.com for more review and practice on the following topics:

◉ **Watch:** Phobias

◉ **Watch:** Posttraumatic Stress Disorder: Sara

Mood Disorders

There have almost certainly been times in your life when you would have described yourself as terribly depressed or incredibly happy. For some people, however, extremes in mood come to disrupt normal life experiences. A **mood disorder** is an emotional disturbance, such as severe depression or depression alternating with mania. Researchers estimate that 20.8 percent of adults have suffered from mood disorders (Kessler et al., 2005a). We will describe two major categories: major depressive disorder and bipolar disorder.

MAJOR DEPRESSIVE DISORDER

Depression has been characterized as the "common cold of psychopathology," both because it occurs so frequently and because almost everyone has experienced elements of the full-scale disorder at some time in his or her life. Everyone has, at one time or another, experienced grief after the loss of a loved one or felt sad or upset when failing to achieve a desired goal. These sad feelings are only one symptom experienced by people suffering from a **major depressive disorder** (see **Table 14.3**). Consider one individual's description of his struggle to carry out normal daily tasks while in the depths of depression:

> It seemed to take the most colossal effort to do simple things. I remember bursting into tears because I had used up the cake of soap that was in the shower. I cried because one of the keys stuck for a second on my computer. I found everything excruciatingly difficult, and so, for example, the prospect of lifting the telephone receiver seemed to me like bench-pressing four hundred pounds. The reality that I had to put on not just one but two socks and then two shoes so overwhelmed me that I wanted to go back to bed. (Solomon, 2001, pp. 85–86)

This excerpt illustrates some vivid consequences of major depressive disorder.

People diagnosed with depression differ in terms of the severity and duration of their symptoms. Many individuals struggle with clinical depression for only several weeks at one point in their lives, whereas others experience depression episodically or chronically for many years. Estimates of the

What are some differences between the occasional feelings of unhappiness that most people feel and the symptoms of major depressive disorder?

prevalence of mood disorders reveal that about 16.6 percent of adults suffer from major depression at some time in their lives (Kessler et al., 2005a).

Depression takes an enormous toll on those afflicted, on their families, and on society. A study undertaken on behalf of the World Health Organization estimated the loss of healthy life years that could be attributed to physical and mental illnesses (World Health Orgnization, 2008). In this analysis, major depressive disorder ranked third (behind lower respiratory infections and diarrheal diseases) in terms of the burden it places on people's lives around the world. For middle- and high-income countries, major depressive disorder ranked first. In the United States, depression accounts for the majority of all mental hospital admissions, but it is still believed to be underdiagnosed and undertreated. The National Comorbidity Study found that only 37.4 percent of individuals sought treatment in the first year after a major depressive episode (Wang et al., 2005). In fact, the median period people waited between experiencing a major depressive episode and seeking treatment was eight years.

BIPOLAR DISORDER

Bipolar disorder is characterized by periods of severe depression alternating with manic episodes. A person experiencing a **manic episode** generally acts and feels unusually elated and expansive. However, sometimes

---

mood disorder A mood disturbance such as severe depression or depression alternating with mania.

major depressive disorder A mood disorder characterized by intense feelings of depression over an extended time, without the manic high phase of bipolar depression.

TABLE 14.3 Characteristics of Major Depressive Disorder	
Characteristics	**Example**
Dysphoric mood	Sad, blue, hopeless; loss of interest or pleasure in almost all usual activities
Appetite	Significant weight loss (while not dieting) or weight gain
Sleep	Insomnia or hypersomnia (sleeping too much)
Motor activity	Markedly slowed down (motor retardation) or agitated
Guilt	Feelings of worthlessness; self-reproach
Concentration	Diminished ability to think or concentrate; forgetfulness
Suicide	Recurrent thoughts of death; suicidal ideas or attempts

the individual's predominant mood is irritability rather than elation, especially if the person feels thwarted in some way. During a manic episode, a person often experiences an inflated sense of self-esteem or an unrealistic belief that he or she possesses special abilities or powers. The person may feel a dramatically decreased need to sleep and may engage excessively in work or in social or other pleasurable activities.

Caught up in a manic mood, the person shows unwarranted optimism, takes unnecessary risks, promises anything, and may give everything away. Consider this first-person account:

> *Manic depression is about buying a dozen bottles of Heinz ketchup and all eight bottles of Windex in stock at the Food Emporium on Broadway at 4:00 A.M., flying from Zurich to the Bahamas and back to Zurich in three days to balance the hot and cold weather, [and] carrying $20,000 in $100 bills in your shoes into the country on your way back from Tokyo . . . . It's about blips and burps of madness, moments of absolute delusion, bliss, and irrational and dangerous choices made in order to heighten pleasure and excitement and to ensure a sense of control. (Behrman, 2002)*

When the mania begins to diminish, people are left trying to deal with the damage and predicaments they created during their period of frenzy. Manic episodes almost always give way to periods of severe depression.

The duration and frequency of the mood disturbances in bipolar disorder vary from person to person. Some people experience long periods of normal functioning punctuated by occasional short manic or depressive episodes. A small percentage of unfortunate individuals go right from manic episodes to clinical depression and back again in continuous, unending cycles that are devastating to them, their families, their friends, and their coworkers. While manic, they may gamble away life savings or give lavish gifts to strangers, acts that later add to guilt feelings when they are in the depressed phase. Bipolar disorder is rarer than major depressive disorder, occurring in about 3.9 percent of adults (Kessler et al., 2005a).

CAUSES OF MOOD DISORDERS

What factors are involved in the development of mood disorders? We will address this question from the biological, psychodynamic, behavioral, and cognitive perspectives. Note that, because of its prevalence, major depressive disorder has been studied more extensively than bipolar disorder. Our review will reflect that distribution of research.

Biological Several types of research provide clues to the contribution of biology to mood disorders. For example, the ability of different drugs to relieve manic and depressive symptoms provides evidence that different brain states underlie the two extremes of bipolar disorder (Thase & Denko, 2008). Reduced levels of two chemical messengers in the brain, serotonin and norepinephrine, have been linked to depression; increased levels of these neurotransmitters are associated with mania.

Researchers are using brain-imaging techniques to understand the causes and consequences of mood disorders (Gotlib & Hamilton, 2008). For example, researchers have

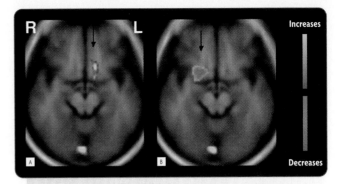

FIGURE 14.2 Brain Activity and Bipolar Disorder

Individuals with bipolar disorder underwent fMRI scans while performing a cognitive task. The brain response was different in an area known as the *caudal ventral prefrontal cortex* (cVPFC) depending on whether the individuals were experiencing elevated, depressed, or balanced moods. As shown in A, individuals in depressed moods showed increased left cVPFC activity by comparison to those in balanced moods. As shown in B, individuals in elevated moods showed reduced right cVPFC activity by comparison to those in balanced moods.

used fMRI to demonstrate that the brains of people who suffer from bipolar disorder respond differently when they are in depressed versus manic states (Blumberg et al., 2003). **Figure 14.2** reports the data from 36 individuals with bipolar disorder. At the time of the study, 11 were in elevated moods, 10 were in depressed moods, and 15 were in *euthymic* (or balanced) emotional states. All of the individuals performed the same cognitive task—naming the colors in which words were printed—while undergoing fMRI scans. Figure 14.2 indicates that particular regions of cortex were more active or less active depending on each individual's particular phase of bipolar disorder.

The contribution of biology to the etiology of mood disorders is also confirmed by evidence that the incidence of mood disorder is influenced by genetic factors (Edvardsen et al., 2008; Kendler et al., 2006). For example, one twin study assessed the likelihood that both twins were diagnosed with bipolar disorder. The correlation was 0.82 for monozygotic twins but only 0.07 for dizygotic twins. These data led to a heritably estimate of 0.77 (Edvarsen et al., 2008). You will see in the *Psychology in Your Life* box on page 460 that researchers have begun to make progress identifying the actual genes that have an impact on individuals' predispositions to experience mood disorders.

Let's see now what the three major psychological approaches can add to your understanding of the onset of mood disorders.

---

bipolar disorder A mood disorder characterized by alternating periods of depression and mania.

manic episode A component of bipolar disorder characterized by periods of extreme elation, unbounded euphoria without sufficient reason, and grandiose thoughts or feelings about personal abilities.

Psychodynamic In the psychodynamic approach, unconscious conflicts and hostile feelings that originate in early childhood are seen to play key roles in the development of depression. Freud was struck by the degree of self-criticism and guilt that depressed people displayed. He believed that the source of this self-reproach was anger, originally directed at someone else, that had been turned inward against the self. The anger was believed to be tied to an especially intense and dependent childhood relationship, such as a parent–child relationship, in which the person's needs or expectations were not met. Losses, real or symbolic, in adulthood reactivate hostile feelings, now directed toward the person's own ego, creating the self-reproach that is characteristic of depression.

Behavioral Rather than searching for the roots of depression in the unconscious, the behavioral approach focuses on the effects of the amount of positive reinforcement and punishments a person receives (Lewinsohn, 1975; Lewinsohn et al., 1985). In this view, depressed feelings result when an individual receives insufficient positive reinforcements and experiences many punishments in the environment following a loss or other major life changes. Without sufficient positive reinforcement, a person begins to feel sad and withdraws. This state of sadness is initially reinforced by increased attention and sympathy from others (Biglan, 1991). Typically, however, friends who at first respond with support grow tired of the depressed person's negative moods and attitudes and begin to avoid him or her. This reaction eliminates another source of positive reinforcement, plunging the person further into depression. Research also shows that depressed people tend to underestimate positive feedback and overestimate negative feedback (Kennedy & Craighead, 1988; Nelson & Craighead, 1977).

Cognitive At the center of the cognitive approach to depression are two theories. One theory suggests that negative *cognitive sets*—"set" patterns of perceiving the world—lead people to take a negative view of events in their lives for which they feel responsible. The second theory, the *explanatory style* model, proposes that depression arises from the belief that one has little or no personal control over significant life events. Each of these models explains some aspects of the experience of depression. Let's see how.

Aaron Beck (1983, 1985, 1988), a leading researcher on depression, has developed the theory of cognitive sets. Beck has argued that depressed people have three types of negative cognitions, which he calls the *cognitive triad* of depression: negative views of themselves, negative views of ongoing experiences, and negative views of the future. Depressed people tend to view themselves as inadequate or defective in some way, to interpret ongoing experiences in a negative way, and to believe that the future will continue to bring suffering and difficulties. This pattern of negative thinking clouds all experiences and produces the other characteristic signs of depression. An individual who always anticipates a negative outcome is not likely to be motivated to pursue any goal, leading to the *paralysis of will* that is prominent in depression.

In the explanatory style view, pioneered by **Martin Seligman,** individuals believe, correctly or not, that they cannot control future outcomes that are important to them. Seligman's theory evolved from research that demonstrated depressionlike symptoms in dogs (and later in other species). Seligman and Maier (1967) subjected dogs to painful, unavoidable shocks: No matter what the dogs did, there was no way to escape the shocks. The dogs developed what Seligman and Maier called **learned helplessness.** Learned helplessness is marked by three types of deficits: *motivational deficits*—the dogs were slow to initiate known actions; *emotional deficits*—they appeared rigid, listless, frightened, and distressed; and *cognitive deficits*—they demonstrated poor learning in new situations. Even when put in a situation in which they could, in fact, avoid shock, they did not learn to do so (Maier & Seligman, 1976).

Seligman believed that depressed people are also in a state of learned helplessness: They have an expectancy that nothing they can do matters (Abramson et al., 1978; Peterson & Seligman, 1984; Seligman, 1975). However, the emergence of this state depends, to a large extent, on how individuals explain their life events. As we discussed in Chapter 11 (see p. 360), there are three dimensions of explanatory style: *internal-external, global-specific,* and *stable-unstable.* Suppose that you have just received a poor grade on a psychology exam. You attribute the negative outcome on the exam to an internal factor ("I'm stupid"), which makes you feel sad, rather than to an external one ("The exam was really hard"), which would have made you angry. You could have chosen a less stable internal quality than intelligence to explain your performance ("I was tired that day"). Rather than attributing your performance to an internal, stable factor that has global or far-reaching influence (stupidity), you could even have limited your explanation to the psychology exam or course ("I'm not good at psychology courses"). Explanatory style theory suggests that individuals who attribute failure to internal, stable, and global causes are vulnerable to depression. This prediction has been confirmed repeatedly (Lau & Eley, 2008; Peterson & Vaidya, 2001).

Once people begin to experience the negative moods associated with major depressive disorder, ordinary cognitive processes make it more difficult for them to escape those moods. Consider a study that demonstrated that depression changes the way in which people attend to information in the world.

Researchers recruited a group of 15 depressed participants and 45 control participants (who had never experienced depression) (Kellough et al., 2008). The participants wore a device that allowed the researchers to monitor eye movements while they viewed visual displays. As you can see in **Figure 14.3,** each display had four photographs that represented the emotion categories sad, threat, positive, and neutral. The participants were told that they were wearing the eye-tracking device so that the researchers could determine the relationship between pupil dilation and emotional images. In fact, the researchers wished to test the hypothesis that depressed individuals would spend more time than control individuals looking at the sad photos and less time looking at the positive photos. The data supported that prediction. The information superimposed on the photographs in Figure 14.3 shows the eye movements of one of the depressed participants. Note that this individual spent most of the trial looking at the crying boy.

---

learned helplessness A general pattern of nonresponding in the presence of noxious stimuli that often follows after an organism has previously experienced noncontingent, inescapable aversive stimuli.

FIGURE 14.3 Attentional Biases in Major Depressive Disorder

Depressed participants and control participants viewed displays with sad, threat, positive, and neutral photographs. Compared to control participants, depressed participants spent more time looking at sad photographs and less time looking at positive photographs. The figure shows eye movement data from a depressed participant. The larger circles indicate that the participant spent more time looking at a particular location.

Kellough, J. L., Beevers, C.G., Ellis, A.J., & Wells, T.T. (2008). Time course of selective attention in clinically depressed young adults: An eye tracking study. *Behaviour Research and Therapy, 46,* 1238–1243.

This research demonstrates that people with major depressive disorder find their attention drawn to sad information in the world. You can understand how this attentional bias could help make depression feel inescapable.

In Chapter 15, we will see that insights generated from cognitive theories of depression have given rise to successful forms of therapy. For now, there are two other important aspects of the study of depression that we will review: the large differences between the prevalence of depression in men and women and the link between depression and suicide.

GENDER DIFFERENCES IN DEPRESSION

One of the central questions of research on depression is why women are afflicted almost twice as often as men (Hyde et al., 2008). Estimates of the prevalence of mood disorders reveal that about 21 percent of females and 13 percent of males suffer a major depression at some time in their lives (Kessler et al., 1994). This gender difference emerges in adolescence, by about ages 13 to 15. One factor that contributes to this difference is, unfortunately, quite straightforward: On average, women experience more negative events and life stressors than men do (Kendler et al., 2004; Shih et al., 2006). For example, women have a greater likelihood of experiencing physical or sexual abuse, and they are more likely to live in poverty while being the primary caregiver for children and elderly parents. Thus women's lives provide more of the types of experiences that lay the groundwork for serious depression.

Research on gender differences has focused on a number of factors that might make women more vulnerable to depression (Hyde et al., 2008). Some of those factors are biological: There might, for example, be hormonal differences that start at puberty that put adolescent girls more at risk for depression than their male peers. Researchers have also looked intensively at cognitive factors that set men and women apart. For example, research by **Susan Nolen-Hoeksema** (2002; Nolen-Hoeksema et al., 1999) contrasts the response styles of men and women once they begin to experience negative moods. On this view, when women experience sadness, they tend to think about the possible causes and implications of their feelings. In contrast, men attempt actively to distract themselves from depressed feelings, either by focusing on something else or by engaging in a physical activity that will take their minds off their current mood state.

This model suggests that the more thoughtful, *ruminative* response style of women—the tendency to focus obsessively on their problems—increases women's vulnerability to depression. Consider a study that examined rumination among a large sample of adolescents.

A group of 1,218 students between the ages of 10 and 17 completed a questionnaire that assessed their responses to life events (Jose & Brown, 2008). The questionnaire included statements like "I sit at home and think about how I feel" and "I think no one will want to be around me if I don't snap out of this mood." The students responded to each statement on a 5-point scale that ranged from "never" to "always." As you can see in **Figure 14.4** on page 458, at the youngest ages there was a modest difference between males and females. However, over the adolescent years the gap grows, with girls engaging in considerably more rumination. The students in the study also completed a measure of depression. For both boys and girls, the students who ruminated the most were also most likely to report the most symptoms of depression. However, the relationship between rumination and depression was even stronger for the girls.

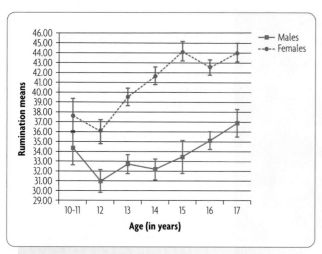

FIGURE 14.4 Gender Differences in Rumination

Across the adolescent years, the gap grows between girls' and boys' reports of rumination.

Jose, P. E., & Brown, I. (2008). When does the gender difference in rumination begin? Gender and age differences in the use of rumination by adolescents. *Journal of Youth and Adolescence, 37*, 180–192. With kind permission of Springer Science + Business Media.

This study supports the hypothesis that rumination is a risk factor for depression: Paying attention to negative moods can increase thoughts of negative events, which eventually increases the quantity and/or the intensity of negative feelings. The study also confirms that men who ruminate are also at risk for depression. The gender difference for depression emerges, in part, because more women ruminate.

SUICIDE

"The will to survive and succeed had been crushed and defeated. . . . There comes a time when all things cease to shine, when the rays of hope are lost" (Shneidman, 1987, p. 57). This sad statement by a suicidal young man reflects the most extreme consequence of any psychological disorder—*suicide*. Although most depressed people do not commit suicide, analyses suggest that many suicides are attempted by those who are suffering from depression (Bolton et al., 2008). In the general U.S. population, the number of deaths officially designated as suicide is around 30,000 each year (Nock et al., 2008). Because many suicides are attributed to accidents or other causes, the actual rate is probably much higher. Because depression occurs more frequently in women, it is not surprising that women *attempt* suicide more often than men do; attempts by men, however, are more often successful (Nock et al., 2008). This difference occurs largely because men use guns more often, and women tend to use less lethal means, such as sleeping pills.

One of the most alarming social problems in recent decades is the rise of *youth suicide*. Although suicide is the eleventh leading cause of death in the United States for all ages, it is third for people ages 15 to 24 (Heron et al., 2008). For every completed suicide, there may be as many as 8 to 20

suicide attempts. To assess the risk of youth suicide, a team of researchers reviewed 128 studies that involved about 500,000 individuals between the ages of 12 and 20 (Evans et al., 2005). Across that broad sample, 29.9 percent of the adolescents had thought about suicide at some point in their lives, and 9.7 percent had actually attempted suicide. Adolescent girls were roughly twice as likely as adolescent boys to have made a suicide attempt.

Youth suicide is not a spur-of-the-moment, impulsive act, but, typically, it occurs as the final stage of a period of inner turmoil and outer distress. The majority of young suicide victims have talked to others about their intentions or have written about them. Thus talk of suicide should always be taken seriously (Rudd et al., 2006). As is the case for adults, adolescents are very likely to attempt suicide when they are experiencing depression (Gutierrez et al., 2004; Nrugham et al., 2008). Feelings of hopelessness and isolation, as well as negative self-concepts, are also associated with suicide risk (Rutter & Behrendt, 2004). Furthermore, gay and lesbian youths are at even higher risk for suicide than are other adolescents (D'Augelli et al., 2005a). These higher suicide rates undoubtedly reflect the relative lack of social support for homosexual orientation. Suicide is an extreme reaction that occurs especially when adolescents feel unable to cry out to others for help. Being sensitive to signs

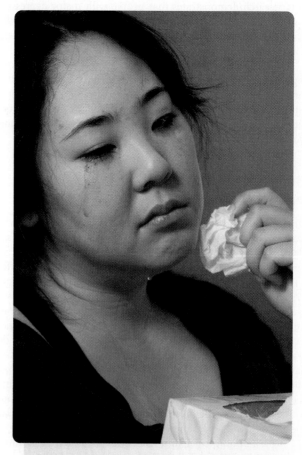

What factors help explain why more women than men experience depression?

Even highly successful individuals, like actor Owen Wilson, are not immune to the feelings of despair that can trigger suicidal thoughts. What has research revealed about the relationship between depression and suicide?

Personality Disorders

A **personality disorder** is a long-standing (chronic), inflexible, maladaptive pattern of perceiving, thinking, or behaving. These patterns can seriously impair an individual's ability to function in social or work settings and can cause significant distress. They are usually recognizable by the time a person reaches adolescence or early adulthood. Personality disorders are coded on Axis II of *DSM-IV-TR*. As shown in **Table 14.4** on page 460, *DSM-IV-TR* organizes 10 types of personality disorders into three clusters.

Diagnoses of personality disorders have sometimes been controversial because of the overlap among the disorders: Some of the same behaviors contribute to diagnoses of different disorders. In addition, researchers have tried to understand the relationship between normal and abnormal personalities. They ask, at what point does an extreme on a particular dimension of personality indicate a disorder (Livesley & Lang, 2005)? For example, most people are somewhat dependent on other people. When does dependence become sufficiently extreme to signal dependent personality disorder? As with other types of psychological disorders, clinicians must understand when and how personality traits become maladaptive—when and how those traits cause either the person or society to suffer. To illustrate that conclusion, we will focus on *borderline personality disorder* and *antisocial personality disorder*.

BORDERLINE PERSONALITY DISORDER

Individuals with **borderline personality disorder** experience great instability and intensity in personal relationships. These difficulties arise in part from difficulties controlling anger. The disorder leads people to have frequent fights and temper tantrums. In addition, people with this disorder display great impulsivity in their behaviors—particularly with respect to behaviors that can relate to self-harm, such as substance abuse or suicide attempts. Among adults in the United States, the prevalence of borderline personality disorder is about 1.6 percent (Lenzenweger et al., 2007).

One important component of borderline personality disorder is an intense fear of abandonment (Lieb et al., 2004). People with this disorder engage in frantic behaviors to prevent abandonment such as frequent phone calls and physical clinging. However, because of their difficulty with emotional control, they are likely to engage in behaviors—angry outbursts and bouts of self-harm—that make it quite difficult to maintain relationships with them. One study that followed people with borderline personality disorder over the course of two years found impaired social functioning across the whole period (Skodol et al., 2005). This research suggests that borderline personality disorder remains stable over time.

Causes of Borderline Personality Disorder As with other disorders, researchers have focused on both the nature and nurture of borderline personality disorder. Twin studies provide strong evidence in favor of a genetic contribution (Distel et al.,

of suicidal intentions and caring enough to intervene are essential for saving the lives of both youthful and mature people who have come to see no exit for their troubles except total self-destruction.

STOP AND REVIEW

① What experiences characterize bipolar disorder?

② In Aaron Beck's theory, what types of negative cognitions make up the cognitive triad?

③ How does the ruminative response style help explain gender differences in depression?

④ What are some suicide risk factors for adolescents?

CRITICAL THINKING Recall the study that demonstrated attentional biases in major depressive disorder. Why might participants have been led to believe the study was about pupil dilation?

Visit MyPsychLab.com for more review and practice on the following topic:

 **Explore:** Bipolar Disorder

---

personality disorder A chronic, inflexible, maladaptive pattern of perceiving, thinking, and behaving that seriously impairs an individual's ability to function in social or other settings.

borderline personality disorder A disorder defined by instability and intensity in personal relationships as well as turbulent emotions and impulsive behaviors.

TABLE 14.4 Personality Disorders

Disorder	Characteristics
Cluster A: People's behavior appears odd or eccentric	
Paranoid	Distrust and suspiciousness about the motives of the individuals with whom they interact
Schizoid	Lack of desire to have social relationships; lack of emotionality in social situations
Schizotypal	Cognitive or perceptual distortions as well as discomfort in social relationships
Cluster B: People's behavior appears dramatic or erratic	
Antisocial	Inability to respect the rights of others; irresponsible or unlawful behavior that violates social norms
Borderline	Instability and intensity in personal relationships; impulsivity, particularly with respect to behaviors that include self-harm
Histrionic	Excessive emotionality and attention seeking; inappropriate sexual or seductive behavior
Narcissistic	Grandiose sense of self-importance and a need for constant admiration; lack of empathy for others
Cluster C: People's behavior appears anxious or fearful	
Avoidant	Avoid interpersonal contact because of risk of rejection; fear criticism and feel inadequate in social situations
Dependent	Need others to take responsibility for major areas of life; feel uncomfortable or helpless without support from other people
Obsessive-Compulsive	Preoccupied with rules and lists; perfectionism interferes with being able to complete tasks

2008). For example, one study compared the rate of concordance for monozygotic versus dizygotic twins (Torgersen et al., 2000). When one MZ twin had borderline personality disorder, 35.3 percent of their siblings also had the disorder; for DZ twins, only 6.7 percent of their siblings also had the disorder. If you recall the discussion in Chapter 13 about the strong heritability of personality traits, you might not be surprised that disorders of those traits are also heritable.

Still, research suggests that environmental factors make a strong contribution in the etiology of borderline personality disorder (Cohen et al., 2008; Lieb et al., 2004). One study compared the incidence of early traumatic events for 66 patients with the disorder to 109 healthy controls (Bandelow et al., 2005). The patients had considerably different lives. For example, 73.9 percent of the patients with borderline personality disorder reported childhood sexual abuse; only 5.5 percent of the controls did so. The patients reported, on average, that the abuse started at age 6 and lasted for 3½ years. That early trauma likely contributed to the incidence of the disorder. However, not all people who endure childhood sexual abuse develop borderline personality disorder—witness the 5.5 percent of control participants in this study who survived childhood sexual abuse but did not develop the disorder. It is likely that a combination of genetic risk and traumatic events explains the etiology of the disorder.

ANTISOCIAL PERSONALITY DISORDER

Antisocial personality disorder is marked by a long-standing pattern of irresponsible or unlawful behavior that violates social norms. Lying, stealing, and fighting are common behaviors. People with antisocial personality disorder often do not experience shame or remorse for their hurtful actions. Violations of social norms begin early in their lives—disrupting class, get-

ting into fights, and running away from home. Their actions are marked by indifference to the rights of others. Among adults in the United States, the prevalence of antisocial personality disorder is about 1.0 percent (Lenzenweger et al., 2007).

Antisocial personality disorder is often comorbid with other pathologies. For example, in one study of adults with histories of alcohol or drug abuse the prevalence of antisocial personality disorder was 18.3 percent for men and 14.1 percent for women—considerably higher than the 1.0 percent prevalence for the general population (Goldstein et al., 2007). In addition, antisocial personality disorder also puts people at risk for suicide, even in the absence of major depressive disorder (Hills et al., 2005). This suicide risk is likely to be a product of the impulsivity and disregard for safety that characterizes the disorder.

Why do people with antisocial personality disorder often have legal difficulties?

---

antisocial personality disorder A disorder characterized by stable patterns of irresponsible or unlawful behavior that violates social norms.

HOW CAN WE PINPOINT INTERACTIONS OF NATURE AND NURTURE?

Throughout this chapter, we have asserted that major types of mental illnesses have a genetic component. The majority of those claims have been based on methods that should be quite familiar to you by this point in *Psychology and Life*. Researchers, for example, compare the rate at which monozygotic and dizygotic twins share the same psychopathology to offer estimates of the heritability of each type of disorder (Coolidge et al., 2001; Hettema et al., 2001). However, in recent years, researchers have begun to move beyond calculations of heritability to pinpoint the actual differences in genetic material that predispose some individuals to experience mental illness. Let's consider a study that establishes an important relationship between genetic variation and life experiences in the etiology of depression.

When we discussed mood disorders, we noted that disruptions in the function of the neurotransmitter serotonin play a role in depression. For that reason, researchers have focused attention on a gene that has an impact on the serotonin system (Caspi et al., 2003). The gene comes in short (s) and long (l) forms. For 847 individuals in a longitudinal study in New Zealand, researchers determined their status for this gene. In the sample, 17 percent had two short versions of the gene (s/s), 51 percent had one short and one long (s/l), and 31 percent had two long versions (l/l). The participants

themselves provided information about the stressors they had weathered in their lives. For ages 21 to 26, they indicated whether they had experienced such events as employment or financial crises, health problems, or relationship issues. Across the genotypes (that is, s/s, s/l, l/l), no one group experienced more life stressors than another. That's an important result: It suggests that any group differences in the prevalence of depression cannot be attributed to easier or harder lives. Instead, we learn that people's genotypes predispose them to respond differently to similar experiences.

The researchers' final step was to determine which participants in the study had suffered from major depressive disorder. As seen in the figure, the pattern that emerged was quite dramatic. In general, people

who had experienced more stressful life events were more likely to experience an episode of major depression. However, as the figure shows, genotypes had an important impact as well. For participants in possession of one or, more so, two copies of the short version of the gene, the impact of negative life events was amplified.

This study makes many of the ideas we've discussed about nature and nurture quite concrete. These researchers have demonstrated that a known genetic difference in combination with negative life events greatly increases the likelihood that people will experience depression. Breakthroughs in the understanding of the human genome allow researchers to determine exactly how nature and nurture interact.

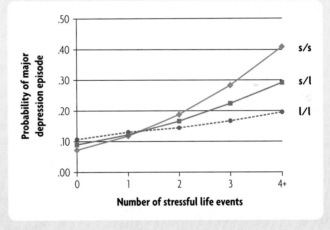

Causes of Antisocial Personality Disorder Researchers have used twin studies to examine genetic components of specific behaviors associated with antisocial personality disorder. For example, one study examined the concordance in behaviors for 3,687 pairs of twins (Viding et al., 2005). Teachers responded to statements about each twin to indicate the presence of callous-unemotional traits (such as "Does not show feelings or emotions") and antisocial behavior (such as "Often fights with other children or bullies them"). The comparisons of MZ and DZ twins suggested that the tendency to display callous-unemotional traits had a strong genetic component. In addition, for twins who displayed high levels of those callous-

emotional traits, genetics also made a strong contribution to antisocial behavior.

Research has also focused on the environmental circumstances that give rise to personality disorders (Paris, 2003). Consider this study of the relationship between parenting practices and antisocial personality traits.

A team of researchers assessed 742 men and women for personality traits that met *DSM-IV* criteria for antisocial personality disorder (Reti et al., 2002). The participants reported on their parents' behaviors toward them during childhood by completing the *Parental Bonding Instrument*

(PBI). The PBI posed a range of questions to which participants responded on a 4-point scale. Some of the questions measured the extent to which parents showed caring for the child (for example, "Could make me feel better when I was upset"). Other questions measured the extent to which parents restricted the child's behavior (for example, "Let me dress in any way I pleased"). A third type of question measured the extent to which parents allowed the child psychological freedom (for example, "Tried to control everything I did"). The researchers looked for relationships between the participants' responses on the PBI and the extent to which they showed antisocial personality traits. The researchers found that the people who reported low levels of parental care had high levels of antisocial personality traits. Also, those individuals who believed that their mothers had been particularly overprotective also had high levels of antisocial personality traits.

The researchers were quick to assert that correlation is not causation. It's possible that parenting behaviors brought about antisocial personality traits; it's also possible that children whose behavior was influenced by antisocial traits negatively affected the way their parents behaved toward them. Still, the results suggest that researchers could observe family patterns to determine what children might be at risk to develop adult forms of antisocial personality disorder.

STOP AND REVIEW

❶ What intense fear do people with borderline personality disorder have with respect to interpersonal relationships?

❷ How do the early lives of people with borderline personality disorder compare to those of healthy controls?

❸ Why are people with antisocial personality disorder at risk for suicide?

CRITICAL THINKING Consider the study that assessed the impact of parenting on antisocial personality traits. Why might the researchers have assessed the three different dimensions of parenting?

Visit MyPsychLab.com for more review and practice on the following topics:

👁 **Watch:** Janna: Borderline Personality Disorder

👁 **Watch:** Antisocial Personality Disorder: Paul

---

somatoform disorder A disorder in which people have physical illnesses or complaints that cannot be fully explained by actual medical conditions.

hypochondriasis A disorder in which individuals are preoccupied with having or getting physical ailments despite reassurances that they are healthy.

somatization disorder A disorder characterized by unexplained physical complaints in several categories over many years.

conversion disorder A disorder in which psychological conflict or stress brings about loss of motor or sensory function.

Somatoform and Dissociative Disorders

As we have reviewed various types of psychological disorders, you have seen how certain everyday experiences can, pushed to the limit, lead to disability or maladaptive behavior. For example, everyone experiences anxiety, but for some people those experiences become so severe that they develop an anxiety disorder. Similarly, many people experience symptoms for physical illnesses that don't have any obvious causes; many people have days when they just "don't feel like themselves." However, when those types of experiences impair individuals' day-to-day life, they may indicate *somatoform disorders* or *dissociative disorders*. We will review the symptoms and etiology of each type of disorder.

SOMATOFORM DISORDERS

A person suffering from a **somatoform disorder** has physical illnesses or complaints that cannot be fully explained by actual medical conditions. To be diagnosed with one of these disorders, people must experience the illnesses or complaints to an extent that they cause sufficient distress to interfere with their everyday functioning. We will focus on *hypochondriasis, somatization disorder*, and *conversion disorder*.

Individuals with **hypochondriasis** believe they have physical illnesses despite assurance from medical practitioners that they do not. Even when they are currently healthy, they may be constantly fearful that they will contact physical illnesses. In addition, this preoccupation with being or getting ill causes such sufficient distress that individuals are impaired in their day-to-day lives. To assess the prevalence of hypochondriasis and other somatoform disorders, researchers often focus on people who present themselves for medical treatment. In that context, the question becomes what proportion of people have physical complaints that don't allow medical explanations. Research suggests that 4.7 percent of adults 18 and older who seek medical treatment meet *DSM-IV-TR* criteria for hypochondriasis (Fink et al., 2004).

Individuals with **somatization disorder** present a long history of physical complaints over many years. Those complaints—which remain medically unexplained—must span several medical categories. To meet *DSM-IV-TR* criteria for the diagnosis, individuals must have experienced four pain symptoms (such as headaches or stomachaches), two gastrointestinal symptoms (such as nausea or diarrhea), one sexual symptom (such as erectile dysfunction or excessive menstrual bleeding), and one neurological symptom (such as paralysis or double vision). Among adults seeking medical treatment, 1.5 percent meet criteria for somatization disorder (Fink et al., 2004).

Both hypochondriasis and somatization disorder are defined by people's complaints about physical symptoms. However, people with hypochondriasis worry about having a specific underlying disease whereas those with somatization disorder focus more on the symptoms themselves. In addition, as you've just seen, to be diagnosed with somatization disorder people must have reported a wide variety of unexplained physical complaints.

Conversion disorder is characterized by a loss of motor or sensory function that cannot be explained by damage to the nervous system or other physical damage. For example, individuals may experience paralysis or blindness without a medical cause. In addition, the onset of the physical symptoms must be preceded by psychological factors such as interpersonal conflict or emotional stressors. Historically, conversion disorder was called *hysteria*—and was believed to represent, in some eras, possession by the devil. Sigmund Freud helped bring about the contemporary understanding of conversion disorder. One of his most enduring insights was that psychological trauma could yield physical symptoms. Conversion disorder is present in 1.5 percent of adults seeking medical treatment (Fink et al., 2004).

Causes of Somatoform Disorders

The defining characteristic of somatoform disorders is that individuals experience physical ailments that have no adequate medical explanation. Researchers have attempted to understand how that could be possible: How, for example, could individuals whose motor systems are intact experience paralysis? Studies have used neuroimaging techniques to discover the brain bases of conversion disorder (Black et al., 2004). Consider a study that demonstrated that individuals with conversion symptoms show different patterns of brain activity than individuals who are only simulating the same symptoms.

> The study focused on four patients who had weakness in one of their ankles that was not the result of any neurological disorder (Stone et al., 2007). The patients underwent fMRI scans while they attempted to flex both the affected ankles and their normal ankles. The researchers also recruited four healthy individuals to serve as controls. The researchers instructed the controls to simulate the conversion symptoms by imagining that one ankle was "too weak and heavy to move" (p. 963). The patterns of brain activity for the patients and controls showed intriguing differences. In particular, the patients' fMRI scans suggested that they were expending greater mental effort than the controls when they tried to flex their weak ankles.

To understand these results, you might take a moment to see what it feels like to simulate an ankle that you cannot flex. It takes some mental effort not to let the ankle bend. However, the study suggests that people with conversion symptoms focus even more effort in their unsuccessful attempts to overcome the weakness.

Researchers have also examined cognitive processes that contribute to somatoform disorders (Brown, 2004). For example, an important aspect of hypochondriasis is an attentional bias in the way that individuals respond to bodily sensations.

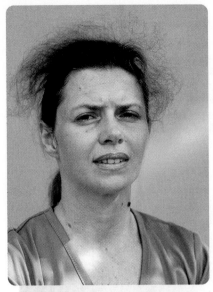

When found in a park in Florida, this woman (dubbed "Jane Doe" by authorities) was emaciated, incoherent, and near death. She was suffering from severe amnesia in which she had lost not only the memory of her name and her past but also the ability to read and write. What types of traumas may lead to dissociative amnesia?

Suppose you wake up one morning with a scratchy throat. If you have an attentional bias that makes it difficult to divert your thoughts from that scratchy throat, you might come to believe that you are seriously ill. In fact, one study demonstrated that people who experience a high level of anxiety about their health find it difficult to disengage their attention even from words such as *cancer*, *tumor*, and *stroke* (Owens et al., 2004). The tight focus on symptoms and illness contributes to a vicious cycle: Stress and anxiety have physical consequences (for example, increased sweating and elevated heart rate) that can feel like the symptoms of illness—providing further proof that the health anxiety is appropriate. Someone who attributes all physical symptoms to illness may perceive a perilous pattern in the co-occurrence of a scratchy throat, excessive sweating, and a swiftly beating heart. Thus the cognitive biases associated with somatoform disorders serve to exaggerate minor bodily sensations.

DISSOCIATIVE DISORDERS

A **dissociative disorder** is a disturbance in the integration of identity, memory, or consciousness. It is important for people to see themselves as being in control of their behavior, including emotions, thoughts, and actions. Essential to this perception of self-control is the sense of selfhood—the consistency of different aspects of the self and the continuity of identity over time and place. Psychologists believe that, in dissociated states, individuals escape from their conflicts by giving up this precious consistency and continuity—in a sense, disowning part of themselves. The forgetting of important personal experiences, a process caused by psychological factors in the absence of any organic dysfunction, called **dissociative amnesia,** is one example of dissociation. For some people, the loss of ability to recall their past is accompanied by an actual flight from their home or place of work. This disorder is called **dissociative fugue.** People may remain in a fugue state for hours, days, or months; they may live with a new identity in a new location.

Dissociative identity disorder (DID), formerly known as *multiple personality disorder,* is a dissociative mental disorder

---

dissociative disorder A personality disorder marked by a disturbance in the integration of identity, memory, or consciousness.

dissociative amnesia The inability to remember important personal experiences, caused by psychological factors in the absence of any organic dysfunction.

dissociative fugue A disorder characterized by a flight from home or work accompanied by a loss of ability to recall the personal past.

dissociative identity disorder (DID) A dissociative mental disorder in which two or more distinct personalities exist within the same individual; formerly known as multiple personality disorder.

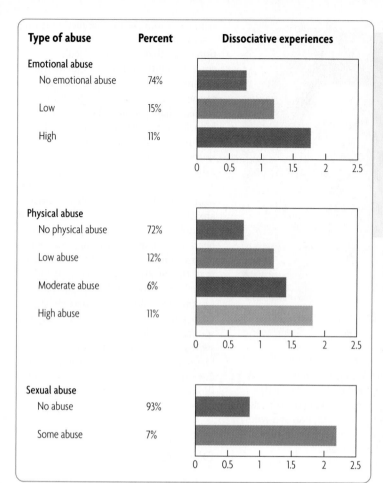

Type of abuse	Percent	Dissociative experiences
Emotional abuse		
No emotional abuse	74%	
Low	15%	
High	11%	
Physical abuse		
No physical abuse	72%	
Low abuse	12%	
Moderate abuse	6%	
High abuse	11%	
Sexual abuse		
No abuse	93%	
Some abuse	7%	

FIGURE 14.5 Victimization and Dissociative Symptoms

Adolescents provided information about their experiences of victimization and their dissociative symptoms. As indicated by the percent figures, the majority of the children had not experienced any abuse. The children who had been abused reported more dissociative symptoms.

Data from Martínez-Taboas, A., Canino, G., Wang, M. Q., Garcías, P., & Bravo, M. (2006). Prevalence of victimization correlates of pathological dissociation in a community sample of youths. *Journal of Traumatic Stress, 19,* 439–448. Reprinted with permission of John Wiley & Sons.

in which two or more distinct personalities exist within the same individual. At any particular time, one of these personalities is dominant in directing the individual's behavior. Dissociative identity disorder is popularly known as *split personality* and sometimes mistakenly called *schizophrenia*, a disorder, as we will see in the next section, in which personality often is impaired but is not split into multiple versions. In DID, each of the emerging personalities contrasts in some significant way with the original self—it might be outgoing if the person is shy, tough if the original personality is weak, and sexually assertive if the other is fearful and sexually naive. Each personality has a unique identity, name, and behavior pattern. In some cases, dozens of different characters emerge to help the person deal with a difficult life situation. Here is an excerpt from a first-person account of a woman who experiences DID (Mason, 1997, p. 44):

> *Just as waves turn the ocean inside out and rearrange the water, different ones of us cycle in and out in an ebb and flow that is sometimes gentle, sometimes turbulent. A child colors with Crayola markers. She moves aside to make way for the administrator, who reconciles the bank statement. A moment later, the dead baby takes over and lies paralyzed on the floor. She remains that way for a while, but no one gets upset—it's her turn. The live baby stops in her crawl, engrossed by a speck of dust. The*

> *cooker prepares meals for three days and packages each separately—we all have different likes and dislikes. A terrified one screams aloud, a wounded one moans, a grieving one wails.*

Can you put yourself in this woman's place, and imagine what it would be like to have this range of "individuals"—the child, the dead baby, the live baby, the cooker, and so on—inside your one head?

Causes of Dissociative Disorders Psychologists who take a psychodynamic perspective have suggested that dissociation serves a vital survival function. They suggest that people who have experienced traumatic stress will sometimes use defense mechanisms to push the traumatic events out of conscious awareness. Consider a study that focused on the life experiences of 891 11- to 17-year-old adolescents in Puerto Rico (Martínez-Taboas et al., 2006). The children completed questionnaires that assessed the presence of victimization experiences and dissociative symptoms in their lives. As you can see in **Figure 14.5,** relatively few of the children in the sample had experienced high levels of victimization. For example, 74 percent of the adolescents had not experienced any emotional abuse. However, Figure 14.5 also reveals that increasing levels of emotional, physical, and sexual abuse were accompanied by higher levels of dissociative symptoms.

Although these data—and personal accounts of the type we quoted earlier—seem compelling, many psychologists remain skeptical about the link between trauma and dissociation (Kihlstrom, 2005). This skepticism has been particularly focused on dissociative identity disorder. No solid data exist about the prevalence of this disorder (*DSM-IV-TR*, 2000). In fact, some critics have suggested that diagnoses of DID have increased because of the media attention paid to individuals who claim to have large numbers of distinct personalities (Lilienfeld & Lynn, 2003). Skeptics have often suggested that therapists who "believe" in DID may create DID—these therapists question their patients, often under hypnosis, in a way that encourages multiple personalities to "emerge." Researchers have tried to find rigorous methods to test the claims people with DID make about the separation between different identities. For example, studies have examined *interidentity amnesia* by assessing the extent to which information acquired by one identity is known to another. Research results fail to support the claim that amnesia occurs between identities (Kong et al., 2008).

Researchers on DID generally acknowledge that not all diagnoses are appropriate. However, many psychologists believe that sufficient evidence has accumulated in favor of the DID diagnosis to indicate that it is not always the product of zealous therapists (Gleaves et al., 2001). The safest conclusion may be that, of the group of people diagnosed with DID, some cases are genuine, whereas other cases emerge in response to therapists' demands.

STOP AND REVIEW

❶ Howard believes that his headaches prove he has a brain tumor, despite his doctor's assurances that he is fine. From which somatoform disorder might Howard suffer?

❷ How is dissociative amnesia defined?

❸ What does research suggest about the life experiences that play a role in the etiology of dissociative identity disorder?

CRITICAL THINKING Recall the study that examined the brain bases of conversion symptoms. Why was it important that the patients with conversion symptoms didn't show differences in brain activity while in a resting state?

Visit MyPsychLab.com for more review and practice on the following topics:

👁 **Watch:** Hypochondriasis: Henry

👁 **Watch:** Dissociative Identity Disorder: The Three Faces of Eve

Schizophrenic Disorders

Everyone knows what it is like to feel depressed or anxious, even though most of us never experience these feelings to the degree of severity that constitutes a disorder. Schizophrenia, however, is a disorder that represents a qualitatively different experience from normal functioning. A **schizophrenic disorder** is a severe form of psychopathology in which personality seems to disintegrate, thought and perception are distorted, and emotions are blunted. The person with a schizophrenic disorder is the one you most often conjure up when you think about madness or insanity. Although schizophrenia is relatively rare—approximately 0.7 percent of U.S. adults have suffered from schizophrenia at some point in their lives (Tandon et al., 2008)—this figure translates to around 2 million people affected by this most mysterious and tragic mental disorder.

Mark Vonnegut, son of novelist Kurt Vonnegut, was in his early 20s when he began to experience symptoms of schizophrenia. In *The Eden Express* (1975), he tells the story of his break with reality and his eventual recovery. Once, while pruning some fruit trees, his reality became distorted:

> *I began to wonder if I was hurting the trees and found myself apologizing. Each tree began to take on personality. I began to wonder if any of them liked me. I became completely absorbed in looking at each tree and began to notice that they were ever so slightly luminescent, shining with a soft inner light that played around the branches. And from out of nowhere came an incredibly wrinkled, iridescent face. Starting as a small point infinitely distant, it rushed forward, becoming infinitely huge. I could see nothing else. My heart had stopped. The moment stretched forever. I tried to make the face go away but it mocked me. . . . I tried to look the face in the eyes and realized I had left all familiar ground. (1975, p. 96)*

Vonnegut's description gives you a glimpse at the symptoms of schizophrenia.

In the world of schizophrenia, *thinking* becomes illogical; associations among ideas are remote or without apparent pattern. *Hallucinations* often occur, involving imagined sensory perception—sights, smells, or, most commonly, sounds (usually voices)—that patients assume to be real. A person may hear a voice that provides a running commentary on his or her behavior or may hear several voices in conversation. **Delusions** are also common; these are false or irrational beliefs maintained in spite of clear contrary evidence. *Language* may become incoherent—a "word salad" of unrelated or made-up words—or an individual may become mute. *Emotions* may be flat, with no visible expression, or they may be inappropriate to the situation. *Psychomotor behavior* may be disorganized (grimaces, strange mannerisms), or posture may become rigid. Even when only some of these symptoms are present, deteriorated functioning in work and interpersonal relationships is likely as the patient withdraws socially or becomes emotionally detached.

Psychologists divide the symptoms between a positive category and a negative category. During *acute* or *active phases* of

---

schizophrenic disorder Severe form of psychopathology characterized by the breakdown of integrated personality functioning, withdrawal from reality, emotional distortions, and disturbed thought processes.

delusion False or irrational belief maintained despite clear evidence to the contrary.

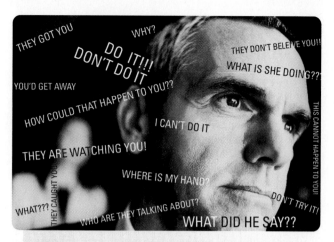

What patterns of thoughts may indicate that a person is experiencing schizophrenia?

Paranoid Type Individuals suffering from this form of schizophrenia experience complex and systematized delusions focused around specific themes:

- *Delusions of persecution.* Individuals feel that they are being constantly spied on and plotted against and that they are in mortal danger.
- *Delusions of grandeur.* Individuals believe that they are important or exalted beings—millionaires, great inventors, or religious figures such as Jesus Christ. Delusions of persecution may accompany delusions of grandeur—an individual is a great person but is continually opposed by evil forces.
- *Delusional jealousy.* Individuals become convinced—without due cause—that their mates are unfaithful. They contrive data to fit the theory and "prove" the truth of the delusion.

Individuals with paranoid schizophrenia rarely display obviously disorganized behavior. Instead, their behavior is likely to be intense and quite formal.

Undifferentiated Type This is the grab-bag category of schizophrenia, describing a person who exhibits prominent delusions, hallucinations, incoherent speech, or grossly disorganized behavior that fits the criteria of more than one type or of no clear type. The hodgepodge of symptoms experienced by these individuals does not clearly differentiate among various schizophrenic reactions.

Residual Type Individuals diagnosed as residual type have usually suffered from a major past episode of schizophrenia but are currently free of major positive symptoms such as hallucinations or delusions. The ongoing presence of the disorder is signaled by minor positive symptoms or negative symptoms like flat emotion. A diagnosis of residual type may indicate that the person's disease is entering *remission*, or becoming dormant.

schizophrenia, the positive symptoms—hallucinations, delusions, incoherence, and disorganized behavior—are prominent. At other times, the negative symptoms—social withdrawal and flattened emotions—become more apparent. Some individuals, such as Mark Vonnegut, experience only one or a couple of acute phases of schizophrenia and recover to live normal lives. Others, often described as chronic sufferers, experience either repeated acute phases with short periods of negative symptoms or occasional acute phases with extended periods of negative symptoms. Even the most seriously disturbed are not acutely delusional all the time.

MAJOR TYPES OF SCHIZOPHRENIA

Because of the wide variety of symptoms that can characterize schizophrenia, investigators consider it not a single disorder but rather a constellation of separate types. The five most commonly recognized subtypes are outlined in **Table 14.5**.

Disorganized Type In this subtype of schizophrenia, a person displays incoherent patterns of thinking and grossly bizarre and disorganized behavior. Emotions are flattened or inappropriate to the situation. Often, a person acts in a silly or childish manner, such as giggling for no apparent reason. Language can become so incoherent, full of unusual words and incomplete sentences, that communication with others breaks down. If delusions or hallucinations occur, they are not organized around a coherent theme.

Catatonic Type The major feature of the catatonic type of schizophrenia is a disruption in motor activity. Sometimes people with this disorder seem frozen in a stupor. For long periods of time, the individual can remain motionless, often in a bizarre position, showing little or no reaction to anything in the environment. At other times, these patients show excessive motor activity, apparently without purpose and not influenced by external stimuli. The catatonic type is also characterized by extreme *negativism*, an apparently unmotivated resistance to all instructions.

TABLE 14.5 Types of Schizophrenic Disorders	
Types of Schizophrenia	**Major Symptoms**
Disorganized	Inappropriate behavior and emotions; incoherent language
Catatonic	Frozen, rigid, or excitable motor behavior
Paranoid	Delusions of persecution or grandeur
Undifferentiated	Mixed set of symptoms with thought disorders and features from other types
Residual	Free from major symptoms but evidence from minor symptoms of continuation of the disorder

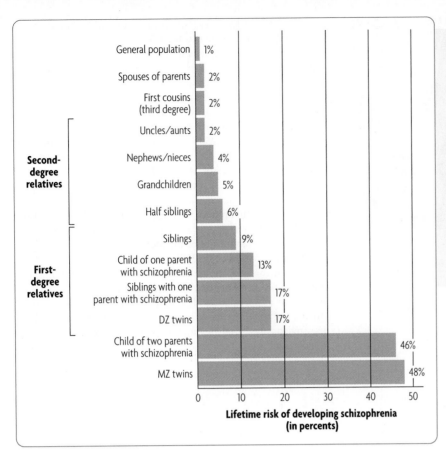

FIGURE 14.6 Genetic Risk of Developing Schizophrenia

The graph shows average risks for developing schizophrenia. Data were compiled from family and twin studies conducted in European populations between 1920 and 1987; the degree of risk correlates highly with the degree of genetic relatedness. Except when the label indicates otherwise, the data reflect the relationship between an individual and someone who has been diagnosed with schizophrenia. For example, the DZ twin of someone diagnosed with schizophrenia has a 17 percent chance of sharing the diagnosis.

CAUSES OF SCHIZOPHRENIA

Different etiological models point to very different initial causes of schizophrenia, different pathways along which it develops, and different avenues for treatment. Let's look at the contributions several of these models can make to an understanding of the way a person may develop a schizophrenic disorder.

Genetic Approaches It has long been known that schizophrenia tends to run in families (Bleuler, 1978; Kallmann, 1946). Three independent lines of research—family studies, twin studies, and adoption studies—point to a common conclusion: Persons related genetically to someone who has had schizophrenia are more likely to become affected than those who are not (Owen & O'Donovan, 2003). A summary of the risks of being affected with schizophrenia through various kinds of relatives is shown in **Figure 14.6.** Schizophrenia researcher **Irving Gottesman** (1991) pooled these data from about 40 reliable studies conducted in Western Europe between 1920 and 1987; he dropped the poorest data sets. As you can see, the data are arranged according to degree of genetic relatedness, which correlates highly with the degree of risk. For example, when both parents have suffered from schizophrenia, the risk for their offspring is 46 percent, as compared with 1 percent in the general population. When only one parent has had schizophrenia, the risk for the offspring drops sharply, to 13 percent. Note also that the probability that identical twins will both have schizophrenia is roughly three times greater than the probability for fraternal twins.

Because the heritability of schizophrenia is so firmly established, researchers have turned their attention toward discovering the specific genes that may put people at risk for the disorder. As you've seen, there are several major types of schizophrenia with a variety of different symptoms. For that reason, researchers believe that a number of genes will have an impact on when and how people will be affected: Research evidence has emerged that associates several candidate genes with the disorder (Shi et al., 2008). Different people's experience of schizophrenia—with respect, for example, to the severity of their symptoms—may depend on exactly the combination of genes they inherit.

Brain Function Another biological approach to the study of schizophrenia is to look for abnormalities in the brains of individuals suffering from the disorder. Much of this research now relies on brain-imaging techniques that allow direct comparisons to be made between the structure and functioning of the brains of individuals with schizophrenia and normal control individuals (Keshavan et al., 2008). For example, as shown in **Figure 14.7,** magnetic resonance imaging has shown that the *ventricles*—the brain structures through which cerebrospinal fluid flows—are often enlarged in individuals with schizophrenia (Barkataki et al., 2006). MRI studies also demonstrate that individuals with schizophrenia have measurably thinner regions in frontal and temporal lobes of cerebral cortex; the loss of neural tissue presumably relates to the disorder's behavioral abnormalities (Kuperberg et al., 2003).

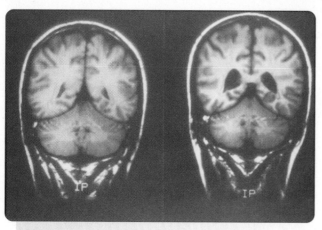

FIGURE 14.7 Schizophrenia and Ventricle Size

Male identical twins underwent MRI scans. The scan of the twin with schizophrenia (on the right) reveals enlarged ventricles compared to the scan of the twin without the disorder (on the left).

Photo courtesy of Drs. E. Fuller Torrey and Daniel Weinberger.

Researchers have also begun to document that some brain abnormalities are related to the progress of the disease (Brans et al., 2008). For example, **Figure 14.8** presents the data from a longitudinal study of 12 individuals who began to experience symptoms of schizophrenia by age 12 (Thompson et al., 2001). The study focused on changes in gray matter (largely the cell bodies and dendrites of nerve cells in the cortex) over a five-year period. The 12 patients underwent repeated MRI scans, as did an age-matched group of healthy control participants. You may recall from Chapter 10 that adolescent brains are still undergoing processes of change. That's why even the normal adolescents experience some loss of gray matter. However, as you can see in Figure 14.8, the loss of gray matter for the adolescents with schizophrenia was quite dramatic. By monitoring for such changes in people at genetic risk for schizophrenia, clinicians may be able to offer diagnosis and treatment earlier in the disorder (Wood et al., 2008).

Given the wide range of symptoms of schizophrenia, you are probably not surprised by the comparably wide range of biological abnormalities that may be either causes or consequences of the disorder. What are the ways in which features of the environment may prompt people who are at risk to develop the disease?

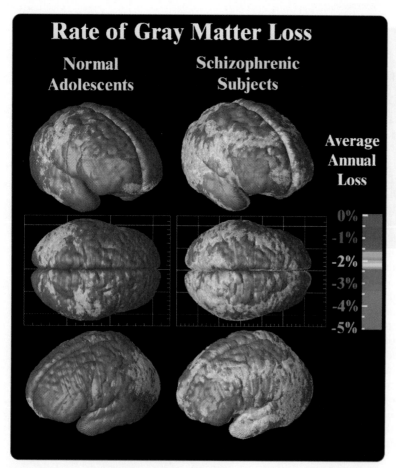

FIGURE 14.8 Gray Matter Loss in Adolescents with Schizophrenia

Researchers carried out MRI scans on 12 adolescents with schizophrenia and 12 age-matched healthy controls. Over a five-year period, the adolescents with schizophrenia showed substantial loss of gray matter in several areas of their brains.

From Thompson, P. M., Vidal, C., Giedd, J. N., Gochman, P., Blumenthal, J., Nicolson, R., Toga, A. W., & Rapoport, J. L. (2001). Mapping adolescent brain change reveals dynamic wave of accelerated gray matter loss in very early-onset schizophrenia. *PNAS, 98*, 11650–11655.

These four genetically identical women each experience a schizophrenic disorder, which suggests that heredity plays a role in the development of schizophrenia. For each of the Genain quadruplets, the disorder differs in severity, duration, and outcome. In general, how do genetics and environment interact to produce instances of schizophrenia?

Environmental Stressors We have been focusing on genetic and biological aspects of schizophrenia. However, as you can see in Figure 14.6, even in the groups with the greatest genetic similarity, the risk factor is less than 50 percent. This indicates that, although genes play a role, environmental conditions may also be necessary to give rise to the disorder. A widely accepted hypothesis for the cause of schizophrenia is the *diathesis-stress hypothesis*. According to the **diathesis-stress hypothesis,** genetic factors place the individual at risk, but environmental stress factors must impinge for the potential risk to be manifested as a schizophrenic disorder. Let's consider some of those factors.

For example, research has demonstrated that people who live in urban settings, people who experience greater economic difficulties, and people who have migrated from one country to another all experience higher rates of schizophrenia (Tandon et al., 2008). Explanations for these relationships often focus on social stressors and social adversity. Research also suggests that people who experience traumatic life events are at higher risk for schizophrenia. One study examined large samples of individuals in both the United States and Great Britain: The more people had experienced traumas such as physical or sexual abuse, the more likely they were to suffer from a schizophrenic disorder (Shevlin et al., 2008).

Researchers have also examined how life events affect changes in people's symptoms once they have been diagnosed with a schizophrenic disorder. Consider a study that demonstrated a relationship between patients' responses to life events and changes in their symptoms.

> Researchers assessed the symptoms of patients with a schizophrenic disorder at the beginning and end of a nine-month period (Docherty et al., 2008). At the study's outset, the researchers also measured each patient's *emotional reactivity*—the intensity of an individual's emotional responses to life events. The patients, for example, responded to statements such as "I have big ups and downs in mood" and "I experience very intense emotions" on a scale ranging from "never, or almost never" to "always, or almost always." Nine months later, the patients gave an account of life events from the preceding month. Based on their reports, the researchers sorted them into categories of people who had experienced moderate or severe life events in the past month and those who hadn't. The researchers predicted that negative life events would lead to greater symptoms of schizophrenia—but only for patients who regularly had intense emotional responses to those events. As you can see in **Figure 14.9,** the data supported the prediction. Only patients who both had negative life events and high emotional reactivity showed increases in symptoms (that is, delusions and hallucinations).

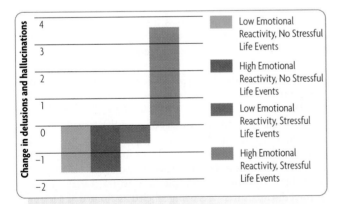

FIGURE 14.9   Changes in Symptoms of Schizophrenic Disorders

Researchers measured patients' emotional reactivity and symptom change over a nine-month-period. Only patients who both had negative life events and high emotional reactivity showed increases in symptoms (that is, delusions and hallucinations).

From Docherty, N. M., St-Hilaire, A., Aakre, J. M., & Seghers, J. P. (2008). Life events and high-trait reactivity together predict psychotic symptom increases in schizophrenia. *Schizophrenia Bulletin.*

We saw earlier that differences in people's responses to life events affects the likelihood that they will experience, for example, major depressive disorder. This study demonstrated a similar pattern for symptoms of schizophrenia.

---

diathesis-stress hypothesis A hypothesis about the cause of certain disorders, such as schizophrenia, that suggests that genetic factors predispose an individual to a certain disorder but that environmental stress factors must impinge in order for the potential risk to manifest itself.

Research has also looked at family stressors that may affect both the likelihood that people develop schizophrenic disorders and the likelihood that they will relapse if the symptoms go into remission (Miklowitz & Tompson, 2003). For example, several studies have focused on the concept of *expressed emotion*. Families are high on expressed emotion if they make a lot of critical comments about the patient, if they are emotionally overinvolved with the patient (that is, if they are overprotective and intrusive), and if they have a generally hostile attitude toward the patient. When patients in remission leave hospitals and return to high-expressed-emotion homes, the risk of relapse is more than twice as high as when they return to low-expressed-emotion homes (Hooley, 2007). If parents are able to reduce their criticism, hostility, and intrusiveness toward an offspring with schizophrenia, the recurrence of acute symptoms and the need for rehospitalization are also reduced (Wearden et al., 2000). The implication is that treatment should be for the entire family as a *system*, to change the operating style toward the disturbed child.

The number of explanations of schizophrenia that we have reviewed—and the questions that remain despite significant research—suggests how much there is to learn about this powerful psychological disorder. Complicating understanding is the likelihood that the phenomenon called schizophrenia is probably better thought of as a group of disorders, each with potentially distinct causes. Genetic predispositions, brain processes, and family interactions have all been identified as participants in at least some cases. Researchers must still determine the exact ways in which these elements may combine to bring about schizophrenia.

STOP AND REVIEW

❶ Are social withdrawal and flattened emotions positive or negative symptoms of schizophrenia?

❷ For what type of schizophrenic disorder would delusions of persecution or grandeur be symptoms?

❸ What impact does family expressed emotion have on relapse for schizophrenic disorders?

CRITICAL THINKING Recall the study that looked at the impact of life events on symptoms of schizophrenia. Why was emotional reactivity measured at the beginning of the nine-month period?

Visit MyPsychLab.com for more review and practice on the following topics:

👁 **Watch:** Schizophrenia: The Case of Georgina

👁 **Watch:** Genetic Schizophrenia

Psychological Disorders of Childhood

Our discussion so far has largely focused on adults who suffer from psychopathology. It is important to note, however, that many individuals begin to experience symptoms of mental illness in childhood and adolescence. Researchers have recently

intensified their study of the time course with which psychopathology emerges in young lives (Zahn-Waxler et al., 2008). Researchers often try to identify behavior patterns that allow for early diagnosis and treatment. For example, problems with social functioning may provide clues that children and adolescents are at risk for schizophrenia (Tarbox & Pogue-Geile, 2008).

DSM-IV-TR also identifies a range of disorders that are "usually first diagnosed in infancy, childhood, or adolescence." We discussed one of these disorders, *mental retardation*, in Chapter 9. Here, we focus on *attention-deficit hyperactivity disorder* and *autistic disorder*.

ATTENTION-DEFICIT HYPERACTIVITY DISORDER

The definition of **attention-deficit hyperactivity disorder** (ADHD) refers to two clusters of symptoms (*DSM-IV-TR*, 2000). First, children must show a degree of *inattention* that is not consistent with their level of development. They might, for example, have difficulty paying attention in school or often lose items such as toys or school assignments. Second, children must show signs of *hyperactivity-impulsivity* that, once again, is not consistent with their developmental level. Hyperactive behaviors include squirming, fidgeting, and excessive talking; impulsive behaviors include blurting out answers and interrupting. A diagnosis of ADHD requires that children have shown these patterns of behavior for at least six months before age 7.

Researchers estimate the prevalence of ADHD to be 3 to 7 percent of school-age children in the United States (Root & Resnick, 2003). Many studies suggest that more boys than girls experience ADHD. However, research also suggests that cultural biases (for example, expectations of gender differences) lead to fewer diagnoses of ADHD among girls than are justified—making it difficult to provide an exact estimate of the gender difference. However, in one large-scale study of adults, 3.2 percent of women and 5.4 percent of men met diagnostic criteria for ADHD (Kessler et al., 2006a). These figures may accurately reflect gender differences across the life span. When they are diagnosed with ADHD, boys and girls show much the same patterns of problematic behavior (Biederman et al., 2005). Some children overcome ADHD as they grow older. In one sample of 133 children diagnosed as hyperactive at ages 4 to 12, 42 percent did not meet criteria for ADHD at age 21 (Fischer et al., 2005). The 58 percent of young adults who still had ADHD performed less well than controls on a variety of cognitive tasks.

The diagnosis of ADHD is complicated by the fact that many children are prone to episodes of inattention, hyperactivity, or impulsiveness. For that reason, the diagnosis has sometimes been controversial: People have worried that children's normal disorderliness was being labeled as abnormal. However, there is now a large consensus among clinicians that some children's behavior reaches a level at which it is maladaptive—the children are unable to control their behavior or complete tasks. Although there has often been a popular perception that ADHD is overdiagnosed, research evidence contradicts that perception (Sciutto & Eisenberg, 2007). In fact, as we noted earlier, ADHD might actually be underdiagnosed for girls.

As with the other disorders we've described, researchers have considered both the nature and nurture of ADHD. Twin and adoption studies have provided strong evidence for the heritability of the disorder (Biederman & Faraone, 2005). Researchers have started to document relationships between

---

attention-deficit hyperactivity disorder (ADHD) A disorder of childhood characterized by inattention and hyperactivity-impulsivity.

What psychological disorders of childhood might lead to classroom disruptions?

specific genes that affect the brain's neurotransmitter function and the symptoms of ADHD (Smoller et al., 2006). There are also important environmental variables associated with ADHD. For example, children who come from families with economic disadvantages or families with high levels of conflict are more likely to experience the disorder (Biederman et al., 2002). Some environmental variables have greater impact on children in different birth positions. For example, the eldest children in families that lack cohesion—families in which members are not committed to providing support to each other—are more at risk for ADHD than are younger siblings in such families (Pressman et al., 2006). Results of this sort suggest that parenting experience has an impact on the incidence of ADHD.

AUTISTIC DISORDER

Children with **autistic disorder** present severe disruption in their ability to form social bonds. They are likely to have greatly delayed and very limited development of spoken language as well as very narrow interests in the world. Consider a report on a child who was diagnosed with this disorder:

> [Audrey] seemed frightened by nearly any changes in her customary routine, including the presence of strange people. She either shrank from contact with other children or avoided them altogether, seemingly content to engage in nonfunctional play by herself for hours at a time. When she was with other children, she seldom engaged in reciprocal play or even copied any of their motor movements. (Meyer, 2003, p. 244)

Many children with autistic disorder also engage in repetitive and ritualistic behaviors: They might, for example, place objects in lines or symmetrical patterns (Greaves et al., 2006).

Research suggests that the prevalence of autistic disorder (and related disorders) is about one out of 150 children (Centers for Disease Control and Prevention, 2007). Because many of the symptoms of autistic disorder relate to language and social interaction, it has often been difficult to diagnose the disorder until parents notice that their children are failing to use language or interact. However, recent research has begun to document behaviors in the first year of life that predict later diagnoses of autistic disorder (Zwaigenbaum et al., 2005). For example, children at risk for autistic disorder are less likely to smile in response to social smiles and respond to their names than are other children.

Causes of Autistic Disorder As with ADHD, autistic disorder has a large genetic component. In fact, researchers have begun to identify the variations in the human genome that may predispose individuals to experience the disorder (Bartlett et al., 2005; Liu et al., 2008). Researchers have also discovered brain markers of the disorder. For example, individuals with autistic disorder experience more rapid brain growth than do their peers (Amaral et al., 2008). The ongoing question is how such brain abnormalities bring about the symptoms of the disorder.

Researchers have suggested that individuals who suffer from autistic disorder have an inability to develop an understanding of other people's mental states (Baron-Cohen, 2008). Under ordinary circumstances, children develop what has been called a *theory of mind*. At first, they interpret the world only from their own perspective. However, with rapid progress between ages 3 and 4, children develop an understanding that other people have different knowledge, beliefs, and intentions than they do. Research suggests that individuals with autistic disorder lack the ability to develop this understanding. Without a theory of mind, it is quite difficult for people to establish social relationships. Individuals with autistic disorder find it virtually impossible to understand and predict other people's behavior, making everyday life seem mysterious and hostile.

STOP AND REVIEW

❶ What types of behaviors characterize ADHD?
❷ Why has it been difficult to diagnose autistic disorder before age 2 or 3?
❸ Why is theory of mind relevant to autistic disorder?

Visit MyPsychLab.com for more review and practice on the following topics:

👁 **Watch:** Attention-Deficit/Hyperactivity Disorder (ADHD): Dr. Raun Melmed

👁 **Watch:** Autism: Dr. Kathy Pratt

The Stigma of Mental Illness

One of our most important goals for this chapter has been to demystify mental illness—to help you understand how, in some ways, abnormal behavior is really ordinary. People with psychological disorders are often labeled as *deviant*. However, the deviant label is not true to prevailing realities: When 46.4 percent of adults in the United States report hav-

---

autistic disorder A developmental disorder characterized by severe disruption of children's ability to form social bonds and use language.

ing experienced some psychiatric disorder in their lifetime (Kessler et al., 2005a), psychopathology is, at least statistically, relatively normal.

Even given the frequency with which psychopathology touches "normal lives," people who are psychologically disordered are often stigmatized in ways that most physically ill people are not. A **stigma** is a mark or brand of disgrace; in the psychological context, it is a set of negative attitudes about a person that places him or her apart as unacceptable (Hinshaw & Stier, 2008). The woman with schizophrenia we quoted at the beginning of the chapter had this to say: "The patient and public, in my [opinion] needs to be educated about mental illness because people ridicule and mistreat, even misunderstand us at crucial times." Another recovered patient wrote, "For me, the stigma of mental illness was as devastating as the experience of hospitalization itself. Repeated rejections, the awkwardness of others around me, and my own discomfort and self-consciousness propelled me into solitary confinement" (Houghton, 1980, pp. 7–8). Negative attitudes toward the psychologically disturbed come from many sources: The mass media portray psychiatric patients as prone to violent crime; jokes about the mentally ill are acceptable; families deny the mental distress of one of their members; legal terminology stresses mental incompetence. People also stigmatize themselves by hiding current psychological distress or a history of mental health care.

Researchers have documented a number of ways in which the stigma of mental illness has a negative impact on people's lives (Hinshaw & Stier, 2008). In one sample of 84 men who had been hospitalized for mental illness, 6 percent reported having lost a job because of their hospitalization; 10 percent reported having been denied an apartment or room; 37 percent reported being avoided by others; and 45 percent reported that others had used their history of mental illness to hurt their feelings. Only 6 percent of the men reported no incidents of rejection (Link et al., 1997). This group of men went through a yearlong course of treatment that resulted in considerable improvement in their mental health. Even so, at the end of that year, there were no changes in their perception of stigma: Despite their improvements in functioning, the patients did not expect to be treated any more kindly by the world. This type of research shows the great duality of many people's experience with mental disorders: Seeking help—allowing one's problems to be labeled—generally brings both relief *and* stigma; treatment improves quality of life at the same time that stigma degrades it (Rosenfield, 1997).

An added difficulty is that people with mental illness often internalize expectations of rejections that may, in turn, bring about negative interactions (Pachankis, 2007). Consider this classic experiment.

Twenty-nine men who had formerly been hospitalized for mental illness volunteered to participate in this study. They believed that the research concerned the difficulties ex-psychiatric patients have with finding jobs. The participants were informed that they would interact with a personnel trainee recruited from a business establishment. Half of the participants were told that the trainee knew of their status as ex-psychiatric patients; the other half were told that the trainee had been led to believe they had been medical or surgical patients at the hospital. In fact, the "trainee" was a confederate of the experimenter who did not have any prior information about the participants' beliefs about his knowledge. That is, he did not know which participants thought that *he* knew that they were ex-patients. Therefore, any differences in the interactions during the time the participants and confederate spent together can be attributed to the participants' *expectations*. In fact, the participants who believed themselves to have been labeled as ex-psychiatric patients talked less during the session and performed worse on a cooperative task. Furthermore, the confederate rated members of this group as more "tense and anxious" without, again, knowing which group each participant was in (Farina et al., 1971).

The important conclusion here is that people who believe that others have attached the "mental illness" label to them may change their interactions in a way that brings about genuine discomfort: The expectation of rejection can create rejection; mental illness can be another of life's unfortunate self-fulfilling prophecies.

A final note on stigma: Research suggests that people who have had prior contact with individuals with mental illnesses hold attitudes that are less affected by stigma (Couture & Penn, 2003). For example, students who read a vignette about a man named Jim who had recovered from schizophrenia were more optimistic about Jim's future prospects when the students had had prior contact with someone who suffered from a mental illness (Penn et al., 1994). Similarly, students' ratings of the dangerousness of patients with schizophrenia were lower when they had had prior contact (Penn et al., 1999). We hope that one consequence of reading this chapter and the next will be to help modify your beliefs about what it means to be mentally ill and what it means to be "cured"—and to increase your tolerance and compassion for mentally ill individuals.

In making sense of psychopathology, you are forced to come to grips with basic conceptions of normality, reality, and social values. In discovering how to understand, treat, and, ideally, prevent psychological disorders, researchers not only help those who are suffering and losing out on the joys of living, they also expand the basic understanding of human nature. How do psychologists and psychiatrists intervene to right minds gone wrong and to modify behavior that doesn't work? We will see in the next chapter on therapies.

STOP AND REVIEW

❶ In the context of mental illness, how does stigma function?
❷ Why does treatment for mental illness often bring about both relief and stigma?
❸ What types of experience reduce stigma?

CRITICAL THINKING Consider the study on ex-psychiatric patients' expectations of rejections. Why was it important that the confederate not know which patients were in which group?

---

stigma The negative reaction of people to an individual or group because of some assumed inferiority or source of difference that is degraded.

Recapping Main Points

The Nature of Psychological Disorders

- Abnormality is judged by the degree to which a person's actions resemble a set of indicators that include distress, maladaptiveness, irrationality, unpredictability, unconventionality, observer discomfort, and violation of standards or societal norms.
- Objectivity is an important problem for discussions of mental illness.
- Classification systems for psychological disorders should provide a common shorthand for communicating about general types of psychopathologies and specific cases.
- The most widely accepted diagnostic and classification system is *DSM-IV-TR*.
- The biological approach to the etiology of mental illness concentrates on abnormalities in the brain, biochemical processes, and genetic influences.
- Psychological approaches include psychodynamic, behavioral, cognitive, and sociocultural models.

Anxiety Disorders

- The five major types of anxiety disorders are generalized, panic, phobic, obsessive-compulsive, and posttraumatic stress.
- Research has confirmed genetic and brain bases for anxiety disorders as well as behavioral and cognitive components of causality.

Mood Disorders

- Major depressive disorder is the most common mood disorder; bipolar disorder is much rarer.
- People have genetic predispositions toward mood disorders.
- Mood disorders change the way people respond to life experiences.
- Women's higher levels of major depressive disorder may reflect differences in negative life experiences as well as cognitive responses to those experiences.
- Suicides are most frequent among people suffering from depression.

Personality Disorders

- Personality disorders are patterns of perception, thought, or behavior that are long-standing and inflexible and impair an individual's functioning.
- Both borderline personality disorder and antisocial personality disorder arise because of genetic and environmental factors.

Somatoform and Dissociative Disorders

- Somatoform disorders such as hypochondriasis, somatization disorder, and conversion disorder are characterized by circumstances in which physical illnesses or complaints cannot be fully explained by actual medical conditions.
- Dissociative disorders involve a disruption of the integrated functioning of memory, consciousness, or personal identity.

Schizophrenic Disorders

- Schizophrenia is a severe form of psychopathology characterized by extreme distortions in perception, thinking, emotion, behavior, and language.
- The five subtypes of schizophrenia are disorganized, catatonic, paranoid, undifferentiated, and residual.
- Evidence for the causes of schizophrenia has been found in a variety of factors including genetics, brain abnormalities, and environmental stressors.

Psychological Disorders of Childhood

- Children with ADHD display inattention and hyperactivity-impulsivity.
- Autistic disorder is characterized by severe disruption of children's ability to form social bonds and use language.

The Stigma of Mental Illness

- Those with psychological disorders are often stigmatized in ways that most physically ill people are not.
- Although treatment for psychological disorders brings about positive changes, the stigma associated with mental illness has a negative impact on quality of life.

KEY TERMS

abnormal psychology (p. 442)
agoraphobia (p. 450)
antisocial personality disorder (p. 460)
anxiety disorder (p. 448)
attention-deficit hyperactivity disorder (ADHD) (p. 470)
autistic disorder (p. 471)
bipolar disorder (p. 454)
borderline personality disorder (p. 459)
comorbidity (p. 445)
conversion disorder (p. 462)
delusion (p. 465)
diathesis-stress hypothesis (p. 469)
dissociative amnesia (p. 463)

dissociative disorder (p. 463)
dissociative fugue (p. 463)
dissociative identity disorder (DID) (p. 463)
DSM-IV-TR (p. 445)
etiology (p. 446)
fear (p. 450)
generalized anxiety disorder (p. 448)
hypochondriasis (p. 462)
insanity (p. 446)
learned helplessness (p. 456)
major depressive disorder (p. 454)
manic episode (p. 454)
mood disorder (p. 454)
neurotic disorder (p. 446)

obsessive-compulsive disorder (OCD) (p. 451)
panic disorder (p. 449)
personality disorder (p. 459)
phobia (p. 450)
psychological diagnosis (p. 444)
psychopathological functioning (p. 442)
psychotic disorder (p. 446)
schizophrenic disorder (p. 465)
social phobia (p. 450)
somatization disorder (p. 462)
somatoform disorder (p. 462)
specific phobia (p. 450)
stigma (p. 472)

Chapter 14 Practice Test

1. *Comorbidity* refers to circumstances in which an individual
   a. cannot be accurately diagnosed using *DSM-IV-TR*.
   b. has a neurotic disorder that cannot be easily cured.
   c. has a psychotic disorder that includes a fear of death.
   d. experiences more than one psychological disorder at the same time.

2. Professor Hexter believes that unconscious conflicts often cause psychological disorders. Which approach to psychopathology does Professor Hexter use?
   a. psychodynamic
   b. sociocultural
   c. cognitive
   d. behavioral

3. Analyses of legal records suggest that the use of the insanity defense is quite_____ and the probability of it succeeding is quite _____ .
   a. rare; low
   b. rare; high
   c. common; low
   d. common; high

4. For binge eating disorder, which criterion is still being researched as a potential part of the diagnosis?
   a. Regular episodes of binge eating without purges
   b. A loss of control during binges
   c. Binges cause great distress
   d. Undue influence of body weight or shape on self-evaluation

5. For over a year, Jane has felt anxious or worried throughout the day. It sounds as though Jane is suffering from
   a. panic disorder.
   b. generalized anxiety disorder.
   c. obsessive-compulsive disorder.
   d. agoraphobia.

6. What attribution style puts people at risk for depression?
   a. internal-specific-stable
   b. external-specific-unstable
   c. internal-global-stable
   d. external-global-unstable

7. When something bad happens, Chris spends a lot of time ruminating about the problem. Based on this behavior, you think it is
   a. more likely that Chris is a man.
   b. equally likely that Chris is a man or a woman.
   c. likely that Chris will develop a specific phobia.
   d. more likely that Chris is a woman.

8. You are trying to assess the probability that Paula will develop major depressive disorder. You would be most concerned if she had the _____ form of a serotonin gene as well as _____ stressful life events.
   a. s/l; two
   b. s/s; three
   c. l/l; four
   d. s/l; three

9. Nadine alternates between yelling at Tricia and begging her to remain friends. Tricia is convinced that Nadine suffers from _____ personality disorder.

   a. schizotypal
   b. narcissistic
   c. borderline
   d. obsessive-compulsive

10. To diagnose conversion disorder, you'd try to find _____ that preceded the appearance of symptoms.
    a. a serious physical illness
    b. psychological conflict or stress
    c. a visit to a medical doctor
    d. both pain and gastrointestinal complaints

11. Although Eve doesn't have any organic dysfunction, she often forgets important personal experiences. This could be an instance of
    a. dissociative amnesia.
    b. hypochondriasis.
    c. somatization disorder.
    d. dependent personality disorder.

12. Which of these is a negative symptom of schizophrenia?
    a. hallucinations
    b. incoherent language
    c. delusions
    d. social withdrawal

13. Which of these behaviors would *not* generally support a diagnosis of attention-deficit hyperactivity disorder?
    a. Manfred blurts out answers during class activities.
    b. Manfred loses his toys and school assignments.
    c. Manfred squirms and fidgets in the classroom.
    d. Manfred cries when other children tease him.

14. Professor Wyatt believes that 1-year-old Brian is at risk for autistic disorder. The professor might observe Brian to determine whether he
    a. fails to respond to his name.
    b. can walk without assistance.
    c. responds appropriately to loud noises.
    d. shows smooth pursuit with his eyes.

15. As part of an introductory psychology class, a professor has her students interview people who have recovered from psychological disorders. This exercise should
    a. prompt the students to be more affected by the stigma of mental illness.
    b. have no impact on the students' experience of stigma.
    c. prompt the students to be less affected by the stigma of mental illness.
    d. decrease the probability that students would seek treatment for mental illness.

Essay Questions

1. Why is it not always possible to be objective about diagnoses of mental illness?

2. What are some benefits of a useful classification system for psychological disorders?

3. What life circumstances lead some people to contemplate suicide?

Discovering Psychology Viewing Guide

Watch the following video by logging on to MyPsychLab (www.mypsychlab.com). After you have watched the video, complete the activities that follow.

Program 21: Psychopathology

KEY TERMS AND PEOPLE

As you watch the program, pay particular attention to these people in addition to those covered in this textbook.

- *Hans Strupp*—argues that psychological factors are of primary importance in the origin of schizophrenia.
- *Fuller Torrey*—studies the psychology and biology of schizophrenia.

PROGRAM REVIEW

1. *Psychopathology* is defined as the study of
   a. organic brain disease.
   b. perceptual and cognitive illusions.
   c. clinical measures of abnormal functioning.
   d. mental disorders.

2. What is the key criterion for identifying a person as having a mental disorder?
   a. The person has problems.
   b. The person's functioning is clearly abnormal.
   c. The person's ideas challenge the status quo.
   d. The person makes other people feel uncomfortable.

3. Which is true about mental disorders?
   a. They are extremely rare, with less than one-tenth of 1 percent of Americans suffering from any form of mental illness.
   b. They are not that uncommon, with about one-fifth of Americans suffering from some form of recently diagnosed mental disorder.
   c. The number of Americans with psychotic disorders fluctuates with the calendar, with more cases of psychosis during the weekends than during weekdays.
   d. The actions of people with mental disorders are unpredictable.

4. Fran is a mental health specialist who has a Ph.D. in psychology. She would be classified as a
   a. psychiatrist.   c. social psychologist.
   b. clinical psychologist. d. psychoanalyst.

5. What happened after David Rosenhan and his colleagues were admitted to mental hospitals by pretending to have hallucinations and then behaved normally?
   a. Their sanity was quickly observed by the staff.
   b. It took several days for their deception to be realized.
   c. In most cases, the staff disagreed with each other about these "patients."
   d. Nobody ever detected their sanity.

6. Olivia is experiencing dizziness, muscle tightness, shaking, and tremors, She is feeling apprehensive. These symptoms most resemble those found in cases of
   a. anxiety disorders.   c. psychoses.
   b. affective disorders.   d. schizophrenia.

7. Agoraphobia is one of the most common phobias. What does a person with this condition fear?
   a. being at the top of a tall building
   b. going out in public
   c. being violently attacked
   d. In this condition, people have a generalized fear of experience.

8. When Freud studied patients with anxiety, he determined that their symptoms were caused by
   a. actual childhood abuse, both physical and sexual.
   b. imbalances in body chemistry.
   c. childhood conflicts that had been repressed.
   d. cognitive errors in the way patients viewed the world.

9. What happens to most people who are suffering from serious clinical depression?
   a. They commit suicide.
   b. They are hospitalized.
   c. They receive treatment outside a hospital.
   d. They receive no treatment at all.

10. People lose touch with reality in cases of
    a. neurosis but not psychosis.
    b. psychosis but not neurosis.
    c. both psychosis and neurosis.
    d. all psychoses and some neuroses.

11. When Hans Strupp speaks of the importance of psychological factors in schizophrenia, he specifically cites the role of
    a. feelings of inadequacy.
    b. antisocial personality.
    c. delayed development.
    d. early childhood experiences.

12. Irving Gottesman and Fuller Torrey have been studying twins to learn more about schizophrenia. If the brain of a twin with schizophrenia is compared with the brain of a normal twin, the former has
    a. less cerebrospinal fluid.
    b. larger ventricles.
    c. a larger left hemisphere.
    d. exactly the same configuration as the latter.

13. For Teresa LaFromboise, the major issue in the treatment of mental disorders among Native Americans is
   a. the prevalence of genetic disorders.
   b. alcohol's impact on family structure.
   c. the effect of imposing white American culture.
   d. isolation due to rural settings.

14. According to experts, what proportion of Americans suffer from some form of mental illness?
   a. about one-fifth
   b. less than 1 in 10,000
   c. about two-thirds
   d. about 1 in a 1,000

15. Which of the following people would argue that psychopathology is a myth?
   a. Philippe Pinel
   b. Thomas Szasz
   c. Teresa LaFromboise
   d. Sigmund Freud

16. What might a severe viral infection do to a woman who has a genetic predisposition toward schizophrenia?
   a. make her schizophrenic
   b. destroy the genetic marker and make her mentally more stable
   c. redirect the predisposition toward a different class of mental illness
   d. kill her with greater likelihood than if she did not have a predisposition toward mental illness

17. Which of the following has been nicknamed "the common cold of psychopathology" because of its frequency?
   a. phobia
   b. personality disorder
   c. schizophrenia
   d. depression

18. All of the following are typically true about schizophrenia, *except* that
   a. fewer than one-third improve with treatment.
   b. the people who have it are aware that they are mentally ill.
   c. about 1 percent of the world's total population is schizophrenic.
   d. it is associated with impaired thinking, emotion, and perception.

19. Who is credited as being the first to introduce the idea that insane people are ill?
   a. Sigmund Freud
   b. Jean Charcot
   c. Emil Kraepelin
   d. Philippe Pinel

20. Which of the following is characterized by boundless energy, optimism, and risk-taking behavior?
   a. a manic episode
   b. paranoid schizophrenia
   c. anxiety disorders
   d. depression

QUESTIONS TO CONSIDER

1. If a person is mentally ill and has violated the law, under what circumstances should he or she be considered responsible for the criminal actions? Under what circumstances should we consider the person to be rehabilitatable?

2. Why has the *DSM* been criticized?

3. Is homosexuality a deviant behavior?

4. Are standards for psychological health the same for men and women? Why are most patients women?

5. How can you tell whether your own behavior, anxieties, and moods are within normal limits or whether they signal mental illness?

ACTIVITIES

1. Collect the advice columns in the daily papers for a week or two (such as "Ann Landers" or "Dear Abby"). What kinds of problems do people write about? How often does the columnist refer people to a psychologist, psychiatrist, or other professional for counseling? Why do people write to an anonymous person for advice about their problems?

2. Ask several people (who are not psychology professionals) to define the terms *emotionally ill*, *mentally ill*, and *insane*. Ask them to describe behaviors that characterize each term. Do some terms indicate more extreme behavior than others? How do their definitions compare with the ones in your text? What can you conclude about the attitudes and understanding of mental illness shown by the people you interviewed?

3. Read through the *DSM-IV-TR* with an eye toward seeing that it is a statistically based manual. The behaviors that define mental illness fall on the same continuum as those that define mental health. Notice whether there are any classifications within the *DSM-IV-TR* for which some of the criteria are a partial match to you.

Therapies for Psychological Disorders

While you were reading Chapter 14, you might at some points have felt overwhelmed by all the ways in which individuals can experience mental illness. Fortunately, psychologists and other providers of mental health care have worked intently to create therapies that address the full range of psychopathology. We will see in this chapter that researchers continue to generate innovations in therapeutic techniques. The more researchers learn about the causes and consequences of psychopathology—the research we described in Chapter 14—the better they are able to fine-tune their repertory of therapies.

In this chapter, we will examine the types of therapies that can help restore personal control to individuals with a range of disorders. We address a number of formidable questions: How has the treatment of psychological disorders been influenced by historical, cultural, and social forces? How do theory, research, and practice interact as researchers develop and test treatment methods? What can be done to influence a mind ungoverned by ordinary reason, to modify uncontrolled behavior, to alter unchecked emotions, and to correct abnormalities of the brain?

This chapter surveys the major types of treatments currently used by health-care providers: psychoanalysis, behavior modification, cognitive alteration, humanistic therapies, and drug therapies. We will examine the way these treatments work. We will also evaluate the validity of claims about the success of each therapy.

The Therapeutic Context

There are different types of therapies for mental disorders, and there are many reasons some people seek help (and others who need it do not). The purposes or goals of therapy, the settings in which therapy occurs, and the kinds of therapeutic helpers also vary. Despite any differences between therapies, however, all are *interventions* into a person's life, designed to change the person's functioning in some way.

GOALS AND MAJOR THERAPIES

The therapeutic process can involve four primary tasks or goals:

1. Reaching a *diagnosis* about what is wrong, possibly determining an appropriate psychiatric *(DSM-IV-TR)* label for the presenting problem, and classifying the disorder.
2. Proposing a probable *etiology* (cause of the problem)—that is, identifying the probable origins of the disorder and the functions being served by the symptoms.
3. Making a *prognosis,* or estimate, of the course the problem will take with and without any treatment.
4. Prescribing and carrying out some form of *treatment,* a therapy designed to minimize or eliminate the troublesome symptoms and, perhaps, their sources.

---

biomedical therapy Treatment for a psychological disorder that alters brain functioning with chemical or physical interventions such as drug therapy, surgery, or electroconvulsive therapy.

psychotherapy Any of a group of therapies, used to treat psychological disorders, that focus on changing faulty behaviors, thoughts, perceptions, and emotions that may be associated with specific disorders.

Biomedical therapies focus on changing the mechanisms that run the central nervous system. Practiced largely by psychiatrists and physicians, these therapies try to alter brain functioning with chemical or physical interventions, including surgery, electric shock, and drugs that act directly on the brain–body connection.

Psychological therapies, which are collectively called **psychotherapy,** focus on changing the faulty behaviors people have learned: the words, thoughts, interpretations, and feedback that direct daily strategies for living. These therapies are practiced by clinical psychologists as well as by psychiatrists. There are four major types of psychotherapies: psychodynamic, behavioral, cognitive, and existential-humanistic.

The *psychodynamic* approach views neurotic suffering as the outer symptom of inner, unresolved traumas and conflicts. Psychodynamic therapists treat mental disorder with a "talking cure," in which a therapist helps a person develop insights about the relation between the overt symptoms and the unresolved hidden conflicts that presumably caused them.

Behavior therapy treats the behaviors themselves as disturbances that must be modified. Disorders are viewed as learned behavior patterns rather than as the symptoms of mental disease. Behaviors are transformed in many ways, including changing reinforcement contingencies for desirable and undesirable responding, extinguishing conditioned responses, and providing models of effective problem solving.

Cognitive therapy tries to restructure the way a person thinks by altering the often distorted self-statements a person makes about the causes of a problem. Restructuring cognitions changes the way a person defines and explains difficulties, often enabling the person to cope with the problems.

Therapies that have emerged from the *humanistic tradition* emphasize the patients' values. They are directed toward self-actualization, psychological growth, the development of more meaningful interpersonal relationships, and the enhancement of freedom of choice. They tend to focus more on improving the functioning of essentially healthy people than on correcting the symptoms of seriously disturbed individuals.

Although we have introduced each type of psychotherapy separately, it is important to note that many psychotherapists

Why do many psychotherapists integrate different theoretical approaches in their clinical practices?

take an *integrative* approach to practice: They integrate different theoretical approaches to provide maximum benefit to their patients or clients. In many cases, psychotherapists begin their careers adhering to a particular theoretical orientation. However, as their careers unfold, they begin to mix together the most effective elements of different therapies (Norcross et al., 2005). Psychotherapists integrate across virtually every pair of orientations (for example, cognitive and humanistic; behavioral and psychodynamic). However, the most prominent integrative therapies combine aspects of the cognitive and behavioral approaches (Goldfried, 2003; Norcross et al., 2005). Later in the chapter, we describe integrative cognitive behavioral therapies.

THERAPISTS AND THERAPEUTIC SETTINGS

When psychological problems arise, most people initially seek out informal counselors who operate in familiar settings. Many people turn to family members, close friends, personal physicians, lawyers, or favorite teachers for support, guidance, and counsel. Those with religious affiliations may seek help from a clergy member. Others get advice and a chance to talk by opening up to bartenders, salesclerks, cabdrivers, or other people willing to listen. In our society, these informal therapists carry the bulk of the daily burden of relieving frustration and conflict. When problems are limited in scope, informal therapists can often help.

Although more people seek out therapy now than in the past, people usually turn to trained mental health professionals only when their psychological problems become severe or persist for extended periods of time. When they do, they can turn to several types of therapists.

A **clinical social worker** is a mental health professional whose specialized training in a school of social work prepares him or her to work in collaboration with psychiatrists and clinical psychologists. Unlike many psychiatrists and psychologists, these counselors are trained to consider the social contexts of people's problems, so these practitioners may also involve other family members in the therapy or at least become acquainted with clients' homes or work settings.

A **pastoral counselor** is a member of a religious group who specializes in the treatment of psychological disorders. Often, these counselors combine spirituality with practical problem solving.

A **clinical psychologist** is required to have concentrated his or her graduate school training in the assessment and treatment of psychological problems, completed a supervised internship in a clinical setting, and earned a PhD or PsyD. These psychologists tend to have a broader background in psychology, assessment, and research than do psychiatrists.

A **counseling psychologist** also typically has obtained a PhD or PsyD. He or she usually provides guidance in areas such as vocation selection, school problems, drug abuse, and marital conflict. Often, these counselors work in community settings related to the problem areas—within a business, a school, a prison, the military service, or a neighborhood clinic—and use interviews, tests, guidance, and advising to help individuals solve specific problems and make decisions about future options.

A **psychiatrist** must have completed all medical school training for an MD degree and also have undergone some postdoctoral specialty training in mental and emotional disorders. Psychiatrists are largely trained in the biomedical basis of psychological problems.

A **psychoanalyst** is a therapist with either an MD or a PhD degree who has completed specialized postgraduate training in the Freudian approach to understanding and treating mental disorders.

These different types of therapists practice in many settings: hospitals, clinics, schools, and private offices. Some humanistic therapists prefer to conduct group sessions in their homes to work in a more natural environment. Community-based therapies, which take the treatment to the client, may operate out of local storefronts or houses of worship. Finally, some therapists work with clients in the life setting that is associated with their problem. For example, they work in airplanes with clients who suffer from flying phobias or in shopping malls with people who have social phobias.

Psychotherapists have also begun to provide mental health care using e-mail or the Internet (King & Moreggi, 1998; Taylor & Luce, 2003). In this type of computer-assisted therapy, individuals often interact with their therapists through exchanges of e-mail. Researchers have been quick to point out both potential dangers and benefits of therapy on the Internet. On the dangers side, researchers worry that patients may be misdiagnosed if they present limited or distorted information without the extra scrutiny that is possible face to face (Bhuvaneswar & Gutheil, 2008; King & Moreggi, 1998). Furthermore, consumers rarely are able to verify the credentials of on-line therapists; in cyberspace anyone can claim to be an expert. Despite these dangers, e-mail therapy may also provide unique opportunities for therapists and their clients. For example, some therapists believe that the relative anonymity of this form of therapy allows clients to reveal their most pressing problems and concerns more quickly and with less embarrassment; individuals may be more honest when they don't have to worry about their therapist's overt reactions to their difficult confessions (Grohol, 1998).

People who enter therapy are usually referred to as either patients or clients. The term **patient** is used by professionals who take a biomedical approach to the treatment of psychological problems. The term **client** is used by professionals who think

---

clinical social worker A mental health professional whose specialized training prepares him or her to consider the social context of people's problems.

pastoral counselor A member of a religious order who specializes in the treatment of psychological disorders, often combining spirituality with practical problem solving.

clinical psychologist An individual who has earned a doctorate in psychology and whose training is in the assessment and treatment of psychological problems.

counseling psychologist Psychologist who specializes in providing guidance in areas such as vocational selections, school problems, drug abuse, and marital conflict.

psychiatrist An individual who has obtained an MD degree and also has completed postdoctoral specialty training in mental and emotional disorders; a psychiatrist may prescribe medications for the treatment of psychological disorders.

psychoanalyst An individual who has earned either a PhD or an MD degree and has completed postgraduate training in the Freudian approach to understanding and treating mental disorders.

patient The term used by those who take a biomedical approach to the treatment of psychological problems to describe the person being treated.

client The term used by clinicians who think of psychological disorders as problems in living, and not as mental illnesses, to describe those being treated.

of psychological disorders as "problems in living" and not as mental illnesses. We will use the preferred term for each approach: *patient* for biomedical and psychoanalytic therapies and *client* for other therapies.

Whatever the form of the treatment, it's important that the individual seeking help enter into an effective therapeutic alliance. A *therapeutic alliance* is a mutual relationship that a client or patient establishes with a therapist: The individual and the therapist collaborate to bring about relief. Research suggests that the quality of the therapeutic alliance has an impact on psychotherapy's ability to bring about improved mental health (Goldfried & Davila, 2005; Joyce et al., 2003). When you enter into therapy, you should believe that you can establish a strong therapeutic alliance with your therapist.

DIVERSITY ISSUES IN PSYCHOTHERAPY

An important goal for clinicians is to provide relief to all people who suffer from psychological disorders. However, that goal is complicated by cultural and gender diversity. To begin, not all cultural groups are equally likely to undergo treatment (Wang et al., 2005). For example, Caucasians in the United States are more likely to seek treatment than are members of minority groups. An important part of that difference is unequal access to both physical and mental health care. However, cultural norms also affect the extent to which people seek psychological care (Snowden & Yamada, 2005). For example, research suggests that African Americans are more likely to interpret mental illness as physical illness. They are, therefore, less likely to obtain psychotherapy when it would be appropriate (Bolden & Wickes, 2005).

Another diversity issue arises once people actually seek therapy: The important question becomes whether particular therapies are equally effective across all cultural groups. Although there are large bodies of research that address the effectiveness of various forms of psychotherapy, only a very small part of the research literature assesses effectiveness in minority groups (Miranda et al., 2005). Fortunately, the limited number studies that do exist are largely optimistic with respect to the broad applicability of standard therapies. For example, one review found that cognitive behavioral therapies (which we review later in the chapter) are mostly effective for adult clients from minority cultures (Voss Horrell, 2008). More research is required to confirm these early results.

Similarly, more research is needed to assess the extent to which men and women benefit from the same therapies (Sigmon et al., 2007). In earlier chapters, we reviewed gender differences in the prevalence of psychological disorders. Recall, for example, that women experience more eating disorders than men do. For that reason, most psychotherapies for eating disorders have been developed for girls and young women (Greenberg & Schoen, 2008). Researchers must determine to what extent the same approaches are effective for men. Similarly, researchers must determine whether therapies that clinicians originated to treat men must be modified to bring relief to women.

A final diversity issue arises with respect to the training of psychotherapists: Therapists must be prepared to provide treatments that are sensitive to cultural differences. Researchers have suggested, in particular, that therapists must have *cultural competence* (Whaley & Davis, 2007). Cultural competence has been defined as having three components (Sue, 2006, p. 238):

- "Cultural awareness and beliefs: Provider's sensitivity to her or his personal values and biases and how these may influence perceptions of the client, client's problem, and the counseling relationship."
- "Cultural knowledge: Counselor's knowledge of the client's culture, worldview, and expectations for the counseling relationship."
- "Cultural skills: Counselor's ability to intervene in a manner that is culturally sensitive and relevant."

Research suggests that therapists with greater cultural competence also have better therapeutic outcomes with patients and clients from diverse groups (Worthington et al., 2008).

Before looking at contemporary therapies and therapists in more detail, we will first consider the historical contexts in which treatment of the mentally ill was developed.

HISTORICAL PERSPECTIVES ON INSTITUTIONAL TREATMENT

What kind of treatment might you have received in past centuries if you were suffering from psychological problems? For much of history, chances are the treatment would not have helped and could even have been harmful. We will trace the institutional treatment of psychological disorders to the 21st century, in which **deinstitutionalization**—the practice of moving people from psychiatric hospitals to other venues for treatment—has become an important issue.

History of Treatment Population increases and migration to big cities in 14th-century Western Europe created unemployment and social alienation. These conditions led to poverty, crime, and psychological problems. Special institutions were soon created to warehouse society's three emerging categories of so-called misfits: the poor, criminals, and the mentally disturbed.

In 1403, a London hospital—St. Mary of Bethlehem—admitted its first patient with psychological problems. For the next 300 years, mental patients of the hospital were chained, tortured, and exhibited to an admission-paying public. Over time, a mispronunciation of Bethlehem—*bedlam*—came to mean chaos because of the horrible confusion reigning in the hospital and the dehumanized treatment of patients there (Foucault, 1975).

It wasn't until the late 18th century that the perception of psychological problems as mental illness emerged in Europe. In 1792, the French physician Philippe Pinel received permission from the government installed after the French Revolution to remove the chains from some of the inmates in mental hospitals. In the United States, psychologically disturbed individuals were confined for their own protection and for the safety of the community, but they were given no treatment. However, by the mid-1800s, when psychology as a field of study was gaining some credibility and respectability, "a cult of curability" emerged throughout the country. Spurred on by her firsthand experience working in prison settings, **Dorothea Dix** (1802–1887) labored continuously between 1841 and 1881 to improve the physical treatment of the mentally ill.

---

deinstitutionalization The movement to treat people with psychological disorders in the community rather than in psychiatric hospitals.

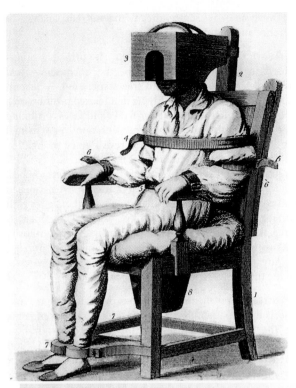

Treatment of mental disorders in the 18th century focused on banishing "ill humors" from the body. Shown here is the "tranquilizing chair" advocated by Philadelphia physician Benjamin Rush. Why did attitudes toward the treatment of the mentally ill change?

In the late 19th and early 20th centuries, many people argued that mental illness arose from the environmental stresses brought on by the turmoil of newly developing cities. To ease those stresses, the disturbed were confined to asylums in rural areas, far from the stress of the city, not only for protection but also for treatment (Rothman, 1971). Unfortunately, many of the asylums that were built became overcrowded. The humane goal of alleviating mental illness was replaced with the pragmatic goal of containing strange people in remote places. These large understaffed state mental hospitals became little more than human warehouses for disturbed individuals (Scull, 1993). Beginning in the 1960s, reformers began to agitate against these warehouses, in favor of the deinstitutionalization of at least those mental patients who could thrive with outpatient treatment and appropriate community supports. Unfortunately, as we'll see next, many deinstitutionalized patients do not obtain adequate assistance in their communities.

Deinstitutionalization and Homelessness In 1969, about 471,000 people in the United States received inpatient treatment for psychological disorders. By 2002, that number had fallen to about 181,000 (Substance Abuse and Mental Health Service Administration, 2006). This reduction for the United States is paralleled in other countries around the world (Fakhoury & Priebe, 2002). As we saw in Chapter 14, it isn't the case that the number of people affected by psychological disorders has fallen. Rather, the change reflects a process of deinstitutionalization: Many people with disorders are now treated outside of hospital settings. Deinstitutionalization arose from both social forces (that is, the movement against the warehousing of people with

mental illness) and genuine advances in treatment. For example, later in this chapter we will describe drug treatments that allowed people with schizophrenia to live outside of institutions.

Many people have been deinstitutionalized with the assumption that they will receive mental health care in some other setting. Unfortunately, that hasn't always proven to be the case. In fact, many people who leave psychiatric hospitals are not able to cope with their psychological disorders once they are in the community. One consequence is that people who leave institutions become homeless. For example, researchers found that 24 percent of a sample of 438 individuals with serious mental illnesses were homeless (Kuno et al., 2000). Among people who were admitted to a major state mental hospital in 1980, 15.3 percent were homeless. By 1996, that figure had risen to 20.2 percent and by 2003 to 29.2 percent (Appleby et al., 2006). Even when deinstitutionalized people are not homeless, ongoing mental health issues can cause substantial problems. For example, researchers examined the rate at which people with severe mental illness are the victims of violent crime such as robbery or assault (Teplin et al., 2005). In a sample of 936 men and women, 25.3 percent had experienced a violent crime—a rate 11 times higher than for individuals in the general population. The researchers suggested that the individuals' mental illnesses may prevent them from recognizing risk or appropriately protecting themselves.

Another consequence of deinstitutionalization is what has sometimes been called the "revolving door": People leave institutions for only brief periods of time before needing help once again. For example, one large-scale study looked at 29,373 patients with schizophrenia who had been released from hospitals. The researchers found that 42.5 percent of the patients were readmitted within 30 days of their initial release (Lin et al., 2006). More generally, approximately 40 to 50 percent of psychiatric patients are readmitted within 1 year after their initial discharge (Bridge & Barbe, 2004). In many of these cases, individuals left institutional care with the symptoms of their psychological disorders at a level that could have allowed them to function in the outside world. Unfortunately, people often do not have appropriate community or personal resources to adhere to treatment outside the structure provided by an institution. In that sense, the problem is not so much with deinstitutionalization as it is with the lack of community resources outside the institutions.

STOP AND REVIEW

❶ What are the primary goals of the therapeutic process?
❷ What special training does a psychoanalyst have?
❸ Why is cultural competence important for therapists?
❹ With respect to deinstitutionalization, what is meant by the "revolving door"?

Visit MyPsychLab.com for more review and practice on the following topics:

👁 **Watch:** Recent Trends in Treatment: Sue Mineka

🔊 **Explore:** Psychotherapy Practitioners and Their Activities

✴ **Simulate:** Overview of Clinical Assessment Methods

👁 **Watch:** Asylum: History of Mental Institutions in America

Psychodynamic Therapies

Psychodynamic therapies assume that a patient's problems have been caused by the psychological tension between unconscious impulses and the constraints of his or her life situation. These therapies locate the core of the disorder inside the disturbed person. We will review the origins of this approach in the work of Sigmund Freud and his followers. We will then describe how contemporary clinicians use psychodynamic therapies.

FREUDIAN PSYCHOANALYSIS

Psychoanalysis, as developed by Sigmund Freud, is an intensive and prolonged technique for exploring unconscious motivations and conflicts in neurotic, anxiety-ridden individuals. As we saw in earlier chapters, Freudian theory views anxiety disorders as inabilities to resolve adequately the inner conflicts between the unconscious, irrational impulses of the *id* and the internalized social constraints imposed by the *superego.* The goal of psychoanalysis is to establish intrapsychic harmony that expands awareness of the forces of the *id,* reduces overcompliance with the demands of the *superego,* and strengthens the role of the *ego.*

Of central importance to a therapist is to understand the way a patient uses the process of *repression* to handle conflicts. Symptoms are considered to be messages from the unconscious that something is wrong. A psychoanalyst's task is to help a patient bring repressed thoughts to consciousness and to gain *insight* into the relationship between the current symptoms and the repressed conflicts. In this psychodynamic view, therapy succeeds and patients recover when they are "released from repression" established in early childhood. Because a central goal of a therapist is to guide a patient toward discovering insights into the relationships between present symptoms and past origins, psychodynamic therapy is often called **insight therapy.**

Traditional psychoanalysis is an attempt to reconstruct long-standing repressed memories and then work through painful feelings to an effective resolution. The psychodynamic approach includes several techniques to bring repressed conflicts to consciousness and to help a patient resolve them (Luborsky & Barrett, 2006). These techniques include free association, analysis of resistance, dream analysis, and analysis of transference and countertransference.

Free Association and Catharsis The principal procedure used in psychoanalysis to probe the unconscious and release repressed material is called **free association.** A patient, sitting comfortably in a chair or lying in a relaxed position on a couch, lets his or her mind wander freely and gives a running account of thoughts, wishes, physical sensations, and mental images. The patient is encouraged to reveal every thought or feeling, no matter how unimportant it may seem.

Freud maintained that free associations are *predetermined,* not random. The task of an analyst is to track the associations to their source and identify the significant patterns that lie beneath the surface of what are apparently just words. The patient is encouraged to express strong feelings, usually toward authority figures, that have been repressed for fear of punishment or retaliation. Any such emotional release, by this or other processes within the therapeutic context, is called **catharsis.**

Resistance A psychoanalyst attaches particular importance to subjects that a patient does *not* wish to discuss. At some time during the process of free association, a patient will show **resistance**—an inability or unwillingness to discuss certain ideas, desires, or experiences. Such resistances are conceived of as *barriers* between the unconscious and the conscious. This material is often related to an individual's sexual life (which includes all things pleasurable) or to hostile, resentful feelings toward parents. When the repressed material is finally brought into the open, a patient generally claims that it is unimportant, absurd, irrelevant, or too unpleasant to discuss. The therapist believes the opposite. Psychoanalysis aims to break down resistances and enable the patient to face these painful ideas, desires, and experiences.

Dream Analysis Psychoanalysts believe that dreams are an important source of information about a patient's unconscious motivations. When a person is asleep, the superego is presumably less on guard against the unacceptable impulses originating in the id, so a motive that cannot be expressed in

---

psychoanalysis The form of psychodynamic therapy developed by Freud; an intensive prolonged technique for exploring unconscious motivations and conflicts in neurotic, anxiety-ridden individuals.

insight therapy A technique by which the therapist guides a patient toward discovering insights between present symptoms and past origins.

free association The therapeutic method in which a patient gives a running account of thoughts, wishes, physical sensations, and mental images as they occur.

catharsis The process of expressing strongly felt but usually repressed emotions.

resistance The inability or unwillingness of a patient in psychoanalysis to discuss certain ideas, desires, or experiences.

Why is psychoanalytic therapy, originally practiced in Freud's study, often called the "talking cure"?

waking life may find expression in a dream. In analysis, dreams are assumed to have two kinds of content: *manifest* (openly visible) content that people remember upon awakening and *latent* (hidden) content—the actual motives that are seeking expression but are so painful or unacceptable that they are expressed in disguised or symbolic form. Therapists attempt to uncover these hidden motives by using **dream analysis,** a therapeutic technique that examines the content of a person's dreams to discover the underlying or disguised motivations and symbolic meanings of significant life experiences and desires.

Transference and Countertransference During the course of the intensive therapy of psychoanalysis, a patient usually develops an emotional reaction toward the therapist. Often, the therapist is identified with a person who has been at the center of an emotional conflict in the past—most often a parent or a lover. This emotional reaction is called **transference.** Transference is called *positive transference* when the feelings attached to the therapist are those of love or admiration and *negative transference* when the feelings consist of hostility or envy. Often, a patient's attitude is ambivalent, including a mixture of positive and negative feelings. An analyst's task in handling transference is a difficult one because of the patient's emotional vulnerability; however, it is a crucial part of treatment. A therapist helps a patient to interpret the present transferred feelings by understanding their original source in earlier experiences and attitudes (Henry et al., 1994).

Personal feelings are also at work in a therapist's reactions to a patient. **Countertransference** refers to what happens when a therapist comes to like or dislike a patient because the patient is perceived as similar to significant people in the therapist's life. In working through countertransference, a therapist may discover some unconscious dynamics of his or her own. The therapist becomes a "living mirror" for the patient and the patient, in turn, for the therapist. If the therapist fails to recognize the operation of countertransference, the therapy may not be as effective (Winarick, 1997). Because of the emotional intensity of this type of therapeutic relationship and the vulnerability of the patient, therapists must be on guard about crossing the boundary between professional caring and personal involvement with their patients. The therapy setting is obviously one with an enormous power imbalance that must be recognized, and honored, by the therapist.

LATER PSYCHODYNAMIC THERAPIES

Freud's followers retained many of his basic ideas but modified certain of his principles and practices. In general, these therapists place more emphasis than Freud did on: (1) a patient's *current* social environment (less focus on the past); (2) the continuing influence of life experiences (not just childhood conflicts); (3) the role of social motivation and interpersonal relations of love (rather than of biological instincts and selfish concerns); (4) the significance of ego functioning and development of the self-concept (less on the conflict between id and superego).

In Chapter 13, we noted two other prominent theorists, Carl Jung and Alfred Adler. To get a flavor of more contemporary

In what ways did the theories of Melanie Klein and Sigmund Freud differ?

psychodynamic approaches, here we will look at the work of Harry Stack Sullivan and of Melanie Klein (see Ruitenbeek, 1973, for a look at other members of the Freudian circle).

Harry Stack Sullivan (1953) felt that Freudian theory and therapy did not recognize the importance of social relationships and a patient's needs for acceptance, respect, and love. Mental disorders, he insisted, involve not only traumatic intrapsychic processes but also troubled interpersonal relationships and even strong societal pressures. Anxiety and other mental ills arise out of insecurities in relations with parents and significant others. Therapy based on this interpersonal view involves observing a *patient's feelings* about the *therapist's attitudes.* The therapeutic interview is seen as a social setting in which each party's feelings and attitudes are influenced by the other's.

Melanie Klein (1975) defected from Freud's emphasis on the Oedipus conflict as the major source of psychopathology. Instead of oedipal sexual conflicts as the most important organizing factors of the psyche, Klein argued that a *death instinct*

---

dream analysis The psychoanalytic interpretation of dreams used to gain insight into a person's unconscious motives or conflicts.

transference The process by which a person in psychoanalysis attaches to a therapist feelings formerly held toward some significant person who figured into past emotional conflict.

countertransference Circumstances in which a psychoanalyst develops personal feelings about a client because of perceived similarity of the client to significant people in the therapist's life.

preceded sexual awareness and led to an innate aggressive impulse that was equally important in organizing the psyche. She contended that the two fundamental organizing forces in the psyche are aggression and love, where love *unites* and aggression *splits* the psyche. On Klein's view, conscious love is connected to remorse over destructive hate and potential violence toward those we love. Thus Klein explained, "one of the great mysteries that all people face [is] that love and hate—our personal heaven and hell—cannot be separated from one another" (Frager & Fadiman, 1998, p. 135). Klein pioneered the use of forceful therapeutic interpretations of both aggressive and sexual drives in analytic patients.

In contemporary practice, psychodynamic therapists continue to draw upon the foundational concepts of Freud and his followers. The core focus for most psychodynamic therapies is interpersonal conflict. Against that background, individual therapists may put more or less emphasis on particular processes such as the interpretation of transference (Gibbons et al., 2008). Therapists also differ with respect to how active a role the therapist plays in interpreting the patient's life experiences. Finally, traditional psychoanalysis often takes a long time (several years at least, with as many as five sessions a week). It also requires introspective patients who are verbally fluent, highly motivated to remain in therapy, and willing and able to undergo considerable expense. Newer forms of psychodynamic therapy are making therapy briefer in total duration.

An important goal of psychodynamic therapy is to provide patients with insights into the interpersonal conflicts that lay at the roots of their psychological disorders. Behavioral therapies, to which we now turn, focus their attention more directly on the maladaptive behaviors that define the disorders.

STOP AND REVIEW

❶ Why is psychodynamic therapy also known as insight therapy?

❷ What is transference?

❸ What role did the death instinct play in Melanie Klein's theory?

Behavior Therapies

Whereas psychodynamic therapies focus on presumed inner causes, behavior therapies focus on observable outer behaviors. Behavior therapists argue that abnormal behaviors are acquired in the same way as normal behaviors—through a learning process that follows the basic principles of conditioning and learning. Behavior therapies apply the principles of conditioning and

---

behavior therapy See behavior modification.

behavior modification The systematic use of principles of learning to increase the frequency of desired behaviors and/or decrease the frequency of problem behaviors.

counterconditioning A technique used in therapy to substitute a new response for a maladaptive one by means of conditioning procedures.

exposure therapy A behavioral technique in which clients are exposed to the objects or situations that cause them anxiety.

reinforcement to modify undesirable behavior patterns associated with mental disorders.

The terms **behavior therapy** and **behavior modification** are often used interchangeably. Both refer to the systematic use of principles of learning to increase the frequency of desired behaviors and/or decrease that of problem behaviors. The range of deviant behaviors and personal problems that typically are treated by behavior therapy is extensive and includes fears, compulsions, depression, addictions, aggression, and delinquent behaviors. In general, behavior therapy works best with specific rather than general types of personal problems: It is better for a phobia than for unfocused anxiety.

The therapies that have emerged from the theories of conditioning and learning are grounded in a pragmatic, empirical research tradition. The central task of all living organisms is to learn how to adapt to the demands of the current social and physical environment. When organisms do not learn how to cope effectively, their maladaptive reactions can be overcome by therapy based on principles of learning (or relearning). The target behavior is not assumed to be a symptom of any underlying process. The symptom itself is the problem. Psychodynamic therapists predicted that treating only the outer behavior without confronting the true, inner problem would result in *symptom substitution,* the appearance of a new physical or psychological problem. However, research has shown that when pathological behaviors are eliminated by behavior therapy, new symptoms are not substituted (Kazdin, 1982; Wolpe, 1986). "On the contrary, patients whose target symptoms improved often reported improvement in other, less important symptoms as well" (Sloane et al., 1975, p. 219).

Let's look at the different forms of behavior therapies that have brought relief to distressed individuals.

COUNTERCONDITIONING

Why does someone become anxious when faced with a harmless stimulus, such as a spider, a nonpoisonous snake, or social contact? The behavioral explanation is that the anxiety arises due to the simple conditioning principles we reviewed in Chapters 6 and 14: Strong emotional reactions that disrupt a person's life "for no good reason" are often conditioned responses that the person does not recognize as having been learned previously. In **counterconditioning,** a new response is conditioned to replace, or "counter," a maladaptive response. The earliest recorded use of behavior therapy followed this logic. **Mary Cover Jones** (1924) showed that a fear could be *unlearned* through conditioning. (Compare with the case of Little Albert in Chapter 6.)

> Her patient was Peter, a 3-year-old boy who, for some unknown reason, was afraid of rabbits. The therapy involved feeding Peter at one end of a room while the rabbit was brought in at the other end. Over a series of sessions, the rabbit was gradually brought closer until, finally, all fear disappeared and Peter played freely with the rabbit.

Following in Cover Jones's footsteps, behavior therapists now use several counterconditioning techniques, including systematic desensitization, implosion, flooding, and aversion therapy.

Exposure Therapies The central component of **exposure therapy** is that individuals are made to confront the object or situation that causes anxiety. The therapeutic principle is that exposure permits counterconditioning—people learn to remain relaxed in circumstances that once would have made them highly anxious. Individual exposure therapies differ with

ARE LIVES HAUNTED BY REPRESSED MEMORIES?

On September 22, 1969, 8-year-old Susan Nason vanished from her northern California neighborhood. In December 1969, her body was found. For 20 years, no one knew who had murdered her. Then, in 1989, Susan's friend Eileen Franklin-Lipsker contacted county investigators. Eileen told them that, with the help of psychotherapy, she had recalled a long-repressed, horrifying memory about what had happened to Susan. In the fall of 1990, Eileen testified that, over two decades earlier, she had witnessed her father, George Franklin, sexually assault Susan and then bludgeon her to death with a rock (Marcus, 1990; Workman, 1990). This testimony was sufficient to have George Franklin convicted of first-degree murder. Because of a technical error at the trial, George Franklin was released after five years in jail. In those five years, strong doubts had also accumulated about the validity of his daughter's memories. Still, a jury had initially found the dramatic recovery of 20-year-old memories quite credible.

How, in theory, had these memories remained hidden for 20 years? The answer to this mystery finds its roots in Sigmund Freud's concept of repressed memories. As we just reminded you, Freud (1923) theorized that some people's memories of life experiences become sufficiently threatening to their psychological well-being that the individuals banish the memories from consciousness—they repress them. Clinical psychologists are often able to help clients

take control of their lives by interpreting disruptive life patterns as the consequences of repressed memories; an important goal of therapy is to achieve catharsis with respect to these repressed memories.

But not all experiences of repressed memories remain in the therapist's office. The media often reports claims of the dramatic recovery of repressed memories. After long intervals of time, individuals report sudden vivid recollections of horrifying events, such as murders or childhood sexual abuse. Could all these claims be real?

Our review of memory research in Chapter 7—particularly research on eyewitness memories—provided you with grounds for skepticism (Loftus & Davis, 2006). You might recall from that research that people will report as true memories information that was provided from an artificial source. They will do so even when, as witnesses, they have been specifically warned that they have been misled. Thus being in confident possession of a memory provides no assurance of the ultimate source of that memory.

Clinicians worry that therapists who believe in repressed memories may, through the mechanisms of psychotherapy, implant those beliefs in their patients (Lynn et al., 2003). Therapists who believe in repressed memories may instigate patients' efforts to find these memories—and verbally rewarded them when the "memories" came to light (de Rivera, 1997). In one study, researchers recruited 128 participants who all claimed that

they had experienced childhood sexual abuse (Geraerts et al., 2007). A majority of the participants (71 of the 128) had continuous memories of the abuse. That is, there were no life periods in which they didn't recall the abuse. The other 57 participants had *discontinuous* memories; they believed that they had forgotten the abuse for some period of time. Of that group, 16 had recovered memories of abuse in therapy, whereas the other 41 had recovered the memories without any special prompting. The researchers sent interviewers into the field to try to find evidence to corroborate the participants' memories of abuse. This was possible for 45 percent of the participants with continuous memories and 37 percent of the participants who had recovered memories on their own. However, for participants who recovered memories during therapy the interviewers found 0 percent corroborating evidence.

This study confirms that some reports of recovered memories are based on real occurrences. However, the study also demonstrates the potential for processes of psychotherapy to lead people to create false memories. Belief in the recovery of repressed memories may provide a measurable benefit for patients in psychotherapy. Even so, if you come to explore the question of whether repressed memories can help explain present discomfort, you should ensure that you are not passively accepting someone else's version of your life.

---

respect to the time course and circumstances in which people are exposed to their sources of anxiety.

For example, **Joseph Wolpe** (1958, 1973) observed that the nervous system cannot be relaxed and agitated at the same time because incompatible processes cannot be activated simultaneously. This insight was central to the *theory of reciprocal inhibition* that Wolpe applied to the treatment of fears and phobias. Wolpe taught his patients to *relax* their muscles and then to *imagine* visually their feared situation. They did so in gradual steps that

moved from initially remote associations to direct images. Psychologically confronting the feared stimulus while being relaxed and doing so in a *graduated* sequence is the therapeutic technique known as **systematic desensitization.**

---

systematic desensitization A behavioral therapy technique in which a client is taught to prevent the arousal of anxiety by confronting the feared stimulus while relaxed.

Why are many therapies for anxiety disorders known as exposure therapies?

session, the student was able to pop the last 115 balloons himself. Another form of flooding therapy begins with the use of imagination. In this procedure, the client may listen to a tape that describes the most terrifying version of the phobic fear in great detail for an hour or two. Once the terror subsides, the client is then taken to the feared situation.

When exposure techniques were first created, therapists brought about exposure through mental imagery or actual contact. In recent years, clinicians have turned to virtual reality to provide exposure therapy (Powers & Emmelkamp, 2008). Consider this study that compared virtual reality therapy to standard exposure therapy for individuals with a fear of flying.

A team of researchers recruited 50 people whose fear of flying was of sufficient intensity to qualify as a psychological disorder (Rothbaum et al., 2006). Half of the group received a standard form of exposure therapy. Much of the treatment took place at an actual airport. Over several sessions, the participants were exposed to aspects of flying that became successively more anxiety provoking—they began by viewing the ticketing area and ended by boarding an airplane. The remainder of the participants experienced exposure through virtual environments. For example, they had virtual experiences of sitting in an airplane, taking off, and landing. As with their peers who went out into the world, they remained in each virtual location until their anxiety had diminished. To measure the effectiveness of each intervention, the researchers assessed the participants' lingering discomfort toward flying on measures such as a *fear of flying inventory*. Both types of therapies yielded consistent and lasting relief for the participants. In fact, when the researchers invited them to take a post-treatment flight, 76 percent of the participants in each treatment group accepted the invitation compared to only 20 percent of individuals in a control group (who had received no treatment).

Desensitization therapy involves three major steps. First, the client identifies the stimuli that provoke anxiety and arranges them in a hierarchy ranked from weakest to strongest. For example, a student suffering from severe test anxiety constructed the hierarchy in **Table 15.1.** Note that she rated immediate anticipation of an examination (No. 14) as more stressful than taking the exam itself (No. 13). Second, the client is trained in a system of progressive deep-muscle relaxation. Relaxation training requires several sessions in which the client learns to distinguish between sensations of tension and relaxation and to let go of tension to achieve a state of physical and mental relaxation. Finally, the actual process of desensitization begins: The relaxed client vividly imagines the weakest anxiety stimulus on the list. If it can be visualized without discomfort, the client goes on to the next stronger one. After a number of sessions, the most distressing situations on the list can be imagined without anxiety.

Systematic desensitization represents a gradual course of exposure to stimuli that provoke anxiety. Therapists have explored a variety of other techniques, some of which bring about exposure with less delay. For example, in a technique known as *flooding,* clients agree to be put directly into the phobic situation. A person with claustrophobia is made to sit in a dark closet, and a child with a fear of water is put into a pool. Researchers successfully treated a 21-year-old student's phobia of balloon pops by having him experience three sessions in which he endured hundreds of balloons being popped (Houlihan et al., 1993). In the third

---

TABLE 15.1 Hierarchy of Anxiety-Producing Stimuli for a Test-Anxious College Student (in order of increasing anxiety)

1. A month before an examination.
2. Two weeks before an examination.
3. A week before an examination.
4. Five days before an examination.
5. Four days before an examination.
6. Three days before an examination.
7. Two days before an examination.
8. One day before an examination.
9. The night before an examination.
10. The examination paper face down.
11. Awaiting the distribution of examination papers.
12. Before the unopened doors of the examination room.
13. In the process of answering an examination paper.
14. On the way to the university on the day of an examination.

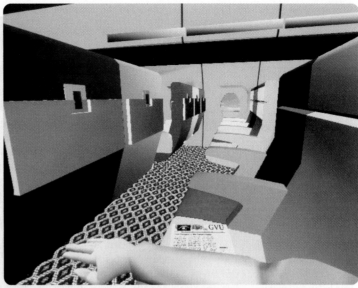

How might a behavior therapist use virtual reality exposure therapy to help a client overcome a fear of flying?

Exposure therapies have proved to be highly effective for treating anxiety disorders. Virtual reality techniques hold out the promise of providing powerful exposure experiences without the time and expense of venturing out into the real world.

Exposure therapy has also been used to combat obsessive-compulsive disorders. However, the therapy adds another component: *response prevention*. Not only are clients exposed to what they fear, but they are also prevented from performing the compulsive behaviors that ordinarily reduce their anxiety. Consider a study of 20 children and adolescents with OCD (Bolton & Perrin, 2008). Because each participant had different obsessions and compulsions, the treatment needed to be tailored to each individual. However, the core components remained the same: Each participant was exposed to the objects of his or her obsession while engaging in exercises to prevent the compulsive behaviors. This program of therapy brought about substantial relief.

Aversion Therapy The forms of exposure therapy we've described help clients deal directly with stimuli that are not really harmful. What can be done to help those who are *attracted* to stimuli that *are* harmful? Drug addiction, sexual perversions, and uncontrollable violence are human problems in which deviant behavior is elicited by tempting stimuli. **Aversion therapy** uses counterconditioning procedures to pair these stimuli with strong noxious stimuli such as electric shocks or nausea-producing drugs. In time, the same negative reactions are elicited by the tempting stimuli, and the person develops an aversion that replaces his or her former desire. For example, aversion therapy has been used with individuals who engage in *self-injurious behaviors,* such as hitting their heads or banging their heads against other objects. When an individual performs such a behavior, he or she is given a mild electric shock. This treatment effectively eliminates self-injurious behaviors in some, but not all, patients (Duker & Seys, 1996).

In the extreme, aversion therapy resembles torture, so why would anyone submit voluntarily to it? Usually, people do so only because they realize that the long-term consequences of continuing their behavior pattern will destroy their health or ruin their careers or family lives. They may also be driven to do so by institutional pressures, as has happened in some prison treatment programs. However, use of aversion therapy in institutional rehabilitation programs has become regulated by ethical guidelines and state laws. The hope is that, under these restrictions, it will be therapeutic rather than coercive.

CONTINGENCY MANAGEMENT

Counterconditioning procedures are appropriate when one response can be replaced with another. Other behavior modification procedures rely on the principles of operant conditioning that arose in the research tradition pioneered by B. F. Skinner. **Contingency management** refers to the general treatment strategy of changing behavior by modifying its consequences. The two major techniques of contingency management in behavior therapy are *positive reinforcement strategies* and *extinction strategies.*

Positive Reinforcement Strategies When a response is followed immediately by a reward, the response tends to be repeated and to increase in frequency over time. This central principle of operant learning becomes a therapeutic strategy

---

aversion therapy A type of behavioral therapy used to treat individuals attracted to harmful stimuli; an attractive stimulus is paired with a noxious stimulus in order to elicit a negative reaction to the target stimulus.

contingency management A general treatment strategy involving changing behavior by modifying its consequences.

when it is used to modify the frequency of a desirable response as it replaces an undesirable one. Dramatic success has been obtained from the application of positive reinforcement procedures to behavior problems.

You might recall from Chapter 6 a technique called *shaping* in which researchers reinforce successive approximations to a desired behavior. Consider how shaping was used to help smokers reduce the number of cigarettes they smoked (Lamb et al., 2007). The researchers measured the participants' breath carbon monoxide (BCO) to determine initial smoking habits. As the study unfolded, the participants received cash incentives if they were able to get their BCO below particular goal levels (which were set for each smoker). Those goals became more demanding over time—shaping participants toward the desired behavior of abstinence from smoking. In Chapter 6, we also described *token economies*, in which desired behaviors (such as practicing personal care or taking medication) are explicitly defined, and token payoffs are given by institutional staff when the behaviors are performed. These tokens can later be exchanged for an array of rewards and privileges (Kazdin, 1994; Martin & Pear, 1999). These systems of reinforcement are especially effective in modifying patients' behaviors regarding self-care, upkeep of their environment, and frequency of their positive social interactions.

In another approach, therapists differentially reinforce behaviors that are incompatible with the maladaptive behavior. This technique has been used successfully with individuals in treatment for drug addiction.

Researchers recruited 142 individuals who were seeking treatment for cocaine and opioid (for example, heroin) dependence into a 12-week study (Petry et al., 2005). All the participants received standard treatment of a series of counseling sessions that imparted strategies and skills for overcoming dependence. In addition to this standard treatment, one group of 53 participants received vouchers each time they produced a urine specimen that was drug free. The first time participants produced a negative urine specimen, they were given a voucher worth $1. The voucher amounts increased by $1.50 with each negative specimen. A positive specimen reset the voucher amount to $1. Another group of 51 participants was given the opportunity to win prizes, contingent on negative urine specimens. To win the prizes, participants pulled cards from an urn. The majority of the cards (62.8 percent) read "good job, try again," but the remainder provided prizes that valued $1, $20, or $100. For the first negative specimen, participants got to pull one card from the urn. For each subsequent negative specimen, they earned an extra one pull. A positive specimen reduced participants back to a single pull. The researchers assessed the efficacy of each treatment program, for example, by measuring the average number of weeks participants in each group were continuously abstinent. For the group that only received standard treatment, that number was 4.6 weeks. For the voucher group, that number was 7.0 weeks, and for the prize group that number was 7.8 weeks. Thus both contingency management treatments increased the likelihood that participants would abstain from drugs.

This study verifies that two different programs of contingency management—vouchers and prizes—can be used successfully to treat drug dependence. You might recognize the same philosophy at work here as the one that motivated the counterconditioning procedures we described earlier: Basic principles of learning are used to increase the probability of adaptive behaviors.

Extinction Strategies Why do people continue to do something that causes pain and distress when they are capable of doing otherwise? The answer is that many forms of behavior have multiple consequences—some are negative, and some are positive. Often, subtle positive reinforcements keep a behavior going despite its obvious negative consequences. For example, children who are punished for misbehaving may continue to misbehave if punishment is the only form of attention they seem to be able to earn.

Extinction strategies are useful in therapy when dysfunctional behaviors have been maintained by unrecognized reinforcing circumstances. Those reinforcers can be identified through a careful situational analysis, and then a program can be arranged to withhold them in the presence of the undesirable response. When this approach is possible, and everyone in the situation who might inadvertently reinforce the person's behavior cooperates, extinction procedures work to diminish the frequency of the behavior and eventually to eliminate the behavior completely. Consider a classroom example. A boy with attention-deficit/hyperactivity disorder was causing problems for his teachers because he frequently engaged in disruptive off-task behaviors. Researchers discovered that the attention the teachers gave to the student when he engaged in off-task behaviors was positively reinforcing those behaviors (Stahr et al., 2006). When the teachers no longer paid attention to him when he behaved inappropriately, the student's behavior improved.

Even symptoms of schizophrenia can be maintained and encouraged by unintentional reinforcement. Consider the following circumstances. It is standard procedure in many psychiatric hospitals for the staff to ask patients frequently, as a form of social communication, "How are you feeling?" Patients often misinterpret this question as a request for diagnostic information, and they respond by thinking and talking about their feelings, unusual symptoms, and hallucinations. Such responding is likely to be counterproductive because it leads staff to conclude that the patients are self-absorbed and not behaving normally. In fact, the more bizarre the symptoms and verbalizations, the more attention the staff members may show to the patient, which reinforces continued expression of bizarre symptoms. In a classic study, dramatic decreases in symptoms were observed when hospital staff members were simply instructed to ignore the behavior and to give attention to the patients only when they were behaving normally (Ayllon & Michael, 1959).

SOCIAL-LEARNING THERAPY

The range of behavior therapies has been expanded by social-learning theorists who point out that humans learn by observing the behavior of other people. Often, you learn and apply rules to new experiences through symbolic means, such as watching other people's experiences in life, in a movie, or on TV. **Social-learning therapy** is designed to modify problematic behavior patterns by arranging conditions in which a client will observe models being reinforced for a desirable form of responding. This vicarious learning process has been

---

social-learning therapy A form of treatment in which clients observe models' desirable behaviors being reinforced.

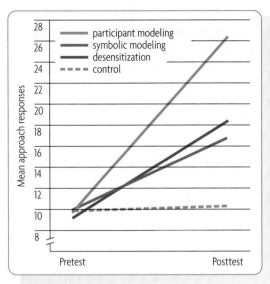

FIGURE 15.1 Participant Modeling Therapy

The subject shown in the photo first watched a model make a graduated series of snake-approach responses and then repeated them herself. She eventually was able to pick up the snake and let it crawl about on her. The graph compares the number of approach responses subjects made before and after receiving participant modeling therapy (most effective) with the behavior of those exposed to two other therapeutic techniques and a control group.

Albert Bandura, from "Modeling Therapy." Reprinted by permission of Albert Bandura.

of special value in overcoming phobias and building social skills. We have noted in earlier chapters that this social-learning theory was largely developed through the pioneering research of Albert Bandura (1977, 1986). Here we will mention only two aspects of his approach: imitation of models and social-skills training.

Imitation of Models Social-learning theory predicts that individuals acquire responses through observation. Thus it should be the case that people with phobias should be able to unlearn fear reactions through imitation of models. For example, in treating a phobia of snakes, a therapist will first demonstrate fearless approach behavior at a relatively minor level, perhaps approaching a snake's cage or touching a snake. The client is aided, through demonstration and encouragement, to imitate the modeled behavior. Gradually, the approach behaviors are shaped so that the client can pick up the snake and let it crawl freely over him or her. At no time is the client forced to perform any behavior. Resistance at any level is overcome by having the client return to a previously successful, less threatening level of approach behavior.

The power of this form of **participant modeling** can be seen in research comparing this technique with symbolic modeling, desensitization, and a control condition. In *symbolic modeling therapy,* individuals who had been trained in relaxation techniques watched a film in which several models fearlessly handled snakes; they could stop the film and try to relax whenever a scene made them feel anxious. In the control condition, no therapeutic intervention was used. As you can see in **Figure 15.1,** participant modeling was clearly the most successful of these techniques. Snake phobia was eliminated in 11 of the 12 individuals in the participant modeling group (Bandura, 1970).

Social-Skills Training A major therapeutic innovation encouraged by social-learning therapists involves training people with inadequate social skills to be more effective. Many difficulties arise for someone with a mental disorder, or even just an everyday problem, if he or she is socially inhibited, inept, or unassertive. *Social skills* are sets of responses that enable people effectively to achieve their social goals when approaching or interacting with others. These skills include knowing *what* (content) to say and do in given situations in order to elicit a desired response (consequences), *how* (style) to say and do it, and *when* (timing) to say and do it.

To help people acquire such skills, many social-learning therapists recommend **behavioral rehearsal**—visualizing how one should behave in a given situation and the desired positive consequences. Rehearsal can be used to establish and strengthen any basic skill, from personal hygiene to work habits to social interactions. Social skills training has proved successful to help the social functioning of diverse groups such as adults with schizophrenia and adolescents with emotional and/or behavioral disorders (Cook et al., 2008; Kurtz & Mueser, 2008).

GENERALIZATION TECHNIQUES

An ongoing issue of concern for behavior therapists is whether new behavior patterns generated in a therapeutic setting will actually be used in the everyday situations faced by their clients (Kazdin, 1994). This question is important for all therapies, because any measure of treatment effectiveness must include maintenance of long-term changes that go beyond a therapist's couch, clinic, or laboratory.

When essential aspects of a client's real-life setting are absent from the therapy program, behavioral changes accomplished through therapy may be lost over time after therapy terminates. To prevent this gradual loss, it has become common practice to build generalization techniques into the therapeutic procedure itself. These techniques attempt to *increase* the similarity of target behaviors, reinforcers, models, and stimulus demands between therapy and real-life settings. For example, behaviors are taught that are likely to be reinforced naturally in

---

participant modeling A therapeutic technique in which a therapist demonstrates the desired behavior and a client is aided, through supportive encouragement, to imitate the modeled behavior.

behavioral rehearsal Procedures used to establish and strengthen basic skills; as used in social-skills training programs, requires the client to rehearse a desirable behavior sequence mentally.

TABLE 15.2 Comparison of Psychoanalytic and Behavioral Approaches to Psychotherapy

Issue	Psychoanalysis	Behavior Therapy
Basic human nature	Biological instincts, primarily sexual and aggressive, press for immediate release, bringing people into conflict with social reality.	Similar to other animals, people are born only with the capacity for learning, which follows similar principles in all species.
Normal human development	Growth occurs through resolution of conflicts during successive stages. Through identification and internalization, mature ego controls and character structures emerge.	Adaptive behaviors are learned through reinforcement and imitation.
Nature of psychopathology	Pathology reflects inadequate conflict resolutions and fixations in earlier development, which leave overly strong impulses and/or weak controls. Symptoms are defensive responses to anxiety.	Problematic behavior derives from faulty learning of maladaptive behaviors. The *symptom* is the problem; there is no *underlying disease*.
Goal of therapy	Psychosexual maturity, strengthened ego functions, and reduced control by unconscious and repressed impulses are attained.	Symptomatic behavior is eliminated and replaced with adaptive behaviors.
Psychological realm emphasized	Motives, feelings, fantasies, and cognitions are experienced.	Therapy involves behavior and observable feelings and actions.
Time orientation	The orientation is discovering and interpreting past conflicts and repressed feelings in light of the present.	Concerned only about client's reinforcement history. Present behavior is examined and treated.
Role of unconscious material	This is primary in classical psychoanalysis and somewhat less emphasized by neo-Freudians.	There is no concern with unconscious processes or with subjective experience even in the conscious realm.
Role of insight	Insight is central; it emerges in "corrective emotional experiences."	Insight is irrelevant and/or unnecessary.
Role of therapist	The therapist functions as a *detective,* searching out basic root conflicts and resistances; detached and neutral, to facilitate transference reactions.	The therapist functions as a *trainer,* helping patients unlearn old behaviors and/or learn new ones. Control of reinforcement is important; interpersonal relationship is minor.

a person's environment, such as showing courtesy or consideration. Rewards are given on a partial reinforcement schedule to ensure that their effect will be maintained in the real world, where rewards are not always forthcoming. Expectation of tangible extrinsic rewards is gradually *faded out* while social approval and more naturally occurring consequences, including reinforcing self-statements, are incorporated.

Behavior therapists, for example, used a fading procedure with a boy (aged 4 years, 10 months) who refused to drink milk (Tiger & Hanley, 2006). To get the boy to drink his milk, the therapists had his teacher mix a small amount of chocolate syrup into a glass of milk. With the chocolate syrup mixed in, the boy drank the milk. Over the next 48 meals, the teacher slowly decreased the amount of chocolate until the boy was offered only plain milk. At the end of this intervention, the boy consistently drank plain milk. This was also true at home, demonstrating generalization from the classroom to an additional setting.

Before we move on to cognitive therapies, take a few minutes to review the major differences between the two psychotherapies outlined thus far—the psychoanalytic and the behavioral—as summarized in **Table 15.2.**

STOP AND REVIEW

❶ What is the basic principle of counterconditioning?
❷ What learning principle is at work when clinicians allow patients to earn vouchers?
❸ What is likely to take place if someone undergoes social-learning therapy?
❹ How does the therapist's role differ between psychoanalysis and behavior therapy?

CRITICAL THINKING Recall the study that used vouchers and prizes to treat drug dependence. Why did the prize amount or the number of urn pulls get set back to the minimum when participants produced positive specimens?

Visit MyPsychLab.com for more review and practice on the following topic:

👁 **Watch:** Anxiety Treatment: Edna Foa

Cognitive Therapies

Cognitive therapy attempts to change problem feelings and behaviors by changing the way a client thinks about significant life experiences. The underlying assumption of such therapy is that abnormal behavior patterns and emotional distress start with problems in *what* people think (cognitive content) and *how* they think (cognitive process). Cognitive therapies focus on changing different types of cognitive processes and providing different methods of cognitive restructuring. We discussed some of these approaches in Chapter 12 as ways to cope with stress and improve health. In this section, we will describe two major forms of cognitive therapy: alteration of false belief systems and cognitive behavioral therapy.

CHANGING FALSE BELIEFS

Some cognitive behavior therapists have, as their primary targets for change, beliefs, attitudes, and habitual thought patterns. These cognitive therapists argue that many psychological problems arise because of the way people think about themselves in relation to other people and the events they face. Faulty thinking can be based on (1) unreasonable attitudes ("Being perfect is the most important trait for a student to have"), (2) false premises ("If I do everything they want me to, then I'll be popular"), and (3) rigid rules that put behavior on automatic pilot so that prior patterns are repeated even when they have not worked ("I must obey authorities"). Emotional distress is caused by cognitive misunderstandings and by failure to distinguish between current reality and one's imagination (or expectations).

Cognitive Therapy for Depression

A cognitive therapist helps a client to correct faulty patterns of thinking by substituting more effective problem-solving techniques. Aaron Beck (1976) has successfully pioneered cognitive therapy for the problem of depression. He states the formula for treatment in simple form: "The therapist helps the patient to identify his warped thinking and to learn more realistic ways to formulate his experiences" (p. 20). For example, depressed individuals may be instructed to write down negative thoughts about themselves, figure out why these self-criticisms are unjustified, and come up with more realistic (and less destructive) self-cognitions.

Beck believes that depression is maintained because depressed patients are unaware of the negative automatic thoughts that they habitually formulate, such as "I will never be as good as my brother"; "Nobody would like me if they really knew me"; and "I'm not smart enough to make it in this competitive school." A therapist then uses four tactics to change the cognitive foundation that supports the depression (Beck & Rush, 1989; Beck et al., 1979):

- Challenging the client's basic assumptions about his or her functioning.
- Evaluating the evidence the client has for and against the accuracy of automatic thoughts.
- Reattributing blame to situational factors rather than to the patient's incompetence.
- Discussing alternative solutions to complex tasks that could lead to failure experiences.

This therapy is similar to behavior therapies in that it centers on the present state of the client.

One of the worst side effects of being depressed is having to live with all the negative feelings and lethargy associated with depression. Becoming obsessed with thoughts about one's negative mood brings up memories of all the bad times in life, which worsens the depressive feelings. By filtering all input through a darkly colored lens of depression, depressed people see criticism where there is none and hear sarcasm when they listen to praise—further "reasons" for being depressed. Cognitive therapy has proved successful at arresting depression's downward spiral (Hollon et al., 2006).

Rational-Emotive Therapy

One of the earliest forms of cognitive therapy was the **rational-emotive therapy (RET)** developed by **Albert Ellis** (1913–2007). RET is a comprehensive system of personality change based on the transformation of irrational beliefs that cause undesirable, highly charged emotional reactions, such as severe anxiety (Ellis, 1962, 1995; Windy & Ellis, 1997). Clients may have core values *demanding* that they succeed and be approved, *insisting* that they be treated fairly, and *dictating* that the universe be more pleasant.

Rational-emotive therapists teach clients how to recognize the "shoulds," "oughts," and "musts" that are controlling their actions and preventing them from choosing the lives they want. They attempt to break through a client's closed-mindedness by showing that an emotional reaction that follows some event is really the effect of unrecognized beliefs about the event. For example, failure to achieve orgasm during intercourse (event) is followed by an emotional reaction of depression and self-derogation. The belief that is causing the emotional reaction is likely to be "I am sexually inadequate and may be impotent because I failed to perform as expected." In therapy, this belief (and others) is openly disputed through rational confrontation and examination of alternative reasons for the event, such as fatigue, alcohol, false notions of sexual performance, or reluctance to engage in intercourse at that time or with that particular partner. This confrontation technique is followed by other interventions that replace dogmatic, irrational thinking with rational, situationally appropriate ideas.

Rational-emotive therapy aims to increase an individual's sense of self-worth and the potential to be self-actualized by getting rid of the system of faulty beliefs that block personal growth. As such, it shares much with humanistic therapies, which we consider later in the chapter.

COGNITIVE BEHAVIORAL THERAPY

You are what you tell yourself you can be, and you are guided by what you believe you ought to do. This is a starting assumption of **cognitive behavioral therapy.** This therapeutic approach

---

cognitive therapy A type of psychotherapeutic treatment that attempts to change feelings and behaviors by changing the way a client thinks about or perceives significant life experiences.

rational-emotive therapy (RET) A comprehensive system of personality change based on changing irrational beliefs that cause undesirable, highly charged emotional reactions such as severe anxiety.

cognitive behavioral therapy A therapeutic approach that combines the cognitive emphasis on thoughts and attitudes with the behavioral emphasis on changing performance.

Suppose you were learning to knit. Assuming you wanted to get better at it over time, what would be the best internal message to give yourself about the activity?

or avoid the cues' impact. Another component of the therapy was for participants to gain confidence that they could control their behavior. The researchers encouraged participants to undermine negative self-statements (for example, "I cannot control my urge to shop") by gathering evidence against such statements and by generating plans to achieve greater control. This program of therapy led to improvement both at the end of treatment and in follow-up assessment six months after treatment ended.

Note that the researchers needed the control group to demonstrate the effectiveness of the treatment (that is, members of the treatment group showed greater improvement than members of the control group). However, members of the control group were also offered treatment once the study came to an end.

As you can see from this example, cognitive behavioral therapy builds expectations of being effective. Therapists know that building these expectations increases the likelihood that people will behave effectively. Through setting attainable goals, developing realistic strategies for attaining them, and evaluating feedback realistically, you develop a sense of mastery and *self-efficacy* (Bandura, 1992, 1997). As we saw in Chapter 13, your sense of self-efficacy influences your perceptions, motivation, and performance in many ways. Self-efficacy judgments influence how much effort you expend and how long you persist in the face of difficult life situations (Bandura, 2006). Researchers have demonstrated the importance of self-efficacy in recovery from psychological disorders (Benight et al., 2008). Consider a study of 108 women with binge eating disorder (Cassin et al., 2008). Women in the control group received a handbook that provided information about the disorder. Women in the treatment group received the handbook but also participated in a therapy session designed to raise self-efficacy. For example, each woman was encouraged to "recall past experiences in which she [had] shown mastery in the face of difficulties and challenges" (p. 421). Sixteen weeks after the treatment, 28 percent of women in the treatment group had refrained from binge eating versus only 11 percent in the control group. Within the treatment group, the women who abstained from binge eating had reported higher levels of self-efficacy. This study provides further evidence that cognitive behavioral approaches to therapy can bring relief.

combines the cognitive emphasis on changing false beliefs with the behavioral focus on reinforcement contingencies in the modification of performance (Goldfried, 2003). Unacceptable behavior patterns are modified by *cognitive restructuring*—changing a person's negative self-statements into constructive coping statements.

A critical part of this therapeutic approach is the discovery by therapist and client of the way the client thinks about and expresses the problem for which therapy is sought. Once both therapist and client understand the kind of thinking that is leading to unproductive or dysfunctional behaviors, they develop new self-statements that are constructive and minimize the use of self-defeating ones that elicit anxiety or reduce self-esteem (Meichenbaum, 1977, 1985, 1993). For example, they might substitute the negative self-statement "I was really boring at that party; they'll never ask me back" with constructive criticism: "Next time, if I want to appear interesting, I will plan some provocative opening lines, practice telling a good joke, and be responsive to the host's stories." Instead of dwelling on negatives in past situations that are unchangeable, the client is taught to focus on positives in the future.

Cognitive behavioral therapy has been used as a successful treatment for a variety of disorders. Let's see how it was used to treat clients with *compulsive buying disorder,* which is defined as "excessive and mostly senseless spending or excessive shopping impulses that cause marked distress, interfere with social or occupational functioning, and often result in financial problems" (Mueller et al., 2008, p. 1131).

Researchers randomly assigned 60 people with compulsive buying disorder to cognitive behavioral therapy or to a control group (Mueller et al., 2008). Participants in the treatment group had one therapy session a week over the course of 12 weeks. The therapy had several components (Burgard & Mitchell, 2000). One component of the therapy was for participants to identify the cues (such as social or psychological situations) in their lives that triggered buying behavior. Once participants identified these cues, the therapists worked with them to develop cognitive strategies to disrupt

STOP AND REVIEW

❶ What is the underlying assumption of cognitive therapy?

❷ With respect to rational-emotive therapy, what is the origin of highly charged emotional reactions?

❸ Why is increased self-efficacy a goal for cognitive behavioral therapy?

CRITICAL THINKING Recall the study that assessed cognitive behavioral therapy for compulsive buying disorder. Why was it important to identify the cues that triggered buying behavior?

Visit MyPsychLab.com for more review and practice on the following topic:

◉ **Watch:** Cognitive Behavioral Therapy

Humanistic Therapies

Humanistic therapies have at their core the concept of a whole person in the continual process of changing and of becoming. Although environment and heredity place certain restrictions, people always remain free to choose what they will become by creating their own values and committing to them through their own decisions. Along with this *freedom to choose,* however, comes the burden of responsibility. Because you are never fully aware of all the implications of your actions, you experience anxiety and despair. You also suffer from guilt over lost opportunities to achieve your full potential. Psychotherapies that apply the principles of this general theory of human nature attempt to help clients define their own freedom, value their experiencing selves and the richness of the present moment, cultivate their individuality, and discover ways of realizing their fullest potential (self-actualization).

In some cases, humanistic therapies also absorbed the lessons of *existentialist* approaches to human experience (May, 1975). This approach emphasizes people's ability to meet or be overwhelmed by the everyday challenges of existence. Existential theorists suggest that individuals suffer from *existential crises:* problems in everyday living, a lack of meaningful human relationships, and an absence of significant goals. A clinical version of existential theory, which integrates its various themes and approaches, assumes that the bewildering realities of modern life give rise to two basic kinds of human maladies. Depressive and obsessive syndromes reflect a retreat from these realities; sociopathic and narcissistic syndromes reflect an exploitation of these realities (Schneider & May, 1995).

The humanistic philosophy also gave rise to the **human-potential movement,** which emerged in the United States in the late 1960s. This movement encompassed methods to enhance the potential of the average human being toward greater levels of performance and greater richness of experience. Through this movement, therapy originally intended for people with psychological disorders was extended to mentally healthy people who wanted to be more effective, more productive, and happier human beings.

Let's examine two types of therapies in the humanistic tradition: client-centered therapy and Gestalt therapy.

How might volunteer work help people to maximize their human potential?

CLIENT-CENTERED THERAPY

As developed by Carl Rogers (1902–1987), *client-centered therapy* has had a significant impact on the way many different kinds of therapists define their relationships to their clients (Rogers, 1951, 1977). The primary goal of **client-centered therapy** is to promote the healthy psychological growth of the individual.

The approach begins with the assumption that all people share the basic tendency to self-actualize—that is, to realize their potential. Rogers believed that "it is the inherent tendency of the organism to develop all its capacities in ways which seem to maintain or enhance the organism" (1959, p. 196). Healthy development is hindered by faulty learning patterns in which a person accepts the evaluation of others in place of those provided by his or her own mind and body. A conflict between the naturally positive self-image and negative external criticisms creates anxiety and unhappiness. This conflict, or *incongruence,* may function outside of awareness, so that a person experiences feelings of unhappiness and low self-worth without knowing why.

The task of Rogerian therapy is to create a therapeutic environment that allows a client to learn how to behave to achieve self-enhancement and self-actualization. Because people are assumed to be basically good, the therapist's task is mainly to help remove barriers that limit the expression of this natural positive tendency. The basic therapeutic strategy is to recognize, accept, and clarify a client's feelings. This is accomplished within an atmosphere of *unconditional positive regard*— nonjudgmental acceptance and respect for the client. The therapist allows his or her own feelings and thoughts to be transparent to the client. In addition to maintaining this genuineness, the therapist tries to experience the client's feelings. Such total empathy requires that the therapist care for the client as a worthy, competent individual—not to be judged or evaluated but to be assisted in discovering his or her individuality (Meador & Rogers, 1979).

The emotional style and attitude of the therapist are instrumental in *empowering* the client to attend once again to the true sources of personal conflict and to remove the distracting influences that suppress self-actualization. Unlike practitioners of other therapies, who interpret, give answers, or instruct, the client-centered therapist is a supportive listener who reflects and, at times, restates the client's evaluative statements and feelings. Client-centered therapy strives to be *nondirective* by having the therapist merely facilitate the client's search for self-awareness and self-acceptance.

Rogers believed that, once people are freed to relate to others openly and to accept themselves, individuals have the potential to lead themselves back to psychological health. This optimistic view and the humane relationship between therapist-as-caring-expert and client-as-person have influenced many practitioners.

---

human-potential movement The therapy movement that encompasses all those practices and methods that release the potential of the average human being for greater levels of performance and greater richness of experience.

client-centered therapy A humanistic approach to treatment that emphasizes the healthy psychological growth of the individual based on the assumption that all people share the basic tendency of human nature toward self-actualization.

GESTALT THERAPY

Gestalt therapy focuses on ways to unite mind and body to make a person whole (recall the Gestalt school of perception, described in Chapter 4). Its goal of self-awareness is reached by helping clients express pent-up feelings and recognize unfinished business from past conflicts that is carried into new relationships and must be completed for growth to proceed. **Fritz Perls** (1893–1970), the originator of Gestalt therapy, asked clients to act out fantasies concerning conflicts and strong feelings and also to recreate their dreams, which he saw as repressed parts of personality. Perls said, "We have to *re-own* these projected, fragmented parts of our personality, and re-own the hidden potential that appears in the dream" (1969, p. 67).

In Gestalt therapy workshops, therapists encourage participants to regain contact with their "authentic inner voices" (Hatcher & Himelstein, 1996). Among the best known methods of Gestalt therapy is the *empty chair technique.* To carry out this technique, the therapist puts an empty chair near the client. The client is asked to imagine that a feeling, a person, an object, or a situation is occupying the chair. The client then "talks" to the chair's occupant. For example, clients would be encouraged to imagine their mother or father in the chair and reveal feelings they might otherwise be unwilling to reveal. The clients can then imagine those feelings in the chair to "talk" to the feelings about the impact they have on the clients' lives. This technique allows clients to confront and explore strong unexpressed feelings that may interfere with psychological well-being.

What are some strengths of group therapies?

STOP AND REVIEW

❶ What is the goal of the human-potential movement?

❷ In client-centered therapy, what is meant by unconditional positive regard?

❸ In Gestalt therapy, what is the purpose of the empty chair technique?

Group Therapies

All the treatment approaches outlined thus far are primarily designed as one-to-one relationships between a patient or client and a therapist. Many people, however, now experience therapy as part of a group. There are several reasons why group therapy has flourished. Some advantages are practical. Group therapy is less expensive to participants and allows small numbers of mental health personnel to help more clients. Other advantages relate to the power of the group setting. The group (1) is a less threatening situation for people who have problems dealing on their own with authority; (2) allows group processes to be used to influence individual maladaptive behavior; (3) provides people with opportunities to observe and practice interpersonal skills within the therapy session; and (4) provides an analogue

of the primary family group, which enables corrective emotional experiences to take place.

Group therapy also poses some special problems (Motherwell & Shay, 2005). For example, some groups establish a culture in which little progress can be made—members create a norm of passivity and limited self-disclosure. In addition, the effectiveness of groups can change dramatically when members leave or join the groups. Both arrivals and departures can change the delicate balance that allows groups to function well as a unit. Therapists who specialize in group therapy must take care to address these group dynamics.

Some of the basic premises of group therapies differ from those of individual therapy. The social setting of group therapies provides an opportunity to learn how one comes across to others, how the self-image that is projected differs from the one that is intended or personally experienced. In addition, the group provides confirmation that one's symptoms, problems, and "deviant" reactions are not unique but often are quite common. Because people tend to conceal from others negative information about themselves, it is possible for many people with the same problem to believe "It's only me." The shared group experience can help to dispel this pluralistic ignorance in which many share the same false belief about their unique failings. In addition, the group of peers can provide social support outside the therapy setting.

COUPLE AND FAMILY THERAPY

Much group therapy consists of strangers coming together periodically to form temporary associations from which they may benefit. Couple and family therapy brings meaningful, existing units into a therapy setting.

Couple therapy for marital problems seeks to clarify the typical communication patterns of the partners and then to improve the quality of their interaction (Snyder et al., 2006). By seeing a couple together, and often by videotaping and replaying their interactions, a therapist can help them appreciate the verbal and nonverbal styles they use to dominate, control, or confuse each other. Each party is taught how to reinforce desirable responding in the other and withdraw

---

Gestalt therapy Therapy that focuses on ways to unite mind and body to make a person whole.

reinforcement for undesirable reactions. They are also taught nondirective listening skills to help the other person clarify and express feelings and ideas. Couple therapy has been shown to reduce marital crises and keep marriages intact (Christensen et al., 2006).

In *family therapy,* the client is a whole nuclear family, and each family member is treated as a member of a *system* of relationships (Fishman & Fishman, 2003). A family therapist works with troubled family members to help them perceive what is creating problems for one or more of them. Consider circumstances in which a child has been diagnosed with an anxiety disorder. Research suggests that certain parenting practices may, unfortunately, maintain the child's anxiety (Wood et al., 2003). For example, if parents do not allow their children sufficient autonomy, the children may never gain enough self-efficacy to cope successfully with novel tasks. Under those circumstances, novel tasks will continue to provoke anxiety. Family therapy can focus on both the child's anxiety and the parent's behaviors that may maintain that anxiety.

> Researchers recruited 40 children, ages 6 to 13, to participate in a treatment study (Wood et al., 2006). All the children had been diagnosed with an anxiety disorder (such as generalized anxiety disorder or social phobia). Half of the children underwent individual cognitive behavioral therapy that included skills training (such as strategies for coping with anxiety) as well as exposure to a hierarchy of feared situations. The other half of the children participated in similar activities, but their parents were also involved for much of the therapy sessions. In these family sessions, parents were taught skills, for example, to increase their children's autonomy and self-efficacy. The two groups of children were comparable in their levels of distress before treatment. At the end of therapy, both groups presented lower levels of anxiety. However, the group whose parents were included in the therapy showed greater improvement than their peers who received individual treatment.

This study illustrates the importance of the family therapy approach. By engaging the whole family, the therapeutic intervention changed environmental factors that may have helped maintain the children's levels of anxiety.

Family therapy can reduce tensions within a family and improve the functioning of individual members by helping clients recognize the positive as well as the negative aspects in their relationships. **Virginia Satir** (1916–1988), a developer of family therapy approaches, noted that the family therapist plays many roles, acting as an interpreter and clarifier of the interactions that are taking place in the therapy session and as influence agent, mediator, and referee (Satir, 1967). Most family therapists assume that the problems brought into therapy represent *situational* difficulties between people or problems of social interaction, rather than *dispositional* aspects of individuals. These difficulties may develop over time as members are forced into or accept unsatisfying roles. Nonproductive communication patterns may be set up in response to natural transitions in a family situation—loss of a job, a child's going to school, dating, getting married, or having a baby. The job of the family therapist is to understand the structure of the family and the many forces acting on it. Then he or she works with the family members to dissolve "dysfunctional" structural elements while creating and maintaining new, more effective structures (Fishman & Fishman, 2003).

COMMUNITY SUPPORT GROUPS

A dramatic development in therapy has been the surge of interest and participation in *mutual support groups* and *self-help groups.* There are over 6,000 of these groups in the United States that focus on mental health issues; self-help groups report over 1 million members (Goldstrom et al., 2006). Also, 5 million people over the age of 12 attend self-help groups for alcohol and illicit drugs each year in the United States (Substance Abuse and Mental Health Services Administration, 2008a). These support group sessions are typically free, especially when they are not directed by a health-care professional, and they give people a chance to meet others with the same problems who are surviving and sometimes thriving. The self-help concept applied to community group settings was pioneered by Alcoholics Anonymous (AA), which was founded in 1935. However, it was the women's consciousness-raising movement of the 1960s that helped extend self-help beyond the arena of alcoholism. Now support groups deal with four basic categories of problems: addictive behavior, physical and mental disorders, life transition or other crises, and the traumas experienced by friends or relatives of those with serious problems. In recent years, people have begun to turn to the Internet as another venue for self-help groups (Barak et al., 2008). In general, Internet self-help groups engage the same range of issues as their physical counterparts (Goldstrom et al., 2006). However, the Internet provides a particularly important meeting place for people who suffer from conditions that limit mobility, such as chronic fatigue syndrome and multiple sclerosis: An inability to attend meetings physically no longer denies people the benefits of self-help.

Researchers have begun to investigate what properties of self-help groups can make them most effective. Self-help groups appear to serve a number of functions for their members: For example, they provide people with a sense of hope and control over their problems, they engage social support for people's suffering, and they provide a forum for dispensing and acquiring information about disorders and treatments (Groh et al., 2008; Schiff & Bargal, 2000). If you consider joining a self-help group, it is important to note that these groups have the most positive impact on people's feelings of well-being when they are satisfied with the group (Schiff & Bargal, 2000). For example, one study found that individuals who affiliated most strongly with AA after treatment for alcoholism showed the lowest levels of continuing substance abuse. Strong affiliation with AA apparently allowed these individuals to maintain their behavioral self-efficacy with respect to the control of their alcoholism (Morgenstern et al., 1997).

A valuable development in self-help is the application of group therapy techniques to the situations of terminally ill patients. The goals of such therapy are to help patients and their families live lives as fulfilling as possible during their illnesses, to cope realistically with impending death, and to adjust to the terminal illness (Kissane et al., 2004). One general focus of such support groups for the terminally ill is to help patients learn how to live fully until they "say goodbye."

The group therapies are our final examples of types of therapies that are based purely on psychological interventions. We will now analyze how biomedical therapies work to alter the brain in order to affect the mind.

❶ How does group therapy help inform participants about the uniqueness of their problems?

❷ What is a common goal for couple therapy?

❸ Under what circumstances are Internet self-help groups particularly valuable?

CRITICAL THINKING Recall the study that used family therapy to treat children's anxiety disorders. Why was it important that the two groups of children had comparable anxiety levels before treatment began?

Biomedical Therapies

The ecology of the mind is held in delicate balance. When something goes wrong with the brain, we see the consequences in abnormal patterns of behavior and peculiar cognitive and emotional reactions. Similarly, environmental, social, or behavioral disturbances, such as drugs and violence, can alter brain chemistry and function. Biomedical therapies most often treat mental disorders as problems in the brain. We will describe four biomedical approaches to alleviating the symptoms of psychological disorders: drug therapies, psychosurgery, electroconvulsive therapy (ECT), and repetitive transcranial magnetic stimulation (rTMS).

DRUG THERAPY

In the history of the treatment of mental disorders, nothing has rivaled the revolution created by the discovery of drugs that can calm anxious patients, restore contact with reality in withdrawn patients, and suppress hallucinations in psychotic patients. This new therapeutic era began in 1953 with the introduction of tranquilizing drugs, notably *chlorpromazine,* into hospital treatment programs. Emerging drug therapies gained almost instant recognition and status as an effective way to transform patient behavior. **Psychopharmacology** is the branch of psychology that investigates the effects of drugs on behavior. Researchers in psychopharmacology work to understand the effect drugs have on some biological systems and the consequent changes in responding.

The discovery of *drug therapies* had profound effects on the treatment of severely disordered patients. No longer did mental hospital staff have to act as guards, putting patients in seclusion or straitjackets; staff morale improved as rehabilitation replaced mere custodial care of the mentally ill (Swazey, 1974). Moreover, the drug therapy revolution had a great impact on the U.S. mental hospital population. Over half a million people were living in mental institutions in 1955, staying an average of several years. The introduction of chlorpromazine and other drugs reversed the steadily increasing numbers of patients. By the early 1970s, it was estimated that fewer than half the country's mental patients actually resided in mental hospitals; those who did were institutionalized for an average of only a few months.

The drugs we will describe that alleviate symptoms of various mental disorders are widely prescribed. As mental health care comes increasingly under the direction of health maintenance organizations (HMOs), cost-cutting practices are limiting the number of patients' visits to therapists for psychological therapies while substituting cheaper drug therapies. Researchers have documented great increases in prescriptions for drug therapies (Stagnitti, 2007). For that reason, it is important to understand the positive and negative features of drug therapies.

Three major categories of drugs are used today in therapy programs: *antipsychotic, antidepressant,* and *antianxiety* medications (see **Table 15.3**). As their names suggest, these drugs chemically alter specific brain functions that are responsible for psychotic symptoms, depression, and extreme anxiety.

Antipsychotic Drugs Antipsychotic drugs alter symptoms of schizophrenia such as delusions, hallucinations, social withdrawal, and occasional agitation (Dawkins et al., 1999). Antipsychotic drugs work by reducing the activity of the neurotransmitter dopamine in the brain. The earliest drugs researchers developed, like *chlorpromazine* (marketed under the U.S. brand name *Thorazine*) and *haloperidol* (marketed as *Haldol*) blocked or reduced the sensitivity of dopamine receptors. Although those drugs functioned by decreasing the overall level of brain activity, they were not just tranquilizers. For many patients, they did much more than merely eliminate agitation. They also relieved or reduced the positive symptoms of schizophrenia, including delusions and hallucinations.

There were, unfortunately, negative side effects of these early antipsychotic drugs. Because dopamine plays a role in motor control, muscle disturbances frequently accompany a course of drug treatment. *Tardive dyskinesia* is a particular disturbance of motor control, especially of the facial muscles, caused by antipsychotic drugs. Patients who develop this side effect experience involuntary jaw, lip, and tongue movements.

Over time, researchers created a new category of drugs, which are called *atypical* antipsychotic drugs, that create fewer motor side effects. The first member of this category, *clozapine* (marketed as *Clozaril*), was approved in the United States in 1989. Clozapine both directly decreases dopamine activity and increases the level of serotonin activity, which inhibits the dopamine system. This pattern of activity blocks dopamine receptors more selectively, resulting in a lower probability of motor disturbance. Unfortunately, *agranulocytosis,* a rare disease in which the bone marrow stops making white blood cells, develops in 1 to 2 percent of patients treated with clozapine.

Researchers have created a range of atypical antipsychotic drugs that act in the brain in a fashion similar to clozapine. Large-scale studies suggest that each of these drugs is effective in relieving the symptoms of schizophrenia—but each also has the potential for side effects (Lieberman et al., 2005). For example, people who take these drugs are at risk for weight gain and diabetes (Nasrallah, 2005; Smith et al., 2008). Unfortunately, the side effects often prompt patients to discontinue the drug therapy. The rate of relapse when patients go off the drugs is quite high—three quarters have new symptoms within one year (Gitlin et al., 2001). Even patients who remain on the newer drugs such as clozapine have about a 15 to 20 percent chance of relapse (Leucht et al., 2003). Thus antipsychotic drugs do not cure schizophrenia—they do not eliminate the underlying psychopathology. Fortunately, they are reasonably effective at controlling the disorder's most disruptive symptoms.

---

psychopharmacology The branch of psychology that investigates the effects of drugs on behavior.

TABLE 15.3 Drug Therapies for Mental Illness		
Disorder	**Type of Therapy**	**Examples**
Schizophrenia	Antipsychotic drug	chlorpromazine (Thorazine) haloperidol (Haldol) clozapine (Clozaril)
Depression	Tricyclic anti-depressant	imipramine (Tofranil) amitriptyline (Elavil)
	Selective serotonin reuptake inhibitor	fluoxetine (Prozac) paroxetine (Paxil) sertraline (Zoloft)
	Serotonin and norepinephrine reuptake inhibitor MAO inhibitor	milnacipran (Dalcipran) venlafaxine (Effexor) phenelzine (Nardil) isocarboxazid (Marplan)
Bipolar disorder	Mood stabilizer	lithium (Eshalith)
Anxiety disorders	Benzodiazepines Antidepressant drug	diazepam (Valium) alprazolam (Xanax) fluoxetine (Prozac)

Antidepressant Drugs Antidepressant drugs work by increasing the activity of the neurotransmitters norepinephrine and serotonin (Thase & Denko, 2008). Recall from Chapter 3 that nerve cells communicate by releasing neurotransmitters into synaptic clefts (the small gaps between neurons). *Tricyclics,* such as *Tofranil* and *Elavil,* reduce the reuptake (removal) of the neurotransmitters from the synaptic cleft (see **Figure 15.2**). Drugs such as *Prozac* are known as *selective serotonin reuptake inhibitors* (SSRIs) because they specifically reduce the reuptake of serotonin. The *monoamine oxidase* (MAO) *inhibitors* limit the action of the enzyme monoamine oxidase, which is responsible for breaking down (metabolizing) norepinephrine. When MAO is inhibited, more of the neurotransmitter is left available. Thus each type of drug leaves more neurotransmitters available to bring about neural signals.

Antidepressant drugs can be successful at relieving the symptoms of depression, although as many as 50 percent of patients will not show improvement (Hollon et al., 2002). (Those patients may be candidates for ECT or rTMS, which we discuss later.) Because antidepressant drugs affect important neurotransmitter systems in the brain, they have the potential for serious side effects. For example, people taking SSRIs such as Prozac may experience symptoms such as nausea, insomnia, nervousness, and sexual dysfunction. Tricyclics and MAO inhibitors may cause dry mouth, difficulty sleeping, and memory impairment. Research suggests that most of the major antidepressant drugs are roughly equal, across individuals, in their ability to bring relief (Hollon et al., 2002). For that reason, it is important for each individual to find the drug that yields the fewest side effects for him or her personally.

Researchers also continue to search for drugs that will help alleviate the symptoms of depression with fewer side effects. The newest class of drugs are called *serotonin and nor-epinephrine reuptake inhibitors,* or *SNRIs.* As that name suggests, these drugs, such as *Effexor* and *Dalcipran,* block the reuptake of both serotonin and norepinephrine. Clinical trials using these drugs indicate that they may be more effective than SSRIs (Stahl et al., 2005). However, researchers still must determine which SNRIs function without serious side effects (Perahia et al., 2008).

In recent years, researchers have examined the important question of whether individuals—and, in particular, children and adolescents—who take antidepressant drugs are at greater risk for suicide. Although conclusions remain controversial, the majority of evidence supports the claim that drug treatment for depression does, in fact, yield a small increase in suicide risk (Möller et al., 2008). The important question is why this is the case. Some researchers believe that the drugs—in particular SSRIs—act in the brain to increase suicidal thoughts. Other researchers suggest that the small increase in suicide risk is an unfortunate consequence of the relief the drugs bring: Because major depressive order impairs motivation, people may be able to carry out suicidal behaviors only once their mental health starts to improve. For that reason, people who start drug treatment for major depressive disorder should receive consistent clinical attention to monitor for possible suicidal thoughts or intentions. Note also that many researchers have argued that, because antidepressant drugs bring relief from depression, they prevent many more suicides than they cause; their benefits outweigh their risks (Bridge et al., 2007).

Lithium salts have proven effective in the treatment of bipolar disorders (Thase & Denko, 2008). People who experience uncontrollable periods of hyperexcitement, when their energy seems limitless and their behavior extravagant and flamboyant,

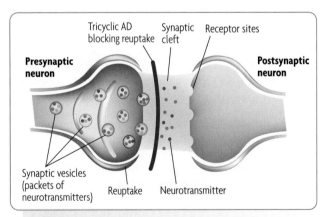

FIGURE 15.2 The Brain Mechanisms of Tricyclic Antidepressants

Tricyclic antidepressants block the reuptake of norepinephrine and serotonin so that the neurotransmitters remain in the synaptic cleft.

From Butcher et al., *Abnormal Psychology,* 13/e, © 2010, 2007 Pearson Education, Inc. Reproduced with permission of Pearson Education, Inc.

are brought down from their state of manic excess by doses of lithium. In addition, if people continue to take lithium when their symptoms are in remission, they are less likely to have recurrences of the disorder (Biel et al., 2007). However, for those people suffering from bipolar disorders who cycle frequently between manic episodes and depression, lithium appears to be less effective than other treatments such as the drug *valproate,* which was originally developed as a drug to prevent seizures (Cousins & Young, 2007).

Antianxiety Drugs Like antipsychotic and antidepressant drugs, antianxiety drugs generally have their effect by adjusting the levels of neurotransmitter activity in the brain. Different drugs are most effective at relieving different types of anxiety disorders (Hoffman & Mathew, 2008). Generalized anxiety disorder is best treated with a *benzodiazepine,* such as *Valium* or *Xanax,* which increases the activity of the neurotransmitter GABA. Because GABA regulates inhibitory neurons, increases in GABA activity decrease brain activity in areas of the brain relevant to generalized anxiety responses. Panic disorders, as well as agoraphobia and other phobias, can be treated with antidepressant drugs, although researchers do not yet understand the biological mechanism involved. Obsessive-compulsive disorder, which may arise from low levels of serotonin, responds particularly well to drugs, like Prozac, that specifically affect serotonin function.

As with drugs that treat schizophrenia and mood disorders, benzodiazepines affect a major neurotransmitter system and therefore have a range of potential side effects (Rivas-Vazquez, 2003). People who begin a course of therapy may experience daytime drowsiness, slurred speech, and problems with coordination. The drugs may also impair cognitive processes such as attention and memory (Stewart, 2005). Furthermore, people who begin treatment with benzodiazepines often experience drug tolerance—they must increase their dosage to maintain a stable effect (see Chapter 5). Discontinuation of treatment might also lead to withdrawal symptoms (O'Brien, 2005). Because of the potential for psychological and physical dependence, people should undertake treatment with antianxiety drugs in careful consultation with a health-care provider.

PSYCHOSURGERY

The headline in the *Los Angeles Times* read, "Bullet in the Brain Cures Man's Mental Problem" (2/23/1988). The article revealed that a 19-year-old man suffering from severe obsessive-compulsive disorder had shot a .22-caliber bullet through the front of his brain in a suicide attempt. Remarkably, he survived, his pathological symptoms were cured, and his intellectual capacity was not affected, although some of the underlying causes of his problems remained.

This case illustrates the potential effects of one of the most direct biomedical therapies: surgical intervention in the brain. Such intervention involves lesioning (severing) connections between parts of the brain or removing small sections of the

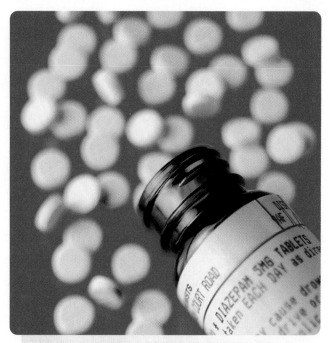

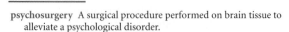 Why should people be cautious when they undertake drug therapies?

brain. These therapies are often considered methods of last resort to treat psychopathologies that have proven intractable to other, less extreme forms of therapy. **Psychosurgery** is the general term for surgical procedures performed on brain tissue to alleviate psychological disorders.

The best known form of psychosurgery is the **prefrontal lobotomy,** an operation that severs the nerve fibers connecting the frontal lobes of the brain with the diencephalon, especially those fibers of the thalamic and hypothalamic areas. The procedure was developed by neurologist **Egas Moniz** (1874–1955), who, in 1949, won a Nobel Prize for this treatment.

The original candidates for lobotomy were agitated patients with schizophrenia and patients who were compulsive and anxiety ridden. The effects of this psychosurgery were dramatic: A new personality emerged without intense emotional arousal and, thus, without overwhelming anxiety, guilt, or anger. However, the operation permanently destroyed basic aspects of human nature. The lobotomy resulted in inability to plan ahead, indifference to the opinions of others, childlike actions, and the intellectual and emotional flatness of a person without a coherent sense of self. (One of Moniz's own patients was so distressed by these unexpected consequences that she shot Moniz, partially paralyzing him).

Because the effects of psychosurgery are permanent, its continued use is very limited. Clinicians only consider psychosurgery when other treatments have repeatedly failed. For example, one study evaluated the effectiveness of a procedure called a *cingulotomy,* in which surgeons create lesions in the limbic system structure called the cingulate gyrus (Shields et al., 2008). The 33 patients in the study had intractable major depression—they had failed to respond to four or more courses of drug treatment as well as other standard treatments. After the surgeries, 75 percent of the patients showed some relief from their symptoms. The cingulotomy procedure has also relieved the symptoms of patients with obsessive-compulsive disorder who were similarly unresponsive to drug treatments (Kim et al., 2003).

psychosurgery A surgical procedure performed on brain tissue to alleviate a psychological disorder.

prefrontal lobotomy An operation that severs the nerve fibers connecting the frontal lobes of the brain with the diencephalon, especially those fibers in the thalamic and hypothalamic areas; best known form of psychosurgery.

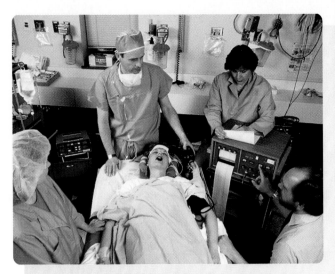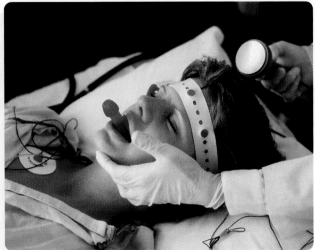

Electroconvulsive therapy has been very effective in cases of severe depression. Why does it remain controversial as a treatment?

ECT AND rTMS

Electroconvulsive therapy (ECT) is the use of electric shock applied to the brain to treat psychiatric disorders such as schizophrenia, mania, and, most often, depression. The technique consists of applying weak electric current (75 to 100 volts) to a patient's temples for a period of time from 1/10 to a full second until a convulsion occurs. The convulsion usually runs its course in 45 to 60 seconds. Patients are prepared for this traumatic intervention by sedation with a short-acting barbiturate and muscle relaxant, which renders the patient unconscious and minimizes the violent physical reactions (Abrams, 1992).

Electroconvulsive therapy has proven quite successful at alleviating the symptoms of serious depression (Lisanby, 2007). ECT is particularly important because it works quickly. Typically, the symptoms of depression are alleviated in a three- or four-day course of treatment, as compared with the one- to two-week time window for drug therapies. Even so, most therapists hold ECT as a treatment of last resort. ECT is often reserved for emergency treatment for suicidal or severely malnourished, depressed patients and for patients who do not respond to antidepressant drugs or can't tolerate their side effects.

If ECT is so effective, why has it so often been demonized? For example, in 1982, the citizens of Berkeley, California, voted to ban the use of electroconvulsive shock in any of their community mental health facilities (the action was later overturned on legal grounds). Scientific unease with ECT centers largely on the lack of understanding of how it works. The therapy was originated when clinicians observed that patients who suffered from both schizophrenia and epilepsy showed improvement in their symptoms of schizophrenia after epileptic seizures. The clinicians conjectured that the same effect could be obtained with artificially induced seizures. Although the conjecture proved correct in part—ECT is much more effective at alleviating depression than schizophrenia—researchers have yet to fit a definitive theory to this chance observation.

Critics have also worried about potential side effects of ECT (Breggin, 1979, 1991). ECT produces temporary disorientation and a variety of cognitive deficits. For example, patients often suffer amnesia for events in the period of time preceding the treatment as well as difficulty forming new memories (Ingram et al., 2008). However, most patients recover from these deficits in the first few weeks after treatment. As a way of minimizing even short-term deficits, ECT is now often administered to only one side of the brain so as to reduce the possibility of speech impairment. Such unilateral ECT alleviates some of the cognitive consequences of the treatment and also remains an effective antidepressant (Fraser et al., 2008).

In recent years, researchers have explored an alternative to ECT called *repetitive transcranial magnetic stimulation (rTMS)*. As you might recall from Chapter 3, people who undergo rTMS receive repeated pulses of magnetic stimulation to the brain. As with ECT, researchers have not yet determined why rTMS can bring relief for major depressive disorder and other forms of psychopathology. However, evidence is mounting that rTMS can be just as effective as some antidepressant drugs (Schutter, 2008). Researchers are working to determine how variables such as the intensity of the magnetic stimulation affect rTMS's ability to bring relief (Daskalakis et al., 2008).

STOP AND REVIEW

❶ What advantages do atypical antipsychotic drugs have over early drug therapies for schizophrenia?

❷ What do SNRIs do in the brain?

❸ What are some effects of prefrontal lobotomies?

❹ What is the rTMS procedure?

Visit MyPsychLab.com for more review and practice on the following topics:

◄●) **Explore:** Drugs Commonly Used to Treat Psychiatric Disorders

● **Watch:** Listening to Blues Test

---

electroconvulsive therapy (ECT) The use of electroconvulsive shock as an effective treatment for severe depression.

Treatment Evaluation and Prevention Strategies

Suppose you have come to perceive a problem in your life that you believe could be alleviated by interaction with a trained clinician. We have mentioned a great variety of types of therapies. How can you know which one of them will work best to relieve your distress? How can you be sure that *any* of them will work? In this section, we examine the projects researchers undertake to test the effectiveness of particular therapies and make comparisons between different therapies. The general goal is to discover the most efficient way to help people overcome distress. We also consider briefly the topic of *prevention:* How can psychologists intervene in people's lives to prevent mental illness before it occurs?

EVALUATING THERAPEUTIC EFFECTIVENESS

British psychologist Hans Eysenck (1952) created a furor some years ago by declaring that psychotherapy does not work at all! He reviewed available publications that reported the effects of various therapies and found that patients who received no therapy had just as high a recovery rate as those who received psychoanalysis or other forms of insight therapy. He claimed that roughly two-thirds of all people with neurotic problems would recover spontaneously within two years of the onset of the problem.

Researchers met Eysenck's challenge by devising more accurate methodologies to evaluate the effectiveness of therapy. What Eysenck's criticism made clear was that researchers needed to have appropriate control groups. For a variety of reasons, *some* percentage of individuals in psychotherapy *does* improve without any professional intervention. This **spontaneous-remission effect** is one *baseline* criterion against which the effectiveness of therapies must be assessed. Simply put, doing something must be shown to lead to a greater percentage of improved cases than doing nothing.

Similarly, researchers generally try to demonstrate that their treatment does more than just take advantage of clients' own expectations of healing. You may recall our earlier discussions of *placebo* effects: In many cases, people's mental or physical health will improve because they expect that it will improve. The therapeutic situation helps bolster this belief by putting the therapist in the specific social role of *healer* (Frank & Frank, 1991). Although the placebo effects of therapy are an important part of the therapeutic intervention,

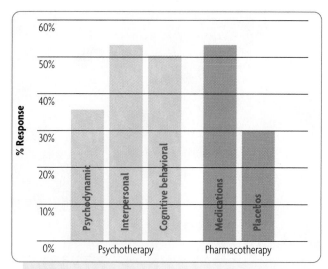

FIGURE 15.3 Treatment Evaluation for Depression

The figure displays the results from meta-analyses of treatments for depression. For each treatment, the figure presents the percentage of patients who typically respond to each category of treatment. For example, about 50 percent of patients taking antidepressant medication experience recognizable symptom relief, whereas 50 percent do not.

researchers typically wish to demonstrate that their specific form of therapy is more effective than a **placebo therapy** (a neutral therapy that just creates expectations of healing) (Hyland et al., 2007).

In recent years, researchers have evaluated therapeutic effectiveness using a statistical technique called meta-analysis. **Meta-analysis** provides a formal mechanism for detecting the general conclusions to be found in data from many different experiments. In many psychological experiments, the researcher asks, "Did most of my participants show the effect I predicted?" Meta-analysis treats experiments like participants. With respect to the effectiveness of therapy, the researcher asks, "Did most of the outcome studies show positive changes?"

Consider **Figure 15.3,** which presents the results of meta-analyses of the research literature on treatments for depression (Hollon et al., 2002). The figure compares results for three types of psychotherapies and medications (averaged across different types of antidepressant drugs) to placebo treatments. We described psychodynamic and cognitive behavioral therapies earlier in the chapter. Interpersonal therapy focuses on a patient's current life and interpersonal relationships. As you can see, across all the studies reviewed in the meta-analyses that contributed to this figure, interpersonal therapy, cognitive behavioral therapy, and drug therapies had a consistently larger impact than did placebos. At least for treatment of depression, classic psychodynamic therapy did not fare well.

Note that these data reflect the impact of each type of treatment alone. Researchers have assessed the effectiveness of psychotherapy alone versus psychotherapy combined with

---

spontaneous-remission effect The improvement of some mental patients and clients in psychotherapy without any professional intervention; a baseline criterion against which the effectiveness of therapies must be assessed.

placebo therapy A therapy interdependent of any specific clinical procedures that results in client improvement.

meta-analysis A statistical technique for evaluating hypotheses by providing a formal mechanism for detecting the general conclusions found in data from many different experiments.

Critical Thinking in Your Life

DOES THERAPY AFFECT BRAIN ACTIVITY?

In this chapter, we've made a number of distinctions among types of therapies. However, our most basic distinction has been between psychological and biomedical approaches to treatment. It has often been the practice to use a computer analogy to motivate this distinction: If we think of the brain as a computer, we can say that mental illness may arise either from the brain's hardware or in the software that programs its actions. With respect to this analogy, biomedical treatments focus on changing the hardware, whereas psychological treatments focus on changing the software. However, cutting-edge research blurs the distinction between hardware and software: There is growing evidence that psychological therapies produce lasting changes in the brain (Frewen et al., 2008).

Consider a study that examined the brain changes that accompanied treatment for social phobia (Furmark et al., 2002). Each of the ten men and eight women in the study met *DSM-IV* criteria for the disorder. The researchers placed them into one of three groups. One group of participants was given the drug citalopram (which has the prescription name *Celexa*). At the end of the nine-week treatment period, the researchers did blood assays to ensure that the participants had adhered to their drug regimen. A second group of participants received eight weekly sessions of therapy. In each three-hour session, participants engaged in simulated exposure to feared situations and cognitive restructuring. The third group of participants was the control group. (After the period of the experiment, they began the drug regimen.)

To assess the impact of the drug and cognitive behavioral therapies, all the participants were asked to deliver brief speeches while they underwent PET scans. The situation was intended to be quite threatening for individuals with social phobia: An audience of six to eight people surrounded the scanner bed while the participants gave their 2 1/2 minute speeches. With respect to behavioral measures (such as the extent to which participants experienced anxiety during their speeches), both treatment groups showed substantial and roughly equivalent improvement as compared to the control group. Moreover, as shown in the figure, the PET scans demonstrated decreased brain activity (again, relative to the control group) in much the same locations in the brain. Of importance, the decreased activity was in areas of the brain (such as the amygdala) that play a role in emotional responses.

Researchers have now demonstrated the brain impact of psychotherapy for several disorders. For example, after patients underwent psychotherapy for PTSD, brain images showed changes in regions associated with symptoms of the disorder (Lindauer et al., 2008). Similarly, patients who experienced cognitive behavior therapy for major depressive disorder showed changes in brain regions that play a causal role in the disorder (Goldapple et al., 2004). In each of these cases, it hasn't been enough to show just that psychotherapies affect particular areas of the brain. Researchers have also argued that changes in those areas are related to the relief that patients experience.

In light of these results, researchers can now shift their attention to *how*: How is it that psychotherapy can restore the brain's balance in the same systems affected by drugs? How, for example, can cognitive therapy have a similar impact on the brain's use of the neurotransmitter serotonin as does a drug that is specifically designated as a selective serotonin reuptake inhibitor (Brody et al., 2002)? These types of questions will help set the research agenda for the first part of the 21st century.

- Why was it important to ensure that the participants in the drug group adhered to the regimen?

- Why did the researchers put a real audience around the scanner?

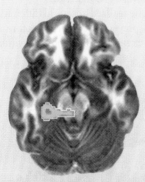

Cognitive behavioral group therapy (compared to control)

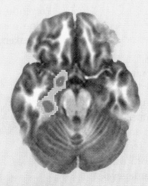

Drug therapy (compared to control)

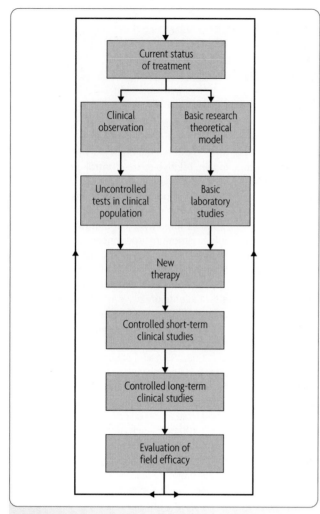

FIGURE 15.4   Building Better Therapies

Flowchart of stages in the development of treatments for mental/physical disorders.

Reprinted with permission from *American Journal of Psychiatry.* Copyright © 1979 American Psychiatric Association.

differences in treatment). Researchers need to ensure that therapies that work in research settings also work out in community settings in which patients and therapists have more diversity of symptoms and experience (Kazdin, 2008). Another important issue for evaluation research is to assess the likelihood that individuals will complete a course of treatment. In almost all circumstances, some people choose to discontinue treatments (Barrett et al., 2008). Researchers seek to understand who leaves treatment and why—with the ultimate hope of creating treatments to which most everyone can adhere.

Figure 15.4 provides a general flowchart for the way theory, clinical observation, and research all play a role in the development and evaluation of any form of treatment (for both mental and physical disorders). It shows the type of systematic research needed to help clinicians discover if their therapies are making the differences that their theories predict. On one side, you see clinical observation—clinicians' own experience with a new procedure. Often, new treatments first get tested without rigorous experimental control. On the other side of the figure, you see a theory being developed. The theory makes predictions about what should work, which may be confirmed in laboratory studies. These two types of insights—clinical and experimental—are combined to yield a new therapy.

In the final section of this chapter, we reflect on an important principle of life: Whatever the effectiveness of treatment, it is often better to prevent a disorder than to heal it once it arises.

PREVENTION STRATEGIES

The traditional therapies we have examined in this chapter share the focus of changing a person who is already distressed or disabled. This focus is necessary because, much of the time, people are unaware that they are at risk for psychological disorders. They present themselves for treatment only once they have begun to experience symptoms. However, as we saw in Chapter 14, researchers have identified a number of biological and psychological factors that put people at risk. The goal of *prevention* is to apply knowledge of those risk factors to reduce the likelihood and severity of distress.

Prevention can be realized at several different levels. *Primary* prevention seeks to prevent a condition before it begins. Steps might be taken, for example, to provide individuals with coping

drug therapy. One study found that combination therapy was most able to bring about full remission from chronic depression (Manber et al., 2008). Of participants who completed a course of treatment, 14 percent of the participants who received only drug therapy met the study's criterion for full remission, as did 14 percent of the participants who received only psychotherapy. For participants who received both drug therapy and psychotherapy, 29 percent showed the same level of improvement.

Because of such findings, contemporary researchers are less concerned about asking *whether* psychotherapy works and more concerned about asking why it works and whether any one treatment is most effective for any particular problem and for certain types of patients (Goodheart et al., 2006). For example, much treatment evaluation has been carried out in research settings that afford reasonable control over patients (often, the studies exclude individuals who have more than one disorder) and procedures (therapists are rigorously trained to minimize

How can prevention strategies encourage people to build "mental hygiene" habits to minimize the need for treatment?

skills so they can be more resilient or to change negative aspects of an environment that might lead to anxiety or depression (Boyd et al., 2006; Hudson et al., 2004). *Secondary* prevention attempts to limit the duration and severity of a disorder once it has begun. This goal is realized by means of programs that allow for early identification and prompt treatment. For example, based on the study we described for depression, a mental health practitioner might recommend a combination of psychotherapy and drug therapy to optimize secondary prevention (Manber et al., 2008). *Tertiary* prevention limits the long-term impact of a psychological disorder by seeking to prevent a relapse. For example, we noted earlier that individuals with schizophrenia who discontinue drug therapy have a very high rate of relapse (Gitlin et al., 2001). To engage in tertiary prevention, mental health practitioners would recommend that their patients with schizophrenia continue their courses of antipsychotic drugs.

The implementation of these three types of prevention has signaled major shifts in the focus and in the basic paradigms of mental health care. The most important of these paradigm shifts are: (1) supplementing treatment with prevention; (2) going beyond a medical disease model to a public health model; (3) focusing on situations and ecologies that put people at risk and away from "at-risk people"; and (4) looking for precipitating factors in life settings rather than for predisposing factors in people.

Preventing mental disorders is a complex and difficult task. It involves not only understanding the relevant causal factors, but overcoming individual, institutional, and governmental resistance to change. A major research effort will be needed to demonstrate the long-range utility of prevention and the public health approach to psychopathology in order to justify the expense in the face of the many other problems that demand immediate solutions. The ultimate goal of prevention programs is to safeguard the mental health of all members of our society.

STOP AND REVIEW

❶ What conclusions can be drawn from meta-analyses of treatments for depression?

❷ Why has research focused on the probability that people will complete courses of treatment?

❸ What is the goal of primary prevention?

Visit MyPsychLab.com for more review and practice on the following topic:

✴ **Simulate:** Ineffective Therapies

Recapping Main Points

The Therapeutic Context

- Therapy requires that a diagnosis be made and a course of treatment be established.
- Therapy may be medically or psychologically oriented.
- The four major types of psychotherapies are psychodynamic, behavior, cognitive, and humanistic.
- A variety of professionals practice therapy.
- Researchers must assess the effectiveness of psychotherapies across diverse groups.
- Harsh early treatment of those with mental illnesses led to a modern movement for deinstitutionalization.
- Unfortunately, many people do not have adequate resources outside the institution, so they may become homeless or quickly are readmitted to institutions.

Psychodynamic Therapies

- Psychodynamic therapies grew out of Sigmund Freud's psychoanalytic theory.
- Freud emphasized the role of unconscious conflicts in the etiology of psychopathology.
- Psychodynamic therapy seeks to reconcile these conflicts.
- Free association, attention to resistance, dream analysis, transference, and countertransference are all important components of this therapy.

- Other psychodynamic theorists place more emphasis on the patient's current social situation and interpersonal relationships.

Behavior Therapies

- Behavior therapies use the principles of learning and reinforcement to modify or eliminate problem behaviors.
- Counterconditioning techniques replace negative behaviors, like phobic responses, with more adaptive behaviors.
- Exposure is the common element in phobia-modification therapies.
- Contingency management uses operant conditioning to modify behavior, primarily through positive reinforcement and extinction.
- Social-learning therapy uses models and social-skills training to help individuals gain confidence about their abilities.

Cognitive Therapies

- Cognitive therapy concentrates on changing negative or irrational thought patterns about the self and social relationships.
- Cognitive therapy has been used successfully to treat depression.

- Rational-emotive therapy helps clients recognize that their irrational beliefs about themselves interfere with successful life outcomes.
- Cognitive behavioral therapy calls for the client to learn more constructive thought patterns in reference to a problem and to apply the new technique to other situations.

Humanistic Therapies

- Humanistic therapies work to help individuals become more fully self-actualized.
- Therapists strive to be nondirective in helping their clients establish a positive self-image that can deal with external criticisms.
- Gestalt therapy focuses on the whole person—body, mind, and life setting.

Group Therapies

- Group therapy allows people to observe and engage in social interactions as a means to reduce psychological distress.
- Family and marital therapy concentrates on situational difficulties and interpersonal dynamics of the couple or family group as a system in need of improvement.

- Community and Internet self-help groups allow individuals to obtain information and feelings of control in circumstances of social support.

Biomedical Therapies

- Biomedical therapies concentrate on changing physiological aspects of mental illness.
- Drug therapies include antipsychotic medications for treating schizophrenia as well as antidepressants and antianxiety drugs.
- Psychosurgery is rarely used because of its radical, irreversible effects.
- Electroconvulsive therapy and repetitive transcranial magnetic stimulation (rTMS) can be effective with depressed patients.

Treatment Evaluation and Prevention Strategies

- Research shows that many therapies work better than the mere passage of time or nonspecific placebo treatment.
- Evaluation projects are helping to answer the question of what makes therapy effective.
- Prevention strategies are necessary to stop psychological disorders from occurring and minimize their effects once they have occurred.

KEY TERMS

aversion therapy (p. 487)
behavioral rehearsal (p. 489)
behavior modification (p. 484)
behavior therapy (p. 484)
biomedical therapy (p. 478)
catharsis (p. 482)
client (p. 479)
client-centered therapy (p. 493)
clinical psychologist (p. 479)
clinical social worker (p. 479)
cognitive behavioral therapy (p. 491)
cognitive therapy (p. 491)
contingency management (p. 487)
counseling psychologist (p. 479)

counterconditioning (p. 484)
countertransference (p. 483)
deinstitutionalization (p. 480)
dream analysis (p. 483)
electroconvulsive therapy (ECT) (p. 499)
exposure therapy (p. 484)
free association (p. 482)
Gestalt therapy (p. 494)
human-potential movement (p. 493)
insight therapy (p. 482)
meta-analysis (p. 500)
participant modeling (p. 489)
pastoral counselor (p. 479)
patient (p. 479)

placebo therapy (p. 500)
prefrontal lobotomy (p. 498)
psychiatrist (p. 479)
psychoanalysis (p. 482)
psychoanalyst (p. 479)
psychopharmacology (p. 496)
psychosurgery (p. 498)
psychotherapy (p. 478)
rational-emotive therapy (RET) (p. 491)
resistance (p. 482)
social-learning therapy (p. 488)
spontaneous-remission effect (p. 500)
systematic desensitization (p. 485)
transference (p. 483)

Chapter 15 Practice Test

1. When Sonja begins treatment, her therapist focuses on her inner conflicts, which he believes remain unresolved. It seems that Sonja's therapist takes a _____ approach.
   a. psychodynamic
   b. cognitive
   c. biological
   d. humanist

2. Which of these topics would you be *least* likely to hear about in a lecture on deinstitutionalization?
   a. homelessness
   b. meta-analysis
   c. readmission rates
   d. violent crime

3. In psychodynamic therapy, _____ refers to a patient's inability or unwillingness to discuss certain topics.
   a. catharsis
   b. transference
   c. countertransference
   d. resistance

4. Research on repressed memories suggests that
   a. recovered memories are never accurate.
   b. people's memories are not subject to therapists' influence.
   c. some memories of abuse are implanted by therapists.
   d. most memories are subject to repression.

5. If Roland undergoes _____, he should expect to have a strong noxious stimulus paired with stimuli to which he is attracted.
   a. systematic desensitization
   b. behavioral rehearsal
   c. social-learning therapy
   d. aversion therapy

6. Every time Janice provides a urine sample that is drug free, she gets vouchers with which she can purchase items she enjoys. This treatment is a form of
   a. systematic desensitization.
   b. contingency management.
   c. participant modeling.
   d. generalization.

7. People can learn the process of _____ to change negative self-statements into positive coping statements.
   a. social learning
   b. self-efficacy
   c. cognitive restructuring
   d. catharsis

8. You hear a therapist talking about how hard he works to communicate unconditional regard. You suspect that he is a _____ therapist.
   a. Gestalt
   b. client-centered
   c. behavioral
   d. psychodynamic

9. In your introductory psychology class, you watch a movie clip of an individual in therapy addressing an empty chair as if it were his abusive boss. This clip demonstrates _____ therapy.
   a. Gestalt
   b. client-centered
   c. aversion
   d. social-learning

10. The particular focus of _____ therapy will often be on poor patterns of communication.
    a. Gestalt
    b. client-centered
    c. couple
    d. psychodynamic

11. _____ drugs largely have their impact in the brain by changing the function of the neurotransmitters serotonin and norepinephrine.
    a. Antidepressant
    b. Antianxiety
    c. Antipsychotic
    d. Antimania

12. In clinical research, _____ proven effective at relieving the symptoms of depression.
    a. only ECT has
    b. only rTMS has
    c. neither ECT nor rTMS have
    d. both ECT and rTMS have

13. _____ therapy is the type of treatment *least* likely to provide relief from major depressive disorder.
    a. Placebo
    b. Interpersonal
    c. Cognitive behavioral
    d. Drug

14. When prevention efforts are intended to prevent relapse, it is called _____ prevention.
    a. primary
    b. regulatory
    c. tertiary
    d. secondary

15. You are looking at PET scans of the brain activity of two people who have undergone treatment for social phobia. One received cognitive behavioral therapy, and one received drug therapy. You expect _____ to show differences in brain activity with respect to people who hadn't received treatment.
    a. only the person who received cognitive behavioral therapy
    b. only the person who received drug therapy
    c. neither person
    d. both people

Essay Questions

1. Why do behavior therapies target adaptive and maladaptive behaviors?

2. What features of self-help groups make them beneficial to mental health?

3. Why are therapies compared to placebos to evaluate their effectiveness?

Discovering Psychology Viewing Guide

Watch the following video by logging on to MyPsychLab (www.mypsychlab.com). After you have watched the video, complete the activities that follow.

Program 22: Psychotherapy

KEY TERMS AND PEOPLE

As you watch the program, pay particular attention to these terms and people in addition to those covered in this textbook.

- *biological biasing*—a genetic predisposition that increases the likelihood of getting a disorder with exposure to prolonged or intense stress.
- *genetic counseling*—counseling that advises a person about the probability of passing on defective genes to offspring.
- *time-limited dynamic psychotherapy*—a form of short-term therapy.
- *Enrico Jones*—investigates which type of treatment is best for which type of problem.
- *Hans Strupp*—a psychodynamic therapist.

PROGRAM REVIEW

1. What are the two main approaches to therapies for mental disorders?
   a. the Freudian and the behavioral
   b. the client-centered and the patient-centered
   c. the biomedical and the psychological
   d. the chemical and the psychosomatic

2. The prefrontal lobotomy is a form of psychosurgery. Though no longer widely used, it was at one time used in cases in which a patient
   a. was an agitated schizophrenic.
   b. had committed a violent crime.
   c. showed little emotional response.
   d. had a disease of the thalamus.

3. Leti had electroconvulsive shock therapy a number of years ago. She is now suffering a side effect of that therapy. What is she most likely to be suffering from?
   a. tardive dyskinesia
   b. the loss of her ability to plan ahead
   c. depression
   d. memory loss

4. Vinnie suffers from manic-depressive disorder, but his mood swings are kept under control because he takes the drug
   a. chlorpromazine.
   b. lithium.
   c. Valium.
   d. tetracycline.

5. The Silverman family is receiving genetic counseling because a particular kind of mental retardation runs in their family. What is the purpose of such counseling?
   a. to explain the probability of passing on defective genes
   b. to help eliminate the attitudes of biological biasing
   c. to repair specific chromosomes
   d. to prescribe drugs that will keep problems from developing

6. In psychodynamic theory, what is the source of mental disorders?
   a. biochemical imbalances in the brain
   b. unresolved conflicts in childhood experiences
   c. the learning and reinforcement of nonproductive behaviors
   d. unreasonable attitudes, false beliefs, and unrealistic expectations

7. Imagine you are observing a therapy session in which a patient is lying on a couch, talking. The therapist is listening and asking occasional questions. What is most likely to be the therapist's goal?
   a. to determine which drug the patient should be given
   b. to change the symptoms that cause distress
   c. to explain how to change false ideas
   d. to help the patient develop insight

8. Rinaldo is a patient in psychotherapy. The therapist asks him to free associate. What would Rinaldo do?
   a. describe a dream
   b. release his feelings
   c. talk about anything that comes to mind
   d. understand the origin of his present guilt feelings

9. According to Hans Strupp, in what major way have psychodynamic therapies changed?
   a. Less emphasis is now placed on the ego.
   b. Patients no longer need to develop a relationship with the therapist.
   c. Shorter courses of treatment can be used.
   d. The concept of aggression has become more important.

10. In the program, a therapist helped a girl learn to control her epileptic seizures. What use did the therapist make of the pen?
    a. to record data
    b. to signal the onset of an attack
    c. to reduce the girl's fear
    d. to reinforce the correct reaction

11. When Albert Ellis discusses with the young woman her fear of hurting others, what point is he making?
    a. It is the belief system that creates the "hurt."
    b. Every normal person strives to achieve fulfillment.
    c. Developing a fear-reduction strategy will reduce the problem.
    d. It is the use of self-fulfilling prophecies that cause others to be hurt.

12. What point does Enrico Jones make about investigating the effectiveness of different therapies in treating depression?
    a. All therapies are equally effective.
    b. It is impossible to assess how effective any one therapy is.
    c. The job is complicated by the different types of depression.
    d. The most important variable is individual versus group therapy.

13. What is the most powerful antidepressant available for patients who cannot tolerate drugs?
    a. genetic counseling
    b. electroconvulsive therapy
    c. psychoanalysis
    d. family therapy

14. All of the following appear to be true about the relation between depression and genetics, *except* that
    a. depression has been linked to a defect in chromosome #11.
    b. depression appears to cause genetic mutation.
    c. most people who show the genetic marker for depression do not exhibit depressive symptoms.
    d. genetic counseling allows families to plan and make choices based on their risk of mental illness.

15. For which class of mental illness would chlorpromazine be prescribed?
    a. mood disorder
    b. psychosis
    c. personality disorder
    d. anxiety disorder

16. Which approach to psychotherapy emphasizes developing the ego?
    a. behavioral
    b. desensitization
    c. humanistic
    d. psychodynamic

17. In behavior modification therapies, the goal is to
    a. understand unconscious motivations.
    b. learn to love oneself unconditionally.
    c. change the symptoms of mental illness through reinforcement.
    d. modify the interpretations that one gives to life's events.

18. Which style of therapy has as its primary goal to make the client feel as fulfilled as possible?
    a. humanistic
    b. cognitive-behavioral
    c. Freudian
    d. social learning

19. Which psychologist introduced rational-emotive therapy?
    a. Carl Rogers
    b. Hans Strupp
    c. Albert Ellis
    d. Rollo May

20. Which type of client would be ideal for modern psychoanalytic therapy?
    a. someone who is smart, wealthy, and highly verbal
    b. someone who is reserved and violent
    c. someone who has a good sense of humor but takes herself seriously
    d. someone who grew up under stressful and economically deprived conditions

QUESTIONS TO CONSIDER

1. How do the placebo effect and the spontaneous remission effect make evaluating the success of therapy difficult?

2. Why might it be that behavioral and medical approaches to the same psychological problem can result in similar effects on the brain? Does this imply that in the future, effective behavioral treatments can be developed for cases that had been successful only through medical intervention?

3. How does someone decide on an appropriate therapy?

4. Can everyone benefit from psychotherapy, or do you think it is only for people with serious problems?

5. Why is there a stigma sometimes associated with seeking professional help for psychological problems? What might be some effective ways to change that?

6. Should we have any concerns about an overreliance on or abuse of drug therapies?

7. If you found that you had a specific phobia, would you be willing to undergo exposure therapy?

ACTIVITIES

1. Identify the services and resources available in your community in case you ever need emotional support in a crisis, want to seek therapy, or know someone who needs this information. How much do these services cost? Look for names of accredited professional therapists and counselors, support groups, hotlines, medical and educational services, and in church and community programs. Is it difficult to find information?

2. Do you have any self-defeating expectations? Do you feel that you might benefit from cognitive therapy? Write out statements of positive self-expectations. Then try to use them in situations in which you feel anxious or insecure. Do they have any effect?

3. Run an Internet search with the goal of finding social support groups for various psychological disorders. In what ways do they serve a therapeutic role? How are they helpful, and how might they potentially be counterproductive?

16

Social Psychology

Imagine circumstances in which you've done everything to get to a job interview on time, but nothing has gone your way. The electricity went off during the night, so your alarm didn't wake you. The friend who was supposed to give you a ride had a flat tire. When you tried to get money for a taxi, the ATM ate your card. When you finally get to the office, you know what the manager is thinking: "Why would I give a job to someone this unreliable?" You want to protest, "It's not me, it's the circumstances!" As you have contemplated this scenario, you have begun to enter the world of *social psychology*—that area of psychology that investigates the ways in which individuals create and interpret social situations.

Social psychology is the study of the ways in which thoughts, feelings, perceptions, motives, and behavior are influenced by interactions and transactions between people. Social psychologists try to understand behavior within its social context. This social context is the vibrant canvas on which are painted the movements, strengths, and vulnerabilities of the social animal. Defined broadly, the social context includes the real, imagined, or symbolic presence of other people; the activities and interactions that take place between people; the features of the settings in which behavior occurs; and the expectations and norms that govern behavior in a given setting (Sherif, 1981).

In this chapter, we will explore several major themes of social psychological research. For the first part of the chapter we focus on **social cognition,** which is the processes by which people select, interpret, and remember social information. We then examine the ways in which situations affect people's behavior and processes by which attitudes and prejudices are formed and changed. We will then consider the social relationships you form with other people. Finally, we will examine aggression and prosocial behaviors. Throughout this chapter, we illustrate how research in social psychology has immediate applications to your life and the society you live in. In this chapter, abstract theory meets the stern test of practicality, as we attempt to answer this question: Does psychological knowledge make a difference in the everyday lives of people and society?

Constructing Social Reality

To open the chapter, we asked you to imagine everything that could go wrong in advance of a job interview. When you finally arrive at the manager's office, you and the manager have very different interpretations of the same event. You know you've been a victim of circumstances. However, at least in the short run, the manager judges you only by what is readily apparent: You are late, and you are disheveled. That's what we mean by *constructing social reality*. The manager considers the evidence you present and makes an interpretation of the situation. If you still wish to get the job, you'll have to get the manager to construct a new interpretation.

Let's look at one classic social psychological example in which people's beliefs led them to view the same situation from different vantage points and make contrary conclusions about what "really happened." The study concerned a football game that took place some years ago between two Ivy League teams.

An undefeated Princeton team played Dartmouth in the final game of the season. The game, which Princeton won, was rough, filled with penalties and serious injuries to both sides. After the game, the newspapers of the two schools offered very different accounts of what had happened.

A team of social psychologists, intrigued by the different perceptions, surveyed students at both schools, showed them a film of the game, and recorded their judgments about the number of infractions committed by each of the teams. Nearly all Princeton students judged the game as "rough and dirty," none saw it as "clean and fair," and most believed that Dartmouth players started the dirty play. In contrast, the majority of Dartmouth students thought both sides were equally to blame for the rough game, and many thought it was "rough, clean, and fair." Moreover, when the Princeton students viewed the game film, they "saw" the Dartmouth team commit twice as many penalties as their own team. When viewing the same film, Dartmouth students "saw" both sides commit the same number of penalties (Hastorf & Cantril, 1954).

This study makes clear that a complex social occurrence, such as a football game, cannot be observed in an objective, unbiased fashion. Social situations obtain significance when observers *selectively encode* what is happening in terms of what they expect to see and want to see. In the case of the football game, people *looked* at the same activity, but they *saw* two different games.

To explain how the Princeton and Dartmouth fans came to such different interpretations of the football game returns us to the realm of *perception*. Recall from Chapter 4 that you often must put prior knowledge to work to interpret ambiguous perceptual objects. The principle is the same for the football game—people bring past knowledge to bear on the interpretation of current events—but the objects for perceptual processing are people and situations. **Social perception** is the process by which people come to understand and categorize the behaviors of others. In this section, we will focus largely on two issues of social perception. First, we will consider how people make judgments about the forces that influence other people's behavior, their *causal attributions*. Next, we will discuss how processes of social perception can sometimes bring the world in line with expectations.

THE ORIGINS OF ATTRIBUTION THEORY

One of the most important inferential tasks facing all social perceivers is to determine the causes of events. You want to know the whys of life. Why did my girlfriend break off the relationship? Why did he get the job and not I? Why did my parents divorce after so many years of marriage? All such whys lead to

---

social psychology The branch of psychology that studies the effect of social variables on individual behavior, attitudes, perceptions, and motives; also studies group and intergroup phenomena.

social cognition The process by which people select, interpret, and remember social information.

social perception The process by which a person comes to know or perceive the personal attributes.

Why are fans who watch their favorite team play likely to perceive more instances of unfair play on the part of the opposing team?

an analysis of possible causal determinants for some action, event, or outcome. **Attribution theory** is a general approach to describing the ways the social perceiver uses information to generate causal explanations.

Attribution theory originated in the writings of Fritz Heider (1958). Heider argued that people continually make causal analyses as part of their attempts at general comprehension of the social world. People, he suggested, are all *intuitive psychologists* who try to figure out what people are like and what causes their behavior, just as professional psychologists do. Heider believed that the questions that dominate most attributional analyses are whether the cause of a behavior is found in the person (internal or *dispositional* causality) or in the situation (external or *situational* causality) and who is responsible for the outcomes. How do people make those judgments?

Harold Kelley (1967) formalized Heider's line of thinking by specifying the variables that people use to make their attributions. Kelly's **covariation model** suggested that people attribute a behavior to a causal factor if that factor was present whenever the behavior occurred but was absent whenever it didn't occur. Suppose, for example, you are walking down a street and you see a friend pointing at a horse and screaming. What evidence would you gather to decide whether your friend is crazy (a dispositional attribution) or danger is afoot (a situational attribution)?

Kelley suggested that people make this judgment by assessing covariation with respect to three dimensions of information relevant to the person whose acts they are trying to explain: distinctiveness, consistency, and consensus:

---

attribution theory A social-cognitive approach to describing the ways the social perceiver uses information to generate causal explanations.

covariation model A theory that suggests that people attribute a behavior to a causal factor if that factor was present whenever the behavior occurred but was absent whenever it didn't occur.

fundamental attribution error (FAE) The dual tendency of observers to underestimate the impact of situational factors and to overestimate the influence of dispositional factors on a person's behavior.

- *Distinctiveness* refers to whether the behavior is specific to a particular situation—does your friend scream in response to all horses?
- *Consistency* refers to whether the behavior occurs repeatedly in response to this situation—has this horse made your friend scream in the past?
- *Consensus* refers to whether other people also produce the same behavior in the same situation—is everyone pointing and screaming?

Each of these three dimensions plays a role in the conclusions you draw. Suppose, for example, that your friend was the only one screaming. Would that make you more likely to make a dispositional or a situational attribution?

Thousands of studies have been conducted to refine and extend attribution theory beyond the solid foundation provided by Heider and Kelley (Försterling, 2001; Moskowitz, 2004). Many of those studies have concerned themselves with conditions in which attributions depart from a systematic search of available information. We will describe four types of circumstances in which bias may creep into your attributions.

THE FUNDAMENTAL ATTRIBUTION ERROR

Suppose you have made an arrangement to meet a friend at 7 o'clock. It's now 7:30, and the friend still hasn't arrived. How might you be explaining this event to yourself?

- I'm sure something really important happened that made it impossible for her to be here on time.
- What a jerk! Couldn't she try a little harder?

We've given you a choice again between a situational and a dispositional attribution. Research has shown that people are more likely, on average, to choose the second type, the dispositional explanation (Ross & Nisbett, 1991). This tendency is so strong, in fact, that social psychologist **Lee Ross** (1977) labeled it the fundamental attribution error. The **fundamental attribution error (FAE)** represents the dual tendency for people to overestimate dispositional factors (blame or credit people) and to underestimate situational factors (blame or credit the environment) when searching for the cause of some behavior or outcome.

Let's look at a laboratory example of the FAE. Ross and his colleagues (1977) created an experimental version of a "College Bowl" type of quiz game in which participants became questioners or contestants by the flip of a coin. After the coin flip, both the questioners- and contestants- to-be listened to the instructions: The experimenters asked the questioners to invent challenging questions based on their own personal knowledge. When the questioners were done, they posed those questions to the contestants. The contestant tried, often in vain, to answer the questions. At the end of the session, the questioner, the contestant, and observers (other participants who had watched the game) rated the general knowledge of both questioner and contestant. The results are shown in **Figure 16.1**. As you can see, questioners seem to believe that both they and the contestants are average. Both contestants and observers, however, rate the questioner as much more knowledgeable than the contestant—and contestants even rate themselves to be a bit below average! Is this fair?

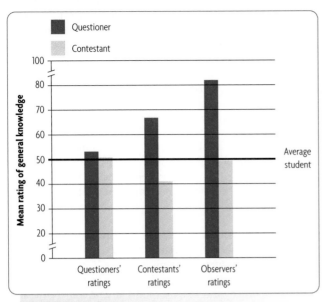

FIGURE 16.1 Ratings of Questioners' and Contestants' General Knowledge

After the quiz game, questioners, contestants, and observers rated each of the participant's general knowledge with respect to a rating of 50 for the average student. Questioners believed that both they and the contestants were average. However, both contestants and observers rated the questioner as much more knowledgeable than the contestant. Furthermore, contestants rated themselves to be a bit below average.

It should be clear that the situation confers a great advantage on the questioner. (Wouldn't you prefer to be the one who gets to ask the questions?) The contestants' and observers' ratings ignore the way in which the situation allowed one person to look bright and the other to look dull. That's the fundamental attribution error.

You should be on a constant lookout for instances of the FAE. However, this may not always be easy: It often takes a bit of "research" to discover the situational roots of behavior. Situational forces are often invisible. You can't, for example, *see* social norms; you can only see the behaviors they give rise to. What can you do to avoid the FAE? Particularly in circumstances in which you are making a dispositional attribution that is negative ("What a jerk!"), you should take a step back and ask yourself, "Could it be something about the situation that is bringing about this behavior?" You might think of such an exercise as "attributional charity." Do you see why? This advice may be particularly important to those of us who live in Western society because evidence suggests that the FAE is due, in part, to cultural sources (Miller, 1984). Recall the discussion in Chapter 13 of cultural differences in construals of the self. As we explained there, most Western cultures embody *independent construals of self*, whereas most Eastern cultures embody *inter-dependent construals of self* (Markus & Kitayama, 1991). Research demonstrates that, as a function of the culture of interdependence, members of non-Western cultures are less likely to focus on individual actors in situations. Let's see how this cultural difference affects media coverage of Olympic athletes.

The researchers compiled television and newspaper reports from the United States and Japan that focused on athletes at the 2000 Summer Olympics and the 2002 Winter Olympics (Markus et al., 2006). Research assistants who were blind to the study's purpose analysed each media report to determine what categories of explanations were used to discuss an athlete's performance: For example, did the articles mention the athletes' strengths or weaknesses, their level of motivation, or the quality of the other competitors? The results showed that U.S. media coverage focused rather tightly on the personal characteristics of the athletes. The Japanese media considered a broader range of factors. The reports didn't ignore the athletes' characteristics, but they also discussed other background factors including the extent to which the athletes met others' expectations. In addition, U.S. media reports focused almost entirely on athletes' positive characteristics whereas Japanese reports mentioned both positive and negative.

An impressive feature of this study is that it captures cultural attributional styles as they are represented on TV and in newspapers. The study makes clear one way in which a cultural style of attribution is transmitted and maintained for all those who are exposed to the media in a particular culture (Morling & Lamoreaux, 2008).

SELF-SERVING BIASES

One of the most startling findings in the College Bowl study was the contestants' negative evaluation of their own abilities. This suggests that people will make the FAE even at their own expense. (In fact, you should recall from Chapter 14 that one theory of the origins of depression suggests that depressed people make too many negative attributions to themselves rather than to situational causes.) In many circumstances, however, people do just the opposite—their attributions err in the direction of being self-serving. A **self-serving bias** leads people to take credit for their successes while denying or explaining away responsibility for their failures. In many situations, people tend to make dispositional attributions for success and situational attributions for failure (Gilovich, 1991): "I got the prize because of my ability"; "I lost the competition because it was rigged."

These patterns of attribution may be good for short-term self-esteem. However, it may often be more important to have an accurate sense of what causal forces are at work in your life outcomes. Consider how you do in your classes. If you get an *A*, what attributions do you make? How about if you get a *C*? Research has demonstrated that students tend to attribute high grades to their own efforts and low grades to factors external to themselves (McAllister, 1996). In fact, professors show the same pattern—they make attributions to themselves for students' successes but not their failures. Once again, can you see what impact this pattern of attributions might have on your GPA? If you don't think about the external causes for your successes (for example, "That first exam was easy"), you might fail to study enough the next time; if you don't think about the dispositional

---

self-serving bias An attributional bias in which people tend to take credit for their successes and deny responsibility for their failures.

causes for failures (for example, "I shouldn't have stayed so long at that party"), you also might never get around to studying hard enough.

We emphasized earlier that you should strive to avoid the FAE when you think about others' behavior. Similarly, you might examine attributions about your own behavior to weed out (non-self-serving) self-serving biases. In fact, research on the brain activity that accompanies dispositional and situational attributions suggests that people need to expend extra mental effort to avoid a reflexive self-serving bias.

> In the study, participants undertook a test of "facial working memory" (Krusemark et al., 2008). The participants viewed "target" faces on a computer screen. After a series of distractor faces, the participants saw a final face and indicated whether it matched or mismatched the previous target. After participants made that judgment, they received feedback about their performance. However, the feedback wasn't accurate. Because the researchers wanted all the participants to have equal numbers of opportunities to provide attributions for successes and failures, they gave them positive feedback for half the trials and negative feedback for the other half (irrespective of actual performance). After each instance of feedback, participants chose between statements that embodied dispositional attributions ("I am dense") versus situational attributions ("It was hard"). The researchers used EEG (see Chapter 3) to monitor participants' brain activity as they made their judgments. The most distinctive brain activity occurred when participants made judgments that were *not* self-serving: When they attributed failure to themselves, rather than to the situation, participants were more likely to engage the areas of the brain that are responsible for monitoring intentions and self control.

These data suggest that participants' self-serving judgments arose without much reflection. When, as indicated by their brain activity, participants engaged in greater deliberation, that deliberation was more likely to yield non-self-serving, dispositional attributions for incorrect judgments.

Why does it matter so much what attributions you make? Recall the example of your tardy friend. Suppose that, because you don't seek information about the situation, you decide that she isn't actually interested in being your friend. Can that incorrect belief actually cause the person to be unfriendly toward you in the future? To address that question, we turn now to the power of beliefs and expectations in constructing social reality.

EXPECTATIONS AND SELF-FULFILLING PROPHECIES

Can beliefs and expectations go beyond coloring the way you interpret experiences to actually shape social reality? Much research suggests that the very nature of some situations can be modified significantly by the beliefs and expectations people have about them. **Self-fulfilling prophecies** (Merton, 1957) are pre-

---

self-fulfilling prophecy A prediction made about some future behavior or event that modifies interactions so as to produce what is expected.

dictions made about some future behavior or event that modify behavioral interactions so as to produce what is expected. Suppose, for example, you go to a party expecting to have a great time. Suppose a friend goes expecting it to be boring. Can you imagine the different ways in which the two of you might behave, given these expectations? These alternative ways of behaving may, in turn, alter how others at the party behave toward you. In that case, which of you is actually more likely to have a good time at the party?

One of the most powerful demonstrations of social expectancy unfolded in elementary school classrooms. Robert Rosenthal, in conjunction with school principal Leonore Jacobson, provided teachers with information to create self-fulfilling prophecies.

> Elementary school teachers in Boston were informed by researchers that their testing had revealed that some of their students were "academic spurters." The teachers were led to believe that these particular students were "intellectual bloomers who will show unusual gains during the academic year." In fact, there was no objective basis for that prediction; the names of these late bloomers were chosen randomly. However, by the end of that school year, 30 percent of the children arbitrarily named as spurters had gained an average of 22 IQ points! Almost all of them had gained at least 10 IQ points. Their gain in intellectual performance, as measured by a standard test of intelligence, was significantly greater than that of their control group classmates who had started out with the same average IQ (Rosenthal & Jacobson, 1968).

How did the teachers' false expectations get translated into such positive student performance? Rosenthal (1974) points to at least four processes that were activated by the teachers' expectations. First, the teachers acted more warmly and more friendly toward the "late bloomers," creating a climate of social approval and acceptance. Second, they put greater demands—involving both quality and level of difficulty of material to be learned—on those for whom they had high hopes. Third, they gave more immediate and clearer feedback (both praise and criticism) about the selected students' performance. Finally, the teachers created more opportunities for the special students to respond in class, show their stuff, and be reinforced, thus giving them hard evidence that they were indeed as good as the teachers believed they were.

What is unusual, of course, about the situation in the Boston classrooms is that the teachers were purposefully given false expectations. This methodology allowed Rosenthal and Jacobson to demonstrate the full potential for self-fulfilling prophecies. In most real-world situations, however, expectations are based on fairly accurate social perceptions (Jussim & Harber, 2005). Teachers, for example, expect certain students to do well because those students arrive in the classroom with better qualifications; and those students, typically, do show the best performance. Research has suggested, in fact, that self-fulfilling prophecies have the greatest effect on the lives of low-achieving students (Madon et al., 1997). When teachers expect them to do poorly, they may do even worse; when teachers expect them to do well, that has the potential to turn their school lives around.

Much of the research on self-fulfilling prophecies has focused on school success. However, researchers have found

How do self-fulfilling prophecies affect the likelihood that children will engage in underage drinking?

evidence in other domains that people's mistaken beliefs and expectations can have an influence on what actually happens. For example, research suggests that when mothers overestimate the amount of alcohol their adolescents will consume, those expectations can become self-fulfilling prophecies (Madon et al., 2008). The data suggest that the adolescents construct a self-image based on their mothers' expectations and consume alcohol to match that self-image.

The research we have described in this section focused on how people explain behaviors with respect to dispositions and situations. In the next section, we provide evidence that people often underestimate the extent to which situations constrain people's actions.

STOP AND REVIEW

❶ What three dimensions did Harold Kelley suggest affect the attribution process?

❷ Why might self-serving biases have a negative impact on a student's GPA?

❸ What limits do ordinary classroom practices place on self-fulfilling prophecies?

CRITICAL THINKING Recall the study that examined cross-cultural differences in media reports. Why might the researchers have focused on Olympic athletes?

Visit MyPsychLab.com for more review and practice on the following topic:

◄●● **Explore:** Internal & External Attributions

The Power of the Situation

Throughout *Psychology and Life,* we have seen that psychologists who strive to understand the causes of behavior look in many different places for their answers. Some look to genetic factors and others to biochemical and brain processes; still others focus on the causal influence of the environment. Social psychologists believe that the primary determinant of behavior is the nature of the social situation in which that behavior occurs. They argue that social situations exert significant control over individual behavior, often dominating personality and a person's past history of learning, values, and beliefs. In this section, we will review both classic research and recent experiments that together explore the effect of subtle but powerful situational variables on people's behavior.

ROLES AND RULES

What *social roles* are available to you? A **social role** is a socially defined pattern of behavior that is expected of a person when functioning in a given setting or group. Different social situations make different roles available. When you are at home, you may accept the role of "child" or "sibling." When you are in the classroom, you accept the role of "student." At other times still, you are a "best friend" or "lover." Can you see how these different roles immediately make different types of behaviors more or less appropriate and also available to you?

Situations are also characterized by the operation of **rules,** behavioral guidelines for specific settings. Some rules are *explicitly* stated in signs (DON'T SMOKE; NO EATING IN CLASS) or are explicitly taught to children (Respect the elderly; Never take candy from a stranger). Other rules are *implicit*—they are learned through transactions with others in particular settings. How loud you can play your music, how close you can stand to another person, when you can call your teacher or boss by a first name, and what is the suitable way to react to a compliment or a gift—all of these actions depend on the situation. For example, the Japanese do not open a gift in the presence of the giver, for fear of not showing sufficient appreciation; foreigners not aware of this unwritten rule will misinterpret the behavior as rude instead of sensitive. Next time you get in an elevator, try to determine what rules you have learned about that situation. Why do people usually speak in hushed tones or not at all?

Ordinarily, you might not be particularly aware of the effects of roles and rules, but one classic social psychological experiment, the *Stanford Prison Experiment,* put these forces to work with startling results (Zimbardo, 2007; replicated in Australia by Lovibond et al., 1979).

On a summer Sunday in California, a siren shattered the serenity of college student Tommy Whitlow's morning. A police car screeched to a halt in front of his home. Within minutes, Tommy was charged with a felony, informed of his constitutional rights, frisked, and handcuffed. After he

social role A socially defined pattern of behavior that is expected of a person who is functioning in a given setting or group.

rule Behavioral guideline for acting in a certain way in a certain situation.

To open or not to open? How do people learn the etiquette for giving and receiving gifts in different cultures?

physically healthy, and "normal-average." The prisoners lived in the jail around the clock; the guards worked standard eight-hour shifts.

What happened once these students had assumed their randomly assigned roles? In guard roles, college students who had been pacifists and "nice guys" behaved aggressively—sometimes even sadistically. The guards insisted that prisoners obey all rules without question or hesitation. Failure to do so led to the loss of a privilege. At first, privileges included opportunities to read, write, or talk to other inmates. Later on, the slightest protest resulted in the loss of the "privileges" of eating, sleeping, and washing. Failure to obey rules also resulted in menial, mindless work such as cleaning toilets with bare hands, doing push-ups while a guard stepped on the prisoner's back, and spending hours in solitary confinement. The guards were always devising new strategies to make the prisoners feel worthless.

As prisoners, psychologically stable students soon behaved pathologically, passively resigning themselves to their unexpected fate. Less than 36 hours after the mass arrest, Prisoner 8412, one of the ringleaders of an aborted prisoner rebellion that morning, began to cry uncontrollably. He experienced fits of rage, disorganized thinking, and severe depression. On successive days, three more prisoners developed similar stress-related symptoms. A fifth prisoner developed a psychosomatic rash all over his body when the Parole Board rejected his appeal.

was booked and fingerprinted, Tommy was blindfolded and transported to the Stanford County Prison, where he was stripped, sprayed with disinfectant, and issued a smock-type uniform with an ID number on the front and back. Tommy became prisoner 647. Eight other college students were also arrested and assigned numbers.

Tommy and his cellmates were all volunteers who had answered a newspaper ad and agreed to be participants in a two-week experiment on prison life. By random flips of a coin, some of the volunteers had been assigned to the role of prisoners; the rest became guards. All had been selected from a large pool of student volunteers who, on the basis of extensive psychological tests and interviews, had been judged as law-abiding, emotionally stable,

By the conclusion of the Stanford Prison Experiment, guards' and prisoners' behavior differed from each other in virtually every observable way (see **Figure 16.2**). However, the figure doesn't completely reveal the extremes of the guards' behavior. On many occasions, the guards stripped their prisoners naked. The guards hooded and chained their prisoners. They denied them food and bedding. Does this list of behaviors sound

The Stanford Prison Experiment created a new "social reality" in which the norms of good behavior were overwhelmed by the dynamics of the situation. Why did the student guards and inmates adopt their roles so powerfully?

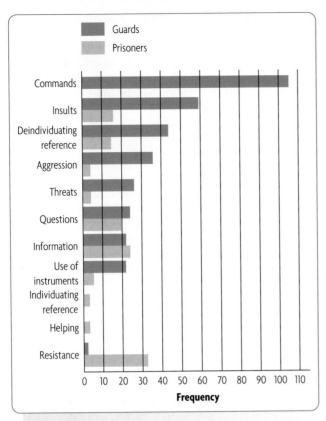

FIGURE 16.2 Guard and Prisoner Behavior

During the Stanford Prison Experiment, the randomly assigned roles of prisoners and guards drastically affected participants' behavior. The observations recorded in the six-day interaction profile show that across 25 observation periods, the prisoners engaged in more passive resistance, while the guards became more dominating, controlling, and hostile.

from the study. Follow-ups over many years revealed no lasting negative effects. Fortunately, the students were basically healthy, and they readily bounced back from this highly charged situation.

As we evaluate the ethical balance of the costs to the participants versus the gains to science and society, we must also consider gains to the participants. Several of the participants have reflected on the long-term consequences of their participation. For example, the student-prisoner who was first to be released with extreme emotional distress became a forensic clinical psychologist and has worked in the San Francisco correctional system. His explicit goal has been to use his experience in the Stanford Prison Experiment to improve prisoner–guard relationships. Similalry, Tommy Whitlow has said that, although he wouldn't want to go through the experiment again, he valued the personal experience because he learned so much about himself and about human nature. (For an extended discussion of the ethical issues raised by this and related research, we recommend reviewing the material in Zimbardo, 2007.)

A critical feature of the Stanford Prison Experiment is that only chance, in the form of random assignment, decided the participants' roles as guards or prisoners. Those roles created status and power differences that were validated in the prison situation. No one taught the participants to play their roles. The student participants had already experienced such power differences in many of their previous social interactions: parent–child, teacher–student, doctor–patient, boss–worker, male–female. They merely refined and intensified their prior patterns of behavior for this particular setting. Each student could have played either role. Many students in the guard role reported being surprised at how easily they enjoyed controlling other people. Just putting on the uniform was enough to transform them from passive college students into aggressive prison guards. What sort of person do *you* become when you slip in and out of different roles? Where does your sense of personal self end and your social identity begin?

familiar? They are among the abuses the guards committed in 2003 at the Abu Ghraib prison in Iraq. The Stanford Prison Experiment helps shed light on this scandal: Situational forces can lead ordinary people to exhibit horrendous behaviors (Fiske et al., 2004; Zimbardo, 2007).

Before the Stanford Prison Experiment began, it underwent a thorough human subjects review of the type we described in Chapter 2. No one anticipated the risks that lay ahead. Even though the researchers believed in the power of the situation, they were nonetheless caught by surprise by the extreme intensity of the situation and the rapidity of the negative psychological processes that emerged. They terminated their two-week study after only six days. They acknowledge, in retrospect, that they should have ended the experiment even sooner: Ethical concerns should have outweighed their scientific agenda. The researchers provided extensive debriefing for the participants. There was a three-hour session directly after the experiment was halted. Data collected after those debriefing sessions suggested that both prisoners and guards were in an emotional state comparable to the positive ones in which they had begun the study. Most participants returned for additional debriefing weeks later, to review and discuss video tapes

How does social psychological research explain some aspects of the guards' behaviors at Abu Ghraib?

SOCIAL NORMS

In addition to the expectations regarding role behaviors, groups develop many expectations for the ways their members *should* act. The specific expectations for socially appropriate attitudes and behaviors that are embodied in the stated or implicit rules of a group are called **social norms.** Social norms can be broad guidelines; if you are a member of Democrats for Social Action, you may be expected to hold liberal political beliefs, whereas members of the Young Republicans will advocate more conservative views. Social norms can also embody specific standards of conduct. For example, if you are employed as a waiter or a waitress, you will be expected to treat your customers courteously no matter how unpleasant and demanding they are to you.

Belonging to a group typically involves discovering the set of social norms that regulates desired behavior in the group setting. This adjustment occurs in two ways: You notice the *uniformities* in certain behaviors of all or most members, and you observe the *negative consequences* when someone violates a social norm.

Norms serve several important functions. Awareness of the norms operating in a given group situation helps orient members and regulate their social interaction. Each participant can anticipate how others will enter the situation, how they will dress, and what they are likely to say and do, as well as what type of behavior will be expected of them to gain approval. You often feel awkward in new situations precisely because you may be unaware of the norms that govern the way you ought to act. Some tolerance for deviating from the standard is also part of the norm—wide in some cases, narrow in others. For example, shorts and a T-shirt might be marginally acceptable attire for a religious ceremony; a bathing suit would almost certainly deviate too far from the norm. Group members are usually able to estimate how far they can go before experiencing the coercive power of the group in the form of ridicule, reeducation, and rejection.

CONFORMITY

When you adopt a social role or bend to a social norm, you are, to some extent, *conforming* to social expectations. **Conformity** is the tendency for people to adopt the behavior and opinions presented by other group members. Why do you conform? Are there circumstances under which you ignore social constraints and act independently? Social psychologists have studied two types of forces that may lead to conformity:

- **Informational influence** processes—wanting to be correct and to understand the right way to act in a given situation.
- **Normative influence** processes—wanting to be liked, accepted, and approved of by others.

---

social norm The expectation a group has for its members regarding acceptable and appropriate attitudes and behaviors.

conformity The tendency for people to adopt the behaviors, attitudes, and values of other members of a reference group.

informational influence Group effects that arise from individuals' desire to be correct and right and to understand how best to act in a given situation.

normative influence Group effects that arise from individuals' desire to be liked, accepted, and approved of by others.

norm crystallization The convergence of the expectations of a group of individuals into a common perspective as they talk and carry out activities together.

We will describe classic experiments that illustrate each type of influence.

Informational Influence: Sherif's Autokinetic Effect

Many life situations in which you must make decisions about behaviors are quite ambiguous. Suppose, for example, you are dining at an elegant restaurant with a large group of people. Each place at the table is set with a dazzling array of silverware. How do you know which fork to use when the first course arrives? Typically, you would look to other members of the party to help you make an appropriate choice. This is *informational influence.*

A classic experiment, conducted by Muzafer Sherif (1935), demonstrated how informational influence can lead to **norm crystallization**—norm formation and solidification.

> Participants were asked to judge the amount of movement of a spot of light, which was actually stationary but that appeared to move when viewed in total darkness with no reference points. This is a perceptual illusion known as the *autokinetic effect.* Originally, individual judgments varied widely. However, when the participants were brought together in a group consisting of strangers and stated their judgments aloud, their estimates began to converge. They began to see the light move in the same direction and in similar amounts. Even more interesting was the final part of Sherif's study—when alone in the same darkened room after the group viewing, these participants continued to follow the group norm that had emerged when they were together.

Once norms are established in a group, they tend to perpetuate themselves. In later research, these autokinetic group norms persisted even when tested a year later and without former group members witnessing the judgments (Rohrer et al., 1954). Norms can be transmitted from one generation of group members to the next and can continue to influence people's behavior long after the original group that created the norm no longer exists (Insko et al., 1980). How do we know that norms can have transgenerational influence? In autokinetic effect studies, researchers replaced one group member with a new one after each set of autokinetic trials until all the members of the group were new to the situation. The group's autokinetic norm remained true to the one handed down to them across several successive generations (Jacobs & Campbell, 1961). Do you see how this experiment captures the processes that allow real-life norms to be passed down across generations?

Normative Influence: The Asch Effect
What is the best way to demonstrate that people will sometimes conform because of *normative influence*—their desire to be liked, accepted, and approved of by others? One of the most important early social psychologists, **Solomon Asch** (1940, 1956), created circumstances in which participants made judgments under conditions in which the physical reality was absolutely clear—but the rest of a group reported that they saw that reality differently. Male college students were led to believe they were in a study of simple visual perception. They were shown cards with three lines of differing lengths and asked to indicate which of the three lines was the same length as the standard line (see **Figure 16.3**). The lines were different enough so that mistakes were rare, and their relative sizes changed on each series of trials.

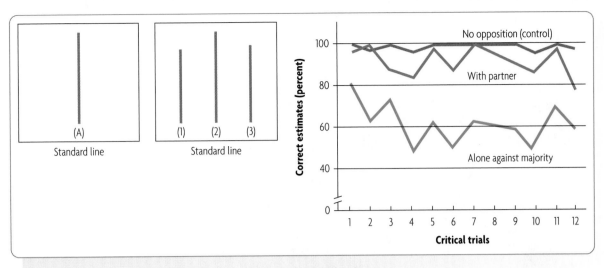

FIGURE 16.3 **Conformity in the Asch Experiments**

In this photo from Asch's study, it is evident that the naive participant, Number 6, is distressed by the unanimous majority's erroneous judgment. The typical stimulus array is shown at the top left. At top right, the graph illustrates conformity across 12 critical trials when solitary participants were grouped with a unanimous majority, as well as their greater independence when paired with a dissenting partner. A lower percentage of correct estimates indicates the greater degree of an individual's conformity to the group's false estimate.

The participants were seated next to last in semicircles of six to eight other students. Unknown to the participants, the others were all experimental confederates—accomplices of the experimenter—who were following a prearranged script. On the first three trials, everyone in the circle agreed on the correct comparison. However, the first confederate to respond on the fourth trial matched two lines that were obviously different. So did all members of the group up to the participant. That student had to decide if he should go along with everyone else's view of the situation and conform or remain independent, standing by what he clearly saw. That dilemma was repeated for the naive participant on 12 of the 18 trials. The participants showed signs of disbelief and obvious discomfort when faced with a majority who saw the world so differently. What did they do?

Roughly one-fourth of the participants remained completely independent—they never conformed. However, between 50 and 80 percent of the participants (in different studies in the research program) conformed with the false majority estimate at least once, and a third of the participants yielded to the majority's wrong judgments on half or more of the critical trials.

Asch describes some participants who yielded to the majority most of the time as "disoriented" and "doubt-ridden"; he states that they "experienced a powerful impulse not to appear different from the majority" (1952, p. 396). Those who yielded underestimated the influence of the social pressure and the frequency of their conformity; some even claimed that they really had seen the lines as the same length, despite their obvious discrepancy.

In other studies, Asch varied three factors: the size of the unanimous majority, the presence of a partner who dissented from the majority, and the size of the discrepancy between the correct physical stimulus comparison and the majority's position. He found that strong conformity effects were elicited with a unanimous majority of only three or four people.

What impact does normative influence have on people's everyday behaviors?

However, giving the naive participant a single ally who dissented from the majority opinion had the effect of sharply reducing conformity, as can be seen in Figure 16.3. With a partner, the participant was usually able to resist the pressures to conform to the majority (Asch, 1955, 1956).

How should we interpret these results? Asch himself was struck by the rate at which participants did *not* conform (Friend et al., 1990). He reported this research as studies in "independence." In fact, two-thirds of the time, participants gave the correct, nonconforming answer. However, most descriptions of Asch's experiment have emphasized the one-third conformity rate. Accounts of this experiment also often fail to note that not all participants were alike: The number of individuals who never conformed, about 25 percent, was roughly equal to the number who always or almost always conformed. Thus Asch's experiment teaches two complementary lessons. On the one hand, we find that people are not entirely swayed by normative influence—they assert their independence on a majority of occasions (and some people always do). On the other hand, we find that people will sometimes conform, even in the most unambiguous situations. That potential to conform is an important element of human nature.

Conformity in Everyday Life Although you've almost certainly never faced the exact circumstances of the Asch experiment, you can no doubt recognize conformity situations in your everyday life. Many of these situations are easy to spot. You might notice, for example, that you are wearing clothes that you find rather silly because someone has declared them to be fashionable. (Certainly that's true of *other* people.) Also, as we noted in Chapter 10, adolescents often conform with their peer groups with respect to risky behaviors such as drug use.

People often resist the idea that their behaviors are influenced by norms. Consider a study that examined the types of messages that work most effectively to bring about reductions in people's energy consumption (Nolan et al., 2007). California residents found one of five types of messages left hanging on

their door knobs. **Table 16.1** provides examples of the types of messages. The researchers later went door-to-door to ask the residents, "How much did the information on these doorhangers motivate you to conserve energy?" Residents' responses could range from 1 (not at all) to 4 (extremely). As you can see in Table 16.1, residents reported that the normative messages provided the *least* motivation. The researchers also read the residents' electricity meters to determine their actual energy consumption one month after the doorhangers were left at their homes. Table 16.1 reveals that the normative message yielded the *lowest* consumption. When you put these pieces together, you'll see why the researchers drew this interesting conclusion: "Despite the fact that participants believed that the behavior of their neighbors—the descriptive norm—had the least impact on their own energy conservation, results showed that the descriptive norm actually had the strongest effect on participants' energy conservation behaviors" (pp. 920–921).

In the domain of energy conservation, it's easy to be comfortable that people are unknowingly influenced by social norms. However, the strong tendency to succumb to normative influence holds out the possibility of considerably more negative consequences. For example, history has provided several instances of *suicide cults*—circumstances in which people have internalized group norms that have led them to take their own lives. Consider events that took place in San Diego, California, in March 1997. The members of a group called "Heaven's Gate" committed mass suicide: The police found 39 bodies wearing identical black uniforms and accompanied by travel bags packed for a journey (Balch & Taylor, 2002). Before their suicides, the cult members had accepted a belief system that required them to shed their earthly bodies so they could board a UFO that would take them to the Kingdom of Heaven. The group had posted much of their belief system to their official Web site. Researchers worry that the Internet will provide a particularly effective means to recruit people into cults and other alternative belief systems (Dawson & Hennebry, 2003). Does this strike you as a legitimate concern? You should consider that

TABLE 16.1 People Are Unaware of Normative Influence

Type of Message	Excerpt from the Message	Motivation to Conserve	Energy Consumption
Descriptive Norm	In a recent survey of households in your community, researchers at Cal State San Marcos found that 77% of San Marcos residents often use fans instead of air conditioning to keep cool in the summer.	1.76	16.10
Self-Interest	According to researchers at Cal State San Marcos, you could save up to $54 per month by using fans instead of air conditioning to keep cool in the summer.	1.86	17.45
Environmental Protection	According to researchers at Cal State San Marcos, you can prevent the release of up to 262 lb of greenhouse gases per month by using fans instead of air conditioning to keep cool this summer!	2.07	16.89
Social Responsibility	According to researchers at Cal State San Marcos, you can reduce your monthly demand for electricity by 29% using fans instead of air conditioning to keep cool this summer!	1.99	17.52
Information Only	Summer is here, and the time is right to conserve energy. How can you conserve energy this summer? By using fans instead of air conditioning!	1.94	17.36

Note: Energy consumption is average daily kilowatt hours.

question in the context of the Asch experiment and other demonstrations of the ease with which conformity arises.

Minority Influence and Nonconformity

Given the power of the majority to control resources and information, it is not surprising that people regularly conform to groups. Yet you know that sometimes individuals persevere in their personal views. How can this happen? How do people escape group domination, and how can anything new (counternormative) ever come about? Are there any conditions under which a small minority can turn the majority around and create new norms?

To address such questions, **Serge Moscovici** and his colleagues conducted a series of studies on minority influence. In one study where participants were given color-naming tasks, the majority correctly identified the color patches, but two of the experimenter's confederates consistently identified a green color as blue. Their consistent minority opposition had no immediate effect on the majority, but, when later tested alone, some of the participants shifted their judgments by moving the boundary between blue and green toward the blue side of the color continuum (Moscovici, 1976; Moscovici & Faucheux, 1972). Eventually, the power of the many may be

When individuals become dependent on a group—such as a religious cult—for basic feelings of self-worth, they are prone to extremes of conformity. Twenty thousand identically dressed couples were married in this service conducted by the Reverend Sun Myung Moon. More recently, in August 1995, Moon simultaneously married 360,000 "Moonie" couples who were linked by satellite in 500 worldwide locations. Why do people find comfort in such large-scale conformity?

undercut by the conviction of the dedicated few (Moscovici, 1980, 1985).

You can conceptualize these effects with respect to the distinction we introduced earlier between normative influence and informational influence (Crano & Prislin, 2006; Wood et al., 1994). Minority groups have relatively little normative influence: Members of the majority are typically not particularly concerned about being liked or accepted by the minority. Conversely, minority groups do have informational influence: Minorities can encourage group members to understand issues from multiple perspectives (Peterson & Nemeth, 1996). Unfortunately, this potential for informational influence may only infrequently allow minorities to overcome majority members' normative desire to distance themselves from deviant or low-consensus views (Wood, 2000).

DECISION MAKING IN GROUPS

If you've ever tried to make a decision as part of a group, you know that it can be quite torturous. Imagine, for example, that you have just seen a movie with a bunch of friends. Although you thought the movie was "OK," by the end of a postmovie discussion you find yourself agreeing that it was "an incredible piece of trash." Is this change after group discussion typical? Are the judgments groups make consistently different from individuals' judgments? Researchers in social psychology have documented specific forces that operate when groups make decisions (Kerr & Tindale, 2004). We will focus on *group polarization* and *groupthink*.

Your postmovie experience is an example of **group polarization**: Groups show a tendency to make decisions that are more extreme than the decisions that would be made by the members acting alone. Suppose, for example, you asked each member of the movie group to provide an attitude rating toward the movie; subsequently, as a group you agree on a single value to reflect your group attitude. If the group's rating is more extreme than the average of the individuals' ratings, that would be an instance of polarization. Depending on the initial group tendency—toward caution or risk—group polarization will tend to make a group more cautious or more risky.

Researchers have suggested that two types of processes underlie group polarization: the *information-influence* model and the *social comparison* model (Liu & Latané, 1998). The information-influence model suggests that group members contribute different information to a decision. If you and your friends each have a different reason for disliking a movie a little bit, all that information taken together would provide the evidence that you should actually dislike the movie a lot. The social comparison model suggests that group members strive to capture their peers' regard by representing a group ideal that is a bit more extreme than the group's true norm. Thus, if you come to decide that everyone was unhappy with a movie, you could try to present yourself as particularly astute by stating a more extreme opinion. If everyone in a group tries to capture the group's esteem in that same fashion, polarization will result.

Group polarization is one consequence of a general pattern of thought called *groupthink*. **Irving Janis** (1982) coined the term **groupthink** for the tendency of a decision-making group to filter out undesirable input so that a consensus may be reached, especially if it is in line with the leader's viewpoint. Janis's theory of groupthink emerged from his historical analysis of the Bay of Pigs invasion of Cuba in 1960. This disastrous invasion was approved by President Kennedy after cabinet meetings in which contrary information was minimized or suppressed by those advisers to the president who were eager to undertake the invasion. From his analysis of this event, Janis outlined a series of features that he believed would predispose groups to fall prey to groupthink: He suggested, for example, that groups that were highly cohesive and insulated from experts and that they operated under directed leadership would make groupthink decisions.

To test Janis's ideas, researchers have turned both to further historical analyses and laboratory experiments (Henningsen et al., 2006). This body of research suggests that groups are particularly vulnerable to groupthink when they embody a collective desire to maintain a shared positive view of a group (Turner & Pratkanis, 1998). Group members must understand that dissent often improves the quality of a group decision even if it may detract, on the surface, from the group's positive feel.

We've just reviewed some of the situational forces that have an impact on the decisions that groups make. We will focus next on one of the most important decisions people make as individuals: When should they obey authority?

OBEDIENCE TO AUTHORITY

What made thousands of Nazis willing to follow Hitler's orders and send millions of Jews to the gas chambers? Why did U.S. soldiers follow the orders of their superiors and massacre hundreds of innocent citizens of the Vietnamese village of My Lai by (Hersh, 1971; Opton, 1970, 1973)? Did character defects lead people to carry out orders blindly? Did they have no moral values? Stanley Milgram (1965, 1974), a student of Solomon Asch, conducted a series of studies that showed that blind obedience is less a product of dispositional characteristics than the outcome of situational forces that could engulf anyone. Milgram's program of obedience research is one of the most controversial because of its significant implications for real-world phenomena and the ethical issues it raises.

The Obedience Paradigm To separate the variables of personality and situation, Milgram used a series of 19 separate controlled laboratory experiments involving more than 1,000 participants. Milgram's first experiments were conducted at Yale University, with male residents of New Haven and surrounding communities who received payment for their participation. In later variations, Milgram took his obedience laboratory away from the university. He set up a storefront research unit in Bridgeport, Connecticut, recruiting through newspaper ads a broad cross-section of the population, varying widely in age, occupation, and education and including members of both sexes.

Milgram's basic experimental paradigm involved individual participants delivering a series of what they thought were extremely painful electric shocks to another person. These volunteers thought they were participating in a scientific

---

group polarization The tendency for groups to make decisions that are more extreme than the decisions that would be made by the members acting alone.

groupthink The tendency of a decision-making group to filter out undesirable input so that a consensus may be reached, especially if it is in line with the leader's viewpoint.

study of memory and learning. They were led to believe that the educational purpose of the study was to discover how punishment affects memory, so that learning could be improved through the proper balance of reward and punishment. In their *social roles* as *teachers*, the participants were to punish each error made by someone playing the role of *learner*. The major rule they were told to follow was to increase the level of shock each time the learner made an error until the learning was errorless. The white-coated experimenter acted as the *legitimate authority* figure—he presented the rules, arranged for the assignment of roles (by a rigged drawing of lots), and ordered the teachers to do their jobs whenever they hesitated or dissented. The dependent variable was the final level of shock—on a shock machine that went up to 450 volts in small, 15-volt steps—that a teacher gave before refusing to continue to obey the authority.

The Test Situation

The study was staged to make a participant think that, by following orders, he or she was causing pain and suffering and perhaps even killing an innocent person. Each teacher had been given a sample shock of 45 volts to feel the amount of pain it caused. The learner was a pleasant, mild-mannered man, about 50 years old, who mentioned something about a heart condition but was willing to go along with the procedure. He was strapped into an "electric chair" in the next room and communicated with the teacher via an intercom. His task was to memorize pairs of words, giving the second word in a pair when he heard the first one. The learner soon began making errors—according to a prearranged schedule—and the teacher began shocking the learner. The protests of the victim rose with the shock level. At 75 volts, he began to moan and grunt; at 150 volts, he demanded to be released from the experiment; at 180 volts, he cried out that he could not stand the pain any longer. At 300 volts, he insisted that he would no longer take part in the experiment and must be freed. He yelled out about his heart condition and screamed. If a teacher hesitated or protested delivering the next shock, the experimenter said, "The experiment requires that you continue" or "You have no other choice, you *must* go on."

As you might imagine, the situation was stressful for the participants. Most participants complained and protested, repeatedly insisting they could not continue. Women participants often were in tears as they dissented. That the experimental situation produced considerable conflict in the participants is readily apparent from their protests:

- 180 volts delivered: "He can't stand it! I'm not going to kill that man in there! You hear him hollering? He's hollering. He can't stand it. What if something happens to him? . . . I mean, who is going to take the responsibility if anything happens to that gentleman?" [The experimenter accepts responsibility.] "All right."
- 195 volts delivered: "You see he's hollering. Hear that. Gee, I don't know." [The experimenter says, "The experiment requires that you go on."] "I know it does, sir, but I mean—huh—he don't know what he's in for. He's up to 195 volts." (Milgram, 1965, p. 67).

Even when there was only silence from the learner's room, the teacher was ordered to keep shocking him more and more strongly, all the way up to the button that was marked "Danger: Severe Shock XXX (450 volts)."

Why Do People Obey Authority?

When 40 psychiatrists were asked by Milgram to predict the performance of participants in this experiment, they estimated that most would not go beyond 150 volts (based on a description of the experiment). In their professional opinions, fewer than 4 percent of the participants would still be obedient at 300 volts, and only about 0.1 percent would continue all the way to 450 volts. The psychiatrists presumed that only those few individuals who were *abnormal* in some way, sadists who enjoyed inflicting pain on others, would blindly obey orders to continue up to the maximum shock.

The psychiatrists based their evaluations on presumed *dispositional* qualities of people who would engage in such abnormal behavior; they were, however, overlooking the power of this special situation to influence the thinking and actions of most people caught up in its social context. The remarkable and disturbing conclusion is just how wrong these experts were: *The majority of participants obeyed the authority fully.* No participant quit below 300 volts. Sixty-five percent delivered the maximum 450 volts to the learner. Note that most people *dissented* verbally, but the majority did not *disobey* behaviorally. From the point of view of the victim, that's a critical difference. If you were the victim, would it matter much that the participants said they didn't want to continue hurting you (they dissented), if they then shocked you repeatedly (they obeyed)?

Milgram's obedience experiment: the "teacher" (participant) with experimenter (authority figure), the shock generator, and the "learner" (the experimenter's confederate). What aspects of the situation affected the likelihood that the teachers would continue to the maximum shock level?

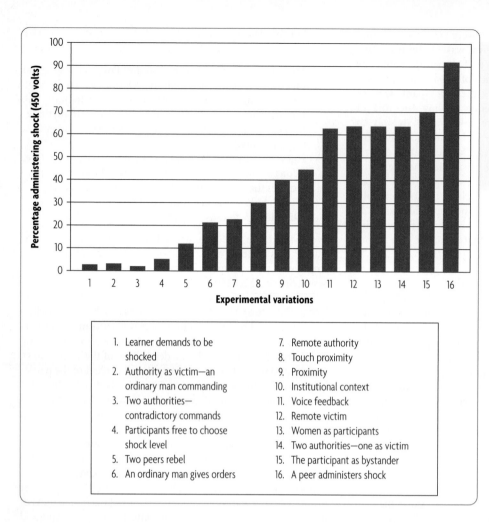

FIGURE 16.4 Obedience in Milgram's Experiments

The graph shows a profile of weak to strong obedience effects across Milgram's many experimental variations.

From *The Obedience Experiments,* by A. G. Miller, 1986, Copyright © 1986 Praeger. Reprinted with permission.

1. Learner demands to be shocked
2. Authority as victim—an ordinary man commanding
3. Two authorities—contradictory commands
4. Participants free to choose shock level
5. Two peers rebel
6. An ordinary man gives orders
7. Remote authority
8. Touch proximity
9. Proximity
10. Institutional context
11. Voice feedback
12. Remote victim
13. Women as participants
14. Two authorities—one as victim
15. The participant as bystander
16. A peer administers shock

Milgram's research suggests that, to understand why people obey authority, you need to look closely at the psychological forces at work in the situation. We saw earlier how often situational factors constrain behaviors; in Milgram's research, we see an especially vivid instance of that general principle. Milgram and other researchers manipulated a number of aspects of the experimental circumstances to demonstrate that the obedience effect is overwhelmingly due to situational variables and not personality variables. **Figure 16.4** displays the level of obedience found in different situations. Obedience is quite high, for example, when a peer first models obedience, when a participant acts as an *intermediary bystander* assisting another person who actually delivers the shock, or when the victim (the learner) is physically remote from the teacher. Obedience is quite low when the learner demands to be shocked, when two authorities give contradictory commands, or when the authority figure is the victim. These findings all point to the idea that the *situation,* and not differences among individual participants, largely controlled behavior.

When we teach contemporary students about Milgram's research, they often express the strong conviction that, because of cultural changes since the early 60s, people would no longer obey. To answer this claim, social psychologist **Jerry Burger** (2009) completed a partial replication of one of

Milgram's experiments. Burger modified the experiment to address ethical concerns present in Milgram's original procedure. Specifically, Burger halted participants if they continued to obey after they believed they had delivered a 150-volt shock. As we noted earlier, 150 volts was the point at which the learner demanded to be released from the experiment. Based on Milgram's original data, Burger reasoned that participants who continued after 150 volts would have been quite likely to continue beyond that point. In Milgram's original experiment, 82.5 percent of the participants continued beyond 150 volts; in Burger's replication, 70.0 percent did so. Thus, in the replication, a large majority of participants continued to obey the experimenter. Burger concluded that "the same situational factors that affected obedience in Milgram's participants still operate today" (p. 9).

Two reasons people obey authority in these situations can be traced to the effects of *normative* and *informational* sources of influence, which we discussed earlier: People want to be liked (normative influence), and they want to be right (informational influence). They tend to do what others are doing or requesting to be socially acceptable and approved. In addition, when in an ambiguous, novel situation—like the experimental situation—people rely on others for cues as to what is the appropriate and correct way to behave. They are more likely to do so when experts or credible communicators tell them what to do. A third factor in the Milgram paradigm is that participants were probably confused about *how to disobey*; nothing they said in dissent satisfied the authority. If they had a simple, direct way out of the situation—for example, by pressing a "quit" button—it is likely more would have disobeyed (Ross, 1988). Finally, obedience to authority in this experimental situation is part of an *ingrained habit* that is learned by children in many different settings—obey authority without question (Brown, 1986). This heuristic usually serves society well when authorities are legitimate and deserving of obedience. The problem is that the rule gets overapplied. Blind obedience to authority means obeying any and all authority figures simply because of their ascribed status, regardless of whether they are unjust or just in their requests and commands.

What is the personal significance to you of this obedience research? What choices will you make when faced with moral dilemmas throughout your life? Take a moment to reflect on the types of obedience to authority situations that might arise in your day-to-day experience. Suppose you were a salesclerk. Would you cheat customers if your boss encouraged such behavior? Suppose you were a member of Congress. Would you vote along party lines, rather than vote your conscience?

Milgram's obedience research challenges the myth that evil lurks in the minds of evil people—the bad "they" who are different from the good "us" or "you," who would never do such things. Our purpose in recounting these findings is not to debase human nature but to make clear that even normal, well-meaning individuals are subject to the potential for frailty in the face of strong situational and social forces.

In this section, we have argued that people are interconnected by the rules, norms, and situations they share. We next consider how people gather and apply information from their day-to-day experiences. We examine the question of how attitudes are formed and changed—and we explore the links among beliefs, attitudes, and actions.

STOP AND REVIEW

❶ What did the Stanford Prison Experiment demonstrate about social roles?

❷ Why are groups able to have normative influence?

❸ What type of influence are minorities able to exert in a group?

❹ How can you recognize circumstances of group polarization?

❺ How did psychiatrists' predictions compare to participants' actual behavior in Milgram's experiments?

CRITICAL THINKING Consider the study that looked at conformity in line judgments. Why was it important that the group members all gave the correct answer on the first few trials?

Visit MyPsychLab.com for more review and practice on the following topics:

👁 **Watch:** Stanford Prison Experiment: Phil Zimbardo

👁 **Watch:** Milgram Obedience Study Today

Attitudes, Attitude Change, and Action

Have you already had a chance today to express an *attitude?* Has someone asked you, "What do you think of my shirt?" or "Was the chicken any good?" An **attitude** is a positive or negative evaluation of people, objects, and ideas. This definition of attitude allows for the fact that many of the attitudes you hold are not overt; you may not be consciously aware that you harbor certain attitudes. Attitudes are important because they influence your behavior and how you construct social reality. Recall the Princeton–Dartmouth football game (p.509). Those people who favored Princeton "saw" a different game from those people who favored Dartmouth; attributions about events were made in line with their attitudes. What are the sources of your attitudes, and how do they affect your behaviors?

ATTITUDES AND BEHAVIORS

We have already defined attitudes as positive or negative evaluations. We'll begin this section by giving you an opportunity to make an evaluation. To what extent do you agree with this statement? (Circle a number.)

I enjoy movies that star Angelina Jolie.

1 —— 2 —— 3 —— 4 —— 5 —— 6 —— 7 —— 8 —— 9
Strongly   Neutral   Strongly
disagree   agree

Let's say that you gave a rating of 3—you disagree somewhat. What is the origin of that judgment? We can identify three types of information that give rise to your attitude:

- *Cognitive.* What thoughts do you have in response to "Angelina Jolie"?
- *Affective.* What feelings does the mention of "Angelina Jolie" evoke?
- *Behavioral.* How do you behave when, for example, you have the opportunity to see one of Angelina Jolie's movies?

Some combination of these types of information most likely guided your hand when you circled "3" (or some other number). Your attitudes also generate responses in the same three categories. If you believe yourself to have a somewhat negative attitude toward Angelina Jolie, you might say, "She isn't a serious actor" (cognitive), "She looked better when she first started out" (affective), or "After *Sky Captain and the World of Tomorrow*, I'm going to wait to read her reviews" (behavioral).

It isn't too hard to measure an attitude, but is that attitude always an accurate indication of how people will actually behave? You know from your own life experiences that the answer is "no": People will say they dislike Angelina Jolie but spend good money to see her anyway. At the same time, sometimes people's behaviors *do* follow their attitudes: They say they won't pay to see Angelina Jolie, and they don't. How can you determine when attitudes will or will not predict behavior? Researchers have worked hard to answer that question—to

---

attitude The learned, relatively stable tendency to respond to people, concepts, and events in an evaluative way.

How does your attitude toward Angelina Jolie affect your willingness to watch her movies?

them to report their attitudes toward blood donations. Of this group, 2,389 people completed the questionnaire. The 1,772 people randomly assigned to the control group did not receive the questionnaire. Six months and 12 months after the time the questionnaires went out, the researchers checked to see how many people had made blood donations. The impact of the questionnaire was clear: Members of the experimental group donated more blood. For example, after six months, 8.6 percent more people in the experimental group had registered to give blood.

There are a whole variety of reasons people might or might not donate blood in six months or a year. However, the very act of rehearsing and reporting their attitudes on a simple questionnaire had a major impact on people's subsequent behavior.

Attitudes also are better predictors of behavior when the attitudes remain stable over time. Suppose, for example, we asked you to agree or disagree with the statement "I trust politicians." Your judgment would depend on which politician or politicians came to mind: Was it George Washington, Winston Churchill, George W. Bush, or Barack Obama? Now, suppose we asked you the same question a week from now. If you called different politicians to mind, your overall attitude toward politicians would likely change (Lord et al., 2004; Sia et al., 1997). Only when the "evidence" for your attitude remains stable over time can we expect to find a strong relationship between your evaluation (thoughts) and what you do (actions).

Another way to improve the match between attitudes and behaviors would be to improve attitude measures. In recent years, researchers have created a number of new attitude measures that attempt to capture people's *automatic* or *implicit* attitudes—the attitudes they hold toward people, objects, or ideas that often remain outside conscious awareness (Greenwald et al., 2002; Stanley et al., 2008). The claim is these implicit attitudes may allow for predictions of behavior. Consider a study that focused on a group of undecided voters in an Italian election (Arcuri et al., 2008). Although these voters did not have a conscious preference, many of them revealed an unconscious preference when they underwent a procedure called the *implicit association test*. The political version of the test assessed how easy people found it to categorize the two candidates in association with positive and negative words. When the participants reported their votes after the election, they were consistently more likely to have voted for the candidate with whom they found it easier to associate positive words. Although these voters were not able to reveal conscious preferences, their implicit attitudes were correlated with future behavior. Across several domains of human experience, researchers continue to examine the ability of implicit measures to predict behavior. Much of that research focuses on the same issues we identified for explicit attitudes such as the stability of implicit attitudes over time (Gawronski & LeBel, 2008).

PROCESSES OF PERSUASION

We've just seen that, under appropriate circumstances, attitudes can predict behavior. That's good news for all the people who spend time and money to affect your attitudes. But quite often others *can't* affect your attitudes when they want to do so. You don't change brands of toothpaste each time you see a peppy new commercial with scads of pearly-toothed actors; you don't change your political affiliation each time a candidate looks into the camera and declares sincerely that he or she deserves your vote. Many people in your life indulge in **persuasion**—deliberate

identify the circumstances in which the link is strongest between people's attitudes and how they act (Ajzen & Fishbein, 2005; Glasman & Albarracín, 2006).

One property of attitudes that predicts behavior is *accessibility*—the strength of the association between an attitude object and a person's evaluation of that object (Fazio & Roskos-Ewoldsen, 2005). When we asked you about Angelina Jolie, did an answer rush to mind or did you have to consider the question for a while? The more quickly an answer rushed in, the more likely it is that your behavior will be consistent with that attitude. But how do attitudes become more accessible? Research suggests that attitudes are more accessible when they are based on *direct experience:* You will have a more accessible attitude about Angelina Jolie movies if you've experienced several of them yourself rather than hearing or reading about them indirectly. Attitudes are also more accessible when they have been rehearsed more often: Just as you might expect, the more often you've formulated an attitude about something (consider "chocolate" versus "kiwi"), the more accessible is the attitude. Let's consider a study that illustrates the behavioral consequences of attitude rehearsal.

The researchers were interested in understanding the factors that lead people to make repeated blood donations (Godin et al., 2008). The study focused on 4,672 people who had previously donated blood. Prior donors are quite likely to have positive attitudes about the importance of donating blood. The researchers reasoned that they could increase the likelihood that people would donate again if they made those attitudes more accessible. To increase attitude accessibility, the researchers randomly selected 2,900 people for the experimental group and mailed a questionnaire that asked

---

persuasion Deliberate efforts to change attitudes.

efforts to change your attitudes. For persuasion to take place, certain conditions must be met. Let's explore some of those conditions.

To begin, we introduce the **elaboration likelihood model,** a theory of persuasion that defines how likely it is that people will focus their cognitive processes to elaborate on a persuasive message (Petty & Briñol, 2008; Petty et al., 2005). This model makes a critical distinction between *central* and *peripheral routes* to persuasion. The central route represents circumstances in which people think carefully about a persuasive communication so that attitude change depends on the strength of the arguments. This careful thought is called *high* elaboration. When someone is trying to convince you that gasoline should cost $5 a gallon, you are likely to process the information in this careful fashion. The peripheral route represents circumstances in which people do not focus critically on the message but respond to superficial cues in the situation. When an attractive model is placed in front of the product someone wishes you to buy, the seller is hoping you'll avoid critical thought. That absence of critical thought is called *low* elaboration. The central or peripheral route that people take depends in large part on their *motivation* with respect to the message: Are they willing and able to think carefully about the persuasive content; will they engage in high or low elaboration?

If you take a close look at the messages that surround you, you will quickly come to the conclusion that advertisers, for example, often count on you to take the peripheral route. Why do advertisers pay celebrities to sell their products? Do you really believe that

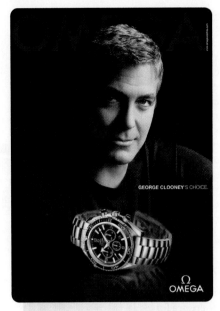

Why do advertisers pay celebrities to endorse their products?

Hollywood actors worry enormously about which long-distance phone service will produce bigger savings? Presumably, the advertisers hope that you won't evaluate the arguments too closely—instead, they hope you'll let yourself be persuaded by your general feelings of warmth toward the actor hawking the product.

Now ask yourself this question: Under what circumstances are you likely to feel sufficiently motivated to take the central route to persuasion? Researchers have undertaken an enormous amount of research to address that question (Petty et al., 2005). Let's consider a study that illustrates how difficult it is to persuade all of the people all of the time. Recall from Chapter 5 that people often label themselves as a *morning person* or an *evening person*. Researchers hypothesized that people are more likely to have the energy and motivation to engage in elaborative processing—the central route to persuasion—when they encounter persuasive messages at their right time of day.

To test their hypothesis, the researchers recruited participants who self-identified their "optimal" time of day as morning or evening (Martin & Marrington, 2005). The study had two sessions: one at 8:30 A.M. and one at 7:00 P.M. Each session included both morning people and evening people. At the start of the session, participants provided attitude ratings (on nine-point scales) on several social issues including the mercy killing of terminally ill people. Next, the participants read the same set of persuasive statements that argued against mercy killing. Finally, participants listed the thoughts they had while reading the statements and provided a second set of attitude ratings. When the participants' session matched their optimal time of day, they listed more thoughts that were focused on the persuasive statements. In addition, as shown in **Figure 16.5,** people showed more attitude change in the direction of the statements when they read the persuasive statements at the optimal time of day.

At their optimal time of day, participants were motivated to elaborate on the persuasive statements. Because the statements provided strong arguments against mercy killing, their attitudes changed in the direction of the statements. If the arguments had been weak, high elaboration should have prevented attitude change.

There are many circumstances in life in which you probably want to resist having your attitudes changed. The elaboration likelihood model suggests that you'll often need to expend some effort to avoid being persuaded. Consider a

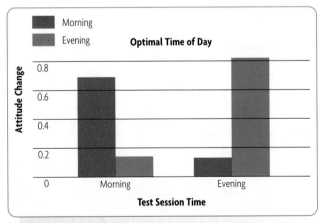

FIGURE 16.5 **Persuasion at the Optimal Time of Day**

When participants read persuasive statements at their optimal time of day, they showed more attitude change in the direction of those statements.

Adapted from Martin & Marrington, *Personality and Individual Differences, 39,* 367–377, 2005.

---

elaboration likelihood model A theory of persuasion that defines how likely it is that people will focus their cognitive processes to elaborate upon a message and therefore follow the central and peripheral routes to persuasion.

study in which a researcher asked students to read an essay that argued that college vacations should be shortened to just one month (Burkley, 2008). The essay suggested, for example, that such a change would allow students to graduate more rapidly. Before reading the essay, some participants engaged in a separate task in which they spent five minutes listing thoughts that came to mind—but they were under explicit instructions *not* to think about a white bear. After doing that task, the participants gave attitude ratings that were more favorable toward the idea of one-month vacations than did control participants. It seemed that the effort they expended trying not to think about white bears had depleted the mental resources they needed to resist the essay's arguments. In your own life, when you know that you're going to face a persuasive appeal, you should try to ensure that you are ready to engage your full mental effort.

PERSUASION BY YOUR OWN ACTIONS

In the last section, we described factors that influence people's ability to change others' attitudes. However, there are forces at work in a number of circumstances that cause people to bring about their *own* attitude change. Imagine a situation in which you've vowed not to eat any extra calories. You arrive at work, and there's a cake for your boss's birthday. You consume a piece. Did you break your vow? That is, should you have a negative attitude about your own behavior? Aren't you likely to think what you did was OK? Why? We describe two analyses of self-persuasion, *cognitive dissonance theory* and *self-perception theory*.

Cognitive Dissonance Theory One of the most common assumptions in the study of attitudes is that people like to believe that their attitudes remain consistent over time. This striving for consistency was explored within the field of social psychology in the theory of *cognitive dissonance*, as developed by **Leon Festinger** (1957). **Cognitive dissonance** is the state of conflict someone experiences *after* making a decision, taking an action, or being exposed to information that is contrary to prior beliefs, feelings, or values. Suppose, for example, you chose to buy a car against a friend's advice. Why might you be overly defensive about the car? It is assumed that when a person's cognitions about his or her behavior and relevant attitudes are dissonant—they do not follow one to the next—an aversive state arises that the person is motivated to reduce. Dissonance-reducing activities modify this unpleasant state. In the case of your car, being defensive—overstating its value—makes you feel better about going against your friend's advice. (Dissonance also might lead you to think less well of your friend.)

Dissonance has motivational force—it impels you to take action to reduce the unpleasant feeling (Wood, 2000). The motivation to reduce dissonance increases with the magnitude of the dissonance created by a cognitive inconsistency. In other words, the stronger the dissonance, the greater the motivation to reduce it. In a classic dissonance experiment, college students told a lie to other students and came to believe in their lie when they got a small, rather than a large, reward for doing so.

What messages might you give yourself to reduce cognitive dissonance if you were aware of the adverse effects of smoking but continued to smoke?

Stanford students participated in a very dull task and were then asked (as a favor to the experimenter because his assistant hadn't shown up) to lie to another participant by saying that the task had been fun and interesting. Half the participants were paid $20 to tell the lie; the others were paid only $1. The $20 payment was sufficient external justification for lying, but the $1 payment was an inadequate justification. The people who were paid $1 were left with dissonant cognitions: "The task was dull" and "I chose to lie by telling another student it was fun and interesting without a good reason for doing so."

To reduce their dissonance, these $1 participants changed their evaluations of the task. They later expressed the belief that they found "it really was fun and interesting—I might like to do it again." In comparison, the participants who lied for $20 did not change their evaluations—the task was still a bore; they had only lied "for the money" (Festinger & Carlsmith, 1959).

As this experiment shows, under conditions of high dissonance, an individual acts to justify his or her behavior after the fact and engages in self-persuasion.

Hundreds of experiments and field studies have shown the power of cognitive dissonance to change attitudes and behavior (Cooper, 2007). Recently, however, researchers have begun to question whether dissonance effects generalize to other cultures. Consider again the way the concept of *self* changes from culture to culture. As we noted earlier, North Americans typically view themselves as *independent,* distinct from others in the environment; members of Asian cultures typically view themselves as *interdependent,* fundamentally interconnected with others. Does the cultural concept of the self affect the experience of cognitive dissonance?

Groups of Canadian and Japanese participants examined a list of entrées for a Chinese restaurant (Hoshino-Browne et al., 2005). Out of list of 25 dishes, they chose the 10 that they most liked (in one condition) or that they thought a friend would most like (in a second condition). Next, they

---

cognitive dissonance The theory that the tension-producing effects of incongruous cognitions motivate individuals to reduce such tension.

rank-ordered those 10 dishes from most to least desirable—again, with respect either to their own or a to friend's preferences. The experimenters then asked the participants to choose between two coupons for free food. The coupons named the participants' fifth- and sixth-ranked choices (for them or their friend). Finally, participants were asked to go through and rate their top 10 choices once again. How might those ratings change from the first to the second time? According to dissonance theory, when you make a tough choice—like the one between your fifth- and sixth-ranked alternatives—you should adjust your attitudes to feel better about the outcome of the choice: "If I chose kung pao chicken [originally no. 5], it really must be a better choice than mu shu pork [originally no. 6]." However, cross-cultural research on the self suggests that Canadian participants should experience more dissonance with respect to their own choices (because of their independent senses of self), whereas Japanese participants should experience more dissonance with respect to their choices for their friends (because of their interdependent senses of self). The data confirmed those expectations: Canadian participants' attitudes changed considerably more for self-judgments; Japanese participants' attitudes changed considerably more for friend judgments.

This research suggests that people experience cognitive dissonance—they seek to maintain consistency within their self-concept—in ways that are specific to their particular senses of self. If you are ever in circumstances in which you must make decisions jointly with members of other cultures, you will want to reflect on the culture's impact on the way you all think and act after the decision has been made.

Self-Perception Theory Dissonance theory describes one way in which people, at least in Western cultures, allow their behaviors ("I chose that CD") to have an impact on their attitudes ("I must like it much better than my other option"). *Self-perception theory,* developed by Daryl Bem (1972), identifies other circumstances in which behaviors inform attitudes. According to **self-perception theory,** you infer what your internal states (beliefs, attitudes, motives, and feelings) are or should be by perceiving how you are acting now and recalling how you have acted in the past in a given situation. You use that self-knowledge to reason backward to the most likely causes or determinants of your behavior. For example, the self-perceiver responds to the question, "Do you like psychology?" by saying, "Sure, I'm taking the basic course and it's not required, I do all the readings, I pay attention during lectures, and I'm getting a good grade in the course." In other words, you answer a question about personal preferences by a behavioral description of relevant actions and situational factors—rather than undertaking an intense search of thoughts and feelings.

One flaw in the process of gaining self-knowledge through self-perception is that people can be insensitive about the extent to which their behavior is influenced by situational forces. You can see this if we return a final time to the College Bowl experiment. Recall that the participants who labored unsuccessfully as contestants rated their own general knowledge relatively low. Imagine what it must have been like to be in their position. Over and over you would hear yourself saying, "I don't know the answer to that question." Can you see how

observation of this behavior—the process of self-perception—could give rise to a negative self-evaluation?

Let's return to the attitudes you might express toward yourself if you eat a slice of cake at your boss's birthday party. According to dissonance theory, you need to resolve the inconsistency between your vow ("I won't consume any extra calories") and your behavior (eating a piece of cake). There are many things you can do to avoid feeling bad: Perhaps you'd reason, "I can't afford to have my boss be angry at me by declining a piece of cake." Similarly, according to self-perception theory, you look at your behavior to calculate your attitude. If you think, "Because I ate cake, my boss's birthday must have been very important," you'll also escape any negative impact on your self-esteem. Self-persuasion can sometimes be useful!

COMPLIANCE

In this section so far, we have discussed what attitudes are and how they might be changed. It should be clear to you, however, that most often what people want you to do is change your *behavior:* People wish to bring about **compliance**—a change in behavior consistent with their direct requests. When advertisers spend a lot of money for TV commercials, they don't want you just to feel good about their products—they want you to march into a store and buy them. Similarly, doctors want you to follow their medical advice. Social psychologists have extensively studied the way in which individuals bring about compliance with their requests (Cialdini, 2009; Cialdini & Goldstein, 2004). We will describe some of those techniques and note how wily salespeople often use them to get you to do things you might not otherwise have done.

Reciprocity One of the rules that dominates human experience is that when someone does something for you, you should do something for that person as well—this is called the **reciprocity norm.** Laboratory research has shown that even very small favors can lead participants to do much larger favors in return (Regan, 1971). Salespeople use reciprocity against you by appearing to do you a favor: "I'll tell you what, I'll take $5 off the price" or "Here's a free sample just for agreeing to talk to me today." This strategy puts you in a position of psychological distress if you don't return the favor and buy the product.

Another compliance technique that arises from the reciprocity norm has often been called the *door-in-the-face technique:* When people say "no" to a large request, they will often say "yes" to a more moderate request.

In one experiment, students were asked to spend two hours every week for two years as counselors for juvenile delinquents. They all said "no." Next, they were asked if they would serve as chaperones for some of the delinquents on a

---

self-perception theory The idea that people observe themselves to figure out the reasons they act as they do; people infer what their internal states are by perceiving how they are acting in a given situation.

compliance A change in behavior consistent with a communication source's direct requests.

reciprocity norm Expectation that favors will be returned—if someone does something for another person, that person should do something in return.

trip to the zoo. When they had previously said "no" to the large request, 50 percent of the students agreed to this smaller request. When a different group of students was approached, who had never been asked the large request, only 17 percent of them agreed to serve as chaperones (Cialdini et al., 1975).

How does this technique invoke the reciprocity norm? When people making requests go from the large to the moderate request, they have done something for you: Now you must do something for them—or risk violating the norm. You agree to the smaller request!

Commitment The door-in-the-face technique moves you from a large to a moderate request. Salespeople also know that if they can get you to *commit* yourself to some small concession, they can probably also get you to commit to something larger. In experiments, people who agreed to small requests (for example, signing petitions) were more likely subsequently to agree to a bigger request (for example, putting large signs on their lawn) (Freedman & Fraser, 1966). This is often called the *foot-in-the-door technique:* Once people get a foot in the door, they can use your sense of commitment to increase your later compliance.

This strategy works because your original behavior makes you think about yourself in a particular way. You want your subsequent behavior to be consistent with that self-image: You become committed to your own sense of what type of person you are. For that reason, foot-in-the-door works better when people make dispositional attributions about their compliance with the original request; it works less well when people make situational attributions about their initial behavior. When, for example, participants were paid $1 to add their comments to a petition, they were less likely to agree to a larger request than were other participants who were just made to feel like good people (Burger & Caldwell, 2003). Salespeople seem to understand that the key to using this technique is to focus you on the sort of person you are. They often use foot-in-the-door against you by getting you to make a decision and then subtly changing the deal: "I know this is the car you want to buy, but my manager will only let me give you a $200 discount"; "I know you're the sort of person who buys quality goods, so I know you won't mind paying a little extra." This strategy makes you feel inconsistent or foolish if you don't go through with the purchase.

In explaining these compliance techniques, we have provided a couple of examples of things you might *want* to do: You might want to volunteer your time or sign petitions for good causes. However, you can see that much of the time people use these techniques to get you to do things you probably *wouldn't* want to do. How can you defend yourself against wily salespeople and their kin? Try to catch them using these strategies—and resist their efforts. Your knowledge of social psychology can make you an all-around wiser consumer.

In this section we have described attitudes and behaviors and the relationships between them. However, we have not yet

What can you do if you want to increase the probability that your neighbors will recycle?

touched on circumstances in which attitudes in the form of *prejudice* may lead to destructive behaviors. We turn now to the topic of prejudice and document both how it comes about and procedures that may be effective to reduce or eliminate it.

STOP AND REVIEW

❶ What three components define attitudes?
❷ What cognitive process discriminates the central and peripheral routes to persuasion?
❸ Why does culture have an impact on processes of cognitive dissonance?
❹ Why does the door-in-the-face technique engage the reciprocity norm?

CRITICAL THINKING Recall the study in which experimental participants filled out a questionnaire about their attitudes toward blood donation. Why was it important that people were randomly assigned to the experimental and control groups?

Visit MyPsychLab.com for more review and practice on the following topic:

✴ **Simulate:** Cognitive Dissonance

Prejudice

Of all human weaknesses, none is more destructive to the dignity of the individual and the social bonds of humanity than prejudice. Prejudice is the prime example of social reality gone awry—a situation created in the minds of people that can demean and destroy the lives of others. **Prejudice** is a learned attitude toward a target object, involving negative feelings (dislike or fear), negative beliefs (stereotypes) that justify the attitude, and a behavioral intention to avoid, control, dominate, or eliminate those in the target group. Nazi leaders, for example, passed laws to enforce their prejudiced beliefs that Jews were subhuman and trying to

---

prejudice A learned attitude toward a target object, involving negative affect (dislike or fear), negative beliefs (stereotypes) that justify the attitude, and a behavioral intention to avoid, control, dominate, or eliminate the target object.

bring about the downfall of Aryan culture. A false belief qualifies as prejudice when it resists change even in the face of appropriate evidence of its falseness. People display prejudice, for example, when they assert that African Americans are all lazy despite their hardworking African American colleagues. Prejudiced attitudes serve as biasing filters that influence the way individuals are perceived and treated once they are categorized as members of a target group.

Social psychology has always put the study of prejudice high on its agenda in an effort to understand its complexity and persistence and to develop strategies to change prejudiced attitudes and discriminatory behavior (Allport, 1954; Nelson, 2006). In fact, the Supreme Court's 1954 decision to outlaw segregated public education was, in part, based on research, presented in federal court by social psychologist **Kenneth Clark,** that showed the negative impact on Black children of their separate and unequal education (Clark & Clark, 1947). In this section, we will describe the progress social psychologists have made in their efforts to understand the origins and effects of prejudice, as well as their efforts to help reverse its effects.

ORIGINS OF PREJUDICE

One of the sad truths from the study of prejudice is that it is easy to get people to show negative attitudes toward people who do not belong to the same "group." **Social categorization** is the process by which people organize their social environment by categorizing themselves and others into groups. The simplest and most pervasive form of categorizing consists of an individual determining whether people are like him or her. This categorization develops from a "me versus not me" orientation to an "us versus them" orientation: People divide the world into **in-groups**—the groups with which they identify as members—and **out-groups**—the groups with which they do not identify.

The most minimal of distinctive cues is sufficient to give people strong feelings of in-groups and out-groups. **Henry Tajfel** and his colleagues (Tajfel et al., 1971) invented a paradigm that demonstrated the impact of what they called *minimal groups.* In one study, students provided estimates of the number of dots in a series of patterns projected on a movie screen. The students were told that, based on their performance, they were "dot overestimators" or "dot underestimators." In reality, the researchers randomly assigned the students to those two groups. Next, each student had the opportunity to allocate monetary rewards to the members of the two groups. The students consistently gave greater rewards to the people who they believed shared their dot estimating tendencies.

Studies of this type illustrate how very easy it is to generate an **in-group bias:** With only a minimal cue to group identity, people begin to favor the members of their own group over the members of other groups (Nelson, 2006). Many experiments have examined the consequences of in-group versus out-group status (Brewer, 2007; Hewstone et al., 2002). This research points to the conclusion that, for the most part, people show favoritism toward those people who are members of their own group rather than bias against members of the other group. For example, people typically rate members of their in-group more highly (on pleasantness, diligence, and so on) than they do members of the out-group. However, that's because they have positive feelings toward the in-group and neutral feelings toward the out-group. Thus, one can have an in-group bias without also having the negative feelings that constitute prejudice.

Unfortunately, in some circumstances people's feelings about out-groups are guided by learned prejudices. In those cases, in-group bias may become more purposeful. Prejudice easily leads to **racism**—discrimination against people based on their skin color or ethnic heritage—and **sexism**—discrimination against people based on their sex. In contemporary times, people are often reluctant to admit to having racist or sexist attitudes. Instead people may express what have been called *modern racism* and *modern sexism.* Measures of modern racism, for example, include statements such as "Blacks are demanding too much from the rest of society" and "Over the past few years, Blacks have gotten more economically than they deserve" (Henry & Sears, 2002). The implicit attitude measures we introduced earlier also measure less open forms of prejudice (Greenwald et al., 2002). These tests identify people whose explicit attitudes are not racist, but whose automatic responses suggest that they hold negative attitudes toward an out-group. Similarly, these tests identify people who accept claims such as "Blacks are demanding too much," but who do not hold negative implicit attitudes toward other races (Son Hing et al., 2008). To have a complete sense of how individuals will respond to members of other groups, we need to measure both explicit and implicit attitudes.

We have seen so far that people's categorization of the world into "us" and "them" can swiftly lead to prejudice. Let's look at the way in which prejudice functions through applications of stereotypes.

EFFECTS OF STEREOTYPES

We can use the power of social categorization to explain the origins of many types of prejudice. To explain how prejudice affects day-to-day interactions, we must explore the memory structures that provide important support for prejudice, stereotypes. **Stereotypes** are generalizations about a group of people in which the same characteristics are assigned to all members of a group. You are no doubt familiar with a wide range of stereotypes. What beliefs do you have about men and women? Jews, Muslims, and Christians? Asians, African Americans, Native Americans, Hispanics, and Whites? How do those beliefs affect your day-to-day interactions with members of those groups? Do you avoid members of some of these groups based on your beliefs?

---

social categorization The process by which people organize the social environment by categorizing themselves and others into groups.

in-group A group with which people identify as members.

out-group A group with which people do not identify.

in-group bias People's tendency to favor members of their own group over members of other groups.

racism Discrimination against people based on their skin color or ethnic heritage.

sexism Discrimination against people because of their sex.

stereotype Generalization about a group of people in which the same characteristics are assigned to all members of a group.

How does prejudice arise, and why is it so difficult to eradicate?

Because stereotypes so powerfully encode *expectations,* they frequently contribute to the types of situations we described earlier in this chapter, in which people construct their own social reality. Consider the potential role stereotypes play to generate judgments about what "exists" in the environment. People are prone to fill in "missing data" with information from their stereotypes: "I'm not going to get in a car with Hiroshi— all Asians are terrible drivers." Those same powerful expectations may cause people to engage in a process called *behavioral confirmation:* Their own actions toward an out-group individual creates a context in which the individual will produce behaviors consistent with the stereotype (Klein & Snyder, 2003). If, for example, someone were noticeably anxious when driving with an Asian friend, that friend might drive less well as a consequence. In addition, to maintain consistency, people are likely to discount information that is inconsistent with their stereotyped beliefs.

At the outset of a study, 210 students indicated the extent to which they agreed with the statement "Homosexuality is a legitimate and acceptable sexual orientation" (Boysen & Vogel, 2007). Next, the students read 1½ pages from an introductory psychology textbook that discussed biological evidence for the origins of homosexuality. After they read the text, participants responded to statements such as "How persuasive was the reading on homosexuality in showing that homosexuality is a legitimate and acceptable sexual orientation?" Participants' responses paralleled their prior attitudes. For example, those participants with negative initial attitudes toward homosexuality did not find the text persuasive with respect to the legitimacy of homosexuality.

Participants also indicated whether the text had changed their attitudes. Although they had read the very same words, participants' responses were now more polarized: Participants with negative initial attitudes were likely to report that their attitudes were now even more negative; participants with positive initial attitudes were likely to report that their attitudes were now even more positive.

This experiment suggests why information alone can typically not reduce prejudice: People tend to devalue information that is inconsistent with their prior stereotype. (We will see in the next section more successful methods for overcoming prejudice.)

Let us remind you about another effect of stereotypes that we introduced in the context of intelligence testing. Recall that in Chapter 9, we discussed racial differences among IQ scores. In that section, we reviewed evidence that members of stereotyped groups experience *stereotype threat* when they are placed in situations to which negative aspects of stereotypes are relevant. Stereotype threat produces a context in which people are not able to make efficient use of their mental resources (Schmader et al., 2008). Although researchers first explored this concept in circumstances of intellectual performance, they have now demonstrated that there is potential for negative effects wherever stereotypes apply. For example, one study examined how a group of women who rated themselves as above average athletes performed on a golf task (Stone & McWhinnie, 2008). Some of the women were told only that the task was a test of "natural ability." Others were told, in addition, that the task had previously yielded differences between men and women. The instructions continued, "So even though there may be gender differences on this test, we ask that you give 100 percent effort on the task so we can accurately measure your natural skills" (p. 448). Despite this request for 100 percent effort, the women who were reminded about gender differences needed more strokes to complete the eight holes of the golf course. This result illustrates how stereotype threat can impair people's performance across several life domains.

Even if you do not believe yourself to be a prejudiced person, you still are likely aware of the stereotypes that exist in contemporary society. Knowledge of these stereotypes might prompt you to use them in some ways, below the level of conscious awareness (Amodio & Devine, 2006; Trawalter et al., 2008). Even people whose explicit beliefs are not prejudiced may produce automatic acts of prejudice as a function of the messages they have unknowingly internalized from many sources in their current and earlier environments. Consider your best friends: Do they belong to the same ethnic group as you do? If so, why might this be the case?

We have come to the rather troubling conclusion that prejudice is easy to create and difficult to remove. Even so, from the earliest days of social psychology, researchers have attempted to reverse the march of prejudice. Let's now sample some of those efforts.

REVERSING PREJUDICE

One of the classic studies in social psychology was also the first demonstration that arbitrary "us" versus "them" divisions could lead to great hostility. In the summer of 1954, **Muzafer Sherif** and his colleagues (1961/1988) brought two groups of boys to a summer camp at Robbers Cave State Park in Oklahoma. The

In the intergroup competition phase of the Robbers Cave experiment, the "Eagles" and "Rattlers" pulled apart—but in the end, they pulled together. What general conclusions about contact and prejudice can be drawn from this study?

two groups were dubbed the "Eagles" and the "Rattlers." Each group forged its own camp bonds—for example, the boys hiked, swam, and prepared meals together—in ignorance of the other group for about a week. The groups' introduction to each other consisted of a series of competitive activities like baseball, football, and a tug-of-war. From this beginning, the rivalry between the groups grew violent. Group flags were burned, cabins were ransacked, and a near-riotlike food fight broke out. What could be done to reduce this animosity?

The experimenters tried a propaganda approach, by complimenting each group to the other. That did not work. The experimenters tried bringing the groups together in noncompetitive circumstances. That did not work either. Hostility seethed even when the groups were just watching a movie in the same place. Finally, the experimenters hit on a solution. What they did was to introduce problems that could be solved only through *cooperative action* on *shared goals*. For example, the experimenters arranged for the camp truck to break down. Both groups of boys were needed to pull it back up a steep hill. In the face of mutual dependence, hostility faded away. In fact, the boys started to make "best friends" across group boundaries.

The Robbers Cave experiment disproved the idea that simple contact between hostile groups alone will reduce prejudice (Allport, 1954). The boys did not like each other any better just by being in each others' company. Instead, the experiment provided evidence for the **contact hypothesis**—a program combating prejudice must foster personal interaction (Pettigrew, 2008).

Researchers have carried out studies around the world to determine what types of contact between people lead to reduced prejudice. A review of 515 studies on the contact hypothesis—studies carried out all over the world—strongly supported the conclusion that contact with out-group mem-

bers lowers prejudice (Pettigrew & Tropp, 2006). Let's consider a concrete example of the effects of contact.

Although Germany was reunited in October 1990, the inhabitants of the former East and West Germany still show important differences: When social scientists assess the level of prejudice and violence toward foreigners, the data consistently show that East Germans are much more hostile. Researchers tested the hypothesis that an important force that contributes to the ongoing hostility arises from East Germany's historic isolation (Wagner et al., 2003): Fewer foreigners reside in East Germany, providing fewer opportunities for the type of contact that reduces prejudice. A study with 2,893 East and West German participants confirmed this hypothesis. Each participant provided information about his or her level of prejudice by responding to statements such as "Foreigners living in Germany are a problem for the social system." Each participant also indicated his or her level of personal contact by responding to questions such as "Are there any foreigners among your friends?" Those individuals who had more foreign friends reported, on average, lower levels of prejudice. Because the inhabitants of East Germany had fewer opportunities to have foreign friends, their prejudice levels remained relatively high.

This study shows the great importance of friendship for prejudice reduction. In fact, people's prejudice is reduced even when the contact is *indirect*—when it's just the case that they have in-group friends who have out-group friends (Pettigrew et al., 2007; Wright

---

contact hypothesis The prediction that contact between groups will reduce prejudice only if the contact includes features such as cooperation toward shared goals.

et al., 1997). Why are both direct and indirect friendships so effective? Friendships allow people to learn to take the perspective of out-group members and empathize with them. Friendships also reduce the anxiety associated with out-group contacts and make the out-group seem less threatening (Pettigrew, 2008).

Social psychology has no great solution to end prejudice all at once. It does, however, provide a set of ideas to eliminate prejudice's worst effects slowly but surely, in each small locality. It is worth taking a moment to contemplate the prejudices you have enforced or endured—to see how you might begin to make adjustments in your own small locality.

We have just considered circumstances in which psychological forces drive individuals apart. We now examine the opposite situations in which people are drawn together in relationships of liking and loving.

STOP AND REVIEW

❶ How does in-group bias affect the distribution of resources?

❷ How does the process of behavioral confirmation support stereotypes?

❸ What has research demonstrated about the impact of contact between members of different groups?

CRITICAL THINKING Recall the study that looked at people's attitudes on homosexuality. Why might the researchers have used an excerpt from an introductory psychology textbook?

Visit MyPsychLab.com for more review and practice on the following topics:

✳ **Simulate:** Prejudice

◉ **Watch:** Prejudice

Social Relationships

How do you choose the people with whom you share your life? Why do you seek the company of your friends? Why are there some people for whom your feelings move beyond friendship to feelings of romantic love? Social psychologists have developed a variety of answers to these questions of *interpersonal attraction*. (But don't worry, no one yet has taken all the mystery out of love!)

LIKING

Have you ever stopped to examine how and why you acquired each of your friends? The first part of this answer is straightforward: People tend to become attracted to others with whom they are in close *proximity*—you see and meet them because they live or work near you. This factor probably requires little explanation, but it might be worth noting that there is a general tendency for people to like objects and people just by virtue of *mere exposure:* As we explained in Chapter 12, the more you are exposed to something or someone, the more you like it (Zajonc, 1968). This mere exposure effect means that, on the whole, you will come to like more and more the people who are nearby. Many people now maintain relationships over networks of computers. Although a friend may be geographically quite distant, daily messages appearing on a computer screen can make the person seem psychologically very close. Let's look now at other factors that can lead to attraction and liking.

Physical Attractiveness For better or worse, *physical attractiveness* often plays a role in the kindling of friendship. There is a strong stereotype in Western culture that physically attractive people are also good in other ways. A review of a large number of studies documented the impact of physical attractiveness on a whole range of judgments (Langlois et al., 2000). For example, people rate both children and adults as more socially competent when they are attractive. In addition, attractive children receive higher competence ratings in school, and attractive adults receive higher competence ratings in their occupations. In light of the social basis of the stereotype, it might not surprise you that physical attractiveness plays a role in liking.

> In one study, researchers randomly assigned incoming University of Minnesota freshmen to couples as blind dates for a large dance. The researchers collected a variety of information about each student along dimensions of intelligence and personality. On the night of the dance and in later follow-ups, the students were asked to evaluate their dates and indicate how likely they were to see the individual again. The results were clear, and very similar for both men and women. Attractiveness mattered more than high IQs, good social skills, or good personalities. Only those matched by chance with attractive blind dates wanted to pursue the relationship further (Walster et al., 1966).

Physical attractiveness may not have as strong a role in other cultures. For example, students at universities in Ghana and the United States viewed the same photographs of attractive and unattractive people (Anderson et al., 2008). They provided ratings of each photograph for several personality traits (such as trustworthy, stable, sensitive, and strong). As you can see in **Figure 16.6,** participants from Ghana made nearly the same attributions to attractive and unattractive photographs. Participants from the United States made less positive attributions to the unattractive photographs. This finding echoes other results we've described in which people with different cultural construals of the self—independent for the United States and interdependent for Ghana—provide different interpersonal judgments.

Similarity A famous adage on *similarity* suggests that "birds of a feather flock together." Is this correct? Research evidence suggests that, under many circumstances, the answer is yes. Similarity on dimensions such as beliefs, attitudes, and values fosters friendship. Why might that be so? People who are similar to you can provide a sense of personal validation because a similar person makes you feel that the attitudes, for example, you hold dear are, in fact, the right ones (Byrne & Clore, 1970). Furthermore, dissimilarity often leads to strong repulsion (Chen & Kenrick, 2002). When you discover that someone holds opinions that are different from yours, you may evoke from memory past

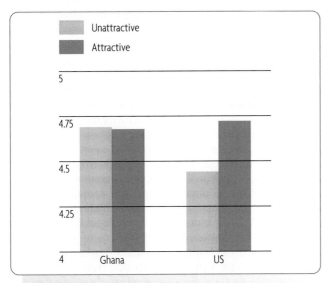

FIGURE 16.6 Cross-Cultural Trait Judgments for Attractive and Unattractive Individuals

Participants in Ghana and the United States made trait judgments based on photographs of attractive and unattractive individuals. Participants from Ghana made nearly the same attributions to attractive and unattractive photographs. U.S. participants made less positive attributions to the unattractive photographs.

From Anderson, S. L., Adams, G., & Plaut, V. C., *Journal of Personality and Social Psychology*, 95, 2008. Copyright © 2008 American Psychological Association. Reprinted with permission.

instances of interpersonal friction. That will motivate you to stay away—and if you stay away from dissimilar people, only the similar ones will be left in your pool of friends.

Similarity appears to play a role in allowing friendships to endure over time. Consider a study that began in 1983, when researchers assessed similarity between 45 pairs of friends (Ledbetter et al., 2007). In 2002, 58 of the 90 original participants provided information about the state of their friendships after the passage of 19 years. The participants indicated, for example, how much contact they still had with each other. The results suggested that those pairs that had been more similar in 1983 were also more likely to remain in contact in 2002. It's also important to note that, just as similarity may lead to attraction, attraction can lead to perceptions of similarity: People tend to believe that the people they like are more similar than they really are. In one study, students rated themselves and cross-sex friends on the same set of personality traits (Morry, 2007). The students rated their friends as being more similar to them than their friends' self-reports indicated they actually were.

Reciprocity Finally, you tend to like people whom you believe like you. Do you recall our discussion of salespeople's use of *reciprocity*? The rule that you should give back what you receive applies to friendship as well. People give back "liking" to people whom they believe have given "liking" to them (Backman & Secord, 1959; Kenny & La Voie, 1982). Furthermore, because of the way your beliefs can affect your behaviors, believing that

someone likes or dislikes you can help bring that relationship about (Curtis & Miller, 1986). Can you predict how you would act toward someone you believe likes you? Toward someone you believe dislikes you? Suppose you act with hostility toward someone you think doesn't like you. Do you see how your belief could become a self-fulfilling prophecy? When we look out at the social world, our judgments about which acquaintances are united by a "liking" relationship tend to be heavily guided by reciprocity. That is, if we know that Person A particularly likes Person B, we infer that Person B has the same feelings toward Person A (Kenny et al., 1996).

The evidence we have reviewed suggests that most of your friends will be people you encounter frequently, and people with whom you share the bonds of similarity and reciprocity. But what have researchers found about more intense relationships people call "loving"?

LOVING

Many of the same forces that lead to liking also get people started on the road to love—in most cases, you will first like the people you end up loving. (However, some people report loving certain relatives that they don't particularly like as individuals.) What special factors have social psychologists learned about loving relationships?

The Experience of Love What does it mean to experience *love*? Take a moment to think how you would define this important concept. Do you think your definition would agree with your friends' definitions? Researchers have tried to answer this question in a variety of ways, and some consistency has emerged (Reis & Aron, 2008). People's conceptualizations of love cluster into three dimensions (Aron & Westbay, 1996):

- *Passion*—sexual passion and desire
- *Intimacy*—honesty and understanding
- *Commitment*—devotion and sacrifice

Would you characterize all your loving relationships as including all three dimensions? You're probably thinking, "not *all* of them." In fact, it is important to make a distinction between "loving" someone and being "in love" with someone (Meyers & Berscheid, 1997). Most people report themselves to "love" a larger category of people than the group with whom they are "in love"—who among us hasn't been heartbroken to hear the words, "I love you, but I'm not *in* love with you"? Being "in love" implies something more intense and special—this is the type of experience that includes sexual passion.

Let us make one more distinction. Many loving relationships start out with a period of great intensity and absorption, which is called *passionate* love. Over time, there is a tendency for relationships to migrate toward a state of lesser intensity but greater intimacy, called *companionate love* (Berscheid & Walster, 1978). When you find yourself in a loving relationship, you may do well to anticipate that transition—so that you don't misinterpret a natural change as a process of falling "out of love." In fact, people who report higher levels of companionate love also generally experience greater satisfaction with their lives (Kim & Hatfield, 2004). Even so, the decline of passionate love may not be as dramatic as the stereotype of

Companionate feelings for someone you were once passionate about do not signal "falling out of love": On the contrary, they are a natural outgrowth of romance and a vital ingredient to most long-term partnerships.

long-committed couples suggests. Researchers find a reasonable level of passionate love as much as 30 years into a relationship (Aron & Aron, 1994). When you enter a loving relationship, you can have high hopes that the passion will endure in some form, even as the relationship grows to encompass other needs.

Note that experiences of romantic relationships are also influenced by cultural expectations (Wang & Mallinckrodt, 2006). At various moments in this chapter, we've alluded to the cultural dimension of independence versus interdependence: Cultures with independent construals of self value the person over the collective; interdependent cultures put greater value on shared cultural goals rather than on individual ones. How does this apply to your love life? If you choose a life partner based on your own feelings of love, you are showing preference for your personal goals; if you choose a partner with an eye to how that individual will mesh with your family's structure and concerns, you are being more attuned to collective goals. Cross-cultural research has led to the very strong generalization that members of independent cultures put much greater emphasis on love (Dion & Dion, 1996). Consider the question, "If a man (woman) had all the other qualities you desired, would you marry this person if you were not in love with him (her)?" Only 3.5 percent of a sample of male and female undergraduates in the United States answered yes; 49 percent of a comparable group of students in India answered yes (Levine et al., 1995). Members of independent cultures are also more *demanding* of their potential partners. Because people in these cultures have stronger ideas about personal fulfillment within relationships, they also expect more from marriage partners (Hatfield & Sprecher, 1995).

What Factors Allow Relationships to Last? It seems likely that everyone reading this text—and certainly everyone *writing* this text—has been in a relationship that didn't last. What happened? Or, to put the question in a more positive light, what can researchers say about the types of situations, and people in those situations, that are more likely to lead to long-term loving relationships?

One theory conceptualizes people in close relationships as having a feeling that the "other" is included in their "self" (Aron et al., 2004). Consider the series of diagrams given in **Figure 16.7.** Each of the diagrams represents a way you could conceptualize a close relationship. If you are in a romantic relationship, can you say which of the diagrams seems to capture most effectively the extent of interdependence between you and your partner? Research has shown that people who perceive the most overlap between self and other—those people who come to view the other as included within the self—are most likely to remain

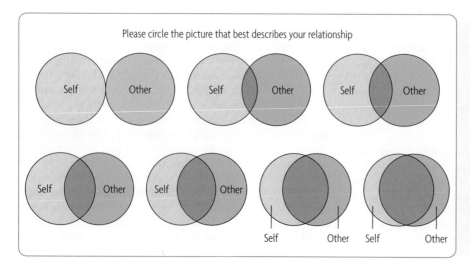

Please circle the picture that best describes your relationship

FIGURE 16.7   The Inclusion of Other in the Self (IOS) Scale

If you are in a romantic relationship, which diagram best captures the interdependence of you and your partner? Research with the IOS scale suggests that people who most perceive the other as included with the self are most likely to stay committed to their relationships.

From Aron, A., Aron, E. N., Smollan, D., IOS Scale, *Journal of Personality and Social Psychology.* Vol 63(4), Oct 1992, 596-612. Copyright © 1992 by the American Psychological Association. Reproduced with committed to their relationships over time (Aron et al., 1992; Aron & Fraley, 1999).

Researchers have also been interested in understanding individual differences in people's ability to sustain loving relationships over an extended period of time. In recent years, attention has often focused on *adult attachment style* (Fraley et al., 2005; Fraley & Shaver, 2000). Recall from Chapter 10 the importance of the quality of a child's attachment to his or her parents for smooth social development. Researchers began to wonder how much impact that early attachment might have later in life, as the children grew up to have committed relationships and children of their own.

What are the types of attachment styles? **Table 16.2** provides three statements about close relationships (Hazan & Shaver, 1987; Shaver & Hazan, 1994). Please take a moment to note which statement fits you best. When asked which of these statements best describes them, the majority of people (55 percent) choose the first statement; this is a *secure* attachment style. Sizable minorities select the second statement (25 percent, an *avoidant* style) and the third (20 percent, an *anxious-ambivalent* style). Attachment style has proven to be an accurate predictor of relationship quality (Mikulincer et al., 2002; Tidwell et al., 1996). Compared with individuals who chose the other two styles, securely attached individuals had the most enduring romantic relationships as adults. Attachment style also predicts the ways in which individuals experience jealousy in relationships (Sharpsteen & Kirkpatrick, 1997). For example, people with an anxious style tend to experience jealousy more frequently and more intensely than do people with a secure attachment style.

In this section, we have considered some of the factors that influence whether people enter into relationships with each other. We next examine the types of behaviors that emerge within the context of those relationships. We discuss the variety of forces that lead people to harm and help each other.

TABLE 16.2 Styles of Adult Attachment for Close Ralationships

Statement 1:
I find it relatively easy to get close to others and am comfortable depending on them. I don't often worry about being abandoned or about someone getting too close to me.

Statement 2:
I am somewhat uncomfortable being close to others; I find it difficult to trust them completely, difficult to allow myself to depend on them. I am nervous when anyone gets too close; and, often, love partners want me to be more intimate than I feel comfortable being.

Statement 3:
I find that others are reluctant to get as close as I would like. I often worry that my partner doesn't really love me or won't want to stay with me. I want to get very close to my partner, and this sometime scares people away.

STOP AND REVIEW

❶ What effect does similarity have on liking?
❷ What three dimensions define love?
❸ Which adult attachment style is generally associated with the highest-quality relationships?

CRITICAL THINKING Recall the study that examined the impact of physical attractiveness on people's liking for randomly assigned dates. Why was it important to assess the impact of physical attractiveness both on the night of the date and in later follow-ups?

Visit MyPsychLab.com for more review and practice on the following topic:

👁 **Watch:** Men, Women, and Attraction: Michael Bailey

Aggression, Altruism, and Prosocial Behavior

If you spend a few minutes reviewing the daily news, you'll almost certainly get reports on the extremes of human behavior: You'll learn both about situations in which people have done each other harm and those in which people have done each other good. In this section, we consider the factors that yield both types of behavior. We begin with acts of **aggression:** People's behaviors that cause psychological or physical harm to other individuals. Psychologists try to understand the causes of aggression with the goal of using that knowledge to help reduce societal levels of aggression. We then turn our attention to the positive extreme: The **prosocial behaviors** that people carry out with the goal of helping other people. We focus, in addition, on **altruism**—the prosocial behaviors people carry out without considering their own safety or interests. We discuss some personal and situational factors that change the likelihood of these helping behaviors.

INDIVIDUAL DIFFERENCES IN AGGRESSION

One major fact of research on aggression is that some people are consistently more aggressive than others. Why might that be so? One type of research has examined genetic contributions to individual differences in rates of aggression. Researchers have used many of the methods we've illustrated in earlier chapters. They have, for example, compared the similarity of identical (monozygotic, MZ) and fraternal (dizygotic, DZ) twins with

aggression Behaviors that cause psychological or physical harm to another individual.

prosocial behavior Behavior that is carried out with the goal of helping other people.

altruism Prosocial behaviors a person carries out without considering his or her own safety or interests.

Psychology in Your Life

IN WHAT WAYS ARE YOU LIKE A CHAMELEON?

Here's something you may have noticed: When you interact with other people, you are quite likely to find yourself mimicking them in certain ways. You may, for example, unconsciously match your friends' speech patterns and accents. Social psychologists **Tanya Chartrand** and **John Bargh** (1999) labeled this type of mimicry the *chameleon effect*. Chameleons automatically change their color to blend in with their environment. Chartrand and Bargh suggested that humans also automatically adjust their behavior to blend with the people around them.

In their original demonstration of the chameleon effect, Chartrand and Bargh had pairs of people interact to describe photographs. However, one member of each pair was actually a confederate of the researchers. Chartrand and Bargh instructed the confederates to perform one of two motor gestures while describing the photographs: Either they rubbed their faces or they shook one foot. If people act like chameleons, we would expect that the experimental participants would mimic those motor gestures. That's exactly what happened. Participants were considerably more likely to rub their faces or shake their feet when the confederates performed those actions.

Chartrand and Bargh speculated that this form of mimicry functions as a type of "social glue." By producing identical motor gestures, people make themselves more similar to the other individuals around them. Recall from our discussion of social relationships that similarity increases liking. For that reason, Chartrand and Bargh hypothesized that people whose gestures were mimicked by a partner would like that partner better. To test that hypothesis, Chartrand and Bargh conducted a second study in which they instructed their confederates to subtly mimic the actions of the experimental participants. Compared to members of the control group, whose gestures were not mimicked, the mimicked participants consistently reported liking the confederates better. Importantly, only one of the 37 participants was aware of having been mimicked. This strongly suggests that the chameleon effect operates outside of conscious awareness.

Even so, these results might lead you to wonder whether you could do better in some social circumstances by consciously mimicking others' behavior. To address this question, researchers provided explicit instructions to a subset of students who were about to carry out a negotiation: "Successful negotiators recommend that you should mimic the mannerisms of your negotiation partner to get a better deal. For example, when the other person rubs his/her face, you should too. If he/she leans back or leans forward in the chair, you should too. However, they say it is very important that you mimic subtly enough that the other person does not notice what you are doing, other-wise this technique completely back-fires" (Maddux et al., 2008, p. 463). The students who received these instructions consistently scored more points in the negotiation than their peers who were not encouraged to mimic.

Of course, there are circumstances in which people might not want to get people to like them more. Suppose someone is already in a romantic relationship. To keep that relationship safe, that individual might want to distance him- or herself from attractive alternatives. That goal might lead to a diminished chameleon effect. To test that hypothesis, researchers recruited some participants who were in romantic relationships and some who were not (Karremans & Verwijmeren, 2008). All the participants interacted with a confederate who rubbed his or her face regularly during a conversation. In support of the hypothesis, participants who were in romantic relationships mimicked the attractive confederate consistently less often. The participants were not aware of their behavior. The researchers concluded that "the goal to maintain one's current romantic relationship nonconsciously guides an individual's behavior during an interaction with a potentially relationship-threatening alternative" (p. 947).

Now that you know about the chameleon effect, do you think you will be more aware of how mimicry affects your social relationships?

---

respect to aggressive personalities; in other cases, they have estimated the contributions of nature and nurture by examining children raised in adoptive homes.

These studies typically demonstrate a strong genetic component for aggressive behavior (DiLalla, 2002). For example, MZ twins consistently show higher correlations for aggressiveness than do DZ twins (Haberstick et al., 2006). However, research suggests that genetics may play a stronger and weaker role for different types of aggression.

Researchers collected data on 234 6-year-old twins to assess genetic and environmental contributions to individual differences in *physical* and *social* aggression (Brendgen et al., 2005). Physical aggression represents circumstances in which children get into fights or hit, bite, or kick other children. Social aggression represents circumstances in which children spread nasty rumors or try to make others dislike particular classmates. To assess the twins' behaviors for both types of aggression, the researchers obtained ratings from the twins' teachers and their peers. These ratings provided converging evidence that the MZ and DZ twins differed with respect to their similarity levels of aggression. The comparison between MZ and DZ twins suggested that 50 to 60 percent of the variation in physical aggression could be explained by genetic factors. For social aggression, 20 percent of the variation was explained by genetics.

Why might genetics have less influence over social aggression? The researchers speculated that children's inclination to use social aggression might follow from the type of parenting they receive: Parents who use shame or guilt to manipulate their children may provide models for the children's later classroom behavior. Overall, this study supports the conclusion that some individuals have a greater genetic predisposition toward aggression than do others.

Researchers have also focused attention on differences in brain function that may mark a predisposition toward aggressive behavior. As we saw in Chapter 12, several brain structures, such as the amygdala and portions of cortex, play roles in the expression and regulation of emotion. With respect to aggression, it is critical that brain pathways function effectively so that individuals can control the expression of negative emotion. If, for example, people experience inappropriate levels of activation in the amygdala, they may not be able to inhibit the negative emotions that lead to aggressive behaviors (Siever, 2008).

Attention has also focused on the neurotransmitter serotonin. Research suggests that inappropriate levels of serotonin may impair the brain's ability to regulate negative emotions and impulsive behavior (Siever, 2008). For example, one study demonstrated that men with higher life histories of aggression showed decreased response in the serotonin system to a drug (fenfluramine) that typically has a considerable impact on that system (Manuck et al., 2002). Recall from Chapter 14 that researchers have begun to explore consequences of variations in the actual genes that underlie serotonin function. In this study as well, the researchers showed that a particular genetic variation was likely to affect serotonin function in a way that put people at risk for high levels of aggressive behavior.

Personality research on aggression has pointed to the importance of differentiating categories of aggressive behaviors: People with different personality profiles are likely to engage in different types of aggression. One important distinction separates *impulsive aggression* from *instrumental aggression* (Little et al., 2003; Ramírez & Andreu, 2006). **Impulsive aggression** is produced in reaction to situations and is emotion driven: People respond with aggressive acts in the heat of the moment. If you see people get into a fistfight after a car accident, that is impulsive aggression. **Instrumental aggression** is goal directed (the aggression serves as the *instrument* for some goal) and cognition based: People carry out acts of aggression, with premeditated thought, to achieve specific aims. If you see someone knock an elderly woman down to steal her purse, that is instrumental aggression. Research has confirmed that those individuals with high propensities toward one or the other of these types of violence have distinct sets of personality traits (Caprara et al., 1996). For example, individuals who reported a propensity toward impulsive aggression were likely, in general, to be characterized as high on the factor of *emotional responsivity*. That is, they were likely, in general, to report highly emotional responses to a range of situations. By contrast, individuals who

Why do some types of day-to-day experiences make even the calmest people contemplate aggressive acts?

reported a propensity toward instrumental aggression were likely to score high on the factor of *positive evaluation of violence.* These individuals believed that many forms of violence are justified, and they also did not accept moral responsibility for aggressive behaviors. You learn from this analysis that not all types of aggression arise from the same underlying personality factors.

Most people are not at the extremes of either impulsive or instrumental aggression: They do not lose their tempers at the least infraction or purposefully commit acts of violence. Even so, in some situations, even the most mild-mannered individuals will perform aggressive acts. We look now at the types of situations that may often provide the triggering conditions for aggression.

SITUATIONAL INFLUENCES ON AGGRESSION

Take a moment now to think back to the last time you engaged in aggressive behavior. It may not have been physical aggression: You may just have been verbally abusive toward some other individual, with the intent of causing psychological distress. How would you explain why that particular situation gave rise to aggression?

Consider a situation in which other people made it impossible for you complete some important task. Did you reach a breaking point? This general relationship is captured by the **frustration-aggression hypothesis** (Dollard et al., 1939). According to this hypothesis, *frustration* occurs in situations in

---

impulsive aggression Cognition-based and goal-directed aggression carried out with premeditated thought, to achieve specific aims.

instrumental aggression Cognition-based and goal-directed aggression carried out with premeditated thought, to achieve specific aims.

frustration-aggression hypothesis According to this hypothesis, frustration occurs in situations in which people are prevented or blocked from attaining their goals; a rise in frustration then leads to a greater probability of aggression.

which people are prevented or blocked from attaining their goals; a rise in frustration then leads to a greater probability of aggression. The link between frustration and aggression has obtained a high level of empirical support (Berkowitz, 1993, 1998). For example, children who are frustrated in their expectation that they will be allowed to play with highly attractive toys act aggressively toward those toys when they finally have an opportunity to play (Barker et al., 1941). Researchers have used this relationship to explain aggression at both the personal and societal levels.

Do you recognize this news story? A man gets fired from a job and goes back to kill the boss who fired him, as well as several coworkers. Could this count as an instance of frustration (that is, the frustrated goal of earning a living) leading to aggression? To provide a general answer to this question, a team of researchers examined the relationship between San Francisco's unemployment rate and the rate at which people in that city were committed for being "dangerous to others." This analysis allows for predictions across a whole community: What unemployment rate is likely to lead to the highest levels of violence? The researchers found that violence increased as unemployment increased, but only to a certain point. When unemployment got too high, violence began to fall again. Why might that be? The researchers speculated that people's fears that they too might lose their jobs helped inhibit frustration-driven tendencies toward violence (Catalano et al., 1997, 2002).

This study suggests how individual and societal forces interact to produce a net level of violence. We can predict a certain level of aggression based on the frustration each individual experiences in an economy with rising unemployment. However, as people realize that expressions of aggression may imperil their own employment, violence is inhibited. You can probably recognize these forces in your day-to-day experiences: There are many situations in which you might feel sufficiently frustrated to express aggression, but you also understand that an expression of aggression will work against your long-term best interest.

It's not going to surprise you that *direct provocation* will also give rise to aggression. That is, when someone behaves in a way that makes you angry or upset—and you think that behavior was intentional—you are more likely to respond with some form of physical or verbal aggression (Johnson & Rule, 1986). The effects of direct provocation are consistent with the general idea that situations that produce negative affect will lead to aggression. The intentionality of the act matters because you are less likely to interpret an unintentional act in a negative way. Consider a study that focused on fourth grade children (Nelson et al., 2008). The researchers asked the children to read scenarios and make judgments about the actors' intentions. For example, in one scenario the children were meant to imagine that a peer's basketball rolled under their feet and caused them to fall during a race. The children indicated whether they believed the peer's actions were intentional or accidental. The researchers also gathered information about the extent of the children's actual physical aggression in the classroom. The two types of data revealed interesting relationships. For example, the boys who perceived the most hostile intent in scenarios like the basketball example were also the most physically aggressive. These data remind you why it matters how people construct social

reality: When people interpret ambiguous situations as provocations, they are more likely to respond with aggression.

We have been focusing on aspects of particular situations that bring about aggression. In addition, broader social norms also affect the likelihood that people will display aggression (Bond, 2004). Recall the research we discussed in Chapter 6 suggesting that children very readily adapt aggressive behaviors from watching adult models. For example, children who watched adult models punching, hitting, and kicking a large plastic BoBo doll later showed a greater frequency of the same behaviors than did children in control conditions who had not observed the aggressive models (Bandura et al., 1963). We also suggested in Chapter 6 that television in the United States beams an enormous number of aggressive models directly into children's homes—exposure to violence is highly related to adult levels of aggression (Comstock & Scharrer, 1999; Huesmann et al., 2003).

Researchers have developed the *general aggression model* to explain the relationship between exposure to violent media (television, movies, and so on) and aggressive behavior. This model suggests that people acquire a general set of aggression-related knowledge structures through their experiences of media violence: On this view, "each violent media episode is essentially one more trial to learn that the world is a dangerous place, that aggression is an appropriate way to deal with conflict and anger, and that aggression works" (Bushman & Anderson, 2002, p. 1680). Consider a study that examined the short-term impact of violent video games.

Researchers asked 224 college undergraduates to play either violent video games (for example, Mortal Kombat) or nonviolent video games (for example, 3D Pinball) (Bushman & Anderson, 2002). After playing for 20 minutes, the participants were asked to complete what they believed to be an unrelated task. The participants read incomplete stories and indicated what they thought would happen next. For example, in one story, Todd was rear-ended when he braked quickly at a yellow light. Participants wrote answers to the question, "What happens next?" Those students who played the violent video games gave consistently more aggressive outcomes for the stories. For example, participants suggested that Todd would kick out a window or stab or shoot the other driver.

Why should parents worry that children who play violent video games may be prone to more real-world aggression?

This study illustrates that those students who had just played violent video games versus nonviolent video games were ready to provide much more aggressive responses. Other research has contrasted the physiological responses of college students who have recently played violent or nonviolent video games (Carnagey et al., 2007). The students who had played violent games produced weaker responses (such as lower heart rate) to videos of real-world violence such as stabbings, shootings, and prison fights. These data suggest that the students' game play had desensitized them to the violent images. Thus, exposure to these violent games both makes the world seem more violent and numbs people's response to that violence.

Unfortunately, for many children the world does present real dangers. Children may be exposed to aggressive acts in their homes (Evans et al., 2008). In addition, many children in the United States grow up in inner-city communities in which violence is daily and chronic (Berkowitz, 2003; Salzinger et al., 2006). Researchers have only begun to explore the consequences of exposure to violence for children's mental health and their inclination to aggressive behavior (Bingenheimer et al., 2005).

In this section we have described too many reasons why people might engage in aggressive behavior. Fortunately, people are also well prepared to provide help to others. We turn now to the roots of helping behavior.

THE ROOTS OF PROSOCIAL BEHAVIOR

In May 2008, an earthquake measuring 8.0 on the Richter scale struck China's Sichuan province. The media was full of images of the devastation the earthquake caused. However, the media also provided images of people risking their lives to save others. People from China and other parts of the world converged on Sichuan province with the hope of finding and aiding survivors. How can we explain why people engage in prosocial behaviors? Researcher **C. Daniel Batson** (1994) suggests that there are four forces that prompt people to act for the public good:

- *Altruism.* Acting in response to a motive to benefit others, as in the case of the driver who saved another person's life.
- *Egoism.* Performing prosocial behaviors ultimately in one's own self-interest; someone might perform a helping behavior to receive a similar favor in return (for example, compliance with a request) or to receive a reward (for example, money or praise).
- *Collectivism.* Performing prosocial behaviors to benefit a particular group; people might perform helping behaviors to improve circumstances for their families, fraternities or sororities, political parties, and so on.
- *Principlism.* Performing prosocial behaviors to uphold moral principles; someone might act in a prosocial manner because of a religious or civic principle.

You can see how each of these motives might apply in different situations.

The same prosocial behavior can serve more than one motive. For example, many colleges and universities now encourage students to participate in *service learning:* "an educational assignment in which students meet the academic

What prosocial motive explains why people band together to protect the environment?

learning goals of a course through an experience working on behalf of others" (Jay, 2008, p. 255). For example, in one service learning project students in an introductory course on gerontology assisted a county agency to gather information about legal issues relevant to older adults (Anstee et al., 2008). Because participation in this project enhanced students' educational experience, we might count this as an instance of egoism (that is, the student's reward is greater learning). However, their participation also provided benefits to older adults and to the county agency, so we might also count this instance of service learning as collectivism. In fact, educators who support service learning often hope that the values service learning instills will lead students to undertake a lifetime of prosocial behavior (Tomkovick et al., 2008).

Among these motives for prosocial behavior, the existence of altruism has sometimes been controversial. To understand why, you must think back to the discussion of evolutionary forces we presented in earlier chapters. According to the evolutionary perspective, the main goal of life is to reproduce so that one can pass on one's genes. How, in that context, does altruism make sense? Why should you risk your life to aid others? There are two answers to this question, depending on whether the "others" are family members or strangers.

For family members, altruistic behaviors makes some sense because—even if you imperil your own survival—you aid the general survival of your gene pool (Burnstein, 2005). Researchers have examined the extent to which genetic overlap influences people's altruistic behaviors.

Participants in an experiment had the opportunity to earn money for themselves and for relatives with whom they had 50 percent genetic overlap (for example, siblings and parents), 25 percent overlap (for example, grandparents, aunts, and nephews), or 12.5 percent overlap (as with cousins) (Madsen et al., 2007). However, to earn the money, the participants had to remain in a painful physical position: The longer they remained in the position, the more money they made for themselves or for their relatives. The participants returned to the laboratory over several days so that the researchers could complete the test for each relatedness category. Participants did not know how long they had held the painful position until the end of each trial. The results demonstrated a clear impact of genetic overlap. On the whole, the greater the genetic overlap, the longer the participants endured the pain. The researchers demonstrated much the same pattern with university students in London and with two South African Zulu populations.

Because the participants endured pain to provide funds to their relatives, their behavior meets the criteria for altruism. The results strongly suggest that people are more willing to engage in altruistic behavior for some relatives than for others. However, the researchers acknowledged that other types of social relationships also affect people's behaviors. In fact, other research suggests that people are most willing to help individuals to whom they feel emotionally close, including their circle of friends (Korchmaros & Kenny, 2006; Stewart-Williams, 2007). For most people, their closest emotional attachments are also to their closest kin. Thus patterns of helping based on emotional closeness indirectly help people's gene pools to survive.

But how about nonkin? The focus on emotional closeness suggests why people might engage in altruistic behaviors toward their closest friends. But why, for example, was the driver willing to risk his own survival to help a stranger? To explain altruism toward acquaintances and strangers, theorists have explored the concept of **reciprocal altruism** (Trivers, 1971). This concept suggests that people perform altruistic behaviors because they, in some sense, expect that others will perform altruistic behaviors for them: I will save you when you are drowning with the expectation that you would save me, in the future, when I am drowning.

Note, however, that the concept of reciprocal altruism cannot explain all facets of cooperation in social species. For example, the guy who stopped the stranger's car surely didn't expect that the stranger would perform a similarly altruistic act in return. To explain acts of this sort, researchers suggest that *indirect reciprocity* is at work: People perform altruistic behaviors because they believe that, in the future, they will become the recipients of altruistic acts. To put it somewhat more plainly, "I scratch your back, and someone else will scratch mine" (Nowak & Sigmund, 2005, p. 1291). An important component of this concept of indirect reciprocity is that people gain the reputation of being altruistic and trustworthy. For example, in one study, participants played a game that gave them several opportunities to behave altruistically by making monetary donations to other players (Wedekind & Braithwaite, 2002). As the game unfolded, the players' "image scores" were posted as a concrete index of their reputations. In a second phase of the study—in a different game—players with the best reputations for being altruistic were themselves the most likely to be rewarded by altruistic actions. Results of this sort suggest that there is long-term value in having a reputation for being a trustworthy source of altruism.

What social forces prompt people—like rescue workers after the deadly earthquake in China's Sichuan Province—to put their lives in jeopardy for the sake of others?

There is also often a social component when people perform altruistic behaviors toward nonkin. The *empathy-altruism hypothesis* suggests a particular relationship: When you feel empathy—feelings of emotional identification—toward another individual those feelings evoke an altruistic motive to provide help (Batson, 1991). Research supports this hypothesis. For example, in one study the researchers asked participants to allocate raffle tickets either to a whole group or to individuals within the group (Batson et al., 1999). In one condition of the experiment, the participants read an autobiographical message from someone they were led to believe was a group member; the message revealed that that person had just been dumped by a long-time romantic partner. When participants experienced empathy, they gave extra tickets to the dumped individual. Across humans and other species, researchers have demonstrated quite general links between empathy and altruism (de Waal, 2008).

We have just reviewed several reasons why people might engage in prosocial and altruistic behaviors. In the next section, we describe a classic program of research that demonstrated fully how much people's willingness to help—their ability to follow through on prosocial motives—depends on characteristics of the situation.

THE EFFECTS OF THE SITUATION ON PROSOCIAL BEHAVIOR

This program of research began with a tragedy. From the safety of their apartment windows, 38 respectable, law-abiding citizens in Queens, New York, for more than half an hour watched a killer stalk and stab a woman in three separate attacks. Two times the sound of the bystanders' voices and the sudden glow of their bedroom lights interrupted the assailant and frightened

---

reciprocal altruism The idea that people perform altruistic behaviors because they expect that others will perform altruistic behaviors for them in turn.

him off. Each time, however, he returned and stabbed the victim again. Not a single person telephoned the police during the assault; only one witness called the police after the woman was dead (Rosenthal, 1964). This newspaper account of the murder of Kitty Genovese shocked a nation that could not accept the idea of such apathy or hard-heartedness on the part of its responsible citizenry.

But is it fair to pin the label of "apathy" or "hard-hearted" on these bystanders? Or can we explain their inaction in terms of situational forces? To make the case for situational forces, **Bibb Latané** and **John Darley** (1970) carried out a classic series of studies. Their goal was to demonstrate that **bystander intervention**—people's willingness to help strangers in distress—was very sensitive to precise characteristics of the situation. They ingeniously created in the laboratory an experimental analogue of the bystander-intervention situation.

The murder of Kitty Genovese, in a pleasant Queens neighborhood, shocked the nation. Why did so many responsible citizens fail to intervene when they heard her cries for help?

discussion about personal problems, he heard what sounded like one of the other students having an epileptic seizure and gasping for help. During the "seizure," it was impossible for the participant to talk to the other students or to find out what, if anything, they were doing about the emergency. The dependent variable was the speed with which the participant reported the emergency to the experimenter.

It turned out that the likelihood of intervention depended on the number of bystanders the participant thought were present. The more people he thought were present, the slower he was in reporting the seizure, if he did so at all. As you can see in **Figure 16.8**, everyone in a two-person situation intervened within 160 seconds, but nearly 40 percent of those who believed they were part of a larger group never bothered to inform the experimenter that another student was seriously ill (Darley & Latané, 1968).

The participants were male college students. Each student, placed in a room by himself with an intercom, was led to believe that he was communicating with one or more students in an adjacent room. During the course of a

This result arises from a **diffusion of responsibility.** When more than one person *could* help in an emergency situation, people often assume that someone else *will* or *should* help—so they back off and don't get involved.

Diffusion of responsibility is only one of the reasons that bystanders may fail to help. Let's explore more of the facets of many emergency situations.

Bystanders Must Notice the Emergency In the seizure study, the situation was rigged so that participants had to notice what was going on. In many real-life circumstances, however, people who are pursuing their own agendas—they may, for example, be on their way to work or an appointment—may not even notice that there is a situation in which they can help. In one dramatic experiment, students at the Princeton Theological Seminary thought they were going to be evaluated on their sermons, one of which was to be about the parable of the Good Samaritan—a New Testament figure who takes time to help a man lying injured by the roadside.

The seminarians had to deliver their lectures in a different building from the one in which they were initially briefed. Some were randomly assigned to a *late* condition, in which they had to hurry to make the next session, others to an *on-time* condition, and a third group to an *early* condition. When each seminarian walked down an alley between the two buildings, he came upon a man slumped in a doorway, coughing and groaning. On their way to deliver a sermon

FIGURE 16.8 Bystander Intervention in an Emergency

The more people present, the less likely that any one bystander will intervene. Bystanders act most quickly in two-person groups.

From Darley & Latané, *Journal of Personality and Social Psychology, 8*(4), 1968. Copyright © 1968 American Psychological Association. Reprinted with permission.

bystander intervention Willingness to assist a person in need of help.

diffusion of responsibility In emergency situations, the larger the number of bystanders, the less responsibility any one of the bystanders feels to help.

Critical Thinking in Your Life

HOW CAN YOU GET PEOPLE TO VOLUNTEER?

Suppose you become a leader in an organization. It's very likely that you'll want to recruit volunteers to help with the organization's activities. To do so, it should help to have an understanding of why people undertake volunteer work and what sustains their interest in the work.

Let's begin with the question of why people volunteer. Researchers have identified several motives that prompt people to get involved (Omoto & Snyder, 2002). For example, people volunteer to express personal values related to altruism, to expand their range of experiences, and to strengthen social relationships. If volunteer positions do not meet these needs, people may not wish to participate. To recruit volunteers, you may need to understand the motives of the people you wish to attract.

People also volunteer because they are required to do so. To increase levels of community service, some schools have instituted mandatory volunteer programs. Unfortunately, these mandatory programs can shift people's causal attributions from an internal locus of control (for example, "I volunteer because it's important to me") to an external locus of control (for example, "I volunteer because I'm required to do so"). When that happens, people become less likely to volunteer in the future (Stukas et al., 1999). People must be sensitive to this possibility when they mandate volunteer activities.

Once people begin to volunteer, what leads them to remain in their positions over time? To answer this question, researchers have engaged in longitudinal studies in which they track volunteers over time. For example, one study followed 238 volunteers in Florida over the course of a year (Davis et al., 2003). The volunteers participated in organizations such as the St. Petersburg Free Clinic and the Center against Spouse Abuse. One of the most important factors that influenced the participants' satisfaction as volunteers was the amount of distress they experienced in their volunteer positions. Although this result may not surprise you, it leads to important practical advice. The researchers note that attention should be given to "training methods that would prepare volunteers for distressing situations or provide them with strategies for coping with the distress they do experience" (p. 259).

Another study of 302 volunteers at a hospice in the southeastern United States focused on individual differences in the extent to which people view "volunteer" as an important social role (Finkelstein et al., 2005). Recall from earlier in the chapter that people's behavior is often highly influenced by social roles. This study addressed the hypothesis that those people for whom the role of volunteer was most part of their personal identity would also be most likely to continue

volunteer work. Participants indicated the extent to which the social role mattered by responding to statements such as "Volunteering for hospice is an important part of who I am." Consistent with the researchers' expectations, they found a positive correlation between the strength of role identity and the length of time people continued to volunteer. These results, once again, lead to concrete advice: "Once an individual begins volunteering, retention efforts might focus on cultivating a volunteer role identity. . . . Items (e.g., T-shirts, license plate holders) that allow volunteers to be recognized publicly for their contributions can help strengthen role identity" (p. 416).

We have offered this analysis from the perspective of a person who wishes to encourage others to volunteer. However, you can also use these analyses to scrutinize your own behavior. What motives apply to your experiences of volunteering? Are you ready to cope with distress? To what extent do you embrace "volunteer" as a respected social role? You can address these questions to increase the personal and societal benefits of your volunteer activities.

- Why is it appropriate to use longitudinal designs to study volunteer behaviors?

- Why might T-shirts and license plate holders help strengthen role identity?

---

about the Good Samaritan, these seminary students now had the chance to practice what they were about to preach. Did they? Of those who were in a hurry because they were late, only 10 percent helped. If they were on time, 45 percent helped the stranger. Most bystander intervention came from those who were early—63 percent of these seminarians acted as Good Samaritans (Darley & Batson, 1973).

How should we evaluate the "late" seminarians? Perhaps the seminarians were so caught up in their own concerns that they failed to even "notice" the emergency situation. Perhaps they noticed; but, in their hurry, they did not pay careful enough attention to determine how serious the situation was. In either case, you see that helping behavior depends on taking the time to evaluate a situation accurately.

Bystanders Must Feel Responsibility We have already seen that an important factor in nonintervention is the diffusion of responsibility. If you find yourself in a situation in which you need help, you should do everything you can to cause bystanders to focus responsibility on themselves and overcome this force. Point directly toward someone and say, "You! I need your help." Consider two studies that involved apparent crimes. In the first study, New Yorkers watched as a thief snatched a women's suitcase in a fast-food restaurant when she left her table. In the second, beachgoers watched as a thief snatched a portable radio from a beach blanket when the owner left it for a few minutes.

> In each experiment, the would-be theft victim (the experimenter's accomplice) asked the soon-to-be observer of the crime either, "Do you have the time?" or "Will you please keep an eye on my bag (radio) while I'm gone?" The first interaction elicited no personal responsibility, and the bystanders simply stood by idly as the thefts unfolded. However, of those who agreed to watch the victim's property, almost every bystander intervened. They called for help, and some even tackled the runaway thief on the beach (Moriarty, 1975).

These experiments suggest that the act of requesting a favor forges a special human bond that involves other people in ways that materially change the situation. This is another instance in which it would be wrong to make an attribution of apathy when people fail to stop the theft. The social psychological power of the small commitment—"Will you watch this for me?"—turned almost every bystander into someone who cared enough to help.

In this section, we have discussed prosocial behaviors—those circumstances in which people come to each others' aid. We have seen that people have several motives that explain prosocial behaviors. However, as we have seen quite often in this chapter, the social situation has a large impact on the extent to which people will act on those motives.

STOP AND REVIEW

❶ Why do researchers believe that genetic factors play a role in aggression?
❷ What is the relationship between frustration and aggression?
❸ What is meant by reciprocal altruism?
❹ Why does diffusion of responsibility occur?

CRITICAL THINKING Recall the experiment that assessed the impact of violent video games. Why was it important that participants believed the task in which they provided endings for stories was unrelated to their video game playing?

Visit MyPsychLab.com for more review and practice on the following topic:

◄●► **Explore:** Bystander Intervention

A Personal Endnote

We have come to the end of our journey through *Psychology and Life*. As you think back, we hope you will realize just how much you have learned on the way. Yet we have barely scratched the surface of the excitement and challenges that await the student of psychology. We hope you will pursue your interest in psychology and that you may even go on to contribute to this dynamic enterprise as a scientific researcher or a clinical practitioner or by applying psychological knowledge to the solution of social and personal problems.

Playwright Tom Stoppard reminds us that "every exit is an entry somewhere else." We'd like to believe that the entry into the next phase of your life will be facilitated by what you have learned from *Psychology and Life* and from your introductory psychology course. In that next journey, may you infuse new life into the psychology of human endeavors while strengthening the connections among all the people you encounter.

Richard Gerrig

Phil Zimbardo

Recapping Main Points

Constructing Social Reality

- Each person constructs his or her own social reality.
- Social perception is influenced by beliefs and expectations.
- Attribution theory describes the judgments people make about the causes of behaviors.
- Several biases, such as the fundamental attribution error, self-serving biases, and self-fulfilling prophecies, can creep into attributions and other judgments and behaviors.

The Power of the Situation

- Being assigned to play a social role, even in artificial settings, can cause individuals to act contrary to their beliefs, values, and dispositions.
- Social norms shape the attitudes and behaviors of group members.
- Classic research by Sherif and Asch illustrated the informational and normative forces that lead to conformity.
- Minority influence may arise as a consequence of informational influence.
- Milgram's studies on obedience are a powerful testimony to the influence of the situational factors that can lead ordinary people to sanction and participate in organized aggression.

Attitudes, Attitude Change, and Action

- Attitudes are positive or negative evaluations of objects, events, or ideas.
- Not all attitudes accurately predict behaviors; they must be highly accessible or highly stable.
- According to the elaboration likelihood model, the central route to persuasion relies on careful analyses of arguments, whereas the peripheral route relies on superficial features of persuasive situations.

- Dissonance theory and self-perception theory consider attitude formation and change that arise from behavioral acts.
- To bring about compliance, people can exploit reciprocity and commitment.

Prejudice

- Even arbitrary, minimal cues can yield prejudice when they define an in-group and an out-group.
- Stereotypes affect the way in which people evaluate behaviors and information in the world.
- Researchers have eliminated some of the effects of prejudice by creating situations in which members of different groups must cooperate to reach shared goals.
- Cross-cultural studies also suggest that friendship plays an important role in eliminating prejudice.

Social Relationships

- Interpersonal attraction is determined in part by proximity, physical attractiveness, similarity, and reciprocity.
- Loving relationships are defined with respect to passion, intimacy, and commitment.
- Adult attachment style affects the quality of relationships.

Aggression, Altruism, and Prosocial Behavior

- Individual differences in aggressive behavior reflect genetics, brain function, and personality profiles.
- Frustration and provocation can lead to aggression
- Cultures provide different norms for aggressive behavior.
- Researchers have tried to explain why people engage in prosocial behaviors, particularly altruistic behaviors that do not serve their own interests.
- Evolutionary explanations focus on kinship and reciprocity.
- Bystander intervention studies show that situations largely determine who is likely or unlikely to help in emergencies.

KEY TERMS

aggression (p. 535)
altruism (p. 535)
attitude (p. 523)
attribution theory (p. 510)
bystander intervention (p. 541)
cognitive dissonance (p. 526)
compliance (p. 527)
conformity (p. 516)
contact hypothesis (p. 531)
covariation model (p. 510)
diffusion of responsibility (p. 541)
elaboration likelihood model (p. 525)
frustration-aggression hypothesis (p. 537)
fundamental attribution error (FAE) (p. 510)

group polarization (p. 520)
groupthink (p. 520)
impulsive aggression (p. 537)
informational influence (p. 516)
in-group (p. 529)
in-group bias (p. 529)
instrumental aggression (p. 537)
norm crystallization (p. 516)
normative influence (p. 516)
out-group (p. 529)
persuasion (p. 524)
prejudice (p. 528)
prosocial behavior (p. 535)
racism (p. 529)

reciprocal altruism (p. 540)
reciprocity norm (p. 527)
rule (p. 513)
self-fulfilling prophecy (p. 512)
self-perception theory (p. 527)
self-serving bias (p. 511)
sexism (p. 529)
social categorization (p. 529)
social cognition (p. 509)
social norm (p. 516)
social perception (p. 509)
social psychology (p. 509)
social role (p. 513)
stereotype (p. 529)

1. Grace wants to help her friend Charlie avoid the fundamental attribution error. She suggests that he focus on _____ causes of behaviors.
   a. situational
   b. dispositional
   c. distinctive
   d. consistent

2. Which of these statements is *not* consistent with a self-serving bias?
   a. I lost because the other guy was probably cheating.
   b. I lost because it was too hot in the room.
   c. I won because I'm a genius.
   d. I won because I got lucky.

3. Self-fulfilling prophecies may be modest in the real world because
   a. most students perform better than their teachers expect them to perform.
   b. teachers usually have accurate expectations about how students will perform.
   c. teachers rarely have expectations about students.
   d. students do not allow teachers to treat them differently from their classmates.

4. In the Stanford Prison Experiment, the guards often abused the prisoners. This result suggests that
   a. people seek situations in which they can indulge their aggressive impulses.
   b. some people are born to play the role of guards.
   c. only aggressive people are willing to assume the role of prison guard.
   d. social roles have an important influence on how people behave.

5. Solomon Asch's experiments on conformity demonstrate the impact of _____ in group situations.
   a. norm crystallization
   b. social rules
   c. normative influence
   d. informational influence

6. In Milgram's experiments on obedience, many people protested that they didn't want to give any more shocks. After that happened,
   a. the experimenter told them the study was over.
   b. most participants asked to leave the experiment.
   c. most participants continued to administer shocks.
   d. the experimenter asked to decrease shocks.

7. When a company hires a celebrity to endorse a product, they are likely hoping that most consumers will follow the _____ route to persuasion and engage in _____ elaboration.
   a. peripheral; low
   b. central; high
   c. peripheral; high
   d. central; low

8. Sam chooses desserts for himself and for his friend Randy. Both desserts turn out to be duds. If Sam has a(n) _____ sense of self, you'd expect him to experience the most cognitive dissonance with respect to the dessert he chose for _____.
   a. independent; Randy
   b. interdependent; himself
   c. interdependent; Randy
   d. dependent; himself

9. Oliver is trying to change his friend Stan's stereotype that women aren't as funny as men. They watch a TV special with a series of women doing comedy routines. Do you think Stan's stereotype will change?
   a. Yes, because he will appreciate Oliver's effort on his behalf.
   b. No, because he will discount information that is inconsistent with his stereotype.
   c. No, because he will convince Stan that the stereotype is true.
   d. Yes, because he will learn a new stereotype from the TV special.

10. Which of these statements suggests that Carmen is exploiting similarity to get Perry to like her more?
    a. "Did you know that we're both Libras?"
    b. "I really enjoy spending time with you."
    c. "Would you like me to get you the newspaper?"
    d. "Your new haircut looks terrific."

11. Which statement is *not* correct?
    a. Companionate love is associated with life satisfaction.
    b. Most relationships have more passionate love at the outset.
    c. Companionate love is characterized by less intensity but greater intimacy.
    d. There is little passionate love in long-term relationships.

12. You are watching a video of Juliet interacting with an attractive man. Because Juliet is mimicking his gestures _____, you guess that she _____ currently in a romantic relationship.
    a. quite a bit, is
    b. continuously, is
    c. very little, is
    d. infrequently, is not

13. According to the frustration-aggression hypothesis, in which of these situations is Brett most likely to act in an aggressive fashion?
    a. Brett has an important job interview, but he's stuck in a traffic jam.
    b. Brett's girlfriend yelled at him all morning for being mean to her.
    c. Brett hates the song playing on his car radio.
    d. Brett thinks his boss has been monitoring the websites he visits.

14. With respect to bystander intervention, it is typically *least* important that bystanders must
    a. notice the emergency.
    b. label events as an emergency.
    c. feel responsibility in the situation.
    d. consider themselves to be helpful people.

15. If you want to increase the likelihood that people will continue to volunteer in the future, which of these measures would you *not* want to try?
    a. Give T-shirts to identify people as volunteers.
    b. Have people start to volunteer as a mandatory assignment.
    c. Help people cope with distressing aspects of the volunteer work.
    d. Determine the motives people have for volunteering.

Essay Questions

1. What properties of attitudes increase the correlations between attitudes and behaviors?

2. How do stereotypes affect behavior?

3. What situational factors affect the likelihood that people will engage in prosocial behaviors?

Discovering Psychology Viewing Guide

Watch the following videos by logging on to MyPsychLab (www.mypsychlab.com). After you have watched the videos, complete the activities that follow.

Program 19: The Power of the Situation

Program 20: Constructing Social Reality

KEY TERMS AND PEOPLE

As you watch the programs, pay particular attention to these terms and people in addition to those covered in this textbook.

- *autocratic*—governed by one person with unlimited power.
- *cognitive control*—the power of beliefs to give meaning to a situation.
- *democratic*—practicing social equality.
- *laissez-faire*—allowing complete freedom, with little or no interference or guidance.
- *legitimate authority*—a form of power exercised by someone in a superior role such as a teacher or president.
- *Pygmalion effect*—the effect of positive and negative expectations on behavior.
- *thought-stopping*—a technique employed by cults to suppress critical thinking by its members.
- *Elliot Aronson*—helped change the way students saw themselves and others in terms of cooperation and not competition through creating the "Jigsaw Classroom" with Alex Gonzalez.
- *Jane Elliot*—conducted an experiment where she induced prejudice in third-graders based on blue-eyed versus brown-eyed children.
- *Steven Hassan*—once a high-ranking member of the Sun Myung Moon Unification Church, he has devoted 25 years to understanding and counseling people on the manipulative techniques used by cults to recruit and retain their members.

PROGRAM REVIEW

1. What do social psychologists study?
   a. how people are influenced by other people
   b. how people act in different societies
   c. why some people are more socially successful than others
   d. what happens to isolated individuals

2. What precipitated Kurt Lewin's interest in leadership roles?
   a. the rise of social psychology
   b. the trial of Adolf Eichmann
   c. Hitler's ascent to power
   d. the creation of the United Nations after World War II

3. In Lewin's study, how did the boys behave when they had autocratic leaders?
   a. They had fun but got little accomplished.
   b. They were playful and did motivated, original work.
   c. They were hostile toward each other and got nothing done.
   d. They worked hard but acted aggressively toward each other.

4. In Solomon Asch's experiments, about what percent of participants went along with the group's obviously mistaken judgment at least once?
   a. 70 percent
   c. 30 percent
   b. 50 percent
   d. 90 percent

5. Before Stanley Milgram did his experiments on obedience, experts were asked to predict the results. The experts
   a. overestimated people's willingness to administer shocks.
   b. underestimated people's willingness to administer shocks.
   c. gave accurate estimates of people's behavior.
   d. believed most people would refuse to continue with the experiment.

6. Which light did Milgram's experiment shed on the behavior of citizens in Nazi Germany?
   a. Situational forces can bring about blind obedience.
   b. Personal traits of individuals are most important in determining behavior.
   c. Cultural factors unique to Germany account for the rise of the Nazis.
   d. Human beings enjoy being cruel when they have the opportunity.

7. Which statement most clearly reflects the fundamental attribution error?
   a. Everyone is entitled to good medical care.
   b. Ethical guidelines are essential to conducting responsible research.
   c. People who are unemployed are too lazy to work.
   d. Everyone who reads about the Milgram experiment is shocked by the results.

8. Why did the prison study conducted by Philip Zimbardo and his colleagues have to be called off?
   a. A review committee felt that it violated ethical guidelines.
   b. It consumed too much of the students' time.

c. The main hypothesis was supported, so there was no need to continue.

d. The situation that had been created was too dangerous to maintain.

9. How did Tom Moriarity get people on a beach to intervene during a robbery?
a. by creating a human bond through a simple request
b. by reminding people of their civic duty to turn in criminals
c. by making the thief look less threatening
d. by providing a model of responsible behavior

10. Which leadership style tends to produce hard work when the leader is watching but much less cooperation when the leader is absent?
a. authoritative
b. autocratic
c. democratic
d. laissez-faire

11. Typically, people who participated in Milgram's study
a. appeared to relish the opportunity to hurt someone else.
b. objected but still obeyed.
c. refused to continue and successfully stopped the experiment.
d. came to recruit others into shocking the learner.

12. Psychologists refer to the power to create subjective realities as the power of
a. social reinforcement.
b. prejudice.
c. cognitive control.
d. the Pygmalion effect.

13. When Jane Elliot divided her classroom of third-graders into the inferior brown-eyed students and the superior blue-eyed students, what did she observe?
a. The students were too young to understand what was expected.
b. The students refused to behave badly toward their friends and classmates.
c. The boys tended to go along with the categorization, but the girls did not.
d. The blue-eyed students acted superior and were cruel to the brown-eyed students, who acted inferior.

14. In the research carried out by Robert Rosenthal and Lenore Jacobson, what caused the performance of some students to improve dramatically?
a. Teachers were led to expect such improvement and so changed the way they treated these students.
b. These students performed exceptionally well on a special test designed to predict improved performance.
c. Teachers gave these students higher grades because they knew the researchers were expecting the improvement.
d. The students felt honored to be included in the experiment and so were motivated to improve.

15. Robert Rosenthal demonstrated the Pygmalion effect in the classroom by showing that teachers behave differently toward students for whom they have high expectations in all of the following ways, *except*
a. by punishing them more for goofing off.
b. by providing them with a warmer learning climate.
c. by teaching more to them than to the other students.
d. by providing more specific feedback when the student gives a wrong answer.

16. What happens to low-achieving students in the Jigsaw Classroom?
a. They tend to fall further behind.
b. They are given an opportunity to work at a lower level, thus increasing the chance of success.
c. By becoming "experts," they improve their performance and their self-respect.
d. By learning to compete more aggressively, they become more actively involved in their own learning.

17. When Robert Cialdini cites the example of the Hare Krishnas' behavior in giving people at airports a flower or other small gift, he is illustrating the principle of
a. commitment.
b. reciprocity.
c. scarcity.
d. consensus.

18. Salespeople might make use of the principle of scarcity by
a. filling shelves up with a product and encouraging consumers to stock up.
b. claiming they have a hard time ordering the product.
c. imposing a deadline by which the consumer must make a decision.
d. being difficult to get in touch with over the phone.

19. Nancy is participating in a bike-a-thon next month and is having a large group of friends over to her house in order to drum up sponsorships for the event. She is capitalizing on the principle of
a. liking.
b. consensus.
c. commitment.
d. authority.

20. An appropriate motto for the principle of consensus would be
a. "I've reasoned it through."
b. "I am doing it of my own free will."
c. "It will be over quickly."
d. "Everyone else is doing it."

21. All of the following manipulation techniques were described as being used by cults to maintain control over their members, *except*
a. sleep deprivation.
b. suggestive questioning.
c. thought-stopping.
d. bribery.

22. Which of the following people would be most likely to advise that you try to understand a cult member by adopting his or her perspective?
a. Hassan
b. Festinger
c. Aronson
d. Cialdini

QUESTIONS TO CONSIDER

1. Some psychologists have suggested that participants in Milgram's research must have suffered guilt and loss of dignity and self-esteem, although they were told later that they hadn't actually harmed the learner. Follow-up studies to the prison experiment revealed that the participants had not suffered long-term ill effects. What psychological principle might explain these outcomes? Did the value of the research outweigh the risks for participants? Was Milgram in a position to weigh the relative value and risks ahead of time? Would you participate in such experiments?

2. In emerging democracies like Iraq, people are faced with freedoms that they previously had not known. When the situation shifts so dramatically and being in a position of submission to power is suddenly removed, what sorts of new risks also emerge?

3. In Zimbardo's prison experiment, students were randomly assigned the role of guard or prisoner. All participants in the study were surprised when the true identities of the guards and prisoners were erased during the course of the experiment. Each of us plays many roles: child, spouse, friend, student, parent, boss, employee, citizen, consumer, sibling. Do you feel that any of the roles you play conflict with your "true identity"? How do you know what your true identity is?

4. How is nationalism used to structure social reality? Does this become a more powerful force for people's attitudes and interaction during times of actual war or cold war than it is during times of peace? How might it be affected by phenomena like globalized economics and common languages across borders?

5. Many of the socially undesirable aspects of human behavior (e.g., violent crime, rudeness, apathy) seem to be more likely in urban than in suburban or rural environments. How can social psychology help to explain this phenomenon?

ACTIVITIES

1. Norms of social behavior include "social distances" that we place between ourselves and friends, acquaintances, and strangers. Observe and compare the social distance you maintain between yourself and family members, friends, and strangers. Purposely change how close to them you would normally stand. Observe their responses. Does anyone mention it? Do others adjust their positions to achieve normal distances?

2. Observe the interactions of several different kinds of pairs of people—for example, a boss speaking with an employee, a minister speaking with a church member, a customer speaking with a clerk, or two close friends speaking with each other. Compare how those conversations differ (for example, in terms of how often each has the floor, how often polite requests versus direct requests are made, and how often each looks the other directly in the eye or physically touches the other person). If you can, observe the same person in many different kinds of situations in which they do or do not have the more powerful position. How does their behavior differ?

3. Look for editorials, news stories, or political cartoons that portray an international situation. Which words, labels, and images promote "us versus them" thinking? How might someone with opposite views have written the articles or drawn the cartoons differently? Do you find that the tendency to present an "us versus them" view changes over time or that it differs across cultures?

4. Think of norms of proper dress or social behavior that you can violate. For example, what would happen if you wore shorts to a formal gathering? Or asked a stranger an extremely personal question? Or arrived at work in your bedroom slippers? Pay attention to your feelings as you think about carrying out these activities. What fears or inhibitions do you have? How likely is it that you could actually carry out these activities?

Answer Appendix

Stop and Review Answers

CHAPTER 1

Stop and Review (What Makes Psychology Unique? p. 5)

1. Psychology is the *scientific* study of the *behavior* of *individuals* and their *mental* processes.
2. The four goals are to describe, explain, predict and control behavior.
3. Researchers regularly try to explain behaviors by identifying underlying causes; successful causal explanations often allow accurate predictions.

Stop and Review (The Evolution of Modern Psychology, p. 13)

1. Structuralism tries to understand mental experiences as the combination of basic components. Functionalism focuses on the purposes of behavioral acts.
2. Wooley argued that sex differences do not reflect natural ability but, rather, differences in men's and men's and women's social experiences.
3. The psychodynamic perspective focuses on powerful, instinctive forces and the behaviorist perspective focuses on how consequences shape behaviors.
4. Researchers in cognitive neuroscience combine the cognitive and biological perspectives to understand the brain bases of mental activities such as memory and language.
5. The evolutionary perspective focuses on the features that all people share as a consequence of human evolution. The sociocultural perspective focuses on the differences brought about by cultures, against that shared evolutionary background.

Stop and Review (What Psychologists Do, p. 15)

1. Research provides new insights that psychologists then try to apply in real-world settings.
2. Academic settings (e.g., colleges and universities) and independent practice.

Stop and Review (How To Use This Text, p. 17)

1. You must be actively involved in the course by developing your own understanding of what you hear in lectures and read in the text.

2. In the *Question* phase you invent questions that direct your attention while you are reading; in the *Read* phase you read the material with an eye to answering your questions.
3. When you attempt to recite explicit answers to questions, you obtain concrete evidence of what you know and what you don't know.

CHAPTER 2

Stop and Review (The Process of Research, p. 31)

1. Theories attempt to explain phenomena. Those explanations should generate new hypotheses—testable consequences of a theory.
2. Researchers can standardize their procedures and provide operational definitions for their variables.
3. Researchers use double-blind controls so that the expectations they bring to the research setting cannot have an impact on their studies' results.
4. When an experiment has a within-subjects design, each participant serves as his or her own control.
5. A correlation coefficient indicates the extent to which two variables are related—it does not give any indication of why that relationship exists.

Stop and Review (Psychological Measurement, p. 35)

1. If a measure is reliable, it means that it yields a comparable value when researchers use it repeatedly. However, that value might still not accurately reflect the psychological variable that the researcher is after. That's why shoe size would be a reliable but not a valid measure of happiness.
2. Interviewers seek to create a context in which people are willing to provide information through self-reports that might be highly personal or sensitive.
3. The researcher is engaged in naturalistic observation of the children's behavior.

Stop and Review (Ethical Issues in Human and Animal Research, p. 38)

1. Research participants must have the opportunity to understand their rights and responsibilities before they choose to engage in an experiment.
2. During debriefing, participants have an opportunity to learn something new about the psychological phenomena that were the topic of the study. In addition, through debriefing researchers can ensure that participants do not leave the study upset or confused.
3. Ethical considerations support a move toward research in naturalistic or seminaturalistic settings.

CHAPTER 3

Stop and Review (Heredity and Behavior, p. 59)

1. The Grants observed that, as a result of changes in the environment, sometimes big-beaked finches were able to survive and reproduce, whereas at other times small-beaked finches were able to survive and reproduce.
2. The genotype is the underlying genetic material that helps determine the phenotype, which is the observable characteristics of an organism.
3. Two critical advances were bipedalism and encephalization.
4. Heritability is a measure of the relative influence of genetics in determining an organism's constellation of traits and behaviors.

Stop and Review (The Nervous System in Action, p. 66)

1. In general, the dendrites receive incoming signals. The soma integrates information from the many dendrites and passes that information along to the axon.
2. The all-or-none law suggests that, once the threshold for firing has been reached, the strength of an action potential is constant.
3. Neurotransmitters are released into synapses when synaptic vesicles rupture; the neurotransmitters then bind to receptor molecules on the receiving neuron.
4. GABA is the brain's most common inhibitory neurotransmitter.

Stop and Review (Biology and Behavior, p. 83)

1. fMRI allows researchers to make claims about both structures and functions.
2. The autonomic nervous system is divided into the sympathetic and parasympathetic divisions.
3. The amygdala plays a role in emotional control and the formation of emotional memories.
4. For most individuals, the processing style of the left hemisphere is relatively more analytic, whereas the right hemisphere is relatively more holistic.
5. The pituitary gland produces hormones that influence the activity of all the other endocrine glands.
6. Neurogenesis is the creation of new neurons.

CHAPTER 4

Stop and Review (Perceptual Knowledge of the World, p. 97)

1. The proximal stimulus is the optical image on the retina.
2. Psychophysics is the study of the relationship between physical stimuli and the psychological experience of those stimuli.

3. An absolute threshold is defined as the stimulus level at which a sensory signal is detected half the time.
4. Judgments are affected both by sensory processes and observers' biases.
5. A difference threshold is the smallest physical difference between two stimuli that observers can recognize.
6. Transduction is the conversion of one form of physical energy into another form.

Stop and Review (The Visual System, p. 105)

1. Accommodation is the process by which the thickness of the lens changes so that focus is achieved on both near and far objects.
2. The fovea is 100 percent cones.
3. Complex cells respond to bars in particular orientations, but those bars must also be moving.
4. This experience is explained by opponent-process theory.

Stop and Review (Hearing, p. 110)

1. You perceive sounds with different frequencies as having different pitches.
2. Hair cells transform the mechanical vibrations of the basilar membrane into nerve impulses.
3. Place theory associates pitch perception with the location of stimulation on the basilar membrane.
4. The sound should reach your right ear before it reaches your left ear.

Stop and Review (Your Other Senses, p. 114)

1. Nerve impulses convey odor information to the olfactory bulb.
2. The basic taste qualities are sweet, sour, bitter, saline, and umami.
3. You have separate types of receptors that encode information about warmth and coolness.
4. The vestibular sense provides information about how the body is oriented in space with respect to gravity.
5. Gate-control theory attempts to explain how experiences of pain are affected by psychological context.

Stop and Review (Organizational Processes in Perception, p. 124)

1. Sometimes stimulus features in the environment—like the abrupt change of a spotlight from red to green—will capture your attention.
2. People tend to fill in small gaps to experience objects as wholes.
3. When someone is walking toward you, the size of the man's image on your retina expands.
4. The angle of convergence is larger when an object is closer to you.
5. Shape constancy is your ability to perceive the true shape of an object even as the shape of the retinal image changes.

Stop and Review (Identification and Recognition Processes, p. 129)

1. People use their knowledge of sounds and words to restore information that is missing from the auditory signal.
2. A stimulus is ambiguous when more than one object or event in the environment could give rise to the same proximal stimulus.
3. A set is a temporary readiness to perceive or react to a stimulus in a particular way.

CHAPTER 5

Stop and Review (The Contents of Consciousness, p. 139)

1. A memory is preconscious when it is not currently part of the content of consciousness but could easily become so.
2. Freud suggested that some ideas or motives are sufficiently threatening they become repressed into the unconscious.
3. Researchers ask experimental participants to report their thoughts while they carry out particular tasks.

Stop and Review (The Functions of Consciousness, p. 141)

1. Consciousness allows you to make explicit decisions about what information you should attempt to commit to memory.
2. A cultural construction of reality is a way of thinking about the world that is shared by most members of a particular group of people.
3. People generally need to use conscious attention to search for objects with a combination of features.

Stop and Review (Sleep and Dreams, p. 148)

1. You experience jet lag because your internal circadian rhythm is out of phase with the temporal environment.
2. Early in the night you experience relatively more NREM sleep; late in the night you experience relatively more REM sleep.
3. NREM sleep serves the functions of conservation and restoration.
4. Sleep apnea is a sleep disorder in which a person stops breathing while asleep.
5. The latent content is the underlying meaning that has been hidden by the mind's censors.

Stop and Review (Altered States of Consciousness, p. 151)

1. The goal of lucid dreaming is for dreamers to become consciously aware that they are dreaming so they can control the content of their dreams.
2. Early twin studies suggested that hypnotizability has a genetic component; researchers have begun to identify specific genes that might underlie this impact.
3. Some people practice concentrative mediation, whereas others practice mindfulness meditation.

Stop and Review (Mind-Altering Drugs, p. 157)

1. Drug tolerance is circumstances in which an individual requires greater doses of a drug to yield the same effect.
2. Drugs like heroin bind to the same receptors sites as the brain's endogenous opiates.
3. Nicotine is an example of a stimulant.

CHAPTER 6

Stop and Review (The Study of Learning, p. 166)

1. The learning-performance distinction acknowledges that people's behaviors might not always reflect everything they have learned.
2. He argued that people's private experiences were too subjective to be studied with scientific rigor.
3. Behavior analysts attempt to discover regularities in learning that occur in all types of animal species.
4. Habituation is a decrease in an organism's behavioral response when a stimulus occurs repeatedly.

Stop and Review (Classical Conditioning: Learning Predictable Signals, p. 174)

1. Classical conditioning begins with behaviors (such as salivation) that are reflex responses to unconditioned stimuli (such as the presentation of food powder).
2. The UCS is the unconditioned stimulus that produces a response prior to conditioning; the CS is the conditioned stimulus that produces a response as a result of conditioning.
3. Stimulus discrimination means that the organism has learned to produce a conditioned response to a more narrow range of conditioned stimuli than would otherwise be the case.
4. It's not enough for the CS and UCS to occur close together in time; the UCS must be contingent upon—be predictable from—the CS.
5. The CR is the body's compensatory response to the drug's effects.

Stop and Review (Operant Conditioning: Learning About Consequences, p. 184)

1. The law of effect states that a response followed by satisfying consequences becomes more probable and a response followed by dissatisfying consequences becomes less probable.
2. Reinforcement makes behaviors more likely; punishment makes behaviors less likely.
3. Animals learn that behaviors will only have consequences (reinforcement or punishment) in the context of particular stimuli—those stimuli are the discriminative stimuli.
4. In FR schedules, a reinforcer is delivered each time the organism has made a fixed number of responses. In FI schedules, a reinforcer is delivered when the organism makes the first response after a fixed amount of time.
5. Shaping is a method that allows an organism to learn a behavior through successive approximations.

Stop and Review (Biology and Learning, p. 187)

1. Instinctual drift is the tendency, over time, for learned behaviors to drift toward instinctual behaviors.
2. Taste aversion will develop with only one pairing of the CS and UCS and with a long lag between the CS and UCS. It will often be permanent after one experience.

Stop and Review (Cognitive Influences on Learning, p. 190)

1. Tolman concluded that his rats developed cognitive maps for the layouts in the mazes.
2. Pigeons can look at photographs of objects and make different responses to categorize them as, for example, "flowers" and "natural stimuli."
3. Vicarious reinforcement occurs when an individual's behavior becomes more probable after he or she observes other people's behaviors being reinforced.
4. Research suggests that children who observe a large number of aggressive acts may learn to be aggressive themselves.

CHAPTER 7

Stop and Review (What Is Memory? p. 199)

1. Explicit uses of memory involve conscious effort, whereas implicit uses of memory do not.
2. Your skill relies more on procedural memory.
3. Because you've previously encoded and stored your password, it's most likely your problem is with retrieval.

Stop and Review (Memory Use for the Short Term, p. 204)

1. Comparisons of the whole- and partial-report procedures indicate that people have very brief access to all the information in a display.
2. Researchers believe that the capacity of STM is in the range of three to five items.
3. Chunking is the process of reconfiguring items into meaningful groups.
4. Working memory includes the phonological loop, the visuospatial sketchpad, the central executive, and the episodic buffer.

Stop and Review (Long-Term Memory: Encoding and Retrieval, p. 216)

1. Recognition generally provides more retrieval cues.
2. This would be an example of the primacy effect in serial recall.
3. Transfer-appropriate processing suggests that memory is best when the type of processing carried out at encoding matches the type of processing carried out at retrieval.
4. These circumstances provide an example of retroactive interference because new information has made it harder to remember older information.
5. Beginning with hydrogen, you would associate each element with a position along a familiar route.
6. The familiarity of the retrieval cue and the accessibility of information related to the cue both contribute to feelings-of-knowing.

Stop and Review (Structures in Long-Term Memory, p. 223)

1. Concepts are the mental representations of the categories you form.
2. The exemplar theory claims that people categorize new objects by comparing them to the exemplars they have stored in memory.
3. Bartlett identified the processes of leveling, sharpening, and assimilating.
4. Loftus and her colleagues demonstrated that people will include incorrect postevent information when they attempt to remember events.

Stop and Review (Biological Aspects of Memory, p. 227)

1. Lashley concluded that the engram did not exist in any localized regions but was widely distributed throughout the brain.
2. Research suggests that important aspects of implicit memory will often be spared for individuals who have amnesia for explicit memories.
3. PET scans reveal that different areas of the brain are disproportionately active for encoding and retrieval—left prefrontal cortex for encoding and right prefrontal cortex for retrieval.

CHAPTER 8

Stop and Review (Studying Cognition, p. 237)

1. Donders's goal was to determine the speed of mental processes by inventing tasks that differed only by specific processes.
2. Serial processes take place one after the other; parallel processes overlap in time.
3. Automatic processes do not generally require attentional resources.

Stop and Review (Language Use, p. 246)

1. The cooperative principle specifies some of the dimensions speakers should consider to design an utterance for a particular listener.
2. Spoonerisms are more likely when the sound exchange yields real words.
3. When representations include more information than the propositions provided by a text, you can conclude that people have encoded inferences.
4. Humans can produce and understand utterances with complex grammatical structures; humans can engage in audience design.
5. Linguistic relativity is the idea that the structure of the language people speak has an impact on the way in which they think about the world.

Stop and Review (Visual Cognition, p. 250)

1. The consistency of the rate of mental rotation suggests that the processes of mental rotation are very similar to those of physical rotation.
2. Brain-imaging research suggests large amount of overlap between the brain regions that people use for perception and the regions people use when they create visual images.
3. Research suggests that you find it easier to say what is in front of you, rather than behind you, in the mental scene.

Stop and Review (Problem Solving and Reasoning, p. 256)

1. An algorithm is a step-by-step procedure that guarantees a correct answer for a particular type of problem.
2. You have overcome functional fixedness if you have been able to find a new function for an object that you previously associated with a different purpose.
3. When people succumb to the belief-bias effect, they have judged conclusions based on their real-world believability rather than on their logical relationship to premises.
4. People often engage in inductive reasoning by forming analogies between the features of current circumstances and past experiences in memory.

Stop and Review (Judgment and Decision Making, p. 263)

1. Heuristics provide people with the shortcuts that allow them to make frequent and rapid judgments.
2. It's likely that you would use the anchoring heuristic—by starting at a plausible anchor (e.g., 100 years old) and adjusting from there.
3. Frames play a large role because they determine, for example, whether people think about the gains or losses associated with particular circumstances.
4. When making a decision, satisficers often choose the first option that is good enough; maximizers keep evaluating options trying to find the absolute best one.

CHAPTER 9

Stop and Review (What is Assessment? p. 274)

1. Galton suggested that differences in intelligence could be measured objectively.
2. To assess split-half reliability, researchers divide a test into two halves. A test with high split-half reliability yields highly similar scores on the two halves.
3. The researcher should determine whether scores on the measure allow for accurate predictions of relevant future outcomes.
4. Norms enable researchers to understand the scores of particular individuals in the context of a broader population's scores.

Stop and Review (Intelligence Assessment, p. 278)

1. The original measure of IQ was mental age divided by chronological age.
2. Wechsler added performance subtests to his IQ measure.
3. Diagnosis of intellectual disability now focuses on both IQ and adaptive skills.
4. The three dimensions are ability, creativity, and task commitment.

Stop and Review (Theories of Intelligence, p. 282)

1. Because Spearman demonstrated that people's performance on a variety of intelligence tests was highly correlated, he concluded that there was a factor of general intelligence.
2. Sternberg proposed that people have analytical, creative, and practical intelligence.
3. Gardner defined "spatial" intelligence as the ability to perceive the visual-spatial world and transform one's initial perceptions—these abilities are relevant to sculpture.

Stop and Review (The Politics of Intelligence, p. 288)

1. Goddard's suggested that IQ tests be used to exclude some immigrants as mentally inferior.
2. Heritability estimates do not allow for comparisons between groups of individuals.
3. Research has demonstrated that people who experience quality preschool programs have higher measured IQs and are more likely to graduate from regular high schools and have better paying jobs.
4. People in the United States were more likely to believe that innate ability matters more than hard work; for people in Asia, the beliefs were reversed.

Stop and Review (Creativity, p. 291)

1. Ideas or products are often considered creative when they are both novel and appropriate to the circumstances.
2. Divergent thinking is defined as a person's ability to generate a variety of unusual solutions to a problem.
3. Research suggests that individuals who are exceptionally creative are risk takers, they have preparation in their domains, and they have intrinsic motivation.

Stop and Review (Assessment and Society, p. 292)

1. If members of particular groups generally test less well than others, that pattern might prevent equal access to jobs.
2. In many school districts, support is based on test scores—forcing teachers to cover only material that will be tested.
3. When tests are used without flexibility to label people as belonging to certain academic or social tracks, those labels can have broad consequences.

CHAPTER 10

Stop and Review (Studying Development, p. 300)

1. Developmental age is the chronological age at which most people are able to achieve a particular physical or mental accomplishment.

2. To study individual differences, researchers often measure variation (on some dimension) among people at one age and then reexamine the same participants later in life to examine the consequences of that variation.
3. For some cross-sectional analyses, researchers have to rule out the possibility that what appear to be age-related changes are really differences brought about by the time at which individuals were born.

Stop and Review (Physical Development Across the Life Span, p. 306)

1. Compared to their noncrawling peers, children who have begun to crawl experience fear on the "deep" end of the visual cliff.
2. Recent studies indicate that the brain continues to mature during adolescence, particularly in areas such as the frontal lobes.
3. As people age, the lenses in their eyes often become yellowed, which is thought to be responsible for diminished color vision.

Stop and Review (Cognitive Development Across the Life Span, p. 312)

1. Assimilation allows children to fit new information to old schemes; accommodation changes schemes to fit new information.
2. A child who can overcome centration is able to ignore surface aspects of a problem to show deeper understanding of a domain such as number or liquid quantity.
3. By inventing more subtle measures of infants' knowledge, researchers have been able to demonstrate that children show evidence of object permanence by age 4 months.
4. Vygotsky emphasized the importance of the social context in the way that children's cognitive development unfolds.
5. Research suggests that people's processing speed slows down as they age.

Stop and Review (Acquiring Language, p. 317)

1. When talking to infants and children, adults tend to slow down, use exaggerated, high-pitched intonation, and produce shorter utterances with simpler structures.
2. Children form hypotheses for the meanings of new words. On some occasions, their hypotheses are broader than the adult category.
3. Deaf children who have not been exposed to either a spoken language or a formal signed language will sometimes begin to use their own signed languages that share structural features with real languages.
4. If a child is overregularizing English past tense constructions, you would expect to hear him or her say words like *doed* and *breaked* rather than *did* and *broke*.

Stop and Review (Social Development Across the Life Span, p. 327)

1. Erikson suggested that the crisis of intimacy versus isolation comes into focus during early adulthood.
2. Research suggests that children who have secure attachments at early ages are, for example, more popular and less socially anxious later in life.
3. Parenting styles are defined by the dimensions of the parent's demandingness and the parent's responsiveness.
4. Adolescents experience peer relationships at the levels of friendships, cliques, and crowds.
5. The birth of a child often has a negative impact on marital satisfaction.

Stop and Review (Sex and Gender Differences, p. 330)

1. Sex differences emerge from biological differences between men and women; gender differences emerge from cultural constructions of different roles for men and women.
2. Research suggests that men and women use somewhat different brain structures to encode and recognize emotional stimuli.
3. Young children prefer the company of peers of the same sex.

Stop and Review (Moral Development, p. 332)

1. The three major levels are preconventional morality, conventional morality, and principled morality.
2. Gilligan argued that men are more focused on justice, whereas women are more focused on caring for others.
3. People may bring concerns related to autonomy, community, and divinity.

CHAPTER 11

Stop and Review (Understanding Motivation, p. 344)

1. You would probably draw some inference about why the student was running, which relates to the idea that motivational concepts can be links between public acts and private states.
2. Homeostasis reflects a state of equilibrium with respect to biological states.
3. Research demonstrated a good deal of variability in behavior between cultures—arguing against biological instincts.
4. Heider made a distinction between dispositional and situational forces as explanations for outcomes.
5. Attachment needs relate to people's needs to belong, to affiliate with others, to love, and to be loved.

Stop and Review (Eating, p. 350)

1. Sense-specific satiety is circumstances in which an individual has become satiated with respect to a particular flavor of food.
2. The dual-center model suggested that the VMH was the "satiety center." However, more recent research suggests that the role of the VMH depends on the type of food.
3. Restrained eaters habitually maintain a low-calorie diet until they become disinhibited, at which point they often will indulge in high-calorie binges.
4. Bulimia nervosa is characterized by the behaviors of binging and purging.

Stop and Review (Sexual Behaviors, p. 358)

1. In most nonhuman species, all members of the species follow the same predictable pattern of sexual behavior.
2. Masters and Johnson identified the phases of excitement, plateau, orgasm, and resolution.
3. Because men can impregnate several women in the same period of time, but women can only have one pregnancy at a time, men seek more sexual partners.
4. Sexual scripts are socially learned programs that define appropriate forms of sexual activity.
5. Concordance rates are higher for MZ twins than for DZ twins, supporting the claim that homosexuality has a genetic component.

Stop and Review (Motivation for Personal Achievement, p. 363)

1. Need for achievement reflects individual differences in the value people place on planning and working toward goals.
2. People make attributions along the dimensions of internal versus external, global versus specific, and stable versus unstable.

3. Expectancy theory proposes that workers are motivated when they expect their effort and performance will yield desirable outcomes.

CHAPTER 12

Stop and Review (Emotions, p. 379)

1. Cross-cultural research suggests there are seven facial expressions that people generally recognize around the world.
2. The autonomous nervous system plays an important role to bring about the physiological aspects of emotions—such as a racing heart and sweaty palms.
3. The Cannon–Bard theory suggests that an emotion stimulus produces concurrently arousal and an emotional feeling.
4. People in negative moods tend to process information in a more detailed and effortful fashion than people in positive moods.
5. Research suggests that good social relationships are the single most important source of happiness.

Stop and Review (Stress and Living, p. 392)

1. The three stages of the GAS are the alarm reaction, resistance, and exhaustion.
2. Participants in the 1990s reported more life-change units, suggesting that they were generally experiencing more stress than people in the 1960s.
3. In general, daily hassles have a negative impact on well-being, and daily pleasures have a positive impact.
4. When people engage in emotion-focused coping, they engage in activities that make them feel better but do not directly change the stressor.
5. When people do not believe they have control over a stressful situation, they are at risk for poor physical and psychological adjustment.
6. People are able to identify positive changes that arise from negative life events.

Stop and Review (Health Psychology, p. 401)

1. Research comparing MZ and DZ twins for the similarity of their tobacco use indicates that there is a genetic component to people's smoking behaviors.
2. Successful AIDS interventions must provide information, instill motivation, and teach behavioral skills.
3. To produce the relation response, people must find a quiet environment in which they can rest in a comfortable position with their eyes closed and use a repetitive mental device.
4. Researchers who study psychoneuroimmunology seek to understand how psychological states have an impact on the immune system.
5. The aspect of Type A personality that puts people at risk for illness is hostility.
6. Job burnout is a state of emotional exhaustion, depersonalization, and reduced sense of personal accomplishment.

CHAPTER 13

Stop and Review (Type and Trait Personality Theories, p. 414)

1. Personality types are defined as all-or-none categories.
2. Neuroticism is defined as a dimension from stable, calm, and contented versus anxious, unstable, and temperamental.
3. To assess the heritability of traits, researchers have conducted studies that compare the trait similarity of monozygotic and dizygotic twins.
4. The consistency paradox refers to finding that people often give consistent personality descriptions for individuals even though the individuals' behavior is not consistent across situations.

Stop and Review (Psychodynamic Theories, p. 420)

1. The individual might engage in oral behaviors such as smoking or overeating; the individual might be overly passive or gullible.
2. The ego is guided by the reality principle to put reasonable choices before the id's demands for pleasure.
3. Leon might be using the defense mechanism of projection—he projects his own motives onto other people.
4. Adler suggested that people are driven to overcome feelings of inferiority.

Stop and Review (Humanistic Theories, p. 422)

1. Self-actualization is a person's constant striving to reach his or her inherent potential.
2. Humanistic theories focus on people's innate qualities, which influence their behaviors.
3. A psychobiography uses psychological theories to give a coherent account of the way in which an individual's life unfolds.

Stop and Review (Social-Learning and Cognitive Theories, p. 427)

1. People who have an external locus of control orientation believe that rewards are largely contingent on environmental factors.
2. Mischel's theory focuses on encodings, expectancies and beliefs, affects, goal and values, and competencies and self-regulatory plans.
3. According to Bandura, the individual's characteristics, the individual's behavior, and the environment all interact to influence and modify the other components.
4. Social intelligence refers to the expertise people bring to their experiences of life tasks.

Stop and Review (Self Theories, p. 431)

1. Possible selves motivate behavior by prompting people to consider what behaviors are consistent with the "self" they wish to achieve or wish to avoid.
2. Self-handicapping applies to circumstances in which people engage in behaviors that allow them to attribute their failures to causes besides lack of ability.
3. People who have interdependent construals of self experience themselves as one element of a larger social structure.

Stop and Review (Comparing Personality Theories, p. 433)

1. Some theories explain individual differences by focusing on each person's genetic endowment, whereas other theories make reference to the life experiences that have shaped individual personalities.
2. Freud's theory stresses the way in which events in early childhood—the past—affect an adult's personality.
3. The relevant dimension of personality theories is consciousness versus unconsciousness.

Stop and Review (Assessing Personality, p. 436)

1. Each of the MMPI's 10 clinical scales is intended to differentiate people who have a specific clinical disorder from those who do not.
2. The NEO-PI measures the five personality traits defined by the five-factor model of personality.
3. Clinicians assess Rorschach responses for location, content, and determinants.

CHAPTER 14

Stop and Review (The Nature of Psychological Disorders, p. 448)

1. The most relevant criteria appear to be "distress or disability" (that is, Jerry's fear causes him personal distress) and "maladaptiveness" (that is, Jerry's fear prevents him from easily pursuing his goals).
2. Classification can provide a common shorthand language, an understanding of causality, and a treatment plan.
3. Behaviors are interpreted in different ways in different cultures—the same behaviors may seem "normal" or "abnormal" in different cultural contexts.

Stop and Review (Anxiety Disorders, p. 453)

1. People who suffer from phobias experience irrational fears in situations that are not objectively dangerous.
2. Obsessions are thoughts, whereas compulsions are acts.
3. Research suggests that the evolutionary history of the human species leaves people "prepared" to experience phobias with respect to certain stimuli.
4. People who are high on anxiety sensitivity are more likely to believe that bodily symptoms will have harmful consequences.

Stop and Review (Mood Disorders, p. 459)

1. Bipolar disorder is characterized by periods of severe depression alternating with manic episodes.
2. The cognitive triad refers to negative views of the person him- or herself, negative views of ongoing experiences, and negative views of the future.
3. Research suggests that women are more likely than men to ruminate on their problems, which has the result of increasing negative feelings.
4. Adolescents are at risk for suicide attempts when they feel depressed, hopeless, or isolated and have negative self-concepts.

Stop and Review (Personality Disorders, p. 462)

1. People with borderline personality disorder have an intense fear of being abandoned.
2. People with borderline personality disorder have experienced substantially more childhood sexual abuse.
3. Antisocial personality disorder is characterized by both impulsive behaviors and a disregard for safety, which creates a risk for suicide.

Stop and Review (Somatoform and Dissociative Disorders, p. 465)

1. Howard's case fits the definition of hyponchondriasis.
2. Dissociative amnesia is an inability to recall important personal experiences, caused by psychological factors in the absence of any organic dysfunction.
3. Research suggests that nearly all the individuals who develop DID have undergone some form of physical or psychological abuse.

Stop and Review (Schizophrenic Disorders, p. 470)

1. Social withdrawal and flattened emotions are negative symptoms of schizophrenia.
2. Delusions of persecution or grandeur would be symptoms of the paranoid type of schizophrenic disorder.
3. Research suggests that patients who return to families with high expressed emotion are more likely to experience relapses.

Stop and Review (Psychological Disorders of Childhood, p. 471)

1. ADHD is characterized by degrees of inattention and hyper-activity-impulsivity that are inconsistent with children's levels of development.
2. Many parents start to have concerns only when children fail to meet developmental norms for social interaction or language use starting in the second year.
3. Researchers have suggested that children with autistic disorder fail to develop a standard theory of mind.

Stop and Review (The Stigma of Mental Illness, p. 472)

1. Negative attitudes about mental illnesses place people apart as unacceptable.
2. When people enter into treatment, they must often publicly acknowledge that they have a mental illness, creating a context for stigma.
3. Research suggests that contact with people who have mental illnesses serves to reduce stigma.

CHAPTER 15

Stop and Review (The Therapeutic Context, p. 481)

1. The goals of the process are to reach a diagnosis, propose a probable etiology, make a prognosis, and carry out a treatment.
2. Psychoanalysts have completed postgraduate training in the Freudian approach to therapy.
3. Research suggests that therapists with greater cultural competence achieve better therapeutic outcomes.
4. Substantial numbers of patients who are released from psychiatric institutions are readmitted after a short amount of time.

Stop and Review (Psychodynamic Therapies, p. 484)

1. Psychodynamic therapy is also known as insight therapy because a central goal is to guide a patient toward insights into the relationships between present symptoms and past conflicts.
2. Transference refers to circumstances in which a patient develops an emotional reaction toward the therapist that often represents an emotional conflict from the patient's life.
3. Klein believed that the death instinct precedes sexual awareness and leads to an innate aggressive impulse.

Stop and Review (Behavior Therapies, p. 490)

1. Treatments using counterconditioning attempt to replace a maladaptive response (such as fear) with a healthy response (such as relaxation).
2. Typically, clinicians use vouchers to provide positive reinforcement for desirable behaviors (such as remaining drug free).
3. In social-learning therapy, clients usually observe models receiving positive reinforcement for desirable forms of responding.
4. In psychoanalysis, the therapist functions as a detective; in behavior therapy, the therapist functions as a trainer.

Stop and Review (Cognitive Therapies, p. 492)

1. The underlying assumption of cognitive therapy is that abnormal behavior patterns and emotional distress arise from problems in what and how people think.

2. RET suggests that irrational beliefs lead to maladaptive emotional responses.
3. A goal of cognitive behavioral therapy is to change people's behaviors—it is important that they believe they have the efficacy to perform adaptive behaviors.

Stop and Review (Humanistic Therapies, p. 494)

1. The goal of the human-potential movement was to enhance individuals' potential toward greater levels of performance and greater richness of experience.
2. A client-centered therapist establishes a setting with unconditional positive regard—nonjudgmental acceptance and respect for the client.
3. In Gestalt therapy, clients imagine that a feeling, person, object, or situation is occupying an empty chair; they talk to the chair's "occupant" to work through issues in their lives.

Stop and Review (Group Therapies, p. 496)

1. Group therapy gives participants an opportunity to understand that the types of problems they have may actually be quite common.
2. The goal of couple therapy is often to help partners clarify and improve the quality of their interactions.
3. Internet self-help groups are particularly valuable for individuals with mobility issues, who might not otherwise have access to these groups.

Stop and Review (Biomedical Therapies, p. 499)

1. Atypical antipsychotic drugs help alleviate the symptoms of schizophrenia without causing severe problems in motor control.
2. SNRIs inhibit the reuptake of both serotonin and norepinephrine.
3. The procedure fundamentally alters personalities: People become less emotional, but they also lose their sense of self.
4. When people undergo the rTMS procedure, repeated pulses of magnetic stimulation are focused on their brains.

Stop and Review (Treatment Evaluation and Prevention Strategies, p. 503)

1. The meta-analyses suggest that many standard treatments for depression (such as cognitive behavioral therapy and drug therapy) provide relief beyond a placebo treatment.
2. Even if treatments bring about relief, they are not particularly valuable if people are often unwilling or unable to complete the course of treatment.
3. The goal of primary prevention is to implement programs that lower the probability that individuals will experience mental illnesses.

CHAPTER 16

Stop and Review (Constructing Social Reality, p. 513)

1. Kelley suggested that people assess distinctiveness, consistency, and consensus when they make attributions.
2. Students are likely to take responsibility for successes and explain away failures—this pattern might prompt them, for example, not to change their study habits when they do poorly on an exam.
3. In most classrooms, teachers have accurate information about their students' potential, which limits the possibility of self-fulfilling prophecies.

Stop and Review (The Power of the Situation, p. 523)

1. The Stanford Prison Experiment demonstrated how quickly people take up the patterns of behaviors that are defined by social roles.
2. Because people want to be liked, accepted, and approved by others, groups are able to have normative influence.
3. Minorities are able to exert informational influence—they can have an impact because of majority group members' desire to correct.
4. When a group's joint decision is more extreme than group members would have made on their own, it suggests that processes of group polarization have been at work.
5. Psychiatrists' predictions vastly underestimated the number of people who would continue to administer shocks up to very high levels.

Stop and Review (Attitudes, Attitude Change, and Action, p. 528)

1. Attitudes include cognitive, affective, and behavioral components.
2. The central route to persuasion is marked by high elaboration—careful thought about the persuasive material.
3. Because dissonance reduction reflects the impulse to be self-consistent, cross-cultural differences in sense of self affect the situations in which people experience dissonance.
4. When people make reductions from large to medium requests, they have done something for you. The reciprocity norm requires that you do something for them—by agreeing to their smaller request.

Stop and Review (Prejudice, p. 532)

1. When distributing resources, people tend to give more resources to members of their own in-groups than to members of the out-group.
2. People often interact with people in ways that do not allow them to behave in ways that disconfirm stereotypes.
3. Research suggests that contact with out-groups members consistently reduces prejudice.

Stop and Review (Social Relationships, p. 535)

1. People tend to like more those individuals who are similar to them.
2. The three dimensions that characterize love are passion, intimacy, and commitment.
3. People with secure attachment styles tend to have the most enduring romantic relationships as adults.

Stop and Review (Agression, Altruism, and Prosocial Behavior, p. 543)

1. Researchers have used twin studies to demonstrate that MZ twins have a higher concordance for forms of antisocial and aggressive behavior than do DZ twins.
2. When people are frustrated in pursuit of their goals, they are more likely to engage in aggression.
3. Reciprocal altruism is the idea that people perform altruistic behaviors because they expect, in return, to be the recipients of such behaviors.
4. When groups of people witness an emergency, members of the group most often assume that someone else has taken the responsibility to provide assistance.

Practice Test Answers

CHAPTER 1	CHAPTER 2	CHAPTER 3	CHAPTER 4
1. b	1. a	1. c	1. b
2. b	2. c	2. b	2. b
3. c	3. b	3. d	3. a
4. a	4. d	4. d	4. b
5. b	5. a	5. c	5. d
6. c	6. b	6. d	6. d
7. d	7. d	7. c	7. b
8. b	8. c	8. b	8. c
9. c	9. b	9. b	9. a
10. c	10. d	10. a	10. c
11. d	11. d	11. c	11. a
12. a	12. c	12. a	12. d
13. d	13. a	13. a	13. c
14. b	14. b	14. b	14. c
15. a	15. c	15. d	15. a

CHAPTER 5

1. a
2. d
3. d
4. d
5. b
6. d
7. b
8. a
9. a
10. b
11. d
12. c
13. c
14. a
15. d

CHAPTER 6

1. b
2. a
3. b
4. d
5. b
6. a
7. c
8. d
9. d
10. c
11. d
12. b
13. c
14. a
15. a

CHAPTER 7

1. b
2. c
3. a
4. a
5. b
6. d
7. b
8. a
9. b
10. d
11. a
12. a
13. b
14. c
15. d

CHAPTER 8

1. c
2. c
3. b
4. a
5. d
6. b
7. c
8. a
9. a
10. a
11. c
12. b
13. d
14. a
15. a

CHAPTER 9

1. d
2. a
3. b
4. d
5. b
6. b
7. c
8. a
9. c
10. b
11. a
12. d
13. c
14. a
15. b

CHAPTER 10

1. c
2. a
3. d
4. b
5. d
6. a
7. d
8. c
9. d
10. d
11. b
12. a
13. c
14. d
15. b

CHAPTER 11

1. c
2. d
3. c
4. d
5. a
6. b
7. b
8. d
9. c
10. b
11. b
12. a
13. c
14. d
15. a

CHAPTER 12

1. a
2. a
3. c
4. c
5. c
6. c
7. d
8. b
9. c
10. a
11. b
12. a
13. d
14. b
15. d

CHAPTER 13

1. b
2. a
3. c
4. c
5. a
6. d
7. c
8. a
9. a
10. c
11. b
12. a
13. d
14. b
15. b

CHAPTER 14

1. d
2. a
3. a
4. d
5. b
6. c
7. d
8. b
9. c
10. b
11. a
12. d
13. d
14. a
15. c

CHAPTER 15

1. a
2. b
3. d
4. c
5. d
6. b
7. c
8. b
9. a
10. c
11. a
12. d
13. a
14. c
15. d

CHAPTER 16

1. a
2. d
3. b
4. d
5. c
6. c
7. a
8. c
9. b
10. a
11. d
12. c
13. a
14. d
15. b

between the two. Because of this complexity, and because the comparison process depends on what one has experienced in the past, this might vary across people. Other perceptual experiences that might differ between people are those that involve evaluation of pleasantness. One person might perceive a shrill, unpleasant shriek, while another experiences a crisp, pleasant high tone. One person might experience pressure, while another might experience an unpleasant level of pain.

7. One possibility is that the tendency in primates to climb and to brachiate through trees required an extremely accurate three-dimensional perceptual system that would allow rapid navigation. Vision seems to serve this function best, although other animals who navigate at night seem to do well by using hearing, rather than vision.

CHAPTER 5

Program Review

1. c, 2. b, 3. d, 4. b, 5. a, 6. b, 7. c, 8. b, 9. b, 10. b, 11. c, 12. a, 13. b, 14. a, 15. d, 16. b, 17. d, 18. b, 19. c, 20. a, 21. a, 22. d, 23. b, 24. c, 25. d, 26. b, 27. a, 28. d, 29. c, 30. d, 31. d

Questions to Consider

1. Filter theory states that there are limits on early stages of perception. Other sensory information is held briefly but not processed. Although attention reduces confusion and sensory overload, it is not an all-or-nothing phenomenon. There is generally some screening of the sensory input for meaningful information and some partial analysis below a level of conscious awareness.

2. In the sense that perception is influenced by norms and expectations, our selective attention can be determined by cultural context. We form concepts based on experience and language. Our perceptual habits are influenced by the environment and by the culture, which communicates what is important to notice and remember. Language helps to categorize elements of experience. But personal motivation and individual characteristics also create enormous variation within cultures.

3. REM sleep is critical, and when one is deprived of it, one generally experiences rebound effects. These can take the form of particularly vivid daydreaming, more rapid onset of the first REM phase when one falls asleep again, and a longer proportion of total sleep time spent in REM sleep.

4. Illness, love, and grief can cause many changes in mental functioning typically associated with altered consciousness. Love and grief particularly can cause people to experience intense or extensive changes in consciousness and behavior.

5. Treatment should take into account social and psychological factors, as well as chemical effects and physiological factors. Drug education programs must prepare students to evaluate the social and psychological components of drug use that lead to dependence and addiction. Some drug education programs aimed at children attempt to establish a certain mindset that counteracts peer and cultural pressures and promotes critical thinking about pro-drug messages.

6. Effects of extensive television viewing include heightened arousal and suggestibility, depression, and lowered motivation, as well as a distorted sense of time, disorientation, impulsivity, and hyperactivity, especially in children. Studies tend to be contradictory. Prolonged inactivity can lead to a kind of stimulus deprivation. Young children do not have the intellectual ability or sufficient experience and information to distinguish fantasy from reality, so they may be confused by the distortions of reality they see on television.

7. People certainly differ in their ability to be hypnotized or the ease with which they can enter meditative states. It may take some practice, but you may well find that the benefits outweigh the investment you have to make up-front to learn to do it. In both cases, exposing oneself to quiet environments, practicing without imposing inappropriate demands on oneself, and following the instructions of an expert should help. You aren't guaranteed success, but it is certainly worth trying.

CHAPTER 6

Program Review

1. b, 2. d, 3. d, 4. a, 5. b, 6. c, 7. c, 8. a, 9. d, 10. c, 11. b, 12. d, 13. c, 14. a, 15. b, 16. d, 17. a, 18. c, 19. b, 20. d

Questions to Consider

1. Compulsive gambling could be considered a disease and a learned behavior. There is an organization called Gamblers Anonymous that is based on the same principles as Alcoholics Anonymous. However, analyzing compulsive gambling in terms of antecedents and consequences might suggest ways to eliminate cues that lead to gambling, thereby leading to extinction. The best policy might be to avoid all settings where gambling takes place. Because any winning would serve to reinforce gambling, the best goal for a behavior change program is no gambling at all. Because it is reinforced intermittently (on a variable ratio schedule), it may be very resistant to extinction.

2. You could provide positive reinforcement for keeping the school clean. For example, students could receive a sticker for every 50 pieces of litter they pick up. They could also be punished (e.g., with extra homework or reduced break periods) if they are caught littering. You might also try integrating other principles, like modeling, shaping, and ideal reinforcement schedules, into your program to increase the likelihood that students' behavior will conform to your goals.

3. Intention is not always a prerequisite for learning. We learn many behaviors without setting out to do so. However, if intention can help us focus attention, learning is enhanced. One exciting aspect of learning principles is that they do not require consent or knowledge of the learner in order for them to work. They can work on pigeons, people with mental retardation, and people who are resistant to change just as well as they can work on intelligent human adults. They are truly a universal phenomenon.

4. Parents generally don't reward or punish their children's grammar. Instead, they model good grammar for their children and do what they can to understand whatever utterances their children produce. So the learning of grammar does not depend on operant principles. Parents do, however, reward and punish other linguistic features, such as content (e.g., "That's right; that IS a doggy") and politeness (e.g., "Did you say 'thank you?' You're such a good girl").

CHAPTER 7

Program Review

1. d, 2. c, 3. b, 4. b, 5. d, 6. a, 7. b, 8. a, 9. b, 10. b, 11. c, 12. d, 13. d, 14. a, 15. b, 16. d, 17. a, 18. a, 19. b, 20. d

Questions to Consider

1. Helpful memory strategies include paying attention, minimizing distractions and interference, and encoding information in

more than one way, such as reading out loud, outlining important points, or chunking information in some personally meaningful way. It is also helpful to add meaning by linking new facts and ideas to familiar information, to use visual imagery, to review material distributed in study sessions, to study before going to sleep, and to overlearn material.

2. The schema we used as children are very different from the ones we have developed as adults. And because young children are lacking in language, which normally helps us to label and organize memories, we may find that memories from our preverbal days are sparse or nonexistent. There is also evidence that early memories may be lost due to physiological maturation. Nevertheless, many memories, particularly from later childhood, are recoverable through good cues, and most people find that cues, such as family stories or photographs, can help in reconstructing memories.

3. The ABC song offers many devices to aid retention. The letters are chunked or grouped in units that conform to the capacity of short-term memory. The letters at the end of each phrase rhyme, which is a mnemonic device. The song encodes the information in sounds, as well as in movements. And the fun of it also motivates multiple rehearsals and performances.

4. Most of us are justifiably impressed with the capacity of our long-term memory. Society rewards people for good memories, starting in early childhood. Playing trivia games can set off a host of associations to events and ideas that we often don't even know we have in memory.

5. There is substantial controversy over what "leading" questions do to memories. The way a person perceives and recalls an event depends on perceptual and cognitive biases that even the eyewitness may not be aware of. Jury members are subject to their own biases when they hear and judge testimony. Jury members need to be especially alert to leading questions that might introduce details or prompt a witness to report an event in a particular way. The more informed a jury member is about how memory works, the better he or she may be able to weigh the value of testimony.

6. Not only does a good memory help in preparing for exams, but so do good metamemory skills. If you know how you learn and know what is most likely to work in your attempts to recall information, you can learn more effectively. Also, if you are good at gauging how well you have learned something so that you don't stop studying too early due to overconfidence, you vastly increase your odds of success on the exam.

CHAPTER 8

Program Review

1. d, 2. c, 3. b, 4. a, 5. b, 6. c, 7. a, 8. c, 9. a, 10. c, 11. b, 12. d, 13. b, 14. a, 15. c, 16. d, 17. b, 18. d, 19. b, 20. c, 21. a, 22. c, 23. c, 24. d, 25. c, 26. b, 27. a, 28. a, 29. a, 30. d, 31. b, 32. a

Questions to Consider

1. To interpret the poem, you need to consider language rules and underlying structure—word order, forms, endings, and sounds and language patterns. Although there are many strange and made-up words, some clearly echo familiar words—so that there are some built-in associations that imply meaning.

2. Scripts might include types of activities and dress, level of education, achievement, income, social status, family patterns, interests, vacation ideas, restaurant preferences, and health status.

3. Pitfalls of problem solving include the inability to define the problem, the tendency to be illogical in situations in which emo-

tions are involved, and the reluctance to consider opposing points of view. People also depend on certain familiar approaches and strategies and often do not recognize when these are no longer useful. Cognitive bias and mental shortcuts also cause people to draw false conclusions or make bad decisions.

4. Although you can certainly perceive more subtleties than your native language has words for, the way in which you think of complex situations, like campaign issues, can be influenced by the details of a situation that are made salient to you. Perhaps the best way to think about this seeming contradiction is to view the two phenomena as occurring at different cognitive levels. Concepts and percepts are more sophisticated than the language used to describe them. More complex cognitive processes involving elaborate knowledge structures can be vulnerable to framing.

5. According to the representativeness heuristic, we are prone to believe that an event is likely if it fits our stereotype of what usually happens. This makes us particularly likely to notice events that fit our stereotype, and it may lead us to overestimate how commonly stereotype-consistent instances are. Similarly, the availability heuristic can perpetuate stereotypes through the cues we provide ourselves with when conjuring up examples of or "typical profiles" of the groups with whom we hold the stereotypes.

CHAPTER 9

Program Review

1. b, 2. d, 3. a, 4. c, 5. d, 6. c, 7. b, 8. d, 9. c, 10. b, 11. c, 12. c, 13. a, 14. b, 15. a, 16. d, 17. a, 18. a, 19. c, 20. c

Questions to Consider

1. No. Environment still has an important influence on the expression of any trait or ability. This is obvious from studies of development in enriched and impoverished environments. Impoverished environments lower a person's test performance. Both heredity and environment play a role.

2. Some might say that people already tend to sort and segregate each other according to intelligence, even if judgments are based on informal, personal assessments. If IQs become public knowledge, this might have the largest effect on those at the top and bottom of the scale, leading to institutionalized forms of discrimination.

3. Both have tremendous value, and often in the same arenas of life (school, job, social success). Luckily, scoring high on one doesn't mean you're lacking in the other!

4. Intelligence tests and psychological assessments attempt to avoid personal bias and to obtain an objective measure of a person's abilities. However, the tests can be used as a shortcut in place of a more thorough and personalized evaluation. Tests are often misunderstood and misapplied. People have an inappropriate reverence for scores. Few people question the authority of a computer printout. Objections to the tests include claims that they are not objective and that they do not measure what they are intended to measure. People often use tests to focus on what is wrong with the individual instead of considering what is wrong with the system. Test scores have been used to argue for the heritability of intelligence, which has important public policy implications for immigration, education, employment, and affirmative action.

5. It is rare for someone to be universally more capable or more intelligent than the average person. A brilliant mathematician may be kinesthetically awkward, and a person with excellent spatial skills may be average or below average on verbal meas-

ures of intelligence. Looking around at our greatest models of mathematical intelligence, body skills, and social intelligence leads to outstanding models for those specific kinds of intelligence that may show no particular excellence on any of the other scales.

CHAPTER 10

Program Review

Program 5

1. c, 2. d, 3. c, 4. b, 5. a, 6. d, 7. c, 8. d, 9. a, 10. a, 11. b, 12. d

Program 6

13. d, 14. a, 15. b, 16. c, 17. a, 18. a, 19. a, 20. d, 21. a, 22. b, 23. d

Program 18

24. b, 25. a, 26. d, 27. b, 28. b, 29. d, 30. a, 31. a, 32. c, 33. b, 34. d, 35. a

Questions to Consider

1. Many very clever techniques for measuring topics, such as memory, perception, and preference, have been developed to study infants, who can have sophisticated abilities but who cannot respond to complex language or answer questions verbally. Some of these techniques can be adapted for use with other nonverbal animals, so long as their behavioral capabilities (such as grasping and looking) are well enough developed.

2. As people age, their interests and activities may need to be modified to fit their capabilities. Their interests may lead them to indoor rather than outdoor activities, and their participation in physical activity may be redirected to watching children play outside. The good news is that, regardless of one's physical limitations, there are plenty of options for occupying one's time and occupying one's mind.

3. Whether gorillas or chimps are truly capable of language is still debated. It really depends on your definition of language. Your textbook definition may include such characteristics as specialization, arbitrariness, displacement, productivity and novelty, and iteration and recursion. Although animals do use symbols, no animal other than humans consistently and naturally organizes symbols according to specific rules. Human language seems to be unique, and humans appear to be uniquely "programmed" to acquire it. Recent research has suggested that gorillas and chimps have higher-level communicative ability, and mothers trained in signs and symbols can transfer their learning to their offspring. The debate goes on.

CHAPTER 11

Program Review

Program 12

1. d, 2. b, 3. b, 4. c, 5. a, 6. c, 7. c, 8. a, 9. b, 10. a, 11. c, 12. d, 13. c, 14. d, 15. b, 16. c

Program 17

17. d, 18. c, 19. a, 20. c, 21. a, 22. a, 23. c, 24. a, 25. a, 26. c, 27. b, 28. c, 29. d, 30. c

Questions to Consider

1. An individual's sexual script is based on a unique combination of personal, social, and cultural beliefs and attitudes. Scripts are influenced by family role models, the media, and feedback from social experiences. Boys and girls are typically treated differently during development. Cultural stereotypes tend to reinforce some personal choices and not others. Sexual scripts are often not overtly expressed and may be a source of friction and disappointment in a relationship. If couples can talk about mismatched role expectations and values, they may be able to negotiate a shared script. The threat of AIDS and other sexually transmitted diseases may change the norms governing sexual activity and thereby rewrite the social scripts that guide sexual behavior. Expect to see changes in what characterizes an acceptable mate, dating patterns, and other relationship issues.

2. Armed with this knowledge, you might couple a diet plan with stress management skills, such as meditation, time management courses, exercise, participation in a support group, and/or individual psychotherapy. You might also frame the diet plan so that the dieter doesn't feel deprived or self-restrained and is therefore less tempted by opportunities to binge.

3. People are typically motivated to approach activities or goals that increase pleasure and to avoid those that cause pain. Although food is generally thought of as something pleasurable, even as a reward or incentive, people with certain eating disorders see food as something to avoid. They modify or inhibit their eating behavior in an attempt to achieve an idealized body shape.

4. Male traits are often perceived as more desirable by both men and women. Being assertive, achieving, and independent seems related to a better self-concept for both men and women. In general, the labels used to describe male traits are more positive. However, in judging the relative merits of masculine and feminine traits for adjustment, it is important to specify exactly what that means. For example, one study suggests that feminine traits contribute to happier marriages.

CHAPTER 12

Program Review

1. c, 2. b, 3. d, 4. b, 5. d, 6. c, 7. a, 8. b, 9. c, 10. d, 11. b, 12. d, 13. a, 14. c, 15. d, 16. c, 17. a, 18. d, 19. b, 20. c

Questions to Consider

1. Friends can help reduce stress in several ways. They can offer practical help. For example, when there is illness or a crisis in a family, friends can relieve temporary concerns about money, child care, food, or transportation needs. They can also offer emotional support, being there to listen and empathize with you about what you are going through and reassuring you that you are not going crazy even when you feel most vulnerable and confused. Friends may also offer advice in an unfamiliar situation, helping you think through decisions. Social support makes people less vulnerable to stress-related problems. Social networks counteract a sense of isolation by providing a sense of belonging. In support groups, individuals help each other by providing a social reference group. They share advice, feelings, and information specific to the situation.

2. Victims of a curse may feel such intense or prolonged fear that it wears down the body's ability to cope. One theory suggests that the body's attempt to counteract an extreme emotional reaction may go too far, slowing down important systems and processes to the point of death.

3. Most people use defense mechanisms at times. Some defenses help us gain time to adjust to a trauma or other type of problem. Rationalization may be a stress-reducing strategy in the face of frustration or failure. Any defense mechanism can be

part of a coping approach, but it may prevent us from confronting and solving our real problems if it becomes habitual.

4. Self-defeating thoughts undermine a person's sense of self-esteem, optimism, efficacy, and control—all necessary for adequate coping.

5. Perfectionists unnecessarily stress themselves by setting impossible goals and standards. They may compare themselves with inappropriate models of achievement, never being satisfied with their own accomplishments. They may feel they have inadequate resources to measure up to their unreasonably high standards. These attitudes can create stress and can undermine their ability to perform.

6. Although the traditional gender roles for running a household have changed over the past several years, men still typically find themselves in more stressful, powerful job situations. Such work conditions are associated with poor lifestyle habits, such as caffeine, nicotine, and alcohol abuse, and with insufficient sleep and lack of exercise. Add to that a cultural tendency to foster aggression in men, and we see that such a combination puts men at risk for cardiovascular disease. Women are also at risk. In the workplace, they may find themselves in situations where they have less control than men do, making them also prone to stress-related health problems, including cardiovascular disease. And as gender roles continue to shift, women become more and more vulnerable to the traditional "male" stress-related risks.

7. Meditation and yoga allow the body to physically relax, making stress responses like rapid heart rate and muscle tensing less likely. Because these practices lower stress and because stress is associated with health outcomes, meditation and yoga improve health and create the experience of greater peace.

CHAPTER 13

Program Review

1. c. 2. b. 3. a. 4. b. 5. a. 6. d. 7. d. 8. b. 9. c. 10. b. 11. a. 12. c. 13. d. 14. a. 15. b. 16. b. 17. a. 18. a. 19. c. 20. d

Questions to Consider

1. To the extent that standardized tests are used to categorize or place people, they pose some risk for inaccuracy and bias. What is normal or average in the larger population may differ from subculture to subculture. If members of a given subculture are compared to the larger population, they may be judged unfavorably, and this may lead to concrete consequences, such as a greater likelihood of being labeled as abnormal, or fewer job or social opportunities.

2. Shy people tend to be pessimistic. They have more social anxieties than those who are not shy. Shy people also tend to anticipate rejection and social failure and to interpret social encounters negatively, thus confirming their sense of inadequacy and helplessness.

3. The id is the driving energy of our passion, curiosity, and excitement. According to Freud, it is the life force that operates on the pleasure principle. On the positive side, it is the drive for self-preservation. It is also the place where sexual urges arise, thus ensuring the survival of the species. The fantasies of the id are the basis for imagination and creative endeavors. The id also contains aggressive and destructive drives that can be turned against the self or against society.

4. Your answer is probably yes, different experiences of success or failure can change your sense of efficacy and your level of self-esteem. But success and failure are relative. If a task is too

easy, it doesn't help a person with low self-esteem. Also, research has suggested that self-esteem is often affected by a social referent. An extremely attractive person sitting next to you before a job interview might make you feel dissatisfied with yourself, but a disheveled or unattractive person might make you feel better about yourself.

5. Although the Internet exposes us to lots of different kinds of people from all around the world, many of the social skills used with the Internet are specific to that particular medium. For people who substitute Internet-based interaction with face-to-face interaction, other critical social skills may be underdeveloped or lost over time. They may feel isolated, awkward in social situations, and shy. This is becoming particularly important as people find that identities are easy to slip into and out of in an Internet-based culture.

CHAPTER 14

Program Review

1. d, 2. b, 3. b, 4. b, 5. d, 6. a, 7. b, 8. c, 9. d, 10. b, 11. d, 12. b, 13. c, 14. a, 15. b, 16. a, 17. d, 18. b, 19. d, 20. a

Questions to Consider

1. Courts differ on how they deal with the insanity defense. In order for a person to be excused from legal responsibility for criminal actions, the defense must demonstrate severely impaired judgment and lack of self-control. A person is not considered legally responsible if he or she is unable to distinguish right from wrong. The definition may vary from country to country, from state to state, even from court to court. It is a highly controversial issue.

2. The *Diagnostic and Statistical Manual* has been criticized for inflating disorders, for basing some criteria on myth instead of empirical evidence, and for stigmatizing people. It is also, clearly, a relative assessment guide subject to cultural forces. For example, homosexuality was once characterized as a disorder. Today, the self-defeating personality has been proposed as a disorder to be included. Women's groups and others are very concerned that such a label will lead to a blaming of the victim.

3. Statistically, homosexuality is relatively less common. However, cultural standards are relative. Psychological assessments show no differences in personality or adjustment between heterosexuals and homosexuals. Today, the DSM-IV does not list homosexuality as a disorder. It is considered a problem only if it causes guilt or self-hate.

4. Women may be more willing to talk about distress and emotional problems. They are more often denied opportunities for independence and achievement and may feel angry, hopeless, or helpless, justifiably. There is a male bias toward traditional concepts of mental health.

5. Many psychological problems are just extreme instances of behavior that most of us exhibit at one time or another. If you are extremely worried about a certain behavior, if the behavior is disruptive to relationships, or if it has become a persistent problem, you might consider getting a professional evaluation.

CHAPTER 15

Program Review

1. c, 2. a, 3. d, 4. b, 5. a, 6. b, 7. d, 8. c, 9. c, 10. d, 11. a, 12. c, 13. b, 14. b, 15. b, 16. d, 17. c, 18. a, 19. c, 20. a

Questions to Consider

1. It is difficult to determine the success of a particular therapy because faith in the effectiveness of any treatment may be enough to bring about changes in a patient's feelings or behavior. Also, some problems resolve themselves over time without professional intervention.

2. A given psychological problem is often associated with clear abnormalities in the functioning of the brain. We know, for example, that depression is associated with the functioning of the neurotransmitter serotonin. We also know that serotonin can be affected in multiple ways, including through either direct manipulation of serotonin re-uptake in the brain, as is accomplished through some antidepressants, or indirectly, through one's psychological experience. Psychotherapy is intended to provide people with the skills and experience that will allow changes in one's behavior, environment, experience, and relationships. Although it is not intended as the ultimate goal, a change in brain functioning co-occurs with these other changes. One's movement toward greater happiness and self-efficacy is reflected in one's brain.

3. Finding the right match between a problem and an approach to therapy starts with how you define the problem and your attitude or beliefs about the kind of help you need. A person might seek assistance in making the decision from a physician or person in the community who is familiar with available resources and services.

4. Unit 22 describes therapies that focus on illness and problem solving, as well as on those designed to address life management issues, self-esteem, relationships, and potential. Most people, at some time, could benefit from professional intervention.

5. In American culture, there is typically a stigma associated with seeking help of any kind. Our culture emphasizes individuality, self-sufficiency, and strength, especially for men. That makes it harder to admit weakness or the need for support.

6. Although drug therapies can be enormously helpful in correcting abnormal neurochemistry, they cannot fix a marriage or magically raise someone's self-esteem. People who expect too much from drug therapies may fail to do the additional work necessary to make headway on their problems. In addition, people may come to be dependent on or addicted to their prescription drugs, creating an additional problem that they'll need to address.

7. Although it is confrontational and can be aversive, exposure therapy is also quite an effective treatment strategy. If you are committed to facing and overcoming a phobia and you trust your therapist, you might consider this very efficient therapeutic strategy.

CHAPTER 16

Program Review

1. a, 2. c, 3. d, 4. a, 5. b, 6. a, 7. c, 8. d, 9. a, 10. b, 11. b, 12. c, 13. d, 14. a, 15. a, 16. c, 17. b, 18. c, 19. a, 20. d, 21. d, 22. a

Questions to Consider

1. The participants in Milgram's research could avoid blaming themselves if they reasoned that the situation was influencing their behavior. They could rationalize that they were only following orders and did not have to accept responsibility for their behavior. Therefore, they could avoid guilt, much as the Nazis did when they claimed they were only following orders.

2. People who have only known oppressive conditions like this may be susceptible to other psychological phenomena, such as pressures toward conformity or toward following new charismatic leaders. They may also lack the sophistication in thinking about controversial issues that have been developed by others who have spent a lifetime debating all sides of them.

3. Roles involve expectations about behavior. Roles and social obligations are sometimes perceived as social traps, especially when behavior is dictated by social expectations and norms rather than by personal feelings and individual tastes. You may conform only to win approval or to avoid social rejection. For example, being respected in the community might require church attendance, even if you are not a believer. When social expectations conflict with feelings, alienation or resentment may result. When behavior coincides with role expectations, it reinforces a sense of true identity.

4. Nationalism can be a source of pride and cohesiveness for a population. However, this is all too often gained at the expense of making certain classes of people into internal or external enemies. These out-groups are used to divert attention from national problems and often become a target for anger. Nationalism can encourage "us versus them" thinking and escalate conflicts. An "us versus them" mentality is simple to create. It depends only on drawing some distinction—relevant or arbitrary—between groups of people. Such opportunities for perceiving differences and exaggerating them are bigger in times of war or cold war, and since people at war tend not to socialize with each other, negative stereotypes and negative interactions aren't easily overridden by positive exchanges. As borders between cultures and economies become blurred, globalization might counteract some of these forces.

5. People who are made aware of their identities and responsibilities are more likely to follow cultural norms. The de-individuation and anonymity of big cities foster irresponsible and aggressive behavior. In addition, in accordance with the principle of diffusion of responsibility, the large number of people who can intervene to help or to correct a situation tends to lower the likelihood that anyone will intervene.

Glossary

abnormal psychology The area of psychological investigation concerned with understanding the nature of individual pathologies of mind, mood, and behavior.

absolute threshold The minimum amount of physical energy needed to produce a reliable sensory experience; operationally defined as the stimulus level at which a sensory signal is detected half the time.

accommodation The process by which the ciliary muscles change the thickness of the lens of the eye to permit variable focusing on near and distant objects.

accommodation According to Piaget, the process of restructuring or modifying cognitive structures so that new information can fit into them more easily; this process works in tandem with assimilation.

acquisition The stage in a classical conditioning experiment during which the conditioned response is first elicited by the conditioned stimulus.

action potential The nerve impulse activated in a neuron that travels down the axon and causes neurotransmitters to be released into a synapse.

acute stress A transient state of arousal with typically clear onset and offset patterns.

addiction A condition in which the body requires a drug in order to function without physical and psychological reactions to its absence; often the outcome of tolerance and dependence.

aggression Behaviors that cause psychological or physical harm to another individual.

agoraphobia An extreme fear of being in public places or open spaces from which escape may be difficult or embarrassing.

AIDS Acronym for acquired immune deficiency syndrome, a syndrome caused by a virus that damages the immune system and weakens the body's ability to fight infection.

algorithm A step-by-step procedure that always provides the right answer for a particular type of problem.

all-or-none law The rule that the size of the action potential is unaffected by increases in the intensity of stimulation beyond the threshold level.

altruism Prosocial behaviors a person carries out without considering his or her own safety or interests.

amacrine cell One of the cells that integrate information across the retina; rather than sending signals toward the brain, amacrine cells link bipolar cells to other bipolar cells and ganglion cells to other ganglion cells.

ambiguity Property of perceptual object that may have more than one interpretation.

amnesia A failure of memory caused by physical injury, disease, drug use, or psychological trauma.

amygdala The part of the limbic system that controls emotion, aggression, and the formation of emotional memory.

analytic psychology A branch of psychology that views the person as a constellation of compensatory internal forces in a dynamic balance.

anchoring heuristic An insufficient adjustment up or down from an original starting value when judging the probable value of some event or outcome.

anorexia nervosa An eating disorder in which an individual weighs less than 85 percent of her or his expected weight but still expresses intense fear of becoming fat.

anterograde amnesia An inability to form explicit memories for events that occur after the time of physical damage to the brain.

anticipatory coping Efforts made in advance of a potentially stressful event to overcome, reduce, or tolerate the imbalance between perceived demands and available resources.

antisocial personality disorder A disorder characterized by stable patterns of irresponsible or unlawful behavior that violates social norms.

anxiety An intense emotional response caused by the preconscious recognition that a repressed conflict is about to emerge into consciousness.

anxiety disorder Mental disorder marked by psychological arousal, feeling of tension, and intense apprehension without apparent reason.

archetype A universal, inherited, primitive, and symbolic representation of a particular experience or object.

assimilation According to Piaget, the process whereby new cognitive elements are fitted in with old elements or modified to fit more easily; this process works in tandem with accommodation.

association cortex The parts of the cerebral cortex in which many high-level brain processes occur.

attachment Emotional relationship between a child and the regular caregiver.

attention A state of focused awareness on a subset of the available perceptual information.

attention-deficit hyperactivity disorder (ADHD) A disorder of childhood characterized by inattention and hyperactivity-impulsivity.

attitude The learned, relatively stable tendency to respond to people, concepts, and events in an evaluative way.

attribution Judgment about the causes of outcomes.

attribution theory A social-cognitive approach to describe the ways the social perceiver uses information to generate causal explanations.

audience design The process of shaping a message depending on the audience for which it is intended.

auditory cortex The area of the temporal lobes that receives and processes auditory information.

auditory nerve The nerve that carries impulses from the cochlea to the cochlear nucleus of the brain.

autistic disorder A developmental disorder characterized by severe disruption of children's ability to form social bonds and use language.

automatic process Process that does not require attention; it can often be performed along with other tasks without interference.

autonomic nervous system (ANS) The subdivision of the peripheral nervous system that controls the body's involuntary motor responses by connecting the sensory receptors to the central nervous system (CNS) and the CNS to the smooth muscle, cardiac muscle, and glands.

availability heuristic A judgment based on the information readily available in memory.

aversion therapy A type of behavioral therapy used to treat individuals attracted to harmful stimuli; an attractive stimulus is paired with a noxious stimulus in order to elicit a negative reaction to the target stimulus.

avoidance conditioning A form of learning in which animals acquire responses that allow them to avoid aversive stimuli before they begin.

axon The extended fiber of a neuron through which nerve impulses travel from the soma to the terminal buttons.

basic level The level of categorization that can be retrieved from memory most quickly and used most efficiently.

basilar membrane A membrane in the cochlea that, when set into motion, stimulates hair cells that produce the neural effects of auditory stimulation.

behavior The actions by which an organism adjusts to its environment.

behavior analysis The area of psychology that focuses on the environmental determinants of learning and behavior.

behavior modification The systematic use of principles of learning to increase the frequency of desired behaviors and/or decrease the frequency of problem behaviors.

behavior therapy See behavior modification.

behavioral data Observational reports about the behavior of organisms and the conditions under which the behavior occurs or changes.

behavioral measure Overt actions or reaction that is observed and recorded, exclusive of self-reported behavior.

behavioral neuroscience A multidisciplinary field that attempts to understand the brain processes that underlie behavior.

behavioral rehearsal Procedures used to establish and strengthen basic skills; as used in social-skills training programs, requires the client to rehearse a desirable behavior sequence mentally.

behaviorism A scientific approach that limits the study of psychology to measurable or observable behavior.

behaviorist perspective The psychological perspective primarily concerned with observable behavior that can be objectively recorded and with the relationships of observable behavior to environmental stimuli.

belief-bias effect A situation that occurs when a person's prior knowledge, attitudes, or values distort the reasoning process by influencing the person to accept invalid arguments.

between-subjects design A research design in which different groups of participants are randomly assigned to experimental conditions or to control conditions.

binge eating disorder An eating disorder characterized by out-of-control binge eating without subsequent purges.

binocular depth cue Depth cue that uses information from both eyes.

biofeedback A self-regulatory technique by which an individual acquires voluntary control over nonconscious biological processes.

biological constraint on learning Any limitation on an organism's capacity to learn that is caused by the inherited sensory, response, or cognitive capabilities of members of a given species.

biological perspective The approach to identifying causes of behavior that focuses on the functioning of the genes, the brain, the nervous system, and the endocrine system.

biomedical therapy Treatment for a psychological disorder that alters brain functioning with chemical or physical interventions such as drug therapy, surgery, or electroconvulsive therapy.

biopsychosocial model A model of health and illness that suggests links among the nervous system, the immune system, behavioral styles, cognitive processing, and environmental domains of health.

bipolar cell Nerve cell in the visual system that combines impulses from many receptors and transmits the results to ganglion cells.

bipolar disorder A mood disorder characterized by alternating periods of depression and mania.

blind spot The region of the retina where the optic nerve leaves the back of the eye; no receptors cells are present in this region.

borderline personality disorder A disorder defined by instability and intensity in personal relationships as well as turbulent emotions and impulsive behaviors.

bottom-up processing Perceptual analyses based on the sensory data available in the environment; results of analysis are passed upward toward more abstract representations.

brain stem The brain structure that regulates the body's basic life processes.

brightness The dimension of color space that captures the intensity of light.

Broca's area The region of the brain that translates thoughts into speech or signs.

bulimia nervosa An eating disorder characterized by binge eating followed by measures to purge the body of excess calories.

bystander intervention Willingness to assist a person in need of help.

Cannon–Bard theory of emotion A theory stating that an emotional stimulus produces two co-occurring reactions—arousal and experience of emotion—that do not cause each other.

case study Intensive observation of a particular individual or small group of individuals.

catharsis The process of expressing strongly felt but usually repressed emotions.

central nervous system (CNS) The part of the nervous system consisting of the brain and spinal cord.

centration Preoperational children's tendency to focus their attention on only one aspect of a situation and disregard other relevant aspects.

cerebellum The region of the brain attached to the brain stem that controls motor coordination, posture, and balance as well as the ability to learn control of body movements.

cerebral cortex The outer surface of the cerebrum.

cerebral hemispheres The two halves of the cerebrum, connected by the corpus callosum.

cerebrum The region of the brain that regulates higher cognitive and emotional functions.

child-directed speech A form of speech addressed to children that includes slower speed, distinctive intonation, and structural simplifications.

chronic stress A continuous state of arousal in which an individual perceives demands as greater than the inner and outer resources available for dealing with them.

chronological age The number of months or years since an individual's birth.

chunking The process of taking single items of information and recoding them on the basis of similarity or some other organizing principle.

circadian rhythm A consistent pattern of cyclical body activities, usually lasting 24 to 25 hours and determined by an internal biological clock.

classical conditioning A type of learning in which a behavior (conditioned response) comes to be elicited by a stimulus (conditioned stimulus) that has acquired its power through an association with a biologically significant stimulus (unconditioned stimulus).

client The term used by clinicians who think of psychological disorders as problems in living, and not as mental illnesses, to describe those being treated.

client-centered therapy A humanistic approach to treatment that emphasizes the healthy psychological growth of the individual based on the assumption that all people share the basic tendency of human nature toward self-actualization.

clinical psychologist An individual who has earned a doctorate in psychology and whose training is in the assessment and treatment of psychological problems.

clinical social worker A mental health professional whose specialized training prepares him or her to consider the social context of people's problems.

cochlea The primary organ of hearing; a fluid-filled coiled tube located in the inner ear.

cognition Processes of knowing, including attending, remembering, and reasoning; also the content of the processes, such as concepts and memories.

cognitive appraisal theory of emotion A theory stating that the experience of emotion is the joint effect of physiological arousal and cognitive appraisal, which serves to determine how an ambiguous inner state of arousal will be labeled.

cognitive behavioral therapy A therapeutic approach that combines the cognitive emphasis on thoughts and attitudes with the behavioral emphasis on changing performance.

cognitive development The development of processes of knowing, including imagining, perceiving, reasoning, and problem solving.

cognitive dissonance The theory that the tension-producing effects of incongruous cognitions motivate individuals to reduce such tension.

cognitive map A mental representation of physical space.

cognitive neuroscience A multidisciplinary field that attempts to understand the brain processes that underlie higher cognitive functions in humans.

cognitive perspective The perspective on psychology that stresses human thought and the processes of knowing, such as attending, thinking, remembering, expecting, solving problems, fantasizing, and consciousness.

cognitive process One of the higher mental processes, such as perception, memory, language, problem solving, and abstract thinking.

cognitive psychology The study of higher mental processes such as attention, language use, memory, perception, problem solving, and thinking.

cognitive science The interdisciplinary field of study of the approach systems and processes that manipulate information.

cognitive therapy A type of psychotherapeutic treatment that attempts to change feelings and behaviors by changing the way a client thinks about or perceives significant life experiences.

collective unconscious The part of an individual's unconscious that is inherited, evolutionarily developed, and common to all members of the species.

comorbidity The experience of more than one disorder at the same time.

comparative cognition The study of the development of cognitive abilities across species and the continuity of abilities from nonhuman to human animals.

complementary colors Colors opposite each other on the color circle; when additively mixed, they create the sensation of white light.

compliance A change in behavior consistent with a communication source's direct requests.

computerized axial tomography (CT or CAT) A technique that uses narrow beams of X-rays passed through the brain at several angles to assemble complete brain images.

concept Mental representation of a kind or category of items and ideas.

conditioned reinforcer In classical conditioning, a formerly neutral stimulus that has become a reinforcer.

conditioned response (CR) In classical conditioning, a response elicited by some previously neutral stimulus that occurs as a result of pairing the neutral stimulus with an unconditioned stimulus.

conditioned stimulus (CS) In classical conditioning, a previously neutral stimulus that comes to elicit a conditioned response.

cone One of the photoreceptors concentrated in the center of the retina that are responsible for visual experience under normal viewing conditions for all experiences of color.

conformity The tendency for people to adopt the behaviors, attitudes, and values of other members of a reference group.

confounding variable A stimulus other than the variable an experimenter explicitly introduces into a research setting that affects a participant's behavior.

consciousness A state of awareness of internal events and the external environment.

conservation According to Piaget, the understanding that physical properties do not change when nothing is added or taken away, even though appearances may change.

consistency paradox The observation that personality ratings across time and among different observers are consistent while behavior ratings across situations are not consistent.

construct validity The degree to which a test adequately measures an underlying construct.

contact comfort Comfort derived from an infant's physical contact with the mother or caregiver.

contact hypothesis The prediction that contact between groups will reduce prejudice only if the contact includes features such as cooperation toward shared goals.

content validity The extent to which a test adequately measures the full range of the domain of interest.

contextual distinctiveness The assumption that the serial position effect can be altered by the context and the distinctiveness of the experience being recalled.

contingency management A general treatment strategy involving changing behavior by modifying its consequences.

control group A group in an experiment that is not exposed to a treatment or does not experience a manipulation of the independent variable.

control procedure Consistent procedure for giving instructions, scoring responses, and holding all other variables constant except those being systematically varied.

controlled process Process that requires attention; it is often difficult to carry out more than one controlled process at a time.

convergence The degree to which the eyes turn inward to fixate on an object.

convergent thinking An aspect of creativity characterized by the ability to gather together different sources of information to solve a problem.

conversion disorder A disorder in which psychological conflict or stress brings about loss of motor or sensory function.

coping The process of dealing with internal or external demands that are perceived to be threatening or overwhelming.

corpus callosum The mass of nerve fibers connecting the two hemispheres of the cerebrum.

correlation coefficient (r) A statistic that indicates the degree of relationship between two variables.

correlational method Research methodology that determines to what extent two variables, traits, or attributes are related.

counseling psychologist Psychologist who specializes in providing guidance in areas such as vocational selections, school problems, drug abuse, and marital conflict.

counterconditioning A technique used in therapy to substitute a new response for a maladaptive one by means of conditioning procedures.

countertransference Circumstances in which a psychoanalyst develops personal feelings about a client because of perceived similarity of the client to significant people in the therapist's life.

covariation model A theory that suggests that people attribute a behavior to a causal factor if that factor was present whenever the behavior occurred but was absent whenever it didn't occur.

creativity The ability to generate ideas or products that are both novel and appropriate to the circumstances.

criterion validity The degree to which test scores indicate a result on a specific measure that is consistent with some other criterion of the characteristic being assessed; also known as predictive validity.

cross-sectional design A research method in which groups of participants of different chronological ages are observed and compared at a given time.

crystallized intelligence The facet of intelligence involving the knowledge a person has already acquired and the ability to access that knowledge; measures by vocabulary, arithmetic, and general information tests.

cutaneous senses The skin senses that register sensations or pressure, warmth, and cold.

dark adaptation The gradual improvement of the eyes' sensitivity after a shift in illumination from light to near darkness.

date rape Unwanted sexual violation by a social acquaintance in the context of a consensual dating situation.

debriefing A procedure conducted at the end of an experiment in which the researcher provides the participant with as much information about the study as possible and makes sure that no participant leaves feeling confused, upset, or embarrassed.

decision making The process of choosing between alternatives; selecting or rejecting available options.

declarative memory Memory for information such as facts and events.

deductive reasoning A form of thinking in which one draws a conclusion that is intended to follow logically from two or more statements or premises.

deinstitutionalization The movement to treat people with psychological disorders in the community rather than in psychiatric hospitals.

delusion False or irrational belief maintained despite clear evidence to the contrary.

dendrite One of the branched fibers of neurons that receive incoming signals.

dependent variable In an experimental setting, a variable that the researcher measures to assess the impact of a variation in an independent variable.

depressant Drug that depresses or slows down the activity of the central nervous system.

descriptive statistics Statistical procedures that are used to summarize sets of scores with respect to central tendencies, variability, and correlations.

determinism The doctrine that all events—physical, behavioral, and mental—are determined by specific causal factors that are potentially knowable.

developmental age The chronological age at which most children show a particular level of physical or mental development.

developmental psychology The branch of psychology concerned with interaction between physical and psychological processes and with stages of growth from conception throughout the entire life span.

diathesis-stress hypothesis A hypothesis about the cause of certain disorders, such as schizophrenia, that suggests that genetic factors predispose an individual to a certain disorder but that environmental stress factors must impinge in order for the potential risk to manifest itself.

difference threshold The smallest physical difference between two stimuli that can still be recognized as a difference; operationally defined as the point at which the stimuli are recognized as different half of the time.

diffusion of responsibility In emergency situations, the larger the number of bystanders, the less responsibility any one of the bystanders feels to help.

discriminative stimulus Stimulus that acts as a predictor of reinforcement, signaling when particular behaviors will result in positive reinforcement.

dissociative amnesia The inability to remember important personal experiences, caused by psychological factors in the absence of any organic dysfunction.

dissociative disorder A personality disorder marked by a disturbance in the integration of identity, memory, or consciousness.

dissociative fugue A disorder characterized by a flight from home or work accompanied by a loss of ability to recall the personal past.

dissociative identity disorder (DID) A dissociative mental disorder in which two or more distinct personalities exist within the same individual; formerly known as multiple personality disorder.

distal stimulus In the processes of perception, the physical object in the world, as contrasted with the proximal stimulus, the optical image on the retina.

divergent thinking An aspect of creativity characterized by an ability to produce unusual but appropriate responses to problems.

DNA (deoxyribonucleic acid) The physical basis for the transmission of genetic information.

double-blind control An experimental technique in which biased expectations of experimenters are eliminated by keeping both participants and experimental assistants unaware of which participants have received which treatment.

dream analysis The psychoanalytic interpretation of dreams used to gain insight into a person's unconscious motives or conflicts.

dream work In Freudian dream analysis, the process by which the internal censor transforms the latent content of a dream into manifest content.

drive Internal state that arises in response to a disequilibrium in an animal's physiological needs.

DSM-IV-TR The current diagnostic and statistical manual of the American Psychological Association that classifies, defines, and describes mental disorders.

ego The aspect of personality involved in self-preservation activities and in directing instinctual drives and urges into appropriate channels.

egocentrism In cognitive development, the inability of a young child at the preoperational stage to take the perspective of another person.

ego defense mechanism Mental strategy (conscious or unconscious) used by the ego to defend itself against conflicts experienced in the normal course of life.

elaboration likelihood model A theory of persuasion that defines how likely it is that people will focus their cognitive processes to elaborate upon a message and therefore follow the central and peripheral routes to persuasion.

elaborative rehearsal A technique for improving memory by enriching the encoding of information.

electroconvulsive therapy (ECT) The use of electroconvulsive shock as an effective treatment for severe depression.

electroencephalogram (EEG) A recording of the electrical activity of the brain.

embryonic stage The second stage of prenatal development, lasting from the third through eighth week after conception.

emotion A complex pattern of changes, including physiological arousal, feelings, cognitive processes, and behavioral reactions, made in response to a situation perceived to be personally significant.

emotional intelligence Type of intelligence defined as the abilities to perceive, appraise, and express emotions accurately and appropriately, to use emotions to facilitate thinking, to understand and analyze emotions, to use emotional knowledge effectively, and to regulate one's emotions to promote both emotional and intellectual growth.

encoding The process by which a mental representation is formed in memory.

encoding specificity The principle that subsequent retrieval of information is enhanced if cues received at the time of recall are consistent with those present at the time of encoding.

endocrine system The network of glands that manufacture and secrete hormones into the bloodstream.

engram The physical memory trace for information in the brain.

episodic memory Long-term memory for an autobiographical event and the context in which it occurred.

equity theory A cognitive theory of work motivation that proposes that workers are motivated to maintain fair and equitable relationships with other relevant persons; also, a model that postulates that equitable relationships are those in which the participants' outcomes are proportional to their inputs.

escape conditioning A form of learning in which animals acquire a response that will allow them to escape from an aversive stimulus.

estrogen The female sex hormone, produced by the ovaries, that is responsible for the release of eggs from the ovaries as well as for the development and maintenance of female reproductive structures and secondary sex characteristics.

etiology The causes of, or factor related to, the development of a disorder.

evolutionary perspective The approach to psychology that stresses the importance of behavioral and mental adaptiveness, based on the assumption that mental capabilities evolved over millions of years to serve particular adaptive purposes.

evolutionary psychology The study of behavior and mind using the principles of evolutionary theory.

excitatory input Information entering a neuron that signals it to fire.

exemplar Member of a category that people have encountered.

expectancy The extent to which people believe that their behaviors in particular situations will bring about rewards.

expectancy effect Result that occurs when a researcher or observer subtly communicates to participants the kind of behavior he or she expects to find, thereby creating that expected reaction.

expectancy theory A cognitive theory of work motivation that proposes that workers are motivated when they expect their efforts and job performance to result in desired outcomes.

experimental group A group in an experiment that is exposed to a treatment or experiences a manipulation of the independent variable.

experimental method Research methodology that involves the manipulation of independent variables to determine their effects on the dependent variables.

explicit use of memory Conscious effort to encode or recover information through memory processes.

exposure therapy A behavioral technique in which clients are exposed to the objects or situations that cause them anxiety.

extinction In conditioning, the weakening of a conditioned association in the absence of a reinforcer or unconditioned stimulus.

fear A rational reaction to an objectively identified external danger that may induce a person to flee or attack in self-defense.

fetal stage The third stage of prenatal development, lasting from the ninth week through birth of the child.

fight-or-flight response A sequence of internal activities triggered when an organism is faced with a threat; prepares the body for combat and struggle or for running away to safety; recent evidence suggests that the response is characteristic only of males.

five-factor model A comprehensive descriptive personality system that maps out the relationships among common traits, theoretical concepts, and personality scales; informally called the Big Five.

fixation A state in which a person remains attached to objects or activities more appropriate for an earlier stage of psychosexual development.

fixed-interval (FI) schedule A schedule of reinforcement in which a reinforcer is delivered for the first response made after a fixed period of time.

fixed-ratio (FR) schedule A schedule of reinforcement in which a reinforcer is delivered for the first response made after a fixed number of responses.

flashbulb memory People's vivid and richly detailed memory in response to personal or public events that have great emotional significance.

fluid intelligence The aspect of intelligence that involves the ability to see complex relationships and solve problems.

formal assessment The systematic procedures and measurement instruments used by trained professionals to assess an individual's functioning, aptitudes, abilities, or mental states.

foundational theory Framework for initial understanding formulated by children to explain their experiences of the world.

fovea Area of the retina that contains densely packed cones and forms the point of sharpest vision.

frame A particular description of a choice; the perspective from which a choice is described or framed affects how a decision is made and which option is ultimately exercised.

free association The therapeutic method in which a patient gives a running account of thoughts, wishes, physical sensations, and mental images as they occur.

frequency distribution A summary of how frequently each score appears in a set of observations.

frequency theory The theory that a tone produces a rate of vibration in the basilar membrane equal to its frequency, with the result that pitch can be coded by the place at which activation occurs.

frontal lobe Region of the brain located above the lateral fissure and in front of the central sulcus; involved in motor control and cognitive activities.

frustration-aggression hypothesis According to this hypothesis, frustration occurs in situations in which people are prevented or blocked from attaining their goals; a rise in frustration then leads to a greater probability of aggression.

functional fixedness An inability to perceive a new use for an object previously associated with some other purpose; adversely affects problem solving and creativity.

functional MRI (fMRI) A brain-imaging technique that combines benefits of both MRI and PET scans by detecting magnetic changes in the flow of blood to cells in the brain.

functionalism The perspective on mind and behavior that focuses on the examination of their functions in an organism's interactions with the environment.

fundamental attribution error (FAE) The dual tendency of observers to underestimate the impact of situational factors and to overestimate the influence of dispositional factors on a person's behavior.

g According to Spearman, the factor of general intelligence underlying all intelligent performance.

ganglion cell Cell in the visual system that integrates impulses from many bipolar cells in a single firing rate.

gate-control theory A theory about pain modulation that proposes that certain cells in the spinal cord act as gates to interrupt and block some pain signals while sending others to the brain.

gender A psychological phenomenon that refers to learned sex-related behaviors and attitudes of males and females.

gender identity One's sense of maleness or femaleness; usually includes awareness and acceptance of one's biological sex.

gender stereotype Belief about attributes and behaviors regarded as appropriate for males and females in a particular culture.

gene The biological unit of heredity; discrete section of a chromosome responsible for transmission of traits.

general adaptation syndrome (GAS) The pattern of nonspecific adaptational physiological mechanisms that occurs in response to continuing threat by almost any serious stressor.

generalized anxiety disorder An anxiety disorder in which an individual feels anxious and worried most of the time for at least six months when not threatened by any specific danger or object.

generativity A commitment beyond one's self and one's partner to family, work, society, and future generations; typically, a crucial state in development in one's 30s and 40s.

genetics The study of the inheritance of physical and psychological traits from ancestors.

genome The genetic information for an organism, stored in the DNA of its chromosomes.

genotype The genetic structure an organism inherits from its parents.

germinal stage The first two weeks of prenatal development following conception.

Gestalt psychology A school of psychology that maintains that psychological phenomena can be understood only when viewed as organized, structured wholes, not when broken down into primitive perceptual elements.

Gestalt therapy Therapy that focuses on ways to unite mind and body to make a person whole.

glia The cells that hold neurons together and facilitate neural transmission, remove damaged and dead neurons, and prevent poisonous substances in the blood from reaching the brain.

goal-directed selection A determinant of why people select some parts of sensory input for further processing; it reflects the choices made as a function of one's own goals.

group polarization The tendency for groups to make decisions that are more extreme than the decisions that would be made by the members acting alone.

groupthink The tendency of a decision-making group to filter out undesirable input so that a consensus may be reached, especially if it is in line with the leader's viewpoint.

gustation The sense of taste.

habituation A decrease in a behavioral response when a stimulus is presented repeatedly.

hallucination False perception that occurs in the absence of objective stimulation.

hallucinogen Drug that alters cognitions and perceptions and causes hallucinations.

health A general condition of soundness and vigor of body and mind; not simply the absence of illness or injury.

health promotion The development and implementation of general strategies and specific tactics to eliminate or reduce the risk that people will become ill.

health psychology The field of psychology devoted to understanding the ways people stay healthy, the reasons they become ill, and the ways they respond when they become ill.

heredity The biological transmission of traits from parents to offspring.

heritability The relative influence of genetics—versus environment—in determining patterns of behavior.

heritability estimate A statistical estimate of the degree of inheritance of a given trait or behavior, assessed by the degree of similarity between individuals who vary in their extent of genetic similarity.

heuristic Cognitive strategies, or "rules of thumb," often used as shortcuts in solving a complex inferential task.

hierarchy of needs Maslow's view that basic human motives form a hierarchy and that the needs at each level of the hierarchy must be satisfied before the next level can be achieved; these needs progress from basic biological needs to the need for self-actualization.

hippocampus The part of the limbic system that is involved in the acquisition of explicit memory.

HIV Human immunodeficiency virus, a virus that attacks white blood cells (T lymphocytes) in human blood, thereby weakening the functioning of the immune system; HIV causes AIDS.

homeostasis Constancy or equilibrium of the internal conditions of the body.

horizontal cell One of the cells that integrate information across the retina; rather than sending signals toward the brain, horizontal cells connect receptors to each other.

hormone One of the chemical messengers, manufactured and secreted by the endocrine glands, that regulate metabolism and influence body growth, mood, and sexual characteristics.

hozho A Navajo concept referring to harmony, peace of mind, goodness, ideal family relationships, beauty in arts and crafts, and health of body and spirit.

hue The dimension of color space that captures the qualitative experience of the color of light.

human behavior genetics The area of study that evaluates the genetic component of individual differences in behaviors and traits.

humanistic perspective A psychological model that emphasizes an individual's phenomenal world and inherent capacity for making rational choices and developing to maximum potential.

human-potential movement The therapy movement that encompasses all those practices and methods that release the potential of the average human being for greater levels of performance and greater richness of experience.

hypnosis An altered state of awareness characterized by deep relaxation, susceptibility to suggestions, and changes in perception, memory, motivation, and self-control.

hypnotizability The degree to which an individual is responsive to standardized hypnotic suggestion.

hypochondriasis A disorder in which individuals are preoccupied with having or getting physical ailments despite reassurances that they are healthy.

hypothalamus The brain structure that regulates motivated behavior (such as eating and drinking) and homeostasis.

hypothesis A tentative and testable explanation of the relationship between two (or more) events or variables; often stated as a prediction that a certain outcome will result from specific conditions.

iconic memory Memory system in the visual domain that allows large amounts of information to be stored for very brief durations.

id The primitive, unconscious part of the personality that represents the internalization of society's values, standards, and morals.

identification and recognition Two ways of attaching meaning to percepts.

illusion An experience of a stimulus pattern in a manner that is demonstrably incorrect but shared by others in the same perceptual environment.

implicit uses of memory Availability of information through memory processes without conscious effort to encode or recover information.

imprinting A primitive form of learning in which some infant animals physically follow and form an attachment to the first moving object they see and/or hear.

impulsive aggression Cognition-based and goal-directed aggression carried out with premeditated thought, to achieve specific aims.

incentive External stimulus or reward that motivates behavior although it does not relate directly to biological needs.

independent construal of self Conceptualization of the self as an individual whose behavior is organized primarily by reference to one's own thoughts, feelings, and actions, rather than by reference to the thoughts, feelings, and actions of others.

independent variable In an experimental setting, a variable that the researcher manipulates with the expectation of having an impact on values of the dependent variable.

inductive reasoning A form of reasoning in which a conclusion is made about the probability of some state of affairs, based on the available evidence and past experience.

infant-directed speech A form of speech addressed to infants that includes slower speed, distinctive intonation, and structural simplifications.

inference Missing information filled in on the basis of a sample of evidence or on the basis of prior beliefs and theories.

inferential statistics Statistical procedures that allow researchers to determine whether the results they obtain support their hypotheses or can be attributed just to chance variation.

informational influence Group effects that arise from individuals' desire to be correct and right and to understand how best to act in a given situation.

informed consent The process through which individuals are informed about experimental procedures, risks, and benefits before they provide formal consent to become research participants.

in-group A group with which people identify as members.

in-group bias People's tendency to favor members of their own group over members of other groups.

inhibitory input Information entering a neuron that signals it not to fire.

insanity The legal (not clinical) designation for the state of an individual judged to be legally irresponsible or incompetent.

insight Circumstances of problem solving in which solutions suddenly come to mind.

insight therapy A technique by which the therapist guides a patient toward discovering insights between present symptoms and past origins.

insomnia The chronic inability to sleep normally; symptoms include difficulty in falling asleep, frequent waking, inability to return to sleep, and early-morning awakening.

instinct Preprogrammed tendency that is essential to a species's survival.

instinctual drift The tendency for learned behavior to drift toward instinctual behavior over time.

instrumental aggression Cognition-based and goal-directed aggression carried out with premeditated thought, to achieve specific aims.

intellectual disability Condition in which individuals have IQ scores of 70 to 75 or below and also demonstrate limitations in the ability to bring adaptive skills to bear on life tasks.

intelligence The global capacity to profit from experience and to go beyond given information about the environment.

intelligence quotient (IQ) An index derived from standardized tests of intelligence; originally obtained by dividing an individual's mental age by chronological age and then multiplying by 100; now directly computed as an IQ test score.

interdependent construal of self Conceptualization of the self as part of an encompassing social relationship; recognizing that one's behavior is determined, contingent on, and, to a large extent organized by what the actor perceived to be the thoughts, feelings, and actions of others.

internal consistency A measure of reliability; the degree to which a test yields similar scores across its different parts, such as odd versus even items.

internalization According to Vygotsky, the process through which children absorb knowledge from the social context.

interneuron Brain neuron that relays messages from sensory neurons to other interneurons or to motor neurons.

intimacy The capacity to make a full commitment—sexual, emotional, and moral—to another person.

introspection Individuals' systematic examination of their own thoughts and feelings.

ion channel A portion of neurons' cell membranes that selectively permits certain ions to flow in and out.

James–Lange theory of emotion A peripheral-feedback theory of emotion stating that an eliciting stimulus triggers a behavioral response that sends different sensory and motor feedback to the brain and creates the feeling of a specific emotion.

job burnout The syndrome of emotional exhaustion, depersonalization, and reduced personal accomplishment, often experienced by workers in high-stress jobs.

judgment The process by which people form opinions, reach conclusions, and make critical evaluations of events and people based on available material; also, the product of the mental activity.

just noticeable difference (JND) The smallest difference between two sensations that allows them to be discriminated.

kinesthetic sense The sense concerned with bodily position and movement of the body parts relative to one another.

language-making capacity The innate guidelines or operating principles that children bring to the task of learning a language.

language production What people say, sign, and write, as well as the processes they go through to produce these messages.

latent content In Freudian dream analysis, the hidden meaning of a dream.

law of effect A basic law of learning that states that the power of a stimulus to evoke a response is strengthened when the response is followed by a reward and weakened when it is not followed by a reward.

learned helplessness A general pattern of nonresponding in the presence of noxious stimuli that often follows after an organism has previously experienced noncontingent, inescapable aversive stimuli.

learning A process based on experience that results in a relatively permanent change in behavior or behavioral potential.

learning disorder A disorder defined by a large discrepancy between individuals' measured IQ and their actual performance.

learning-performance distinction The difference between what has been learned and what is expressed in overt behavior.

lens The flexible tissue that focuses light on the retina.

lesion Injury to or destruction of brain tissue.

levels-of-processing theory A theory that suggests that the deeper the level at which information was processed, the more likely it is to be retained in memory.

libido The psychic energy that drives individuals toward sensual pleasures of all types, especially sexual ones.

life-change unit (LCU) In stress research, the measure of the stress levels of different types of changes experienced during a given period.

lightness constancy The tendency to perceive the whiteness, grayness, or blackness of objects as constant across changing levels of illuminations.

limbic system The region of the brain that regulates emotional behavior, basic motivational urges, and memory, as well as major physiological functions.

linguistic relativity The hypothesis that the structure of the language an individual speaks has an impact on the way in which that individual thinks about the world.

locus of control People's general expectancy about the extent to which the rewards they obtain are contingent on their own actions or on environmental factors.

longitudinal design A research design in which the same participants are observed repeatedly, sometimes over many years.

long-term memory (LTM) Memory processes associated with the preservation of information for retrieval at any later time.

loudness A perceptual dimension of sound influenced by the amplitude of a sound wave; sound waves in large amplitudes are generally experienced as loud and those with small amplitudes as soft.

lucid dreaming The theory that conscious awareness of dreaming is a learnable skill that enables dreamers to control the direction and content of their dreams.

magnetic resonance imaging (MRI) A technique for brain imaging that scans the brain using magnetic fields and radio waves.

major depressive disorder A mood disorder characterized by intense feelings of depression over an extended time, without the manic high phase of bipolar depression.

manic episode A component of bipolar disorder characterized by periods of extreme elation, unbounded euphoria without sufficient reason, and grandiose thoughts or feelings about personal abilities.

manifest content In Freudian dream analysis, the surface content of a dream, which is assumed to mask the dream's actual meaning.

maturation The continuing influence of heredity throughout development; the age-related physical and behavioral changes characteristic of a species.

mean The arithmetic average of a group of scores; the most commonly used measure of central tendency.

measure of central tendency A statistic, such as a mean, median, or mode, that provides one score as representative of a set of observations.

measure of variability A statistic, such as a range or standard deviation, that indicates how tightly the scores in a set of observations cluster together.

median The score in a distribution above and below which lie 50 percent of the other scores; a measure of central tendency.

meditation A form of consciousness alteration designed to enhance self-knowledge and well-being through reduced self-awareness.

medulla The region of the brain stem that regulates breathing, waking, and heartbeat.

memory The mental capacity to encode, store, and retrieve information.

menarche The onset of menstruation.

mental age In Binet's measure of intelligence, the age at which a child is performing intellectually, expressed in terms of the average age at which normal children achieve a particular score.

mental set The tendency to respond to a new problem in the manner used to respond to a previous problem.

meta-analysis A statistical technique for evaluating hypotheses by providing a formal mechanism for detecting the general conclusions found in data from many different experiments.

metamemory Implicit or explicit knowledge about memory abilities and effective memory strategies; cognition about memory.

mnemonic Strategy or device that uses familiar information during the encoding of new information to enhance subsequent access to the information in memory.

mode The score appearing most frequently in a set of observations; a measure of central tendency.

monocular depth cue Depth cue that uses information from only one eye.

mood disorder A mood disturbance such as severe depression or depression alternating with mania.

morality A system of beliefs and values that ensures that individuals will keep their obligations to others in society and will behave in ways that do not interfere with the rights and interests of others.

motion parallax A source of information about depth in which the relative distances of objects from a viewer determine the amount and direction of their relative motion in the retinal image.

motivation The process of starting, directing, and maintaining physical and psychological activities; includes mechanisms involved in preferences for one activity over another and the vigor and persistence of responses.

motor cortex The region of the cerebral cortex that controls the action of the body's voluntary muscles.

motor neuron Neuron that carries messages away from the central nervous system toward the muscles and glands.

myelin sheath Insulating material that surrounds axons and increases the speed of neural transmission.

narcolepsy A sleep disorder characterized by an irresistible compulsion to sleep during the daytime.

natural selection Darwin's theory that favorable adaptations to features of the environment allow some members of a species to reproduce more successfully than others.

naturalistic observation A research technique in which unobtrusive observations are made of behaviors that occur in natural environments.

need for achievement (n Ach) An assumed basic human need to strive for achievement of goals that motivates a wide range of behavior and thinking.

negative punishment A behavior is followed by the removal of an appetitive stimulus, decreasing the probability of that behavior.

negative reinforcement A behavior is followed by the removal of an aversive stimulus, increasing the probability of that behavior.

neurogenesis The creation of new neurons.

neuromodulator Any substance that modifies or modulates the activities of the postsynaptic neuron.

neuron A cell in the nervous system specialized to receive, process, and/or transmit information to other cells.

neuroscience The scientific study of the brain and of the links between brain activity and behavior.

neurotic disorder Mental disorder in which a person does not have signs of brain abnormalities and does not display grossly irrational thinking or violate basic norms but does experience subjective distress; a category dropped from DSM-III.

neurotransmitter Chemical messenger released from a neuron that crosses the synapse from one neuron to another, stimulating the postsynaptic neuron.

nightmare A frightening dream that usually wakes up the sleeper.

nonconscious Not typically available to consciousness or memory.

non-REM (NREM) sleep The period during which a sleeper does not show rapid eye movement; characterized by less dream activity than during REM sleep.

norm Standard based on measurement of a large group of people; used for comparing the scores of an individual with those of others within a well-defined group.

norm crystallization The convergence of the expectations of a group of individuals into a common perspective as they talk and carry out activities together.

normal curve The symmetrical curve that represents the distribution of scores on many psychological attributes; allows researchers to make judgments of how unusual an observation or result is.

normative influence Group effects that arise from individuals' desire to be liked, accepted, and approved of by others.

normative investigation Research effort designed to describe what is characteristic of a specific age or developmental stage.

object permanence The recognition that objects exist independently of an individual's action or awareness; an important cognitive acquisition of infancy.

observational learning The process of learning new responses by watching the behavior of another.

observer bias The distortion of evidence because of the personal motives and expectations of the viewer.

obsessive-compulsive disorder (OCD) A mental disorder characterized by obsessions—recurrent thoughts, images, or impulses that recur or persist despite efforts to suppress them—and compulsions—repetitive, purposeful acts performed according to certain rules or in a ritualized manner.

occipital lobe Rearmost region of the brain; contains primary visual cortex.

olfaction The sense of smell.

olfactory bulb The center where odor-sensitive receptors send their signals, located just below the frontal lobes of the cortex.

operant Behavior emitted by an organism that can be characterized in terms of the observable effects it has on the environment.

operant conditioning Learning in which the probability of a response is changed by a change in its consequences.

operant extinction When a behavior no longer produces predictable consequences, it returns to the level of occurrence it had before operant conditioning.

operational definition A definition of a variable or condition in terms of the specific operation or procedure used to determine its presence.

opponent-process theory The theory that all color experiences arise from three systems, each of which includes two "opponent" elements (red versus green, blue versus yellow, and black versus white).

optic nerve The axons of the ganglion cells that carry information from the eye toward the brain.

organizational psychologist Psychologist who studies various aspects of the human work environment, such as communication among employees, socialization or enculturation of workers, leadership, job satisfaction, stress and burnout, and overall quality of life.

out-group A group with which people do not identify.

overregularization A grammatical error, usually appearing during early language development, in which rules of the language are applied too widely, resulting in incorrect linguistic forms.

pain The body's response to noxious stimuli that are intense enough to cause, or threaten to cause, tissue damage.

panic disorder An anxiety disorder in which sufferers experience unexpected, severe panic attacks that begin with a feeling of intense apprehension, fear, or terror.

parallel forms Different versions of a test used to assess test reliability; the change of forms reduces effects of direct practice, memory, or the desire of an individual to appear consistent on the same items.

parallel processes Two or more mental processes that are carried out simultaneously.

parasympathetic division The subdivision of the autonomic nervous system that monitors the routine operation of the body's internal functions and conserves and restores body energy.

parental investment The time and energy parents must spend raising their offspring.

parenting style The manner in which parents rear their children; an authoritative parenting style, which balances demandingness and responsiveness, is seen as the most effective.

parietal lobe Region of the brain behind the frontal lobe and above the lateral fissure; contains somatosensory cortex.

partial reinforcement effect The behavioral principle that states that responses acquired under intermittent reinforcement are more difficult to extinguish than those acquired with continuous reinforcement.

participant modeling A therapeutic technique in which a therapist demonstrates the desired behavior and a client is aided, through supportive encouragement, to imitate the modeled behavior.

pastoral counselor A member of a religious order who specializes in the treatment of psychological disorders, often combining spirituality with practical problem solving.

patient The term used by those who take a biomedical approach to the treatment of psychological problems to describe the person being treated.

perceived control The belief that one has the ability to make a difference in the course of the consequences of some event or experience; often helpful in dealing with stressors.

perception The processes that organize information in the sensory image and interpret it as having been produced by properties of objects or events in the external, three-dimensional world.

perceptual constancy The ability to retain an unchanging percept of an object despite variations in the retinal image.

perceptual organization The processes that put sensory information together to give the perception of a coherent scene over the whole visual field.

peripheral nervous system (PNS) The part of the nervous system composed of the spinal and cranial nerves that connect the body's sensory receptors to the CNS and the CNS to the muscles and glands.

personality The psychological qualities of an individual that influence a variety of characteristic behavior patterns across difference situations and over time.

personality disorder A chronic, inflexible, maladaptive pattern of perceiving, thinking, and behaving that seriously impairs an individual's ability to function in social or other settings.

personality inventory A self-report questionnaire used for personality assessment that includes a series of items about personal thoughts, feelings, and behaviors.

personality type Distinct pattern of personality characteristics used to assign people to categories; qualitative differences, rather than differences in degree, used to discriminate among people.

persuasion Deliberate efforts to change attitudes.

phenotype The observable characteristics of an organism, resulting from the interaction between the organism's genotype and its environment.

pheromone Chemical signal released by an organism to communicate with other members of the species; pheromones often serve as long-distance sexual attractors.

phi phenomenon The simplest form of apparent motion, the movement illusion in which one or more stationary lights going on and off in succession are perceived as a single moving light.

phobia A persistent and irrational fear of a specific object, activity, or situation that is excessive and unreasonable, given the reality of the threat.

phoneme Minimal unit of speech in any given language that makes a meaningful difference in speech and production and reception; r and r.

photoreceptor Receptor cell in the retina that is sensitive to light.

physical development The bodily changes, maturation, and growth that occur in an organism starting with conception and continuing across the life span.

physiological dependence The process by which the body becomes adjusted to or dependent on a drug.

pitch Sound quality of highness or lowness; primarily dependent on the frequency of the sound wave.

pituitary gland Located in the brain, the gland that secretes growth hormone and influences the secretion of hormones by other endocrine glands

place theory The theory that different frequency tones produce maximum activation at different locations along the basilar membrane, with the result that pitch can be coded by the place at which activation occurs.

placebo control An experimental condition in which treatment is not administered; it is used in cases where a placebo effect might occur.

placebo effect A change in behavior in the absence of an experimental manipulation.

placebo therapy A therapy interdependent of any specific clinical procedures that results in client improvement.

plasticity Changes in the performance of the brain; may involve the creation of new synapses or changes in the function of existing synapses.

polygenic trait Characteristic that is influenced by more than one gene.

pons The region of the brain stem that connects the spinal cord with the brain and links parts of the brain to one another.

population The entire set of individuals to which generalizations will be made based on an experimental sample.

positive psychology A movement within psychology that applies research to provide people with the knowledge and skills that allow them to experience fulfilling lives.

positive punishment A behavior is followed by the presentation of an aversive stimulus, decreasing the probability of that behavior.

positive reinforcement A behavior is followed by the presentation of an appetitive stimulus, increasing the probability of that behavior.

positron emission tomography (PET) scan Brain image produced by a device that obtains detailed pictures of activity in the living brain by recording the radioactivity emitted by cells during different cognitive or behavioral activities.

possible self One of the ideal selves that a person would like to become, the selves a person could become, and the selves a person is afraid of becoming; components of the cognitive sense of self.

posttraumatic stress disorder (PTSD) An anxiety disorder characterized by the persistent reexperience of traumatic events through distressing recollections, dreams, hallucinations, or dissociative flashbacks; develops in response to rapes, life-threatening events, severe injury, and natural disasters.

preconscious memory Memory that is not currently conscious but that can easily be called into consciousness when necessary.

predictive validity The degree to which test scores indicate a result on a specific measure that is consistent with some other criterion of the characteristic being assessed; also known as predictive validity.

prefrontal lobotomy An operation that severs the nerve fibers connecting the frontal lobes of the brain with the diencephalon, especially those fibers in the thalamic and hypothalamic areas; best known form of psychosurgery.

prejudice A learned attitude toward a target object, involving negative affect (dislike or fear), negative beliefs (stereotypes) that justify the attitude, and a behavioral intention to avoid, control, dominate, or eliminate the target object.

primacy effect Improved memory for items at the start of a list.

primary reinforcer Biologically determined reinforcer, such as food and water.

priming In the assessment of implicit memory, the advantage conferred by prior exposure to a word or situation.

proactive interference Circumstances in which past memories make it more difficult to encode and retrieve new information.

problem solving Thinking that is directed toward solving specific problems and that moves from an initial state to a goal state by means of a set of mental operations.

problem space The elements that make up a problem: the initial state, the incomplete information or unsatisfactory conditions the person starts with; the goal state, the set of information or state the person wishes to achieve; and the set of operations, the steps the person takes to move from the initial state to the goal state.

procedural memory Memory for how things get done; the way perceptual, cognitive, and motor skills are acquired, retained, and used.

projective test A method of personality assessment in which an individual is presented with a standardized set of ambiguous, abstract stimuli and asked to interpret their meanings; the individual's responses are assumed to reveal inner feelings, motives, and conflicts.

prosocial behavior Behavior that is carried out with the goal of helping other people.

prototype The most representative example of a category.

proximal stimulus The optical image on the retina; contrasted with the distal stimulus, the physical object in the world.

psychiatrist An individual who has obtained an MD degree and also has completed postdoctoral specialty training in mental and emotional disorders; a psychiatrist may prescribe medications for the treatment of psychological disorders.

psychic determinism The assumption that mental and behavioral reactions are determined by previous experiences.

psychoactive drug Chemical that affects mental processes and behavior by temporarily changing conscious awareness of reality.

psychoanalysis The form of psychodynamic therapy developed by Freud; an intensive prolonged technique for exploring unconscious motivations and conflicts in neurotic, anxiety-ridden individuals.

psychoanalyst An individual who has earned either a PhD or an MD degree and has completed postgraduate training in the Freudian approach to understanding and treating mental disorders.

psychobiography The use of psychological (especially personality) theory to describe and explain an individual's course through life.

psychodynamic personality theory Theory of personality that shares the assumption that personality is shaped by and behavior is motivated by inner forces.

psychodynamic perspective A psychological model in which behavior is explained in terms of past experiences and motivational forces; actions are viewed as stemming from inherited instincts, biological drives, and attempts to resolve conflicts between personal needs and social requirements.

psychological assessment The use of specified procedures to evaluate the abilities, behaviors, and personal qualities of people.

psychological dependence The psychological need or craving for a drug.

psychological diagnosis The label given to psychological abnormality by classifying and categorizing the observed behavior pattern into an approved diagnostic system.

psychology The scientific study of the behavior of individuals and their mental processes.

psychometric function A graph that plots the percentage of detections of a stimulus (on the vertical axis) for each stimulus intensity on the horizontal positions of corresponding images in the two eyes.

psychometrics The field of psychology that specializes in mental testing.

psychoneuroimmunology The research area that investigates interactions between psychological processes, such as responses to stress, and the functions of the immune system.

psychopathological functioning Disruptions in emotional, behavioral, or thought processes that lead to personal distress or block one's ability to achieve important goals.

psychopharmacology The branch of psychology that investigates the effects of drugs on behavior.

psychophysics The study of the correspondence between physical simulation and psychological experience.

psychosocial stage Proposed by Erik Erikson, one of the successive developmental stages that focus on an individual's orientation toward the self and others; these stages incorporate both the sexual and social aspects of a person's developmental and the social conflicts that arise from the interaction between the individual and the social environment.

psychosomatic disorder Physical disorder aggravated by or primarily attributable to prolonged emotional stress or other psychological causes.

psychosurgery A surgical procedure performed on brain tissue to alleviate a psychological disorder.

psychotherapy Any of a group of therapies, used to treat psychological disorders, that focus on changing faulty behaviors, thoughts, perceptions, and emotions that may be associated with specific disorders.

psychotic disorder Severe mental disorder in which a person experiences impairments in reality testing manifested through thought, emotional, or perceptual difficulties; no longer used as diagnostic category after DSM–III.

puberty The process through which sexual maturity is attained.

punisher Any stimulus that, when made contingent on a response, decreases the probability of that response.

pupil The opening at the front of the eye through which light passes.

racism Discrimination against people based on their skin color or ethnic heritage.

random assignment A procedure by which participants have an equal likelihood of being assigned to any condition within an experiment.

random sampling A procedure that ensures that every member of a population has an equal likelihood of participating in an experiment.

range The difference between the highest and the lowest scores in a set of observations; the simplest measure of variability.

rapid eye movement (REM) A behavioral sign of the phase of sleep during which the sleeper is likely to be experiencing dreamlike mental activity.

rational-emotive therapy (RET) A comprehensive system of personality change based on changing irrational beliefs that cause undesirable, highly charged emotional reactions such as severe anxiety.

reasoning The process of thinking in which conclusions are drawn from a set of facts; thinking directed toward a given goal or objective.

recall A method of retrieval in which an individual is required to reproduce the information previously presented.

recency effect Improved memory for items at the end of a list.

receptive field The area of the visual field to which a neuron in the visual system responds.

reciprocal altruism The idea that people perform altruistic behaviors because they expect that others will perform altruistic behaviors for them in turn.

reciprocal determinism A concept of Albert Bandura's social-learning theory that refers to the notion that a complex reciprocal interaction exists among the individual, his or her behavior, and environmental stimuli and that each of these components affects the others.

reciprocity norm Expectation that favors will be returned—if someone does something for another person, that person should do something in return.

recognition A method of retrieval in which an individual is required to identify stimuli as having been experienced before.

reconstructive memory The process of putting information together based on general types of stored knowledge in the absence of a specific memory representation.

reflex An unlearned response elicited by specific stimuli that have biological relevance for an organism.

refractory period The period of rest during which a new nerve impulse cannot be activated in a segment of an axon.

reinforcement contingency A consistent relationship between a response and the changes in the environment that it produces.

reinforcer Any stimulus that, when made contingent on a response, increases the probability of that response.

relaxation response A condition in which muscle tension, cortical activity, heart rate, and blood pressure decrease and breathing slows.

reliability The degree to which a test produces similar scores each time it is used; stability or consistency of the scores produced by an instrument.

repetitive transcranial magnetic stimulation (rTMS) A technique for producing temporary inactivation of brain areas using repeated pulses of magnetic stimulation.

representative sample A subset of a population that closely matches the overall characteristics of the population with respect to the distribution of males and females, racial and ethnic groups, and so on.

representativeness heuristic A cognitive strategy that assigns an object to a category on the basis of a few characteristics regarded as representative of that category.

repression The basic defense mechanism by which painful or guilt-producing thoughts, feelings, or memories are excluded from conscious awareness.

resistance The inability or unwillingness of a patient in psychoanalysis to discuss certain ideas, desires, or experiences.

response bias The systematic tendency as a result of nonsensory factors for an observer to favor responding in a particular way.

resting potential The polarization of cellular fluid within a neuron, which provides the capability to produce an action potential.

reticular formation The region of the brain stem that alerts the cerebral cortex to incoming sensory signals and is responsible for maintaining consciousness and awakening from sleep.

retina The layer at the back of the eye that contains photoreceptors and converts light energy to neutral responses.

retinal disparity The displacement between the horizontal positions of corresponding images in the two eyes.

retrieval The recovery of stored information from memory.

retrieval cue Internally or externally generated stimulus available to help with the retrieval of a memory.

retroactive interference Circumstances in which the formation of new memories makes it more difficult to recover older memories.

retrograde amnesia An inability to retrieve memories from the time before physical damage to the brain.

rod One of the photoreceptors concentrated in the periphery of the retina that is most active in dim illumination; rods do not produce sensation of color.

rule Behavioral guideline for acting in a certain way in a certain situation.

sample A subset of a population selected as participants in an experiment.

saturation The dimension of color space that captures the purity and vividness of color sensations.

schedule of reinforcement In operant conditioning, a pattern of delivering and withholding reinforcement.

schema General conceptual framework, or cluster of knowledge, regarding objects, people, and situations; knowledge package that encodes generalizations about the structure of the environment.

scheme Piaget's term for a cognitive structure that develops as infants and young children learn to interpret the world and adapt to their environment.

schizophrenic disorder Severe form of psychopathology characterized by the breakdown of integrated personality functioning, withdrawal from reality, emotional distortions, and disturbed thought processes.

scientific method The set of procedures used for gathering and interpreting objective information in a way that minimizes error and yields dependable generalizations.

selective optimization with compensation A strategy for successful aging in which one makes the most gains while minimizing the impact of losses that accompany normal aging.

self-actualization A concept in personality psychology referring to a person's constant striving to realize his or her potential and to develop inherent talents and capabilities.

self-concept A person's mental model of his or her abilities and attributes.

self-efficacy The set of beliefs that one can perform adequately in a particular situation.

self-esteem A generalized evaluative attitude toward the self that influences both moods and behavior and that exerts a powerful effect on a range of personal and social behaviors.

self-fulfilling prophecy A prediction made about some future behavior or event that modifies interactions so as to produce what is expected.

self-handicapping The process of developing, in anticipation of failure, behavioral reactions and explanations that minimize ability deficits as possible attributions for the failure.

self-perception theory The idea that people observe themselves to figure out the reasons they act as they do; people infer what their internal states are by perceiving how they are acting in a given situation.

self-report measure A self-behavior that is identified through a participant's own observations and reports.

self-serving bias An attributional bias in which people tend to take credit for their successes and deny responsibility for their failures.

semantic memory Generic, categorical memory, such as the meaning of words and concepts.

sensation The process by which stimulation of a sensory receptor gives rise to neutral impulses that result in an experience, or awareness, of conditions inside or outside the body.

sensitization An increase in behavioral response when a stimulus is presented repeatedly.

sensory adaptation A phenomenon in which receptor cells lose their power to respond after a period of unchanged stimulation; allows a more rapid reaction to new sources of information.

sensory neuron Neuron that carries messages from sense receptors toward the central nervous system.

sensory receptor Specialized cell that converts physical signals into cellular signals that are processed by the nervous system.

serial position effect A characteristic of memory retrieval in which the recall of beginning and end items on a list is often better than recall of items appearing in the middle.

serial processes Two or more mental processes that are carried out in order, one after the other.

set A temporary readiness to perceive or react to a stimulus in a particular way.

sex chromosome Chromosome that contains the genes that code for the development of male or female characteristics.

sex difference One of the biologically based characteristics that distinguish males from females.

sexism Discrimination against people because of their sex.

sexual arousal The motivational state of excitement and tension brought about by physiological and cognitive reactions to erotic stimuli.

sexual script Socially learned program of sexual responsiveness.

shape constancy The ability to perceive the true shape of an object despite variations in the size of the retinal image.

shaping by successive approximations A behavioral method that reinforces responses that successively approximate and ultimately match the desired response.

short-term memory (STM) Memory processes associated with preservation of recent experiences and with retrieval of information from long-term memory; short-term memory is of limited capacity and stores information for only a short length of time without rehearsal.

shyness An individual's discomfort and/or inhibition in interpersonal situations that interferes with pursuing an interpersonal professional goal.

signal detection theory A systematic approach to the problem of response bias that allows an experimenter to identify and separate the roles of sensory stimuli and the individual's criterion level in producing the final response.

significant difference A difference between experimental groups or conditions that would have occurred by chance less than an accepted criterion; in psychology, the criterion most often used is a probability of less than 5 times out of 100, or $p < .05$.

size constancy The ability to perceive the true size of an object despite variations in the size of its retinal image.

sleep apnea A sleep disorder of the upper respiratory system that causes the person to stop breathing while asleep.

sleep terrors Episodes in which sleepers wake up suddenly in an extreme state of arousal and panic.

social categorization The process by which people organize the social environment by categorizing themselves and others into groups.

social cognition The process by which people select, interpret, and remember social information.

social development The ways in which individuals' social interactions and expectations change across the life span.

social intelligence A theory of personality that refers to the expertise people bring to their experience of life tasks.

social norm The expectation a group has for its members regarding acceptable and appropriate attitudes and behaviors.

social perception The process by which a person comes to know or perceive the personal attributes.

social phobia A persistent, irrational fear that arises in anticipation of a public situation in which an individual can be observed by others.

social psychology The branch of psychology that studies the effect of social variables on individual behavior, attitudes, perceptions, and motives; also studies group and intergroup phenomena.

social role A socially defined pattern of behavior that is expected of a person who is functioning in a given setting or group.

social support Resources, including material aid, socioemotional support, and informational aid, provided by others to help a person cope with stress.

socialization The lifelong process whereby an individual's behavioral patterns, values, standards, skills, attitudes, and motives are shaped to conform to those regarded as desirable in a particular society.

social-learning theory The learning theory that stresses the role of observation and the imitation of behaviors observed in others.

social-learning therapy A form of treatment in which clients observe models' desirable behaviors being reinforced.

sociobiology A field of research that focuses on evolutionary explanations for the social behavior and social systems of humans and other animal species.

sociocultural perspective The psychological perspective that focuses on cross-cultural differences in the causes and consequences of behavior.

soma The cell body of a neuron, containing the nucleus and cytoplasm.

somatic nervous system The subdivision of the peripheral nervous system that connects the central nervous system to the skeletal muscles and skin.

somatization disorder A disorder characterized by unexplained physical complaints in several categories over many years.

somatoform disorder A disorder in which people have physical illnesses or complaints that cannot be fully explained by actual medical conditions.

somatosensory cortex The region of the parietal lobes that processes sensory input from various body areas.

somnambulism A disorder that causes sleepers to leave their beds and wander while still remaining asleep; also known as sleepwalking.

sound localization The auditory processes that allow the spatial origins of environmental sounds.

specific phobia Phobia that occurs in response to a specific type of object or situation.

split-half reliability A measure of the correlation between test takers' performance on different halves (such as odd- and even-numbered items) of a test.

spontaneous recovery The reappearance of an extinguished conditioned response after a rest period.

spontaneous-remission effect The improvement of some mental patients and clients in psychotherapy without any professional intervention; a baseline criterion against which the effectiveness of therapies must be assessed.

standard deviation (SD) The average difference of a set of scores from their mean; a measure of variability.

standardization A set of uniform procedures for treating each participant in a test, interview, or experiment, or for recording data.

stereotype Generalization about a group of people in which the same characteristics are assigned to all members of a group.

stereotype threat The threat associated with being at risk for confirming a negative stereotype of one's group.

stigma The negative reaction of people to an individual or group because of some assumed inferiority or source of difference that is degraded.

stimulant Drug that causes arousal, increased activity, and euphoria.

stimulus discrimination A conditioning process in which an organism learns to respond differently to stimuli that differ from the conditioned stimulus on some dimension.

stimulus generalization The automatic extension of conditioned responding to similar stimuli that have never been paired with the unconditioned stimulus.

stimulus-driven capture A determinant of why people select some parts of sensory input for further processing; occurs when features of stimuli—objects in the environment—automatically capture attention, independent of the local goals of a perceiver.

storage The retention of encoded material over time.

stress The pattern of specific and nonspecific responses an organism makes to stimulus events that disturb its equilibrium and tax or exceed its ability to cope.

stress moderator variable Variable that changes the impact of a stressor on a given type of stress reaction.

stressor An internal or external event or stimulus that induces stress.

structuralism The study of the structure of mind and behavior; the view that all human mental experience can be understood as a combination of simple elements or events.

subjective well-being Individuals' overall evaluation of life satisfaction and happiness.

superego The aspect of personality that represents the internalization of society's values, standards, and morals.

sympathetic division The subdivision of the autonomic nervous system that deals with emergency response and the mobilization of energy.

synapse The gap between one neuron and another.

synaptic transmission The relaying information from one neuron to another across the synaptic gap.

systematic desensitization A behavioral therapy technique in which a client is taught to prevent the arousal of anxiety by confronting the feared stimulus while relaxed.

taste-aversion learning A biological constraint on learning in which an organism learns in one trial to avoid a food whose ingestion is followed by illness.

temperament A child's biologically based level of emotional and behavioral response to environmental events.

temporal lobe Region of the brain found below the lateral fissure; contains auditory cortex.

tend-and-befriend response A response to stressors that is hypothesized to be typical for females; stressors prompt females to protect their offspring and join social groups to reduce vulnerability.

teratogen Environmental factors such as diseases and drugs that cause structural abnormalities in a developing fetus.

terminal button A bulblike structure at the branched ending of an axon that contains vesicles filled with neurotransmitters.

test–retest reliability A measure of the correlation between the scores of the same people on the same test given on two different occasions

testosterone The male sex hormone, secreted by the testes, that stimulates production of sperm and is also responsible for the development of male secondary sex characteristics.

thalamus The brain structure that relays sensory impulses to the cerebral cortex.

Thematic Apperception Test (TAT) A projective test in which pictures of ambiguous scenes are presented to an individual, who is encouraged to generate stories about them.

theory An organized set of concepts that explains a phenomenon or set of phenomena.

think-aloud protocol Report made by an experimental participant of the mental processes and strategies he or she uses while working on a task.

three-term contingency The means by which organisms learn that, in the presence of some stimuli but not others, their behavior is likely to have a particular effect on the environment.

timbre The dimension of auditory sensation that reflects the complexity of a sound wave.

tolerance A situation that occurs with continued use of a drug in which an individual requires greater dosages to achieve the same effect.

top-down processing Perceptual processes in which information from an individual's past experience, knowledge, expectations, motivations, and background influence the way a perceived object is interpreted and classified.

trait Enduring personal quality or attribute that influences behavior across situations.

transduction Transformation of one form of energy into another; for example, light is transformed into neutral impulses.

transfer-appropriate processing The perspective that suggests that memory is best when the type of processing carried out at encoding matches the processes carried out at retrieval.

transference The process by which a person in psychoanalysis attaches to a therapist feelings formerly held toward some significant person who figured into past emotional conflict.

trichromatic theory The theory that there are three types of color receptors that produce the primary color sensations of red, green, and blue.

two-factor theory of emotion The theory that emotional experiences arise from autonomic arousal and cognitive appraisal.

Type A behavior pattern A complex pattern of behaviors and emotions that includes excessive emphasis on competition, aggression, impatience, and hostility; hostility increases the risk of coronary heart disease.

Type B behavior pattern As compared to Type A behavior pattern, a less competitive, less aggressive, less hostile pattern of behavior and emotion.

unconditional positive regard Complete love and acceptance of an individual by another person, such as a parent for a child, with no conditions attached.

unconditioned response (UCR) In classical conditioning, the response elicited by an unconditioned stimulus without prior training or learning.

unconditioned stimulus (UCS) In classical conditioning, the stimulus that elicits an unconditioned response.

unconscious The domain of the psyche that stores repressed urges and primitive impulses.

validity The extent to which a test measures what it was intended to measure.

variable In an experimental setting, a factor that varies in amount and kind.

variable-interval (VI) schedule A schedule of reinforcement in which a reinforcer is delivered for the first response made after a variable period of time whose average is predetermined.

variable-ratio (VR) schedule A schedule of reinforcement in which a reinforcer is delivered for the first response made after a variable number of responses whose average is predetermined.

vestibular sense The sense that tells how one's own body is oriented in the world with respect to gravity.

visual cortex The region of the occipital lobes in which visual information is processed.

volley principle An extension of frequency theory, which proposes that when peaks in a sound wave come too frequently for a single neuron to fire at each peak, several neurons fire as a group at the frequency of the stimulus tone.

Weber's law An assertion that the size of a difference threshold is proportional to the intensity of the standard stimulus.

wellness Optimal health, incorporating the ability to function fully and actively over the physical, intellectual, emotional, spiritual, social, and environmental domains of health.

Wernicke's area A region of the brain that allows fluent speech production and comprehension.

wisdom Expertise in the fundamental pragmatics of life.

within-subjects design A research design that uses each participant as his or her own control; for example, the behavior of an experimental participant before receiving treatment might be compared to his or her behavior after receiving treatment.

working memory A memory resource that is used to accomplish tasks such as reasoning and language comprehension; consists of the phonological loop, visuospatial sketchpad, and central executive.

zygote The single cell that results when a sperm fertilizes an egg.

References

Abdallah, R. T., & Simon, J. A. (2007). Testosterone therapy in women: Its role in the management of hypoactive sexual desire disorder. *International Journal of Impotence Research, 19*, 458–463.

Abrams, R. (1992). *Electroconvulsive therapy.* New York: Oxford University Press.

Abramson, L. Y., Seligman, M. E. P., & Teasdale, J. D. (1978). Learned helplessness in humans: Critique and reformulation. *Journal of Abnormal Psychology, 87*, 32–48, 49–74.

Adams, J. L. (1986). *Conceptual blockbusting* (3rd ed.). New York: Norton.

Adams, J. S. (1965). Inequity in social exchange. In L. Berkowitz (Ed.), *Advances in experimental social psychology* (Vol. 2, pp. 267–299). New York: Academic Press.

Adams, R. E., & Laursen, B. (2007). The correlates of conflict: Disagreement is not necessarily detrimental. *Journal of Family Psychology, 21*, 445–458.

Ader, R., & Cohen, N. (1981). Conditioned immunopharmacological responses. In R. Ader (Ed.), *Psychoneuroimmunology* (pp. 281–319). New York: Academic Press.

Ader, R., & Cohen, N. (1993). Psychoneuroimmunology: Conditioning and stress. *Annual Review of Psychology, 44*, 53–85.

Adler, A. (1929). *The practice and theory of individual psychology.* New York: Harcourt, Brace & World.

Adolphs, R., & Damasio, A. R. (2001). The interaction of affect and cognition: A neurobiological perspective. In J. P. Forgas (Ed.), *Handbook of affect and social cognition* (pp. 27–49). Mahwah, NJ: Erlbaum.

Adolphs, R., & Tranel, D. (2004). Impaired judgments of sadness but not happiness following bilateral amygdala damage. *Journal of Cognitive Neuroscience, 16*, 453–462.

Ahmed, S. H., & Koob, G. F. (2004). Changes in response to a dopamine receptor antagonist in rats with escalating cocaine intake. *Psychopharmacology, 172*, 450–454.

Ainsworth, M. D. S., Blehar, M., Waters, E., & Wall, S. (1978). *Patterns of attachment.* Hillsdale, NJ: Erlbaum.

Ajzen, I., & Fishbein, M. (2005). The influence of attitudes on behavior. In D. Albarracin, B. T. Johnson, & M. P. Zanna (Eds.), *The handbook of attitudes* (pp. 173–221). Mahwah, NJ: Erlbaum.

Akiskal, H. S., & Akiskal, K. K. (2007). In search of Aristotle: Temperament, human nature, melancholia, crea-tivity and eminence. *Journal of Affective Disorders, 100*, 1–6.

Akmajian, A., Demers, R. A., Farmer, A. K., & Harnish, R. M. (1990). *Linguistics.* Cambridge, MA: The MIT Press.

Albarracín, D., Durantini, M. R., Earl, A., Gunnoe, J. B., & Leeper, J. (2008). Beyond the most willing audiences: A meta-intervention to increase exposure to HIV-prevention programs by vulnerable populations. *Health Psychology, 27*, 638–644.

Allan, C. A., Forbes, E. A., Strauss, B. J. G., & McLachlan, R. I. (2008). Testosterone therapy increases sexual desire in ageing men with low-normal testosterone levels and symptoms of androgen deficiency. *International Journal of Impotence Research, 20*, 396–401.

Allen, J. P., & Land, D. (1999). Attachment in adolescence. In J. Cassidy & P. R. Shaver (Eds.), *Handbook of attachment: Theory, research, and clinical applications.* New York: Guilford Press.

Allen, J. P., Porter, M. R., & McFarland, F. C. (2006). Leaders and followers in adolescent close relationships: Susceptibility to peer influence as a predictor of risky behavior, friendship instability, and depression. *Development and Psychopathology, 18*, 155–172.

Allport, G. W. (1937). *Personality: A psychological interpretation.* New York: Holt, Rinehart & Winston.

Allport, G. W. (1954). *The nature of prejudice.* Cambridge, MA: Addison-Wesley.

Allport, G. W. (1961). *Pattern and growth in personality.* New York: Holt, Rinehart & Winston.

Allport, G. W. (1966). Traits revisited. *American Psychologist, 21*, 1–10.

Allport, G. W., & Odbert, H. S. (1936). Trait-names, a psycholexical study. *Psychological Monographs, 47*(1, Whole No. 211).

Amabile, T. M. (1983). *The social psychology of creativity.* New York: Springer-Verlag.

Amaral, D. G., Schumann, C. M., & Nordahl, C. W. (2008). Neuroanatomy of autism. *Trends in Neurosciences, 31*, 137–145.

Amato, P. R., & Hohmann-Marriott, B. (2007). A comparison of high- and low-distress marriages that end in divorce. *Journal of Marriage and Family, 69*, 621–638.

American Association on Mental Retardation. (2002). *Mental retardation: Definition, classification, and systems of supports* (10th ed.). Washington, DC: American Association on Mental Retardation.

American Psychological Association. (2002). Ethical principles of psychologists and code of conduct. *American Psychologist, 57,* 1060–1073.

American Psychological Association. (2008). Summary report of journal operations, 2007. *American Psychologist, 63,* 490.

Amodio, D. M., & Devine, P. G. (2006). Stereotyping and evaluation in implicit race bias: Evidence for independent constructs and unique effects on behavior. *Journal of Personality and Social Psychology, 91,* 651–661.

Anderson, J. R. (1987). Skill acquisition: Compilation of weak-method problem-solutions. *Psychological Review, 94,* 192–210.

Anderson, J. R. (1996). ACT: A simple theory of complex cognition. *American Psychologist, 51,* 355–365.

Anderson, J. R., Bothell, D., Byrne, M. D., Douglass, S., Lebiere, C., & Qin, Y. (2004). An integrated theory of mind. *Psychological Review, 111,* 1036–1060.

Anderson, S. L., Adams, G., & Plaut, V. C. (2008). The cultural grounding of personal relationship: The importance of attractiveness in everyday life. *Journal of Personality and Social Psychology, 95,* 352–368.

Anliker, J. A., Bartoshuk, L., Ferris, A. M., & Hooks, L. D. (1991). Children's food preferences and genetic sensitivity to the bitter taste of 6-*n*-propylthiouracil (PROP). *American Journal of Clinical Nutrition, 54,* 316–320.

Anstee, J. L. K., Harris, S. G., Pruitt, K. D., & Sugar, J. A. (2008). Service-learning projects in an undergraduate gerontology course: A six-stage model and application. *Educational Gerontology, 34,* 595–609.

Anthony, D. B., Holmes, J. G., & Wood, J. V. (2007). Social acceptance and self-esteem: Tuning the sociometer to interpersonal value. *Journal of Personality and Social Psychology, 92,* 1024–1039.

Appleby, D. C. (2006). Defining, teaching, and assessing critical thinking in introductory psychology. In D. S. Dunn & S. L. Chew (Eds.), *Best practices for teaching introduction to psychology* (pp. 57–69). Mahwah, NJ: Erlbaum.

Appleby, L., Luchins, D. J., & Freels, S. (2006). Homeless admissions and immigration in a state mental hospital. *Psychiatric Services, 57,* 144.

Arcuri, L., Castelli, L., Galdi, S., Zogmaister, C., & Amadori, A. (2008). Predicting the vote: Implicit attitudes as predictors of the future behavior of decided and undecided voters. *Political Psychology, 29,* 369–387.

Arendt, J., & Skene, D. J. (2005). Melatonin as a chronobiotic. *Sleep Medicine Reviews, 9,* 25–39.

Arkin, R. M. (Ed.). (1990). Centennial celebration of the principles of psychology. *Personality and Social Psychology Bulletin, 16*(4).

Armour, B. S., Woollery, T., Malarcher, A., Pechacek, T. F., & Husten, C. (2005). Annual smoking attributable mortality, years of potential life lost, and productivity losses—United States, 1997–2001. *Morbidity and Mortality Weekly Report, 54,* 626–628.

Arnett, J. J. (1999). Adolescent storm and stress reconsidered. *American Psychologist, 54,* 317–326.

Aron, A., & Aron, E. N. (1994). Love. In A. L. Weber & J. H. Harvey (Eds.), *Perspectives on close relationships* (pp. 131–152). Boston: Allyn & Bacon.

Aron, A., Aron, E. N., & Smollan, D. (1992). Inclusion of other in the self scale and the structure of interpersonal closeness. *Journal of Personality and Social Psychology, 63,* 596–612.

Aron, A., Aron, E. N., Tudor, M., & Nelson, G. (1991). Close relationships as including other in the self. *Journal of Personality and Social Psychology, 60,* 241–253.

Aron, A., & Fraley, B. (1999). Relationship closeness as including other in the self: Cognitive underpinnings and measures. *Social Cognition, 17,* 140–160.

Aron, A., Mashek, D., McLaughlin-Volpe, T., Wright, S., Lewandowski, G., & Aron, E. N. (2004). Including close others in the cognitive structure of self. In M. W. Baldwin (Ed.), *Interpersonal cognition* (pp. 206–232). New York: Guilford Press.

Aron, A., & Westbay, L. (1996). Dimensions of the prototype of love. *Journal of Personality and Social Psychology, 70,* 535–551.

Aruguete, M. S., DeBord, K. A., & Yates, A., & Edman, J. (2005). Ethnic and gender differences in eating attitudes among black and white college students. *Eating Behaviors, 6,* 328–336.

Asch, S. E. (1940). Studies in the principles of judgments and attitudes: II. Determination of judgments by group and by ego standards. *Journal of Social Psychology, 12,* 433–465.

Asch, S. E. (1952). *Social psychology.* Englewood Cliffs, NJ: Prentice Hall.

Asch, S. E. (1955). Opinions and social pressure. *Scientific American, 193*(5), 31–35.

Asch, S. E. (1956). Studies of independence and conformity: A minority of one against a unanimous majority. *Psychological Monographs, 70*(9, Whole No. 416).

Ayduk, O., Rodriguez, M. L., Mischel, W., Shoda, Y., & Wright, J. (2007). Verbal intelligence and self-regulatory competencies: Joint predictors of boys' aggression. *Journal of Research in Personality, 41,* 374–388.

Ayllon, T., & Michael, J. (1959). The psychiatric nurse as a behavioral engineer. *Journal of the Experimental Analysis of Behavior, 2,* 323–334.

Baars, B. J. (1992). A dozen completing-plans techniques for inducing predictable slips in speech and action. In B. J. Baars (Ed.), *Experimental slips and human error: Exploring the architecture of volition* (pp. 129–150). New York: Plenum Press.

Baars, B. J., Motley, M. T., & MacKay, D. G. (1975). Output editing for lexical status in artificially elicited slips of the tongue. *Journal of Verbal Learning and Verbal Behavor, 14,* 382–391.

Baas, M., De Creu, C. K. W., & Nijstad, B. A. (2008). A meta-analysis of 25 years of mood-creativity research: Hedonic tone, activation, or regulatory focus? *Psychological Bulletin, 134,* 779–806.

Back, M. D., Schmukle, S. C., & Egloff, B. (2008). How extraverted is honey.bunny77@hotmail.de? *Journal of Research in Personality, 42,* 1116–1122.

Backman, C. W., & Secord, P. F. (1959). The effect of perceived liking on interpersonal attraction. *Human Relations, 12,* 379–384.

Baddeley, A. D. (2002). Is working memory still working? *European Psychologist, 7,* 85–97.

Baddeley, A. D. (2003). Working memory: Looking back and looking forward. *Nature Reviews Neuroscience, 4,* 829–839.

Bahrick, H. P., Bahrick, P. O., & Wittlinger, R. P. (1975). Fifty years of memory for names and faces: A cross-sectional approach. *Journal of Experimental Psychology: General, 104,* 54–75.

Bailey, B. A., & Sokol, R. J. (2008). Pregnancy and alcohol use: Evidence and recommendations for prenatal care. *Clinical Obstetrics and Gynecology, 51,* 436–444.

Baker, C. I., Liu, J., Wald, L L., Kwong, K. K., Benner, T., & Kanwisher, N. (2007). Visual word processing and experiential origins of functional selectivity in human extrastriate cortex. *PNAS, 104,* 9087–9092.

Balch, R. W., & Taylor, D. (2002). Making sense of the Heaven's Gate suicides. In D. G. Bromley & J. G. Melton (Eds.), *Cults, religion, and violence* (pp. 209–228). Cambridge, UK: Cambridge University Press.

Balsam, K. F., Beauchaine, T. P., Rothblum, E. D., & Solomon, S. E. (2008). Three-year follow-up of same-sex couples who had civil unions in Vermont, same-sex couples not in civil unions, and heterosexual married couples. *Developmental Psychology, 44,* 102–116.

Baltes, P. B. (1993). The aging mind: Potential and limits. *The Gerontologist, 33,* 580–594.

Baltes, P. B., & Kunzmann, U. (2003). Wisdom. *Psychologist, 16,* 131–133.

Baltes, P. B., Smith, J., & Staudinger, U. M. (1992). Wisdom and successful aging. In T. B. Sonderegger (Ed.), *The Nebraska Symposium on Motivation: Vol. 39. The psychology of aging* (pp. 123–167). Lincoln: University of Nebraska Press.

Baltes, P. B., & Staudinger, U. M. (1993). The search for a psychology of wisdom. *Current Directions in Psychological Science, 2,* 75–80.

Baltes, P. B., & Staudinger, U. M. (2000). Wisdom: A meta-heuristic (pragmatic) to orchestrate mind and virtue toward excellence. *American Psychologist, 55,* 122–136.

Bandelow, B., Krause, J., Wedekind, D., Broocks, A., Hajak, G., & Rüther, E. (2005). Early traumatic life events, parental attitudes, family history, and birth risk factors in patients with borderline personality disorder and healthy controls. *Psychiatry Research, 134,* 169–179.

Bandura, A. (1970). Modeling therapy. In W. S. Sahakian (Ed.), *Psychopathology today: Experimentation, theory and research.* Itasca, IL: Peacock.

Bandura, A. (1977). *Social learning theory.* Englewood Cliffs, NJ: Prentice-Hall.

Bandura, A. (1986). *Social foundations of thought and action: A social cognitive theory.* Englewood Cliffs, NJ: Prentice-Hall.

Bandura, A. (1992). Exercise of personal agency through the self-efficacy mechanism. In R. Schwarzer (Ed.), *Self-efficacy: Thought control of action* (pp. 3–38). Washington, DC: Hemisphere.

Bandura, A. (1997). *Self-efficacy: The exercise of control.* New York: Freeman.

Bandura, A. (1999). Social cognitive theory of personality. In L. A. Pervin & O. P. John (Eds.), *Handbook of personality: Theory and research* (2nd ed., pp. 154–196). New York: Guilford Press.

Bandura, A. (2006). Toward of psychology of human agency. *Perspectives on Psychological Science, 1,* 164–180.

Bandura, A., Ross, D., & Ross, S. A. (1963). Imitation of film-mediated aggressive models. *Journal of Abnormal and Social Psychology, 66,* 3–11.

Banks, S., & Dinges, D. F. (2007). Behavioral and physiological consequences of sleep restriction. *Journal of Clinical Sleep Medicine, 3,* 519–528.

Banyai, E. I., & Hilgard, E. R. (1976). Comparison of active-alert hypnotic induction with traditional relaxation induction. *Journal of Abnormal Psychology, 85,* 218–224.

Barak, A., Boniel-Nissim, M., & Suler, J. (2008). Fostering empowerment in online support groups. *Computers in Human Behavior, 24,* 1867–1883.

Bárez, M., Blasco, T., Fernández-Castro, J., & Viladrich, C. (2007). A structural model of the relationships between perceived control and the adaptation to illness in women with breast cancer. *Journal of Psychosocial Oncology, 25,* 21–43.

Bar-Hillel, M., & Neter, E. (1993). How alike is it versus how likely is it: A disjunction fallacy in probability judgments. *Journal of Personality and Social Psychology, 65,* 1119–1131.

Barkataki, I., Kumari, V., Das, M., Taylor, P., & Sharma, T. (2006). Volumetric structural brain abnormalities in men with schizophrenia and antisocial personality disorder. *Behavioural Brain Research, 169*, 239–247.

Barker, L. M., Best, M. R., & Domjan, M. (Eds.). (1978). *Learning mechanisms in food selection.* Houston: Baylor University Press.

Barker, R., Dembo, T., & Lewin, D. (1941). Frustration and aggression: An experiment with young children. *University of Iowa Studies in Child Welfare, 18*(1).

Baron-Cohen, S. (2008). Theories of the autistic mind. *The Psychologist, 21*, 112–116.

Barrett, L. F., Tugade, M. M., & Engle, R. W. (2004). Individual differences in working memory capacity and dual-process theories of mind. *Psychological Bulletin, 130*, 553–573.

Barrett, M. S., Chua, W.-J., Crits-Christoph, P., Gibbons, M. B., & Thompson, D. (2008). Early withdrawal from mental health treatment: Implications for psychotherapy practice. *Psychotherapy Theory, Research, Practice, Training, 45*, 247–267.

Bartlett, C. W., Gharani, N., Millonig, J. H., & Brzustowicz, L. M. (2005). Three autism candidate genes: A synthesis of human genetic analysis with other disciplines. *International Journal of Developmental Neuroscience, 23*, 221–234.

Bartlett, F. C. (1932). *Remembering: A study in experimental and social psychology.* Cambridge, UK: Cambridge University Press.

Barton, N. (2000). The rapid origin of reproduction isolation. *Science, 290*, 462–463.

Bartoshuk, L. M. (1993). The biological basis of food perception and acceptance. *Food Quality and Preference, 4*, 21–32.

Bartoshuk, L. M., & Beauchamp, G. K. (1994). Chemical senses. *Annual Review of Psychology, 45*, 419–449.

Bartz, J. A., & Hollander, E. (2006). The neuroscience of affiliation: Forging links between basic and clinical research on neuropeptides and social behavior. *Hormones and Behavior, 50*, 518–528.

Basso, E. B. (1987). The implications of a progressive theory of dreaming. In B. Tedlock (Ed.), *Dreaming: Anthropological and psychological interpretations* (pp. 86–104). Cambridge, UK: Cambridge University Press.

Batson, C. D. (1991). *The altruism question: Toward a social-psychological answer.* Hillsdale, NJ: Erlbaum.

Batson, C. D. (1994). Why act for the public good? Four answers. *Personality and Social Psychology Bulletin, 20*, 603–610.

Batson, C. D., Ahmad, N., Yin, J., Bedell, S. J., Johnson, J. W., Templin, C. M., & Whiteside, A. (1999). Two threats to the common good: Self-interested egoism and empathy-induced altruism. *Personality and Social Psychology Bulletin, 25*, 3–16.

Baumeister, R. F. (2000). Gender differences in erotic plasticity: The female sex drive as socially flexible and responsive. *Psychological Bulletin, 126*, 347–374.

Baumeister, R. F., Campbell, J. D., Krueger, J. I., & Vohs, K. D. (2003). Does high self-esteem cause better performance, interpersonal success, happiness, or healthy lifestyles? *Psychological Science in the Public Interest, 4*, 1–44.

Baumeister, R. F., & Twenge, J. M. (2002). Cultural suppression of female sexuality. *Review of General Psychology, 6*, 166–203.

Baumgartner, T., Heinrichs, M., Vonlanthen, A., Fischbacher, U., & Fehr, E. (2008). Oxytocin shapes the neural circuitry of trust and trust adaptation in humans. *Neuron, 58*, 639–650.

Bauminger, N., Finzi-Dottan, R., Chason, S., & Har-Even, D. (2008). Intimacy in adolescent friendship: The roles of attachment, coherence, and self-disclosure. *Journal of Social and Personal Relationships, 25*, 409–428.

Bayley, N. (1956). Individual patterns of development. *Child Development, 27*, 45–74.

Beauchaine, T. P., Webster-Stratton, C., & Reid, M. J. (2005). Mediators, moderators, and predictors of 1-year outcomes among children treated for early-onset conduct problems: A latent growth curve analysis. *Journal of Counseling and Clinical Psychology, 73*, 371–388.

Beck, A. T. (1976). *Cognitive therapy and emotional disorders.* New York: International Universities Press.

Beck, A. T. (1983). Cognitive theory of depression: New perspectives. In P. J. Clayton & J. E. Barrett (Eds.), *Treatment of depression: Old controversies and new approaches* (pp. 265–290). New York: Raven Press.

Beck, A. T. (1985). Cognitive therapy. In H. I. Kaplan & J. Sandock (Eds.), *Comprehensive textbook of psychiatry* (4th ed.). Baltimore: Williams & Wilkins.

Beck, A. T. (1988). Cognitive approaches to panic disorders: Theory and therapy. In S. Rachman & J. D. Maser (Eds.), *Panic: Psychological perspectives.* New York: Guilford Press.

Beck, A. T., & Emery, G. (1985). *Anxiety disorders and phobias: A cognitive perspective.* New York: Basic Books.

Beck, A. T., & Rush, A. J. (1989). Cognitive therapy. In H. I. Kaplan & B. Sadock (Eds.), *Comprehensive textbook of psychiatry* (Vol. 5). Baltimore: Williams & Wilkins.

Beck, A. T., Rush, A. J., Shaw, B. F., & Emery, G. (1979). *Cognitive therapy of depression.* New York: Guilford Press.

Becker, M. W., Pashler, H., & Anstis, S. M. (2000). The role of iconic memory in change-detection tasks. *Perception, 29*, 273–286.

Becker, S. W., & Eagly, A. H. (2004). The heroism of women and men. *American Psychologist, 59,* 163–178.

Behrman, A. (2002). *Electroboy.* New York: Random House.

Béïque, J.-C., Imad, M., Mladenovic, L., Gingrich, J. A., & Andrade, R. (2007). Mechanism of the 5-hydroxytryptamine 2A receptor-mediated facilitation of synaptic activity in prefrontal cortex. *PNAS, 104,* 9870–9875.

Bell, D. C. (2001). Evolution of parental caregiving. *Personality and Social Psychology Review, 5,* 216–229.

Belsky, J., Vandell, D. L., Burchinal, M., Clarke-Stewart, K. A., McCartney, K., Owen, M. T., & The NICHD Early Child Care Research Network. (2007). Are there long-term effects of early child care? *Child Development, 78,* 681–701.

Bem, D. (2000). The exotic-becomes-erotic theory of sexual orientation. In J. Bancroft (Ed.), *The role of theory in sex research* (pp. 67–81). Bloomington: Indiana University Press.

Bem, D. J. (1972). Self-perception theory. In L. Berkowitz (Ed.), *Advances in experimental social psychology* (Vol. 6, pp. 1–62). New York: Academic Press.

Bem, D. J. (1996). Exotic becomes erotic: A developmental theory of sexual orientation. *Psychological Review, 103,* 320–335.

Bem, S. L. (1981). *The Bem Sex Role Inventory: Professional manual.* Palo Alto, CA: Consulting Psychology Press.

Bem, S. L. (1974). The measurement of psychological androgyny. *Journal of Consulting and Clinical Psychology, 42,* 155–162.

Benedetti, F., Mayberg, H. S., Wager, T. D., Stohler, C. S., & Zubieta, J. K. (2005). Neurobiological mechanisms of the placebo effect. *Journal of Neuroscience, 25,* 10390–10402.

Benedict, R. (1938). Continuities and discontinuities in cultural conditioning. *Psychiatry, 1,* 161–167.

Benedict, R. (1959). *Patterns of culture.* Boston: Houghton Mifflin.

Benenson, J. F., Apostoleris, N. H., & Parnass, J. (1997). Age and sex differences in dyadic and group interaction. *Developmental Psychology, 33,* 538–543.

Benenson, J. F., & Heath, A. (2006). Boys withdraw from one-on-one interactions, whereas girls withdraw more in groups. *Developmental Psychology, 42,* 272–282.

Benhamou, S., & Poucet, B. (1996). A comparative analysis of spatial memory processes. *Behavioural Processes, 35,* 113–126.

Benight, C. C., Cieslak, R., Molton, I. R., & Johnson, L. E. (2008). Self-evaluative appraisals of coping capability and posttraumatic distress following motor vehicle accidents. *Journal of Consulting and Clinical Psychology, 76,* 677–685.

Benjamin, A. S. (2005). Response speeding mediates the contributions of cue familiarity and target retrievability to metamnemonic judgments. *Psychonomic Bulletin & Review, 12,* 874–879.

Benjet, C., & Kazdin, A. E. (2003). Spanking children: The controversies, findings, and new directions. *Clinical Psychology Review, 23,* 197–224.

Bennett, D. S., Bendersky, M., & Lewis, M. (2008). Children's cognitive ability from 4 to 9 years old as a function of prenatal cocaine exposure, environmental risk, and maternal verbal intelligence. *Developmental Psychology, 44,* 919–928.

Benson, H. (2000). *The relaxation response* (Updated ed.). New York: HarperCollins.

Bergman, E. T., & Roediger, H. L., III. (1999). Can Bartlett's repeated reproduction experiments be replicated? *Memory & Cognition, 27,* 937–947.

Bering, J. M., & Bjorklund, D. F. (2007). The serpent's gift: Evolutionary psychology and consciousness. In P. D. Zelazo, M. Moscovitch, & E. Thompson (Eds.), *The Cambridge handbook of consciousness* (pp. 597–629). New York: Cambridge University Press.

Berkowitz, L. (1993). *Aggression: Its causes, consequences, and control.* New York: McGraw-Hill.

Berkowitz, L. (1998). Affective aggression: The role of stress, pain, and negative affect. In R. G. Geen & E. Donnerstein (Eds.), *Human aggression: Theories, research, and implications for public policy* (pp. 49–72). San Diego, CA: Academic Press.

Berkowitz, S. J. (2003). Children exposed to community violence: The rationale for early intervention. *Clinical Child and Family Psychology Review, 6,* 293–302.

Berlin, B., & Kay, P. (1969). *Basic color terms: Their universality and evolution.* Berkeley: University of California Press.

Berlyne, D. E. (1960). *Conflict, arousal, and curiosity.* New York: McGraw-Hill.

Bernard, L. L. (1924). *Instinct.* New York: Holt, Rinehart & Winston.

Berscheid, E., & Walster, E. H. (1978). *Interpersonal attraction* (2nd ed.). Reading, MA: Addison-Wesley.

Bersoff, D. N. (Ed.) (2008). *Ethical conflicts in Psychology* (4th ed.). Washington, DC: American Psychological Association.

Bhuvaneswar, C. G., & Gutheil, T. G. (2008). E-mail and psychiatry: Some psychotherapeutic and psychoanalytic perspectives. *American Journal of Psychotherapy, 62,* 241–261.

Biederman, J., & Faraone, S. V. (2005). Attention-deficit hyperactivity disorder. *The Lancet, 366,* 237–248.

Biederman, J., Faraone, S. V., & Monteaux, M. C. (2002). Differential effect of environmental adversity by gender: Rutter's index of adversity in a group of boys and girls with and without ADHD. *American Journal of Psychiatry, 159,* 1556–1562.

Biederman, J., Kwon, A., Aleardi, M., Chouinard, V.-A., Marino, T., Cole, H., Mick, E., & Faraone, S. V. (2005). Absence of gender effects on attention deficit hyperactivity disorder: Findings in nonreferred subjects. *American Journal of Psychiatry, 162*, 1083–1089.

Biehl, M., Matsumoto, D., Ekman, P., Hearn, V., Heider, K., Kudoh, T., & Ton, V. (1997). Matsumoto and Ekman's Japanese and Caucasian facial expressions of emotion (JACFEE): Reliability data and cross-national differences. *Journal of Nonverbal Behavior, 21*, 3–21.

Biel, M. B., Preselow, E., Mulcare, L., Case, B. G., & Fieve, R. (2007). Continuation versus discontinuation of lithium in recurrent bipolar illnesss: A naturalistic study. *Bipolar Disorders, 9*, 435–442.

Bielak, A. A. M., Hughes, T. F., Small, B. J., & Dixon, R. A. (2007). It's never too late to engage in lifestyle activities: Significant concurrent but not change relationships between lifestyle activities and cognitive speed. *Journal of Gerontology: Psychological Sciences, 62B*, P331–P339.

Biglan, A. (1991). Distressed behavior and its context. *Behavior Analyst, 14*, 157–169.

Bilder, R. M., Volavka, J., Lachman, H. M., & Grace, A. A. (2004). The Catechol-O-Methyltransferase polymorphism: Relations to the tonic-phasic dopamine hypothesis and neuropsychiatric phenotypes. *Neuropsychopharmacology, 29*, 1943–1961.

Billings, A. G., & Moos, R. H. (1982). Family environments and adaptation: A clinically applicable typology. *American Journal of Family Therapy, 20*, 26–38.

Binet, A. (1911). *Les idées modernes sur les enfants.* Paris: Flammarion.

Bingenheimer, J. B., Brennan, R. T., & Earls, F. J. (2005). Firearm violence exposure and serious violent behavior. *Science, 308*, 1323–1326.

Black, D. N., Seritan, A. L., Taber, K. H., & Hurley, R. A. (2004). Conversion hysteria: Lessons from functional imaging. *Journal of Neuropsychiatry and Clinical Neurosciences, 16*, 245–251.

Blatter, K., & Cajochen, C. (2007). Circadian rhythms in cognitive performance: Methodologocial constrains, protocols, theoretical underpinnings. *Physiology & Behavior, 90*, 196–208.

Bleuler, M. (1978). The long-term course of schizophrenic psychoses. In L. C. Wynne, R. L. Cromwell, & S. Mattysse (Eds.), *The nature of schizophrenia: New approaches to research and treatment* (pp. 631–636). New York: Wiley.

Blond, A. (2008). Impacts of exposure to images of ideal bodies on male body dissatisfaction: A review. *Body Image, 5*, 244–250.

Bloom, K., Delmore-Ko, P., Masataka, N., & Carli, L. (1999). Possible self as parent in Canadian, Italian, and Japanese young adults. *Canadian Journal of Behavioural Science, 31*, 198–207.

Blos, P. (1965). *On adolescence: A psychoanalytic interpretation.* New York: The Free Press.

Blumberg, H. P., Leung, H. C., Skudlarski, P., Lacadie, C. M., Fredericks, C. A., Harris, B. C., Charney, D. S., Gore, J. C., Krystal, J. H., & Peterson, B. S. (2003). A functional magnetic resonance imaging study of bipolar disorder. *Archives of General Psychiatry, 60*, 601–609.

Blustein, D. L. (2008). The role of work in psychological health and well-being: A conceptual, historical, and public policy perspective. *American Psychologist, 63*, 228–240.

Boardman, J. D., Saint Onge, J. M., Haberstick, B. C., Timberlake, D. S., & Hewitt, J. K. (2008). Do schools moderate the genetic determinants of smoking? *Behavioral Genetics, 38*, 234–246.

Bock, K. (1990). Structure in language: Creating form in talk. *American Psychologist, 45*, 1221–1236.

Bock, K., Dell, G. S., Chang, F., & Onishi, K. H. (2007). Persistent structural priming from language comprehension to language production. *Cognition, 104*, 437–458.

Bogle, K. A. (2008). *Hooking up: Sex, dating, and relationships on campus.* New York: New York University Press.

Bohannon, J. N. III, Gratz, S., & Cross, V. S. (2007). The effects of affect and input source on flashbulb memories. *Applied Cognitive Psychology, 21*, 1023–1036.

Bohlin, G., Hagekull, B., & Rydell, A.-M. (2000). Attachment and social functioning: A longitudinal study from infancy to middle childhood. *Social Development, 9*, 24–39.

Boivin, D. B., Tremblay, G. M., & James, F. O. (2007). Working on atypical schedules. *Sleep Medicine, 8*, 578–589.

Bolden, L., & Wicks, M. N. (2005). Length of stay, admission types, psychiatric diagnoses, and the implications of stigma in African Americans in the nationwide inpatient sample. *Issues in Mental Health Nursing, 26*, 1043–1059.

Bolhuis, J. J., & Honey, R. C. (1998). Imprinting, learning and development: From behaviour to brain and back. *Trends in Neurosciences, 21*, 306–311.

Bolino, M. C., & Turnley, W. H. (2008). Old faces, new places: Equity theory in cross-cultural contexts. *Journal of Organizational Behavior, 29*, 29–50.

Bolton, D., & Perrin, S. (2008). Evaluation of exposure with response-prevention for obsessive compulsive disorder in childhood and adolescence. *Journal of Behavior Therapy and Experimental Psychiatry, 39*, 11–22.

Bolton, J. M., Belik, S.-L., Enns, M. W., Cox, B. J., & Sareen, J. (2008). Exploring the correlates of suicide attempts among individuals with major depressive disorder: Findings from the national epidemiologic survey on alcohol and related conditions. *The Journal of Clinical Psychiatry, 69*, 1139–1149.

Bond, C. F., Jr., Pitre, U., & van Leeuwen, M. D. (1991). Encoding operations and the next-in-line effect. *Personality and Social Psychology Bulletin, 17,* 435–441.

Bond, M. H. (2004). Culture and aggression—from context to coercion. *Personality and Social Psychology Review, 8,* 62–78.

Bonnano, G. A., & Mancini, A. D. (2008). The human capacity to thrive in the face of potential trauma. *Pediatrics, 121,* 369–375.

Bornstein, M. H., & Arterberry, M. E. (2003). Recognition, discrimination and categorization of smiling by 5-month-old infants. *Developmental Science, 6,* 585–599.

Bostrom, N. (2005). In defense of posthuman dignity. *Bioethics, 19,* 202–214.

Bouchard, T. J. Jr. (2004). Genetic influence on human psychological traits: A survey. *Current Directions in Psychological Science, 13,* 148–151.

Bouchard, T. J. Jr., & Loehlin, J. C. (2001). Genes, evolution, and personality. *Behavior Genetics, 31,* 243–273.

Boutin, P., & Frougel, P. (2005). GAD2: A polygenic contribution to genetic susceptibility for common obesity? *Pathologie Biologie, 53,* 305–307.

Bovbjerg, D. H. (2006). The continuing problem of post chemotherapy nausea and vomiting: Contributions of classical conditioning. *Autonomic Neuroscience: Basic and Clinical, 129,* 92–98.

Bovbjerg, D. H., Montgomery, G. H., & Raptis, G. (2005). Evidence for classically conditioned fatigue responses in patients receiving chemotherapy treatment for breast cancer. *Journal of Behavioral Medicine, 28,* 231–237.

Bowden, E. M., & Beeman, M. J. (2003). Normative data for 144 compound remote associates problem. *Behavior Research Methods, Instruments, and Computers, 35,* 634–639.

Bowers, J. S., & Marsolek, C. J. (Eds.). (2003). *Rethinking implicit memory.* London: Oxford University Press.

Bowlby, J. (1969), *Attachment and loss, Vol 1. Attachment.* New York: Basic Books.

Bowlby, J. (1973), *Attachment and loss, Vol 2. Separation, anxiety and anger.* London: Hogarth.

Boyd, R. C., Diamond, G. S., & Bourolly, J. N. (2006). Developing a family-based depression prevention program in urban community mental health clinics: A qualitative investigation. *Family Process, 45,* 187–203.

Boysen, G. A., & Vogel, D. L. (2007). Biased assimilation and attitude polarization in response to learning about biological explanations of homosexuality. *Sex Roles, 57,* 755–762.

Brainerd, C. J. (1996). Piaget: A centennial celebration. *Psychological Science, 7,* 191–195.

Branje, S. J. T., Frijns, T., Finkenaer, C., Engels, R., & Meeus, W. (2007). You are my best friend: Commitment and stability in adolescents' same-sex friendships. *Personal Relationships, 14,* 587–603.

Brans, R. G. H., van Haren, N. E. M., van Baal, C. M., Schnack, H. G., Kahn, R. S., & Hulshoff, H. E. (2008). Heritability of changes in brain volume over time in twin pairs discordant for schizophrenia. *Archives of General Psychiatry, 65,* 1259–1268.

Braun, K. A., Ellis, R., & Loftus, E. F. (2002). Make my memory: How advertising can change our memories of the past. *Psychology & Marketing, 19,* 1–23.

Breen, F. M., Plomin, R., & Wardle, J. (2006). Heritability of food preferences in young children. *Physiology & Behavior, 88,* 443–447.

Breggin, P. R. (1979). *Electroshock: Its brain disabling effects.* New York: Springer.

Breggin, P. R. (1991). *Toxic psychiatry.* New York: St. Martin's Press.

Breland, K., & Breland, M. (1951). A field of applied animal psychology. *American Psychologist, 6,* 202–204.

Breland, K., & Breland, M. (1961). A misbehavior of organisms. *American Psychologist, 16,* 681–684.

Brendgen, M., Dionne, G., Girard, A., Boivin, M., Vitaor, F., & Pérusse, D. (2005). Examining genetic and environmental effects on social aggression: A study of 6-year-old twins. *Child Development, 76,* 930–946.

Breslin, P. A. S., & Spector, A. C. (2008). Mammalian taste perception. *Current Biology, 18,* R148–R155.

Bretherton, I. (1996). Internal working models of attachment relationships as related to resilient coping. In G. G. Noam & K. W. Fischer (Eds.), *Development and vulnerability in close relationships* (pp. 3–27). Mahwah, NJ: Erlbaum.

Brewer, M. B. (2007). The importance of being *we*: Human nature and intergroup relations. *American Psychologist, 62,* 728–738.

Bridge, J. A., & Barbe, R. P. (2004). Reducing hospital readmission in depression and schizophrenia: Current evidence. *Current Opinion in Psychiatry, 17,* 505–511.

Bridge, J. A., Iyengar, S., Salary, C. B., Barbe, R. P., Birmaher, B., Pincus, H. A., Ren, L., & Brent, D. A. (2007). Clinical response and risk for reported suicidal ideation and suicide attempts in pediatric antidepressant treatment: A meta-analysis of randomized controlled trials. *JAMA, 297,* 1683–1696.

Briggs, C. J., Reis, S. M., & Sullivan, E. E. (2008). A national view of promising programs and practices for culturally, linguistically, and ethnically diverse gifted and talented students. *Gifted Child Quarterly, 52,* 131–145.

Briones, T. L., Klintsova, A. Y., & Greenough, W. T. (2004). Stability of synaptic plasticity in the adult rat visual cortex induced by complex environment exposure. *Brain Research, 1018*, 130–135.

Broadbent, D. E. (1958). *Perception and communication.* London: Pergamon Press.

Brody, A. L., Saxena, S., Stoessel, P., Gillies, L. A., Fairbanks, L. A., Alborzian, S., Phelps, M. E., Huang, S. C., Wu, H. M., Ho, M. L., Ho, M. K., Au, S. C., Maidment, K., & Baxter, L. R. Jr. (2002). Regional brain metabolic changes in patients with major depression treated with either paroxetine or interpersonal therapy. *Archives of General Psychiatry, 58*, 631–640.

Broman, S. H., Nichols, P. I., & Kennedy, W. A. (1975). *Preschool IQ: Prenatal and early developmental correlates.* Hillsdale, NJ: Erlbaum.

Bronfenbrenner, U. (Ed.) (2004). *Making human beings human: Bioecological perspectives on human development.* Thousand Oaks, CA: Sage Publications.

Brown, F. B., & Klute, C. (2003). Friendships, cliques, and crowds. In G. R. Adams & M. D. Berzonsky (Eds.), *Blackwell handbooks of developmental psychology* (pp. 330–348). Malden, MA: Blackwell Publishing.

Brown, N. R., & Siegler, R. S. (1992). The role of availability in the estimation of national populations. *Memory & Cognition, 20*, 406–412.

Brown, R. (1976). Reference: In memorial tribute to Eric Lenneberg. *Cognition, 4*, 125–153.

Brown, R. (1986). *Social psychology: The second edition.* New York: The Free Press.

Brown, R., & Kulik, J. (1977). Flashbulb memories. *Cognition, 5*, 73–99.

Brown, R. J. (2004). Psychological mechanisms in medically unexplained symptoms: An integrative conceptual model. *Psychological Bulletin, 130*, 793–812.

Bruni, O., Ferri, R., Novelli, L., Finotti, E., Miano, S., & Guilleminault, C. (2008). NREM sleep instability in children with sleep terrors: The role of slow wave activity interruptions. *Clinical Neurophysiology, 119*, 985–992.

Brunyé, T. T., Rapp, D. N., & Taylor, H. A. (2008). Representational flexibility and specificity following spatial descriptions of real-world environments. *Cognition, 108*, 418–443.

Buchler, N. E. G., & Reder, L. M. (2007). Modeling age-related memory deficits: A two-parameter solution. *Psychology and Aging, 22*, 104–121.

Buckner, J. C., Mezzacappa, E., & Beardslee, W. R. (2003). Characteristics of resilient youths living in poverty: The role of self-regulatory processes. *Development and Psychopathology, 15*, 139–162.

Buckworth, J., Lee, R. E., Regan, G., Schneider, L. K., & DiClemente, C. C. (2007). Decomposing intrinsic and extrinsic motivation for exercise: Application to stages of motivational readiness. *Psychology of Sport and Exercise, 8*, 441–461.

Buckworth, J., Lee, R. E., Regan, G., Schneider, L. K., & DiClemente, C. C. (2007). Decomposing intrinsic and extrinsic motivation for exercise: Application to stages of motivational readiness. *xi,* 441–461.

Buffardi, L. E., & Campbell, W. K. (2008). Narcissism and social networking web sites. *Personality and Social Psychology Bulletin, 34*, 1303–1314.

Burgard, M., & Mitchell, J. E. (2000). Group cognitive behavioral therapy for buying disorder. In A. L. Benson (Ed.), *I shop therefore I am: Compulsive buying and the search for self* (pp. 367–397). Northvale, NJ: Jason Aronson.

Burger, J. M. (2009). Replicating Milgram: Would people still obey today? *American Psychologist, 64*, 1–11.

Burger, J. M., & Caldwell, D. F. (2003). The effects of monetary incentives and labeling on the foot-in-the-door effect: Evidence for a self-perception process. *Basic and Applied Social Psychology, 25*, 235–241.

Burkley, E. (2008). The role of self-control in resistance to persuasion. *Personality and Social Psychology Bulletin, 34*, 419–431.

Burnett, R. C., Medin, D. L., Ross, N. O., & Blok, S. V. (2005). Ideal is typical. *Canadian Journal of Experimental Psychology, 59*, 3–10.

Burnstein, E. (2005). Altruism and genetic relatedness. In D. M. Buss (Ed.), *The handbook of evolutionary psychology* (pp. 528–551). Hoboken, NJ: Wiley.

Bushman, B. J., & Anderson, C. J. (2002). Violent video games and hostile expectations: A test of the general aggression model. *Personality and Social Psychology Bulletin, 28*, 1679–1686.

Buss, D. M. (1995). Evolutionary psychology: A new paradigm for psychological science. *Psychological Inquiry, 6*, 1–30.

Buss, D. M. (2008). Evolutionary psychology: *The new science of mind* (3rd ed.), Boston, MA: Allyn & Bacon.

Buss, D. M. (2000). The evolution of happiness. *American Psychologist, 55*, 15–23.

Butcher, J. N., Graham, J. R., Ben-Porath, Y. S., Tellegen, A., Dahlstrom, W. G., & Kaemmer, B. (2001). *Minnesota Multiphasic Personality Inventory-2 (MMPI-2): Manual for administration and scoring* (2nd ed.). Minneapolis: University of Minnesota Press.

Butcher, J. N., Mineka, S., & Hooley, J. M. (2008). *Abnormal Psychology* (13th ed.). Boston, MA: Allyn & Bacon.

Butcher, J. N., & Rouse, S. V. (1996). Personality: Individual differences and clinical assessment. *Annual Review of Psychology, 47,* 87–111.

Bykov, K. M. (1957). *The cerebral cortex and the internal organs.* New York: Academic Press.

Byrne, D., & Clore, G. L. (1970). A reinforcement model of evaluative processes. *Personality: An International Journal, 1,* 103–128.

Cabeza, R. (2002). Hemispheric asymmetry reduction in older adults: The HAROLD model. *Psychology and Aging, 17,* 85–100.

Cabeza, R., Daselaar, S. M., Dolcos, F., Prince, S. E., Budde, M., & Nyberg, L. (2004). Task-independent and task-specific age effects on brain activity during working memory, visual attention and episodic retrieval. *Cerebral Cortex, 14,* 364–375.

Cahill, L., Uncapher, M., Kilpatrick, L., Alkire, M. T., & Turner, J. (2004). Sex-related hemispheric lateralization of amygdala function in emotionally influenced memory: An fMRI investigation. *Learning & Memory, 11,* 261–266.

Cahn, B. R., & Polich, J. (2006). Meditation states and traits: EEG, ERP, and neuroimaging studies. *Psychological Bulletin, 132,* 180–211.

Cameron, C. L., Cella, D. C., Herndon, E. E., II, Kornblith, A. B., Zucerkman, E., Henderson, E., Weiss, R. B., Cooper, M. R., Silver, R. T., Leone, L., Canellos, G. P., Peterson, B. A., & Holland, J. C. (2001). Persistent symptoms among survivors of Hodgkin's disease: An explanatory model based on classical conditioning. *Health Psychology, 20,* 71–75.

Camras, L. A., Oster, H., Bakeman, R., Meng, Z., Ujiie, T., & Campos, J. L. (2007). Do infants show distinct negative facial expressions for fear and anger? Emotional expression in 11-month-old European American, Chinese, and Japanese infants. *Infancy, 11,* 131–155.

Camras, L. A., Oster, H., Campos, J., Campos, R., Ujiie, T., Miyake, K., Wang, L., & Meng, Z. (1998). Production of emotional facial expressions in European American, Japanese, and Chinese infants. *Developmental Psychology, 34,* 616–628.

Canli, T., Desmond, J. E., Zhao, Z., & Gabrieli, J. D. E. (2002a). Sex differences in the neural basis of emotional memories. *Proceedings of the National Academy of Sciences, 99,* 10789–10794.

Canli, T., Desmond, J. E., Zhao, Z., Glover, G., & Gabrieli, J. D. E. (1998). Hemispheric asymmetry for emotional stimuli detected with fMRI. *NeuroReport, 9,* 3233–3239.

Canli, T., Sivers, H., Whitfield, S. L., Gotlib, I. H., & Gabrieli, J. D. E. (2002b). Amygdala response to happy faces as a function of extraversion. *Science, 296,* 2191.

Cannon, W. B. (1927). The James–Lange theory of emotion: A critical examination and an alternative theory. *American Journal of Psychology, 39,* 106–124.

Cannon, W. B. (1929). *Bodily changes in pain, hunger, fear, and rage* (2nd ed.). New York: Appleton-Century-Crofts.

Cannon, W. B. (1934). Hunger and thirst. In C. Murchison (Ed.), *A handbook of general experimental psychology.* Worcester, MA: Clark University Press.

Cannon, W. B., & Washburn, A. L. (1912). An explanation of hunger. *American Journal of Physiology, 29,* 441–454.

Cantor, N., & Kihlstrom, J. R. (1987). *Personality and social intelligence.* Englewood Cliffs, NJ: Prentice Hall.

Cappelletti, M., Fregni, F., Shapiro, K., Pascual-Leone, A., Caramazza, A. (2008). Processing nouns and verbs in the left frontal cortex: A transcranial magnetic stimulation study. *Journal of Cognitive Neuroscience, 20,* 707–720.

Caprara, G. V., Barbaranelli, C., & Zimbardo, P. G. (1996). Understanding the complexity of human aggression: Affective, cognitive, and social dimensions of individual differences in pro-pensity toward aggression. *European Journal of Personality, 10,* 133–155.

Carazo, P., Sanchez, E., Font, E., & Desbilis, E. (2004). Chemosensory cues allow male *Tenebrio molitor* beetles to assess the reproductive status of prospective mates. *Animal Behaviour, 68,* 123–129.

Carducci, B. J., & Zimbardo, P. G. (1995, November/December). Are you shy? *Psychology Today, 28,* 34–40.

Carey, S. (1978). The child as word learner. In M. Hale, J. Bresnan, & G. A. Miller (Eds.), *Linguistic theory and psychological reality* (pp. 265–293). Cambridge, MA: MIT Press.

Carey, S. (1985). *Conceptual change in childhood.* Cambridge, MA: MIT Press.

Carlier, P., & Jamon, M. (2006). Observational learning in C57BL/6j mice. *Behavioural Brain Research, 174,* 125–131.

Carnagey, N. L., Anderson, C. A., & Bushman, B. J. (2007). The effect of video game violence on physiological desensitization to real-life violence. *Journal of Experimental Social Psychology, 43,* 489–496.

Carroll, M. E., & Overmier, J. B. (Eds.). (2001). *Animal research and human health: Advancing human welfare through behavioral science.* Washington, DC: American Psychological Association.

Carstensen, L. L., & Freund, A. M. (1994). The resilience of the aging self. *Developmental Review, 14,* 81–92.

Carter, J. H. (1982). The effects of aging on selected visual functions: Color vision, glare sensitivity, field of vision, and accommodation. In R. Sekuler, D. Kline, & K. Dismukes (Eds.), *Aging and human visual function* (pp. 121–130). New York: Liss.

Carter, S. J., & Cassaday, H. J. (1998). State-dependent retrieval and chlorpheniramine. *Human Psychopharmacology, 13,* 513–523.

Casey, B. J., Getz, S., & Galvan, A. (2008). The adolescent brain. *Developmental Review, 28,* 62–77.

Caspi, A., Sugden, K., Moffitt, T. E., Taylor, A., Craig, I. W., Harrington, H., McClay, J., Mill, J., Martin, J., Braithwaite, A., & Poulton, R. (2003). Influence of life stress on depression: Moderation by a polymorphism in the 5-HTT gene. *Science, 301,* 386–389.

Cassel, J.-C., Riegert, C., Rutz, S., Koenig, J., Rothmaier, K., Cosquer, B., Lazarus, C., Birthelmer, A., Jeltsch, H., Jones, B. C., & Jackisch, R. (2005). Ethanol, 3,4-methylenedioxymethamphetamine (Ecstasy) and their combination: Long-term behavioral, neurochemical and neuropharmacological effects in the rat. *Neuropsychopharmacology, 30,* 1870–1882.

Cassin, S. E., von Ranson, K. M., Heng, K., Brar, J., & Wojtowica, A. E. (2008). Adapted motivational interviewing for women with binge eating disorder: A randomized controlled trial. *Psychology of Addictive Behaviors, 22,* 417–425.

Catalano, R., Novaco, R., & McConnell, W. (1997). A model of the net effect of job loss on violence. *Journal of Personality and Social Psychology, 72,* 1440–1447.

Catalano, R., Novaco, R. W., & McConnell, W. (2002). Lay-offs and violence revisited. *Aggressive Behavior, 28,* 233–247.

Caterina, M. J., Leffler, A., Malmberg, A. B., Martin, W. J., Trafton, J., Petersen-Zeitz, K. R., Koltzenburg, M., Basbaum, A. I., & Julius, D. (2000). Impaired nociception and pain sensation in mice lacking the capsaicin receptor. *Science, 288,* 306–313.

Cattell, R. B. (1963). Theory of fluid and crystallized intelligence: A critical experiment. *Journal of Educational Psychology, 54,* 1–22.

Cattell, R. B. (1979). *Personality and learning theory.* New York: Springer.

Centers for Disease Control and Prevention. (2007, February 9). Prevalence of autism spectrum disorders—Autism and Developmental Disabilities Monitoring Network, 14 Sites, United States, 2002. *Morbidity and Mortality Weekly Report, 56,* 12–28. Retrieved from www.cdc.gov/mmwr/PDF/ss/ss5601.pdf.

Ceschi, G., van der Linden, M., Dunker, D., Perroud, A., & Brédart, S. (2003). Further exploration memory bias in compulsive washers. *Behaviour Research and Therapy, 41,* 737–748.

Chapman, P. D. (1988). *Schools as sorters: Lewis M. Terman, applied psychology, and the intelligence testing movement, 1890–1930.* New York: New York University Press.

Chartrand, T. L., & Bargh, J. A. (1999). The chameleon effect: The perception-behavior link and social interaction. *Journal of Personality and Social Psychology, 76,* 893–910.

Chase, W. G., & Ericsson, K. A. (1981). Skilled memory. In J. R. Anderson (Ed.), *Cognitive skills and their acquisition.* Hillsdale, NJ: Erlbaum.

Chaves, J. F. (1999). Applying hypnosis in pain management: Implications of alternative theoretical perspectives. In I. Kirsch, A. Capafons, E. Cardeña-Buelna, & S. Amigó (Eds.), *Clinical hypnosis and self-regulation: Cognitive-behavioral perspectives* (pp. 227–247). Washington, DC: American Psychological Association.

Chen, F. F., & Kenrick, D. T. (2002). Repulsion or attraction? Group membership and assumed attitude similarity. *Journal of Personality and Social Psychology, 83,* 111–125.

Chen, S., Boucher, H. C., & Tapias, M. P. (2006). The relational self revealed: Integrative conceptualization and implications for interpersonal life. *Psychological Bulletin, 132,* 151–179.

Chen, Z., & Cowan, N. (2005). Chunk limits and length limits in immediate recall: A reconciliation. *Journal of Experimental Psychology: Learning, Memory, and Cognition, 31,* 1235–1249.

Cheney, D. L., & Seyfarth, R. M. (1990). *How monkeys see the world.* Chicago: University of Chicago Press.

Cheney, D. L., & Seyfarth, R. M. (2007). *Baboon metaphysics.* Chicago: The University of Chicago Press.

Cheng, P. W., & Holyoak, K. J. (1985). Pragmatic reasoning schemas. *Cognitive Psychology, 17,* 391–416.

Child Welfare Information Gateway. (2007). *Foster Care Statistics.* Retrieved from www.childwelfare.gov/pubs/factsheets/foster.pdf.

Cho, S., Holyoak, K. J., & Cannon, T. D. (2007). Analogical reasoning in working memory: Resources shared among relational integration, interference resolution, and maintenance. *Memory & Cognition, 35,* 1445–1455.

Chomsky, N. (1965). *Aspects of a theory of syntax.* Cambridge, MA: MIT Press.

Chomsky, N. (1975). *Reflections on language.* New York: Pantheon Books.

Chorover, S. (1981, June). *Organizational recruitment in "open" and "closed" social systems: A neuropsychological perspective.* Conference paper presented at the Center for the Study of New Religious Movements, Berkeley, CA.

Christensen, A., Atkins, D. C., Yi, J., Baucom, D. H., & George, W. H. (2006). Couple and individual adjustment for 2 years following a randomized clinical trial comparing traditional versus integrative behavioral couple therapy. *Journal of Consulting and Clinical Psychology, 74,* 1180–1191.

Christensen, A. J., & Johnson, J. A. (2002). Patient adherence with medical treatment regimens: An interactive approach. *Current Directions in Psychological Science, 11,* 94–97.

Christensen, B. T., & Schunn, C. D. (2007). The relationship of analogical distance to analogical function and preinventive structure: The case of engineering design. *Memory & Cognition, 35,* 29–38.

Christie, B. R., & Cameron, H. A. (2006). Neurogenesis in the adult hippocampus. *Hippocampus, 16,* 199–207.

Cialdini, R. B. (2009). *Influence: Science and practice* (5th ed.). Boston, MA: Allyn & Bacon.

Cialdini, R. B., & Goldstein, N. J. (2004). Social influence: Compliance and conformity. *Annual Review of Psychology, 55,* 591–621.

Cialdini, R. B., Vincent, J. E., Lewis, S. K., Catalan, J., Wheeler, D., & Darby, B. L. (1975). Reciprocal concessions procedure for inducing compliance: The door-in-the-face technique. *Journal of Personality and Social Psychology, 31,* 206–215.

Clamp, M., Fry, B., Kamal, M., Xie, X., Cuff, J., Lin, M. F., Kellis, M., Lindblad-Toh, K., & Lander, E. S. (2007). Distinguishing protein-coding and noncoding genes in the human genome. *PNAS, 104,* 19428–19433.

Clark, E. V. (2003). *First language acquisition.* Cambridge, UK: Cambridge University Press.

Clark, H. H. (1996). *Using language.* Cambridge, UK: Cambridge University Press.

Clark, H. H., & Clark, E. V. (1977). *Psychology and language: An introduction to psycholinguistics.* New York: Harcourt Brace Jovanovich.

Clark, H. H., & Van Der Wege, M. M. (2002). Psycholinguistics. In H. Pashler & D. Medin (Eds.), *Stevens' handbook of experimental psychology: Vol. 3. Memory and cognitive processes* (pp. 209–259). New York: Wiley.

Clark, K., & Clark, M. (1947). Racial identification and preference in Negro children. In T. M. Newcomb & E. L. Hartley (Eds.), *Readings in social psychology* (pp. 169–178). New York: Holt.

Clark, M. D., & Carroll, M. H. (2008). Acquaintance rape scripts of women and men: Similarities and differences. *Sex Roles, 58,* 616–625.

Clarke-Stewart, A., & Alhusen, V. D. (2005). *What we know about childcare.* Cambridge, MA: Harvard University Press.

Clarke-Stewart, K. A. (1993). *Daycare.* Cambridge, MA: Harvard University Press.

Clopton, N. A., & Sorell, G. T. (1993). Gender differences in moral reasoning: Stable or situational? *Psychology of Women Quarterly, 17,* 85–101.

Clore, G. L., & Huntsinger, J. R. (2007). How emotions inform judgment and regulate thought. *Trends in Cognitive Sciences, 11,* 393–399.

Coan, J. A., Schaefer, H. S., & Davidson, R. J. (2006). Lending a hand: Social regulation of the neural response to threat. *Psychological Science, 17,* 1032–1039.

Coates, T. J., & Szekeres, G. (2004). A plan for the next generation of HIV prevention research: Seven key policy investigative challenges. *American Psychologist, 59,* 747–757.

Coe, C. L. (1999). Psychosocial factors and psychoneuroimmunology within a lifespan perspective. In D. P. Keating & C. Hertzman (Eds.), *Developmental health and the wealth of nations: Social, biological, and educational dynamics* (pp. 201–219). New York: Guilford Press.

Cohen, A., & Avrahami, A. (2005). Soccer fans' motivation as a predictor of participation in soccer-related activities: An empirical examination in Israel. *Social Behavior and Personality, 33,* 419–434.

Cohen, P., Chen, H., Gordon, K., Johnson, J., Brook, J., & Kasen, S. (2008). Socioeconomic background and the developmental course of schizotypal and borderline personality disorder symptoms. *Development and Psychopathology, 20,* 633–650.

Cohen, S., Tyrrell, D. A. J., & Smith, A. P. (1993). Negative life events, perceived stress, negative affect, and susceptibility to the common cold. *Journal of Personality and Social Psychology, 64,* 131–140.

Cole, D. A., Ciesla, J. A., Dallaire, D. H., Jacquez, F. M., Pineda, A. Q., LaGrange, B., Truss, A. E., Folmer, A. S., Tilghman-Osborne, C., & Felton, J. W. (2008). Emergence of attributional style and its relation to depressive symptoms. *Journal of Abnormal Psychology, 117,* 16–31.

Collins, M. A., & Amabile, T. M. (1999). Motivation and creativity. In R. J. Sternberg (Ed.), *Handbook of creativity* (pp. 297–312). Cambridge, UK: Cambridge University Press.

Collins, W. A., Maccoby, E. E., Steinberg, L., Hetherington, E. M., & Bornstein, M. H. (2000). Contemporary research on parenting: The case for nature and nurture. *American Psychologist, 55,* 218–232.

Comstock, G., & Scharrer, E. (1999). *Television: What's on, who's watching, and what it means.* San Diego, CA: Academic Press.

Congdon, E., & Canli, T. (2006). The endophenotype of impulsivity: Reaching consilience through behavioral, genetic, and neuroimaging approaches. *Behavioral and Cognitive Neuroscience, 4,* 1–20.

Conway, A. R., Kane, M. J., Bunting, M. F., Hambrick, D. Z., Wilhelm, O., & Engle, R. W. (2005). Working memory span tasks: A methodological review and user's guide. *Psychonomic Bulletin & Review, 12,* 769–786.

Cook, C. R., Gresham, F. M., Kern, L., Barreras, R. B., Thornton, S., & Crews, S. D. (2008). Social skills training for secondary students with emotional and/or behavioral disorders: A review and analysis of the meta-analytic literature. *Journal of Emotional and Behavioral Disorders, 16,* 131–144.

Coolidge, F. L., Thede, L. L., & Jang, K. L. (2001). Heritability of personality disorders in childhood: A preliminary investigation. *Journal of Personality Disorders, 15,* 33–40.

Cooper, J. (2007). *Cognitive dissonance: Fifty years of a classic theory.* Thousand Oaks, CA: Sage Publications.

Cooper, J. O., Heron, T. E., & Heward, W. L. (2007). *Applied behavior analysis.* Upper Saddle River, NJ: Prentice-Hall.

Coren, S., Ward, L. M., & Enns, J. T. (1999). *Sensation and perception* (5th ed.). Fort Worth, TX: Harcourt Brace.

Corr, P. J., & Gray, J. A. (1996). Attributional style as a personality factor in insurance sales performance in the UK. *Journal of Occupational and Organizational Psychology, 69,* 83–87.

Corso, J. F. (1977). Auditory perception and communication. In J. E. Birren & K. W. Schaie (Eds.), *Handbook of the psychology of aging* (pp. 535–553). New York: Van Nostrand Reinhold.

Coslett, H. B., & Lie, G. (2008). Simultanagnosia: When a rose is not red. *Journal of Cognitive Neuroscience, 20,* 36–48.

Costa, P. T. Jr., & McCrae, R. R. (1985). *The NEO Personality Inventory manual.* Odessa, FL: Psychological Assessment Resources.

Costa, P. T. Jr., & McCrae, R. R. (1992). Four ways five factors are basic. *Personality and Individual Differences, 13,* 653–665.

Cota, D., Marsicano, G., Lutz, B., Vicennati, V. Stalla, G. K., Pasquali, R., & Pagotto, U. (2003). Endogenous cannabinoid system as a modulator of food intake. *International Journal of Obesity, 27,* 289–301.

Cota, D., Tschöp, M. H., Horvath, T. L., & Levine, A. S. (2006). Cannabinoids, opioidis and eating behavior: The molecular face of hedonism? *Brain Research Reviews, 51,* 85–107.

Council, J. R., & Green, J. P. (2004). Examining the absorption-hypnotizability link: The roles of acquiescence and consistency motivation. *International Journal of Clinical and Experimental Hypnosis, 52,* 364–377.

Cousins, D. A., & Young, A. H. (2007). The armamentarium of treatments for bipolar disorder: A review of the literature. *International Journal of Neuropsychopharmacology, 10,* 411–431.

Couture, S., & Penn, D. (2003). Interpersonal contact and the stigma of mental illness: A review of the literature. *Journal of Mental Health, 12,* 291–306.

Cowan, C. P., & Cowan, P. (2000). *When partners become parents: The big life change for couples.* Mahwah, NJ: Erlbaum.

Cowan, N. (2001). The magical number 4 in short-term memory: A reconsideration of mental storage capacity. *Behavioral and Brain Sciences, 24,* 87–185.

Cowan, W. M. (1979, September). The development of the brain. *Scientific American, 241,* 106–117.

Cowles, J. T. (1937). Food tokens as incentives for learning by chimpanzees. *Comparative Psychology Monographs, 74,* 1–96.

Cox, J. J., Reimann, F. Nicholas, A. K., Thornton, G., Roberts, E., Springell, K., Karbani, G., Jafri, H., Mannan, J., Raashid, Y., Al-Gazali, L., Hamamy, H., Valente, E. M., Gorman, S., Williams, R., McHale, D. P., Wood, J. N., Gribble, F. M., & Woods, C. G. (2006). An SCN9A channelopathy causes congenital inability to experience pain. *Nature, 444,* 894–898.

Craik, F. I. M., & Lockhart, R. S. (1972). Levels of processing: A framework for memory research. *Journal of Verbal Learning and Verbal Behavior, 11,* 671–684.

Crano, W. D., & Prislin, R. (2006). Attitudes and persuasion. *Annual Review of Psychology, 57,* 345–374.

Crocco, M. S., & Costigan, A. T. (2007). The narrowing of curriculum and pedagogy in the age of accountability: Urban educators speak out. *Urban Education, 42,* 512–535.

Cryder, C. H., Kilmer, R. P., Tedeschi, R. G., & Calhoun, L. G. (2006). An exploratory study of posttraumatic growth in children following a natural disaster. *American Journal of Orthopsychiatry, 76,* 65–69.

Curci, A., & Luminet, O. (2006). Follow-up of a cross-national comparison on flashbulb and event memory for the September 11th attacks. *Memory, 14,* 329–344.

Curt, G. A., Breitbart, W., Cella, D., Groopman, J. E., Horning, S. J., Itri, L. M., Johnson, D. H., Miaskowski, C., Scherr, S. L., Portenoy, R. K., & Vogelzang, N. J. (2000). Impact of cancer-related fatigue on the lives of patients: New findings from the Fatigue Coalition. *Oncologist, 5,* 353–360.

Curtis, R. C., & Miller, K. (1986). Believing another likes or dislikes you: Behaviors making the beliefs come true. *Journal of Personality and Social Psychology, 51,* 284–290.

Cutting, J. C., & Proffitt, D. (1982). The minimum principle and the perception of absolute, common and relative motions. *Cognitive Psychology, 14,* 211–246.

Cvengros, J. A., Christensen, A. J., Hillis, S. L., & Rosenthal, G. E. (2007). Patient and physician attitudes in the health care context: Attitudinal symmetry predicts patient satisfaction and adherence. *Annals of Behavioral Medicine, 33,* 262–268.

Czeisler, C. A., Duffy, J. F., Shanahan, T. L., Brown, E. N., Mitchell, J. F., Rimmer, D. W., Ronda, J. M., Silva, E. J., Allan, J. S., Emens, J. S., Dijk, D. J., & Kronauer, R. E. (1999). Stability, precision, and near-24-hour period of the human circadian pacemaker. *Science, 284,* 2177–2181.

Dahlman, I., & Arner, P. (2007). Obesity and polymorphisms in genes regulating human adipose tissue. *International Journal of Obesity, 31,* 1629–1641.

Dahlstrom, W. G., Welsh, H. G., & Dahlstrom, L. E. (1975). *An MMPI handbook, Vol. 1: Clinical interpretation.* Minneapolis: University of Minnesota Press.

Darley, J. M., & Batson, C. D. (1973). From Jerusalem to Jericho: A study of situational and dispositional variables in helping behavior. *Journal of Personality and Social Psychology, 27,* 100–108.

Darling, N., & Steinberg, L. (1993). Parenting style as context: An integrative model. *Psychological Bulletin, 113,* 487–496.

Darwin, C. (1965). *The expression of emotions in man and animals.* Chicago: University of Chicago Press. (Original work published 1872)

Daselaar, S. M., Rice, H. J., Greenberg, D. L., Cabeza, R., LaBar, K. S., & Rubin, D. C. (2008). The spontaneous dynamics of autobiographical memory: Neural correlates of recall, emotional intensity, and reliving. *Cerebral Cortex, 18,* 217–229.

Daskalakis, Z. J., Levinson, A. J., & Fitzgerald, P. B. (2008). Repetitive transcranial magnetic stimulation for major depressive disorder: A review. *Canadian Journal of Psychiatry, 53,* 555–566.

D'Augelli, A. R., Grossman, A. H., Salter, N. P., Vasey, J. J., Starks, M. T., & Sinclair, K. O. (2005a). Predicting the suicide attempts of lesbian, gay, and bisexual youth. *Suicide and Life-Threatening Behavior, 35,* 646–660.

D'Augelli, A. R., Hershberger, S. L., & Pilkington, N. W. (2001). Suicidality patterns and sexual orientation-related factors among lesbian, gay, and bisexual youths. *Suicide and Life-Threatening Behavior, 31,* 250–264.

Davidson, R. J., Jackson D.C., & Kalin, N. H. (2000). Emotion, plasticity, context, and regulation: Perspectives for affective neuroscience. *Psychological Bulletin, 126,* 890–909

Davis, J. L., Byrd, P., Rhudy, J. L., & Wright, D. C. (2007). Characteristics of chronic nightmares in a trauma-exposed treatment-seeking sample. *Dreaming, 17,* 187–198.

Davis, M. H., Hall, J. A., & Meyer, M. (2003). The first year: Influences on the satisfaction, involvement, and persistence of new community volunteers. *Personality and Social Psychology Bulletin, 29,* 248–260.

Dawkins, K., Lieberman, J. A., Lebowitz, B. D., & Hsiao, J. K. (1999). Antipsychotics: Past and future. *Schizophrenia Bulletin, 25,* 395–405.

Dawson, L. L., & Hennebry, J. (2003). New religions and the Internet: Recruiting in a new public space. In L. L. Dawson (Ed.), *Cults and new religious movements* (pp. 271–291). Oxford, UK: Blackwell.

Dean, K. L., Viglione, D. J., Perry, W., & Meyer, G. J. (2007). A method to optimize the response range while maintaining Rorschach comprehensive system validity. *Journal of Personality Assessment, 89,* 149–161.

Deaux, K., Bikmen, N., Gilkes, A., Ventuneac, A., Joseph, Y., Payne, Y. A., & Steele, C. A. (2007). Becoming American: Stereotype threat effects in Afro-Caribbean immigrant groups. *Social Psychology Quarterly, 70,* 384–404.

De Bellis, M. D., Keshavan, M. S., Beers, S. R., Hall, J., Frustaci, K., Masalehdan, A., Noll, J., & Boring, A. M. (2001). Sex differences in brain maturation during childhood and adolescence. *Cerebral Cortex, 11,* 552–557.

DeCasper, A. J., & Prescott, P. A. (1984). Human newborns' perception of male voices: Preference, discrimination, and reinforcing value. *Developmental Psychology, 17,* 481–491.

De Cock, R., & Matthysen, E. (2005). Sexual communication by pheromones in a firefly, *Phosphaenus hemipterus* (Coleoptera: Lampyridae). *Animal Behaviour, 70,* 807–818.

De Corte, W., Lievens, F., & Sackett, P. R. (2007). Combining predictors to achieve optimal trade-offs between selection quality and adverse impact. *Journal of Applied Psychology, 92,* 1380–1393.

Dehaene, S., & Akhavein, R. (1995). Attention, automaticity, and levels of representation in number processing. *Journal of Experimental Psychology: Learning, Memory, and Cognition, 21,* 314–326.

Dejin-Karlsson, E., Hsonson, B. S., Oestergren, P.-O., Sjoeberg, N. O., & Karel, M. (1998). Does passive smoking in early pregnancy increase the risk of small-for-gestational age infants? *American Journal of Public Health, 88,* 1523–1527.

de Kruijk, J. R., Leffers, P., Menheere, P. P. C. A., Meerhoff, S., Rutten, J., & Twijnstra, A. (2003). Olfactory function after mild traumatic brain injury. *Brain Injury, 17,* 73–78.

DeLamater, J. D., & Sill, M. (2005). Sexual desire in later life. *The Journal of Sex Research, 42,* 138–149.

Delgado, M. R., Olsson, A., & Phelps, E. A. (2006). Extending animal models of fear conditioning to humans. *Biological Psychology, 73,* 39–48.

Dell, G. S. (2004). Speech errors in language production: Neuropsychological and connectionist perspectives. In

B. H. Ross (Ed.), *The psychology of learning and motivation* (Vol. 44, pp. 63–108). New York: Elsevier.

Dennerstein, L., Dudley, E., & Guthrie, J. (2003). Empty nest or revolving door? A prospective study of women's quality of life in midlife during the phase of children leaving and re-entering the home. *Psychological Medicine, 32,* 545–550.

Dennett, D. C. (1987). Consciousness. In R. L. Gregory (Ed.), *The Oxford companion to the mind* (pp. 160–164). New York: Oxford University Press.

De Oliveira Alvares, L., Genro, B. P., Diehl, F., & Quillfeldt, J. A. (2008). Differential role of the hippocampal endocannabinoid system in the memory consolidation and retrieval mechanisms. *Neurobiology of Learning and Memory, 90,* 1–9.

De Pascalis, V, Cacace, I., & Massicolle, F. (2008). Focused analgesia in waking and hypnosis: Effects on pain, memory, and somatosensory event-related potentials. *Pain, 134,* 197–208.

DePaulo, B. M., Ansfield, M. E., Kirkendol, S. E., & Boden, J. M. (2004). Serious lies. *Basic and Applied Social Psychology, 26,* 147–167.

DePaulo, B. M., Lindsay, J. J., Malone, B. E., Muhlenbruck, L., Charlton, K., & Cooper, H. (2003). Cues to deception. *Psychological Bulletin, 129,* 74–118.

de Rivera, J. (1997). The construction of false memory syndrome: The experience of retractors. *Psychological Inquiry, 8,* 271–292.

De Santis, M., Cavaliere, A. F., Straface, G., & Caruso, A. (2006). Rubella infection in pregnancy. *Reproductive Toxicology, 21,* 390–398.

Després, J.-P., Golay, A., & Sjöström, L. (2005). Effects of rimonabant on metabolic risk factors in overweight patients with dyslipidemia. *The New England Journal of Medicine, 353,* 2121–2134.

De Valois, R. L., & Jacobs, G. H. (1968). Primate color vision. *Science, 162,* 533–540.

Dew, M. A., Hoch, C. C., Buysse, D. J., Monk, T. H., Begley, A. E., Houck, P. R., Hall, M., Kupfer, D. J., & Reynolds, C. F. (2003). Healthy older adults' sleep predicts all-cause mortality at 4 to 19 years of follow-up. *Psychosomatic Medicine, 65,* 63–73.

de Waal, F. B. M. (2008). Putting the altruism back into altruism: The evolution of empathy. *Annual Review of Psychology, 59,* 279–300.

Dewsbury, D. A. (1981). Effects of novelty on copulatory behavior: The Coolidge effect and related phenomena. *Psychological Bulletin, 89,* 464–482.

Dhawan, N., Roseman, I. J., Naidu, R. K., Thapa, K., & Rettek, S. I. (1995). Self-concepts across two cultures: India and the United States. *Journal of Cross-Cultural Psychology, 26,* 606–621.

Dickerson, F. B., Tenhula, W. N., & Green-Paden, L. D. (2005). The token economy for schizophrenia: Review of the literature and recommendations for future research. *Schizophrenia Research, 75,* 405–416.

Dickens, W. T., & Flynn, J. R. (2006). Black Americans reduce the racial IQ gap: Evidence from standardization samples. *Psychological Science, 17,* 913–920.

Dickinson, C. A., & Intraub, H. (2008). Transsaccadic representation of layout: What is the time course of boundary extension? *Journal of Experimental Psychology: Human Perception and Performance, 34,* 543–555.

Dietrich, A. (2004). The cognitive neuroscience of creativity. *Psychonomic Bulletin & Review, 11,* 1011–1026.

Digman, J. M. (1990). Personality structure: Emergence of the five-factor model. *Annual Review of Psychology, 41,* 417–440.

DiLalla, L. F. (2002). Behavior genetics of aggression in children: Reviews and future directions. *Developmental Review, 22,* 593–622.

Di Marzo, V., & Cristino, L. (2008). Why endocannabinoids are not all alike. *Nature Neuroscience, 11,* 124–126.

DiMatteo, M. R. (2004). Social support and patient adherence to medical treatment: A meta-analysis. *Health Psychology, 23,* 207–218.

DiMatteo, M. R., Haskard, K. B., & Williams, S. L. (2007). Health beliefs, disease severity, and patient adherence: A meta-analysis. *Medical Care, 45,* 521–528.

Dion, K. K., & Dion, K. L. (1996). Cultural perspectives on romantic love. *Personal Relationships, 3,* 5–17.

Dirkzwager, A. J. E., Bramsen, I., & van der Ploeg, H. M. (2003). Social support, coping, life events, and posttraumatic stress symptoms among former peacekeepers: A prospective study. *Personality and Individual Differences, 34,* 1545–1559.

Distel, M. A., Trull, T. J., Derom, C. A., Thiery, E. W., Grimmer, M. A., Martin, N. G., Willemsen, G., & Boomsma, D. I. (2007). Heritability of borderline personality disorder features is similar across three countries. *Psychological Medicine, 38,* 1219–1229.

Dixon, R. A. (2003). Themes in the aging of intelligence: Robust decline with intriguing possibilities. In R. J. Sternberg, J. Lautrey, & T. I. Lubart (Eds.), *Models of intelligence: International perspectives* (pp. 151–167). Washington, DC: American Psychological Association.

Dixon, R. A., & de Frias, C. M. (2004). The Victoria longitudinal study: From characterizing cognitive aging to illustrating changes in memory compensation. *Aging Neuropsychology and Cognition, 11,* 346–376.

Do, A. M., Rupert, A. V., & Wolford, G. (2008). Evaluations of pleasurable experiences: The peak-end rule. *Psychonomic Bulletin & Review, 15,* 96–98.

Docherty, N. M., St-Hilaire, A., Aakre, J. M., & Seghers, J. P. (2008). Life events and high-trait reactivity together predict psychotic symptom increases in schizophrenia. *Schizophrenia Bulletin.* Dollard, J., Doob, L. W., Miller, N., Mower, O. H., & Sears, R. R. (1939). *Frustration and aggression.* New Haven: Yale University Press.

Domhoff, G. W. (1999). Drawing theoretical implications from descriptive empirical findings on dream content. *Dreaming, 9,* 201–210.

Domhoff, G. W. (2005). Refocusing the neurocognitive approach to dreams: A critique of the Hobson versus Solms debate. *Dreaming, 15,* 3–20.

Domjan, M. (2005). Pavlovian conditioning: A functional perspective. *Annual Review of Psychology, 56,* 179–206.

Donnellan, M. B., Trzesniewski, K. H., Conger, K. J., & Conger, R. D. (2007). A three-wave longitudinal study of self-evaluations during young adulthood. *Journal of Research in Personality, 41,* 453–472.

Donnellan, M. B., Trzesniewski, K. H., Robins, R. W., Moffitt, T. E., & Caspi, A. (2005). Low self-esteem is realted to aggression, antisocial behavior, and delinquency. *Psychological Science, 16,* 328–335.

Donovan, W., Leavitt, L., Taylor, N., & Broder, J. (2007). Maternal sensitivity, mother-infant 9-month interaction, infant attachment status: Predictors of mother-toddler interaction at 24 months. *Infant Behavior & Development, 30,* 336–352.

Douglas, K. S., & Skeem, J. L. (2005). Violence risk assessment: Getting specific about being dynamic. *Psychology, Public Policy, and Law, 11,* 347–383.

Downing, P. E., Chan, A. W.-Y., Peelen, M. V., Dodds, C. M., & Kanwisher, N. (2006). Domain specificity in the visual cortex. *Cerebral Cortex, 16,* 1453–1461.

Drake, C. L., & Roth, T. (2006). Predisposition in the evolution of insomnia: Evidence, potential mechanisms, and future directions. *Sleep Medicine Clinics, 1,* 333–349.

DSM-IV. (1994). *Diagnostic and statistical manual of mental disorders* (4th ed.). Washington, DC: American Psychiatric Association.

DSM-IV-TR. (2000). *Diagnostic and statistical manual of mental disorders* (4th ed., Text revision). Washington, DC: American Psychiatric Association.

DuBois, P. H. (1970). *A history of psychological testing.* Boston: Allyn & Bacon.

Dudycha, G. J. (1936). An objective study of punctuality in relation to personality and achievement. *Archives of Psychology, 204,* 1–53.

Duker, P. C., & Seys, D. M. (1996). Long-term use of electrical aversion treatment with self-injurious behavior. *Research in Developmental Disabilities, 17,* 293–301.

Duncker, D. (1945). On problem solving. *Psychological Monographs, 58* (No. 270).

Durkin, S. J., & Paxton, S. J. (2002). Predictors of vulnerability to reduced body image satisfaction and psychological well-being in response to exposure to idealized female media images in adolescent girls. *Journal of Psychosomatic Research, 53,* 995–1005.

Dusek, J. A., Hibberd, P. L., Buczynski, B., Chang, B.-H., Dusek, K. C., Johnston, J. M., Wohlhueter, A. L., Benson, H., & Zusman, R. M. (2008). Stress management versus lifestyle modification on systolic hypertension and medication elimination: A randomized trial. *The Journal of Alternative and Complementary Medicine, 14,* 129–138.

Dutton, D. G., & Aron, A. P. (1974). Some evidence for heightened sexual attraction under conditions of high anxiety. *Journal of Personality and Social Psychology, 30,* 510–517.

Dweck, C. S. (1975). The role of expectations and attributions in the alleviation of learned helplessness. *Journal of Personality and Social Psychology, 31,* 674–685.

Eastwick, P. W., Eagly, A. H., Glick, P., Johannesen-Schmidt, M. C., Fiske, S. T., Blum, A. M. B., Eckes, T., Freiburger, P., Huang, L.-L., Fernández, M. L., Manganelli, A. M., Pek, J. C. X., Rodríguez Castro, Y., Sakalli-Ugurlu, N., Six-Materna, I., & Volpato, C. (2006). Is traditional gender ideology associated with sex-typed mate preferences? A test in nine nations. *Sex Roles, 54,* 603–614.

Ebbinghaus, H. (1973). *Psychology: An elementary text-book.* New York: Arno Press. (Original work published 1908)

Edinger, J. D., Fins, A. I., Glenn, D. M., Sullivan, R. J., Jr., Bastian, L. A., Marsh, G. R., Dailey, D., Hope, T. V., Young, M., Shaw, E., & Vasilas, D. (2000). Insomnia and the eye of the beholder: Are there clinical markers of objective sleep disturbances among adults with and without insomnia complaints? *Journal of Consulting and Clinical Psychology, 68,* 593–596.

Edvardsen, J., Torgersen, S., Røysamb, E., Lygren, S., Skre, I., Onstad, S., & Øien, P. A. (2008). Heritability of bipolar spectrum disorders. Unity or heterogeneity. *Journal of Affective Disorders, 106,* 229–240.

Ekman, P. (1972). Universal and cultural differences in facial expressions of emotion. In J. Cole (Ed.), *Nebraska symposium on motivation.* Lincoln: University of Nebraska Press.

Ekman, P. (1984). Expression and the nature of emotion. In K. R. Scherer & P. Ekman (Eds.), *Approaches to emotion.* Hillsdale, NJ: Erlbaum.

Ekman, P. (1994). Strong evidence for universals in facial expressions: A reply to Russell's mistaken critique. *Psychological Bulletin, 115,* 268–287.

Ekman, P., & Friesen, W. V. (1971). Constants across cultures in the face and emotion. *Journal of Personality and Social Psychology, 17,* 124–129.

Ekman, P., & Friesen, W. V. (1986). A new pan-cultural facial expression of emotion. *Motivation and Emotion, 10,* 159–168.

Elbert, T., Pantev, C., Wienbruch, C., Rockstroh, B., & Taub, E. (1995). Increased cortical representation of the fingers of the left hand in string players. *Science, 270,* 305–307.

Elias, S. M., & MacDonald, S. (2007). Using past performance, proxy efficacy, and academic self-efficacy to predict college performance. *Journal of Applied Social Psychology, 37,* 2518–2531.

Ellis, A. (1962). *Reason and emotion in psychotherapy.* New York: Lyle Stuart.

Ellis, A. (1995). *Better, deeper, and more enduring brief therapy: The rational emotive behavior therapy approach.* New York: Brunner/Mazel.

Elms, A. C. (1988). Freud as Leonardo: Why the first psychobiography went wrong. *Journal of Personality, 56,* 19–40.

Elsabagh, S., Hartley, D. E., Ali, O., Williamson, E. M., & File, S. E. (2005). Differential cognitive effects of *Ginkgo biloba* after acute and chronic treatment in healthy young volunteers. *Psychopharmacology, 179,* 437–446.

Endler, N. S., Macrodimitris, S. D., & Kocovski, N. L. (2000). Controllability in cognitive and interpersonal tasks: Is control good for you? *Personality & Individual Differences, 29,* 951–962.

Epley, N., & Gilovich, T. (2006). The anchoring-and-adjustment heuristic. *Psychological Science, 17,* 311–318.

Epstein, L. H., Nandley, E. A., Dearing, K. K., Cho, D. D., Roemmich, J. N., Paluch, R. A., Raja, S., Pak, Y., & Spring, B. (2006). Purchases of food in youth: Influence of price and income. *Psychological Science, 17,* 82–89.

Ericsson, K. A., & Chase, W. G. (1982). Exceptional memory. *American Scientist, 70,* 607–615.

Ericsson, K. A., & Simon, H. A. (1993). *Protocol analysis: Verbal reports as data* (rev. ed.). Cambridge, MA: MIT Press.

Erikson, E. (1963). *Childhood and society.* New York: Norton.

Erlacher, D., & Schredl, M. (2008). Cardiovascular responses to dreamed physical exercise during REM lucid dreaming. *Dreaming, 18,* 112–121.

Ervik, S., Abdelnoor, M., Heier, M. S., Ramberg, M., & Strand, G. (2006). Health-related quality of life in narcolepsy. *Acta Neurologica Scandiavica, 114,* 198–204.

Eshbaugh, E. M., & Gute, G. (2008). Hookups and sexual regret among college women. *The Journal of Social Psychology, 148,* 77–89.

Espelage, D. L., Aragon, S. R., Birkett, M., & Koenig, B. W. (2008). Homophobic teasing, psychological outcomes, and sexual orientation among high school students: What influence do parents and schools have? *School Psychology Review, 37,* 202–216.

Espie, C. A. (2002). Insomnia: Conceptual issues in the development, persistence, and treatment of sleep disorder in adults. *Annual Review of Psychology, 53,* 215–243.

Estrada, C. A., Isen, A. M., & Young, M. J. (1994). Positive affect improves creative problem solving and influences reported source of practice satisfaction in physicians. *Motivation and Emotion, 18,* 285–299.

Evans, E., Hawton, K., Rodham, K., & Deeks, J. (2005). The prevalence of suicidal phenomena in adolescents: A systematic review of population-based studies. *Suicide and Life Threatening Behavior, 35,* 239–250.

Evans, J. St. B. T. (2008). Dual-processing accouts of reasoning, judgment, and social cognition. *Annual Review of Psychology, 59,* 255–278.

Evans, J. St. B. T., & Curtis-Holmes J. (2005). Rapid responding increases belief bias: Evidence for the dual-process theory of reasoning. *Thinking & Reasoning, 11,* 382–389.

Evans, S. E., Davies, C., & DiLillo, D. (2008). Exposure to domestic violence: A meta-analysis of child and adolescent outcomes. *Aggression and Violent Behavior, 13,* 131–140.

Exner, J. E. Jr. (1974). *The Rorschach: A comprehensive system.* New York: Wiley.

Exner, J. E. Jr. (2003). *The Rorschach: A comprehensive system* (4th ed.). New York: Wiley.

Exner, J. E. Jr., & Weiner, I. B. (1994). *The Rorschach: A comprehensive system: Vol. 3. Assessment of children and adolescents* (2nd ed.). New York: Wiley.

Eysenck, H. J. (1952). The effects of psychotherapy: An evaluation. *Journal of Consulting Psychology, 16,* 319–324.

Eysenck, H. J. (1973). *The inequality of man.* London: Temple Smith.

Eysenck, H. J. (1990). Biological dimensions of personality. In L. A. Pervin (Ed.), *Handbook of personality theory and research* (pp. 244–276). New York: Guilford Press.

Fabian, J. M. (2006). A literature review of the utility of selected violence and sexual violence risk assessment instruments. *The Journal of Psychiatry & Law, 34,* 307–350.

Fagan, J. F., & Holland, C. R. (2007). Racial equality in intelligence: Predictions from a theory of intelligence as processing. *Intelligence, 35,* 319–334.

Fahey, C. D., & Zee, P. C. (2006). Circadian rhythm sleep disorders and phototherapy. *Psychiatric Clinics of North America, 29,* 989–1007.

Fakhoury, W., & Priebe, S. (2002). The process of deinstitutionalization: An international overview. *Current Opinion in Psychiatry, 15,* 187–192.

Fantz, R. L. (1963). Pattern vision in newborn infants. *Science, 140,* 296–297.

Farina, A., Gliha, D., Boudreau, L. A., Allen, J. G., & Sherman, M. (1971). Mental illness and the impact of believing others know about it. *Journal of Abnormal Psychology, 77,* 1–5.

Farmer, T. A., Anderson, S. E., & Spivey, M. J. (2007). Gradiency and visual context in syntactic garden-paths. *Journal of Memory and Language, 57,* 570–595.

Farrell, M., & Gibson, S. (2007). Age interacts with stimulus frequency in the temporal summation of pain. *Pain Medicine, 8,* 514–520.

Fattore, L., Spano, M. S., Deiana, S., Melis, V., Cossu, G., Fadda, P. & Fratta, W. (2007). An endocannabinoid mechanism in relapse to drug seeking: A review of animal studies and clinical perspectives. *Brain Research Reviews, 53,* 1–16.

Fazio, R. H., & Roskos-Ewoldsen, D. R. (2005). Acting as we feel: When and how attitudes guide behavior. In T. C. Brock & M. C. Green (Eds.), *Persuasion: Psychological insights and perspectives* (2nd ed.) (pp. 41–62). Thousand Oaks, CA: Sage.

Feather, N. T. (1961). The relationship of persistence at a task to expectation of success and achievement related motives. *Journal of Abnormal and Social Psychology, 63,* 552–561.

Fechner, G. T. (1966). *Elements of psychophysics* (H. E. Adler, Trans.). New York: Holt, Rinehart & Winston. (Original work published 1860)

Federal Interagency Forum on Aging-Related Statistics. (2008). *Older Americans 2008: Key indicators of well-being.* Washington, DC: U. S. Government Printing Office. Retrieved from http://agingstats.gov/agingstatsdotnet/Main_Site/Data/Data_2008.asp.

Feldman, D. H. (2004). Piaget's stages: The unfinished symphony of cognitive development. *New Ideas in Psychology, 22,* 175–231.

Fernald, A., & Hurtado, N. (2006). Names in frames: Infants interpret words in sentence frames faster than words in isolation. *Developmental Science, 9,* F33–F40.

Fernald, A., & Morikawa, H. (1993). Common themes and cultural variations in Japanese and American mothers' speech to infants. *Child Development, 64,* 637–656.

Fernández-Dávila, P., Salazar, X., Cáceres, C. F., Maiorana, A., Kegeles, S., Coates, T. J., & Martinez, J. (2008). Compensated sex and sexual risk: Sexual, social and economic interactions between homosexually- and heterosexually-identified men of low income in two cities of Peru. *Sexualities, 11,* 352–374.

Ferrari, M. C. O., & Chivers, D. P. (2008). Cultural learning of predator recognition in mixed-species assemblages of frogs: The effect of tutor-to-observer ratio. *Animal Behaviour, 75,* 1921–1925.

Ferster, C. B., & Skinner, B. F. (1957). *Schedules of reinforcement.* New York: Appleton-Century-Crofts.

Festinger, L. (1957). *A theory of cognitive dissonance.* Stanford, CA: Stanford University Press.

Festinger, L., & Carlsmith, J. M. (1959). Cognitive consequences of forced compliance. *Journal of Abnormal and Social Psychology, 58,* 203–211.

Fields, R. D., & Stevens-Graham, B. (2002). New insights into neuro-glia communication. *Science, 298,* 556–562.

Fillmore M. T., Blackburn, J. S., & Harrison, E. L. R. (2008). Acute disinhibiting effects of alcohol as a factor in risky driving behavior. *Drug and Alcohol Dependence, 95,* 97–106.

Fink, P., Hansen, M. S., & Oxhøj, M. L. (2004). The prevalence of somatoform disorders among internal medical inpatients. *Journal of Psychosomatic Research, 56,* 413–418.

Finkelstein, M. A., Penner, L. A., & Brannick, M. T. (2005). Motive, role identity, and prosocial personality as predictors of volunteer activity. *Social Behavior and Personality, 33,* 403–418.

Fiore, M. C., Jaén, C. R., & Baker, T. B. (2008). *Treating tobacco use and dependence: 2008 update.* Rockville, MD: U.S. Department of Health and Human Services. Public Health Service.

Fischer, M., Barkley, R. A., Smallish, L., & Fletcher, K. (2005). Executive functioning in hyperactive children as young adults: Attention, inhibition, response perseveration, and the impact of comorbidity. *Developmental Neuropschology, 27,* 107–133.

Fisher, B. S., Cullen, F. T., & Turner, M. G. (2000). *The sexual victimization of college women.* Washington, DC: National Institute of Justice.

Fishman, H. C., & Fishman, T. (2003). Structural family therapy. In G. P. Sholevar & L. D. Schwoeri (Eds.), *Textbook of family and couples therapy: Clinical applications* (pp. 35–54). Washington, DC: American Psychiatric Publishing.

Fitch, W. T., & Hauser, M. D. (2004). Computational constraints on syntactic processing in a nonhuman primate. *Science, 303,* 377–380.

Flavell, J. H. (1985). *Cognitive development* (2nd ed.). Englewood Cliffs, NJ: Prentice Hall.

Flavell, J. H. (1996). Piaget's legacy. *Psychological Science, 7,* 200–203.

Fleming, I. (1959). From a view to a kill. In *For your eyes only* (pp. 1–30). New York: Charter Books.

Foa, E. B., & Riggs, D. S. (1995). Posttraumatic stress disorder following assault: Theoretical considerations and empirical findings. *Current Directions in Psychological Science, 4,* 61–65.

Folkard, S. (2008). Do permanent night workers show circadian adjustment? A review based on endogenous melatonin rhythm. *Chronobiology International, 25,* 215–224.

Folkman, S. (1984). Personal control and stress and coping processes: A theoretical analysis. *Journal of Personality and Social Psychology, 46,* 839–852.

Ford, C. S., & Beach, F. A. (1951). *Patterns of sexual behavior.* New York: Harper & Row.

Forgas, J. P. (2008). Affect and cognition. *Perspectives on Psychological Science, 3,* 94–101.

Forgas, J. P., & East, R. (2008). On being happy and gullible: Mood effects on skepticism and detection of deception. *Journal of Experimental Social Psychology, 44,* 1362–1367.

Forooqi, I. S., & O'Rahilly, S. (2007). Genetic factors in human obesity. *Obesity Reviews, 8,* 37–40.

Förster, J., Friedman, R. S., & Liberman, N. (2004). Temporal construal effects on abstract and concrete thinking: Consequences for insight and creative cognition. *Journal of Personality and Social Psychology, 87,* 177–189.

Försterling, F. (2001). *Attributions: An introduction to theories, research and applications.* New York: Psychology Press.

Foster, R. G., & Wulff, K. (2005). The rhythm of rest and excess. *Nature Reviews Neuroscience, 6,* 407–414.

Foucault, M. (1975). *The birth of the clinic.* New York: Vintage Books.

Foulkes, D. (1962). Dream reports from different states of sleep. *Journal of Abnormal and Social Psychology, 65,* 14–25.

Fowler, H. (1965). *Curiosity and exploratory behavior.* New York: Macmillan.

Frager, R., & Fadiman, J. (1998). *Personality and personal growth.* New York: Longman.

Fraley, R. C., Brumbaugh, C. C., & Marks, M. J. (2005). The evolution and function of adult attachment: A comparative and phylogenetic analysis. *Journal of Personality and Social Psychology, 89,* 731–746.

Fraley, R. C., & Shaver, P. R. (2000). Adult romantic attachment: Theoretical developments, emerging controversies, and unanswered questions. *Review of General Psychology, 4,* 132–154.

Frank, J. D., & Frank, J. B. (1991). *Persuasion and healing: A comparative study of psychotherapy* (3rd ed.). Baltimore: Johns Hopkins University Press.

Frank, M. E., & Nowlis, G. H. (1989). Learned aversions and taste qualities in hamsters. *Chemical Senses, 14,* 379–394.

Franklin, N., & Tversky, B. (1990). Searching imagined environments. *Journal of Experimental Psychology: General, 119,* 63–76.

Frans, Ö., Rimmö, P. A., Åberg, L., & Fredrikson, M. (2005). Trauma exposure and post-traumatic stress disorder in the general population. *Acta Psychiatrica Scandinavica, 111,* 291–299.

Fraser, L. M., O'Carroll, R. E., & Ebmeier, K. P. (2008). The effect of electroconvulsive therapy on autobiographical memory: A systematic review. *The Journal of ECT, 24,* 10–17.

Freedman, J. L., & Fraser, S. C. (1966). Compliance without pressure: The foot-in-the-door technique. *Journal of Personality and Social Psychology, 4,* 195–202.

Fresco, D. M., Williams, N. L., & Nugent, N. R. (2006). Flexibility and negative affect: Examining the associations of explanatory flexibility and coping flexibility to each other and to depression and anxiety. *Cognitive Therapy and Research, 30,* 201–210.

Freud, A. (1946). *The ego and the mechanisms of defense.* New York: International Universities Press.

Freud, A. (1958). Adolescence. *Psychoanalytic Study of the Child, 13,* 255–278.

Freud, S. (1923). *Introductory lectures on psychoanalysis* (J. Riviera, Trans.). London: Allen & Unwin.

Freud, S. (1957). Leonardo da Vinci and a memory of his childhood. In J. Strachey (Ed. and Trans.), *The standard edition of the complete psychological works of Sigmund Freud* (Vol. 11, pp. 59–137). London: Hogarth Press. (Original work published 1910)

Freud, S. (1965). *The interpretation of dreams.* New York: Avon. (Original work published 1900)

Freund, A. M., & Baltes, P. B. (1998). Selection, optimization, and compensation as strategies of life management: Correlations with subjective indicators of successful aging. *Psychology and Aging, 13,* 531–543.

Frewen, P. A., Dozois, D. J. A., & Lanius, R. A. (2008). *Clinical Psychology Review, 28,* 228–246.

Friedman, M., & Rosenman, R. F. (1974). *Type A behavior and your heart.* New York: Knopf.

Friend, R., Rafferty, Y., & Bramel, D. (1990). A puzzling misinterpretation of the Asch "conformity" study. *European Journal of Social Psychology, 20,* 29–44.

Fromkin, V. A. (Ed.). (1980). *Errors in linguistic performance: Slips of the tongue, pen, and hand.* New York: Academic Press.

Furmark, T., Tillfors, M., Marteinsdottir, I., Fischer, H., Pissiota, A., Långström, B., & Fredrikson, M. (2002). Common changes in cerebral blood flow in patients with social phobia treated with citalopram or cognitive-behavioral therapy. *Archives of General Psychiatry, 59,* 425–433.

Furnham, A., Crump, J., & Whelan, J. (1997). Validating the NEO Personality Inventory using assessor's ratings. *Personality & Individual Differences, 22,* 669–675.

Gale, C. R., Batty, G. D., & Deary, I. J. (2008). Locus of control at age 10 years and health outcomes and behaviors at age 30 years: The 1970 British Cohort Study. *Psychosomatic Medicine, 70,* 397–403.

Gallace, A., Tan, H. Z., Haggard, P., & Spence, C. (2008). Short term memory for tactile stimuli. *Brain Research, 1190,* 132–142.

Gallo, L. C., & Matthews, K. A. (2003). Understanding the association between socioeconomic status and physical health: Do negative emotions play a role? *Psychological Bulletin, 129,* 10–51.

Galton, F. (1907). *Inquiries into human faculty and its development.* London: Dent Publishers. (Original work published 1883)

Ganis, F., Thompson, W. L., & Kosslyn, S. M. (2004). Brain areas underlying visual imagery and visual perception: An fMRI study. *Cognitive Brain Research, 20,* 226–241.

Ganor-Stern, D., Tzelgov, J., & Ellenbogen, R. (2007). Automaticity and two-digit numbers. *Journal of Experimental Psychology: Human Perception and Performance, 33,* 483–496.

Gao, Q., & Horvath, T. L. (2007). Neurobiology of feeding and energy expenditure. *Annual Review of Neuroscience, 30,* 367–398.

Garb, H. N., Wood, J. M., Lilienfeld, S. O., & Nezworski, M. T. (2005). Roots of the Rorschach controversy. *Clinical Psychology Review, 25,* 97–118.

Garcia, J. (1990). Learning without memory. *Journal of Cognitive Neuroscience, 2,* 287–305.

Garcia, J., & Koelling, R. A. (1966). The relation of cue to consequence in avoidance learning. *Psychonomic Science, 4,* 123–124.

Gardner, H. (1993). *Creating minds.* New York: Basic Books.

Gardner, H. (1999). *The disciplined mind.* New York: Simon & Schuster.

Gardner, H. (2006). *Multiple intelligences: New Horizons.* New York: Basic books.

Gardner, M., & Steinberg, L. (2005). Peer influence on risk taking, risk preference, and risky decision making in adolescence and adulthood: An experimental study. *Developmental Psychology, 41,* 625–635.

Gardner, R. A., & Gardner, B. T. (1969). Teaching sign language to a chimpanzee. *Science, 165,* 664–672.

Gassió, R., Artuch, R., Vilaseca, M. A., Fusté, E., Boix, C., Sans, A., & Campistol, J. (2005). Cognitive functions in classic phenylketonuria and mild hyperphenylalaninaemia: Experience in a paediatric population. *Developmental Medicine & Child Neurology, 47,* 443–448.

Gatchel, R. J. (2004) Comorbidity of chronic pain and mental health disorders: The biopsychosocial perspective. *American Psychologist, 59,* 784–805.

Gatchel, R. J., Peng, Y. B., Peters, M. D., Fuchs, P. N., & Turk, D. C. (2007). The biopsychosocial approach to chronic pain: Scientific advances in future directions. *Psychological Bulletin, 133,* 581–624.

Gawronksi, B., & LeBel, E. P. (2008). Understanding patterns of attitude change: When implicit measures show change, but explicit measures do not. *Journal of Experimental Social Psychology, 44,* 1355–1361.

Gazzaniga, M. (1970). *The bisected brain.* New York: Appleton-Century-Crofts.

Gazzaniga, M. S. (1985). *The social brain.* New York: Basic Books.

Gelman, S. A. (2003). *Origins of essentialism in everyday thought.* London: Oxford University Press.

Gelman, S. A., & Raman, L. (2002). Folk biology as a window into cognitive development. *Human Development, 45,* 61–68.

Gelman, S. A., & Wellman, H. M. (1991). Insides and essences: Early understandings of the non-obvious. *Cognition, 38,* 213–244.

Gentner, D., & Goldin-Meadow, S. (Eds.). (2003). *Language in mind: Advances in the study of language and thought.* Cambridge, MA: MIT Press.

Geraerts, E., Schooler, J. W., Merckelbach, H., Jelicic, M., Hauer, B. J. A., & Ambadar, Z. (2007). The reality of recovered memories: Corroborating continuous and discontinuous memories of childhood sexual abuse. *Psychological Science, 18,* 564–568.

Gergen, K. J., Gulerce, A., Lock, A., & Misra, G. (1996). Psychological science in a cultural context. *American Psychologist, 51,* 496–503.

Gerrig, R. J., & O'Brien, E. J. (2005). The scope of memory-based processing. *Discourse Processes, 39,* 225–242.

Gershkoff-Stowe, L., & Hahn, E. R. (2007). Fast mapping skills in the developing lexicon. *Journal of Speech, Language, and Hearing Research, 50,* 682–697.

Gershoff, E. T., & Bitensky, S. H. (2007). The case against corporal punishment for children: Converging evidence from social science research and international human rights law and implications for U. S. public policy. *Psychology, Public Policy, and Law, 13,* 231–272.

Gibbons, A. (2002). Hot spots of brain evolution. *Science, 296,* 837.

Gibbons, A. (2007). Food for thought. *Science, 316,* 1558–1560.

Gibbons, M. B. C., Crits-Christoph, P., & Hearon, B. (2008). The empirical status of psychodynamic therapies. *Annual Review of Clinical Psychology, 4,* 93–108.

Gibbs, J. C., Basinger, K. S., Grime, R. L., & Snarey, J. R. (2007). Moral judgment development across culture: Revisiting Kohlberg's universality claims. *Developmental Review, 27,* 443–500.

Gibson, E. J., & Walk, R. D. (1960). The "visual cliff." *Scientific American, 202,* 64–71.

Gibson, J. J. (1979). *An ecological approach to visual perception.* Boston: Houghton Mifflin.

Gidron, Y., Davidson, K., & Bata, I. (1999). The short-term effects of a hostility-reduction intervention on male coronary heart disease patients. *Health Psychology, 18,* 416–420.

Gigerenzer, G. (2008). Why heuristics work. *Perspectives on Psychological Science, 3,* 20–29.

Gilbert, D. T., Morewedge, C. K., Risen, J. L., & Wilson, T. D. (2004). Looking forward to looking backward: The misprediction of regret. *Psychological Science, 15,* 346–350.

Gilligan, C. (1982). *In a different voice: Psychological theory and women's development.* Cambridge, MA: Harvard University Press.

Gilovich, T. (1991). *How we know what isn't so: The fallibility of human reason in everyday life.* New York: The Free Press.

Gitlin, M., Nuechterlein, K., Subotnik, K. L., Ventura, J., Mintz, J., Fogelson, D. L., Bartzokis, G., & Aravagiri, M. (2001). Clinical outcome following neuroleptic discontinuation in patients with remitted recent-onset schizophrenia. *American Journal of Psychiatry, 158,* 1835–1842.

Glasman, L. R., & Albarracín, D. (2006). Forming attitudes that predict behavior: A meta-analysis of the attitude-behavior relation. *Psychological Bulletin, 132,* 778–822.

Gleaves, D. H., May, M. C., & Cardeña, E. (2001). An examination of the diagnostic validity of dissociative identity disorder. *Clinical Psychology Review, 21,* 577–608.

Goddard, H. H. (1914). *The Kallikak family: A study of the heredity of feeble-mindedness.* New York: Macmillan.

Godden, D. R., & Baddeley, A. D. (1975). Context-dependent memory in two natural environments: On land and under water. *British Journal of Psychology, 66,* 325–331.

Godin, G., Sheeran, P., Conner, M., & Germain, M. (2008). Asking questions changes behavior: Mere measurement effects on frequency of blood donation. *Health Psychology, 27,* 179–184.

Goel, V. (2007). Anatomy of deductive reasoning. *Trends in Cognitive Science, 11,* 435–441.

Goldapple, K., Segal, Z., Garson, C., Lau, M., Bieling, P., Kennedy, S., & Mayberg, H. (2004). Modulation of cortical-limbic pathways in major depression. *Archives of General Psychiatry, 61,* 34–41.

Goldberg, A. E., & Perry-Jenkins, M. (2007). The division of labor and perceptions of parental roles: Lesbian couples across the transition to parenthood. *Journal of Social and Personal Relationships, 24,* 297–318.

Goldberg, A. E., & Sayer, A. (2006). Lesbian couples' relationship quality across the transition to parenthood. *Journal of Marriage and Family, 68,* 87–100.

Goldfried, M. R. (2003). Cognitive-behavior therapy: Reflections on the evolution of a therapeutic orientation. *Cognitive Therapy and Research, 27,* 53–69.

Goldfried, M. R., & Davila, J. (2005). The role of relationship and technique in therapeutic change. *Psychotherapy: Theory, Research, Practice, Training, 42,* 421–430.

Goldin-Meadow, S. (2003). *The resilience of language: What gesture creation in deaf children can tell us about how all children learn language.* New York: Psychology Press.

Goldin-Meadow, S., & Mylander, C. (1990). Beyond the input given: The child's role in the acquisition of language. *Language, 66,* 323–355.

Goldrick, M., & Larson, M. (2008). Phonotactic probability influences speech production. *Cognition, 107,* 1155–1164.

Goldstein, D., Hahn, C. S., Hasher, L., Wiprzycka, U. J., & Zelazo, P. D. (2007). Time of day, intellectual performance, and behavioral problems in morning versus evening type adolescents: Is there a synchrony effect? *Personality and Individual Differences, 42,* 431–440.

Goldstein, E. B. (1999). *Sensation & perception* (5th ed.). Pacific Grove, CA: Brooks/Cole.

Goldstein, J. M., Seidman, L. J., Horton, N. J., Makris, N., Kennedy, D. N., Caviness, V. S., Jr., Faraone, S. V., & Tsuang, M. T. (2001). Normal sexual dimorphism of the human brain assessed by in vivo magnetic resonance imaging. *Cerebral Cortex, 11,* 490–497.

Goldstein, R. B., Compton, W. M., Pulay, A. J., Ruan, W. J., Pickering, R. P., Stinson, F. S., & Grant, B. F. (2007). Antisocial behavioral syndromes and DSM-IV drug use disorders in the United States: Results from the National Epidemiologic Survey on Alcohol and Related Conditions. *Drug and Alcohol Dependence, 90,* 145–158.

Goldstrom, I. D., Campbell, J., Rogers, J. A., Lambert, D. B., Blacklow, B., Henderson, M. J., & Manderscheid, R. W. (2006). National estimates for mental health support groups, self-help organizations, and consumer-operated services. *Administration and Policy in Mental Health and Mental Health Services Research, 33,* 92–103.

Golombok, S., Rust, J., Zervoulis, K., Croudace, T., Golding, J., & Hines, M. (2008). Developmental trajectories of sex-typed behavior in boys and girls: A longitudinal general population study of children aged 2.5–8 years. *Child Development, 79,* 1583–1593.

Goodheart, C. D., Kadzin, A. E., & Sternberg, R. J. (2006). *Evidence-based psychotherapy: Where practice and research meet.* Washington, DC: American Psychological Association.

Goodyn, H., Callaerts-Vegh, Z., Stroobants, S., Dirikx, T., Vansteenwegen, D., Hermans, D., van der Putten, H., & D'Hooge, R. (2008). Deficits in acquisition and extinction of conditioned responses in mGluR7 knockout mice. *Neurobiology of Learning and Memory, 90,* 103–111.

Gotlib, I. H., & Hamilton, J. P. (2008). Neuroimaging and depression: Current status and unresolved issues. *Current Directions in Psychological Science, 17,* 159–163.

Gottesman, I. I. (1991). *Schizophrenia genesis: The origins of madness.* New York: Freeman.

Gottfredson, L. S. (1997). Mainstream science on intelligence: An editorial with 52 signatories, history, and bibliography. *Intelligence, 24,* 13–23.

Gottfredson, L. S. (2002). Where and why *g* matters: Not a mystery. *Human Performance, 15,* 25–46.

Gouin, J.-P., Kielcolt-Glaser, J. K., Malarkey, W. B., & Glaser, R. (2008). The influence of anger expression on wound healing. *Brain, Behavior, and Immunity, 22,* 699–708.

Gould, E., & Gross, C. G. (2002). Neurogenesis in adult mammals: Some progress and problems. *Journal of Neuroscience, 22,* 619–623.

Gould, S. J. (2002). *The structure of evolutionary theory.* Cambridge, MA: Belknap Press.

Grady, C. L., McIntosh, A. R., & Craik, F. I. M. (2005). Task-related activity in prefrontal cortex and its relation to recognition memory performance in young and old adults. *Neuropsychologia, 43,* 1466–1481.

Grady, C. L., Springer, M. V., Hongwanishkul, D., McIntosh, A. R., & Winocur, G. (2006). Age-related changes in brain activity across the adult lifespan. *Journal of Cognitive Neuroscience, 18,* 227–241.

Granic, I., & Patterson, G. R. (2006). Toward a comprehensive model of antisocial development: A dynamic systems approach. *Psychological Review, 113,* 101–131.

Grant, A. M. (2008). The significance of task significance: Job performance effects, relational mechanisms, and boundary conditions. *Journal of Applied Psychology, 93,* 108–124.

Grant, P. R., & Grant, B. R. (2006). Evolution of character displacement in Darwin's finches. *Science, 313,* 224–226.

Grant, P. R., & Grant, B. R. (2008). *How and why species multiply.* Princeton, NJ: Princeton University Press.

Gray, M. R., & Steinberg, L. (1999). Unpacking authoritative parenting: Reassessing a multidimensional construct. *Journal of Marriage and the Family, 61,* 574–587.

Greaves, N., Prince, E., Evans, D. W., & Charman, T. (2006). Repetitive and ritualistic behaviour in children with Prader-Willi syndrome and children with autism. *Journal of Intellectual Disability Research, 50,* 92–100.

Green, D. M., & Swets, J. A. (1966). *Signal detection theory and psychophysics.* New York: Wiley.

Greenberg, S. T., & Schoen, E. G. (2008). Males and eating disorders: Gender-based therapy for eating disorder recovery. *Professional Psychology: Research and Practice, 39,* 464–471.

Greene, J. D., Morelli, S. A., Lowenberg, K., Nystrom, L. E., & Cohen, J. D. (2008). Cognitive load selectively interferes with utilitarian moral judgment. *Cognition, 107,* 1144–1154.

Greene, J. D., Sommerville, R. B., Nystrom, L. E., Darley, J. M., & Cohen, J. D. (2001). An fMRI investigation of emotional engagement in moral judgment. *Science, 293,* 2105–2108.

Greenfield, P. M. (1997). You can't take it with you: Why ability assessments don't cross cultures. *American Psychologist, 52,* 1115–1124.

Greenwald, A. G., Banaji, M. R., Rudman, L A., Farnham, S. D., Nosek, B. A., & Mellott, D. S. (2002). A unified theory of implicit attitudes, stereotypes, self-esteem, and self-concept. *Psychological Review, 109,* 3–25.

Greenwald, A. G., Spangenber, E. R., Pratkanis, A. R., & Eskenazi, J. (1991). Double-blind tests of subliminal self-help audiotapes. *Psychological Science, 2,* 119–122.

Gregory, R. (1966). *Eye and brain.* New York: McGraw-Hill.

Grice, H. P. (1968). Utterer's meaning, sentence-meaning, and word-meaning. *Foundations of Language, 4,* 1–18.

Grice, H. P. (1975). Logic and conversation. In P. Cole & J. L. Morgan (Eds.), *Syntax and semantics: Vol. 3. Speech acts* (pp. 41–58). New York: Academic Press.

Grieger, T. A., Waldrep, D. A., Lovasz, M. M., & Ursano, R. J. (2005). Follow-up of Pentagon employees two years after the terrorist attack of September 11, 2001. *Psychiatric Services, 56,* 1374–1378.

Griffin, A. S. (2008). Socially acquired predator avoidance: Is it just classical conditioning? *Brain Research Bulletin, 76,* 264–271.

Grigorenko, E. L. (2000). Heritability and intelligence. In R. J. Sternberg (Ed.), *Handbook of intelligence* (pp. 53–91). Cambridge, UK: Cambridge University Press.

Grigorenko, E. L., Meier, E., Lipka, J., Mohatt, G., Yanez, E., & Sternberg, R. J. (2004). Academic and practical intelligence: A case study of the Yup'ik in Alaska. *Learning and Individual Differences, 14,* 183–207.

Grilo, C. M., Hrabosky, J. I., White, M., Allison, K. C., Stunkard, A. J., & Masheb, R. M. (2008). Overvaluation of shape and weight in binge eating disorder and overweight controls: Refinement of a diagnostic construct. *Journal of Abnormal Psychology, 117,* 414–419.

Grodner, D., Gibson, E., & Watson, D. (2005). The influence of contextual contrast on syntactic processing: Evidence for stong-interaction in sentence comprehension. *Cognition, 95,* 275–296.

Groh, D. R., Jason, L. A., & Keys, C. B. (2008). Social network variables in alcoholics anonymous: A literature review. *Clinical Psychology Review, 28,* 430–450.

Grohol, J. M. (1998). Future clinical directions: Professional development, pathology, and psychotherapy on-line. In J. Gackenbach (Ed.), *Psychology and the Internet: Intrapersonal, interpersonal, and transpersonal implications* (pp. 111–140). San Diego, CA: Academic Press.

Grüsser, S. M., Thalemann, C. N., Platz, W., Gölz, J., & Partecke, G. (2006). A new approach to preventing relapse in opiate addicts: A psychometric evaluation. *Biological Psychiatry, 71,* 231–235.

Guéraud, S., Tapiero, I., & O'Brien, E. J. (2008). Context and the activation of predictive inferences. *Psychonomic Bulletin & Review, 15,* 351–356.

Guilleminault, C., Poyares, D., Aftab, F., & Palombini, L. (2001). Sleep and wakefulness in somnambulism: A spectral analysis study. *Journal of Psychosomatic Research, 51,* 411–416.

Gur, R. C., Gunning-Dixon, F., Bilker, W. B., & Gur, R. E. (2002). Sex differences in temporo-limbic and frontal brain volumes of healthy adults. *Cerebral Cortex, 12,* 998–1003.

Gutierrez, P. M., Watkins, R., & Collura, D. (2004). Suicide risk screening in an urban high school. *Suicide and Life-Threatening Behavior, 34,* 421–428.

Haas, S. M., & Stafford, L. (2005). Maintenance behaviors in same-sex and marital relationships: A matched sample comparison. *Journal of Family Communication, 5,* 43–60.

Haberstick, B. C., Schmitz, S., Young, S. E., & Hewitt, J. K. (2006). Genes and developmental stability of aggressive behavior: Problems at home and school in a community sample of twins aged 7–12. *Behavior Genetics, 36,* 809–819.

Habib, R., Nyberg, L., & Tulving, E. (2003). Hemispheric asymmetries of memory: the HERA model revisited. *TRENDS in Cognitive Sciences, 7,* 241–245.

Haddock, G. (2002). It's easy to like or dislike Tony Blair: Accessibility experiences and the favourability of attitude judgments. *British Journal of Psychology, 93,* 257–267.

Haidt, J. (2007). The new synthesis in moral psychology. *Science, 316,* 998–1002.

Haier, R. J., Jung, R. E., Yeo, R. A., Head, K., & Alkire, M. T. (2004). Structural variation and general intelligence. *NeuroImage, 23,* 425–433.

Hajcak, G., & Olvet, D. M. (2008). The persistence of attention to emotion: Brain potentials during and after picture presentation. *Emotion, 8,* 250–255.

Hall, G. S. (1904). *Adolescence: Its psychology and its relations to physiology, anthropology, sociology, sex, crime, religion and education* (Vols. 1 and 2). New York: D. Appleton.

Hamilton, M., & Rajaram, S. (2001). The concreteness effect in implicit and explicit memory tests. *Journal of Memory and Language, 44,* 96–117.

Hamilton, N. A., Gallagher, M. W., Preacher, K. J., Stevens, N., Nelson, C. A., Karlson, C., & McCurdy, D. (2007). Insomnia and well-being. *Journal of Consulting and Clinical Psychology, 75,* 939–946.

Hamlin, J. K., Hallinan, E. V., & Woodward, A. L. (2008). Do as I do: 7-month-old infants selectively reproduce other's goals. *Developmental Science, 11,* 487–494.

Han, J.-S. (2004). Acupuncture and endorphins. *Neuroscience Letters, 361,* 258–261.

Harbluk, J. L., Noy, Y. I., Trbovich, P. L., & Eizenman, M. (2007). An on-road assessment of cognitive distraction: Impacts on drivers' visual behavior and braking performance. *Accident Analysis and Prevention, 39,* 372–379.

Harder, J. W. (1991). Equity theory versus expectancy theory: The case of major league baseball free agents. *Journal of Applied Psychology, 76,* 458–464.

Hardy, J., & Selkoe, D. J. (2002). The amyloid hypothesis of Alzheimer's disease: Progress and problems on the road to therapeutics. *Science, 297,* 353–356.

Hare, B. (2007). From nonhuman to human mind: What changed and why? *Current Directions in Psychological Science, 16,* 60–64.

Hargadon, R., Bowers, K. S., & Woody, E. Z. (1995). Does counterpain imagery mediate hypnotic analgesia? *Journal of Abnormal Psychology, 104,* 508–516.

Harlow, H. F. (1958). The nature of love. *American Psychologist, 13,* 673–685.

Harlow, H. F., & Zimmerman, R. R. (1958). The development of affectional responses in infant monkeys. *Proceedings of the American Philosophical Society, 102,* 501–509.

Harlow, H. F., & Zimmerman, R. R. (1959). Affectional responses in the infant monkey. *Science, 130,* 421–432.

Harlow, J. M. (1868). Recovery from the passage of an iron bar through the head. *Publications of the Massachusetts Medical Society, 2,* 327–347.

Harris, B. (1979). Whatever happened to Little Albert? *American Psychologist, 34,* 151–160.

Harrison, P. J., Lyon, L., Sartorius, L. J., Burnet, P. W. J., & Lane, T. A. (2008). The group II metabotropic glutamate receptor 3 (mGluR3, mGlu3, GRM3): Expression, function and involvement in schizophrenia. *Journal of Pharmacology, 22,* 308–322.

Hart, J. T. (1965). Memory and the feeling-of-knowing experience. *Journal of Educational Psychology, 56*, 208–216.

Hartshorne, H., & May, M. A. (1928). *Studies in the nature of character: Vol. 1. Studies in deceit.* New York: Macmillan.

Hartsuiker, R. J., Corley, M., & Martensen, H. (2005). The lexical bias effect is modulated by context, but the standard monitoring account doesn't fly: Related reply to Baars et al. (1975). *Journal of Memory and Language, 52,* 58–70.

Hasson, U., Furman, O., Clark, D., Dudai, Y., & Davachi, L. (2008). Enhanced intersubject correlations during movie viewing correlate with successful episodic encoding. *Neuron, 57*, 452–462.

Hastorf, A. H., & Cantril, H. (1954). They saw a game: A case study. *Journal of Abnormal and Social Psychology, 49,* 129–134.

Hatcher, C., & Himelstein, P. (Eds.). (1996). *The handbook of Gestalt therapy.* Northvale, NJ: Jason Aronson.

Hatfield, E., & Sprecher, S. (1995). Men's and women's preferences in marital partners in the United States, Russia, and Japan. *Journal of Cross-Cultural Psychology, 26,* 728–750.

Hathaway, S. R., & McKinley, J. C. (1940). A multiphasic personlaity schedule (Minnesota): I. Construction of the schedule. *Journal of Psychology, 10,* 249–254.

Hathaway, S. R., & McKinley, J. C. (1943). *Minnesota Multiphasic Inventory manual.* New York: Psychological Corporation.

Hazan, C., & Shaver, P. (1987). Romantic love conceptualized as an attachment process. *Journal of Personality and Social Psychology, 52,* 511–524.

Hazeltine, E., & Ivry, R. B. (2002). Can we teach the cerebellum new tricks? *Science, 296,* 1979–1980.

Hearst, E. (1988). Fundamentals of learning and conditioning. In R. C. Atkinson, R. J. Herrnstein, G. Lindzey, & R. D. Luce (Eds.), *Stevens' handbook of experimental psychology: Vol. 2. Learning and cognition* (2nd ed., pp. 3–109). New York: Wiley.

Heatherington, L., & Lavner, J. A. (2008). Coming to terms with coming out: Review and recommendations for family systems-focused research. *Journal of Family Psychology, 22,* 329–343.

Hebl, M. R., & Heatherton, T. F. (1998). The stigma of obesity in women: The difference is black and white. *Personality and Social Psychology Bulletin, 24,* 417–426.

Heider, F. (1958). *The psychology of interpersonal relationships.* New York: Wiley.

Hektner, J. M., & Csikszentmihalyi, M. (2002). The experience sampling method: Measuring the context and the content of lives. In R. B. Bechtel & A. Churchman (Eds.), *Handbook of environmental psychology* (pp. 233–243). New York: Wiley.

Hektner, J. M., Schmidt, J. A., Csikszentmihaly, M. (2007). *Experience sampling method: Measuring the quality of everyday life.* Thousand Oaks, CA: Sage.

Helgeson, V. S., Reynolds, K. A., & Tomich, P. L. (2006). A meta-analytic review of benefit finding and growth. *Journal of Consulting and Clinical Psychology, 74,* 797–816.

Heller, M. A., Bracket, D. D., Salik, S. S., Scroggs, E., & Green, S. (2003). Objects, raised lines, and the haptic horizontal-vertical illusion. *Quarterly Journal of Experimental Psychology, 56A,* 891–907.

Helms, J. E. (2006). Fairness is not validity or cultural bias in racial-group assessment: A quantitative perspective. *American Psychologist, 61,* 845–859.

Hendriksen, E. S., Pettifor, A., Lee, S.-J., Coates, T. J., & Rees, H. V. (2007). Predictors of condom use among young adults in South Africa: The reproductive health and HIV research unit national youth survey. *American Journal of Public Health, 97,* 1241–1248.

Henningsen, D. D., Henningsen, M. L. M., Eden, J., & Cruz, M. G. (2006). Examining the symptoms of groupthink and retrospective sensemaking. *Small Group Research, 37,* 36–64.

Henry, P. J., & Sears, D. O. (2002). The symbolic racism 2000 scale. *Political Psychology, 2,* 253–283.

Henry, W. P., Strupp, H. H., Schacht, T. E., & Gaston, L. (1994). Psychodynamic approaches. In A. E. Bergin & S. L. Garfield (Eds.), *Handbook of psychotherapy and behavior change* (4th ed., pp. 467–508). New York: Wiley.

Herek, G. M. (2002). Gender gaps in public opinion about lesbians and gay men. *Public Opinion Quarterly, 66,* 40–66.

Herek, G. M. (2006). Legal recognition of same-sex relationships in the United States: A social science perspective. *American Psychologist, 61,* 607–621.

Herholz, K., Weisenbach, S., & Kalbe, E. (2008). Deficits of the cholinergic system in early AD. *Neuropsychologia, 46,* 1642–1647.

Herman, C. P., Roth, D. A., & Polivy, J. (2003). Effects of the presence of others on food intake: A normative investigation. *Psychological Bulletin, 129,* 873–886.

Hernnstein, R. J., & Murray, C. (1994). *The bell curve.* New York: The Free Press.

Heron, M. P., Hoyert, D. L., Xu, J., Scott, C., & Tejada-Vera, B. (2008). *Deaths: Preliminary data for 2006.* Washington, DC: National Vital Statistics Reports.

Hersh, S. M. (1971). *My Lai 4: A report on the massacre and its aftermath.* New York: Random House.

Hertwig, R., Herzog, S. M., Schooler, L. J., & Reimer, T. (2008). Fluency heuristic: A model of how the mind exploits a by-product of information retrieval. *Journal of Experimental Psychology: Learning, Memory, and Cognition, 34,* 1191–1206.

Hess, T. M. (2005). Memory and aging in context. *Psychological Bulletin, 131,* 383–406.

Hess, T. M., & Hinson, J. T. (2006). Age-related variation in the influences of aging stereotypes on memory in adulthood. *Psychology and Aging, 21,* 621–625.

Hettema, J. M., Neale, M. C., & Kendler, K. S. (2001). A review and meta-analysis of the genetic epidemiology of anxiety disorders. *American Journal of Psychiatry, 158,* 1568–1578.

Hettema, J. M., Prescott, C. A., Myerse, J. M., Neale, M. C., & Kendler, K. S. (2005). The structure of genetic and environmental risk factors for anxiety disorders in men and women. *Archives of General Psychiatry, 62,* 182–189.

Hewstone, M., Rubin, M., & Willis, H. (2002). Intergroup bias. *Annual Review of Psychology, 53,* 575–604.

Hibbard, J. H., Peters, E., Dixon, A., & Tusler, M. (2007). Consumer competencies and the use of comparative quality information: It isn't just about literary. *Medical Care Research and Review, 64,* 379–394.

Hickok, G., Love-Geffen, T., & Klima, E. S. (2002). Role of the left hemisphere in sign language comprehension. *Brain & Language, 82,* 167–178.

Higgie, M., Chenoweth, S., & Blows, M. W. (2000). Natural selection and the reinforcement of mate recognition. *Science, 290,* 519–521.

Higgins, E. T., & Pittman, T. S. (2008). Motives of the *human* animal: Comprehending, managing, and sharing inner states. *Annual Review of Psychology, 59,* 361–385.

Hilgard, E. R. (1986). *Psychology in America: A historical survey.* San Diego, CA: Harcourt Brace Jovanovich.

Hills, A. L., Cox, B. J., McWilliams, L. A., & Sareen, J. (2005). Suicide attempts and externalizing psychopathology in a nationally representative sample. *Comprehensive Psychiatry, 46,* 334–339.

Hilsenroth, M. J., Charnas, J. W., Zodan, J., & Streiner, D. L. (2007). Criterion-based training for Rorschach scoring. *Training and Education in Professional Psychology, 1,* 125–134.

Hinshaw, S. P., & Stier, A. (2008). Stigma as related to mental disorders. *Annual Review of Clinical Psychology, 4,* 367–393.

Hobara, M. (2005). Beliefs about appropriate pain behavior: Cross-cultural and sex differences between Japanese and Euro-Americans. *European Journal of Pain, 9,* 389–393.

Hobson, J. A. (1988). *The dreaming brain.* New York: Basic Books.

Hobson, J. A., & McCarley, R. W. (1977). The brain as a dream state generator: An activation-synthesis hypothesis of the dream process. *American Journal of Psychiatry, 134,* 1335–1348.

Hodgkinson, G. P., & Healey, M. P. (2008). Cognition in organizations. *Annual Review of Psychology, 59,* 387–417.

Hoekstra, R. A., Bartels, M., & Boomsma, D. I. (2007). Longitudinal genetic study of verbal and nonverbal IQ from early childhood to young adulthood. *Learning and Individual Differences, 17,* 97–114.

Hoelzle, J. B., & Meyer, G. J. (2008). The factor structure of the MMPI-2 Restructured Clinical (RC) Scales. *Journal of Personality Assessment, 90,* 443–455.

Hoffman, E. J., & Mathew, S. J. (2008). Anxiety disorders: A comprehensive review of pharmacotherapies. *Mount Sanai Journal of Medicine, 75,* 248–262.

Hoffer, T. B., Hess, M., Welch, V. Jr., & Williams, K. (2007). *Doctorate Recipients from United States Universities: Summary Report 2006.* Chicago: National Opinion Research Center.

Hoffmann, A. A., & Willi, Y. (2008). Detecting genetic responses to environmental change. *Nature Reviews Genetics, 9,* 421–432.

Hoge, C. W., Castro, C. A., Messer, S. C., McGurk, D., Cotting, D. I., & Koffman, R. L. (2004). Combat duty in Iraq and Afghanistan, mental health problems, and barriers to care. *New England Journal of Medicine, 351,* 13–22.

Holahan, C. K., & Sesrs, R. R. (1995). The gifted group in later maturity. Stanford, CA: Stanford University Press.

Holen, M. C., & Oaster, T. R. (1976). Serial position and isolation effects in a classroom lecture simulation. *Journal of Educational Psychology, 68,* 723–725.

Hollon, S. D., Stewart, M. O., & Strunk, D. (2006). Enduring effects for cognitive behavior therapy in the treatment of depression and anxiety. *Annual Review of Psychology, 57,* 285–315.

Hollon, S. D., Thase, M. E., & Markowitz, J. C. (2002). Treatment and prevention of depression. *Psychological Science in the Public Interest, 3,* 39–77.

Holmbeck, G. N., & O'Donnell, D. (1991). Discrepancies between perceptions of decision making and behavioral autonomy. In R. L. Paikoff (Ed.), *Shared views in the family during adolescence* (pp. 51–69). San Francisco: Jossey-Bass.

Holmes, T. H., & Rahe, R. H. (1967). The social readjustment rating scale. *Journal of Psychosomatic Research, 11*(2), 213–218.

Homer, B. D., Solomon, T. M., Moeller, R. W., Mascia, A., DeRaleau, L., & Halktis, P. N. (2008). Methamphetamine abuse and impairment of social functioning: A review of the underlying neurphysiological causes and behavioral implications. *Psychological Bulletin, 134,* 301–310.

Hooley, J. M. (2007). Expressed emotion and relapse of psychopathology. *Annual Review of Clinical Psychology, 3,* 329–352.

Hope, L., Ost, J., Gabbert, F., Healey, S., & Lenton, E. (2008). "With a little help from my friends . . .": The role of co-witness relationship in susceptibility to misinformation. *Acta Psychologia, 127,* 476–484.

Hopson, J. L. (1979). *Scent signals: The silent language of sex.* New York: Morrow.

Horgen, K. B., & Brownell, K. D. (2002). Comparison of price change and health message interventions in promoting healthy food choices. *Health Psychology, 21,* 505–512.

Horney, K. (1937). *The neurotic personality of our time.* New York: Norton.

Horney, K. (1939). *New ways in psychoanalysis.* New York: Norton.

Horney, K. (1945). *Our inner conflicts: A constructive theory of neurosis.* New York: Norton.

Horney, K. (1950). *Neurosis and human growth.* New York: Norton.

Horton, J. E., Crawford, H. J., Harrington, G., & Downs, J. H. III. (2004). Increased anterior corpus callosum size associated positively with hypnotizability and the ability to control pain. *Brain, 127,* 1741–1747.

Horton, W. S. (2007). The influence of partner-specific memory associations on language production: Evidence from picture naming. *Language and Cognitive Processes, 22,* 1114–1139.

Horton, W. S., & Gerrig, R. J. (2005). The impact of memory demands on audience design during language production. *Cognition, 96,* 127–142.

Horwitz, B., Amuntsb, K., Bhattacharyya, R., Patkin, D., Jeffries, K., Zilles, K., & Braun, A. R. (2003). Activation of Broca's area during the production of spoken and signed language: A combined cytoarchitectonic mapping and PET analysis. *Neuropsychologia, 41,* 1868–1876.

Hoshino-Browne, E., Zanna, A. S., Spencer, S. J., Zanna, M. P., Kitayama, S., & Lackenbauer, S. (2005). On the cultural guises of cognitive dissonance: The case of Easterners and Westerners. *Journal of Personality and Social Psychology, 89,* 294–310.

Hosking, R. D., & Zajicek, J. P. (2008). Therapeutic potential of cannabis in pain medicine. *British Journal of Anaesthesia, 101,* 59–68.

Houghton, J. (1980). One personal experience: Before and after mental illness. In J. G. Rabkin, L. Gelb, & J. B. Lazar (Eds.), *Attitudes toward the mentally ill: Research perspectives* (pp. 7–14). Rockville, MD: National Institutes of Mental Health.

Houlihan, D., Schwartz, C., Miltenberger, R., & Heuton, D. (1993). The rapid treatment of a young man's balloon (noise) phobia using in vivo flooding. *Journal of Behavior Therapy and Experimental Psychiatry, 24,* 233–240.

Howe, C. Q., & Purves, D. (2005). The Müller-Lyer illusion explained by the statistics of image-source relationships. *PNAS, 102,* 1234–1239.

Howell, R. T., & Howell, C. J. (2008). The relation of economic status to subjective well-being in developing countries: A meta-analysis. *Psychological Bulletin, 134,* 536–560.

Hublin, C., Partinen, M., Koskenvuo, M., & Kaprio, J. (2007). Sleep and mortality: A population-based 22-year follow-up study. *Sleep, 30,* 1245–1253.

Hudson, J. I., Hiripi, E., Pope, H. G. Jr., & Kessler, R. C. (2007). The prevalence and correlates of eating disorders in the national comorbidity survey replication. *Biological Psychiatry, 61,* 348–358.

Hudson, J. L., Flannery-Schroeder, E., & Kendall, P. (2004). Primary prevention of anxiety disorders. In D. J. A. Dozois, & K. S. Dobson (Eds.), *The prevention of anxiety and depression: Theory, research, and practice* (pp. 101–130). Washington, DC: American Psychological Association.

Huesmann, L. R., Moise-Titus, J., Podolski, C. L., & Eron, L. D. (2003). Longitudinal relations between children's exposure to TV violence and their aggressive and violent behavior in young adulthood: 1977–1992. *Developmental Psychology, 39,* 201–221.

Hughes, S. C., & Boakes, R. A. (2008). Flavor preferences produced by backward pairing with wheel running. *Journal of Experimental Psychology: Animal Behavior Processes, 34,* 283–293.

Huizink, A. C., & Mulder, E. J. H. (2006). Maternal smoking, drinking or cannabis use during pregnancy and neurobehavioral and cognitive functioning in human offspring. *Neuroscience and Biobehavioral Reviews, 30,* 24–41.

Hull, C. L. (1943). *Principles of behavior: An introduction to behavior theory.* New York: Appleton-Century-Crofts.

Hull, C. L. (1952). *A behavior system: An introduction to behavior theory concerning the individual organism.* New Haven, CT: Yale University Press.

Hume, D. (1951). In L. A. Selby-Bigge (Ed.), *An enquiry concerning human understanding.* London: Oxford University Press. (Original work published 1748)

Hunt, E., & Carlson, J. (2007). Considerations relating to the study of group differences in intelligence. *Perspectives on Psychological Science, 2,* 194–213.

Hurvich, L., & Jameson, D. (1974). Opponent processes as a model of neural organization. *American Psychologist, 29,* 88–102.

Huston, A. C. (2005). The effects of welfare reform and poverty policies on children and families. In D. B. Pillemer & S. H. White (Eds.), *Developmental psychology and social change: Research, history, and policy* (pp. 83–103). New York: Cambridge University Press.

Hyde, J. S., & Durik, A. M. (2000). Gender differences in erotic plasticity—evolutionary or sociocultural forces? Comment on Baumeister (2000). *Psychological Bulletin, 126,* 375–379.

Hyde, J. S., Mezulis, A. H., & Abramson, L. Y. (2008). The ABCs of depression: Integrating affective, biological, and cognitive models to explain the emergence of the gender difference in depression. *Psychological Review, 115,* 291–313.

Hyland, M. E., Whalley, B., & Geraghty, A. W. A. (2007). Dispositional predictors of placebo responding: A motivational interpretation of flower essence and gratitude therapy. *Journal of Psychosomatic Research, 62,* 331–340.

Ingram, A., Saling, M. M., & Schweitzer, I. (2008). Cognitive side effects of brief pulse electroconvulsive therapy: A review. *The Journal of ECT, 24,* 3–9.

Insko, C. A., Thibaut, J. W., Moehle, D., Wilson, M., Diamond, W. D., Gilmore, R., Solomon, M. R., & Lipsitz, A. (1980). Social evolution and the emergence of leadership. *Journal of Personality and Social Psychology, 39,* 431–448.

Irvine, J. T. (1990). Registering affect: Heteroglossia in the linguistic expression of emotion. In C. A. Lutz & L. Abu-Lughod (Eds.), *Language and the politics of emotions* (pp. 126–161). Cambridge, UK: Cambridge University Press.

Iyengar, S. S., Wells, R. E. & Schwartz, B. (2006). Doing better but feeling worse: Looking for the "best" job undermines satisfaction. *Psychological Science, 17,* 143–150.

Izard, C. E. (1993). Four systems for emotion activation: Cognitive and noncognitive processes. *Psychological Review, 100,* 68–90.

Izard, C. E. (1994). Innate and universal facial expressions: Evidence from developmental and cross-cultural research. *Psychological Bulletin, 115,* 288–299.

Jackson, V. A., Mack, J., Matsuyama, R., Lakoma, M. D., Sullivan A. M., Arnold, R. M., Weeks, J. C., & Block, S. D. (2008). A qualitative study of oncologists' approaches to end-of-life care. *Journal of Palliative Medicine, 11,* 893–906.

Jacob, B. R., & Levitt, S. D. (2003). Rotten apples: An investigation of the prevalence and predictors of teacher cheating. *The Quarterly Journal of Economics, 118,* 843–877.

Jacobs, R. C., & Campbell, D. T. (1961). The perpetuation of an arbitrary tradition through several generations of a laboratory microculture. *Journal of Abnormal and Social Psychology, 62,* 649–658.

Jaffee, S., & Hyde, J. S. (2000). Gender differences in moral orientation: A meta-analysis. *Psychological Bulletin, 126,* 703–726.

Jager, G., de Win, M. M. L., van der Tweel, I., Schilt, T., Kahn, R. S., van den Brink, W., van Ree, J. M., & Ramsey, N. F. (2008). Assessment of cognitive brain function in ecstasy users and contributions of other drugs of abuse: Results from an fMRI study. *Neuropsychopharmacology, 33,* 247–258.

Jahnke, J. C. (1965). Primacy and recency effects in serial-position curves of immediate recall. *Journal of Experimental Psychology, 70,* 130–132.

Jain, S., Mills, P. J., von Känel, R., Hong, S., & Dimsdale, J. E. (2007). Effects of perceived stress and uplifts on inflammation and coagulability. *Psychophysiology, 44,* 154–160.

James, W. (1882). Subjective effects of nitrous oxide. *Mind, 7,* 186–208.

James, W. (1892). *Psychology.* New York: Holt.

James, W. (1950). *The principles of psychology* (2 vols.). New York: Holt, Rinehart & Wilson. (Original work published 1890)

Janis, I. (1982). *Groupthink* (2nd ed.). Boston: Houghton Mifflin.

Janis, I. L., & Frick, F. (1943). The relationship between attitudes toward conclusions and errors in judging logical validity of syllogisms. *Journal of Experimental Psychology, 33,* 73–77.

Janofsky, J. S., Dunn, M. H., Roskes, E. J., Briskin, J. K., & Rudolph, M. S. L. (1996). Insanity defense pleas in Baltimore city: An analysis of outcome. *American Journal of Psychiatry, 153,* 1464–1468.

Janowitz, H. D., & Grossman, M. I. (1950). Hunger and appetite: Some definitions and concepts. *Journal of the Mount Sinai Hospital, 16,* 231–240.

January, D., & Kako, E. (2007). Re-evaluating evidence for linguistic relativity: Reply to Boroditsky (2001). *Cognition, 104,* 417–426.

Jay, G. (2008). Service learning, multiculturalism, and the pedagogies of difference. *Pedagogy, 8,* 255–281.

Jedrej, M. C. (1995). *Ingessana: The religious institutions of a people of the Sudan–Ethiopia borderland.* Leiden: Brill.

Jensen, A. R. (1962). Spelling errors and the serial position effect. *Journal of Educational Psychology, 53,* 105–109.

Jensen, L A. (2008). Through two lenses: A cultural-developmental approach to moral psychology. *Developmental Review, 28,* 289–315.

Jo, H., Chen, Y. J., Chua, S. C., Jr., Talmage, D. A., & Role, L. W. (2005). Integration of endocannabinoid and leptin signaling in an appetite-related neural circuit. *Neuron, 48,* 1055–1066.

Joh, A. S., & Adolph, K. E (2006). Learning from falling. *Child Development, 77,* 89–102.

Johnson, T. E., & Rule, B. G. (1986). Mitigating circumstances, information, censure, and aggression. *Journal of Personality and Social Psychology, 50,* 537–542.

Johnson-Laird, P. N., & Wason, P. C. (1977). A theoretical analysis of insight into a reasoning task. In P. N. Johnson-Laird & P. C. Wason (Eds.), *Thinking* (pp. 143–157). Cambridge, UK: Cambridge University Press.

Jones, E. (1953). *The life and works of Sigmund Freud.* New York: Basic Books.

Jones, M. C. (1924). A laboratory study of fear: The case of Peter. *Pedagogical Seminary and Journal of Genetic Psychology, 31,* 308–315.

Jose, P. E., & Brown, I. (2008). When does the gender difference in rumination begin? Gender and age differences in the use of rumination by adolescents. *Journal of Youth and Adolescence, 37,* 180–192.

Joyce, A. S., Ogrodniczuk, J. S., Piper, W. E., & McCallum, M. (2003). The alliance as mediator of expectancy effects in short-term individual therapy. *Journal of Consulting and Clinical Psychology, 71,* 672–679.

Joyce, L. (1990). Losing the connection. *Stanford Medicine,* pp. 19–21.

Jung, C. G. (1959). The concept of the collective unconscious. In *The archetypes and the collective unconscious, collected works* (Vol. 9, Part 1, pp. 54–74.). Princeton, NJ: Princeton University Press. (Original work published 1936)

Jung, C. G. (1973). *Memories, dreams, reflections* (rev. ed., A. Jaffe, Ed.). New York: Pantheon Books.

Jusczyk, P. W. (2003). Chunking language input to find patterns. In D. H. Rakison & L. M. Oakes (Eds.), *Early category and concept development.* London: Oxford University Press.

Jusczyk, P. W., & Aslin, R. N. (1995). Infants' detection of the sound patterns of words in fluent speech. *Cognitive Psychology, 29,* 1–23.

Jussim, L., & Harber, K. D. (2005). Teacher expectations and self-fulfilling prophecies: Knowns and unknowns, resolved and unresolved controversies. *Personality and Social Psychology Review, 9,* 131–155.

Just, M. A., Keller, T. A., & Cynkar, J. (2008). A decrease in brain activation associated with driving when listening to someone speak. *Brain Research, 1205,* 70–80.

Kabat-Zinn, J. (1990). *Full catastrophe living: Using the wisdom of your body and mind to face stress, pain, and illness.* New York: Dell.

Kagan, J. (1994). *Galen's prophesy: Temperament in human nature.* New York: Basic Books.

Kagan, J., & Snidman, N. (1991). Infant predictors of inhibited and uninhibited profiles. *Psychological Science, 2,* 40–44.

Kagan, J., & Snidman, N. (2004). *The long shadow of temperament.* Cambridge, MA: Belknap Press.

Kahneman, D. (1992). Reference points, anchors, norms, and mixed feelings. *Organizational Behavior and Human Decision Processes, 51,* 296–312.

Kahneman, D., & Frederick, S. (2002). Representativeness revisited: Attribute substitution in intuitive judgment. In T. Gilovich, D. Griffin, & D. Kahneman (Eds.), *Heuristics and biases: The psychology of intuitive judgment* (pp. 49–81). Cambridge, UK: Cambridge University Press.

Kahneman, D., Frerickson, B. L., Schreiber, C. A., & Redelmeier, D. A. (1993). When more pain is preferred to less: Adding a better end. *Psychological Science, 4,* 401–405.

Kahneman, D., & Tversky, A. (1973). On the psychology of prediction. *Psychological Review, 80,* 237–251.

Kallmann, F. J. (1946). The genetic theory of schizophrenia: An analysis of 691 schizophrenic index families. *American Journal of Psychiatry, 103,* 309–322.

Kalueff, A. V., & Nutt, D. J. (2007). Role of GABA in anxiety and depression. *Depression and Anxiety, 24,* 495–517.

Kamil, A. C., & Balda, R. P. (1990). Spatial memory in seed-caching corvids. In G. H. Bower (Ed.), *The psychology of learning and motivation* (Vol. 26, pp. 1–25). San Diego: Academic Press.

Kamil, A. C., Balda, R. P., Olson, D. P., & Good, S. (1993). Returns to emptied cache sites by Clark's nutcrackers, *Nucifraga columbiana:* A puzzle revisited. *Animal Behaviour, 45,* 241–252.

Kamin, L. J. (1969). Predictability, surprise, attention, and conditioning. In B. A. Campbell & R. M. Church (Eds.), *Punishment and aversive behavior* (pp. 279–296). New York: Appleton-Century-Crofts.

Kammrath, L. K., Mendoza-Denton, R., & Mischel, W. (2005). Incorporating *if . . . then . . .* personality signatures in person perception: Beyond the person–situation dichotomy. *Journal of Personality and Social Psychology, 88,* 605–618.

Kane, M. J., Brown, L. H., McVay, J. C., Silvia, P. J., Myin-Germeys, I., & Kwapil, T. R. (2007). For whom the mind wanders, and when: An experience-sampling study of working memory and executive control in daily life. *Psychological Science, 18,* 614–621.

Kangas, M., Henry, J. L., & Bryant, R. A. (2005). Predictors of posttraumatic stress disorder following cancer. *Health Psychology, 24,* 579–585.

Kaplan, C. A., & Simon, H. A. (1990). In search of insight. *Cognitive Psychology, 22,* 374–419.

Káradóttir, R., Hamilton, N. B., Bakiri, Y., & Attwell, D. (2008). Spiking and nonspiking classes of oligodendrocyte precursor glia in CNS white matter. *Nature Neuroscience, 11,* 450–456.

Karavasilis, L., Doyle, A. B., & Markiewicz, D. (2003). Associations between parenting style and attachment to mother in middle childhood and adolescence. *International Journal of Behavioral Development, 27,* 153–164.

Karremans, J. C., & Verwijmeren, T. (2008). Mimicking attractive opposite-sex others: The role of romantic relationship status. *Personality and Social Psychology Bulletin, 34,* 939–950.

Kassebaum, N. L. (1994). Head Start: Only the best for America's children. *American Psychologist, 49,* 1123–1126.

Kazdin, A. E. (1982). The token economy: A decade later. *Journal of Applied Behavior Analysis, 15,* 431–445.

Kazdin, A. E. (1994). *Behavior modification in applied settings* (5th ed.). Pacific Grove, CA: Brooks/Cole.

Kazdin, A. E. (2008). Evidence-based treatment and practice: New opportunities to bridge clinical research and practice, enhance the knowledge base, and improve patient care. *American Psychologist, 63,* 146–159.

Kazdin, A. E., & Benjet, C. (2003). Spanking children: Evidence and issues. *Current Directions in Psychological Science, 12,* 99–103.

Keiger, D. (1993, November). Touched with fire. *Johns Hopkins Magazine,* pp. 38, 40–44.

Keller, M. C., & Miller, G. (2006). Resolving the paradox of common, harmful, an heritable mental disorders: Which evolutionary genetic models work best? *Behavioral and Brain Sciences, 29,* 385–452.

Kelley, H. H. (1967). Attribution theory in social psychology. In D. Levine (Ed.), *Nebraska symposium on motivation* (Vol. 15). Lincoln: University of Nebraska Press.

Kellough, J. L., Beevers, C. G., Ellis, A. J., & Wells, T. T. (2008). Time course of selective attention in clinically depressed young adults: An eye tracking study. *Behaviour Research and Therapy, 46,* 1238–1243.

Kempermann, G. (2008). The neurogenic reserve hypothesis: What is adult hippocampus neurogenesis good for? *Trends in Neurosciences, 31,* 163–169.

Kendler, H. H. (1987). *Historical foundations of modern psychology.* Chicago: Dorsey Press.

Kendler, K. S., Gatz, M., Gardner, C. O., & Pedersen, N. L. (2006). A Swedish national twin study of lifetime major depression. *American Journal of Psychiatry, 163,* 109–114.

Kendler, K. S., Kuhn, J. W., & Prescott, C. A. (2004). Childhood sexual abuse, stressful life events and risk for major depression in women. *Psychological Medicine, 34,* 1475–1482.

Kendler, K. S., Thornton, L. M., Gilman, S. E., & Kessler, R. C. (2000a). Sexual orientation in a U.S. national sample of twin and nontwin sibling pairs. *American Journal of Psychiatry, 157,* 1843–1846.

Kennedy, R. E., & Craighead, W. E. (1988). Differential effects of depression and anxiety on recall of feedback in a learning task. *Behavior Therapy, 19,* 437–454.

Kenny, D. A., Bond, C. F., Jr., Mohr, C. D., & Horn, E. M. (1996). Do we know how much people like one another? *Journal of Personality and Social Psychology, 71,* 928–936.

Kenny, D. A., & La Voie, L. (1982). Reciprocity of interpersonal attraction: A confirmed hypothesis. *Social Psychology Quarterly, 45,* 54–58.

Keren, G. (2007). Framing, intentions, and trust-choice incompatibility. *Organizational Behavior and Human Decision Processes, 103,* 238–255.

Kermer, D. A., Driver-Linn, E., Wilson, T. D., & Gilbert, D. T. (2006). Loss aversion is an affective forecasting error. *Psychological Science, 17,* 649–653.

Kerr, N. L., & Tindale, R. S. (2004). Group performance and decision making. *Annual Review of Psychology, 55,* 625–655.

Kershaw, T. C., & Ohlsson, S. (2004). Multiple causes of difficulty in insight: The case of the nine-dot problem. *Journal of Experimental Psychology: Learning, Memory, and Cognition, 30,* 3–13.

Kesebir, P., & Diener, E. (2008). In pursuit of happiness: Empirical answers to philosophical questions. *Perspectives on Psychological Science, 3,* 117–125.

Keshavan, M. S., Tandon, R., Boutros, N. N., & Nasrallah, H. A. (2008). Schizophrenia, "Just the Facts": What we know in 2008. Part 3: Neurobiology. *Schizophrenia Research, 106,* 89–107.

Kessel, N. (1989). Genius and mental disorder: A history of ideas concerning their conjunction. In P. Murray (Ed.), *Genius: The history of an idea* (pp. 196–212). London: Basil Blackwell.

Kessler, R. C., Adler, L., Barkley, R., Biederman, J., Conners, C. K., Demler, O., Faraone, S. V., Greenhill, L. L., Howes, M. J., Secnik, K., Spencer, T., Ustun, T. B., Walters, E. E., & Zaslavsky, A. M. (2006a). The prevalence and correlates of adult ADHD in the United States: Results form the National Comorbidity Survey Replication. *American Journal of Psychiatry, 163,* 716–723.

Kessler, R. C., Berglund, P., Demler, O., Jin, R., Merikangas, K. R., & Walters, E. E. (2005a). Lifetime prevalence and age-of-onset distributions of *DSM-IV* disorders in the National Comorbidity Survey Replication. *Archives of General Psychiatry, 62,* 593–602.

Kessler, R. C., Chiu, W. T., Demler, O., & Walters, E. E. (2005b). Prevalence, severity, and comorbidity of 12-month *DSM-IV* disorders in the National Comorbidity Survey Replication. *Archives of General Psychiatry, 62,* 617–627.

Kessler, R. C., Chiu, W. T., Jin. R., Ruscio, A. M., Shear, K., & Walters. E. E. (2006b). The epidemiology of panic attacks, panic disorder, and agoraphobia in the National Comorbidity Survey Replication. *Archives of General Psychiatry, 63,* 415–424.

Kessler, R. C., McGonagle, K. A., Zhao, S., Nelson, C. B., Hughes, M., Eshleman, S., Wittchen, H. U., & Kendler, K. S. (1994). Lifetime and 12-month prevalence of *DSM-III-R* psychiatric disorders in the United States. *Archives of General Psychiatry, 51,* 8–19.

Kiecolt-Glaser, J. K., Marucha, P. T., Malarkey, P. T., Mercado, A. M., & Glaser, R. (1995). Slowing of wound healing by psychological stress. *Lancet, 346,* 1194–1196.

Kiecolt-Glaser, J. K., McGuire, L., Robles, T. F., & Glaser, R. (2002). Psychoneuroimmunology: Psychological influences on immune function and health. *Journal of Consulting and Clinical Psychology, 70,* 537–547.

Kihlstrom, J. F. (2005). Dissociative disorders. *Annual Review of Clinical Psychology, 1,* 227–253.

Kihlstrom, J. F. (2007). Consciousness in hypnosis. In P. D. Zelazo, M. Moscovitch, & E. Thompson (Eds.), *The Cambridge handbook of consciousness* (pp. 445–479). New York: Cambridge University Press.

Kihlstrom, J. F., & Cantor, N. (2000). Social intelligence. In R. J. Sternberg (Ed.), *Handbook of intelligence* (pp. 359–369). New York: Cambridge University Press.

Kilpatrick, D. G., Ruggiero, K. J., Acierno, R., Saunders, B. E., Resnick, H. S., & Best, C. L. (2003). Violence and risk of PTSD, major depression, substance abuse/dependence, and comorbidity: Results from a national survey of adolescents. *Journal of Consulting and Clinical Psychology, 71,* 692–700.

Kilpatrick, L. A., Zald, D. H., Pardo, J. V., & Cahill, L. F. (2006). Sex-related differences in amygdala functional connectivity during resting conditions. *NeuroImage, 30,* 452–461.

Kim, C.-H., Chang, J. W., Koo, M.-S., Kim, J. W., Suh, H. S., Park, I. H., & Lee, H. S. (2003). *Acta Psychatrica Scandinavica, 107,* 283–290.

Kim, H. S., Sherman, D. K., & Taylor, S. E. (2008). Culture and social support. *American Psychologist, 63,* 518–526.

Kim, J., & Hatfield, E. (2004). Love types and subjective well-being: A cross-cultural study. *Social Behavior and Personality, 32,* 173–182.

Kim, J. J., & Jung, M. W. (2006). Neural circuits and mechanisms involved in Pavlovian fear conditioning: A critical review. *Neuroscience and Biobehavioral Reviews, 30,* 188–202.

Kimura, D. (1999). *Sex and cognition.* Cambridge, MA: MIT Press.

King, S. A., & Moreggi, D. (1998). Internet therapy and self-help groups—The pros and cons. In J. Gackenbach (Ed.), *Psychology and the Internet: Intrapersonal, interpersonal, and transpersonal implications* (pp. 77–109). San Diego, CA: Academic Press.

Kinsey, A. C., Martin, C. E., & Pomeroy, W. B. (1948). *Sexual behavior in the human male.* Philadelphia: Saunders.

Kinsey, A. C., Pomeroy, W. B., Martin, C. E., & Gebhard, R. H. (1953). *Sexual behavior in the human female.* Philadelphia: Saunders.

Kintsch, W. (1974). *The representation of meaning in memory.* Hillsdale, NJ: Erlbaum.

Kinzler, K. D., & Shutts, K. (2008). Memory for "mean" over "nice": The influence of threat on children's face memory. *Cognition, 107,* 775–783.

Kirkham, T. C. (2005). Endocannabinoids in the regulation of appetite and body weight. *Behavioural Pharmacology, 16,* 297–313.

Kirschner, S. M., & Galperin, G. J. (2001). Psychiatric defenses in New York County: Pleas and results. *Journal of the American Academy of Psychiatry and the Law, 29,* 194–201.

Kisilevsky, B. S., & Low, J. A. (1998). Human fetal behavior: 100 years of study. *Developmental Review, 18,* 1–29.

Kisilevsky, B. S., Hains, S. M. J., Lee, K., Xie, X., Huang, H., Ye, H. H., Zhang, K., & Wang, Z. (2003). Effects of experience on fetal voice recognition. *Psychological Science, 14,* 220–224.

Kissane, D. W., Grabsch, B., Clarke, D. M., Christie, G., Clifton, D., Gold, S., Hill, C., Morgan, A., McDermott, F., & Smith, G. C. (2004). Supportive-expressive group therapy: The transformation of existential ambivalence into creative living while enhancing adherence to anticancer therapies. *Psycho-Oncology, 13,* 755–768.

Kitayama, S., Markus, H. R., & Lieberman, C. (1995). The collective construction of self-esteem: Implications for culture, self, and emotion. In J. A. Russell, J. Fernandez-Dols, T. Manstead, & J. Wellenkamp (Eds.), *Everyday conceptions of emotion* (pp. 523–550). Dordrecht: Kluwer.

Klein, D. N. (2008). Classification of depressive disorders in *DSM-V:* Proposal for a two-dimension system. *Journal of Abnormal Psychology, 117,* 552–560.

Klein, K. E., & Wegmann, H. M. (1974). The resynchronization of human circadian rhythms after transmeridian flights as a result of flight direction and mode of activity. In L. E. Scheving, F. Halberg, & J. E. Pauly (Eds.), *Chronobiology* (pp. 564–570). Tokyo: Igaku.

Klein, M. (1975). *The writings of Melanie Klein* (Vols. 1–4). London: Hogarth Press and the Institute of Psychoanalysis.

Klein, O., & Snyder, M. (2003). Stereotypes and behavioral confirmation: From interpersonal to intergroup perspectives. In M. P. Zanna (Ed.), *Advances in experimental social psychology* (Vol. 35, pp. 153–234). New York: Academic Press.

Klump, K. L., Burt, A., McGue, M., & Iacono, W. G. (2007). Changes in genetic and environmental influences on disordered eating across adolescence. *Archives of General Psychiatry, 64,* 1409–1415.

Knickmeyer, R., Baron-Cohen, S., Raggatt, P., & Taylor, K. (2005). Foetal testosterone, social relationships, and restricted interests in children. *Journal of Child Psychology and Psychiatry, 46,* 198–210.

Knobloch, L. K., Miller, L. E., Bond, B. J., & Mannone, S. E. (2007). Relational uncertainty and message processing in marriage. *Communication Monographs, 74,* 154–180.

Kobiella, A., Grossmann, T., Reid, V. M., & Striano, T. (2008). The discrimination of angry and fearful facial expressions in 7-month-old infants: An event-related potential study. *Cognition and Emotion, 22,* 133–146.

Koffka, K. (1935). *Principles of Gestalt psychology.* New York: Harcourt Brace.

Kohen, D. E., Leventhal, T., Dahinten, V. S., & McIntosh, C. N. (2008). Neighborhood disadvantage: Pathways of effects for young children. *Child Development, 79,* 156–169.

Kohlberg, L. (1964). Development of moral character and moral ideology. In M. L. Hoffman & L. W. Hoffman (Eds.), *Review of child development research* (Vol. 1). New York: Russell Sage Foundation.

Kohlberg, L. (1981). *The philosophy of moral development.* New York: Harper & Row.

Köhler, W. (1947). *Gestalt psychology.* New York: Liveright.

Kolb, B. (1989). Development, plasticity, and behavior. *American Psychologist, 44,* 1203–1212.

Konen, C. S., & Kastner, S. (2008). Two hierarchically organized neural systems for object information in human visual cortex. *Nature Neuroscience, 11,* 224–231.

Kong, L. L., Allen, J. J. B., & Glisky, E. L. (2008). Interidentity memory transfer in dissociative identity disorder. *Journal of Abnormal Psychology, 117,* 686–692.

Korchmaros, J. D., & Kenny, D. A. (2006). An evolutionary and close-relationship model of helping. *Journal of Social and Personal Relationships, 23,* 21–43.

Koriat, A., & Fischoff, B. (1974). What day is today? An inquiry into the process of time orientation. *Memory & Cognition, 2,* 201–205.

Koriat, A., & Levy-Sadot, R. (2001). The combined contributions of cue-familiarity and accessibility heuristics to feelings of knowing. *Journal of Experimental Psychology: Learning, Memory, and Cognition, 27,* 34–53.

Kortegaard, L. S., Hoerder, K., Joergensen, J., Gillberg, C., & Kyvik, K. O. (2001). A preliminary population-based twin study of self-reported eating disorder. *Psychological Medicine, 31,* 361–365.

Kotovsky, K., Hayes, J. R., & Simon, H. A. (1985). Why are some problems hard? Evidence from Tower of Hanoi. *Cognitive Psychology, 17,* 248–294.

Kounios, J., Fleck, J. I., Green, D. L., Payne, L., Stevenson, J. L., Bowdend, E. M., Jung-Beeman, M. (2008). The origins of insight in resting-state brain activity. *Neuropsychologia, 46,* 281–291.

Kousta, S.-T., Vinson, D. P., & Vigliocco, G. (2008). Investigating linguistic relativity through bilingualism: The case of grammatical gender. *Journal of Experimental Psychology: Learning, Memory, and Cognition, 34,* 843–858.

Kraepelin, E. (1921). *Manic-depressive disorder and paranoia.* London: Churchill Livingstone.

Krahé, B., Bieneck, S., Scheinberger-Olwig, R. (2007). Adolescents' sexual scripts: Schematic representations of consensual and nonconsensual heterosexual interactions. *Journal of Sex Research, 44,* 316–327.

Krämer, N. C., & Winter, S. (2008). Impression management 2.0: The relationship of self-esteem, extraversion, self-efficacy, and self-presentation within social networking sites. *Journal of Media Psychology, 20,* 106–116.

Krebs, D. L. (2008). Morality: An evolutionary account. *Perspectives on Psychological Science, 3,* 149–172.

Kristensen, P., & Bjerkedal, T. (2007). Explaining the relation between birth order and intelligence. *Science, 316,* 1717.

Krohne, H. W., & Slangen, K. E. (2005). Influence of social support on adaptation to surgery. *Health Psychology, 24,* 101–105.

Krueger, J., & Stanke, D. (2001). The role of self-referent and other-referent knowledge in perceptions of group characteristics. *Personality & Social Psychology Bulletin, 27,* 878–888.

Kruger, J., Wirtz, D., & Miller, D. T. (2005). Counterfactual thinking and the first instinct fallacy. *Journal of Personality and Social Psychology, 88,* 725–735.

Krusemark, E. A., Campbell, W. K., & Clementz, B. A. (2008). Attributions, deception, and event related potentials: An investigation of self-serving bias. *Psychophysiology, 45,* 511–515.

Kuest, J., & Karbe, H. (2002). Cortical activation studies in aphasia. *Current Neurology and Neuroscience Reports, 2,* 511–515.

Kuhn, M. H., & McPartland, T. S. (1954). An empirical investigation of self-attitudes. *American Sociological Review, 19,* 68–76.

Kujawski, J. H., & Bower, T. G. R. (1993). Same-sex preferential looking during infancy as a function of abstract representation. *British Journal of Developmental Psychology, 11,* 201–209.

Kuno, E., Rothbard, A. B., Averyt, J., & Culhane, D. (2000). Homelessness among persons with serious mental illness in an enhanced community-based mental health system. *Psychiatric Services, 51,* 1012–1016.

Kuperberg, G. R., Broome, M. R., McGuire, P. K., David, A. S., Eddy, M., Ozawa, F., Goff, D., West, W. C., Williams, S. C. R., van der Kouwe, A. J. W., Salat, D. H., Dale, A. M., & Fischl, B. (2003). Regionally localized thinning of the cerebral cortex in schizophrenia. *Archives of General Psychiatry, 60,* 878–888.

Kuppens, P., Realo, A., & Diener, E. (2008). The role of positive and negative emotions in life satisfaction judgment across nations. *Journal of Personality and Social Psychology, 95,* 66–75.

Kurtz, M. M., & Mueser, K. T. (2008). A meta-analysis of controlled research on social skills training for schizophrenia. *Journal of Consulting and Clinical Psychology, 76,* 491–504.

LaBar, K. S. (2007). Beyond fear: Emotional memory mechanisms in the human brain. *Current Directions in Psychological Science,* 16, 173–177.

LaBerge, S. (2007). Lucid dreaming. In D. Barret & P. McNamara (Eds.), *The new science of dreaming: Vol 2. Content, recall, and personality correlates* (pp. 307–328). Westport, CT: Praeger.

LaBerge, S., & Levitan, L. (1995). Validity established of DreamLight cues for eliciting lucid dreaming. *Dreaming: Journal of the Association for the Study of Dreams, 5,* 159–168.

LaBerge, S., Nagle, L., Dement, W., & Zarcone, V. (1981). Lucid dreaming verified by volitional communication during REM sleep. *Perceptual & Motor Skills, 52,* 727–732.

LaBerge, S., & Rheingold, H. (1990). *Exploring the world of lucid dreaming.* New York: Ballantine Books.

Lachman, M. E. (2004). Development in midlife. *Annual Review of Psychology, 55,* 305–331.

Lachman, R., Lachman, J. L., & Butterfield, E. C. (1979). *Cognitive psychology and information processing.* Hillsdale, NJ: Erlbaum.

Lachter, J., Forster, K. I., & Ruthruff, E. (2004). Forty-five years after Broadbent (1958): Still no indentification without attention. *Psychological Review, 111,* 880–913.

Lamb, R. J., Morral, A. R., Kirby, K. C., Javors, M. A., Galbicka, G., & Iguchi, M. (2007). Contingencies for change in complacent smokers. *Experimental and Clinical Psychopharmacology, 15,* 245–255.

Lambert, T. A., Kahn, A. S., & Apple, K. J. (2003). Pluralistic ignorance and hooking up. *The Journal of Sex Research, 40,* 129–133.

Lampinen, J. M., Copeland, S. M., & Neuschatz, J. S. (2001). Recollections of things schematic: Room schemas revisited. *Journal of Experimental Psychology: Learning, Memory, and Cognition, 27,* 1211–1222.

Lander, E. S., & Weinberg, R. A. (2000). Genomics: Journey to the center of biology. *Science, 287,* 1777–1782.

Langlois, J. H., Kalakanis, L., Rubenstein, A. J., Larson, A., Hallam, M., & Smoot, M. (2000). Maxims or myths of beauty? A meta-analytic and theoretical review. *Psychological Bulletin, 126,* 390–423.

Langton, S. R. H., Law, A. S., Burton, A. M., & Schweinberger, S. R. (2008). Attention capture by faces. *Cognition, 107,* 330–342.

Lanius, R. A., Williamson, P. C., Hopper, J., Densmore, M., Boksman, K., Gupta, M. A., Neufeld, R. W. J., Gati, J. S., & Menon, R. S. (2003). Recall of emotional states in post-traumatic stress disorder: An fMRI investigation. *Biological Psychiatry, 53,* 204–210.

Lashley, K. S. (1929). *Brain mechanisms and intelligence.* Chicago: University of Chicago Press.

Lashley, K. S. (1950). In search of the engram. In *Physiological mechanisms in animal behavior: Symposium of the Society for Experimental Biology* (pp. 454–482). New York: Academic Press.

Latané, B., & Darley, J. M. (1970). *The unresponsive bystander: Why doesn't he help?* New York: Appleton-Century-Crofts.

Lau, I. Y., Chiu, C., & Hong, Y. (2001). I know what you know: Assumptions about others' knowledge and their effects on message construction. *Social Cognition, 19,* 587–600.

Lau, J. Y. F., & Eley, T. C. (2008). Attributional style as a risk marker of genetic effects for adolescent depressive symptoms. *Journal of Abnormal Psychology, 117,* 849–859.

Lauronen, E., Veijola, J., Isohanni, I., Jones, P. B., Nieminen, P., & Isohanni, M. (2004). Links between creativity and mental disorder. *Psychiatry, 6,* 81–98.

Lawrence, E., Nylen, K., & Cobb, R. J. (2007). Prenatal expectations and marital satisfaction over the transition to parenthood. *Journal of Family Psychology, 21,* 155–164.

Lay, C. H. (1986). At last my research article on procrastination. *Journal of Research in Personality, 20,* 474–495.

Lazar, S. W., Kerr, C. E., Wasserman, R. H., Gray, J. R., Greve, D. N., Treadway, M. T., McGarvey, M., Quinn, B. T., Dusek, J. A., Benson, H., Rauch, S. L., Moore, C. I., & Fischl, B. (2005). Meditation experience is associated with increased cortical thickness. *NeuroReport, 16,* 1893–1897.

Lazareva, O. F., Freiburger, K. L., & Wasserman, E. A. (2004). Pigeons concurrently categorize photographs at both basic and superordinate levels. *Psychonomic Bulletin & Review, 11,* 1111–1117.

Lazarus, R. S. (1981, July). Little hassles can be hazardous to your health. *Psychology Today,* pp. 58–62.

Lazarus, R. S. (1984a). On the primacy of cognition. *American Psychologist, 39,* 124–129.

Lazarus, R. S. (1984b). Puzzles in the study of daily hassles. *Journal of Behavioral Medicine, 7,* 375–389.

Lazarus, R. S. (1991). Cognition and motivation in emotion. *American Psychologist, 46,* 352–367.

Lazarus, R. S. (1993). From psychological stress to the emotions: A history of changing outlooks. *Annual Review of Psychology, 44,* 1–21.

Lazarus, R. S. (1995). Vexing research problems inherent in cognitive-mediational theories of emotion—and some solutions. *Psychological Inquiry, 6,* 183–196.

Lazarus, R. S., & Folkman, S. (1984). *Stress, appraisal, and coping.* New York: Springer.

Lazarus, R. S., & Lazarus, B. N. (1994). *Passion and reason: Making sense of our emotions.* New York: Oxford University Press.

Lecci, L., & Myers, B. (2008). Individual differences in attitudes relevant to juror decision making: Development and validation of the Pretrial Juror Attitude Questionnaire (PJAQ). *Journal of Applied Social Psychology, 38,* 2010–2038.

Ledbetter, A. M., Griffin, E., & Sparks, G. S. (2007). Forecasting "friends forever": A longitudinal investigation of sustained closeness between best friends. *Personal Relationships, 14,* 343–350.

Lee, H. S., & Holyoak, K. J. (2008). The role of causal models in analogical inference. *Journal of Experimental Psychology: Learning, Memory, and Cognition, 34,* 1111–1122.

Lee, M., Zimbardo, P., & Bertholf, M. (1977, November). Shy murderers. *Psychology Today,* pp. 68–70, 76, 148.

Leen-Feldner, E. W., Feldner, M. T., Reardon, L. E., Babson, K. A., & Dixon, L. (2008). Anxiety sensitivity and posttraumatic stress among traumatic event-exposed youth. *Behaviour Research and Therapy, 46,* 548–556.

Legrand, D. (2007). Pre-reflective self-as-subject from experiential and empirical perspectives. *Consciousness and Cognition, 16,* 583–599.

Leiter, M. P., & Maslach, C. (2005). *Banishing burnout: Six strategies for improving your relationship with work.* San Francisco: Jossey-Bass.

Lennon, R. T. (1985). Group tests of intelligence. In B. B. Wolman (Ed.), *Handbook of intelligence* (pp. 825–847). New York: Wiley.

Lenroot, R. K., Gogtay, N., Greenstein, D. K., Wells, E. M., Gregory L. Wallace, G. L., Clasen, L. V., Blumenthal, J. D., Lerch, J., Zijdenbos, A. P., Evans, A. C., Thompson, P. M., & Giedda, J. N. (2007). Sexual dimorphism of brain developmental trajectories during childhood and adolescence. *NeuroImage, 36,* 1065–1073.

Lenzenweger, M. F., Lane, M. C., Loranger, A. W., & Kessler, R. C. (2007). DSM-IV personality disorders in the National Comorbidity Survey Replication. *Biological Psychiatry, 62,* 553–564.

Lesku, J. A., Bark, R. J., Martinez-Gonzalez, D., Rattenborg, N. C., Amlaner, C. J., & Lima, S. L. (2008). Predator-induced plasticity in sleep architecture in wild-caught Norway rats (*Rattus norvegicus*). *Behavioural Brain Research, 189,* 298–305.

Leucht, S., Barnes, T. R. E., Kissling, W., Engel, R. R., Correll, C., & Kane, J. M. (2003). Relapse prevention in schizophrenia with new-generation antipsychotics: A systematic review and exploratory meta-analysis of randomized, controlled trials. *American Journal of Psychiatry, 160,* 1209–1222.

Leung, A. K.-Y., Maddux, W. W., Galinsky, A. D., & Chiu, C.-Y. (2008). Multicultural experience enhances creativity: The when and how. *American Psychologist, 63,* 169–181.

Levenson, R. W., Carstensen, L. L., & Gottman, J. M. (1993). Long-term marriage: Age, gender, and satisfaction. *Psychology and Aging, 8,* 301–313.

Levenson, R. W., Ekman, P., Heider, K., & Friesen, W. V. (1992). Emotion and autonomic nervous system activity in the Minangkabau of West Sumatra. *Journal of Personality and Social Psychology, 62,* 972–988.

Leventhal, A. M., Martin, R. L., Seals, R. W., Tapia, E., & Rehm, L. P. (2007). Investigating the dynamics of affect: Psychological mechanisms of affective habituation to pleasurable stimuli. *Motivation and Emotion, 31,* 145–157.

Leventhal, H. (1980). Toward a comprehensive theory of emotion. In L. Berkowitz (Ed.), *Advances in experimental social psychology* (Vol. 13, pp. 139–207). New York: Academic Press.

Levine, R., Sato, S., Hashimoto, T., & Verma, J. (1995). Love and marriage in eleven cultures. *Journal of Cross-Cultural Psychology, 26,* 544–571.

Lewin, K. (1936). *Principles of topological psychology.* New York: McGraw-Hill.

Lewinsohn, P. M. (1975). The behavioral study and treatment of depression. In M. Hersen, R. M. Eisler, & P. M. Miller (Eds.), *Progress in behavior modification* (pp. 19–64). New York: Academic Press.

Lewinsohn, P. M., Hoberman, H. M., Teri, L., & Hautzinger, M. (1985). An integrative theory of depression. In S. Reiss & R. Bootzin (Eds.), *Theoretical issues in behavior therapy* (pp. 331–359). San Diego, CA: Academic Press.

Lewis, R. J., Derlega, V. J., Clarke, E. G., & Kuang, J. C. (2006). Stigma consciousness, social constraints, and lesbian well-being. *Journal of Counseling Psychology, 53,* 48–56.

Li, J.-Y., Christophersen, M. S., Hall, V., Soulet, D., & Brundin, P. (2008). Critical issues of clinical human embryonic stem cell therapy for brain repair. *Trends in Neurosciences, 31,* 146–153.

Li, M., Chen, L., Lee, D. H. S., Yu, L.-C., & Zhang, Y. (2007). The role of intracellular amyloid β in Alzheimer's disease. *Progress in Neurobiology, 83,* 131–139.

Liang, C. T. H., & Alimo, C. (2005). The impact of white heterosexual students' interactions on attitudes toward lesbian, gay and bisexual people: A longitudinal study. *Journal of College Student Development, 46,* 237–250.

Liao, S. M. (2005). The ethics of using genetic engineering for sex selection. *Journal of Medical Ethics, 31,* 116–118.

Licata, S. C., & Rowlett, J. K. (2008). Abuse and dependence liability of benzodiazepine-type drugs: GABA$_A$ receptor modulation and beyond. *Pharmacology, Biochemistry and Behavior, 90,* 74–89.

Lieb, K., Zanarini, M. C., Schmahl, C., Linehan, M. M., & Bohus, M. (2004). Borderline personality disorder. *The Lancet, 364,* 453–461.

Lieberman, J. A., Stroup, T. S., McEvoy, J. P., Swartz, M. S., Rosenheck, R. A., Perkins, D. O., Keefe, R. S. E., Davis, S. M., Davis, C. E., Lebowitz, B. D., Severe, J., & Hsiao, J. K. (2005). Effectiveness of antipsychotic drugs in patients with chronic schizophrenia. *New England Journal of Medicine, 353,* 1209–1223.

Lilienfeld, S. O., & Lynn, S. J. (2003). Dissociative identity disorder: Multiple personalities, multiple controversies. In S. O. Lilienfeld, S. J. Lynn, & J. M. Lohr (Eds.), *Science and pseudoscience in clinical psychology* (pp. 109–142). New York: Guilford Press.

Lilienfeld, S. O., Wood, J. M., & Garb, H. N. (2001). The scientific status of projective techniques. *Psychological Science in the Public Interest, 1,* 27–66.

Lim, M. M., & Young, L. J. (2006). Neuropeptidergic regulation of affiliative behavior and social bonding in animals. *Hormones and Behavior, 50,* 506–517.

Lin, H., Tian, W., Chen, C., Liu, T., Tsai, S., & Lee, H. (2006). The association between readmission rates and length of stay for schizophrenia: A 3-year population based study. *Schizophrenia Research, 83,* 211–214.

Lindau, S. T., Schumm, L. P., Laumann, E. O., Levinson, W., O'Muircheartaigh, C. A., & Waite, L. J. (2007). A study of sexuality and health among older adults in the United States. *The New England Journal of Medicine, 357,* 762–775.

Lindauer, R. J. L., Booij, J., Habraken, B. A., van Meijel, E. P. M., Uylings, H. B. M., Olff, M., Carlier, I. V. E., den Heeten, G. J., van Eck-Smit, B. L. F., & Gersons, B. P. R. (2008). Effects of psychotherapy on regional cerebral blood flow during trauma imagery in patients with post-traumatic stress disorder: A randomized clinical trial. *Psychological Medicine, 38,* 543–554.

Link, B. G., Struening, E. L., Rahav, M., Phelan, J. C., & Nuttbrock, L. (1997). On stigma and its consequences: Evidence from a longitudinal study of men with dual diagnoses of mental illness and substance abuse. *Journal of Health and Social Behavior, 38,* 177–190.

Lipkus, I. M., Barefoot, J. C., Williams, R. B., & Siegler, I. C. (1994). Personality measures as predictors of smoking initiation and cessation in the UNC Alumni Heart Study. *Health Psychology, 13,* 149–155.

Lisanby, S. H. (2007). Electroconvulsive therapy for depression. *New England Journal of Medicine, 357,* 1939–1945.

Little, T. D., Jones, S. M., Henrich, C. C., & Hawley, P. H. (2003). Disentangling the "whys" from the "whats" of aggressive behavior. *International Journal of Behavioral Development, 27,* 122–123.

Littlewood, R. A., Venable, P. A., Carey, M. P., & Blair D. C. (2008). The association of benefit finding to psychosocial and health behavior adaptation among HIV+ men and women. *Journal of Behavioral Medicine, 31,* 145–155.

Liu, J. H., & Latané, B. (1998). Extremitization of attitudes: Does thought- and discussion-induced polarization cumulate? *Basic and Applied Social Psychology, 20,* 103–110.

Liu, W., Vichienchom, K., Clements, M., DeMarco, S. C., Hughes, C., McGucken, E., Humayun, M. S., de Juan, E., Weiland, J. D., & Greenberg, R. (2000). A neuro-stimulus chip with telemetry unit for retinal prosthetic device. *IEEE Journal of Solid-State Circuits, 35,* 1487–1497.

Liu, Z.-Q., Paterson, A. D., Szatmari, P., & The Autism Genome Project Consortium. (2008). Genome-wide linkage analyses of quantitative and categorical autism subphenotypes. *Biological Psychiatry, 64,* 561–570.

Livesley, W. J., & Lang, K. L. (2005). Differentiating normal, abnormal, and disordered personality. *European Journal of Personality, 19,* 257–268.

Lloyd-Jones, T. J., & Luckhurst, L. (2002). Effects of plane rotation, task, and complexity on recognition of familiar and chimeric objects. *Memory & Cognition, 30,* 499–510.

Lobo, I. A., & Harris, R. A. (2008). GABAA receptors and alcohol. *Pharmacology, Biochemistry and Behavior, 90,* 90–94.

LoBue, V., & DeLoache, J. (2008). Detecting the snake in the grass: Attention to fear-relevant stimuli by adults and young children. *Psychological Science, 19,* 284–289.

Locher, P., Frens, J., & Overbeeke, K. (2008). The influence of induced positive affect and design experience on aesthetic responses to new product designs. *Psychology of Aesthetics, Creativity, and the Arts, 2,* 1–7.

Locke, J. (1975). *An essay concerning human understanding.* Oxford, UK: P. H. Nidditch. (Original work published 1690)

Lockhart, R. S., & Craik, F. I. M. (1990). Levels of processing: A retrospective commentary on a framework for memory research. *Canadian Journal of Psychology, 44,* 87–122.

Loehlin, J. C. (2000). Group differences in intelligence. In R. J. Sternberg (Ed.), *Handbook of intelligence* (pp. 176–193). Cambridge, UK: Cambridge University Press.

Loftus, E. F. (1979). *Eyewitness testimony.* Cambridge, MA: Harvard University Press.

Loftus, E. F. (2005). Planting misinformation in the human mind: A 30-year investigation of the malleability of memory. *Learning & Memory, 12,* 361–366.

Loftus, E. F., & Davis, D. (2006). Recovered memories. *Annual Review of Clinical Psychology, 2,* 469–498.

Loftus, E. F., Miller, D. G., & Burns, H. J. (1978). Semantic integration of verbal information into a visual memory. *Journal of Experimental Psychology: Human Learning and Memory, 4,* 19–31.

Loftus, E. F., & Palmer, J. C. (1974). Reconstruction of automobile destruction: An example of the interaction between language and memory. *Journal of Verbal Learning and Verbal Behavior, 13,* 585–589.

Logan, G. D. (2002). Parallel and serial processes. In H. Pashler & J. Wixted (Eds.), *Stevens' handbook of experimental psychology: Vol 4. Methodology in experimental psychology* (pp. 271–300). New York: Wiley.

Logue, A. W. (1991). *The psychology of eating & drinking: An introduction* (2nd ed.). New York: Freeman.

London, B., Nabet, B., Fisher, A. R., White, B., Sammel, M. D., & Doty, R. L. (2008). Predictors of prognosis in patients with olfactory disturbance. *Annals of Neurology, 63,* 159–166.

Loomis, A. L., Harvey, E. N., & Hobart, G. A. (1937). Cerebral states during sleep as studied by human brain potentials. *Journal of Experimental Psychology, 21,* 127–144.

Lord, C. G., Paulson, R. M., Sia, T. L., Thomas, J. C., & Lepper, M. R. (2004). Houses built on sand: Effects of exemplar stability on susceptibility to attitude change. *Journal of Personality and Social Psychology, 87,* 733–749.

Lourenço, O., & Machado, A. (1996). In defense of Piaget's theory: A reply to 10 common criticisms. *Psychological Review, 103,* 143–164.

Lovibond, S. H., Adams, M., & Adams, W. G. (1979). The effects of three experimental prison environments on the behavior of nonconflict volunteer subjects. *Australian Psychologist, 14,* 273–285.

Luborsky, L., & Barrett, M. S. (2006). The history and empirical status of key psychoanalytic concepts. *Annual Review of Clinical Psychology, 2,* 1–19.

Lucas, R. E. (2007). Adaptation and the set-point model of subjective well-being: Does happiness change after major life events? *Current Directions in Psychological Science, 16,* 75–79.

Luchins, A. S. (1942). Mechanization in problem solving. *Psychological Monographs, 54* (No. 248).

Lumpkin, E. A., & Caterina, M. J. (2007). Mechanisms of sensory transduction in the skin. *Nature, 445,* 858–865.

Luo, M., Fee, M. S., & Katz, L. C. (2003). Encoding pheromonal signals in the accessory olfactory bulb of behaving mice. *Science, 299,* 1196–1201.

Luong, A., & Rogelberg, S. G. (2005). Meetings and more meetings: The relationship between meeting load and daily well-being of employees. *Group Dynamics: Theory, Research, and Practice, 9,* 58–67.

Lynch, D. J., McGrady, A., Alvarez, E., & Forman, J. (2005). Recent life changes and medical utilization in an academic family practice. *The Journal of Nervous and Mental Disease, 193,* 633–635.

Lynch, J. W., Kaplan, G. A., & Shema, S. J. (1997). Cumulative impact of sustained economic hardship on physical, cognitive, psychological, and social functioning. *New England Journal of Medicine, 337,* 1889–1895.

Lynch, W. C., Heil, D. P., Wagner, E., & Havens, M. D. (2008). Body dissatisfaction mediates the association between body mass index and risky weight control behaviors among White and Native American adolescent girls. *Appetite, 51,* 210–213.

Lynn, S. J., & Kirsch, I. (2006). *Essentials of clinical hypnosis: An evidence-based approach.* Washington, DC: American Psychological Association.

Lynn, S. J., Lock, T., Loftus, E. F., Krackow, E., & Lilienfeld, S. O. (2003). The remembrance of things past: Problematic memory recovery techniques in psychotherapy. In S. O. Lilienfeld, S. J. Lynn, & J. M. Lohr (Eds.), *Science and pseudoscience in clinical psychology* (pp. 205–239). New York: Guilford Press.

Lyubomirsky, S., King, L., & Diener, E. (2005). The benefits of frequent positive affect: Does happiness lead to success? *Psychological Bulletin, 131,* 803–855.

Ma, V., & Schoeneman, T. J. (1997). Individualism versus collectivism: A comparison of Kenyan and American self-concepts. *Basic and Applied Social Psychology, 19,* 261–273.

Macchi Cassia, V., Turati, C., & Simion, F. (2004). Can a non-specific bias toward top-heavy patterns explain newborns' face preference? *Psychological Science, 15,* 379–383.

Maccoby, E. E. (2002). Gender and group processes: A developmental perspective. *Current Directions in Psychological Science, 11,* 54–58.

Maccoby, E. E., & Martin, J. A. (1983). Socialization in the context of the family: Parent–child interaction. In E. M. Hetherington (Ed.), *Handbook of child psychology: Vol. 4. Socialization, personality, and social development* (pp. 1–101). New York: Wiley.

Macknik, S. L., King. M., Randi, J., Robbins, A., Teller, Thompson, J., & Martinez-Conde, S. (2008). Attention and awareness in stage magic: Turning tricks into research. *Nature Research Neuroscience,*

Maddux, W. W., Mullen, E., & Galinsky, A. D. (2008). Chameleons bake bigger pies and take bigger pieces: Strategic behavioral mimicry facilitates negotiation outcomes. *Journal of Experimental Social Psychology, 44,* 461–468.

Madon, S., Fuyll, M., Spoth, R., & Willard, J. (2004). Self-fulfilling prophecies: The synergistic accumulative effect of parents' beliefs on children's drinking behaviors. *Psychological Science, 15,* 837–845.

Madon, S., Guyll, M., Buller, A. A., Scherr, K. C., Willard, J., & Spoth, R. (2008). The mediation of mothers' self-fulfilling effects on their children's alcohol use: Self-verification, informational conformity, and modeling processes. *Journal of Personality and Social Psychology, 95,* 369–384.

Madsen, E. A., Tunney, R. J., Gieldman, G., Plotkin, H. C., Dunbar, R. I. M., Richardson, J.-M., & McFarland, D. (2007). Kinship and altruism: A cross-cultural experimental study. *British Journal of Psychology, 98,* 339–359.

Maguen, S., Floyd, F. J., Bakeman, R., & Armistead, L. (2002). Developmental milestones and disclosure of sexual orientation among gay, lesbian, and bisexual youths. *Applied Developmental Psychology, 23,* 219–233.

Mahowald, M. W., & Schenck, C. H. (2005). Insights from studying human sleep disorders. *Nature, 437,* 1279–1285.

Maier, N. R. F. (1931). Reasoning in humans: II. The solution of a problem and its appearance in consciousness. *Journal of Comparative Psychology, 12,* 181–194.

Maier, S. F., & Seligman, M. E. P. (1976). Learned helplessness: Theory and evidence. *Journal of Experimental Psychology, 105,* 3–46.

Male, L. H., & Smulders, T. V. (2007). Memory for food caches: Not just retrieval. *Behavioral Ecology, 18,* 456–459.

Malinowski, B. (1927). *Sex and repression in savage society.* London: Routledge & Kegan Paul.

Manber, R., Kraemer, H. C., Arnow, B. A., Trivedi, M. H., Rush, A. J., Thase, M. E., Rothbaum, B. O., Klein, D. N., Kocsis, J. H., Gelenberg, A. J., & Keller, M. E. (2008). Faster remission of chronic depression with combined psychotherapy and medication than with each therapy alone. *Journal of Consulting and Clinical Psychology, 76,* 459–467.

Mandel, D. R., Jusczyk, P. W., & Pisoni, D. B. (1995). Infants' recognition of the sound patterns of their own names. *Psychological Science, 5,* 314–317.

Manoussaki, D., Dimitriadis, E. K., & Chadwick, R. S. (2006). Cochlea's graded curvature effect on low frequency waves. *Physical Review Letters, 96,* 088701.

Manuck, S. B., Flory, J. D., Muldoon, M. F., & Ferrell, R. E. (2002). Central nervous system serotonergic responsivity and aggressive disposition in men. *Physiology & Behavior, 77,* 705–709.

Marcus, A. D. (1990, December 3). Mists of memory cloud some legal proceedings. *Wall Street Journal,* p. B1.

Marecek, J., Kimmel, E. B., Crawford, M., & Hare-Mustin, R. T. (2003). Psychology of women and gender. In D. K. Freedheim (Ed.), *Handbook of Psychology: Vol. 4. History of Psychology* (pp. 249–268). Hoboken, NJ: Wiley.

Mares, M. L., & Woodard, E. (2005). Positive effects of television on children's social interactions: A meta-analysis. *Media Psychology, 7,* 301–322.

Marian, V., & Kaushanskaya, M. (2007). Language contexts guides memory content. *Psychonomic Bulletin & Review, 14,* 925–933.

Markman, K. D., Lindberg, M. J., Kray, L. J., & Galinsky, A. D. (2007). Implications of counterfactual structure for creative generation and analytic problem solving. *Personality and Social Psychology Bulletin, 33,* 312–324.

Markou, A. (2007). Metabotropic glutamate receptor antagonists: Novel therapeutics for nicotine dependence and depression? *Biological Psychiatry, 61,* 17–22.

Markowitsch, H. J. (2000). Neuroanatomy of memory. In E. Tulving & F. I. M. Craik (Eds.), *The Oxford handbook of memory* (pp. 465–484). Oxford, UK: Oxford University Press.

Markus, H., & Nurius, P. (1986). Possible selves. *American Psychologist, 41,* 954–969.

Markus, H. R., & Kitayama, S. (1991). Culture and the self: Implications for cognition, emotion, and motivation. *Psychological Review, 98,* 224–253.

Markus, H. R., Mullally, P. R., & Kitayama, S. (1997). Self-ways: Diversity in modes of cultural participation. In U. Neisser & D. A. Jopling (Eds.), *The conceptual self in context* (pp. 13–61). Cambridge, UK: Cambridge University Press.

Markus, H. R., Uchida, Y., Omoregie, H., Townsend, S. S. M. & Kitayama, S. (2006). Going for the gold: Models of agency in Japanese and American contexts. *Psychological Science, 17,* 103–112.

Marshall, G. D., & Zimbardo, P. G. (1979). Affective consequences of inadequately explained physiological arousal. *Journal of Personality and Social Psychology, 37,* 970–988.

Martin, C. L., & Ruble, D. (2004). Children's search for gender cues: Cognitive perspectives on gender development. *Current Directions in Psychological Science, 13,* 67–70.

Martin, C. L., Ruble, D. N., & Szkrybalo, J. (2002). Cognitive theories of early gender development. *Psychological Bulletin, 128,* 903–933.

Martin, G., & Pear, J. (1999). *Behavior modification: What it is and how to do it* (6th ed.). Upper Saddle River, NJ: Prentice Hall.

Martin, P. Y., & Marrington, S. (2005). Morningness-eveningness orientation, optimal time-of-day and attitude change: Evidence for the systematic processing of a persuasive communication. *Personality and Individual Differences, 39,* 367–377.

Martin-Fardon, R., Lorentz, C. U., Stuempfig, N. D., & Weiss, F. (2005). Priming with BTCP, a dopamine reuptake blocker, reinstates cocaine-seeking and enhances cocaine cue-induced reinstatement. *Pharmacology, Biochemistry, and Behavior, 92*, 46–54.

Martínez-Taboas, A., Canino, G., Wang, M. Q., Garcías, P., & Bravo, M. (2006). Prevalence of victimization correlates of pathological dissociation in a community sample of youths. *Journal of Traumatic Stress, 19*, 439–448.

Maslach, C. (1979). Negative emotional biasing of unexplained arousal. *Journal of Personality and Social Psychology, 37*, 953–969.

Maslach, C., & Leiter, M. (2008). Early predictors of job burnout and engagement. *Journal of Applied Psychology, 93*, 498–512.

Maslow, A. H. (1968). *Toward a psychology of being* (2nd ed.). Princeton, NJ: Van Nostrand.

Maslow, A. H. (1970). *Motivation and personality* (rev. ed.). New York: Harper & Row.

Mason, L. E. (1997, August 4). Divided she stands. *New York,* pp. 42–49.

Mason, R. A., & Just, M. A. (2007). Lexical ambiguity in sentence comprehension. *Brain Research, 1146*, 115–127.

Mason, T. B. A. II, & Pack, A. I. (2007). Pediatric parasomnias. *Sleep, 30*, 141–151.

Masters, W. H., & Johnson, V. E. (1966). *Human sexual response.* Boston: Little, Brown.

Masters, W. H., & Johnson, V. E. (1970). *Human sexual inadequacy.* Boston: Little, Brown.

Masters, W. H., & Johnson, V. E. (1979). *Homosexuality in perspective.* Boston: Little, Brown.

Maxwell, J. C. (2005). Party drugs: Properties, prevalence, patterns, and problems. *Substance Abuse & Misue, 40*, 1203–1240.

Maxwell, J. S., & Davidson, R. J. (2007). Emotion as motion: Asymmetries in approach and avoidant actions. *Psychological Science, 18*, 1113–1119.

May, R. (1975). *The courage to create.* New York: Norton.

Mayer, J. D., Roberts, R. D., & Barsade, S. G. (2008a). Human abilities: Emotional intelligence. *Annual Review of Psychology, 59*, 507–536.

Mayer, J. D., Salovey, P., & Caruso, D. R. (2008b). Emotional intelligence: New ability or eclectic traits. *American Psychologist, 63*, 503–517.

Mays, V. M., Chochran, S. D., & Barnes, N. W. (2007). Race, race-based discrimination, and health outcomes among African Americans. *Annual Review of Psychology, 58*, 201–225.

McAdams, D. P. (1988). Biography, narrative, and lives: An introduction. *Journal of Personality, 56*, 1–18.

McAdams, D. P. (2001). The psychology of life stories. *Review of General Psychology, 5,* 100–122.

McAdams, D. P., Bauer, J. J., Sakaeda, A. R., Anyidoho, N. A., Machado, M. A., Magrino-Failla, K., White, K. W., & Pals, J. L. (2006). Continuity and change in the life story: A longitudinal study of autobiographical memories in emerging adulthood. *Journal of Personality, 74*, 1371–1400.

McAdams, D. P., & de St. Aubin, E. (Eds.). (1998). *Generativity and adult development: How and why we care for the next generation.* Washington, DC: American Psychological Association.

McAllister, H. A. (1996). Self-serving bias in the classroom: Who shows it? Who knows it? *Journal of Educational Psychology, 88*, 123–131.

McClelland, D. C. (1961). *The achieving society.* Princeton, NJ: Van Nostrand.

McClelland, D. C., Atkinson, J. W., Clark, R. A., & Lowell, E. L. (1953). *The achievement motive.* New York: Appleton-Century-Crofts.

McClelland, D. C., Atkinson, J. W., Clark, R. A., & Lowell, E. L. (1976). *The achievement motive* (2nd ed.). New York: Irvington.

McClelland, D. C., & Franz, C. E. (1992). Motivational and other sources of work accomplishments in mid-life: A longitudinal study. *Journal of Personality, 60*, 679–707.

McClelland, J. L., & Elman, J. L. (1986). The TRACE model of speech perception. *Cognitive Psychology, 18*, 1–86.

McCrae, R. R., & Costa, P. T. Jr. (1997). Personality trait structure as a human universal. *American Psychologist, 52*, 509–516.

McCrae, R. R., Costa, P. T. Jr., & Martin, T. A. (2005). The NEO-PI-3: A more readable revised NEO Personality Inventory. *Journal of Personality Assessment, 84*, 261–270.

McCrae, R. R., Costa, P. T. Jr., Martin, T. A., Oryol, V. E., Rukavishnikov, A. A., Senin, I. G., Hrˇebícˇková, M., & Urbánek, T. (2004). Consensual validation of personality traits across cultures. *Journal of Research in Personality, 38*, 179–201.

McCrae, R. R., Costa, P. T. Jr., Ostendorf, F., Angleitner, A., Hrˇebícˇková, M., Avia, M. D., Sanz, J., Sanchez-Bernardos, M. L., Kusdil, M. E., Woodfield, R., Saunders, P. R., & Smith, P. B. (2000). Nature over nurture: Temperament, personality, and life span development. *Journal of Personality and Social Psychology, 78*, 173–186.

McCrae, S. M., Hirt, E. R., & Milner, B. J. (2008). She works hard for the money: Valuing effort underlies gender differences in behavioral self-handicapping. *Journal of Experimental Social Psychology, 44*, 292–311.

McCrae, S. M., & Hirt, E. R. (2001). The role of ability judgments in self-handicapping. *Personality & Social Psychology Bulletin, 27,* 1378–1389.

McGovern, K., & Baars, B. J. (2007). Cognitive theories of consciousness. In P. D. Zelazo, M. Moscovitch, & E. Thompson (Eds.), *The Cambridge handbook of consciousness* (pp. 177–205). New York: Cambridge University Press.

McGregor, H. A., & Elliott, A. J. (2002). Achievement goals as predictors of achievement-relevant processes prior to task engagement. *Journal of Educational Psychology, 94,* 381–395.

McGue, M., Elkins, I., Walden, B., & Iacono, W. G. (2005). Perceptions of the parent-adolescent relationship: A longitudinal investigation. *Developmental Psychology, 41,* 971–984.

McCabe, C., & Rolls, E. T. (2007). Umami: A delicious flavor formed by convergence of taste and olfactory pathways in the human brain. *European Journal of Neuroscience, 25,* 1855–1864.

McHale, S. M., Crouter, A. C., & Whiteman, S. D. (2003). The family contexts of gender development in childhood and adolescence. *Social Development, 12,* 125–148.

McKone, E., Kanwisher, N., & Duchaine, B. C. (2007). Can generic expertise explain special processing for faces? *Trends in Cognitive Science, 11,* 8–15.

McNeil, B. J., Pauker, S. G., Sox, H. C., Jr., & Tversky, A. (1982). On the elicitation of preferences for alternative therapies. *New England Journal of Medicine, 306,* 1259–1262.

Mead, M. (1928). *Coming of age in Samoa.* New York: Morrow.

Mead, M. (1939). *From the South Seas: Studies of adolescence and sex in primitive societies.* New York: Morrow.

Meador, B. D., & Rogers, C. R. (1979). Person-centered therapy. In R. J. Corsini (Ed.), *Current psychotherapies* (2nd ed., pp. 131–184). Itasca, IL: Peacock.

Meece, J. L., Anderman, E. M., & Anderman, L. H. (2006). Classroom goal structure, student motivation, and academic achievement. *Annual Review of Psychology, 57,* 487–503.

Meichenbaum, D. (1977). *Cognitive-behavior modification: An integrative approach.* New York: Plenum.

Meichenbaum, D. (1985). *Stress inoculation training.* New York: Pergamon Press.

Meichenbaum, D. (1993). Changing conceptions of cognitive behavior modification: Retrospect and prospect. *Journal of Consulting and Clinical Psychology, 61,* 202–204.

Melzack, R. (1973). *The puzzle of pain.* New York: Basic Books.

Melzack, R. (1980). Psychological aspects of pain. In J. J. Bonica (Ed.), *Pain.* New York: Raven Press.

Melzack, R. (2005). Evolution of the neuromatrix theory of pain. *Pain Practice, 5,* 85–94.

Merton, R. K. (1957). *Social theory and social structures.* New York: The Free Press.

Mesquita, B., & Leu, J. (2007). The cultural psychology of emotion. In S. Kitayama & D. Cohen (Eds.), *Handbook of cultural psychology* (pp. 734–759). New York: Guilford Press.

Metcalfe, J. (2000). Metamemory: Theory and data. In E. Tulving & F. I. M. Craik (Eds.), *The Oxford handbook of memory* (pp. 197–211). Oxford, UK: Oxford University Press.

Meyer, R. G. (2003). *Case studies in abnormal behavior* (6th ed.). Boston: Allyn & Bacon.

Meyers, S. A., & Berscheid, E. (1997). The language of love: The difference a preposition makes. *Personality and Social Psychology Bulletin, 23,* 347–362.

Michael, R. T., Gagnon, J. H., Laumann, E. O., & Kolata, G. (1994). *Sex in America: A definitive survey.* Boston: Little, Brown.

Miklowitz, D. J., & Tompson, M. C. (2003). Family variables and interventions in schizophrenia. In G. P. Sholevar & L. D. Schwoeri (Eds.), *Textbook of family and couples therapy: Clinical applications* (pp. 585–617). Washington, DC: American Psychiatric Publishing.

Mikulincer, M., Florian, V., Cowan, P. A., & Cowan, C. P. (2002). Attachment security in couple relationships: A systematic model and its implications for family dynamics. *Family Process, 41,* 405–434.

Milar, K. S. (2000). The first generation of women psychologists and the psychology of women. *American Psychologist, 55,* 616–619.

Milgram, S. (1965). Some conditions of obedience and disobedience to authority. *Human Relations, 18,* 56–76.

Milgram, S. (1974). Obedience to authority. New York: Harper & Row.

Miller, G. A. (1969). Psychology as a means of promoting human welfare. *American Psychologist, 24,* 1063–1075.

Miller, G. A. (1956). The magic number seven plus or minus two: Some limits in our capacity for processing information. *Psychological Review, 63,* 81–97.

Miller, J. G. (1984). Culture and the development of everyday social explanation. *Journal of Personality and Social Psychology, 46,* 961–978.

Miller, J. G., Bersoff, D. M., & Harwood, R. L. (1990). Perceptions of social responsibilities in India and in the United States: Moral imperatives or personal decisions? *Journal of Personality and Social Psychology, 58,* 33–47.

Miller, K. A., Fisher, P. A., Fetrow, B., & Jordan, K. (2006). Trouble on the journey home: Reunification failures in foster care. *Children and Youth Services Review, 28,* 260–274.

Miller, M. A., & Rahe, R. H. (1997). Life changes scaling for the 1990s. *Journal of Psychosomatic Research, 43,* 279–292.

Miller, N. E. (1978). Biofeedback and visceral learning. *Annual Review of Psychology, 29,* 373–404.

Mindell, J. A. (1997). Children and sleep. In M. R. Pressman & W. C. Orr (Eds.), *Understanding sleep: The evaluation and treatment of sleep disorders* (pp. 427–439). Washington, DC: American Psychological Association.

Miranda, J., Bernal, G., Lau, A., Kohn, L., Hwang, W.-C., & LaFromboise, T. (2005). State of the science on psychosocial interventions for ethnic minorities. *Annual Review of Clinical Psychology, 1,* 113–142.

Mischel, W. (1968). *Personality and assessment.* New York: Wiley.

Mischel, W. (1973). Toward a cognitive social learning reconceptualization of personality. *Psychological Review, 80,* 252–283.

Mischel, W. (2004). Toward an integrative science of the person. *Annual Review of Psychology, 55,* 1–22.

Mischel, W., & Shoda, Y. (1995). A cognitive-affective system theory of personality: Reconceptualizing situations, dispositions, dynamics, and invariance in personality structure. *Psychological Review, 102,* 246–268.

Mischel, W., & Shoda, Y. (1999). Integrating dispositions and processing dynamics within a unified theory of personality: The cognitive-affective personality system. In L. A. Pervin & O. P. John (Eds.), *Handbook of personality: Theory and research* (2nd ed., pp. 197–218). New York: Guilford Press.

Mishra, J., & Backlin, W. (2007). The effects of altering environmental and instrumental context on the performance of memorized music. *Psychology of Music, 35,* 1–20.

Mitchell, K. J., & Johnson, M. K. (2000). Source monitoring: Attributing mental experiences. In E. Tulving & F. I. M. Craik (Eds.), *The Oxford handbook of memory* (pp. 179–195). London: Oxford University Press.

Miyashita, T., Kubik, S., Lewandowski, G., & Guzowski, J. F. (2008). Networks of neurons, networks of genes: An integrated view of memory consolidation. *Neurobiology of Learning and Memory, 89,* 269–284.

Modirrousta, M., & Fellows, L. K. (2008). Medial prefrontal cortex plays a critical and selective role in "feeling of knowing" meta-memory judgments. *Neuropsychologia, 46,* 2958–2965.

Mohamed, F. B., Faro, S. H., Gordon, N. J., Platek, S. M., Ahmad, H., & Williams, J. M. (2006). Brain mapping of deception and truth telling about an ecologically valid situation: Functional MR imaging and polygraph investigation—initial experience. *Radiology, 238,* 679–688.

Möller, J.-J., Baldwin, D. S., Goodwin, G., Kasper, S., Okasha, A., Stein, D. J., Tandon, R., Versiani, M., & the WPA section on Pharmacopsychiatry. (2008). Do SSRIs or antidepressants in general increase suicidality? WPA Section on Pharmacopsychiatry: Consensus statement. *European Archives of Psychiatry and Clinical Neuroscience, 258* (Suppl. 3), 3–23.

Moncrieff, R. W. (1951). *The chemical senses.* London: Leonard Hill.

Morgan, A. H., Hilgard, E. R., & Davert, E. C. (1970). The heritability of hypnotic susceptibility of twins: A preliminary report. *Behavior Genetics, 1,* 213–224.

Morgenstern, J., Labouvie, E., McCrady, B. S., Kahler, C. W., & Frey, R. M. (1997). Affiliation with Alcoholics Anonymous after treatment: A study of its therapeutic effects and mechanisms of action. *Journal of Consulting and Clinical Psychology, 65,* 768–777.

Moriarty, T. (1975). Crime, commitment and the responsive bystander: Two field experiments. *Journal of Personality and Social Psychology, 31,* 370–376.

Morin, S. F., & Rothblum, E. D. (1991). Removing the stigma: Fifteen years of progress. *American Psychologist, 46,* 947–949.

Morling, B., & Lamoreaux, M. (2008). Measuring culture outside the head: A meta-analysis of individualism-collectivism in cultural products. *Personality and Social Psychology Review, 12,* 199–221.

Morris, J. A., Jordan, C. L., & Breedlove, S. M. (2004). Sexual differentiation of the vertebrate nervous system. *Nature Neuroscience, 7,* 1034–1039.

Morris, J. S., Frith, C. D., Perrett, D. I., Rowland, D., Young, A. W., Calder, A. J., & Dolan, R. J. (1996). A differential neural response in the human amygdala to fearful and happy facial expressions. *Nature, 383,* 812–815.

Morry, M. M. (2007). The attraction-similarity hypothesis among cross-sex friends: Relationship satisfaction, perceived similarities, and self-serving perceptions. *Journal of Social and Personal Relationships, 24,* 117–138.

Moscovici, S. (1976). *Social influence and social change.* New York: Academic Press.

Moscovici, S. (1980). Toward a theory of conversion behavior. In L. Berkowitz (Ed.), *Advances in experimental social psychology* (Vol. 13, pp. 209–239). New York: Academic Press.

Moscovici, S. (1985). Social influence and conformity. In G. Lindzey & E. Aronson (Eds.), *The handbook of social psychology* (3rd ed., pp. 347–412). New York: Random House.

Moscovici, S., & Faucheux, C. (1972). Social influence, conformity bias, and the study of active minorities. In L. Berkowitz (Ed.), *Advances in experimental social psychology* (Vol. 6). New York: Academic Press.

Moskowitz, G. B. (2004). *Social cognition: Understanding self and others.* New York: Guilford Press.

Motherwell, L., & Shay, J. J. (2005). (Eds.). *Complex dilemmas in group therapy.* New York: Brunner-Routledge.

Mueller, A., Mueller, U., Silbermann, A., Reinecker, H., Bleich, S., Mitchell, J. E., & de Zwaan, M. (2008). A randomized, controlled trial of group cognitive-behavioral therapy for compulsive buying disorder: Posttreatment and 6-month follow-up results. *Journal of Clinical Psychiatry, 69,* 1131–1138.

Mulvaney, M. K., & Mebert, C. J. (2007). Parental corporal punishment predicts behavior problems in early childhood. *Journal of Family Psychology, 21,* 389–397.

Munafò, M. R., & Johnstone, E. C. (2008). Genes and cigarette smoking. *Addiction, 103,* 893–904.

Munsterberg, H. (1908). *On the witness stand.* New York: McClure.

Murphy, G. L. (2002). *The big book of concepts.* Cambridge, MA: MIT Press.

Murphy, K. J., Troyer, A. K., Levine, B., & Moscovitch, M. (2008). Episodic, but not semantic, autobiographical memory is reduced in amnestic mild cognitive impairment. *Neuropsychologia, 46,* 3116–3123.

Mussweiler, T., & Bodenhausen, G. V. (2002). I know you are, but what am I? Self-evaluative consequences of judging in-group and out-group members. *Journal of Personality and Social Psychology, 82,* 19–32.

Narayan, V. M., Narr, K. L., Phillips, O. R., Thompson, P. M. Toga, A. W., Szeszko, P. R. (2008). Greater regional cortical gray matter thickness in obsessive-compulsive disorder. *NeuroReport, 19,* 1551–1555.

Nash, J. R., Sargent, P. A., Rabiner, E. A., Hood, S. D., Argyropoulos, S. V., Potokar, J. P., Grasby, P. M., & Nutt, D. J. (2008). Serotonin 5-HT$_{1A}$ receptor binding in people with panic disorder: positron emission tomography study. *The British Journal of Psychiatry, 193,* 229–234.

Nasrallah, H. A. (2005). Factors having impact on the tolerability of antipsychotic agents. *Journal of Clinical Psychiatry, 66,* 131–133.

National Institute on Aging. (2006). *Alzheimer's Disease Fact Sheet.* Retrieved from www.nia.nih.gov/Alzheimers/ Publications/adfact.htm.

Neath, I., Brown, G. D. A., McCormack, T., Chater, N., & Freeman, R. (2006). Distinctiveness models of memory and absolute identification: Evidence for local, not global, effects. *Quarterly Journal of Experimental Psychology, 59,* 121–135.

Neath, I., & Crowder, R. G. (1990). Schedules of presentation and temporal distinctiveness in human memory. *Journal of Experimental Psychology: Learning, Memory, and Cognition, 16,* 316–327.

Neath, I., & Surprenant, A. M. (2003). *Human memory: An introduction to research, data, and theory* (2nd ed.). Belmont, CA: Wadsworth.

Neiss, M. B., Sedikides, C., & Stevenson, J. (2006). Genetic influences on level and stability of self-esteem. *Self and Identity, 5,* 247–266.

Neisser, U. (1967). *Cognitive psychology.* New York: Appleton-Century-Crofts.

Nelson, D. A., Mitchell, C., & Yang, C. (2008). Intent attributions and aggression: A study of children and their parents. *Journal of Abnormal Child Psychology, 36,* 793–806.

Nelson, R. E., & Craighead, W. E. (1977). Selective recall of positive and negative feedback, self-control behaviors and depression. *Journal of Abnormal Psychology, 86,* 379–388.

Nelson, T. D. (2006). *The psychology of prejudice* (2nd ed.). Boston: Allyn & Bacon.

Nes, R. B., Røysamb, E., Tambs, K., Harris, J. R., & Reichborn-Kjennerud, T. (2006). Subjective well-being: Genetic and environmental contributions to stability and change. *Psychological Medicine, 36,* 1033–1042.

Nettle, D. (2006). The evolution of personality variation in humans and other animals. *American Psycholgist, 61,* 622–631.

Nettelbeck, T., & Wilson, C. (2005). Intelligence and IQ: What teachers should know. *Educational Psychology, 25,* 609–630.

Nevéus, T., Cnattingius, S., Olsson, U., & Hetta, J. (2001). Sleep habits and sleep problems among a community sample of schoolchildren. *Acta Paediatr, 90,* 1450–1455.

Newcomb, T. M. (1929). *The consistency of certain extrovert-introvert behavior traits in 50 problem boys* (Contributions to Education, No. 382). New York: Columbia University Press.

Newell, A., & Simon, H. A. (1972). *Human problem solving.* Englewood Cliffs, NJ: Prentice Hall.

Newman, T. K., Syagailo, Y. V., Barr, C. S., Wendland, J. R., Champoux, M., Grassele, M., Suomi, S. J., Higley, J. D., & Lesch, K.-P. (2005). Monoamine oxidase: A gene promoter variation and rearing experiences influence aggressive behavior in rhesus monkeys. *Biological Psychiatry, 57,* 167–172.

Niaura, R., Todaro, J. F., Stoud, L., Sprio, A., III, Ward, K. D., & Weiss, S. (2002). Hostility, the metabolic syndrome, and incident coronary heart disease. *Health Psychology, 21,* 588–593.

Niccols, A. (2007). Fetal alcohol syndrome and the developing socio-emotional brain. *Brain and Cognition, 65,* 135–142.

NICHD Early Child Care Research Network. (1997). The effects of infant child care on infant-mother attachment security: Results of the NICHD Study of Early Child Care. *Child Development, 68,* 860–879.

NICHD Early Child Care Research Network. (2006). Infant-mother attachment classification: Risk and protection in relation to changing maternal caregiving quality. *Developmental Psychology, 42*, 38–58.

Nicoll, C., Russell, S., & Katz, L. (1988, May 26). Research on animals must continue. *San Francisco Chronicle*, p. A25.

Nielsen, B. D., Pickett, C. L., & Simonton, D. K. (2008). Conceptual versus experimental creativity: Which works best on convergent and divergent thinking tasks? *Psychology of Aesthetics, Creativity, and the Arts, 2*, 131–138.

Nielsen, T. A., & Stenstrom, P. (2005). What are the memory sources of dreaming? *Nature, 437*, 1286–1289.

Nigg, C. R., Borrelli, B., Maddock, J., & Dishman, R. K. (2008). A theory of physical activity maintenance. *Applied Psychology: An International Review, 57*, 544–560.

Nock, M. K., Borges, G., Bromet, E. J., Cha, C. B., Kessler, R. C., & Lee, S. (2008). Suicide and suicidal behavior. *Epidemiologic Reviews, 30*, 133–154.

Nolan, J. M., Schultz, P. W., Cialdini, R. B., Goldstein, N. J., & Griskevicius, V. (2007). Normative social influence is underdetected. *Personality and Social Psychology Bulletin, 34*, 913–923.

Nolen-Hoeksema, S. (2002). Gender differences in depression. In I. H. Gotlib & C. L. Hammen (Eds.), *Handbook of depression* (pp. 492–509). New York: Guilford Press.

Nolen-Hoeksema, S., Larson, J., & Grayson, C. (1999). Explaining the gender difference in depressive symptoms. *Journal of Personality and Social Psychology, 77*, 1061–1072.

Nooteboom, S., & Quené, H. (2008). Self-monitoring and feedback: A new attempt to find the main cause of lexical bias in phonological speech errors. *Journal of Memory and Language, 58*, 837–861.

Norcross, J. C., Karpiak, C. P., & Lister, K. M. (2005). What's an integrationist? A study of self-identified and (occasionally) eclectic psychologists. *Journal of Clinical Psychology, 61*, 1587–1594.

Nordberg, A. (2008). Amyloid imaging in Alzheimer's disease. *Neuropsychologia, 46*, 1636–1641.

Norman, G. J., Velicer, W. F., Fava, J. L., & Prochaska, J. O. (1998). Dynamic topology clustering within the stages of change for smoking cessation. *Addictive Behaviors, 23*, 139–153.

Norman, G. J., Velicer, W. F., Fava, J. L., & Prochaska, J. O. (2000). Cluster subtypes within stage of change in a representative sample of smokers. *Addictive Behaviors, 25*, 183–204.

Norman, W. T. (1963). Toward an adequate taxonomy of personality attributes: Replicated factor structure in peer nomination personality ratings. *Journal of Abnormal and Social Psychology, 66*, 574–583.

Norman, W. T. (1967). *2,800 personality trait descriptors: Normative operating characteristics for a university population* (Research Rep. No. 083101-T). Ann Arbor: University of Michigan Press.

Nosofsky, R. M., & Stanton, R. D. (2005). Speeded classification in a probabilistic category structure: Contrasting exemplar-retrieval, decision-boundary, and prototype models. *Journal of Experimental Psychology: Human Perception and Performance, 31*, 608–629.

Novick, L. R., & Bassok, M. (2005). Problem solving. In K. J. Holyoak & R. G. Morrison (Eds.), *Cambridge handbook of thinking and reasoning* (pp. 321–349). New York: Cambridge University Press.

Nowak, M. A., & Sigmund, K. (2005). Evolution of indirect reciprocity. *Nature, 437*, 1291–1298.

Nrugham, L., Larsson, B., & Sund, A. M. (2008). Predictors of suicidal acts across adolescence: Influences of family, peer and individual factors. *Journal of Affective Disorders, 109*, 35–45.

Nyberg, L., & Cabeza, R. (2000). Brain imaging of memory. In E. Tulving & F. I. M. Craik (Eds.), *The Oxford handbook of memory* (pp. 501–519). Oxford, UK: Oxford University Press.

O'Brien, C. P. (2005). Benzodiazepine use, abuse, and dependence. *Journal of Clinical Psychiatry, 66* (Suppl. 2), 28–33.

O'Connor, M. G., & Lafleche, G. (2005). Amnesic syndromes. In P. J. Snyder, P. D. Nussbaum, & D. L. Robins (Eds.), *Clinical neuropsychology: A pocket handbook for assessment* (2nd ed.) (pp. 463–488). Washington, DC: American Psychology Association.

Ogden, C. L., Carroll, M. D., Curtin, L. R., McDowell, M. A., Tabak, C. J., & Flegal, K. M. (2006). Prevalence of overweight and obesity in the United States, 1999–2004. *Journal of The American Medical Association, 295*, 1549–1555.

Öhman, A., & Mineka, S. (2001). Fears, phobias, and preparedness: Toward an evolved module of fear and fear learning. *Psychological Review, 108*, 483–522.

Okamoto-Barth, S., Call, J., & Tomasello, M. (2007). Great apes' understanding of other individuals' line of sight. *Psychological Science, 18*, 462–468.

Olsson, I. A. S., Hansen, A. K., & Sandøe, P. (2007). Ethics and refinement in animal research. *Science, 317*, 1680.

Olszewski-Kubilius, P., & Lee, S. Y. (2004). The role of participation in in-school and outside-of-school activities in the talent development of gifted students. *Journal of Secondary Gifted Education, 15*, 107–123.

Olton, D. S. (1992). Tolman's cognitive analyses: Predecessors of current approaches in psychology. *Journal of Experimental Psychology: General, 121*, 427–428.

Oman, D., Hedberg, J., & Thoresen, C. E. (2006). Passage meditation reduces perceived stress in health professionals: A randomized, controlled trial. *Journal of Consulting and Clinical Psychology, 74*, 714–719.

Omoto, A. M., & Snyder, M. (2002). Considerations of community: The context and process of volunteerism. *American Behavioral Scientist, 45,* 846–867.

Oppenheimer, D. M., & Frank, M. C. (2008). A rose in any other font would not smell as sweet: Effects of perceptual fluency on categorization. *Cognition, 106,* 1178–1194.

Opton, E. M. Jr. (1970). Lessons of My Lai. In N. Sanford & C. Comstock (Eds.), *Sanctions for evil.* San Francisco: Jossey-Bass.

Opton, E. M. Jr. (1973). "It never happened and besides they deserved it." In W. E. Henry & N. Stanford (Eds.), *Sanctions for evil* (pp. 49–70). San Francisco: Jossey-Bass.

Orban, G. A., van Essen, D., & Vandeuffel, W. (2004). Comparative mapping of higher areas in monkeys and humans. *Trends in Cognitive Science, 8,* 315–324.

Orbuch, T. L., Veroff, J., Hassan, H., & Horrocks, J. (2002). Who will divorce: A 14-year longitudinal study of black couples and white couples. *Journal of Social and Personal Relationships, 19,* 179–202.

Orth, U., Robins, R. W., & Roberts, B. W. (2008). Low self-esteem prospectively predicts depression in adolescence and young adulthood. *Journal of Personality and Social Psychology, 95,* 695–708.

Ou, S.-R., & Reynolds, A. J. (2006). Early childhood intervention and educational attainment: Age 22 findings from the Chicago Longitudinal Study. *Journal of Education for Students Placed at Risk, 11,* 175–198.

Owen, M. J., & O'Donovan, M. C. (2003). Schizophrenia and genetics. In R. Plomin, J. C. DeFries, I. W. Craig, & P. McGuffin (Eds.), *Behavioral genetics in the postgenomic era* (pp. 463–480). Washington, DC: American Psychological Association.

Owens, K. M. B., Asmundson, G. J. G., Hadjistavropoulos, T., & Owens, T. J. (2004). Attentional bias toward illness threat in individuals with elevated health anxiety. *Cognitive Therapy and Research, 28,* 57–66.

Ozer, D. J., & Reise, S. P. (1994). Personality assessment. *Annual Review of Psychology, 45,* 357–388.

Pachankis, J. E. (2007). The psychological implications of concealing a stigma: A cognitive-affective-behavioral model. *Psychological Bulletin, 133,* 328–345.

Packer, I. K. (2008). Specialized practice in forensic psychology: Opportunities and obstacles. *Professional Psychology: Research and Practice, 39,* 245–249.

Pagel, J. F. (2008). The burden of obstructive sleep apnea and associated excessive sleepiness. *Journal of Family Practice, 57,* S3–S8.

Pagnoni, G., & Cekic, M. (2007). Age effects on gray matter volume and attentional performance in Zen meditation. *Neurobiology of Aging, 28,* 1623–1627.

Paivio, A. (2006). *Mind and its evolution: A dual coding theoretical interpretation.* Mahwah, NJ: Lawrence Erlbaum Associates, Inc.

Paller, K. A., & Voss, J. L. (2004). Memory reactivation and consolidation during sleep. *Learning & Memory, 11,* 664–670.

Pandi-Perumal, S. R., Srinivasan, V., & Spence, D. W., & Cardinali, D. P. (2007). Rold of the melatonin system in the control of sleep: Therapeutic implications. *CNS Drugs, 21,* 995–1018.

Papafragou, A., Li, P., Choi, Y., & Han, C.-H. (2007). Evidentiality in language and cognition. *Cognition, 103,* 253–299.

Paris, J. (2003). *Personality disorders over time: Precursors, course, and outcome.* Washington, DC: American Psychiatric Publishing.

Parker, A., Ngu, H., & Cassaday, H. J. (2001). Odour and Proustian memory: Reduction of context-dependent forgetting and multiple forms of memory. *Applied Cognitive Psychology, 15,* 159–171.

Parker, A. M., Bruine de Bruin, W., & Fischhoff, B. (2007). Maximizers versus satisficers: Decision-making styles, competence, and outcomes. *Judgment and Decision Making, 2,* 342–350.

Parr, W. V., & Siegert, R. (1993). Adults' conceptions of everyday memory failures in others: Factors that mediate the effects of target age. *Psychology and Aging, 8,* 599–605.

Parsons, L. M., & Osherson, D. (2001). New evidence for distinct right and left brain systems for deductive versus probabilistic reasoning. *Cerebral Cortex, 11,* 954–965.

Patterson, C. J. (2002). Lesbian and gay parenthood. In M. H. Bornstein (Ed.), *Handbook of parenting: Vol. 3. Being and becoming a parent* (2nd ed., pp. 317–338). Mahwah, NJ: Erlbaum.

Pauli, P., Dengler, W., Wiedemann, G., Montoya, P., Flor, H., Birbaumer, N., & Buchkremer, G. (1997). Behavioral and neuropsychological evidence for altered processing of anxiety-related words in panic disorder. *Journal of Abnormal Psychology, 106,* 213–220.

Paus, T. (2005). Mapping brain maturation and cognitive development during adolescence. *Trends in Cognitive Sciences, 9,* 60–68.

Pavlov, I. P. (1927). *Conditioned reflexes* (G. V. Anrep, Trans.). London: Oxford University Press.

Pavlov, I. P. (1928). *Lectures on conditioned reflexes: Twenty-five years of objective study of higher nervous activity (behavior of animals)* (Vol. 1, W. H. Gantt, Trans.). New York: International Publishers.

Penick, S., Smith, G., Wienske, K., & Hinkle, L. (1963). An experimental evaluation of the relationship between hunger and gastric motility. *American Journal of Physiology, 205,* 421–426.

Penke, L., Denissen, J. J. A., & Miller, G. F. (2007). The evolutionary genetics of personality. *European Journal of Personality, 21,* 549–587.

Penn, D. L., Guynan, K., Daily, T., Spaulding, W. D., Garbin, C. P., & Sullivan, M. (1994). Dispelling the stigma of schizophrenia: What sort of information is best? *Schizophrenia Bulletin, 20,* 567–578.

Penn, D. L., Kommana, S., Mansfield, M., & Link, B. G. (1999). Dispelling the stigma of schizophrenia: II. The impact of information on dangerousness. *Schizophrenia Bulletin, 25,* 437–446.

Pennebaker, J. W. (1990). *Opening up: The healing power of confiding in others.* New York: Morrow.

Pennebaker, J. W. (1997). Writing about emotional experiences as a therapeutic process. *Psychological Science, 8,* 162–166.

Perahia, D. G. S., Pritchett, Y. L., Kajdasz, D. K., Bauer, M., Jain, R., Russell, J. M., Walker, D. J., Spencer, K. A., Froud, D. M., Raskin, J., & Thase, M. E. (2008). A randomized, double-blind comparison of duloxetine and venlafaxine in the treatment of patients with major depressive disorder. *Journal of Psychiatric Research, 42,* 22–34.

Perkins, D. N. (1988). Creativity and the quest for mechanism. In R. J. Sternberg & E. E. Smith (Eds.), *The psychology of human thought* (pp. 309–336). Cambridge, UK: Cambridge University Press.

Perls, F. S. (1969). *Gestalt therapy verbatim.* Lafayette, CA: Real People Press.

Peters, E., Västfjäll, D., Slovic, P., Mertz, C. K., Mazzocco, K., & Dickert, S. (2006). Numeracy and decision making. *Psychological Science, 17,* 407–413.

Peterson, C., & Seligman, M. E. P. (1984). Causal explanations as a risk factor for depression: Theory and evidence. *Psychological Review, 91,* 347–374.

Peterson, C., & Vaidya, R. S. (2001). Explanatory style, expectations, and depressive symptoms. *Personality and Individual Differences, 31,* 1217–1223.

Peterson, H. M., & Kemp, R. I. (2006). Co-witness talk: A survey of eyewitness discussion. *Psychology Crime & Law, 12,* 181–191.

Peterson, L. R., & Peterson, M. J. (1959). Short-term retention of individual verbal items. *Journal of Experimental Psychology, 58,* 193–198.

Peterson, R. S., & Nemeth, C. J. (1996). Focus versus flexibility: Majority and minority influence can both improve performance. *Personality and Social Psychology Bulletin, 22,* 14–23.

Petrie, K. J., Booth, R. J., & Pennebaker, J. W. (1998). The immunological effects of thought suppression. *Journal of Personality and Social Psychology, 75,* 1264–1272.

Petrie, K. J., Fontanilla, I., Thomas, M. G., Booth, R. J., & Pennebaker, J. W. (2004). Effect of written emotional expression on immune function in patients with human immunodeficiency virus infection: A randomized trial. *Psychosomatic Medicine, 66,* 272–275.

Petry, N. M., Alessi, S. M., Marx, J., Austin, M., & Tardif, M. (2005). Vouchers versus prizes: Contingency management treatment of substance abusers in community settings. *Journal of Consulting and Clinical Psychology, 73,* 1005–1014.

Pettigrew, T. F. (2008). Future directions for intergroup contact theory and research. *International Journal of Intercultural Relations, 32,* 187–199.

Pettigrew, T. F., Christ, O., Wagner, U., & Stellmacher, J. (2007). Direct and indirect intergroup contact effects on prejudice: A normative interpretation International. *Journal of Intercultural Relations, 31,* 41–425.

Pettigrew, T. F., & Tropp, L. R. (2006). A meta-analytic test of intergroup contact theory. *Journal of Personality and Social Psychology, 90,* 751–783.

Petty, R. E., & Briñol, P. (2008). Persuasion: From single to multiple to metacognitive processes. *Perspectives on Psychological Sciences, 3,* 137–147.

Petty, R. E., Cacioppo, J. T., Strathman, A. J., & Priester, J. R. (2005). To think or not to think: Exploring two routes to persuasion. In T. C. Brock & M. C. Green (Eds.), *Persuasion: Psychological insights and perspectives* (2nd ed., pp. 81–116). Thousand Oaks, CA: Sage.

Pfeifer, M., Goldsmith, H. H., Davidson, R. J., & Rickman, M. (2002). Continuity and change in inhibited and uninhibited children. *Child Development, 73,* 1474–1485.

Piaget, J. (1929). *The child's conception of the world.* New York: Harcourt, Brace.

Piaget, J. (1954). *The construction of reality in the child.* New York: Basic Books.

Piaget, J. (1965). *The moral judgment of the child* (M. Gabain, Trans.). New York: Macmillan.

Piaget, J. (1977). *The development of thought: Equilibrium of cognitive structures.* New York: Viking Press.

Piccione, C., Hilgard, E. R., & Zimbardo, P. G. (1989). On the degree of stability of measured hypnotizability over a 25-year period. *Journal of Personality and Social Psychology, 56,* 289–295.

Pilkonis, P. A., & Zimbardo, P. G. (1979). The personal and social dynamics of shyness. In C. E. Izard (Ed.), *Emotions in personality and psychopathology* (pp. 131–160). New York: Plenum Press.

Pines, A., & Zimbardo, P. G. (1978). The personal and cultural dynamics of shyness: A comparison between Israelis, American Jews and Americans. *Journal of Psychology and Judaism, 3,* 81–101.

Piotrowski, C., Keller, J. W., & Ogawa, T. (1993). Projective techniques: An international perspective. *Psychological Reports, 72,* 179–182.

Pischke, C. R., Scherwitz, L., Weidner, G., & Ornish, D. (2008). Long-term effects of lifestyle changes on well-being and cardiac variables among coronary heart disease patients. *Health Psychology, 27,* 584–592.

Pitts, D. G. (1982). The effects of aging on selected visual functions: Dark adaptation, visual acuity, stereopsis, and brightness contrast. In R. Sekuler, D. Kline, & K. Dismukes (Eds.), *Aging and human visual function* (pp. 131–159). New York: Liss.

Plazzi, G., Vertugno, R., Provini, F., & Montagna, P. (2005). Sleepwalking and other ambulatory behaviours during sleep. *Neurological Sciences, 26,* s193–s198.

Plomin, R., DeFries, J. C., Craig, I. W., & McGuffin, P. (2003). Behavioral genetics. In R. Plomin, J. C. DeFries, I. W. Craig, & P. McGuffin (Eds.), *Behavioral genetics in the postgenomic era* (pp. 3–15). Washington, DC: American Psychological Association.

Plomin, R., & Petrill, S. A. (1997). Genetics and intelligence: What's new? *Intelligence, 24,* 53–77.

Plomin, R., & Spinath, F. M. (2004). Intelligence: Genetics, genes, and genomics. *Journal of Personality and Social Psychology, 86,* 112–129.

Plous, S. (1996a). Attitudes toward the use of animals in psychological research and education: Results from a national survey of psychology majors. *Psychological Science, 7,* 352–358.

Plous, S. (1996b). Attitudes toward the use of animals in psychological research and education: Results from a national survey of psychologists. *American Psychologist, 51,* 1167–1180.

Polivy, J., & Herman, C. P. (1999). Distress and eating: Why do dieters overeat? *International Journal of Eating Disorders, 26,* 153–164.

Porter, L. W., & Lawler, E. E. (1968). *Managerial attitudes and performance.* Homewood, IL: Irwin.

Posada, R., & Wainryb, C. (2008). Moral development in a violent society: Columbian children's judgments in the context of survival and revenge. *Child Devleopment, 79,* 882–898.

Poucet, B. (1993). Spatial cognitive maps in animals: New hypotheses on their structure and neural mechanisms. *Psychological Review, 100,* 163–182.

Powers, M. B., & Emmelkamp, P. M. G. (2008). Virtual reality exposure therapy for anxiety disorders: A meta-analysis. *Journal of Anxiety Disorders, 22,* 561–569.

Powley, T. (1977). The ventromedial hypothalamic syndrome, satiety, and a cephalic phase hypothesis. *Psychological Review, 84,* 89–126.

Preckel, F., Holling, H., & Wiese, M. (2006). Relationship of intelligence and creativity in gifted and non-gifted students: An investigation of threshold theory. *Personality and Individual Differences, 40,* 159–170.

Premack, D. (1965). Reinforcement theory. In D. Levine (Ed.), *Nebraska symposium on motivation* (pp. 128–180). Lincoln: University of Nebraska Press.

Premack, D. (1971). Language in chimpanzee? *Science, 172,* 808–822.

Pressman, L. J., Loo, S. K., Carpenter, E. M., Asarnow, J. R., Lynn, D., McCracken, J. T., McGough, J. J., Lubke, G. H.,

Yang, M. H., & Smalley, S. L. (2006). Relationship of family environment and parental psychiatric diagnosis to impairment in ADHD. *Journal of the American Academy of Child and Adolescent Psychiatry, 45,* 346–354.

Prosser, D., Johnson, S., Kuipers, E., Szmukler, G., Bebbington, P., & Thornicroft, G. (1997). Perceived sources of work stress and satisfaction among hospital and community mental health staff, and their relation to mental health, burnout, and job satisfaction. *Journal of Psychosomatic Research, 43,* 51–59.

Quine, W. V. O. (1960). *Word and object.* Cambridge, MA: The MIT Press.

Quittner, A. L., Modi, A., Lemanek, K. L., Ievers-Landis, C. E., & Rapoff, M. A. (2008). Evidence-based assessment of adherence to medical treatments in pediatric psychology. *Journal of Pediatric Psychology, 33,* 916–936.

Rachlin, H. (1990). Why do people gamble and keep gambling despite heavy losses? *Psychological Science, 1,* 294–297.

Radvansky, G. A. (2006). *Human memory.* Boston: Allyn & Bacon.

Rahman, Q., & Wilson, G. D. (2003). Born gay? The psychobiology of human sexual orientation. *Personality and Individual Differences, 34,* 1337–1382.

Rahman, R. A., & Melinger, A. (2007). When bees hamper the production of honey: Lexical interference from associates in speech production. *Journal of Experimental Psychology: Learning, Memory, and Cognition, 33,* 604–614.

Rajaram, S., & Roediger, H. L. III (1993). Direct comparison of four implicit memory tests. *Journal of Experimental Psychology: Learning, Memory, and Cognition, 19,* 765–776.

Ramey, C. H., & Weisberg, R. W. (2004). The "poetical activity" of Emily Dickinson: A further test of the hypothesis that affective disorders foster creativity. *Creativity Research Journal, 16,* 173–185.

Ramírez, J. M., & Andreu, J. M. (2006). Aggression, and some related psychological constructs (anger, hostility, and impulsivity): Some comments from a research project. *Neuroscience and Biobehavioral Reviews, 30,* 276–291.

Rapoport, J. L. (1989, March). The biology of obsessions and compulsions. *Scientific American,* pp. 83–89.

Rasch, B., & Born, J. (2008). Reactivation and consolidation of memory during sleep. *Current Directions in Psychological Science, 17,* 188–192.

Rasmussen, T., & Milner, B. (1977). The role of early left-brain injury in determining lateralization of cerebral speech functions. *Annals of the New York Academy of Sciences, 299,* 355–369.

Ratcliff, R., & McKoon, G. (1978). Priming in item recognition: Evidence for the propositional structure of sentences. *Journal of Verbal Learning and Verbal Behavior, 17,* 403–418.

Rau, H., Bührer, M., & Wietkunat, R. (2003). Biofeedback of R-wave-to-pulse interval normalizes blood pressure. *Applied Psychophysiology and Biofeedback, 28,* 37–46.

Rawson, R. A., Maxwell, J., & Rutkowski, B. (2007). OxyContin abuse: Who are the users? *The American Journal of Psychiatry, 164,* 1634–1636.

Ray, W. J., Keil, A., Mikuteit, A., Bongartz, W., & Elbert, T. (2002). High resolution EEG indicators of pain responses in relation to hypnotic susceptibility and suggestion. *Biological Psychology, 60,* 17–36.

Raynor, H. A., & Epstein, L. H. (2001). Dietary variety, energy regulation, and obesity. *Psychological Bulletin, 127,* 325–341.

Raz, A. (2005). Attention and hypnosis: Neural substrates and genetic associations of two converging processes. *International Journal of Clinical and Experimental Hypnosis, 53,* 237–258.

Reb, J. (2008). Regret aversion and decision process quality: Effects of regret salience on decision process carefulness. *Organizational Behavior and Human Decision Processes, 105,* 169–182.

Recanzone, G. H., & Sutter, M. L. (2008). The biological basis of audition. *Annual Review of Psychology, 59,* 119–142.

Regalado, M., Sareen, H., Inkelas, M., Wissow, L. S., & Halfon, N. (2004). Parents' discipline of young children: Results from the national survey of early childhood health. *Pediatrics, 113,* 1952–1958.

Regan, R. T. (1971). Effects of a favor and liking on compliance. *Journal of Experimental Social Psychology, 7,* 627–639.

Reilly, T., Atkinson, G., Edwards, B., Waterhouse, J., Farrelly, K., & Fairhurst, E. (2007). Diurnal variation in temperature, mental and physical performance, and tasks specifically related to football (soccer). *Chronobiology International, 24,* 507–519.

Reis, H. T., & Aron, A. (2008). Love: What is it, why does it matter, and how does it operate? *Perspectives on Psychological Science, 3,* 80–86.

Renzulli, J. S. (2005). The three-ring conception of giftedness: A developmental model for promoting creative productivity. In R. J. Sternberg & J. E. Davidson (Eds.), *Conceptions of giftedness* (2nd ed.) (pp. 246–279). New York: Cambridge University Press.

Rescorla, R. A. (1966). Predictability and number of pairings in Pavlovian fear conditioning. *Psychonomic Science, 4,* 383–384.

Rescorla, R. A. (1988). Pavlovian conditioning: It's not what you think it is. *American Psychologist, 43,* 151–160.

Reti, I. M., Samuels, J. F., Eaton, W. W., Bienvenu, O. J. III, Costa, P. T. Jr., & Nestadt, G. (2002). Adult antisocial personality traits are associated with experiences of low paternal care and maternal overprotection. *Acta Psychiatrica Scandinavica, 106,* 126–133.

Reyna, C., & Weiner, B. (2001). Justice and utility in the classroom: An attributional analysis of the goals of teachers' punishment and intervention strategies. *Journal of Educational Psychology, 93,* 309–319.

Reynolds, J. S., & Perrin, N. A. (2004). Mismatches in social support and psychosocial adjustment. *Health Psychology, 23,* 425–430.

Ribeiro, S. C., Kennedy, S. E., Smith, Y. R., Stohler, C. S., & Zubieta, J. K. (2005). Interface of physical and emotional stress regulation through the endogenous opioid system and μ-opioid receptors. *Progress in Neuro-Psychopharmacology & Biological Psychiatry, 29,* 1264–1280.

Richards, M. H., Crowe, P. A., Larson, R., & Swarr, A. (1998). Developmental patterns and gender differences in the experience of peer companionship during adolescence. *Child Development, 69,* 154–163.

Rinck, M. (2008). Spatial situation models and narrative comprehension. In M. A. Gluck, J. R. Anderson, & S. M. Kosslyn (Eds.), *Memory and mind: A festschrift for Gordon H. Bower* (pp. 359–370). Mahwah, NJ: Erlbaum.

Ritchie, P. L.-J. (2007). Annual report of the International Union of Psychological Science (IUPsyS) to the International Council for Science. *International Journal of Psychology, 42,* 353–360.

Rivas-Vazquez, R. A. (2003). Benzodiazepines in contemporary clinical practice. *Professional Psychology: Research and Practice, 34,* 424–428.

Roberson, D., Davidoff, J., Davies, I. R. L., & Shapiro, L. R. (2005). Color categories: Evidence for the cultural relativity hypothesis. *Cognitive Psychology, 50,* 378–411.

Roberts, A., Cash, T. F., Feingold, A., & Johnson, B. T. (2006). Are Black–White differences in females' body dissatisfaction decreasing? A meta-analytic review. *Journal of Consulting and Clinical Psychology, 74,* 1121–1131.

Roberts, A. H., Kewman, D. G., Mercier, L., & Hovell, M. (1993). The power of nonspecific effects in healing: Implications for psychosocial and biological treatments. *Clinical Psychology Review, 13,* 375–391.

Rode, J. C., Mooney, C. H., Arthaud-Day, M. L., Near, J. P., Baldwin, T. T., Rubin, R. S., & Bommer, W. H. (2007). Emotional intelligence and individual performance: Evidence of direct and moderated effects. *Journal of Organizational Behavior, 28,* 399–421.

Roediger, H. L. III, Gallo, D. A., & Geraci, L. (2002). Processing approaches to cognition: The impetus from the levels-of-processing framework. *Memory, 10,* 319–332.

Roenneberg, T., Kuehnle, T., Juda, M., Kantermann, T., Allebrandt, K., Gordijn, M., & Merrow, M. (2007). Epidemiology of the human circadian clock. *Sleep Medicine Reviews, 11,* 429–438.

Roese, N. J., & Summerville, A. (2005). What we regret most . . . and why. *Personality and Social Psychology Bulletin, 31,* 1273–1285.

Rogers, C. R. (1947). Some observations on the organization of personality. *American Psychologist, 2,* 358–368.

Rogers, C. R. (1951). *Client-centered therapy: Its current practice, implications and theory.* Boston: Houghton Mifflin.

Rogers, C. R. (1959). A theory of therapy, personality, and interpersonal relationships, as developed in the client-centered framework. In S. Koch (Ed.), *Psychology: A study of a science* (Vol. 3). New York: McGraw-Hill.

Rogers, C. R. (1977). *On personal power: Inner strength and its revolutionary impact.* New York: Delacorte.

Rogers, M., & Smith, K. (1993). Public perceptions of subliminal advertising: Why practitioners shouldn't ignore this issue. *Journal of Advertising Research, 33*(2), 10–18.

Rogers, S. (1993). How a publicity blitz created the myth of subliminal advertising. *Public Relations Quarterly, 37,* 12–17.

Rogoff, B. (1990). *Apprenticeship in thinking: Cognitive development in social context.* New York: Oxford University Press.

Rogoff, B. (2003). *The cultural nature of human development.* London: Oxford University Press.

Rogoff, B., & Chavajay, P. (1995). What's become of research on the cultural basis of cognitive development? *American Psychologist, 50,* 859–877.

Rohrer, J. H., Baron, S. H., Hoffman, E. L., & Swinder, D. V. (1954). The stability of autokinetic judgment. *Journal of Abnormal and Social Psychology, 49,* 595–597.

Roid, G. (2003). *Stanford-Binet intelligence scale* (5th ed.). Itasca, IL: Riverside Publishing.

Roisman, G. I., Clausell, E., Holland, A., Fortuna, K., & Elieff, C. (2008). Adult romantic relationships as contexts of human development: A multimethod comparison among same-sex couples with opposite-sex dating, engaged, and married dyads. *Developmental Psychology, 44,* 91–101.

Rolls, E. T. (2000). Memory systems in the brain. *Annual Review of Psychology, 51,* 599–630.

Rolls, E. T. (2005). Taste, olfactory, and food texture processing in the brain, and the control of food intake. *Physiology & Behavior, 85,* 45–56.

Romer, M., Lehrner, J., Wymelbeke, V. V., Jiang, T., Deecke, L. & Brondel, L. (2006). Does modification of olfacto-gustatory stimulation diminish sensory-specific satiety in humans? *Physiology & Behavior, 87,* 469–477.

Root, R. W. II, & Resnick, R. J. (2003). An update on the diagnosis and treatment of attention-deficit/hyperactivity disorder in children. *Professional Psychology: Research and Practice, 34,* 34–41.

Rorschach, H. (1942). *Psychodiagnostics: A diagnostic test based on perception.* New York: Grune & Stratton.

Rosch, E., & Mervis, C. B. (1975). Family resemblances: Studies in the internal structure of categories. *Cognitive Psychology, 7,* 573–605.

Rosch, E. H. (1973). Natural categories. *Cognitive Psychology, 4,* 328–350.

Rosch, E. H. (1978). Principles of categorization. In E. Rosch & B. B. Lloyd (Eds.), *Cognition and categorization* (pp. 27–48). Hillsdale, NJ: Erlbaum.

Rosch, E. H., Mervis, C. B., Gray, W. D., Johnson, D. M., & Boyes-Braem, P. (1976). Basic objects in natural categories. *Cognitive Psychology, 8,* 382–439.

Rose, A. J., & Rudolph, K. D. (2006). A review of sex-differences in peer relationship processes: Potential trade-offs for the emotional and behavioral development of girls and boys. *Psychological Bulletin, 132,* 98–131.

Rose, M. E., & Grant, J. E. (2008). Pharmacotherapy for methamphetamine dependence: A review of the pathophysiology of methamphetamine addiction and the theoretical basis and efficacy of pharmacotherapeutic interventions. *Annals of Clinical Psychiatry, 20,* 145–155.

Rosenfield, S. (1997). Labeling mental illness: The effects of received services and perceived stigma on life satisfaction. *American Sociological Review, 62,* 660–672.

Rosenhan, D. L. (1973). On being sane in insane places. *Science, 179,* 250–258.

Rosenhan, D. L. (1975). The contextual nature of psychiatric diagnoses. *Journal of Abnormal Psychology, 84,* 462–474.

Rosenthal, A. M. (1964). *Thirty-eight witnesses.* New York: McGraw-Hill.

Rosenthal, R., & Fode, K. L. (1963). The effect of experimenter bias on the performance of the albino rat. *Behavioral Science, 8,* 183–189.

Rosenthal, R., & Jacobson, L. F. (1968). *Pygmalion in the classroom: Teacher expectations and intellectual development.* New York: Holt.

Rosenzweig, M. R. (1996). Aspects of the search for neural mechanisms of memory. *Annual Review of Psychology, 47,* 1–32.

Rosenzweig, M. R. (1999). Effects of differential experience on brain and cognition throughout the life span. In S. H. Broman & J. M. Fletcher (Eds.), *The changing nervous system: Neurobehavioral consequences of early brain disorders* (pp. 25–50). New York: Oxford University Press.

Ross, L. (1977). The intuitive psychologist and his shortcomings. In L. Berkowitz (Ed.), *Advances in experimental social psychology* (Vol. 10, pp. 173–220). New York: Academic Press.

Ross, L. (1988). Situational perspectives on the obedience experiments. [Review of the obedience experiments: A case study of controversy in social science]. *Contemporary Psychology, 33,* 101–104.

Ross, L., Amabile, T., & Steinmetz, J. (1977). Social roles, social control and biases in the social perception process. *Journal of Personality and Social Psychology, 37,* 485–494.

Ross, L., & Nisbett, R. E. (1991). *The person and the situation: Perspectives of social psychology.* New York: McGraw-Hill.

Rothbart, M. K. (2007). Temperament, development, and personality. *Current Directions in Psychological Science, 16,* 207–212.

Rothbaum, B. O., Anderson, P., Zimand, E., Hodges, L., Lang, D., & Wilson, J. (2006). Virtual reality exposure therapy and standard (in vivo) exposure therapy in the treatment of fear of flying. *Behavior Therapy, 37,* 80–90.

Rothman, D. J. (1971). *The discovery of the asylum: Social order and disorder in the new republic.* Boston: Little, Brown.

Rotter, J. B. (1954). *Social learning and clinical psychology.* Englewood Cliffs, NJ: Prentice-Hall.

Rotter, J. B. (1966). Generalized expectancies for internal versus external locus of control of reinforcement. *Psychological Monographs, 80* (Whole No. 609).

Rouse, S. V., Greene, R. L., Butcher, J. N., Nichols, D. S., & Williams, C. L. (2008). What do the MMPI-2 Restructured Clinical Scales reliably measure? Answers from multiple research settings. *Journal of Personality Assessment, 90,* 435–442.

Roussi, P. (2002). Discriminative facility in perceptions of control and its relation to psychological distress. *Anxiety, Stress, & Coping: An International Journal, 15,* 179–191.

Roussi, P., Krikeli, V., Hatzidimitriou, C., & Koutri, I. (2007). Patterns of coping, flexibility in coping and psychological distress in women diagnosed with breast cancer. *Cognitive Therapy and Research, 31,* 97–109.

Rozin, P., & Fallon, A. E. (1987). A perspective on disgust. *Psychological Review, 94,* 23–41.

Rozin, P., Millman, L., & Nemeroff, C. (1986). Operation of the laws of sympathetic magic in disgust and other domains. *Journal of Personality and Social Psychology, 50,* 703–712.

Rubin, D. C., & Kontis, T. C. (1983). A schema for common cents. *Memory & Cognition, 11,* 335–341.

Ruch, R. (1937). *Psychology and life.* Glenview, IL: Scott, Foresman.

Rudd, M. D., Berman, A. L., Joiner, T. E. Jr., Nock, M. K., Silverman, M. M., Mandrusiak, M., Van Orden, K., & Witte, T. (2006). Warning signs for suicide: Theory, research, and clinical applications. *Suicide and Life-Threatening Behavior, 36,* 255–262.

Ruitenbeek, H. M. (1973). *The first Freudians.* New York: Jason Aronson.

Rule, N. O., & Ambady, N. (2008). The face of success: Inferences from chief executive officers' appearance predict company profits. *Psychological Science, 19,* 109–111.

Runco, M. A. (1991). *Divergent thinking.* Norwood, NJ: Ablex.

Runco, M. A. (2007). *Creativity: Theories and themes: Research, development, and practice.* San Diego, CA: Elsevier Academic Press.

Runco, M. A. (2008). Commentary: Divergent thinking is not synonymous with creativity. *Psychology of Aesthetics, Creativity, and the Arts, 2,* 93–96.

Ruscio, A. M. Brown, T. A., Chiu, W. T., Sareen, J., Stein, M. B., & Kessler, R. C. (2008). Social fears and social phobia in the USA: Results from the National Comorbidity Survey Replication. *Psychological Medicine, 38,* 15–28.

Russo, F. A., & Thompson, W. F. (2005). An interval size illusion: The influence of timbre on the perceived size of melodic intervals. *Perception & Psychophysics, 67,* 559–568.

Russo, N. F., & Denmark, F. L. (1987). Contributions of women to psychology. *Annual Review of Psychology, 38,* 279–298.

Rutter, P. A., & Behrendt, A. E. (2004). Adolescent suicide risk: Four psychosocial factors. *Adolescence, 39,* 295–302.

Ryder, R. D. (2006). Speciesism in the laboratory. In P. Singer (Ed.), *In defense of animals: The second wave.* Oxford, UK: Blackwell.

Ryff, C. D. (1989). In the eye of the beholder: Views of psychological well-being among middle-aged and older adults. *Psychology and Aging, 4,* 195–210.

Sachdev, P., Mondraty, N., Wen, W., & Gulliford, K. (2008). Brains of anorexia nervosa patients process self-images differently from non-self-images: An fMRI study. *Neuropsychologia, 46,* 2161–2168.

Saffran, J., Hauser, M., Seibel, R., Kapfhamer, J., Tsao, F., & Cushman, F. (2008). Grammatical pattern learning by human infants and cotton-top tamarin monkeys. *Cognition, 107,* 479–500.

Sak, U. (2004). A synthesis of research on psychological types of gifted adolescents. *Journal of Secondary Gifted Education, 15,* 70–79.

Salihu, H. M., & Wilson, R. E. (2007). Epidemiology of prenatal smoking and perinatal outcomes. *Early Human Development, 83,* 713–720.

Salloway, S., Mintzer, J., Weiner, M. R., & Cummings, J. L. (2008). Disease-modifying therapies in Alzheimer's disease. *Alzheimer's & Dementia, 4,* 65–79.

Salthouse, T. A. (2006). Mental exercise and mental aging: Evaluating the validity of the "use it or lose it" hypothesis. *Perspectives on Psychological Science, 1,* 68–87.

Salvy, S.-J., Jarrin, D., Paluch, R., Irfan, N., & Pliner, P. (2007). Effects of social influence on eating in couples, friends and strangers. *Appetite, 49,* 92–99.

Salvy, S.-J., Kieffer, E., & Epstein, L. H. (2008). Effects of social context on overweight and normal-weight children's food selection. *Eating Behaviors, 9,* 190–196.

Salzinger, S., Ng-Mak, D. S., Feldman, R. S., Kam, C. M., & Rosario, M. (2006). Exposure to community violence: Processes that increase the risk for inner-city middle school children. *Journal of Early Adolescence, 26,* 232–266.

Samuel, A. G. (1981). Phonemic restoration: Insights from a new methodology. *Journal of Experimental Psychology: General, 110,* 474–494.

Samuel, A. G. (1991). A further examination of attentional effects in the phonemic restoration illusion. *Quarterly Journal of Experimental Psychology: Human Experimental Psychology, 43A,* 679–699.

Samuel, A. G. (1997). Lexical activation produces potent phonemic percepts. *Cognitive Psychology, 32,* 97–127.

Sanderson, C. A., Rahm, K. B., & Beigbeder, S. A. (2005). The link between pursuit of intimacy goals and satisfaction in close same-sex friendships: An examination of the underlying processes. *Journal of Social and Personal Relationships, 22,* 75–98.

Sandstrom, M. J., & Cramer, P. (2003). Girls' use of defense mechanisms following peer rejection. *Journal of Personality, 71,* 605–627.

Santhi, N., Aeschbach, D., Horowitz, T. S., & Czeisler, C. A. (2008). The impact of sleep timing and bright light exposure on attentional impairment during night work. *Journal of Biological Rhythms, 23,* 341–352.

Santosa, C. M., Strong, C. M., Nowakowska, C., Wang, P. W., Rennicke, C. M., & Ketter, T. A. (2007). Enhanced creativity in bipolar disorder patients: A controlled study. *Journal of Affective Disorders, 100,* 31–39.

Sapir, E. (1964). *Culture, language, and personality.* Berkeley: University of California Press. (Original work published 1941)

Sapolsky, R. M. (1994). *Why zebras don't get ulcers: A guide to stress, stress-related disease, and coping.* New York: Freeman.

Satir, V. (1967). *Conjoint family therapy* (rev. ed.). Palo Alto, CA: Science and Behavior Books.

Savage-Rumbaugh, S., Shanker, S. G., & Taylor, T. J. (1998). *Apes, language, and the human mind.* New York: Oxford University Press.

Savic, I., & Lindström, P. (2008). PET and MRI show differences in cerebral asymmetry and functional connectivity between homo- and heterosexual subjects. *PNAS, 105,* 9403–9408.

Scaramella, L. V., Neppl, T. K., Ontai, L. L., & Conger, R. D. (2008). Consequences of socioeconomic disadvantage across three generations: Parenting behavior and child externalizing problems. *Journal of Family Psychology, 22,* 725–733.

Scarborough, E., & Forumoto, L. (1987). *Untold lives: The first generation of women psychologists.* New York: Columbia University Press.

Schachter, S. (1971a). *Emotion, obesity and crime.* New York: Academic Press.

Schaie, K. W. (2005). *Developmental influences on adult intelligence: The Seattle longitudinal study.* New York: Oxford University Press.

Schick, B., Marschark, M., & Spencer, P. E. (Eds.) (2006). *Advances in the sign language development of deaf children.* New York: Oxford University Press.

Schiff, M., & Bargal, D. (2000). Helping characteristics of self-help and support groups: Their contribution to participants' subjective well-being. *Small Group Research, 31,* 275–304.

Schalock, R. L., Luckasson, R. A., & Shogren, K. A. (2007). The renaming of *Mental Retardation:* Understanding the change to the term *Intellectual Disability. Intellectual and Developmental Disabilities, 45,* 116–124.

Schlenger, W. E., Caddell, J. M., Ebert, L., Jordan, B. K., Rourke, K. M., Wilson, D., Thalji, L., Dennis, J. M., Fairbank, J. A., & Kulka, R. A. (2002). Psychological reactions to terrorist attacks: Findings from the National Study of Americans' reactions to September 11. *JAMA, 288,* 581–588.

Schlitz, M. (1997). *Dreaming for the community: Subjective experience and collective action among the Anchuar Indians of Ecuador.* Research proposal. Marin, CA: Institute of Noetic Sciences.

Schmader, T., Johns, M., & Forbes, C. (2008). An integrated process model of stereotype threat effects on performance. *Psychological Review, 115,* 336–356.

Schmitt, D. P. (2003). Universal sex differences in desire for sexual variety: Tests from 52 nations, 6 continents, and 13 islands. *Journal of Personality and Social Psychology, 85,* 85–104.

Schneider, K., & May, R. (1995). *The psychology of existence: An integrative, clinical perspective.* New York: McGraw-Hill.

Scholz, U., Schüz, B., Ziegelmann, J., Lippke, S., & Schwarzer, R. (2008). Beyond behavioural intentions: Planning mediates between intentions and physical activity. *British Journal of Health Psychology, 13,* 479–494.

Schousboe, K., Visscher, P. M., Erbas, B., Kyvik, K. O., Hopper, J. L., Henriksen, J. E., Heitmann, B. L., & Sørensen,

T. I. A. (2004). Twin study of genetic and environmental influences on adult body size, shape, and composition. *International Journal of Obesity, 28,* 39–48.

Schredl, M., & Erlacher, D. (2008). Relation between waking sport activities, reading, and dream content in sports students and psychology students. *The Journal of Psychology, 142,* 267–275.

Schutter, D. J. L. G. (2008). Antidepressant efficacy of high-frequency transcranial magnetic stimulation over the left dorsolateral prefrontal cortex in double-blind sham-controlled designs: A meta-analysis. *Psychological Medicine*

Schwab, C., Bugnyar, T., Schloegl, C., & Kotrschal, K. (2008). Enhanced social learning between siblings in common ravens, *Corvus corax. Animal Behaviour, 75,* 501–508.

Schützwohl, A. (2006). Sex differences in jealousy: Information search and cognitive preoccupation. *Personality and Individual Differences, 40,* 285–292.

Schwartz, B., Ward, A., Monterosso, J., Lyubomirsky, S., White, K., & Lehman, D. R. (2002). Maximizing versus satisficing: Happiness is a matter of choice. *Journal of Personality and Social Psychology, 83,* 1178–1197.

Schwarz, N., Bless, H., Wänke, M., & Winkielman, P. (2003). Accessibility revisited. In G. V. Bodenhausen & A. J. Lambert (Eds.), *Foundations of social cognition: A festschrift in honor of Robert S. Wyer* (pp. 51–77). Mahwah, NJ: Erlbaum.

Schweinhart, L. J. (2004). *The High/Scope Perry preschool study through age 40: Summary, conclusions, and frequently asked questions.* Retrieved from www.highscope.org/Research/PerryProject/PerryAge40SumWeb.pdf.

Sciutto, M. J., & Eisenberg, M. (2007). Evaluating the evidence for and against the overdiagnosis of ADHD. *Journal of Attention Disorders, 11,* 106–113.

Scott, D., Scott, L. M., & Goldwater, B. (1997). A performance improvement program for an international-level track and field athlete. *Journal of Applied Behavior Analysis, 30,* 573–575.

Scull, A. (1993). *A most solitary of afflictions: Madness and society in Britain 1700–1900.* London: Yale University Press.

Seamon, J. G., Philbin, M. M., & Harrison, L G. (2006). Do you remember proposing marriage to the Pepsi machine? False recollections from a campus walk. *Psychonomic Bulletin & Review, 13,* 752–756.

Seal, D. S., Smith, M., Coley, B., Perry, J., & Gamez, M. (2008). Urban heterosexual couples' sexual scripts for three shared sexual experiences. *Sex Roles, 58,* 626–638.

Sear, R., & Mace, R. (2008). Who keeps children alive? A review of the effects of kin on child survival. *Evolution and Human Behavior, 29,* 1–18.

Searle, J. R. (1979). Literal meaning. In J. R. Searle (Ed.), *Expression and meaning* (pp. 117–136). Cambridge, UK: Cambridge University Press.

Sears, S. R., Stanton, A. L., & Danoff-Burg, S. (2003). The yellow brick road and the Emerald City: Benefit finding, positive reappraisal coping, and posttraumatic growth in women with early-stage breast cancer. *Health Psychology, 22,* 487–497.

Sedikides, C., Gaertner, L., & Toguchi, Y. (2003). Pancultural self-enhancement. *Journal of Personality and Social Psychology, 84,* 60–79.

Sedikides, C., & Gregg, A. P. (2008). Self-enhancement: Food for thought. *Perspectives on Psychological Science, 3,* 102–116.

Segerstrom, S. C. (2005). Optimism and immunity: Do positive thoughts always lead to positive effects? *Brain, Behavior, and Immunity, 19,* 195–200.

Segerstrom, S. C. (2006). How does optimism suppress immunity? Evaluation of three affective pathways. *Health Psychology, 25,* 653–657.

Segerstrom, S. C. (2007). Stress, energy, and immunity. *Current Directions in Psychological Science, 16,* 326–330.

Seidenberg, M. S., & Petitto, L. A. (1979). Signing behavior in apes: A critical review. *Cognition, 7,* 177–215.

Seidler, R. D., Purushotham, A., Kim, S. G., Ugurbil, K., Willingham, D., & Ashe, J. (2002). Cerebellum activation associated with performance change but no motor learning. *Science, 296,* 2043–2046.

Selfridge, O. G. (1955). Pattern recognition and modern computers. *Proceedings of the Western Joint Computer Conference.* New York: Institute of Electrical and Electronics Engineers.

Seligman, M. E. P. (1975). *Helplessness: On depression, development, and death.* San Francisco: Freeman.

Seligman, M. E. P. (1991). *Learned optimism.* New York: Norton.

Seligman, M. E. P., & Maier, S. F. (1967). Failure to escape traumatic shock. *Journal of Experimental Psychology, 74,* 1–9.

Seligman, M. E. P., Steen, T. A., Park, N., & Peterson, C. (2005). Positive psychology progress: Empirical validation of interventions. *American Psychologist, 60,* 410–421.

Selye, H. (1976a). *Stress in health and disease.* Reading, MA: Butterworth.

Selye, H. (1976b). *The stress of life* (2nd ed.). New York: McGraw-Hill.

Serpell, R. (2000). Intelligence and culture. In R. J. Sternberg (Ed.), *Handbook of intelligence* (pp. 549–577). Cambridge, UK: Cambridge University Press.

Serpell, R., & Boykin, A. W. (1994). Cultural dimensions of cognition: A multiplex, dynamic system of constraints and possibilities. In R. J. Sternberg (Ed.), *Handbook of perception and cognition: Vol. 2. Thinking and problem solving* (pp. 369–408). Orlando, FL: Academic Press.

Sevdalis, N., & Harvey, N. (2007). Biased forecasting of post-decisional affect. *Psychological Science, 18,* 678–681.

Shafir, E. (1993). Choosing versus rejecting: Why some options are both better and worse than others. *Memory & Cognition, 21,* 546–556.

Sharpsteen, D. J., & Kirkpatrick, L. A. (1997). Romantic jealousy and adult romantic attachment. *Journal of Personality and Social Psychology, 72,* 627–640.

Shaver, P. R., & Hazan, C. (1994). Attachment. In A. L. Weber & J. H. Harvey (Eds.), *Perspectives on close relationships* (pp. 110– 130). Boston: Allyn & Bacon.

Shaw, M., & Black, D. W. (2008). Internet addiction: Definition, assessment, epidemiology and clinical management. *CNS Drugs, 22,* 353–365.

Sheehan, E. P. (1993). The effects of turnover on the productivity of those who stay. *Journal of Social Psychology, 133,* 699–706.

Sheehy, R., & Horan, J. J. (2004). Effects of stress inoculation training for 1st-year law students. *International Journal of Stress Management, 11,* 41–55.

Sheets, V. L., & Lugar, R. (2005). Sources of conflict between friends in Russia and the United States. *Cross-Cultural Research, 39,* 380–398.

Sheldon, W. (1942). *The varieties of temperament: A psychology of constitutional differences.* New York: Harper.

Shepard, R. N. (1978). Externalization of mental images and the act of creation. In B. S. Randhawa & W. E. Coffman (Eds.), *Visual learning, thinking, and communicating.* New York: Academic Press.

Shepard, R. N. (1984). Ecological constraints on internal representation: Resonant kinematics of perceiving, imagining, thinking and dreaming. *Psychological Review, 91,* 417–447.

Sheppard, L. D., & Vernon, P. A. (2008). Intelligence and speed of information-processing: A review of 50 years of research. *Personality and Individual Differences, 44,* 535–551.

Sher, K. J., Bartholow, B. D., & Wood, M. D. (2000). Personality and substance use disorders: A prospective study. *Journal of Consulting and Clinical Psychology, 68,* 818–829.

Sherif, C. W. (1981, August). *Social and psychological bases of social psychology.* The G. Stanley Hall Lecture on social psychology, presented at the annual convention of the American Psychological Association, Los Angeles, 1961.

Sherif, M. (1935). A study of some social factors in perception. *Archives of Psychology, 27*(187).

Sherif, M., Harvey, O. J., White, B. J., Hood, W. R., & Sherif, C. W. (1988). *The Robbers Cave experiment: Intergroup conflict and cooperation.* Middletown, CT: Wesleyan University Press. (Original work published 1961)

Sherwood, C. C., Subiaul, F., & Zawidzki, T. W. (2008). A natural history of the human mind: Tracing evolutionary changes in brain and cognition. *Journal of Anatomy, 212,* 426–454.

Shevlin, M., Houston, J. E., Dorahy, M. J., & Adamson, G. (2008). Cumulative traumas and psychosis: An analysis of the National Comorbidity Study and the British Psychiatric Morbidity Survey. *Schizophrenia Bulletin, 34,*193–199.

Shi, J., Gershon, E. S., & Liu, C. (2008). Genetic associations with schizophrenia: Meta-analyses of 12 candidate genes. *Schizophrenia Research, 104,* 96–107.

Shields, D. C., Asaad, W., Eskandar, E. N., Jain, F. A., Cosgrove, G. R., Flahtery, A. W., Cassem, E. H., Prince, B. H., Rauch, S. L., & Dougherty, D. D. (2008). Prospective assessment of stereotactic ablative surgery for intractable major depression. *Biological Psychiatry, 64,* 449–454.

Shiffrar, M. (1994). When what meets where. *Current Directions in Psychological Science, 3,* 96–100.

Shiffrin, R. M. (2003). Modeling memory and perception. *Cognitive Science, 27,* 341–378.

Shiffrin, R. M., & Schneider, W. (1977). Controlled and automatic human information processing: II. Perceptual learning, automatic attending, and a general theory. *Psychological Review, 84,* 127–190.

Shih, J. H., Eberhart, N. K., Hammen, C. L., & Brennan, P. A (2006). Differential exposure and reactivity to interpersonal stress predict sex differences in adolescent depression. *Journal of Clinical Child and Adolescent Psychology, 35,* 103–115.

Shmueli-Goetz, Y., Target, M., Fonagy, P., & Datta, A. (2008). The child attachment interview: A psychometric study of reliability and discriminant validity. *Developmental Psychology, 44,* 939–956.

Shneidman, E. S. (1987, March). At the point of no return. *Psychology Today,* pp. 54–59.

Shoda, Y., Mischel, W., & Wright, J. C. (1993a). The role of situational demands and cognitive competencies in behavior organization and personality coherence. *Journal of Personality and Social Psychology, 65,* 1023–1035.

Shorter, L., Brown, S. L., Quinton, S. J., & Hinton, L. (2008). Relationships between body-shape discrepancies with favored celebrities and disordered eating in young women. *Journal of Applied Social Psychology, 38,* 1364–1377.

Shuwairi, S. M., Albert, M. K., & Johnson, S. P. (2007). Discrimination of possible and impossible objects in infancy. *Psychological Science, 18,* 303–307.

Sia, T. L., Lord, C. G., Blessum, K. A., Ratcliff, C. D., & Lepper, M. R. (1997). Is a rose always a rose? The role of social category exemplar change in attitude stability and attitude-behavior consistency. *Journal of Personality and Social Psychology, 72,* 501–514.

Siegel, J. M. (2005). Clues to the functions of mammalian sleep. *Nature, 437,* 1264–1271.

Siegel, P. H., Schraeder, M., & Morrison, R. (2008). A taxonomy of equity factors. *Journal of Applied Social Psychology, 38,* 61–75.

Siegel, S. (1984). Pavlovian conditioning and heroin overdose: Reports by overdose victims. *Bulletin of the Psychonomic Society, 22,* 428–430.

Siegel, S. (2005). Drug tolerance, drug addiction, and drug anticipation. *Current Directions in Psychological Science, 14,* 296–300.

Siegel, S., Hinson, R. E., Krank, M. D., & McCully, J. (1982). Heroin "overdose" death: The contribution of drug-associated environmental cues. *Science, 216,* 436–437.

Siever, L. J. (2008). Neurobiology of aggression and violence. *American Journal of Psychiatry, 165,* 429–442.

Sigmon, S. T., Pells, J. J., Edenfield, T. M., Hermann, B. A., Scharter, J. G., LaMattina, S. M., & Boulard, N. E. (2007). Are we there yet? A review of gender comparisons in three behavioral journals through the 20th century. *Behavior Therapy, 38,* 333–339.

Sillitoe, R. V., & Vogel, M. W. (2008). Desire, disease, and the origins of the dopaminergic system. *Schizophrenia Bulletin, 34,* 212–219.

Silventoinen, K., Pietiläinen, K. H., Tynelius, P., Sørensen, T. I. A., Kaprio, J., & Rasmussen, F. (2007). Genetic and environmental factors in relative weight from birth to age 18: The Swedish young male twins study. *International Journal of Obesity, 31,* 615–621.

Silventoinen, K., Posthuma, D., van Beijsterveldt, T., Bartels, M., Boomsma, D. I. (2006). Genetic contributions to the association between height and intelligence: Evidence from Dutch twin data from childhood to middle age. *Genes, Brain and Behavior, 5,* 585–595.

Silverman, A. B., Reinherz, H. Z., & Giaconia, R. M. (1996). The long-term sequelae of child and adolescent abuse: A longitudinal community study. *Child Abuse & Neglect, 20,* 709–723.

Simmons, J. A., Ferragamo, M. J., & Moss, C. F. (1998). Echodelay resolution in sonar images of the big brown bat, *Eptesicus fuscus. Proceedings of the National Academy of Sciences of the United States, 95,* 12647–12652.

Simon, H. A. (1973). The structure of ill-structured problems. *Artificial Intelligence, 4,* 181–202.

Simon, H. A. (1979). *Models of thought* (Vol. 1). New Haven: Yale University Press.

Simon, H. A. (1989). *Models of thought* (Vol. 2). New Haven: Yale University Press.

Simons, D. J., & Levin, D. T. (1998). Failure to detect changes to people during a real-world interaction. *Psychonomic Bulletin & Review, 5,* 644–649.

Sinclair, R. C., Hoffman, C., Mark, M. M., Martin, L. L., & Pickering, T. L. (1994). Construct accessibility and the misattribution of arousal: Schachter and Singer revisited. *Psychological Science, 5,* 15–19.

Singer, L. T., Arendt, R., Minnes, S., Farkas, K., Salvator, A., Kirchner, H. L., & Kliegman, R. (2002). Cognitive and motor outcomes of cocaine-exposed infants. *Journal of the American Medical Association, 287,* 1952–1960.

Singer, T., Verhaegen, P., Ghisletta, P., Lindenberger, U., & Baltes, P. B. (2003). The fate of cognition in very old age: Six-year longitudinal findings in the Berlin Aging Study (BASE). *Psychology & Aging, 18,* 318–331.

Sireteanu, R. (1999). Switching on the infant brain. *Science, 286,* 59–61.

Skinner, B. F. (1938). *The behavior of organisms.* New York: Appleton-Century-Crofts.

Skinner, B. F. (1953). *Science and human behavior.* New York: Macmillan.

Skinner, B. F. (1957). *Verbal behavior.* New York: Appleton-Century-Crofts.

Skinner, B. F. (1966). What is the experimental analysis of behavior? *Journal of the Experimental Analysis of Behavior, 9,* 213–218.

Skinner, B. F. (1990). Can psychology be a science of mind? *American Psychologist, 45,* 1206–1210.

Skodol, A. E., Pagano, M. E., Bender, D. S., Shea, M. T., Gunderson, J. G., Yen, S., Stout, R. L., Morey, L. C., Sanislow, C. A., Grilo, C. M., Zanarini, M. C., & McGlashan, T. H. (2005). Stability of functional impairment in patients with schizotypal, borderline, avoidant, or obsessive-compulsive personality disorder over two years. *Psychological Medicine, 35,* 443–451.

Slivia, P. J. (2008a). Discernment and creativity: How well can people identify their most creative ideas? *Psychology of Aesthetics, Creativity, and the Arts, 2,* 139–146.

Slivia, P. J. (2008b). Another look at creativity and intelligence: Exploring higher-order mental models and probable confounds. *Personality and Individual Differences, 44,* 1012–1021.

Sloane, R. B., Staples, F. R., Cristol, A. H., Yorkston, N. J., & Whipple, K. (1975). *Psychotherapy versus behavior therapy.* Cambridge, MA: Harvard University Press.

Slobin, D. I. (1985). Crosslinguistic evidence for the language-making capacity. In D. Slobin (Ed.), *The crosslinguistic study of language acquisition: Vol. 2. Theoretical issues* (pp. 1157–1256). Hillsdale, NJ: Erlbaum.

Sloman, S. A., Hayman, C. A. G., Ohta, N., Law, J., & Tulving, E. (1988). Forgetting in primed fragment completion. *Journal of Experimental Psychology: Learning, Memory, and Cognition, 14,* 223–239.

Slovic, P., Monahan, J., & MacGregor, D. G. (2000). Violence risk assessment and risk communication: The effects of using actual cases, providing instruction, and employing probability versus frequency formats. *Law and Human Behavior, 24,* 271–296.

Smetana, J. G., Campione-Barr, N., & Metzger, A. (2006). Adolescent development in interpersonal and societal contexts. *Annual Review of Psychology, 57,* 255–284.

Smith, C. T., Nixon, M. R., & Nader, R. S. (2004). Posttraining increases in REM sleep intensity implicate REM sleep in memory processing and provide a biological marker of learning potential. *Learning & Memory, 11,* 714–719.

Smith, J., & Baltes, P. B. (1990). Wisdom-related knowledge: Age/cohort differences in response to life-planning problems. *Developmental Psychology, 26,* 494–505.

Smith, M., Hopkins, D., Peveler, R. C., Holt, R. I. G., Woodward, M., & Ismail K. (2008). First- v. second-generation antipsychotics and risk for diabetes in schizophrenia: Systematic review and meta-analysis. *The British Journal of Psychiatry, 192,* 406–411.

Smith, S. L., & Donnerstein, E. (1998). Harmful effects of exposure to media violence: Learning of aggression, emotional desensitization, and fear. In R. G. Geen & E. Donnerstein (Eds.), *Human aggression: Theories, research, and implications for public policy* (pp. 167–202). San Diego, CA: Academic Press.

Smith, T. W., & Ruiz, J. M. (2002). Psychosocial influences on the development and course of coronary heart disease: Current status and implications for research and practice. *Journal of Consulting and Clinical Psychology, 70,* 548–568.

Smoller, J. W., Biederman, J., Arbeitman, L., Doyle, A. E., Fagerness, J., Perlis, R. H., Sklar, P., & Faraone, S. V. (2006). Association between the 5HT1B receptor gene (*HTR1B*) and the inattentive subtype of ADHD. *Biological Psychiatry, 59,* 460–467.

Sniehotta, F. F., Scholz, U., & Schwarzer, R. (2006). Action plans and coping plans for physical exercise: A longitudinal study in cardiac rehabilitation. *British Journal of Health Psychology, 11,* 23–37.

Snowden, L. R., & Yamada, A.-M. (2005). Cultural differences in access to care. *Annual Review of Clinical Psychology, 1,* 143–166.

Snyder, D. K., Castellani, A. M., & Whisman, M. A. (2006). Current status and future directions in couple therapy. *Annual Review of Psychology, 57,* 317–344.

Soderstrom, M. (2007). Beyond babytalk: Re-evaluating the nature and content of speech input to preverbal infants. *Developmental Review, 27,* 501–532.

Solomon, A. (2001). *The noonday demon.* New York: Scribner.

Son Hing, L. S., Chung-Yan, G., A., Hamilton, L. K., & Zanna, M. P. (2008). A two-dimensional model that employs explicit and implicit attitudes to characterize prejudice. *Journal of Personality and Social Psychology, 94,* 971–987.

Sonnad, S. S., Moyer, C. A., Patel, S., Helman, J. I., Garetz, S. L., & Chervin, R. D. (2003). A model to facilitate outcome assessment of obstructive sleep apnea. *International Journal of Technology Assessment in Health Care, 19,* 253–260.

Sonnadara, R. R., & Trainor, L. J. (2005). Perceived intensity effects in the octave illusion. *Perception & Psychophysics, 67,* 648–658.

Soska, K. C., & Johnson, S. P. (2008). Development of three-dimensional object completion in infancy. *Child Development, 79,* 1230–1236.

Southwick, S. M., Vythilingam, M., & Charney, D. S. (2005). The psychobiology of depression and resilience to stress: Implications for prevention and treatment. *Annual Review of Clinical Psychology, 1,* 255–291.

Spangler, W. D. (1992). Validity of questionnaire and TAT measures of need for achievement: Two meta-analyses. *Psychological Bulletin, 112,* 140–154.

Spearman, C. (1927). *The abilities of man.* New York: Macmillan.

Spence, M. J., & DeCasper, A. J. (1987). Prenatal experience with low-frequency maternal-voice sounds influences neonatal perception of maternal voice samples. *Infant Behavior and Development, 10,* 133–142.

Spence, M. J., & Freeman, M. S. (1996). Newborn infants prefer the maternal low-pass filtered voice, but not the maternal whispered voice. *Infant Behavior and Development, 19,* 199–212.

Sperling, G. (1963). A model for visual memory tasks. *Human Factors, 5,* 19–31.

Sperling, G. (1960). The information available in brief visual presentations. *Psychological Monographs, 74,* 1–29.

Sperry, R. W. (1968). Mental unity following surgical disconnection of the cerebral hemispheres. *The Harvey Lectures,* Series 62. New York: Academic Press.

Spiers, H. J., & Maguire, E. A. (2007). Decoding human brain activity during real-world experiences. *Trends in Cognitive Sciences, 11,* 356–365.

Spitz, R. A., & Wolf, K. (1946). Anaclitic depression. *Psychoanalytic Study of Children, 2,* 313–342.

Springer, M. V., McIntosh, A., Wincour, G., & Grady, C. L. (2005). The relation between brain activity during memory tasks and years of education in young and older adults. *Neuropsychology, 19,* 181–192.

Stafford, B. L., Balda, R. P., & Kamil, A. C. (2006). Does seed-caching experience affect spatial memory performance by pinyon jays? *Ethology, 112,* 1202–1208.

Stagnitti, M. N. (2007). *Trends in the Use and Expenditures for the Therapeutic Class Prescribed Psychotherapeutic Agents and All Subclasses, 1997 and 2004.* Rockville, MD: Agency for Healthcare Research and Quality. Retrieved from www.meps.ahrq.gov/mepsweb/data_files/publications/st163/stat163.pdf.

Stahl, S. M., Grady, M. M., Moret, C., & Briley, M. (2005). SNRIs: Their pharmacology, clinical efficacy, and tolerability in comparison with other classes of antidepressants. *CNS Spectrums, 109,* 732–747.

Stahr, B., Cushing, D., Lane, K., & Fox, J. (2006). Efficacy of a function-based intervention in decreasing off-task behavior exhibited by a student with ADHD. *Journal of Positive Behavior Interventions, 8,* 201–211.

Stanley, D., Phelps, E., & Banaji, M. (2008). The neural basis of implicit attitudes. *Current Directions in Psychological Science, 17,* 164–170.

Stanton, A. L., Revenson, T. A., & Tennen, H. (2007). Health psychology: Psychological adjustment to chronic disease. *Annual Review of Psychology, 58,* 565–592.

Starace, F., Massa, A., Amico, K. R., & Fisher, J. D. (2006). Adherence to antiretroviral therapy: An empirical test of the information-motivation-behavioral skills model. *Health Psychology, 25,* 153–162.

Steele, C. M. (1997). A threat in the air: How stereotypes shape intellectual identity and performance. *American Psychologist, 6,* 613–629.

Steele, C. M., & Aronson, J. (1995). Stereotype threat and the intellectual test performance of African Americans. *Journal of Personality and Social Psychology, 69,* 797–811.

Steele, C. M., & Aronson, J. (1998). Stereotype threat and the test performance of academically successful African Americans. In C. Jencks & M. Phillips (Eds.), *The black–white test score gap* (pp. 401–427). Washington, DC: Brookings Institution Press.

Steger, M. F., Hicks, B. M., Kashdan, T. B., Krueger, R. F., & Bouchard, T. J. Jr. (2007). Genetic and environmental influences on positive traits of the values in action classification, and biometric covariance with normal personality. *Journal of Research in Personality, 41,* 524–539.

Stein, M. B., Jang, K. L., Taylor, S., Vernon, P. A., & Livesley, W. J. (2002). Genetic and environmental influences on trauma exposure and posttraumatic stress disorder symptoms: A twin study. *American Journal of Psychiatry, 159,* 1675–1681.

Steinberg, L. (2008). A social neuroscience perspective on adolescent risk-taking. *Developmental Review, 28,* 78–106.

Stern, W. (1914). The psychological methods of testing intelligence. *Educational Psychology Monographs* (No. 13).

Sternberg, R. J. (1986). *Intelligence applied.* San Diego: Harcourt Brace Jovanovich.

Sternberg, R. J. (1994). Intelligence. In R. J. Sternberg (Ed.), *Handbook of perception and cognition: Vol. 2. Thinking and problem solving* (pp. 263–288). Orlando, FL: Academic Press.

Sternberg, R. J. (1999). The theory of successful intelligence. *Review of General Psychology, 3,* 292–316.

Sternberg, R. J. (2006). The Rainbow Project: Enhancing the SAT through assessments of analytical, practical, and creative skills. *Intelligence, 34,* 321–350.

Sternberg, R. J. (2007). Who are the bright children? The cultural context of being and acting intelligent. *Educational Researcher, 36,* 148–155.

Sternberg, R. J., & Grigorenko, E. L. (2003). Teaching for successful intelligence: Principles, procedures, and practices. *Journal for the Education of the Gifted, 27,* 207–228.

Sternberg, R. J., & Grigorenko, E. L. (2007). The difficulty of escaping preconceptions in writing an article about the difficulty of escaping preconceptions: Commentary on Hunt and Carlson (2007). *Perspectives on Psychological Science, 2,* 221–226.

Sternberg, R. J., Grigorenko, E. L., & Kidd, K. K. (2005). Intelligence, race, and genetics. *American Psychologist, 60,* 46–59.

Sternberg, R. J., & Lubart, T. I. (1996). Investing in creativity. *American Psychologist, 51,* 677–688.

Sternberg, R. J., & Lubart, T. I. (1999). The concept of creativity: Prospects and paradigms. In R. J. Sternberg (Ed.), *Handbook of creativity* (pp. 3–15). Cambridge, UK: Cambridge University Press.

Stevens, J. A., Fonlupt, P., Shiffrar, M., & Decety, J. (2000). New aspects of motion perception: Selective neural encoding of apparent human movements. *Neuroreport, 11,* 109–115.

Stevenson, H. W., Chen, C., & Lee, S. Y. (1993). Mathematics achievement of Chinese, Japanese, and American children: Ten years later. *Science, 259,* 53–58.

Stewart, S. A. (2005). The effects of benzodiazepines on cognition. *Journal of Clinical Psychiatry, 66* (Suppl. 2), 9–13.

Stewart-Williams, S. (2007). Altruism among kin vs. nonkin: Effects of cost of help and reciprocal exchange. *Evolution and Human Behavior, 28,* 193–198.

Stockhorst, U., Steingrueber, H.-J., Enck, P., & Klosterhalfen, S. (2006). Pavlovian conditioning of nausea and vomiting. *Autonomic Neuroscience: Basic and Clinical, 129,* 50–57.

Stone, J., & McWhinnie, C. (2008). Evidence that blatant versus subtle stereotype threat cues impact performance through dual processes. *Journal of Experimental Social Psychology, 44*, 445–452.

Stone, J., Zeman, A., Simonotto, E., Meyer, M., Azuma, R., Flett, S., & Sharpe, M. (2007). fMRI in patients with motor conversion symptoms and controls with simulated weakness. *Psychosomatic Medicine, 69*, 961–969.

Storbeck, J., & Clore, G. L. (2007). On the interdependence of cognition and emotion. *Cognition and Emotion, 21*, 1212–1237.

Story, L. B., & Bradbury, T. N. (2004). Understanding marriage and stress: Essential questions and challenges. *Clinical Psychology Review, 23*, 1139–1162.

Strauch, I. (2005). REM dreaming in transition from late childhood to adolescence: A longitudinal study. *Dreaming, 15*, 155–169.

Strauch, I., & Lederbogen, S. (1999). The home dreams and waking fantasies of boys and girls between ages 9 and 15: A longitudinal study. *Dreaming, 9*, 153–161.

Strayer, D. L., & Drews, F. A. (2007). Cell-phone-induced driver distraction. *Current Directions in Psychological Science, 16*, 128–131.

Strayer, D. L., Drews, R. A., & Johnston, W. A. (2003). Cell phone-induced failures of visual attention during simulated driving. *Journal of Experimental Psychology: Applied, 9*, 23–32.

Streiner, D. L. (2007). Criterion-based training for Rorschach scoring. *Training and Education in Professional Psychology, 1*, 125–134.

Striegel-More, R. H., & Bulik, C. M. (2007). Risk factors for eating disorders. *American Psychologist, 62*, 181–198.

Striegel-Moore, R. H., Dohm, F. A., Kraemer, H. C., Taylor, C. B., Daniels, S., Crawford, P. B., & Schreiber, G. B. (2003). Eating disorders in white and black women. *American Journal of Psychiatry, 160*, 1326–1331.

Striegel-Moore, R. H., & Franko, D. L. (2008). Should binge eating disorder be included in *DSM-V*? A critical review of the state of the evidence. *Annual Review of Clinical Psychology, 4*, 305–324.

Stukas, A. A., Snyder, M., & Clark, E. G. (1999). The effects of "mandatory volunteerism" on intentions to volunteer. *Psychological Science, 10*, 59–64.

Substance Abuse and Mental Health Services Administration. (2006). *Mental Health, United States 2004.* Retrieved from http://download.ncadi.samhsa.gov/ken/pdf/SMA06-4195/CMHS_MHUS_2004.pdf.

Substance Abuse and Mental Health Services Administration. (2008a). *Participation in self-help groups for alcohol and illicit drug use: 2006 and 2007.* Retrieved from http://oas.samhsa.gov/2k8/selfHelp/selfHelp.pdf.

Substance Abuse and Mental Health Service Administration (SAMHSA). (2008b). *Results from the 2007 national survey on drug use and health: National findings.* Available: www.oas.samhsa.gov/nsduh/2k7nsduh/2k7Results.pdf.

Sue, S. (2006). Cultural competency: From philosophy to research and practice. *Journal of Community Psychology, 34*, 237–245.

Sullivan, H. S. (1953). *The interpersonal theory of psychiatry.* New York: Norton.

Sulloway, F. J. (1996). *Born to rebel: Birth order, family dynamics, and creative lives.* New York: Pantheon.

Summerville, A., & Roese, N. J. (2007). Dare to compare: Fact-based versus simulation-based comparison in daily life. *Journal of Experimental Social Psychology, 44*, 664–671.

Suzuki, M., Hagino, H., Nohara, S., Zhou, S., Kawasaki, Y., Takahashi, T., Matsui, M., Seto, H., Ono, T., & Kurachi, M. (2005). Male-specific volume expansion of the human hippocampus during adolescence. *Cerebral Cortex, 15*, 187–193.

Swann, W. B., Chang-Schneider, C., & McClarty, K. L. (2007). Do people's self-views matter? Self-concept and self-esteem in everyday life. *American Psychologist, 62*, 84–94.

Swazey, J. P. (1974). *Chlorpromazine in psychiatry: A study of therapeutic innovation.* Cambridge, MA: MIT Press.

Szasz, T. S. (1974). *The myth of mental illness* (rev. ed.). New York: Harper & Row.

Szasz, T. S. (2004). *Faith in freedom: Libertarian principles and psychiatric practices.* Somerset, NJ: Transaction Publishers.

Tacon, A. M., McComb, J., Caldera, Y., & Randolph, P. Mindfulness meditation, anxiety reduction, and heart disease: A pilot study. *Family and Community Health, 26*, 25–33.

Tajfel, H., Billig, M., Bundy, R., & Flament, C. (1971). Social categorization and intergroup behavior. *European Journal of Social Psychology, 1*, 149–178.

Talarico, J. M., & Rubin, D. C. (2003). Confidence, not consistency, characterizes flashbulb memories. *Psychological Science, 14*, 455–461.

Talarico, J. M., & Rubin, D. C. (2007). Flashbulb memories are special after all; in phenomenology, not accuracy. *Applied Cognitive Psychology, 21*, 527–578.

Tandon, R., Keshavan, M. S., & Nasrallah, H. A. (2008). Schizophrenia, "Just the Facts": What we know in 2008. 2. Epidemiology and etiology. *Schizophrenia Research, 102*, 1–18.

Tanofsky-Kraff, M., Wilfley, D. E., & Spurrell, E. (2000). Impact of interpersonal and ego-related stress on restrained eaters. *Inter national Journal of Eating Disorders, 27*, 411–418.

Tarbox, S. I., & Pogue-Geile, M. F. (2008). Development of social functioning in preschizophrenic children and adolescents: A systematic review. *Psychological Bulletin, 34,* 561–583.

Taylor, C. B., & Luce, K. H. (2003). Computer- and Internet-based psychotherapy interventions. *Current Directions in Psychological Science, 12,* 18–22.

Taylor, S. E. (2006). Tend and befriend: Biobehavioral bases of affiliation under stress. *Current Directions in Psychological Science, 15,* 273–277.

Taylor, S. E., Klein, L. C., Lewis, B. P., Gruenewald, T. L., Gurung, R. A. R., & Updegraff, J. A. (2000). Biobehavioral responses to stress in females: Tend-and-befriend, not fight-or-flight. *Psychological Review, 107,* 411–429.

Tedeschi, R. G., & Calhoun, L. G. (2004). Posttraumatic growth: Conceptual foundations and empirical evidence. *Psychological Inquiry, 15,* 1–18.

Tedlock, B. (1992). The role of dreams and visionary narratives in Mayan cultural survival. *Ethos, 20,* 453–476.

Tellegen, A. & Ben-Porath, Y. S. (2008). *MMPI-2-RF Technical Manual.* Minneapolis: University of Minnesota Press.

Templin, M. (1957). Certain language skills in children: Their development and interrelationships. *Institute of Child Welfare Monograph,* Series No. 26. Minneapolis: University of Minnesota Press.

Tennen, H., Affleck, G., Armeli, S., & Carney, M. A. (2000). A daily process approach to coping: Linking theory, research, and practice. *American Psychologist, 55,* 626–636.

Teplin, L. A., McClelland, G. M., Abram, K. M., & Weiner, D. A. (2005). Crime victimization in adults with severe mental illness. *Archives of General Psychiatry, 62,* 911–921.

Terman, L. M. (1916). *The measurement of intelligence.* Boston: Houghton Mifflin.

Terman, L. M., & Merrill, M. A. (1937). *Measuring intelligence.* Boston: Houghton Mifflin.

Terman, L. M., & Merrill, M. A. (1960). *The Stanford-Binet intelligence scale.* Boston: Houghton Mifflin.

Terman, L. M., & Merrill, M. A. (1972). *Stanford-Binet intelligence scale—manual for the third revision, Form L-M.* Boston: Houghton Mifflin.

Terrace, H. S., & Metcalfe, J. (2005). *The missing link in cognition: Origins of self-reflective consciousness.* Oxford, UK: Oxford University Press.

Tetlock, P. E. (2005). *Expert political judgment: How good is it? How can we know?* Princeton, NJ: Princeton University Press.

Thase, M. E., & Denko, T. (2008). Pharmacotherapy of mood disorders. *Annual Review of Clinical Psychology, 4,* 53–91.

Thiessen, E. D., Hill, E. A., & Saffran, J. R. (2005). Infant-directed speech facilitates word segmentation. *Infancy, 7,* 53–71.

Thomas, A., & Chess, S. (1977). *Temperament and development.* New York: Brunner/Mazel.

Thomas, E., & Wingert, P. (2000, June 19). Bitter lessons. *Newsweek,* pp. 50, 51–52.

Thomas, E. L., & Robinson, H. A. (1972). *Improving reading in every class: A sourcebook for teachers.* Boston: Allyn & Bacon.

Thompson, P. M., Vidal, C., Giedd, J. N., Gochman, P., Blumenthal, J., Nicolson, R., Toga, A. W., & Rapoport, J. L. (2001). Mapping adolescent brain change reveals dynamic wave of accelerated gray matter loss in very early-onset schizophrenia. *PNAS, 98,* 11650–11655.

Thompson, W. L., Kosslyn, S. M., Hoffman, M. S., & van der Koolj, K. (2008). Inspecting visual mental images: Can people "see" implicit properties as easily in imagery and perception. *Memory & Cognition, 36,* 1024–1032.

Thorndike, E. L. (1898). Animal intelligence. *Psychological Review Monograph Supplement, 2*(4, Whole No. 8).

Thorndike, R. L., Hagen, E. P., & Sattler, J. M. (1986). *Stanford-Binet intelligence scale* (4th ed.). Chicago: Riverside.

Thorpe, S. K. S., Holder, R. L., & Crompton, R. H. (2007). Origin of human bipedalism as an adaptation for locomotion on flexible branches. *Science, 316,* 1328–1331.

Tice, D. M., & Baumeister, R. F. (1997). Longitudinal study of procrastination, performance, stress, and health: The costs and benefits of dawdling. *Psychological Science, 8,* 454–458.

Tidwell, M. C. O., Reis, H. T., & Shaver, P. R. (1996). Attachment, attractiveness, and social interaction: A diary study. *Journal of Personality and Social Psychology, 71,* 729–745.

Tiger, J. H., & Hanley, G. P. (2006). Using reinforcer pairing and fading to increase the milk consumption of a preschool child. *Journal of Applied Behavior Analysis, 39,* 399–403.

Tijus, C. A., & Reeves, A. (2004). Rapid iconic erasure without masking. *Spatial Vision, 17,* 483–495.

Timberlake, W., & Allison, J. (1974). Response deprivation: An empirical approach to instrumental performance. *Psychological Review, 81,* 146–164.

Todd, P. M., & Gigerenzer, G. (2007). Environments that make us smart: Ecological rationality. *Current Directions in Psychological Science, 16,* 167–171.

Todrank, J., & Bartoshuk, L. M. (1991). A taste illusion: Taste sensation localized by touch. *Physiology & Behavior, 50,* 1027–1031.

Tolman, E. C. (1948). Cognitive maps in rats and men. *Psychological Review, 55,* 189–208.

Tolman, E. C., & Honzik, C. H. (1930). "Insight" in rats. *University of California Publications in Psychology, 4,* 215–232.

Tomasello, M. (2008). *Origins of human communication.* Cambridge, MA: MIT Press.

Tombu, M., & Jolicœur, P. (2005). Testing the predictions of the central capacity sharing model. *Journal of Experimental Psychology: Human Perception and Performance, 31,* 790–802.

Tomkins, S. (1962). *Affect, imagery, consciousness* (Vol. 1). New York: Springer.

Tomkins, S. (1981). The quest for primary motives; Biography and autobiography of an idea. *Journal of Personality and Social Psychology, 41,* 306–329.

Tomkovick, C., Lester, S. W., Flunker, L., & Wells, T. A. (2008). Linking collegiate service-learning to future volunteerism: Implications for nonprofit organizations. *Nonprofit Management and Leadership, 19,* 3–26.

Tomoyasu, N., Bovbjerg, D. H., & Jacobsen, P. B. (1996). Conditioned reactions to cancer chemotherapy: Percent reinforcement predicts anticipatory nausea. *Physiology & Behavior, 59,* 273–276.

Tong, S. T., Van Der Heide, B., Langwell, L., & Walther, J. B. (2008). Too much of a good thing? The relationship between number of friends and interpersonal impressions on Facebook. *Journal of Computer-Mediated Communication, 13,* 531–549.

Torgersen, S., Lygren, S., Øien, P. A., Skre, I., Onstad, S., Edvardsen, J., Tambs, K., & Kringlen, E. (2000). A twin study of personality disorders. *Comprehensive Psychiatry, 41,* 416–425.

Torrance, E. P. (1974). *The Torrance tests of creative thinking: Technical-norms manual.* Bensenville, IL: Scholastic Testing Services.

Tranter, L. J., & Koustaal, W. (2008). Age and flexible thinking: An experimental demonstration of the beneficial effects of increased cognitively stimulating activity on fluid intelligence in healthy older adults. *Aging, Neuropsychology, and Cognition, 15,* 184–207.

Trautner, H. M., Ruble, D. N., Cyphers, L., Kirsten, B., Behrendt, R., & Hartmann, P. (2005). Rigiditiy and flexibility of gender stereotypes in childhood: Developmental or differential? *Infant and Child Development, 14,* 365–381.

Trawalter, S., Todd, A. R., Baird, A. A., & Richeson, J. A (2008). Attending to threat: Race-based patterns of selective attention. *Journal of Experimental Social Psychology, 44,* 1322–1327.

Trescot, A. M., Datta, S., Lee, M., & Hansen, H. (2008). Opiod pharmacology. *Pain Physician, 11,* S133–S153.

Triandis, H. C. (1990). Cross-cultural studies of individualism and collectivism. In J. Berman (Ed.), *Nebraska Symposium on Motivation, 1989* (pp. 41–133). Lincoln: University of Nebraska Press.

Triandis, H. C. (1994). *Culture and social behavior.* New York: McGraw-Hill.

Triandis, H. C. (1995). *Individualism and collectivism.* Boulder, CO: Westview.

Trivers, R. L. (1971). The evolution of reciprocal altruism. *Quarterly Review of Biology, 46,* 35–57.

Trzesniewski, K. H., Donnellan, M. B., Moffitt, T. E., Robins, R. W., Poulton, R., & Caspi, A. (2006). Low self-esteem during adolescence predicts poor health, criminal behavior, and limited economic prospects during adulthood. *Developmental Psychology, 42,* 381–390.

Tulving, E. (1972). Episodic and semantic memory. In E. Tulving & W. Donaldson (Eds.), *Organization of memory.* New York: Academic Press.

Tulving, E., & Thomson, D. M. (1973). Encoding specificity and retrieval processes in episodic memory. *Psychological Review, 80,* 352–373.

Tupes, E. G., & Christal, R. C. (1961). *Recurrent personality factors based on trait ratings* (Tech. Rep. No. ASD-TR–61–97). Lackland Air Force Base, TX: U.S. Air Force.

Turner, C. F., Villarroel, M. A., Chromy, J. R., Eggleston, E., & Rogers, S. M. (2005). Same-gender sex among U.S. adults: Trends across the twentieth century and during the 1990s. *Public Opinion Quarterly, 69,* 439–462.

Turner, M. E., & Pratkanis, A. R. (1998). A social identity maintenance model of groupthink. *Organizational Behavior and Human Decision Processes, 73,* 210–235.

Turner, M. L., & Engle, R. W. (1989). Is working memory capacity task dependent? *Journal of Memory and Language, 28,* 127–154.

Tversky, A., & Kahneman, D. (1973). Availability: A heuristic for judging frequency and probability. *Cognitive Psychology, 5,* 207–232.

Tversky, A., & Shafir, E. (1992). Choice under conflict: The dynamics of deferred decision. *Psychological Science, 3,* 358–361.

Twenge, J. M., Campbell, W. K., & Foster, C. A. (2003). Parenthood and marital satisfaction: A meta-analytic review. *Journal of Marriage and Family, 65,* 574–583.

Tyler, L. E. (1965). *The psychology of human differences* (3rd ed.). New York: Appleton-Century-Crofts.

Ullman, S. E., Filipas, H. H., Townsend, S. M., & Starzynski, L. L. (2007). Psychosocial correlates of PTSD symptom severity in sexual assault survivors. *Journal of Traumatic Stress, 20,* 821–831.

Underwood, B. J. (1948). Retroactive and proactive inhibition after five and forty-eight hours. *Journal of Experimental Psychology, 38,* 28–38.

Underwood, B. J. (1949). Proactive inhibition as a function of time and degree of prior learning. *Journal of Experimental Psychology, 39,* 24–34.

U.S. Census Bureau (2008a). *2007 American community survey.* Retrieved from www.census.gov/acs/www/index.html.

U.S. Census Bureau (2008b). *Families and living arrangements: 2007.* Retrieved from www.census.gov/population/www/socdemo/ hh-fam.html.

U. S. Department of Agriculture. (2005). *Dietary guidelines for Americans.* Retrieved from www.health.gov/dietaryguidelines/dga2005/document.

U.S. Department of Health and Human Services. (2008a). *Child maltreatment 2006.* Washington, DC: U.S. Government Printing Office. Retrieved from www.acf.hhs.gov/programs/cb/pubs/cm06/cm06.pdf.

U.S. Department of Health and Human Services. (2008b). *2008 Physical Activity Guidelines for Americans.* Retrieved from www.health.gov/PAGuidelines/pdf/paguide.pdf.

Urban, J., Carlson, E., Egeland, B., & Stroufe, L. A. (1991). Patterns of individual adaptation across childhood. *Development and Psychopathology, 3,* 445–460.

Urbszat, D., Herman, C. P., & Polivy, J. (2002). Eat, drink, and be merry, for tomorrow we diet: Effects of anticipated deprivation on food intake in restrained and unrestrained eaters. *Journal of Abnormal Psychology, 111,* 396–401.

Vaillant, G. E. (1977). *Adaptation to life.* Boston: Little, Brown.

Vallabha, G. K., McClelland, J. L., Pons, F., Werker, J. F., & Amano, S. (2007). Unsupervised learning of vowel categories from infant-directed speech. *PNAS, 104,* 13273–13278.

van der Sluis, S., Willemsen, G., de Geus, E. J. C., Boomsma, D. I., & Posthuma, D. (2008). Gene-environment interaction in adults' IQ scores: Measures of past and present environment. *Behavior Genetics, 38,* 348–360.

van Dijk, E., & Zeelenberg, M. (2005). On the psychology of "if only": Regret and the comparison between factual and counterfactual outcomes. *Organizational Behavior and Human Decision Processes, 97,* 152–160.

Van Gelder, R. N. (2003). Making (a) sense of non-visual ocular photoreception. *Trends in Neurosciences, 26,* 458–461.

Van IJzendoorn, M. H., & Kroonenberg, P. M. (1988). Cross-cultural patterns of attachment: A meta-analysis of the Strange Situation. *Child Development, 59,* 147–156.

Vansteensel, M. J., Michel, S., & Meijer, J. H. (2008). Organization of cell and tissue circadian pacemakers: A comparison among species. *Brain Research Reviews, 58,* 18–47.

Van Zeijl, J., Mesman, J., Van IJzendoorn, M. H., Bakermans-Kranenburg, M. J., Juffer, F., Stolk, M. N., Koot, H. M., & Alink, L. R. A. (2006). Attachment-based intervention for enhancing sensitive discipline in mothers of 1- to 3-year-old children at risk for externalizing behavior problems: A randomized controlled trial. *Journal of Consulting and Clinical Psychology, 74,* 994–1005.

Vartanian, L. R., Herman, C. P., & Wansink, B. (2008). Are we aware of the external factors that influence our food intake? *Health Psychology, 27,* 533–538.

Velicer, W. F., Redding, C. A., Sun, X., & Prochaska, J. O. (2007). Demographic variables, smoking variables, and outcome across five studies. *Health Psychology, 26,* 278–287.

Vemuri, V. K., Janero, R., & Makriyannis, A. (2008). Pharmacotherapeutic targeting of the endocannabinoid system: Drugs for obesity and the metabolic syndrome. *Physiology & Behavior, 93,* 671–686.

Verfaelli, M., Martin, E., Page, K., Parks, E., & Keane, M. M. (2006). Implicit memory for novel conceptual associations in amnesia. *Cognitive, Affective, and Behavioral Neuroscience, 6,* 91–101.

Vezina, P., McGehee, D. S., & Green, W. N. (2007). Exposure to nicotine and sensitization of nicotine-induced behaviors. *Progress in Neuro-Psychopharmacology & Biological Psychiatry, 31,* 1625–1638.

Viding, E., Blair, J. R., Moffitt, T. E., & Plomin, R. (2005). Evidence for substantial genetic risk for psychopathy in 7-year-olds. *Journal of Child Psychology and Psychiatry, 46,* 592–597.

Vignoles, V. L., Regalia, C., Manzi, C., Golledge, J., & Scabini, E. (2006). Beyond self-esteem: Influence of multiple motives on identity construction. *Journal of Personality and Social Psychology, 90,* 308–333.

Vohs, K. D., & Schooler, J. W. (2008). The value of believing in free will: Encouraging a belief in determinism increases cheating. *Psychological Science, 19,* 49–54.

Vonnegut, M. (1975). *The Eden express.* New York: Bantam.

Vonofakou, C., Hewstone, M., & Voci, A. (2007). Contact with out-group friends as a predictor of meta-attitudinal strength and accessibility of attitudes toward gay men. *Journal of Personality and Social Psychology, 92,* 804–820.

Voorspoels, W., Vanpaemel, W., & Storms, G. (2008). Exemplars and prototypes in natural language concepts: A typicality-based evaluation. *Psychonomic Bulletin & Review, 15,* 630–637.

Voss, J. L., & Paller, K. A. (2008). Brain substrates of implicit and explicit memory: The importance of concurrently acquired neural signals of both memory types. *Neuropsychologia, 46,* 3021–3029.

Voss Horrell, S. C. (2008). Effectiveness of cognitive-behavioral therapy with adult ethnic minority clients: A review.

Professional Psychology: Research and Practice, 39, 160–168.

Vroom, V. H. (1964). *Work and motivation.* New York: Wiley.

Vu, H., Kellas, G., Metcalf, K., & Herman, R. (2000). The influence of global discourse on lexical ambiguity resolution. *Memory & Cognition, 28,* 236–252.

Wade, T. D., Tiggemann, M., Bulik, C. M., Fairburn, C. G., Wray, N. R., & Martin, N. G. (2008). Shared temperament risk factors for anorexia nervosa: A twin study. *Psychosomatic Medicine,* 70, 239–244.

Wagner, U., van Dick, R., Pettigrew, T. F., & Christ, O. (2003). Ethnic prejudice in East and West Germany: The explanatory power of intergroup contact. *Group Processes & Intergroup Relations, 6,* 23–37.

Walach, H., Nord, E., Zier, C., Dietz-Waschkowski, B., Kersig, S., & Schüpbach, H. (2007). Mindfulness-based stress reduction as a method for personnel development: A pilot evaluation. *International Journal of Stress Management, 14,* 188–198.

Walker, M. P., & Stickgold, R. (2006). Sleep, memory, and plasticity. *Annual Review of Psychology, 57,* 139–166.

Wallach, M. A., & Kogan, N. (1965). *Modes of thinking in young children.* New York: Holt, Rinehart & Winston.

Wallis, D. J., & Hetherington, M. M. (2004). Stress and eating: The effects of ego-threat and cognitive demand on food intake in restrained and emotional eaters. *Appetite, 43,* 39–46.

Walster, E., Aronson, V., Abrahams, D., & Rottman, L. (1966). Importance of physical attractiveness in dating behavior. *Journal of Personality and Social Psychology, 5,* 508–516.

Walton, G. M., & Cohen, G. L. (2007). A question of belonging: Race, social fit, and achievement. *Journal of Personality and Social Psychology, 92,* 82–96.

Wang, C., & Mallinckrodt, B. S. (2006). Differences between Taiwanese and U.S. cultural beliefs about ideal adult attachment. *Journal of Counseling Psychology, 53,* 192–204.

Wang, P. S., Berglund, P., Olfson, M., Pincus, H. A., Wells, K. B., & Kessler, R. C. (2005). Failure and delay in initial treatment contact after first onset of mental disorders in the national comorbidity survey replication. *Archives of General Psychiatry, 62,* 603–613.

Wang, S., Baillargeon, R., & Brueckner, L. (2004). Young infants' reasoning about hidden objects: Evidence from violation-of-expectation tasks with test trials only. *Cognition, 93,* 167–198.

Wann, D. L., Royalty, J. L., & Rochelle, A. R. (2002). Using motivation and team identification to predict sport fans' emotional responses to team performance. *Journal of Sport Behavior, 25,* 207–216.

Ward, C. D., & Cooper, R. P. (1999). A lack of evidence in 4-month-old human infants for paternal voice preference. *Developmental Psychobiology, 35,* 49–59.

Warker, J. A., & Dell, G. S. (2006). Speech errors reflect newly learned phonotactic constraints. *Journal of Experimental Psychology: Learning, Memory, & Cognition, 32,* 387–398.

Warren, C. S. (2008). The influence of awareness and internalization of Western appearance ideals on body dissatisfaction in Euro-American and Hispanic males. *Psychology of Men & Masculinity, 9,* 257–266.

Warren, R. M. (1970). Perceptual restoration of missing speech sounds. *Science, 167,* 392–393.

Wasserman, E. A., & Zentall, T. R. (Eds.). (2006). *Comparative cognition: Experimental explorations of animal intelligence.* New York: Oxford University Press.

Waterhouse, J., Reilly, T., Atkinson, G., & Edwards, B. (2007). Jet lag: Trends and coping strategies. *Lancet, 369,* 1117–1129.

Watson, J. B. (1924). *Behaviorism.* New York: Norton.

Watson, J. B. (1913). Psychology as the behaviorist views it. *Psychological Review, 20,* 158–177.

Watson, J. B. (1919). *Psychology from the standpoint of a behaviorist.* Philadelphia: Lippincott.

Watson, J. B., & Rayner, R. (1920). Conditioned emotional reactions. *Journal of Experimental Psychology, 3,* 1–14.

Wax, M. L. (2004). Dream sharing as social practice. *Dreaming, 14,* 83–93.

Wearden, A. J., Tarrier, N., Barrowclough, C., Zastowny. T. R., & Rahill, A. A. (2000). A review of expressed emotion research in health care. *Clinical Psychology Review, 20,* 633–666.

Wechsler, D. (1997). *Manual for the Wechsler Adult Intelligence Scale-III.* San Antonio, TX: Psychological Corporation.

Wechsler, D. (2002). *WPPSI-III manual.* San Antonio, TX: Psychological Corporation.

Wechsler, D. (2003). *WISC-IV manual.* San Antonio, TX: Psychological Corporation.

Wedekind, C., & Braithwaite, V. A. (2002). The long-term benefits of human generosity in indirect reciprocity. *Current Biology, 12,* 1012–1015.

Weeks, J. W., Heimberg, R. G., Rodebaugh, T. L., & Norton, P. J. (2008). Exploring the relationship between fear of positive evaluation and social anxiety. *Journal of Anxiety Disorders, 22,* 386–400.

Weidner, R., & Find, G. R. (2007). The neural mechanisms underlying the Müller-Lyer illusion and its interaction with visuospatial judgments. *Cerebral Cortex, 17,* 878–884.

Weinberger, L. E., Sreenivasan, S., Garrick, T., & Osran, H. (2005). The impact of surgical castration on sexual recidivism risk among sexually violent predatory offenders. *The Journal of the American Academy of Psychiatry and the Law, 33,* 16–36.

Weiner, B. (2006). *Social motivation, justice, and the moral emotions: An attributional approach.* Mahwah, NJ: Erlbaum.

Weinfield, N. S., Ogawa, J. R., & Sroufe, L. A. (1997). Early attachment as a pathway to adolescent peer competence. *Journal of Research on Adolescence, 7,* 241–265.

Weisberg, R. W. (1986). *Creativity: Genius and other myths.* New York: Freeman.

Weiss, A., Bates, T. C., & Luciano, M. (2008). Happiness is a personal(ity) thing: The genetics of personality and well-being in a representative sample. *Psychological Science, 19,* 205–210.

Weissenborn, R., & Duka, T. (2000). State-dependent effects of alcohol on explicit memory: The role of semantic associations. *Psychopharmacology, 149,* 98–106.

Wellman, H. M., & Inagaki, K. (1997). *The emergence of core domains of thought.* San Francisco: Jossey-Bass.

Wells, G. L., & Loftus, E. F. (2003). Eyewitness memory for people and events. In A. M. Goldstein (Ed.), *Handbook of psychology: Forensic psychology* (Vol. 11, pp. 149–160). New York: Wiley.

Werker, J. F. (1991). The ontogeny of speech perception. In I. G. Mattingly & M. Studdert-Kennedy (Eds.), *Modularity and the motor theory of speech perception* (pp. 91–109). Hillsdale, NJ: Erlbaum.

Werker, J. F., & Lalond, F. M. (1988). Cross-language speech perception: Initial capabilities and developmental change. *Developmental Psychology, 24,* 672–683.

Werker, J. F., & Tees, R. C. (1999). Influences on infant speech processing: Toward a new synthesis. *Annual Review of Psychology, 50,* 509–535.

Wertheimer, M. (1923). Untersuchungen zur lehre von der gestalt, II. *Psychologische Forschung, 4,* 301–350.

Wever, E. G. (1949). *Theory of hearing.* New York: Wiley.

Whaley, A. L., & Davis, K. E. (2007). Cultural competence and evidence-based practice in mental health services. *American Psychologist, 62,* 563–574.

White, L., & Edwards, J. N. (1990). Emptying the nest and parental well-being: An analysis of national panel data. *American Sociological Review, 55,* 235–242.

Whorf, B. L. (1956). In J. B. Carroll (Ed.), *Language, and reality: Selected writings of Benjamin Lee Whorf.* Cambridge, MA: MIT Press.

Widom, C. S., Dutton, M. A., Czaja, S. J., & DuMont, K. A. (2005). Development and validation of a new instrument to assess lifetime trauma and victimization history. *Journal of Traumatic Stress, 18,* 519–531.

Wiggins, J. S. (1973). *Personality and prediction: Principles of personality assessment.* Reading, MA: Addison-Wesley.

Wiggins, J. S., & Pincus, A. L. (1992). Personality: Structure and assessment. *Annual Review of Psychology, 43,* 473–504.

Williamson, P., McLeskey, J., Hoppey, D., & Rentz, T. (2006). Educating students with mental retardation in general education classrooms. *Exceptional Children, 72,* 347–361.

Wilson, R. I., & Nicoll, R. A. (2002). Endocannabinoid signaling in the brain. *Science, 296,* 678–682.

Wilson, T. D., Houston, C. E., Etling, K. M., & Brekke, N. (1996). A new look at anchoring effects: Basic anchoring and its antecedents. *Journal of Experimental Psychology: General, 125,* 387–402.

Winarick, K. (1997). Visions of the future: The analyst's expectations and their impact on the analytic process. *American Journal of Psychoanalysis, 57,* 95–109.

Windy, D., & Ellis, A. (1997). *The practice of rational emotive behavior therapy.* New York: Springer.

Winner, E. (2000). The origins and ends of giftedness. *American Psychologist, 55,* 159–169.

Wismer Fries, A. B., Ziegler, T. E., Kurian, J. R., Jacoris, S., & Pollak, S. D. (2005). Early experience in humans is associated with changes in neuropeptides critical for regulating social behavior. *Proceedings of the National Academy of Sciences, 102,* 17237–17240.

Witherington, D. C., Campos, J. J., Anderson, D. I., Lejeune, L., & Seah, E. (2005). Avoidance of heights on the visual cliff in newly walking infants. *Infancy, 7,* 285–298.

Witt, J. K., & Proffitt, D. R. (2005). See the ball, hit the ball: Apparent ball size is correlated with batting average. *Psychological Science, 16,* 937–938.

Witte, K., & Noltemeier, B. (2002). The role of information in mate-choice copying in female sailfin mollies (*Poecilia latipinna*). *Behavioral Ecology and Sociobiology, 52,* 194–202.

Wittmann, M., Dinich, J., Merrow, M., & Roenneberg, T. (2006). Social jetlag: Misalignment of biological and social time. *Chronobiology International, 23,* 497–509.

Wolcott, S., & Strapp, C. M. (2002). Dream recall frequency and dream detail as mediated by personality, behavior, and attitude. *Dreaming, 12,* 27–44.

Wolfe, J. M. (2003). Moving towards solutions to some enduring controversies in visual search. *Trends in Cognitive Science, 7,* 70–76.

Wolfe, J. M., Friedman-Hill, S. R., & Bilsky, A. B. (1994). Parallel processing of part-whole information in visual search tasks. *Perception & Psychophysics, 55,* 537–550.

Wolpe, J. (1958). *Psychotherapy by reciprocal inhibition.* Stanford, CA: Stanford University Press.

Wolpe, J. (1973). *The practice of behavior therapy* (2nd ed.). New York: Pergamon Press.

Wolpe, J. (1986). Misconceptions about behaviour therapy: Their sources and consequences. *Behaviour Change, 3,* 9–15.

Wong, S. C. P., & Gordon, A. (2006). The validity and reliability of the violence risk scale: A treatment-friendly violence risk assessment tool. *Psychology, Public Policy, and Law, 12,* 279–309.

Wood, E., Desmarais, S., & Gugula, S. (2002). The impact of parenting experience of gender stereotyped toy play of children. *Sex Roles, 47,* 39–49.

Wood, J. J., McLeod, B. D., Sigman, M., Hwang, W. C., & Chu, B. C. (2003). Parenting and childhood anxiety: Theory, empirical findings, and future directions. *Journal of Child Psychology and Psychiatry, 44,* 134–151.

Wood, J. J., Piacentini, J. C., Southam-Gerow, M., Chu, B. C., & Sigman, M. (2006). Family cognitive behavioral therapy for child anxiety disorders. *Journal of the American Academy of Child and Adolescent Psychiatry, 45,* 314–321.

Wood, J. M., Bootzin, R. R., Rosenhan, D., Nolen-Hoeksema, S., & Jourden, F. (1992). Effects of the 1989 San Francisco earthquake on frequency and content of nightmares. *Journal of Abnormal Psychology, 101,* 219–224.

Wood, N., & Cowan, N. (1995a). The cocktail party phenomenon revisited: How frequent are attention shifts to one's name in an irrelevant auditory channel? *Journal of Experimental Psychology: Learning, Memory, and Cognition, 21,* 255–260.

Wood, N., & Cowan, N. (1995b). The cocktail party phenomenon revisited: Attention and memory in the classic selective listening procedure of Cherry (1953). *Journal of Experimental Psychology: General, 124,* 243–262.

Wood, S. J., Pantelis, C., Velakoulis, D., Yücel, M., Fornito, A., & McGorry, P. D. (2008). Progressive changes in the development toward schizophrenia: Studies in subjects at increased symptomatic risk. *Schizophrenia Bulletin, 34,* 322–329.

Wood, W. (2000). Attitude change: Persuasion and social influence. *Annual Review of Psychology, 51,* 539–570.

Wood, W., Lundgren, S., Ouellette, J. A., Busceme, S., & Blackstone, T. (1994). Minority influence: A meta-analytic review of social influence processes. *Psychological Bulletin, 115,* 323–345.

Woolley, H. T. (1910). Psychological literature: A review of the recent literature on the psychology of sex. *Psychological Bulletin, 7,* 335–342.

Workman, B. (1990, December 1). Father guilty of killing daughter's friend, in '69. *San Francisco Examiner-Chronicle,* pp. 1, 4.

World Health Orgnization. (2008). *The global burden of disease: 2004 update.* Retrieved from www.who.int/healthinfo/global_burden_disease/GBD_report_2004update_full.pdf.

Worthington, R. L., Soth-McNett, A. M., & Moreno, M. V. (2007). Multicultural counseling competencies research: A 20-year content analysis. *Journal of Counseling Psychology, 54,* 351–361.

Wright, S. C., Aron, A., McLaughlin-Volpe, T., & Ropp, S. A. (1997). The extended contact effect. *Journal of Personality and Social Psychology, 73,* 73–90.

Yamagata, S., Suzuki, A., Ando, J., Ono, Y., Kijima, N., Yoshimura, K., Osendorf, F., Angleitner, A., Riemann, R., Spinath, F. M., Livesley, W. J., & Jang, K. L. (2006). Is the genetic structure of human personality universal? A cross-cultural twin study from North America, Europe, and Asia. *Journal of Personality and Social Psychology, 90,* 987–998.

Yang, Y., Raine, A., Lencz, T., Bihrle, S., Lacasse, L., & Coletti, P. (2005). Prefrontal white matter in pathological liars. *British Journal of Psychiatry, 187,* 320–325.

Yantis, S. (1993). Stimulus-driven attentional capture. *Current Directions in Psychological Science, 2,* 156–161.

Yegneswaran, B., & Shapiro, C. (2007). Do sleep deprivation and alcohol have the same effects of psychomotor performance? *Journal of Psychosomatic Medicine, 63,* 569–572.

Zadra, A., & Donderi, D. C. (2000). Nightmares and bad dreams: Their prevalence and relationship to well-being. *Journal of Abnormal Psychology, 109,* 273–281.

Zahn-Waxler, C., Shirtcliff, E. A., & Marceau, K. (2008). Disorders of childhood and adolescence: Gender and psychopathology. *Annual Review of Clinical Psychology, 4,* 275–303.

Zajonc, R. B. (1968). Attitudinal effects of mere exposure. *Journal of Personality and Social Psychology. Monograph Supplement, 9* (2, Part 2), 1–27.

Zajonc, R. B. (2000). Feeling and thinking: Closing the debate over the independence of affect. In J. P. Forgas (Ed.), *Feeling and thinking: The role of affect in social cognition* (pp. 31–58). New York: Cambridge University Press.

Zajonc, R. B. (2001). Mere exposure: A gateway to the subliminal. *Current Directions in Psychological Science, 10,* 224–228.

Zeanah, C. H., Smyke, A. T., Koga, S. F., & Carlson, E. (2005). Attachment in institutionalized and community children in Romania. *Child Development, 76,* 1015–1028.

Zeineh, M. M., Engel, S. A., Thompson, P. M., & Bookheimer, S. Y. (2003). Dynamics of the hippocampus during encoding and retrieval of face-name pairs. *Science, 299*, 577–580.

Zelazo, P. D., Helwig, C. C., & Lau, A. (1996). Intention, act, and outcome in behavioral prediction and moral judgment. *Child Development, 67*, 2478–2492.

Zelinski, E. M., Gilewski, M. J., & Schaie, K. W. (1993). Individual differences in cross-sectional and 3-year longitudinal memory performance across the adult life span. *Psychology and Aging, 8*, 176–186.

Zenderland, L. (1998). *Measuring minds: Henry Herbert Goddard and the origins of American intelligence testing.* Cambridge, UK: Cambridge University Press.

Zimbardo, P. G. (1991). *Shyness: What it is, what to do about it* (rev. ed.). Reading, MA: Addison-Wesley. (Original work published 1977)

Zimbardo, P. G. (2007). *The Lucifer effect: Understanding how good people turn evil.* New York: Random House.

Zimbardo, P. G., & Montgomery, K. D. (1957). The relative strengths of consummatory responses in hunger, thirst, and exploratory drive. *Journal of Comparative and Physiological Psychology, 50*, 504–508.

Zimbardo, P. G., & Radl, S. L. (1999). *The shy child* (2nd ed.). Los Altos, CA: Malor Press.

Zimmerman, B. J., Bandura, A., & Martinez-Pons, M. (1992). Self-motivation for academic attainment: The role of self-efficacy beliefs and personal goal setting. *American Educational Research Journal, 29*, 663–676.

Zuckerman, M. (2007). *Sensation seeking and risky behavior.* Washington, DC: American Psychological Association.

Zwaigenbaum, L., Bryson, S., Rogers, T., Roberts, W., Brian, J., & Szatmari, P. (2005). Behavioral manifestations of autism in the first year of life. *International Journal of Developmental Neuroscience, 23*, 143–152.

Name Index

Dell, G. S., 239
DeLoache, J., 452
Denko, T., 455, 497
Denmark, F. L., 8
Dennerstein, L., 325
Dennett, D. C., 138
De Oliveira Alvares, L., 153
De Pascalis, V., 150
DePaulo, B. M., 246
de Rivera, J., 485
De Santis, M., 301
Descartes, R., 60, 70
de St. Aubin, E., 326
DeValois, R. L., 105
Devine, P. G., 530
Dew, M. A., 144
de Waal, F. B. M., 540
Dewey, J., 8
Dewsbury, D. A., 351
Dhawan, N., 430
Dickens, W. T., 284
Dickenson, C. A., 117
Dickerson, F. B., 180
Diener, E., 324, 378
Dietrich, A., 291
DiLalla, L. F., 536
Di Marzo, V., 153
DiMatteo, M. R., 396
Dinges, D. F., 145
Dion, K. K., 534
Dion, K. L., 534
Dirkzwager, A. J. E., 390
Distel, M. A., 459–460
Dix, D., 480
Dixon, R. A., 298, 311
Do, A. M., 260
Docherty, N. M., 469
Dollard, J., 537
Domhoff, G. W., 148
Domjan, M., 184
Donderi, D. C., 146
Donders, F. C., 234
Donnellan, M. B., 428
Donnerstein, E., 189
Donovan, W., 320
Douglas, K. S., 16
Downing, P. D., 101
Drake, C. L., 145
Drews, R. A., 126
DuBois, P. H., 433
Dudycha, G. J., 412
Duka, T., 207

Duker, P. C., 487
Duncker, D., 253
Durik, A. M., 354
Durkin, S. J., 349
Dusek, J. A., 396
Dutton, D. G., 376
Dweck, C. S., 343

Eagly, A. H., 34
East, R., 377
Eastwick, P. W., 354
Ebbinghaus, H., 5, 211–212
Edinger, J. D., 145
Edwards, J. N., 325
Einstein, A., 247
Eisenberg, M., 470
Ekman, P., 371–372
Elbert, T., 83
Eley, T. C., 456
Elias, S. M., 426
Elliott, A. J., 362
Ellis, A., 491
Elman, J. L., 127
Elms, A. C., 422
Elsabagh, S., 28
Emery, G., 453
Emmelkamp, P. M. G., 486
Endler, N. S., 390
Engle, R. W., 204
Enns, J. T., 121
Epley, N., 260
Epstein, L. H., 345, 346
Ericsson, K. A., 203, 251
Erikson, E., 317–319, 324, 327
Erlacher, D., 148
Ervik, S., 146
Esbaugh, E. M., 354
Espelage, D. L., 357
Espie, C. A., 146
Estrada, C. A., 377
Evans, E., 458
Evans, J. St. B. T., 140, 253, 254, 258
Evans, S. E., 539
Evardsen, J., 455
Exner, J. E., Jr., 435
Eysenck, H., 407, 410, 500

Fabian, J. M., 16
Fadiman, J., 420, 484
Fagan, J. F., 287

Fahey, C. D., 141
Fakhoury, W., 481
Fallon, A. E., 172
Faraday, M., 247
Faraone, S. V., 470
Farina, A., 472
Farmer, T. A., 242
Farrell, M., 165
Fattore, L., 154
Faucheux, C., 519–520
Fazio, R. H., 524
Feather, N. T., 358
Fechner, G., 93
Feldman, D. H., 309
Fellows, L. K., 225
Fernald, A., 314
Fernández-Dávila, P., 395
Ferster, C. B., 183
Festinger, L., 343, 526
Fields, R. D., 62
Fillmore, M. T., 155
Find, G. R., 124
Fink, P., 462, 463
Fiore, M. C., 395
Fischer, M., 470
Fischoff, B., 208
Fishbein, M., 524
Fisher, B. S., 355
Fishman, H. C., 495
Fishman, T., 495
Fiske, S. T., 515
Fitch, W. T., 244
Flavell, J. H., 309
Fleming, I., 248
Flynn, J. R., 284
Foa, E. B., 386
Fode, K. L., 27
Folkman, S., 387, 388
Ford, C. S., 351
Forgas, J. P., 377
Forooqi, I. S., 346
Förster, J., 292
Försterling, F., 510
Forumoto, L., 8
Foster, R. G., 144
Foucault, M., 480
Foulkes, D., 146
Fowler, H., 341
Fox, M. J., 66
Frager, R., 420, 484
Fraley, B., 535
Fraley, R. C., 535

Frank, J. B., 500
Frank, J. D., 500
Frank, M. C., 258
Frank, M. E., 111
Franklin, G., 485
Franklin, N., 248
Franklin-Lipsker, E., 485
Franko, D. L., 449
Frans, Ö., 451
Franz, C. E., 358–359
Fraser, L. M., 499
Fraser, S. C., 528
Frederick, S., 259
Freedman, J. L., 528
Fresco, D. M., 388
Freud, A., 9, 315, 323
Freud, S., 9–10, 12, 137–138, 147, 290, 317, 322, 323, 324, 414–420, 421–422, 427, 447, 456, 463, 482–483, 485
Freund, A. M., 327, 332
Frewen, P. A., 501
Frick, F., 254
Friedman, M., 398–399
Friend, R., 518
Friesen, W. V., 371–372
Fromkin, V. A., 239
Frougel, P., 346
Furmark, T., 501
Furnham, A., 434

Gage, P., 68, 76
Gale, C. R., 423
Galen, 407, 410
Gallace, A., 199
Gallo, L. C., 386
Galperin, G. J., 446
Galton, F., 271–272
Ganis, F., 248, 249
Ganor-Stern, D., 236
Gao, Q., 345
Garb, H. N., 435
Garcia, J., 170, 185–186
Garcías, P., 463
Gardner, B. T., 244
Gardner, H., 281–282, 290, 422
Gardner, M., 324, 325
Gardner, R. A., 244
Gassió, R., 277
Gatchel, R. J., 113

Subject Index

Amnesia, 223–224. *See also* Anterograde amnesia dissociative amnesia, 463
Amphetamines, 153, 156
state-dependent memory and, 207
Amplitude, 105–106
Amygdala, 73–74, 75
aggression and, 537
dreams and, 148
emotions and, 374
extraversion and, 411
five-factor model and, 411
homosexuality and, 356
memory and, 223, 224
Amyloid B-peptide (AB), 225
Anagrams, 210
Analogical problem solving, 255
Analogies, 255
Analytical intelligence, 279–280, 280, 281
Analytic psychology, 420
Analyzing data, 45–51
Anandamide, 153
Anchoring heuristic, 260
Androgens, 350
Anger
and borderline personality disorder, 459
MMPI-2 content scale, 434
NEO-PI dimension for, 434
Anima, 419–420
The Animal Mind (Washburn), 8, 9
Animals
cognition and, 187
instincts and, 342
language and, 244
phobia, animal-type specific, 450
research, ethical issues of, 37–38
sexual behaviors in, 350–351
Animus, 419–420
Anorexia nervosa, 348–349
Anosmia, 110
Anterior chamber of eye, 97
Anterior parahippocampal cortex (aPHG), 227

Anterior pituitary gland, 82
Anterograde amnesia, 224
implicit memory and, 224–225
Antianxiety drugs, 498
Anticipated diets, 347–348
Anticipatory coping with stress, 388
Antidepressant drugs, 497–498
Antihistamines and state-dependent memory, 207
Antipsychotic drugs, 496
Antisocial behavior
coercion model for, 179
observational learning and, 189
Antisocial personality disorder, 460–462
Anvil of ear, 108
Anxiety
Freudian theory and, 417–418
hierarchy of, 486
NEO-PI dimension for, 434
Anxiety disorders, 448
behavioral explanations of, 453
biology and, 452
causes of, 451–453
cognitive perspectives on, 453
GABA (gamma-aminobutyric acid) and, 65
generalized anxiety disorder, 448
psychodynamic model of, 452–453
Anxiety sensitivity, 453
Anxious-ambivalent attachment style, 535
Aphasia, Broca's, 77
Appetite and marijuana, 154
Application and research, 15
Appraisal of stress, 387–388
Approach-related emotional responses, 374, 411
Appropriate Pain Behavior Questionnaire (APBQ), 373
Aqueous humor, 97
Archtype, 419–420

Archur Indians, Ecuador, 147
Arcuate nucleus (ARC), 345
Asch effect, 516–518
Assessment, 271–274. *See also* Intelligence assessment
content validity, 273
criterion validity, 273
ethics and, 291–292
formal assessment, 272–274
history of, 271–272
norms, 274
of personality, 433–436
reliability and, 272
and society, 291–292
standardization and, 274
validity and, 272–273
Assimilation, 306–307
Association cortex, 76–77
Association for Psychological Science (APS), 15
journals from, 24
Athletics and shaping, 184
Attachment, 319–321
contact comfort and, 322
cupboard theory of, 321
day care and, 321
needs, 343–344
Strange Situation Test, 320–321
Attention. *See also* Consciousness
benzodiazepines and, 498
extinction strategies and, 488
observational learning and, 189
processes of, 114–116
working memory and, 204
Attentional processes, 235–236
Attitudes, 523–524
survey research and, 32
Attractiveness, 532
Attributional styles, 359–360
Attributions for success and failure, 359–361
Attribution theory, 509–510
fundamental attribution error (FAE) and, 510–511

Atypical antipsychotic drugs, 496
Audience design and evolution, 244
Auditory cortex, 76, 108
Auditory nerve, 108–109
Auditory system, 107–108
Australopithecus, 55, 57
Authoritarian parents, 321
Authoritative parents, 320–321
Authority, obedience to, 520–523
Autistic disorder, 471
Autokinetic effect, 516
Automatic attitudes, 524
Automatic processes, 236
Automobile accidents, alcohol and, 155–156
Autonomic nervous system (ANS), 71–72
diagram of, 73
and emotions, 373–374
stress response and, 380–381
Autonomy
moral development and, 331
vs. self-doubt stage, 317
Availability heuristic, 258–259
Aversion therapy, 487
Avoidance conditioning, 177
Avoidant attachment style, 535
Awareness and consciousness, 136–138
Axons, 61
Aztec culture, 152

Backward conditioning, 168
Balanced time perspective, 401
Barbiturates, 153, 155
Bar graphs, 46–47
Basic level hierarchies, 218
Basilar membrane, 107–108
place theory and, 108
Bathers (Seurat), 3, 4
Bats, echolocation by, 109
Bedlam, 480
Behavior. *See also* Behaviorism; Behavior therapies; Prosocial behavior

Brain stem, 72–73, 75
and memory, 224
Brightness, 102
Broca's aphasia, 77
Broca's area, 68, 76
Bulimia nervosa, 348
Bystander intervention, 541–543
responsibility, feeling of, 543

Caffeine, 153, 157
Cancer, 175
Cannabinoids, 153, 346
Cannabis. *See* Marijuana
Cannon-Bard theory of central neural processes, 375
Cardinal personality traits, 409
Case studies, 35
Cataplexy, 146
Catatonic type of schizophrenia, 466
Catecholamines, 66
Catharsis, 482
Caudal ventral prefrontal cortex (cVPFC), 455
Causal attributions, 360, 509
Causality and psychological diagnosis, 444
Causation
behaviors and, 4
correlation and, 29
Celexa, 501
Cell phones, distraction and, 126
Cells
and action potential, 62–64
receptive fields of, 100–101
Central executive, 203, 204
Central nervous system (CNS), 70–72
hypothalamus and, 81
psychoneuroimmunology, 398
Central neural processes theory, 375
Central personality traits, 409
Central responses and eating, 345
Central route to persuasion, 525

Centration, 307
Cerebellum, 72–73, 75, 76
memory and, 223, 224
Cerebral cortex, 74–75, 76
and aggression, 537
and emotions, 374
and memory, 223
and schizophrenia, 468
Cerebral hemispheres, 74–75
Cerebrum, 74–77
Challenge to objectivity
and experimental method, 26–27
observer biases and, 24–27
Chameleon affect, 536
Change blindness, 118
Chemotherapy, 175
"Chicken" game, 324
Child abuse
attachment and, 323
borderline personality disorders and, 460
dissociative disorders and, 464–465
Child-directed speech, 314
Children. *See also* Infants
ADHD (attention deficit hyperactivity disorder) and, 470–471
attachment, 319–320
autistic disorder, 471
birth order and personality, 408, 409
coercion model for, 179
day care and development, 321
eating, social context and, 347
family therapy and, 495
foundational theories, 310
gender development in, 328–329
and homosexuality, 357
internal working model, 320
language acquisition in, 314
moral development in, 330–331
nightmares and, 146
parenting styles, 320–321
photographic memory in, 200

physical development in, 302–303
Piaget's stage of development, 306–309
psychological disorders of, 470–471
social development in, 319–322
spanking, effect of, 182
as supertasters, 115
temperament in, 319
unconditional positive regard and, 420
Children's Activities Inventory (CAI), 329
Chimpanzees, language and, 244
China, formal assessment in, 271
Chlopromazine, 496
Chloride, 63
Chromosomes, 56–57
color blindness and, 104
at conception, 59
Down syndrome, 277
Chronic stress, 379
general adaptation syndrome (GAS) and, 382–383
psychological reactions to, 386
Chronological age, 275
Chronotypes, 142
Chunking, 202–203
Cigarette smoking
and health, 393–395
nicotine and, 157
quitting, stages of, 394–395
taste receptors and, 111
teratogen, smoke as, 301
Cingulate gyrus, 498
Cingulotomy, 498
Circadian rhythms, 141
morning/night people, 142
Citalopram, 501
Classical conditioning, 166–174
acquisition and, 171–172
applications of, 172–174
cancer treatment and, 175
extinction, 168–169
informative stimulus, 172

stimulus discrimination, 170
stimulus generalization, 169–170
Client, defined, 479–480
Client-centered therapy, 493
Clinical psychologists, 15, 479
Clinical scales of MMPI-2, 433
Clinical social workers, 479
Cliques and adolescence, 324
Closure, law of, 117
Clozapine, 496
Clozaril, 496
Cocaine, 153, 157
as teratogen, 301
Cochlea, 107–108
Cochlear nucleus of brain, 108
Cocktail party phenomenon, 137
Coding scheme reliability, 272
Coercion model, 179
Cognition, 233. *See also* Language; Problem solving; Reasoning; Visual cognition
benzodiazepines and, 498
comparative cognition, 187–188
conceptual behavior and, 188
deductive reasoning, 253–255
inductive reasoning, 255–256
infant cognition, 309–310
learned helplessness and, 456
mental resources and, 234–237
mood and, 377
motivation and, 342–343
social cognition, 509
and somatoform disorders, 463
speed of mental processes, 234
Cognitive-affective personality theory, 423–424

Cognitive appraisal theories of emotion, 375–376
Cognitive behavioral therapy, 491–492
Cognitive development, 306–312
in adulthood, 311–312
cultural influences on, 310–311
Piaget, Jean on, 306–309
schemes and, 306–307
social influences on, 310–311
stages of, 307–309
Cognitive dissonance theory, 526–527
Cognitive maps, 187–188
Cognitive neuroscience, 11
Cognitive perspective, 11
and aggression, 13
on anxiety disorders, 453
on mood disorders, 456
Cognitive psychology, 2, 13, 233
and psychological disorders, 447
Cognitive sets, 456
Cognitive social-learning theory, 424–426
Cognitive therapies, 478, 491–492
cognitive behavioral therapy, 491–492
false beliefs, changing, 491
rational-emotive therapy (RET), 491
Cold fibers, 112
Collective unconscious, 419–420
Collectivism, 539
Collectivist cultures, 430
Color blindness, 104
Color circle, 103
Colors
color blindness, 104
seeing color, 101–105
simultanagnosia and, 100
Commitment
and compliance, 528
and loving, 533
Common fate, law of, 117
Common ground
and language, 238

Community
language and, 238, 239
moral development and, 331
support groups, 495
Comorbidity, 445–446
Companionate love, 533–534
Comparative cognition, 187–188
Compensation and brain, 313
Compensatory response, 174
Competence v. inferiority stage, 318
Competencies in cognitive-affective personality theory, 424
Competition
and phenotypes, 55
Complementary colors, 102–103
Complex cells, 101
Compliance, 527–528
commitment and, 528
reciprocity and, 527–528
Compulsions, 451. *See also* Obsessive-compulsive disorder (OCD)
buying disorder, compulsive, 492
Computerized axial tomography (CT/CAT), 69–70
Concentrative meditation, 151
Conceptual behavior, 188
conceptually-driven processing, 126
Conclusions from research, 24
Concrete operations stage, 307–308
Conditional reinforcers, 180
Conditioned response (CR), 166–169
Conditioned stimulus (CS), 166–169
Conditioning. *See also* Classical conditioning; Operant conditioning
avoidance conditioning, 177
escape conditioning, 177
taste-aversion learning, 168, 185–187

Conduction deafness, 108
Cones. *See* Rods and cones
Conformity, 516–520
Asch effect, 516–518
in everyday life, 518
informational influence, 516
minority influence and, 519–520
nonconformity, 519–520
normative influence, 516–520
Confounding variables, 26
Conscience and superego, 417
Conscientiousness, 411
NEO-PI dimension, 434
Consciousness
altered states of, 148–152
awareness and, 136–138
comparing theories, 432
functions of, 139–141
hypnosis and, 149–151
lucid dreaming, 148–149
meditation, 151
studying contents of, 138
survival and, 139
uses of, 139–140
Consensus and attribution theory, 510
Conservation, sleep and, 144
Consistency
and attribution theory, 510
paradox, 412, 413
Constructing social reality, 509–513
Constructive criticism, 401
Construct validity, 273
Contact comfort and attachment, 322
Contact hypothesis, 531–532
Content validity, 273
Context
-dependent memory, 207
and encoding, 206–209
influence of, 127–129
Contextual distinctiveness, 208–209
Contingency
acquisition and, 171–172
classical conditioning and, 169, 172
management, 487–488

reinforcement contingencies, 176–179
Control
defined, 5
locus of control, 423
perceived control and stress, 390
procedures, 27–28
Control group, 28
Controllable/uncontrollable stressors, 388
Controlled processes, 236
Conventional morality, 331
Convergence cues, 119, 120
Convergent thinking, 289
Conversation, Piaget on, 308
Conversion disorder, 462–463
Conversion hysteria, 434
Cooperative principle, 237–238
Coping
optimism and, 400
positive reappraisal coping, 392
with stress, 387–391
Copresence and language, 238
Copulation, 351
Co-relations, 271
Cornea, 97
Coronary heart disease, 399
Corpus callosum, 74–76, 79
hypnotizability and, 150
Correlational methods, 29–30
Correlation coefficient (r), 29, 48–49
Correlations, 271
in statistics, 48–49
and test-retest reliability, 272
Cortex. *See* Cerebral cortex
Cortical cells, receptive fields of, 101
Counseling psychologists, 479
Counterconditioning, 484–487
Countertransference, 483
Couple therapy, 494–495
Covariation model, 510
Crack cocaine, 157

Hierarchy
and long-term memory, 217–218
of needs (Maslow), 343–344
High-distress relationships, 326
High/Scope Perry program, 286–287
High self-esteem, 428–429
Hippocampus, 73–74, 75
dreams and, 148
memory and, 223, 224
neurogenesis in, 83
Histograms, 46–47
History of psychology, 5–8
women researchers, 8–9
HIV/AIDS, 395
emotional writing and, 398, 399
psychological impact on outcomes, 398
HMOs (health maintenance organizations) and drug therapies, 496
HMS *Beagle,* 53
Holistic view, 10
of personality, 421, 422
Homelessness, 481
Homeostasis, 74, 341
Homo erectus, 55, 57
Homo sapiens, 55, 57
Homophobia, 357
Homosexuality, 325, 355–358. *See also* Prejudice
awareness of, 357
nature *vs.* nurture and, 356–357
society and, 357
suicide and, 458
Hooking up, 355
Horizontal cells, 99
Hormones, 81–82
sexual arousal and, 350
Hostility
and health, 399
NEO-PI dimension for, 434
Hot/spicy foods, 115
Hozho concept, 393
Hue, 102
Human deprivation, 322–323
Human development. *See* Development

Human Genome Project (HGP), 57, 58–59, 67
Humanistic perspective, 10
and aggression, 13
of personality, 420–422
Humanistic therapies, 478, 493–494
client-centered therapy, 493
Gestalt therapy, 494
Human-potential movement, 493
Humors, 407
Hunger and marijuana, 154
Hunger center, 345
Hyperactivity-impulsivity, 470
Hypercomplex cells, 101
Hypnosis, 149–151
effects of, 150–151
Hypnotic induction, 149
Hypnotizability, 149–150
Hypochondriasis, 434, 462
Hypomania, 434
Hyposmia, 110
Hypothalamus, 73–74, 75
eating and, 345
and endocrine system, 81–82
stress response and, 380
Hypotheses, 24
with behavior measures, 34
perceptual processes and, 93
testing, 31
and word meanings, 315
hypothesis-driven processing, 126
Hysteria, 463

Iconic memory, 199–200
Id, 417
psychoanalysis and, 482
psychological disorders and, 447
Identical twins, 58. *See also* Twin studies
Identification, 418
Identification
and recognition, 91, 93
bottom-up processing, 125–127
contexts, influence of, 127–129

expectations, influence of, 127–129
top-down processing, 126–127
Identity *vs.* role confusion stage, 318
Ill-defined problem, 250
Illness. *See* Health
Illusions, 124
Ames room illusion, 122, 123
of ease, 91
Müller-Lyer illusion, 124, 125
Ponzo illusion, 122
Imagination
flooding therapy and, 486
visual imagination, 247–248
Imitation of models, 489
Immigration
intelligence quotient (IQ) and, 287
and selective exclusion, 283
Immune system
optimism and, 400
psychoneuroimmunology, 398
Implicit association test, 524
Implicit attitudes, 524
Implicit memory, 196–197
anterograde amnesia and, 224–225
priming and, 210
processes and, 210–211
Imprinting, 319–320
Impulse behavior, 67
Impulsive aggression, 537
Impulsiveness
ADHD (attention deficit hyperactivity disorder) and, 470
NEO-PI dimension for, 434
Incentives, 341–342
Incongruence, 493
Independence and adolescence, 324
Independent construals of self, 430, 511
Independent variables, 25
Indirect reciprocity, 540
Individualist cultures, 430
Inductive reasoning, 255–256

Indulgent parents, 321
Industrial-organizational psychology, 15
Infants
cognition in, 309–310
human deprivation and, 322–323
imprinting, 319–320
language acquisition in, 314
physical development in, 301–302
Piaget, Jean on, 306–307
premature infants, 146
speech, infant-directed, 314
survival capabilities of, 301–302
temperament of, 319
universality of emotions and, 370
Inferences, 243
Inferential statistics, 45, 49–51
Inferiority, feelings of, 419
Infidelity, 353
Informational influence, 516
group polarization and, 520
and obedience to authority, 522–523
Information processing, 196
Informative stimulus, 172
Informed consent, 36
In-group bias, 529
In-groups, 529
Inhibitory inputs, 62
Initial state of problem, 250
Initiative *vs.* guilt stage, 317–318
Inkblot tests, 435
Innate emotional responses, 370–371
Inner ear, 107–108
Insanity. *See also* Psychological disorders
concept of, 446
Insight therapy, 482
Insomnia, 145–146
opiate addiction and, 154–155
Instincts, 342
Instinctual drift, 184–185
Institution-reared children, 322–323
Instrumental aggression, 537

Positive reappraisal coping, 392

Positive reinforcement/reinforcers, 177
    response deprivation and, 181
    strategies, 487–488

Positive transference, 483

Positron emission tomography (PET) scans, 69–70

Possible selves, 428

Posterior parahippocampal gyrus (pPHG), 227

Posterior pituitary gland, 82

Postevent information, 222

Posttraumatic growth, 392

Posttraumatic stress disorder. *See* PTSD (posttraumatic stress disorder)

Potassium and action potentials, 63–64

Poverty
    intelligence quotient (IQ) and, 286
    social development and, 317

Power of the situation, 513–523

PQ4R (Preview, Question, Read, Reflect, Recite, Review) technique, 17

Practical intelligence, 281

Practice index, 429

Pragmatics, 314

Preconscious memories, 136, 137

Preconventional morality, 331

Predictability. *See* Contingency

Predictions, 4–5

Predictive validity, 273

Preferences and classical conditioning, 172–173

Prefrontal cortex
    and memory, 224
    and pathological liars, 246

Prefrontal lobotomy, 498

Pregnancy
    intellectual disability and, 277
    teratogens and, 301

Prejudice, 528–532
    origins of, 529

reversing, 530–532
    stereotypes and, 529–530

Premature infants, 146

Prenatal development, 300–301

Preoperational stage, 307

Preparedness hypothesis, 452

Preschool Activities Inventory (PSAI), 329

Pressure on skin, 112

Pretrial Juror Attitude Questionnaire (PJAQ), 273

Prevention strategies, 502–503

Primacy effect, 208

Primary appraisal of stress, 387–388

Primary colors, 104

Primary prevention, 502–503

Primary reinforcers, 180

Priming and implicit memory, 210–211

Principled morality, 331

Principle of contrast, 315

Principles of Physiological Psychology (Wundt), 7

The Principles of Psychology (James), 7

Principlism, 539

Proactive interference, 212

Problem-directed coping with stress, 388, 390

Problem solving, 250–253
    analogical problem solving, 255
    functional fixedness and, 253
    improving, 252–253
    inductive reasoning and, 255

Problem spaces, 250

Procedural knowledge, 312

Procedural memory, 197–198

Procrastination, 385

Production of language, 237–240

Prognosis, 478

Progressive education, 8

Projection, 418, 419

Projective test for personality, 434–436

Propositions and language, 242

Prosocial behavior, 530–543, 535
    bystander intervention, 541–543
    observational learning and, 189
    situational effects on, 540–543
    volunteering, 542

Prototypes and memory, 218

Provocation and aggression, 538

Proximal stimulus, 92–93

Proximity, law of, 117

Prozac, 66, 497, 498

Psilocybe mushrooms, 152

Psychedelics, 153

Psychiatrists, 479

Psychic determinism, 416

Psychic energy, 414

Psychoactive drugs. *See* Drugs

Psychoanalysts, 479, 482–483

Psychobiographies, 421–422

Psychodynamic model, 9–10, 447
    and aggression, 12
    and anxiety disorders, 452–453
    and mood disorders, 456
    of personality, 414–420
    for therapies, 478

Psychodynamic therapy, 482–484
    behavioral therapy compared, 490
    later therapies, 483–484

Psychological dependence, 152–153

Psychological diagnosis, 444, 478

Psychological disorders. *See also* specific types
    abnormal, labeling behavior as, 442–443
    ADHD (attention deficit hyperactivity disorder), 470–471
    behavioral model, 447
    biological approaches, 447
    of children, 470–471
    classifying, 444–446

cognitive perspective on, 447

creativity and, 290–291

dissociative disorders, 462–463

etiology of, 446–448

history of classification, 444–445

and homelessness, 481

interactionist perspective, 448

nature of, 442–448

nature *vs.* nurture, explaining, 461

objectivity and, 443–444

panic disorder, 449–450

phobias, 450

prevention strategies, 502–503

psychodynamic model, 447

Rorschach inkblot tests and, 435

sociocultural perspective and, 447–448

somatoform disorders, 462–463

stigma of, 471–472

Psychological measurement. *See* Measurement

Psychologists
    clinical psychologists, 15, 479
    counseling psychologists, 479
    forensic psychologists, 16
    health psychologists, 370
    intuitive psychologists, 510

Psychology, defined, 2

Psychology from the Standpoint of a Behaviorist (Watson), 165

Psychometric curve, 94

Psychometric function, 94

Psychometric theory of intelligence, 279

Psychomotor behavior and schizophrenia, 465

Psychoneuroimmunology, 398

Psychopathic deviate, 434

Psychopharmacology, 496–498

Psychophysics, 93–96

Psychosexual development, 414–418
  evaluation of theory, 418–419
Psychosocial maturity, 326
Psychosocial stages, 317–319
Psycho somatic disorders, 383
Psychosurgery, 74, 498
Psychotherapy, 478. *See also* Therapies
Psychotic disorders, 446
Psychotism, 410
PTSD (posttraumatic stress disorder), 385, 451
  anxiety sensitivity and, 453
  biology and, 452
  brain changes and treatment of, 501
  social support and, 390
Puberty, 303
  depression and, 457
Pubescent growth spurt, 303
Public verifiability, 24
Punishers, 178
Punishment
  operant conditioning and, 178
  reducing the sentence behavior, 179–180
  spanking, effect of, 182
  vicarious punishment, 188
Pupil of eye, 97–98
Pure tones, 106–107

Questionnaires
  as self-reports, 33
Questions
  with fixed alternatives, 33
  open-ended questions, 33

Race. *See also* African Americans; Prejudice
  body dissatisfaction and, 349–350
  controversy of, 285
  intelligence quotient (IQ) and, 284–285
  slavery and, 443
  social development and, 317
Racism, 529
Random assignment, 28

Random sampling, 28
Range, 48
Rank-ordered scores, 46
Rape, 355
Rapid eye movement (REM) sleep, 142–143
  dreams and, 146
  functions of, 144–145
  lucid dreaming, 148–149
  narcolepsy and, 146
Rapport in interviews, 33
Rational-emotive therapy (RET), 491
Rationalization, 418
Ratio schedule of reinforcement, 181
Raw data, 45
  from Sudden Murderers Study, 46
Reaction formation, 418
Reaction time, 234, 235
Reality
  cultural constructions of, 139–140
  expectations and, 343
  personal construction of, 139
Reality principle, 417
Real-word reasoning, 254–255
Reasoning
  and brain, 255–256
  deductive reasoning, 253–255
  inductive reasoning, 255–256
Recall, 205–206
Recency effect, 208
Receptive fields of cells, 100–101
Receptor molecules, 64–65
Receptors
  for pain, 113–114
  for smell, 110–111
  for taste, 111–112
Recessive genes, 57
Reciprocal altruism, 540
Reciprocal determinism, 425
Reciprocal inhibition theory, 485
Reciprocity
  and altruism, 540
  and compliance, 527–529
  and liking, 533
Reciprocity norm, 527–529

Recognition, 205–206
  process, 91
Reconstructive memory, 219–223
  accuracy of, 220–221
  eyewitness memory, 222–223
  flashbulb memories, 221–222
Red-green color blindness, 104
Reducing the sentence behavior, 179–180
Reflexes, 166–168
  infant survival and, 301–302
Refractory period, 64
Regression, 418
Regret, 262–263
Rehearsal, 201–202
  elaborative rehearsal, 213
Reinforcement. *See also* Positive reinforcement/reinforcers
  contingencies, 176–179
  history, 422
  schedules of, 181–183
  spanking and, 182
  vicarious reinforcement, 188
Reinforcers. *See also* Positive reinforcement/reinforcers
  properties of, 180–181
  response deprivation and, 181
Relative refractory period, 64
Relative size, 120
Relaxation response, 396–397
Reliability
  formal assessment and, 272
  and measurement, 33
  validity and, 273
Remembering: A Study in Experimental and Social Psychology (Bartlett), 220
Remission and schizophrenia, 466
Remote associates test, 289
REM sleep. *See* Rapid eye movement (REM) sleep
Repeated pairings, 166–167

Repetitive transcranial magnetic stimulation (rTMS), 68–69, 499
Representations
  language and, 242
  memory and, 218
  mental representations, 198
  problem-solving and, 252
  verbal and visual representations, combining, 248–249
  visual representations, 247–248
Representativeness heuristic, 259–260
Representative samples, 28
Repression
  and ego, 417–418
  of memories, 485
  of motives, 137–138
  psychoanalysis and, 482
Reproduction
  observational learning and, 189
  sexual behaviors and, 353
Research. *See also* Adoption studies; Experimental methods; Statistics; Twin studies
  application and, 15
  challenge to objectivity, 24–27
  correlational methods, 29–30
  debriefing, 37
  designs, 28–29
  on development, 298–300
  ethics and, 35–38
  informed consent requirements, 36
  intentional deception and, 37
  on plasticity, 82
  process of, 23–31
  risk/gain assessment, 36–37
  subliminal messages and, 30–31
  survey research, 32
Residual type of schizophrenia, 466

Valence, 362
Validity
    and assessment, 272–273
    construct validity, 273
    intelligence assessment
        and culture, 287–288
    and measurement, 33
    MMPI scales, 433
    reliability and, 273
Valium, 65, 153, 155, 498
Valproate, 498
Variability, measures of, 48
Variable-interval (VI)
    schedules, 183
Variable-ratio (VR)
    schedules, 182–183
Variables, 25. *See also*
    Statistics
Variations
    in genotypes, 56–59
    of populations, 54
Ventricles of brain and
    schizophrenia, 467–468
Ventromedial hypothalamus
    (VMH), 345
Verbal Behavior (Skinner),
    11
Vervet monkeys, 244
Vestibular senses, 112–113
Viagra, 354
Vicarious punishment, 188
Vicarious reinforcement,
    188
Victimization and dissocia-
    tive symptoms, 464
Video games and aggression,
    538–539

Violence. *See* Aggression and
    violence
Violence Risk Scale (VRS),
    16
Visual cliff research, 302, 303
Visual cognition, 247–249
    brain and, 249
    in infants, 302
    mental rotation, 247–248
    verbal and visual repre-
        sentations, combining,
        248–249
    visual representations,
        247–248
Visual cortex, 76, 100–101
Visual imagination, 247–248
Visual memory, 199
Visual reality techniques, 487
Visual system, 97–105. *See
    also* Blindness; Retina
    accommodation process,
        97–98
    in adulthood, 305
    blind spot, 99–100
    brain processes, 100–101
    color, seeing, 101–105
    of infants, 302
    neural pathways for, 79
    structures of eye, 97–100
    visual cortex and, 76,
        100–101
Visuospatial sketchpad, 203
Vitreous humor, 97
Volley principle, 109
Volunteering, 542
Vomiting and opiate
    addiction, 154–155

Vulnerability, NEO-PI
    dimension for, 434

Warm fibers, 112
Wason selection task,
    254–255
Wavelengths of light,
    102–103
Wealth
    intelligence quotient (IQ)
        and, 286
    subjective well-being and,
        379
Weber's law, 96
*Wechsler Adult Intelligence
    Scale (WAIS)*, 275–276
*Wechsler Intelligence Scale for
    Children - Fourth Edition
    (WISC-IV)*, 276
*Wechsler Preschool and Pri-
    mary Scale of Intelligence -
    Third Edition (WPPSI-
    III)*, 276
Well-being, subjective,
    378–379
Well-defined problem, 250
Wellness, 393. *See also*
    Health
Wernicke's area, 76
Whole-report procedure,
    200
WHO (World Health
    Organization) depression,
    study on, 454
    International Classifica-
        tion of Diseases (ICD),
        445

Wisdom, 312
Wish-fulfillment, 147
Withdrawal-related emo-
    tional responses, 374, 411
Withdrawal symptoms, 152
Within-subjects design, 28
Wolof people, Senegal, 372
Womb envy, 419
Women. *See* Gender
Woodworth Personal Data
    Sheet, 433
Words
    fragment completion, 210
    identification, 210
    meanings, learning, 315
    perceiving, 313
Word stem completion, 210
Work and organizational
    psychology, 361–363
Working memory, 203–204
World Trade Center attacks.
    See September 11th
    attacks
World War I, intelligence
    assessment in, 275

Xanax, 65, 155, 498
X chromosome, 57
    color blindness and, 104

Y chromosome, 57
    color blindness and, 104
Young-Helmholtz trichro-
    matic theory, 104
Youth suicide, 458

Zygotes, 300

Photo Credits

Chapter 1:

p. 1: MediaMagnet/SuperStock Royalty Free; p. 3, tl: Myrleen Ferguson Cate/PhotoEdit, Inc.; p. 3, tr: Tony Savino/The Image Works; p. 3, bl: David Young-Wolff/PhotoEdit, Inc.; p. 3, br: Michael Schwarz/The Image Works; p. 3, t: George S. Seurat, *Bathers at Asnieres*. National Gallery, London. Copyright Erich Lessing/Art Resource, NY; p. 4, b: Jeff Greenberg/PhotoEdit, Inc.; p. 7: Archives of the History of American Psychology/University of Akron; p. 8: Michael Newman/PhotoEdit, Inc.; p. 9, t: The Granger Collection, New York; p. 9, b: Archives of the History of American Psychology/University of Akron; p. 10: Benjamin Harris, Ph.D; p. 11: Roger Ressmeyer/Corbis; p. 12: Wolfgang Kaehler/Corbis; p. 15: David Kelly Crow/PhotoEdit, Inc.

Chapter 2:

p. 22: Photodisc/SuperStock Royalty Free; p. 24: AP Images/Amy Sancetta; p. 27: Edouard Berne/Stone/Getty Images; p. 30: David Young-Wolff/Alamy; p. 34: Dan McCoy/Rainbow; p. 35, l: Courtesy of Dorothy Cheney, Ph D; p. 35. R: Courtesy of Dr. Robert Seyfarth; p. 37: Richard T. Nowitz/Phototake; p. 38: Ethan Miller/Getty Images.

Chapter 3:

p. 52: ©Mads Abildgaard/iStockPhoto; p. 53: VLC/Antonio Mo/Taxi/Getty Images; p. 54, t: Science Photo Library/Photo Researchers, Inc.; p. 57, all: ©Jeffrey H. Schwartz; p. 58: Dan Mc-Coy/Rainbow; p. 60: D. W. Fawcett/Komuro/Photo Researchers, Inc.; p. 66, t: AP Images/Joe Marquette; p. 66, b: Dr. Colin Chumbley/Photo Researchers, Inc.; p. 68: Reprinted with permission from Damasio H, Grabowski T, Frank R, Galaburda, AM, Damasio AR: The Return of Phineas Gage: Clues about the brain from a famous patient. *Science*, 264:1102–1105, © 1994, American Association for the Advancement of Science. Photo courtesy of H. Damasio, Human Neuroanatomy and Neuroimaging Laboratory, Department of Neurology, University of Iowa; p. 69: Jiang Jin/SuperStock; p. 70: Stone/UHB Trust/Getty Images; p. 80: AP Images/Roadell Hickman/*The Plain Dealer*.

Chapter 4:

p. 90: Meg Takamura/IZA Stock/Getty Images Royalty Free; p. 91: Christina Kennedy/Getty Images; p. 94: Stefan May/Stone Allstock/Getty Images; p. 98, both: Tony Freeman/PhotoEdit, Inc.; p. 102: © Downing et. al. 2006. Published by Oxford University Press. All rights reserved. Image provided by Dr Paul E. Downing.; p. 106: Richard T. Nowitz/Corbis; p. 108: Ted Streshinsky/Corbis; p. 109: Juniors Bildarchiv/Alamy; p. 111: Norbert Schwerin/The Image Works; p. 113, t: POPPER-FOTO/Alamy; p. 113, b: David Ball/Index Stock/Photolibrary; p. 114: Fuji Photos/The Image Works; p. 115: Scott Foresman; p. 116: Reprinted from Cognition, Vol 107/Edition 1, Stephen R.H. Langton, Anna S. Law, A. Mike Burton, and Stefan R. Schweinberger, Attention capture by Faces/©2008, with permission from Elsevier.; p. 118: Federico Veronesi/Gallo Images/Getty Images; p. 119: Dennis O'Clair/Stone/Getty Images; p. 121: moodboard/Corbis Royalty Free; p. 122, t: Martin Barraud /Stone/Getty Images; p. 122, b: Naki Kouyioumtzis/Axiom Photographic Agency/Getty Images; p. 123: David Wells/The Image Works; p. 124: Bob Rowan/Corbis; p. 128: SuperStock; © 2009

Salvador Dali, Gala-Salvador Dali Foundation/Artists Rights Society (ARS), New York.; p. 129: USDA/APHIS Animal And Plant Health Inspection Service.

Chapter 5:

p. 135: Hummer/Lifesize/Getty Images Royalty Free; p. 136: David Young-Wolff/PhotoEdit, Inc.; p. 137, l: Bonnie Kamin/PhotoEdit, Inc.; p. 137, tr: N. Durrell/McKenna/Photo Researchers, Inc.; p. 137, br: Ulrike Welsche/PhotoEdit, Inc.; p. 145, both: Spencer Grant/PhotoEdit, Inc.; p. 149: Courtesy of Dr. Philip G. Zimbardo; p. 151: Peter Hvizdak/The Image Works; p. 152: Doug Menuez/Getty Images Royalty Free; p. 155: Ace Stock Limited/Alamy; p. 156: Faces of Meth/Multnomah County Sheriff.

Chapter 6:

p. 163: Andersen Ross/Blend Images/Getty Images Royalty Free; p. 164: Topham/The Image Works; p. 165: Ken Heyman /Woodfin Camp & Assoc.; p. 166: Bettmann/Corbis; p. 169: Richard Heinzen/SuperStock; p. 173, t: Archives of the History of American Psychology; p. 173, bl: Bill Aron/PhotoEdit, Inc.; p. 173, br: Maya Barnes/The Image Works; p. 176: SuperStock; p. 179, #4: Visuals Unlimited/Corbis; p. 180, t: Cindy Charles/PhotoEdit, Inc.; p. 180, b: Yerkes Regional Primate Research Center, Emory University; p. 183: Rita Nannini/Photo Researchers, Inc.; p. 185: John Warden/Stone/Getty Images; p. 186: Dr. Stuart R. Ellins, California State University, San Bernadino; p. 189: Dr. Albert Bandura, Stanford University.

Chapter 7:

p. 195: Digital Vision/Alamy Royalty Free; p. 196: AP Images; p. 198: Michael Newman/PhotoEdit, Inc.; p. 202: Corbis Royalty-Free; p. 203, t: Marty Heitner/The Image Works; p. 203, b: Frank Chmura/Alamy; p. 206: Jeff Greeberg/PhotoEdit, Inc.; p. 207: Spencer Grant/Photo Researchers, Inc.; p. 213: Josef Polleross/The Image Works; p. 216: Hemera Technologies/Alamy Royalty Free; p. 220: Rolf Bruderer/Corbis; p. 222: Lon C. Diehl/PhotoEdit, Inc.; p. 227: Reprinted from Neuron, Vol 57/Edition 3, Uri Hasson, Orit Furman, Dav Clark, Yadin Dudai and Lila Davachi, Enhanced Intersubject Correlations during Movie Viewing Correlate with Successful Episodic Encoding/p. 11©2008, with permission from Elsevier.

Chapter 8:

p. 232: Philippe Garo/Photo Researchers, Inc.; p. 236: David Young-Wolff/PhotoEdit, Inc.; p. 237: Tony Savino/The Image Works; p. 240: Joel Sartore /National Geographic/Getty Images; p. 242: "Reprinted from Brain Research, 1146/Issue 3, Robert A. Mason and Marcel Adam Just, Lexical ambiguity in sentence comprehension / © 2007, with permission from Elsevier.; p. 244: The Great Ape Trust of Iowa, www.greatapetrust.org; p. 245: Karl Muller/Woodfin Camp & Assoc.; p. 253: Will & Demi McIntyre/Photo Researchers, Inc. p. 257: Alan Abraham/Corbis Royalty Free.

Chapter 9:

p. 270: Digital Vision Ltd./SuperStock Royalty Free; p. 272: Science Library/Photo Researchers, Inc.; p. 276: Mary Kate Denny/PhotoEdit, Inc.; p. 283: Brown Brothers; p. 285, t: Bettmann/Corbis; p. 285, b: Robert Beck/Time Life Pictures/Getty Images; p. 286,